P9-CJG-845

Percussion Anthology

A Compendium of Articles
From *The Instrumentalist*

Fourth Edition
(articles from 1946-1995)

200 Northfield Road • Northfield, Illinois

Introduction

The articles in this volume are reprinted from issues of *The Instrumentalist* from the past 49 years. This fifth edition of the Percussion Anthology includes articles from 1946 through April 1995. Each article is indexed by title, author, and subject matter. To facilitate finding an article about a particular person, the author index lists articles about a person as well as those written by him. The interview with Lionel Hampton is listed under his name and the author's. Some article titles have been changed to fit the the columns of the index.

Table of Contents

Index of Articles by Years

1946-1947

What Size Drums?

John P. Noonan

WELCOME to the drum section of the INSTRUMENTALIST! We are glad to be here, and hope you will shoot in your questions, or any ideas you may have on drums or drumming.

The first subject I would like to look into is the matter of drum sizes for the band and orchestra. From my own playing experience as well as observation and discussion with many top drummers, I should say that the general tendency is to use drums that are too large for best results.

What Size Drums?

First, in the orchestra, a 6½x14 or 6½x15 inch snare drum is the best all-around size. In the major symphony orchestra, the usual size is 6½x 14 and they have only one snare drummer. Upon occasion a field drum is used for military effect, or when called for in the score, but not so often. Thus it is fairly safe to assume that the 6½x14 is a fine size for orchestra, regardless of size.

The bass drum for orchestra can be 14x30 for the small orchestra, 16x32 for medium orchestra and 16x34 for large orchestra.

The band presents a little different problem. Many band drummers in professional bands use a 6½x14 drum for concert with excellent results. For the large band a 6½x15 is a little better. Drum makers of late years have featured a 7x15 or 8x15 size which is very good.

These sizes are for concert of course. For parade purposes the 12x15 is the ideal size for the adult and high school player. For the younger chap of grade school age a 10x14 parade drum serves well as he can carry such a drum better than the larger 12x15.

Bass Drums

From a practical standpoint the marching band should use a 14x30 bass drum when it is carried by the player. The marching band wants the bass drum to have volume (tone is secondary), so a large bass drum isn't really necessary unless a cart is used. Use a smaller bass drum and a harder beater than is used in concert.

For concert work the small band can use the 14x30 bass drum, and for a band of from forty-five to sixty pieces, a 16x30 or 16x32 is ideal. From sixty to eighty pieces and up, the 16x32 is still good, a 16x34 can be used, as can a 16x36; but don't go "overboard" on a big bass drum. They don't always do what you think they will. Too often a bass drum has too much resonance and "ring" and does not give the solid boom the concert band requires.

It is also obvious that too small a drum can be used also. Below thirty inches in diameter, drums are for the "double-drummer" who uses a foot pedal and are too sharp toned for concert band or orchestra.

Good cymbals also are required to "sharpen up" the bass drum. A 14″ or 15″ is fine for average use where the bass drummer plays cymbals, while for the separate cymbal player 14″, 15″ or 16″ can be used with fine results.

Tension

As to the type of drums I will make this blanket statement: "Whenever possible, drums should be separate tension and of best quality." You all know this, but too many "skimp" on the budget when it comes to drums, and it is a mistake.

If separate tension snare drums are used, gut snares are best for concert, if single tension,—*no*. A single tension drum can not be adjusted properly for good gut snare tone. If the drum is single tension, silk wire or coiled wire snares are the best bet.

The bass drum should be separate tension, with fairly heavy heads. Do not tune the bass drum to definite pitch. The word BASS is pertinent, in that it should be low in pitch, but not definite. The beating head should be tighter than the opposite head, about one-fourth. This prevents kickback or "bark".

The general thought, then, is to be reasonable on sizes and above all use the best separate tension models.

Snare Drum Stick Grip

John P. Noonan

As mentioned in our last article we should like to devote some attention to the matter of the "stick grip", that is, the approved manner of holding the snare drum sticks. We say "approved" rather than "correct" for it would be a matter of opinion to say that a certain way of holding the sticks would be correct and all other ways incorrect.

From a mechanical standpoint there is hardly any single factor in drumming that is more important than a proper grip of the sticks. If the grip is scientifically accurate it is reasonable to say that rapid precise manipulation of the sticks will be attained more easily and with less effort, and finally with controlled relaxation, which is the secret of facile technic upon percussion instruments.

The orthodox rudimental grip.

The stick grip shown in the majority of drum instruction methods is the orthodox rudimental grip, and is the grip probably best adapted to playing upon a large field drum for "open" military type playing. It is characterized principally by a full hand grip in the right hand, i.e., the right stick is held in the palm of the hand, with the middle finger curled around the stick into the palm to retain the stick in this position, and with the remaining fingers curled loosely about the stick. In the left hand the stick is held in the crotch of the thumb and forefinger with the stick resting on the second joint of the third finger. The first two fingers are curled about the stick with the first finger resting on the stick for control. Example 1 shows the "open" position of the hands for this stick grip, while example 2 shows the "closed" position of the hands employing this grip. Such a stick grip is, as noted before, the grip for the field drummer and is excellent for use upon a large drum for street work, military solos and open precise playing where the pure double-stroke roll and open "stroke rolls," flams, etc., are to be used.

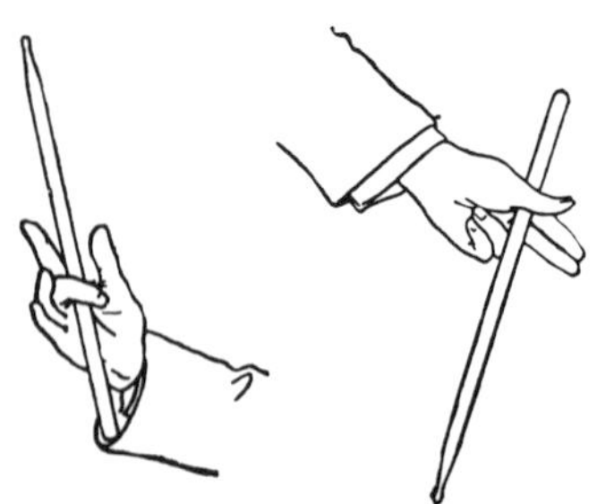

EXAMPLE I

Modern Delicacy

But one must take into consideration that this type of drumming is not always desired, for as a matter of fact there are few times when such open, robust playing of the drum is musically in good taste. Today's needs, and for that matter yesterday's needs in the band or orchestra call for closer grained, more delicate drumming with fine shadings and accurate, precise rhythms. The ardent rudimentalist sees "red" at this last statement and "rants" all over the place about his rudiments and his shadings etc., but alas, it is wishful thinking upon his part and he is still thinking about the Three Camps and the Downfall of Paris and not of modern requirements.

Mind you, I do not say the rudimental stick grip is wrong, but I do say it is not adaptable to band and orchestral requirements of today where *"pp"* means very soft and not "pretty powerful." I have yet to hear a drummer who uses this strict rudimental grip who can do a fine job of concert drumming!

The preferred grip.

Now let us see what is a more logical stick grip for band and orchestral use. We will use a 2B model stick for this illustration. The 2B stick is approximately $15\frac{7}{8}''$ long overall. In the right hand the gripping point is approximately $4\frac{1}{2}$ inches from the butt end. The stick is held between the thumb and the *first* joint of the middle finger with the remaining fingers curled loosely about the stick, with the palm of the hand down. Another adaptation is with the stick held between the thumb and *first* finger with the first finger curved to meet the thumb, with remaining fingers curled inward and using pressure of the second finger only in extreme *forte* passages. Either of these modifications of the strict rudimental right hand grip is practical. In the left hand the gripping point is again $4\frac{1}{2}''$ from the butt end, with the stick held in

EXAMPLE II

the crotch of the left hand between the thumb and forefinger, the first and second fingers curved over, but not gripping the stick. The third and fourth fingers are curved inward under the stick with the stick resting on the "shelf" of the second joint of the third finger. Example 3 shows this grip in closed playing position. Example 4, the position on the drum.

EXAMPLE III

The difference is small but Eminently Important.

We can see that there isn't a lot of difference in these various grips, but close attention will show the following differences between the strict rudimental grip and the modified concert grip. *In the right hand the grip is not in the palm of the hand, but is closer to the end of the fingers* allowing more finesse and delicacy. In the left hand the grip is substantially the same except in the modified grip the first finger does *not* grip the stick.

Much can be said for the strict rudimental grip from the standpoint of practice. It is such a "rigid" grip comparatively that it is fine for practice purposes and clean open playing. The student should use it and practice with its employment, and for "open" rudimental solos it is fine, but the modified grip is more adaptable to practical band and orchestra use.

Quality vs. Quantity

Remember that when this strict rudimental grip was developed and used the drum was a marching instrument used outdoors where volume was the primary requisite. As the drum became more "lady-like" and percussion instruments more and more the fine "effect" instruments that they are today a modification of the stick grip was necessary to produce these fine grained effects. Then too, for the bulk of playing today we use a smaller snare drum with thinner heads and lighter snares which necessitate a more delicate manipulation of the sticks.

With the modified stick grip one doesn't have to worry about adequate volume which might appear to be a problem in view of my stressing finesse and delicacy. Sufficient volume is a minor problem and easily attained.

The important point is that most instruction books show the strict rudimental grip for most of the books are strict rudimental methods.

Thus the teacher is apt to get the idea that the grip shown is the only correct one. In my opinion this "outdoor" stick grip is one of the big reasons so many of our drummers play rough and overly loud. They are "trying to drive a tack with a sledge hammer" and it simply does not work!

EXAMPLE IV

The Long Roll

John P. Noonan

THE PRODUCTION of the long roll on the snare drum is the highest form of the drummer's skill. It is the most difficult of all the drum rudiments. It proves to be a stumbling block to many a student and many a professional drummer.

In theory, the long roll is not difficult. There are two methods of producing a drum roll; first, a rapid reiteration of single strokes; and second, a reiteration of double strokes. The latter is employed on the snare drum while the first is used with tympani, bells, etc. It is evident that the first method, i.e., single strokes, is best, for in it the strokes are all wrist actuated. It is the more perfect roll of the two, and while not easy, is more quickly acquired than a good double-stroke snare drum roll.

The inherent crispness and short lived tone of the snare drum makes it necessary that we use double strokes to produce the roll on this instrument; and to create the effect of sustentation we employ speed, which calls for a stroke and a *rebound*. Here is where we run into difficulty, for it is the control of the rebound that causes all the trouble.

No Short Cuts

Many teachers and students have talked to me about roll production, and I wish I could provide a simple, quick and effective expedient to solve the problem. Twenty years experience has proved to me, however, that there is no easy way—no short cut method of gaining an even, rapid drum roll. Few have the patience to devote monotonous hours to practicing for long roll perfection, but there is no other way. Factors increasing the difficulty for long roll practice are the inherent weakness and awkwardness of the left hand, and the fact that we know what a closed roll sounds like and are overly anxious to gain this speed. This second factor is the one that causes the student to push, scrape, and dig in order to produce some semblance of a roll. This bad habit once acquired is likely to remain with the drummer. As a result, very few drummers play a fast, even roll.

Single Stroke

I believe that before the drum student can play a double stroke roll, he should be thoroughly adept at single stroke combinations, with particular emphasis on the single stroke roll. In order to even up the hands, single stroke combinations should be practiced three ways: first, with the right hand alone; next, with the left hand alone; and finally, from hand to hand. The left-hand-alone exercise is of great value. It helps strengthen the left hand and tends to make the left stick lift faster. Example I (opposite page) shows a typical exercise for this type of practice. Stress the fact that the student should be able to play any figure with his left hand alone which he can play with his right alone. If he is serious, he will see immediately that he has a job on his hands.

Next, the single stroke roll should be developed as shown in Example II. This can be practiced two ways from a mechanical standpoint. First, start with raising the sticks over the head with a free arm movement, lowering the strokes as speed is increased; second, with the arms at the side in playing position, raising the sticks only as far as the wrist will turn. Practice for evenness first, speed second. Work through all levels from *pp* to *ff* and vice versa, *crescendo* and *decrescendo*.

Double Stroke

The pure double stroke roll can be started and practiced in four ways.

1. Begin with the sticks over the head, strike a "right" with an arm blow, and before the stick returns to the up position, strike an accented blow with wrist action—then follow with the left in the same manner. Gradually increase speed until the roll is closed. This procedure is outlined in Example III, and involves an arm and wrist movement as indicated by the letters A and W.

2. Follow the same procedure as in the first case, but without accent on the second blow as shown in Example IV.

3. Production of double stroke roll. Use only wrist action, keeping the arms at the side in playing position, allowing sticks to rise only as far as the wrists will turn, and accenting the second blow with each hand (shown

DRUM EXERCISES

in Example V). In this exercise the second blow becomes a rebound as speed is gained. Then we have a "two for one" proposition. The stick strikes a blow, rebounds once, and is picked up ready for the next blow. Example Va shows wrist and rebound indicated by letters W and R.

4. A stroke and rebound based on a single stroke pattern. Here the rebound is used immediately, not as speed is gained. It is doubling the pattern by the addition of a rebound. This exercise is invaluable and should be used in all forms. Example VI shows several forms of this type of practice. All of these should be practiced diligently and during each practice period. These forms employ only double strokes and the combination of stroke and rebound; in other words, series of "twos." To further facilitate wrist action groups of "threes" should be worked out as in Example VII and groups of "fours" as in Example VIII.

It is obvious that the strokes and rebounds must be even and clean if the slight pressure is to produce a fine, close roll. This should be "put over" to the drum student, constantly warning him that the old adage of "Haste makes waste" applies truly to the production of a good snare drum roll.

March-April 1947

Teaching the Rudiments

JOHN P. NOONAN

Perhaps the easiest part of the drum teacher's task is teaching his students the drum rudiments. If the student is an average one and works even fairly hard during his practice periods he will in due time become reasonably proficient with all of the drum rudiments.

There is certainly nothing mysterious about the essential drum rudiments. While many teachers disagree upon the methods of teaching these fundamentals, they are nevertheless well established and well defined. Upon several different occasions I have known of young drummers who have secured books of rudiments, pads and sticks, and without any help at all worked the rudiments out remarkably well. In one of these cases the youngster, who had no knowledge of note values. even had figured those out pretty well and could do a creditable job on the first thirteen rudiments.

Unfortunately, the task of a teacher does not end at the point where the rudiments are well in hand, but rather his job has just started. He must now begin the application of these drum rudiments to musical forms—and that is a real job!

The bulk of drum students do not have the services of a specialist in drumming, so we will assume from this point on that the teacher is a band director whose own instrument is the trumpet, trombone, clarinet or any of the wind instruments.

Rhythm and Rudiments

This teacher should of course understand the drum rudiments, and, in general, their application. If he has not had any work along this line while in school he should, if at all possible, take a few lessons from a drum teacher during summer sessions, or attend a clinic session on percussion to "iron out" his ideas on the subject and to secure suggestions on a course of study for the drum student.

With an elementary drum method, the study of common time should be started at once, employing only single strokes as shown in illustration. Here is where the player of a wind instrument can really help the student. The teacher should improvise melodies to fit the drum part given, first playing the exact note values as given in the drum part, next filling in these parts, thus showing the drum student why he must count and be constantly alert. The manuscript example given below shows a sample drum part with two improvised melodies to be employed. I truly believe this to be a tremendous aid in drum teaching. It does several things: it helps the student with rhythm, accustoms the student to playing with someone, and keeps the *teacher* busy and interested!

Simultaneously with this rhythm study the rudiments should be started, with a careful explanation of what the long roll is, how it can be attained and put over the idea of the "imitation of sustentation"—explain how the drummer can not "hold" a tone, but can only imitate the effect, and why this imitation must be as perfect as possible. Keep your horn constantly at hand so the pupil can be shown what a certain rhythmic figuration sounds like. It is pretty certain that if he uses the orthodox sticking shown in the book, he will be correct.

Musical Terms

Next, stress dynamics—always keep after him about dynamics—explain to him carefully why he above all others in the band or orchestra must understand and use all shadings. Explain

that the drummer has only rhythm to work with and that shadings are his greatest aid in making his playing interesting and musically correct.

Next, require him to learn a reasonable number of musical terms. Assign several each lesson to write out and define, so that he will know the meaning of *andante, presto,* etc.

Explain to him the basic patterns of conducting, in the common rhythms and allow him to "lead" a phrase or two while the teacher plays on the trumpet or trombone.

Then give him the upswing and downbeat only, in various rhythms and require him to count aloud the remainder of the measure. Explain to him how the speed of the upswing and downbeat plainly shows the tempo. Then require him to memorize the first two bars of each exercise so that he can watch the leader for absolute accuracy of tempo.

All of these things help in the development of drumming routine, and the earlier started the better. The average youngster today is pretty intelligent—don't talk "down" to him—talk to him like you would to an adult and try and keep abreast of his ideas.

Dance Bands

I believe it to be an excellent idea to encourage the drummer to play in every type of organization that uses drums: band, orchestra and dance band. The dance band offers a lot to the drummer.

Almost invariably the drum student likes to play in a dance unit and it certainly does no harm; it even helps him, for here he gets an opportunity to "play". The teacher can turn this to good stead by making the student write out some of the tom tom "licks," etc., so dear to the drummer's heart, and help him analyze some of the ideas he hears over the radio and on records.

Yes—indeed the rudiments are simple, when one considers all the other phases of turning out a good drummer.

Part of the task is to make as good a musician as possible out of the drum student. As early as is practicable start him on the bells and/or xylophone to further aid this idea of musicianship. This phase of the drummer's study is almost invariably neglected, but it should not be, for it is invaluable in his training. The student should really have this background for the ultimate study of the timpani.

Thus the drum teacher has a pretty well defined task ahead of him aside from teaching the mechanics of the drum rudiments, and the band leader can do an excellent job if he will employ the same methods used in teaching the other instruments, as affecting good musicianship.

May-June 1947

New Instruments - Snares - New Solos - Heads

John P. Noonan

THE END of the school year leaves this column with a few odds and ends of "drum beats" which we pass on for your consideration.

The drum production picture is indeed much better than it has been since the war days. While still not able to serve the demand the drum makers should be in good shape by fall. Almost every type of percussion equipment can be supplied now within a reasonable delivery time, but with timpani, xylophones, bells, marimbas, vibraharps and chimes still trickling through pretty slowly. It is best therefore, to order what you will need as soon as possible, lest you be disappointed on delivery.

✦

Speaking of timpani, the W. F. L. Drum Company and the Leedy Drum Company, are both showing new models of pedal timpani. The W. F. L. Co. is showing new models with suspended bowls for increased resonance, as well as several other models. The Leedy Co. has an improved pedal mechanism with a clutch device to prevent pedal slippage.

✦

The most complete timpani method available is probably the Seitz Timpani Method published by the Leedy Mfg. Co. of Elkhart, Indiana.

✦

On a recent clinic date I used three concert type snare drums, one with gut snares, one with silk wire snares, and one with heavy coiled wire snares. Before the audience was informed of this fact, we played the same beats on each drum and asked for a vote on the best sounding of the three drums. The drum with coiled wire snares was the unanimous choice. It shows that our ears are becoming attuned to a lighter, more crisp drum tone. There is a lot to be said in favor of coiled wire snares. They respond well, are not subject to atmospheric changes, and are easy to take care of. Just recently I heard a concert by one of our major symphony orchestras where coiled wire snares were used on the snare drum and it seemed to me to "cut through" very well.

✦

Just received eight new drum solos by Acton Ostling who has been writing some fine things for percussion. All of these solos are "drumistic;" i.e., characteristic of the drum and heartily recommended for solo use. The numbers, published by Gamble Hinged Music Company of Chicago are:

First Competition, Grade I
Young Contestant, Grade I
Den Chief, Grade II
Heads Up, Grade II

Drummers Delight, Grade III
Rolling Alone, Grade III
Rudimental Rhythm, Grade IV
Rudimental Review, Grade IV

The grade I and II solos are fine for the young student and help to keep up the youngster's interest.

✦

When storing drums and timpani for the summer do not loosen the heads until the skins are flabby. Leave some tension on the heads to prevent shrinkage. If possible place covers on the instruments or wrap with cloth or paper to prevent dust and dirt from gathering on the heads and rods.

✦

If you have a solo drummer who can tackle something difficult, secure a copy of Alan Abel's solo, "2040'S SORTIE". But I warn you it is tough and a definite challenge to the above average drummer. For your copy write Alan Abel, 32 15th Street, Columbus, Ohio. The price of the solo is 50c.

✦

Beyond question the world's largest drum studio is the Roy C. Knapp School of Percussion, Kimball Hall, Chicago, under the personal direction of Mr. Knapp who has given instruction to many of our top flight drummers. Roy is thoroughly conversant with all types of orchestral and band routine and has served as timpanist, drummer and xylophonist with many crack musical organizations. Knapp-trained percussionists are active in symphony, radio, concert bands and orchestras and in dance bands.

Mr. Knapp is the author of several brochures, one on the fundamentals of Modern Drumming and the other on the fundamentals of Timpani playing, both published by Ludwig and Ludwig of Elkhart, Indiana.

✦

I repeat, a drum must have good live heads if it is to sound well. Drum heads have been scarce but are beginning to come through again in better quantity. When heads become old, hard and "beat out" no one can obtain good clean tone.

In adjusting and testing many snare drums I have found that one of the most important factors is the selection of a good snare side head. Many drummers and school band leaders feel that "any old head" will do. That certainly has not been my experience. My slogan is very simple as regards drum heads. Only the best are good enough! Timpani heads must be of the finest and fresh stock. Remember here we have definite pitch and need plenty of resonance.

Assign your principal drummer to oversee the care of the school drum equipment. Make him responsible for it. His duties are to see that it is kept in good condition, put away carefully after rehearsal and on hand for concerts. He checks new numbers for instruments and accessories, triangle, tambourine, etc nd has them out and ready for use. .ves time and money.

✦

In numbers where snare drum, triangle, tambourine, castanets and other traps are used in rapid succession, allocate one or more effects to each player, depending on how many drummers you have. Initial the parts so each person will know what part he is to handle. This prevents "scrambling" and indecision within the section.

The High School and College Timpanist

John P. Noonan

I THINK we will all agree that there has been a marked improvement in the work of percussion sections in the high school and college bands and orchestras. Critical musicians, however, still seem to feel that generally speaking this section is still the weakest from a sectional viewpoint. So many directors have agreed on this, that I suppose it is true, although it is vastly improved over a few years back. Pedal timpani are standard in most bands today, but there are many that do not have them, and who really need them.

Timpani are like any other instrument. One can devote a lifetime to their study and can become, within the limits of the instrument, a virtuoso. Let any one who doubts this lend a critical ear to the Henry Morgan show, an ABC network feature on Wednesday nights, this past season. This crack comedy show uses a sensational orchestra for background and incidental music, directed by Bernie Green, top arranger and conductor, who composes some, and arranges all of the music. We salute Mr. Green for his fine work in general, but in particular for his projection of percussion instruments, and his imaginative use of the timpani as solo melodic instruments. This would not be possible except for the art of Mr. George Gaber, the timpanist on the program, who, I guarantee, will astonish you as he did me with some of the finest timpani playing I have ever heard. To illustrate the type of thing George does, take a look at this, an excerpt from the Liszt Hungarian Rhapsody, played on the program recently.

Note the tempo, no allowance made for pedaling, and absolutely a solo passage. It was as "clean as a hound's tooth." You can see now why his work has caused such critical artists as Roy Knapp to exclaim, "The finest timpani playing ever heard on the air."

Mr. Gaber tells me he uses four pedal timpani, and on rare occasions, five. He illustrates better than thousands of words what can be done with study.

Pedals vs. Hands

Now back to school! First, there is no comment needed as concerns pedal versus hand timpani. Hand screw timpani are practically obsolete, and it is a waste of money to pay even fifty dollars for a pair. My good friend, Wm. F. Ludwig, Sr., who has spent a lifetime developing timpani to the highest point of perfection, becomes almost uncontrollable at the mention of hand timpani, and his son, Wm. F., Jr., formerly timpanist with the famed University of Illinois band, just simply sighs and shakes his head when he hears about hand timpani.

The timpanist should be carefully chosen. Select as good a musician as can be had for the post. If the applicant is a drummer, fine; but he must be made to realize that being a drummer isn't all that is required. If he doesn't have a good ear, he must develop one and study some harmony and ear training, for his difficulty will be tuning accurately and rapidly. If no trained drummer is available or suitable for the chair, it is best to select a good violinist or pianist and train him to be a timpanist, but above all select someone who will take the job seriously and work at it. There isn't much training literature for timpani. Here are the materials with which I am familiar, that the timpanist should have:

Seitz Timpani Method
Leedy, Elkhart, Ind.

Ludwig Timpani Method
Ludwig & Ludwig, Elkhart, Ind.

Rubank Elementary Timpani Method
Rubank, Chicago

Timpani Passages, BKS I, II, III
Belwin, Inc., N. Y.

Timpani Tips
Metzenger, W.F.L., Chicago (free)

The History of Timpani
W. F. L., Chicago (free)

Fundamentals of Timpani Playing
Knapp, L & L, Elkhart (free).

This, plus ear training, harmonic study and practice, plus playing experience, should develop a pretty good timpanist.

How Many Drums?

Next, have adequate drums. The literature played by university groups, and, in many cases, high school groups, is becoming more and more complex. The timpanist will have plenty of grief trying to do the work on two drums, even if they are pedal drums. He should have three, and, in many cases, four, pedal drums to do a good job.

If you have a standard set of 28 and 25 inch drums, you can add a single 30 inch drum, or a 32 inch, and later a 24 inch drum to complete the set of four. The 30 inch and 24 inch can be purchased singly. I just bought a new 30 inch, latest type suspended bowl pedal drum for $320.00. The 24 inch pedal drum is $280.00. They can be added as the budget allows.

The reason for three or four pedal drums is obvious. Fewer tuning changes are required, and, more important, better tone. For example, the range of the regular 28 inch kettle is F to C, but the F and G are not too good, with the F "flabby" and "boardy," under volume. On the 30 inch drum the F is big and resonant. On the 25 inch drum the range is from B*b* to F, but the high F is too stiff, due to the tautness of the head. The 24 inch drum remedies this, so that on four drums you have not only extended your range but you have fine tone throughout the regular F to F compass.

If your band or orchestra is fairly large, but you do not use numbers requiring more than two pedal drums, or you cannot afford to buy three or four at first, consider a regular pair of pedal timpani, but in the 29 inch and 26 inch sizes. For all around purposes, when only two drums are used, much can be said for the 29 inch and 26 inch sizes.

Many symphony orchestras like the 29 and 26 for the two middle drums. Edward Metzenger, ace timpanist with the Chicago Orchestra, just purchased a set of four latest model suspended bowl timpani in 32 inch, 29 inch, 26 inch and 24 inch sizes (see the INSTRUMENTALIST for May, 1947, page 29), and he tells me they are really excellent. His work calls for a large range, but he says aside from this, he can secure all the normal range tones in a full resonant way.

The student must practice pedal manipulation long and arduously, and constantly work towards rapid, accurate tuning. Added to this must be the science of drumming or "sticking," and good tone production. It is not an easy task, but it can be done, if the student will approach the work seriously, and devote as much time to practice as other instrumentalists do. The director's job is to see that the student studies ear training and harmony, (and this is most important) to make sure that the student plays rhythmically correct at all times. A good timpanist must not be shy or backward in his playing. Rather he must be sure and confident and play that way. There must be no hesitancy in rhythm. It must be certain and dominant. It is a big job and requires a lot of work.

NEW LOCKING DEVICE PREVENTS SLIPPING

The first fool-proof tension locking device developed for tympani is "standard equipment" on the improved precision tympani manufactured by Leedy Drums of Elkhart, Indiana. The proven ball-bearing clutch mechanism is designed to prevent pedal slippage, a problem that has always vexed the tympanist. It is a distinct forward step in tension control construction, both because it locks positively at any position, and because the clutch is practically wear proof and completely silent.

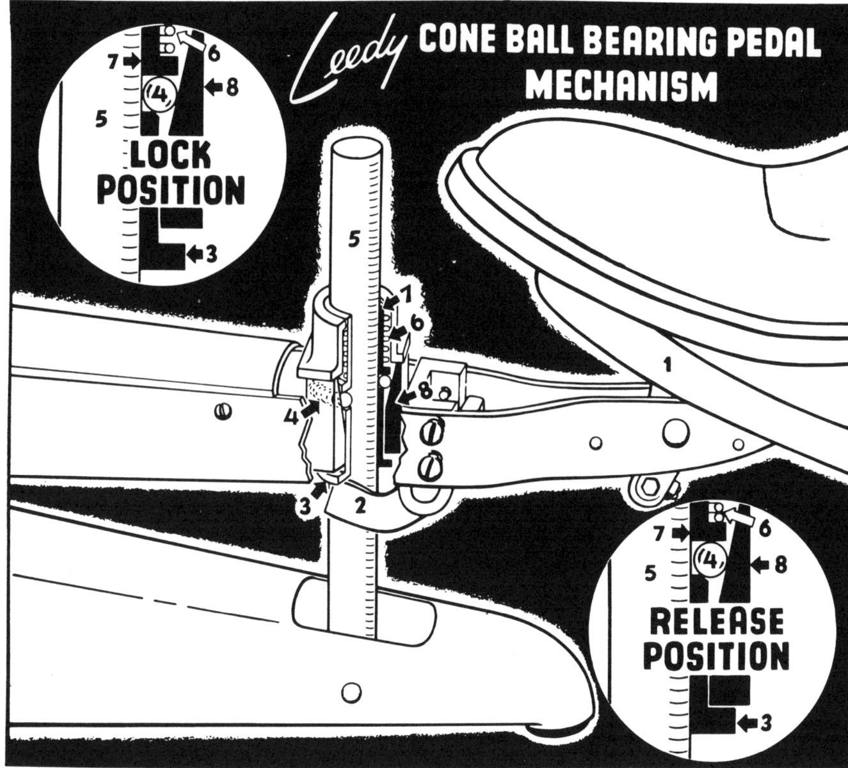

The accompanying sketch shows how manipulation of the pedal both releases and locks the ball bearings in the cone clutch device. Step by step. this is what happens:

Release—Pushing toe forward on pedal (1) lifts finger (2), raising sleeve (3) and pushing precision ball bearings (4) up and away from hardened steel rod (5).

Lock—Releasing toe pressure on pedal allows downward pressure of spring (6) against sleeve (7), which pushes precision ball bearing (4) against wedge-like housing (8), causing balls to grip hardened steel rod (5) without slippage at any position.

Smooth, relaxed, and silent control is achieved throughout the extreme range of each bowl through use of this outstanding mechanism.

November-December 1947

THE MARCHING BAND DRUM SECTION

JOHN P. NOONAN

THERE is one place where the drum section can be "large and loud", and that is in the marching band. Here we want plenty of volume, snap, and martial character that drums can supply so well.

There are several problems, as there always are in almost every situation, and we will try to be practical in this discussion as well as theoretical.

If you have what you consider a good drum section in a forty-five to sixty piece band, the ideal set-up would be four snare drums, one bass drum, and one cymbal player. The snare drums would be 12 in. x 15 in. separate tension models with gut snares; the bass drum, your regular concert drum on a cart (or 14 x 28, or 14 x 30) if slung from the player, and a pair of 15 in. best quality cymbals. The section could, of course, be proportionately larger or smaller, depending upon the band.

A good grade school section would be the same number equipped with 10 x 14 or 10 x 15 snare drums with wire snares, and 13 in. cymbals.

Now let's tear that down a little. First the high school group. The ideal drums are 12 x 15's with gut snares. The size is the best, really better than 12 x 16. The 12 x 15's are snappier, hold head tension better, are lighter in weight and easier to carry.

What Kind of Snares?

The snares should be gut *if* your drummers play well and understand how to care for and adjust gut snares. If they don't, and few do, it is best to use heavy gauge coiled wire snares. I really believe this, although I am personally a gut snare advocate; but years of experience have taught me that too many high school drummers do not understand the care and use of gut. Gut snares are made from sheep gut, are an animal substance, and thus shrink or become loose, depending on the weather. They must be properly set, kept straight, constantly realigned, *and* tightened up tight when the drum is not in use. This latter procedure keeps them from excessive shrinking and becoming too short and binding. If all this is watched, and the weather is dry on parade day, and the drummers all play well, the drums will sound marvelous.

You will notice a lot of "ifs" and "ands" there,—too many, I believe, for the average section. Silk-wire snares are OK, but sound a little "tubby"; so I think heavy coiled wire is the best bet in most cases. A well-known dealer showed me some separate tension 12 x 15's with heavy coiled wire snares that really sounded fine, played easily, and kept in adjustment without any trouble—so—that's the story.

The grade school kid should have the 10 x 14 with coiled wire snares by all means.

Put leg rests on all the snare drums, and be sure they are all "slung" at the right height. Not under the chin nor at the knees, but with the batter head about 6 inches below the waist line.

The bass drum on parade is for one principal purpose: a loud, steady beat. Tone is secondary. If you have a cart, use a 16 x 32, or whatever size drum you have. If not, get a 14 x 30 preferably, and a hard felt beater, for good results.

Beats for Street Use

Now the street beats. Thousands of them have been written, many of them good. Here is where you can really use rudiments, flamadiddles, drags, and many of the rest. The determining factor here, I think, is the ability of your section. Fancy beats of all kinds are fine if the section can play them and the band march to them. If not, better keep them simple. A good high school section can work up some good ones. Material for ideas is available: "Drummers on Parade," Wilcoxson Drum Shop, 349 The Arcade, Cleveland, Ohio, 75c; and "Novel Street Beats," Berryman, Frank's Drum Shop, 226 S. Wabash, Chicago 4, Illinois, 20c, are two good publications for ideas, and they can be worked out without too much trouble.

Drummers get a kick out of playing street beats. It gives them a chance to be heard and to be "the show" on the street. Play up this angle to them and encourage them to work out street beats of their own. Many times they will come up with novel ideas that are practical as well.

Work out the sticking on all street beats so that it is uniform and put all the flash possible in the playing. Here we can raise the sticks up and do anything necessary to make it more spectacular. The public is greatly impressed with what they see—unfortunately, in most cases, more than with what they hear. We do know that "eye appeal" is a big factor in the parade band, so don't be a "die-hard". Do the best you can with what you have.

November-December 1947

Which Instrument Is Best For Schools?

James Dutton

WHILE playing concerts throughout the Middle West, I have been asked by many band directors which mallet-played instrument should be purchased to obtain the maximum value for the music department. If I were to make a choice of one instrument, it would have to be a marimba.

A vibraharp is more expensive than the marimba and its use is limited. Its lush, ringing tone is adaptable only to certain types of compositions—like the slow ballad (Adrian Rollini style), or the popular tune with a bounce (Lionel Hampton style). There are occasions for it in the classics, such as Debussy's "Clair de Lune" or Loeffler's "Evocation," but certainly not enough of them to warrant the investment of five or six hundred dollars in such an instrument. If, however, a vibraharp is available, it can be used as the substitute for the celesta, or vice versa, depending upon the particular passage.

An interesting note regarding the celesta concerns its construction, which is very similar to the vibraharp. It consists of a series of small steel bars struck by hammers, controlled from an ordinary pianoforte keyboard. An accurately tuned resonator of wood is attached to each bar. To Tschaikowsky goes the distinction of introducing the celesta into the symphony orchestra in his "Casse-Noisetti."

Xylophone?

The xylophone is similar to the vibraharp in that its use is also limited. Its shrill, piercing, woody quality functions well only to produce an effect, or perhaps as a solo to overbalance an unusully loud band which is incapable of providing the proper accompaniment for a solo instrument. It is almost impossible to make this instrument blend into the orchestration so that it may be used as an integral part of the band or orchestra.

Marimba Endorsed

The full, resonant tone of the marimba, with its fine blending qualities, enables it to overcome the shortcomings of the above mentioned instruments. With a little experimentation and ingenuity on the part of the conductor, the marimba will prove itself to be one of the most valuable instruments in the high school musical organization. For example, J. Irving Talmadge of Proviso High School, Maywood, Illinois, uses a five-octave marimba (which he himself designed) in every selection which the band plays.

The marimba adds color to an orchestration which is weak. It also can take over any solo parts which may be lacking in the individual band instrumentation, such as oboe, flute, clarinet, trumpet, etc. A more complete discussion with specific illustrations will be given in following articles. As a solo instrument, the marimba has no peer. Time and again a marimba soloist, regardless of talent, has made the band concert an outstanding success.

Imitating Church Bell

A method for reproducing the actual harmonic effect of a bell in the orchestra as suggested by Frederic Corder "consists of a single f (4th line—bass clef), forte and sostenuto, played by four horns and three trombones in unison. Below it a cello sounds the b-natural a diminished fifth lower, molto vibrato; while above it two flutes hold the chord pianissimo. See Fig. 1.

"A more simple scheme consists of a mezzo-forte unison of horns, bassoon, and clarinet on a fairly low note with the addition of a cello pizzicato and a soft-stick roll on the cymbal, while a harp or a glockenspiel sets the note free in the octave above. The additional "ppp" brass with flutes above materially helps the illusion."

Safonofs's recipe for "Parsifal" bells needs only a grand piano behind the scenes and the music of Fig. 2.

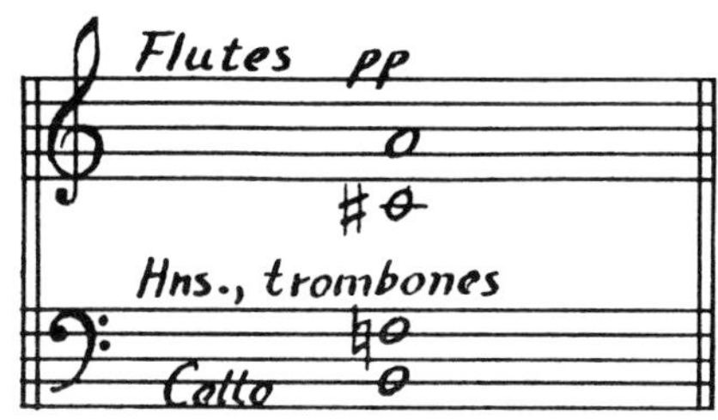

Figure 1

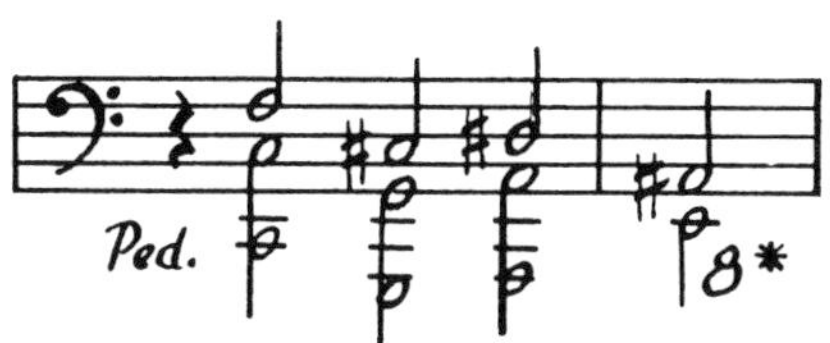

Figure 2

1948-1949

16	Developing Drummers	Roy C. Knapp	January-February
17	Marimba Musings	James Dutton	January-February
18	The Story of the Marimba	James Dutton	March-April
19	Stroke Rolls	John P. Noonan	March-April
20	Flams	John P. Noonan	May-June
21	Your Drum Questions Answered	John P. Noonan	September-October
22	Marimba Repertory	James Dutton	November-December
23	The Tympani Section	John P. Noonan	January-February
24	The Snare Drummer	John P. Noonan	March-April
26	Effective Use of the Marimba	James Dutton	March-April
27	Street Beats	John P. Noonan	May-June
28	Percussion Procedures in Florida	Arved M. Larsen	May-June
29	How to Play the Marimba, Part I	James Dutton	November-December
29	Drum Rolls	Haskell W. Harr	November-December

DEVELOPING DRUMMERS

ROY C. KNAPP

THE high school and college Band Director, as I see it, has an important, and, incidentally, a very tough job. His task is to turn out a good concert band, a good marching band, and aside from this, his basic job is to give the members of his organizations as good a musical foundation as is possible in the time that he has. Thus, very often he has to forego everything to prepare a concert or get ready for a football game. In many cases, the band is composed of some who study privately and who are serious students, and of others who look upon the band as a student activity only and are in the band as a hobby.

Much has been written about the percussion section, and the fact that it is usually the poorest section in the band or orchestra. In many cases this is true. The average band director is quick to admit that he knows less about drums than he does about the other instruments, unless he happened to study privately with a competent drum teacher while preparing for his career as a director. In many cases no drum course was available in the music school which he attended, and he may find himself lost when he begins teaching the requirements of the percussion player.

Being a competent drummer is not an easy job. It takes many years of study and routine to handle the task expertly. A great number of school band players do not intend to follow music as a career, and after leaving school seldom play their instruments. Others pursue their music study and reach the top.

Drummer Musicianship

If the Band Director can "sell" his drummers on the true facts, i.e., that the drummer should be as good a musician as the other instrumentalists, he has won half his battle. Any major instrument of the drum section is really a specialized study: snare drum, bass drum, timpani and/or mallet played instruments. Yet the competent drummer is expected to do a reasonably good job on all, and to do so calls for a lot of practice and study.

The band director can at least do one thing. He can guide the drum student in rhythmic and harmonic analysis, and, by doing so, help his musicianship. A drummer can be an expert rudimentalist and not a good musician—don't forget that! I am not knocking the rudiments. They are merely fundamentals, and every drummer, therefore, is expected to learn them and play them reasonably well. This is just the groundwork. The real job is applying them to musical forms.

The band director and teacher can help the drummer immeasurably by guiding his study through rhythmic analysis. The student should thoroughly understand all rhythms, and how to count them correctly, for the drummer's stock in trade is RHYTHM. In 6/8 for example, the drummer must know more than the two basic rhythms of the Flam-accents Nos. 1 and 2. Likewise, 12/8 and 9/8 should not baffle the drummer as it usually does. His study should include analysis of *all* rhythms.

On mallet played instruments the student should at least learn all he can about keyboard harmony, and on tympani he has to devote some time to ear-training and tuning.

Study Jazz (!)

The average drummer is also a jazz-enthusiast. Most of them spend a lot of time "knocking themselves out" on hi-hats and tom-toms, and so forth, and they can all tell you about Krupa, Rich, et al, and what they do. Nothing wrong with that! It is the music of the day and must be considered. If correctly done, it is excellent training for the drummer. If, however, the drummer wants to play jazz intelligently, he must, or should, know what he is trying to do. The answer? Rhythm analysis again, and a thorough understanding of "cut" time. If you can get him interested here it will help to guide him in all rhythmic forms.

Many band directors have complained to me of the paucity of good drum literature for study. That is true. There is not as much material as for, say, the cornet. But there is a lot of work to be done aside from the mechanics of the drum rudiments. The general purpose of the school music program is fundamentally to give the student a good musical background. Thus, the idea to put over to your drummers is that there is more to being a percussion player than slugging out paradiddles and hitting everything he touches so hard it sounds like he is "building a garage".

Insist that the drummer study rhythms, thoroughly memorize all musical markings, and pursue some harmonic study.

Its a hard task and must be handled temperately. It takes time, but it can be done, even with the very young students. There is no reason why a child of ten years shouldn't learn about music in general as he works out the problems of the "daddy-mammy" roll. A little time given to his general music education along with his drumming will undoubtedly help to produce a better drummer.

MARIMBA MUSINGS

James Dutton

SOME band and orchestra directors have been using the marimba in such a way that it has become an indispensable instrument in their musical organizations. Unfortunately, however, many others have a marimba or xylophone at their disposal but have made little use of it. These instruments can be used in many ways.

Before any of these instruments can be of real value there must be available from eight to twelve pairs of good, carefully selected mallets. These should include yarn wound mallets, ranging from extra soft to medium hard; and rubber mallets, of both soft and medium hardness. As of this writing, I have not seen any mallet handles that are satisfactory other than those made of wood, (bamboo, rattan, etc.). The handles should be about twelve inches long, as sticks of any shorter length have little resiliency. A stick with too much spring is also poor, because it is practically impossible to play accurately with it. What reason is there to have a fairly expensive marimba if it is made to sound like a "pile of wood" by the use of cast-off glockinspiel, xylophone, and bell hammers? The instrument will become as versatile as the performer's variety of mallets.

Versatility

The instrument can be given a great many shadings, from a complete blend to a prominent solo, depending upon the variety of mallets used. In this respect, the marimba is a much more satisfactory instrument than a piano, because the latter always sounds like a piano regardless of how loudly or softly it is played; whereas the marimba, with several changes of mallets, can take on the character of many different instruments, from the organ-like qualities obtained with soft four mallet work, to the staccato skeleton effect that results when hard rubber mallets are used.

The mallet number should be marked in the score at each spot where a change is desired. A piece with three or four mallet changes is not unusual. Different mallets should be used in different registers. For example: in the octave below middle C a very large, soft, yarn-wound mallet around three inches in diameter can be used that will give the instrument a sustained quality. This type of mallet is of little value in the second octave above middle C because it is not hard enough to produce an effective tone. Similarly, only fairly hard yarn mallets can be used in the third octave above middle C. If two players are available, it is quite possible to use a combination of rubber and yarn mallets simultaneously.

Duplicate Parts

Assuming that one has the marimba, adequate mallets and players (suggestions will be given for obtaining these), we are confronted with the obstacle of sufficient marimba or xylophone parts. The directors that obtain the maximum use of these instruments solve this problem by buying an extra piano conductor's score for each orchestration. This is given to the marimbist, who can sometimes be allowed to choose his own parts, the director suggesting the parts the remainder of the time. Or, the director can select the parts all of the time, if this arrangement seems more desirable. Whenever a solo for oboe, bassoon, English horn, clarinet, etc. occurs, and part needs strengthening, the student at the marimba marks in his score that he is to play the desired part. The marimba can handle a melody and up to eight part chords if there are two players.

One in Every School

If possible, each school should have a marimba. Under proper guidance, it will become the most versatile instrument in the organization, and will also develop and make available a fine soloist for all concerts. It provides the band with a glockinspiel, bells and chimes, and all of the other percussion accessories as well. Ability to play the piano is definitely not a pre-requisite to becoming a marimbist; but if a pianist is available, it is very simple for him to play the marimba, due to the identical keyboards and wrist movements.

The marimba is one of the best means of teaching rhythm and ear training to children of all ages. It is a fascinating musical instrument—*not* a novelty. It requires genuine musicianship to display its effectiveness.

THE STORY OF THE MARIMBA

James Dutton

Storms and delayed trains make all passengers neighbors. The noted pianist who sat opposite me in the diner was no exception. He seemed happy to find that I could understand the "language of music." I listened to his views on composers, conductors and contemporary artists. When he asked me my part in the music world and I told him I was a marimbist, his look was blank. The instrument was clearly outside the realm of his musical knowledge. After my explaining that it is somewhat similar to the dulcimer, the Russian stringed instrument played with mallets, we were able to discuss it. He suggested, as have numerous other musicians, including orchestra and band directors, that the main problem in securing acclaim for the marimba is caused by the fact that few of the people even know what it is and where it came from. Thus I am writing the following article.

THE STORY of the marimba is an ancient and colorful one. Few people realize that the marimba is one of the oldest instruments in the world—that it preceded the violin by about 2,000 years.

Instruments similar to marimbas have been found in tombs near the Pyramids, which were built more than 5000 years ago. We can find even in the Bible, in the books of Genesis and Job, references to instruments which were early ancestors of our present-day marimba. Old sculptures at Nineveh and Babylon show musicians playing on such instruments.

The marimba is a member of the Harmonicon family and in some countries is referred to as a harmonica—not to be confused with today's mouth organ. It is so old an instrument that we are not sure where it was first used; some think in Africa; others say it may have originated in South or Central America. As proof, they tell of a mountain in Guatemala which is called, in the native dialect of the country, "the marimba of the ravines".

In Latin America

A Latin American marimba can readily be recognized by its unique buzzing tone quality. This is effected by the resonators, each of which has two holes, one at the top and a tiny one at the bottom, in the resonator wall. The bottom hole is covered with a thin film of spider's skin. When the marimba is played, it is this film which causes the peculiar identifying sound. The Guatemalan "marimberos" go from place to place carrying their marimbas with them on their backs.

In some sections of Africa the marimba is built on a curved frame, almost in a semi-circle. To each end a cord is attached which passes around the player's neck. Thus the marimba becomes portable. Gourds of varying sizes are suspended below the keys for resonators.

Ancient China

Chinese history tells us that the Chinese had a form of the marimba as long ago as 2000 years before the birth of Christ. At that time it was considered a sacred instrument and was used to accompany songs of praise. At the moment in the religious ceremony when the instrument was sounded, sticks of incense were burned. The Chinese marimba was not only a holy but a royal instrument. It was used early in the morning as a musical alarm clock to awaken the Emperor.

For the keys of the instrument, the Chinese used a type of stone which was very hard, held its pitch well, and was beautiful with many colors. These stones were often cut into odd shapes. Some represented animals, such as a bat with outstretched wings, or two fishes side by side. Others were in the shape of an ancient Chinese bell.

Popular in Java

In Java, the marimba was made in the shape of a dragon, beautifully carved and painted. In that country, the marimba, not the strings, forms the nucleus of the orchestra. The Javanese musicians use six different types of marimbas—three with wooden keyboards, and three with metal.

In Europe the marimba for many years was used only by wandering, gypsy-like peoples. Then, around 1830, Michael Joseph Gusikov played it with skill and made it known in all the musical centers of Europe. He made many tours, during which he was heard and praised by such famous musicians as Chopin, Liszt and Mendelssohn. The latter so admired Gusikov that he arranged a Paganini work for marimba and piano, and played the piano part himself.

The differences between the marimba and xylophone are significant. The latter, being much higher in range, plays the music an octave higher than written. The improved method of suspending the marimba bars, the use of thinner pieces of wood, better methods of tuning, more accurate resonators, the use of yarn and vulcanized rubber rather than hard material in the mallets—all add to the make-up of the fine concert marimba of today.

OLD SIAMESE BELL TYPE MARIMBA

STROKE ROLLS

JOHN P. NOONAN

STROKE ROLLS, or short rolls, are those containing a definite number of strokes, as we know, and generally are considered fives, sevens, nines and thirteens. In all probability, the fives, sevens and nines should really be the only stroke rolls, as such, and all rolls of a notation longer than nines should be considered long rolls. I wouldn't argue that point especially, but would like to look at stroke roll notation and what it means.

Example 1 shows typical stroke roll notation in 2/4 rhythm. At a regular march tempo five-stroke rolls are indicated. Example 1A shows the single stroke hand motions for the five-stroke roll. The addition of a rebound on each sixteenth note produces the five-stroke, and is musically the true number of strokes called for in Example 1 notation. However, we can't say that this notation makes the five-stroke roll absolutely mandatory, for the *tempo* would govern. At a regular allegro, fives would fit very well, but if the tempo were slower, the seven-stroke roll would fit better, and if the tempo were slower yet, nine-stroke rolls may have to be used to give the effect of the closed roll. Conversely, it would not work to force a nine or seven into a very fast 2/4 rhythm for the rolls would be too "tight" and "scratchy".

Example 2 shows the same notation as before, while Example 2A shows the hand pattern in triplet form single strokes to produce the seven-stroke rolls.

Example 3 shows again the same notation, with Example 3A showing the single stroke hand patterns to produce the nine-stroke rolls. Thus this could be carried out up to seventeen stroke rolls all on the same notation depending entirely upon the tempo. However, if the tempo were slow enough to play comfortably over the nine-stroke, then I believe it would be best to conceive the rolls as long rolls.

Function of "Trimmings"

Stroke rolls, as such, are really drum "trimmings" and are effective as a carry-over from one pulse to the next. Used thus, stroke rolls are most "drummistic," or characteristic of the snare drum.

Example 4 shows the five-stroke ruff, wherein the strokes are considered as an embellishment to the principal notes. Many drummers play these types of ruffs, instead of the regular five-stroke rolls, and there is some justification for this, but I wouldn't recommend it for all uses. In the last strain of a march, these ruffs are effective, crisp, short, solid, and sound fine for martial effects.

Example 5 shows the anticipated sevens in true notation and not to be confused with Example 2. Many drummers play Example 2 as shown in Example 5, which is incorrect. The sevens in Example 2 are attached on the "and" count while the rolls in Example 5 are "anticipated" or started before the "and" count. Example 5A shows the hand motions with the rebounds started on the second sixteenth of each group.

Example 6 shows another way of writing anticipated sevens, with a "drag," or two grace notes, ahead of the regular five-stroke rolls, with Example 6A showing the hand motions involved.

Example 7 shows stroke rolls on the beat in 2/4 rhythm. Here again, the number of strokes depends upon tempo and the strong attack is on the first note of each stroke roll, rather than on the last stroke of each group. 7A is the same problem in *alla breve*. 7B and 7C are similar problems. Measures 7D and 7E show a typical figuration wherein stroke rolls are used, the length depending upon the tempo. 7F shows a 6/8 figuration calling for stroke rolls.

Let's Make It Musical

Unfortunately, we cannot always give these notations from Example 7 through 7F their full value as a player

of, say, the trumpet could; but we can, by playing the proper stroke rolls, give a precise, musical effect, which is what we strive for. It is this type of thing that distinguishes the expert drummer, and helps him to gain the title of musician. The unskilled drummer must "scratch-roll" his way through figurations of this kind, which results in a nonmusical interpretation.

Thus, interpretation also has a place in drumming. Let us take as an example a typical march containing successive measures of five stroke rolls, played as in Example 1. That is correct and authentic, but let us say that in one strain the leader likes the five-stroke ruff as shown in Example 4 better. O.K.—fine. If in the last strain the second time through he wants anticipated sevens for a full military effect, O.K., nothing better, and used by Sousa and many other fine bands with thrilling effect. The drummer should know exactly what he is playing and why, however, or nothing much can happen.

May-June 1948

FLAMS

(1) How to do them, (2) How to take them or leave them

JOHN P. NOONAN

A FLAM is defined as a principal note preceded by a grace note, and is used in drumming to broaden or "thicken" the inherent stacatto of the snare drum.

To illustrate by use of words, if a single stroke would sound the monosyllable "tick" a flam would sound "click." You will note, of course, that "click" is a one syllable word; and thus a closed, applied flam sounds as one syllable, and not as "ca-lick" in two syllables. This latter is the sound of the "open" flam when done slowly. The flams are right or left flams, depending upon which stick hits the principal note; thus LR is a right flam, RL a left flam.

The usual procedure for flam production practice is first to assume stick position for a right flam. The left stick is placed two inches above the pad, the right stick eight inches above the pad. The left stick strikes the pad (grace note) and is immediately raised to the eight inch height. The right stick strikes the pad as quickly as possible after the left, but *stays* down in the two inch position, which places the sticks in the reverse of their original position and in proper position for the left flam. To produce the left flam then, the right stick strikes the pad for the grace note, and is instantly raised, while the left stick immediately strikes the principal note and stays down, placing the sticks in position for another right flam.

Practice Slowly at First

The beginner will almost always fail to keep the stick that hits the principal note down, ready to use it for the grace note of the next flam; but he will invariably raise both sticks up, which places the sticks out of position. Therefore, to assure plenty of time to check stick position, start with a quarter note flam in common time, followed by three quarter note rests, so that position can be checked. After control is fairly well attained, add a flam on the third beat, and finally on each of the four beats. The tempo in each instance can gradually be increased until the flam is under control.

Bear in mind, however, that the above method of flam production, done slowly, will produce the open flam, and will say "ca-lick." The next step is to gain speed until the sticks are striking the pad almost simultaneously and sound "click," as one syllable or the applied "closed" flam. This will require a great deal of practice, as it is very difficult to make the right and left flams sound the same width (usually the left sounds more open than the right, and also lighter than the right).

Arrangers are usually of two types as concerns the scoring of flams. The first scores flams "all over the place" while the second scores none, leaving it up to the drummer to place them where they will serve best. I know of many instances where flams have been indiscriminately written and, together with being almost unplayable, add nothing but a distortion of the rhythm, which is certainly not desired. The principal notes are, of course, the rhythmic patterns desired, and must predominate. If flams can "broaden" the pattern, well and good. If not, they are out of place.

Use Flams Judiciously

In the exhibition or drum contest solo, a more free use can be made of flams; but in the band or orchestra they can play havoc with clean-cut rhythm unless first properly written, and then properly played. It is significant that in most big orchestral works flams are sparingly written. In the band and orchestra, however, and especially the band where the tone color is heavier, flams can be used with fine results if properly understood.

In other words, I am trying to convey the idea that they can be left out as well as added. The simple rule is that whenever flams distort the rhythm or "muddy-up" the sounds, then some or all had best be cut out; for clarity of rhythm is the drummer's stock in trade.

It follows that the better the drummer becomes in flam production, the more flams he can add without rhythmic distortion. Even granting this, there are times when the addition of this embellishment is not desired, even though written. Conversely, when a broad, "wide" effect is desired, flams can well be added even though they are not scored.

If we acknowledge, as we must, that the three principal beats in snare drum playing are rolls, single strokes and flams, we can readily see that a lot of practice time must be given to flams. If we can get them to the point where they are evenly spaced and clean, the drummer will experience little difficulty in placing them correctly. The director is the one who can determine if the flams are out of place by the above simple rules.

For the preparation of other rudiments, flam-tap, flam accents, flamadiddle, and so on, it is apparent that clean single flams must be first adequately prepared.

September-October 1948

YOUR DRUM QUESTIONS ANSWERED

JOHN P. NOONAN

SINCE the last issue of The INSTRUMENTALIST we have received a few questions about drums and drumming which we will answer at this time.

Q—Is there any way I can keep my drummers from "pounding" on the snare drum?—A.E.W.

A—Usually this is caused by too much arm movement. I suggest that you make your students practice their lesson assignments without any arm movements whatsoever, just wrist motions, and yet observe dynamics. If no dynamics are shown, suggest "pp" through "f" with emphasis on the "pp" always. As you well know, the difficulty is to play softly enough on the snare drum. The forte passages are usually no problem. I believe that for almost every purpose very little arm movement is required in playing the snare drum. If terrific volume is required, some arm movement will augment the volume, and for "show" on the street raised arms are fine. For concert work, however, the use of flailing arms is bound to give a "boiler maker" touch.

Q—In modern concert band arrangements of popular numbers such as "Stardust", the drum parts do not seem too well arranged. Would you recommend filling in?—R.S.

A—In most cases the arranger of popular tunes really writes only a "guide" part for drums. Usually the introduction and endings are O.K. and should be so played. I do recommend filling in the chorus parts of the arrangement, for usually only straight beats and afterbeats are scored for bass and snare drum. If more than one snare drummer is used, obviously they will have to get together on the ad lib'ing. Wire brushes can be used to good effect for many of the "light" passages, as in the Stardust number you mentioned. I know several band drummers who use a regular hi-hat pedal with 14-inch cymbals for these popular tunes. Why not? The hi-hat is one of the dance band drummer's most important rhythm instruments and great for "pop" tunes. The bass drummer can play four light beats in a measure on the drum with the cymbal "pressed" lightly against the cymbal on the bass drum on the afterbeat instead of the beat. (Obviously this can be done only where one player plays both bass drum and cymbals).

Q—Do you feel that the vibraphone should be classified separately in contests? As it is, it is classified with xylophone and marimba, and I feel it is a separate and different instrument. —R.D.

A—I agree with you entirely. I have had this situation arise at a state contest and I believe they should be classified separately. I can see the marimba and xylophone in the same general grouping, but the vibraphone should be in a different class, in my opinion. I suppose the "powers that be" just grouped them all under mallet-played instruments and let it go at that. Usually from the judge's standpoint it isn't any problem as there are few vibraphones entered in contests; but there are a few more now than formerly and the instrument deserves a separate classification. Perhaps this will happen before too long.

Q—A well known drummer told me that practicing upon a pad is not good, and that the drum should be used for all practice. What do you say?—S.G.

A—If we could practice on the drum at all times I am sure it would be better, so I suppose your informant is right—if we just take that as a statement without any qualifications. From a practical standpoint I do not agree for several reasons. First, if you practice on a drum at all times you will not be too popular with your neighbors. (If you live in an apartment the landlord will soon curtail your practice!) More important, though, is the fact that the volume of the drum also distracts you and you will not keep at it very long. The snares, especially wire snares, tend to cover up defects in the rolls. A good drum pad will give excellent results and has the advantage of little noise. You can hear better what you are actually doing. The action of the pad is a little different than the drum head, but certainly not a serious drawback. If you are practicing a solo for contest work some practice sessions should be done on the drum, but not until the solo is memorized and all set. Then work it out on the drum. Thus I should say from a practical standpoint practice on the pad will bring excellent results.

It is the purpose of this column to help out in any way possible with your percussion problems. I would like very much to hear from many of you who have problems and further, if you have any ideas that have worked out for you, let me know about them so we can pass them on.

MARIMBA Repertory

JAMES DUTTON

MANY inquiries have been sent to me about good numbers for the Marimba. Following is a compilation of lists received from four outstanding specialists (see footnote).

Grading

E—easy, M—moderate, D—difficult.

Key to Publishers

Order from publisher or your local dealer. Abbreviations: Bel—Belwin, BH—Boosey & Hawkes, CF—Carl Fischer, Cht—Chart, EMB—Educational Music Bureau, FDS—Frank's Drum Shop, For—Forster, GHM—Gamble Hinged Music Co., Mar—Edw. B. Marks, Ru—Rubank, SMC—Southern Music Co., Wit—Witmark.

BURTON JACKSON played 1,300 performances, marimba, in 38 states in three and one-half years. Soloist with 100-piece European Marimba Symphony. A native of Illinois, he received his training at Northwestern University and Chicago conservatories. All marimba training from Clair Musser.

ART JOLLIF is director of the Quigley Music Studios, Kansas City, Mo., has many marimba students, and conducts Hogan High School Band, Kansas City. Educated at Northwestern, University of Kansas, and private conservatories. Composer of Marimba literature.

DOROTHY HEICK JORGENSON teaches marimba and piano in Madison, Wis. Starting marimba at five, she worked with several teachers, competed in national contests, and won scholarship at Interlochen. Attended University of Wisconsin. Traveled three years in vaudeville.

CLAIR MUSSER is faculty member of Northwestern University and president of Musser Marimbas, Inc., Chicago. Director of World's Fair and Imperial Marimba Symphonies. Many of the outstanding marimbists have been under his tutelage at one time or another.

A new publication is "Music for Marimba," Books I, II, and III, by Art Jolliff (Rubank, each $1.00). Book I

TWO MALLETS

Title	Composer	Publisher	Accompaniment	Grade
Country Gardens	Grainger-Quick	GHM	Pia	E
Dancing Tambourine	Polla-Quick	Harr	Pia	E
Dark Eyes	arr. Quick	Ru	Pia	E
Le Secret	Gautier-Quick	Ru	Pia	E
A La Valse	Von Weber-Sifert	Bel	Pia	M
Al Fresco	Herbert-Klickmann	Wit	Pia	M
Capricetto	Schipa-Musser	For	Pia	M
Caprice Viennois	Kreisler-Green	CF	Pia	M
Chiu Chiu	Milinare-Breuer	Cht	Pia	M
Dance of the Queen Swan	Tschaikowsky-Sifert	Bel	Pia	M
Danse Russe Trepak	Tschaikowsky-Wallace	CF	Pia	M
Eighteenth Century Theme	Mozart-Jolliff	Ru	Pia	M
Elfentanz	Grieg-Peterson	Mills	Pia	M
Hungarian Dance No. 5	Brahms-Quick	Ru	Pia	M
Liebesfreud	Kreisler-Green	CF	Pia	M
Norwegian Dance No. 2	Grieg-Green	CF	Pia	M
Rain	Green	CF	Pia	M
Schon Rosmarin	Kreisler-Green	CF	Pia	M
Valse in E Flat	Durrand-Namaro	Mar	Pia	M
Zita	Charrosin	BH	Pia	M
Brilliant, Valse	Von Weber-Sifert	Bel	Pia	D
Etude, Op. 6, No. 2	Musser	GHM	Pia	D
Fantasie Impromptu	Chopin-Sifert	Bel	Pia	D
Hora Stacatto	Dinicu-Heifetz-Goldenberg	CF	Pia	D
Invitation to the Dance	Von Weber-Sifert	Bel	Pia	D
Master Works for the Marimba	Musser	For	Pia	D
Mignon Overture	Thomas-Green	EMB	Pia	D
Minuet in G	Paderewski-Edwards	Ru	Pia	D
Polonaise Brilliante	Von Weber-Musser	GHM	Pia	D
Prelude, Op. 11, No. 3	Musser	GHM	Pia	D
Rhapsodic Fantasie	Liszt-Edwards	Ru	Pia	D
Rondo Capriccioso	Green		Pia	D
	Mendelssohn		or Orch	
Rondo Capriccioso	(Solo violin part)		Pia	D
	Saint Saens		or Orch	
Spanish Waltz	(Solo violin part)	CF	Pia	D
Tambourin Chinois	Kreisler-Green	CF	Pia	D
Tico Tico	Abreu-Bethancourt	SMC	Pia	D

THREE MALLETS

Title	Composer	Publisher	Accompaniment	Grade
Prelude in A Major	Chopin (Piano part)		None	E
Ave Maria	Schubert-Edwards	Ru	Pia	M

FOUR MALLETS

Title	Composer	Publisher	Accompaniment	Grade
Barcarolle	Offenbach-Quick	GHM	Pia	E
Dreams	Wagner	FDS	None	E
Adagio	Beethoven-Peterson	Mills	Pia	M
Ave Maria	Schubert	FDS		M
Ave Maria	Gounod	FDS		M
Berceuse (Jocelyn)	Godard	FDS	None	M
Chanson Triste	Tschaikowsky	FDS	None	M
Estrallita	Tonce	FDS	None	M
Finlandia	Sibelius	FDS	None	M
Liebestraum	Liszt	FDS	None	M
Londonderry Air (Danny Boy)	Irish	FDS	None	M
Melody in F	Rubinstein	FDS	None	M
Simple Aveu	Thome	FDS	None	M
Song to the Evening Star	Wagner	FDS	None	M
The Swan	Saint Saens	FDS	None	M
Andante Cantabile	Tschaikowsky (from string quartet)	FDS	None	D
Ase's Death (Peer Gynt Suite)	Greig	FDS	None	D
Cavatina	Raff	FDS	None	D
Celeste Aida	Verdi	FDS	None	D
Etude, Op. 11, No. 3	Musser	GHM	None	D
Humoresque	Dvorak	FDS	None	D
Intermezzo (Cavalleria Rusticana)	Mascagni	FDS	Pia	D
Kammenoi Ostrow	Rubinstein	FDS	None	D
Largo (New World Symphony)	Dvorak	FDS	None	D
My Heart at Thy Sweet Voice	Saint Saens	FDS	None	D
Romance	Rubinstein	FDS	None	D
Romeo and Juliet	Tschaikowsky	FDS	None	D
Scarf Dance	Chaminade	FDS	None	D

is arranged in duet form for pupil and teacher. Three-mallet playing is introduced. Book II contains easy two- and three-mallet solos. Book III consists of easy to moderate four-mallet solos.

BRASS SEXTET—ONE OR TWO MARIMBAS

Capriccio Italian	Tschaikowsky-Tallmadge	Bel	D
Eri Tu (Masked Ball)	Verdi-Tallmadge	CF	M
Kammenoi-Ostrow	Rubinstein-Tallmadge	Bel	E
Prelude and Finale (Lake of the Swans)	Tschaikowsky-Tallmadge	Bel	D

The TYMPANI Section

JOHN P. NOONAN

I WISH all school drummers could have been with Roy Knapp and me recently when we heard the New York Philharmonic Symphony Orchestra in Chicago and visited with the boys in the percussion section. It would have been a fine opportunity to hear and see one of the best percussion sections in action.

Saul Goodman is the timpanist. (He started with this orchestra at 19 years of age. Who says there is no opportunity for youth?) Mr. Goodman is a superb timpani player, a real artist, and plays all other percussion instruments as well. The other percussionists are Samuel Borodkin, the "boss" of the section; Arthur Layfield, one time crack jazz drummer with Paul Ash and Isham Jones, and William (Billy) Dorn. Here are indeed four "real" drummers. All of them are experts on all percussion instruments. "Billy" Dorn, for instance, was recording for phonograph records on xylophone when he was seventeen years old, and you should hear and see him sight read now. Borodkin and Layfield are also expert on all phases of percussion. "Boss" Borodkin has served for over thirty years in the orchestra under most of the world's renowned conductors.

It certainly proved beyond all doubt that the percussion section, when manned by "musician-drummers" is indeed one of the outstanding sections of the band or orchestra.

Famous drummers discuss new music and instruments. Seated, Saul Goodman, timpanist, New York Philharmonic; from left to right, Arthur Layfield, also of the New York Philharmonic; John Noonan, Associate director, Knapp School of Percussion; Allen Kimmey, staff drummer, CBS, Chicago; William Dorn, New York Philharmonic; Roy C. Knapp, director, Knapp School; Don R. Knapp, Knapp School; Samuel Borodkin, New York Philharmonic.

Mr. Goodman, the timpanist, has written a timpani instruction method: "The Saul Goodman Timpani Method," published by Mills Music, 1619 Broadway, New York City, price $5.00. It is the best of its kind that I have seen. It is complete in every respect from elementary exercises to advanced studies, with a section devoted to "Complete Timpani Parts" to standard works. It is a complete graded course of study with many fine illustrations to guide the student and teacher. I think it would be a fine book, particularly where the band leader is not a timpanist himself and must develop a timpanist. Using this method with its many photographs and clear instruction material, the band leader could do a good job teaching the timpanist.

Mr. Knapp, after carefully looking over the method, agrees heartily with the above.

Tone From Sticks

Now, about timpani sticks! Long a tough question, I believe Mr. Goodman has developed the best all around timpani sticks I have ever used. Most professional timpanists will tell you that much of the tone comes from proper sticks. Many drummers, including myself, have had "stick-trouble" and have tried all kinds, including home-made ones, for the proper, full, round tone desired. Mr. Goodman, after years of experimenting, has developed the "Goodman All-Purpose Sticks," which, in my opinion, solve the problem. I have tried them out thoroughly and am delighted with the results. Most timpani sticks have heads (discs or balls) that are too large, and thus are fluffy and too light, and give a "woolly" tone, or else they are too heavy and the blows are discernable. Goodman sticks are comparatively small as regards the heads, have properly shaped and balanced hickory handles, and give a fine solid tone, without either the hard tone or the "woolly" tone. The sticks sell for $6.00 a pair, and can be had from your dealer. If your dealer cannot supply you, address Saul Goodman, 151 Kneeland Ave., Yonkers, New York. Mr. Knapp and I have both tried these sticks and have shown them to many timpanists. All agree they are tops.

Three Tympani Minimum

Mr. Goodman was using four timpani—30", 28", 25", and 23". I think the next move in high school and college band and orchestras as regards timpani is the addition first of the 30" drum to the regular pair of 28" and 25". In most cases the 23" isn't too badly needed unless you get into pretty extensive repertoire, but the 30" is really needed. A properly made 30" drum will go down to D and up to A natural. While the low D is not required much, it is really fine to have this 30" drum for the F, F♯ and G, and, of course, it is indispensable where three tones are called for. At present I am using a 30", 28" and 25" (all pedal), and I would certainly hate to dispense with the 30". Any of the makers will quote you on a single 30" kettledrum, and I am sure you will consider it a fine investment, as I have, after you have used it in the band or orchestra, especially in the band where the tone color requires a little more volume from timpani.

THE SNARE DRUMMER

JOHN P. NOONAN

In the percussion department we are often reminded that the snare drum section is the most neglected of the band and orchestra section. Generally speaking, this is true; but I don't think it is too serious, for at the risk of being too optimistic I really believe the last several sections I heard at clinics were better than average and better than the same sections a year before.

I do feel, however, that specifically the snare drummers are the most neglected and least proficient of the percussion section. I hear pretty good bass drummers, good tympani players, excellent marimbas, "vibes," etc., but the snare drums are rarely expert. This is true in most grade, high school and college bands and even extends into the professional field. A leader can take a pianist or violinist, for example, and with a little work make a pretty good bass drummer, tympanist or xylophone player out of that person in direct ratio to his musical background, due to the fact that all of these instuments employ single stroke technique, have inherent resonance, and no not necessarily require a finished mechanical technique.

I do not wish to under-rate the amount of work necessary to become, for example, a proficient tympanist. That is truly a life-time job, as is that of an expert xylophonist; but the point I am trying to bring out is that the snare drum is also a tough job, far more so than is ordinarily supposed.

This is caused, I believe, by the natural, short, staccato sound of the drum, the embellishments used, viz: flams, ruffs, stroke rolls, etc., and the absolute requirement of clean, even technique to produce the desired results. The production of the sustained tone (long roll) in an even, rapid manner requires a tremendous amount of patience and practice; and employing as it does, double strokes of a primary and secondary (bounce) nature, it is apparent instantly that it can never be absolutely perfected, for it is, at best, an imitation of a sustained tone, and the secondary stroke (bounce) is of necessity weaker than the primary stroke.

Thus the matter of even strokes and speed to convey the impression of a even unbroken sound is quite a job.

Rolls Take Practice

We say that double-strokes are used, thus the old Daddy-Mammy roll is the answer to this problem. However, due to the fact that finally the secondary beat becomes a bounce, the student should practice and perfect the single roll (a single primary beat with each hand) to build a foundation for the bounce beats.

It will take years, not months, to develop these two rolls on the snare drum to a high point of perfection. In the final analysis we actually "close down" this double stroke roll by adding a slight degree of pressure to "fine-grain" the sound, BUT unless the double strokes are present in even form we do not produce the sound desired here—hence the bulk of the practice is best done using pure double strokes.

The same is true of all stroke rolls, fives, sevens, etc.; striving for clarity and even tone. The left hand is always the offender, and particular attention must be given to this offending hand. Other embellishments (flams, ruffs, etc.) require the same attention, always working towards clean "un-smudgy" strokes.

The average drummer practices, and should, mostly on a practice pad. In order to gain wrist control and speed, he raises his sticks high—for example—he starts the Daddy-Mammy roll with the arm fully extended up, and comes down with a blow that on a drum would have to be scored FFFFZZZ*!!??. (That's the only dynamic mark I can think of that describes the sound.) As he gains speed his arms come down closer to the pad and finally (in most cases) he is playing a "smudgy" too close roll at a *mp* dynamic. I have no quarrel particularly with the fully raised arm. I just do not think it is necessary, and see no point in doing it, and do not intend to waste my own energy trying it!

What is Proper Height?

Without raising the arms at all, we can easily bend the wrists and place the sticks 15 inches from the pad. That is almost twice as high as the actual playing level, for a powerful roll of the *ff* variety can be produced with about an 8 inch travel of the sticks. The 15 inch practice level allows us to lift the sticks quickly (and here's the secret, in my opinion, of good drumming); and subconsciously when we play, we try to swing them back and up to this 15 inch level, but only allow them to travel as far as the dynamic level wanted. So on the pad practice we must logically allow that the pad is only half as loud, at the best, as the same degree of force on the drum head. With the actual playing levels of maximum 8 inch height we can easily adjust our full dynamic range and help to produce touch.

Is Touch Required?

This "touch" is just as surely required on percussion instruments as it is on piano. It is best illustrated in the words of an excellent musician who told me that "most drummers play by the pound," and that is surely correct. A professional tympanist for example, speaks of "drawing tone." He means that the touch must pull out the tone. He uses a variety of "touches." The legato (loose), staccato (tight), the precise rhythmical (stiff), for the effects he wants. The snare drummer uses a little different idea. He has a small head surface—his problem is to play crisp, quick, sharp, and so the whole technique revolves, in my opinion, on one important factor,—the instant raising of the sticks after the blow is made. The idea here is to strike UP, and one of our finest teachers suggests saying the word "UP" as single blows are made.

It's HOT!

The idea of this UP stroke should be put across in several ways. For example, the pad is a red hot stove, the stick is your finger—another example, watch a woman test an iron to see if its hot enough—how does she do it? By pulling her finger away from the iron almost before it touches. I think this latter way is an almost perfect example of a percussion blow. One-half of all drum strokes finds the stick or sticks in the air away from the drum, thus raising them quickly is half the battle. This will have to be watched especially in the left hand, as the lifting is done with wrist turning only and employs no arm movement.

Lift 'Em for Flash!

I like to see band drummers on parade lift their arms and put all the flash possible in their work. This is a spectacle and the crowds love it. The fancier the better; and here too, we need all the volume we can get. But this flashing of the arms has little to do with orchestral or band concert playing.

Practice!

The only way a fine mechanical snare drum technique can be mastered is by long, tedious hours of practice. The twenty-six rudiments? Certainly! At a moment's notice and at rapid tempo. That's only the beginning. A drummer should be able to do all of them evenly and rapidly. Then his rhythmic study must start. All rhythms, all combinations, drum solos, duets, trios, quartets—anything that is of a drummistic nature.

Write Solos!

I find one good way to help develop good musicianship in the drum student is to have him write street beats, solos, duets, etc.: Start the habit in grade school students by having them write simple street beats gradually requiring longer solos, etc. The high school drummer can write solos, duets, and don't forget jazz!

Nearly all high school kids like dance music. The drummers are nearly always "Bop-guys" and aspiring Krupas. That's natural, but too often it's a little irritating as they pound away merrily with their hair hanging over their eyes in a rather brutal interpretation of one of Mr. Krupa's imaginative solos. There is no use to discourage them. If you do you are promptly and surely labelled a "square." Tell them the idea is great, but let's write out one of these things—a solo tom-tom stint for instance. At first they will write some strange things! No semblance of what they play, but after a while they get so they come closer, and every once in a while they will surprise you. I suggest to them a "build-up" idea, starting in quarter note form, then eights, triplets, and sixteenths with accents, and a lot of attention to dynamics for effect. It's like anything else, some do poorly, others average, and a few excellent things are uncovered, but it all is of value in developing the good drummer. This definitely shows one thing—how the student thinks rhythmically.

I've noticed in almost every case, a tendency to think along certain lines in a rhythmic way. Some have a natural sense of phrasing, others have difficulty with it. The teacher can find out many things by this writing business.

Like Other Instruments

The teaching of snare drum is along the same lines as any other instrument, requires as much time, and certainly as much practice. To some extent the thought that percussion is easy has been caused by the habit of using other players in the section for numbers requiring more drummers. It is apparent that any musician who can read can hit a triangle or a gong, or tap out rhythm on tambourine, etc. (it seldom sounds as well as when a skilled drummer does it though!) but "look out" for that snare drum. It's a simple looking thing and looks harmless, but to play it well and make it an integral part of the band or orchestra requires a tremendous amount of work and patience. The teacher whether a specialized one or band-leader teacher can develop good drummers through the same amount of attention given to other instruments, but so far as I know it can be done in no other way.

Effective Use of the MARIMBA

JAMES DUTTON

THOUGH the marimba is an ideal solo instrument, it serves other functions which are of great importance to any music department. Because the marimba cannot be played out of tune, it serves as a stabilizer of pitch regardless with what group of players or singers it is used. A few of the ways and means in which the marimba will fulfill its function are:

A. For Special Occasions.

Every year there are several occasions for which our best efforts are required in setting up an interesting program. Programs such as for Christmas, Easter, Baccalaureate, Commencement, and Armistice Day are important affairs. The marimba can be used to great advantage especially at these times, as, for example, for a prelude or so-called "mood music." It also provides an excellent vehicle for connecting the program divisions to give a program continuity, or to provide a medium for a recurring motive. For an Armistice program, for instance, a marimba is very effective if used between each tune in Groffe's "Over There."

It is effective to have the marimba played where it cannot be seen by the audience. Christmas carols played back stage or from a balcony give an extra touch to a program that will be remembered. A suitable selection can be used as an opening prayer for an Easter assembly. For special occasions, one needs special effects.

B. To "dress up" a concert.

At the band concert, showmanship, without question, is an important factor. A marimba used either as a solo instrument or as a part of the organization is intriguing to watch. It adds color to the appearance of the group; it points up the concert.

C. As a training instrument for all.

The marimba is unsurpassed for the development of rhythm, and ear training. It must be played with a definite stroke that is large enough for the student to feel strong pulsating muscular movement. It also has fixed pitch. Consequently, it has the advantages of the drum and the piano combined. Several experiments have been conducted in grade schools in which each student in several test classes was given a small eight-note xylophone. At the end of six weeks, with one or two exceptions, each child could not only play a melody on his xylophone, but *also sing it.*

D. To enrich repertoire.

A school marimba makes the enlargement of repertoire possible by including numbers such as "Dance Macabre," many works of Percy Grainger, and selections of modern composers.

For special arrangements, the type in which a school arranger is interested, striking effects can be obtained with the marimba in combination. It can also be used to "revitalize" old standard pieces; e.g., "William Tell" as a marimba solo with band accompaniment.

The "fluttering" of the marimba roll as heard in a band or an orchestra adds a unique type of intensity. It can be compared somewhat with vocal or string tremolo, but it is much less distinguishable.

E. To strengthen and enrich parts.

Use the marimba in unison with clarinets or flutes when reinforcement is desired—it will make the runs and arpeggios much cleaner. It can be used to emphasize a desired part.

Use it to fill in for missing instruments, as oboe, bassoon, violas, and so on, in solo or harmony parts. Use it on the horn parts for the chords on the weak beats. Frequently the tuba or bass parts are lacking in resonance or sustaining power. By using the marimba on these parts played in octaves, a marvelous foundation in the bass line can be obtained.

A school marimba will also help to provide the indispensable glockenspiel player for the marching band. A marimba is a good substitute for a harp.

F. With strings and voices.

With a string orchestra, an interesting effect can be achieved by using two marimba players reading from the piano part (one on the treble and one on the bass part).

The marimba will provide a rich foundation for any A Cappella choir number. It will sustain the pitch and provide balance. If used on the humming parts, it will make the choir sound more richly resonant. It can be used to great advantage to provide continuity between numbers or groups of numbers. Hymns sound strikingly different when done antiphonally with one verse by the choir followed by one on the marimba.

We could go on. It would probably be impossible to exhaust the possibilities of the marimba, depending upon the ingenuity of the conductor and the players.

The first requisite is a good marimba. After the school has acquired one, there will be little difficulty in finding able applicants and extensive use for the instrument in band, orchestra, and vocal groups. The marimba will last a lifetime. It is an investment that will prove productive of much good.

STREET BEATS!

JOHN P. NOONAN

STREET beats or marching taps are an important part of the marching bands routine. They can be made very simple or very complex, the determining factor being the ability of the drum section to play the various beats with accuracy and precision.

It is obvious however, that the fundamental purpose of the drum section is to maintain a steady cadence, that will enable the band to march easily and without complications. I have always felt that there is no point in trying to produce street beats that are beyond the capabilities of the performers resulting in a "blurry" sound that doesn't do much but bother the rest of the band and cause them to worry about where the beat is going to be!

Better Keep 'Em Simple!

If the drum section isn't too sharp, it is far better to keep the most simple cadence that will give assurance and confidence to the marchers.

On the other hand, if the section is of average ability a little practice on fairly simple beats will "liven" up the proceedings and put a little flash in the band. Several times in this column I have decried the use of flailing arms, etc., and I still feel the same way when it is done at the expense of rhythmic accuracy; but in the marching band I really believe the drummers should "put on a show" and take advantage of every appeal to the eye as well as the ear.

Use Flashy Beats!

On the march the drummers can raise their arms high at every opportunity; and should, if at all possible, use fairly simple or the more complex "tricky beats," to impress the public as to the band's ability. I have jotted down six easy street beats, that I give my grade and high school students for practice material, using "stick clicks" to sharpen up the beats. On the "X" notes the right stick strikes the left stick. The regular notes are on the drum. The stick clicks stand out and can be heard plainly at some distance. No flams are scored, but can be added if desired. With these as a guide I ask my students to write out others and some have come up with some good ones and used them in the band. The bandleader may want to write his own individual ideas which is also a good idea.

Vary the Beats!

In one of the sections I worked with, the drummers memorized three beats in 2/4 and three in 6/8 (similar to those shown). They will start on No. 1, for example, and play that until the first drummer calls No. 2; then upon completion of the phrase, they play No. 2 until he calls No. 3, etc. If the march to be played on the roll-off is in 6/8 they change to No. 4, for example, and proceed to 5 and 6 etc., until the roll-off. It works out very well and seems to interest the drummers and keep them alert.

Dynamics!

On all street beats, dynamics (none marked on examples) can be varied for fine effects. For instance, first time through soft, second time loud; crescendos, diminuendos, and accents can be placed as wanted. Don't overlook the accents, they make the street beats. Place 'em where you like, but stress them. Just playing at one dynamic level is pretty tiresome.

Originality of Beats!

The point is, that aside from the published street beats, there are hundreds that can be written out. Employ all tricks, some stick clicks (both shaft and butt end), rim shots, some beats on the hoop of the drum; and use of cymbals and bass drum that will certainly "point up" the section, and by so doing sharpen up the entire band.

Percussion Procedures in Florida

Seventy Florida Band Directors Inventory their Rhythm Business

ARVED M. LARSEN

HERE is an opportunity to look over your neighbor's fence. Seventy-eight percent of the school band directors in the Sunshine State have reported on their percussion methods and how they integrate them in the actual school music situation.

The typical Florida instrumental instructor:

1. Starts the percussion student on the 5.22 grade level.
2. Selects the percussion student by rhythm tests.
3. Teaches the percussion student in a homogeneous instrumental class.
4. Uses drumming rudiments and emphazies them.
5. Uses the Victor Method Book (State adopted).
6. Has regularly scheduled drum section rehearsals.

Methods of Selection

There are eleven different methods used by the Florida school band directors in selecting their beginning percussion students. An overwhelming majority use a rhythm test, with a consideration of the pupil's choice and general ability rating second and third, respectively.

After the pupil has been tested and selected from the fifth grade his instruction might be started under any one of the following classifications:

1. Homogeneous class, used by 50 directors.
2. Individual instruction, used by 37 directors.
3. Heterogeneous class, 25 directors.
4. Private instruction outside of school, which is recognized by 8 directors.

The frequent use of the drum class suggests that for most children this method is efficient, as has been advocated by many educational authorities. The eight instances of private instruction outside of school were found to be in the most densely populated areas in the state, probably indicating that the use of the private teacher is determined by availability.

Rudiments are taught by all seventy of the instructors, but only fifty-two intentionally emphasize them. There are seventeen different method books used throughout the state. The most popular is used by 40 of the directors reporting; others by 13, 12, 9, 8, 6, etc., on down to one, including original exercises.

The typical Florida high school has in—

Marching Band:

1. 56.2 members
2. A 137.5 cadence
3. 3.67 snare drummers
4. 1.27 glockenspiels
5. A separate cymbal player

Concert Band:

1. 53.8 members
2. 2.68 snare drummers
3. .74 glockenspiel
4. Separate cymbal player
5. Pedal tympani

Integration

The marching band is undoubtedly the greatest vehicle with which to integrate and display effectiveness of methods. The importance of the marching band is even further realized in our state, where the weather permits marching activity the year around. Band sizes range from twenty to one hundred-fifty members; and although there are a number of marching organizations that have a membership of more than a hundred, only three concert bands include more than eighty students. Marching cadences fall between the extremes of 120 and 180 with the smaller band generally employing the slower cadence.

It can be discerned from the previously stated summary that a good proportion of the difference in size between the marching and concert band is due to the reduction of the number of snare drummers and glockenspiel players when concert work is begun.

We Florida band directors are pleased to know that others are interested in our activities. Percussion work is most certainly receiving its share of attention. Twenty-one different high school bands featured drum solos on concerts during the past year alone. To realize the extent of the school instrumental movement in Florida one needed only to witness the Fuller Warren inaugural parade in January when more than forty Florida high school bands passed the reviewing stand.

HOW TO PLAY THE MARIMBA

Part I

JAMES DUTTON

There is little cause for argument about the use of the marimba as compared with the xylophone. The latter has not been produced for a number of years. It is probably the great versatility of the marimba that accounts for the gradual disuse of its higher pitched relative.

Learning Not Difficult

A tone that is produced by striking a bar is easier to play than a tone which is made by bowing or blowing. Furthermore, the familiar pattern of the marimba keyboard makes learning easy. To achieve evenly developed hands and relaxed wrists is the primary concern.

The First Lesson

Correct holding of the mallets is essential. Here is an easy way to achieve this. Place the mallets on the marimba so that the student can pick them up with his thumb and *1st* finger. The end of the stick should not extend beyond the base of the palm. Next, allow the remaining fingers to fall around the stick and then turn the wrist flat. See illustration.

Avoid these common faults: (1) placing index finger on top of stick, and (2), gripping the handle like a club instead of using just the fingers.

Exercise 1. With the left hand play a long series of notes on any one bar. Repeat this with the right hand.

Exercise 2. With L H play 8 notes on any one bar; then 6 notes, then 4 notes. Repeat with R H.

Exercise 3. With L H play Ex. 2 up and down C Major, G Major, and F Major scales. Repeat with R H. To stimulate interest arrange melodies that can be played by striking each note four times per beat. Use L H only. Some good tunes for this are: "Faith of Our Fathers," "Joyful, Joyful," "Twinkle, Twinkle, Little Star."

Exercise 4. Using alternate hands, repeat Ex. 2 and 3; i.e. play 8 notes with L H, then 8 with R H; 6 with L H, then 6 with R H; etc.

Caution: Watch wrists and hands. This is very important in the first lesson. If the left hand is weaker than the right, use a proportionate number of left hand exercises to correct this. The opposite is true if the right hand is weak.

References to Previous Articles

1. For marimba History, see page 22 of September-October, 1947 issue and page 34, March-April, 1948.
2. For effective uses of the marimba, see page 52, March-April, 1949.
3. For repertory, see page 34, November-December, 1948.

November-December 1949

DRUM ROLLS

HASKELL W. HARR

THE ONE PHASE of drumming which seems to cause the most confusion is the playing and application of the stroke rolls. There are seven rolls plus the long roll which I think all drummers should master. They are the 5, 7, 9, 11, 13, 15, and 17 stroke rolls. The long roll is used only for contest and exhibition work. By mastering all of the stroke rolls, the drummer will be able to start and stop at any time, with either hand, and give any sustained note its correct time value. The rolls are based on 32nd notes, and the rate of speed is set on the metronome for 120 quarter notes per minute. We use this speed to develop a good smooth roll. Once a drummer has developed such a roll, he will not change the speed of his roll to fit the tempo, but will add or subtract the number of strokes to or from the note to be sustained, according to the tempo.

The rolls consist of a primary and secondary beat with each hand, played in rapid succession. The secondary beat is a controlled rebound. The roll, I believe, that is used most in our school band scores is the 5-stroke roll. Let us analyze it:

The roll is designated by two 8th notes tied together, two lines through the stem of the first 8th note (1). To give a sticking pattern, break it down to two 16ths for the first 8th note and count it "1 e &" (2). Now to develop the five strokes, we replace the first 16th note with two 32nd notes and play them with a stroke and rebound of the right stick, replace the second 16th the same way, but play with the left stick, then play the second 8th note with a single stroke. We now have (3).

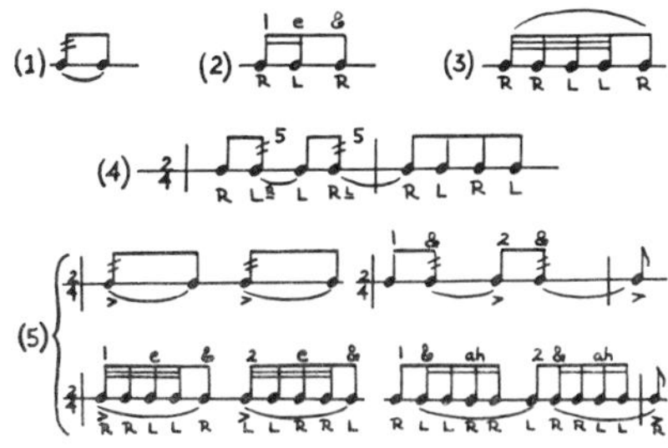

You have probably noticed that I divided the first 8th note but not the second. The rule is that the roll will consist of the number of 32nd notes contained in the first note, but the note to which it is tied will be played with a single stroke, regardless of its length.

When 5-stroke rolls are played in succession, they are played from "hand to hand." That is, if the first roll started with the right hand, the second one would start with the left hand (4).

Another important rule in the application of rolls is that if a roll starts on a beat, the accent should

be on the first beat; but if the roll ends on the beat, the accent must be on the last beat (5).

The 7-stroke roll is another much discussed roll. It is designated by two 8th notes tied together, the same as the five, or by a quarter note. In all drum solos of the rudimental type, the seven starts on the after-beat and ends on the beat. It will start with the left hand and end with the right (6).

When applying the 7-stroke roll to our band scores, if it is designated by a quarter note on the beat, I would start with the right hand and end with the left (7).

In 6/8 march rhythm, I make it a rule to start the seven with the right hand if it starts on the first beat of the measure, with the left hand if it starts on the second beat of the measure (8).

I use a slightly more open roll in 6/8 rhythm than I do in 2/4 rhythm to establish a definite sticking pattern for school drummers.

The 15-stroke roll is another that will have to be reversed to apply to our drum scores. In the score, it is designated by a half note. As it fills one complete measure, 2/4 time, it should start with the right hand and end with the left. When written in a drum solo such as the "Downfall of Paris," it is designated by a dotted quarter note, the usual notation for a 13-stroke roll (9), and is started with the left and ended with the right hand; written (10) and played (11).

Of the balance of the rolls, the 9-stroke and the 17-stroke (not listed as a rudiment) are the most commonly used in band scores. The following is a chart I use to show the various rolls.

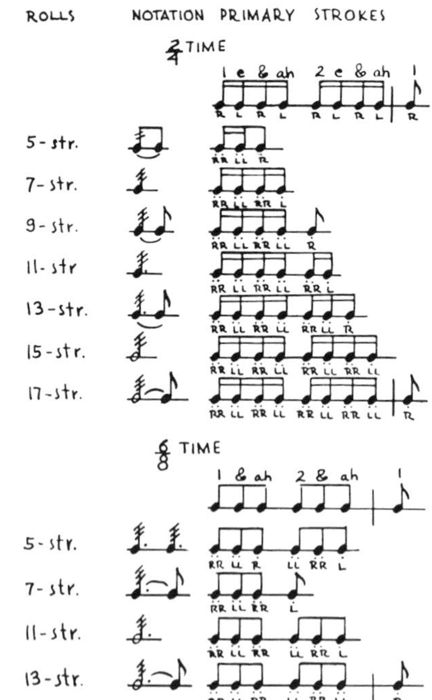

Practice starting all rolls with either hand, also practice playing rolls first by starting with an accent, then by ending with an accent.

When applying the various rolls in march tempo, if you keep the hands moving in strict rhythm, you will have little difficulty in playing the correct roll, example:

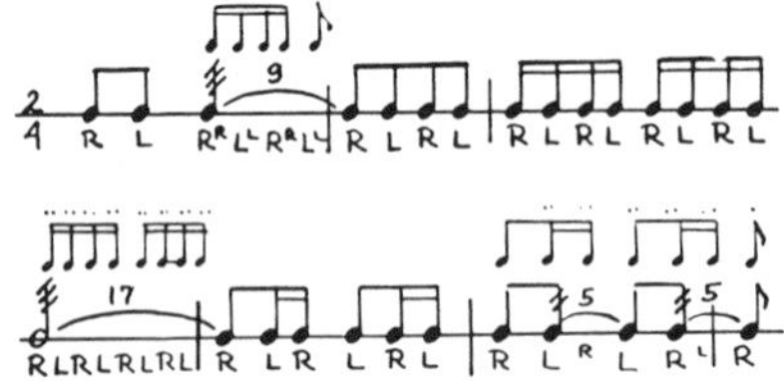

1950-1951

33	How to Play the Marimba, Part II	James Dutton	January-February
33	The South American Way of Drumming	John P. Noonan	January-February
35	How to Play the Marimba, Part III	James Dutton	March-April
36	The Timpanist	Edward M. Metzenger	March-April
38	How to Play the Marimba, Part IV	James Dutton	May-June
38	"It's All in The Head"	John P. Noonan	May-June
40	Survey of Mallet Instruments	James Dutton	September
43	The Beginning Drummer	John P. Noonan	September
45	Continuing With the Drummer	John P. Noonan	October
47	The Intermediate and Advanced Drummer	John P. Noonan	November
48	Care and Repair of Percussion Instruments	Paul Price	January-February
49	Traps and Accessories	John P. Noonan	March-April
51	Odds and Ends	John P. Noonan	May-June
52	The "Hi Hat" and How It Grew	John P. Noonan	September
53	The Concert Bass Drum	John P. Noonan	October
55	Percussion Problems in High School Bands	Richard P. Scherer	November-December

HOW TO PLAY THE MARIMBA

JAMES DUTTON

Part II

THE ease of learning to play the marimba is an attractive asset. Any student can make excellent progress each week if the habit of a regular practice period is established. It should be brief but daily.

Lesson I of *How To Play The Marimba* appeared in the last issue of the INSTRUMENTALIST.

Use the following exercises as a continuation of the wrist control work begun in the first lesson:

Exercise 1. Begin by using the C scale. Play 8 notes on C, then 8 notes on D, then 8 notes on E and so on, up and down the scale for one octave. Use alternate sticking, e.g.,

|| c c c c c c c c |
|| l r l r l r l r |
d d d d d d d d: ||
l r l r l r l r: ||

Repeat this exercise, playing 6 notes per bar up and down the octave, then play 4 notes per bar, 2 notes per bar, and finally strike each bar only once. The primary concern in this exercise is smoothness through wrist control. This can be achieved only by constant slow practice! It is desirable that the student write and learn all major scales. To attain the maximum value from this exercise, it should be played in all keys. Begin 1st with C, then take C♯, D, E♭, E and so on.

Exercise 2. This is the 1st of a series of exercises gaged to develop speed and facility. The 1st 5 notes of each scale are used. Play in eighth notes:

	c d e f g f e d	c d e f g f e d
	l r l r l r l r	l r l r l r l r
	c d e f g f e d	c d e f g f e d
	l r l r l r l r	l r l r l r l r
c c c c c: ||
l r l r l: ||

Play in all keys. Caution the student not to raise the mallets over four or five inches high. Both hands must sound the same. The proper holding of mallets and the development of smoothly functioning wrists are very important. These habits should be set in the first lessons. The mallets should be held well back on the end. Use the thumb and first two fingers (see cut). To produce a fine tone quality, the grip should be quite free and easy—without tension. The arm has three hinges; one at the shoulder, one at the elbow, and one at the wrist. The wrist hinge is essentially the only one used in playing the marimba. The other two joints in the arm remain motionless but without tension. Practice playing with one hand and holding your "hinges" with the other to impress the idea.

Exercise 3. Play the chromatic scale, using the full range of the instrument in the following manner: Step 1: With the left hand only hit each note once. Play up and down the keyboard. Facility will be no problem if the raised bars are struck on the tips nearest the player and the lower bars are struck close to the tips of the raised bars. Do not strike the bars at the point through which the string passes. This is true of all scales and arpeggios in which the raised bars are used. Step 2: Repeat the first step with the right hand only. Step 3: Play the entire scale using alternate left and right. Step 4: Repeat Step 3 but strike each note twice; ll rr ll rr, etc. Step 5: Strike each note twice with alternate sticking; lr lr lr lr, etc. There is only one *correct* place to strike each bar. In order to obtain a smooth, rippling scale, they should all be struck in the same relative position. Foot work enters the picture with the use of this exercise. Side stepping is more desirable than crossing the feet.

January-February 1950

The South American Way of Drumming

JOHN P. NOONAN

THE LATIN-AMERICAN type of music has been finding its way on to concert programs of bands and orchestras with increasing frequency during the past few years, and as we all know has met with terrific audience acceptance. Many fine arrangements of rhumbas, beguines and other forms of this type of music are available both for band and orchestra.

Here again we find the need for a good drum section for the rhythmic effects called for in these arrangements. The arranger is up against a tough problem in writing the drum parts, for to write the authentic and best sounding effects would entail complicated scoring, very difficult to read and a bit misleading. Actually, therefore, I believe the arranger usually writes a "guide" part for the drum section and hopes they will be able to interpret it by filling it in a little to secure the real Latin-American flavor.

Proper Instruments Important

I suppose all the "instruments" used by the rhythm section could be placed in the "trap" category. (I wonder who first called drummers' effects "traps?" I have never seen a trap—bear, rat or fish—among a drummer's effects, but that seems to be the word!) The usual scoring calls for timbales (or bongos), maracas, guiro (gourd), claves, and one or two cowbells (cencerro).

Timbales are two single head drums usually about 6½ x 11 and 6½ x 13, mounted on a floor stand. The shells may be of wood or metal. I prefer metal, copper or brass. The heads are calf or goat skins. The timbales are played with straight rattan sticks or small snare drum sticks (7A). Bongos consist of two smaller single head drums about 6 and 8 inches in diameter, with varying shell depths from 4 to 10 inches. The bongos are mounted on a block of wood close together and held between the knees, played with the fingers. I think for practical purposes the timbales are best for concert use as they supply more volume and do not require the more intricate finger technique of the bongos. American drum makers are now listing well made timbales at from $55.00 to $75.00, and bongos from $40.00 to $65.00.

Maracas are familiar to everyone. They are round ball-like shells of different sizes with handles attached and filled with seeds, buck-shot, pits or beads. One maraca is higher pitched than the other, or should be. The lower pitched one is held in the left hand, the higher in the right. The Cuban maracas are of vegetable origin, and must be handled carefully lest they break or crack. The price is around $2.50. There are Mexican made maracas of wood that sell for about $7.50 that are better and last longer.

The guiro, or gourd, is vegetable in origin. It looks like a squash, is hollowed out and ridges are cut across the face of it. It is played by rubbing a "scraper" across the ridges. The Cuban variety sells for $6.50 to $7.50. Again the Mexican variety of wood runs around $10.00 to $12.00, and is a better buy.

Claves consist of two sticks of resonant wood, ebony, or rosewood, etc. They are about 1 inch in diameter and 8 inches long. They sell from $1.50 to $6.50. The better ones give a sharp, definite click and are the best buy.

Cowbells (cencerro) are the regular cowbell minus clapper. The bell is held in one hand and struck with a light stick.

You Must Be Subtle

The above "traps" are the principal ones used. A substitute for timbales is a muffled (snares off) snare drum. It will work pretty well, but not as effectively as the timbales.

Now as to the function of these various instruments. It would require many, many pages to score examples and give instructions on the manipulation of these "traps." A very excellent book on the subject is "Latin-American Rhythms for the Drummer" by Phil Rale, published by Remick Music Corporation, price $1.00. Your dealer can easily obtain it for you. Here you will find photos and instructions as well as the rudiments required, plus many examples of authentic rhythms. When I say authentic, I mean, at least, practical. It would require intense study and "feel" to secure the effects the native instrumentalists do so easily. Our best bet is to simulate these effects in the best and most practical way. The above mentioned book will enable us to do this. There are several cardinal rules for the rhythm section. First, be subtle; nice and easy, in a lazy, detached manner. While the part should be followed for rests, stops and so forth, a good deal of ad-libbing is called for. The maracas, claves, gourd and cowbell are the "persistent" rhythmists, the timbale player is the "prima-donna" who can add color and effect by ad-lib patterns, BUT he must know what he is doing, and by studying and practicing from the aforementioned book he can soon do a creditable job.

Don't "Clown"

I notice a tendency on the part of rhythm sections to "clown around," and by so doing spoil the entire Cuban effect. Take it seriously. Work for soft underlying persistent rhythm, and the results will intrigue your audience. On a regular rhumba it produces a fine effect to start with the rhythm only for 8 or 16 bars, nice and soft, and then bring in the band.

The Rale method also gives excellent illustrations of the rhythmic structure of the beguine, samba, conga, etc., and should be carefully studied. Latin-American music is becoming increasingly popular, and the drummer is most important in proper interpretation of this music form. I have found the study of this type of drumming very, very interesting, and my students have had a lot of fun working it out.

"Ya Gotta Read"

Again we find the necessity of the drummer learning to read well and accurately. While I have mentioned the lazy, ad-lib, etc., obviously the rhythms must also be precise. If drum students would only learn that the key to smart, intelligent improvising is a good musical background and a thorough knowledge of their instruments! Some of these Latin-American rhythms are hard to read "at sight," or, rather I should say, hard to play at sight. The better the reader, the easier it is for him to work out the real effects.

It's Worth the Effort

I am sure of one thing. It is definitely worth the time, money and study to secure the Cuban type instruments and learn how to play them.

The results are always worthwhile. Don't be afraid of it. Even the simple things go over big with an audience, and I am sure you will enjoy the work as well. A few sectional rehearsals of the rhythm section will help a lot. It may be necessary to add a player or two to the section. Timbales, claves, maracas, gourd and cowbell would call for five players, and you might need the timpanist and bass drummer, so select several from other sections to fill in. Put these substitutes on claves, gourd and cowbell. Keep your drummers on timbales and maracas. Just a little coaching will bring out the best effects on the gourd, claves and cowbell, but the timbales and maracas players should be as skilled as possible, particularly the timbale player. The point I wish to stress is that although all this may sound complicated, it can be done in a simple, effective way. Like any other skill it becomes more complex if you really want to go into it, and you may want to, for it is pretty interesting.

March-April 1950

How To Play the Marimba

Part III

James Dutton

THE most important concern in the first few marimba lessons is probably the problem of wrist control. A habit that will seriously limit the student's progress will become set if rigidity is allowed to take the place of controlled tension. Other points (such as hitting incorrect notes) can be overlooked until suppleness has been developed in *both* wrists. Practice Exercise 1 with this in mind. Play in all keys: C, C♯, D, E♭, etc.

Try the scale exercise, No. 2. Limiting this exercise to one octave will make it easier to handle for the very young beginner. This will be an effective exercise if special attention is given to the natural triplet accents. Make them sound the same with either hand. It is necessary that all major and minor scales be practiced—the above exercise and others of your own invention should be used for this. To gain the maximum effectiveness, try playing each scale twice consecutively without a mistake before proceeding to the next one.

Try the arpeggio exercise. Limit to one octave if necessary in beginning.

If one wrist needs more attention than the other, play the exercise with that hand only. Strike each note 2, 3, or 4 times if more emphasis is desired.

First it is advisable to work on all the scales and arpeggios before attempting the single stroke roll of the marimba. This will bring about the properly developed wrist control which is necessary before an evenly controlled roll can be accomplished. The roll is the most difficult technic to master. The discussion of it follows in the next lesson.

More Exercises

This list of 20 technical problems is suggested as additional exercise material.

1. Major scales.
2. Natural minor scales.
3. Harmonic minor scales.
4. Melodic minor scales.
5. Major arpeggios (c e g).
6. Minor arpeggios (c e♭ g).
7. Diminished arpeggios (c e♭ g♭).
8. Augmented arpeggios (c e g♯).
9. Major triad with major seventh arpeggios (c e g b).
10. Major triad with minor seventh arpeggios (c e g b♭).
11. Major triad with diminished seventh arpeggios (c e g b♭♭).
12. Minor triad with major seventh arpeggios (c e♭ g b).
13. Minor triad with minor seventh arpeggios (c e♭ g b♭).
14. Minor triad with diminished seventh arpeggios (c e♭ g b♭♭).
15. Diminished triad with major seventh arpeggios (c e♭ g♭ b).
16. Diminished triad with minor seventh arpeggios (c e♭ g♭ b♭).
17. Diminished triad with diminished seventh arpeggios (c e♭ g♭ b♭♭).
18. Augmented triad with major seventh arpeggios (c e g♯ b).
19. Augmented triad with minor seventh arpeggios (c e g♯ b♭).
20. Augmented triad with diminished seventh arpeggios (c e g♯ b♭♭).

Master the above, and most of your 2-mallet facility will have been achieved.

THE TIMPANIST

EDWARD M. METZENGER

The timpanist of the orchestra and band is an important member of the group, and should be very carefully trained for this position. It is not an easy task to produce a good timpani player, for several reasons. First, in those cases where the school band leader must do the teaching, it is a pretty tough job, unless he has had some private instruction on the instruments; and secondly, there is not very much good instruction material published on timpani.

Must Know Instruments

As hand tuned timpani are practically obsolete, we will speak only of machine, or pedal, timpani. The student should first understand the mechanical principles of the kind of drums he uses. That is, he should understand what happens when the pedal is depressed or raised, so that he can visualize the mechanical operation. This is important in proper adjustment, so that easy tuning can be had.

Next, he should understand fully the heads on the instruments, and by this I mean he should be carefully taught that the heads are calfskin, left in the transparent state to produce the utmost resonance; the necessity of a "collar," or pull-down, over the edges of the bowls to provide sufficient slack for tuning; how to re-set the heads when they become too tight; how the heads react to temperature changes, i.e., a damp cold or a damp heat will cause them to loosen, a dry cold or dry heat will cause them to tighten; why the necessity of never loosening the heads clear down when the drums are put away, and all other pertinent facts concerning the physical makeup of the timpani.

The size of the timpani is important if best results are to be obtained. In symphonic work we use four timpani, and for this I recommend as the best sizes 32, 29, 26, and 24-inch drums. Some use 30, 28, 25, and 23-inch drums, which are also good.

In those cases when only two drums can be had, I believe the 29-inch and 26-inch would be the best choice, with the standard 28-inch and 25-inch next. If you already have a 28-inch and 25-inch set, the addition of a 30-inch drum would help a lot, as it is becoming very difficult to try to play modern timpani parts on two timpani. In some cases, it is, of course, impossible. Some notes have to be left out. In the case of the standard 28-inch and 25-inch drums, the range is from F to F (F to C on the large, B♭ to F on the small kettle).

The quality of the low F on the large kettle is not good. The head surface is not large enough to give it solidity, and under power it is "flabby" sounding, and the F♯ and G are not too good when played *forte*. The quality of the tones from the small kettle are pretty good, although the high F is apt to sound "stuffy" and stiff due to the head's tightness in producing this tone. For this reason I recommended above the 29-inch and 26-inch sizes where but two drums are used (playing range same as 28- and 25-inch). I realize that in many cases for budget reasons only two drums can be had, but the director should always aim to have at least three, and, better, four timpani. The better university bands are fast realizing the necessity for a complete set as their playing repertoire widens.

Heads and Sticks Important

The timpani must have good, live heads, for the heads are the tone producing medium. Don't buy cheap heads! Get the best ones obtainable from a recognized maker of good heads. Then impress on the player that a set of good heads is expensive and must be taken care of. Then select good sticks. I see many timpanists in school bands trying to get along with one pair of "dog-eared" sticks. That certainly cannot bring good results.

Either ball end or disc (cart-wheel) sticks are acceptable. The heads should be good wool felt, firm enough to produce or "pull" a good tone from the drums. You can play s o f t passages better, strangely enough, with a fairly firm stick than with the soft, fluffy type, for the sticks must have firm heads to bring out the tone. Control the volume with your wrists! Several pairs are necessary for good results, and many timpanists have five or six pairs including one pair with wooden heads (for special effects) at hand to produce the best possible effects in good timpani playing.

There are several methods of holding the sticks, but I am convinced that the best way is as follows. The stick is held about four inches from the butt end with the thumb and forefinger, the remaining fingers curled around the stick, and the thumb on the *top* of the stick, *not* on the side of the stick as in holding xylophone mallets. Both sticks are held the same. The thumb on top of the shaft of the stick is very important in producing a good blow, and in dynamic control from *pp* to *ff*. Many players hold the sticks as xylophone mallets are held, thumbs on the side of stick, but I am convinced that the best results are not obtainable with this grip.

To produce good tone on timpani calls for much practice in proper blow production. Timpanists speak of "pulling" or "drawing" tone from the drums, and by this they mean that the proper strike, a quick elastic blow, tends to produce a good, round tone. These things are why, if at all possible, the young timpanist should study privately with a professional, for many of these factors are extremely difficult to write down, but easier to demonstrate.

Sound Your "A"

Let's see, however, if we can't help the band leader who must teach timpani. As I mentioned before, there isn't a lot of instructional material available. The Saul

Goodman method is a recent and good method. The Ludwig and Ludwig Timpani Instructor is good. The Seitz Method is good, but I believe has been discontinued, and is possibly out of print. There is a Carl E. Gardner method that is good, in fact, all of the available methods are satisfactory. There is always one big headache among students of timpani, and that is *tuning.* Obviously, there is nothing more important than the tuning in playing timpani; obviously, too, the better natural (or developed) ear the player has, the easier it becomes to tune well.

Provide the student with an A tuning fork or accurate pitch pipe, and start him to learn the tone A. He should carry the fork or pipe with him at all times, and sound this A many times a day. Then he should start sounding the A vocally, checking with the fork until he can sound A at any time. This gives him a starting point to begin hearing intervals. It will take a little time, but persistence will reward the patient ones.

When this is well in hand, start on the intervals, using the fourth and fifth to get started. Then work on all intervals, until the student can hear and tune rapidly and accurately. There is no short-cut method. The better the ear, the better the tuning. Harmony and ear-training is a great aid in developing a "crack" timpanist. The above listed books will give photographs and instructions on the method of "flipping" the head with the finger, and lightly tapping the head with the stick to test pitch.

At the same time the ear-training is started, the study of stick technic and the roll can be started as well. The successful timpanist must have a fine, well controlled roll, and this takes arduous, concentrated practice to play correctly. The timpani roll consists of even *single strokes* to produce sustentation. The speed of the roll varies to some extent with the pitch of the drum. For example, the roll is slower on the low F than it is on the C above. The goal here is to set the head in vibration, and keep it vibrating at the speed it starts; thus, as you can see, the head will vibrate in a slower wave on the low F than it does on the C above, and the roll is slower. On the high F, a much faster roll is required.

However, at first, evenness of the roll is the goal. This can be practiced on a pillow, to develop the wrists, or on a cane bottomed chair where there is a little give, and then on the timpani. Careful attention is given to rolls in all dynamics from *ppp* to *fff* and *crescendo* and *decrescendo,* watching that the evenness of sound is the same, especially in the *crescendo* and *decrescendo.*

The methods listed above give explanatory and practice material on roll production.

Learn all "Fingerings"

The instruction books give exercises and parts from standard compositions, which will provide quite a little practice material. Study it all carefully. Some of the exercises are extremely difficult to play with good tone and clean sticking (or fingering). Cross stickings are used sparingly in actual playing, but work them all out as they might be needed. Watch dynamic markings carefully, for they are extremely important to the timpanist.

Rhythm

In addition to all the aforementioned requirements, the timpanist must acquire a faultless sense of rhythm. There can be no rhythmic hesitancy here. The timpanist must be sure of himself. He dare not "sneak" along on a difficult rhythmic passage, for even his lightest *pp* is distinctly audible, and he can't get by with anything but perfection. The student must have a thorough understanding of all rhythms, and how to count them. Do not allow guessing in this respect. It must be absolutely perfect. The young timpanist should always be rhythm conscious, and curious about any rhythm he hears. He should acquaint himself with all the seldom-used rhythms, for he never knows when he will run up against one of them and turn red with embarrassment over his inability to properly play his part.

Study Music!

While we mentioned earlier that there are not too many timpani instruction methods, there are enough to help the timpanist with the fundamentals of his art. From this point on, all the field of music is open to the aspiring timpanist. Any study in the field of music will help him to be a better timpani player. As mentioned, harmony and ear training is almost endless in its possibilities. Arranging, score reading, listening to records, watching other timpanists and conductors at concerts,— any of this type of study is of great value. It is these things that help any instrumentalist learn to interpret the part at hand. It is this extra "know-how" that distinguishes the top flight timpanist from a "tub-thumper."

My parting advice is to choose your timpanist carefully. He must be made to realize that he has a tough job ahead of him. I have had the pleasure of playing under most of the world's renowned conductors, and I know the requirements of these top-flight men. They expect the timpanist to know all phases of his craft thoroughly and well, and will not tolerate second grade work. The teacher can never tell but that one of his students might finally reach the major symphony orchestra, as many school band players have, and so he is responsible for giving the best instruction he can.

If you develop a talent as far as you can, don't be ashamed to admit it. Send him where he can go on, and should he reach the top, he will be ever grateful to you.

HOW TO PLAY THE MARIMBA

Part IV

JAMES DUTTON

THE marimba roll is accomplished by striking the keyboard rapidly with a series of alternating single strokes. The method of producing the roll on the xylophone and marimba is identical. Glockenspiel and vibraharp players do not need to learn this technique because of the sustaining power of the metal keyboard.

Mastering the roll is one of the biggest and most important problems confronting the beginning marimbist. Without this technique sustained or legato playing of any kind is impossible. There is no rule governing the use of the roll. Tempo and phrasing will give the main indications for application. The stroke roll as on the drum does not exist for marimba. The number of strokes is of no concern. The value of the note must be fulfilled. Make the roll even but not measured.

Exercises

To develop the roll:

1. Begin a long series of alternating strokes very slowly, gradually increase speed until tension begins in the wrists, and gradually decrease speed to original starting point. This exercise should sound somewhat similar to a long freight train starting up from a dead stop, gaining speed, etc. *It must be done smoothly. Both hands must sound the same.* Practice this on the notes of the C scale for three to five minutes at a time.

2. Practice playing a steady roll for four counts on each note throughout major scales: (a) begin all rolls with the right hand, (b) begin all rolls with the left hand, (c) practice legato playing. Connect the rolls when moving from bar to bar by starting rolls with the right hand when moving to the right, and with the left hand when moving to the left. Arpeggios and octave jumps provide excellent patterns for this.

When playing with three or four mallets, the roll is accomplished in the same manner as with two—by alternating the hands. The technique of playing with three or four mallets should be introduced early in the marimbist's training. This will be the subject of our next article.

Marimba Repertory List

A complete list of over 300 published selections for marimba, xylophone and vibraharp will soon be available; also, lists of transcribable material, method books, collections and ensemble repertory. Write the Instrumentalist if interested!

Original Work for Marimba

A *Sonata for Marimba and Piano* by Eloise Matthies has just been completed. It had its first performance by the composer at a National Composer's Symposium at Cincinnati on April 20, 1950.

"IT'S ALL IN THE HEAD"

JOHN P. NOONAN

THERE have been a number of questions directed to this column concerning drum heads and their care. I will try and make some points about heads in a crisp, concise manner, based on my personal experience in the "field of calfskin."

Kinds of Heads to Use

1. *Snare drum. Batter (beating) side.*

Buy medium weight white heads for orchestra or concert drum, medium heavy to heavy for parade drums. Do not use transparent heads for batter side use. They are not as tough as the white calf and have too much "ring." It is usually better to buy heads already tucked on hoops. If they arrive pulled out of shape, do not force them on shell. Dampen the head thoroughly on both sides with room temperature water until head is soft, mop off water, place on shell. Put on hoop and rods and pull head down about one-half inch and allow to dry for twenty-four hours.

2. *Snare drum. Snare side.*

Buy thin transparent snare side heads for concert, medium for parade drum. Follow above rules as regards tucking and procedure if head arrives pulled out of shape.

3. *Bass drum.*

Buy medium to medium heavy white calf heads for bass drum 28″ to 32″, heavy weight for 32″ to 36″, extra heavy for above 36". Above rules as to placing on drum.

4. *Timpani.*

Transparent first grade heads for timpani. Be careful here. Always buy factory tucked heads, the best grade obtainable. If they arrive tight on hoop and produce a "ping" to the snap of the finger, they must be stretched to allow slack for low notes. Dampen thoroughly as in case of snare drum batter head, place on kettle and pull down 3/4" evenly all the way around. Allow to dry slowly for 24 hours. Watch this carefully. The head *must* have slack or "collar" at all times.

Heat and Humidity

It's the condition of the atmosphere that affects drum heads.

A dry heat will cause heads to tighten.

A dry cold will cause heads to tighten.

A damp heat will cause heads to loosen.

A damp cold will cause heads to loosen.

Thus the section of the country has some bearing on the condition of drum heads and their care.

Dry climates. Here heads have a tendency to be tight and become tighter. Do not loosen drums after use (except for long storage, then only a turn or two), and watch them closely. If they "climb" up the shell or kettle, dampen thoroughly and pull down as described before to restore and maintain slack. This may be necessary three or four times a year.

Damp climates. Here heads have a tendency to become soft and pull down too fast. Loosen the heads several turns after playing to allow them to shrink a little. If the air is extremely damp, it may be necessary to retuck heads, i.e., soak heads off flesh hoops and retuck to take up excessive slack.

Cardinal Rules

In general I think the best all around rule is to leave drum heads alone as much as possible. In Illinois where I live I handle my own drum heads as follows:

Snare drum. Tension heads to suit, then leave them alone as much as possible. I do *not* loosen after each use unless damp weather has caused me to tighten them way up, then I let down to where I started.

Bass drum. Same as above.

Timpani. Have approximately 3/4" pull down over edge of kettles and maintain it. During winter season I may have to dampen heads thoroughly and pull down a little due to drums being kept in dry, hot room. I leave heads under tension at all times. Large kettle tuned to A, small kettle to D, to maintain "collar," or "pull down."

Following this procedure I have very little trouble with heads, and haven't broken a head in many a moon (where's some wood!). It so happens I dislike dirty drum heads, so I clean them. How? Soap (Ivory) and water. I use nothing else, do it just as I wash my hands. Use soap and water, rinse off soap and dry by gently mopping off water, then (unlike my hands) I let them set for 24 hours before using. There is one thing I have noticed and that is the less you fool with drum heads, the better they behave.

You can easily find out if a drum head has become too tight. Loosen the rods clear down on drum or kettle drum. When all tension is off the head should "ripple" and be dead to the snap of the finger against it. If this doesn't happen, and the head is tight and produces a "ping" to the finger, it has no slack and should be dampened and pulled down.

Tighten Evenly

I hear much discussion about whether to go around the drum or across the drum to the opposite rod, etc. I don't think it makes any difference. No one ever proved to me that it did. I (through habit) go clockwise around the drum, a quarter turn on each rod and try to pull the head down as evenly as possible (the *evenly* is the pertinent word here, not how you do it). The selection of proper weight heads for a certain drum can be, and often is, a fixation with drummers. I admit certain weight heads work better for certain individuals, depending on size of drum, purpose, weight of sticks, touch, etc., but I don't believe in worrying too much about it. Select the heads as outlined earlier in this article for good all around results. I tell my "professional worriers" to spend the time they waste worrying about heads in *practicing*, and they will find a lot of these troubles disappear.

Change Heads How Often?

Well, drum heads will last for years under ordinary care and use. I don't think anyone can set a definite time to change. Therefore, it is not altogether "It's all in the head," as per the title of this article, but "Some of it is in the ear." When the timpani sounds false and "tired," and the drums sound flabby and not snappy, then it is time to think about new heads. It is up to the individual drummer or director to listen and determine this. Ordinary good musical judgment will do the trick.

Survey of Mallet Instruments

James Dutton

Last July we visited exhibits of mallet-played instruments shown in connection with the annual music industry trade show in Chicago sponsored by the National Association of Music Merchants. All the makes of marimbas, xylophones, vibra-harps and bells were shown to good advantage, in a variety of styles to suit every purpose and pocketbook.

Peripole Products offers rhythm bells with 20 bars and a chromatic scale C-G, mounted in a Keratol carrying case, for $16.50. These bells, without the case, are priced at $8.50. Others, varying in size from 8 to 25 bars, are priced from $1.25 to $11.50. All have bronze finished bars, made from finely tempered steel and stamped with the scale letters. One set of mallets is included. These bells are especially desirable for the very young beginner as they are sturdy and easy to carry.

Leedy & Ludwig "Challenger" marimba has tapered bars for speed

Leedy & Ludwig "Challenger" marimba has tapered bars for speed

Deagan "Performer" vibra-harp, polished aluminum bars, wide pedal

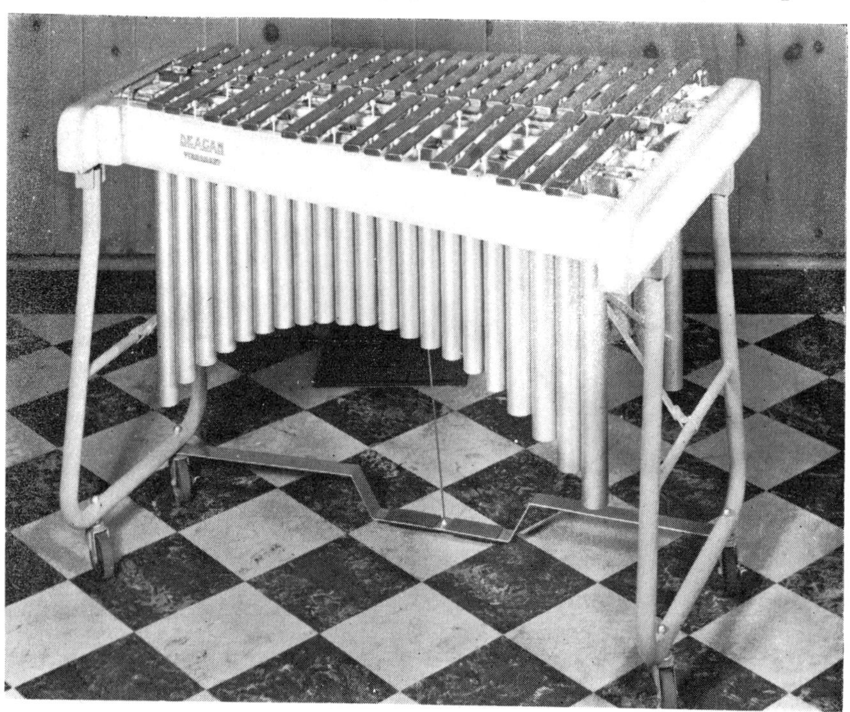

Jen-Co Musical Products makes a 3-octave xylophone, No. 625-L, which can be removed from the legs and set on a table if desired, at $57.50, and a 3½-octave xylophone (F to C), No. 628, at $240, which has a portable folding stand and detachable aluminum resonators. The bars are 1½" x ⅞". The Leedy & Ludwig model 5634 is a 4-octave xylophone (C to C). Bars are 1⅝" x ⅞". The price is $435, and fibre hand carrying cases are available.

Marimbas

For beginning marimbists, 2½-octave (C to F) instruments are available. The Musser "Prep" marimba, Model 20, at $95, has 1⅜" x ⅝" bars, removable resonators and strong tubular legs which snap on and off. Others, which have bars of Honduras rosewood, include Musser's "Prep Deluxe," Model 20D, at $150, with arched tone pipes and permanently mounted keyboard. J. C. Deagan, Inc., presents Model 333, the "Studette," priced at $105. The resonators are of tempered aluminum. The "Studette" is made easily portable by the carrying handle provided, and by removing the legs and placing them in clips provided between the resonators. Jen-Co shows model 634, with all aluminum resonators and portable type folding stand at $110. The "Juniorimba," Leedy & Ludwig's model 5649, has 1¼″ bars, ¾″ thick, and is priced at $99.50.

In 3-octave marimbas (F to F), Jen-Co's model 630 is a good number for the semi-professional or young amateur looking for an instrument between the prices of the beginner's and the concert models. The stand is a portable folding type (bars do not come off). The price is $240. Deagan's model 410, the "Wellington," is equipped with hinged end frames which lock in position when folded, and so is easy to move. The "Wellington" is listed at $295. Leedy & Ludwig's "Marimbanette," No. 5623-A, has bar rails and resonator frames which fold at the center for easy moving. The price of this marimba is $275, and fibre hand carrying cases are available. The bars on each of the three models described above are of Honduras rosewood.

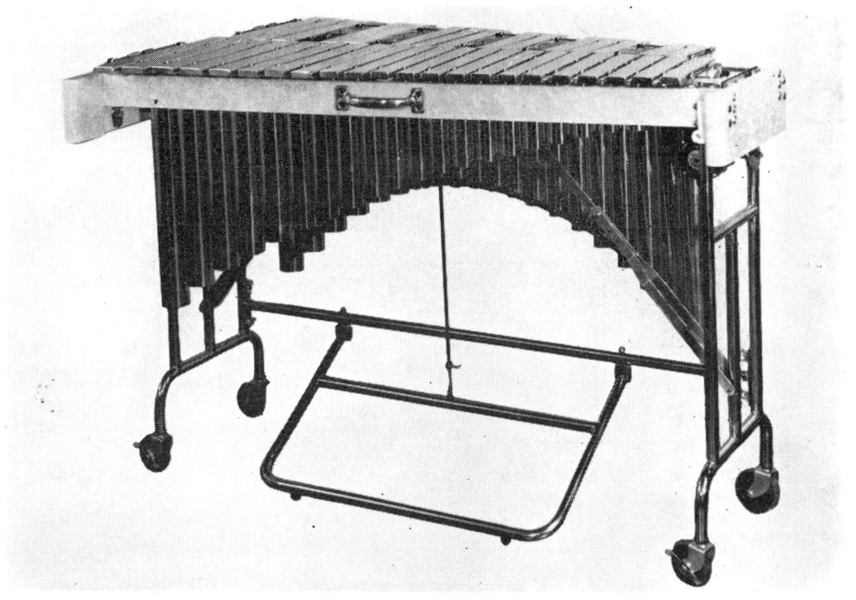

Jen-Co model "620" 3-octave vibra-bells feature heavy, rounded bars

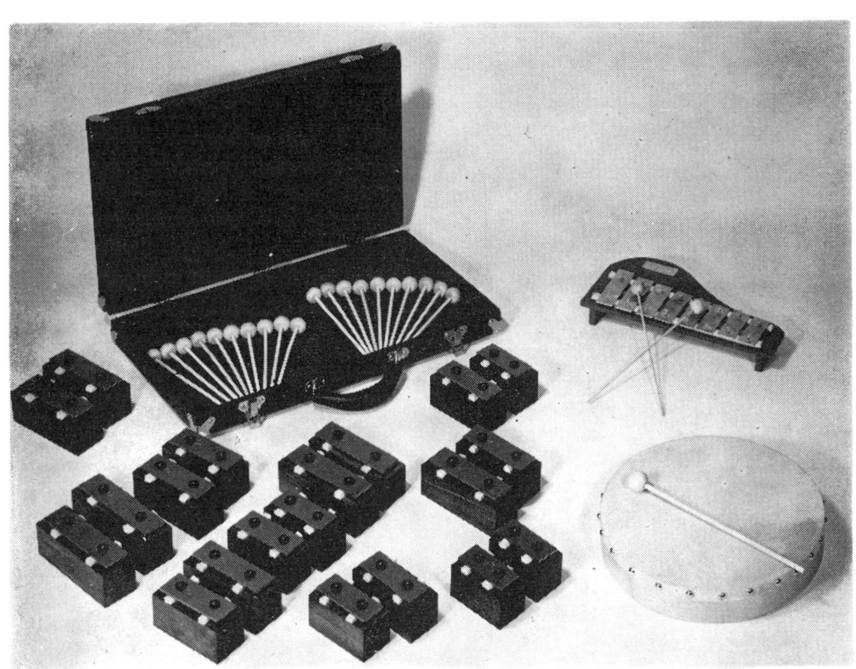

Peripole tuned resonator bells, junior metalophone, rhythm drum.

Above, the 1950 class of the marimba department, Northwestern U. Contra-bass in center designed by class director, Clair Omar Musser. Monster instrument has been heard over ABC network; used by Stokowski in concert, when it replaced ten string basses. Marimba courses are accredited in many universities; popular in schools.

Four Octaves

In 4-octave marimbas (C to C), Leedy & Ludwig's "Challenger," No. 5640, at $399.50, features a new bar design on the top keyboard with increased length and tapered ends for faster execution and reduction of mallet reach. The concert size bars of Honduras rosewood are 7/8" thick and of three widths—2 1/8", 1 7/8", and 1 5/8". The grill front is of modern design. The frame of Jen-Co's model 632, at $390, divides in the center and folds in two parts. The "Windsor," made by Musser, model 30, has graduated bars, 2" x 15/16" to 1 3/8" x 5/8". The tone pipes, which are mitered and arched, break in the middle for convenient assembly. The "Windsor" is priced at $395. The larger "Century" also by Musser, model 100, at $575, is unusual in its curved parabolic end contour bars. They are 2 1/4" x 15/16" to 1 5/8" x 3/4". Rails are hinged, and the tone-pipes are hinged in the center to fold for convenient packing. One of the other good 4-octave models shown at the convention was Deagan's No. 490, the "Imperial Bolero," of blonde mahogany. This marimba, priced at $645, has Honduras rosewood bars graduated from 2 1/4" x 15/16" to 1 5/8" x 3/4" in size. Mounting rails are hinged in the middle, and resonators separate into two sections each for easy dis-assembly and transportation.

The 4 1/2-octave (A to C) marimba made by Musser, the "Canterbury," model 500, has a temperature control to assure perfect resonance, balance and tonal clarity at all times. This impressive instrument is priced at $965.

Bass Marimba

Musser's contra-bass is a unique marimba, with a physical register of 1 1/2 octaves, and musical register of 2 1/2 octaves through compound octave tuning and resonance. This is used as a real bass instrument and is equivalent in volume to several string basses.

Vibra-Bells

Jen-Co Musical Products has several electric vibra-bells. Nos. 606 and 612 are 2 1/2-octave (C to F) vibes with bars 1 1/4" wide. No. 606, which has folding legs with rubber crutch tips, is priced at $235. No. 612 has arched resonators. The price, including bar covers and mallets, is $295. Musser's 2 1/2-octave "Prep" vibe, No. 25, has bars 1 1/2" x 1/2"; 30-second assembly time is claimed for this $295 vibe.

Resonators on the Deagan 3-octave vibra-harps are mounted in live, shockproof rubber. The "Performer," No. 510, listed at $395, has polished aluminum bars 1/2" thick, and from 1 3/8" to 1 1/4" wide, a special lightweight 110-volt AC motor, and a wide pedal bar for good damper control. The "Imperial Nocturne," Deagan's No. 590, has durable non-reflecting gold-finished bars, two 110-volt AC beltless drive motors (one for each pulsator shaft). The 1/2"-thick bars are from 1 1/2" to 2" wide, octavely tuned. The instrument is listed at $775.

In 3-octave vibra-bells (F to F), Jen-Co 615, with 1 3/4" x 1/4" bars, is $360; No. 618, with uniform 1 1/2" x 1/2" rounded bars, is $425, white or black pearl covered; and No. 620, with heavy rounded bars, 1/2" x 2", is $525. Leedy & Ludwig's 3-octave "Challenger" vibraphone, No. 5646, at $495, is distinguished for its extra "booster" resonators. These are three additional resonator tubes under lower sharp bars and five additional

DIMENSIONS AND WEIGHT OF INSTRUMENTS NOTED

Model	Height (inches)	Length (inches)	Width (inches)	Weight (pounds)
XYLOPHONES:				
Jen-Co 625-L			Not given	
Jen-Co 628	34	53	31	Not given
Leedy 5634			Not given	
MARIMBAS:				
(2½-octave)				
Musser 20	33	36	27	22
Musser 20D	33	36	27	24
Deagan 333	32	36	25	23
Jen-Co 634			Not given	
Leedy 5649	30	35	22	18
(3-octave)				
Jen-Co 630	34	45½	30	65
Deagan 410	32⅜	47	15¼ to 30	62
Leedy 5623-A	32	48	29	49
(4-octave)				
Leedy 5640	33	66	30	83
Jen-Co 632	34	67	34½	Not given
Musser 30	35	68	14 to 29½	70
Musser 100	35	70	15 to 31	110
Deagan 490	33½	72	16 to 32½	149
(4½-octave)				
Musser 500	36½	81	16 to 34	190
(Bass)				
Musser	65		Not given	
VIBES:				
(2½-octave)				
Jen-Co 606			Not given	
Jen-Co 612			Not given	48
Musser 25	32	39	27½	40
(3-octave)				
Jen-Co 615 }				
Jen-Co 618 }			Not given	
Jen-Co 620 }				
Leedy 5646	33	46	30	86
Deagan 510	33⅞	45¼	16¼ to 30	74
Deagan 590	34¾	53	16 to 30½	143
Musser 35	34	53	15 to 29	80
Musser 75	33½	57	14½ to 29½	125
(3½-octave)				
Musser 775			Not given	

MANUFACTURERS

J. C. Deagan, Inc. .... 1770 W. Berteau Ave., Chicago 13
G. C. Jenkins Co. (Jen-Co) .... Decatur, Illinois
Leedy & Ludwig .... Elkhart, Indiana
Musser Marimbas, Inc. .... 5115 Ravenswood Ave., Chicago 40
Peripole Products, Inc. .... 2917 Avenue R, Brooklyn, N.Y.

tubes under lower natural bars. The bars, all of which are 1¼″ wide, are ½″ thick. The grill front is similar to that used on the "Challenger" marimba.

The Musser 3-octave vibes are the "Windsor," model 35, bars 1½″ x ½″, and the "Century," model 75, bars 2¼″ x ½″ to 1½″ x ½″. These are priced at $495 and $785, respectively. Each of these incorporates self-aligning shafts and a well engineered dampening mechanism.

The "Canterbury," Model 775 is a 3½″-octave (middle C to F) vibraharp made by Musser. This is the first standardized vibe of this musical register. It has automatic tremolo control, both by foot and manual hand switch. This feature makes possible a variable-speed vibrato. The instrument has a starter booster to attain tremolo speed immediately, and a pilot light. It is priced at $1495.

The excellent and wide selection shown is gratifying evidence of growing interest in these instruments.

September 1950

THE BEGINNING DRUMMER

JOHN P. NOONAN

"All's well that* starts *well" is a good slogan for the beginning of a student's drumming career

STARTING a drummer from "scratch" is a problem I've been asked about a lot. What books to use, the pad, type of sticks, and so forth. I am glad to pass on a few tips picked up in my own teaching experience.

First, the materials required. In elementary methods any of the following will serve, as well as many others, depending upon the teacher's personal preference:

1. Rubank Elementary Drum Method
2. Haskell Harr Method No. 1
3. Gardner Method Part 1
4. Progressive Studies for Snare Drum—Gardner
5. Reading Lessons for 1st Year Drummer—Gardner
6. Music Educators Basic Method —Berryman

For the other materials:

1. A good practice pad, $3.50 to $4.00
2. 2B drum sticks
3. Music blank book
4. Music folder (9x12 band folio)

A good pad is recommended. I notice many teachers feel the cheapest pad will serve, but I do not agree. Cheap pads have a poor rubber beating surface, no resonance, hard action, and a hard sound. Buy the best. The drum sticks of the 2B style are usually okay, but if the student has small hands, use a 2A or similar stick, which is smaller in diameter. The music blank book will be used from the first, so have the student buy one of about fifty pages. Then secure a regular band music cardboard music folio, concert size, with pocket to carry the instruction method and blank book. The folio discourages rolling up the drum book and putting it in the pocket, resulting in a very soggy and dog-eared treatise on the art of drumming.

Down to Business

The first lesson should be a relaxed and easy one, to gain the student's confidence and not build any mental barriers about the difficulty of the skill.

Although all drum books contain the rudiments of music, I have found that it is better to start by using the notebook. Start with common time and write out the note valuations, rests, and so forth. Then immediately show the student how to write notes and assign him to copy what you have written. In most cases the beginner grasps this quickly, and at the first lesson can tap out a page of simple notes.

Now, the all-important mechanical phase of the art is started. First the stick grip. This must be very carefully considered. In almost every case the drum methods show a stick grip that is impractical for band and orchestra drumming, but well adapted to the drum corps player. This, in my opinion, is certainly not the stick grip to use in *starting* a student. Remember that habit is a forceful influence; start, therefore, to build a habit pattern that insures the correct wrist and arm motion. In methods where the field drum grip is illustrated, I cross it out immediately with a heavy pencil and write "*Disregard*" over it.

I stress this point always, and keep repeating it in this column. I see evidence of the results of using the field drum grip at contests and among students; as I observe professional players I am thoroughly convinced that, since drumming technic is a mechanical skill, this grip problem is a most vital one.

I attach so much importance to it that we are reproducing here pictures by courtesy of the Knapp School of Percussion. These pictures, posed by Donald Roy Knapp, show a good, practical stick grip for all types of drumming in the band and orchestra. Study this grip carefully and insist that the student use it. Watch any departure (and there will be many) from this grip. You may rest assured that such attention will pay dividends.

Step-by-Step

After the grip is explained, start the first exercises slowly and carefully, and proceed through the various whole, half, and quarter note forms. Opinions differ as to when to start the roll, i.e., the double-stroke roll. If one wants to be pretty technical, all drum beats narrow down to single and double strokes. The double-stroke closed roll is the "long tones" of other instruments, the sustaining characteristic of the drum, so start it at once. But a word of caution here. Start it slow, start it evenly. Write out the fundamentals in quarter note form, as in Example 1. Take it as slow

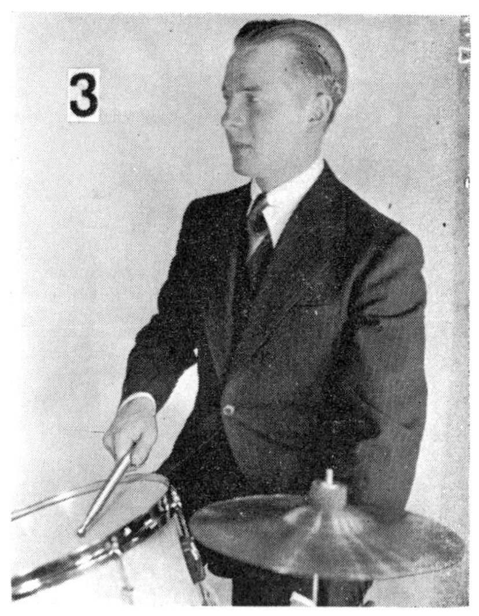

as necessary, starting sometimes with left hand, and gradually work it up to the notation of Ex. 2.

In the meantime, keep up the single stroke patterns as in the book, and have the student copy some of them in his note book. As soon as possible, write a simple street beat (just single taps will do), so that the student can read and play a phrase that means something to him rhythmically. Then invite him to write one each week as he progresses.

Introducing the Roll

So far no rolls have been introduced into the reading but part of each lesson is devoted to the double stroke roll until the bounce beat (or secondary beat) enters as speed is gained. Explain to the student that this practice of the double-stroke roll is a "must" as long as he plays the drum.

Then also (and this is extremely important) develop a roll of single strokes, to the highest point of efficiency possible, as in Ex. 3.

It is immediately apparent that we cannot play rapid, even double strokes unless we have clean, even single strokes; for the secondary, or bounce, beat must have a single stroke as its basis.

Good single strokes, fast and even, are the key to all rudiments. Don't let the student, therefore, "crush" out double-stroke rolls, but devote the first few lessons to single patterns. with the beginning work on slow single and double-stroke roll forms.

Right Stick Grip and Stroke

Photos 1, 2, and 3 show the grip of the right drum stick. Gripped between the thumb and first finger curved to meet the thumb, with a firm, but not tensioned grip. The second, third, and fourth fingers curved inward near the stick, using pressure of second finger only in the extreme forte passages; the butt end of stick extending just beyond the end of the center of the palm of the hand. Also illustrated is the flexible wrist action, using necessary movement of arm.

Left Stick Grip and Stroke

Photos 4, 5, and 6 show the grip of left drum stick. Gripped in the crotch of left hand, between thumb and first finger, with a firm, but not tensioned grip, and first and second fingers curved over, but not gripping the stick. Third and fourth fingers curved inward under the stick, with stick resting above first joint of third finger; the butt end of stick extending from crotch of hand, the same distance as in position of holding the right stick, to equal the balance of stroke and volume of both sticks. Also illustrated is the flexible wrist action, using necessary movement of arm, with the left stick following the wrist action, in a downward, upward side movement of the wrist.—From *Fundamentals of Modern Drumming*, by Roy C. Knapp.

Continuing with the Drummer

JOHN P. NOONAN

To continue with our young drummer, keep on with the single note patterns in the various rhythms, and be sure you stress a counting system, with each note accounted for. Also, encourage foot-tapping, as this will help develop the coordination required later in manipulating the foot pedal. Continue with the study and practice of the single and double stroke rolls, and insist that this be kept up, always stressing evenness of the strokes.

The next step, I believe, should be the flams. Most methods give the correct procedure with flams, so it will not be repeated here. The purpose of flams is to give a legato or broadening effect to drum strokes. Flams also lend a solidity to the drumming, and are extremely important. They must be done crisply and cleanly lest they "muddy" the sound of the rhythmic pattern in which they are used. Allow the student to play the open flam at first, the beat sounding two distinct syllables "fa-lam." Check stick positions carefully after each flam so that one stick is up, the other down, after each one. Finally, the flams sound one syllable "flam," very close to the principal note.

The closeness of the grace note to the principal note depends on the type of music, but generally speaking it should be played in the time value of the principal note, with the grace note as close as possible to the principal note. If flams are not done well, it would be best not to "clutter" up the rhythm with their use; thus they must be practiced with close attention to stick positions, and be done cleanly. It is obvious that the more rapidly one plays, the fewer the flams used. Most instruction books cover this adequately, and little trouble should be had here.

The drag or ruff can be taught next. Stick positions same as for flams. A rebound on a single grace note produces the two grace notes, with the opposite stick striking the principal note. The words go-to-bed can be used for the sound of the beat. This beat is a "drummism" and is highly characteristic of the snare drum. The two grace notes should be evenly spaced and very close to the principal note. At first the drags can be played "open" as in the case of the flams; later, closed down. Open drags can be used in military or street beats as desired. Some writers call the "open" beat a drag, and refer to the closed beat as the ruff. This is a good distinction and can be used to advantage in describing the beats.

By this time we are ready to start the stroke rolls, starting with the fives. I have had good results with the use of "frames" in producing the stroke rolls. For example, in the notation of Fig. I, Ex. 1, break down the eighths which are marked with rolls, and we have two sixteenths to serve as the primary strokes or frames for the five strokes, making our primary pattern, as in Ex. 2.

With rebounds added to these sixteenths tied over to the following eighths, we have five stroke rolls, as shown in Ex. 3. *Pre-Roll Studies for the First Year Drummer* by Carl E. Gardner, published by B. F. Wood, Boston, elaborates on the problems of Fig. I.

The stroke rolls' most effective use are as "trimmings" between beats, and again are very drummistic. The notations and frames for such use are shown in Ex. 4.

Be sure the "frames" are played hand to hand and exactly in time. Then with the *same hand motion* and count, the rebounds are added to produce the strokes. It is imperative that the *exact* number of strokes are played, for pressure or "digging" will destroy the number and result in a "smear."

For the seven, nine, thirteen and seventeen stroke rolls, use the same formula. First, break down the roll rate into sixteenths to produce the thirty-seconds in the roll, as in Fig. II, Ex. 1-4.

These illustrations are in 2/4 rhythm. In cut time, the frames are eighth notes, the roll valuations in sixteenths, as in Ex. 5-6.

To go further into this system, it would seem that every time we see the notation of Fig. I, Ex. 4, it would indicate a five stroke roll. Such notation, say at a standard march tempo, would sound close and well with five stroke rolls. But at a slower tempo, the fives would be too "open" and would not "sound" as rolls. Obviously, the slower the tempo the more strokes required to "fill" the above notation. To do this we add strokes to the "frames" to produce above fives, sevens or nines, in the manner of Fig. III.

This is advanced work and not important at this point, for in elementary teaching we can set our tempos to suit, and the first playing of the student is usually easy marches, so no difficulty is encountered at this point.

The tempo "set" for these stroke rolls should be one where clarity of the stroke roll is best. Actually it is, I suppose, impossible to produce a rebound as strong as the primary stroke. Some systems call this rebound a secondary stroke, producing the primary blow with the arm, the secondary blow with the wrist. In either case, the rebound (secondary) stroke will not be of the same force as the initial blow, so if it were practical to play all rolls single strokes (as on timpani, bells, etc.), the results would be better musically, but as the snare drum is inherently very staccato, we use double strokes (actually a stroke and rebound) to imitate sustentation.

So with this handicap to begin with, we must be careful to strive always for evenness in sound. I have been criticized, in the words of the estimable critics, for "making it sound pretty difficult to play the drum." Well, it *is* really difficult if

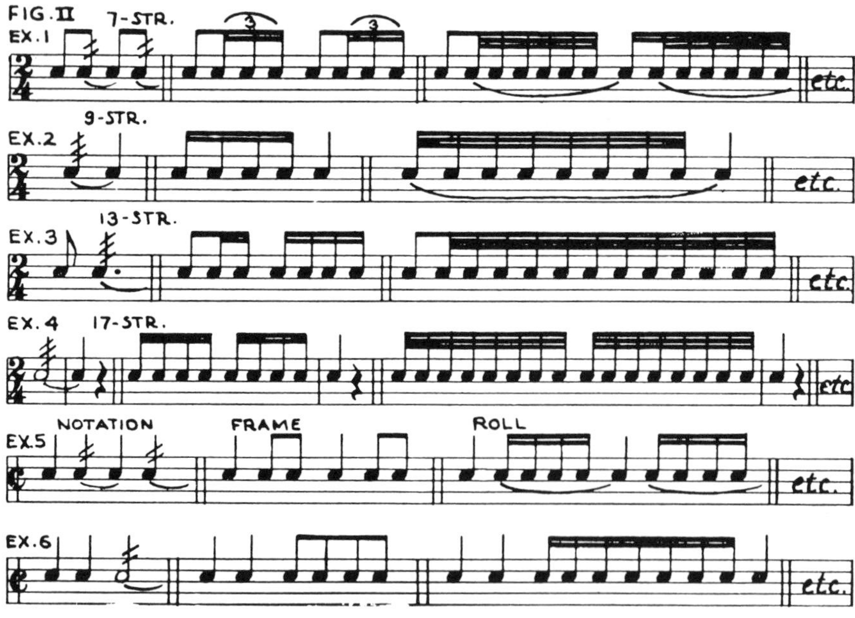

we aspire to do it well. It is extremely hard technically, and calls for a lot of practice if the student is to play musically. It is not difficult to grasp the idea, nor for that matter to teach, but like any other instrument, it requires a lot of perseverance and perspiration.

As regards the student's practice time, it is hard to set a definite length of time. An hour a day total will bring good results. If the student can spend more—good. If he becomes interested he will do it without prodding. I tell my students this, "You do not have the difficulty of pitch, big tone, and so forth, but your problems are similar. A good roll (long tones), rudiments (scales), and your rhythmic sense should be developed to the highest point possible. On top of this, anything you learn about music will help you immeasurably in becoming a fine drummer."

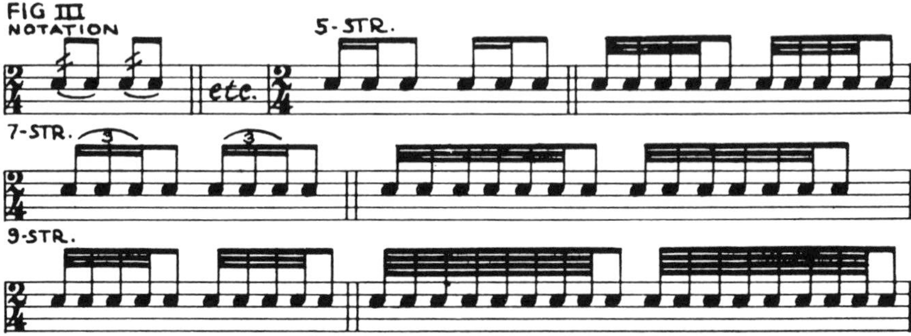

The Intermediate and Advanced DRUMMER

JOHN P. NOONAN

THE intermediate stage of a drum student's training is a difficult one. There aren't too many exercise methods for reading material of that grade. The average drum teacher has a little problem here in selecting materials that will suffice to bring the student gradually up to the advanced stage of learning.

Obviously, in the intermediate stage the student should learn all of the rudiments and their application, and as he nears the advanced classification. he should be given some theory and started on bells and/or xylophone. I have found a stumbling block here. A lot of young drummers are not interested in bells, timpani and the rest of "the business," and they definitely resist work along these lines.

I do not insist that they do it. If they are serious, it begins to dawn on them in a little while that they need this additional work, and once it is their own idea, the results are much better. I do not mean to imply that I am indifferent about this matter of the student's lack of interest in "tuned percussion." It seems to me that it is not good to insist on it, but rather to go along for awhile and see what happens.

Specialization in Order

Although some may not agree, it is my own opinion that it is extremely difficult to become an artist in the three branches of percussion, i.e. (1) snare drum, etc., (2) bells and xylophone, and (3) timpani. I have known quite a few who were very good at all three, but only a handful who could really qualify as expert in all classes. This is a natural situation because any one of the three is a full time job. Therefore, specialization in one field is the best answer, but with some attention also to the others. Thus in the intermediate and early advanced stages there is plenty of work for snare drum without anything else.

During the intermediate stage, when the student has worked out a few of the rudiments, is really the time to get after all of the rudiments and their application. At this point the student should be reading better and should have a pretty fair idea of the long roll, stroke rolls, flams and so forth. The teacher, therefore, can more easily explain the remaining rudiments and their place in music. Here is the point, in my opinion, to use the regular rudimental methods.

The Harr Book No. 2 continues with rudiments, the Moeller Book, "The Art of Drumming" by Burns Moore, and "Drumology" by A. V. Scott, are three books that can be used to excellent advantage here. These books outline all of the rudiments well and show how they are used. Care must be taken, however. that the student does not become a strict "rudiment mechanic." That is, he should not conceive every rhythmical grouping as a certain rudiment and let it go at that. This can be a dangerous habit resulting in stilted and unmusical playing of the snare drum.

Reading Big Factor

From this point on, it is a matter of securing additional reading material and constantly trying to improve the student's ability to read rapidly and accurately. I am listing herewith some books I have found useful in teaching:

1. The Straight System
   Book I Lesson File 2/4
   Book II Analysis 6/8 Time
   Book III Modern Syncopated Rhythms
2. Standard Drum Method—Podemski
3. Modern Drum Studies—Sternberg
4. Musical Drummer—Bellson Book II
5. Sensational Drum Method—Cole-Kessler
6. Wilcoxson Drum Method

These are a few that contain very good reading material. In addition to these there are many others of merit, and the student should go through as many as he can afford to buy, for in almost every instance there is something of value to be found in each one.

Swing, Too!

For the dance band approach, the "Swing Drumming Method" by W. F. Ludwig, Jr., is very good and contains some Latin-American work as well. The Krupa Method is very good, also. In the Latin-American field the "Latin-American Rhythms for the Drummer" by Phil Rale, and the "Humberto Morales Instructor for Latin-American Rhythms" are both good. (The Morales work is the more advanced of the two). There is a fine book called "Stick Control" by Geo. L. Stone, which is, as the name implies, a book helping to balance up the hands. It can be used right along with any instruction book.

In addition to all books, drum parts from numbers being used in the band or orchestra can be worked out carefully, and march books are well utilized for reading purposes.

For drum section use, the employment of duets, trios, ensembles, etc. are very good training materials. I don't know of a better way to develop a good drum section than to have them spend a lot of time on this work. It teaches them the all-important phases of counting rests, dynamic control, and so forth, and is time well spent in section development. It tends, also, to make one or more of the participants realize that they are weak and should get to work to be up with the others.

All solo material is good, if carefully worked out with the correct tempo and expression marks closely watched. The matter of "correct" tempo is a relative one for student use. Very often the metronome marking is given, but this does not mean it must be played at that speed by the student. It is something for him to work on with the indicated speed only a goal, rather than a "must."

"Pad Drummers"

Another important factor here is dynamics. I think most teachers agree that a practice pad is best for the great bulk of practicing, but I have noticed that many of my students have had one peculiar trait. They are "pad drummers." That is, they play twice as well on a pad as they do on a drum.

At first I thought it was merely an adjustment that would take care of itself, but I finally noticed another very important reason why this happens. It is a difference in the travel of the sticks. For example, on a 6½ x 14 concert drum in the average band, the stick heights from the head in the various degrees of volume isn't very much. In a *pp* the sticks leave the head, but about ½ inch; and at an *ff*, if they raise 8″—brother, you're loud enough! But this isn't true on a practice pad, for the sticks go higher relatively on a pad than they do on a drum. So it happens that when the change over to the drum is made, the player becomes "muscle-bound" trying to hold down the volume.

The answer here must be that some practice should be on the drum itself; but this isn't always practical, so the only other answer to it is to find out the approximate stick travel on the drum (depending on size) and practice considerably on the pad at these levels. This means that the *pp* is almost inaudible, but that is good. That is where it should be to sound just about right on the drum. We must realize that raising the sticks to eye-level for rudimental practice, while a fine mechanical exercise, is not the situation when we play in a band or orchestra.

I think this is the real answer to "pad drumming." By all means, if practical, the student should devote some time to practice on the drum, so he may hear the true sound at various stick levels. There is also a slight difference in "feel" between the pad and the drum, but this seems to be overcome rapidly. In the case of the parade drum this is still another factor. Here, the player can "rip into it" with the more volume the better. The old saying, "if you can play soft you can play loud" doesn't fit very well here. I know from experience that it isn't true.

Not long ago I made a parade (the first in some years, and I might add the last, I hope, for some more years!), with a big 12 x 17 field drum and heavy snake wood sticks. All went well for several blocks, and then it wasn't so easy. I wasn't conditioned to swinging those heavy sticks, and it amazed me how quickly my wrists gave out. For this is again a specialized type of work. The point here is that most drummers are expected to do diversified types of work reasonably well. This street "slugging" is necessary once in awhile, but it can't be done in the concert band and orchestra. Too often it is, with pretty sad results.

The phase that is hard to develop is the smooth, clean-cut, close-grained drumming required for band and orchestra, and I believe close attention to the raising of the sticks to the proper actual level on the pad while practicing, the same as on the drum, will do a lot toward developing good technic. Notice this one of those times and you will notice that when playing on the pad the sticks go lots higher than on the drum. Correct this, and, in my opinion, the results are a lot better.

CARE and REPAIR of Percussion Instruments

PAUL PRICE

In many schools the condition of percussion equipment is appalling. There is no rational excuse for such a situation, and despite the frequent neglect and abuse, performers are still expected to produce typical and characteristic sounds on the instruments.

Keeping percussion equipment in good playing condition is really a minor task. Music directors should acquaint themselves with the essentials of proper percussion care, pass this information along to their students, and then follow up to see that instructions are carried out regularly.

Proper care of equipment is as important as technical proficiency. It is of no avail to perform difficult technical passages on instruments that will not respond properly.

In many schools that I have visited, I have found bass drum and snare drum brace rods rusted in place to the extent that any amount of adjustment was impossible. I have seen kettle-drum tuning posts, pedals, and heads in such poor condition that careful tuning was impossible. Very often, the audible creaking of kettle-drum heads makes tuning a non-musical highlight to be enjoyed by the performing unit and audience alike.

Improper handling has made the triangle a target for much misuse. This instrument has the distinction of being an extremely delicate sounding one. The holder and beaters play an important part in the production of the delicate sound. Too often, the triangle takes on the sound of a fire-bell, and the effect upon the listener is completely misleading. The following check-list is suggested to help keep percussion equipment in good playing condition. *At least twice each year:*

1. Oil all moving parts, including rods, pedals, snare strainer, etc. One drop of light machine oil is sufficient for each rod. This permits easy adjustment of heads, etc.
2. Clean grit from under counter-hoops. This will prevent heads from becoming damaged from the constant pressure of the counterhoops.
3. Replace and tighten any nuts, screws, and washers which have come loose from vibration, either inside or outside the drum shells.
4. Inspect all heads. Kettle-drum and bass drum heads may need "wetting down" or re-tucking.
5. Inspect the mounting cord on xylophone, marimba, and vibraphone. Renew if necessary.

Other Suggestions

Triangle tone may be improved a great deal by using a gut string holder. This may be attached to a music clip or spring clothespin, thus permitting the instrument to be suspended from the music rack until needed. Three different weight steel beaters should be used, approximately 3/16, 1/8, and 1/16 of an inch in diameter, and ten inches in length.

The creaking of timpani heads may be prevented by rubbing new heads with paraffin-wax on that part of the head coming in contact with the edge of the kettle bowl. Dents may be removed by using a rawhide or padded hammer, and tapping gently.

Small traps, wood block, castanets, tambourine, sleigh bells, whip crack, etc., may be kept together in a card-board container, or trap case. The presence of this container at rehearsal assures having any desired effect handy.

Cover timpani, xylophone, and bells, etc., whenever these are not being used. This prevents unnecessary handling, and cuts down repair bills. Small traps and snare drums should be placed out of sight, or at least a safe distance out of the path of the curious.

Drum head care is all-important in achieving correct and characteristic drum sounds. The crisp, perky, and brittle snare drum sound is best obtained by subjecting the heads to a fair amount of tension, and keeping them there, except in damp weather, when they should be tightened temporarily, and returned to original tension after use.

The low "boom" tones of the concert bass drum are best obtained by tightening the drum somewhat after use, being sure, of course, to release this tension for the next performance. The "thud" sound of the bass drum used for marching is best obtained from a fairly taut head.

To insure being able to obtain lower tones on the timpani, the heads should be left under tension, in order that they can easily be released when needed. When timpani or bass drum heads become too tight to obtain lower sounds, they may be "wet down," or re-tucked. Wetting down a head involves removing it and sponging with a damp cloth or sponge, on both sides, being careful not to permit water to get under the flesh hoop.

The above material includes no out-of-the-ordinary suggestions, but consists only of the essential procedures for proper percussion care, all of which is necessary for good playing.

March-April 1951

Traps and Accessories

John P. Noonan

Aside from regular drum instruction, the student should be taught the use of all the so-called "traps." Some of you may remember the silent movie days when the drummer was really a "trap-drummer." The number of traps the drummer had and his skill with them was an important factor in obtaining a job. Many a drummer who was a "fly-boy,"—a term applied to self-taught drummers—could hold a movie job, even though he wasn't too good, if he was quick and adept at sound effects.

The trap-artist had to catch everything: storms, wind, pistol shots—every bit of "screen business"—and all else was a sacrifice on the altar of realism. Many drummers had elaborate cabinets with space for dry cell batteries, push buttons, and so forth, to make their work quicker and easier. After the talkies, such sound effects were used in radio and movie studios for realistic effects. Many of these were sold by drum makers, but some had to be homemade affairs. In the last few years recordings of actual sounds have replaced effects. Some are still used, however, as the actual sound of a certain thing doesn't always record as such, and in some cases a "trap" does a better job of producing a more realistic effect.

Space would hardly permit including all the drummer's effects. Here is a fairly complete list of the most important ones:

Sleigh-bells	Rooster-crow
Ratchet	Cow-bawl
Thunder-sheet	Hen-cackle
Steamboat whistle	Baby-cry
Locomotive whistle	Bird whistles
Bell plate	Cricket
Anvil	Slap-stick
Train imitation	Wood blocks
Bells, all kinds	Temple-blocks
Telephone, door, etc.	Jingle-clogs
Cuckoo whistle	Shot-pad
Lion-roar	Horse-hoofs
Wind-whistle	

Boy, what a field day the trap artist had "catching" the old silent slap-stick comedies! Many uninhibited drummers disdained the use of mechanical traps for baby-cries, roosters, hens and so forth. They were actually very good at doing these things vocally.

Most manufacturers have discontinued the traps, but they can be obtained from drum shops. Two such shops who specialize in such effects are: *Carroll Drum Service*, 339 W. 43rd St., New York City, and *Frank's Drum Shop*, 226 S. Wabash Ave., Chicago, Ill.

No Substitutions

The cardinal rule in the use of traps is: *do not substitute.* It doesn't work out well. For example, the number "Sleigh Ride" calls for sleigh bells and temple-blocks. A triangle and a wood block will *not* produce the effect. It is better to leave out all effects than to substitute.

Traps and accessories today are used principally by concert bands. The traps can be bought a few at a time until a fairly complete collection is acquired. Keep them in a *locked* box or cabinet, and never, never throw one away! (You'll be looking all over for just that one three years later.)

In many cases the use of traps is for a humorous effect (Spike Jones, et al), but the skilled use of the various gadgets—attention to correct sound, proper entrance, duration, and so forth—is *not* funny. In any composition where traps are called for they are as important as any part of the arrangement. The audience appeal of such descriptive numbers is always great. Sometimes a really fine effect can be "dreamed up" with amazing results.

Not long ago I had such an experience. In a symphonic tone poem for orchestra, several little effects were carefully scored. One of these was a cricket effect, and the regular cricket trap, a small metal affair, was not at all satisfactory. The number was "Tombstone," by K. W. Bradshaw, a contemporary writer, and it was the composer himself who really hit upon the idea of the better effect.

We searched my drum shop and found a small, high-pitched wood block. We then took a very small 7A snare drum stick and filed notches along the shaft, experimenting until we had them spaced correctly. Then we merely scraped the notched stick across the lip of the wood block, and we had a cricket sound far more genuine than any cricket I ever heard! (We are seriously considering giving lessons to crickets on how to sound like a cricket!)

It is certainly a tribute to this composer that he would spend a lot of time on such a little thing. He also spent hours listening to me "gallop" and "make like a horse." I galloped all over the place on everything I could think of until he found and scored the effect he wanted. And, mind you, this "Tombstone" is *not* a "funny" piece of music, but a brilliantly scored tone-poem of the old west.

I did not list triangle, tambourine, and castanets in the trap category. I think accessories is a better word. These are important percussion accessories, and require practice to play well. The skill of good playing of these things is practically a "father-to-son" proposition. Very little has been written on it, for it is hard to describe and illustrate with photographs. Perhaps one day some one will attempt a brochure or booklet on it (what's the matter, Noonan, are you lazy?) but in the meantime it has to be acquired from a percussionist who is adept at it, and it is a highly important branch of the drummer's skill.

Get Organized!

The physical aspects of accessories, like drum equipment, are the same, i.e.: well made and adaptable to the use. I have noticed many school band drummers who invariably will place all the accessories and traps on the floor. They then proceed to disappear for a few seconds, and we hear a "clatter" in the rear flank, letting us all know a few bars ahead of time what is going to happen. The "silent side" of drumming is as important as the "noisy side" of it. The best solution here is to use a table, padded on top with felt. Place accessories to be used on this table within easy reach and pick them up and put them back *noiselessly.*

The triangle is a powerful little thing and will cut through heavy and loud tone color. Several should be on hand: small, medium, and large, and at least three metal beaters of different diameters. A triangle is not always supposed to sound like a ranch hand's call to chow!

For castanets I prefer to have one double set on a handle, and two single sets, each on a handle. The double set can be used for simple rhythms, and where a quick change-over to drums is required. The two single sets can be used for rapid or complicated rhythms, playing them on the knees or against a pillow.

For tambourines, I prefer several, one small with a single set of jingles, and one large, with a double set of jingles.

When the drummer "sets-up" he should look through the program and lay out the things needed. This will prevent "panics" later.

If your audiences aren't responsive, try a good descriptive number, work out the effects, and listen to them applaud vigorously. A little spice always adds to the enjoyment of a good meal! It's a good way to lay the groundwork for presenting fine music. I am told that in the early days of the great Chicago Symphony Orchestra, Theodore Thomas, the founder, used such devices as a piece called the "Midnight Fire Alarm," complete with redshirted men running out on stage with buckets and axes. Such tunes were to lure the "civilians" to hear the better music which was carefully administered in small doses. We have just as many "civilians" today —don't forget that!

In conclusion, remember that traps are not difficult to use. A little imagination will help, and the player must be an extrovert. The effects are for the enjoyment of the audience, as in the case of all music, so do it right.

Odds and Ends

JOHN P. NOONAN

This is a recital of percussive happenings that have interested me during the past year. As the title indicates, "anything can happen," so here we go.

Had a letter from my old friend, Louis Goucher, the famous drummer of the U.S. Navy Band, who is retiring after thirty years of service. Lou was xylophone soloist with the band as well as being one of the good drummers. He also taught at the Navy School of Music, where he was highly respected by his colleagues as a splendid teacher and a fine gentleman. He is now teaching and playing in the Washington, D.C., area, giving many young people valuable and authentic instruction.

Many of you probably have heard Goucher playing. I remember the first time I heard him. I was a youngster, and he really scared me with his fine drumming. The Navy will miss one of its valued players and teachers.

Heard an unusual and extremely interesting recital (Yes, you heard right—programs and everything) at the University of Illinois on March 1. The percussion ensemble under the direction of Paul Price presented an hour's program of percussion numbers, including "Ionization" by Edgar Varese as the serious work of the concert. This piece, which requires thirteen players using some thirty instruments, ranging from a triangle to a red fire siren, was presented with precision and finesse. Other selections, like "Invention for Four Percussion Players" and "Auto Accident," demonstrated percussion "color" rather than being just a noisy jangle. The music certainly proved the value of good work and was greatly liked and applauded by a large audience.

I recall a Chicago recital a few years back when Bobby Christian and Jose Bethancourt used a double quartet of voices and an English horn, with a Hammond organ as backing. These two famous percussionists wrote their own compositions to illustrate the "color" of percussion, and even hard-boiled music critics were a bit amazed at the results.

Don't forget the value of all duets, trios, and other ensembles for drum sections. A few rudimentary compositions not too difficult for practice and presentation are available. As in the case of strings, woodwind, and brass, the value of such practice and experience is invaluable.

Here are some things I've noticed about school band sections.

1. Many band leaders try to get the two or three snare bands in a section to sound alike. Hm-m-m! Well, I doubt that they'll succeed. Drums may be the same size and make, but differences in head thickness make the attempt to get tonal uniformity impractical. Tension may be corrected, but there's no need to worry about one being higher pitched, for the sound will blend to produce good drum tone.

2. Timpani sticks. What passes for these is really amazing! A timpani stick, like a good fiddle bow, is extremely important in drawing good tone. Budget or no budget, you've got to have at least two pairs. Use one pair for rehearsal and save the other for performance. Why spend six hundred dollars for a fine set of pedal drums and then pound them with a "shoe dauber"? And, while on this subject, please do not permit a double stroke roll on timpani. It is bewildering to find so many timpanists in school bands playing a "squashy" double stroke roll.

(Please turn to page 45)

3. In playing "pop" tunes in bands where more than one snare drummer is used, the choruses are usually best played *ad lib.* Keep the wire bush beats simple and be sure that they are done the same. They provide a nice easy backdrop to the number and do not clutter up the rhythm. Promiscuous every-man-for-himself ad libbing is, in the modern idiom, "nowhere." High-hat cymbals are being used on "pop" tunes, too. They are the trademark of rhythm in a dance band: their judicious use in concert production points up the rhythm. Obviously the device is no better than the cymbals used. Ninety per cent of the dance men use a 14- or 15-inch pair of medium Zildjians on their high-hats. The same kind will work well for the average concert band.

4. Drum heads are becoming increasingly hard to obtain. Price freezes, the large number of skins taken by the government, and other factors, are having an effect on availability and price. Probably there will be enough to go around. Buy good heads and take care of them. Remember the rules for obtaining good results with them. Keep some tension on the heads: do not loosen them entirely. You can wash them with soap and water; "trick" preparations are of no value.

5. Clean cymbals sound and look better. The Zildjians agree that dirt filling the "sound tracks" of cymbals can dampen vibrations to some extent. To clean, use any good metal polish. They may be lightly machine buffed, but do not let the metal heat up to a degree that will destroy its temper.

6. I do considerable judging at contests on percussion. I believe that good manners and a clean neat appearance are universally respected. In training your contestants, stress the importance of posture, neatness, and politeness. About a month before a contest it is not a bad idea to make your own weekly judging sheets on contestants, even to division ratings. Be super-critical in order to help acquaint them with the problems they will encounter at the real contest.

Did you read in the last issue the Sousa statement concerning bass drummers? Be sure to show that to your bass drummer. Many of you doubtless recall Gus Helmecke, the famous bass drummer with the Sousa organization. I remember hearing the band while I was a youngster. The timpanist and xylophone soloist was George Carey, now with the Cincinnati Symphony Orchestra. The snare drummer was Howard Goulden, who is now, I believe, doing radio work in New York City.

The band had a jazz band of thirteen men within its ranks, and Goulden had a little specially made drum outfit in one unit which he could use while standing. I even recall one of the tunes this jazz group used, "Follow the Swallow Back Home." How many others remember that? I do not know what year it was, but it must have been about 1925-26 or so. John Dolan was cornet soloist at that time.

I noted the statement also that Sousa often directed school bands, for I was in one of them. He came out to a football game and directed our band. Boy! were we scared! So, you see, I, too, have played with Sousa. (Two numbers, "Washington Post" and "Semper Fidelis"!) As I recall, Mr. Sousa wasn't too "knocked out" by my artistic rendition of the drum solo in "Semper Fidelis." I was so scared that I may have played it in 2/4!

Since that time I've talked to many ex-Sousa men now in symphony orchestras, radio, etc., and without exception all have glowing praise for the "old master." He certainly merits his immortality, for when all the common side-men give the leader the accolade, that is really something.

Well, there are a thousand things I could tell about, but space will not allow. I would like to stress that I will be glad to give my opinion on any of your questions. If you like to hear about various percussion sections in famous bands and orchestras, I can discuss many of them, telling the size and type of their equipment and other information that might prove helpful to directors.

September 1951

The "Hi-HAT"

–and how it grew

JOHN P. NOONAN

SEVERAL band leaders and drummers have asked me about the drummer's "hi-hat" pedal and the proper cymbals to be used. I remember the birth of this device, as do many of you. It was originally an invention for the dance drummer, as we all know.

When I first started playing in a dance orchestra, both hands and the right foot were occupied while the left foot led a life of ease and idleness. Suddenly a contraption known as the Snowshoe Charleston Cymbals hove into view. This instrument consisted of a flat board about 14 inches long, on the end of which was affixed a small 8-inch brass cymbal with the cup inverted. Another flat matching board had a second 8-inch brass cymbal on one end and was attached on the other end to the first board with a hinged spring. Across the top board was a 4-inch web strap to place the foot in stirrup fashion. Thus the term "snowshoe pedal" was an apt term for the device.

Each of us bought one of these immediately and attempted to use it on the after-beat, with disastrous results, I can assure you. Bass players threatened us with mayhem, for it was quite a trick to clamp this board-like affair together exactly on the after-beat. The drum makers began to improve this new drummer's "trap" at once, as it became instantly apparent that it was to stay. After a few weeks' use, the drummer found he could co-ordinate his hands and both feet, and sales of the sock-cymbal (by now it was a sock-cymbal) zoomed. Came a period of evolution, and out of it developed the hi-hat sock pedal in use today.

During all this time, remember, brass cymbals were being used. Soon the "sharp" drummers started to use deep cup cymbals 10 inches in diameter, still of brass, for a more pronounced "sock." Shortly before the "Krupa Era," as I recall it, some pioneer drummer placed two good Zildjian cymbals on the hi-hat and started to use one or both sticks on the top cymbal.

New Tone Color

This practice of using the sticks on the top cymbal caught on instantly. It produced an entirely new tone color with a powerful rhythmic influence, and, in my opinion, will always be with us in the popular orchestra field. I think most dance drummers will agree that a good hi-hat pedal with good cymbals is about as important a single factor as they have at their command.

The modern hi-hat pedal has an adjustable top section of tubing to place the cymbals where desired, and the action of the pedal is fast and accurate. Cymbals used are, of course, tremendously important. The effect desired helps determine the type and size of cymbals chosen.

As a result of experimenting with and using different set-ups, I will go out on a limb and say that for general all-around use, a pair of 14-inch or 15-inch A. Zildjian matched medium weight hi-hat cymbals is very good. In such a pair of matched cymbals the top one is a trifle thinner and higher pitched than the bottom. They are stamped "top" and "bottom" and produce the desired tonal effect. No two pairs will sound exactly alike, and the pitch and "feel" are a matter of preference, but in my experience, none of them in this aforementioned set-up is bad.

Small cymbals of the 11 and 12-inch size are seldom used now except for a special effect desired. Many drummers use, for example, a 15-inch top cymbal and a 14-inch bottom cymbal, or vice versa. Some use a pair of 16-inch and so on, but I really feel that a matched pair of A. Zildjian, both 14 or both 15-inch, is the best all-around selection.

There are two general types of hi-hat cymbal sounds; one is the solid sock, which is produced with slightly heavy cymbals; and the other, the "swish" sound produced with cymbals a little more on the thin side. Thus our original selection of medium hi-hat cymbals gives the best all-around results, with enough sock and enough swish to keep everybody happy.

The number of felt washers underneath the bottom cymbal is a determining factor also. A single felt will produce more of a sock, while additional felts give more "spring" or cushion to lighten up the sock sound. Generally about four felt washers under the bottom cymbal or two on either side of the top cymbal will work well, but one must experiment for the sound desired.

There are several "sounds" to be used on the hi-hat. First is the "chi-yumpta-chi" sound, written as follows:

O C C O C C O C C O C C

etc.

The figure "O" indicates that the cymbals are open or up, and the figure "C" indicates closed. This happens automatically if the cymbals are struck together on the after-beat with the foot pedal. The right stick, crossed either over or under the left stick, plays the notated rhythm.

Then there is the "click" sound produced by clamping the cymbals tightly together by use of the pedal and keeping them there, playing the same rhythm as before or a straight four in a bar. The "ching" sound is produced by letting the cymbals barely meet, by using the pedal to produce a hissing "ching" sound, sustaining through, using the first rhythm, four in a bar straight, or both sticks for barrel-house rhythmic figures. In controlling volume the tip or the shaft of the right stick is used. For a light tone use the tip about 3 inches from the edge; for more volume, the shaft of the stick against the edge of the top cymbal.

Now, what about the hi-hat in the concert band? Yes, yes, by all means on pop tunes. More and more, better pop arrangements are being written and played in dance band style. I notice that many leaders are trying hard to achieve more of a dance band effect on their popular tunes in the concert band. The bass drummer used to do it by playing four in a bar on the drum and clamping the cymbal down on the after-beat. Why do that when the hi-hat gives the genuine effect? It is definitely coming, for I know of quite a few instances where schools are adding a hi-hat set-up owned by the school. A good hi-hat pedal with 15-inch A. Zildjian cymbals will run in price about $75, but it is indispensable to the orchestra drummer, and I wager will soon be so to the band drummer.

The use of the hi-hat is "ad lib" in pop tunes. The rhythmic pattern notated earlier will fit practically every pop tune in the repertoire. Thus in the average ballad or jazz type tune the rhythm as shown is used throughout except for introductions and endings, which are played "as is." The rhythm need not be loud, just nice and easy to balance the combination of instruments being used in the various parts of the arrangement.

One final word of caution. Don't try to save ten or eleven dollars or more by substituting cheap cymbals and pedal. You're just throwing money away and not getting the real effect. This hi-hat rhythmic structure is the very backbone of pop music, and the sound of it is known to musicians and public alike. So far as I know, it can't be approached with cheap cymbals. Rather than waste money, wait until you can buy the best.

October 1951

The Concert Bass Drum

Separate tensioning of heads—height of drum—cymbal player—place, direction of strokes

John P. Noonan

Although much has been written about the bass drum and cymbals, I receive so many questions that I feel more should be said on the subject. There are several things in this regard that have not been touched upon, to my knowledge, and I'll take up a few of them here.

The drum should be separate tension. Some call the separate tension drums "double tension," but "separate tension" is the correct terminology. The term means that each head is tensioned separately.

For grade school bands the 14x28 size or 14x30 size is good; for high school the 14x30 to 16x32 size is common; while for college bands the 16x32 to 16x36 size is indicated. A little judgment only is required here; the number of players will influence the choice. I believe the listed sizes are the most common. There is also, as you know, the single tension model, where both heads are tightened by the same rod. This model is not too bad, but only slightly cheaper. Thus the separate tension is the better buy and the better drum, as finer head adjustment is possible.

Both heads of the bass drum are of the same type, white calfskin (some cheap drums use goatskin; not so good, so watch that!). There is not an indicated "batter" or beating head, as either head can be used. Try both sides and select the one that seems better to you, and that's it.

Now we tension the drum. We do

not want definite pitch but rather a low solid "boom" tone; the heads must be adjusted to best secure this pitch. Most expert bass drummers tension the batter head about four tones higher than the opposite or "carry" head to prevent a "kick-back." Therefore, tension the beating side not too low in sound, about medium, and adjust the other head to sound about a fourth below.

It is immediately apparent that this process will take a little experimenting. If the batter side is too low to start with, one can't obtain the fourth below. The opposite head will "ripple" and lose all its tension in going that low; therefore, the batter head, as mentioned, must be about medium low to secure the interval between the two. Obviously, as we have said before, one should tension the drum by going around it clockwise, giving each rod the same number of turns to keep the tension evenly distributed.

Best Height

Here is something else that I have noticed, especially in school bands. In almost every case the bass drum is too high off the floor for the player to secure best results. In some instances I have seen the drum so high that the player had to "peek" around the side of it to see the conductor!

The best height really is to have the top of the shell even with the player's chest. The bass drum stands made commercially do not seem to adjust low enough to make this possible, especially with a large drum. A satisfactory stand can be made of wood to hold the drum low enough for effective use. I have never seen a professional bass drummer place his drum as high as I see most of them used in school bands.

Should the bass drummer also play the cymbals? This is a tough question but one that I think is extremely important in getting the correct "sound" of the bass drum. In a symphony orchestra there is, as you know, a separate cymbal player. Such an arrangement is necessary for symphonic interpretation.

Now let's look at the concert band of average size and think about marches, selections, etc. The bass drum tone is very "dark" in color, and in marches, for example, needs "pointing up" to make it "brighter," more precise, and more solid.

With one man playing both bass drum and cymbals on marches, this "point up" really gives excellent results, and is, in my opinion, better than a separate cymbal player. The cymbalist can "catch" the crashes, but for the regular pulse beats it is hard to improve on having one man play both. A single player can secure a light "zing" with each bass drum note that really "brightens up" the beat and makes it more definite at all dynamics. If you don't have my booklet, "Notes on Band and Orchestra Cymbals," secure a copy*. It discusses the subject, giving illustrations to show positions, etc.

Remember that I am not advising this procedure for symphonic type compositions but for marches and the lighter type music. In the symphonic type, e.g., the Finale to Tchaikovsky's *Fourth Symphony*, play "as is" with a separate cymbalist.

There are many different ideas on how to strike the drum. Many prefer, as, for example, any 2 in a bar military march, to strike the first beat with a down blow and the second with an up blow. First, let's look at note values on the drum, assuming that we have a 16x32 bass drum. About five inches from the rim of the drum, the beat will produce notes of long duration (half notes, whole notes, etc.) Quarter and eighth notes sound about 12 inches from the rim. A *sforzando* or heavy accent comes from the center of the head. The distances from the hoop are arbitrary; the head weight will be a qualifying factor, but I believe I'm close, anyway.

Down Blow Preferred

My idea of the correct blow is a down blow for *every note*, with a glancing motion of the stick. In this way the same stress can be placed on each note. On the street or for any fancy sticking, "anything goes." Scotch type is excellent or twirling the stick is great for effect, but for regular concert, a down blow of each note is better controlled.

*Published by Avedis Zildjian Co., 39 Fayette St., North Quincy, Mass.

It is not easy to get the best sticks. I firmly believe that the best bass drum stick for concert use would be a double-end one covered with piano felt, like an over-grown ball type tympani stick. I don't believe, however, that such a stick is made commercially. The double-end lambswool stick is very good, but it should be made of good quality and changed or re-covered when all the wool surface is gone. A pair of tympani sticks also should be used for rolls wherever there is time to change over to them and back.

There is one swell rule for bass drum and snare drum heads, and that is: "Let them alone as much as possible!"

In the case of the bass drum, if it is to be put away for several days, tighten each rod a couple of turns. Then you can easily loosen it to obtain the low pitch you want. Here is another circumstance. At a concert the weather is humid, and during the concert you have tightened each rod four turns to keep the head at playing level. At the end of the concert you should loosen it back about two turns of each rod to keep the head in good shape. You will note that you tightened the head four turns and loosened it but two. When you next use the drum, the day may be dry, and you will have to loosen it the extra two (maybe three) turns.

If the weather is not too changeable, leave the drum alone as long as it sounds good. Any drum head acts the same. When it's dry, the head tightens; when it's damp, the head loosens. Bear that fact in mind, and you will have no trouble.

Let's have a little test now. Let's say it's extremely hot and dry, and the drum has a tendency to climb higher in pitch during the concert. Then you want to leave it in an extremely hot instrument room. What should you do? That's right; loosen it a few turns. The rule here is that it is all right to loosen a head, but never to loosen it to the point where it "ripples."

I would certainly like to have band leaders try out cymbals on the bass drum for marches, and let me know how they like the idea. I suggest also that they get my booklet and study the illustrations.

Percussion Problems In High School Bands

can be solved if players are required to follow their music, to execute rolls, and to learn all percussion instruments

RICHARD P. SCHERER

THE past few years have seen an increasing number of music education programs, clinics, and demonstrations placing discussion of percussion instruments on their programs. Undoubtedly the reason behind this heightened interest in the drums is the desire of band directors and area music leaders to improve the general playing level of the percussion instruments, particularly at the high school level.

Perhaps this interest in the playing of percussion instruments is an indication that the average band director is now finding out what every drummer has known for a long time—that the percussion instruments are the most sadly neglected of all and that if we are to have top-notch musical organizations, we cannot afford to overlook the drum section.

Foremost among the problems confronting the average drum section is the inability to read music with enough facility to play the score properly. That this is a problem at all is astonishing because the majority of the composers who write for high school bands write drum parts so simplified that they are a matter of utter dismay to the drummer who can read! That it is a problem is, however, a matter of record. When I was once requested to audition drummers for entrance into a university band, I found that out of the ten applicants there was only one who could make musical sense out of a few bars of simple binary time. And yet I knew that the high school bands in which these applicants had played were in many cases fine organizations which had produced excellent players on other instruments.

Why is it that drummers are unable to read the music that their cornet and clarinet playing fellow-bandsmen can play with little difficulty? The answer, to my mind, is two-fold. First of all, most directors have a decided tendency to overlook the drum section as a playing unit, not only in actual playing but also in band work. Some time ago I was discussing this subject with a director friend of mine who declared that his attention was so taken up with the more apparent problems of the band that he did not get around to the drum part until the rest of the players had achieved at least partial mastery of the selection.

It is this lack of attention to the drum section that is one of the prime reasons for the players' inability to read. If the director does not insist that the drummers adhere to the written music, they will feel free to ad-lib their parts. Once they have been successful at this without the director's taking notice, they will continue, not seeing any reason for being able to read the music. It is this freedom in the percussion section that is responsible for poor reading. When these drummers are required to read their parts accurately, they cannot do so. Instead, they attempt to fake the passage, often with disastrous results.

There are methods of overcoming this problem, however. The director must devise a way of constantly checking the drum part so that he can insist that the music be followed faithfully. This can be done by having an extra drum part on the podium, by part study, by consistent sectional rehearsal, or by having a responsible person in the drum section who will insist that the music be played correctly.

Impractical Training

A second reason for the drummers' inability to read is found in their method of training. Many times when drummers have approached me about playing in a band, they have immediately started talking about playing the rudiments, sounding quite scholarly in the matter. And frequently they can play the rudiments well. However, once the band commences to rehearse or these drummers are asked to play the music set before them, it is amazing how little they can read in relationship to the technique that they have developed in their hands.

What has happened in their training to bring about such a paradox? I believe that the reason is to be found in the method by which the rudiments are presented to the student. He has been schooled in the playing of these rudiments in such a manner as to present them as an end in themselves instead of as a means to an end. In this case the end to be achieved is the proper execution of the written music. The rudiments are good only to the extent that they aid the drummer in executing his part.

It is the author's conviction that the rudiments of drumming can be more successfully utilized if they are presented in connection with reading exercises instead of as a meaningless bag of tricks. Many times I feel that we "get the cart before the horse." First the student is taught to play the rudiments as meaningless exercises, and then without further training he is expected to read music on the basis of those same exercises. How much better it would be if those rudiments were introduced as the student encountered them in a series of well-planned reading exercises! In this method reading ability would be developed along with technical ability. and at the same time the whole process would become more meaningful to the student.

Rudiments in Exercises

I follow this method by using the reading exercises contained in the HARRY A. BOWER SYSTEM, introducing the rudiments as they appear in the exercises. The ability to read and play these exercises is a prerequisite to first band membership.

As the reading ability of the drum section increases, the director will find that many of the problems in the section will tend to disappear. That bass drummer who doesn't follow the baton will tend to be more accurate because of his ability to read ahead. and the general rhythm of the section will be improved because the notation becomes less of a problem. Without a doubt, the inability to read and interpret music is the strongest single factor in the weakness of the drum section in relationship to the rest of the band. Without this ability they are merely guessing or deliberately ad-libbing, and this at its best results in uneven rhythms harmful to the entire ensemble.

Perhaps the greatest difficulty that drummers have in actually executing music is to play the roll in a musical manner. The most difficult technique the student must perfect is to develop the speed necessary to "close" the roll. I have used every method I can invent in an attempt to facilitate this development, and each time I come to the same conclusion. The long roll is a slow development and any attempt to rush it will only result in a scratch or a buzz roll. The roll must be built from a very slow tempo, being careful to accent the second beat. Once the "hump" is reached, the student must not be permitted merely to let the sticks bounce off the head. If he is, nothing good will result, and a fine roll will never develop. The second beat in the actual roll must be as strong as the first or the roll will tend to become lop-sided or uneven.

Controlled Bounce

The drummer must not merely bounce the stick on the head. The bounce must be controlled so that the second or bounce beat has just enough force behind it to make it equal to the first or primary blow. Actually. the stick rebounds from the primary blow and is stopped by the thumb, or finger, which acts as a spring, sending the stick back to the drum head for the secondary blow. *There is no such thing as a free bounce in drumming.* If there is, it stands to reason that the bounce must be weaker than the original blow. The bounce must be fortified in some manner. Many drummers achieve this by placing the first finger of the left hand over the stick, while others make use of the thumb. I have always favored the thumb in producing this effect. In the right hand the fingers necessarily do the job.

Of course, a great deal of practice is necessary to perfect this technique as it requires a high degree of coordination on the part of the drummer. Nevertheless, there is no substitute for a roll well played.

Once the roll has been developed so that it can be closed adequately, the rhythmic approach of its use in music should be instituted. It is disturbing, to say the least, to hear a drummer who is doing a fairly nice job of playing a drum solo completely lose sight of the rhythm when he commences a roll of a few beats' duration. I have heard this many times, particularly in a 6/8 solo when the drummer will roll something akin to a 2/4 rhythm. The absence of the rhythmic roll completely destroys the desired effect.

Tempo of Roll

Many times I have been asked at clinics, "How do you know how many beats to put into a roll, particularly when that roll is played at many different tempos?"

Actually the roll is. played in the same manner as eighth or sixteenth notes, depending on the tempo. The movement of the right hand should always represent the eighth notes in a measure, whether in 2/4, 3/4, or 6/8 time. The right hand should start the measure, playing two beats for each note, with the left hand playing alternately to the right. If this method is followed, the roll becomes as much a part of the rhythm as any other portion of the solo, and the entire composition becomes an even flow rather than a series of disconnected phrases.

During the past few years a great deal has been said about whether the right or the left hand should lead at the beginning of a measure. The left-hand method has some advocates, and a few instruction books have been published, definitely marked for the first beat to be played with the left. The primary theory behind this seems to be that if the left hand is utilized to a greater extent, it will develop more readily.

Right or Left?

However, some drummers are inclined to regard this left-hand-first principle as erroneous because of the natural tendency of the right hand to follow the left foot while marching. While many advanced drummers can probably use either hand without noticeable change, observation of the student will show definite awkwardness if street beats are started with the left hand. As far as the left hand development is concerned, there are innumerable exercises which can be used to insure proper development without changing what would seem to many to be a natural aspect of drumming. I would like to cite George L. Stone's STICK CONTROL as a method of achieving equal hand development as efficiently as any I have found up to this time.

Tonal Snap

When comparing students and professionals on any instrument, the tone is usually the distinguishing factor. Drummers can readily be divided into two groups by the "snap" with which they play. This snap corresponds to the tone of the instrument and makes a world of difference in the actual sound that is emitted from the drum. Most high school drummers play with a noticeable lack of this snap, and their playing sounds dull and uninteresting.

The basis of the snap is in the primary blow; it must be brought out as soon as the student starts to play. As the stick descends toward the drum, the wrist must snap the stick toward the drum head. At a recent clinic W. F. Ludwig, Jr., spoke at some length concerning this matter. He compared the action of the left hand with that of flinging drops of water off the fingers. The action of the right hand might be compared to snapping a whip. At any rate, the sticks cannot merely be dropped to the head. They must be directed with force and power behind the action. The amount of this power, of course, is determined by the loudness of sound required, but there is still snap in good drumming even in the most pianissimo passages. This statement is applicable to the preceding remarks in connection with the development of the double roll, wherein the secondary or "bounce" beat must have snap as well as the primary blow in order to make the two beats even.

Rotation System

Often while listening to bands, I have noticed that the drummers are saddled to a particular percussion instrument, and there they stay. The snare drummer never plays the bass drum; the bass drummer never plays the traps. In some of the bands of which I have been a member, and certainly in my own bands, a system of rotation has been used so that each player plays each of the percussion instruments in turn. In all of these instances there has been a noticeable increase in the general ability of the section. Many snare drummers dislike to play the bass drum, but once they have done so for a period of time, there is definite improvement in their snare drumming. The same is true of the bass drummer and the bell player.

Needless to say, if such a system of rotation is to be at all efficient, the individual members of the section will need instruction on the various instruments before they are allowed to play them. This involves the over-all training of the percussion section for a number of years. *Each member of the section should be trained to play all the percussion instruments and then be allowed to specialize on the instrument that seemingly suits him best.*

I have attempted this training in my bands by instituting a course for all drummers. They get three years of training on the snare drum, bass drum, and cymbals, then one year on orchestra bells or xylophone, and finally one year of timpani. The remaining traps are worked in at random when they are needed for the music. The completion of this course will insure each student a good fundamental knowledge of the snare drum and a working knowledge of the bells and timpani. Any student may continue with private lessons on any of the instruments, and many do. It will be found that one student will want to play timpani, another bells, and another snare drum. Advanced studies can be given these students, and they can be permitted to specialize. Still, they have completed a comprehensive course in the percussion instruments and have a working knowledge of each of them.

Drums an Asset

While many of our high school drum sections are indescribably weak, there isn't any conceivable reason why they cannot be a decidedly efficient asset to the band. Careful training as to musicianship, along with "physical education," can make the drum section the strong point in our ensembles. With the same care and consideration which is many times lavished on our other sections, we can easily change the drum section from the "most sadly neglected" to the firm foundation upon which good bands are built.

1952-1953

61	Drumming Standards as I Have Observed Them	Alan Abel	January-February
63	Triangle, Tambourine, and Castanets	Sidney Berg	January-February
65	Confusion Confounds as Authorities Argue	John P. Noonan	March-April
66	'Sticking' Methods Cause Controversy	John P. Noonan	May-June
67	Developing the Clean Roll	Bill Muehler	September
69	Advice on Selecting, Training Drummers for Marching Band	James D. Salmon	October
70	Learning to Apply the Drum Rudiments	Acton E. Ostling	November-December
72	Tympani Study Needs Basis of Musicianship	Joe Barry Mullins	January-February
73	Percussion Ensemble Class Gives Training in 'New Style' Music	Paul Price	March-April
74	Hints on Care and Use of Tympani	Saul Goodman	May-June
76	Drums on The March	Haskell W. Harr	September
77	Drums on The March	Haskell W. Harr	October
79	Music Now Available for Drum Ensembles	Haskell W. Harr	November
80	Does Your Percussion Meet High Standards?	H.E. Nutt	December

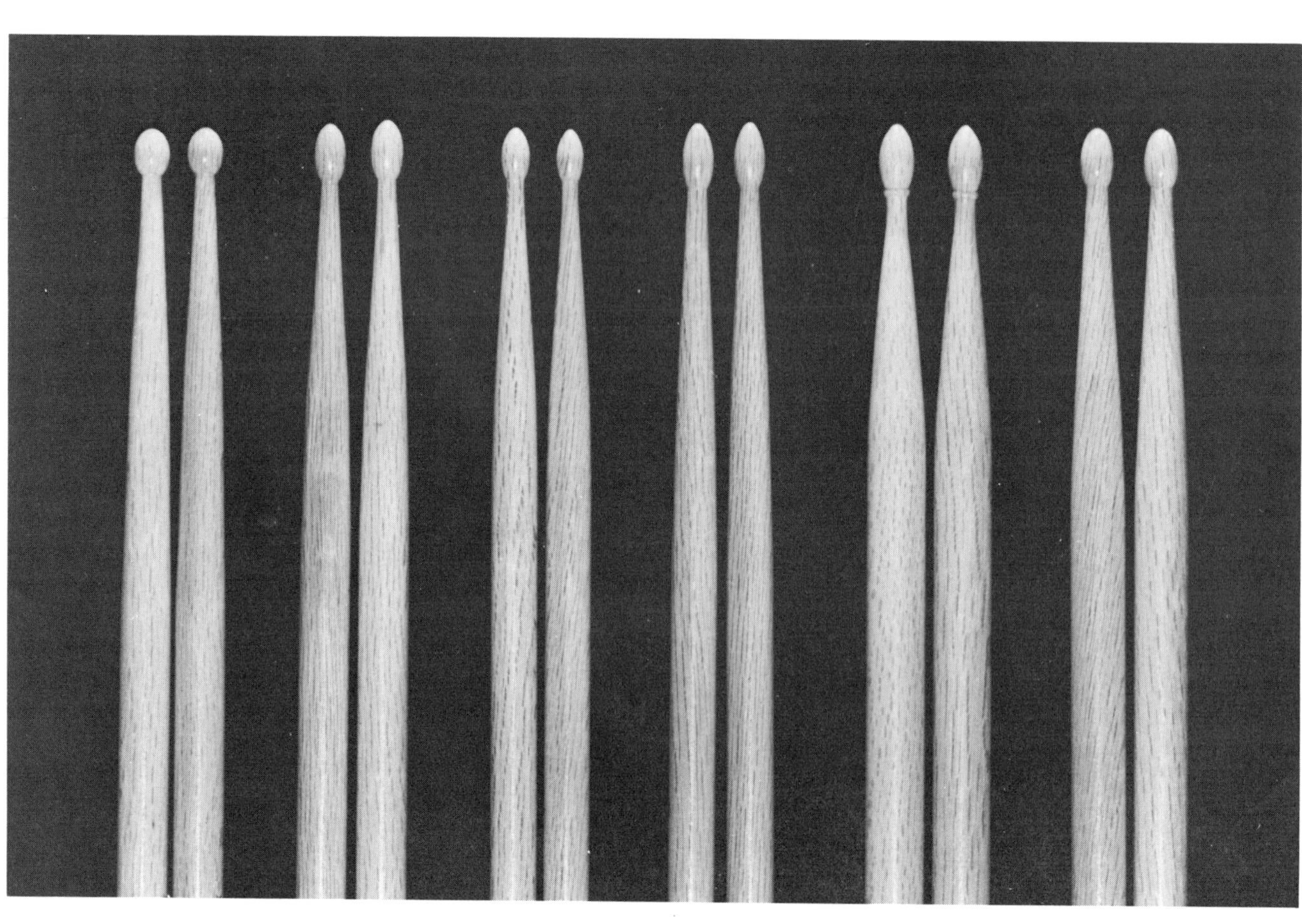

Drumming Standards As I Have Observed Them

Players content to get by rather than to raise performance standards and exploit instrument

ALAN ABEL

According to many musicians, the field of percussion is always in the rear when it is compared with other instruments on the basis of techniques and literature. By techniques we mean usage as performing instruments; in literature we include what has been written to display the performance possibilities of the instruments.

Only recently have many drummers been conscious of the tremendous potentialities of the snare drum, tympani, and mallet instruments as solo media in their own right. The interest and enthusiasm that a drummer can generate in exploiting his field are infinite.

That drumming has lagged behind other instruments we drummers cannot deny. One strong reason is that far too many drummers have been content to learn just enough to get by. Far too many teachers have been teaching just enough to permit the student to join the band. Far too many percussion classes have been teaching just enough to their potential high school teachers to maintain the minimum standard or perhaps to lower it another notch.

Notable Weaknesses

Thus, most drummers in high school and college are not sharing in the vast amount of drumming knowledge that is rightfully theirs. Last summer I auditioned one hundred high school drummers to fill the ten percussion berths in the two-hundred member All Ohio Boys' Band. All of the candidates had been recommended by their respective band directors as being outstanding; yet I found only two who could play the drum score of "Semper Fidelis." The others were pathetic in reading and technical ability. The section was finally filled with students of two drum teachers, Charles Wilcoxon of Cleveland and Louis Swigert of Cincinnati.

Since 1941 I have kept a series of notes on the hundreds of high school and college bands that I have observed, with particular emphasis on percussion sections. Nine out of ten drum sections in these organizations sounded like so many cement mixers! The chief flaws were poor rhythm, lack of dynamics, "dirty" flams, "smudgy" rolls, and poor tuning.

Universities at Fault

Who is to blame for all this drumming chaos? Musicians and laymen blame the drummer. The drummers blame their teachers. I say that all are wrong, or at least partially so. The real fault lies in the universities who supply the drumming knowledge to the educators who do most of the drum teaching in this country. In effect, the music educator has been the victim of unfortunate circumstances. He "covers" the field of percussion in a three-month course at a college that refuses to recognize percussion as a major field of study.

I firmly believe that no institution not offering percussion as a major can effectively transmit up-to-date and legitimate drumming knowledge to potential music teachers. Far too many sincere and well-meaning educators have been supplied with inadequate and distorted drumming knowledge. The result has been a chain reaction that has produced our present-day level of drumming, which often fails to reach a minimum standard.

Young drummers who are anxious to excel in the field can look forward to a wrong start from their school music directors—a wrong start burdened with bad habits in an art that demands skilful teaching and constant coaching as the student progresses. Today, unless a drummer seeks one of the few dozen drum authorities in the country, his chances for correct learning are small. If he remains loyal to music and enters a university, he must seek refuge in a field other than percussion, thus adding to the pressure which is cramping the art of drumming.

University band and orchestra directors often cry and moan because of their "sad" drum sections. They blame high school directors for improper teaching of drumming when these same high school instructors had been graduated from those very universities!

Two of twenty graduating seniors in music education in a Mid-West college knew the difference between the marimba and the vibra-harp. All of them could name and open the first thirteen rudiments. None of them was sure of the role these thirteen rudiments would play in their future drum teaching. They felt that their two-and-a-half months drum class had given them a bundle of confused notions. Had they gained anything from the class? Yes, they had; a pair of drumsticks and a passing grade!

Young Drummers Cheated

One can readily see that enough music educators have left, are leaving, and will continue to leave schools and universities with little more than a vague idea about percussion, not to mention usable knowledge of practical drum teaching. The net result is that a young drummer is exposed to an uninformed teacher—a situation that is unfair to teaching ethics, the teacher, the student, his parents, musical organizations, and the arrangers who are not getting their drum parts played properly.

The drummer today who is fortunate enough to survive the educational trial and error method of teaching is lucky indeed to get by. Paradoxically, he is unlucky, for should he want to go on and make drumming his vocation or even a life-long interest, he would find how much he had failed to get and would probably suffer ultimate frustration. Today's professional drummer in the best jobs is a thoroughly trained rudimentalist, skilful on tympani and the mallet instruments, and at home with Bach or boogie-woogie. If he was "thrown for a loss" by his high school music teacher, the chances are that he made up for the wasted time by getting the help of a professional drummer or by working out his own training the hard way.

Our unhealthy drumming situation can and should be rectified. Regardless of whether the student is interested in playing an instrument in order to get into the football games free or for the fun of playing music, the educator has a moral responsibility for teaching the best ways and means of playing. How can he meet the responsibility when he himself has been denied proper training?

School administrations and the people heading music departments need to be awakened to the need. A good start would be made by university and college recognition of drumming; by having competent drum teachers in the universities; and by sponsoring many more drum clinics and contests.

LET YOUR DRUMMERS TRY THESE FANFARES

Submitted by Al Wright, Miami, Fla.

Triangle, Tambourine, and Castanets

SIDNEY BERG

THE TRIANGLE is one of the most used of all the traps. There is no substitute for it; a bell or a cymbal will not be a satisfactory replacement. Good triangles are not expensive; every school should have at least two of them of different sizes.

One five-inch and one seven-inch would be satisfactory. The triangle beater is of the utmost importance; the player should have an ample supply of different pairs of beaters matched exactly as to size, weight, and composition. Softer passages should be played with lighter beaters and loud ones with heavy. The beater must be metal; a snare drum stick should never be used as a substitute.

The triangle should be suspended by a short piece of fishing tackle or a strong thin cord. The cord should be tied in such a way that the triangle will not spin around when it is struck. Cut off a piece of cord about 8 inches long. Wrap the middle part of it around the triangle, tying a very tight knot on the very top. Now move the knot to the under side of the triangle. Bring the string on each side of the triangle and tie a knot about two inches above the instrument. (See Fig. I.)

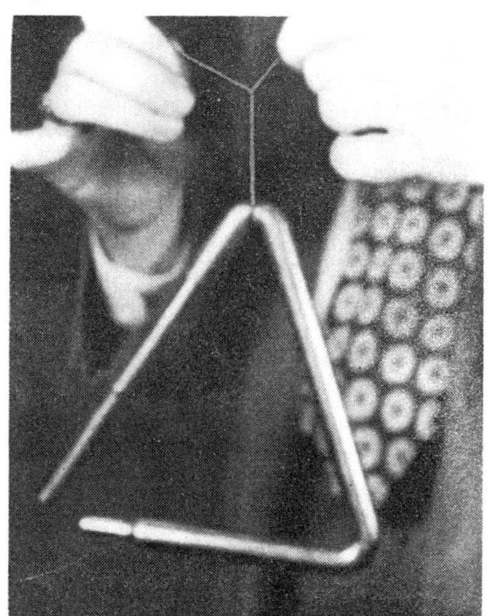

Fig. I

In playing the triangle, suspend it from the thumb just back of the thumb nail, not on the first joint, and let the remaining fingers go around the triangle. The fingers are not to touch the triangle (Fig. II) except to dampen it or to stop it from ringing.

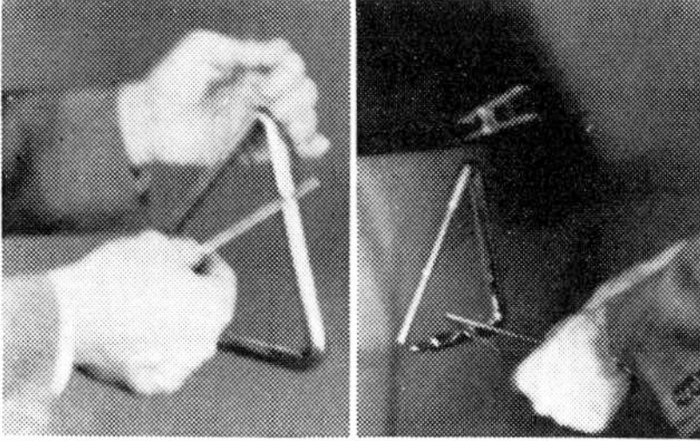

Fig. II Fig. III

The triangle should be struck on the upper third of the right side (the corner with the opening being to the left) or on the bottom (Fig. III).

When playing the instrument, hold it up to shoulder height. Before you play the first note, *lay the beater on the triangle.* This act will eliminate "missed" strokes and is especially important for soft beats. It is the same principle a carpenter uses when driving a nail. The triangle should sound for the exact value of the note written. Thus in 4/4 time two quarter notes followed by rests would not sound the same as two half notes.

In the first example you would dampen the triangle on the rests. Occasionally parts become too technical to be played with one beater. Use of two depends upon the speed the individual performer can play and the tempo taken by the conductor. The following excerpt from the "Meistersinger Overture" by Wagner is one that is often found to be difficult to play accurately.

In such a case, suspend the triangle from a music rack by means of a triangle holder (Fig. III). Check carefully to see that everything is set in a manner that will not permit the stand to topple over or the triangle to drop. A triangle holder can be purchased from any drum company or one may be made from a music rack clip. Play the figure with two beaters on the bottom bar. The trill or roll is done in either of the closed corners with a single beater.

Tambourine

Known as the Tambour de Basque in French and as Tambourino in Italian, the tambourine is a very effective instrument when properly played. Like triangles, good tambourines are inexpensive, and every school should have at least two of different sizes. Tambourines should not be too thick as a thick one will tend to cramp the hand in which it is held.

The instrument is held in the left hand between the thumb and the fingertips, and it is struck by the fingers of the right hand. In very soft passages only the very outside rim needs to be tapped. If the head itself is tapped very softly, a sort of tom-tom tone rather than the tone of the jingles will be produced. For very loud parts, however, the player may close the hand in a fist and strike the head with the knuckles.

Two types of rolls are used for the tambourine. The wrist roll, which actually is not done by the wrist, is made by holding the tambourine as described before and shaking it by turning the arm rapidly in a twisting or rotating motion for loud or long rolls.

The thumb roll is a little more difficult and requires practice for perfection. The player first moistens the fleshy part of the thumb by sucking it for at least a minute. He then rubs the thumb along the edge of the tambourine, pressing very gently. (See Fig. IV.)

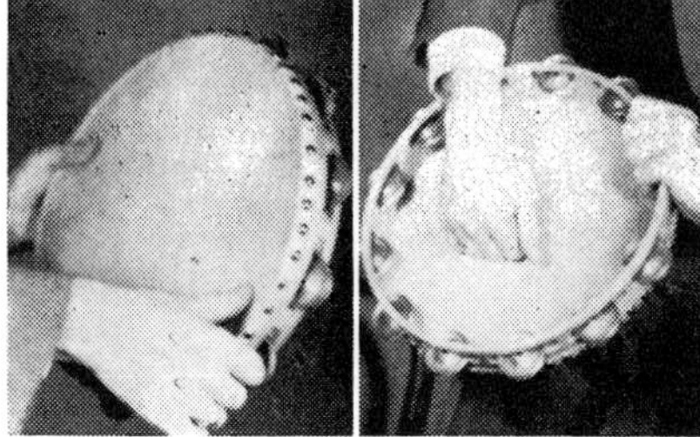
Fig. IV **Fig. V**

Crescendos are made by added pressure of the thumb against the head and by moving the thumb faster as the pressure is increased. Obviously, the size of the instrument and the speed of the roll will have to determine the length of thumb roll that can be made. A beginner who has trouble in producing a thumb roll may try rubbing a bit of rosin on the edge of the head where the thumb will rub. Once the roll has been mastered, the rosin should not be used.

The thumb can be very effectively used in the Polovetsian Dances from "Prince Igor" by Borodin. (See Example 1.)

In the same composition the wrist roll also may be used. The very last note is struck with the right hand in a closed fist with the knuckles striking the center of the tambourine. (See Example 2.)

The reader will note that neither of these excerpts shows the roll tied to the following note. This should be indicated; in many cases the drummer or the director must edit the parts. Example 2 should be played as a continuous roll.

In playing the excerpt in Example 3, I have always found it best to place one foot on a chair and rest the tambourine on the leg while playing with both hands. Such a procedure should be followed for all passages which are too difficult to be played with one hand.

In the Russian Sailor's Dance from "The Red Poppy" by Gliere, (Example 4) the leg is placed on a chair and the tambourine is struck against the knee for the first note and with the fist for the next note, continuing alternately. (Fig. V) This technic is used only for loud passages which are too difficult to play with one hand. Actually, the left hand is almost stationary while the right hand moves the tambourine back and forth between the left hand and the knee.

The head of the tambourine must be tight. It should be given a coat of shellac. The tambourine is a fragile instrument and must be given careful treatment. Once the head begins to slacken or the jingles come loose, it is time to get a new instrument.

Castanets

Playing castanets is not very difficult; with a bit of practice the percussion student should become proficient in their use. The single pair of castanets attached to a handle is the best to buy.

The handle is held by the thumb and fingers of the right hand with the castanets toward the floor. The instrument is played against the palm of the left hand with the fingers closing around them to stop them at the end of the rolls and on the rests, similar to the technic described for the triangle.

Castanet parts written by master composers should be played exactly as written. The figure in Example 5 is very difficult for castanets. One way of playing it is to use two pairs of castanets, closely matched in pitch, with the bottom clapper of each pair taped so that it cannot sound, and played against the leg. It is also possible just to hold the bottom clapper with the index finger of each hand.

In very soft passages it is possible to tap the rhythm with a triangle beater against the clapper if the speed is not too fast. Many times arrangers and composers write this figure, but actually desire the figure shown in Example 6. Unless the composition is by a great composer, or by one who wants that exact rhythm, it would be best to change the figure to a roll.

In traps, as in many other instruments, there is no set or only way. Many of the examples used would be played differently by different drummers. The important thing is that the results be what the composer or arranger intended. The best possible way to learn how to play these instruments is to watch the artists in symphony orchestras as they perform at concerts, on television, or in movies.

Confusion Confounds As Authorities Argue

Percussion teachers need only to follow good elementary drum method on proper instruments

JOHN P. NOONAN

IN THE TEACHING of percussion as well as of other instruments, the tendency seems to be to look for a quick short-cut method of achieving good results.

I have in the past written articles and made statements about drum rudiments and their shortcomings, and I have read articles by other writers along the same line. For example, I have said that there are only three drum rudiments, the Roll, the Single Stroke, and the Flam. I have heard of others who have gone even further and stated that there is only one, the Single Stroke! It is pretty obvious that we can't get it lower than that!

These statements by myself and by many other writers and speakers on the subject should not be misconstrued by the band leader-teacher. I want here to attempt to straighten out the matter a bit. First, as a specialist in percussion, I will go along with the one rudiment, the Single Stroke. I believe, however, that it can be realized only after a tremendous amount of work has been accomplished and the whole picture, so to speak, unfolds and can be viewed as a whole.

There are, as you know, twenty-six rudiments or first principles of drumming. Thirteen of these are deemed the essential rudiments and are accepted as such by educators everywhere. Contests are based on them. As with any other established system, however, someone sooner or later has to quarrel with the idea in whole or in part. Such disagreement is good, for thus do we finally achieve progress.

We must always keep in mind that the basic purpose of school music is education. I do not have statistics on how many students go on to be fine professional players, but I imagine that the percentage is small. On the other hand, I presume that the percentage of professionals who had school music training is very high. The teacher, therefore, should be guided by the principle that he must give the student a legitimate music education and provide an effective approach to the instrument chosen.

Non-Specialist

My ideas are stated for the teacher who is not a specialist on percussion but who has had some work on the subject. Such a teacher, of course, can do as good a job as the "specialist" in teaching the student the fundamentals of music. He can use almost any of the elementary drum methods to start the young player on his way. Practically all the first methods for drums are good. He can do a good job of guiding the beginner on the production of the thirteen essential rudiments.

I believe that every teacher will agree that it would be best to have a specialized teacher for each instrument from the very beginning of the child's training. One day this ideal will probably be realized and become customary; then the school band leader will actually be a conductor and a music adviser to the teacher. (Utopian, what?) It certainly isn't that way now, but we need not go into that, for the many problems are well known.

Every teacher has his own ideas as to how to put across the problem at hand, for such is the difference in teachers. This factor, added to knowledge and experience, is what produces the fine teacher of any instrument. A student can go to any drum teacher anywhere, and he will be instructed in the Roll, Stroke Rolls, Flams, and other rudiments rather than in the Single Stroke alone. As I said at the beginning, however, I firmly believe that perfect control of Single Strokes is the answer to the whole business. It is pretty obvious, though, that if we taught nothing but Single Strokes, we would have nothing but a Single-Stroke drummer!

Bewilderment

Thus it happens that the non-specialist becomes a bit confused. He doesn't know exactly what to do. The sincere teacher wants to do as good a job as possible with the beginning drum student, but all these ideas "louse up the act," and he wonders if he is doing the right thing. Well, let me allay his fears along this line. The teacher who starts the student along the rudimental lines as outlined in practically every elementary method is doing a good job.

There is no excuse for the band leader to ignore the drummers in his band, but many do. I have heard such leaders tell their bass drummers, "Never mind the music; watch me!"

That is good advice, I suppose, where the band is having a little trouble staying together, but as a general practice I can certainly see no excuse at all for it. The drummers should have the same training and lesson periods as the other instrumentalists. Unless they do, they are not receiving music education but are merely trying to play in the band. The greatest band leaders we have had have all remarked many times on the importance of the drum section; some have even said that the most important single player in the organization is the bass drummer. I will not argue that point, but I will say that the bass drummer should be very good, as should also the snare drummers and the timpanist.

The drum section can be a good one if the leader will devote a little time and attention to it. If he will but follow a good drum method and insist that the drummers learn the rudiments and read their parts, he will get them on their way. Then, if they do go to a specialized instructor, they can move right along.

I suppose that this "voice in the wilderness" will not accomplish much along the line of equipment, but it has to be mentioned. In visiting many bands throughout the country, I am amazed to see and hear the drums in some of these groups. I quite realize that a fully equipped drum section costs money, but there is little excuse for not having at least a good bass drum, cymbals, and snare drums.

By the word "good" I do not imply that they must be fancy, but I do insist that they can be of the school grade of reputable manufacturers, that the heads can be changed occasionally, and that the drums be kept in good condition. Even first-line instruments cost less than good clarinets, for example, but the school grade is adequate. Like everything else, it is a matter of budgeting.

I believe that many teachers are afraid of the drum work they should do and feel a little confused about what to teach. I can see no reason for this feeling. Just teach the rudiments with a clear conscience.

If some "authority" tells you, "Naw, that ain't the way," let him tell you about his way, and perhaps you can pick up a few pointers.

Go ahead with your rudimental instruction, and you can be sure that no good percussion man will in the future call down the wrath of heaven on your head. Rather, he will have a healthy respect for the good start that you have given the student that he must now guide further along the way toward being a good percussion player.

May-June 1952

'Sticking' Methods Cause Controversy

DRUMMERS DISAGREE ON USE OF HAND-TO-HAND FINGERING COMPARED TO SINGLE STICK METHOD

JOHN P. NOONAN

A HIGHLY CONTROVERSIAL subject among percussion players is the correct sticking or "fingering" of certain rhythmical figures in various compositions. The cardinal rule in drumming has always been a hand-to-hand proposition; that is, one stick follows the other in executing rhythmic passages. It is a condition devoutly to be wished, one that should be the aim of every drummer.

Now we come to the "however" or "but" that is bound to creep in whenever such a matter is discussed. First, we have our old pal, the left hand, to consider. I shall speak throughout this article of the right-handed drummer. The left is the awkward hand, and I seriously doubt if it ever equals the right in either speed or power. We all know the difficulties of producing either a double stroke or a single stroke roll on the snare drum and a fine even single stroke roll on the bells, xylophone, and timpani.

There is no question that evenness of sound is to be acquired before speed. All any drummer has to do is simply to try to play successive bars of quarter notes in common time *evenly*, using RLRL sticking and playing at a slow tempo to convince himself that it is possibly as difficult a feat as can be done on the snare drum. Almost anyone can tell the difference from the same exercise played with the right stick RRRR. First, there is the difference in stick weights and pitch; next, it is extremely difficult to give each stroke exactly the same amount of force. I believe any drummer will admit this if he is frank about it.

I am convinced that the factor that causes all the faults in drum technique is the failure to raise the left hand quickly enough after the blow has been produced. Our right stick goes down, makes a blow and comes back; our left stick goes down fine, but it doesn't seem to get back up quickly enough, causing our eventual downfall in speed, finesse, and power, not to mention evenness of sound.

Always Hand-to-Hand?

However, let us assume that the drummer plays well, has a good roll and good control of single strokes, and does play with fairly even strokes on the drum. Such performance is not a miracle. It can be acquired by anyone who will practice, but the question arises as to the advisability of actually playing always in a hand-to-hand manner. Most instruction books show the sticking below the notes and usually hand-to-hand, whether for single strokes, flams, ruffs, or a combination of strokes.

Drum solos also frequently show the sticking. All well and good, but I do not feel that hand-to-hand sticking is always the best. I believe it depends on several factors—the speed of the composition being played, the sound desired, and the way the figuration fits in the ensemble. Let's take a four-bar example in 2/4 time (Fig. I).

FIG. I.

No. 1 sticking is hand-to-hand and can be done at any tempo. Note that there are ten right strokes and ten left strokes. In No. 2 the right hand predominates with eleven rights and nine lefts. No. 3 has fifteen right strokes and but five lefts. No. 4 has again ten rights and ten lefts. Which is correct?

Try all four and you will note that each sounds differently although the rhythmic structure is unchanged. Try No. 3, for example, at a slow tempo and see if it isn't "cleaner" and more definite. Try No. 4 at a presto one-in-a-bar speed and see if it also doesn't come out a little more clearly. Try No. 2 sticking as a march tempo and notice it also is pretty definite and crystal clear. Now, let's look at flams (Fig. II and III).

FIG. II

FIG. III

Play No. 1 hand-to-hand and then No. 2, trying to make them sound the same. Pretty tough to do! If the passage is important or rapid or soft, I think No. 2 works out better. Another example may be seen in Fig. III.

There is nothing new about all this Such sticking is taught by many teachers, and much of it is outlined in the Straight System of Drumming by Edward B. Straight. I have also seen illustrations of it in other methods, and I know that many of the country's finest drummers use these variations of the orthodox hand-to-hand method, depending upon speed, importance, etc.

I believe that many band leaders are afraid to change the orthodox sticking even though the sound isn't really what they would like to hear. However, there is no reason for not changing, for the final results are what we are after. A student of mine once complained that in watching and listening to a famous timpanist he noted that the artist had played a solo figure as indicated in Fig. IV.

FIG. IV

Obviously so, for the player and the conductor had probably tried it several ways and found that the single stick method was best and much cleaner. However, if this figure is fast and forte, use hand-to-hand or RLRR RLRR for certain effects.

Every good drum teacher agrees that hand-to-hand stroke production must be perfected. It should be done that way and every effort made to perfect it, but there is certainly no reason that it must be done that way when playing in a band or an orchestra. Thus, for example, in the playing of a military march at a snappy tempo, hand-to-hand works fine and looks well. However, for an overture, symphony, or programmatic selection where an important part or solo is to be executed, it is best to think over the sticking and try it several ways for the desired sound and effect.

Everyone knows the Bolero drum rhythm of Ravel. Several fine percussionists have told me of changes in the sticking required by their conductors in order to achieve the clarity and preciseness required in a fine musical organization. The drummer can't say, "Look, Pop, that's hand-to-hand," and hold his job. The idea is to try to get the best possible results, regardless of what the sticking may be.

I suggest that you band leaders experiment a little, and I believe that you will be able to get some good musical results.

September 1952

Developing the Clean Roll

Unorthodox grips and the buzz roll are the downfall of many drum sections

BILL MUEHLER

IN DISCUSSING DRUM problems with band directors I have found that because of their need of a drum section in a hurry they often thrust sticks into a student's hands and tell him to play even though he knows nothing of the theory behind the principles of drumming.

In order to avoid such advanced playing for beginners we have hit upon the idea of starting the drum section two or three months ahead of the other instruments. Thus, the student develops sufficiently to be able to play the material in the so-called "beginner's" books without doing him any harm.

A majority of the method books written for bands start the drummer out on quarter notes. Five-stroke rolls, paradiddles, and the other rudiments follow much too quickly for him to grasp. Technique, control, and speed must be built up just as gradually in drumming as must fingering, etc., in other instruments.

Early Correction

If the beginner starts out with unorthodox grips and improper knowledge of how to get clean rolls, he has three strikes against him. It is very important to correct such faults in the beginning since it is next to impossible to break them later, when too many students accept the "easy way out," feeling that the "old way" is good enough.

Four main factors in the development of a good roll should be mastered by the beginner.

1. Take position. The student should have one stick in the air and one stick low to the drum. Thus he is physically ready to execute the more important steps of learning.

2. Keep sticks in motion like the pistons in an engine to develop even and smooth coordination. One stick goes up as the other goes down; therefore, the student is preparing with one stick while playing with the other. In applying this method to rolls, the sticks will be coming off the head quickly enough to prevent them from bouncing more than they should, thus creating a buzz or sloppy roll.

Uniform Speed

3. Move sticks at the same speed as you are playing. By doing so the student will be moving his sticks in a fashion that will enable him to keep relaxed; therefore, he will avoid getting a tight grip on the sticks which would prevent him from rebounding freely.

Aside from helping develop the roll, the above factor has a great deal to do with developing a good beat, which is the first quality a player must have to be considered a good drummer.

4. Raise sticks the same height. If this rule is followed by a beginner he will develop the same volume and power in each hand. It is safe to say that many drummers who have weak left hands are victims of teachers who have let a natural tendency go too far. If every person who started drums looked for the easy way, we would all have weak left hands.

Raising the sticks the same height has a bearing on the player's coordination, for when one stick goes higher than the other, it will require longer for it to play, and unevenness will result.

To establish the four factors in a beginner I assign an exercise of four quarter notes, R L R L, very slowly so that he may study and apply them.

After the student has mastered single strokes, using the above method, I start him on an exercise called single strokes into rebounds, illustrated in Fig. I.

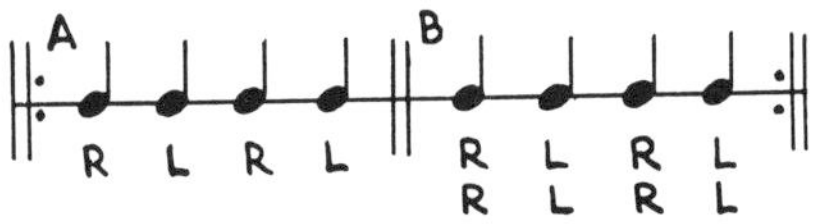

A R L R L B R L R L R L R L

Fig. I

It should be impressed upon a student's mind that Part B of Fig. I should be played with the same idea in mind as Part A. By moving the sticks the same way on both, the sticks will be coming up off the head to develop a clean roll.

The principle of the above exercise can be applied to all the various roll rudiments shown in Fig. II.

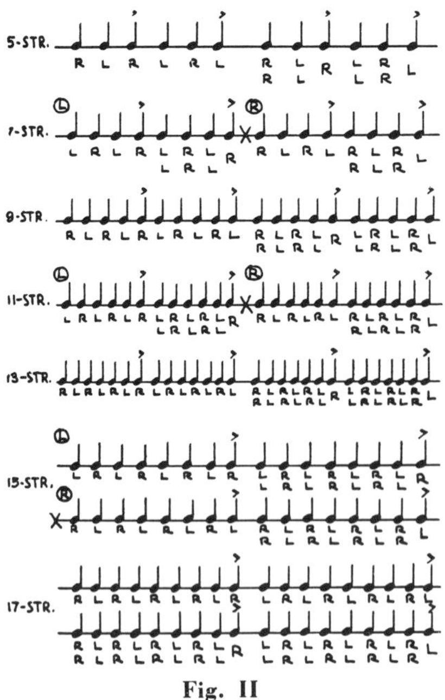

Fig. II

To help the beginner develop a consistent accent on the end of the roll it is necessary to keep the sticks low except where accents are indicated, as in Fig. III.

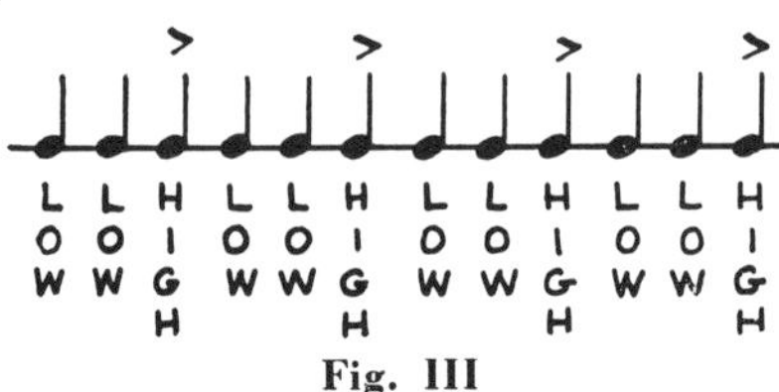

Fig. III

The aim of the preceding exercises is to improve the cleanness of the roll rudiments. To prepare the student for solo contests, "open and closed" practice would have to be stressed as well.

If the band director is working to develop his drum section strictly for band music and street beats, he would not necessarily have to follow the rudimental pattern. Instead, he could apply the rolls by dividing the various rolls found in everyday band music by sixteenth notes, as shown below in Fig. IV.

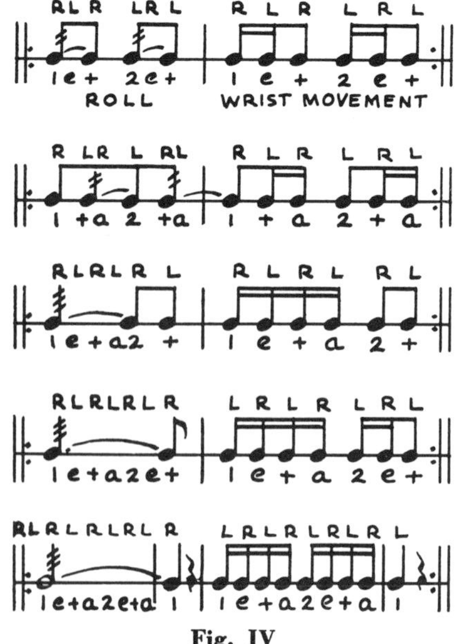

Fig. IV

The above are the rolls most commonly used in band music. I have not gone into detail in the above exercise but have merely tried to show a few patterns which the student may practice in order to get his band work clean while studying the rudiments shown in Fig. II.

Rolls applied in the above fashion are called rhythm rolls, which are used extensively by the professional show drummer. The subject of rolling to various rhythms is a highly controversial one that would take a complete article in itself.

Application of the various methods described in this article may test the patience, but the finished product will be far superior to the "quick easy method."

Advice on Selecting, Training Drummers for Marching Band

Drum section can be heart of group if properly chosen, taught and drilled

JAMES D. SALMON

THE HEART of any good marching band is the drum section. Its steady tempo and even cadence can be yours if you take the time to guide your drummers toward this goal. This just doesn't happen; it takes lots of patience, careful planning and organization to achieve it. However, it can be done!

First of all, pick your drummers for their leadership qualities as well as their playing potential. Select those who are alert and are adaptable to any given situation; choose them as you would your solo cornetist. Put very reliable people on the bass drum and the cymbals as this will save you lots of rehearsal time and trouble in the long run. The best of equipment in the hands of careless players who are not interested in drumming is just so much wasted time, energy and money.

Good bass drummers and cymbal players are usually good snare drummers, and a well trained percussion rank will contain drummers that can play every percussion part reasonably well. A good drummer is also a good musician! It is wise to appoint your most experienced drummer as your section leader or drum sergeant. Outline your plans to him and let him rehearse the drum section accordingly.

Next, insist that your drummers be trained to play as well as possible. It is essential to good drumming that the various rhythms be played with the same sticking patterns by *all* the drummers, much in the same manner as bowing patterns are worked out in the string sections of symphony orchestras. In order to do this, every drummer should be prepared to play at least half of the first thirteen rudiments of drumming and *apply them to music.* Have them practice their routines on practice pads before transferring them to drums to help cut down on the over-all band rehearsal time later on. Simplify any of the drum parts when necessary, but do not allow anyone to "fake" a part. The section must do everything the same way at the same time for best results.

March Cadences

Select your street beats or marching cadences for their "footlifting appeal." Don't use rhythms that might mislead the band into a disorganized step. It is also suggested that marching cadences be used that will lead the band into its next playing sequence as smoothly as possible. I recommend the use of a 6/8 cadence before a 6/8 march and a 2/4 or ¢ cadence before a 2/4 or ¢ march. This will help to prepare the band rhythmically for the music that is to follow. Have several cadences prepared and use them alternately for variety in performance. Cadences that are easy to play and march to will use rolls sparingly. Let the cymbals punctuate the phrases; the snare drum part should emphasize all accents quite heavily. The bass drum should strive for steady rhythm with accents at the half and full cadence points.

Practice Routines

Your drummers should practice marching maneuvers *without* drums at first until they can execute *all* turns, facings and commands smoothly. Then have them go through the same routines while carrying but not playing their drums. It takes practice to carry a drum as well as to play it properly. When all drummers can do this satisfactorily, then let them combine the marching and playing. Start them at about MM 120 and let them increase their speed gradually until your regular marching tempo is reached.

It also helps if the drummers can sing, whistle or hum the melody line of all the music used in the football band. How can they expect to play a melody they cannot recognize? A new song can be learned every practice period if the director will insist upon it since most football show routines are made up of the trios or the popular theme of most songs. This takes a little time, but it will produce results. The drum section can be working at this while the conductor is working with other sections of the band.

Because good drumming demands a certain amount of showmanship, I recommend the choosing of drummers that lean toward the "extrovert" side—not the rowdy "show-off" type but rather those who like to demonstrate their playing abilities with enthusiasm in public performances and who thoroughly enjoy themselves while doing so.

I have also found that use of silk ribbons in the school colors attached to the ends of the various drumsticks helps to show off the percussion rank to good advantage. Use ribbons 1″ by 10″ attached with Scotch tape to the thick ends of the snare drumsticks and sewed into the felt or lamb's wool tips of bass drum or tenor drumsticks. Work out sticking patterns carefully; raise the sticks about chin level over the drums; and the breeze on the streamers will complete the picture.

Pride in Achievement

Teach your drummers to take pride in their work and to take care of their equipment properly so that it will be in the best possible playing condition at all times. If they are careful with their equipment, they will usually be careful in their playing.

Drummers should be taught to set a tempo with a stop watch or any watch with a sweep-second hand. The following formula may be helpful in teaching them to do this:

$$\frac{\text{Cadence of music}}{4} = \text{steps per 15 seconds;}$$

$$\text{e.g., } \frac{140}{4} = 35 \text{ (steps per 15 sec.)}$$

By counting in 15-second periods instead of the full minute, the drummers will have a shorter period of time to clock and fewer steps to count. They can practice this at any free time or when walking to and from school. Your drum major and your drum sergeant can cooperate in this routine in order to establish and maintain steadier marching tempi.

Sousa became the "March King" because of his meticulous attention to the rhythmic content and the flawless adaptation of musically written drum parts. He knew that the spark that gives that specific drive to any well organized band has to come from the drum section because the melody and the harmony instruments cannot produce it.

I hope that the above suggestions may prove helpful to the conductors and drummers of the many school bands that are marching on gridirons from coast to coast.

November-December 1952

Learning To Apply the Drum Rudiments

ACTON E. OSTLING

Method dependent on wishes of conductor, type of music and experience of drummer

At the present time there are few band directors who do not know about the rudiments of drumming; they are demonstrated and discussed at nearly every band clinic and workshop. It is when the director takes a drum part of a band selection and tries to determine when and where to play the rudiments that he is likely to become confused.

Some drum parts have the rudiments clearly indicated, leaving little doubt as to how they should be played. Sousa marches, for instance, are written with all rudiments shown so that a trained drummer has little trouble with the parts. However, many

Application of Rudiments

Fig. I

FLAMS may be substituted for quarter and eighth notes in some types of music. They help "broaden" the effect of afterbeats and are especially effective in marches, waltzes, etc. They may be used to reinforce certain accents.

Fig. II

FLAM ACCENTS may be substituted for groups of three eighth notes. The sticking of the flam accent may be, at times, advantageously applied to other rhythmic patterns.

arrangers do not understand drums and score the drum parts with rhythms only, leaving to the individual drummer the application of the rudiments to the parts.

Substitution Desirable

Which rudiments to apply and when to apply them depend on the type of music, the experience of the drummer and the wishes of the conductor. Single sticking is often preferred in soft strains, delicate passages and fast tempo. However, in certain types of music there are places where the judicious substitution of rudiments for the written rhythmic patterns adds greatly to the parts by giving them a distinctly "drummistic" effect which cannot be obtained with single sticking.

Not One Best

In discussing with different drummers the application of rudiments I have not been able to find any "one" way which is universally recognized as correct. In fact, there is considerable disagreement on some points. For instance, one outstanding drummer told me that he frequently uses the sticking of the paradiddle for groups of sixteenth notes; another told me that he would never do so. It would be much easier if we could say that one should ALWAYS use THIS rudiment in THAT place. Although we cannot do this, the examples which follow show some of the places where rudiments can be applied advantageously.

It should be stressed to young drummers that they should be consistent in the substituting of rudiments. If flams are used for a pattern, they should be applied in like places throughout the number. Conversely, if an arranger has scored any flams in a number, he probably wanted them only in those places, and the drummer should not substitute but should play the part as written.

Stressing again that the type of music and the wishes of the conductor must always be considered, the examples on the opposite page show some ways in which rudiments may be applied to make drum parts more effective.

Special Drill

To reiterate, drum parts of band music should not always be played as written; there are many individual

Fig. III

FLAM TAPS may be applied to groups of two eighth notes. This sticking may be applied to the quarter and eighth (sometimes called Flam Accent No. II) and the dotted eighth and sixteenth (sometimes called the Flam and Feint).

Fig. IV

FLAM ACCENTS I and II may be much more effective for the drum parts of six-eight marches when played as indicated in Fig. IV.

Fig. V **Fig. VI**

RUFFS are usually played only when written, but one fine drummer stated that he used them on afterbeats of waltzes to "broaden" the quarter notes. (See Fig. V.)

FLAMACUES may be effectively substituted, with accent, in drum solos of various marches, as in Fig. VI. This sticking may be applied to one group of sixteenths; however, the distinctive accent of this rudiment

should not be played unless indicated.

George L. Stone, the fine Boston drummer, once told me he felt that a band with a drummer that used accented flamacues would be comparable to a male quartet having a tenor with the hiccoughs.

Fig. VII

PARADIDDLES and FLAMADIDDLES are especially effective when applied to drum solos in marches to obtain a distinctive martial effect. Sticking, without accent, may be used when playing one or more groups of sixteenths.

band numbers—in fact, even whole books of marches—without a single rudiment other than rolls being indicated on the drum parts. To make these more effective, band directors should work with their drummers and give them positive directions as to how they want the parts played. Special drill regarding the substituting of rudiments at specified places will do much to develop more precision, more uniform sticking and a more effective and better sounding drum section in the band.

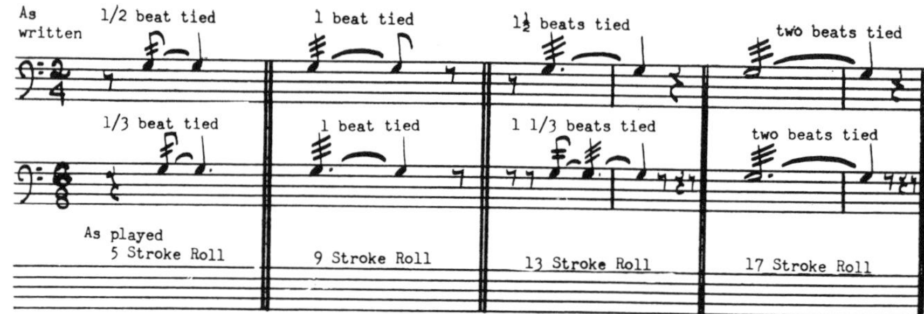

Fig. VIII

SHORT ROLLS as shown in the roll chart (Fig. VIII) work satisfactorily when the tempo is not too slow or too fast. Young drummers usually get along better when they are taught to execute a definite roll for a certain notation.

January-February 1953

Tympani Study Needs Basis of Musicianship

Adjustments necessary in roll speeds, volume, dynamics and values of notes

JOE BARRY MULLINS

TO ARRIVE AT THE CONCEPT of good tympani tone, it is necessary to understand that tympani possess greater resonance than any other percussion instrument. The characteristic of resonant tone at any desired pitch within range renders them the most important and the most musical of all percussion instruments.

Tympani tone is semi-sustaining, as opposed to the staccato quality of the snare drum, for instance. The elements of sostenuto and resonance are, paradoxically, the reasons for the difficulty of good tone production. Like other percussion instruments, tympani are struck with sticks and mallets, tone being produced by impact and direct attack. If such attack is improperly made, both resonance and quality are hindered and impaired, and poor tone results.

In general, tympani tone is "drawn" or "pulled" from the instruments; thus the tympanist must possess good physical control together with a satisfactory aural concept of the tone desired. Tympani "attack" is comparable with the function of the tongue in releasing the breath which produces tone on a wind instrument. In the same manner that the tongue moves backward, the ball of the tympani stick produces its tone almost on the upstroke and not directly on the down blow.

Though correct holding position of the sticks, proper playing form, and mental and physical preparation are of great importance, the final criterion is the actual sound produced; as with all other instruments, the ear is of primary importance and often "directs" the physical motions involved. Good tone quality is produced with a minimum of audible attack or other extraneous sound. Acceptable tympani tone is largely dependent upon the type of impact which the ball of the stick makes when striking the head. The sound of attack must be reduced to the barest minimum so that more or less "pure tone" results.

Relaxation Needed

The natural resonance of tympani suggests legato style. Such style further indicates that relaxation is necessary in order that maximum tone and smoothness may be effected.

A finely controlled legato style is required for the development of a good tympani roll, which, of course, is produced with alternating single strokes. The roll imperfectly simulates the true sostenuto of wind instruments. The method of producing the tympani roll is perhaps the least understood element in tympani playing. As previously mentioned, tone is always of first importance, and the best quality and greatest resonance is attained through controlled stick attacks and relaxation. The roll is merely a somewhat more rapid legato style having the above characteristics; the roll must be *tonal*.

Controlled Speed

For the best possible tone in the roll, the stick sound must be kept under careful control. This idea serves to reveal the little-known fact that a good tympani roll is not extremely rapid. The actual speed of the stick impacts varies slightly on tones of different pitch. Low tones, such as the low F on the 28-inch kettle, require that the roll be considerably slower than, for instance, the C taken on the 25-inch drum.

The lower tones do not need as much "assistance" from the sticks; whereas higher pitches demand a faster roll in order to keep the head in constant vibration. In order to get the best tone possible, an experienced tympanist will make slight adjustments in his roll speed on almost every tone of different pitch. The higher tones played on the smaller kettles, though demanding more rapid stick movement in the roll, are often distorted by exceeding the speed which produces the best quality and resonance. High tones can usually be "relieved" by slight modification of volume and roll speed and by concentrating on relaxation.

As mentioned before, the only really dependable factor is the ear, coupled with considerable sensitivity and manual finesse.

In addition to subtle adjustments in roll speed and method of attack on tones at various levels of pitch, changes are often desirable in connection with alterations in dynamics. Tone often suffers in quality at each end of the dynamic range (as with many other instruments) so that care should be exercised when playing extremely softly or very loudly.

Tonal Fluency

If the tympanist has not developed a fluent technic which is always *tonal*, it may be better to modify extreme volume toward a more controllable level. Excessively loud playing usually removes the tympani from the realm of "musical percussion." Powerful stick impacts which are required for great volume are sometimes so lacking in control that both pitch and tone quality are lost, momentarily placing the tympani among the "indeterminate" percussion.

Loss of tone through excessive volume and a too-rapid roll speed, especially on low tones, sometimes occurs with many otherwise excellent tympanists.

Although quality of tone is the most important factor in tympani playing (together with tuning accuracy, which will not be discussed here), another important factor is that of articulation and note values or the shortness and length of tones. The length of time which single tones or rolls are allowed to sustain must coincide with the articulation and note values as played by other sections of the band or orchestra.

Unfortunately, many tympani parts give no indication of either note values or articulation in the printed part. It is necessary that the tympanist be encouraged to listen carefully to the music as played by the other instruments and learn to perform his part in appropriate style insofar as articulation and length of tones are concerned.

The inexperienced player may need much guidance from the conductor in matters of tone, balance and general dynamic adjustment. It should be the conductor's responsibility either to edit the tympani part carefully or to convey his wishes through verbal instruction in rehearsal. It has been the writer's experience that many high school percussion players are capable of considerable musical insight and finesse in such details if given frequent guidance and suggestion.

It is necessary that the tympanist be able to play staccato on his instruments as well as legato, which has been previously discussed. In staccato playing, each tone must be clearly sounded in semi-detached style; all of the tones in a particular staccato passage must be heard distinctly. Such effects are secured by assuming in the fingers, wrists or forearms a certain amount of muscular tension. The physical movements thus appear to be somewhat mechanical. The "stiffening" produces a different type of attack, the sound is less tonal, and the effect is more articulate.

In staccato playing, the impact of the sticks must be more pronounced than in the legato style. For even more staccato sounds, the beating spot may be moved more toward the center of the drum, where there is less natural resonance.

It is the writer's opinion that more satisfactory results from student percussion players—and from tympanists in particular—could be attained if the emphasis in instruction could be placed on musicianship rather than on technic, mechanics and virtuosity. Instruction in tympani especially must be toward musical playing and literature since, in general, there is no technically complex system of technic and fingering. The difficulties are musical, and for the benefit of the students a more musical approach should be employed. It is hoped that the few comments and suggestions herein will serve to promote that end.

Percussion Ensemble Class Gives Training in 'New Style' Music

PAUL PRICE

THE PERCUSSION ENSEMBLE has as its purpose the performance of music written for percussion instruments.

In addition to providing an organization readily available for presenting percussion works, the percussion ensemble class affords students the opportunity to acquire playing experience in small groups such as duets, trios, and quartets as well as in larger combinations, and to become acquainted with percussion ensemble literature.

Besides learning the usual percussion instruments the player must add to his technical facility new techniques for obtaining musical sounds from such unorthodox "instruments" as bottles, glass plates, tin cans, auto brake drums, boxes, electric buzzers, pieces of wood and a variety of Oriental drums, bells and gongs as well as primitive drums, rattles, etc.

Creative ingenuity is exercised by constructing instruments that cannot be easily purchased. Such a class not only arouses the analytical and experimental curiosity of the participants but inspires many of them toward original composition.

The interest in percussion instruments, their variety and their construction has resulted in the production of many new works for such instruments, running the gamut from concert hall calibre to high school contest material. Composers have, however, been writing for and experimenting with percussion since the eighteenth century craze-influence of Turkish music.

World War I is a convenient association landmark for the period beginning a new thought for percussion instruments. Perhaps the spirit of wild abandon which followed in the wake of the war and the popular animated rhythmic pulsations of the period were responsible for the importance given percussion instruments both in and out of the concert hall.

New Style

Small chamber works with percussion appeared first in the early 1920's, and these became a strong influence toward the so-called *New Style*. Stravinsky and Milhaud were significant in this connection.

Concert music in the form of ensembles of all sizes written for percussion alone began appearing in the early 1930's. Through 1942 an abundance of percussion music was written by such composers as Roldan, Varese, Ardevol, Beyer, Russell, Cowell, Strang, Davidson, Green, Becker, Cage, Harrison and Chavez.

During the past ten years John Cage, Lou Harrison, Henry Cowell and others have been instrumental in bringing percussion music before the listening public. Performed works include their own as well as other "old" and new percussion ensembles. The opportunities to hear percussion music have brought about renewed interest and many new ideas for this idiom.

Many of the more recent works include such other instruments as clarinet, bass clarinet, trombone and trumpet, as well as voice. In this connection Carlos Surinach, Virgil Thompson, Peggy Glanville-Hicks, Henry Cowell, Paul Bowles, Fred Noak, and J. H. McKenzie should be mentioned.

Percussion players have not been idle or disinterested in the *New Style* but have contributed many works. The technical knowledge of the percussion-player-composer permits production of functional as well as purely academic compositions. Michael Colgrass, Ben Johnston and Paul Price, in addition to those mentioned above, have been active in this field.

Influence on Schools

Recently school contest materials have been noticeably influenced by percussion ensemble music. Such works have been written in an attempt to break away from the usual "military" type ensemble comprising bass drum, cymbals and snare drums. Ensembles including timpani, tambourine, claves, wood blocks, bells, tom-toms, etc., in addition to the usual percussion offer participants an opportunity to become acquainted with a variety of percussion instrument techniques and afford a decidedly different kind of enjoyment for players and listeners.

Colgrass, McKenzie and Noak, previously mentioned, have contributed functional works for school use, as have Mervin Britton, Elliot Carter, Rudolph Ganz, Daniel Jones, Richard Kamm, Donovan Olson, Truman Shoaff and Eugene Weigel.

May-June 1953

Hints on Care and Use of Tympani

SAUL GOODMAN

FOR MANY YEARS THE PERCUSSION sections of our bands and orchestras were looked upon as a sort of last refuge for those who had tried every other instrument without success or who had tired of one instrument and resorted to the drums as a final testing ground for their musical ability. The section was often referred to as the "Kitchen," which did not further enhance its prestige.

The situation is different today. Playing of percussion has become a most exacting art, one which requires highly specialized training for mastery. Composers are more and more inclined to assign important parts to percussion instruments, especially the tympani, which have emerged in modern music as instruments possessing rhythmic, harmonic and melodic values.

Hence, tympani must be accepted as important musical instruments requiring the understanding and care accorded other instruments. One of the outstanding faults in care of tympani in schools is lack of knowledge of the requirements for keeping the instruments sounding well. I have often come into a school and found drums stored in a hot room or shunted off to some damp corner in the basement. Both conditions are bad for the drum head.

When not in use, tympani should be stored in a dry cool atmosphere away from heat of any kind unless the head is damp. As soon as it has dried, it should be stored with the other drums in a cool dry place. During the winter months when in overheated buildings, the head continually tends to contract, but it can be revived by placing it in a cool spot. Another point is to tune the drums carefully before putting them away. Thus even tension all around is insured, the head will set evenly and sound its best and the finest possible intonation will result.

The Collar

Maintaining an even collar or shoulder in the head is of vital importance. The ability to retain the collar will rest to a large extent on the manner in which the head was originally tucked on the flesh hoop. The manner of tucking the head will be determined by the atmospheric and room conditions under which it is to be used.

For example, in a dry cold climate like Denver, Colorado, the head should be tucked with a large amount of slack to allow for excessive contraction. A ball of newspaper rolled to the desired size and placed under the exact center of the head will do.

Conversely, under extremely damp conditions the head should be tucked with no slack at all. The amount of slack, therefore, should be determined between these extreme conditions. Very often when I have visited a school during the dry cold months of the year, the musical director has asked me why the large tympani would not go below A. Of course, the cause was that the proper collar had not been maintained or that the head had not been properly tucked in the first place. The head may be wet down on both sides, avoiding wetting the skin closer than a half inch to the edge. It should then be allowed to sit for several hours in order to get the range of the lower tones. Too much wetting of the head, however, causes it to overstretch and ultimately to go toneless and dull.

Another important method is to keep the drums tuned high when not in use. I have found that leaving the large drum tuned to C and the small one to high F will greatly assist in maintaining the proper collar under extremely dry conditions. Under damp conditions very little tension should be applied; the large drum may be tuned to low F and the small one to B♭. I do not advocate leaving the drum heads completely limp.

The Sticks

The type of tympani sticks one uses is a very important factor in the results obtained. In many schools I have seen large-balled lamb's wool sticks being used. They produce a tubby inarticulate tone not at all related to the tympani although they are excellent for rolling on the bass drum.

Nothing can equal an outer covering of soft damper felt for tympani. It must be properly applied to the stick. The ball for either the cartwheel or ball type should be constructed so that the felt is firmly sewed around the ball itself with no excess of felt bulging out or lapping over.

Firm Inner Core

A good firm inner core is essential for a good stick. Proper stick dimensions are difficult to establish because of differing preferences of individual players. One fact can be stated, however: a ball that is too large will not give good results. To satisfy normal conditions of playing the following types may be considered:

1. Sticks for full round tone and general all-purpose use.
2. Small-headed sticks for staccato and sharp rhythmical passages.
3. Sticks for loud playing.
4. Specialized sticks like wood ball ends where this type is required.

Since the drum head is an organic material affected by varying conditions of weather, temperature, animal heat, etc., its vibrating quality will depend largely on the effect of such conditions. If the head is hard and dry from too much heat, a large-balled stick is indicated. If the head is moister, a smaller type stick is required.

Tuning

Tuning of tympani requires great skill and experience, even when the head is even and a good tensioning system is used. Because the head on a pedal tympani has hand screws for adjustment, it is easily thrown out of gear by improper turning of the screws. Every individual screw must be adjusted in order to obtain the required range and individually checked for accuracy so that true pitch will prevail. Although the pedal does the work of automatically tightening the entire head at once, the important factor is the adjustment of each individual screw point around the head to prevent the collar's becoming uneven and thus making the head sound false.

From a theoretical point of view, given a head of even texture all around, turning each screw the same amount should produce clear intonation on every note. The human hand cannot always be so accurate; therefore, the ear takes over to check correctness of tuning. Unless the player has a good ear, uneven intonataion results.

Several mechanical devices have been put forth to correct tuning defects. The writer has devised a system using a sprocket and chain principle (U.S. Patent 2,587,310) whereby the turning of any individual screw turns all the screws in absolute unison, thereby insuring even tension of the head throughout.*

Before the head chain is attached to the sprocket, the head is pulled down evenly by means of the individual sprockets so that the desired collar in the head is obtained. Then each screw point around the circumference of the head is tuned carefully to a note in the range of the particular drum. The chain is then attached and the drum is ready for use.

The writer has found over a long period of time that it is a rare occurrence indeed when an individual screw has to be adjusted. If it does, it is a simple matter to remove the chain and make the adjustment. Since the chain is endless, the range of the drum is increased and no special adjustment is necessary for weather changes. Tightening or loosening the chain assembly is all that is required to obtain any note in the range under any and all conditions. When the head is subjected to this type of even tensioning and individual screw points remain undisturbed, the tone keeps getting better and better. Tuning by ear is not necessary since the mechanical device insures correct tension.

The Heads

Choice of heads is made easier by the fact that American drum head manufacturers produce the finest in the world. They have choice raw materials, specialized machinery and technical knowledge.

---

*Additional information concerning the chain tuning device and the tympani sticks may be obtained from the Goodman Drum Company, 141 Knelland Avenue, Yonkers, New York.

Heads are classified as thin, medium heavy and heavy. A thin head usually sounds well immediately after being installed, but with rough use it soon becomes stretched and loses its tone. For the average 25-inch and 28-inch tympani, my experience has shown that a good medium head will do an acceptable job although it may be slightly thicker for the larger drum. A heavier head should be used in dry weather. Breaking it in will take longer, but it will last longer, take more rough use and sound better than a thin head. For drums of special sizes, like 30-inch or 22-inch, I recommend heavy for the larger and medium for the smaller size. In very damp climates heavy heads will not work well; therefore such a condition will influence choice.

September 1953

Drums on the March

Percussion section must go into action in marching band early in school year

HASKELL W. HARR

At the beginning of each school year comes the problem of getting the percussion section ready for the marching band. Among the problems that the director faces are choice of equipment, decision on the size of drums, training of auxiliary drummers, and other related questions.

Selection of Drums

For the grade school marching band I would suggest the 10-inch by 14-inch parade drum with wire snares and separate tension rods. Separate tension rods permit each head to be tightened individually.

Let me say a few words about tensioning the heads. When adjusting them, make about two turns of the key for the batter (top) head to one turn for the snare (bottom) head. When the heads are fairly tight, snap off the snares and tap the head with the finger about two inches from each post. If the head has been tensioned evenly, the tone will be the same at all posts. Heads may be tensioned clockwise. When the drum is in playing condition, one should be barely able to dent the top head by applying pressure to the center with the forefinger. A little more give should be allowed to the snare head so that the snares can vibrate freely.

The high school marching band will find 12-inch by 15-inch parade drums more suitable. These should be equipped with gut or combination wire-gut snares. Every parade drum should be equipped with a leg rest as it keeps the drum more steady and permits a natural even stride.

Drumsticks should be the size recommended by the manufacturer; 2B is good for the smaller drum and 1S for the larger one.

In bass drums I recommend the 10-inch by 26-inch Scotch bass drum for the grade school band and the 10-inch by 30-inch Scotch drum for the high school band. These drums are lighter and easier to carry than the regular ones and yet give about the same amount of volume. Two bass drums may be used with the marching band if the drummers are well trained and alert to each other's playing. Some bands that carry two bass drums have the drummers take turns playing during the parade.

Where additional flash is desired, tenor drums are becoming very popular. They are oversized parade drums without snares; the junior size is 10 by 15 inches and the large size 12 by 17 inches. They are played with sticks similar to bass drum beaters. One tenor drum is used for each two parade drums. With tenor drums I would use the Scotch style of bass drumming. The up-and-down rhythmic movement of the arms of the entire section adds much flash to the band. A pamphlet on the style of Scotch drumming may be had by writing the WFL Drum Company, 1728 North Damen Avenue, Chicago, Illinois.

The name of the band should be painted on both sides of the drum. Nothing is more exasperating than to watch a band march past with no identification of the organization which it represents. Use regular sign painters' paint and cover with spar varnish.

Slinging the Drum

Drummers must spend considerable time practicing marching with their drums; this subject brings us to the proper method of slinging drums. The sling should be over the right shoulder and fastened together at the waist on the left side. The top of the drum should be just far enough below the waist to permit the right arm to hang nearly straight down and the left arm below the elbow to be at about a 30-degree angle. The drum rests in front of the left leg, and the lower counter hoop just above the left knee. (See Fig. I.)

The bass drum should be carried on the chest so that the eyes just clear the top of the drum. (See Fig. II.)

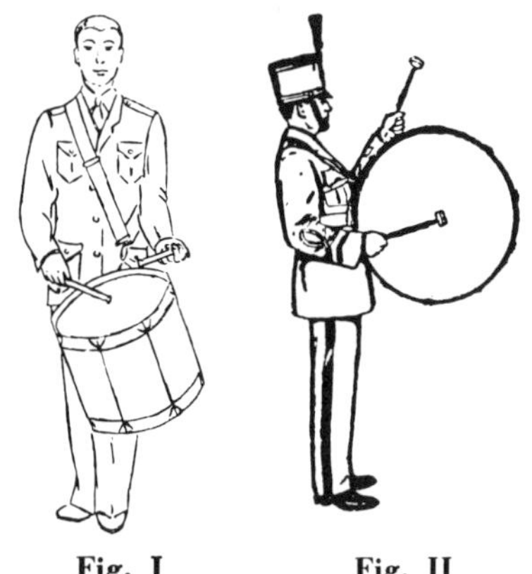

Fig. I **Fig. II**

A good pair of cymbals adds to the tonal quality of the band. The 14, 15 or 16-inch medium-heavy cymbals are best to use, depending upon the size of the player. To get the best tone out of your cymbals use the felt pad and finger loop. Avoid the wooden cymbal handle with a bolt because it not only stops the tone and breaks cymbals but tires the player as well.

To grip the cymbal, insert the third finger through the loop and close the hand; then play with the fingertips, knuckles and wrist, as shown in Figures III and IV.

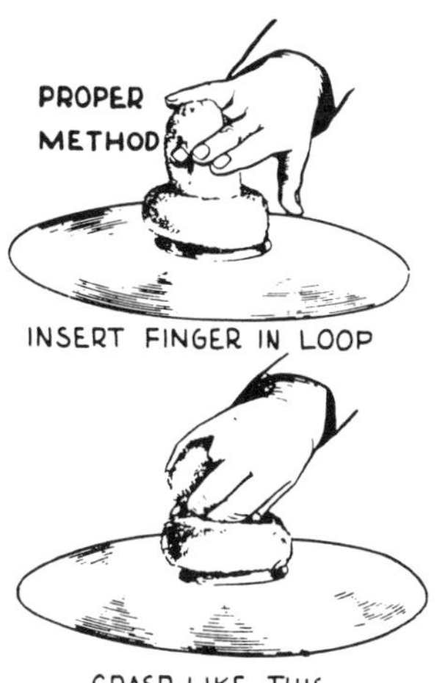

Fig. III and Fig. IV

Figure V shows the position of the cymbals when they are not being played.

Figure VI shows the up-and-down stroke; the height is governed by the volume desired. The stroke is always made with a glancing blow. The left cymbal is raised and the right cymbal lowered. With an up blow the uppermost edge of the right cymbal makes the initial attack at a point three inches from the top of the left cymbal as the left one starts down. If you wish the cymbals to

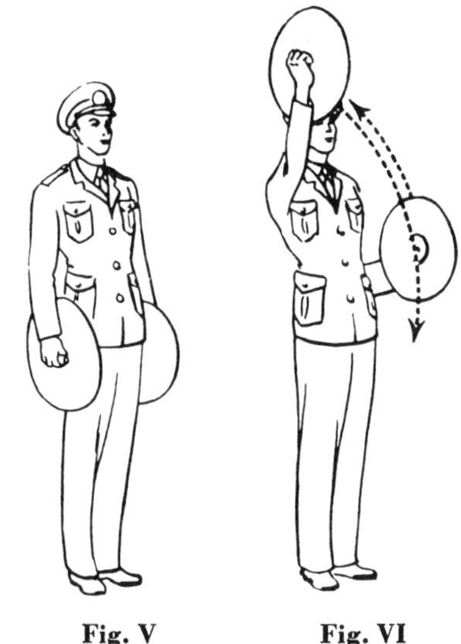

Fig. V **Fig. VI**

vibrate at the end of the crash, hold them at arms' length for maximum vibration.

Best results are obtained when the cymbals are used with every beat of the bass drum. In this case the second beat is played in reverse of the beat just described.

A restful flashy cymbal beat that may be used in soft passages is the cymbal roll shown in Figures VII and VIII. To play, hold the left cymbal almost stationary, strike the right against it with a glancing blow and then reverse the procedure.

Street Beats

Drum sections should memorize a series of street beats. Several books on the subject have been published. *Fifty Street Beats* by Wilcoxon; *Forty Street Cadences*, published by Southern Music Company; and *Berryman Street Beats*, published by Gamble, are especially helpful.

Many band leaders like to have more drummers in the marching band than in the concert band. My suggestion is to train oboe players,

Fig. VII **Fig. VIII**

bassoonists or other instrumentalists that can be spared to fill in the drum section. It will not take them long to master the fundamentals of drumming.

October 1953

Drums on the March

Percussion section must go into action in marching band early in school year

HASKELL W. HARR

THE ARTICLE WHICH FOLLOWS is the second in a series by Mr. Harr, the new conductor of the percussion clinic. At the close of the first discussion Mr. Harr suggested that players of other instruments be trained to fill in the drum section of the marching band. Then he gives suggestions on teaching these auxiliary drummers.

Holding the Sticks

First teach them to hold the sticks correctly. Each student should be equipped with a pair of heavy drumsticks of the style used for parade drumming and a good drum pad. Heavy sticks are best as they are more easily controlled, and they help to build up the wrist. In holding the left stick, extend the left arm and hand with the palm down and fingers extended. Place the stick well up in the socket between the first finger and the thumb. Have about one third of the stick (from the butt end) extend above the hand.

Close the third and fourth fingers so that the tips just touch the palm of the hand; then turn the arm to the left until the stick falls into position across the third finger between the first and second joints. The third finger will act as a bumper. Draw the arm toward the body and allow the first two fingers to curl lightly over the stick to serve as a guide. (See Fig. I.)

To hold the right stick turn the palm of the right hand up and place the stick diagonally across the hand so that it will rest on the second joint

of the first finger. Place the thumb

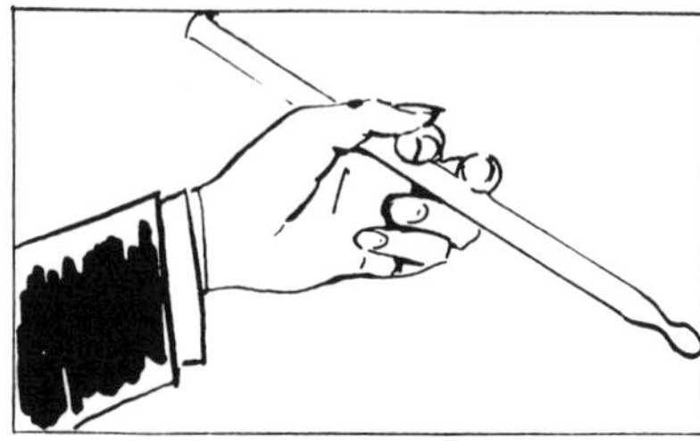

Fig. I

opposite the second joint of the finger, turn the hand over, and you have the playing position. Notice that the stick now pivots between the thumb and the first finger. Close the rest of the fingers loosely around the stick. Retain a slight grip with the second finger for better control. (See Fig. II.)

Principal Strokes

The marching drummer should have flash; therefore, he should be

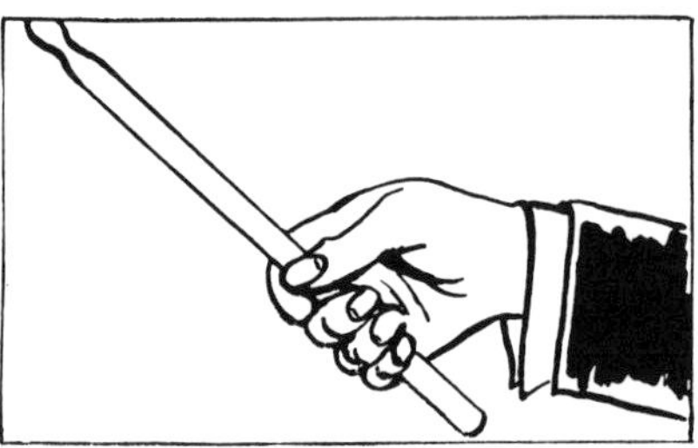

Fig. II

taught the four principal strokes of drumming—the full stroke, the upstroke, the down-stroke and the tap.

The full stroke is started with the stick in the high position. In this position the hand is on a level with the chin and the bead (point) of the stick about three feet above the drum. The drum is struck and the stick allowed to rebound to high position. (Fig. III.)

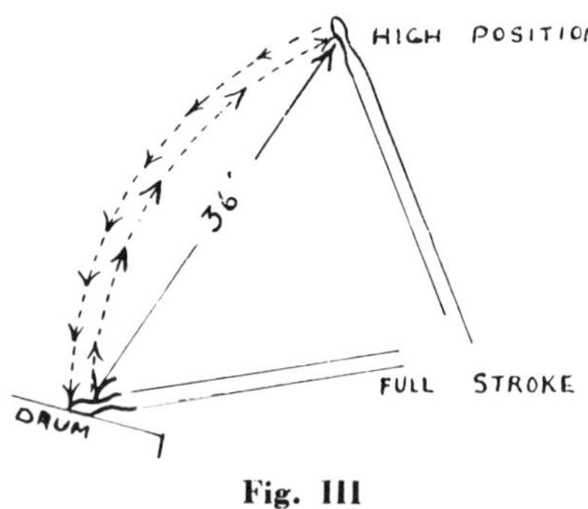

Fig. III

The down stroke is started from high position, the same as the full stroke, but the rebounce is stopped at low position on the way back about four inches from the head. (See Fig. IV.) To stop the rebounce, grip the stick tighter between the thumb and finger, at the same time pulling the

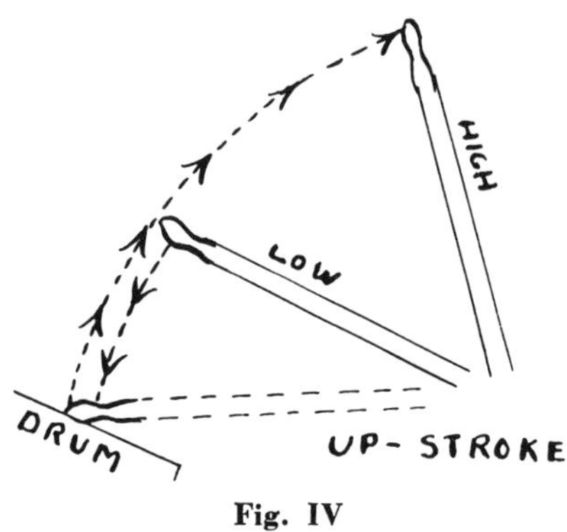

Fig. IV

stick into the palm of the hand with the second finger. To stop the rebounce with the left hand, apply more pressure with the thumb.

The upstroke is started at low position where the down stroke ended. It is struck with and the stick allowed to rebound to the high position. The stick is struck while the hand is rising. Turn the elbow out as you start to raise the arm, and this will force the hand to turn in, striking the drum. As you continue raising the arm, the stick will travel in a graceful arc. (Fig. V.)

The tap is started at the low position, is struck and then is allowed to rebounce to the low position as in

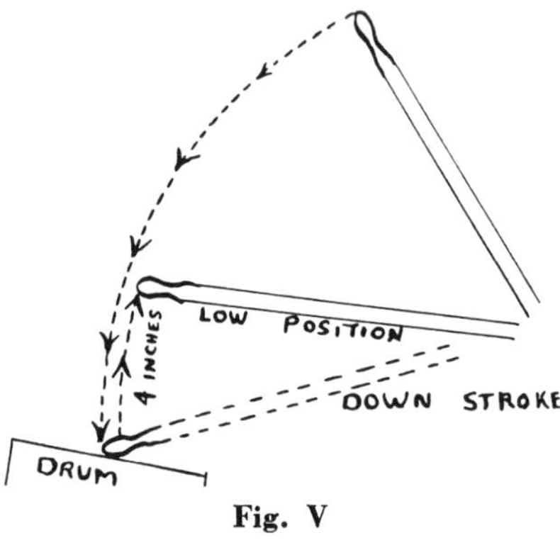

Fig. V

Figure VI. The tap is a wrist movement only.

In rapid tempos the sticks will not

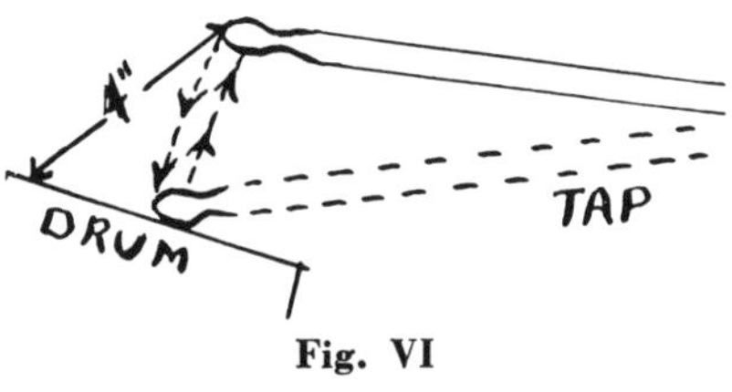

Fig. VI

be raised quite so high as they are at the slower tempos.

Time Figures and Rolls

The preliminary work of learning the various strokes and rhythm figures should be done on the drum pad. A few time figures such as the following ones will fit nicely in most marches.

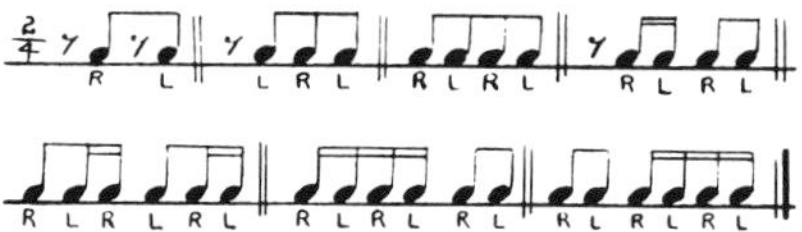

In 6/8 time the most common figures are as follows:

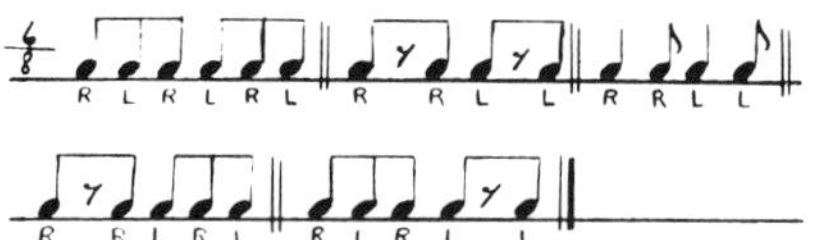

Just a few rolls are needed—the 5, 9 and 17 strokes in 2/4 time and the 5, 7, 11 and 13 strokes in 6/8 time. If you wish to use the drummer before he can play the rolls, have him play the fundamental or primary beats until he can master the roll.

The shortest of the rolls is the five stroke, designated by two eighth notes tied together.

The number of times the stick strikes the drum is determined by the number of thirty-second notes contained in the first note of the roll, plus a single tap or stroke for the second note. Divide the first eighth note into sixteenths and you have the primary strokes and sticking pattern.

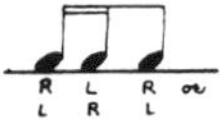

To complete the roll, play a stroke on the first sixteenth note and let it bounce, a stroke and bounce on the second sixteenth, and a single stroke for the eighth note.

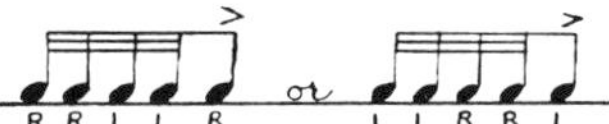

The five is played from "hand to hand." That means that when played in series, if one roll ends with the right hand, the next roll will start with the left hand.

The nine stroke roll is designated by a quarter note tied to an eighth note.

It has five primary strokes.

When you bounce the first four notes, you have the thirty-second notes of the quarter note; then add a single stroke for the eighth note.

The designation for the seventeen stroke roll is

It has nine primary strokes, as follows:

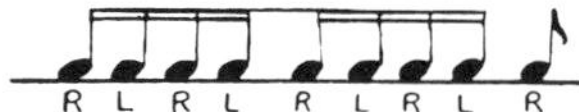

When the first eight are bounced, you have the sixteen beats; then add one for the eighth note.

All rolls can be counted in march rhythm.

In 6/8 time bounce the eighth notes for a roll. It will be more open than in 2/4, but you can stay in rhythm. The five stroke

is played

The seven stroke

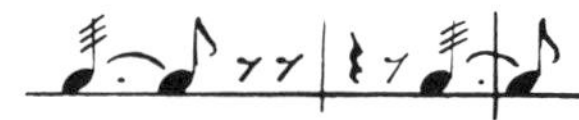

is played

The eleven stroke

is played

The thirteen stroke

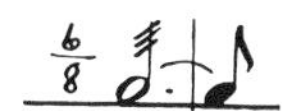

November 1953

Music Now Available for Drum Ensembles

Valuable training in precision, dynamics and teamwork gained from group playing

HASKELL W. HARR

FOR THE PAST FEW YEARS much interest has been shown among drummers in the development of drum ensembles, which have value in many ways. They encourage precision, teamwork and better appreciation of dynamics. As it is impossible to play melody and harmony parts on a drum, it is necessary to have catchy rhythmic beats and flash to make a successful ensemble.

When playing in ensembles, drums should be as near the same pitch as possible to make them sound as one drum. All movements of arms and sticks should be uniform, and every movement should be done with a great deal of showmanship. Drum ensembles make excellent program features, for everyone likes to hear good snappy drum beats. They also fill an emergency need, as they do not require a band background.

Music is now available for any combination of drums of from two to seven players. For the encouragement of school drum ensembles, I am submitting a list of available music from the stocks of Carl Fischer, Lyon and Healy and Frank's Drum Shop.

Addresses of publishers will be found at the end of the article. Grading was done on the following basis: E for Easy, suitable for grade school level; M for Medium, suitable for advanced elementary and high school; and D for Difficult, suitable for advanced students.

Title	Composer	Publisher	Grade
	DRUM DUETS		
Admiral Byrd	John J. Heney	C. Fischer	E
Admiral Dewey	John J. Heney	C. Fischer	M
Admiral Farragut	John J. Heney	C. Fischer	M
Admiral Sims	John J. Heney	C. Fischer	M
Victory Forever	E. V. Clark	Chart	E
Alphonso and Gaston	J. Berryman	Beihoff	E
Tip and Tap	Rehfeldt	Rehfeldt	M
Joe and Joe	George Lawrence Stone	Stone	M
Before Breakfast	George Lawrence Stone	Stone	D
Double Bubble	Phil Grant	Mercury	M
Two of Us	Robert Buggert	Rubank	E
You and I	Robert Blount	C. Fischer	D
Queen's Choice	Robert Blount	C. Fischer	D
A Pair of Diddlers	Acton Ostling	Belwin	D
Rudimental Repartee	Acton Ostling	Belwin	M
A Two-four for Two	Acton Ostling	Belwin	D
Variations on London Bridge	Acton Ostling	Belwin	D
	DRUM TRIOS		
	(Three snare drums)		
Rataplan	Haskell W. Harr	Cole	M
Suite for Drums	S. A. Smith	C. Fischer	D
Three Competitors	Acton Ostling	Gamble	M
We Three	Robert Buggert	Rubank	E
Captain Blount	John J. Heney	Barnhouse	M
Drummers Courageous	Robert Blount	C. Fischer	M
Three Gals	Arthur Hayek	Havek	E
Bolero	John J. Heney	C. Fischer	D
The Conquerors	Robert Blount	C. Fischer	M
Dawn Patrol	John J. Heney	Barnhouse	D
Drummers' Canzonetta	Robert Buggert	Rubank	M
The Drummers' Farewell	H. E. Firestone	Belwin	D
Drumming in Triplicate	Acton Ostling	Belwin	M
Flinging It Threefold	Robert Buggert	Rubank	M
Jessie, Johnny and Mary	John J. Heney	C. Fischer	D
	DRUM QUARTETS		
	(Two snare drums, cymbals, bass drum)		
Submarine Express	John J. Heney	C. Fischer	M
Uncle Gus	Phil Grant	Mercury	M
Parading the Drum Section	L. Jessel	Marks	M
Tom, Dick and Jerry	Shlimovitz	Mills	E
Chasing the Beat	Phil Grant	Mercury	M
Drummers' Patrol	Acton Ostling	Belwin	M
Listen to the Drummers Play (also band arrangement)	Acton Ostling	Gamble	D
	DRUM QUARTETS		
	(Four snare drums)		
The Midnight Express	John J. Heney	C. Fischer	M
The Pony Express	John J. Heney	C. Fischer	M
	DRUM QUINTETS		
	(Three snare drums, cymbals, bass drum)		
The Big Show	John J. Heney	C. Fischer	D
The Black Cat Quintette	Haskell W. Harr	Cole	D
Colonel Irons	Haskell W. Harr	Cole	M
Lieutenant Donna	Haskell W. Harr	Cole	E
The Downfall of Paris	Haskell W. Harr	C. Fischer	M
Five of Us	Arthur Hayek	Hayek	E
Men of Marlborough	George Lawrence Stone	Stone	D
Military Men	John J. Heney	C. Fischer	M
Modulation	Robert Blount	C. Fischer	D
Newport	Haskell W. Harr	Cole	M
A Soldier's Life	John J. Heney	C. Fischer	D
The United Allies	E. V. Clark	Chart	E
Parade of the Quints	John J. Heney	C. Fischer	M
Rudimental Roulade	Robert Buggert	Rubank	M

Addresses of Publishers

C. L. Barnhouse Co., Music Publishers, Oskaloosa, Iowa
Belwin, Inc., Rockville Centre, Long Island, N.Y.
Beihoff Music Co., 5040 W. North Ave., Milwaukee, Wisc.
Chart Music Publishing House, Inc., 506 South Wabash Ave., Chicago 5, Ill.
M. M. Cole Publishing Co., 823 South Wabash Ave., Chicago, Ill.
Carl Fischer, Inc., 62 Cooper Square, New York 3, N.Y.
Frank's Drum Shop, 226 South Wabash Ave., Chicago, Ill.
Gamble Hinged Music Co., 308 South Wabash Ave., Chicago, Ill.
Hayek Drum Shop, 5710 West Vliet St., Milwaukee, Wis.
Edward B. Marks, RCA Building, Radio City, New York
Mercury Music Corporation, 47 West 63rd Street, New York 23, N.Y.
Mills Music, Inc., 1619 Broadway, New York 19, N.Y.
Herb Rehfeldt, Stevens Point, Wisc.
Rubank Inc., 5544 West Armstrong Ave., Chicago 30, Ill.
G. B. Stone and Son, 61 Hanover St., Boston, Massachusetts

December 1953

Does Your Percussion Meet High Standards?

Certain definite techniques can increase effectiveness of training and playing.

H. E. NUTT

THE PURPOSE OF THIS ARTICLE is to present ideas on increasing the efficiency of percussion as a section of the band rather than to discuss performance techniques on the instruments.

To begin with, the location of this section in the band is very important. Experience and experimentation indicate that the best location is to the director's left with the bass drum next to the bass horns. In this location the tone of the bass drum carries into the bass horn section and helps steady the rhythm in many passages. Tympani should be located at the other end of the bass horn section for good balance. Both bass drum and tympani are really bass instruments.

Experience and considerable experimentation also indicate that percussion players SHOULD BE SEATED as they play. A sitting position makes for better blend with the rest of the band and modifies much of the usual "rawness" and noisiness heard in the average band. Percussion players not only see better from the seated position but find it much less tiring both in rehearsal and in concert. Discipline problems are avoided as are audience distractions due to unnecessary moving about of players.

If the bass drum stand will not adjust to bring the drum within a few inches of the floor, a special wooden cradle should be made. If a very large bass drum is used, the player may have to sit on a stool somewhat higher than a regular chair. Stands for concert size snare drums are adjustable for putting the drum at the proper playing height when the player is seated, but for field drums it may be necessary to make a wooden cradle to bring them low enough. Cymbal players have no trouble playing in seated position. Tympani players should use an adjustable stool and slant the kettles at an angle to get the best playing position. Bell lyra holders are usually adjustable as to height.

Location of Stands

Music stands must be of proper height and in direct line with the director for best results. The bass drummer should have a separate stand for his music. If a separate cymbal player is used, he should read with the bass drummer. Snare drummers should NOT be reading from this stand. The bass drummer must be very sure that his stand and music are in direct line with the director's hands and face. For better vision march-size music should be fastened at the top of the music stand with a clothespin.

When the director raises his arms, wind players form embouchure. How do percussion players form "embouchure"? By silently placing the ends of the sticks against the drum head at the striking spot; by pressing cymbals silently together; by placing bell lyra mallet head on the first bar to be played. As the director makes the preliminary upbeat, percussion players move sticks away from the drum head in rhythm with director's baton motion and back again to strike the head as he makes the first downbeat. This procedure helps players feel the rhythm of the attack and insures precision. "Embouchure" should be formed for all entrances after measures of rest in a number.

Director's Signals

Percussion players (especially the bass drummer) must be extremely sensitive to changes in speed and volume as indicated by the director. Special training and special signals are necessary to insure best results. The bass drummer is often spoken of as the "second leader" of the band. If the director has a good signal system and the bass drummer understands and is skilled in responding, speed and volume changes are easily controlled. To indicate acceleration the director looks at the bass drummer, inclines his head slightly forward, and moves his lips as though saying "faster, faster, come on, let's go," etc. The bass drummer gradually increases the speed of his beat until the director quits moving his lips, straightens his head to the usual position and quits looking at the player.

To indicate slowing down, the director tilts his head slightly backward and holds the lips still as though saying "whoa." The bass drummer gradually slows the speed of his beat until the director closes his lips, brings his head to the usual position and quits looking at the player. All members of the percussion section should be trained in this system. It gets results without confusion.

For volume signals use facial expression and the left hand. To indicate more volume, look at the players, firm the facial muscles, clench the left fist and move it slightly on the beats. For less volume raise the eyebrows slightly, form the lips as though whispering "sh," and extend the fingers of the left hand palm down. In both cases resume usual facial expression and left-hand position as soon as the desired volume is secured.

Volume Control

This matter of volume control is very important in building good balance. No matter how the music is marked, the drums must play with volume that fits the situation. How loud is loud? How soft is soft? The drums have no way of judging how strongly they are coming through, so that the director must judge for them and signal changes that will create good balance. As a rule it is better to train a percussion section to UNDERPLAY its part as to volume and to wait for the director's signals for an increase if he feels it is called for. This does not mean that it should play insipidly. On the contrary it should stress accents and other volume changes, but at a reduced volume level. In the case of the percussion section, volume contrasts are the most important factors in playing with expression.

As mentioned before, the bass drummer must be extremely sensitive to speed and volume changes and to accents. His music looks rather dumb and dry, but his playing must not sound so. It would be well for him to study the score or solo parts and to sing the melodies so that he will instinctively make the accents and volume changes called for.

Study of Parts

In rehearsals it is often effective to have the percussion players study their music without playing as the rest of the band plays a passage. In this way they get the "sound" of the passage and a better idea of what to do with their parts. The bass drummer should listen closely to the bass horns, for his part is quite similar to theirs. Another way to get at this is to have the drum section play on sponge rubber head covers or special pads. (Robinson Drumette is fine for snare drummers.) This form of "dummy drumming" helps the band and also helps the percussion section.

Cymbals Player

Should the bass drummer also play cymbals, or should there be a separate cymbal player? This seems to be a matter of personal opinion among directors. The double cymbal tone as heard when played by a separate player is richer and more effective in some passages and on certain solos but seems too rich for other passages. For routine work it is usually easier to get balanced cymbal-bass drum effect when the bass drummer plays both.

The logical plan is to use both forms of cymbal playing. This means that two or more sets of good cymbals should be available. (Do not use wooden handles on cymbals.) The set to be played by the separate cymbal player should be somewhat larger, lighter and more responsive. By experimentation the director can determine which type of tone best fits a given passage. He should then mark this on his score and on the drum music.

Another question that bothers some directors is the question as to when to use cymbals with the bass drum. Unless music is marked "B D only," cymbals should be used on all notes written for the bass drum. This rule applies to all forms of music, including marches. On final holds where a bass drum roll is indicated, the cymbals should be played on the release and quickly choked. It should be mentioned here that bass drums should be equipped with adjustable mutes for both heads to assist in control of unpleasant reverberation and to get better precision in tone effect. The bass drummer should always use a soft-headed beater and put on a new cover when the beater becomes worn.

Ensembles Valuable

Percussion ensembles (to include all members of the section) are a fine way to develop balance, good style, precision and musicianship in the section. Insist that performers play musically with contrast and expression and that all rolls be played as "measured rolls." Keep the volume down and avoid noisy playing. Also avoid exaggerated stick motions. Gum chewing should be absolutely forbidden.

In closing, here are a few additional suggestions for the director. If the score does not include percussion parts, study the parts themselves. Then, using red pencil, cue important entrances, rhythm patterns, solos, etc., in your score, or have an extra drum part on your stand at rehearsal with the measures numbered for reference.

During rehearsal use a lead pencil to circle spots that need special attention at section drill. Be sure you know when the drums are to come in, give them advance warning with the eyes and cue them carefully at the exact point of entrance. Simplify parts for younger players so that they will play well on what they do and not get into bad habits trying to play music that is beyond them. When drums have rests, don't hesitate to use them to "fill in" and assist other sections on rhythm patterns and effects.

Teach your percussion section to be alert and quick to sense ways in which it can be helpful. Sell players the idea that they are important, because they really are. Good percussion for the band is like icing on a cake. It adds the zip and pep that everyone likes.

1954-1955

85	Facts About Chimes	Haskell W. Harr	January
86	Care of Drum Heads Is Important Factor in Length of Service	Haskell W. Harr	February
88	The Percussionist's Problem — Phrasing	Jack Lee	March
89	Drum Rolls	Bill Muehler	April
91	Training in Rudiments Essential to Drumming	John P. Noonan	May
92	Drumming With Just Eight Rudiments	Haskell W. Harr	September
93	From Just Eight Rudiments to Many Different Rhythms, Part I	Haskell W. Harr	October
95	From Just Eight Rudiments to Many Different Rhythms, Part II	Haskell W. Harr	December
96	Marching Band Drum Section, Asset or Liability?	Robert W. Buggert	January
98	Is Your Bass Drum an Uncontrolled Monster?	Joe Berryman	February
99	What is Your Tympani IQ?	Haskell W. Harr	March
100	Rudimental Bass Drumming	Acton Ostling	April
102	What Is Your Marimba IQ?	Haskell W. Harr	May
103	Drums, Drummers and Drumming	John P. Noonan	September
104	Materials for Drumheads	Howard P. Emery	September
104	The Fall Semester	Robert W. Buggert	October
105	The Edward B. Straight Books	Robert W. Buggert	November
106	Organize for Efficiency	Charles L. Spohn	December

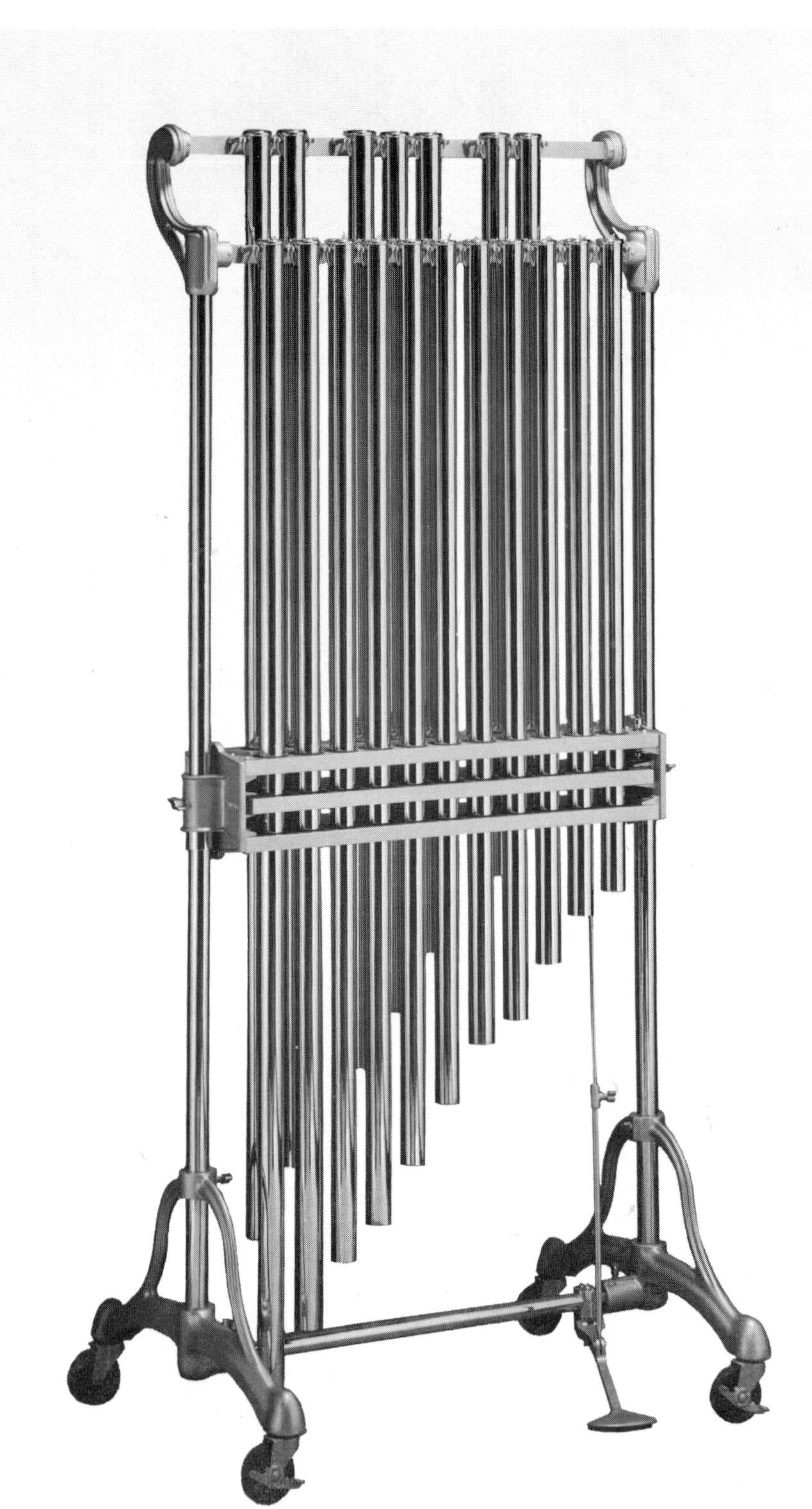

Facts About Chimes

Drummer faces peculiar problems in tone characteristics and range

HASKELL W. HARR

THE DRUMMER IS OFTEN called upon to play the chimes because of his experience in playing bells, xylophone and similar instruments.

Chimes parts are written in the treble clef. They are mounted in a double row with the natural tones in front and the sharps elevated in the back row to facilitate playing. Only one mallet is used for chimes as the very nature of their tone prohibits any rapid execution such as would require the use of two mallets.

To bring out the maximum tone, the chime should be struck on the end, as shown in Figure I. To produce the best tone, soften the hard rawhide mallet that is sent with each set by making cross-cuts on one end or covering one striking surface with soft leather. The soft end produces the best tone.

Fig. I

It is a good idea to silence one chime at the precise time that the next one is struck. Silencing is done with the free hand. On chimes equipped with a damper pedal, passing notes of a chord are silenced with the hand and the damper pedal is depressed when chord changes are made. As no rapid execution is possible, it will not be necessary to practice any intricate passages. However, it is necessary that the letters of the various tones be learned and their positions be fixed firmly in the mind.

Register

The register of a regulation set of eighteen chimes is from C 52 to F 69. It is possible to build chimes with a greater range, but the one and one-half octave set (C in third space of treble clef to F above the staff) has proven most efficient.

Very often we find musicians of the highest calibre who harbor wrong impressions regarding chimes tones and tuning. It is not unusual for those in the most prominent positions to condemn a perfect set of chimes as being out of tune. Such conclusions do not reflect on the ability of the musician; they are natural because of the peculiar characteristics of the instrument, which are vastly different from most others. Until the mystery of chime tone construction has been explained, wrong conclusions may continue to be made.

Marked Differences

Chimes differ greatly from most musical instruments. Generally speaking, other instruments have true harmonics or overtones, being usually spaced in fifths, fourths, thirds, etc., above the fundamental tone and being rather feeble and hardly perceptible. In chimes the desired tone is one of the overtones (the fourth of the series) and is the predominating tone, but instead of being accompanied by true harmonics as in most other instruments it has three lower overtones and any number above this predominating tone with none of the overtones in any true harmonic relation. There are near octaves, sixths, fifths, fourths, etc., but all are too badly out of tune to sound well with the harmony of an accompanied melody unless heard from a more or less distant point, whereupon they lose the discordant effect of the overtones. This situation is natural and cannot be altered.

In testing chimes, octaves should

CHART OF THE A CHIME

Showing All Overtones and Their Pitch

Pitch found		Partial	Tune pitch
1772	A	6	1760
1308	E	5	1318
880	A	4	880 (Partial Tuned)
537	C	3	523
273	C#	2	277
	G	1	Fundamental

Fig. II

not be attempted, for every chime has a sixth partial which sounds nearly an octave with the fourth or predominating tone and yet is always sharp. When listening to octaves for comparison (as is usually the custom with other instruments) we unconsciously use this sixth partial of the lowest octave chime to judge the fourth or predominant tone of the upper octave; therefore we imagine the upper octave chime to be flat.

Another peculiarity of chimes which helps to explain why they are difficult to understand is the fact that the A (read in the second space) in an ordinary set of chimes is the A on the first line above the staff. In listening to it, this does not seem possible because of the prominence of the three lower partials, which are very intense (the lowest of the three partials or overtones sounding more than two octaves lower), especially when standing close. Therefore, they are misleading at a short distance but are hardly noticeable at a greater distance from the chimes.

Beauty of Tone

Almost without exception chimes are complimented by audiences on their beauty of tone. Such compliments verify the explanations in the foregoing paragraph that overtones, partials and harmonics are noticeable and sometimes annoying near the instrument but inaudible at a distance.

The tone A-880 is the fourth partial of the series and also the predominant; therefore, it is not the fundamental tone, as sounds from a piano or violin string would be called, because all partials are above the predominating or fundamental tone on these instruments. The diagram shows that to sound an A chime one octave higher with a four-octave comparison, one would unknowingly use the fourth partial of the 880 chime, whose sixth sounds 1772 against 1760 or a partial of the higher octave chime with an out-of-tune effect of twelve beats, which is about 1/8 of a semitone.

When setting up or taking down chimes, one should be very careful not to drop or bump the tubes, for if they get the slightest bit out of round, their tone will be affected.

Technical data and chart for the above article were used with permission of the Leedy and Ludwig Drum Company.

February 1954

Care of Drum Heads Is Important Factor in Length of Service

Amount of tension and degree of dampness affect condition and performance of head

HASKELL W. HARR

THE BEST DRUMHEADS are made of hides taken from cattle. The hides range in size from that of the small unborn calf, used for snare heads, to that of the large bull, used for oversize bass drums. Sheep and goat skin have been used at times but have not proved as successful as calf skin.

Fresh skins make the best hides. Heads selected by the manufacturers are usually being processed in the tanneries within two days after removal from the animal. After processing, the hides are dried before cutting into sizes for drums. The thin heads used for the snare side of the drum are dried loosely to avoid damaging the fibers of the skin and when dry are transparent. The skins to be used for batter heads are slightly thicker than the snare heads. These skins are stretched very tight before drying in order to break down the fibers. Breaking the fibers makes the skin white and takes all of the stretch out of the head so that it will remain firm to withstand the terrific beating it receives.

Hides are uneven when taken from the animal, for they are more thickened at the neck and rump than at the ribs. All manufacturers of drum heads buff the hides to make them a uniform thickness throughout. The transparent spots sometimes found on white heads are a sign of quality rather than a defect; they are caused by the hide rubbing over the shoulders of the animal. If they are still there when the head is finished, one may know that the head was not kept in the lime solution long enough to weaken it. Thin heads are used for orchestra drums, medium thick for band, and thick heads for tom-toms.

Tucking the Head

Factory-tucked heads should be used whenever possible. The few pennies saved by doing your own tucking is small when compared with the time required and the risk of spoiling the drum head. However, knowing how to tuck a head may be valuable in an emergency. When purchasing untucked heads allow an extra four inches for snare drum, five inches for bass drum and six inches for timpani. To get the drum size, measure across the outside of the shell; do not include the counterhoops. Have a container large enough to hold the head for soaking. Do not try to fold a head to get it into a small container.

The steps of procedure listed below should be followed.

1. Soak the head in water of room temperature until it is pliable like a chamois. This will take about ten minutes for a snare drum head and twenty minutes for bass drum and timpani heads.

2. Lay the soaked head out on a flat clean table with the smooth or grain side facing down on the table. The smooth side is the side to be played upon. It is not hard to determine the difference between the smooth side and the rough side on the thicker heads, but it is sometimes difficult on the thin snare heads. The manufacturer's trade mark is usually stamped on the grain side. If it is not, then look for the veins; they are sunken on the smooth side.

3. Place the flesh hoop on the head (Figure I).

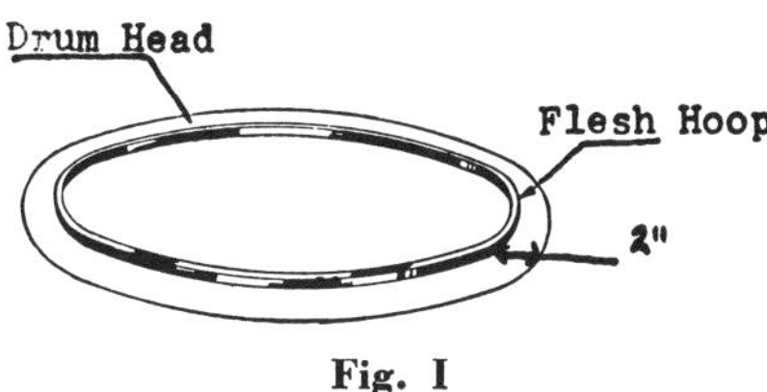

Fig. I

Proceed to tuck the head as in Figure II.

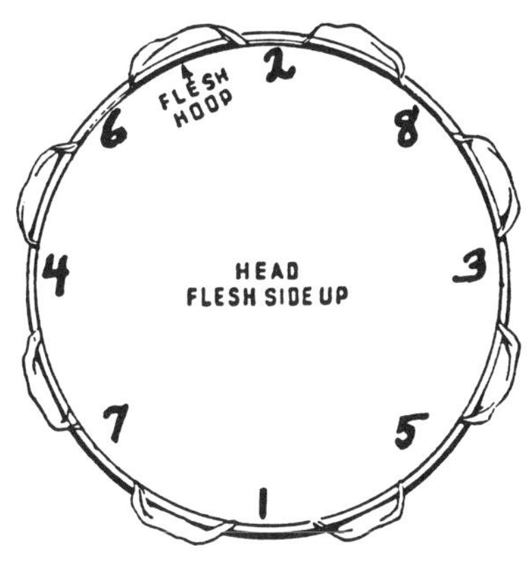

Fig. II

The best tool to use is one made especially for that purpose (Figure III).

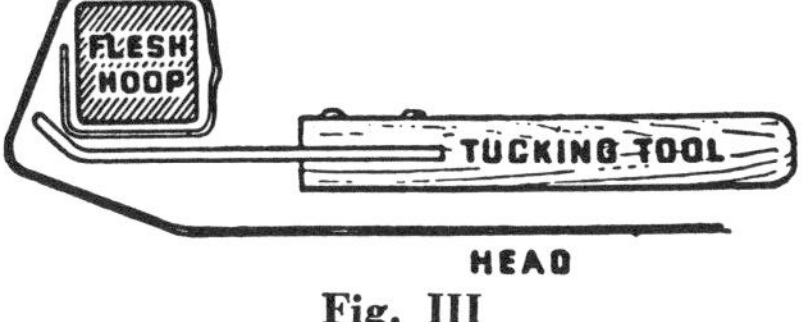

Fig. III

Begin tucking at the point nearest to you, at 1, Figure II. Carefully fold the head over the hoop and tuck it under the lower inside edge at four equal spots, numbered 2, 3 and 4 in the illustration. Complete the tucking all around the hoop as shown in the diagram.

4. After the head has been tucked run the tucking tool around the flesh hoop to smooth out any bumps. Batter heads may be tucked rather tight as the stretch has been taken out of the head, but snare heads must be tucked loosely. I would suggest placing a small object about an inch or so high under it for slack. For timpani heads use a soup bowl or other object 3½ inches high.

5. Wipe excess water off the head with a rag. Place the head on the drum. If it is a tympani head, put the counterhoop on and tighten the rods so that the head is pulled down about one-fourth of an inch. Then allow the head to dry.

6. Tympani heads should be permitted to dry before they are put on the kettle. Place two strips of wood across the kettle, wipe excess water off the head, and then place it on top of the strips to dry. Do not allow the head to touch anything else while drying.

After it has dried, moisten the center of the head to about four inches from the flesh hoop. Put the head in the counter hoop and set it on the kettle. Place the foot pedal in the relaxed position and tighten the rods so that the top of the counterhoop is about a half inch below the edge of the kettle. Then allow the moistened tympani head to dry.

To be safe, I would allow the snare drum head to dry about twenty-four hours before using and the bass drum and the tympani heads about forty-eight hours.

Tensioning the Head

7. When the head is thoroughly dry, it should be tensioned for playing. If it is a batter head, tighten it until you can barely dent the head when pressure is applied to the center with the forefinger. Next, snap off the snares and strike the head lightly with a stick all around the drum about two inches from the hoop and between each pair of rods. The tone must be the same; if it is not, adjust with the key until you have the same tone.

Uneven tension is the direct cause of more playing dissatisfaction in regard to "feel" and poor sound than any other quality. It requires a little more time and patience to procure even head tension, but it can be done systematically and is well worth the trouble. If the fibers of the head are tighter in some spots than in others, they do not vibrate in unison. One spot fights the other in the upward and downward movements of the head, creating a choking, hard-playing and dull-sounding drum.

The snare head should not have as much tension applied as the batter head, for it must assist the snares in vibrating. It is not possible to tighten the snare head so that all points will sound the same because of the two snare beds, which place more tension at those points than at others. Evenness, however, can be brought into approximately the same tone areas by the method described above. It is agreed that the batter head should be tighter than the snare head. The amount of difference between the two is based on the style of playing and weight of sticks used and can only be arrived at by the individual, who must learn from experience.

After you have your drum adjusted to the point where it plays nicely in dry weather, let it alone. Do not loosen the heads after every job. Weather conditions will make readjustment necessary at times. However, it is not the heat and cold that affect the heads, but the dampness or dryness; both damp heat and damp cold will make a drum head go down or slacken. Both dry heat and dry cold will make a drumhead tighten. Therefore, watch the humidity of the atmosphere rather than the temperature, and you will avoid a lot of head breakage. If you tighten the heads during damp weather, let them out after the job to the point where you started to take them up. This will slacken the heads and allow for contraction should the atmosphere dry out the next day.

Heads are a product of nature and no guarantee can be given as to their length of service. However, by keeping them in good condition at all times, you will extend their life of usefulness.

The Percussionist's Problem–Phrasing

Key to 'dynamic following' of phrasing is found in well-rounded musicianship

JACK LEE

THROUGHOUT THE ENTIRE FIELD OF MUSIC an individual's musicianship may generally be determined by his ability to phrase. Regardless of the technique and tone an instrumentalist may display, his performances will be meaningless if the music does not unify itself into sections of sound. These sections we refer to as phrases, and it is the interpretation of these phrases which changes tone into the art of music.

Certainly an advanced technical knowledge in any musical medium offers the instrumentalist greater finesse in his phrasing. The violinist learns certain bowing techniques that aid his phrasing; the trumpeter learns different styles of tonguing which help him interpret legato and staccato passages; and the percussionist is sometimes aided by rudiments which have been arranged to offer natural sequences of sticking.

However, technique is only a means to the end and is not a determining factor in the knowledge or art of phrasing. The percussionist, like any other instrumentalist, must learn this art of phrasing if he is to be known as a good musician. How then does he learn it? Since many excellent drummers are unable to describe how they achieved their knowledge, a discussion of the subject may prove profitable.

Military history has had a profound influence on the percussionist. The entire system of rudimental drumming has stemmed from a method of preparing uneducated men to be field drummers in military service. The terms we identify as flams, paradiddles, ratamacues, etc., are actually auditory sounds which the percussionist has imitated to achieve a variety of percussive sounds. This was an excellent system, as it enabled the drum instructor to set patterns of rudiments together, thus giving recognizable street beats or war signals such as "Call to Arms."

Even today many drum and bugle corps employ this same learning device since it does not require the percussionist to be able to read music. Furthermore, such training can be justified musically since the rudiments are grouped together into excellent rhythmic patterns. These patterns offer a most natural phrasing.

Composers' Influence

Unfortunately, teaching the percussionist by rote, in the manner previously discussed, presents an entirely different problem from that of teaching him to read music. Perhaps the reason lies not in the system of teaching but in the manner in which the music is written. After examining numerous newly-published works, it is obvious that rudimental drumming knowledge is a thing of the past insofar as our modern composers are concerned. Incidentally, many of the percussion parts to our great symphonic works also apparently were written without a rudimental drumming knowledge.

There are, however, a few composers, such as Sousa, who have written their percussion parts with the rudiments clearly in mind. These parts are, perhaps, the best examples of percussion phrasing. It is unfortunate that they are in the minority.

Therefore, it is apparent that we cannot rely on the printed page to set up patterns which will offer natural sticking and phrasing. Most composers are writing their drum parts purely by the rhythmic sound, and, although the percussionist may not approve of the writing, he nevertheless must phrase the part.

Phrasing by Stickings

In recent years there has been a general trend toward teaching a system of alternate (LRLR) sticking. This particular style of drumming has been used by many professional percussionists who have successfully demonstrated that it affords excellent phrasing.

However, a few percussionists argue that phrasing and reading are easier if each measure is started with the right stick. Many former pit-orchestra drummers from the old days of vaudeville used this system because of the importance of "on the spot" sight reading and phrasing. It would be wise for all percussionists to acquaint themselves with the system, for it presents a very logical approach for both teaching and playing rhythm passages.

Whether or not phrasing is made easier by sticking methods, I cannot say, for I am not a percussionist. As a conductor I can judge the percussion field only by what I hear. My ears lead me to believe that every drumming system has placed its emphasis entirely on rhythm patterns, rudiments or stickings, completely neglecting phrasing. Undoubtedly many fine percussionists have solved the phrasing problem, but their methods have not made an impression on their colleagues. The time has come when we must consider phrasing if we are to advance the percussion field.

Phrasing Aids

Many people have advocated that a melodic line should be written above or with the percussion part, thus enabling a drummer to follow his music more easily. This would certainly make his phrasing more accurate. Although the idea would work, it is not practical since the majority of our music has been written without this aid. Perhaps a more simple method of notation would be to bracket each phrase in the same manner as the average published dance-band arrangement is phrased. The author has frequently used this technique to improve the phrasing of his band's percussion section. Perhaps the reason that phrasing is so often misunderstood in the entire music field is that we have not developed a system of notation to indicate phrasing accurately.

As I analyze the method I use in interpreting a melodic line, it is apparent why phrasing in percussion is so difficult. A melodic line may suggest a style purely from its sound. "When Johnny Comes Marching Home Again" and "I Dream of Jeannie with the Light Brown Hair" suggest two dissimilar styles of playing, but the printed page gives no clue to this important part of phrasing. Many instrumentalists who frequently play melodic lines still have not learned to read style into a printed page of music.

To cope with this factor is even more difficult for the percussionist. Frequently the direction of a melodic line will give us the "tip-off" as to the dynamic line. The instrumentalist soon learns that when the notes go up he can usually crescendo, and as they descend, he can diminuendo, thus improving his musical phrasing. But, again, the percussionist doesn't have this printed clue to phrasing, for his notes are on a straight line.

It is true that our musical system of notation leaves much to be desired, for sensitive phrasing must be felt. Accents, tempo markings and dynamics cannot be clearly notated. Our phrasing problem now becomes one of feeling percussion parts. I do not believe there are any short cuts.

One thing becomes clear—percussion training must embody more than sticking, rudiments and rhythm. These factors are only a very small portion of what we call musicianship. When we teach the percussionist the other factors, then and only then do we teach him phrasing. To place all our efforts on technique is not to see the forest for the trees. The percussion section gives us a series of trees, big ones, small ones, oaks and palms. Sometimes we even get a well-lighted Christmas tree.

These glittering examples of poor musicianship are characteristic not only of percussion but of the entire music field. In a recent band contest I judged, only three of fourteen bands used dynamic phrasing. If the score did not indicate a dynamic change, the conductors permitted their bands to play on one monotonous dynamic level. Furthermore, the use of *rubato tempi* was never considered an aid to most of these bands in their phrasing. Therefore, it becomes evident that others besides the percussionist need to improve upon their phrasing knowledge.

In questioning several percussionists I consider to have excellent phrasing ability, I have learned that most of them phrase by following the rest of the band or orchestra. Unlike the belief that the ensemble follows the percussion section, I have found the reverse situation. Certainly, following one another's tempi will never allow precision. This is not the type of "following" the good percussionist does but rather "dynamic following." To have a dynamic curve in the phrase requires the percussionist to apply his phrasing in accordance with the other instruments. Good musicianship is therefore necessary to understand what can be expected in ensemble playing.

General Musicianship

I know this article has not answered any particular problems in phrasing percussion parts, but I sincerely hope it will stimulate the reader in his consideration of the matter. My best advice to the percussionist is to become a well-rounded musician through the study of theory, music history, melodic line, etc. At present this seems to be the accepted method of increasing musical understanding.

Although my early training was in the instrumental field, I feel that my greatest awakening to phrasing came as a result of my college voice training. The text of a song offers a very obvious insight into interpretation and phrasing. Since this approach to phrasing is basic and easy, it is perhaps an excellent starting point for all instrumentalists. In this way, one can easily learn various ways to phrase. Then, as the instrumentalist is exposed to pure music without clue-bearing words, he will have a better background to aid him in the proper choice of his phrasing.

In like manner the study of melodic line will undoubtedly contribute to the phrasing ability of the percussionist. We must face the fact that the average percussionist has fewer clues to phrasing than any other musician and thus finds himself confused regarding it. There is only one obvious conclusion to reach: we must stop training ourselves as trumpeters, violinists, percussionists, etc., and concentrate on becoming musicians.

April 1954

Drum Rolls

Applying rolls to various rhythm patterns and speeds ranks high among problems

BILL MUEHLER

THE BEGINNING DRUMMER must get a good fundamental background on methods of developing a good clean roll and he must take ample time to perfect it before he goes on to further training.

If the student is rolling "buzzy" to begin with, this article will not help the drum section too much, for one of its purposes is to prevent the drummer from developing a "buzz."

After the roll has been developed to a certain degree of efficiency, the step that must follow is applying the rolls to music. I have seen many students who have learned to roll with a degree of cleanness but still do not seem to understand how to apply the rolls to music. Knowing the rolls, such as the 5-7-9, etc., is only half the job. If drummers do not know when and

how to apply rolls, they are at just as much of a loss as if they did not know them at all.

The drummer does not necessarily have to be rudimental to follow the exercises in this article, although it would help him to execute them if he has studied all the rolls, open and close.

My main purpose is to point out that in order to have a good drum section, it must roll together, like that of a brass or reed section playing with matching vibratos. If rolling to rhythm is not used, the drum section will be very much disorganized as each drummer may be playing his roll at a different speed. As the tempo varies, the speed of the roll should change in order to have a clean-sounding roll. Many drummers, both schooled and unschooled, try to crowd as many strokes as they possibly can into a roll, thereby making even a good roll sound "buzzy."

Following are patterns to roll to at the suggested tempos in 2/4, which would also apply to 4/4, 3/4, etc.

The reader will notice that in the first bar of Figure VI I have inserted ruffs instead of a roll. It would be physically impossible to play a clean five-stroke roll at such a fast tempo. Figure VI should be more applicable to 3/4 met. dotted half equals 80 or cut-time at whole note equals 100.

The student should become efficient at one pattern before attempting to roll to other patterns. Trying to teach all the various ways too close together only adds confusion. One method should be mastered at a time.

If the student tried to roll to sixteenth notes at too fast a speed, his roll would automatically be too crowded or "buzzy." On the other hand, rolling to triplets at too slow a speed would cause the roll to be too open. Therefore, the player should listen carefully and let his ear be the deciding factor in choosing the type of roll to suit his needs.

Applying rolls to 6/8, 3/8, 12/8, etc., runs closely parallel to 2/4 although I have heard other ideas on this phase of rolling. Following are suggestive patterns to roll to at suggested tempos in 6/8; they also apply to 3/8, 9/8, 12/8, etc.

Some instructors have the idea that the student should roll to 1&A, 2&A to keep the 6/8 feel. In my estimation, he needs more practice if he wishes to get a definite rhythm in rolls. A roll should sound like a sustained note on a horn. If he were to roll to 1&A, 2&A, at dotted quarter equals 112-120, the roll would sound like hailstones hitting on a tin roof.

Some argue that by rolling to 1&A, 2&A in 6/8, the student keeps the R hand on count 1 and the L hand in count 2. However, I believe that a student should be taught to use both hands equally well and not have to figure out the sticking ahead of time to favor the right hand. It is safe to say that many drummers who have weak left hands are victims of teachers who have let a natural tendency go too far. If every person who started drums looked for the easy way, we should all have weak left hands.

A student taught by the method

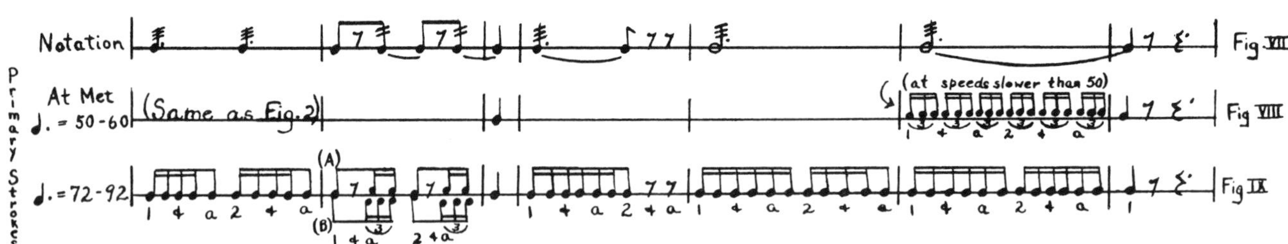

Fig. III could be used for Fig. VII for a different effect at speeds between 72 and 92.

For interpreting Fig. VII between speeds 112 and 132, follow the interpretation of Fig. IV. Note that the speed of playing determines where the roll is cut off.

At speed 132 to 160, see Fig. V. At 132, cut off on "ah." At 160, cut off on 2.

At 160 to 210, follow Fig. VI. "Men of Marlbrough" by Stone puts this tempo and rhythm pattern to test.

that I have suggested is capable of meeting any director's requirements in regard to the degree of close or open he may want the roll. In dealing with students from fifteen or twenty different bands I have found that this method works with great success. No matter what band a student is in, he is equipped to roll as the director wishes. Some directors like open rolls; others prefer more of a close roll.

I suggest that drummers secure a copy of "The Big Show" by John T. Heney, which necessitates applying rolls to the various rhythms mentioned in the article.

May 1954

Training in Rudiments Essential to Drumming

Players must master reading of music and principal and single-stroke patterns

JOHN P. NOONAN

IN TALKING WITH A NUMBER of band leaders I notice that many of them seem to be trying to achieve ensemble results that are a bit ahead of the possibilities of individual players. Strangely enough, it is almost always true that the sound of the band or orchestra is better than it actually should be according to the limitations of the individuals.

This circumstance is especially true in the drum section, and it is a tough problem to iron out. It is imperative that the student of the drum be taught the principal rudiments first, the long roll, the five-stroke roll, the nine-stroke roll, the thirteen-stroke roll, the seventeen-stroke roll, flams and ruffs. In addition, he should be given all the single-stroke patterns available. With this technical equipment he can play well almost any drum part, and, in addition, will be well prepared for the rest of the rudiments.

Now about the other rudiments, the single and double drags, flam-paradiddles, etc. There is certainly no excuse for a drummer who will not learn these rudiments, regardless of what kind of playing he does or intends to do. I cannot understand why drummers resist them, but we all know that many do.

First, let me say that I do not recall ever having used a single or double drag, as such, in any band or orchestra I've played in, and I do not remember playing any rudimental flam-paradiddles in any composition for band or orchestra. I tell students these facts frankly, and almost always they ask, "Why fool with them?"

The answer is really simple. These twenty-six rudiments, or first principles of drumming, are traditional. They are an important part of the drummer's training, and to neglect them is ridiculous.

Objections

Some of our critics say the rudiments are military in scope, are really limited to marching groups, and have little place in the modern band or orchestra. Granted! I'll buy that! But I stoutly maintain that they must be taught, for beyond question these rudiments give the drummer control of the sticks and an understanding of the instrument.

To say, conversely, that with the playing of the twenty-six rudiments a drummer has mastered the drum is equally absurd. He has acquired only technical facility with little regard for the musical aspects involved.

Every instrument has its category and, like it or not, the drum is essentially a military instrument. Its uses for color, effect, rhythmical patterns, unbroken crescendos, etc., are many, but fundamentally it is a military instrument. Thus, it follows that this aspect of playing the instrument is basic, but only basic, for any student can be taught to play all of the rudiments by rote. With this in hand, the student must develop musicianship like any other musician.

Now, a word about the drummer who refuses to learn to read music. You all know this lad! He will *not* learn to read. He is the "cat" of the band, the real cool character who hits everything in sight (including the leader!) The only one to blame here *is* the leader. There is only one answer to this problem. The leader, or teacher, must have a talk with the student and tell him that if he does not wish to learn to read, there is no place in the band or orchestra for him.

A clarinet or trumpet player would not be permitted to remain in the group if he persisted in "faking" his way along. If the drummer refuses to try to learn to read music, then he should be dismissed from the band.

Definite Requirements

The requirements should be outlined to all drum students when they start to take lessons, and rules should be followed through religiously. The first procedure is the reading and playing of simple single-stroke patterns, then the start of learning the long roll, followed by the principal rudiments as outlined at the beginning of this article, and then the remainder of the rudiments. If one expects to have a good drum section, this method is good, and it will work.

All this is particularly true in those cases in which the band leader is forced to teach all instruments and has no private teachers available to help him. He really has a tough job. Amazingly enough, many of these men obtain marvelous results.

Good Foundation

It is to those men in particular that this advice is directed. The job at hand is to give the students the proper foundation. I feel that most band-leaders today have a pretty good idea of the thirteen essential rudiments. If these are properly taught, the drum student has his foundation, and there is no limit to how far he can go. Without it he is simply not a well-equipped drummer.

I have had many students who resisted the rudiments, but to a man they later say they are glad they were forced to learn them. In some cases the only way it could be done was by issuing an ultimatum—either get the rudiments under control or seek lessons elsewhere. A tough attitude? Yes, but a necessary one to produce good drummers.

Over a period of many years I have heard of, and investigated, many "new" ideas on how to play the drum. Some of the ideas set forth in these "methods" I thought good, others not so good. A top-flight percussion player with one of the world's great symphony orchestras said to me, "In my opinion, being a good snare drummer is part rudimental, part your own ideas, a lot of somebody else's ideas and part vaudeville, plus a lot of nerve."

A pretty good practical observation from a great player! I recalled that, years before, I had judged this man in a high school rudimental contest, and he had got a "Superior" on rudiments. He seldom plays a flam-paradiddle or a double drag today, but he can whip all of them off at a moment's notice.

All of your drummers will not play in a great orchestra, but you can give every last one of them the same rudimental foundation this chap had. That's the marvelous thing about a standard in any field; it's there; it's traditional; it will work; therefore, use it. It's foolish not to require high standards.

September 1954

Drumming with Just Eight Rudiments

HASKELL W. HARR

At this time of year when reorganizing our bands, one of the most important subjects to consider is just how much ability is necessary for our drummers to have in order to play the percussion parts correctly.

Drum parts in band and orchestra arrangements do not require a knowledge of many of the 26 drum rudiments. If the drummer can play single strokes, rolls, flams, ruffs and flam accents, he can play any drum part. Flam accents are characteristic of 6–8 meter marches.

Rhythmic Figures

The study of rhythmic figures is most important. The various figures are the fundamental beats for rolls and rudiments. As soon as the student is able to hold the sticks correctly and make a good stroke, the study of figures should begin. He should be taught to analyze each figure he studies, in order to be able to play it correctly whenever it will appear before him in the future. Too many students proceed to forget one lesson as soon as a new one is presented.

All rhythmic figures should be memorized. Memorization of these figures will help the player to become a good sight reader. When discussing sight reading, I often think of Mr. H. A. VanderCook who said: "There is no such thing as sight reading. If you are well versed in your fundamentals, you will encounter nothing new when playing."

Playing Rolls

After a student feels at home with a pair of drum sticks in his hands and can play rhythmic figures well, he should be taught to play the short rolls. In march music, which is generally encountered first, he will need to know three rhythmic rolls—the five stroke, the nine stroke and the seventeen stroke. For some reason the seventeen stroke roll is not included among the 26 drum rudiments, although it is used very much.

The five stroke roll is designated by two eighth notes tied together with three lines through the stem of the first eighth note. All rolls are designated by three lines through the stem of the first note, regardless of tempo. If the student has played the

primary strokes of the five stroke roll. In 2-4 march tempo the number of strokes in a roll is determined by the number of 32nd notes in the first note of the roll plus one tap for the note to which it is tied.

If the student plays a stroke and a rebound on the *1*, a stroke and rebound on *e* and a single stroke on *&*, he will have the five stroke roll. When playing this roll in series, it should be alternated, *i. e.*, since the first roll started and ended with the right hand, the next should start and stop with the left hand. This is called playing from hand to hand.

After the student has mastered the five stroke roll, it is quite simple for him to learn to play the other rolls. Strokes and rebounds added to the five make other stroke rolls.

The next common roll in march tempo is the nine, written ♩♪. Count the number of 16th notes in the quarter note, counting *1-e-&-a*, and play a stroke and a rebound for each. Play a single stroke for the 8th note and you have the nine stroke roll (1 e & a 2; R R L L R R L L R).

The third important roll to learn is the seventeen stroke. It is designated by a half note tied to an 8th note. This roll has nine primary strokes, counted *1-e-&-a-2-e-&-a-1.* Playing a stroke and rebound on each of the primary strokes except the last which is a single stroke, you have the seventeen.

All of the other rolls, the seven, eleven, thirteen and fifteen should be learned later. They will be used in concert music wherein the rules governing the number of strokes for rolls in marches do not apply. The rudimental long roll should be taught prior to the student's participation in contests.

The Flam

After the single stroke and the rolls have been learned, the next important rudiment is the flam, a combination of tap and stroke. The flam is written by placing a small grace note before a large note. The grace note is played with a tap, the large note with a stroke. To teach the right flam—a flam gets its name from the hand that plays the large note—start with both sticks about three inches from the drumhead, low position. Let both sticks strike the head at the same time.

After a few up and down movements together, start raising the right stick higher and higher until it is about chin high, high position. Be sure to keep the left stick low during the exercise. The beat should sound FLAM, not FA-LAM. Sticks should not strike together when the flam is accomplished, yet not far enough apart to register as two separate sounds. The purpose of the flam is to broaden the sound.

The left flam is played just the opposite of the right flam. When alternating flams, play the grace note of the first flam with a snap of the wrist. As soon as the stick strikes the head, raise the stick chin high, up-stroke. Start the right stick chin high. After it strikes the drumhead, stop the rebound about three inches above the head, down-stroke. The sticks are now in position for the next flam.

The Ruff

The ruff is designated by placing two grace notes before a large note. Both grace notes are played with the same hand. When playing the ruff, both hands must travel up and down together, as when playing a flam. Play the two grace notes with a little bounce, the same as in a roll, and follow immediately with the stroke. The three notes should be spaced evenly.

Flam Accent No. 1

For the flam accent No. 1, start by playing the 6–8 (R L R L R L) figure. Place a grace note before the first note and the fourth note (L R L R R L R L). Play a right flam for the first note, a left tap for the second and a right tap on the third note. Raise the stick high on the second note, up-stroke. Your sticks are now in position for the next note, a left flam. Play the left flam, a right tap and then a left tap. Raise the stick high on the second note. The sticks are now in position to start another flam accent. When playing say, *Flam-left-right-Flam-right-left.*

Flam Accent No. 2

Flam accent No. 2 is notated (L R R R L L). Play the grace note of the first flam with a left up-stroke and the large note with a down-stroke. Play the second note with a right tap. The hands are now in position for the left flam. Play the grace note with a right up-stroke, the large note with a left down-stroke and then play the next note with a left tap.

October 1954

From Just Eight Rudiments To Many Different Rhythms

Part I

HASKELL W. HARR

In the September issue "Drumming with Just Eight Rudiments" was presented. In the next two articles we will show how these rudiments grow into many different rhythmic figures by adding a grace note here and there and by combining these fundamentals.

Basic Rhythm No. 1

This time figure is the rhythm for the FIVE STROKE ROLL. Play a stroke and a rebound on each of the sixteenth notes and a single stroke on the eighth note while counting, 1-e-&, 2-e-& for the rhythm:

This roll is played

from hand to hand. If the roll starts on the beat the accent will be on the first note of the roll, , if it ends on a beat the accent will be on the last note of the roll.

Place two grace notes before the first note of the same rhythm figure,

to make a ruff. The accent will be on the eighth note. The sticking does not reverse. In solos you will find the notes mostly written in the reversed position:

Notice that the accent is then on the beat. Be careful not to accent the ruff.

Rhythm No. 2

The SEVEN STROKE ROLL is derived from this figure by playing a stroke and a rebound on each of the first three sixteenth notes and a single stroke on the fourth note

1 e & a
L L R R L L R

It is written . Rudimentally this roll always starts with the left hand and ends with the right. Playing the roll in the concert band it may be started with *either* hand, depending on its location in the measure.

By applying a special sticking pattern to the same figure we have a rudiment called a SINGLE PARADIDDLE

R L R R

. When PARADIDDLES are played in series, the sticking of the second one is reversed:

R L R R L R L L

Play a grace note before the first note of the figure and you change the paradiddle to a FLAM PARADIDDLE

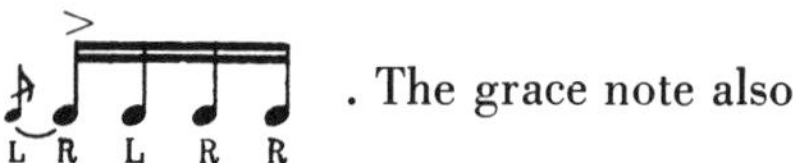

. The grace note also adds technical difficulties to the playing of the rudiment in that, when playing in series, the drummer now has three notes to play with one hand, namely, the last two notes of the first paradiddle and the grace note of the second one:

A grace note before the first and third notes of the figure:

changes it to a FLAM TAP. Notice the sticking—a right flam and right tap, a left flam and left tap. Rudimentally the main beats are played with single strokes, not a stroke and rebound.

Another rudiment built on this same time figure is the SINGLE DRAG, formed by adding two grace notes to the first and third notes:

The accent is on the second note, which is played with the hand opposite from the one playing the first note. This rudiment may be substituted for the five stroke roll in extremely rapid passages.

The DRAG PARADIDDLE also uses the same basic rhythm. Place a grace note before the first note and use paradiddle sticking:

L L R L R R

The DRAG PARADIDDLE NO. I is formed by placing a single note and two grace notes before the figure:

R L L R L R R

This rudiment is often used in solos in rhythm and when played in series is played from hand to hand

R L L R L R R L R R L R L L

This rudiment is also called the Stroke and Drag Paradiddle.

The DRAG PARADIDDLE NO. II, a very flashy beat, is made by adding another stroke and two grace notes to drag paradiddle no. 1. It is played from hand to hand:

Basic Rhythm No. 3

This is the basic rhythm pattern for the nine stroke roll, written .

Play a stroke and a rebound on each of the sixteenth notes and a single stroke for the eighth note while counting 1-e-&-ah-2,

1 e & a 2
R R L L R R L L R

The nine stroke roll is played hand to hand.

The FLAMACUE is formed by placing a grace note before the first and the fifth notes:

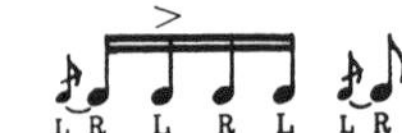

Play the second note with a heavy accent, this gives character to the rudiment. Play the first grace note with an upstroke of the left hand to get the hand in position to make this heavy accent. Count the rudiment 1-E-&-ah 2.

The teacher who has never had any drum lessons should first master the eight basic rudiments given in the September issue. Then by actually *performing* the foregoing rhythmic figures they will be understood clearly, and what is even more important, they will be remembered.

If there is any doubt as to how these rudiments should sound, the writer has made a record which explains these rudiments and provides the sound too. There is no substitute for performing them yourself and actually *feeling* the rhythms. All that is needed is a pair of fairly heavy drum sticks and preferably a practice pad or snare drum.

From Just Eight Rudiments To Many Different Rhythms

Part II

HASKELL W. HARR

THE ARTICLE "DRUMMING WITH Just Eight Rudiments" appeared in the September issue. The embellishments which produce the many different rhythmic figures are usually made by adding a grace note here and there and by combining two different rudimental figures. The first part was presented in the October issue. In this issue we conclude this subject.

Rhythm No. 4 

One of the most important rudiments used in 6/8 tempo is FLAM ACCENT No. 1. Place a grace note before the first and fourth notes for this beat, and stick as shown:

In most cases, grace notes are played with the same stick that plays the beat ahead. When practicing say — Flam-left-right-Flam-right-left.

In 6/8 march tempo when dotted quarter notes are to be rolled, rhythmic five stroke rolls may be used.

Written: ; played:

When a dotted half note is to be played with a roll, bounce five of the six eighth notes of the figure and play the last one with a single stroke. The accent will be on the first note.

Start with the right hand: played

The DOUBLE DRAG may also be made from this time figure. Place two grace notes before the first, second, fourth and fifth notes and accent the third and sixth notes:

The first two ruffs are played from left to right, the first accented note with the left hand. The next two ruffs are played from right to left and the second accented note with the right hand. This rudiment is best played at a tempo of 110.

The FLAM-PARADIDDLE-DIDDLE also uses the same time figure. Place a grace note before the first note and use the special sticking shown:

LR L R R L L

When played in series the sticking is reversed:

LR L R R L L RL R L L R R

Rhythm No. 5

This common 6/8 figure becomes FLAM ACCENT NO. 2 when a grace note is placed before the first and third notes:

LR R RL L

Notice that the first two main notes are played with the right hand, the second two main notes played with the left hand. Always stick this rudiment in the prescribed way for smooth rhythm. If sticks are alternated one has a tendency to play unevenly or to swing into 2/4 time.

Rhythm No. 6

This rhythmic pattern will develop three rudiments. The first, the TEN STROKE ROLL, written, (L R R) is played with a stroke and a rebound on each of the first four notes, a single accented beat for the fifth note and a single accented beat for the sixth note. This last accented note should be played with the hand opposite from the one playing the fifth note and should be struck with the same amount of force:

The ELEVEN STROKE ROLL written: is made by playing a stroke and rebound on the first five notes and a single stroke on the sixth note. Count 1-e-&-ah-2-e.

The third rudiment from this same figure, the DOUBLE PARADIDDLE, is made by using special sticking as shown: (R L R L R R) The rudiment is played from hand to hand:

Rhythm No. 7

From this time figure we develop the SINGLE RATAMACUE by placing two grace notes before the triplet:

LLR L R L

This rudiment is also played from hand to hand:

To form the DOUBLE RATAMACUE place a ruff before the single ratamacue:

This rudiment is played from hand to hand. It is used in 3/4 and 6/8 time.

The TRIPLE RATAMACUE is made by adding two ruffs to the single ratamacue. It is played from hand to hand:

You will notice that whenever ruffs are added to a beat, they are all played with the same hand. Care must be taken in playing the Ratamacues, or any other rudiment using ruffs, that the grace notes are not played so open that they will sound like separate beats. When playing ruffs, start with one hand high, one low. Start both hands down at the same time so the high hand strikes right after the low hand. Some drummers make the mistake of starting with both hands at practically the same level. They drop the hand that plays the grace notes but raise the other hand before striking the main blow. This makes a space between the grace notes and the main beat. Try to make the rudiment sound like the word RATAMACUE would sound if you pronounced it by rolling the R.

There are many more rudiments than the twenty-six adopted by the National Association of Rudimental Drummers. Years ago when drumming was taught by rote, many other combinations of notes were needed to cover various rhythms. Some of the other rudiments, taken from Mr. Sousa's "Trumpet and Drum", Sanford A. Moeller's book, and Bruce and Emmet include the FLAM AND STROKE: LR L RL R, the FLAM AND FEINT: LR L RL R, the FEINT AND FLAM: L RL R LR, the STROKE AND SINGLE DRAG: R LLR L RRL | R, the FLAM AND DRAG PARADIDDLE: L R L R R LLR L R R, the FOUR-STROKE RUFF: L R L R L R L R, the DOUBLE FLAM PARADIDDLE: LR L LR L R R RL LR RL R L L, the FULL DRAG: LLR R RRL L.

COMPOUND STROKE NUMBER ONE: L LR L R LLR L R | LLR L R L R LLR

COMPOUND STROKE NUMBER TWO:

Upon reading this article, you probably noticed that the biggest percentage of the rudiments are not usable in concert band scores. In many cases where the time figure could be used, the addition of a flam or ruff would make the drum part much too heavy, especially when two or three drummers are trying to play the parts. The written drum part just does not give the drummer the opportunity to use them.

Every drummer should learn to play all twenty-six drum rudiments up to tempo for the development of technic. They are interesting to play and, when mastered, provide enjoyment and satisfaction for the performer.

January 1955

Marching Band Drum Section, Asset or Liability?

ROBERT W. BUGGERT

No PERCUSSION CLASS, clinic, demonstration or lecture is ever completed without the instructor or lecturer receiving the following questions: "How can one develop an adequate marching band drum section? Will you write some street beats?" The answer is not simple but attention to the following principles will help bring about a more desirable result.

Esprit de Corps

The members of the drum section must realize that their section is the *heart* of any marching unit. From this they should achieve a willingness to work together for one general objective: becoming the greatest asset to the band. Once a sincere attitude is developed, the achievement of desirable techniques will have purpose. Leadership depends, to some extent, on the personalities involved. The band director usually will be responsible for rehearsals, training and coaching. If the drummers are mature and someone in the group has qualities of leadership, the section may function with less direct supervision. A third factor helping to establish unity is the recognition of achievement. A section should be allowed to feature and demonstrate its accomplishments; if these are exceptional, the public should know their school is above average in this field of endeavor. Good *esprit de corps* depends upon the development of purpose, good leadership and recognition of results.

Tempo

The drum section is not the assistant director of the band. It is a vital but integrated part. No drum section can function efficiently if it must lead, drag or force the band to play the desired tempo. To do this it must play at an unmusical dynamic level. The point is this: teach the drum section to establish and maintain the correct cadence, but also teach the band to do this without depending solely on the drum section. Creation and maintenance of correct tempo depend upon (1) conception of cadence, (2) technical facility and (3) use of material suited to the established tempo. The section should have a correct metronomic conception of the cadence which is expected and, in addition, know the melodic content of all the music to be played. These melodies, learned at the correct tempo, will help unify the approach to steadiness. The drum part should be written to correlate with the music, the tempo and the technility facility of the drummers. Simplicity is often the answer to cadential efficiency.

Accompaniment Parts

A drum section cannot perform effectively and play the written parts of most published marching band music. This statement must not be misinterpreted; irrational improvisation is not the answer. The drum part must be revised to fit the melody as well as the accompaniment. It must also be expressive, have rhythmic continuity and emphasize the forward motion of the music. Afterbeats do not fulfill these requirements. In addition, the bass drum and cymbals must accent to help create a rhythmic-melodic unity in expressiveness. For example, play the trio of *On Wisconsin* using the written part; repeat and use the following part:

Which creates the better rhythmic drive and sounds the more effective? Which is easier for the drummers? Apply this principle to any 2/4 or 2/2 march.

Unique Qualities

No section sounds unique if it plays something which has been done previously. It is better to establish a few formulas and write variations of these. Most four-measure or eight-measure beats and variations have a good sound but at the same time are very routine. The following seems to underlie all of them:

A first step toward a new pattern is the extension of this to five measures:

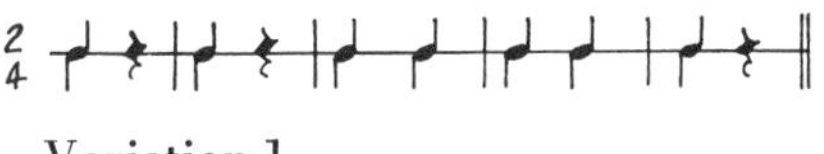

Variation 1.

Variation 2.

A second step is the use of variants in the bass drum and cymbal parts:

Variation 3. (Add the following)

Variation 4. (Intricate but effective)

The above seem quite intricate but when thoroughly analyzed are not too difficult. However, one must note that they are ineffective if the tempo is too slow. Their usage is not recommended at less than metronome marking, quarter note equals 140.

A third step is that of mixed meter. For example, mix 2/4 and 3/4 measures in a manner that will create an effect of cross rhythms:

In effect:

The University of Wichita Marching Band Drum Section uses the following cadence for leaving the field:

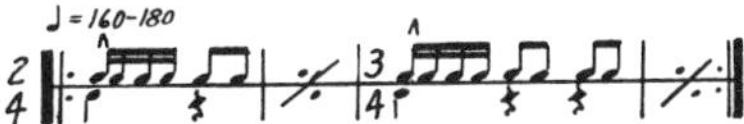

It has never failed to create a feeling of excitement. For additional interest the following variations are used:

Variation 1. (Add cymbals)

Variation 2.

In closing one might summarize as follows:

1. Establish a spirit
2. Set the tempo
3. Make the parts better
4. Challenge the players
5. Use imagination

Is Your Bass Drum an Uncontrolled Monster?

Joe Berryman

LIKE MANY OTHER DIRECTORS AND percussionists I feel that everyone in the percussion section should be able to play acceptably on most, if not all, of the percussion instruments. If they have been taught that way, there is little likelihood that at least one of them will not be a very good bass drummer. Of course, selecting the best person available for the instrument is not only the first step but, perhaps, the most important step.

The technic of playing the bass drum is relatively simple, as compared with the other instruments; but good rhythmic sense, good musical taste and good judgment are most essential. A steady, dependable student is likewise desirable. Good bass drum material can often be found among the piano, vocal and string students who are not in the band.

Next in importance is proper equipment. Most bands now use one or two Scotch drums for marching and a larger, deeper drum for concert. This is fine. If your budget will not stand it, however, and you must use one drum for all purposes, select a 28″ or 30″ for the average size band. Avoid using hard felt sticks. They last longer, which is about the only point in their favor; but they also break more heads and produce a most disagreeable sound, regardless of the drum or the ability of the player.

"To tune or not to tune?, that IS the question". and I might add a most controversial question. Many people in the past few years have advocated tuning the bass drum to a certain pitch. Some say F, some G, some E♭, some A♭; and still others say one head to F, the other to E♭.

Without making too many enemies, I'd like to suggest that you strike your drum halfway between center and rim. Note the pitch. Now move 6 inches nearer the rim and strike again. Now from the point you struck first, move 6 inches nearer the center. You will undoubtedly have three different pitches. Conclusion: to get the same pitch each time you must strike the drum in the same place each time. Next, strike the drum about 4 inches from the rim. Slowly play alternately loud and soft. You will find you get different predominate pitches as the volume is changed. Further conclusion: to get the same pitch you must play at the same volume all the time. So I suggest we forget *pitch* and look for a good, acceptable *tone* on the bass drum.

Many good band performances—both in concert and marching—are spoiled by a roaring, ringing bass drum that ruins all phrasing of the wind instruments by a continuous, unmusical long tone that runs one phrase into the next with no regard for the release of other instruments. I do not advocate a box-like *thud* as is so prevalent in dance bands; however, there is a happy medium. In the concert band, try a muffler on the head you do NOT beat upon and dampen the beating head with your left hand at the completion of each phrase. A good rule is: Whenever possible, have the left hand on the head on every rest. The composer or arranger put the rest there for only one purpose, *silence;* the previous tone ringing over into the rest is *not* silence. If the bass drummer also plays cymbals on top of the drum, touch the head with the fingers of the right hand to silence the drum. This also applies equally well to tympani. Some drummers use the right knee for this purpose and quite successfully, even if it is rather awkward.

Another point that has caused much confusion is the advice that you should not strike the bass drum in the center. The average student interprets this to mean that he is to strike near the rim all the time. This produces a long tone that at times, in legato passages, is very desirable; but in marches and other extremely rhythmic passages, a shorter tone produces a much better effect. The nearer the center you strike, the shorter the tone; the nearer the rim, the longer the tone. Try striking a distance from the rim that is $\frac{1}{3}$ of the diameter of the head—on a 30″ drum, strike 10″ from the rim for most playing. For a more legato tone, move a few inches toward the rim; for a staccato tone, move a few inches toward the center.

Most professional concert bands use one player for both bass drum and cymbals, except in some cymbal solos or where very heavy cymbal tone is desired. There is coordination and tonal effect thus produced that cannot be achieved with two separate players. In this case, a pair of slightly smaller cymbals (15″) with the top cymbal of slightly lighter weight (medium or perhaps med-heavy) than the one on the bottom is preferable. Accented notes and rhythmic effects are much enhanced by playing in this manner. It is, naturally, much more difficult and should be attempted only if you have a good, serious student.

Try putting your BEST student on bass drum instead of using the old custom of making a bass drummer of the person who has been the most outstanding failure every place else in the band. Then spend some time with him, helping and showing what can be done with a little attention to detail and serious study. It will pay big dividends in your band's performance.

What Is Your Tympani IQ?

HASKELL HARR

1. *What is considered the standard size set of tympani?* The standard set of tympani or kettle drums consists of a 25-inch drum and a 28-inch drum.

2. *What is their range?* The overall range of the set is one octave, from F2 to F3. The large 28-inch drum has a range of a fifth, from F2 to C3. The 25-inch drum range is from B♭2 to F3. Under favorable conditions the range may be extended. However, if notes above or below this octave are needed, it is best to use more drums. The 23-inch drum will have a range from D3 to A3, while the 30-inch drum will give you E2 to B♭2.

3. *What is the "collar" of the tympani head?* The portion of the tympani head that turns downward over the bowl is called the *collar*. A reasonable amount of collar must be kept on the tympani head at all times, especially when not in use, so that there will be enough *let out* to reach the lower notes.

4. *How do you keep the collar on the head?* When you are through playing the instruments, the pedals should be left up as high as they will go. (This applies to the Leedy-Ludwig and the Slingerland.) This loosens the heads. Then the tension handles should be turned until there is at least a half inch collar over the edge of the bowl. It doesn't matter which note this happens to be. Of course, this will mean that at all times the heads will be very tight when not in use, but if they are evenly tensioned there is no danger of breaking—if the heads are of good quality. When ready to play again, loosen the tension handles until you have the lowest note for each drum, F2 or B♭2. You will find that you have the full scope of the tympani when you press down on the pedal.

If you have the W. F. L. or the Ludwig-Ludwig tympani, apply full pressure on the heads when through playing, by pressing the toe of the pedal as far as it will go. When ready to play again, press the heel of the pedal to the floor, then make whatever adjustments are necessary to get B♭2 and F2 by using the tension handles. You will then find that you have full range of the drums when you press down on the toe of the pedal.

5. *I have a new set of tympani but am unable to get the low tones. Can you give me the reason for this and information about how to remedy the situation?* Apparently you have not kept pressure on the heads when not in use. Remove the heads from the kettles and sponge them carefully with a damp cloth on both sides to within an inch and a half of the flesh hoop. Be sure not to get water under the hoop. Place the head back on the kettle and pull down slowly and evenly so that you have a quarter of an inch of collar. Allow to dry slowly. Take off the head again and repeat until you have obtained the full half inch collar. Go slowly, using two or three operations to prevent breakage.

6. *I left the pressure on my tympani heads as instructed, but when I pressed the heel to the floor to get ready to play, it came right back to the first position. Is the tension spring out of adjustment?* Do not disturb the adjustment of the tension spring. Atmospheric conditions have caused the head to become damp and flabby. Hold the heel of the pedal to the floor and tighten the tension screws until you have F2 on the large drum and B♭2 on the small drum. Then you will have full range of the tympani when you press on the pedals. The only time the tension spring has to be adjusted is when the pedal will not stay on the highest note.

7. *When I move the pedal up and down, the head of my tympani creaks. What is the cause?* The bowl of the kettle needs lubrication. Remove the head from the kettle, and with a strip of fine emery cloth clean the rounding edge of the bowl. Wipe the edge of the bowl with a clean cloth, then apply paraffin to the edge. Replace head and adjust.

8. *Where is the "beating spot" on a tympani?* The beating spot is about one-eighth of the diameter of the head from the rim. That will average about three to five inches from the rim.

Occasionally an area of six or eight inches will develop in a tympani head which resists the bounce of the sticks at this point more than on other parts of the surface. Tympanists call this a *stiff* spot. It is caused by Nature placing more closely-knit fibers in the calf skin in one place than in another. It does not harm the overall tone of the instrument unless the area happens to cover at least one-fourth of the head surface. In this case, the head should not be used. It is, however, a simple matter to get away from a small spot merely by turning the kettle slightly to the right or left. If the kettle does not turn, remove the head and change the position of the spot.

9. *Why is the single stroke roll used on the tympani while the double roll is used on the snare drum?* The snare drum head, being much smaller in diameter and stretched much tighter than the tympani, vibrates faster and responds to lightning-like speed under the sticks, whereas the larger and more slack tympani head (plus the softer sticks) takes a little longer to *answer* the blows of the sticks. If a second blow is struck before the previous one has had time to *speak* out in full tone, the result is that the vibrations of the two strokes become confused and an imperfect tone is produced. This is known, mechani-

cally, as *choking the tone* and is the reason why the somewhat more open single stroke is necessary for the tympani.

10. *How are the tympani sticks held?* There are two basic methods for holding tympani sticks: (1) In the same manner that one holds marimba or xylophone mallets, palms down, backs of hands up, gripping the sticks between the cushion of the thumb and the first inside joint of the index finger. This provides the hinge. Control is divided between the second and third fingers, using one or the other (or both) at the same time—whichever suits the player best. (2) Thumbs up, palms and backs of the hands perpendicular, sticks held as described in the first method. Control is obtained in the same manner.

The finest of teachers, of course, advocate slight variations of both methods.

11. *What is meant by "flipping the head"?* When the band or orchestra is playing, it is necessary to tune the tympani quietly. To strike the head with the stick, even slightly, would cause a disturbance of the head, the tone of which would travel and be heard. A more quiet and satisfactory method is to flip the head with the tip of the middle finger. The tone will be loud enough for you to hear by placing the ear close to the head, and not enough of the head will have been set in motion to cause a disturbance. Flipping the head may be done while holding the stick in the hand. It is done by placing the tip of the finger on the head just enough to adhere to it slightly. Quickly snap the finger forward; that will set a small portion of the head in motion. Form the habit of tuning in this manner; do not use the stick. Practice flipping with both the right hand and the left hand, so that you can hold the sticks in either hand and still tune.

12. *How do you stop the tone after a blow has been struck?* To stop the vibration of the head when necessary, place the little finger on the head and immediately drop all fingers in place. Try rolling the fingers in rapid succession, making contact with the head one at a time. This will avoid the slap tone you get when you place the entire hand on the head at one time.

The stopping of the tone after a note has been struck is very important; thus, the tone of the tympani will not interfere with the possible chordal changes in the composition being played.

April 1955

Rudimental Bass Drumming

ACTON OSTLING

MOST MUSICAL GROUPS USE ONE OF two types of bass drumming while on parade: either the one-stick *on the beat* style, or the *Scotch* style, played with two felt beaters. There is another style which is used a great deal in the Eastern part of the country and is generally referred to as the *rudimental* style. Fife and drum corps have used this for many years, but it is now being used in corps of other types, and has recently been used by some bands.

In earlier days, most corps bass drummers used sticks with heads of soft materials. The only reference to bass drumming that I have found in early American drum methods is the following, which is in *The Drummer's Instructor or Martial Musician* by J. L. Rumrille and H. Holton, published in 1817: "The Bass Drum must be tuned to chord with the Music with which is plays—The right hand stick must not exceed ten inches in length, with a ball at the end six inches in circumference, composed of spunge properly wound with woolen yarn and covered with Cloth or Wash-Leather—the Left hand Stick may be of the length and size of a common beating Drum Stick". I found this of interest because the old corps of Moodus, Connecticut (org. 1860) used two chamois-covered beaters *of different sizes* on the bass drums. They had their own style of playing and the bass drummers *filled in* extra beats with the smaller (left hand) stick. Another reference to the type of beater used in earlier days is given in a newspaper account of the first Drummer's Convention (Wallingford, Conn., September 3, 1885) which stated that "tall drummers and short drummers in gorgeous uniforms smote big and little drums with their *padded potato mashers . . .*"

At the present time most drummers use two solid wooden beaters for playing the *rudimental* style. These beaters vary in size and shape, but an average size might be 11-12 inches in length with a head, either round or egg-shaped, about 2 inches in diameter. Most drummers turn out their own sticks, shaped to suit their own

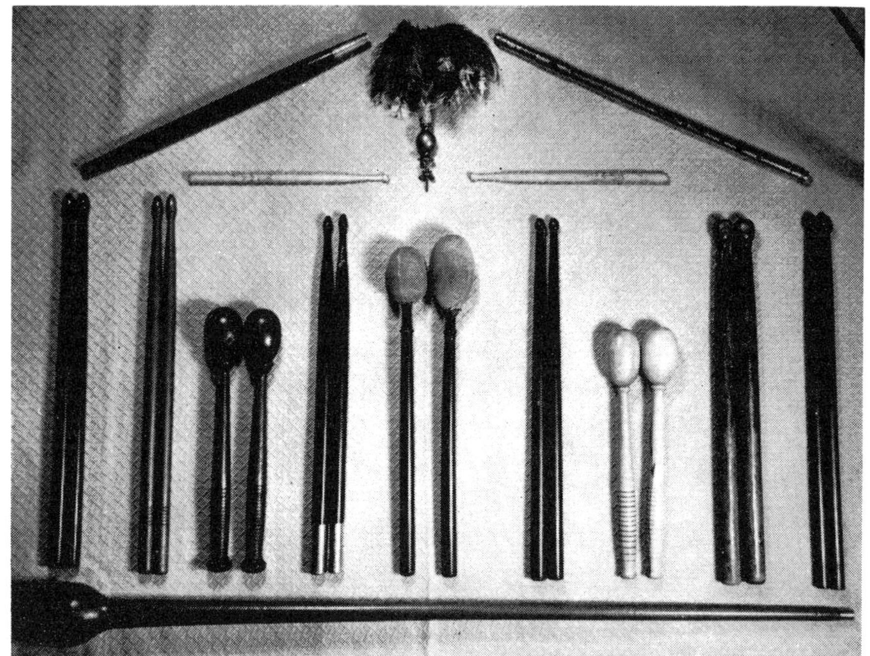

Various type drum sticks. The 3rd pair from the left and the 3rd pair from the right are wooden beaters used in rudimental bass drumming.

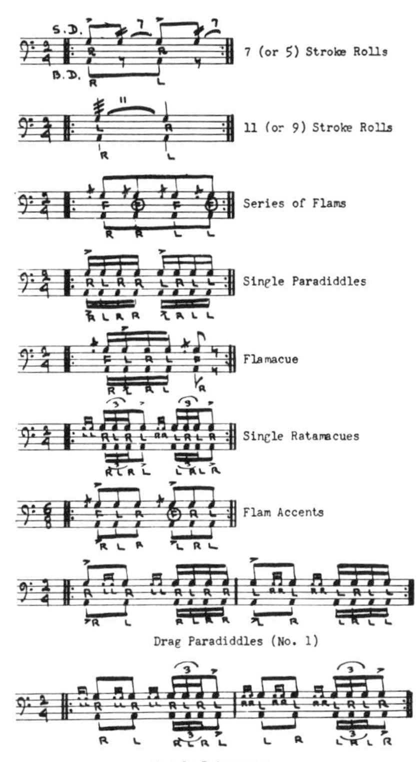

Nine representative snare drum rudiments and the rudimental bass drum figures which are generally used to accompany them.

individual taste. It is these wooden beaters which give the unique *solidity* which is so typical of this style of playing.

In the *rudimental* style, bass drummers play figures which are the same as, or similar to, the snare drum rudiments, except that no rolls or embellishments (single or double grace notes) are performed. Most bass drummers play basic beats, but add little flourishes and mannerisms while playing them. Generally, they use an easy, balanced, swinging arm motion, with one beater always moving up high as the other comes down. A rather colorful description of this style of playing was given in *Martial Music* when the writer of an article told of watching a corps pass a reviewing stand: "They were rudimental bass drummers, four of them, as near alike as four peas in a pod. As they marched away, throwing their two wooden beaters high and low with precision, grace, and power . . . they were a sight you could not forget." This type of playing appeals to the spectator as well as to the performer.

At Eastern field days, competition for individual bass drumming is held as it is for snare drumming, baton swinging, fifing and bugling. The bass drummer is usually called upon to play one or two drum beats, accompanied by one snare drummer. Usually the beats are played twice through—once in a *straight* or easier manner, and then *filled up* with more intricate figures (rudiments) to demonstrate the performer's ability. Drummers are judged on such things as correct sticking, balance between hands, style and cadence. These contests are among the most interesting from the standpoint of the spectator and there is always an interested group around the individual bass drum stand.

Charles Peters, conductor of the nationally-famous Joliet Grade School Band, uses rudimental bass drumming with his band when they are on parade. Between marches, his drummers use two series of four 8-bar cadences; each cadence is repeated four times—first FFF, then PP. His four bass drummers use solid wooden beaters which he made from bowling

A short excerpt from a melody with parts included for both *rudimentary* and *regular* bass drumming for comparison.

pins. The Joliet Legion Band has also used wooden beaters for parade work and has found playing to be easier with these than with regular felt beaters.

Sanford A. Moeller, the well-known New York drummer, recently wrote me that, at times, the U.S. Army Band uses two-stick bass drumming while on parade.

School band directors who would like to introduce something a little different might consider using rudimental bass drumming in one of the following ways:

(1) With drum cadences on parade.

(2) As a concert novelty, using snare drums, bass drums, and piccolos and flutes—a la *fife and drum corps.*

(3) Concert demonstration, having one snare drummer and one bass drummer play a beat together as it is done at contests (explain to audience —either verbally or with program notes).

Any school woodshop can turn out wooden beaters, and these can be used on any type bass drum. Material, with all sticking indicated for both snare and bass drum, is available*; or, a director can arrange his own. These are easy to work up, boys enjoy this type of playing, and the spectators will enjoy the *novel* angle—especially in sections of the country where rudimental bass drumming has not been seen.

**Music of '76* books, published by Remick Music Corp.

Belwin Fife and Drum Corps Builder, I & II, available about May 1.

May 1955

What Is Your Marimba IQ?

HASKELL HARR

1. *To what other instrument does the keyboard of the marimba correspond?* There is a very close similarity between the piano keyboard and that of the marimba.

2. *How does the pitch of the marimba compare with that of the xylophone?* The top note of the xylophone is one octave higher than that of the marimba. The top C of the xylophone is C8, while the top C of the marimba is C7.

3. *Which C on the marimba corresponds with middle C on the piano?* The lowest C on the marimba is C3. The C one octave above that would be C4, middle C on the piano.

4. *Is there any difference in the wood used for the bars of the marimba and the xylophone?* The wood used for the bars of marimbas and xylophones is Honduras rosewood, carefully graded. Xylophone bars are taken from the core of the log where the wood is much harder. Marimba bars are cut from the outer, softer part of the log.

5. *What is the purpose of the resonator?* The resonator amplifies the tone.

6. *Would adding a larger resonator to a bar give it more tone?* No, the air column encased in the tube must be of exact size according to the pitch of the bar. The bar, when struck, gives out a definite sound wave. The resonator, being in tune with the bar, simply boosts the sound wave.

7. *What measures are used to compensate for the effects of changing weather conditions?* Provision is made on marimbas and xylophones whereby the resonators may be raised or lowered as needed. Instructions are given on a plate at the bass end of the instrument.

8. *What kind of mallets are best suited for playing the marimba?* The most common mallets used are made of yarn, wound on rubber balls. They are graded in size from the heavy 2″ ball down to the small 1½″ size. Rubber mallets may also be used.

9. *When selecting mallets to play a marimba solo what factors must be taken into consideration?* First, determine the range, and then see what register it will cover on the instrument. Also study the character of the selection. If it is a four mallet number, you will need heavier mallets in the left hand than you do in the right hand, to balance the tones. It is best to have the hardest mallet in the outside position of the right hand to bring out the melody. For a rapid number using the upper register, use a mallet hard enough to bring out the upper notes, yet not hard enough to impair the tone of the middle register.

10. *Where should the bars of the xylophone or marimba be struck to produce the best tone?* The bars should be struck in the center over the resonators to produce the best tone. The sharps and flats may be struck on the end closest to the player in rapid passages to avoid long reaches. Avoid striking the node, where the string passes through the bar, as the tone there is dead.

11. *What kind of a roll is used?* The roll used is a single stroke, open roll. The bars must be struck with a lifting motion to permit full tone of the bar.

12. *Do you play a roll with the same speed on the high notes of the marimba that you do on the low notes?* No. The vibrations of the bars on the lower end of the marimba are much slower, and call for a slower roll. A rapid roll will become uneven. You will have to experiment to determine how much slower to play.

13. *How do you tell which notes are to be rolled on the marimba?* Roll any note that has to be sustained.

14. *If no marimba part is available, what part is best suited for the band marimba player?* Give him or her the conductor's score and mark the parts you wished played. If the player is not accustomed to reading scores, give him the oboe part or write a special one.

Drums, Drummers and Drumming

A retrospective glance over the percussion picture of the past few years.

John P. Noonan

I AM GLAD to be back for the 10th Anniversary issue of *The Instrumentalist* and think it would be a good idea to report on the "percussion picture" as I have viewed it during my absence from these pages.

I was tremendously interested in the various foreign musical organizations heard in Chicago; and, very naturally, my primary interest was in the percussion sections.

Garde Républicaine Band

First, the *Garde Republicaine Band* from France. In this group one timpanist and three percussionists were employed. The timpanist used the French revolving kettledrums, i.e. the entire kettle is turned to the right to raise the pitch and to the left to lower the pitch.

Results were good, but there are several obvious disadvantages. First. the beating spot is changed constantly, and pitch changes cannot be made as quickly as with the pedal timpani. (This type of kettledrum has been made in America, but was discontinued in the 1930's). The bass drum had a metal shell, about 14" x 30", and the snare was a 5" x 14" metal drum, and I'm quite sure, the only American-made instrument in the band. In the concert arrangements, the section was one timpanist, one snare drum, one bass drum and one cymbal player, doubling when required on xylophone, bells, etc. On the marches the timpanist and the snare drum man played "Tambour Militaires" (field drums) with marvelous effect. At the trio of the march they would play the following figure

all the way through the first time and halfway through the second time, building a long roll into

for the second half, marvelously effective. The thing that impressed me the most was the fact that the drummers play almost exactly as we do here in this country.

Danish Orchestra

Next came the Danish State Radio Symphony Orcestra, a fine orchestra in a modern program that brought the percussion into the limelight. Here equipment was German pedal timpani, and again metal snare drums, two $6\frac{1}{2}$" x 14", and a metal shell bass drum. This percussion section was the closest to a top American section of any I've heard. During a Carl Nielsen Symphony the score calls for about thirty-two bars of snare drum improvising. During it the snare drummer "ran down" as fine a single stroke roll as I've heard. During the orchestra's stay in Chicago, the timpanist tried some of our American-made pedal timpani, and was quite astonished at the easy manipulation of the pedals, and more so at the quality of our timpani heads. Again, the Danish Orchestra percussionists played much like Americans do.

Concertgebouw Orchestra

Then came the Concertgebouw Orchestra of Amsterdam, by reputation one of the world's finest orchestras. The timpanist was using five German timpani at the program I heard, all pedal. Drums were a $5\frac{1}{2}$" x 14" modern pearl snare drum, and a wood shell bass drum. The timpani playing was excellent, the percussion not so effective as in the other groups. A different approach than the American style, lacking the "drive" and color our sections achieve.

Berlin Philharmonic

Then the Berlin Philharmonic Orchestra. Percussion instruments: a new set of four German pedal timpani made especially for the American tour. Fine drums, with the world's *worst* heads, and once more, metal snare and bass drums. The solo timpanist, Werner Tharicen has written a concerto for timpani and orchestra that is a remarkable work. When he first showed it to me I dismissed it as, "Nice, but too difficult." Then he played most of it for me, wow! The drummers are very interested in our American school of drumming, although these men didn't quite understand our approach. During their stay they picked up some American drumheads to take back.

American Percussion Leadership

After hearing all of the above groups, I heard a concert by the New York Philharmonic, and several by the Chicago Symphony Orchestra, which proved again that America leads the world in producing fine drummers.

Simon Sternburg, for thirty-two years first percussion with the Boston Symphony Orchestra and the Boston Pops, has written a new beginner's method for the drummer called *Five Easy Steps to Drumming*. Looks very good. Published by Charles Colin, N. Y. C. Every advanced drummer should have Sternburg's *Modern Drum Studies*, which is a "work-book" of *alla-breve* drum studies that is very good and is widely used by many of our finest drum teachers.

A letter from Fred D. Hinger, solo timpanist of the Philadelphia Orchestra, tells of his European trip with the Orchestra. He mentioned the fact that many timpanists and drummers in Europe marvelled at our fine American drums, and especially the drumheads!!!

Additional Thoughts

It may soon be possible to buy drumheads in color! I have seen several samples. For example, if the school colors are blue and gold, one gold and one blue head on the bass drum! Colorful? Looks good for marching bands.

A third kettledrum is fast becoming a necessity, and in colleges, a full set of four. To the standard 28" and 25", a 30" or 32", is next in line. Then a 24" or 23". Better allover tone as well as increased range.

At the last school contests, drumming was a little better. Also a few good timpanists were heard. Marimbas were excellent and in general better than drummers. Same old answer — NOT ENOUGH EMPHASIS ON RUDIMENTS!

September 1955

Materials for Drumheads

Will there ever be a good substitute for calfskin? We asked a well-known manufacturer of drumheads; his answer follows—

Dear Mr. Rohner:

In reply to your letter asking about other materials which might replace calfskin for drumheads in the future, I wish to say that many products have been tried but none of them have been completely successful. We have been manufacturing drumheads from calfskins for twenty-seven years and have seen many substitutes come in for a short period of time but do not believe that any of these synthetic materials can completely replace all of the qualities found in natural calfskin.

There have been plastic heads, synthetic-coated cloth heads, and both of these in many different varieties. The only quality they have been able to improve upon is that on rainy parade days they do not get wet or soft as calfskin will. The problem of dampness can be solved with the calfskin by covering it with a round plastic cover for parade use. These covers are made with an elastic edge that fits snugly around the drum.

Natural vs. Substitute

In recent years we seem to be going through a phase of thinking that all natural products are less valuable than synthetics for some reason or other. A rawhide calfskin has a natural hide fiber and texture that lends itself to greater resiliency, volume and tone than any man-made product we have ever found.

As you know, rawhide always has a tendency to stretch and pull back; and a very few minutes after a drum has been played upon, the skin again tightens and there is no pocket left where the drummer has been playing. There are some types of plastic that have this quality also, but the stretch and pull does not last nearly as long as this quality found in calfskin. Also, in the natural calfskin there are the animal oils and gelatin which form a very tight textured material that furnishes the essential quality of resiliency and tone.

Moisture and Breakage

I suppose with most drummers, the two qualities of calfskin which they would like to have improved would be less moisture effect and less breakage. With reasonable care calfskin drumheads will not break easily; to eliminate the pulling quality of rawhide, which sometimes causes breakage, would take away the required resiliency and pull back quality which is so essential for a drumhead. The problem of moisture, as stated before, can be temporarily solved by using a plastic cover. There are also waterproofing materials that could be applied to the surface of the skin which will, under temporary conditions, eliminate the moisture problem.

Tone Quality

About ten years ago we were told by several of our leading drum shops to get ready to close the tannery because plastic heads were proving very successful. However, after a few weeks drummers were returning the plastic heads because the tone and volume produced from synthetic heads could not equal that of the drummer using a calfskin head. These drummers also found that the plastic material did not continue to pull back after playing and left a pocket which produced a much deader tone.

In our opinion there are many qualities in natural calfskin which are essential to a drumhead. There are substitute materials that will produce some of these qualities, but there is no material that will match all of the qualities of calfskin. Our feeling, therefore, is that calfskin is the standard by which anything else must be compared. We do not believe there is too great a chance to substitute all of nature's qualities as found in rawhide calfskin as used for drumheads today.—*Howard P. Emery*, American Rawhide Mfg. Co.

October 1955

The Fall Semester

Robert W. Buggert

WITH THE BEGINNING of the fall semester, instrumental instructors face at least two immediate problems: marching band percussion, and beginners. It seems logical, then, to make a few suggestions regarding these problems.

Concerning marching band percussion, rather than be redundant, attention might be called to the January (1955) "Percussion Clinic" in *The Instrumentalist*. Some comments were made in that article which may help. At that time were stated the necessity for establishing a spirit, working for unity, and experimenting with the unique. In addition, attention to the following will aid in the improvement of the drum section *per se*.

Equipment Problems

The condition of the equipment affects the sound of the section as well as its appearance. Although a manual for repair cannot be stated within the scope of this article, directors and students should check the status of the equipment.

Field drums should be taken apart, cleaned and painted or varnished if necessary. Any bent lugs, tension rods or parts with worn threads should be replaced. Snares should be adjusted to equal lengths and replaced if necessary. Heads which are stretched out of shape should be sponged and adjusted. Moving parts should be lubricated. The aforementioned items seem obvious; however, when was the last time your equipment was overhauled? Do it now!

With certain limitations, bass drums should be exposed to the same process. Regarding cymbals, there is one major factor, the type of holder. Remove wooden handles and use straps. Although many nationally known percussionists have commented on this fact, some doubt evidently remains. Wooden handles limit vibration, impairing the tone; eventually they ruin the cymbals.

Players of Unequal Ability

One of the most prevalent problems is that of having several drummers of unequal experience and ability. How can they function efficiently in the same section? Rewrite the drum parts and street beats to suit the general technical level of the section. Furthermore, all players need not play the same parts. In the following street beat, which is moderately difficult, the more experienced may play Example 1 while the younger players perform Example 2.

Such a method allows for gradations of technical efficiency while giving more clarity of sound with better precision. Use bass drum and cymbals sparingly on street beats as the players of these instruments must work extensively while the band is playing.

Start Right

The future of many school musicians often depends upon their "beginning". A correct beginning implies good teaching and successful motivation. No textbooks of which I know give incorrect methods for holding sticks. There may be some variance but all seem to agree on certain fundamentals. However, it is possible to find many high school drummers holding sticks in a manner making it impossible to play correctly. Adopt a correct basic method and insist upon adherence to it.

Although methods of motivation vary among students and teachers, it is necessary to show the beginner some of the path he is to travel. It is also necessary to travel this path securely and at an interesting pace.

November 1955

The Edward B. Straight Books

His permanent contribution to percussion teaching.

Robert W. Buggert

EDWARD B. STRAIGHT—musician, percussionist, educator, philosopher, writer—was known for his excellence of performance and his great interest in the development of musical percussion playing. Four books constitute his contribution to the percussion field: *The Lesson File*, *Analysis 6/8 Time*, *The American Drummer*, and *Modern Syncopated Rhythms*. Commentary here will be limited to the first two books.

The Lesson File

Original publication by Mr. Straight, 1923; copyright owned for a period by Chart Music Co.; present publisher is Frank's Drum Shop, 226 So. Wabash Ave., Chicago. 45 exercises in 2/4, 102 pages, 52 pages of commentary.

The 45 exercises are progressive in scope. Each presents a new problem except occasionally certain exercises (Nos. 10, 24, 25, 32, 38, 42, 43 & 44) culminate with the inclusion of most preceding problems.

Although the book progresses at a rather rapid pace, the development is—for the most part—very logical. Sixteenth notes are introduced in Ex. 4, rolls in Ex. 6, flams in Ex. 9, drags in Ex. 20, dotted notes in Ex. 26, and the sixteenth-note triplets in Ex. 33. From Ex. 33 to the end only one new problem is introduced: dotted sixteenths followed by thirty-seconds.

The approach to learning is through logically developed reading material. The only rudiments used are rolls, flams, and drags. Several introductory pages explain the system and recommend a very plausible philosophy of professional ethics. Each exercise is preceded by one page of commentary explaining the problem and suggesting a solution.

Analysis 6/8 Time

Publishing data is the same as for *The Lesson File*. 57 exercises in 6/8. 117 pages, 58 pages of commentary. The development of materials parallels *The Lesson File*. The exercises which include a culmination of preceding problems are #13, 14, 18, 21, 32, 37, 42, 47 & 52. Detailed discussion here would be redundant.

The Problem of Method

These books are not used by some teachers because of disagreement with patterns of sticking, description of rolls, and the lack of hand-to-hand or alternating projection of rudimental playing. If such is the case with a particular teacher, I recommend using the exercises but revising the method or system to suit pedagogical preferences. These books can be played with alternate sticking as desired by the teacher. I believe it is correct to assume that the system *per se* is not presently used by the majority of music educators in this country.

The music educator for whom percussion is not a major performing medium may note the following chart for clarification of roll designation:

Straight System	Rudimental System
1. 3 stroke roll	5 stroke roll
2. 5 stroke roll	9 stroke roll
3. 7 stroke roll	13 stroke roll
4. 9 stroke roll	17 stroke roll

The application of the present prevalent sticking patterns and new roll designation will make these exercises as contemporary as you like.

Evaluation

In most teaching situations these books might not be classified as adequate material for beginning instruction. However, for the intermediate or advanced student they are first-rate. Players who can correctly perform the exercises contained in these two books will not be confused by many 2/4 or 6/8 parts. These books, on the other hand, will not serve to develop technical facility to its greatest potential.

It is the writer's opinion that a student's interest, musicianship, and snare drum performance will improve in direct relation to his sensitive and serious study of these two books. Whether or not you agree with this system, the books can be used. You can edit the exercises as you wish.

The late Mr. Straight's dedication, "Yours for better drumming," rings true and these books offer the second or third year player many enjoyable hours of practice. Simultaneously, they will make him more competent.

December 1955

Organize for Efficiency

Charles L. Spohn

WHILE WORKING with and observing many different instrumental organizations, I have found that many times the members of the percussion section — even though they might be well trained — are not performing up to the high standards of which they are capable. The fault frequently lies with the director. When working with young and relatively inexperienced percussionists, it is easy to fall into the habit of emphasizing only the seemingly important items, such as technique and musicianship. However, the percussion student must be taken several steps farther in order to make him a useful and producing member of an instrumental group.

The average music student learns to play one instrument so that he may participate in an instrumental organization. It is reasonable then for the beginning percussionist to expect to study only the snare drum, or, perhaps, only bass drum and cymbals. Therefore, the first big step toward improving the percussion section is to develop the attitude that percussionists should be all-around performers, capable of playing a variety of instruments.

Benefits of All-Round Performance

The percussion sections that can be started or directed toward this attitude benefit in several ways. First, through the variety of the many percussion instruments, there will be a better musical experience for the individual student. Second, there is enough transfer of training from one instrument to another to effect improvements in individual techniques. Third, there will be more opportunity for more people to play. And fourth, the percussion section will act and function as a single unit and will increase its efficiency thereby.

Organizing

Of course, just a change in attitude is not enough. The second big step is the direct organization of the percussion section.

Due to the many different types of instrumental groups, with each one having its particular staging problems, there is no one standard arrangement for the placing of the many percussion instruments. However, the placement of the instruments within a section should be effected in such a manner that all are easily accessible.

The arrangement should include a table of proper standing height for bells and another table to be used for the smaller instruments and sticks. I feel, also, that it is very important that the timpani be included with the rest of the section instead of being placed on the opposite side of the stage. In this way the timpanist can often help with other percussion parts.

Assigning Parts

The third essential step in getting the percussion section to produce to capacity is the assignment of parts. At the junior high and senior high levels, the director should assign the players to *definite* parts. After studying the score he can determine very quickly which students should play which parts. In this way he can also control the varying of assignments from one composition to another.

The assignments should be written inside the music folder or on separate sheets that can be given to each drummer. Careful part assignments can avoid instrument changes that are awkward. Whereas other instrumentalists usually perform on a single instrument, a percussionist may have to play three or four different instruments during one selection.

In addition to all this preparation the percussion section should be given a schedule of the music to be rehearsed each day. This will enable the players to have the needed instruments available. Consequently, there need be no confusion or loss of time during the rehearsal.

Percussion sections are often the target of much criticism, and rightly so. However, careful training and planning in developing and organizing the section can work wonders.

1956-1957

109	Rudimental System and Straight System	Robert W. Buggert	January
109	Percussion Pointers	James D. Salmon	February
110	Timpani Sticks	Fred William Noak	March
112	Applications of Various Types of Stick Technique	Robert W. Buggert	April
113	Dear Band Director:	Betty Masoner	May
114	Solo Literature for Timpani	Fred William Noak	September
116	Developing Precision in the Marching Band Drum Section	Robert W. Buggert	October
117	The Beginning Drummer	Robert W. Buggert	November
118	The Percussion Ensemble	Jack McKenzie	December
119	It Started as a Gourd	William J. Murdoch	January
121	Solo Literature for the Beginning Snare Drummer	Robert W. Buggert	February
122	Latin American Instruments and Rhythms, Part I — Rhumbas	Robert W. Buggert	April
123	Latin American Instruments and Rhythms, Part II — Sambas, Congas, Tangos, and Beguines	Robert W. Buggert	May
124	All Plastic Drum Heads	William F. Ludwig	September
125	Percussion Pointers	Lawrence White	September
126	Variety in Cadences	Robert W. Buggert	October
127	Drums for the Marching Band	Betty Masoner	November
128	Percussion Recordings	Charles A. Irick	December

January 1956

Rudimental System and Straight System

Robert W. Buggert

THE NOVEMBER *Percussion Clinic* has given rise to several questions. The most prevalent of these has been a request to explain differences between the Rudimental System of drumming and the Straight System.

Rudimental Approach

The Rudimental System finds its foundation in the *Thirteen Essential Rudiments* as codified by the National Association of Rudimental Drummers. Although twenty-six rudiments are now listed, the NARD requires the execution of the first thirteen only for membership.

These might be considered the snare drummers' counterpart of the scales and chords used to develop facility on melodic instruments. Such patterns, then, form rhythmic-technical formulas for ultimate application in the execution of the printed score. In this way players are able to apply pre-learned patterns to music, and, as such, they read by group rather than by individual notes. Emphasis is placed upon a style of drumming called *hand to hand* which places somewhat of a premium on ambidexterity.

From the pedagogical viewpoint, the drummer learns rudiments by practicing them from open (slow) style and by gradually accelerating until they are closed (fast). While gaining some facility with the basic rudiments, the drummer is taught to read and to permeate his reading of music with the application of the rudiments.

Although each teacher may vary his approach, the philosophy of rudimental teaching indicates the following:

1. Learn the rudiments.
2. Learn to read music.
3. Apply the rudiments.
4. Play *hand to hand.*

Straight Approach

The Straight approach finds its foundation in the books of Edward B. Straight discussed in the November, 1955 issue. This system emphasizes the use of the right or preferred hand and an approach to snare drum technic via the medium of reading music.

All rolls are executed beginning and ending with the right or preferred hand; each measure begins with the right; most flams are executed with the right; and repeated figures are always played with the same sticking pattern. Ambidexterity is not basic to the system.

Three rudiments — flams, rolls, and ruffs (drags) — are incorporated into the system. The paradiddles, single and double drags, flamacue, and others are not taught. Basically, then, the Straight System approach indicates the following pattern:

1. Learn to read music.
2. Utilize the preferred hand (usually the right) predominantly.
3. Play the same patterns the same way.
4. Emphasize unity of sound.

Variations in Terminology

Variances in terminology exist in the identification of rolls. The Straight System considers only the alternating strokes, whereas the Rudimental System accounts for each note. Therefore, we have the following differences in terminology although the number of actual notes remains the same in both systems:

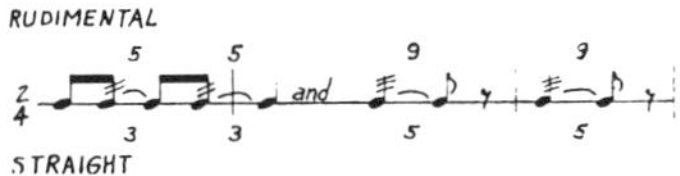

The following examples show differences in sticking patterns between the two systems. The sticking above the notes indicates the application of rudiments and the sticking below indicates the Straight pattern.

R—R L R LR L R L R L RLRRLRLL R L—L
R—R L R RL RL R R L RLRLRLRL R R-R

R—R R L L R L—L L RLR LRL R
R—R L R L R R-R L RLR RLR R

February 1956

Percussion Pointers

James D. Salmon

THE EFFICIENCY OF your percussion section can be improved a great deal by careful attention to the details that seem to be ignored by so many band directors. The following suggestions are presented to assist the drummers in school bands to perform in a more professional manner.

Bass Drum

To get a proper *musical boom* from the bass drum, the heads must be tensioned evenly; and a proper beater must be used. Tension bass drum heads as a timpanist tunes his kettledrums, i.e. get the same quality of sound at each tension bolt on both heads. Personally, I prefer more tension on the head played upon than on the opposite head; this seems to curtail the roar and rumble associated with too loose head tensioning.

The lamb's wool double-end bass drum beater is the most practical for concert playing; and each beater should be replaced with a new model as soon as bare leather spots begin to show on the wool tips.

To get a cleaner articulation of rhythmic patterns, such as triplet figures or rolls of several measures duration, a set of timpani sticks of soft felt or lamb's wool tips should be used. The bass drum can be placed on its side and played in timpani style, or the player, standing at the side of the drum (normal position), can use a single stroke snare drum technique on the top third of the drumhead.

Snare Drum

The snare drum, too, should be tensioned in timpani style. Release the snares and tap the drumhead lightly at each tension bolt to check quality of sound. More tension should be used on the batter (top) head than on the snare (bottom) head for a more sensitive response. The snares should not be pulled too tightly against the snare head.

If several snare drums are to be used, they should all be tensioned alike so that the sound of each drum blends with that of the others in the same manner that brass and woodwind instruments blend for good section playing.

I suggest that the following models of drumsticks be used to allow for variance in music styles and dynamics: 1S or 2S (to produce f to fff), for all outdoor performances on parade drums; 2B or 5B (to produce p to ff), for normal concert playing on concert drums; 3A, 5A, or 7A (to produce pp to f), for performance of light concert, dance band, and Latin-American selections.

Cymbals

I believe that most bands should have a pair of 16 inch or 17 inch cymbals with leather straps and pads for most "crash" effects, and a separate 18 inch cymbal on a suitable floor rack for playing long rolls, crash solos, and choked cymbal effects.

A roll on a suspended cymbal will sound fuller if the player uses the felt-tipped sticks on opposite sides of the plate, rather than placing the stick tips together. This will also prevent the cymbal from swaying from side to side.

Triangles

Two sizes of triangles permit greater observance of dynamics. The 8 to 10 inch size should be used for heavier sounds, and the 4 to 5 inch size should be used for lighter playing. Always play with a metal beater, never with wooden drumsticks.

Triangles should be suspended with stout cord or with gut strings for best results. A metal spring clamp or a spring clothespin can be an effective substitute for the more conventional holder.

Castanets

Castanets can be purchased with either a single or a double set of shells on a wooden handle. For normal playing, hold the castanets firmly in one hand and strike the shells in the open palm, or on the knuckles of the closed fist on the free hand. To execute a tremolo use a fast wrist shake; in fact, a set of castanets in each hand will definitely give a smoother tremolo and a cleaner articulation for fast rhythmic passages.

Tambourines

Use a smaller tambourine with a single row of jingles for soft dynamics and a larger tambourine with a double row of jingles for loud dynamics. For long rolls and very loud playing, use two tambourines. For fast rhythmic passages, set the tambourine head down on a soft pad and play the part with timpani sticks, hitting the edge of the wood shell. For normal playing, remember always to bring the *free* hand *to* the tambourine in order to lessen the extraneous sounding of the jingles.

Monthly Review

Salmon, James D., *The Percussion Section for the Concert Band*, 1955. Hal Leonard Music, Inc., Winona Minn., $2.50.

The article by Mr. Spohn in the December issue of *The Instrumentalist* emphasized the necessity for organization within the percussion section. Mr. Salmon's new book is an excellent handbook which will assist the director with these problems. It contains the answers to numerous questions frequently asked at clinics and workshops. The commentary is clarified by illustrations.

Information includes playing techniques, care and repair, and numerous suggestions regarding all of the percussion instruments. Special attention is given to the playing of the more common percussion accessories. The following topics represent only a few of the twenty-two categories of subject material: castanets, claves, maracas, sectional seating charts, tambourines, gong, etc.

This book is a welcome addition to the published materials about percussion playing, and it should be read by drummers and directors alike.—R. W. Buggert.

March 1956

Timpani Sticks

Fred William Noak

MUSICALLY, the important instrument of the percussion section is the timpani. Its earliest use was particularly in religious services. Later it was used in secular festivals, and still later it found its way into the activities of war.

Fundamentally the shape of the drums has not changed very much. The mechanical devices have been developed to a high degree and with them have come more demands upon the player. As a result, sticks, too, became more important when particular shadings were required.

Tuning is accomplished by the mechanisms, although the ear with perfect pitch is still almost a necessity. The quality of tone produced is up to the musician and his sticks. So we come to the importance of stick technique. If you use bass drum sticks, you will have a tone, but you might as well play bass drum as far as quality is concerned.

Choose Sticks Carefully

I would warn that care should be taken in choosing sticks. Just as a violinist buys a good bow, so a timpanist should consider his sticks. It is as essential for one as for the other to have good tools to do a good job. Usually a school instrumental teacher will leave it up to the special teacher of timpani to suggest types of sticks. Music dealers who sell instruments also sell standard sticks at a nominal price. Later, when a student becomes more conscious of the qualities he can achieve, he begins to ask about professional handmade materials.

Most of the timpanists in major orchestras make their own sticks. There are countless stories about how they make them and what they put into them. It is said that they use anything from rabbit's feet to sheep's wool! They make them with great care and I should say with love, and they often guard their findings jealously. In such cases the sticks are usually not for sale. However, many players do make excellent sticks which they will sell.

Soft vs. Medium Sticks

The beginner should use two pair of timpani sticks, soft and medium hard. The former are used for a soft roll. Often when the mood of sadness or mystery is to be expressed the timpanist can add to this by using soft sticks. The timpani is just as important in the soft passages as in the louder ones. A fine crescendo roll with a good contrast between the *piano* and the *forte* can be a great help to the orchestra. The conductor feels the strength of a good roll and appreciates the support he gets from it. No matter if it is a soft roll or a loud one, it will become more effective through the use of correct sticks.

If a fast roll is required going from a *pianissimo* to a *fortissimo*, medium sticks should be used. They are also used for most effective rhythmical patterns. In a college orchestra of fifty to seventy-five players it is not necessary to play as heavily as would be the case in a larger group. A band of thirty-five brasses is again a different matter.

If a band overblows its fortissimo, it becomes brassy and out of tune. If a violin is played too loud, a harsh quality is produced. If a timpani is played too loud, it too will be out of tune. Everything is relative. In Italian *forte* means strong but not loud. If a timpanist plays with a string or brass group, he should never dominate the situation but should feel his way, fitting himself into the ensemble.

Hard Sticks

Hard sticks should be used very seldom. Only when a terrific crash is expected is it necessary to turn to them. Usually the score will be marked that wood sticks are wanted. A few examples will show how special the situation should be to indicate the use of wooden sticks: when the hero in Richard Strauss' symphonic poem *Don Juan* breaks through a window into the room of Donna Anna: when Death takes hold of the victim in Strauss' *Death and Transfiguration*.

Another example is in Wagner's *Die Walkure* when Siegfried and Sieglinde realize their love as they look into each other's eyes. They are sitting before the fireplace in her husband's house. With a crash from the timpani, the huge door at the back of the room suddenly opens inviting them to flee. In Mozart's *Don Giovanni* the Stone Statue is invited to supper by the Don. When he arrives the Don must shake hands with him. At this moment the timpani carries a long D with hard sticks while the scene changes into a holocaust of fire and smoke as if the world were coming to an end, as it truly does for the Don.

In Verdi's *Aida* when Amonasro, the Ethiopian king, exclaims that Aida is his daughter, the moment is a shock to the people of Egypt; hard sticks dramatize the shock. In Puccini's *Madam Butterfly* the heroine thinks of hari-kari to the accompaniment of a timpani passage which can be interpreted as the excited heartbeat of those last moments which lead to suicide. But even in this last example, medium hard sticks give a better quality. The use of hard sticks makes the same impression as a shot when heard in the distance.

From the examples given above, you can see that we use hard sticks for very special, highly dramatic effects.

The beginner should use two pairs of sticks, soft and medium hard. As he develops, he may add other sticks to his liking. The variety will help the player in getting a passage performed the way a composer has imagined it. Sometimes he can improve on a composer (that is, if the conductor also happens to be the composer himself) and he will be grateful for this. It is after all, the musicianship of the timpanist which will help him find out what certain sticks will do for him in order to render a good performance.

Applications of Various Types of Stick Technique

Robert W. Buggert

FROM A STUDY of various methods and systems of drumming one finds that a passage may often be played with several different patterns of sticking. Likewise, it is often difficult to decide upon the most satisfactory pattern. Two factors must be considered. First, is the material being played an exercise to develop a certain technique? Second, is this passage an excerpt which must conform to the style of music being performed?

Dexterity

Relative to the first factor cited above, the development of good rudimental technique and the improvement of ambidextrous facility are most essential. When training a person to develop good alternating rolls, the following exercise is best played as marked:

When developing technique in playing paradiddles, the following exercise is best played as indicated:

When working to play flams, the following is applicable:

These examples should suffice to indicate desirable sticking patterns for the development of rudimental technique and ambidexterity.

Applications

Although a drummer must know rudimental patterns and have equal facility with both the right and left hands, alternation, rudimental application, and hand-to-hand playing do not always serve the best musical purpose. If the material cited in the first example was *pianissimo* and played with a passage by muted trumpets, it would probably sound more even if the rolls were all played the same way, i.e., R—R or L—L. The second measure might also be R L R RL.

In symphonic playing the sixteenth notes of the second example would be more stylistic if played with alternating sticking, i.e., RLRLRLRL, etc.

If the third example were the trio of a concert march, the tone, syntax, rhythm, and musical essence would be better if the flams were played all R or all L.

Although the above is by no means complete, the hypothesis is this: although ambidexterity is necessary, although rudimental technique is mandatory, a percussion passage should always be interpreted to portray the musical implications of such a passage.

Style

To decide sticking patterns it is necessary to understand the style of music being performed. As string players, wind players, and pianists vary their styles and techniques when playing music of different composers and different periods, thus must the drummer vary his style and technique when going from symphonic, to military, to dance music, etc.

The passage in the following exercise could be interpreted in several ways: *a* indicates a possibility as a *pianissimo* solo in an orchestra; *b* a possibility for marching band at a tempo of a quarter note equal to 144; *c* a probable application in drum and bugle corps when a quarter note equals 128; and *d* a probable interpretation for a solo in a Dixieland style dance band.

Conclusions

Drummers should learn to play the rudiments, work at the technique of ambidexterity, and be able to apply such techniques. However, in the final analysis, let the volume, purpose, and especially the style of the music dictate the final interpretation. It must be remembered that the rudiments are a means to an end and not end in themselves; the desired result should be rhythm, tone, and a musical sound indicative of the style of the music being performed.

Monthly Review

Price, Paul, *Beginning Snare Drum Method*, 1955, Edwin H. Morris and Company, N. Y., $5.00.

It would be impossible in a short review to note the many useful facets of this book. Many new ideas are represented in the presentation of a drum method. The approach is unique. It is logical and musical. Sections deal with the function of the snare drum in band and orchestra, holding sticks, position, and pitch notation, as well as rhythm notation. One of its noteworthy features is the illustrative method showing "stroke pathways." There are some 250 exercises, and the final pages include several challenging solos. This book is a welcome addition to the teaching material available for percussion.

Dear Band Director:

Letter from a drummer to his Director

Betty Masoner

WHY DO YOU neglect me so? Whether I am in a small band or a large one, a good band or a poor one, you treat me as an intruder — as a sixth finger—as something always there but not really necessary.

Won't you please show me how to hold my sticks? In the left hand the stick should be held as far back as possible between the thumb and first finger and not out by the first knuckle of the finger; and in the right hand it should be held between the second finger and the thumb.

And, by the way, I will gladly buy the proper sticks if only you will tell me I need 2B or 5B for concert work and heavier sticks for street work. And how much I would appreciate it, if you would put a set of concert and a set of street drums in your budget. After all, the two wouldn't cost nearly as much as some of your other school-owned instruments, and then I could do a much better job for you.

Need Attention Like Other Instruments

You spend hours working on intonation during rehearsals, and then comes the concert appearance and you carefully tune each individual instrument. But what about us? Our drums should be tensioned evenly, snares adjusted to produce a crisp live tone instead of a sound like pounding on an old cardboard box.

You spend your working day teaching the arts of breath control, tonguing, and articulation to your brass and woodwind students. But you don't teach us a thing; you just give us a book and a pair of sticks and tell us to go to it. Why don't you explain the rudiments to us and teach us how to read music? *Help* us so we can really play well. And maybe we could even play in ensembles like the other band members do.

And please help us to get the desired tone colors from the many varied traps you ask us to play. Often, of course, we aren't even supplied with the proper traps, or we are likely to throw them around because you don't designate a proper place for us to store them.

And, please teach ALL of us to play ALL of the percussion instruments, instead of having bass drummers and snare drummers and cymbals players, etc., who can't or won't play anything else. I want to be a DRUMMER—not just an extra man to fill in another rank in your marching band.

Proper Equipment and Use

If I am to play bass drum, please get me a short double end lamb's wool covered beater instead of an old war club somebody has discarded. As for cymbals, please buy the best with straps so I won't crack these expensive instruments, and it wouldn't cost much to furnish a little brass polish to clean them once in a while; I'll gladly supply the elbow grease! And *do* teach me to play them gracefully and to produce a tone of quality instead of a clang like a couple of kettle lids banged together.

They should be played with a sliding motion rather than a to and fro motion, and the straps should be grasped like the right hand snare drum stick—not like a fist full of paper.

And the timpani, which should be the aristocrat of the drum section, is usually completely forgotten—unless you have a few notes in your score that must be played but aren't cued for anyone else. Let the timpani be the final step in my journey through the maze of percussion instruments rather than the one least desired and least understood. But don't think that just because I play the piano I will be an expert at the control of the roll, which is so important on the timpani!

Proper position and attitude condition the effectiveness of any percussion section. Photos 1 and 3 show incorrect bass drum and cymbals positions; photos 2 and 4 illustrate desirable positions. Photos posed by Wayne Wegge.

Asset to Band

Dear director, PLEASE help me! I want to help you improve your band, be it large or small, but I *can't* unless you give me the same individual instruction, time, and patience you give your other instrumentalists.

And, *Do* encourage me to practice. I can't develop a fine sounding roll without practice, and it is so monotonous to beat on an old practice pad all the time while my friends practice on their nice shiny horns.

So again I say, please help me help you! You will be surprised and thrilled to learn what a well-organized and efficient drum section can do for your band!—One of your drummers.

Incorrect and correct methods for holding snare drum sticks.

September 1956

Solo Literature for Timpani

Fred William Noak

In 1795 there appeared a little 6x8 inch book dealing with the playing of the trumpet and the timpani. From the title it appeared to be a printed "method." Upon examination, as a result of looking for the earliest material on timpani available, we found pages 125 to 132 devoted to the playing of these tuned drums.

Seven whole pages of explanation, the first three of these being history of the instrument. The other four gave a few hints about tuning the drums (one to the tonic and the second to the dominant), a few remarks about holding the sticks, and some comments about the materials of which the sticks are made. Nothing else was given which would stimulate the player to do more than drum as his instinct told him.

Parallel Today

Today we have somewhat of a parallel in the modern dance band drummer, except that he is farther advanced, being attuned not only to his own national influence but also to that of other peoples. This we see in the *rhumba, mamba, cha-cha,* or any other foreign rhythms which have been adapted.

The pattern of the tonic and the dominant was the forerunner of the early works of Handel, Haydn, Mozart, and Beethoven. Haydn first used the rhythmic phrase in the first or sometimes the last movement of his symphonies. As a youngster he heard the timpanists in the military parades. He also saw them at the festivals for royalty when they rode on elaborately decorated horses with their drums strapped on each side of the animal.

At the same time, Handel was making special use of the timpani in England. He actually borrowed the "Great Kettledrums of the Artillery" for his oratorios. These were larger and more effective than the regular drums which were being used on the orchestra stage at that time. The Artillery Drums are the ones which are so often pictured on carts drawn by horses. They were used as early as 1655 in Sweden, the Prussian Artillery used them in 1689, and the chariot in the Marlborough Train is dated 1702. These great drums were taken into the field where action was taking place.

Use of Timpani by Handel

Handel liked the timpani. He scored them with great effect in martial and triumphant moments in the *Dettingen Te Deum* (1743), the *Occasional Oratorio,* and *Judas Maccabaeus* (1746). For all these he borrowed the "Great Kettledrums of the Artillery" as they were called in London. Later he used them also for the *Fireworks Music.* This was written for a very special occasion and was scored for wind band of "warlike instruments," as the journals of the day described them.

Dr. Charles Burney in his famous *History of Music* also describes the borrowing of the "Artillery Drums" by Handel for this last important great occasion. It was the famous Handel Commemoration Festival of 1748 in Westminster Abbey. There was also a still larger set of kettledrums made for this occasion by John Asbridge. So it seems that Handel, at this time, used the regular size orchestra drums of the era, a set of artillery drums, and others still larger which were especially made. There were either four or five kettledrummers present for the occasion. There seems to be a bit of a controversy as to which number it was. To us, four kettledrummers, each with a pair of different sized drums, seems more than plenty for the greatest festival.

Handel's *Messiah* is another good example. The "Hallelujah Chorus" is not only great for the chorus but for the whole orchestra—again trumpet and timpani shine.

Haydn and Rossini

We may turn again to Haydn who was writing his symphonies in Austria. In the *Drum Symphony* he opens with a timpani solo. This may have been to attract the people who still wandered into the audience, possibly chatting as they came. The drums called for quiet and made them ready to listen. Another effect Haydn used was the timpani "crash" in the *Surprise Symphony*. This we know was to wake up the sleepers in the audience!

In Italy, Rossini used an opening for the whole orchestra with timpani in full force because people came in—even peasants with baskets—talking and making noise. So the music had to be very loud at first. The *Barber of Seville* opens this way.

Use by Mozart

From Handel's loudly dramatic effects through Haydn's more practical use of the timpani, we come to Mozart. Here the composer, for the first time, uses the kettledrum and gives it a phrase as a solo which is thrown back and forth between basses, cellos, and timpani in imitation. His symphonies are full of artistic use of the kettledrums.

The last movement of the *Jupiter Symphony* is a fine example. Here is one of the greatest contrapuntal developments in music literature. Mozart himself may not have realized the extent of the power in what he wrote. Conductors like Richard Strauss, who was a great exponent of Mozart, and Bruno Walter went to great pains to fill in the expressions which Mozart left to the individual artists to work out for themselves.

Development

Beethoven wrote remarkable passages in his *Symphonies, No. 2 and No. 4*, the *Pastoral Symphony*, and in his great *Ninth Symphony*. Meyerbeer gives us a fine timpani solo in his opera *Robert the Devil*. Berlioz, in his *Symphony Fantastique*, and, indeed, in all his compositions, is a master in scoring for instruments, not forgetting the timpani.

Gustave Mahler treats the timpani as a solo instrument in all his symphonies. Richard Strauss wrote the *Burlesca* for piano and four timpani with orchestral accompaniment. In his opera literature he excells, each player becomes a soloist, the timpanist not excluded. In *Salome* he has harmonic chords, broken and to be played on four drums. The timpanist must show technical skill in eight measures solo played before the cistern is opened on the stage and the henchman descends to decapitate Johanaan. The chord must be played

Timpani Solos and Ensembles

Composer	*Title*	*Grade*
Unaccompanied solos—		
Carter	Six Pieces for Four Kettle Drums	D
Colgrass	12 Easy Solos for Contest	E
Harr	The Downfall of Paris (for Timpani)	M
Harr	Newport	M
Harr	Cuckoo Quickstep	M
Jones	Sonata for Three Kettle Drums	D
McKenzie	6 Graded Solos	E, M, D
Price	12 Graded Solos for Contest	E, M, D
With piano accompaniment—		
Bigot	Timpiana	D
Britton	Solo Pieces for Contest	E
Clark	Concertino	M
Harr	"The Four Hundred"	M
Harr	The Green Diamond	M
McKenzie	Concertino for E Kettle Drums	M
Noak	Around the table	M, D
Noak	Big Ben	M, D
Noak	Burial Ceremony of an Indian Chief	M, D
Noak	Fantasia	D
Noak	Rondo	D
Noak	Skeppy and the Tree Drum	M, D
Noak	Shadow Boxing	M, D
Payson	The Sphinx (for 2 Kettle Drums)	M
Striegler	Scherzo Capriccioso (for 4 or 5 Kettle Drums)	D
Tcherepnin	Sonatine for Timpani and Piano	M
Tomasi	Concert Asiatique	D
Vito	Concerto	M
With instrumental accompaniment—		
Adler	Concert Piece (with brass)	D
Altenberg	Concerto for Clarini and Timpani (with brass)	D
Bach	March (Fanfare) (with three trumpets)	E
Beadell	Introduction and Allegro (Brass)	D
Beckhelm	Tragic March (brass, side drum, cymbals)	D
Britton	One Over Three (with bells, tambourine, and bass drum)	M
Colgrass	Concerto for Timpani with Brass	D
Colgrass	Three Brothers (for percussion ensemble)	D
Hartmeyer	Negev (for brass)	D
Marks	Introduction and Passacaglia (for brass)	D
Noak	Fantasy for Percussion Orchestra	D
Noak	Rondo (piano or band arrangement)	D
Noak	Scherzo Fantasy	D
Read	Sound Piece for Brass and Percussion	D
McKenzie	Song (4 timpani, vibraphone, xylophone, percussion, trombone)	D
McKenzie	Three Dances for Timpani and Percussion	M
Tschaikowsky	Romance (brass, timpani, cymbals)	D
Weinberger	Concerto for Four Timpani	M
Weigel	Piece for Percussion Ensemble	M

with four sticks on four different drums.

Delibes used the timpani to dominate the rhythm in the *Bacchanal* for the third act of *Samson and Delilah.* We could go on and on through the great literature of music and find Rimsky-Korsakoff and his *Boris Godunov,* Shostakovitch and his symphonies, Randall Thompson, William Schumann, Howard Hanson, Eugene Goossens, Franchotti, Henry Cowell, and many more who are making use of the percussion section for highly effective drama.

All these composers placed the timpanist in a high position. With this came greater recognition and better standards. The timpanist has to have technique, a fine ear and explicit rhythm, and be able to blend into any ensemble. This requires an elusive thing called musicianship.

Finally composers wrote timpani concertos for five or more timpani with piano or orchestra accompaniment. There are now many solos and the variety is most satisfying.

We now have a good repertoire of timpani solos and ensembles for percussion. The accompanying list is taken, by permission of Paul Price, from the University of Illinois Bulletin No. 18, "Percussion Methods." A few numbers have been added to this original list.

October 1956

Developing Precision in the Marching Band Drum Section

Robert W. Buggert

ONE OF THE FOREMOST problems in the training of the marching band drum section is that of achieving articulate precision. Several factors must be taken into account in the treatment of this problem.

First and probably most important is the acquiring of absolute accuracy in the execution of simple rhythms. It is wise to test a section on these rhythms, note any discrepancy, and correct it immediately. Usually the high school drum section tends to anticipate the beat after any short rests which may occur. Test a section using Example 1 and observe any hurrying which may exist. There will be tendency to play the last three notes ahead of time, thereby creating a rhythmic distortion as illustrated in Example 2.

Two solutions are possible: 1) use a metronome, and 2) make the students count aloud subdividing each beat as follows—*1 and 2 and,* etc. Continued practice with constant attention to a steady beat will improve the section's precision. It is also very likely that if this basic rhythm is inaccurate, other more complicated patterns will be carelessly played and such inaccuracies will pass by unnoticed.

Causes of Poor Precision

Poor precision often results when players are trying to execute patterns which are too difficult for them. Any street beats used should be within the technical grasp of all the members of the section. In addition, parts should be altered when the written part does not adequately suit the music being played. Avoid long passages of after-beats and use rhythmic patterns which are flowing and solid.

Another factor in the improvement of precision is the establishing of uniform and logical sticking patterns. Drummers will not play well if a certain street beat is played with a different pattern each time it is executed. Decide upon a pattern feasible for the section and then dogmatically adhere to it. The sticking patterns used should be easily executed, uniform, logical, and technically coherent.

Many drum sections play poorly, unrhythmically, and without precision simply because they are trying to play too loud. A section which plays correct rhythmically and well together will carry farther and sound louder than a section playing *fffff* but not playing together. Precision and accuracy should be more important than sheer volume for the sake of volume.

Appearance

A drum section which plays well and correctly will look good; therefore, emphasis upon style without articulate playing renders the section inefficient. Good style can be achieved only as a result of accurate position, correct stroking, and proper playing.

Excessive flaunting of the sticks hampers the precision, while at the same time it creates an awkward appearing section.

An incorrect position of the slinging of the drum may cause undue hardship for the physical movements of the player, thus rhythm and precision might suffer. Figure 8 in the *Beginning Snare Drum Method* by Paul Price is representative of a good position for the field drum on a sling.

Director's Part

To obtain precision from the drum section the director must be consistent and work toward the establishment of an *absolute tempo*. He must not allow a band to march a different cadence at successive rehearsals.

Much lack of precision in the marching band is not the sole fault of the drum section. The drummers cannot be expected to be the "assistant director;" if the band as a whole is rhythmically inaccurate, the drum section can do little to remedy the situation. The section must not lead and superimpose itself upon the band; it must be an integral part of a musical ensemble.

From the technical point of view, the drum section must have the facility to execute the basic rudiments used and, above all, must be well acquainted with the fundamentals of marching. The drummer has little time to think about marching maneuvers. He must know them well enough to execute them spontaneously.

Concentration on these points will improve a marching band drum section and aid in the development of top-notch precision.

November 1956

The Beginning Drummer

Robert W. Buggert

Each fall instrumental music instructors in communities throughout the country prepare to instruct groups of novice drummers. The problems of the teacher are many and among the foremost are those of selection, equipment, method, scheduling, etc., as they apply to the training of future drummers or percussionists for the school's band or orchestra.

Selecting Students

Very often the request for drum instruction is so great that if the director started and developed all those who wished to express themselves in this medium he would have to eliminate much of the music program and merely maintain a drum corps. Sometimes, then, the process of elimination of aspiring drummers becomes a major one.

To the young, interested seeker of drumming ability, the picture is a deceiving one. His conception of drumming is often obtained thru seeing drummers on TV, at a theater, at a circus, or by some other such contact. The drummers he sees are professional and, from outward appearances, the task looks enjoyable and easy.

Selection, therefore, should be based upon the student's desire to become a sincere worker. This cannot be measured by any test; probably, a trial period of instruction is the only valid method of selecting. Following current educational principles, the teacher should give each student a chance if he exhibits desire and sincerity. At any rate, the student should be made aware of the challenge that faces him in his pursuit of this task.

Equipment Needed

The basic equipment is easily obtained: a practice pad, a pair of sticks, a method book, and one is ready to begin. However, the answer is not always quite so simple. Interest is not easily maintained when only the practice pad is used. Therefore, the begining drummer should have some opportunity to play on a drum. It is even wiser if he owns his own drum. It has been my experience that student interest, parent concern, and the rate of progress are all improved when the beginner has an instrument of his own. If, for various reasons, this is not possible, arrangements should be made for these potential drummers to use school instruments periodically.

Although snare drum seems to be basic to the percussion section, students will often want to begin on either timpani or marimba. I suggest that in public school systems, where the time of the director is at a premium, that students should not be started on these two instruments unless if they have some previous musical experience, preferably piano, string instrument, or, in the case of timpani, voice.

Grouping

Due to the difference in the nature of drum instruction as compared with other instruments, it is wise if the beginning drummers are able to meet separately in a homogeneous group. Progress will be faster for the drummers and also for the other instrumentalists. This homogeneous group should not be maintained too long for the real desire of the young student is to play with a band or an orchestra. Most group method parts, however, are not of great interest to the beginning drummer. Thus, it is feasible, if one has an abundance of drummers, to let them take turns playing with heterogeneous groups.

Music

Although the rudiments are important for the eventual attainment of satisfactory technical facility, a method book which emphasizes reading is usually best for such an elementary class. However, basic rudiments should be introduced by the director so that drumming facility progresses along with reading ability and musicianship. The director should examine the basic elementary instruction books and decide on one which he thinks he can use to best advantage for his particular situation. In addition to the one used in class, others should be placed in the school library for remedial, reference, and supplementary material.

The Director

The progress of the beginning drum class will be in proportion to the experience and ability of the director. It is his responsibility, then, to equip himself to teach these people. Much information can be obtained from nearby colleges or universities, clinics, conventions, camps, or private instruction. Well schooled percussion instructors are more readily available than twenty years ago and, in addition, are available in most parts of the country.

Although this article has not given specific instruction in the procedure to follow for beginners, such information is now available in many books; also, teachers of percussion are within reach of nearly everyone, if a little effort is put forth. The purpose of this article is to challenge all directors to improve their status relative to percussion instruction.

December 1956

THE PERCUSSION ENSEMBLE

Jack McKenzie

DURING THE LAST FORTY years or so a new concept has arisen regarding the importance and use of percussion instruments. A school of thought, which includes most of the better composers for orchestras and bands as well as the writers of percussion ensembles, has maintained that percussion instruments do not have to be, and indeed should not be, relegated to a function of mere time beating. They believe that percussion, carefully handled, can be made to evolve definite qualities of musical expression.

Along with the changing concepts of the use of these instruments, performance has become a more difficult and involved art. A percussion player should be just that, *a percussionist*, not just a drummer.

It is generally agreed that a good ensemble program is one sound way to develop better players for the larger groups. The same holds true for the percussion player. Some of the most valuable training he can receive is that gained by performance in percussion ensembles.

Before continuing with this line of thought a description of the two categories of ensembles for percussion instruments is in order. They are: (1) drum ensembles which use only snare drums, bass drums, and cymbals in various combinations and have as their basic impetus the street beat or drum corps types of rhythms; and (2) percussion ensembles which use any or all the instruments of the percussion family and generally are written with an avoidance of the drum corps patterns.

Drum ensembles are a definite aid in developing snare drummers, but are of limited value in producing well rounded percussionists. Percussion ensembles, while offering challenging parts for the snare drummer, also afford valuable training on all the other various instruments of the percussion family.

Whereas drum ensembles are for the most part written in 2/4, 4/4, or 6/8 time, percussion ensembles utilize these plus many of the not-so-common time signatures. There are several written in the changing-meter idiom. In many cases the performer must play on two, three, or more instruments in the same work. This has a direct carry-over value into the performance of much of the contemporary literature for orchestras and bands.

Aside from the technical proficiency to be gained, the musical and interpretative challenge which these works offer is of even greater worth to the student. These musical skills must be mastered in order to achieve correct performance of percussion ensembles.

The ensembles may be found in almost any degree of difficulty: from near beginner level thru some of the most difficult rhythmic inspirations written; from novelty numbers, thru technique building etudes, to serious concert works. There is a wide choice available in the number of players required, and the number of instruments to be used.

A look at a few ensembles which have achieved fairly wide performance will better illustrate the above points.

Concert Works

Medium - difficult. *Three Brothers,* Michael Colgrass, published by Music for Percussion. Nine players—bongos, snare drum, and timpani, (2), cow bell, maracas, tambourine, suspended cymbal, three tom-toms, second timpani (2). This work requires four advanced percussionists. It offers technical displays on the bongos, snare drum, and timpani players with the other six instruments being used as background.

Medium. *Piece,* Eugene Weigel, published by University of Illinois, Division of Music Extension. Five players—2 snare drums and 2 tenor drums, timpani, suspended cymbal, bass drum, wood block, triangle and crash cymbals. Playable by intermediate level students, this work includes a short fugue for all the instruments.

Easy. *First Quartet,* Mervin Britton, Music for Percussion. Four players—triangle, suspended cymbal, tambourine, and bass drum. This work, written for beginners is playable by grade school level students. It utilizes most of the techniques necessary for the correct playing of these instruments.

Technical Etudes

Sextet, Donovan Olson, Music for Percussion. Six players—tambourine, claves, triangle, bass drum, tenor drum, snare drum. This piece is a good example of percussion ensembles written to exploit certain problems. It is a study in divided triplets and in 5/16 time. It is playable by intermediate level students.

Novelty

Auto Accident, Harold G. Davidson, New Music Editions. Fourteen players—trap drum, bass drum, siren, rachet, wood block, temple bells, three timpani, chimes, musical tumblers, xylophone, piano, and glass plates. This is perhaps one of the better known novelty percussion ensembles. It is playable by intermediate high school students. The piece contains the following measure signatures: 5/8, 4/4, 10/8, 3/4, and 5/4.

The above list is not intended to be an inclusive one. It is included in order to give a representative idea of the types of works available for this media.

Percussion ensembles are securing for themselves a rightful place in the literature, not only as training devices for developing better percussionists, but also as concert-recital music, music which conveys aesthetic qualities.

Percussion ensembles should be as much a part of the training of a percussionisst as are woodwind, brass, and string ensembles a part of the training of these instrumentalists.

Percussion Music Review

McKenzie, Jack, *Introduction and Allegro,* published by Music for Percussion. Score and four parts—$3.00. This is an interesting but fairly difficult work. However, the efforts dispensed in its preparation are well worth the time spent. It is actually a quartet in which player 1 plays a low tom-tom, snare drum, wood block, and triangle; player 2 a medium tom-tom, snare drum, and large suspended cymbal; player 3 a medium tom-tom, temple blocks, tamtams, small cymbal, and marimba; player 4 a high tom-tom and vibraphone. This work approaches a chamber music concept in its texture; dynamics must be carefully observed. Rhythmic changes from 4/4 to 9/8, 3/4, 5/8, 6/8, 7/8, and 3/8 with the eighth remaining constant offers wonderful experience for the percussionist. It is a very satisfying concert piece. R.W.B.

It Started as a Gourd

William J. Murdoch

Now it's music from oil drums. A magazine circulated by one of the major oil companies relates that musically-inclined natives of certain Caribbean isles are converting empties into tin timpani—super deluxe kettledrums.

What these people do, after they have sawed the empty drum down to desired size and thrown away the top, is hammer the bottom smooth; and in this surface they cut tongues of various length and shape. Next they bend the tongues up just enough to permit free vibration, adjust them here and there for proper pitch, and there it is — a musical drum that gives off not just one but many different notes in unison.

It looks like a drum, has tongues like jew's harps', and it's played like a marimba. That's putting up with a lot, even for an instrument that is as accustomed to taking a beating as the kettledrum is.

The kettledrum—timpanum, if you prefer—is one of the oldest and most honored instruments you'll see in the modern orchestra. It started out as a small, truncated gourd equipped with a tight head of skin. It ballooned up in size and acquired a metal jacket, developed into an exclusive organ for promulgating the pomp of royalty, and finally took its place in the orchestra as, in the opinion of Hector Berlioz, "the most valuable of all instruments of percussion."

Instrument of Royalty

In medieval Europe the kettledrum was considered so important that it was denied to the common man. It was a prerogative of the privileged, not a music instrument of the people. Princes and dukes and such had hirelings announce their comings and goings, their battles and banquets, with thunderous thumps on the drums.

In 17th century Germany no one below the rank of baron was permitted to own one, and sometimes even the nobility were deprived of their noisy rights. For example, there was the French nobleman who, grievously affronted by the swaggering of a certain visiting German baron, gave the offending tourist his come-uppance by ordering his kettledrum smashed.

King Ladislas Posthumus of Hungary used kettledrums in his courting. Desiring the hand of Princess Madeleine, daughter of Charles VII of France, he sent his petition via emissaries accompanied by a troop of kettledrummers on horseback—the better, presumably, to sound her out. He never did get the girl, if that's any criticism.

Henry VIII of England liked his kettledrums on horseback, too. When he heard of the dashing hussars of Hungary who pranced on parade and raced into battle to the rumbling and bumbling of mounted kettledrummers, he sent to the Continent for drums of his own.

Thus, by introducing them to the British Isles this monarch, who was something of a musician himself and wrote church music that is said to be not without merit, made it possible for Henry Purcell to be among the first to write for timpani in orchestral music. He included them in his overture to his opera *Fairy Queen*. His countryman Locke was also a pioneer in using the kettledrum orchestrally, as were Lully and Graupner.

Use by Composers

Haydn had a thumping good time with the drum. At the court of Prince Esterhazy he made the staid ladies and gentlemen fairly jump out from under their powdered wigs by the explosive burst of the kettledrums in the *Andante* of his *Surprise Symphony*. He got in another good stroke in his *Symphony No. 103 in E♭* which opens with the rumble of timpani and since has become known as the *Drum Roll Symphony*.

Most authorities agree, however, that is was under the genius of Beethoven that the kettledrum grew to real musical stature. To him it was more than a means of producing a loud noise at a definite pitch: it was an instrument that could contribute musical value as well as mere dynamics. He proved it in his *Ninth Symphony*.

Others took it from there. Berlioz sometimes used them by the dozen. In his *Requiem* he scored for 16 timpani manned by 10 players. And they didn't just make noise, either. They played chords, some of them of the most delicate texture. Berlioz himself played timpani more than passing well and did so at the premiere of his *Fantastic Symphony*. There is a story that whenever he caught the bewitching eye of his beloved who sat out in the audience and probably could not understand this feverish music any more than she could understand the impetuous man who created it, he sounded a furious roll on the drums. A writer has pointed out the unlikelihood of this incident, however. Berlioz would hardly mar the first public hearing of his masterpiece with indiscriminate mutterings and banging from the timpani.

Development

If there was any one man who did more for kettledrums than any other, it was probably Ernest Pfund. He it was who pioneered the mechanically tuned timpanum whose pitch can be altered simply by stepping on a pedal. Pfund was kettledrummer for Mendelssohn in the Gewandhaus Orchestra at Leipzig.

He was a virtuoso, but one night he got more effects out of his drum than even he bargained for. He had made the mistake of lending a fellow musician money, and compounded the error by hounding him for payment. At last the exasperated debtor paid up, but in his own way. Just before a concert, while Pfund was temporarily absent from his chair, the fellow put the amount due on Pfund's drums in small coins. When Pfund returned, his first mighty stroke sent a shower of coins jingling over the orchestra members' heads.

Speaking of coins, one of the most unusual kettledrum techniques involves them. It is said some timpanists use coins on the drumheads rather than sticks to simulate the restlessness of the ocean in the *Romanza* of Elgar's *Enigma Variations*. But the most extraordinary drum solo must be credited to Handel. Things were not going well at a rehearsal. The choleric Handel, incensed at a player, threw a kettledrum at him. Let us hope it was a *pianissimo* stroke.

Solo Literature for the Beginning Snare Drummer

Robert W. Buggert

THE DEVELOPMENT of music instrument study in the schools has brought forth some type of solo literature for all instruments. Even tho the snare drum is not basically a solo instrument except for relatively short passages and in parades, the student learning to play this instrument gains much from the playing of solos. In addition, the use of solo literature has benefits for the music teacher.

First, the playing of a solo can be a worth-while motivating force challenging a young drummer. It is common knowledge that the use of a drum solo, although nothing more than an exercise with a name, will receive more attention from the student than merely another page in a method book. Second, the completion of a solo is a goal toward which a student will work for a longer period of time. Third, the performance of a solo in public or before other students can give to the performer a sense of accomplishment gained in no other way. Fourth, solo playing offers opportunity for measurement and evaluation of work accomplished. Fifth, memorization is important in the development of a percussionist, and the use of solo literature aids in this respect. Drummers, must memorize street beats and solo passages; sight-reading can be greatly improved by the expansion of memorization horizons.

Solos

The remainder of this article is a thumb-nail sketch, including teaching suggestions, concerning six solos which have served me well.

1. Buchtel, *Marines Hymn*, 2/4, Kjos, 40¢.

2. Buchtel, *Caissons Go Rolling Along*, 4/4 or cut-time, Kjos, 40¢.

3. Buchtel, *When Johnny Comes Marching Home*, 6/8, Kjos, 40¢.

Although these solos read drum with piano accompaniment, any intelligent performer would realize that they are actually drum accompaniments to the piano. However, this is not adverse criticism because this is often the type of musical situation a young drummer should experience.

Solos such as these are interesting to the beginner because of the melodic content in the piano part. The drummer and his *solo* become a part of a real musical situation. Often I use these arrangements before a drummer can adequately play *flams;* I merely omit the *flams.*

Although these solos do contain some *flams* they have no rolls. It might be wise for the instructor to add some accents and dynamic marks which have been omitted. The three above-cited solos give to the young drummer reading experience as well as a good musical and ensemble experience.

The *tap-flam* used in two of these solos is sometimes difficult. Stick-beats add interest and variety to *When Johnny Comes Marching Home.* Probably the use of *Flam accent No. 2* would be easier if both *flams* were used rather than merely the one on the first beat.

4. Ostling, *First Competition*, 2/4, Remick, 40¢.

This solo uses only *flams* and *five-stroke rolls.*

Attention should be called to the manner of indicating sticking: *right flam* is indicated by an F, and *left flam* by an encircled F. Dynamic contrasts add musical quality to the solo. Sticking is very logical although not completely alternating. Double bars for repeats are placed in the middle of measures and this creates a slight reading problem but one which students should learn to solve.

5. Ostling, *Den Chief*, 2/4, Remick, 40¢.

This solo uses *paradiddles* in addition to *flams* and *five-stroke rolls.* Stick-beats and rim playing add interest. Young drummers are particularly fascinated by the use of paradiddles with the accents on the *rim.*

6. Ostling, *Rolling Along*, cut-time, Remick, 40¢.

This solo is more difficult than those mentioned above. Necessary rudiments are the *long roll* (closed to open), *five* and *seventeen-stroke rolls, flams, flamacue,* and *ruff.* Stick-beats and syncopated accents add interest. Dynamic markings are good. The *long roll* is developed in a rhythmical concept.

These six solos are merely representative of possible achievements for young snare drummers. There are many others and I encourage you to investigate solo possibilities.

Latin-American Instruments and Rhythms

Part I — Rhumbas

Robert W. Buggert

A PERUSAL OF A percussion score for the typical Latin-American style composition brings to mind immediately the fact that a straightforward performance of the part would be dull and uncharacteristic of the many sounds emanating from the rhythm section of a professional group. At once two facts are realized: (1) special instruments are necessary, and (2) the percussionist must be schooled in the art of proper improvisation for the specific style.

Instruments

First, drawing attention to specific instruments, is a list of basic instruments. They will not be described in this article as reference to any current catalog of the major percussion manufacturers will clarify the point.

1. Timbales (two muffled snare drums may be used as substitutes, but any sensitive drummer or conductor will know that substitutions are sometimes necessary for expediency but are never really adequate.)

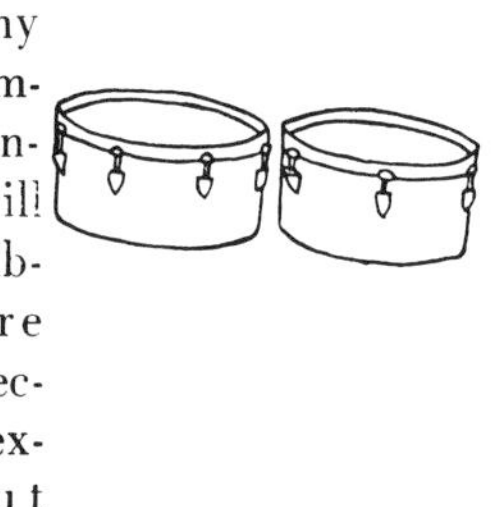

2. Claves

3. Maracas

4. Cow-bell

5. Bongos

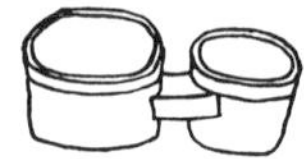

6. Conga drum or large tom-tom

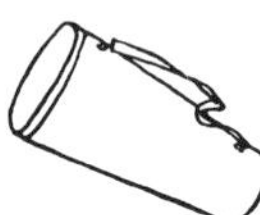

Other instruments are also used but these are basic and readily obtainable.

Playing Timbales

To play timbales the drummer, although using the right stick in the conventional manner, needs a different grip on the left stick. It should be held over the drum, palm down. (For illustrations of this position see *Latin-American Rhythms* by Phil Rale, Remick Music Corporation.) The basic rhythm played on timbales can be achieved by studying and practicing the following patterns:

After these patterns are learned, combine the two. The next step is to play a short one-stick roll with the right on the second note: begin this roll with an accent near the edge of the timbale and move the stick rapidly toward the center of the drum.

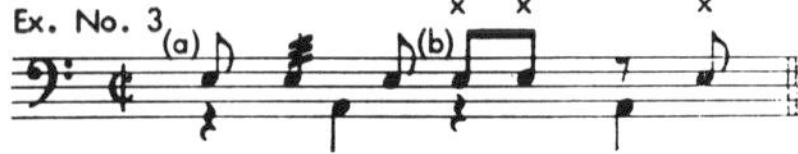

Although this pattern is basic, many variations are necessary. Some suggestions are: (1) play the first half of the measure, "a," on the large timbale and the second half, "b," on the small timbale; (2) play the notes marked "x" on rim; (3) play the notes "x" with the right stick striking the left; (4) play on different areas of the drum achieving a variety of sounds; and (5) play the notes "x" on the shell of the drum. The use of these variations gives a typical Latin-American flavor to the music.

As is easily noted, a composer could not efficiently indicate these variations; therefore, the drummer must improvise intelligently.

Playing Maracas, etc.

The rhythm indicated for maracas is often distorted to one of irregular accents. Actually the maracas should play a very even pattern. Example 4 shows the common maraca pattern

which should be used. At the point marked "x" it is desirable to have the *R* maraca cross over the left.

The rhythm of the claves is steady and usually remains unchanged except for "breaks" in the rhythmic pattern. See Example 5.

The cow-bell is an ever-present instrument in the performance of rhumbas. In slow rhumbas it is played very simply using either a steady on-the-beat rhythm or the second rhythm shown in Example 6. For changes in quality the cow-bell

is usually struck alternately with the tip of the stick on the surface or with the shoulder of the stick on the lip.

When playing a fast rhumba the cow-bell plays intricate patterns as the one shown in Example 7.

Usually parts for bongos are not written. These parts are freely improvised and of a soloistic, virtuoso-like character. The player uses fast, free rhythms, accents, and short, machine-gun like rolls which are single stroke. Thus, color is added to the performance.

May 1957

Part II — Sambas, Congas, Tangos, and Beguines

As was noted last month in Part I of this article, specific instruments and improvisatory techniques are needed by the drummer when he is to play Latin-American music.

The Samba

For the *samba*, however, one may turn to the more basic bass drum and snare drum. The unique factor for the performance of sambas lies in the fact that the drummer usually uses a regular drum stick in the right hand while using a wire brush with the left. The right stick may play several variant rhythms but must not change the pattern frequently, as is done in the *rhumba*. The most simple pattern for the right stick is that of merely playing on the beat.

The first note should be played near the edge of the drum or as a rim-shot; the second note should be played in the center of the drum (snares off). The bass drum plays this same rhythm with an accent on the second beat.

Added to this on the afterbeat is a brush stroke with the left hand.

When this basic concept has been established, the patterns which are played by the right stick may include the following:

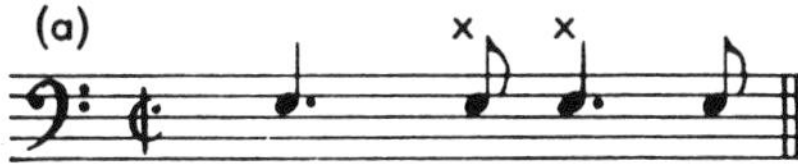

Notes marked "x" should be played in the center of the drum. In a high school group where three players are available, one could do the bass drum, one the wire brush, and one the muffled snare drum.

Straight quarter note rhythms may be played by maracas if so desired, and the same drum part may be doubled by tambourine. Basically, however, the rhythmic element should change as little as possible.

The Conga

Congas offer only the problem of the syncopated measure. The conga drum should be used as well as timbales and, often, the cowbell. The basic pattern is a syncopated meas-

ure followed by a measure of steady quarter notes. The syncopation is accented. Many rhythmical variants may be utilized on timbales, cowbells, or tom-toms.

The Tango

Tango drum parts must be accurately written and the drummer must observe the part carefully. If the part is well written, no improvisation is

necessary. The rolls on the afterbeats should be accented at their beginnings, and the drum should be used with the snares on.

The Beguine

The parts for most *beguines* are written as follows:

However, since the drum tone has little sustaining quality this type of part usually sounds "march-like." It should be altered as follows, with the result being more effective, more musical, and easier to play:

The foregoing ideas and examples are by no means exhaustive but they do give some basic conceptions for these often-used rhythms. The potential variants are limitless.

September 1957

All-Plastic Drum Heads

William F. Ludwig

Ever since I can remember, the dream of all drummers has been to have a good pair of heads that would be responsive and play consistently well in all sorts of weather. I suppose that this dream may be centuries old. To date, animal skins have provided us with the most practical membranes for drum heads but, as is well known, because they are animal skins they are extremely susceptible to every weather change.

Thus, the drummer whether playing inside or out is at the mercy of the elements—particularly changes in humidity. And the drummer playing out-of-doors is especially vulnerable to these frustrating weather changes which make proper drum tuning so difficult.

Plastics

Now, there may be an answer. This answer may be found in the new plastics being produced by the large chemical companies. The idea of a "weather-proof" head is not new by any means; in fact, there have been at least a half dozen attempts during my life-time to produce acceptable "weather-proof" heads. All these attempts ended in failure because they were based on cloth woven heads doped with various forms of acetone and acetates.

The acetate would chip off in use exposing the raw cloth; thus, a pocket would form and spread over the entire head making further use impossible.

The new plastics now coming on the market are pure plastics; they are not cloth or doped but 100% plastic. They have great durability and are particularly unaffected by weather changes. Being strong enough for drum playing, yet durable and weather-proof, they may be the answer we all have been looking for. We have mounted many on our drums over a period of the past two years of experimentation, and so far the results do look promising.

Test Results

At the present time, we are field-testing these new plastic heads by supplying them to a limited number of dance bands, concert bands, and of course, top-flight marching bands and drum corps. So far, they have not stood up as well in drum corps because they do not stand the severe pounding and tensions found in corps playing; but the results in concert and dance band have been favorable. Their uniformity makes them ideal snare heads.

One of the great problems facing us is mounting this tough, unyielding material on the flesh hoops. The solution to date has only been partial. We continue to experiment, seeking new and better methods of mounting to achieve what all of us want—the *perfect* drum head.

The new plastic drum head is shown above after it was thoroughly wetted. Since it is impervious to water, it can be used without danger of breaking; furthermore, it sounds as well wet as dry.

Percussion Pointers

Lawrence White

PERCUSSION INSTRUMENTS can be compared to the weather, abstract art, and ultra-modern music; they are talked about a great deal, but not very much is done about them.

Essentially, they are *musical* noises and *noisy* noises which align themselves into four basic groups: the snare drum, mallet instruments, the timpani, and the various non-pitch pulsatile instruments. In a discussion of any of these divisions the instruments should be observed from the *stand*point, the *sound*point, and the *view*point of the conductor and of the student player. In handling a percussion instrument, does it look right? Is it being played correctly? And is the resultant sound characteristic of the instrument?

Percussion Tone

The piano is our greatest percussion instrument. The hammer action of the modern piano is the key and vital clue to the production of right and proper percussion tone on any "hit" instrument. Think this over and retain it. No matter what the speed and intensity with which you strike or press the piano key—slow, fast, loud, or soft—the hammer strikes the string and *gets away*.

This is the basic concept of percussion tone. Now, what takes the place of the hammer action with the player? One thing and one thing only, the wrist and its motion. The arm and the fingers have their place in the handling of a stick or mallet, but the wrist with its spring-like tension controls the speed and lightness of the stick and mallet stroke.

Rudiments

Our basic snare drum rudiments are the result of a project by the United States Army. Many years ago the Army sent out a call for material to be used in a training manual for field music. A Mr. Strube was assigned the task of preparing in modern notation the jiggles and hen tracks submitted by Army drummers of that day. Thus, he earned for himself a sort of immortality with his 26 Basic Rudiments.

There are many excellent methods available with which to teach the beginning snare drummer, and a band director—even with no actual percussion training—can do an adequate job. One thing is well worth keeping in mind; each hand, especially the left, has its own aptitude level and too strict an insistence on an exact reproduction of the teacher's hand position can lead to frustration and lack of control.

Left Hand

A fortunate and workable bypass of "finger clutching" for the beginning left hand can be accomplished as follows: place the left hand stick in proper balance firmly in the cradle of the left thumb and first finger. Again, *firm* is the word, and a little muscle training is in order for the thumb and wrist to control the arc of the stick. Instead of allowing the stick to rest on the supposedly relaxed fourth and fifth fingers, keep four fingers *away* from the stick—not rigid, but in a relaxed manner.

Naturally, the control of the stick by the thumb alone will at first be a bit awkward, but the thumb grip and flexing of the wrist and forearm under proper muscle memory will get a good high rebound in a wonderfully short time.

In using this little maneuver, if the thumb grip loosens the other fingers cannot clutch over the stick since they are extended away from it. By the third or fourth lesson the cradle between the left hand thumb and the first finger is strengthened to control the stroke, and the fourth and fifth fingers can be relaxed under the stick in the orthodox left hand position.

By doing the beginner's grip in this way, you can save yourself the agony of "unlearning" a cramp-fingered, stick-clutching fiasco—brought about by the inability of the student to control, at one time, the various fingers and factors involved in the left hand drum stroke.

Right Hand

The balance point of the right hand stick should match that of the left, and the line of the stick should follow that of the right wrist and arm. The stick should always be picked up as tho it were going to be thrown, and any tendency toward holding it like a club or turning it at a right angle "fiddle bow" position should be corrected.

Variety in Cadences

The use of four basic rudiments in 2/4 street beats.

Robert W. Buggert

THE APPROACH of the fall season, football, marching band activities, pep rallies, etc., poses for the school band director the recurring problem of cadences. Many times the frequency of performance forces upon the director the use of the same old street beats. However, a little ingenuity and a bit of creative urge can do wonders for the sound and spirit of the marching band drum section.

Elementary-Intermediate Street Beats

It seems wise to offer a series of street beats using a limited number of rudiments: therefore, I have chosen four, the 5-*stroke roll*, the *flam*, the *single paradiddle*, and the *double paradiddle*. These can be used in a various number of ways, thus offering many cadences based upon only a few fundamentals. Bass drum and cymbals parts can be added for the sake of variety and additional color.

It should be noted that the following patterns do not follow the typical 4-measure and 8-measure phrasing so commonly used. Many percussion sections attract attention by being unique in some way, such as by using odd-numbered cadence phrases.

Probably the simplest street beats are those based upon the 5-stroke roll. A simple variation is achieved by adding a 5th measure to the usual 4-measure pattern and by using a single paradiddle in this measure:

The addition of flams gives this beat a little more continuity and additional fullness of sound:

The use of 16th notes, applying the first half of a single paradiddle in measures 1 and 2, adds more life to the beat, therefore gives more action:

The use of the double paradiddle in a pseudo-syncopated style lends additional rhythmic effect:

Another use of these rudiments is as follows:

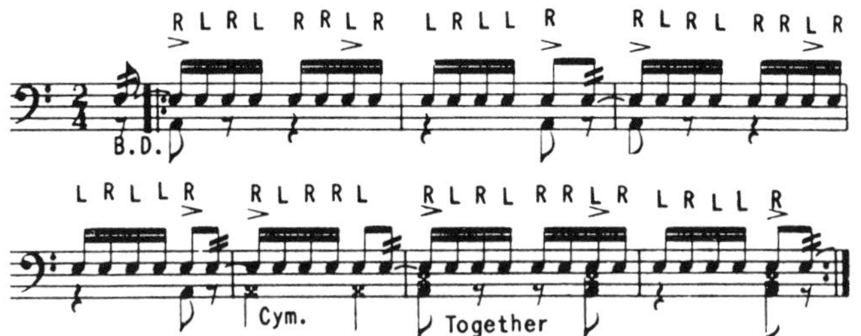

The foregoing examples are representative of what can be done with 4 elementary rudiments. Each may be used as a street beat in its own right, or two or more may be used in alternating fashion. This is merely a beginning. Many additional variations can be worked out.

Advanced Street Beats

For the experienced percussion section more complicated rhythms may be used. The four rudiments I would suggest for them are the *flam accent #1*, the *flamacue*, the *single drag*, and the *double drag*. It might be wise to note that these rudiments, being adapted to street beats, are not always used in the conventional manner found in rudimental solos and rudiment charts. They undergo a certain amount of permutation and are used in various ways.

The use of flam accent #1 may imply the use of triplets:

But if this rudiment is used on a series of even 8th notes, a syncopated effect is created:

The flamacue adds a desirable lilt to the playing of four 16th notes by adding an accent to the second one of the group. By beginning the flamacue at various places in the measure a unique cross-accent pattern can be obtained:

The single drag used in its most conventional manner is not usually too suitable for cadence application. However, as used in the following example, a desirable effect can be achieved:

The double drag, usually used in 6/8, is not easily applicable to usage in cadences. Nevertheless, it's use in 2/4—although not conventional—can create some interesting patterns:

Most of the patterns are fairly difficult. However, diligent practice, a mastering of the rudiments in question, and a good knowledge of counting time will place these street beats within the grasp of many marching band drum sections.

November 1957

Drums for the Marching Band

Betty Masoner

By all means, secure *parade* drums for your marching band. They sound like a drum should for martial music. they produce a more colorful appearance. and they are so much easier to carry. Of course. they should be equipped with leg rests.

You quickly say. "They cost too much!" Stop to think a minute. and you will realize that the cost of the parade drum *and* the concert drum together do not exceed the usual cost of other school-owned instruments. And. if the budget will not cover the cost of both. why not have the students buy one or the other?

Choice of Equipment

As to choice of drums. the 12 inch by 15 inch separate tension is probably the most practical. although for high school students a smaller drum may be used—especially if junior high school youngsters will be carrying them. In regard to snares use anything but the coiled wire: save them for the concert drum. Gut snares are the best for parade use. but they also require the most care and best technique on the part of the performer. Wire wound will give the best all around service for school use.

When buying a new set of drums the most economical shell is the plastic finish: its initial cost is more, but the upkeep is nil, and it will wear longer with less sign of the abuse it must endure. Of course. the appearance is an added reason for purchasing the plastic shells.

After one goes to the expense of equipping the section with parade drums, be sure to have the students use a stick labeled "S" not "A." (These are U.S. markings: if you are using the English made "Premier" equipment, the equivalent marching stick is labeled "H.") The heavier sticks will sound better and help the students play more smoothly. It is next to impossible to get a drum *sound* from a parade drum with "toothpick" size sticks. It is somewhat like a carpenter trying to drive six inch spikes with a toy hammer.

On the market today are slings of many colors. one of which should match your uniforms. However. the standard colors will always be khaki and white. A little soap and water never hurt the white ones. or the khaki either for that matter.

The sling should put the drum approximately three inches below the waist: this should be varied so that the drums of different height students will fall in a straight line. The strap goes over the right shoulder unless you use concert drums, then you will have to put it over the left shoulder and hook each end separately to the drum.

If you have short jackets a nice appearance is created if the sling is put under the jacket; and if you have Sam Brown belts, get a belt hook instead of using an extra strap.

Maintenance

As far as maintenance is concerned. any drum that is used should be in proper mechanical operation and *clean.* If the drums are in really bad shape the best method is to take them apart and clean each part separately.

All metal parts should be cleaned of any rust spots with steel wool followed by a coat of light oil. To clean the shells. use furniture polish on the wood. metal polish on the metal. and wipe off the plastic shell with a damp cloth. When clean, the shells may be given a coat of wax to make the cleaning process easier the next time it needs to be done.

The best method for keeping the drum looking its best is to provide a dust proof cover for it when it is not in use. When reassembling the drum, be sure to put a little grease on the moving parts. In case you don't have a key holder and a leg rest on the drum, now, when the drum is apart, would be a good time to add these necessities. Also replace all bent or broken hardware. If the snares are bent or worn so they will not lay flat, they should be replaced. When replacing the heads on the shell be sure to pull the hoops down evenly all the way around the drum.

Bass Drum and Cymbals

The bass drum on parade may be the popular Scotch style or the usual concert bass drum. If the Scotch drum is used, be sure it is slung at chin level, not down by the player's knees. The thongs on the sticks should be threaded thru the fingers, not hung around the wrist. (See any drum corps manual!)

For a very authentic drum section spend a little time working out some routines for your Scotch drummer, and add a pair or quartet of tenor drums. Median size Scotch bass drum for high school use is the 10 inch by 28 inch; for the tenor drums the 12 inch by 17 inch size is almost standard equipment. Any concert drum above the 30 inch diameter will prove to be very cumbersome to carry unless two people are employed.

For real flash, ribbons may be fastened to the tenor and bass drum sticks by unscrewing the plastic nut on the end of the sticks, tying the ribbon to the sticks, and replacing the nut.

Cymbals add considerably to the marching band. They should be as large as the performer can handle—band weight, of course. They should be played when the drum section is working out alone and also during the marches.

In regard to the holding of the cymbals, they should be equipped with leather straps and grasped as one would a snare drum stick in the right hand—fingers curled over the strap with the thumb on top. Any good copper or brass polish and a little elbow grease will keep the discs glistening in the sun or under the lights.

The other little "extra" which undoubtedly does belong to the drum section is the often forgotten bell lyre. It can add much to the section by providing short ditties interspersed with the drummers' cadences. There are several books on the market covering this field. For the bell player, during the playing of marches, the oboe part is traditionally used; don't however, try to play runs. The tones just run together and create an illusion of wrong notes. One or two notes per beat, depending on the tempo at which you are marching, is plenty to add that extra dash of spice and still not detract from the overall playing of the composition.

December 1957

Percussion Recordings

A valuable aid in teaching percussionists.

Charles A. Irick

CERTAIN CONCEPTS of percussion performance can be obtained only thru listening to live performances or recorded works. These ideas can be acquired more quickly and will become more definitely established thru the use of recordings which may be studied at leisure, with or without a score. Repetitions of all or part may be executed as many times as desired.

A student can obtain a more complete feeling for the mood and spirit of a composition with a better understanding of all of the elements of artistic percussion performance thru the use of recordings. By using them to present to the student a better understanding of the tone qualities of the various percussion instruments, as well as a concept of the versatility of these instruments, there is an excellent opportunity to motivate the young percussionist to become more than just a time beater.

Following is a list of long play recordings which are presently available and which can be very useful in training percussionists. Only those recordings which are recorded by professional or college performers have been included. Additional recordings of other percussion solos or ensembles are available from On the Spot Recording Co., Box 314, Addison, Illinois.

Percussion Records Available

Antheil, George, *Ballet Mechanique*, New York Percussion Group, Columbia ML-4956.

Bach, J. S., *Bach for Percussion*, New York Percussion Ensemble, Audio Fidelity 1812.

Bartok, Bela, *Sonata for Two Pianos and Percussion*, Stuttgart Pro Musica Orchestra, Vox PL-9600.

Bartok, Bela, *Sonata for Two Pianos and Percussion*, Marcus and Goodman, Dial 1.

Bartok, Bela, *Sonata for Two Pianos and Percussion*, Westminster XWN 18425.

Blomdahl, Karl-Birger, *Chamber Concerto for Piano, Winds, Percussion*, MGM Chamber Orchestra, MGM 3371.

Chavez, Carlos, *Toccata for Percussion*, Boston Percussion Group, Boston 207.

Chavez, Carlos, *Toccata for Percussion*, Concert Arts Percussion Group, Capitol P-8299.

Chavez, Carlos, *Toccata for Percussion*, Gotham Percussion Group, Urania A-7144.

Chavez, Carlos, *Toccata for Percussion*, University of Illinois Percussion Ensemble, Custom Recording Series 3.

Colgrass, Michael, *Three Brothers*, University of Illinois Percussion Ensemble, Custom Recording Series 3.

Donovan, Richard, *Soundings for Trumpet, Bassoon, Percussion*, MGM Chamber Orchestra, MGM 3371.

Farberman, Harold, *Evolution*, Boston Percussion Group, Boston 207.

Glanville-Hicks, Peggy, *Sonata for Piano and Percussion*, New York Percussion Ensemble, Columbia ML-4990.

Harrison, Lou, *Canticle No. 3*, University of Illinois Percussion Group, Custom Recording Series 3.

McKenzi, Jack H., *Introduction and Allegro*, University of Illinois Percussion Ensemble, Custom Recording Series 3.

Milhaud, Darius, *Concerto for Percussion and Small Orchestra*, Concert Arts Orchestra, Capitol P-8299.

Ruffles and Flourishes, Eastman Symphonic Wind Ensemble, Mercury MG 50112.

The Spirit of '76 and *Music for Fifes and Drums*, Eastman Symphonic Wind Ensemble, Mercury MG 50111.

Varese, Edgard, *Ionisation*, University of Illinois Percussion Ensemble, Custom Recording Series 3.

Wolpe, Stefan, *Percussion Quartet*, Baron Chamber Group, Esoteric 530.

The following three records are listed separately since they are an explanatory or study type of record. They do contain some snare drum solos which are excellent for solo or contest use.

Goodman, Sam, *Bell, Drum and Cymbal*, Angel 35629.

Harr, Haskell, *Drum Method, Book II* (with record), M. M. Cole Publishing Co. (4 solos and 26 rudiments).

Ludwig, William F., *Rudimental Drum Record No. 1* (with book), Ludwig Drum Co. (9 solos and 13 rudiments).

Many Advantages

The use of recordings to teach percussionists will not only increase the students' interest and appreciation of professional playing but will also serve as a stimulus to improve their own performance of music.

Recently publishers of band music and the manufacturers of phonograph records have been combining efforts by making more and more recordings available which can be studied with the score. These can be a real timesaver and a valuable motivating factor for the instrumental instructor who will use them.

Percussionists can play in a much shorter time after listening to a recording than with a much longer period of explanation and drill. The student can have an improved concept of percussion musicianship and thereby be aware of an increase in the importance of percussion parts.

Percussionists need the same kind of solo and ensemble experience that is available to the remainder of the instrumentalists. Using recordings as a learning device and motivating factor can save much valuable time. Why not give them a chance?

Percussion Music Review

Quintet in Five. Truman Shoaff. Music for Percussion. score and 5 parts—$2.00.

This is an interesting quintet written in A-B-A form and in 5/4 with the exception of seven measures which alternate between 3/4 and 2/4. The instrumentation is as follows: player 1, Tambourine and Triangle; player 2, Temple Blocks and Temple Bells; player 3, Cymbal, Cowbell, 2 Tom-Toms; player 4, Snare Drum and Wood Block; and player 5, Bass Drum, Rachet, and Sandpaper.

Most of the instruments can be obtained by the average high school group without too much trouble, and most of the parts are not individually difficult. The Snare Drum and Temple Blocks parts are the most complicated. This ensemble can be performed by high school students and the experience will be rewarding to them, to their director, and to the public.

Evolution of Drumming, Vincent L. Mott, 1957, Music Textbook Co., Paterson, N. J., 129 pp., bibliography, diagrams, $3.00.

Mr. Mott's purpose is "to present the rudiments of drumming concisely, thoroughly, and effectively." Therefore, most of the book is used to present the rudiments and applications of them. It should be noted that the 26 rudiments are not exactly the same as those adopted by the N.A.R.D. This is not a negative criticism, but it makes one wonder regarding any standardization of the rudiments. The author mentions them in a "new, systematic" order which is very logical. He compares them to a basic vocabulary or alphabet. Diagrams throughout are clear. There are sections on solos, professional pointers, and popular music. Among strong features of the book are its bibliography and a suggested library of music. The book itself is well printed and bound with a plastic spiral.—R.W.B.

1958-1959

Snare Drum Roll

Exercises and Special Techniques

Emil Sholle

FOR YEARS I USED the method of teaching the roll as suggested in most drum study books, i.e., by starting slowly and hitting two left hand strokes and two right hand strokes, controlling each hit until a certain speed was reached and then going into the "hit-bounce" in the fast speed. Inasmuch as thousands of drummers have learned to make the roll in this manner, there must be some merit in following this procedure.

New Approach

I still feel it is good practice. However, I have come to the conclusion that it is wiser for the drum teacher to introduce the study of the roll in a different way and use this "old method" only after the student has reached a certain stage of development as far as the roll is concerned.

If you analyze the movements involved in the making of the roll, you find the most important things to be: (1) evenness in the stroking, left hand as well as right; (2) an equal volume of sound made by both sticks; and (3) an equal number of taps made by each thrust of the stick.

By an equal number of taps I mean two taps with the left and two with the right, or three with each stick, or even four with each. Of course, they must be the same in speed, volume, and number. An absolute matching in all of these things is the aim. When considering exercises for the study of the roll, these items listed must be kept in mind. The improvement and perfection of each of these should be the result of such exercises if practiced correctly.

Exercises

When I decided to write my book, *The Study of the Snare Drum Roll,* I corresponded with many teachers and received some fine suggestions. I was happy to hear that many others felt as I did regarding the study of the roll.

In Ex. 1 the rolls in the top line are made with the right hand stick, and in the bottom line they're made with the left hand stick. All notes are played at the same speed regardless of the number of notes in a measure. Every 8th note or rest receives the same value.

First time thru, play the right stick on the drum and the left stick on your knee. Listen to the even bouncing of the right stick. Second time, use the left hand on the drum and right on your knee, and listen to the even bouncing of the left stick. Third time, use both sticks on the drum.

In this exercise, the roll—made first with one stick and then the other—does not necessarily mean two notes with the left and two with the right. It could be three with each, or four with each; but it is better for the student to start with two.

In Ex. 2 let each stroke be a pressing in of the stick, about the same way a person who never held a pair of sticks would do when trying to make a roll. Play slowly and let the sticks lie on the head of the drum without bouncing each stroke. *Be sure to* watch accents. Then try a continuous roll, paying attention to the accents. Finally, play the exercise very softly (ppp) with very delicate accents. Feel the accents without actually making them.

Ex. 3 is designed to develop control by much repetition of one stick.

These are just three examples of different ways to practice a roll apart from the old *daddy-mammy* way.

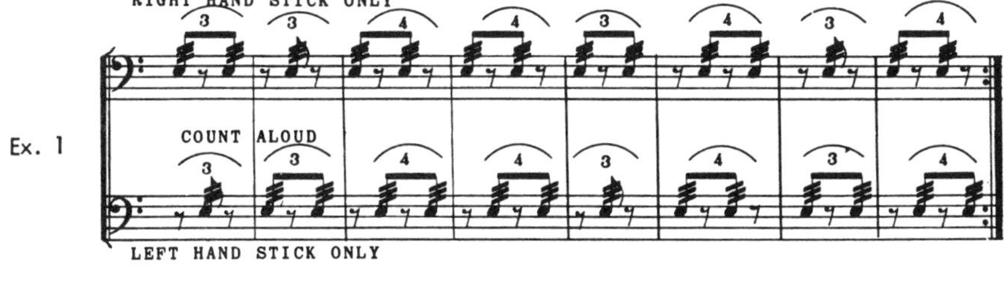

Percussion Music Review

Sholle, Emil
The Big 230, 1957, Brook Publishing Co., Cleveland Heights, Ohio, $1.25, 40 pp.

This is a new book of 230 short studies for the snare drum by Emil Sholle. They are designed for the improvement of speed and control. The studies are well organized and divided into several sections. Each section contains material emphasizing a specific rudiment. Although a sticking pattern is indicated for the rudiment which precedes the section, the exercises contain no indication of sticking. They are thoroughly conceived and very interesting to play. The printing job is excellent. Percussion players should enjoy this as supplementary reading material during the intermediate stages.—R.W.B.

Let's Have Percussion Ensembles

Thomas L. Davis

THE PERCUSSION ENSEMBLE is a relatively recent development in the field of music. The first pure percussion music was written in the early 1930's, and since 1950 this means of musical expression has gained tremendous recognition throughout the country. If handled properly, percussion music can be as effective as music of any other type.

Definition and Goals

By way of explanation, a Percussion Ensemble is a group of *percussionists,* not just drummers, who make authentic music by using those instruments which come under the classification of percussion. Incidentally, there are over 110 music instruments in the group, including mallet instruments! An ensemble which contains just a few of these various instruments is capable of traveling the musical cycle from Bach to Kenton, and it's absolute music all the way. Imagine the varieties of rhythmic and tonal combinations possible with so many instruments from which to choose!

The goal of the percussion ensemble movement is two-fold. First and more important, it represents an effort to give the greatest amount of practical playing experience possible to the members. This means that each person has a chance to learn the proper way to play the countless indefinite-pitched instruments, as well as mallet instruments. In the course of one composition a performer may play three or four different instruments. Think of the opportunities that are offered here: in short, the percussion ensemble makes percussionists out of ordinary drummers!

The second goal is to produce absolute music, with percussion instruments, thereby gaining for the percussion section the respect and recognition it rightly deserves. The members of the percussion section are entitled to a playing experience equal to that enjoyed by the members of other instrumental ensembles.

Instruments Needed

It is relatively easy to start a percussion ensemble, and it is not necessary to spend large sums of money for the purchase of instruments. Most of our schools own a snare drum, bass drum, a pair of cymbals, and at least two timpani. These are the basic instruments, and if they are available the ensemble is on its way. A sizable amount of literature is available which requires the use of these instruments only. Also considered to be standard equipment for most schools are orchestra bells, triangle, wood blocks, tambourine, and castanets. Should the ensemble have the use of these instruments, a considerable amount of playable literature is at its disposal.

Should there be a desire to increase the size of the percussion section by the purchase of additional instruments, some suggestions in the order of their importance are: xylophone, chimes, tunable tom-toms, tam-tam (gong), and temple blocks. Of course, the use of other small "traps" is advisable. Among the most useful are: cow bells, sleighbells, ratchet, slapstick (whip), sand blocks, etc.

Latin American percussion instruments are playing an increasingly important part in our band literature, and are of great value to both the band and the ensemble. The most important of these are: maracas, claves, guiro (gourd), bongo drums, conga drums, and timbales.

Some of the advanced literature for percussion ensemble calls for the use of more expensive definite-pitched instruments such as marimba, vibraharp, and celeste. Like the Latin American instruments, these are not absolute necessities, but their use adds greatly to the versatility and effectiveness of the ensemble.

Practical substitution of instruments will often enable the ensemble to play compositions calling for instruments which are not ordinarily at its disposal. For instance, where a composition might be written for xylophone and marimba and only a xylophone is available, both parts could conceivably be played by two players on the xylophone—the player with the xylophone part using harder mallets than the player with the marimba part.

Celeste parts can be effectively reproduced by playing them on piano two octaves higher than written. Similarly, muffled field and snare drums can be used to replace tom-toms if they are tuned properly. Usually some member of the school percussion section owns a set of dance drums, and the tom-toms for a dance set can be put to very good use in the percussion ensemble. Incidentally, piano players make excellent mallet performers if given the opportunity to practice on the various instruments.

Frequency of Use

The following is a list of the most commonly used instruments in percussion ensembles, numbered according to the frequency of their appearance in ensemble literature:

1. Snare Drum
2. Bass Drum
3. Double Cymbals
4. Timpani
5. Suspended Cymbals
6. Field Drums
7. Tenor Drums
8. Orchestra Bells
9. Triangles
10. Wood Blocks
11. Tambourine
12. Castanets
13. Hi-Hat Cymbals
14. Xylophone
15. Tunable Tom-Toms
16. Tam-Tam (Gong)
17. Temple Blocks
18. Maracas
19. Claves
20. Guiro (Gourd)
21. Bongo Drums
22. Conga Drums
23. Timbales
24. Cow Bell

25. Chimes
26. Sleighbells
27. Ratchet
28. Whip (Slapstick)
29. Sandpaper Blocks
30. Vibraharp
31. Marimba
32. Celeste (Magnaharp)
33. Dance Drums
34. Siren Whistle
35. Slide Whistle
36. Bird Whistle
37. Auto Horns
38. Marching Machine
39. Antique Finger Cymbals
40. Piano
41. String Bass
42. Guitar

Selected Literature

Below is a listing of selected percussion ensemble literature. The numbers immediately following each composition indicate the instrumentation according to the frequency list above:

Parade, by Morton Gould; published by C & G Music Corp; Grade II; 3 players. Instrumentation: 1, 2, 3, 39.

Three Dances, by Jack McKenzie; published by Music for Percussion; Grade III; 3 players. Instrumentation: 1, 4, 9, 10, 11, 15, 20.

Trio for Snare Drum, Bass Drum, and Tom-Tom, by Frank Ward; published by Chaz. Colin; Grade III; 3 players. Instrumentation: 1, 2, 15.

First Quartet, by Mervin Britten; published by Music for Percussion; Grade I; 4 players. Instrumentation: 2, 5, 9, 11.

Introduction and Allegro, by Jack McKenzie; published by Music for Percussion; Grade IV; 4 players. Instrumentation: 1, 5, 9, 10, 15, 16, 17, 31, 32.

Percussion Music, by Michael Colgrass; published by E. H. Morris; Grade V; 4 players. Instrumentation: 15, 17.

Quartet, by Frank Ward; published by Chaz. Colin; Grade I; 4 players. Instrumentation: 1, 9, 10, 15.

The Frustrated Percussionist, by Richard Schory; published by Creative Music; Grade III; 6 players; Instrumentation: 1, 3, 4, 5, 8, 10, 14, 17, 24, 34, 35, 36, 38.

Piece, Eugene Weigel; published by University of Illinois Division of Music Extension; Grade II; 5 players. Instrumentation: 1, 2, 3, 4, 5, 7, 9, 10.

Percussional Melee, by Rudolph Ganz; published by Mills Musico Co.; Grade III; 6 players. Instrumentation: 1, 2, 3, 8, 9, 11, 14, 16, 17, 26, 28, 29, 30, 33, 35, 37.

Sextet, by Donovan Olson; published by Music for Percussion; Grade II; 6 players. Instrumentation: 1, 2, 7, 9, 11, 19.

Sextet, by Thomas Siwe; published by Music for Percussion; Grade III; 6 players. Instrumentation: 4, 10, 18, 19, 21, 23, 24.

Toccata for Percussion Instruments, by Carlos Chavez; published by Mills Music Co.; Grade V; 6 players. Instrumentation: 1, 2, 4, 7, 8, 14, 15, 16, 18, 19, 26.

Two For Six, Thos. L. Davis; published by Creative Music; Grade II; 6 players. Instrumentation: 1, 9, 11, 15, 18, 19.

Invasion, by A. E. McDonell; published by Ludwig Publishing Co.; Grade III; 7 players. Instrumentation: 1, 2, 5, 7, 8, 9, 10, 11, 16, 18, 19.

Introduction & Allegro, by Richard Schory; published by Creative Music; Grade IV; 8 players. Instrumentation: 1, 2, 3, 4, 5, 7, 10, 11, 12, 14, 15, 16, 17.

Nonet, by Jack McKenzie; published by Music for Percussion; Grade III; 8 players. Instrumentation: 2, 5, 15, 16, 17, 18, 19, 20, 21, 22, 24.

Cloud Nine, Schory-Davis; published by Creative Music; Grade IV; 9 players. Instrumentation: 4, 5, 8, 10, 14, 15, 16, 17, 26, 31, 32, 34.

Octet for Percussion, by Frank Ward; published by Chaz. Colin; Grade IV; 9 players. Instrumentation: 1, 2, 3, 4, 7, 9, 10, 11, 13, 15, 16, 29, 32.

Omoo, by Willis Charkovsky; published by Creative Music; Grade IV; 9 players. Instrumentation: 4, 5, 9, 11, 18, 19, 20, 21, 22, 23, 24, 31, 32, 33, 41. (optional String Bass part included)

Pentatonic Clock, by Willis Charkovsky; published by Creative Music; Grade III. 9 players. Instrumentation: 5, 8, 9, 10, 14, 15, 17, 26, 28, 32, 33. (optional Guitar part included)

Woodpile Polka, by Willis Charkovsky; published by Creative Music; Grade IV; 9 players. Instrumentation: 2, 3, 8, 10, 14, 31, 32, 34, 41.

Three Brothers, by Michael Colgrass; published by Music for Percussion; Grade IV; 9 players. Instrumentation: 1, 4, 5, 11, 15, 18, 21, 24.

Amazon Tributary, by Willis Charkovsky; published by Creative Music; Grade IV; 10 players. Instrumentation: 1, 2, 4, 5, 6, 8, 14, 15, 16, 21, 31.

Oriental Mambo, by Thos. L. Davis; published by Creative Music; Grade III; 10 players. Instrumentation: 2, 4, 13, 14, 15, 16, 18, 19, 20, 21, 24, 31, 32.

Mau Mau Suite, by Thos. L. Davis; published by Creative Music; Grade IV; 12 players. Instrumentation: 1, 4, 14, 15, 16, 17, 18, 19, 20, 21, 22, 23, 31, 32, 41. (optional Guitar part is included)

This is by no means an all-inclusive listing. There are many more excellent numbers available for groups of various sizes.

Let's make Percussion Ensembles a part of the regular program, and make percussionists out of our drummers! !

Calfskin vs. Plastic Drumheads

An Experiment to Determine Some of the Qualities of Each Type.

Arthur E. Neumann
Consulting Engineer

IT ALL STARTED on December 20th, 1957, in the offices of the American Rawhide Mfg. Co. of Chicago. The event was a series of scientific tests to determine some of the differences between the traditional calfskin drumheads and the newer plastic variety.

Howard and Munson Emery of American Rawhide asked me to design equipment which could determine some of the differences between the two types of heads. The Company's interest stems from the fact that it manufactures the calfskin product and also acts as distributor for the plastic product.

Howard Emery stated, "Since the advent last year of all-plastic heads, various claims have been made as to their playing quality and strength, many of which have not been substantiated. In trying to give percussionists the best playing heads possible, we felt that it was necessary to determine objectively and scientifically just what properties are found in each of the types."

Acoustical Tests

Simultaneously with the tests that I was to conduct with mechanical equipment, Howard C. Hardy & Associates, an acoustical consulting firm in Chicago, was retained to conduct acoustical tests.

In the Hardy laboratories, technicians made graphs with recorded drum beats and the comparative acoustical responses of calfskin and plastic heads. The graphs showed that greater volume was possible with calfskin, about 5 decibels more on the bass drum, for example. They also indicated that with calfskin, a drummer can produce a crisper staccato tone.

Mechanical Tests

The mechanical tests were made on equipment which permits two heads to be locked evenly into position face to face, four inches apart. A drumstick on an electrically controlled arm located exactly between the two heads, automatically snaps back and forth at the rate of six beats per second on each head. The striking force of the stick can be adjusted; and, in the first test, it simulated a light, normal roll.

Great care was taken to assure identical conditions for both heads, including the pitch of the heads and striking force of the stick. Inside the heavily insulated box, resting on rubber cushions to deaden vibration, each of the heads began to absorb 21,000 beats per hour.

Periodically, the heads were examined, and at the end of the 4th day the plastic head was found to have developed a *pocket.*

After seven days and 3½ million strokes the equipment was stopped momentarily. The plastic head was found to be one octave lower in pitch and a slight crack was appearing at the point of impact. Its pitch was adjusted and the test resumed.

Six days after this the test was again stopped, and this time the calfskin head was found to be one note low. Pitch was adjusted and test resumed. Then, a week later the plastic head broke and the first test was halted.

Second Test

During the second test, with a different plastic head but the same calfskin head, the striking force of the stick was increased four times. After 24 hours and 49 minutes the plastic head broke. Two more have broken at the time of this writing, but the calfskin head is still intact. The test will continue until it breaks.

In the early stages of the second test, the pin holding the stick broke; and in repairing it, we noted that the side of the stick hitting the plastic head was wearing flat—probably due to the difference in resiliency.

Another characteristic discovered during the tests is a tendency of the plastic head to *cold flow,* a technical term applied to materials meaning to *loosen internally,* resulting in a lowering of pitch and volume.

More Research

The Hardy Laboratories also went beyond the initial tests in their acoustical analysis. They made extensive tape recordings in a Chicago sound studio. They analyzed the response of both heads, which were played for the demonstration by Roy Knapp, head of the School of Percussion in Chicago, and himself a well-known drummer. The tapes were analyzed for playing qualities such as sustained response, fall-off patterns, etc.

Mr. Emery says, "Both the acoustical and strength tests will continue until we have definitely and accurately determined the characteristics of both types of heads."

Arthur E. Neumann, Consulting Engineer, and Howard Emery of the American Rawhide Manufacturing Company with the equipment used to test the strength of plastic and calfskin drumheads.

Teacher-Training in Percussion

An analysis of the percussion instruction offered by colleges and universities.

Michael B. Lamade

THE MUSIC PROFESSION has long been aware of a shortage of well-trained percussionists, not only in secondary school organizations, but also on the university and college level. It is felt that the source of this inadequacy may be found in the agencies involved in teacher preparation. One researcher provided evidence which upheld the validity of this statement.[1] He was concerned with the opinions of high school music teachers regarding what they felt were the major weaknesses in their undergraduate teacher-training institutions. One hundred and fifty teachers offered suggestions, and the following conclusion was reached: "High school instrumental music teachers singled out the lack of training in percussion instruments as the greatest weakness in college training programs . . ."[2]

In the present study seeking to elucidate the question of percussion training, a questionnaire was distributed to the member schools of the National Association of Schools of Music in order to determine to what extent a need exists in our teacher-training institutions for improvement in the facilities, processes, and personnel concerning instruction of percussion instruments.

Two hundred and ten schools were contacted in this survey and questionnaires were returned from 116. Interest in the problem is clearly shown by this fact alone, as a questionnaire return of 55.2% is considered to be well above average. Sixteen of the schools did not offer percussion instruction of any kind. In determining the statistics and percentages of the questionnaire these 16 institutions were not considered.

Non-Percussion Music Education Majors

An *average* of one semester hour of percussion is required of these students, although 25% do not receive instruction in percussion at all; at least, they are not required to take it. In nearly all of the cases percussion is taught in a class, with the number of students in the class ranging from 3 to 50. Approximately one-third of the schools teach percussion as a segment or part of another class, such as brass or woodwind.

How much time is actually spent on percussion under these circumstances is difficult to ascertain, but a feeling exists that it is very often neglected. Only half of the schools provide the student with an opportunity to perform on the instruments with a "laboratory" band or orchestra. In many cases the student is limited to the use of the practice pad. This is as undesirable as the piano student spending all his time on a silent keyboard.

Latin American rhythms, instruments, and dance forms, which are playing an important part in the musical culture of today, are grossly neglected. Over half of the schools do not include this area in the training of their students. It is also surprising to note that the majority of students are not receiving instruction in the basic fundamentals of the xylophone, marimba, and vibraphone, although the timpani are considered in nearly all of the cases. A performing examination is required of most of the students, and about half of the institutions require a written examination.

Percussion Music Education Majors

At the present time 57% of our colleges and universities do not have a music education major who is a percussionist. Compare this with the number of brass and woodwind students and it becomes more apparent why our school organizations are suffering. A few larger colleges with outstanding percussionists on the faculty are the exception, with one school having over a dozen students in this classification.

In order to estimate more accurately the number of music education students majoring in percussion, we have studied the situation over a four-year period. The picture should look brighter considering this longer period of time, but it does not. The fact is that over half of our colleges and universities have not had a percussion major in music education in the past four years! The school mentioned above has had 40 during this time, but again we point out that this is a rare exception.

Applied Percussion Majors

Here we are concerned with the student who is preparing for a career in music on the professional performance level. These people will be playing in symphony orchestras, professional bands, radio and television studios, and teaching in colleges, universities, and private studios.

Nearly three-fourths (74%) of the schools accredited by the National Association of Schools of Music do not even offer a degree with a major in percussion! Of the remaining one-fourth, nearly half of the schools which do offer the degree do not have any students enrolled at the present time. Of the small number of schools which remain, an average of one percussion major per school is the common figure at the present time. These schools have graduated an average of two students during a four year period.

Percussion Personnel

Music cannot be taught effectively without well-trained and competent teachers. A person who has had very limited training in a specific area cannot possibly qualify to teach the subject on the college level. We would not allow brass, woodwind, theory, or composition to be taught under these circumstances. We are constantly stating that we must maintain high standards, and pride ourselves in the quality of our faculties. But do we maintain these standards when it comes to percussion instruction? Definitely not.

Examine a few of the facts. 67% of the persons teaching percussion in American colleges and universities today are not percussionists at all, but instructors in another area, such as brass or woodwind. They have been given this area to teach either because there is no one else qualified to teach the subject or in order to fill out their schedule.

Only 10% of the schools questioned possess a full-time instructor who has a college degree with percussion as his major instrument, although 8% of the schools had a part-time instructor with a college degree with emphasis in percussion. The remaining 15% of the schools employed part-time teachers who play percussion professionally but do not have college training. These men come from our symphonies and studios in and around our larger cities.

It is felt that this shortage of well-trained and qualified teachers is one of the main reasons for the lack of competent students in the percussion sections of our secondary school and college organizations. If the person who is teaching is improperly trained, it stands to reason that he cannot instruct others as effectively as he might do otherwise. Thus we find that our colleges are producing teachers with inadequate training in percussion, who cannot effectively train their students when they go into the field. It produces a never-ending circle which restrains progress.

Equipment and Facilities

In the majority of cases practice facilities are very limited for percussion students. More specifically, only 36% of the participating schools provide percussion practice rooms. This is of major importance, as it is very difficult to carry timpani and other heavy percussion instruments from place to place. In many cases the instruments are kept in the auditorium and are not available for the use of the student.

Another inadequacy which was noted was the lack of provision for proper storage space. Instruments which are left on the stage or in the hallway without proper cases and protection soon become abused. Timpani heads which are left uncovered become dirty and have a tendency to dry out. Producing a good tone on this instrument is difficult under the best conditions, but next to impossible on one which has been treated improperly. Seventy-two per cent of the schools interviewed did not feel that they had adequate storage facilities.

Percussion Ensembles

An interesting observation is the appearance of percussion ensembles in a number of our colleges and universities.[3] Twenty-four per cent stated that they were operating, or in the process of forming, an organization of this type. There are great possibilities for ensembles of this nature, as anyone who has heard an outstanding one will testify. These organizations can do a great deal in helping people understand the great potential of the percussion instruments.

Recommendations

The main responsibility for better percussion training lies with the individual institution engaged in teacher-training, and it is up to the administration and staff of these schools to see that their program is satisfying the needs of the student.

Music teachers in our secondary schools can also help the situation by demanding a higher degree of performance ability from the percussionists in their organizations, with private study encouraged. Selection of students to play percussion instruments should be done more carefully and the idea, "if he can't learn to blow a horn, give him a drum," should be abolished.

The secondary school teacher can also become better informed on the subject by attending percussion clinics offered at state and national conventions, and if possible, arrange for an outstanding percussionist to visit his school for the purpose of conducting a clinic for the local students. By keeping alert to the materials available from drum companies and publishing houses, the music director who has had limited background in percussion can increase his understanding and improve his teaching method.

An awareness of the problem is not enough—action must be taken before improvement can occur.

---

1. Wilbur J. Peterson, "The Place of the Performance Area in Training High School Music Teachers," *Journal of Research in Music Education,* IV (Spring, 1956), p. 52.
2. *Ibid.*, p. 55.
3. For a very informative article on this subject see: Jack McKenzie, "The Percussion Ensemble," *The Instrumentalist,* XI (December, 1956), p. 58.

The Timpanist, Ideas and Suggestions

Part 1

William Sebastian Hart

The kettledrums or timpani are kings of the percussion hierarchy. The timpanist is occupant of the first chair in the percussion section. He should be master of the many percussion instruments, as well as the kettledrums, to reach this position. The player who progresses in study from the snare drum, to the accessories, to the mallet played instruments, to the timpani, has approached the top instrument properly. One who plays the timpani only with little knowledge of the others is truly an amateur percussionist.

Tuning the Timpani

The kettledrums are hemispheres of copper over which are stretched heads of calf skin of the best quality and texture. The head is tucked while wet on a metal hoop and allowed to dry. When dry it is placed on the open bowl of copper and the counter-hoop placed on top and thru its openings; handles are inserted and screwed into connecting sockets in the kettle. When this has been done, the head is then made wet again by applying water to its entire circumference, with the exception of about one inch from the edge. As the head becomes slack, the handles are tightened until a "collar" forms on the rim.

When the "collar" reaches about ½ inch, the excess moisture is wiped away from the head and the handles should be left even all around the rim, i.e. *even to the eye*—parallel to the rim at each particular point. When the head dries (about 12 hours later) the skin will have an even sound at every point on the head. This is tremendously important and the heart of all timpani tuning.

If only more timpanists observed this there would be fewer problems about "tensioning" the head. If the handles are even to the eye, they will be *even to the sound.* Whenever the handles are turned in every direction on a kettle, the player has a jungle-like maze of sound to worry about and doubtless he lives a lifetime with his instruments and never truly gets a clear tone.

After the handles are set in this even manner, they can be turned evenly in either direction and the head will go up or down in pitch, evenly and clearly. This is the basis of good clear tone in tuning—the point being that the head is allowed to dry to an even tone with the handles arranged evenly around the edge.

Heads should be replaced on timpani every year for best tone quality. At the very longest, heads should not be retained on the kettle beyond two years. Every timpanist should learn his instruments by first mastering the "hand screw" type of kettledrums. He should learn to tune proficiently by hand; then he can go on to pedal tuning by one large handle or other mechanical means.

Too often in our schools today, the band or orchestra director assigns some pianist or other instrumentalist to the timpani—pedal timpani at that. The student pushes his foot down, the head tightens; he hears some sort of squeal and believes that he is a timpanist, because he counts his rests correctly and "comes in," generally in a loud manner.

Nothing could be further from the truth. Yet we see and hear these misguided players thumping away in our high schools, truly believing that the instrument is a "snap" to play. To make matters worse, the school player usually uses *one pair* of timpani sticks—not for one piece—but for the *entire concert.*

Timpani Sticks

Sticks are of paramount importance in good timpani playing. Just as an oboist worthy of the name makes his own reeds, good timpanists make their own sticks, at least the felt ball portions. This is an art. Sewing of varying degrees of thicknesses of felt onto a hard felt core and then screwing that core onto the wooden portion of the stick produces various weights, sizes, and shapes of sticks. These in turn, bring out different tone colors from the kettles.

A good rule to follow, generally, is: When the music is marked pianissimo and great delicacy and crispness is desired from the timpani, then the *hardest felt ball* stick should be used. When the music is louder, a felt ball of greater weight and body is to be used. This is a highly individual problem. Timpanists who use hard sticks almost exclusivley sound brittle and "drummy" in their playing.

If the pitch is obviated by hard sticks in loud passages, why tune at all? Why not play on the bass drum, or on the wall of the concert hall? Naturally, great care and taste must be exercised in stick selection. This matter must be gone into in great detail by the teacher when the pupil has reached an advanced degree of proficiency on the instruments.

A good timpanist, in performance, uses several pairs of sticks in each composition. Fine players change sticks often, as the music warrants it in their opinion. No sign in the music tells the player to change sticks, it is usually left to the discretion of the player and the conductor.

There are times when directions are given to the player by some composers. These instances are rare and they center around the two phrases "wooden sticks" (baguettes de bois) and felt sticks (baguettes d'eponge) used frequently by Berlioz. Berlioz was a timpanist himself, and these terms may be the clue to some attempt at different colors to be sought after from the kettledrums. The general run of parts, however, leave stick selection to the player. Yet the wrong stick may actually ruin the performance.

Timpani Parts

Much must be said about the timpani "part." Generally speaking, *every* timpani part in the classical repertoire—by all the master composers—is erroneously written. If the performer were actually to play what is printed with exact attention to the rhythmic notation, especially concerning the rests, the effect would be disastrous. For example, in the music of Mozart, the composer used the timpani simply to strengthen the sound of the trumpets which played tonic—dominant figures throughout the work. The strings carry the burden and the woodwinds embroider on the principal choir. The brasses are to be supported by timpani.

If the composition is in "common time" and the trumpets are assigned 2 half notes in a particular measure followed by a whole note, the "strengthener" for this is the timpani. The rhythm in the timpani part balancing that trumpet figure is 8th note, 8th rest, quarter rest; 8th note, 8th rest, quarter rest; followed in the next measure by a quarter note, quarter rest, and half rest. Thus, we have the trumpets resounding in half notes and the timpani thumping away on 8th notes, supposedly matching them.

If the timpanist actually dampened the notes of the ketttle to allow it to ring for an 8th note only, the effect would be bad. The intelligent timpanist, therefore, forgets the actual written rhythmic figure and allows the tones to ring as if they were half notes or whole notes as the trumpets suggest.

Today the intelligent timpanist must use his good sense to "interpret" every part that comes before him, to find out what the composer *intended*, and play it so. The conductor who insists that every note be played exactly as the composer wrote it is mistaken. Generally speaking, timpanists should play every part with a ringing quality of sound. A rule to remember is "never dampen unless a general cut-off occurs."

But a word must be said about the

"unwanted note." In a passage between two or more timpani, the tone to be struck *last* in a particular phrase should be the one to "ring" and the notes leading up to this one should be dampened. If this is not done, and *all* are allowed to ring, a general roar of sound takes place. Only the *last note* should ring, whichever it may be.

This is an intricate problem and must be gone into during actual instruction periods. Suffice it to say **that discretion must be used in many ways in playing the timpani, in stick selection, in tuning, and in dampening or not dampening as the case may be.**

May 1958

Part II

IT SHOULD BE obvious that a fine musician in the field of percussion is one who is well trained in the broad scope of music. The best hypothetical example is that of a young person trained in early life on the piano, since this is the basic instrument and will simplify his future progress. A musician majoring on *any* orchestral instrument should have sufficient piano training to enable him to play a simple accompaniment and to be able to read easy pieces without hesitation.

With this early training under the guidance of a good teacher, the future percussionist has a reserve upon which to draw all his life. The piano is the key to the understanding of all music. Also, early tendencies of the person to have little or no trouble with rhythm are beacons pointing to the desirability of training in the field of percussion.

Training

A person with piano background should then "be put in the hands" of an excellent teacher of percussion, and a *course of study* should be taken up. The snare drum is the instrument to be studied first. After sufficient skill has been demonstrated here, both in reading and playing, the mallet-played instruments should be undertaken. Interspersed with these and while study of both previously mentioned instruments is proceeding, the various accessories should be explained and undertaken.

Finally, after skill has been shown on all of the preceding, the teacher should guide the student to the timpani. Here great understanding and knowledge of these instruments should be carefully set forth. While all this training is going on, the player should be a member of one or more orchestras or bands, or both, getting the training in ensemble playing which is the very heart of the future role he will play as a percussionist.

The student will be specially fortunate at this time if he is under the guidance of a thorough orchestral conductor, patient enough to teach routine to all of the players. It is not too much to ask that the piano be kept up during all this percussion training. It is also not too much to ask that courses in theory and ear training be undertaken. All of this will be of value to the student when he reaches the part in his training program which deals with timpani.

At this point, to train his ear, the young player should carry an "A 440" tuning fork in his pocket. To train his ear the student should listen to all the sounds around him and try to tell the pitches of them. He can help himself with the tuning fork. Whenever he hears a shrill squeak, an auto horn, train whistle, or school bell, he can decipher what the pitch of these sounds is if he has an "A" from which to start.

It is advised that whenever possible, a full course of study, such as that offered by a leading conservatory of music, should be sought to give the young student the beginnings of artistic stature.

Heretofore much stress has been laid on the piano. This is not to say that only pianists or those who study the piano make good percussionists. Good percussionists have the desire and the talent and the insatiable urge for rhythm in their blood. The player of *any* instrument can be a good potential percussionist.

Opportunities for Players

There was a time when a person showing reasonable ability, even mediocre ability, on a music instrument, could find a job in the music field. Instrumental groups or ensembles were to be found in restaurants, hotels, resorts, theater pits playing for silent pictures, vaudeville theaters, dancing schools, opera houses, and there were many symphony orchestras, ballet companies, etc.

At the present time, the opportunities in radio have diminished almost to the vanishing point, being succeeded by recorded music. In the theater there are no orchestras, the sound coming from the sound track on the motion picture screen. The other sources mentioned above have almost vanished as employers of live music. The opportunities in symphony, opera, and ballet are slim.

Many musicians have turned to the teaching field exclusively in order to keep in music. This narrows the musical activity to the radius of the schools and colleges. What, then, is the career opportunity for a percussion artist thoroughly trained and eager to earn his living in music?

If the player is good, he'll have opportunities; if he is extraordinary, he will be sought after. If there is an absolute vacuum of opportunities, the player then has the challenge of making the opportunity for himself. He can do this by organizing a musical unit within his community and becoming a part of it.

Where there is a will there is a way, and a way will be found by the man who seeks it. There may come a time when the arts will be more recognized and job opportunities will arise. If that time comes, the fine percussionist and all good musicians will find places suitable to them. In the meantime, the experienced percussionist who has been thru a rigorous period of training and who really wishes to pursue music can proceed with the knowledge that his talent can be used to promote an art of such an uplifting nature as to make sacrifices worthwhile.

Preparation for Popular Music

Robert W. Buggert

THE PERFORMANCE of limited amounts of popular music has become standard practice in many school music situations, and this literature poses some unique problems for the percussion section. When performing, the director must often decide whether to use the entire section, or limit the percussion part to one player using a complete "drum-outfit."

Unless the organization is a large one, I feel that the best arrangement is to use one drummer; however, if two drummers play, one should play hi-hat and snare while the other one plays bass drum; if three play, one may play bass drum, one snare drum, and the other a hi-hat. Cymbals on the bass drum might be substituted for hi-hat, but if an organization performs popular music with any frequency the pedal cymbals are essential. Because unique techniques are required for playing popular music, this article will be limited to exercises to be played by one person playing a drum outfit.

Equipment and Materials

Although percussion equipment has little limitation, the percussionist should have at least a bass drum with pedal, a snare drum, a hi-hat with cymbals, and—if possible—a tom-tom and one large cymbal on the drum outfit. A field drum without snares might substitute for the floor tom-toms.

Although there are many basic books and materials which deal with popular music, swing, etc., some good ones at the beginning level are: (1) A card by H. E. Nutt called common musical figures and published by the VanderCook Bookstore; (2) *Rudimental Swing Solos* by Wilcoxson; (3) *Advanced Techniques for the Modern Drummer* by Chapin; and (4) *110 Progressive Etudes for Snare Drum* by Buggert.

Exercises

Before beginning the basic study of the rhythms of popular music a drummer should have good control of the rudiments and should be a well-schooled reader. The following new problems are involved:

1. Independence of hands and feet
2. Use of different instruments
3. Versatility and ambidexterity
4. Musical taste
5. Intelligent improvisation

First the feet must be controlled so their function is practically automatic. The following basic patterns should be learned and practiced until completely controlled: Exercise I—a, b, c, d, e, and f.

The left hand should keep the basic beat and be able to do the following on the snare drum with ease: Exercise II—a, b, and c.

After the feet and left hand work adequately and independently, combine Exercises I and II as follows: Ic with IIc, Id with IIa, Id with IIb, Ie with IIc, and If with IIa. Other combinations might be used but these five will form adequate basic beats for 4-beat playing, 2-beat style, and Dixieland.

The right hand must now be able to play rhythms which are executed independently from the other three appendages. With the right stick play such patterns as the following: Exercise III—a, b, c, and d. These are merely a few. Then learn to play all the rhythms on the card by H. E. Nutt, and play all etudes that do not have rolls or flams from *110 Progressive Etudes for Snare Drum.*

The Wilcoxson book gives exercises and solos to use for decorative playing and the Chapin book develops the advanced stages. The completion of these give one a basic background for the execution of popular music and the suggestions in this article will certainly help the novice percussionist get a start toward learning these patterns.

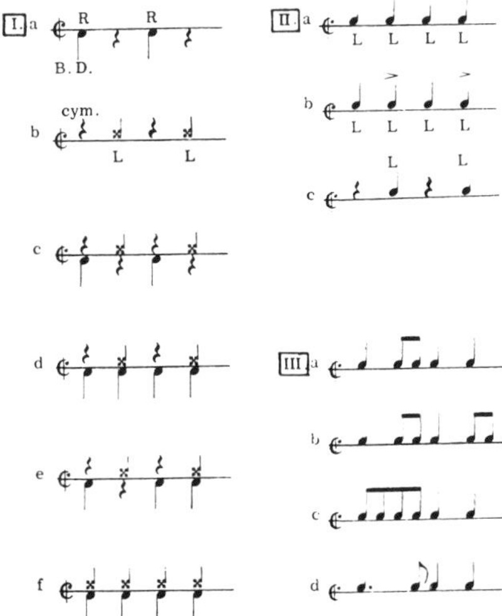

Basic exercises for developing popular music percussion patterns.

Percussion in Football Band

Thomas L. Davis

That the percussion section is an important part of any marching band is common knowledge. What most of us fail to realize is just how important this section really is in the complete picture of our bands. The percussion section can actually "make or break" a marching band. One that is well-co-ordinated, plays together, and functions as a closely-knit team can add the precision and sparkle to your band that will put it in that coveted top-notch category. Just how does one develop this type of group? Let's do a little examining.

Section Status

First, the percussion section must be treated *as a section,* just like the brass or woodwinds. The drums must be tuned to each other. That is, the tension on the snare drum heads and snares themselves must be matched. If tenor drums are employed and more than one bass drum is used, these too should be tuned alike. A percussion section that is not properly tuned sounds just as bad as a brass or woodwind section where faulty intonation exists.

Secondly, when treating the percussion section as such, you should write for it as a section. If your school does not own tenor drums, you can easily substitute by using regular field drums with the snares off. Tenor drums add balance to your section by filling the gap that exists between snare and bass drums. With this balance, you can write for your section just as you would for a brass section—the snares corresponding to cornets or trumpets, the tenors corresponding to trombones and baritones, and the bass drums corresponding to sousaphones. A balanced percussion section is a powerfully effective unit.

Sectional Rehearsals

Of utmost importance are sectional rehearsals for the drums alone. During these drills you will have an opportunity to be sure the right people are playing the right drums. A weak snare drummer may make an excellent tenor drummer if given the opportunity to work. At these drills, the regular music should be rehearsed just as much as the cadences or street beats. In the long run, your percussion section is only as good as its weakest player, so individual practice should always be stressed. The section must function as a well-co-ordinated team, and each person must carry his share of the load.

In the current era when bands are marching at faster tempos, certain problems confront the drummer which did not exist a few years ago. Snare drummers find that they can no longer execute the rudiments properly at these fast tempos. Further, they have great difficulty in trying to stay together and play with precision. Some of these problems are not altogether the fault of the technique of the individuals, but more properly they arise as a result of the music and cadences the drummers are forced to play. When writing cadences and drum parts, keep the following things in mind:

Arranging Suggestions

1. Use single strokes in fast cadences and avoid double strokes and bounces. The following rhythmic pattern should be sticked as indicated:

R L R L | R L R L R L | R L R L R L | R L R

2. Avoid excessive use of flams as they tend to make the section sound ragged and not precise. A heavy, single-handed accent will sound much cleaner and is easier to play at fast tempos.

3. Drummers should roll in rhythm, using rather open double bounces. Rolling in rhythm will tend to make the section more precise.

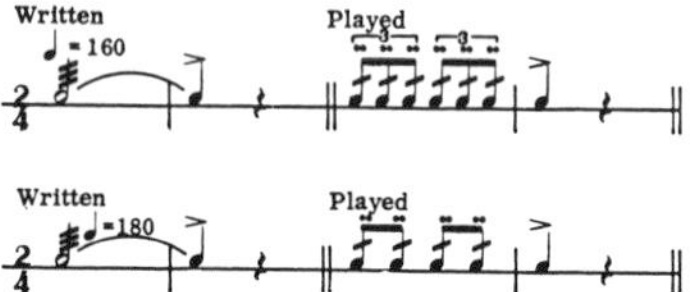

4. All rolls of duration should be played as if they were marked "forte-piano & crescendo." This increases the dynamic effect of all rolls.

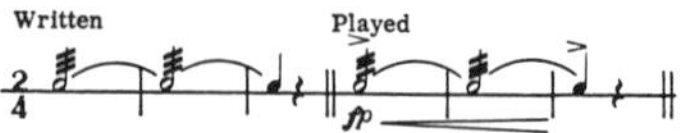

5. Cadences should be concluded with first and second endings, so that the final note of the cadence is on beat *one*. This enables the drummers to get a brief, well-deserved rest on beat *two*, and also gives form to your cadence.

6. Avoid the use of after-beats in fast tempo playing. They are tiring as well as difficult to play rapidly, and they are rather ineffective. Develop rhythmic patterns to play in marches, and be sure that all snare drummers use the same sticking.

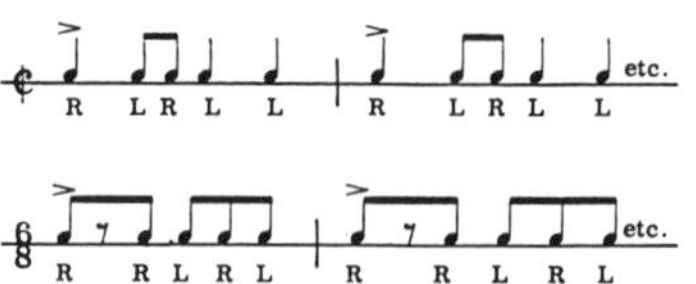

7. Use cymbals sparingly in cadences, or not at all. Save them for heightening effects in the actual music.

8. When the band plays syncopated rhythmic figures, the whole percussion section should play the figure too.

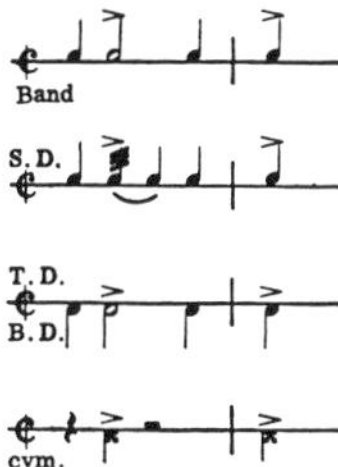

9. Keep tenor and bass drum parts simple. Complicated rhythmic figures tend to cause a muddled sound and do not enhance the precision of the section.

10. Flash sticking and twirling routines for tenor and bass drummers should be kept fairly simple. Complicated routines are good only if everyone can do them. The twirls should be so simple that the weakest man in the section can execute them with ease. Stick twirls look good only when they are precise. The sound must not suffer!

Additional Ideas

At one time or another, most directors have to face the problem of whether or not to use the leg rest. Their drummers usually complain that they do more harm than good. This is generally because the leg rests are not being used correctly. The drum should be slung high enough so that the leg rest hits the thigh midway between knee and hip. In this position the drum will not bounce against the leg, nor will it sway when the drummer executes flank movements.

Another suggestion is the use of the verti-holder for tenor drums. This attachment puts the drum on the chest, away from the lower body and leaves both legs free to move. Another advantage of this holder is that it puts the tenor drum in the same position as the bass drums, and twirling and sticking routines can then be matched with those of the bass drummers.

One of the most important psychological aspects of the outstanding percussion section is the spirit that exists among its members. Even if you feel that your section is only average, each individual should feel and *believe* that he is a member of a top-notch outfit. With this in mind, plus plenty of work, both individually and as a group, in time your percussion section will be one of the best!

October 1958

Tenor & Scotch Bass Drums

Haskell W. Harr

In the past, the drum sections of drum and bugle corps consisted mainly of snare and bass drums. Then the tenor drum was added to the ensemble, primarily because it added an intermediate tone between the crisp, sharp tones of the snare drums and the deep, resonant tones of the bass drums.

During the last few years the Scotch bass drum has gradually been replacing the concert bass drum in our school marching bands, due to the fact it is carried more easily. This also eliminates the boy needed to carry the front of the concert bass drum.

The tenor drum is also finding its way into the drum section of the marching band, doing its bit to help the director have something new to present to the public. Because of the great possibilities for "flash" as well as tone color, it is almost a desecration to both the tenor and Scotch bass drums to use them as "straight" instruments. Intelligent application of stick figurations, cross-arm technique, and stick twirling can and do make the drum section of the band outstanding.

The tenor drum primarily was carried the same as the snare drum. Since it is larger than the snare drum, it is harder to control at the fast pace of our school and college bands. Also, the cross-over technique used is nearly lost to the audience. The trend now is to carry the tenor drums with the heads in a vertical position, like the bass drums. For carrying the tenor drum in this position, a special harness has been devised, called a vertical tenor drum holder. When used in this style, the drum should have a batter head, top and bottom, as both heads are used when playing.

From the "flash" angle, every tenor drum played in the vertical position adds another pair of arms to twirl sticks and do cross-over techniques. But due to the width of the drum in that position, it is rather difficult to reach across the drum for some of the beats.

To facilitate easier playing of these flashy cross-overs on the tenor drum in the vertical position, one company (Slingerland Drum Company) has developed a new type tenor drum 6½ by 18 inches, called a Tenor-Scotch bass drum. The regular bass drum sling may be used for carrying. With this thinner drum the player can easily reach over the shell to play on the opposite head. This permits use of the same routine beats being used on both tenor and Scotch drums.

Interlude Playing

Did you ever stand on the curb to watch a parade and have nearly every band stop playing a half block before it gets to you? Did you ever notice how many people start yelling, "Why don't you play something?" as soon as your band stops playing? With the addition of bell lyras and tenor drums to your drum section, you can form a section to play during these intervals. With a special section of this type, you not only add "flash" to your band but you furnish music and entertainment for your audience during the time when the band is not playing. If you do not have drummers enough for a separate section, take some of the extra people who do not ordinarily march and teach them to play the tenor and scotch drums.

Al Wright, Director of Bands at Purdue University, uses such a group with his band, as does W. A. Gill of New Orleans. Don Cuthbert, Beloit (Wis.) High School, has a special group, and has featured it at football half-time shows.

Write Your Own Interludes

There is not too much music available for such a combination at the present time. But any bandleader should be able to write a few interludes for these instruments by using the suggested routines accompanying this article. When writing parts, the bell lyra part should not have too many notes, as only one mallet is used. Ordinarily the melody alone is satisfactory, but if an alto or harmony part is desired, it should be executed by another player. Write your parts for cymbals, tenor drums, and scotch bass drums so that all players perform their technique together. For added "flash" tie ribbons of school colors to the beater handles and do all of the playing as high as possible.

"Flash" routines for tenor and Scotch drums. The note above the line indicates the Right stick and the note below the Left stick. Other symbols: D—down stroke, U—up stroke; kinky line—twirl; X—cross over drum and strike opposite head; O—swing arm behind back and strike opposite head.

October 1958

Starting the Beginners' Drum Section

Bill Muehler

One of the major projects at the beginning of school is always the planning and starting of the year's beginners' band.

What do you give the beginning drummers? What books do you use? How do you start them out and how is the drum problem treated in other areas?

Reading and Rudiments

At least for the first few months we should look at drumming as two separate subjects, *rudiments* and *reading*. Most of the beginners' band method books now on the market are trying to do both jobs at the same time. For the students who do not study privately, this method gives a false conception of drumming. For the students who do study privately, this method adds up only to confusion.

First, let us take the student who does not study privately. He goes to band and sees, in part, the following music:

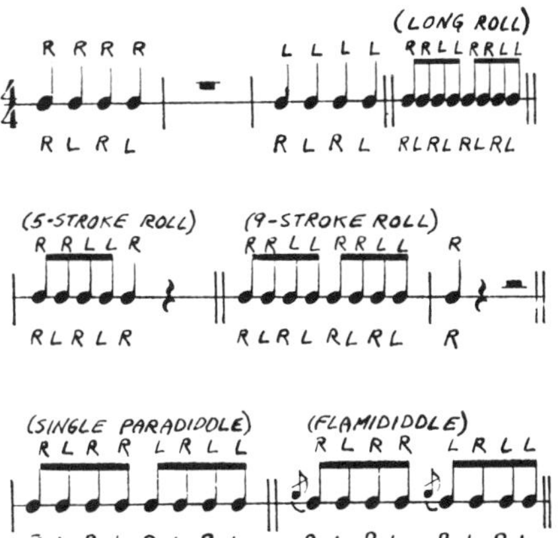

Here he gets the idea that simple rhythmic passages are played in rudimental sticking (indicated above the notes) rather than in alternating sticking (indicated below the notes). He also gets the idea that rudiments are applied to music in this fashion which, of course, is incorrect in both cases.

Don't try to teach a beginner how to play rhythmic patterns with rudimental sticking applied, such as several beginners' books advocate. Most beginners are struggling to read the notes, let alone apply a rudimental sticking at the same time.

The beginner is pushed ahead at such a rapid pace that he is merely exposed to the various rudiments with little time to develop them, which is a job half done. One book introduces flams before the student has ever been taught to bounce a stick.

It is actually humorous to see a beginner's drum part with flams worked in. At this level, single strokes would sound as good as flams; besides, the student cannot yet play good flams, so he is hurting himself, present and future, and isn't helping the band either.

This past summer I taught a summer session of eight weeks' duration, in which 90% of the high school students did not know what a good flam sounded like. In giving the demonstration I played a series of good flams and a series of bad flams. During the discussion period most of the students called good flams bad and bad flams good. Before anyone can develop, he has to know the sound he is striving for.

In many cases the band is composed of some who study privately and who are serious students, and of others who look upon band as a hobby. Whichever the case may be, I think we should stress the importance of doing a good job of what we start out to do.

Now let's take the student who studies privately. He goes to band and plays rudimental sticking as indicated in his method book. Then he takes his private lesson and sees the same thing, in part, in a regular drum method book, and the teacher says, "all rhythm passages are alternated." And there we have a conflicting condition of beginners' band books vs. beginners' lesson books. It goes without saying that the student is getting his rudiments in open and close fashion.

How to Correct Problem

In trying to correct this condition I have suggested, in many areas, starting the beginning drum section in June (at the close of school), thereby giving the drummers three months to develop a proper concept of drumming. It is imperative that the student be taught the basic rudiments first, such as the long roll, 5-stroke roll, 9-stroke roll, flams, flam accents No. 1 and No. 2, open and close.

This can be done either by a private instructor, or if you are not set up with a private program it can be worked in by the band director along with his regular summer program. In the three months the student will get a chance to develop a clean long roll, 5-7-9 stroke rolls and a good flam. Also, he will see that drum music is played in an alternating fashion.

If your program is not set up in such a manner that you can start the beginning drummers ahead of the rest of the band, I would suggest taking the drummers aside and rehearsing them as a separate section. At this rehearsal the emphasis should be placed on alternating all drum parts and assigning each rudiment, open and close. If you are going to use the book you are currently using at band, I would suggest changing the sticking to an alternating method. However, a good book that would be suitable for such a rehearsal would be *Haskell Harr Book No. 1.*

For rudiment assignments I would secure copies of the *26 Drum Rudiments*, which can be obtained from the Ludwig Drum Company. Your students will develop more this way than by letting them struggle along in a beginners' band rehearsal. Most of the conductor scores do not have the drum parts cued in; therefore the director does not know what the drummers are supposed to be doing anyway.

The point I am trying to make is that the *beginner* should start out learning to *read* and to *develop* the rudiments separately. If anyone is going to develop properly he cannot do everything at the same time and do justice to himself, the material, or the organization he belongs to.

Drumming in 6/8 Time

Haskell W. Harr

When playing in the school band the drummer finds a very limited number of time figures and rolls in a 6/8 march. Much discussion is had about the proper sticking to use, and the number of strokes to use in the rolls.

As band directors, we are required to teach our drummers a method of playing what they see on the printed sheet, not something that should be there. We must teach them to start and stop all rolls at exactly the same time other instrumentalists start and stop their notes. If we don't, the professional fault finders judging our bands at contests will mark us down on precision.

When playing in 2/4 time, or "cut time," the sticking and the number of strokes in each roll work out very well rhythmically. Why not apply the same idea to 6/8 marches? In studying 6/8 marches written for fife and drum, I find that in different marches the same roll notations have a varied number of strokes suggested. However, the tempo of the march at the time those numbers were written was much slower that the tempos we use with our school bands today. This will necessitate fewer strokes in the rolls. One thing that was noticeable is that every march started off with the right hand playing the first beat of the measure, which conforms with the marching code of stepping off with the left foot, swinging the right arm.

Sticking Patterns

To establish a sticking pattern for a 6/8 march, and we must have a pattern if we wish our young drummers to play uniformly, I believe the drum rudiment, Flam Accent Number One,

to be the proper rudiment to use for this purpose. It starts the measure with a right hand flam as we step off with the left foot, and it starts the second beat (fourth note) with a left flam as we step with the right foot.

The next rudiment to use would be Flam Accent Number Two. It carries out the same pattern. When forming this rudiment, the second and fifth notes were left out, as was the sticking for those notes.

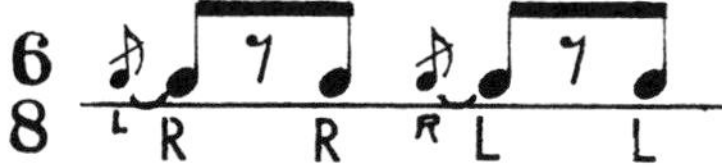

The sticking for Flam Accent Number two should always be played as written. Never alternate the sticks; you loose the swing of the rudiment.

The four main time figures found in 6/8 marches are shown below, with the most practical sticking.

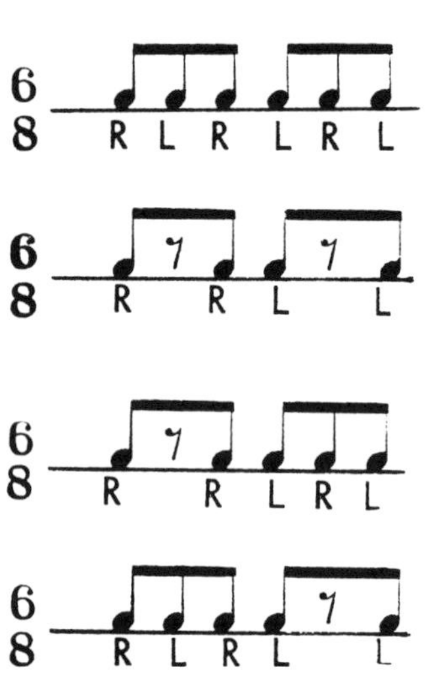

Rolls

Now let's work out a rhythmic pattern for the rolls. The notes designated by most writers to be played as rolls in 6/8 time are the dotted quarter notes, the dotted quarter tied to an eighth, the dotted half note. and the dotted half note tied to an eighth. Three lines thru the stem of a note normally designate 32nd notes. In drum terminology they designate a role, regardless of tempo. Also, in drum terminology, each time the bead of the stick hits the drum is called a stroke. For example, the four 32nd notes contained in an eighth note would be played, stroke-bounce, stroke-bounce, but called four strokes when playing a roll.

In 2/4 time for each beat (two eighth notes) one will play eight 32nd notes. In 6/8 march time, where three eight notes are played for each count, it would require twelve strokes on the same basis. That is extremely fast and would sound like a press or buzz. If you use a 2/4 roll in 6/8 time you are playing two eighth notes per count against three eighth notes, which the band is playing. That throws the drummer out of rhythm with the band.

Sanford A. Moeller states in his book, "When playing a roll you should avoid buzzing," so in order to play a nice clean rhythmic roll, I suggest that we play a stroke and bounce (sixteenth notes) for each eighth note contained in the note to be rolled, with the exception of the last eighth, which should be a single stroke. This will make the roll slightly more open than when playing in 2/4 time, but the drummer will be playing in rhythm. As the student must have a definite method of playing what he sees on the score, let's study the four rolls given above.

Roll Analysis

The dotted quarter note roll, equal to the three eighth notes of the first beat in the measure, should be sticked in rhythm, R-L-R. The first two notes are bounced, the third played with a single stroke. If the same dotted quarter is marked for a roll starting on the second beat (4th, 5th, & 6th eighth notes) it should be sticked L-R-L, conforming with the original sticking pattern on the measure, R-L-R-L-R-L. Of course, when playing rolls in this manner, the accent *must* be on the first beat of the roll, not the last. Count, ONE & ah, TWO & ah; not, one & AH, two & AH. If a drummer has been properly trained he should have no difficulty in starting the rolls with an accent.

An open seven stroke roll fits nicely in rhythm for the dotted quarter note tied to an eighth note. Bounce each of the three eighth notes contained in the dotted quarter and play a single stroke for the fourth eighth. If the roll starts on the second beat, start it with the left stick.

For the dotted half note roll I would suggest the eleven stroke pattern be used. The eleven has six primary strokes, equal to the six eighth notes in the measure. The first five are bounced, the sixth played with a single stroke. It fits perfectly in the rhythm. Rudimentally, the eleven should always start with the left hand, end with the right. In recommending the eleven, which in this case will start with the right hand (the seven comes in the same category), I would again like to refer to Mr. Moeller who says, "If not influenced by anything that precedes, this roll, singly or in succession, would start with the left hand because it is not a hand to hand roll. But let us suppose that the preceding beats have left the right hand free. If he is not able to start the eleven stroke roll with the right hand the drummer is unable to play the roll called for."

The thirteen stroke roll, with its seven primary beats, fits perfectly in the rhythm of the dotted half note tied to an eighth note. Start this roll with the right hand, end it with the right, as the roll starts on the first beat of the measure and ends on the first beat of the next measure. Many drummers form the habit of playing a 2/4 seventeen stroke roll for this measure of 6/8, but the roll does not fit rhythmically because they are playing a duple rhythm against a triple rhythm.

December 1958

Interpreting Rolls

James D. Salmon

The snare drum roll seems to be the most difficult of all the percussion stick techniques that the school music director has to teach, particularly if he is not a percussionist himself. Actually it is not beyond the reach of those who are not percussionists, and the following suggestions and roll charts are presented for the consideration of our fellow teachers "in the field", with the hope that this information will enable them to teach their students a proper application of the various roll patterns to their band and orchestra music.

Too Many Problems

The music educator, who is not a percussionist, frequently falls into a trap by attempting to teach *too much material* to the beginning drummer. The rudiments of drumming, plus other pertinent musical information —in addition to the use of the percussion instruments for the student's first participation in the junior ensemble—is just too large a load for the beginner to handle.

We must always remember that the drummer has but two small wooden sticks to accomplish any and all playing that can be done. It is therefore suggested that emphasis on a careful control of alternate single taps be the first goal before attempts to play complicated sticking patterns are presented as lesson material. This will also be a foundation for the building of our sustained sound which we call *the long roll.*

It might prove helpful to those who are having difficulty along this line if the following suggestions could be included in their own school instrumental music program:

Roll Chart I

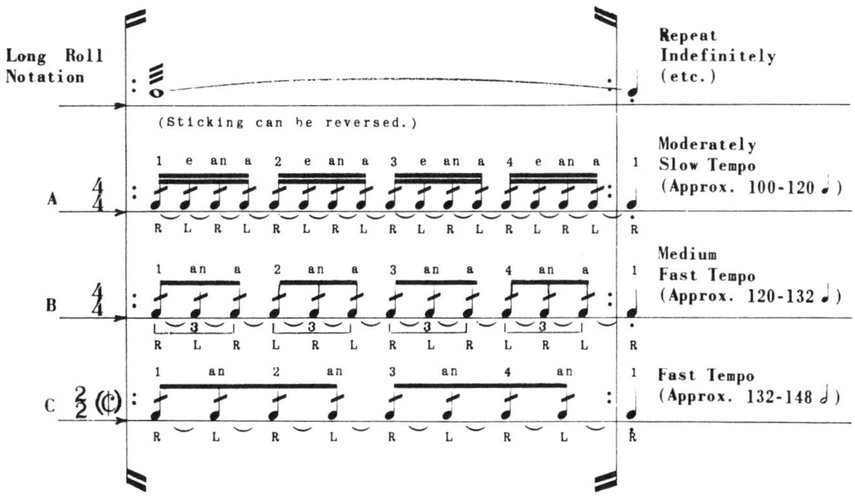

Long Roll Notation — Repeat Indefinitely (etc.)

(Sticking can be reversed.)

A — 1 e an a 2 e an a 3 e an a 4 e an a 1 — R L R L R L R L R L R L R L R L R — Moderately Slow Tempo (Approx. 100-120 ♩)

B — 1 an a 2 an a 3 an a 4 an a 1 — R L R L R L R L R L R L R — Medium Fast Tempo (Approx. 120-132 ♩)

C — 1 an 2 an 3 an 4 an 1 — R L R L R L R L R — Fast Tempo (Approx. 132-148 𝅗𝅥)

Ex. 1a:

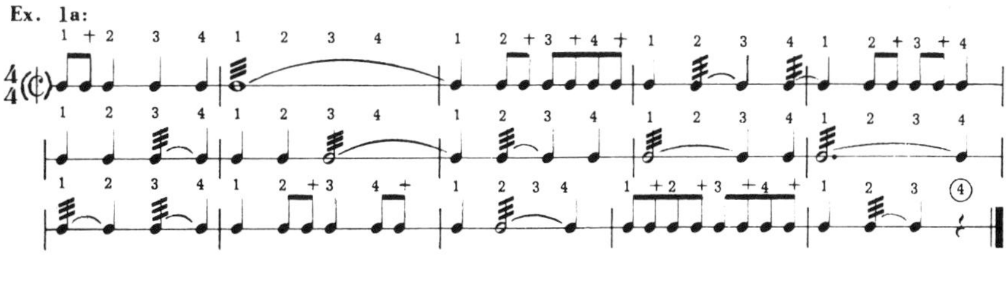

Suggestions

1. All primary work should be played on a regular practice pad, with performance on the drums coming at a later date when the student can play and read simple rhythmic lines.

2. Select drum sticks to fit the size of the young student's hands: 3A or 5B for smaller hands: 2B or 1S for larger hands.

3. More attention should be given to the holding of the drum sticks in each hand: most of the published texts on drumming have adequate pictures to help establish this important part of stick technique in drumming.

4. Develop more wrist action than exaggerated arm action at this time, as it will tend to hold down the student's urge to *pound.*

5. Stay well within single note rhythmic notation for a longer period of time before beginning work with rudiments. Remember, the rudiments are only sticking patterns to standard rhythmic notations, and if the young drummer cannot read and play the single note patterns with alternated stickings he's not likely to get very far.

6. The matched alternated single tap is probably the most difficult stick technique to develop. Without this the snare drum roll cannot be executed properly; imitated, *yes*—properly played, *no*!

7. Try introducing the *long roll* only after sixteenth notes can be played, alternating evenly at approximately a quarter note equal to MM 120 beats per minute. Let each stick get more than a double tap at first, and let them bounce loosely. The double taps will develop much more easily if you don't force them.

8. Basically, a good roll will consist of alternated double taps at the louder dynamic levels: and it will consist of more than these double taps at the softer dynamic levels. Most text books on drumming refer to the former as the *open roll,* and to the latter as the *closed roll.*

Roll Chart I

Check the rhythmic bases in Roll Chart I, at the various speed markings, and then try the exercises that follow, using the roll-base patterns at the speeds indicated above in examples *A*, *B*, and *C*. We find that rolls should be played on a definite count and in a steady tempo. This steadiness can be developed by having the alternation of the drum sticks occur on a given rhythmic pattern. (The sixteenth note roll base is probably the most usable by the average school drummer.)

A rule to remember is: the tempo and the time signature will control the actual number of strokes in the roll. *The drummer actually plays the same type of roll, but will add or subtract strokes only in proportion to the rate of speed of his playing.*

As the tempo increases the number of strokes in any roll will decrease; and as the tempo decreases the number of strokes in any roll will increase. The key to correct phrasing of rolls will be found in the use of a steady counting system with the proper roll base for the particular tempo in which you are playing.

Roll Chart II

If you have trouble adapting rolls to music, try the examples of rolled notation in Roll Chart II using the suggested tempo markings, and you should begin to improve your playing in just a few practice sessions. When you have control of these examples, then these same rules can be applied to the regular band and orchestra music. The general playing technique should improve, and sight reading should be less of a problem for you.

Roll Chart II

Type of Roll	No. of Hand Strokes	2/4 Using the 1/16th note Roll Base	Usual Notation is:
Buzz *	1	① ②	(or)
Drag	2	e an	
5 Stroke	3	1 e an	
7 Stroke	4	1 e an a 2 - - an (or)	(or)
9 Stroke	5	1 e an a 2	
11 Stroke	6	1 e an a 2 e	
13 Stroke	7	1 e an a 2 e an	
15 Stroke	8	1 e an a 2 e an a	
17 Stroke	9	1 e an a 2 e an a	

Ex. 2a: (Type of roll encircled at rolled notation.)

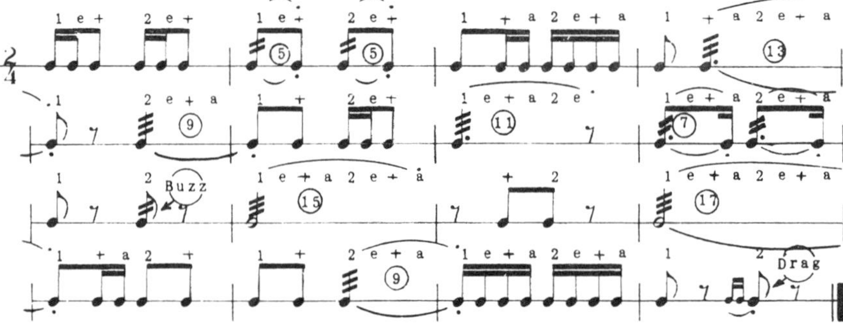

*To get the "Buzz Roll," let both sticks double-tap at the same time.

Rolls in Rhythm

James L. Moore

QUITE A FEW OF the students who come to me with previous rudimental instruction, or in some cases self-taught, have the ability to execute a roll of 9 strokes, 17 strokes, etc.; however, when it comes to applying these rolls to a definite rhythmic notation and to interpreting a page of drum music, they seem quite unable to make maximum use of the "tools of their trade."

As any bandmaster or musician will testify, the rhythmic pulse of the percussion instruments is of utmost importance to the ensemble, whether it be in the concert band or a dance music ensemble. This feeling of rhythmic stability must not be established by the bass drummer alone; it must also be done by a well-executed rhythmic snare drum roll.

Rolling in Rhythm

The most basic factor in determining the use of the proper roll is *tempo*. It is a prerequisite to all rhythmic rolling to develop the following *roll bases*:

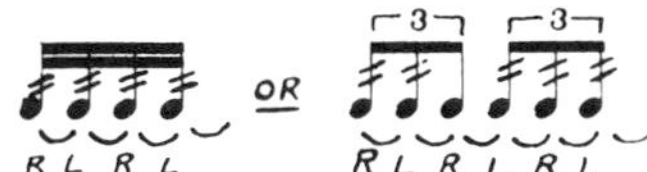

All rolls can be executed basically in some form of groups of three or four pulses per beat. The possible roll bases are numerous; however, all of them are derived from the basic duple or triple pulsation.

Specific roll indications may leave some question in the reader's mind as to how many bounces of the stick are executed per pulse. The rudimental drummer would answer, strictly two per stick; whereas many fine concert band and orchestral percussionists now use a "multiple tap" roll. I believe that the multiple tap is the most musical roll and that its smoothness will blend with an ensemble best; however, with many authorities using both methods, it is sufficient to say that the principle of rolling in rhythm will work well regardless of whether the player uses a strict "Da Da-Ma Ma" roll or whether he strives for multiple bounces.

Stroke Rolls

Now that the student is able to execute the roll bases, let us take the most common meter signature of 2/4 at a standard march tempo of m.m. 120 and apply the rudimental rolls. It should be understood that these be learned at a tempo considerably slower than m.m. 120, which is the "finished product" speed. Also, in the accompanying chart I have commenced all of the rolls on the first beat of the measure, although many of them may start and end on other beats. Also, as will be discussed under Advanced Roll Interpretation, the experienced percussionist often plays some of the rolls slightly different than the exact notation indicates. The ability to execute rolls and to recognize them when they appear in the drum part of a piece of music is basic to understanding the further interpretation of roll figures.

In the accompanying chart, you will notice that the right hand lead system is used. This system is used by the majority of outstanding percussionists in this country, although many European drummers and some American rudimental drummers still commence rolls with the left hand. The angle at which the snare drum is carried or placed, and the need for a definite pattern of sticking are the primary reasons that the R.H. lead is the most effective.

The roll bases in 6/8 march tempo present some choice to the drummer. Following are a few of the most common notations and some possible rolls to use. Again, the exact tempo and the texture of roll desired are factors that the player has to consider in selecting the best roll. These are for 6/8 at a m.m. of 120.

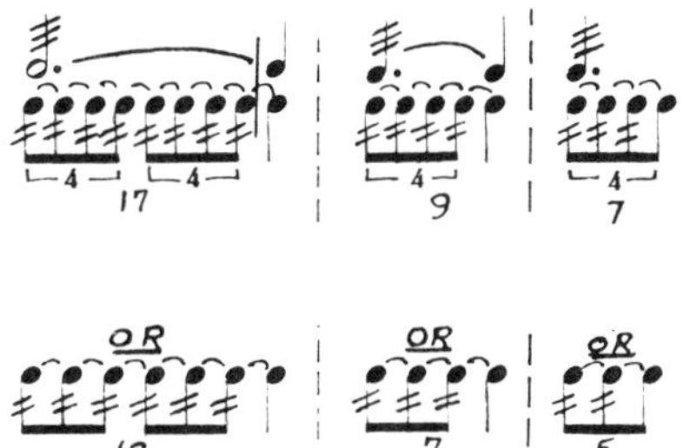

It might be added here that the 6/8 roll, or triplet 2/4 roll, is an excellent roll for field work where a powerful roll of long duration is needed.

The drummer should be able to determine the best roll to use in each piece of music; as shown in the following examples there may be several interpretations of the same written notation. The student should first play thru an entire march or exercise using only the roll base rhythms as shown and then play it adding the bounces to form the rolls.

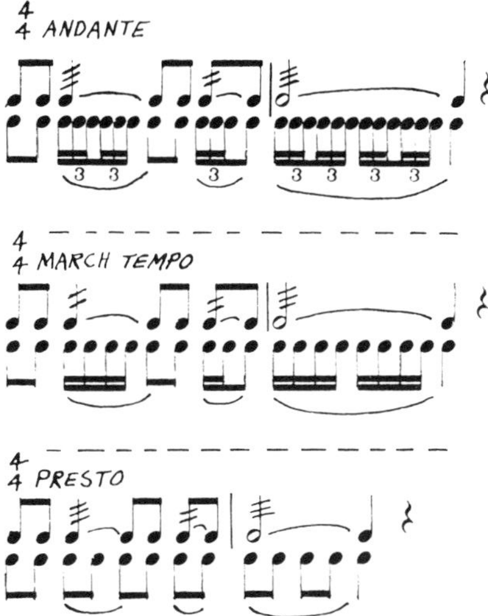

Advanced Roll Interpretation

Due to the fact that many composers and arrangers often are less familiar with percussion writing than that of other instruments, they tend to write figures that require some special attention by the experienced percussionist. Following are a few figures that present some interpretation problems:

The above is the correct notation for a 13-stroke roll; however, often in rudimentary solos a 15-stroke roll is indicated as follows:

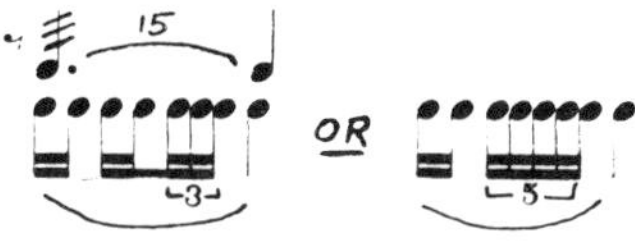

Roll Chart

*If a roll starts and ends with the same hand, it ALTERNATES. If a roll starts with one hand and ends with the opposite hand, it DOES NOT alternate.

In march tempo the following are examples of full beat rolls:

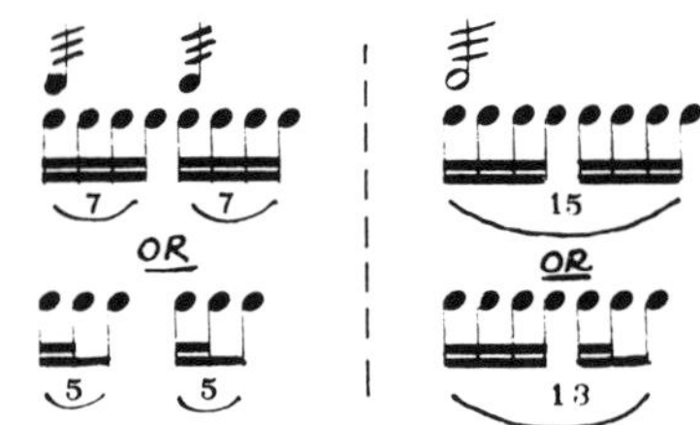

Seven Stroke Roll

Special attention should be given the 7-stroke roll, as it is a very useful and versatile roll and can be played five different ways:

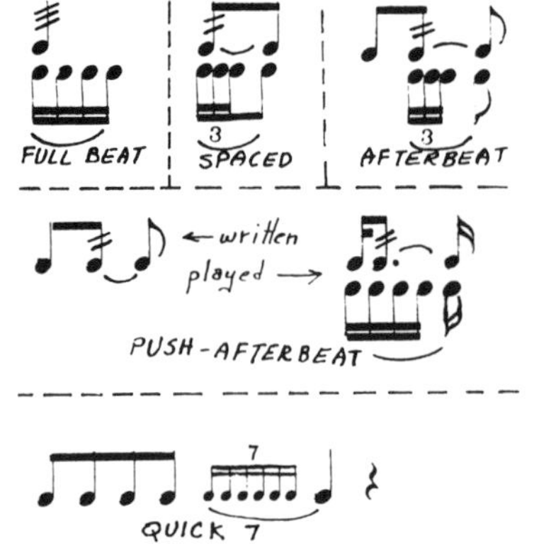

Grace Notes

Grace notes that decorate the beginnings of rolls should usually be omitted on the snare drum parts.

These notes are easily executed on some wind instruments, but are awkward to play on a drum and they tend to cause a lack of precision to the entry of the snare drum part.

In closing, if one general point can be made concerning snare drum rolls, it is this: Regardless of what rudimental number name could be assigned to a roll, the important point is that the roll must be in rhythm with the tempo of the music being played.

Review of Percussion Materials

4 Fundamentals Of Snare Drumming, Grace and Joe Berryman, c/o The Band Shed, Itta Bena, Miss., 75¢, 15 pp. A very good text on the development of the *tap, stroke, crushed stroke,* and the *double tap.* Many good exercises to develop each of the four fundamental strokes in building technique in handling snare drum sticking.

The Snare Drum Roll, Emil Sholle, c/o Brook Pub. Co., 3602 Cedarbrook Rd., Cleveland Hts. 18, Ohio, $1.25, 26 pp. Over 80 exercises of interesting material to help the student develop the snare drum roll.

William Sebastian Hart

The Neglected TRIANGLE

THE TRIANGLE IS THE most neglected of the percussion instruments. Practically every conductor, arranger, and composer imagines that it is the easiest to play and that anyone can play it satisfactorily. Truly, anyone can play it—but not everyone can make satisfactory sounds on it.

Equipment Needed

The triangle is a piece of metal shaped in the form of its geometrical description with one corner open. If this corner were closed, the metal would not produce the particular ring that is expected of it. A triangle holder, i.e., a clamp which attaches to the music stand and which has two holes bored thru a projecting prong, should be secured by the player for good results. A string is placed thru the two holes making a loop. The triangle is placed within this loop and allowed to hang and resound freely. It is suggested that the string which is used be a violin gut "A" string. Only a bit is needed to make the loop.

After a portion of the string is plunged thru the one hole and then thru the other producing a loop, the ends protruding above the clamp are then to be burned with a match flame until they swell up enough to *make their own knot* above each hole. Assuming that the triangle is hanging on the violin gut string (not cloth or ordinary string which prevents true resonance), the open end should be to the left of the player.

The player should have at least three single mallets of different sizes and weights and one pair of matched mallets. The matched mallets can be secured at any hardware store, simply by asking for the largest nails available. For normal playing the musician uses the single mallet of his choice and plays on the right portion of the instrument—near the very top for pianissimo work, toward the middle of the right hand bar for louder work, and directly in the middle for loudest effect.

The *roll* is produced by placing the metal mallet within the triangle and rapidly striking the edges in the top corner. The left hand is above the instrument, meanwhile, resting on the clamp, to be ready to dampen the triangle at appropriate intervals. Much color can be brought out by changing mallets. Mallets may be arrayed in order from thick bits of pipe to the thin strands of a metal hair pin.

Correct Interpretation

These are a few examples of interesting writing for the triangle by various master composers:

1. As an example of triangle writing where no great or unusual effects are required, the player is referred to Tschaikowsky's *Symphony No. 4, Fourth Movement.* Here the player follows the procedure outlined directly above using the left hand to dampen the tone wherever necessary for good effect.

2. In the Third Movement of Dvorak's *New World Symphony*, the triangle part is written in $\frac{3}{4}$ and has a repeated pattern of a double triplet followed by a quarter note. This is to be played as one beat to the bar and the pattern should be played on the bottom prong of the triangle with two matched mallets, one in each hand, so that the rhythm can be well articulated to good effect. Usually this passage is erroneously played by placing one mallet in the upper corner of the instrument and *rolling*—with the hope that the roll will consist of six strokes as the composer has written. This method leaves much to guess work and is typical of the amateur view of playing the triangle.

3. In the *Concerto for Piano and Orchestra* (in E♭) by Franz Liszt, the triangle part is very prominent. Some critics have humorously described it the "Triangle Concerto" since the triangle announces the principal theme of the piano. For this music, a very large triangle should be used because this is an example of solo playing which is unique. Again, two mallets are to be used and the rhythm beaten out on the lower prong *except* where single beat entrances are written. These are to be played on the side prong. Tho the dynamic marking is *piano,* it is to be noted that these passages are to be played with *solo* tone.

4. In *Pantomime* by Lukas Foss, the composer writes that the triangle is to be struck with a cotton stick. A paper napkin may be wound around the regular iron mallet for this effect.

Variety Necessary

Naturally, throughout the entire literature, it is inadvisable to play each piece with the same size triangle. The player should have at least three triangles among his percussion lineup—small, medium, and large. One would not think of playing *Capriccio Espagnol* by Rimsky Korsakoff with the same size triangle as that required for some dainty waltz by Waldteufel.

Finally, the triangle which produces a true musical pitch is a poor instrument. If a true musical note is desired, the composer writes for bells, but when an ambiguous sound is called for, tho with a bell-like quality, the triangle is employed. The sound of the triangle is a *tinkle.* This can be frivolous, thunderous, exciting, melancholy, according to the taste and artistry of the person playing it.

Teaching Basic Rhythm

Planned method solves rhythm problems for beginners

Robert Slider

I WONDER HOW many times a band director has heard this statement: "If you would just sing it for me I can play it." A lot of students don't know how long or how short to make the various notes. Until they hear the rhythm sung or played they are at a loss to know the exact time values of the notes. Although they know how many beats there are in a measure and even how many beats certain notes get, they still cannot easily and quickly place the beats under the proper notes in the measure.

Aims

It is therefore very important for the teacher to find a quick and easy method of teaching the beginning student:

1. Where the beat is in the most difficult of rhythms.
2. To read one beat rhythms as a group.
3. The relationship of foot movement to the rhythmic pattern.
4. To play and understand more interesting rhythmic problems earlier in his playing career.
5. The relationship of one note to another.
6. Why and how the note values in 6/8 time are changed when he plays a 6/8 march.

After using a system designed to accomplish these aims—taken in part from *Teaching the High School Band* by H. A. Vander Cook—I find most beginning students are able to see a rhythmic figure and to know immediately how it is supposed to sound. In some cases with the faster students, I am able to reverse the procedure and they are able to take a form of rhythmic dictation. I sing the rhythm, and the student is able to visualize the rhythmic pattern. In almost all cases the students are able to play more music earlier and to sight read faster.

In using this method the teacher should take up very little of the regular class time. This material should be used every class period and occasionally a period of oral testing is recommended. Total class time in a one-half hour lesson should not exceed 7 minutes.

What and How

The teaching of this material should be done in the following order:

1. The students should learn the relationship of one note to another. The following chart should be placed on the board each day until the student knows it forwards and backwards and can write it without reference to the blackboard. In teaching the relationship of notes, compare the notes to the usual apples, pies, money, or in any other way to get the point across.

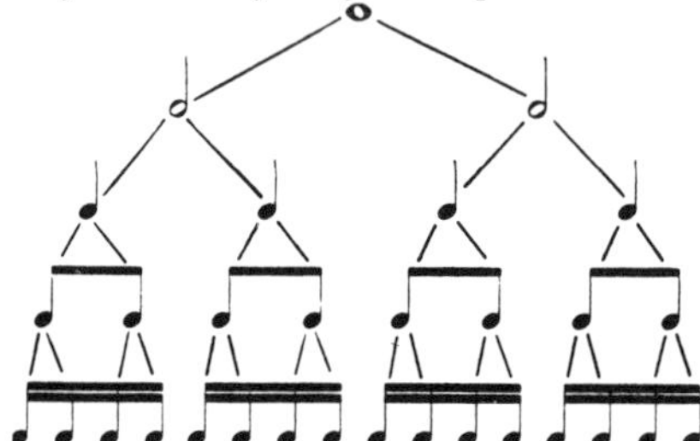

Orally quizzing the individual students by asking how many quarters in a half and how many eights in a quarter is usually a good procedure.

2. Next, the teacher should drill the student on the counts that each of the notes will receive. We should not assume that the student knows that a half note gets two beats. The logical conclusion a student will reach is that a half note gets a half beat, that a whole note gets a whole beat, etc. Therefore, it is very important that the student understands this difference between the name of a note and the value the note actually gets.

𝅝 = 4 beats
𝅗𝅥 = 2 beats
♩ = 1 beat
♪ = 1/2 beat
𝅘𝅥𝅯 = 1/4 beat

3. The teacher should next show the value of the dot in relationship to its preceding note. The student should visualize the dot as the next smaller note tied to the one that preceded it.

𝅝. = 𝅝‿𝅗𝅥 = 6 beats
𝅗𝅥. = 𝅗𝅥‿♩ = 3 beats
♩. = ♩‿♪ = 1-1/2 beats
♪. = ♪‿𝅘𝅥𝅯 = 3/4 beat

4. Then the students themselves should guess all of the combinations of notes that go to make up one beat in 4/4 time. This is a lot of fun for the students as they try to outguess the others. After the one-beat rhythms are well established in everyone's mind then the process of teaching the *sound* starts.

In teaching the sound of the one-beat rhythms the teacher should write the particular rhythm on the board and sing it several times moving the arm up and down thus subdividing the beats. The next step should be for the students to repeat the sound also moving the arm and foot together up and down as the teacher did previously. Next the teacher should ask for solo volunteers until eventually each member of the class has sung all nine rhythms.

5. The explanation of 6/8 time played in two beats is very hard for some students to grasp. Taken separately and explained as a rhythm completely different from what we have had previously the student can start fresh. The teacher should first explain that all 6/8 time is based on the triplet, and two triplets make up a complete measure in that time.

After this has been explained, each one of the common 6/8 rhythms should be simplified. For instance, a dotted half note has how many eight notes in it? The student should answer six. Then the teacher should explain that six eighth notes can be divided into two triplets. Since two triplets get 2 beats, a dotted half note in 6/8 time must also get 2 beats. The same procedure is taken with the dotted quarter note, the quarter and an eighth, etc; until the student realizes that each of these rhythms gets one beat because there is a triplet represented in each.

Many gimmicks can be used to speed up the learning process and make the whole system more enjoyable to the students and to the teacher. If you have not worked on a completely objective and planned procedure for teaching rhythm problems to the beginning student, I suggest you try the above plan as one that has been *tried and works.*

April 1959

Passing Inspection

Betty Masoner

WITH THE PASSING of the winter solstice the days begin to lengthen, and spring is not too far in the offing. Spring is synonymous for the band director with contest and concert time. Now is the time to think about whether or not your drum section will pass inspection, come that important performance.

From attending numerous contests and festivals each year, one is left with the feeling that most band directors use the drum section as a dumping ground for the students who don't make the grade on other instruments. We all know that this is a poor practice, as the drummer must be as much, or perhaps more, of a musician than the other members of the successful ensemble.

The most disheartening aspect of this problem is the number of times the young drummers are found to be "faking," literally playing what they feel like playing when they feel like doing it. This can easily be remedied by checking the drum parts themselves, if a full score is not available.

Proper Equipment

After the part is analyzed, it is important that the proper instruments are made available for the use of the student drummers. It is true that in some cases substitutions must be made, but in an intelligent way, not just on the spur of the moment; and, of course, such things as snare drum sticks on triangles, etc., should not be tolerated.

Speaking of equipment, it is always a good idea to check on your drummers to see that the instruments are in good working order. A little grease on the threads of the rods never hurt a drum and a thorough wash-up job on those autographed heirlooms would put the true character back in the heads of the instruments. Snares should be in good condition, and if they have frayed (wire wound) or bent (coiled wire) they can be replaced for a nominal fee.

Sticks should match the drum in use, and a good solid stand will minimize the cost of drum heads. Also, the angle and height of the drums should be uniform and not too extreme.

Along with the bass drum, a sturdy stand—one that does not "walk"—should be supplied. Also of importance is the supplying of the bass drummer with a good bass drum stick, not one used by his grandparents in the old town band. These things do wear out. In fact, it would not strain the average budget too much to supply the section with several different styles of sticks for use in playing the various types of music. It has even been recommended by some authorities that Scotch sticks be used for playing marches; they add a little extra flash. Speaking of playing marches, did you ever try using field drums on the marches for concert use? It really adds that military solidity to the performance.

Cymbals

Cymbals have always been a sore eye at contest time. I remember a band that had stretched its budget to the breaking point in order to purchase a new set of high quality cymbals. Contest time came, and it played the usual march and overture. The cymbal player stood and held the nice new shiny cymbals throughout both numbers . . . playing only on the final note on the overture.

It is true that cymbal parts are not designated as such in most drum music . . . a policy which is being greatly improved in recent editions. But it is customary in professional bands to play along with the bass drum unless otherwise marked.

It is usually advocated to have a separate cymbal player along with the cymbals attached to the bass drum to add the accents. If two pairs of cymbals are not available, best results with high school students will probably be achieved by using two youngsters, one on bass drum and one on cymbals. But, whatever your decision, do use the cymbals and bass drum simultaneously, especially on marches. You will find that it will cut the tone of the bass drum and make rhythmically precise playing come more easily for the rest of the band.

Traps

In regard to the proper playing of the traps, it is a wise idea to experiment a little and determine just what sound is desired. There are many ways to strike a triangle; there are many sizes of triangle, and there are many weights of beaters. Several tambourines, as well as castanets, and the other traps should be supplied and taken care of. Obviously, ample and desirable storage facilities must be provided.

Each of these instruments should be studied seriously, as a music instrument, and not as a piece of junk to be thrown in a heap on the floor when finished. One should remember that these instruments are to be played at eye level, not behind a chair or on the floor. In regard to the "imitations" which the drummers are called upon to play, they should be semi-concealed.

Latin-American Instruments

The Latin-American rhythm instruments are probably the most abused of the lot. Many times I have witnessed a number in which they are used while a half dozen teen-agers with an equal number of such instruments held a contest to see which one could play the loudest and most "original." These instruments take study just as any other music instrument.

It may be permissible, even advisable on occasion, to add or change the written parts (with copyright O.K.). Some parts are written *ad. lib.*, but they shouldn't be played differently every time the number is done. There are definite beats for these instruments, such as the pace-setting claves beat, and they should be played as the originators of the rhythmical ideas intended them to be played, not some way that the player decides is "easier" or "just as good."

Final Considerations

One of the weaknesses encountered most often with drum sections is their lack of stage deportment. Nowhere have I ever seen a drum instruction book that recommends standing on one foot, chewing gum or sticks, and giggling when a mistake is made. The finale is reached when a player scrambles for a trap and misses the cue.

There are several means of holding the sticks while counting rests and, of course, the players may sit down during lengthy rests, but there should be a uniform pattern for this behavior.

Do you have a drum section that plays at just one dynamic level? Too loud! The drum section should be the backbone of the band as far as reading and interpreting nuances is concerned. Work with your drummers and explain that it is possible to play softly, and that it is often desirable to do so; on the other hand, if they have a sforzando let them play it.

June 1959

Bass Drumming

Vincent B. Mottola

Concert bass drumming has long been a subject of much controversy. Essentially, the bass drum is used to maintain the tempo of the band. The question is, how can this be done musically? First, we must accept the fact that bass drumming is not "a simple task and can be done by mostly anyone." It is an art in itself and requires a person with intelligence and musical ability.

Type of Drum

The bass drum itself has always been a problem to band directors when it comes to choosing the right size and the right type. The size of your band should determine the size of the bass drum used. A band which averages anywhere from 30 to 50 members should use a 14″ x 30″ to 16″ x 36″ double tension bass drum. The intensity of the drum should not be greater than that of the band.

Any group having more than 50 members should use an 18″ x 40″ to 20″ x 40″ double tension bass drum. In any event, avoid using a Scotch bass drum as a concert drum; this type of drum lacks the required tone for concert work. The double tension bass drum is preferred because both drumheads can be tuned separately.

Tuning

There are many theories concerning the tuning of a bass drum, such as tuning the heads in fourths or fifths. And there are some who say, "Why bother to tune a bass drum when you know perfectly well that it has no true pitch?" Granted, there is no specific pitch or "true" pitch that a bass drum can be tuned to, but anyone who has a relatively good ear can come fairly close to an actual pitch when tuning the heads of the drum.

The pitch of the drum should be determined by the particular register in which the band happens to be playing: it should be neither too high nor too low, but such that it will blend with the band and not create an obvious sound, revealing its presence. Like the timpanist, a good bass drummer changes the pitch of his drum throughout a performance.

In controlling the pitch of the drum, the player should place (in the case of the right-handed drummer) his right knee against the side of the head he plays on. The palm of the left hand should be placed against the opposite head so that the pitch can be controlled with various amounts of pressure. The reverse procedure is applied in the case of the left-handed bass drummer. Thru practice, rehearsals, and experience, the drummer will discover the techniques of pitch control by the amount of pressure he applies to the drumheads with his hand and knee.

It isn't always so easy to place one knee against the drumhead and stretch across the drum to place a hand against the opposite head, particularly for the drummer who lacks sufficient height. I suggest you have the drummer stand on a small wooden box, or something comparable, so that he can have complete control over the drum. The drum should be set on a regulation bass drum stand, not on the floor or in a box enclosure as this distorts the tone of the drum.

Only a certain amount of tension can be applied to the large heads of the bass drum; because of this, the drum is subject to drastic changes in pitch, particularly in damp weather. Temperature changes occur frequently, creating much difficulty in maintaining a pitch. Drum companies have been experimenting for the last few years with plastic drumheads that will not be affected by the weather.

The plastic head will produce some difference in sound, but the big difference will be in the way the drummer performs: he will have to make some compensation when applying pressure with his hand and knee. After a few rehearsals, he should be able to cope with these changes.

Bass Drum Beaters

With numerous assortments of bass drum beaters on the market today, band directors often choose the wrong type. I suggest that the bass drummer use two double-end beaters made of lamb or sheep skin. One beater should be slightly heavier than the other for large symphonic works. The lighter beater should be used for marches and other quick tempos.

The double-end beater is preferable because, quite often, the bass drummer is required to play a roll, either as a substitute or reinforcement of the timpani. Whenever possible, the beater should be made to meet the specification of the performer, according to the size of his hand and grip. The importance here is stressed on the balance of the beater so that an even roll can be obtained and controlled.

The idea of having a special beater for each bass drummer may sound ridiculous, but it no more so than a clarinet player choosing a reed to his liking. For the drummer who has a small hand, I recommend the Ludwig No. 319 double-end beater.

The wood of most beaters is covered with a coat of shellac to guard against splitting. Although this is an advantage in most respects, it can also be a hindrance. The shellac creates a condition causing the fingers to blister. To prevent this mishap use adhesive tape on the part of the wood that is used as a grip, or sand down this area with sandpaper. The latter of the two suggestions is preferred.

Technique

Band directors find that it's a difficult task trying to get the attention of the bass drummer who "buries his nose in the music." Have your drummer memorize his music as often as possible. By memorizing his music he can concentrate on the *way* he plays, and he'll have an opportunity to listen to the rest of the band. Listening to the different musical colors and phrase patterns, observing the important factors that surround him, the bass drummer will learn how to make his own instrument blend with the rest of the band.

The bass drummer must know the proper way to strike a drum in order to obtain balance, a steady beat, and "musical taste." In maintaining a steady beat, the head of the drum should be struck in an upward motion—as if "plucking" a harp—drawing the tone from the drum. Tone control is carried on with the use of the hand and knee. The head should be struck on the upper third of the drum. The center is used mainly for specific effects, such as a loud thud, and is struck in a downward or parallel motion.

Don't hesitate to use the terms *legato* or *staccato* to your bass drummer; familiarize him with these terms. Musical terms should be related to the bass drum as they are to brass and woodwind instruments. It is in the soft, legato passages that the heavy beater is used, the reason being that less effort is required in obtaining a big tone because of the weight of the beater. The staccato, or short, quick passages requiring much speed should be performed with the light beater. The lighter the beater, the less effort is used in maintaining speed. You'll be surprised at the great difference in sound when two beaters are used. Your bass drummer will take a new interest in his performance; he'll take pride in his ability to choose the proper beater for particular compositions, adding balance and a suitable blend to your organization.

The *accent* is often abused by the drummer. It should be played in accordance with the intensity which produces this effect. Most bass drummers have a tendency to overplay the accent by striking a hard blow to the center of the drumhead. Instead, the drummer should continue to play on the upper third of the head and apply a little more pressure to his upward stroke, thus creating the accent.

Another abused technique is the roll. An uneven, "muddled" sound is produced when executing the roll at the center of the drumhead. The reason for this is that there is less tension in the center of the drum, causing less bounce of the double-end beater. To produce an even roll, the beater should be directed fairly close to the rim of the drum, where there is more tension, causing the beater to bounce with ease.

Sometimes, timpani sticks are used to create the roll. When this is done the bass drum is tilted enough so that the drummer will have better control. Again, the roll should be executed close to the rim of the drum for a better effect.

Maintenance

Actually, there is very little time and effort in keeping the bass drum in playable condition. The director can save himself a few headaches and his school some money if he pays heed to a few suggestions.

After every rehearsal the rods on the bass drum should be loosened so that all the tension is released from the heads; this prevents the hoops from warping. The bass drum should be taken apart and cleaned at least twice a year. Dust accumulates between the hoops and the heads, causing much difficulty when trying to distribute even tension. Use a damp cloth to remove dust and particles. The rods should be removed and oiled at least four times a year, a caution against rusting. The shell and hoops of the drum should be painted or varnished at least once a year. To keep your drumheads in a "lively" condition, apply a damp cloth to them at least three or four times a year.

No doubt, there is a good deal more that can be said about bass drumming. The important fact is that the bass drummer's position in the band is just as important as that of the solo cornetist.

Significant Percussion Facts

William D. Olive

FIVE HUNDRED percussion questionnaires were sent to a cross-section of high schools throughout the United States as part of my Master's thesis. Over 240 were returned with the following interesting and significant results (not all questions were answered on all questionnaires, thus resulting in different totals):

QUESTION	YES	NO
1. Does your school band equipment now include?		
a. Bass Drum	231	
b. Snare Drum	236	2
c. Cymbals	239	3
d. Timpani	179	33
e. Triangle	224	8
f. Tambourine	208	15
g. Maracas	186	29
h. Castanets	165	43
i. Additional instruments	46	7
2. Do the students own any major drum equipment used in the school?	74	166
3. Would you be interested in a percussion pedagogy class to be available for instrumental music teachers?	179	47
4. Do you have access to a music studio where percussion is taught?	92	145
5. a. Do you teach your school drummers now?	226	13
b. Have you ever taught your school drummers?	167	7
6. Do you refer your percussion students to private teachers?	113	114
7. Does your percussion section get about an equal amount of time or attention as the woodwind and brass?	119	122
8. a. Do you feel the drum part should be a regular part of a conductor's score?	241	2
b. If the drum part were omitted from the conductor's score, have you ever added it?	153	76
9. Does each percussion section member have an opportunity to play both tuned and untuned percussion instruments?	112	123
10. How do you augment your percussion section in marching band?		
No need	99	19
Double reeds	76	8
Pianists	31	7
String bass	22	8
Other	36	2
11. Are any of your regular drum section members able to play a band melody instrument (wind or string) well enough to call it a double?	87	147
12. Are school-owned percussion instruments available to take home?		
Occasionally	103	7
Never	10	16
Weekdays	6	4
Weekends	18	2
Anytime	108	4
Other	5	3
13. Do you use either the same snare drum(s) or bass drum in both marching and concert work?	108	130
14. Do you have or use a trap table (for small drum equipment) in concert band?	104	138
15. a. Can you now do repair emergencies on some percussion equipment?	200	33
b. Can anyone in your drum section do repair emergencies on some percussion equipment now?	141	89
16. About how often do you check your drums to see what condition they are in?		
Once a year	17	
Twice a year	33	
Six times a year	28	
Every month	62	
Every week	63	
More than once a week	20	
17. Does the music firm with which you do business offer drum repairs?	219	20
18. Does your band use these drum accessories?		
Drum key	218	24
Tucking tool	25	125
Internal mufflers	95	77
Cymbal stands	89	83
Practice pads	187	34
19. Are you familiar with any of the following percussion organizations?		
American Drummers Association	31	131
National Association of Rudimental Drummers	115	100
Guild of American Percussionists	7	140
National Association of College Wind and Percussion Instructors	43	124
International Association of Modern Drummers	8	139

20. Rate your present school band sections as a whole as to achievement and capability.

	Excellent	Good	Average	Fair	Poor
a. Woodwind	39	110	74	13	2
b. Brass	42	116	55	16	2
c. Percussion	21	76	90	40	10

21. Which percussion methods or texts are your personal preference (rate: 1-2-3)?

	1	2	3
a. Haskel Harr—M. M. Cole	136	21	7
b. Paul Yoder—Rubank	43	38	18
c. Ed Straight—Frank's Drum Shop	5	7	5
d. Charles Wilcoxon—C. Wilcoxon	4	3	2
e. Fred Weber—Belwin	35	30	15
f. Gerald Prescott—Schmitt	7	10	10
g. Myron Collins—Johnson & Hoffman	3		1
h. Carl Gardner—Carl Fischer	23	14	10
i. Paul Price—Edwin H. Morris	5	5	10

Conclusions

Since these results are based on all kinds of schools from all sections of the country, some with large bands and some with small bands, differences should be expected in some areas. Nevertheless, for comparative purposes the results are significant.

It is unusual that only 31% of the school drummers "own any major drum equipment used in the school." Only 38% of the directors have "access to a music studio where percussion is taught." Evidently, most band directors have to teach everything their drummers need to know.

"The drum part should be a regular part of a conductor's score," according to 99% of the directors surveyed. Also interesting is that 45% of the schools let their drummers take percussion instruments home "anytime." Unfavorable is that 45% of the schools uses the *same* snare and bass drums for both marching and concert work. Also unfavorable is that most directors consider the "achievement" and "capability" as inferior in the percussion section when compared to other sections of the band.

How does your band compare in these and other areas of the survey?

Correct Sticking

LaVerne R. Reimer

IT IS NOT ENOUGH for the drummer to know the correct sticking for a rudiment or for a rhythmic phrase. By reading ahead and preparing in advance for forthcoming accents or rolls, he can take all the guesswork out of his playing.

Sticking

There are several ways of sticking the snare drum, just as there are several ways of bowing a violin. When the various strokes are used in correct combinations, not only will the drummer achieve good sounds, but he will achieve a rudimental style that will look very good.

The Down Stroke starts in high position, elbow bent, stick pointing upward. The stick strikes the drum and is held down (not allowed to bounce up) about ½ inch from the head.

The Up Stroke starts about ½ inch from the head and the stick taps the head and continues up to the high position (a reverse of the down stroke).

The Full Stroke starts in high position, strikes the drum, and returns to the original high position.

The Tap starts and stops about ½ inch above the head.

Alternate Flams

In making hand to hand flams, combine the down stroke and the up stroke for correct sound and good form.

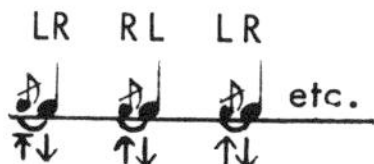

The up stroke of the first flam is then ready for the down stroke of the second flam.

When a flam is followed by a roll, do not use the up stroke, rather a tap.

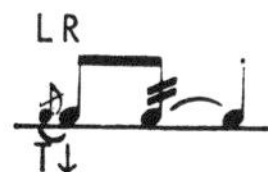

Then you will be in position for the roll.

The same can be said for the last flam in a series of flams preceding a roll.

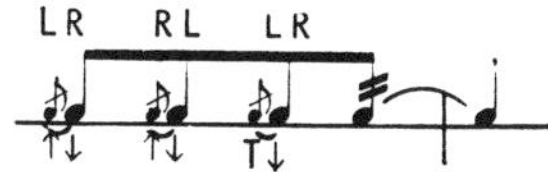

Flam Accents

For *Flam Accent No. 1* use a tap for the grace note, to be in correct position for the second note which

should be a slow up stroke. The third note is a tap which leaves the stick in position for the grace note of the next flam. Notice that you must prepare for strokes in advance, i.e., the second note of Flam Accent No. 1 is an up stroke for the down stroke on the flam (fourth note).

For *Flam Accent No. 2* use the combined up stroke and down stroke flam. This will place the sticks in correct position for each flam.

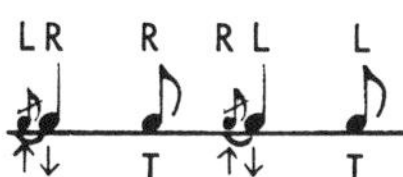

Flamadiddle and Flamacue

The Flamadiddle is played the same as the single paradiddle, with the exception of a grace note placed before the first tap, making it a flam. The grace note is a tap and the main note of the flam is a down stroke. The second note is a slow up stroke, preparing for the flam in the second group. The difficulty of this rudiment lies in the fact that we must play three notes on the same hand. At slow speeds the three taps can be made fairly easily,

but at fast speeds they must be played as controlled bounces.

For the *Flamacue* the grace note of the first flam should be a tap. If it is played as an up stroke, the second accented note will be late. In order to accent the second (tap) note, use a wrist and forearm snap. The third note is then an up stroke, preparing for the final flam.

Drags

For the *Single Drag* play the grace notes with an upstroke, the first note with a tap, and the second or accented note with a down stroke.

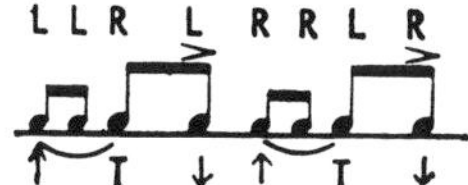

For the *Double Drag* start with both hands low. Play the first set of grace notes low, followed by a tap. Then play the next set of grace notes with an up stroke, preparing for the accented note which should be a down stroke.

Ratamacues

There are two ways of stroking the *Single Ratamacue*, depending on accents and preference. First way: The two grace notes are played with the left hand, the first note with a tap by the right hand, the second note with the up stroke of the left hand, the third

note as a tap, and the fourth note as a down stroke.

Second way: The two grace notes are light taps, the first note is a down

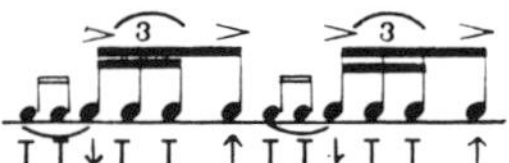

stroke, the next two notes are taps, and the fourth note is an accented up stroke (use wrist snap), preparing for the first note of the next group.

As the speed of the rudiment is increased, the grace note taps become controlled bounces on all drag combinations.

The *Triple Ratamacue* can also be played two ways. First way: Triple the first movement of the single rata-

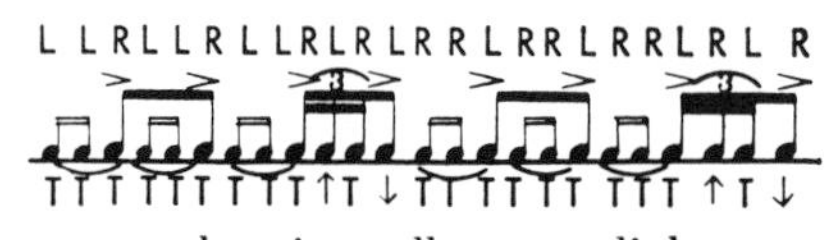

macue, keeping all notes light taps until the second note of the triplet, which should be an up stroke, preparing for the last note which is accented.

Second way: Play the first and second notes as full strokes, the third note as a down stroke, and the last

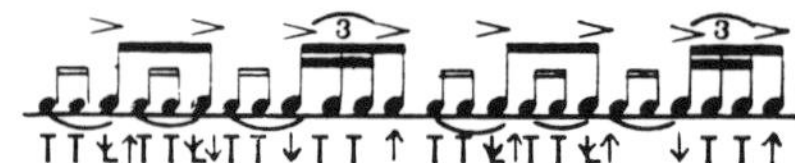

note of the group as an accented up stroke (wrist snap).

December 1959

Temple Blocks; The Gong

William Sebastian Hart

TEMPLE BLOCKS are fascinating instruments of Oriental origin which come in a series of sizes, shapes, and sounds. They are round blocks of resonant wood of a hollowed-out construction with a gaping slit resembling an up-turned mouth. Generally fastened to a rack, side by side, according to size, five of these wood blocks make up the usual set.

When the temple blocks are struck with hard rubber mallets, they produce a "wooden" sound which resembles definite pitch. They also resemble the sound of horse hoofs to many a listener.

Special Effects

Indeed, the temple blocks were employed in a solo capacity in the early 1920's in Fred Grofé's *Grand Canyon Suite* to simulate the tread of a burro. Deems Taylor used them in *Marco Takes a Walk* where he wanted the sound of horse hoofs. Aaron Copland uses two blocks—one high and one low—in *El Salon Mexico.*

The temple blocks are used frequently in symphony orchestra performances today. The wonderful compositions by George Kleinsinger especially for children—*Adventure in the Zoo, Tubby the Tuba, Peewee the Piccolo, Story of Celeste,* and many others—employ diverse percussion instruments. The temple blocks are used here to denote such things as a falling coconut, a closed door, the tick tock of a clock, etc. Leroy Anderson used the blocks for the tick tock effect in *Syncopated Clock.*

Erroneous Assumption

The possibilities of the temple blocks are many. When struck—on their tops—with hard rubber mallets, they produce sounds which blend with many orchestral compositions. The *Violin Concerto* by Paul Hindemith has a percussion part written in the bass clef for "vier Trommeln." I once appeared under the personal direction of Paul Hindemith in a performance of this work. Since the part was written in the bass clef within the range of the kettle drums, the assumption was made that the intention of the composer was for his percussion part to be played on the timpani. However, "vier Trommeln" in this case meant *four temple blocks* of varying pitches; and the performance took place with these instruments playing the intricate part which often was an obligato to the solo violin.

The mistaken notion that this part was to be played on the timpani materialized by having the very same part included in the "orchestral studies section" of a leading timpani instruction book which is on sale in most music stores today.

Many composers are discovering the wide uses which can be made of the temple blocks. Their deep-throated sounds are centuries old to the Oriental peoples who used them originally in their temples of worship, along with other percussion instruments such as gongs and cymbals.

The Gong

The main fact that the performer must remember about the gong is that each instrument must be tested long before it is played in rehearsal or concert. It is to be tested for its best tone spot by striking it with a heavily padded mallet at various points on its surface. The point where the tone is the most resonant is where the instrument should be struck.

Most gongs are set up on an iron hanger or bar and swing freely. The cord which clasps the gong to the hanger should be a gut bass violin string, not an ordinary piece of rope since rope has a tendency to dampen the true ringing sound. If the gong is suspended about three feet from the floor, the player's free hand and knee may be used in dampening the ringing quality when necessary. Various sizes of gongs are to be used throughout the orchestral literature. Generally speaking, however, the deep-toned gong is the one used most frequently.

Use of Mallets

Gong mallets are a great source of varying the tone quality. Various degrees of hardness and softness of the felt ball change the sound. The mallet which consists of a metal core around which yarn is wound produces the best sonority. For special mysterious and weird effects, the gong is sometimes scraped with a metallic object such as a nail or a coin.

When the gong is struck with a mallet, this principle should be made vividly clear: Before the gong is struck it should be set in motion by the player, so that it is already vibrating when the first tone is heard. This can be done by touching the instrument inaudibly several times before the first blow. When the gong is struck without this precaution, it must set itself into vibration with its first blow and the tone is consequently "cold." If the instrument is set into vibration by gentle touching previous to its first entrance, the effect is warm and full-bodied. The roll is produced on the gong by playing the normal timpani roll on the surface of the instrument, with padded sticks.

Notable examples in the orchestral literature of gong solos are: *Symphony No. 6—Movement IV* by Tschaikovsky; *Death and Transfiguration,* Tone Poem by Richard Strauss; Overture *Francesca da Rimini* by Tschaikovsky: and for unusual effects, *Le Sacre du Printemps* by Stravinsky.

1960-1961

163	The Three Camps	LaVerne R. Reimer	January
163	Bass Drum and Its Player	Kenneth C. Krause	February
164	Use of Percussion by Some Great Composers	Lawrence White	March
166	Drummers Can Be Good Neighbors Too!	Fred Begun	April
167	Changing Concepts	Richard Schory	April
169	Quality of Percussion Instruments	Fred D. Hinger	May
171	The Physical Approach to Drumming, Part I	Fred D. Hinger	June
172	The Concert Snare Drum	John P. Noonan	September
173	The Physical Approach to Drumming, Part II	Fred D. Hinger	October
175	Using the Tenor Drum	Kenneth Krause	November
176	Selection and Use of Cymbals	William Sebastian Hart	December
177	13 Fundamental Drum Rudiments	Rex Morgan Longyear	January
179	A Test of Percussion IQ	James L. Moore	February
181	The Physical Approach to Drumming, Part III	Fred D. Hinger	March
182	Improving Snare Drum Instruction	Maxine Lefever	April
183	Bass Drum Celebrity	John M. Crawford	May
184	Same Grip with Both Hands	Jack McKenzie	May
186	The Differences among Xylophone — Marimba — Vibraphone	Vida Chenoweth	June
186	Suggestions for Drummers	Marvin Rosenberg	September
188	Starting Percussion Students on Mallet Instruments	Rex Morgan Longyear	October
190	Discovering Mallet Instruments, Part I	Wallace Barnett	November
191	Discovering Mallet Instruments, Part II Their Use in Concert Band Performance	Wallace Barnett	December

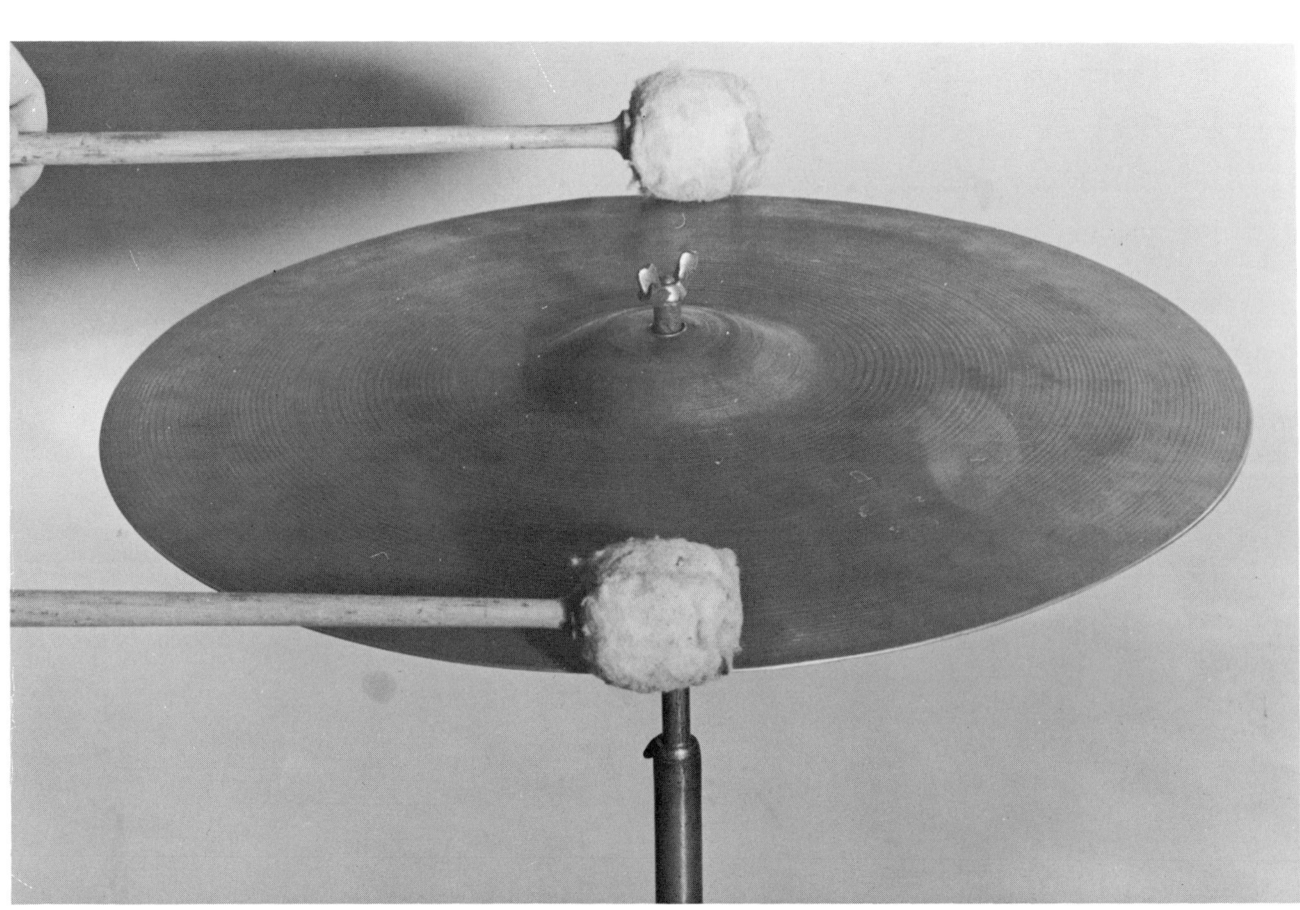

January 1960

The Three Camps

LaVerne R. Reimer

THE DRUM WAS THE PRIMARY instrument for official duty in the Continental Army, and all camp life was ordered by drum beats. Occasionally, fifes were added. The series of calls or beats used was known as "The Camp Duty."

Some of the more familiar beats from The Camp Duty are: The Three Camps, The Slow Scotch, The Quick Scotch, Dawning of the Day, and The Austrian. Of these The Three Camps is the most familiar and popular with today's students.

One of the reasons for this is that The Three Camps is a very fine way to demonstrate ability to play the five, ten, and eleven stroke rolls clearly and distinctly. However, some students when playing The Three Camps perform it as a continuous crush roll and simply accent the principal rhythm.

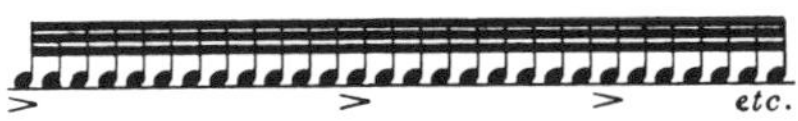

Others play the accents and number of strokes per roll correctly but leave too much space between the accented notes and the roll that follows.

Notation Problems

What the drummers in the camps of the Continental Army learned has been passed down from player to player by rote. Finally efforts were made to notate it. But in checking various drum method books we find different ways of notating The Three Camps. However, in spite of the different notations, the authors all intended the same sound.

In the *Harr* and *Moeller Books* the notation is as follows:

As in the *Gardner Book* (top line—Military Notation; bottom line—Orchestra Notation):

As in the *Ludwig Collection of Drum Solos:*

Practice Suggestions

In order to overcome the continuous roll or the roll with too much space, write out the entire exercise in 12/8 time and make all rolls in triplet rhythm rather than duple rhythm.

First Camp:

Second Camp:

Third Camp:

Think of the roll as a 9-stroke roll with the first note of the next group tacked on.

If your drummers are interested in traditional rudimental drumming, I recommend two records by Frederick Fennell and members of the Eastman Symphonic Wind Ensemble: The Spirit of '76, and Ruffles and Flourishes.

February 1960

Bass Drum and its Player

Kenneth C. Krause

IF YOUR BASS drummer (and/or bass drum) is problematic, the following suggestions might prove helpful. These may not be the most "artistic" suggestions ever offered, but as one who has "had it from both ends," as a professional percussionist and as a high school band director, I can attest to their practicality.

Selecting the Player

The bass drummer need not be a whiz of a snare drummer, but to the extent that he possesses certain characteristics, he will be a good performer. Naturally a "good sense of rhythm," or the ability to keep a steady beat is the most essential quality. This trait is usually found in someone with an even-tempered personality, and who is good natured, not excited easily, but not sluggish. He must be one you could describe as "The Rock." I must admit at this point that I have never "selected" a bass drummer: someone has always appointed himself, and those who did a good job of it seemed to possess all or most of the above traits.

Selecting the Drum

Keep in mind that the *sound* of the bass drum is the most important factor. The size of the drum should not be affected in any way by the size of the organization in which it is to be used (although it may be affected somewhat by the size of the budget). This does not preclude the use of Scotch bass drums for marching. However, it is no more logical to use a smaller bass drum for a smaller band than it is to use a smaller trumpet or clarinet.

I believe that the optimum size for a bass drum lies within certain definite limits (except for special effects). Too large a drum gives a *roar* rather than a *boom* and is very difficult to control with respect to volume and duration. I can remember once when playing bass drum with a concert band, it sometimes became necessary to lean my entire body against one drumhead while another percussionist muffled the opposite head in a similar manner—to keep the drum from imitating thunderstorms. If your bass drummer has to use his knee or body to muffle the drum, trade it in on a smaller one or at least get a pad.

On the other hand, too small a drum sounds *tenor* instead of *bass*, and does not give a satisfactory *boom*. I recommend a size somewhere between 14x30 and 16x36, depending on the amount of money available. Remembering that the bass drum is conspicuous by its size, it is wise to get the best finish you can afford. Pearl finishes last longer and add much to the appearance of your organization.

Sticks

To obtain the full range of tonal effects possible on the bass drum, it is necessary to have at least one lamb's wool beater, one hard felt beater, and a pair of large timpani sticks. The wool and felt beaters may be single-end sticks, as the timpani sticks should be used for rolls. In an emergency, the wool beater and one timpani stick can be used.

Tuning the Drum

The purpose of the bass drum is *not* to produce a definite pitch. It should produce a *boom* of indefinite pitch. To tune the drum properly, first tighten the heads to a medium tension, tight enough to make the heads resilient, but loose enough to produce a boom. The batter head should be somewhat tighter than the opposite one. If the drum produces a definite pitch, loosen *every other lug* on each head.

Training the Player

Since most bass drum parts are not overly complicated, it should not be hard for the bass drummer to memorize his music. This will enable him to watch the conductor faithfully, and I'm sure all directors are aware of this necessity. Of course, one should stress the necessity of a steady beat, and it might be advisable to give the player a pocket metronome to use on the field and occasionally in rehearsals—especially on marches and other numbers where a perfectly steady beat must be maintained.

It is also a requisite of bass drumming that the player understand the inherent sluggishness of the instrument and learn to stay "on top" of the beat. He should anticipate it slightly, in order to keep from dragging the tempo.

Tonal Effects

In striking the drum forget about up-stroke, down-stroke, figure "8," etc.; the main object is to *hit* the drum. After the stick makes contact with the head, you can wave it around any way you want to, and it won't change the tone one bit. I have found that better control is developed by using a straight-in stroke. First, teach the drummer to play straight rhythm, on a beating-spot about half way from the rim to the center. Then have him play thru a march in this manner, playing the accents closer to the center.

For music in dance style, play rhythm in dead center and muffle the opposite head with the left hand or a bass drum muffler.

Many directors think that to play very softly on the bass drum (or timpani) you should use a softer, furrier beater, but actually the contrary is true. The soft beater "muddies" the soft parts, so these parts should be played with the *hard felt* stick in order to be either heard or felt. For a loud, ringing *boom*, use the lamb's wool beater and strike halfway from center to edge. For a *boom* with less ring, tilt the drum and hit nearer center. Since tilting the drum changes its tone quality, it is a good idea to have it mounted so it can be tilted easily.

For a *crack* or *shot* effect, use hard beater and strike dead center. For a *thump*, strike softly with hard stick in center and muffle. For a *roar*, strike hard near the edge with wool beater. To *roll*, use timpani sticks near edge and tilt for ease of playing and for various effects. For a sharp *staccato*, use hard beater or timpani sticks in dead center.

By using different beaters, different beating spots, and tilting to various angles, other effects can be obtained. The best judge of the right effect for a specific instance is the director's ear.

March 1960

Use of Percussion by Some Great Composers

Lawrence White

It is a curious fact that in the opera scores and symphonic works of Richard Wagner there is not a single note scored for the xylophone, which in various forms emerges from great antiquity. The characteristic use of the side drum and tenor drum in the *Rienzi Overture;* the blending of bass piano octaves, deep gongs, and massive chimes in *Parsifal;* the insouciance of the glockenspiel in the *Forest Murmurs* excerpts; the icy glitter of the small bells in the *Rhine Journey*—these examples are classic in the selection of the exact instruments for an exact sound. Their removal or substitution in the score fogs the whole picture.

Richard Strauss further led the way in the use of both xylophone and glockenspiel. The rapid scale passages for xylophone in *Salomé's Dance* serve to filigree the oriental drum's punctuated rhythms. In the *Domestic Symphony* and *Don Quixote* he becomes aware of the lyric sound of the glockenspiel, played softly and legato; the penetrating quality of the sustained bell tones covers the entire orchestra during the few seconds of exposure.

In *Zarathustra* the jangling fortissimo of the steel mallets on the metal bars combined with the high frequencies of the triangle and screeching stridency of the high woodwinds produce a frosty sound in the ear. How differently Strauss uses the bells in *Don Juan* (introduction) where the softly tapped intervals appear as pinpoints of light.

Percussion Instrument Terms

English	French	German	Italian
snare drum	tambour militaire	kleine Trommel	tamburo piccolo
bass drum	caisse (grosse)	grosse Trommel	tamburo grande
wood block	bois-secco	Holztrommel	travolette
triangle	triangle	Triangel	triangolo
cymbals	cymbales	Becken	piatti
tam-tam	—	—	—
tom-tom	—	—	—
tambourine	tambour de Basque	Schellentrommel	tambourino
castanets	—	Holz Klapper	castanetta
sleigh bells	—	Schellen	—
kettledrums	timbales	Pauken	timpani
chimes (large bells)	cloches	Glocken	campagna
orchestra bells	jeux de timbres	Glockenspiel	campanelli
xylophone	—	Holz-harmonica	xilofono
marimba	—	—	—
celesta	—	—	—
vibraphone	—	—	—
vibraharp	—	—	—

This reference chart may be used in studying the percussion parts of the composers referred to in the accompanying article. The spelling of the names of these instruments, in some cases, is not correct, but spellings are given as found on the scores and percussion parts themselves.

Timpani

With the advent of Wagnerian chromaticism, the constantly shifting tonalities are of such a complete nature that the scores require two timpanists with three drums each. It is possible to make the changes in pitch on two pairs of drums but a third large kettle is insurance for the lower tones in an auditorium where there is a minimum of moisture in the air.

There are many passages in the Wagnerian orchestra where the tonality of the music is determined by the spacing of the timpani notes *solo*, and it is often the case that these patterns change with such rapidity that the technique of two players on separate sets of drums is put to a severe test for accuracy and speed in pitch changes.

It must be remembered that all but a minute fraction of pitch changes on timpani are to a key often at complete variance with that in which the orchestra is playing at the time the change is made. This requires in the player a highly developed ear and an ability to keep his place in the score while becoming temporarily oblivious to what is sounding around him.

Other than the kettledrums, the orchestra of Haydn, Mozart, and Schubert offers little in the use of percussion instruments. Beethoven, with his thundering octaves for kettledrums in the *Scherzo* to the *Ninth Symphony*, liberated them in one gigantic leap from the bold 4ths and 5ths of his earlier works; the impact is still unspent in modern scoring. In the last movement of the same symphony he used the large drum, triangle, and cymbals—this being their introduction as a group into the Beethoven orchestra.

Berlioz' statement that it took 70 years of composition to produce a third kettledrum in the orchestra testifies to the long gestation of the medium as we know it today. In the *Roman Carnival* overture he uses a triangle, cymbals fortissimo, and two *tambourini*. The *Symphonie Fantastique* marshalls two pair of timpani, cymbals, bass drum, and snare drum roar, and in the *Witches' Sabbath* a new color emerges, a *tremolando* on the bass drum in contrast to thuds on the kettle heads, with large chimes in the distance.

With Wagner the foundation of modern percussion technique was clearly blocked out; with the exception of the timpani little advance has been made in the originality of scoring percussion instruments—until well after the turn of the 20th century. Rimsky-Korsakoff made no particular innovation in the use of percussion instruments, but he was a pioneer in the preciseness of notation.

Later Composers

There is nothing of a particularly enigmatic nature in Edward Elgar's use of percussion. The lack of subtlety in his use of bass drum, cymbals, triangle, and bells is partly responsible for their charm. He did, however, present the trick of the ponticello effect on the timpani (even tho it is usually accredited to Bax) in *Variations for Orchestra* (variation 13).

Gustav Mahler was, in many ways, as conservative in his use of percussion as was Richard Strauss. In his *Second Symphony*, tho, he introduced the *Ruthe*, a birch rod or broom which is applied to the bass drum head and metal sheet. He had a curious and arresting partiality toward the bass drum; one of his favorite devices to darken the color of his orchestration was to use the bass drum in extended soft rolls and to punctuate musical phrases with soft strokes having no relationship to the rest of the orchestration.

Debussy inherited the same battery of percussion as was used by Strauss, Wagner, and their contemporaries, but he was strongly influenced by the sounds of the Javanese orchestra which he heard in concerts at the Paris Exposition. In *La Mer* he scored for bass drum, triangle, cymbals (clashed, and struck with soft mallets), glockenspiel or celesta, and tam tam. These instruments are used to reinforce the primary undulations of the melodic line.

The genius of Maurice Ravel was so acute that in his search for *la note juste* in percussion sound, he never failed to achieve his mark. His *Bolero* required a composer of great courage and audacity, being a veritable concerto for snare drum in the exhausting repetitions of its primitive two-bar rhythmic phrase.

With Alexander Scriabin it is difficult to reconcile the aesthetic vapors of his music with anything so mundane as the production of tone by hitting an object. Yet in a work such as *Poéme de l'Extase* he employs timpani, bass drum, cymbals, tam tam, triangle, small keyboard bells, large chimes, and celesta.

In Stravinsky's curious and powerful work for chamber orchestra and reader, *The Soldier's Tale,* he presented as far back as 1918 some highly original and extremely fresh viewpoints in scoring for percussion instruments. This daring and original work presents a new idea in the execution of the percussion parts, a single performer! The result is a set of traps and gives the player the feeling of an early Dixieland set-up. There are two snare drums of different sizes (without snares), a larger drum without snares, a drum with snares, a bass drum, cymbals (attached to the bass drum), tambourine, and triangle. Precise instructions are given in *where* and *how* to strike the instruments.

Still, it is in *Le Sacre du Printemps* hat Stravinsky presents his most daring and colorful percussion scoring. Two unusual effects are: a large gong is scraped with a steel triangle stick; a cheese grater is scratched with a steel fork.

Among other composers in the 20th century school whose percussion effects are interesting are Dimitri Shostakovich (very similar to Mahler), Ottorino Respighi (masterful use of percussion completely in keeping with the broad pictures he paints), Charles Loeffler (impeccable taste and superb craftsmanship), Serge Prokofieff (as many as ten percussionists are suggested by the composer for some passages), and George Gershwin (adaptation of dance band percussion technique to the symphony orchestra).

April 1960

Drummers Can Be Good Neighbors Too!

Fred Begun

DURING THE SUMMER of 1959, the 97 members of the National Symphony Orchestra toured 19 Latin American countries covering 17,000 miles in 12 weeks. Under our regular conductor, Howard Mitchell, we played for adult and student audiences, averaging two concerts a day in most of the cities we visited. Besides the standard symphonic repertory the orchestra's programs included a generous proportion of contemporary music by composers from North and South America. I know, because the timpanist gets a good workout in most of these pieces.

While we were on tour I tried to keep a daily diary of our adventures. The following account is based on my notes and jottings in most cases hastily put down late at night or while traveling from one strange new city to the next.

We embarked by air from Washington on May 20th when, before we knew what was happening, we had given our wives that last kiss and found ourselves zooming skyward. Panama was our first stop. It was hot, and our first encounter with a tropical climate really took us by surprise. Before the tour was over we experienced all kinds of weather from tropical to autumn.

Meeting the Climate

Not only the percussion section but each player had fears and worries about how his instrument was going to react to extreme temperature and humidity changes. The percussion instruments came thru pretty well—which is good tribute to the quality of our instruments.

As most musicians know, drumheads do not take kindly to humidity changes. I decided to leave on the four kettledrums the heads that I had been using all season and to bring a set of spare heads. I would like to pay tribute to the American Rawhide Company (Amrawco) for the excellent quality of their product. I did not have to use my spares. We had plastic heads on the snare drums and they likewise came thru unscathed.

Before the tour I had "damp chasers" installed in all four timpani and they really saved the day for me in humid tropical climates. The heat that these clever electric rings throw really dries up the excess moisture in the heads and allows you to get your high notes. Unfortunately, this heat also makes the player 20° warmer on a stage already 95°—but such is life!

We had some amusing experiences with the damp chasers such as almost setting fire to a couple of stages. My talents are largely restricted to the performing aspect of music, meaning that I am a pretty bad mechanic and electrician. "Do it yourself" is not my dish. Our stage technician warned me that we might have trouble in adapting damp chasers to the electric current in some countries. They had converters and some of the better equipped theaters had transformers, but there were times when we were unable to use them because we had burned out our converters in places where we were not really sure of the current. In Asuncion, Paraguay, we hooked up the wires so that the drums could "cook" for a while before the concert. They cooked, all right, and I am very glad I saw the smoke in time. After that we were more careful.

Tour Personnel

Besides myself, the National Symphony's regular percussion section consists of Joseph Leavitt (snare drum and mallets), Frank Sinatra (cymbals), and my assistant and bass drummer, Jesse Kregal. For the tour our orchestra was fortunate in being able to add extra players. Each of the soloists had an assistant. Our section was fortunate to have the services of Ronald Barnett, a talented student from the Eastman School of Music, who was assistant to Joseph Leavitt and extra man in our bigger productions. Jesse Kregal joined the orchestra before the tour.

Having an assistant timpanist is a very good thing, especially on a tour where you can get awfully sick if you're not careful. The funny thing about it is that none of us was ever sick enough to miss a performance, although we had some uncomfortable bouts with "tourista." Even so, one Sunday in Salvador, Brazil, Jesse and I both almost didn't make the concert. Being devotees of the gastronomical arts, we went for a pre-concert luncheon to a French restaurant that had been well recommended to us. The service was *molto adagio*, but the food was superb. We knew we would have to rush back to the hotel to get the bus. Then—bang—all of a sudden, a parade! Not only couldn't we walk; we couldn't breathe. We finally made it back to the hotel, and a kind citizen gave us a ride to the hall. Luckily the parade had thrown everyone else off schedule. From then on we decided that we had better not travel together before a concert so that the chances of one of us making the performance would be better.

Latin American Percussionists

Meeting our Latin colleagues was always a happy, heart-warming experience. The percussion men in every city went overboard to entertain us and make us feel at home. In turn, we gave them some of our good sticks and mallets, and they were overwhelmed. They are so hungry for good instruments to replace their own which, in general, seem to be held together by Scotch tape and chewing gum. We would like to have done so much more for them than we could.

In some cities, I saw interesting antique European timpani that somehow had made their way to Latin America. I did not find any of the Dresden pedal type, but I saw manually-operated master screw types and manual revolving bowl types where the tension is regulated by spinning the bowl in either direction.

One of the things our Latin colleagues would appreciate is drumheads. They simply do not have good ones, and they use them until they fall apart. The average symphony musician that we met has to work a far longer day than we do to make much less of a living than his North American counterpart. On the other hand, in terms of social status Latin American musicians are regarded by the public as very special people and highly respected citizens.

Until the summer of 1958 when the New York Philharmonic made its Latin American tour, it is doubtful that the Latin percussion men had ever heard or seen the likes of Saul Goodman's playing. He evidently made a phenomenal impression on them, since one of the first things they would say to me after hearing the National Symphony play was, "You studied with Goodman!" In the period of a year they had tried to adapt his technique and style. I can think of no better tribute to pay to Saul Goodman than to pass this on. He has lived in their minds and musical imaginations. By his example, percussion playing in Latin America has been given a shot in the arm.

In San José, Costa Rica, I had one of my memorable experiences. The timpanist of the San José Symphony, José Antonio Méndez, was crazy about my "modern technique!" He spoke about as much English as I spoke Spanish, so we had communication problems. After our concert he took me to a small café and insisted on entertaining me. We started singing timpani excerpts from different works to each other; then he tried to show me how he thought I would play it. After a while, he really caught on. He even wanted to give me his wrist watch as a token of friendship. It was this way everywhere. The fellowship of musicians was a living, vivid emotional experience. Our Latin American colleagues are truly wonderful people, and we shall never forget them.

Our Latin percussion colleague is, in general, a talented player. We only wish he could have the economic good fortune of owning better instruments to work with. The percussionists we met made our tour truly memorable by their hospitality and fellowship. Meeting them broadened our outlook on percussion playing also. We were able to see what really first-class results can be obtained with a minimum of technique provided there is that prime requisite: an *X* quantity in creative art, a maximum of heart.

April 1960

Changing Concepts

Richard Schory

DURING THE PAST decade we have enjoyed one of the richest periods of growth and development in the history of instrumental music. One area in particular in the instrumental program which has made exceptional advances is that of *percussion*. Today, percussion instruments are being given ever-increasing importance in our musical organizations.

Marching bands are now featuring large sections of snare drums, tenor drums, scotch bass drums, cymbals, and bell lyras—with special three and four-way parts being employed. On occasion such traps as wood blocks, temple blocks, cow bells, and suspended cymbals are mounted on the snare drum for special effects. Even timpani, chimes, gongs, and all of the Latin percussion instruments are making their appearance on the football fields at half-time.

To the standard school concert band and orchestra percussion sections, we have added such instruments as various sizes and weights of suspended cymbals, tenor drums, various sets of high, medium, and low pitched tom-toms, antique finger cymbals, temple blocks, gongs, bongo drums, conga drums, timbales, and the Latin traps. More and more of the new scores are calling for the use of three and four timpani instead of the standard set of two. The melodic mallet-played instruments, such as xylophone, orchestra bells, vibraphone, and marimba, are being employed more than ever before. There are many new works calling for the use of several sizes of snare drums, and there are also some directors in the band field who advocate the use of two sizes of bass drums for the concert organization.

There are no limits when it comes to instrumentation in the amazing new field of percussion ensembles. Everything from auto brake drums, inverted rice bowls, and even a manifold from a '46 Chevrolet are included with surprisingly good musical results. If it can be struck and can be classified as a percussion instrument, someone, somewhere has scored for it.

In searching for new areas of expression, contemporary composers and arrangers are now just beginning to take advantage of the vast potential of percussion. No longer is percussion relegated to strictly a time keeping or supporting role. Now many of the instruments are being given extensive solo passages of major importance. Entire numbers featuring solo percussion, or the full section, have appeared in recent years. A fine example of the serious approach to writing for percussion is the outstanding work of Clifton Williams, *Concertino for Percussion and Band.*

All Is Not Bright

Despite the great advances that have been made in the percussion field in recent years, these instruments are still the most abused and least understood of all. This can be attributed to several factors, but the primary one is simply a lack of knowledge or outdated teaching theories. The average director was probably never exposed to percussion properly.

The majority of our teacher-training institutions still do not have qualified full or part-time percussion instructors on the faculty. This situation is improving, however, and many of our leading schools of music have added highly qualified percussionists to the teaching staff in the past few years. In many cases where there is a percussion instructor available for private students, the music education department does not take full advantage of his expert experience in training future instrumental teachers.

It is highly recommended, and has proved very successful where employed, that a regular course of percussion lasting a full quarter or semester be required of all music education majors. The regular instrumental methods courses too often devote so much time to the wind and string instruments that there is little or no time left for percussion. When time *is* allowed, instruction is usually provided by one who has little real knowledge of the instruments.

Director's Attitude

Unfortunately there are still too many directors in the field who continue to regard the percussion section as a haven for the "misfits" who cannot quite make it on any other instrument. With the growing demands placed on the percussion section and the increased versatility required of the performer, it is essential that some of the very best students be put in this section.

The attitude on the part of the director toward the percussion section has a lot to do with the results he will achieve. Too often he will look upon the section as something he must tolerate and will do everything he can to keep it "out of the way" of the rest of the band or orchestra. With this approach it is no wonder that the percussion section is the poorest in his organization. An appreciation for the real potential of these instruments and how they can add to, not detract from, the musical performance will aid in improving the entire group.

Outmoded theories and teaching methods should be replaced with an approach to the instruments that best fills the requirements of today's music. No longer can a drummer's education end with the "mastery" of the Standard American Drum Rudiments. The rudiments are important in the early development of the student but are not intended to be the ultimate end in drumming achievement.

A *musical* approach aimed at developing a well-rounded musical personality and technical mastery of the instrument is the desired result. There are too many drummers winning a "first" year after year in our contests who have a fairly good technical command of the instrument but who are very poor readers. It is essential that more time be spent in developing good reading habits and less time learning to play like a machine.

We are just beginning a *new era* in percussion. Much has been done in every phase to improve percussion, and there is much to be done in the future. Before we can progress further in the school field, it is going to be necessary for many of those responsible for training our young percussionists to review their approach to teaching these instruments. Perhaps this review will provide a fresh, new concept of percussion.

Quality of Percussion Instruments

Fred D. Hinger

Ed. Note: This is the first of several articles by Mr. Hinger. Subsequent articles will deal with the physical and the mental approaches to percussion performance.

UNTIL QUITE RECENTLY the *art* of percussion playing was not developed in proportion to that of other instruments. Of course, there have always been outstanding percussionists, but relatively there should have been many more *musical* drummers. In the past, many of the students who did not have enough musicality to play violin, trumpet, etc., were placed in the drum section. Fortunately, some progressive music educators realized the importance of a good drum section and thru their efforts percussion education is finally being given its proper importance.

The objective of percussion performance is "a pleasant musical sound to be derived from a naturally obtrusive instrument." Of course, this is a general statement and—as in other art forms—there are deviations from the general and times when the *obtrusive* sound might be desirable. However, since the *obtrustive* sound is always available, it is the *musical* sound which must be developed. How is a musical sound developed on a percussion instrument? To me the answer is in "playing" the instrument and not "hitting" it.

It is of the utmost importance for the school musician to play as good an instrument as can be procured. If a professional musician cannot play well on inferior equipment, how then can a novice or amateur be expected to produce on inferior equipment? If purchase of top-line drums is prohibitive, one item that is *absolutely necessary* is top-quality heads for the membrane family. Later, under selection, tucking and care of heads, this subject will be discussed further.

Snare Drum

This is one of the most staccato-sounding instruments of the percussion family. The sound of the snare drum should be sharp but vibrant enough to blend with the other instruments of the band or orchestra. This means if the head is too tight, the sound will rise above the band or orchestra; if too loose, the character of the snare drum will be lost.

Gut snares have been the preference of most professionals who play serious music. This type of snare is not as desirable for popular music, so wire snares are used. Although drums with wire snares are easier to play, the gut snare is recommended. This will result in a more proficient technique for the performer.

Snare drum sizes are varied. I prefer one which is 6½ by 14 inches for concert orchestra and band, and 12 by 15 inches for parade. Separate tension drums are desirable.

The heads are of the most importance. The snare head should always be very thin or else the snares will not vibrate properly. The batter head is usually white, or fully stretched, although a used timpani skin can be extremely satisfactory. In fact, many symphony drummers actually prefer the transparent head. The new plastic heads being produced are very good, especially where humidity is excessive. Although I am a "dyed in the wool" naturalist, I am convinced of the worth of plastic snare drum heads.

It is very seldom that there is any need of a music teacher having to tuck a snare drum head since factory tucking is very inexpensive; however, if the occasion arises he should be able to do so. The skin should be soaked until pliable. This usually takes at least twenty minutes. After soaking, the skin should be placed on a flat surface and cut at least 1½ inches larger than the outside of the flesh-hoop. (A novice should try tucking on wooden flesh-hoops *only.*)

Using the handle end of a spoon when a tucker is not available, the head should be shoved under the hoop at opposite sides until the entire head is tucked. The flesh-hoop is then put on the drum shell and the counter hoop screwed lightly down to keep the flesh-hoop from warping and the head from pulling out.

After drying, the heads can be tensioned. Tensioning of the heads must be as even as possible and should be measured accurately with a ruler or any other device that can be contrived. This is done in relation to the counter hoop.

Snare drum sticks can contribute a great deal of assistance to the performer. It is recommended that sticks of sufficient weight be used since this is an important factor in tone production and ease of playing.

The manner in which the drum is held is important because an awkward angle can cause bad habits in technique. If a stand is used, it should be able to be raised to the right playing height and tilt. A field drum on a sling should always be low enough that the arms will be able to perform naturally. The sling should cross the right shoulder.

Bass Drum and Cymbals

The sound of the bass drum is a very important factor in giving a "lift" to the musical beat; therefore, knowing what size to use and what kind of a sound is desired is important. The size can be governed to a certain extent by the size of the organization and the humidity factor. In a dry climate a large diameter is desirable because of the difficulty in keeping a collar (stretch). In humid climates the head stretches, hence a larger collar and the desirability of a smaller diameter head.

Cymbals can be one of the most intriguing instruments of all the percussion family. The variation of color to be obtained by these powerful "plates" is fabulous and it is a wise conductor who is very particular about selecting cymbals and a talented person to play them. Some small cymbals have a bigger and lower sound than larger ones. This is often because a thin cymbal will be lower in pitch than a thick one. Recommended sizes are as follows:

1. Junior High School
   a. 15-inch for smaller players
   b. 16-inch for average players
   c. 17-inch only for the physically strong
2. Senior High School
   a. 16-inch for smaller players
   b. 17-inch for average players
   c. 18-inch for larger players

A suspended cymbal of 16 or 17 inches in diameter is desirable and should be *suspended,* not placed on a post. A "goose neck" can be made by bending a length of pipe and attaching a heavy base to the bottom. Cooperation of the shop teacher is helpful in projects of this sort.

Tam-Tam and Gong

The tam-tam should be of indefinite pitch, and as deep in sound as is possible. There is no ideal size, however, and if it is possible a tam-tam from 28 to 32 inches in diameter is desirable. Although the term "gong" is often used to name the tam-tam, it is not truly the same. Gongs are usually of definite pitch and are not used as extensively as are tam-tams.

Timpani

Timpani are probably the most abused instruments of the percussion family. In order to produce a musical sound it is most necessary to have the best heads available, and today it is possible for any school to procure heads good enough to be used in a symphony orchestra. The selection, tucking, and care of the heads is very important to the tuning and quality of sound produced, therefore, these steps will be outlined.

Selection: In order that a head be of top quality the back bone of the calf should run directly thru the middle, and thickness should be uniform. Large drum heads should be slightly thinner than the smaller ones, the following being recommended for each size drum: .0011-inch thickness for 23 and 25-inch diameters, and .0010-inch thickness for 28 and 30-inch diameters.

If the head is purchased untucked, the diameter should be 4 inches larger than the flesh hoop and 5 inches larger if a great deal of slack is desired. In the dry climates a head should be tucked with some slack in it. This is accomplished by placing a bowl under the head before tucking and not removing it until the entire head is tucked. The skin will dry taut but will stretch again when put on the kettle, wet, and pulled down evenly at all screws.

Care must be taken not to get water too near to the flesh hoop since there is a great amount of pull in this area and there is a danger of the head tearing. Also, if the head is soaked too much at one time and pulled down too quickly, the fibers will stretch and white spots might appear in transparent heads. In humid climates the bowl should not be used in tucking since the dampness keeps the head stretched.

Observation of most school timpani leads to the conclusion that problems encountered in being unable to tune the drums are usually due to the lack of a tuning collar. Use of water will not hurt the heads, and after a new head is on a drum for a few weeks it should set well and not require too much more stretching. (This statement is strictly a generalization because atmospheric conditions can play havoc with a skin.) Each head has a spot which sounds best, and it is only after the head has been pulled down that the beating spot can be found. If the timpani is revolvable to the playing spot, the player is in luck. If the drum is not revolvable, then the head should be loosened and turned.

Lubrication of the head: After trying graphite, vaseline, talcum powder, soap, and paraffin, I find that a product called "door-ease" works best. After applying the door-ease on the head, all the excess should be wiped off or the vibrations might be muffled.

Pedal tuned drums are desirable but cause problems when the mechanism principles are not understood. If the pedal gets out of adjustment it is alway due to change in the head, therefore, if the pedal pushes hard on the high notes, the head should be loosened slightly and if it reaches the high notes too easily, the head should be tightened. The only time the spring screw on the drums should be touched is when the *range* of the drums is to be changed. Ordinarily, the pedals should be adjusted so that the following range can be played: 28-inch drum, from F to D; 25-inch drum, from B♭ to F♯. If hand drums are used, be sure that the heads stay pulled down evenly by instructing the player to turn each handle the same number of revolutions.

Keyboard Instruments

It is desirable to have as complete a family of keyboard instruments as is possible. In order of importance these instruments are: Bells—2½ octaves, Chimes—1½ octaves, Xylophone—3½ octaves, Vibraphone,—3 octaves, and Marimba—4 octaves.

It is necessary for the modern percussionist to recognize that he should become proficient in playing all the percussion instruments; therefore, introduction of any keyboard instruments into the school band or orchestra is very worthwhile.

Mallets and Accessories

The snare drum stick was mentioned previously. Timpani sticks are of two types, commercial and custom-made. If possible, it is advisable to get a professional timpanist to make the type mallet desired.

The commercial keyboard mallets are quite good. The importance of a weighty stick is again mentioned because it gets more tone from the instruments.

The *triangle* is most used of all the accessories. The sound of this "loudest" of all instruments is one of indefinite pitch and high timbre and although triangles are inexpensive, care should be taken in selection. Various size beaters can be fashioned from spikes, darning needles, etc.

A *tambourine* with German-type jingles is most useful since it is sensitive enough for *pianissimos* and heavy and resonant for the *fortes.* The head should be quite tight and if it is not it should be replaced. Replacing is done as follows: An old bass drum or timpani head can be used. Cut it at least an inch larger than the shell of the tambourine. After soaking, the head is placed over the shell and a wire is pulled around it and twisted tightly. The edges of the head are pulled down until the head is taut and fastened down with broad-headed tacks. The tacking is done at opposite sides until the entire head is mounted. After drying, the wire is removed and the excess skin trimmed with a razor or sharp knife.

Castanets can be either mounted on a stick or on a platform. The stick mounted type are more available and quite adequate. Bakelite castanets are acceptable but rosewood is desirable.

The Physical Approach to Drumming

Fred D. Hinger

Ed. Note: This is the second of several articles by Mr. Hinger. "Quality of Percussion Instruments" was his topic last month.

THE PHYSICAL approach as applied to the percussion family can best be described as *playing*, not hitting or beating, the drum. This can be compared to addressing a person as "Hey, you!" instead of by his proper name. The entire conception of drum technique should be built around an artistic core, and by thinking correctly the playing can be artistic.

What Is Correct?

Percussion instruments are naturally obtrusive. In order to overcome this obtrusive sound a method of *placing* the sticks must be devised in order to get the complete head, bar, or cymbal to vibrate. This can best be accomplished by insisting that the student always play *out* of the drum. This idea is certainly not new but is in need of renewing.

The speed with which the player leaves the vibrating body is a determining factor in the degree of sharpness with which the instrument will sound. For a very staccato stroke a quick motion is made. If the drawing motion is slower, a more legato sound is obtained.

The angle at which the instrument is struck will also give various sounds. The glancing blow will produce a smoother sound than one which comes perpendicularly from the instrument. The reason that the glancing blow is smooth is that it is part of a circular motion, the characteristic being continuous.

The circle plays an important part in musical thinking. It is a figure without end and supplies a feeling of movement. This movement is then related to time. Time and motion have always been interesting to study in any form of endeavor, and the application of this principle in drumming is no exception. For example: there is twice as much motion used for 8th notes as for 16th notes, etc. This type of teaching leads to a very smooth and natural style of drumming, the results of which will produce a musical sound.

The Snare Drum

The snare drum should be the first instrument of the percussion family to be studied. This study embodies two schools of thought which only too often are not compatible with each other. However, it is necessary for the student to learn both *rudimental* and *orchestral* techniques since both schools of thought have value and contribute to each other.

The rudimental school of drumming deals with 26 rhythmical figures which coincide with scales, arpeggios, etc., played by melodic instruments. Each rudiment is to be played open so that each stroke, tap, and bounce is distinctly heard. It is a beautiful experience to hear rudiments played correctly.

Orchestral technique is employed in ensemble playing to effect blend. Rudiments are not used ordinarily unless a certain phrasing is desired. It is thru the thorough study of rudimental playing that the orchestra or band player will be able to execute properly.

Physical approach to the snare drum begins with position of the body and arms in relation to the drum and position of the sticks above the drum. It is an accepted fact that it is best to accomplish a point naturally, therefore let this be our guide. Instruction should begin by the student observing the position of his relaxed fingers as they hang by his sides. With but very little change they should remain as observed.

Right hand: Fingers curl naturally around stick with basic hold between thumb and first two fingers. (There are variations for the more advanced students as there are in any field of learning.)

Left hand: Stick held basically in crotch of thumb with first finger over the stick. When stick is in the air it rests on the third finger. Since this is an unnatural position, sometimes difficulty is experienced in teaching it. Two factors, if adhered to, will be of great help—the thumb should always touch the first joint of the first finger and the third finger should assume its natural position. If the third finger is not operated in this fashion it will keep the stick from traveling in a straight line.

The position of both sticks on the drum should form a right angle. This is a rule that should not be broken, even tho it is possible to drum with different degrees of angle. The playing spot on the drum head is usually about half way between the center of the head and the hoop across from the player. The closer to the center, the louder the sound. Rudimental players very often prefer to play in the middle of the head. Orchestral or band technique seldom requires this type of sound.

The most difficult execution on the snare drum is an even roll. There are those who are endowed by nature with an even roll. These are of a small percentage, therefore it is necessary to analyze completely the physical aspects of the roll.

The *rudimental roll* is composed of two beats for each stick. No matter what speed is attained the two beats remain and should always be heard. It is a mistake to add more when the roll is closed. The students should learn the rudimental roll well before progressing to the orchestral roll.

The *orchestral roll* is the type which gives the aural illusion of sustained sound. It is an illusion since the ear cannot hear as fast as the sticks bounce. This roll differs from the rudimental type in that there are more bounces, and the individual beats are not controlled as much. It comes as a surprise to most people that there are seldom more than three bounces in each stick, but this is true. To prove it have a proficient drummer play his roll and tape record it at normal speed, then play it back at half speed. The number of beats can easily be counted. The same results can be obtained by playing across a clean sheet of paper with carbon paper, face up, under it.

Since the roll contains three beats or bounces in each stick, it is necessary to find a way to equalize these bounces. Since the primary beat is the strongest, the remaining two beats are much weaker because they are all bounce. In order to make these two stronger, the sticks can move toward the center after the primary beat hits closer to the edge. This will help even the roll. It is necessary to keep the spaces between the bounces as large as possible. The spaces between, rather than the points themselves, are the important thing.

The speed of the roll depends very much upon the type music being played. For intense sound a fast speed is desired. For average playing a relaxed speed is used. Contrary to a preponderance of opinion, the slowest possible speed should be used for soft playing. Fewer strokes give less intensity, and the player can relax.

The roll, when used in a musical composition, is most often started with a single stick. This is advisable for average players; however, the advanced player should also learn to start with both sticks at once. This will give an added impetus which, in effect, is the same as supplying more gas to a starting automobile.

The next article will deal with the many stroke rolls and various ruffs with examples of application of these rudiments.

September 1960

The Concert Snare Drum

John P. Noonan

During the past few years I have done a considerable amount of experimenting with snare drums of all sizes and types and have reached a few conclusions as to the kind of instrument best suited to concert band and orchestra use. This article is devoted to the concert field, and does not apply to dance band or parade drums.

Drum Sizes

The most common sizes for concert snare drums available today are as follows:

Wood Shell		*Metal Shell*
5″x14″	6½″x15″	5″x14″
5½″x14″	7″x15″	6½″x14″
6½″x14″	8″x15″	
7″x14″		
8″x14″		

The problem today is that in many school bands there are really too many drummers for the size of the band. But usually that can't be helped. The situation occurs in other sections as well, for instance, too many cornets, and usually the director has to live with the situation and do the best he can.

Looking first at the drum sizes of the wood shell drums listed, you will note there are 5″ x 14″ and 5½″ x 14″ sizes, 6½″ x 14″ and 7″ x 14″ sizes, and 6½″ x 15″ and 7″ x 15″ sizes. Why the ½″ difference? Well, there isn't any real reason for it, just one of those things. Thus in the 14″ and 15″ drums, let's narrow down the field to the following:

Wood Shell	*Metal Shell*
5″ x 14″	5″ x 14″
6½″ x 14″	6½″ x 14″
8″ x 14″	
7″ x 15″	

For concert band, symphony orchestra, and school orchestra, the most logical size is the 6½″ x 14″ drum. This drum is ideal for any concert use. It has adequate volume, is crisp sounding, and is a fine size. If there are only two snare drums in the band, some like a 7″ x 15″. The extra inch of head surface will produce more volume. Obviously a 6½″ x 15″ will do the same, but I have found little to be desired in the 8″ x 15″ size. This size drum is to me hard to adjust, too noisy, and requires very careful matching of heads.

The 5″ x 14″ is a fine little drum also. With a good 5″ x 14″ drum, a drummer can do almost any job well. It is good for orchestra, and will also work in band. It is the ideal size when your instrumentation is "drum-heavy."

The 8″ x 14″ size listed is good where there are one or two drummers and they happen to like the size. Actually, I can't see much reason for it. So now we have only the 5″ x 14″, the 6½″ x 14″, and the 7″ x 15″ sizes, which will handle almost any drum job.

Wood or Metal Shell?

Until the 1930's metal shell drums were widely used by most professional drummers. When pearl finishes became popular, the metal shell died out, but is now making a strong comeback. Many people well versed in acoustics have told me that whether a shell is made of wood or metal is of little consequence, so long as the shell is properly made, and will hold its "round."

With this I do not agree. I feel there is considerable difference between the two. A good wood shell snare drum is thoroughly satisfactory, but to me does not compare with a good metal shell snare drum. A 6½″ x 14″ well-made metal shell of the right gauge of brass is in my opinion the best size and type of snare drum for concert use. I have tried drums with aluminum, copper, and brass shells, and the brass seems superior. (The brass shell is usually nickel or chrome plated, but is made of brass, and not of steel, as many people believe). Such a drum speaks quickly, is very crisp, and covers the dynamic range wonderfully well. The 5″ x 14″ metal shell is also excellent. Drum makers are again offering these drums, and they really are fine.

Heads and Snares

Heads used today are made from calfskin or plastic. The new type of plastic heads have been on the market several years now, and calfskin as we all know, has been used for many years.

In my opinion, nothing serves as well as a good calfskin drum head. On the concert snare drum a medium batter head and a medium thin snare head are ideal for snare drum use. With heads of this type, minute adjustment of tension can be had, the drum responds at the edge of the shell, it has great power under *fortes* and, most of all, it has good projection.

Plastic heads have several good points, the most important being that weather does not affect them much. They play "hard" to me, but some who use them say this is an adjustment to be made by the player.

I have tried all types of plastic heads, and also combinations of calfskin and plastic. Of these combinations, I find a calfskin batter head and a plastic snare head to be best. The best results I have found with plastic heads is when they are used on a good metal shell snare drum.

Snares

The snares available today are coiled wire, silk wire wound, and gut. For many years gut snares were used by most drummers for professional use; a few used silk wire wound, and very few used coiled wire. During the 1930's coiled wire started to become popular, and I would guess is used today on 90% of all snare drums made.

Gut snares produce a good solid drum tone, but are difficult to keep in adjustment, and "play" quite differently than wire. To handle gut snares a drummer must have a "clean" technique. Also, the gut should be of good quality, thin gauge, stretched, and shellacked. When gut is used a parallel snare strainer is almost a "must." This is a strainer that throws off at both ends of the shell, keeping the snares under tension whether the snares are on or off. The snares do not bend over the shell, and further individual adjustment of each snare strand is possible. Such a parallel strainer is desirable on all drums, but especially necessary for gut snares. Gut snares produce a different sound, and one must now become accustomed to this sound. I would recommend gut snares only in those cases where not more than two snare drummers are used, and when both are excellent players.

Silk wire wound snares are seldom used today for concert snare drums. They are satisfactory, and some like them; the majority, however, do not.

Coiled wire, as stated before, is now the most widely used of the snares. Coiled wire requires little attention, and on a good drum produces a crisp and very responsive tone.

The number of strands of wire varies from 10 (in the case of the parallel strainer drum) thru 12, 16, 18, and 20 strands. For the concert snare drum the 10, 12, and 16 strand seem best to me. The 18 and 20 strand, while good for the dance band, are too "snarey" for concert.

Summary

It would seem, then, that the best snare drum for concert use would be a 6½″ x 14″ metal snare drum with the parallel strainer and coiled wire snares. Next would be the regular strainer metal drum, and then a good wood shell drum.

Where four or more snare drums are used, the 5″ x 14″ metal (or wood) drum would be indicated, and for large concert groups, the 7″ x 15″ wood drum (not made in metal). Heads in all cases, matched calfskin, tho I am quite sure not all drummers will agree.

October 1960

The Physical Approach to Drumming

Fred D. Hinger

Part II

Ed Note: This is the third in a series of articles by Mr. Hinger. "Quality of Percussion Instruments" appeared in the May issue and Part I of "The Physical Approach to Drumming" was printed in the June issue.

THE PURPOSE of the various measured stroke rolls is to supply sounds of short duration. There have been those who would have students circumvent the rudimental type rolls. I disagree with this method of teaching since the rudiments are the girders of orchestral execution. It is perfectly permissible to try to get a student to play more than two beats in each stick, in order to fill out the short rolls, even at the same time as the rudimental rolls are developing. This is done so that the player may participate in the orchestra or band; however, if it is too complicated for the player to work on both the orchestral rolls and rudimental rolls at the same time, then the rudimental roll should take precedence.

Ruff

The number of strokes in the short rolls is usually an odd number; therefore, the smallest number to be used is three. This sound is so short that it is given the name *Ruff*. It should "sound" just as it is "said" and should be played rudimentally, from hand to hand, LLR RRL, etc. It is sometimes desirable to play a series LLR LLR LLR, etc., in order to keep the pulse constant. Dragging or pressing the stick that plays the "diddle" (doubling) creates an undesirable sound making it necessary for the student to understand once again that it is not the points of measurement that are important, rather the spaces between. Each space should be exactly the same.

The position of the hands when playing the ruff is one hand high, the other low. It is important that both hands start playing at the same time, although the low hand will hit first. After the low hand has played the diddles it is snapped up and the former high hand stays down close to the drum. A danger here is letting the high hand play into the drum. Even when the stroke is a down stroke the stick should be "placed." Another sticking for this type of ruff is RLR LRL, etc., but is not used to a great extent. Its use is advisable when an accent is placed on the first grace note.

The application of the ruff can occur as "beautifully rough" as used in rudimental solos or as the "delicately crisp" grace notes of the French School of Debussy, Ravel, etc.

Determination of when the grace notes should precede the beat or be played on it is sometimes indicated by the grace notes being placed before or after the bar line. However, most often it is left to the discretion of the conductor or the player.

Four Stroke Ruff

It is necessary to include the four stroke ruff in this discussion because it is sometimes used as a roll. There is some controversy as to whether a crushed ruff should be played by both sticks at the same time or by using a four stroke ruff, LRLR, completely bounced in one motion of the arms. The latter system gives a more definite beginning and ending.

Other type four stroke ruffs are executed so that the figure is clean and the spaces between are wide. For pianissimo playing, a desirable method of sticking is RLLR. The reason for more clarity with this method is that the doubling takes more energy to execute, therefore the leading sound (second L in RLLR) is amplified.

When the four stroke ruff is played with the accent on the grace notes, a natural strength is exhibited if the figure is played RLRL (accenting first R) by those who are right handed and LRLR (accenting first L) by others.

Rolls of Longer Duration

Each of the following stroke rolls are related by the fact that each is played in the same amount of time as the other. Variance is not in time but in the number of strokes used.

1. Five = Seven (in time)
2. Nine = Eleven (in time)
3. Thirteen = Fifteen (in time)

Upon examination of one example we find that the primary beats in a five stroke roll equal 3, RR LL R; and in a seven stroke roll the primary beats equal 4, LL RR LL R. It is concluded, therefore, that the pulse of the five stroke roll is duple and that of the seven, triple.

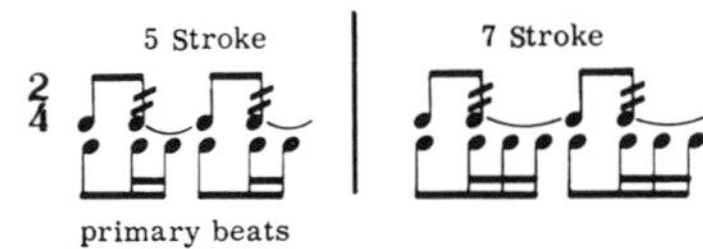

For each of the rolls the primary beats are alternated.

Observe that the final primary beat in the 5 is on the right hand one time and on the left hand the next. This is not so with the 7. It usually begins on the left, ends on the right, then repeats the pattern. If the weight is desired at the beginning of the 7, the sticking can be reversed — RRLLRRL RRLLRRL. This rule can be applied to orchestral technique where the tempo demands a series of 5 stroke rolls RRLLR RRLLR. The pulse is then kept in one hand.

The above formula is applicable to all the other stroke rolls.

An extremely useful short roll is the flam 5 stroke roll. This starts and ends with single beats, thereby giving it a decisive sound LRRLLR. The spaces between the notes here again should all be equal.

Rudiments Applied to Orchestral Playing

It is not my purpose to name and describe each rudiment. They can be learned from many fine instruction books. There are many instances where rudiments are used partially just as a melodic instrument might use a partial scale. If the pattern to be played is in ensemble with other instruments then often it can be played hand to hand to give it a moving "lilt."

It is important to note that the stroke before a doubling in almost any rudiment is snapped upward to a height approximately twice as high as each stroke of the doubling. This is to get the preceding single stroke out of the way of the doubling and also to follow the pattern of the relationship between time and motion.

Examples:

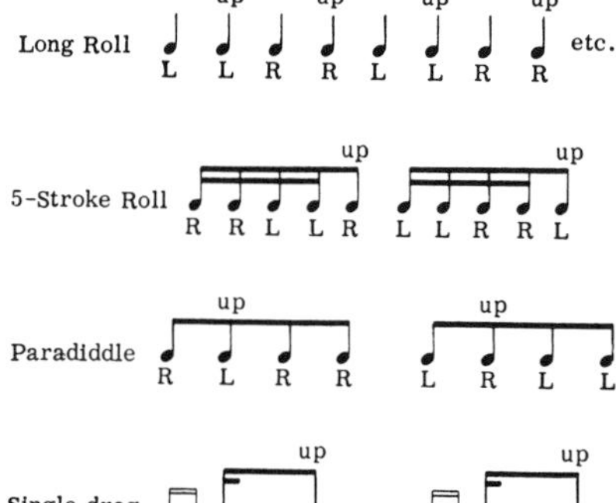

Exceptions to this rule occur when doublings are played in the same hand. Examples:

Double Ratamacue

up up

LL R LL R L R L RR L RR L R L R

Double Drag

Not only can rudiments apply to snare drum but also to the mallet instruments and timpani. Here, they are used many times as doublings to facilitate stickings (usually to eliminate cross sticking). The timpani part in the first movement of the Beethoven *Seventh Symphony* is a fine example of the pattern of double drags, eliminating the ruffs:

When quadruplets moving from one kettle to the other are notated, paradiddles are in order. It is a more modern belief that cross-sticking should be kept at a minimum. One striking exception is a figure illustrated in the final movement of Berlioz' *Symphonie Fantastique*:

This can be doubled RRL RRL but is not as effective.

One of the finest instruction books published is one written by Sanford Moeller. It contains a system of sticking that can be followed with confidence.

Bass Drum Sound and Technique

The school music director realizes the importance of a good bass drummer. This is evidenced often by the assignment of violinists to that post in the band. It is not enough that the player be able to "keep time." As much thought should be given to tone production from the bass drum as from any other instrument. The heads should be on the loose side so that an indeterminate pitch is ever present. The sound should be blended into and underneath the total picture. This can be best achieved by using a heavy soft felt or lambs' wool beater and striking the drum about 6 inches off center. The striking spot is not always the same for all effects. The closer the drum is struck toward the center, the more pronounced the beat will sound. The tighter the stick is held, the more staccato the sound will be. When the roll is indicated, it is executed closer to the rim.

Since the bass drum is very important to the integration of the musical whole, it should be mandatory that the player be very musical, capable of rhythmic astuteness and colorful shadings.

November 1960

Using the Tenor Drum

Kenneth Krause

The tenor drum is probably the most misused (or perhaps *unused*) instrument in the percussion section. In its early days it served mainly as a prop to give the player an excuse to twirl the sticks, which added to the appearance of the organization but contributed little to the sound.

The tenor drummer played a "simplified" bass drum part (if there is such a thing), usually only one note per measure, and spent the rest of his time twirling the sticks and smiling. Today, however, the tenor drum is coming into its own. New things have been added, such as the lateral holder that puts the drum in a position similar to the bass drum, enabling the player to play on both heads. And harder sticks make faster passages more distinct.

The drum and bugle corps are developing more and more intricate tenor drum parts, proving that these drums can be used with imagination, depending on the skill of the players. My purpose here is to survey the possible ways of using the tenor drum in the marching drum section.

Examples

Assuming a usual marching drum section consisting of snare drums, tenor drums, bass drum(s) and cymbals, several ways of utilizing the tenor drums come to mind. The tenor drum, by definition, is a "voice" between the snare (soprano) and bass drum, and it can be related to either or it can be independent of both.

Since the tenor drum is a voice between the snare and bass, the most obvious use would be to play a simplified snare drum part (or an embellished bass drum part, if you wish), using the tenor to reinforce the accents in the snare part.

Another use of the tenor is to echo the snare drum part. The echo may be carried thru from snare to tenor to bass or the reverse, or you may play two-against-one, using snare and tenor echoed by the bass, and so on. This is assuming that you use scotch bass drums.

A newer conception of the drum section would be to consider the snare drums, tenor drums, scotch bass drums, and cymbals as four tonal planes across which rhythms can be produced much in the same manner as the dance drummer utililizing his complete set. With this conception, plus a co-ordinated system of notation, many more possibilities are opened up for consideration, such as the following:

Independent but related parts: Exploiting each tone individually.

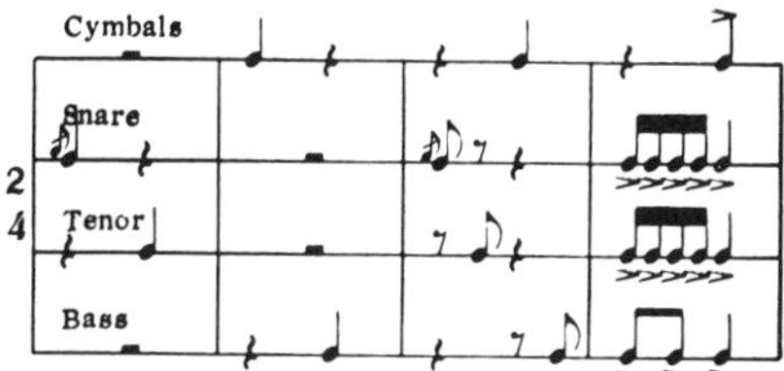

Imitation: Similar to echo but carried thru to all parts, or re-echoed.

Cross Rhythms: This necessitates the use of a system of co-ordinated notation in order to increase the ease of reading.

Polyrhythms: While this example may be a little far-fetched, it will nevertheless suggest some additional possibilities.

The imaginative director can use these short examples as a starting point for creating a great variety of cadences for use on parade, as interludes on the football field, or as feature numbers for percussion. If you want to go to extremes, you may be inspired by this last example to let the percussion section imitate the tunes played by the band. Take *Old MacDonald,* for instance.

December 1960

Selection and Use of Cymbals

William Sebastian Hart

Cymbals are ancient instruments. They are mentioned in the Bible, and their sounds have punctuated the victories of many early armies. The art of cymbal making comes from the tempering and beating out of the metal into the desired shape, the fashioning of the finished product to produce the desired quality of tone. Cymbals that are struck together, known as *crash cymbals,* form a major facet of the percussion section in any band or orchestra.

Cymbals should be chosen in pairs, judging the pairs by their diameter, weight, consistency, tone, and ringing quality, when each is struck alone. In a matched pair of cymbals, one disk should have a slightly lower ring than the other, so that when struck well, a diffused crashing quality results.

Playing Cymbals

As cymbal *manufacture* is an art, so too the *playing* of the cymbals is an art. Rarely is there to be found any mention in the percussion part as to what type cymbals are to be used. The diameter and weight of the metal disks to be struck are left to the discretion of the conductor or the player. The player who uses the same cymbals to play the *Ride of the Valkyries* by Wagner as he would to play *Festivals* by Debussy shows the application of an amateur. The cymbals must satisfy the character of the music. The same cymbals should *not* be used to play every piece in the repertoire. It would be desirable for the percussionist to have at least three pairs of cymbals at his disposal: light, medium, and heavy in weight. These, of course, would have diameters ranging from small, large, to largest. The percussion *artist* has cymbals of various kinds, producing shadings and colorings that are a delight to the conductor.

Crash cymbals often come from the factory with wooden handles held snugly by a metal bolt attachment. These are delivered to our high schools and are used in that manner by the students. When a pair of cymbals is struck together, great force is exacted on the edges and on the area near the handles. If wooden handles are used, the area near the bolt attachment is subjected to such force as to have a tendency to crack the disks. However, if *leather* handles are inserted in the cymbals, the force of the blow is diffused thru the instruments allowing the entire disk to vibrate freely and produce a better sound, not choked or deadened.

The best effect can be secured when cymbals are struck together by keeping one cymbal relatively stationary, while the other cymbal is the active participant. Both hands do not collide into one another—for good effect. After the blow has been struck, the two cymbals should then be waved gracefully in the air to allow the waves of sound to project effectively. A dramatic coloration to the concert is materialized when the cymbals player performs his task tastefully.

Many cymbal parts concern themselves with single isolated beats allowing plenty of time for the player to get ready and to enter. The following are technical examples that require skill:

1. *Roumanian Rhapsody No. 1* by Georges Enesco. Here the cymbals are required to play a quick rhythmic fortissimo. Crash cymbals are to be used.

2. *Carnival Overture* by Antonin Dvorak. In the beginning of this piece large crash cymbals are to be used and played in the normal manner. However, toward the end of the opening fast movement, there occurs a passage for high strings and cymbals "soli." The dynamic indication is *piano—diminuendo.*

3. *Academic Festival Overture* by Johannes Brahms. The first measures of this composition require the cymbals to be played *pianissimo.* Small cymbals should be used and struck gently, with their edges touching slightly. The passage is slow, accompanying the strings in the low register. Later, the largest cymbals should be used in the glorious finale.

Suspended Cymbals

Rarely does the composer write the cymbals part with directions as to *how* the notes are to be played. A suspended cymbal is often required. The suspended cymbal is one that hangs from a strap or holder. In modern orchestras, the cymbal is to be found resting on a rubber holder made for this purpose. This rubber-topped cup is attached to a long metal bar that rests on the floor. A suspended cymbal may be struck with a wooden stick, such as a timpani stick, to produce an entirely different sound. When the cymbal is struck with a wooden stick the attack should be made on its very edge with a glancing blow. Other interesting effects may be obtained by touching the cymbal with the tip of the snare drum stick near the cymbal's cup or center. A snare drum roll played on the cymbal's cup is an entirely different effect from a roll played by striking near the edge of the surface with timpani sticks (one beat in each hand).

Generally, the cymbal roll is produced on the suspended cymbal by using the hardest core felt timpani sticks and playing the ordinary timpani roll on the surface of the cymbal. It is advisable that the hands be placed apart on the surface of the cymbal so that one ball of the mallet will balance the ball of the other mallet and, when a roll is executed, the instrument will remain relatively stationary. If the balls of the mallets are placed together on one point on the surface of the cymbal and a roll is played, the cymbal will tend to dip out and away from the player's hands—and in some cases, actually fall off the stand. By balancing the weight of the blows on opposite sides of the surface, this cannot happen.

Special Effects

The following are some interesting effects that may be produced on the suspended cymbal:

1. If metallic objects are allowed to rest on the surface and the cymbal is struck with a padded stick, a *sizzling* effect results. Such an effect is called for in *Symphony in E♭* by Paul Hindemith. The metallic objects may be bits of iron filings, a set of keys, etc.

2. If the player places one snare drum stick lightly beneath the surface of the cymbal and holds it there so that the edges may touch the wood, and at the same time strikes the upper edge with another snare drum stick, an interesting sizzling sound results of a different *non-metallic* quality.

3. If the player takes a coin and *scrapes* the surface of the instrument, another interesting effect is brought forth. Such a scraping effect would be satisfactory for the cymbal note written in the 1st two measures of *Festivals* by Debussy where the dynamic indication is "pppp" but *solo.*

4. When two cymbals are grasped by the player and their edges placed together, a special sound will occur if the player rubs the edges one against the other. This has been described in some quarters as the swish of angels' wings.

Antique Cymbals

Antique cymbals are tiny cymbals that possess definite pitch. They are to be struck singly with bell mallets so that their musical tone can be heard for what it is: A bell tone with a metallic cymbal-like ring.

A notable example in the orchestral literature for antique cymbals is in the *Afternoon of a Faun* by Debussy. Chromatic sets of antique cymbals are available and any notes can be written by arrangers and composers. However, if antique cymbals are not available orchestra bells can be substituted. The chromatic arrangement of cymbals stems from the instruments used in the Balinese Islands where tuned cymbals and tuned gongs are used in their ceremonial dances and music.

January 1961

13 Fundamental Drum Rudiments

Rex Morgan Longyear

TEACHERS OF PERCUSSION have found that a considerable difference exists between the so-called "13 standard rudiments" of drumming and the snare drum parts in the orchestral, band, and studio literature. In fact, only 8 of the "26 standard rudiments" recognized by the National Association of Rudimental Drummers are applicable in all musical situations and only 4 more are practicable with a high school or college drum section in drum cadences.

There is no substitute for rudimental study in developing the flexibility and co-ordination that an excellent drummer needs, and the rudimental solo literature should be an important ingredient of his musical background. The rudimental style, however, does not lend itself to most musical situations, much as a dance band trumpet tone cannot be used to best effect in the symphony orchestra or concert band.

Place of Rudiments

A considerable amount of misunderstanding exists in the educational world concerning the place of rudiments and rudimental playing. The problem first arises in the percussion methods class given in our schools of music to prospective band directors. This course is, more often than not, taught by a woodwind or brass man who has picked up a smattering of percussion, frequently in a class taught under similar circumstances. Lacking experience as practical percussion teachers, these instructors are forced to rely on traditions that are fallacious if applied to all musical circumstances.

Available to these teachers are charts showing the "13 standard rudiments," and the belief is regrettably prevalent that mastery of these rudiments automatically confers a mastery of drumming. Thus the students are kept — often for the entire term — on these 13 rudiments, with little if any instruction on timpani, the mallet instruments, the accessory percussion instruments, or the "indoor" style of snare drumming. The students in these classes who go out to become band directors teach what they have been taught. The results in the drum sections of their concert and marching bands are evident to anyone who has judged contests.

A second problem occurs at many state contests. Students are often constrained to waste valuable time in learning how to play double drags because the contest judges — often the same brass or woodwind men who teach "percussion" classes — refuse to award superior ratings unless the students can play the "13 standard rudiments."

The crux of the matter is that the instrumental teacher in the elementary and secondary schools has little time to spend with an individual student. What lesson time is available is spent on what the teacher hopes will help his band, and on preparing his students for contests. If the instrumental teacher has to occupy the limited time with the "13 standard rudiments" and their application in what actually is a limited facet of the percussion repertoire, his band or orchestra will accordingly suffer.

Fundamentals

As a result, the adoption of the *Fundamental Rudiments* is proposed. These rudiments are truly applicable to all musical situations. Concentration on them will enable the director to spend more time in teaching his drummers how to play musically. Mastery of these rudiments and how to apply them will guarantee a snare drum section to be effective on the field as well as in the concert hall. Study of the other rudiments can be left to the advanced drummers who have already mastered these fundamentals and how to use them.

The thirteen fundamental rudiments (see examples) are as follows:

(1) *Single-Stroke Roll.* This is played hand-to-hand, that is, the student should be able to start with either his left or his right hand.

(2) *Long Roll.* This is the most difficult of all the rudiments. The student should learn not only to play the "open" or "Connecticut" style long roll, with every rebound distinctly audible, but also the "closed" or "buzz" roll since the "open" roll is inadmissable in the concert band or symphony orchestra. Such expedients as rolling with the sticks on opposite sides of the drum should not be tolerated.

(3) *5-Stroke Roll.* This is played hand to hand, and should be studied as a roll that occurs ON the beat (with the first note accented) and in its most common form as an upbeat (with the last note accented).

(4) *7-Stroke Roll.* This begins with the left hand in musical contexts, and should be practiced hand-to-hand only as a technical exercise. This roll occurs as an upbeat pattern and provides a more intense upbeat, es-

pecially where a crescendo is desired, than does the 5-stroke roll.

(5) *9-Stroke Roll.* This rudiment is played hand-to-hand. Its most familiar occurrence is as a quarter-note roll in 2/4 or 3/4 time or as a half-note in 2/2 time, the tempo for all these meters being *allegro.*

These rolls should be practiced, like the long roll, in both their "open" and "closed" forms, and the student should know which roll to select for a given musical effect.

(6) *Flam.* This should be practiced hand to hand. The sound, except in rudimental solos, should be that of two sticks striking almost simultaneously (the "closed" flam).

(7) *Flam Accent.* The National Association of Rudimental Drummers recognizes only one flam accent, which consists of a group of 6 eighth notes with flams on the first and fourth notes. Customarily the first flam is a right flam and the second flam is a left flam. It is useful in 6/8 marches and as an exercise to develop the left flam and manual co-ordination.

(8) *Ruff.* This is a hand-to-hand rudiment. Care should be taken that it is not regarded as a 3-stroke roll; the first two notes are an upbeat to the final stroke.

(9) *4-Stroke Ruff.* These are played as *single strokes,* and are upbeat patterns except in some rudimental solos (*e.g.* C. S. Wilcoxon's *Elyria Four-Stroke*). As in all upbeat patterns, only the final note is accented; thus this rudiment begins with the left hand. Study of this rudiment is also an excellent preparation for the 7-stroke roll.

For Outdoors

After the preceding rudiments are mastered, the next 4 may be studied. Their application is in outdoor music, on the street, and on the gridiron, seldom in the concert hall.

(10) *Paradiddle.* This is one of the best rudiments for the development of co-ordination between hands. It is used where strong accents on the beat are desired without precise articulation of the intervening notes. Great care must be taken that the student does not regard all groups of 4 (or 6) sixteenth notes as paradiddles. Such groups of notes in concert music are almost invariably intended to be groups in which the precise articulation of every note is desired, and should thus be played as single strokes. Variants of the paradiddle, such as the double paradiddle and flam paradiddle, may be studied if time permits.

(11) *Flam Tap.* This is also excellent for the development of co-ordination. This rudiment is sometimes found in concert music (e.g. Suppé's *Pique Dame Overture*) and the accomplished snare drummer should know how to execute it.

(12) *Flamacue.* Flamacues make very "swinging" cadences and the experienced drummer should be able to play these.

(13) *Downfall of Paris.* This rudiment is not played hand-to-hand. It is effective in 2/4 drum cadences and occurs frequently in rudimental solo literature.

These 13 rudiments—the first 9 of which occur in all musical contexts—will create an excellent, all-round, versatile snare drum section for the street and gridiron—as well as for the concert stage. These are the rudiments on which the emphasis should be placed in drum teaching. The various forms of ratamacues, extended rolls, drags, and their combinations with other rudiments should be known and mastered by the student who intends to make a career in percussion, but they are not essential to the drum section of the high school, college, or university band.

These latter rudiments are of limited use. They appear almost exclusively in the rudimental solo literature, and valuable time should not be spent in learning these at the expense of studying the fundamental rudiments or musicianship. The snare drum is as much a music instrument as is the clarinet, the trumpet, or the violin, and the musical standards of the percussionist should be at least as high as those of the string, wind, brass, or keyboard player.

A test of—

Percussion I. Q.

James L. Moore

THIS SHORT QUIZ should prove interesting to band directors and students of percussion instruments. Study all of the choices carefully; there is but *one best answer* for each question.

In rating your Percussion I. Q., use the following scale: 12-14 correct, excellent; 10-11, good; 8-9, fair; 7 or less—Study man!

Questions

1. *How Many Standard Rudiments of Snare Drumming have been adopted by the National Association of Rudimental Drummers?*

(a) 24 (b) 13 (c) 40 (d) 26

2. *The three most important rudiments of snare drumming are:*

(a) Single stroke roll, flam, flam accent.

(b) Five stroke roll, nine stroke roll, flam.

(c) Single stroke roll, long roll, flam.

(d) Paradiddle, ruff, single ratamacue.

3. *In this figure,*

C

a well-trained snare drummer will:

(a) Stop rolling right on beat 4 of the 1st measure.

(b) Roll thru to the end of beat 1 of the 2nd measure.

(c) Stop rolling on the last 16th note of beat 4 of the 1st measure.

(d) Play a single stroke roll.

4. *The head diameters of the two basic timpani should be:*

(a) 25″ and 35″

(b) 25″ and 28″

(c) 23″ and 25″

(d) 21″ and 25″

5. *The practical playing range of a pedal timpani is:*

(a) one octave

(b) a perfect 5th

(c) a minor 3rd

(d) one and one-half octaves

6. *The drum part indicates a ffz note for Bass Drum (well dampened) with a hard mallet. The player should:*

(a) Muffle the bass drum with a mechanical device or with his free hand and strike the drum with a snare drum stick.

(b) Strike near the rim of the drum with a hard felt mallet.

(c) Be sure to wet the head with a sponge before striking it.

(d) Muffle the drum with a mechanical device or with his free hand, and strike the drum at the center of the head with a hard felt mallet.

7. *Which of the following diameter sizes of cymbals would be best for a set of dance drums?*

(a) 18″ hi-hats and 30″ ride

(b) 14″ hi-hats and 20″ ride

(c) 8″ hi-hats and 14″ ride

(d) 20″ hi-hats and 14″ ride

8. *A composer has written the same printed notes for marimba and xylophone. Which one of the following is correct?:*

(a) They will sound a unison, but the tone qualities will be different because the marimba has wooden keys and the xylophone has metal keys.

(b) The words marimba and xylophone are both meant to indicate the same instrument.

(c) The xylophone notes will sound one octave higher than the marimba notes.

(d) The marimba should be played with hard mallets to obtain a brittle, staccato sound, and the xylophone should be played with yarn mallets for a smoother, mellow sound.

9. *The "collar" of a drum or timpani head is:*

(a) The thickness of the head material.

(b) The portion of the head pulled down over the shell by the tension of the counterhoop.

(c) The head material that is tucked around the flesh hoop.

(d) The diameter of the playing surface.

10. *"Tambourin" and "Tambour de Basque" are:*

(a) French words meaning snare drum and bass drum.

(b) German and French spellings of tambourine.

(c) French words meaning snare drum and tambourine.

(d) French words meaning tenor drum and tambourine.

11. *The temperature of a rehearsal room is 75° and the humidity is 90%; this changes overnight to 65° and 50%. You may expect the drums and timpani with calfskin heads to:*

(a) Break, even tho you loosened them a turn after yesterday's rehearsal.

(b) Sound the same as they did at yesterday's rehearsal.

(c) Sound higher in pitch, much crisper and "snappy" sounding.

(d) Be very low pitched and "muddy" sounding.

12. *In playing a Latin-American tango, the percussion section should:*

(a) Use bass drum, cymbals, muffled snare drum, and claves.

(b) Punctuate the rhythm sharply with *ad lib* bongo drums, cowbell, and timbales.

(c) Play a subdued, steady rhythm using mainly muffled snare drum and bass drum.

(d) Accent the last half of beat one of each measure.

13. *Don Gillis is a modern American composer of works for band. In performing one of his works, you may anticipate that:*

(a) One or more percussion players will be needed to play mallet instruments (i.e., bells, xylophone, etc.).

(b) A complete set of membrane and indefinite-pitched idiophone percussion instruments—but no melodic percussion instruments — will be needed.

(c) Five pedal timpani will be needed.

(d) The percussion part will be very light and often tacet.

14. *In a band transcription of a Mozart overture, you may expect the percussion section to have:*

(a) The traditional bass drum, snare drum, and cymbal parts as used in Mozart's time.

(b) The original pedal timpani part and such percussion as Mozart originally scored in the piece.

(c) The original timpani part; and parts for bass drum, cymbals, and snare drum often added by the arranger.

(d) No parts, as Mozart did not write for snare drum, and the timpani had not been accepted into the orchestra of his time.

Answers

1. (d) 26.

2. (c) Single stroke roll, long roll, flam.

All of the rudiments are derived from combinations of the above three rudiments.

3. (c) Stop rolling on the last 16th note of beat 4 of the 1st measure.

Often, after hearing the passage, the correct phrasing may dictate that this roll be tied over to end right on beat 1 of the 2nd measure.

4. (b) 25″ and 28″.

Some models are now 26″ and 29″.

5. (b) A perfect 5th.

6. (d) Muffle the drum with a mechanical device or with the free hand, and strike the drum at the center of the head with a hard felt mallet.

7. (b) 14″ hi-hats and 20″ ride.

8. (c) The xylophone will sound one octave higher than the marimba.

9. (b) The portion of the head pulled down over the shell by the tension of the counterhoop.

10. (d) French words meaning tenor drum and tambourine.

11. (c) Sound higher in pitch, much crisper and "snappy" sounding.

Humidity has the greatest effect on calfskin heads; the lower the humidity, the tigher the heads will become.

12. (c) Play a subdued, steady rhythm using mainly muffled snare drum and bass drum.

The tango is one of the quieter dance rhythms and *ad lib* percussion effects are not appropriate.

13. (a) One or more percussion players will be needed to play mallet instruments.

14. (c) The original timpani part; and parts for bass drum, cymbals, and snare drum often added by the arranger.

Pedal timpani had not been invented, and the other percussion instruments such as snare drum, and bass drum were rarely, if ever, used in orchestral music of that period.

March 1961

The Physical Approach to Drumming

Fred D. Hinger

Part III

Editor's Note: This is the fourth in an intermittent series of articles by Mr. Hinger. The others appeared last May, June, and October.

Cymbals

The person selected to play cymbals must display a confidence in his ability to assert himself. To quote the late Benjamin Podemski, one of the finest cymbal players I have ever known, "The cymbalist holds dynamite in his hands."

Since each cymbal has its own characteristics, it is possible to obtain a great variety of colors by selecting the proper cymbals for specific compositions. There are definitely limitations for the school situation since the cost of obtaining many cymbals is prohibitive; however, there are still a variety of sounds that can be obtained from one pair that is usually the norm for a school organization.

Contrary to some opinion, it is the energy expended by the player that should get each entire cymbal vibrating to its utmost, not the greatness of motion preceding the crashes of two cymbals. To understand this principle the following outline can be a guide:

1. Hold the straps (never use wooden handles, these stop the vibration) firmly and close enough to the hole to keep the cymbal from getting out of control.

2. Place the cymbals together and rest them on the chest in a slanted position so that the beating cymbal will be on top.

3. When the player has relaxed *completely*, then the preparation for the stroke and the stroke itself should all occur in one continuous motion; in other words, the motion to prepare, which is the separating of the plates, should not stop after the separation and start again for the stroke. Needless to say, when the strokes are repeated the cymbals cannot be placed together each time and, therefore, must be played with the same "feeling" of drawing away when the actual contact has been made.

It is a common occurrence to have the inexperienced player very often "cup" the cymbals. When this happens it is because both cymbals are crashed with the edges exactly corresponding. This captures air and causes a suction. To remedy this fault, have the player practice with the lower far edge of one cymbal hitting a very short time before the upper far edge. This is much like a flam. After the technique has been understood and mastered the actual "flam" should be so subtle that it should not be actually heard.

More brilliance and presence of the cymbal crash is possible if the inside of each plate is faced to the audience after the crash. If too much time lapses between the crash and the turning of the cymbals the effectiveness is lost.

The glissando, or slide, is being used quite extensively in the more modern compositions. This is accomplished by sliding the edge of one cymbal *around* the edge of the other. When the ridges in the cymbals are not worn smooth, then these also can be used for a louder glissando. Then the edge of one cymbal should slide perpendicularly to the ridges of the opposing cymbal.

The suspended cymbal is a very effective ally of many orchestral colors and effects. Some of these are as follows:

1. Cymbal roll with yarn mallets played opposite each other so that the plate stays level.
2. Cymbal played with wooden sticks, giving the timbre a glassy quality.
3. Brushes on cymbal.
4. Coin rubbed across the ridges.

Antique cymbals are very scarce and since there is not much call for them orchestra bells are often used as a substitute.

Timpani

The kettledrums have long been fascinating both for the player and the audience. It is very seldom that the heads have exactly the correct moisture content in them, and it is only thru much familiarity with heads that the player can recognize changes in humidity. With this thought in mind it is necessary to establish a norm with which the music director can operate.

The size of the collar is best determined by measurement in depth rather than pitch, since with variations of humidity the pitch might vary even tho the depth of collar might remain constant. When use of the drums is concluded the heads should be left loose in high humidity and tight in low humidity. The collar should be measured not more than one-half inch perpendicularly down from the shell bridge to the top of the counter-hoop.

Using one-half inch as a median, the collar will even so vary at the whim of Mother Nature. One remedy for heads that have been stretched a great deal is to invert the head (keeping it intact on the flesh hoop) from its original position on the drum, thereby effecting slightly more range by raising the counter-hoop. When this procedure is followed it is best to wet the head, take it off the drum, and let it dry before putting it back upside down. The same procedure is followed as that of putting on a new head.

Timpani Technique

There are as many physical methods being used and taught as there are approaches to any field that uses muscular energy as a means to an end. In this case the end is most important, the correct musical sound to complement the many colors that the art demands.

An explanation of the word "correct" must immediately be defined because a great deal of antagonism can result from misunderstanding. "Correct" in this case carries with it *personal preference* that is the essence of individuality. Some people like the hard sound of timpani in which there is not so much depth but which will carry above the orchestra or band. Others prefer the softer sound that produces more depth and blends better. It is my belief that all these sounds should be used to produce an unlimited range of color and effect.

Whether the method used playing the timpani be finger, wrist, or forearm, the same technique of *playing* the drum — not *hitting* it — should prevail. Exaggerating the stick motion, but playing as softly as possible, will give the player the feeling of "self-resistance" that is so necessary for control. After each hand has been trained to make a *continuous* motion (with absolutely no stop at M.M. 60) with the quickest part of the motion at the moment of contact with the head, then each hand is played alternately.

This training is preliminary to the roll which is a reiteration of single strokes. A word of caution must be added here. The beating spot should be approximately 3 inches from the edge of the drum. This spot will vary with the size of the drum and also personal preference. However, playing too close to the edge might break the head, and playing too far toward the center will give a dead sound.

It is important for the student to understand the roll as being composed of individual strokes. This method will give the roll a "healthy" sound, one which will not call attention to a fall in the musical line that happens when the roll is not strong.

After the long roll has been developed to a fairly fast degree on one drum, then rolling on one drum and ending on the other with one stroke should be attempted. This introduces passage of one drum to the other during the roll. If difficulty occurs in getting the last part of the roll as strong as the last beat that is played on the other drum, then have the student accent the last stroke of the roll before leaving the drum.

The speed of the roll is governed by the pitch, size of the drum, and character of music. If the pitch is low, the roll is slow, if high, fast. If the pitch C3 is played on a 25-inch drum the roll would be slightly slower than if this pitch were tuned on the 28-inch drum. During intense passages the roll will tend to be faster than during more relaxed ones.

Tuning

Tuning the timpani has always seemed a tremendous hurdle for the novice to overcome. Indeed it is and it is advisable that only a student with inherent pitch recognition should attempt to play the kettles. This does not mean perfect pitch, but good relative pitch. There are a number of means that are usable in tuning the timpani.

The interval method is the first that should be taught to the student. The range of the drums should be understood. Normally the range on the 28-inch is from F2 to C3. The range of the 25-inch drum is from B♭2 to F3. There are times when it is necessary to play outside this range; however, if this occurs too often the tension created in the high drum is often detrimental to the head and even to the drum itself. Pitch recognition can best be taught by singing and if the student can sing the pitches his problem is reduced to a minimum.

Key tuning is another method. After the student can recognize intervals and can recognize key centers, he then can relate the tunings of the timpani to the key being played or to a future modulation. Cues in the melodic line can be guides; however, it is not always a good policy to follow cues without actually counting the measures, since it is possible for the instrumentalist playing the cue to be wrong.

The feel of the drum can be helpful, especially during fast tuning passages. The pressure of the head can be felt thru the handles of hand tuned drums. When pedals are used the position of the pedal can give an approximate indication of pitch.

Pitch awareness becomes increasingly acute with experience and although it is a God-given quality it must be exercised with attention.

April 1961

Improving Snare Drum Instruction

Maxine Lefever

TWO RATHER DIVERSE methods have been proposed for initial snare drum instruction; and most instruction is based upon one or the other of these methods, occasionally upon some modification or combination. Much discussion may be heard among precussionists pertaining to the relative merits of these methods, but the problem of actually setting forth in writing the faults and virtues of the various methods still exists.

Rudimental vs. Straight

Most initial snare drum instruction is based primarily upon mastery of the drum rudiments. The opposing method of snare drum instruction is the Straight method. The foundation of the Straight system is based upon several principles:

Always commence every measure with your right hand.

Always have your right hand come on the count ONE, TWO in every bar.

Always flam with your left hand.

Always commence your rolls with the right hand.

Always play the same beat the same way.

Perhaps the most important principle set forth by Straight is that which states that the same beat must always be played the same way. The rudimental system is primarily alternating.

Each of these systems has rather obvious advantages and disadvantages. The rudimental system will produce snare drummers who are fine technicians, but often somewhat lacking in the more musical qualities. This assumption is logically supported by the fact that most drummers are trained via this method and that most drummers do indeed fall into this category. The Straight system, on the other hand, should provide drummers with a more intensive musical background, but may neglect the more technical aspects, particularly the development of ambidexterity which is so necessary to any percussionist.

Rudimental Plus Straight

Here, then, is a situation which demands more formal research than has been undertaken to support the assumptions and the accusations made by proponents of these two methods. And if research should support that which has been suggested, it would seem necessary to develop new methods of snare drum instruction, perhaps combining the best of the two schools of thought.

Some steps have been taken in this direction: directors and composers are expressing verbal dissatisfaction with the performances of snare drummers, articles are appearing in the music publications concerning the merits of various methods of instruction, and a few method books combining the better qualities of each system are being published. Technical ability and ambidexterity can be developed together with an awareness that different styles of music call for different styles of performance. The young student must be taught to listen to the music being played by the rest of the organization and to the melodic line, and to adapt his style of performance accordingly.

No musician will deny that technique and musicianship are essential qualities for any instrumental performance. Is it then logical that we percussionists stress one aspect, more or less neglecting the other? Would it not be better to examine the existing methods of instruction, to carry on research to ascertain the strengths and weaknesses of these methods, and then to combine—in intelligent and comprehensive instruction books—the best that each method has to offer?

If our bands and orchestras are important, then every section, including the percussion, is also important; and if we who are percussionists would like also to be considered as musicians, on a par with other members of these organizations, then we must soon find a way to improve upon existing methods of instruction, and raise the quality of the young drummers being trained.

May 1961

Bass Drum Celebrity

The story of Big Bertha's participation in the Presidential Inauguration Parade

John M. Crawford

HOME AND STILL resting from her triumphal tour of the East is Big Bertha, the 10-foot high, 500-pound deep-voiced "sweetheart" of the University of Texas Longhorn Band in Austin, Texas. Believed to be the world's largest bass drum, she is eight feet in diameter and 44 inches in width.

You would have thought that Bertha was a traveling movie star. Wherever she went, the radio mikes and TV cameras were turned on her; photographers' flashbulbs popped, and reporters scribbled away busily. Governors and other VIP's turned out to meet her and to drum away at her bulk.

Along the highways, train crews on passing freights waved and tooted as Bertha went by, and passengers craned their necks at the windows. School children forgot their games at recess, and ran to the fences to wave and yell at Bertha.

Irene Reeb, featured twirler with the University of Texas Longhorn Band, is shown with "Big Bertha," claimed to be the world's largest drum, in front of the main building on the Texas campus in Austin.

I guess we'll never have any way to know accurately how many thousands of people saw Bertha, either in person or on TV, nor any way to measure the reams of newspaper publicity she received on her two-week trip.

Everyone was tickled at the idea of treating a drum as a celebrity. Holiday Inns of America gave Bertha and her four handlers free lodging all across the country; Humble Oil Company provided the gasoline for the 3,500-mile drive; and Bankston Oldsmobile of Dallas furnished a 1961 automobile to pull the big drum along on its specially-built trailer.

She made a governor jealous. Orville Faubus came out to see Bertha in Little Rock, and beat a rhythm on her side: "Boom, boom, boom, Yea Razorbacks!" Then he declared that Arkansas ought to get itself a drum —"bigger than this one." This despite the fact that Governor Price Daniel had declared her an "unofficial ambassadress of good will from the state of Texas" and requested all courtesies for her.

In Nashville, Tennessee, the motel marquee said "Welcome, Big Bertha!" on its front, facing the state capitol. Governor Buford Ellington and Lieutenant Governor William Baird came over to welcome Bertha, and made a radio tape playing on her, which was wired to CBS in New York.

Narrow Escapes

Bertha had a couple of narrow squeaks; her companions thought two or three times that some of the hastily-procured collision, act-of-God, bridge-collapsing, fire, or tornado insurance might be needed.

She got lost on a steep, narrow, curving mountain road between Nashville and Knoxville in a blinding fog. We couldn't see another car 10 feet in front of us; it took us five hours to make a two-hour drive.

She almost flipped, to her eternal disgrace, on Washington's icy streets in the inauguration day blizzard, but righted herself with ponderous dignity. That's when we bought $19 worth of ice-chains, and learned to use them.

And twice Bertha had to detour around too-low underpasses in historic Charlottesville, Virginia. She stood 12 feet high on her trailer, and several other times one or the other of the handlers had to get out and watch as the driver inched her thru low passes.

But Bertha got to Washington and home again, passing thru every one of the Confederate states except Florida. The excitement she created, the interest she roused lingered long after Bertha herself had passed from view; she fulfilled her mission as a Texas ambassadress.

And her presence at the inauguration of a Texan as Vice President was indeed fitting.

May 1961

Same Grip with Both Hands

Can we have more and better percussionists if we hold the left snare drum stick in the same manner as the right?

Jack McKenzie

Editor's Note: Since Mr. McKenzie is a superior percussion artist and is teaching in one of our major schools of music, serious attention should be given to this controversial article.

Why do we continue to hold snare drum sticks the way we do? In particular I refer to the left hand grip.

Timpani is played with both hands using the identical grip. Marimba, xylophone, and vibraphone are played with both mallets held alike. With snare drum, however, we use one set of muscular motions in the right hand-wrist-arm, and a different set of muscle actions in the left. With these two dissimilar sets of movements we then try to achieve an equal and even snare drum sound.

Why not hold both sticks the same? That is, why not hold both sticks with the grip that we now use only in the right hand?

As far as the author has been able to determine, the left hand grip (or variation of the grip that we *now* use) came about either from the drum being placed on a table, with the head vertical, and played in this manner; or because the drum was hung from a belt or sling in the fashion we now use for marching.

Today, with the use of the drum stand, the first reason (placement on a table) is no longer valid. The second reason (marching) is still very much with us today. However, is it of sufficient importance in the over-all outlook of percussion to warrant the exclusion of any consideration of a variance from the so-called norm? The flimsiest justification of anything is, "It has always been this way."

It would seem that nearly 75% to 90% of our problems in teaching snare drum techniques stem from the unnatural left hand position. It seems that we are forever having to correct young students on wrong or bad left hand positions. If the time that is necessary in training the left hand to work correctly, and the time used in breaking bad left hand habits, were devoted to other musical and technical aspects of snare drum playing, could not much more be accomplished with a student?

Advantages and Disadvantages

Let's examine some of the advantages and disadvantages of each grip. From the traditional methods of supporting the drum we have, as an end result, one grip for snare drum, one for timpani, and one for the mallet instruments. Within each of these there are, of course, probably as many variations as there are teaching methods. However, there is an average basic grip for each.

With this diversity of holding positions, comparatively little muscular action transference takes place among the three basic percussion instrument families. Practicing snare drum does not greatly aid one's timpani playing. Playing marimba does not greatly aid one's snare drumming. However, if all three of these basic percussion instruments were played with the same grip, it is felt that much transfer of training could take place. If we accept the premise that students should strive to become well-rounded percussionists and not just dummers, or marimba players, or timpanists, then this point becomes very important. It is important not only in the actual playing but also in the *time* involved in training them to become performers.

Evenness of sound is much easier to achieve when both sticks are held alike. When both sticks are striking the drum at the same angle and with the same muscular action, a matching of sound in the right and left hands becomes a good deal easier. With the present grip we know that to attain an equalization between the right hand and the left hand is a rather long and arduous process.

The efficient execution of many contemporary percussion parts (calling for multiple drums) is easier with a matched grip. The type of parts referred to here are: the 4 tom-tom part in Clifton William's *Concertino for Percussion and Band*, the 6 drum part in *Canticle No.* 3 by Lou Harrison, the 3 tom-tom part from Michael Colgrass's *Three Brothers*, and the percussion part in *L'Historie du Soldat* by Stravinsky. Composers have begun to realize the potentialities in the effective use of multiple percussion and are writing more challenging parts even in many of the so-called easier works.

Both hands using the same grip for holding snare drum sticks.

The main advantages of the present grip seem to be that playing a marching drum suspended from a sling is somewhat easier and less tiring than with a matched grip, and that a student performing in a contest with other than recognized hand positions would stand a good chance of being disqualified. The use of the matched grip is not completely foreign, however, in the playing of a marching drum. Tenor drums in marching bands and in many drum and bugle corps are occasionally played using the matched method of holding sticks. This is true in many cases where the sticks used are tenor drum sticks (timpani type—ball or cartwheel head) or snare drum type sticks.

In the final analysis the essential difference between the two methods seems to be in control of the bounce and/or roll. The main change one must make in learning to utilize the matched grip is *left hand control of the roll.* An interesting experiment is to ask a percussionist to play a simple part over three or four drums, such as on four tom toms, using snare drum sticks; then give him a

pair of timpani, marimba, or xylophone mallets and ask him to play the same part again. Almost invariably the grip will change with the type of stick or mallet used even tho the music is essentially the same.

Results of Experiment

For the past year I have been conducting an experiment on the matched grip in the following manner. Four of my percussion major students who were interested in trying this idea have been studying various lengths of time on all instruments using the matched grip. I feel that their playing is progressing better in less time than would otherwise have been the case. Both the students and I feel that improvement has been made, and we can say that at least it is not worse than before the change.

In the undergraduate and graduate level percussion methods courses for music education majors, I have been teaching the matched grip to half of each class. In this way the students can see for themselves the advantages and disadvantages of each, and all will still know the traditional way of holding sticks from observing if not from actually playing that method themselves.

Note that a common grip can be used for snare drum, timpani, and mallet instruments —effecting a transfer of training not otherwise possible.

None of the four students, mentioned before, were playing any of the snare drum positions in our football band. However, I do not think that marching snare drum is going to present an insurmountable obstacle. There are holders on the market today that hold the marching drum in a position so that the head is *not* angling across the player. I have not used one of these enough to be able to say that it is superior to the sling. However, the possibility in these holders looks very good.

For anyone interested in trying the matched grip the following points should be considered.

1. The drum should be set so that the head is horizontal.
2. Both hands should be held alike, matching the present right hand grip as much as possible.
3. Hands, wrists, and arms should match as much as possible in their muscular actions.
4. Practice for left hand control of the bounce-rebound-roll.
5. Probably the most difficult playing factor to master will be the control of the loud closed roll.

I realize that the idea of a matched percussion grip goes counter to many years of tradition and that further investigation is necessary. I am not at this time advocating a mass changeover in snare drum grips, but I do think that serious consideration should be given the idea of a matched percussion grip.

June 1961

The differences among –

Xylophone – Marimba – Vibraphone

Vida Chenoweth

THE XYLOPHONE, marimba, and vibraphone are three music instruments that are often mistaken for one another, the most apparent similarity being that all three have keyboards that are played with mallets. Because the tone is produced by striking with a mallet, all three belong to the percussion family.

On examining the word *xylophone* —composed of two Greek words, *xylos* meaning wood and *phono* meaning sound—we see that it means wood sound. Both the xylophone and the marimba have wooden keyboards. On the other hand, the vibraphone or vibraharp has metal keys and belongs to the classification known as metallaphones. Just as *xylophones* include those percussion instruments whose keyboards are made of wood, *metallaphones* include those percussion instruments whose keyboards are made of metal. Incidentally, the vibraphone is the only one of the three that is electrically amplified.

Xylophone/Marimba Differences

If the xylophone and the marimba both have wooden keyboards, in what way do they differ? Even tho the keyboards may be identical, there is still a major difference in the matter of tone production, the marimba being an improvement upon the xylophone principle.

Below each marimba key there is a hollow chamber that sustains and amplifies the tone once the key has been struck. Whether the hollow chamber is a tube, a gourd, a wooden box, etc., the function of the chamber is that of a resonator.

Any hollow vessel is capable of producing a tone, but to act in the capacity of a resonator, it must produce exactly the same tone as its corresponding key. When the key is struck, the air inside the resonator is set in motion sympathetically.

The marimbas manufactured in the United States and in Europe have tubular resonators of metal, while some Central American and African resonators are gourds. Other types of Central American marimbas have wooden box resonators, while some in Indonesia and in Ecuador are of bamboo. Although these instruments differ drastically in appearance their acoustical principal is the same. All are types of marimbas.

Any wooden keyboard, regardless of its scale or range, qualifies as a xylophone. Sometimes it will have flats and sharps, and sometimes not, depending upon the culture of those who made it. Whether there are 5 notes or 55 notes, the instrument is a xylophone if the keys are of wood and played with mallets. Some people mistakenly identify the xylophone as a treble marimba, perhaps because the first marimbas manufactured in the United States were confusingly called "xylophones."

Like those of xylophones, marimba keyboards may also vary in shape, size, scale, or range. The basic difference between the xylophone and the marimba is that each marimba key has its own resonator.

In short; (1) the xylophone is a percussion instrument with a wooden keyboard; (2) the marimba is a xylophone with resonators; and (3) the vibraphone or vibraharp does not belong to the xylophone classification.

September 1961

A professional lists 21–

Suggestions for Drummers

Marvin Rosenberg

THIS LIST of tips or hints has been compiled from my experience as a professional percussionist in the highly competitive New York City music business. It is by no means a complete list, but it covers the most glaring defects in percussion performance I've seen.

Care of Drumheads

(1) The sound of all drums is affected adversely by heads that are unevenly tensioned. This is most evident in timpani, but it is also the case with bass and even snare drums. It is true that the snares tend to hide this a little, but to hear the difference even up the head on a snare drum and listen. The way to equalize the tension is to "throw off" the snares first, then—by tapping lightly with a drumstick about 2 inches in from each tuning screw—adjust each screw so that the same pitch is obtained at each tuning

point. Do this for all your drums and notice how much better your drum section sounds.

(2) Many drummers feel that loosening the head of a snare drum after each rehearsal and then tightening it wears out the head much more quickly than if it were kept at a constant tension. The incessant tightening and loosening seems to affect its pliability. The only time a snare drum head should be tightened and loosened is in damp or humid weather.

The Timpani

(3) Even head tension is an absolute must on the timpani. It is impossible to hear a clear tone on a drum with an uneven head. *Before each rehearsal* the timpanist should adjust each tuning screw so that the pitch is the same at each point. This is the key to easy tuning and good tone on the timpani.

(4) Hand-tuned drums require that all adjustments of the screws be made evenly, and to this purpose many directors teach that the opposite screws be turned together. They feel that this takes care of the problem. Not so! It makes no difference in which order the screws are turned, as long as the even tension is maintained. If there is time, the evening-up procedure should be done *after each change of tension.*

(5) A trick that really helps a beginner to hear pitch on the timpani is to ask him to put his ear close to the head, and with the tension loosened, sing the desired pitch into the head. As the pedal raises the pitch of the drum, the head will begin to vibrate in sympathy with the voice. At the point of maximum vibration, the drum is tuned to the same pitch as the note sung. With a little practice, tuning a drum can be done by even a comparative beginner. But remember, the head must be equalized.

(6) Many times I have warned students against touching the spring adjuster that controls the pedal tension. This is very dangerous, as the spring is extremely powerful and under great tension. While the chances of its breaking out are very small, it has happened.

(7) While directors insist on correct pitch and rhythm, not too many insist on good tone from their timpanist. To obtain good tone on the drums, the same procedure as on any other instrument should be followed. First, the instrument should be in good shape, then the correct technique should be practiced until the desired sound is produced. The key to a good tone is the proper mental concept; I call the concept the "hot stove" idea. This "hot stove" refers to the fact that the stick should be in actual contact with the head for the briefest possible time, and that the blow should be a twisting one rather than an up and down motion. To help keep the contact as brief as possible, use a sweeping or twisting motion. This twisting motion is accomplished by having the wrist snap *as the stick is coming into contact with the head.*

(8) Another factor affecting tone on the timpani is the speed of the roll. Ideally, in a roll the first stroke starts the sound and the other strokes serve only to keep the head vibrating. As a loose head will vibrate longer than a tight one, a lower pitch requires a slower roll. Once this concept is understood, a great deal of practice is needed to make it operational in the playing situation.

The Snare Drum

(9) For any group larger than a dance or stage band, I prefer that the snare drum have gut snares. The depth and fullness of tone that gut gives cannot be duplicated by metal or snappy snares. Because the latter are bent wire, they should be loosened after use to retain the bend. Gut snares present a different problem in that they are mounted individually; the problem is to keep them all at the same tension. The best way to maintain this stability (assuming they are even to start), is to tighten them after each use and loosen them to playing tension each time.

(10) For my own use, I have found that preparing my own gut snares is superior to using the commercial product. I start with high quality gut cello A strings, and very carefully mount them on the drum so that each snare is stretched exactly even. I then tighten the strainer as much as possible and leave it for a day or so. Then the strainer is again tightened to take up any slack that may have developed. This procedure is repeated a few times until the gut is well stretched. I have, of course, watched to see that

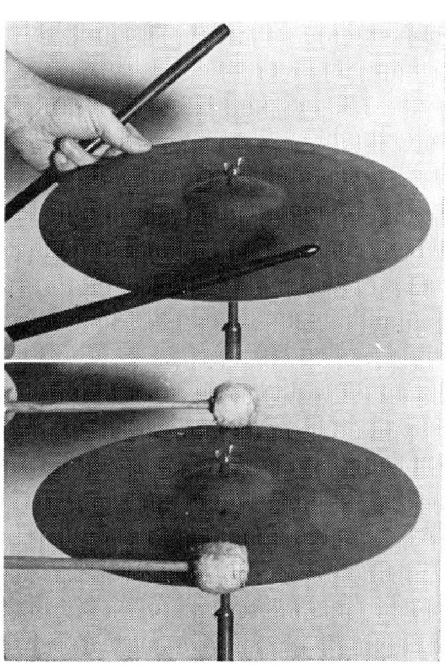

A crash on a suspended cymbal should be played on the edge, not on the top of the cymbal. The shank of the stick, not the bead, should be used. Rolls on a suspended cymbal should be played on opposite edges, and slowly.

the snares remain absolutely even during this operation. At this point paper is slipped between the snares and the head, and the snares are given a few coats of pure shellac. After a thorough drying, the drum is ready for use.

(11) I believe that clear playing of the snare drum, soft as well as loud, requires heavier sticks than most student drummers use. Contrary to what most youngsters believe, control for soft playing is easier with heavier sticks than with the 7A's many use. For general use I like a stick similar to the #21 or at least the 1B.

(12) Another failing of young drummers is not realizing that a gut snare drum requires a more open style of playing than do drums with snappy snares. The roll, especially, must not be the press roll so favored by dance band drummers, but should be a *true double-stroke roll.* Only in this way will the drum sound clean and clear, free of muddiness. Young drummers seem to feel that an open roll on gut snares is not "closed" enough to be good. It is true that because the player is right over the drum, it may seem so, but a few feet away it sounds quite "closed," and is infinitely cleaner.

(13) Too many directors, for whatever reason, allow their snare drummer to use a drum stand that is much too low. A stand is not

suitable for playing while standing unless it brings the drum up well above the waist. A strained position leads to all sorts of bad habits and poor playing.

Bass Drum

(14) Fortunately, this type of thing is now vanishing, but I still see some directors allowing their bass drummer to rest his drum on the floor. The position necessary to read music and look at the conductor while playing in this way is not conducive to either sight or sound. A sturdy bass drum stand should be used at all times.

(15) Most symphonic percussionists prefer that the bass drum be placed at an angle on the stand, not straight up. This facilitates fine control, especially in two-handed playing, rolls, etc.

(16) A good bass drum has some reverberation after the initial impact. In cases where this is not desired, the bass drummer may place his other hand on the head to stop the vibration. With a large drum this may not be enough. In that case the player should place his knee and thigh against the other head. In combination with the free hand, this usually can make the largest bass drum behave.

(17) As in No. 8, the speed of rolls on the bass drum should be suited to the head tension.

The Cymbals

(18) In playing a pair of cymbals for crashes, too many players spoil the tone quality by moving both hands, one moving up and the other down. This is not the best way. The way for best tone is to keep one hand, usually the left, absolutely still, while the other moves in to make contact. As with the timpani stroke, the wrist should snap into the point of contact. I find best control and tone by keeping my left hand stationary and moving my right *down from above*, snapping my wrist into the point of contact.

(19) When soft cymbal crashes are required, the cymbal player should not attempt to crash the entire circumference of the cymbals, but should use the edges or a small portion of the circumference. As above, only one hand should move.

(20) For a loud crash on a suspended cymbal, the stick should not hit the top of the cymbal but should hit the edge a glancing blow. The best part of the stick for this is not the tip (bead) but the shank. Rolling on a suspended cymbal should be on opposite edges, and not too fast.

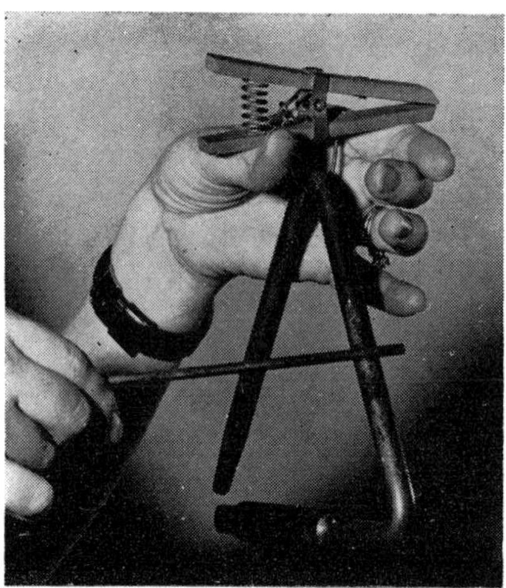

An effective triangle holder can be made easily from an ordinary wooden spring clip and a piece of gut or string. The holder should be suspended between the thumb and the first finger so that the triangle will hang down for easy playing. Damping is achieved with the second and third fingers and the palm. The clip holder is especially useful in fast passages; it can be fastened to the music stand and two beaters can be used on the triangle.

The Triangle

(21) Most triangle problems are caused by using an improper holder for the instrument. An ideal triangle holder can be made from an ordinary wooden spring clip. Two small holes should be drilled along the length of the clip, and a piece of gut from a broken violin string should be looped thru them. The loop should be just large enough for the triangle to fit in without touching the clip. If the clip is then rested on the thumb and first finger, the triangle will hang down between the thumb and other fingers. It will remain in one position and not rotate, and the 2nd, 3rd, and 4th fingers will be able to dampen it when necessary. The clip can also be attached to the edge of a music stand, so that a player can play the triangle with one hand while playing the other traps. It is also possible then to use two beaters to facilitate fast rhythms.

October 1961

Starting Percussion Students on Mallet Instruments

Rey M. Longyear

It is regrettable that so many students with a desire to major in percussion enter colleges and conservatories with insufficient preparation. The incoming freshman may know his 26 "standard" rudiments and may have had some experience with a trap set or with the timpani, but often he has had no piano, has never touched the bells or xylophone, cannot read treble clef, reads bass clef with extreme difficulty, knows few, if any scales or key-signatures, and is quite hazy about the correct techniques of playing the accessory instruments such as the cymbals, the tambourine, or the bass drum.

The solution is for directors of instrumental music in our junior and senior high schools to discover talented percussion students and to guide them in a direction whereby they can make vital contributions to the organizations in which they perform, thus preparing these students, if they so desire, to pursue careers in music and music education with percussion as their major instrument. A percussion student is adequately prepared for college or conservatory work in music if he is familiar with the four families of percussion instruments (snare drum, timpani, mallet-played instruments, and the accessories) and has enough musical background to enable him to compete on relatively equal terms with piano, woodwind, brass, and string majors in theory classes.

Encouragement Must be Given

A serious, well-motivated, budding percussionist should be encouraged along these lines:

1. He should begin the study of piano as early as possible and continue it as long as possible. Knowledge of the piano keyboard is essential for the performer of mallet-played instruments. The student will become cognizant of the fact that music consists of melody, harmony, counterpoint, and form as well as rhythm, and the piano is an invaluable teaching aid for the music educator at any level. The theoretical concepts of scales, chords, and tonalities take on a concrete rather than an abstract meaning to the student well grounded in piano.

2. After the student has studied piano and snare drum for at least a year, he should be introduced to the mallet instruments. The marimba is the best instrument on which to begin, but the xylophone, bells, or vibraphone may be substituted. There is a large amount of transfer from one instrument to another.

3. The student should begin his work on the mallet instruments with scales and arpeggios. These will acquaint him with the "keyboard," provide a vocabulary of melodic patterns which he will encounter, and aid in training the ear.

4. Technical facility can be developed by having the student play scales and arpeggios in the following "sticking" patterns:

(a) Single strokes.

(b) Rebounds, or two strokes to a note made with the same stick, analogous to the rebounds used in snare drum playing. The student should work for speed, as several mallet passages in the literature (*e.g.*, Khachaturian *Gayne* ballet; Hovhaness, *Suite for Violin, Piano, and Percussion*) require rapid rebound facility.

(c) Three strokes per note, played hand to hand.

(d) Four strokes per note, played hand to hand.

(e) Rolls, which are single-stroke, not double-stroke. Care must be taken that the sticks stay on one note and that trills, owing to imperfect control, do not result.

5. The student should be encouraged to pick out familiar tunes by ear. After he has mastered his scales, he should be able to play tunes in any key. This will improve his ear and tonal memory and give him the skills needed to play jazz on the vibraphone.

6. Correct hand position should be observed. The student should bend over the instrument, should hold his sticks in a relaxed but controlled grip, the sticks should form a 45° angle with each other, and he must play in the center (not on the edge) of the bars. Playing on the edge of the bar can be excused only when, in doing three or four-mallet work, both the "white" and "black" keys of the instrument must be played in a given chord.

7. Concerning the choice of a method book, the following points should be kept in mind:

(a) It should not get too difficult too soon.

(b) There should be passages of drill and repetition, especially in the more commonly used keys.

(c) There should be repertory passages or at least many technical exercises in the style of the mallet parts the student is likely to encounter.

8. Playing with three and four mallets should not be begun until the student has acquired considerable facility with two mallets.

9. There is a serious dearth of respectable solo literature for the mallet instruments. Most of the mallet solos on the high school level fall into the "traditional" or "semi-classical" category. Collections of flute, oboe, or violin solos of Grades II to V difficulty contain excellent material which can be transferred to the mallet instruments.

10. The teacher must expect a certain amount of resistance from some of his students. Progress is slow in the initial stages, and the snare drum, the timpani, and the trap set offer more immediate rewards. However, if the student expects to major in percussion in college, he must acquire a certain facility with the mallet instruments, and no one who aspires to the title of percussionist in either the professional or the educational field can get by without being able to perform acceptably on them. Having the student hear recordings of the Benny Goodman sextet, Kabalevsky's *Comedians* (especially the prologue and galop), Khachaturian's *Gayne* ballet, the "Bell Song" from Delibes' *Lakme*, and other works with prominent mallet parts may motivate him to increased efforts.

If the budding percussionist puts in half an hour a day with the mallets, at least an equivalent time with the snare drum and with the timpani, continues his piano study, gets experience in playing instruments in all four percussive families, has a deep love of music and wants to hear and perform as much of it as possible, he will enter college or conservatory with an excellent background for advanced study which will lead him to a career either as a professional musician or as an artist teacher in some phase of music education.

Discovering Mallet Instruments

Wallace Barnett

For many years we have ignored a group of very versatile instruments—the mallet percussions, particularly the vibraharp and marimba. Fortunately the scene is rapidly changing and we now see many records being released using these instruments. Listen to the albums of Milt Jackson, Terry Gibbs and the longtime favorite, Red Norvo; or hear Dick Shory's recordings in which he uses vibes, marimba and xylophone. Today, some stage band arrangements include vibe parts.

Mallet instruments are interesting and easy to work with and not difficult to teach. Their sounds are effective and there are no embouchure or bowing problems!

When used properly mallet percussions add immeasurably to the sound of various groups. Of course, they can be used to "up stage" other instruments because of their striking appearance and distinctive sounds. When the Vibraharp was first introduced in 1927, many dance bands bought one to use *after* the last chord of an arrangement. Although the vibes played one note or one chord only, the effect on the audience was a lasting one.

Percussion sections of symphony orchestras, as well as many high school and college groups include orchestra bells, chimes and xylophone. Who can forget the xylophone's crisp sound in the Shostakovitch *Polka* from *The Golden Age*?

Most bands and orchestras have a set of some kind of bells—bell-lyra, or orchestra bells. These instruments are often used during low-register clarinet passages in march trios.

Most of us use a drummer who has had some piano lessons—and after 32 bars on bells—back to the drums! This has been the extent of much of the use of the instrument. If the arrangement has any other mallet percussion part it rarely is even passed out when the music is put into the students' folders. Get a marimba for use in band and orchestra and obtain a vibraharp especially for stage band work and for *tuning*—and use them!

What to Do When There is No Printed Part

What to do if the arrangement does not include parts for marimba? Take a few minutes to write a part to strengthen some of the weaker sections, or get another "C" score and red pencil the parts to be played. For example, the marimba blends beautifully with sustained horn parts. It can play counter-melodies with baritone or cellos. The instrument fits very well when used with strings and can play from the treble clef part of the piano score, the 2nd violin part, or the added 3rd violin (viola) part if strength is needed here. This instrumentation will give much fuller scope to the sound of any group.

Many arrangements can be used for marimba or vibes with little or no arranging of parts. In a stage band group, the vibes can be used on solo parts, or double with trumpet or tenor sax. Another effective combination heard recently is string bass and vibes in unison. Count Basie used this treatment in the movie *Cinderfella*. A chord background on vibes (with or without piano) provides colorful support for any solo.

Speaking of the tone color potential of mallet percussions, a good number for a Christmas Concert is Leroy Anderson's *Christmas Festival*. This arrangement includes an organ part that can be played on marimba, and a harp part that can be played on vibes.

The Song of the Bells (also by Anderson and a Mills publication) is a natural for mallet instruments; but it is unbelievable how many times this composition is played without bells, even though the instrument and the written part are available. In addition to orchestra bells, the vibes (using medium-soft mallets and vibrato) are effective with the strings after the introduction. As the interlude of the composition is reached, medium-hard to hard vibe mallets should be used to achieve the tonal character indicated. At this point, the vibrato should be off to allow the "bell" effect to come thru with a full, resonant sound.

Another successfully used, but entirely different type of work, is the *Nocturne* from *A Midsummer Night's Dream*. The Reibold arrangement (Fox) is simple and effective. A marimba student can play from piano copy, and the sound of strings, horns and marimba will be very pleasant.

Useful in Tuning

Any sustained, organ-like sounds are effective on marimba, such as the sustained tremolo effect at the beginning of Massenet's *Angelus*. This may be achieved by using soft mallets and striving for a smooth, sustained roll.

The problem of major concern to every instrumental music director is that of *tuning*. Not just "tuning up", but of hearing individual notes as played in a group. Using Ralph R. Pottle's book, *Tuning the School Band*, as a guide, another giant step toward solving some of these problems can be made.

A stroboscope shows *pitch* difficulties. A tuning bar is used to match one tuning note. Carrying this one step further, the Vibraharp can be used as a set of chromatic tuning bars (vibrato off, naturally). Tuned to A-440, a fixed-pitch percussion instrument of this range enables one to match notes throughout the scale, then tune to 5ths, octaves, etc. By following this procedure, students soon learn to hear and identify correct intervals.

Mallet percussions offer endless possibilities in school music, but for the most part they are still either ignored or neglected. These instruments are not new to the musical world. The marimba dates back to prehistoric times. The vibraharp is the most recent addition to the family, yet it pre-dates the fantastic growth of instrumental music in the schools.

At the Trade Show of the National Association of Music Merchants last summer, it was pleasant to see a new trend toward increased use of mallet percussion instruments. Some publishers have indicated that parts for vibes soon will be included with their scores. One manufacturer already has several new stage band arrangements with vibe parts being scored for release to music directors here and abroad. In addition to special performance material, some method and teaching aids are becoming available from mallet instrument manufacturers. Exciting, too, are the new vibraharp technique books being prepared by top professional vibists.

These signs indicate that mallet percussion instruments are destined to have a much greater significance in the sounds of the future. These instruments no longer are used only among the ranks of the professional musician but are beginning to play an important part in the school music field.

Using this group of instruments can be interesting, challenging and rewarding. Do not be afraid of a little experimentation—it will do *you* good, and can do wonders for your group.

Percussion Workshop of America Organized

From Colorado and the Rocky Mountain area comes a new concept in the improvement and perpetuation of the percussion arts, the Percussion Workshop of America. With clinics, workshops, and concerts in every phase of percussion performance this recently organized group is dedicated to the needs of percussion pedagogy, to the improvement of percussion performance, and the uplifting of its position in music organizations.

Members of the staff of Percussion Workshop of America are: Jim Sewrey, Instrumental Music Director, Englewood, Colorado, Public Schools; Jerry Kent, outstanding Rocky Mountain area percussionist and instructor; J. Durward Morsch, Director of Music Education, Sheridan Union High School, Sheridan, Colorado; and Vaughn Jaenike, Instrumental Music Director, Englewood, Colorado, Public Schools.

The aims and objectives of this new concept in percussion betterment are implemented thru workshops in concert percussion, marching percussion, jazz and stage band percussion, orchestra percussion, mallet instruments, teaching techniques, literature and materials, percussion ensembles, scoring for percussion, etc.

A unique offering of the workshop is private instruction by tape recording designed for those students living in areas where no qualified percussion instructor is available.

The workshop specializes in three-day or longer clinics, with specialized curricula, highlighted by a concert performance of scores arranged for large percussion groups with brass or woodwinds.

An outstanding service of the workshop is the augmenting of the staff with such outstanding percussion personalities as Dick Shory, RCA recording artist; George Gabor, percussion instructor, Indiana University; Frank Arsenault, national rudimental champion; Joe Morello; drummer with the Dave Brubeck Quartet; Haskell Harr, dean of American percussion authorities, and many other important figures.

Complete information may be obtained by writing: Vaughn Jaenike, Manager, Percussion Workshop of America, 28 West Broadmoor Drive, Littleton, Colorado.

December 1961

Discovering Mallet Instruments (Part II)

Their Use in Concert Band Performance

Wallace Barnett

New and interesting tone color can be obtained in concert band performance by making use of the versatile family of mallet percussion instruments. More and more composers and arrangers are including these instruments in the complete tonal concept of their scores.

Easily available material makes it possible to use mallet percussion instruments with good balance throughout an entire concert. In the following suggested program the majority of the arrangements were published within the last year and all but three were written within the past three years.

If the band has recently acquired mallet percussion instruments and is introducing them in concert for the first time, *Meet the Band* by Bernard Green (Leeds) is a bright arrangement that appeals to both band and audience. For effective staging the curtain opens on the percussion section, which includes vibraharp, orchestra chimes, orchestra bells, timpani and drums. Since the number is so written that one section at a time is added, each section enters the stage on cue just before its turn to play. Properly rehearsed, this selection makes an excellent opening number.

This can be followed with Paul Yoder's new concert march *First Fed-*

eral on Parade (Kjos). The bells in this march have an interesting part of their own rather than being used merely to double the melody. Although this part is well suited for vibraharp, a fuller sound can be achieved by using both vibes and bells.

Ein Heldenleben by Richard Strauss, as arranged by A. A. Harding, (Kjos) uses marimba to good advantage. Sections of the harp part are effective when played on vibes. If this number seems too challenging, a good substitution is the Merle Isaac arrangement of *Holiday in Paris* by Offenbach (Fischer). This has colorful bell, marimba, and xylophone parts. The second movement (*Valse*) is particularly good with vibes doubling the melody.

Interesting for Students

Studio One by Glenn Osser (Leeds) is a solid number that makes a hit with students. The arrangement includes effective, but not difficult, parts for both vibes and bells.

Midway Gaiety, a bright march by Donald Moore, (Mills) contains an *optional* bell part; but certainly a much fuller sound dimension is obtained when the part is *used*—either on vibes, bells or both.

A standard program number, that becomes more effective with the use of vibraharp, is Ketelby's *Bells Across the Meadows* (Boosey and Hawkes). This is also worthwhile study material, particularly for the clarinet section where the use of six notes per beat is introduced.

Pastels by William McRae (Summy-Birchard) is a beautiful work for band. Written in rubato waltz tempo, the composition begins with vibes, flute, and clarinet playing a melody in unison. Students will enjoy the modern chord progressions and changes in this work and will find the recording by Herman Clebanoff and the Chicago Symphonic Band to be valuable listening.

An excellent march with which to close the first half of the program is Donald Luckenbill's *Sagamore Hill* (Associated Music). The instrumentation includes both marimba and bell parts.

Use of Stage Band

If the instrumental music department includes a stage band, this group can be used during intermission, between halves of the regular concert, or at a convenient place in the second part of the concert. Many fine new arrangements are becoming available for stage bands, and more composers and arrangers are beginning to include mallet percussion instruments in their instrumentation. For example, some of the Berklee Press arrangements make effective use of vibes by doubling the melody with any *one* of the other instruments, and by using the instrument on countermelodies and "fills," as well as in solo parts.

The second half of the concert might begin with Frank Loesser's *Greenwillow*, arranged by Alfred Reed (Frank Music Corporation). Orchestra chime and bell parts are included with the arrangement. If chimes are not available, the vibraharp can play the chime part as well as the indicated cues.

Pentagon by Bernard Green (Leeds) includes parts for xylophone and bells and is well scored. Vibraharp also may be included. If the band has a marimba but not a xylophone, hard mallets should be used to create a "xylophone-like" effect. As the name *Pentagon* implies, this composition is written in a 5/4 meter. The last half of the work is written in D major and is well worth the extra rehearsal time necessary to achieve something a bit different in the way of program material.

For a change of pace, *Coleman Stomp* by James Handlon (Boosey and Hawkes) is fun for band and audience alike. It is easy to play and the bell part is equally effective on vibraharp.

Change of Pace

An interesting change of pace can be achieved by following the *Coleman Stomp* with *Under Paris Skies*, an appealing waltz scored by Harold Walters (Leeds). A vibes part is included with the arrangement and is written for two mallets, over clarinets, basses, and horns. The sounds are pleasing and the vibes are again heard in the beautiful ending.

To display the tone quality of the band, Gerald Tolmage has an exceptionally well-scored arrangement of *Loch Lomond* (Staff). The top line of the score can be used on vibes, doubling the melody in the clarinets and alto saxophones following the introduction.

A good closing number for this type of program is the new concert march *New Horizons* by Harold Walters (Rubank). Chimes are indicated in the score, but bells and vibraharp can be used instead.

This suggested program is merely an example of some of the varied effects that can be obtained with mallet percussion instruments. Many other equally interesting compositions also are available.

Over Exposure?

Could this type of concert result in over-exposure of this group of instruments? If they were used in a solo context, the answer would have to be yes, but the same would be true if brasses, reeds, or any other homogeneous group of instruments were to be used in a solo capacity throughout a full length concert.

Mallet percussion instruments are colorful in appearance and in tone. Proper staging and good instrumental balance when using them will increase the performance potential of a band or orchestra.

1962-1963

195 Better Drummers in Thirty Minutes	Kenneth Krause	January
196 Improving the Percussion Section	Maxine Lefever	February
198 Discovering Mallet Instruments, Part III Chimes in Instrumental Music	Wallace Barnett	March
199 Why Percussion Ensembles?	Gordon Peters	April
200 A Closer Look at an Important Instrument	William S. Hart	May
202 Practice Hints for Vibists	Wallace Barnett	June
204 Drums and Drumming	William Ludwig, Sr.	June
205 Those Confusing 5- and 7-Stroke Rolls	Haskell W. Harr	June
207 The Thinking Drummer	Louis Bellson	June
208 Literature for Timpani	Mervin Britton	August
210 Big Bertha Booms Again	Harold B. Bachman	September
212 The Enchanted Third	Serge de Gastyne	September
214 The Marimba in the Concert Band	Gordon Peters	October
215 The School Percussion Section	Larry W. McCormick	November
216 The Mallet Percussions	Wallace Barnett	December
218 Intonation and Percussions	Ralph R. Pottle	December
219 The Marching Band Percussion Section	Maxine Lefever	December
220 A Likehand Grip for Holding Snare Drum Sticks	Neal Fluegel	January
222 Percussion Class	David A. Tobias	February
223 Just Three Weeks	Kenneth Krause	March
224 The Bass Drummer	Betty Masoner	April
225 Mallet Percussions	James D. Salmon	May
227 Tambourine Technique	William S. Hart	June
228 Instrument Care and Repair	Roy Markle	August
229 Timpani Tuning in Difficult Weather Conditions	Roland Kohloff	September
230 Purposeful Practice for Drummers	Charles Perry	October
231 Harnessing the Student Drummer	Nicholas Tawa	November
232 Detached Rolls in Snare Drumming	Mitchell Peters	December

Three tips to help you develop

Better Drummers in Thirty Minutes

Kenneth Krause

HERE ARE THREE TIPS which require only a half hour of your time, but which should result in an improved drum section within a week.

Tuning the Drum

Nearly everything written about tuning a snare drum says that the batter head should be tighter than the snare head. The opposite is more nearly true. A loose or even semi-loose snare head does not give a crisp, sensitive response, so it is therefore necessary to have the snare head very tight for a good drum tone. One top-flight professional says, "I tighten the snare head as tight as I can without breaking it, and then adjust the batter head for a good response." So, Tip No. 1 is: *Check the snare heads and see that they are really tight, and then make sure that the batter heads are tight enough for a good bounce and a crisp response.*

Wrist Action

Improper wrist action will prevent your drummers from obtaining the best tone and from acquiring technical facility. To check their wrist action, have them play single strokes slowly (RLRL, etc.) while you observe them from the front. When the stick comes up off the drum head, it should point toward the ceiling. For most concert playing, it should not be necessary to use the arm in making the stroke, but the wrist should turn until the stick points up. If the arm goes up and down and the stick remains in a horizontal position, the drummer has improper wrist action— in fact he has *no* wrist action. If the stick grips are correct, the key to proper wrist action is to point the sticks toward the ceiling after each stroke. When the drummer has achieved the proper wrist action, he may use his arm at times, especially when marching, but the wrist action will always be the same whether the arm is used or not. Tip No. 2, then, is: *Make the drum sticks point up after each stroke.*

Dynamics

Excessive volume is probably the greatest cause for altercations between the director and the drum section. It is advisable for the parties involved to come to some sort of gentlemen's agreement on the issue in order to avoid further conflict.

The following method for solving this problem will work successfully for a performer in the band or orchestra. It is based on the following statements: (1) As far as dynamics are concerned, the difference between the amateur and the professional is usually that the professional has a much greater range of volume at his command than the amateur. That is, the professional can play both louder and softer than the amateur, without being offensive. (2) A *forte* (or any other dynamic indication) near the end of a piece should be the same as one near the beginning; that is, the same marking should always produce the same volume. (3) A simple but accurate system for reproducing dynamics with precision will lead to an increased range and greater consistency in interpretation.

In order to reproduce dynamics accurately and consistently, establish the following two rules with your students: (1) *Always hit the drum as hard as possible.* (Don't let this shock you—read Rule No. 2 first.) (2) *To play louder, lift the sticks higher,* (by pointing them up with the wrist, not the arm) and *to play softer, hold the sticks closer to the drum.*

Stick Height Important

Using these two rules, all dynamic contrasts can be controlled by setting a specific height for each dynamic level. If the drummer always hits as hard as he can from any given height, he will always be sure of getting the same volume for each marking. The following measurements have proven successful in actual practice:

ff—lift the tips of the sticks 12 inches from the head.

f—lift the tips of the sticks 8 inches from the head.

mf—lift the tips of the sticks 6 inches from the head.

mp—lift the tips of the sticks 4 inches from the head.

p—lift the tips of the sticks 2 inches from the head.

pp—lift the tips of the sticks 1 inch from the head.

To teach the students to measure dynamics this way, have them start playing slow single strokes from the 12-inch level, and then come down to eight inches, then down one level at a time, playing for about thirty seconds at each level. Next, have them start at the one-inch level and come up one level at a time in the same manner. Then try skipping around from one level to another. The markings may be written on the chalk board and a pointer used to select various levels. When they understand the single stroke idea, try the same thing with rolls. Instruct them to practice these various levels until they become automatic. That is, they should be able to "feel" each level in their wrists without having to look at the sticks. That way, they can keep their eyes on the music and the director.

Rebound to Same Height

Occasionally, you find a drummer who will hold the sticks two inches high, but will lift them higher just before making the stroke. You can cure this by holding your hand at the proper height over the tips of his sticks while he plays.

There is another great advantage to this system which may not be immediately obvious: Suppose there is a section of music where the drummers are always too loud. "But our part is marked *ff*, they protest. All that needs to be done is to cross out the *ff*, write in an *f*, and insist that they lift the sticks only eight inches high. Now they know *exactly* how loud to play this section, and there is no chance of an error due to guesswork.

Still another advantage to having

a measured, consistent set of dynamics is in producing accents. Many students find it difficult to achieve the proper relationship between accented and unaccented notes; that is, the accented notes may be either too loud or too soft in relation to the others. I have found that playing accented notes one dynamic level louder than the volume indicated for unaccented notes usually gives the right contrast. So for Tip No. 3: *Establish a set of accurate, consistent dynamic levels to improve interpretation, increase the dynamic range, and eliminate guesswork.*

In order to get this done in thirty minutes, schedule yourself this way:

Checking the heads—five minutes. (Let the students do the adjusting.)

Working on wrist action—5 to 10 minutes. (It depends on how long it takes them to catch on.)

Dynamics—15 to 20 minutes.

If the students will then practice these rules for 30 minutes a day, (well, there had to be *some* catch to it) you should notice the improvement within a week. Try it!

February 1962

Improving the Percussion Section

Maxine Lefever

Although small in size, the percussion section plays a significant role in band and orchestra literature. Because of its prominence, any lack of technical or musical ability is readily noticed. Unfortunately for all concerned, the poor performance of many percussion sections evokes a considerable amount of criticism, and all too often this section is regarded as a sometimes noisy, yet necessary nuisance.

Why is the percussion section a favorite target for unfavorable comments? Is too much being demanded of percussionists? Is the music, particularly that which is being written today, too difficult? Or, to look at the question from another viewpoint, are we producing drum sections that are on a par, musically as well as technically, with other sections of the band? Are directors and composers satisfied with the percussion sections that are being developed? And, perhaps more significantly, are percussionists themselves pleased with the results?

Section Often Weak

Numerous verbal comments and what few writings exist on the subject lead to the conclusion that the answer to these questions is a definite *no.* Brief excerpts from the preface to a percussion manual recently written by Robert W. Buggert well sum up the situation:

Teachers of instrumental music readily admit that the percussion section is one of the weakest in the band or orchestra. In addition, probably due to lack of information, this section often receives the least amount of attention. . . . knowledge of percussion techniques is lacking and there is confusion as well as misunderstanding.[1]

Criticism of snare drummers has been leveled from all directions and blame has been assigned, in varying degrees, to all concerned. And just who is to blame? The high school drummer who is so lacking in ability? The band director who often instructs the drummer? The colleges and universities who prepare the band director? Or the drum authorities who, through their writings and studies—or lack of same—greatly influence the methods by which the schools instruct future music educators and, through them, the elementary and high school students?

It hardly seems fair to attach all the blame to the young percussionist. It may well be that he has begun the study of the drum with the hope of becoming a member of the band with a minimum of effort. But surely the band director should be able to dispel such a fallacy. Students who display musical talent and a willingness to work towards mastery of percussion instruments can and must be found.

Need Adequate Training

Nor does it seem fair to affix the blame entirely upon the band director who is, more often than not, one whose major instrument does not lie in the percussion field. This person's preparation for the teaching of percussion instruments frequently consists of a short course in percussion methods. This is, of course, hardly adequate—nor could it be expected that he become a master of this segment of his teaching.

Would the blame, then, be centered upon the institutions engaged in the training of the band director? A recent study by Michael B. Lamade would indicate that this might well be the case:

. . . we find that our colleges are producing teachers with inadequate training in percussion, who cannot effectively train their students when they go into the field. It produces a never-ending circle which restrains progress.

The main responsibility for better percussion training lies with the individual institution engaged in teacher training, and it is up to the administration and staff of these schools to see that their program is satisfying the needs of the student . . .[2]

But can all colleges be expected to employ a well-trained percussionist, full-time, for the benefit of these students? It is more likely that the services of such a person would be required on a part-time basis, but is every college so located that the services of such a person can be obtained? And just how much percussion training, in addition to all the other areas which must be mastered, is it feasible to require of a student?

What about the professional percussionists themselves? Are these people doing all that they might to encourage the development of fine young drummers? Many of these people are engaged in teaching, full- or part-time, but they of course cannot, because of limitations of time and location, reach all interested students. Many of these people are producing new methods and articles pertaining to the subject, but the quality and quantity of these writings is still insufficient.

Is, then, the problem a hopeless one? Is it, as Lamade suggests, a "never-ending circle which restrains progress"? A cursory examination might lead to the opinion that this, indeed, is the case, but no one is suggesting that the problem is completely insoluble.

Must Be Aware of Problems

The first steps toward the solution of any problem must involve an awareness of the problem which exists, and recent writings (such as the above quotes) suggest that this awareness is growing. What can each person concerned with this problem contribute? Remedies have been suggested, all worthy of consideration.

It would seem logical that if a solution is to be found, it must be begun not with the young student who is just embarking upon the study of percussion instruments, but at the other end of the scale—with the well-trained, professional percussionists. These persons constitute the greatest source of information upon this subject, but they cannot hope personally to reach all who are anxious to learn. They must make available intelligent method books which can be employed by those who are *not* experts in the field. Practically any existing method can be used successfully by the well-trained percussionist, but relatively few of these methods can be used *with complete understanding* by the average band director. More articles *about* the various approaches to snare drum instruction must be written by the authorities of this field. Much discussion can be heard among these authorities concerning the relative merits of various methods of snare drum instruction; it would seem that research to advance these opinions is indicated.

The teacher-training institutions can contribute much. If it is not practical to employ a full-time percussionist on the staff and if part-time assistance (symphony performers, etc.) is not available, the college can at least see to it that the brass or woodwind person who also instructs the percussion students receives as much training as possible; the college should insist that this person study all percussion instruments with an expert, and should provide whatever time and financial assistance is necessary. The services of students seeking post-graduate degrees who are proficient percussionists could possibly be more fully utilized. Also, the services of clinicians should be obtained from time to time to supplement the regular curriculum. Each college should be able to provide, without undue difficulty, means such as these (or others which better fit their particular circumstance) to increase the quality and amount of percussion instruction available to both teachers and students.

Mastery Not Necessary

If our band directors can be better trained, much of their problem is solved. Though they may not have developed a great proficiency in percussion instruments themselves, they will at least be better equipped to deal with the problem. Realizing that mastery of percussion instruments requires as much study and talent as the mastery of the wind instruments, they will select their students carefully and instruct them meaningfully. They will encourage private study where such is available, be aware of books and articles which exist on the student's level (and several have appeared in the music publications), secure the services of qualified clinicians whenever possible, and encourage attendance at music camps where expert instruction is available. And, perhaps most important, being now more aware of the problems and of their own deficiencies, they will, it is hoped, take advantage of every opportunity to improve themselves, thus improving the quality of their instruction.

If some of these steps are taken, the quality of school drummers will improve. And they, in turn, will be better qualified to become band instructors themselves or even to specialize in the study of percussion instruments. Thus the direction of the never-ending circle could be gradually reversed.

---

[1]Robert W. Buggert, *Teaching Techniques for the Percussions.* (New York: Belwin, Inc., 1960), p. 2.

[2]Michael B. Lamade, *"Teacher-Training in Percussion," The Instrumentalist,* Vol. XII, No. 7. (March, 1958), pp. 74-77.

Vibraharp or Vibraphone

The mounting popularity of vibes brings from vibists, dealers, teachers, and others the constant question: "How do the vibraharp and vibraphone differ?" The answer is: They don't! They are identical in functional design and apparatus. But this was not always true—the vibraphone of today bears scant resemblance to its original namesake.

It happened this way: In 1926 a manufacturer introduced a new instrument with thin, flat steel bars with motor-driven pulsators in the resonators. Essentially, *vibrato* had been added to a steel marimba*phone;* hence, the *vibraphone.* The instrument evoked interest at the time but it was difficult to play and had other shortcomings so the design was abandoned with only a few instruments having been produced.

Meanwhile another manufacturer was experimenting in another direction. They had long been making huge harp celestes for pipe organs and aluminum-bar song bells for orchestras. The organ harp often was installed with a motor-driven paddle vibrator and was called a *vibrato harp.* It had pneumatic-action dampers to control the ring-time of the bars. Extruded aluminum bars on the popular song bells had a more mellow tone and better overtone structure than the steel bars. So in 1927 the second manufacturer introduced the *vibraharp* which had aluminum bars with the fundamental and octave partial tuned, motor-driven pulsators, and pedal-operated damper bar. When the first company re-introduced its vibraphone it was essentially the same instrument. Since that time all vibes have been functionally identical to the original model *vibraharp.*

The word vibraharp is a registered trade name, but in reality all instruments are the same regardless of who manufacturers them. Partly as a reaction against the confusion in names the shorter generic term *vibes* is now being used more and more in all parts of the world.

Discovering Mallet Instruments (Part III)

Chimes in Instrumental Music

Wallace Barnett

ORCHESTRA CHIMES are a distinctive addition to the mallet percussion section and new possibilities for using this colorful voice may be found in the many arrangements (both old and new) which include good chime parts. Also, there are ample opportunities for the use of chimes in numerous other scores.

Although closely linked with religious and program music such as *The Angelus* by Massenet, orchestra chimes are by no means limited to this type of performance.

The usual range of tubular orchestra chimes is one and one-half octaves, C-F, chromatic. While instruments with extended ranges occasionally are built, only the standard 18-note range provides a fully portable set of chimes. Several bands and orchestras have added a half-octave of lower notes (especially built for their use); however, the lowest chime in this increased range is about nine feet in length, necessitating a "step-ladder" device to enable the player to strike the chime properly.

Dimensions and Acoustics

Orchestra chimes are available in three different diameters—1 inch, 1¼ inches and 1½ inches—the most popular size being the 1¼ inch diameter. For maximum tonal depth, resonance, and carrying power, the 1½ inch diameter chime is in demand by large bands and orchestras. The wall thickness of the chime tube should be increased as the diameter is increased to insure proper control of overtones, freedom from "wavers," and the best possible tone quality.

A chime has an overtone partial series which differs from the overtone pattern of other instruments. Additionally, the partials are sufficiently predominant that, literally, five tones are heard when one chime is struck. Since the partials decay much more rapidly than the fundamental or "strike tone," these overtones are rarely heard a few feet away from the instrument. However, when standing close to the instrument, the overtones can be disturbing to the player with an exceptional ear.

The lowest note in the orchestra chime range is written C4 but the partial structure of this chime causes the note to sound one octave higher. The predominant partials are shown in relation to the strike note:

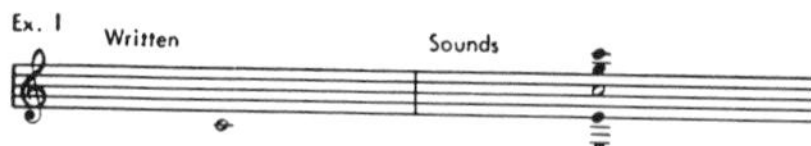

In writing for chimes this partial structure must be taken into consideration. Since the instrument essentially is designed for playing melodic lines harmony is seldom effective.

Orchestra chimes are made of a special brass alloy, and with reasonable care will outlast the director! Such care consists of using only the rawhide mallet supplied by the manufacturer for striking the chime. If after years of service a hanger (holding the chime to the suspension rack) should break, do not improvise with shoelaces, leather thongs or similar material. Such hangers can cause the chimes to sound out of tune. Write to the manufacturer for the proper hangers for the instrument.

Playing the Chimes

Full, resonant tone is produced when the chime is properly struck on its striking head or cap. The chime tube itself is never struck.

Before the advent of the damper pedal, chimes were played with one mallet (usually in the right hand while the other hand was used to dampen the chime. Today, the damper pedal can be used to dampen all chimes, or the damper may be held open by its locking device which allows each chime to be hand dampened. A chime should be hand dampened at the same point where struck—at the cap, or top of the chime—this dampens the tone faster than if the chime tube is grasped.

This new damper pedal innovation opened the way to further exploration of the instrument's possibilities, particularly the flexibility of performance that could be obtained by using two mallets.

The late Adrian Rollini, bass saxophonist turned vibist, was world famous for his two-mallet artistry on chimes which became a trademark of his jazz group.

Some expert two-mallet chime work was observed at the Mid-West Band Clinic last December during the concert played by Harry Begian's Cass Technical High School Band of Detroit.

When a true pianissimo effect is desired, the method used by Jose Bethancourt, a leading mallet instrument authority, is a good one: pad the mallet with chamois, cloth, or similar material (even Band-Aids can be used) to the softness necessary to produce the desired effect. Even a folded handkerchief (held tightly over the mallet head) reduces the usual metallic brilliance when required for certain passages.

Performance Material Using Chimes

Some of the famous peals known the world over can be effectively used in various types of programs. Probably the most familiar of all is the Westminster Peal, Example 2. Two other familiar peals are The Magdalen Chimes (Oxford, 1713), Example 3, and The Whittington Chimes (First rung in the Church of St. Mary-le-Bow in the 14th Century), Example 4.

Other Material

An Easter Concert has greater significance when opened with the chimes alone playing one of the traditional hymns of the season such as *Christ the Lord Is Ris'n Today.*

The following music for band is listed only as an example of the many types of music in which chimes can be utilized effectively:

March Carillon by Howard Hanson, arr. Leidzen (Presser) gives an entirely new impression of a march. (In many other marches a chime tone frequently can be sounded instead of the usual cymbal crash).

Prelude in C Minor (Original C# Minor) by Rachmaninoff, arr. C. Johnson (Rubank) uses chimes to good effect in the last section.

Don Gillis in his suite *The Land of Wheat* (Kjos) writes for many of the mallet percussions (including chimes) in the First Movement (*The Land and the People*) and in the Sixth Movement (*Harvest Celebration*).

Spring Magic by Applebaum (Fox) which includes optional piano with band, uses chimes throughout the first half of the work.

In the Leidzen arrangement of *Where or When* by Rodgers (Chappell), the chimes are heard in unison with the clarinets.

The Rosary by Nevin, arr. Walters (Rubank) uses the instrument in the type of musical setting we so closely associate with chime tone. What a difference when the chime player is absent from rehearsal!

Naturally, many Christmas numbers include important parts for chimes such as the beautiful arrangements of the traditional carols by Morton Gould (Chappell).

Colorful effects can be obtained with orchestra chimes and new ways of using them are to be found in many arrangements as in the following examples:

1. Chimes emphasize dramatic passages with brass (especially unison passages) and opening thematic statements.
2. Chimes may be used in place of the usual cymbal crashes in many marches.
3. Chimes sound well with trombone and baritone counter-melodies.
4. Chimes may occasionally be substituted for orchestra bells.

For proper tone production and timbre, a chime must be struck sharply on the striking cap with a rawhide mallet.

Why Percussion Ensembles?

Gordon Peters

When we look in upon the music world today and glance at the field of percussion, we are confronted with a family of instruments whose use and popularity is growing by leaps and bounds. However, we often find our music educators lacking in training and experience in this area of instrumental music. (This was pointed out recently by Maxine Lefever in these columns in the February, 1962, issue of *The Instrumentalist.*[1]) It is not necessary to be a percussionist to initiate and sustain a percussion ensemble program in the school. It basically boils down to the educator being convinced of the *assets* of such a program before embarking on an *investment* of time, music, and, eventually additional instruments.

Let us examine some of the objectives of percussion ensemble programs.

Objectives

To provide a more personal musical expression for percussionists thru a regulated and constant chamber ensemble experience.

To supplement the most important aspect of percussionists' training: private lessons and studies with competent and experienced instructors.

To acquaint percussion students with the existing percussion ensemble literature.

To promote a greater degree of musicianship, versatility, and flexibility.

To further imbue the percussion student with the concepts of color, imagination, sensitivity, phrasing, artistry, and ensemble as pertains to the playing of his instruments and hence inspire him to greater confidence, pride, and enthusiasm.

To improve sight-reading.

To provide an organized and functional laboratory where percussion parts to orchestra, band, and wind ensemble repertory can be studied and rehearsed.

To improve the organization and efficiency of the percussion section in the band and orchestra.

To acquaint the percussion performer with a wider variety of playing techniques and to make use of developed skills on percussion instruments infrequently used in band and orchestra scores.

To improve percussion playing in the larger organizations thru the transfer of training acquired in the percussion ensemble.

To develop a greater sense of group-responsibility thru group-participation.

To promote greater interest among young talented percussionists to inspire them to serious study of all the percussion instruments.

To help expose the student percussionists to as many different styles of music as is possible, including the rudimental-military types of ensembles but only to the degree that a balanced percussion ensemble program will permit.

To focus particularly on the melodic and harmonic aspects of percussion instruments (the marimba, xylophone, vibraphone, glockenspiel, chimes, and timpani) to compensate for many students receiving only rhythmic training on the snare drum.

To serve as a step toward marimba ensemble work thru which medium the percussion student can experience the finest literature of other instrumental ensembles, including the orchestra (thru transcriptions). Herein lies the key to achieving the highest degree of musical development, appreciation, and reward for the percussion student.

To provide an ensemble experience for jazz arrangements. Many percussionists never get an opportunity to participate in this significant area of musical experience; the "jazz feeling" is learned only thru actual experience and participation; abilities of jazz techniques and "feeling" are now expected of the concert (sometimes called "legit") percussionist and vice-versa.

To give the instructor more opportunity to observe his students' performance in relation to each other and thereby enable him to improve the effectiveness of their performance in the larger instrumental ensembles.

To promote the employment of bona-fide percussionists to teach percussion rather than another person whose major instrument is other than percussion.

To initiate an activity which can be extended throughout life.

To focus the student's attention on the pedagogic value of percussion ensemble training in his own learning situation and in his future work as a teacher.

To stimulate the formation of percussion ensemble programs in other school instrumental music programs.

To encourage percussion students to compose percussion ensemble works in order to gain a deeper insight into understanding their instruments. The development of percussionists' imaginations as pertains to the functional-aesthetic-coloristic roles of this family of instruments is too frequently overlooked.

To raise the standards of percussion ensemble repertory by educating percussionists to the existing repertory; this will raise their threshold of musical discrimination and ultimately result in a demand for more profound compositions for percussion ensemble.

To encourage the composition of percussion ensemble works and compositions for percussion with band and orchestra accompaniments by composers in the community.

To encourage percussion instrument manufacturers to improve the quality of their instruments and sticks.

To bring to audiences a "new" musical experience and entertainment that is both aurally and visually fascinating.

Students Need Program

In weighing the potential benefits to be derived thru the fulfillment of these objectives, it should become evident that a percussion ensemble program is essential to any balanced music program. The young percussion student, particularly, is *entitled* to the experience of chamber music for his family of instruments.

Only after being thoroughly convinced of the validity and importance of percussion ensembles can a music educator's senses of organization, imagination, and perseverance be called upon to implement such a program.

[1] It might stimulate college and university administrators to commence or expand their existing percussion education curriculums were music educators to petition those institutions awarding music education degrees with letters urging more adequate courses in percussion education. There is a list of colleges and universities awarding music degrees in the April, 1961, issue of *The Instrumentalist*.

May 1962

A Closer Look at
An Important Instrument

William Sebastian Hart

CYMBALS ARE ANCIENT instruments. They are mentioned in the Bible and their sounds helped herald the victories of many early armies. The art of cymbal making involves the tempering and beating out of the metal into the desired shape and the aging of the finished product to produce the desired quality of tone.

Cymbals which are struck together, known also as crash cymbals, form a major facet of the percussion section in any band or orchestra. The player chooses cymbals in pairs, judging the pairs by their diameter, weight, consistency, tone, and ringing quality, when each is struck alone. In a matched pair of cymbals, one disk is to have a slightly lower ring than the other, so that when struck correctly, a diffused crashing quality results.

Player Must Make Proper Choice

As cymbal manufacture is an art resembling that of violin making, so too the playing of the cymbals is an art. Rarely is there to be found any mention in the percussion part as to what type cymbals are to be used. The diameter and weight of the metal disks to be struck are left to the discretion of the player. The player who uses the same cymbals to play *Ride of the Valkyries* by Wagner as he would to play *Festivals* by Debussy shows the application of an amateur. The cymbals must satisfy the character of the music. The same cymbals can not be used to play every piece in the repertoire. It is advisable for the percussionist to have at least three pairs of cymbals at his disposal: light, medium, and heavy weight. These, of course, will be small, medium, and large in diameter. The percussion artist will have a trunk full of cymbals of every kind, producing shadings and colorings that will be a delight to the conductor.

Crash cymbals often come from the factory with wooden handles held snugly by a metal bolt attachment. These are delivered to our high schools and are used in that manner by the students. When a pair of cymbals is struck together, great force is exacted on the edges and on the area near the handles. If wooden handles are used, the area near the bolt attachment is subjected to such force as to have a tendency to crack the instruments. However, if leather handles are inserted in the cymbals, the force of the blow is diffused thru the instruments allowing the entire disk to vibrate freely and produce a truer sound, not sounding choked or deadened. The best effect can be secured if the player will remember that one cymbal is to be relatively stationary, while the other cymbal is to be the active participant. Both hands do not collide into one another! On the contrary, one hand which grasps the one cymbal, must play a relatively passive role, while the other hand assumes the active role. After the blow has been struck, the two cymbals must be waved gracefully in the air in a manner to allow the waves of sound to reach the audience effectively. A supreme dramatic coloration to a concert performance is materialized when the cymbal player tastefully performs his task.

Many cymbal parts concern themselves with single isolated beats allowing sufficient time for the player to get ready and to enter. The following are some technical examples from the symphonic repertoire which require skill to perform well: (1.) *Roumanian Rhapsody No. 1* by Georges Enesco. Here the cymbals have a quick rhythmic figure, fortissimo. Crash cymbals are to be used. (2.) *Carnival Overture* by Antonin Dvorak. In the beginning of this piece, large crash cymbals are to be used and played in the normal manner. However, toward the end of the opening fast movement, there occurs a passage for high strings and cymbals *soli.* The dynamic is *piano-diminuendo.* (3.) *Academic Festival Overture* by Johannes Brahms. The first measures of this composition require the cymbals to be played *pianissimo.* Tiny cymbals should be used and struck gently—with their edges touching only slightly. The passage is slow, with strings in the low register. Later on, in this composition, the largest cymbals should be used in the glorious finale.

Suspended Cymbal

Rarely does the composer write the cymbal part with directions as to *how* the notes are to be played. A suspended cymbal is often required. The suspended cymbal is one which hangs from a strap or holder. In modern orchestras it rests on a rubber holder made for this purpose. This rubber topped cup is attached to a long metal bar, the legs of which rest on the floor. A suspended cymbal may be struck with a wooden stick (such as a snare drum stick) to produce an entirely different sound than that of the crash cymbal. When it is struck with a wooden stick (such as a snare a wooden stick, the attack should be made on the very edge with a glancing blow. Other interesting effects may be obtained by touching the cymbal with the tip of the snare drum stick near the cup or center.

A snare drum roll played on the cup of the suspended cymbal gives an entirely different effect from a roll played near the edge of the surface with timpani sticks. Generally, the cymbal roll is produced on the suspended cymbal by using hard core, felt timpani sticks and playing the ordinary timpani roll on the surface of the cymbal. It is advised that the hands be placed apart on the surface of the cymbal so that one ball of the mallet will balance the ball of the other mallet and when a roll is executed, the instrument will remain, for the most part, stationary. If the balls of the mallets are placed together on the surface of the cymbal and a roll is played, the cymbal will tend to dip out and away from the player's hands, and in some cases, actually fall off the stand. By balancing the weights of the blows on opposite sides of the surface this cannot happen. The following are some interesting effects **that** may be produced on the suspended cymbal:

(1.) If metallic objects are allowed to rest on the surface and the cymbal is struck with a padded stick—a sizzling effect results. Such an effect is called for in *Symphony in E♭* by Paul Hindemith. The metallic objects may be bits of iron filings, a set of keys, etc.; (2.) If the player places one snare drum stick lightly beneath the surface of the cymbal and holds it there so that the edges may touch the wood, and at the same time strikes the upper edge with another snare drum stick, the result is an interesting sizzling sound of a different, non-metallic quality; (3.) If the player takes a wire or nail or triangle mallet and scrapes the edge of the suspended cymbal a mysterious sound results; (4.) If the player takes a coin and scrapes the surface of the instrument, another fine effect is brought forth. Such a scraping effect would be satisfactory for the cymbal note written in the last two measures of *Festivals* by Debussy when the dynamic is *pppp* but *solo.*

When two cymbals are grasped by the player and their edges placed together, a wonderful sound will occur if the player rubs the edges one against the other. This has been described in some quarters, as the "swish of angels' wings."

Antique Cymbals

Tiny cymbals which possess definite pitch are known as *crotales* or antique cymbals. They are to be struck singly with hard rubber bell mallets so that their musical tone can be heard for what it is: A bell tone with a metallic, cymbal-like ring. A notable example in the orchestral literature for antique cymbals is in the *Afternoon of a Faun* by Debussy. Here the pitches are to be E and B. Chromatic sets of antique cymbals are available and any notes can be written by arrangers and composers. When antique cymbals are not available, orchestra bells are substituted. The chromatic arrangement of cymbals stems from the instruments used in the Balinese Islands where tuned cymbals and tuned gongs are used in their ceremonial dances and music.

June 1962

Practice Hints for Vibists

Wallace Barnett

THE VIBRAHARP (or vibraphone—the names are synonymous) was introduced in the late 1920's. Similar to other mallet percussion instruments in design, its sound differs markedly. The bars are made of a special aluminum alloy instead of the British Honduras rosewood used for the finest marimba and xylophone bars. Also, the vibraharp is equipped with a damper pedal for control of "ring-time," whereas sustained tones are obtained on wood-bar instruments by using the "roll" technique. The characteristic tone of vibes results when the motor-driven pulsators turn above the resonators, and beneath the bars, to produce a *vibrating* sound.

The damper pedal operates much the same as the sustaining pedal on the piano. Tones will continue to sound while the pedal is depressed. All tones may be stopped simultaneously by releasing the pedal, or individual tones may be dampened with a mallet while the pedal is down.

The range of the vibraharp is usually three octaves, beginning at F3 and sounding where written. The tonal color blends well with all orchestral voices and the range is sufficient to allow interesting passages with flutes, trombones, and low-register clarinets.

No Substitute Available

Morton Gould said recently in a clinic on band arranging, "Bells are not a substitute for vibraphone nor the xylophone for the marimba." Vibes were not designed to sound like orchestra bells. The tone quality of the instrument is much more full and resonant.

Basically, there are two types of vibes: those with variable vibratos and those with one vibrato speed. (Methods of controlling the vibrato speed vary according to the manufacturer.) In performance, use of the vibrato is a matter of individual preference. For example, Milt Jackson uses a very slow vibrato as one of his "trademarks," while Red Norvo plays vibes with the motor (or vibrato) turned off. When using the instrument without the vibrato, the pulsators should be in a vertical position leaving the resonators open to produce a full sound. Many vibists vary the vibrato speed to fit the mood and tempo of the music.

Choosing Players for Instrumental Groups

Although a knowledge of piano may be of some help (as it is in learning any band or orchestra instrument), it is by no means essential. Many students transfer from other instruments because of an interest in vibes and do exceptionally well as a result of their desire to play the instrument. Still others begin their music training on marimba or xylophone. While a mallet percussion background is a technical asset, it is not a pre-requisite to learning vibes.

Choice of Mallets

Most mallets have hard rubber cores and are wound with yarn or cord. These are available in several degrees of hardness. Orchestra bell mallets of hard rubber or brass are unsatisfactory for use on vibes since the initial striking sound is too brittle. Marimba mallets may be used but, generally speaking, are too soft to extract good tone quality. Rattan handles are recommended for four-mallet playing and are excellent for two-mallet work; however, some vibists prefer using short mallets with wire handles. These are very comfortable but not as convenient for three or four mallet playing because short mallets limit the stretch required by certain intervals. Modern slap effects can be obtained with the Red Norvo brand Slap Mallets. These are made of felt covered with lambskin and are for two-mallet work only.

Four Basic Hand Positions

Two mallets, palms down.

Two mallets, palms up.

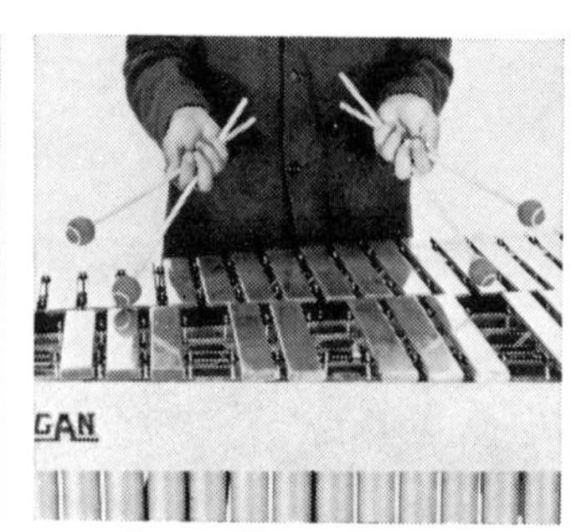

Four mallets, palms up.

Four mallets, palms down.

Holding the Mallets

In two-mallet work the mallets are held as one would hold timpani sticks. The following illustrations are from the new book of Julius Wechter, *Play Vibes—Modern Vibraharp Technique for Musicians,* published by Henry Adler, Inc., New York.

When only three mallets are used, two are held in the left hand and one in the right for better control of the melodic line.

Playing the Vibes

Unlike other instrumentalists, mallet percussion students are tempted to "look before playing the notes." A major problem with beginning vibists playing in the band or orchestra is that of looking at the music, looking at the vibes, *and* looking at the director. One of these three will be ignored and we all know which one! It is as necessary for the vibist to learn to play without hunting for each note as it is for the flutist to change fingering without taking the flute out of position "to look," as most beginners do. This is not an insurmountable problem but the feeling of motion thru space while learning interval distances is different from the sense of touch by which other instruments are learned.

Scales are Important

Practicing scales and chords is a "must" for the vibist. As soon as a scale can be memorized, it should be played over and over with eyes closed; then, played while looking at the director's stand.

The bars must be struck in the center or at either end. Striking above the suspension cords will not produce a live, full tone.

Scales in thirds beginning with the left mallet ascending and the right descending are good exercises. Reversing this order is a challenging and wonderful practice routine.

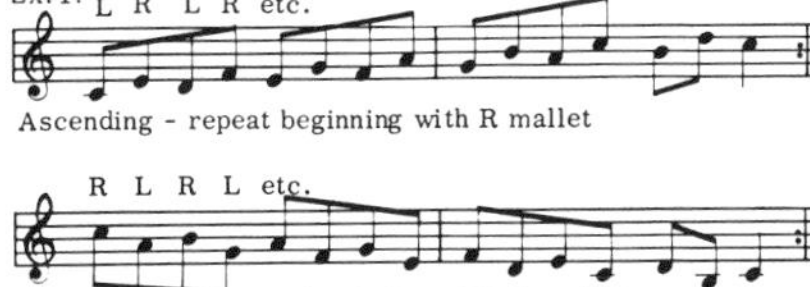

The exercise in the following example will prepare the student for some of the more difficult mallet movements he will encounter.

The usual playing procedure is to use alternate mallets, but sometimes this is unnatural and a repeat with one mallet becomes necessary, eliminating an extended cross-over. Naturally, crossing hands is often required but when a wide skip must be played, it is better to prepare for it by repeated mallet movements. Wide intervals need to be practiced many times until they can be played without looking at the bars. One of the best series of exercises uses a scale such as the following examples:

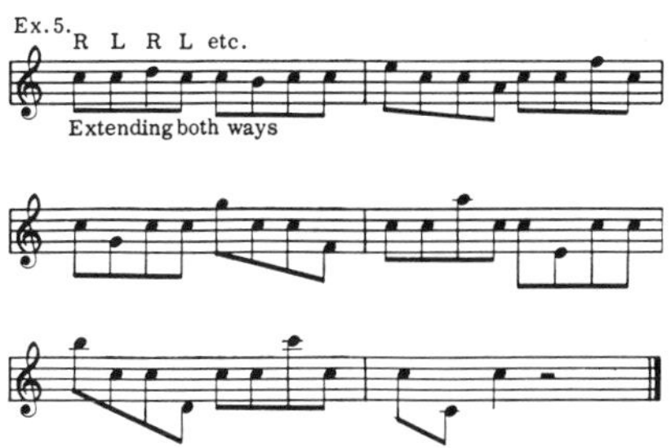

Music for Vibes

Kendor Music, Inc. is currently adding vibes parts to all of the arrangements listed in their Prom Series. New releases by this firm automatically include parts for mallet percussions. The Berklee Press has released the Johnny Richards series of stage band arrangements incorporating vibes, and J. C. Deagan, Inc. has prepared six scores for stage bands in which the vibes form an integral part of the arrangement.

The most comprehensive courses and practice materials available for mallet percussion instruments are published by Henry Adler, Inc. These include:

Modern Mallet Method, Vol. 1, 2, 3 by Phil Kraus;

Lesson Play for Mallet Instruments by George Devens;

Jazz Phrasing for Mallets by Johnny Rae;

15 Bach Inventions for Mallet Instruments (in duet form) by Morris Lang;

Vibes for Beginners by Phil Kraus;

Play Vibes—Modern Vibraharp Technique for Musicians by Julius Wechter.

Drums and Drumming

William F. Ludwig Sr.

Editors Note: Wm. F. Ludwig, Founder and President of the Ludwig Drum Co., Chicago, retraces the development of percussion manufacturing thru his 65 years experience as performer and manufacturer.

IN REVIEWING THE PAST fifty years, I am surprised at the changes that have taken place. I would like to go back sixty-five years, when I started as a drummer, and tell about the equipment we had to work with and how we got it, because in those days there were no drum catalogs and only a very few small manufacturers.

At the age of fourteen I had my first opportunity to try for a job as drummer. It was at the 1893 Columbian Exposition in Chicago, and when I arrived on the job I learned that I was supposed to play not only snare drum in a small Ballyhoo Band on the midway but actually to play double drums, as they called them then. But I had no foot pedal—had never even heard of one. So I lost that job for lack of equipment. I learned then that drummers who used a pedal made their own or had them made by a carpenter. All pedals then were made of wood. (See Example 1.)

Ex. 1. A drawing from an old catalog shows Mr. Ludwig's first bass drum and home made pedal. The curved wire attached just below the head of the bass drum beater struck the cymbal at the same time the beater struck the drum head.

The heel pedal you see here with my old bass drum was made by the bass player of the Sam T. Jacks Theatre Orchestra and cost me $4.00. The bass drum, slightly used, cost $11.00. This rope bass drum with the heel pedal, a 6″ x 14″ second-hand snare drum shown below, and a pair of ebony sticks was the complete outfit I used with the Wood Brothers Circus for the 1895 and 1896 seasons.

The rope bass drum was made by the Excelsior Drum Company of Camden, New Jersey. This Company was started by Joseph Soistman about 1885 and as near as I can learn was the first drum factory in America. Previous to this drums were imported, mostly military rope drums from England and some concert drums from Germany that used a clumsy square nut rod. One of that type was my first snare drum.

Ex. 2. This second-hand snare drum, the bass drum in Example 1, and a pair of ebony sticks constituted Mr. Ludwig's first "set" of drums.

Eagle Drum Adopted by Army

Joseph Soistman was a famous Civil War drummer who designed and induced the Federal Government to adopt the Civil War Eagle Drum for all military use. Previous to this the drummers used a variety of types and sizes, many home-made; all were rope tensioned.

My next snare drum, a Duplex 3″ x 15″ cost $18.00. Emil Boulanger started the Duplex Manufacturing Company in St. Louis in 1887. In their small catalog, dated 1897, appears this sentence: "Our house is probably the only one in the world devoting its entire attention to benefit the double drummer." And in that catalog they showed the first swing pedal. My first Duplex drum featured separate tension with twenty small key rods on each side. This was the first drum to use transparent heads on the snare side. They were called kangaroo heads. With the Duplex snare drum, Excelsior bass drum, and the home-made heel pedal I played the Omaha Exposition in 1897.

Ex. 3. Until 1906 this was the drum issued to percussionists of the United States Marine Band. It was 6″x15″ and featured single tension, wood hoops, heavy gut snares, calf skin heads, a brass shell, and a large shield of the Marine Corps.

In Omaha I also purchased my first set of timpani, size 24″ and 26″ hand screw type, made by Duplex. They cost $85.00 new. Duplex made and patented the first machine timpani of the revolving kettle type in America in 1887. The Ludwig Company built the first pedal timpani in America in 1910 and patented it in 1911. They featured hydraulic tuning with tuning gauges.

It seems that timpani and snare drums made better progress than the foot pedal. I had to use my old circus heel pedal until 1908. I played the Auditorium Theater in Chicago for a musical from New York called *Follies of 1907*. This was my first introduction to ragtime syncopation and kicks of all kinds. My heel pedal simply would not do. I started experimenting and before the season was over I had a new home-made pedal. It was somewhat crude and still made of wood but it did the job. That pedal turned into the Ludwig pedal patented in 1909 and really revolutionized pedal construction. Drummers that saw or heard of it wanted this new pedal.

Lyon & Healy Sell Drum Department

The only drum factory in Chicago at that time was Wilson & Jacobs who purchased the drum department from Lyon & Healy who preferred making harps to drums. Wilson & Jacobs made only drums, mostly rope, including the then famous Monarch Military Drums. They made no pedals.

On tour with the Henry W. Savage English Grand Opera Company I played Indianapolis in 1904. We used house musicians to augment our orchestra. Eugene Leedy was the drummer and I was the timpanist, using three hand timpani 24″, 26″, and 28″. Mr. Leedy showed me the snare drum that his father, a cabinet maker, had made for him and a few other accessories including a swing pedal and a drum stand. These items started the Leedy Drum Company in business. I tried the swing pedal which was much better than my old wooden one, but it did not satisfy the musical director of the *Follies of 1907.* That is why I had to make my own, the Ludwig Pedal, and in 1908 with the help of my brother, Theodor, who was nine years younger, I opened a small shop on the West Side of Chicago to make pedals and other accessories. This was the start of the Ludwig Drum Company.

Now there was rivalry among both manufacturers and drummers. Each wanted to outdo the other and this, of course, was healthy for the progress and development of drummers and instruments.

First Catalog Appears

Drum catalogs began to appear. The Duplex catalog published in 1892 was the first. The first Excelsior catalog I saw was in 1899 and unfortunately the last. That firm went out of business about 1904.

Then came a series of catalogs: George B. Stone and Son, of Boston, about 1900; the Dodge Bros., also of Boston, about the same period; Yerks Mfg. Co., of New York, about 1905; Novak Drum Supply Co., of Chicago; Frank Rice Drum Co., of Chicago; and Dixie Music House, of Chicago, all published about 1910.

Hammond and Gerlack started a drum shop in Pittsburgh about 1906. This firm did not build drums, but assembled and repaired drums, or served drummers generally with parts from various specialty manufacturers. All this inspired drummers and put them on a constant lookout for new and better equipment.

About 1910 the first ragtimers hit Chicago. We called them "fakers" because they improvised and would not stick to the written part. But these progressives inspired manufacturers to a point where one helped the other to a degree that to this day America leads the world in drums and drummers.

Until 1906 for many years the United States Marine Band drum shown in Example 3 was the standard issue. The Marine Corps and Marine Band now, however, use the very latest equipment and make their selection from any of the modern catalogs. This is a clear example of the progress made during the last fifty years and no doubt is one reason why the United States has the finest service bands in the world. We can be proud of America's preeminence in both percussion instruments and percussion players.

Ex. 4. Percussionists in the Service Bands are now free to choose any instrument they prefer. Here SP6 Jim O'Leary, SFC Vincent Romeo, and SGM Bill Callander of the U.S. Army Field Band, Fort Meade, Washington, D.C., select a snare drum with the help of William F. Ludwig.

June 1962

Those Confusing 5- and 7-Stroke Rolls

Haskell W. Harr

So many times young drummers ask, "When do we use a five-stroke and when do we use a seven-stroke roll?" They are both written the same way, and to the young drummer just entering the school band it is confusing. Here are a few suggestions that will help these young students.

One thing that governs which roll is to be played is tempo. In slower music more strokes are used than in fast tempos. For purposes of explanation let us look at some excerpts from the old Bruce and Emmett *Self-Instructor.*

For study purposes, the rolls are all written out, then under the heading *Recapitulation of the Preceding Rolls and Beats* Bruce says, "As the object of all beats is to represent the style of music, and it is utterly impossible to put every roll or beat in its proper place within the 'bars' without extending this work to unusual dimensions, therefore it becomes necessary for the scholar to commit to memory the following abbreviations. He will observe the difference between the number of taps in an open beat or roll, and those required to represent the same when brought to a close. The rolls are designated by figures being placed over or under them, to indicate the number of taps to be made, and the beats are made to conform as much as possible to the style of the tune. He must always begin with a right-hand beat or roll. The rest must follow in the most easy manner (always beating from hand to hand if possible), closing with the right hand to make a good finish. But this rule (*i.e.* the right hand) will not always apply." Bruce then shows the following notations:

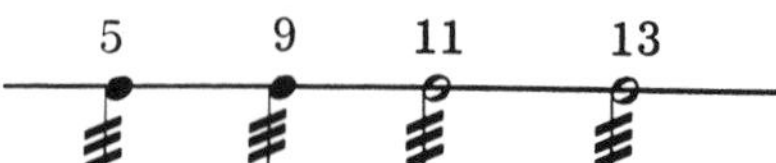

Tempo Governs Strokes

In my interpretation, the various numbers over the same kind of note indicate different tempos and the tempo governs the number of strokes to be played in a roll.

J. Burns Moore, in his book *The Art of Drumming* shows both the five and seven-stroke rolls written the same:

Gardner shows both rolls written the same, but states that, "Mathematical correctness is usually ignored in notating the seven-stroke roll."

Sanford A. Moeller also shows the five and seven written the same, but gives an explanation which does indicate something definite. He says the seven-stroke roll is written:

but played:

In analyzing the playing of the roll notice that it starts between the one and the "and," or on the second 16th note of the first count:

This bears out the statement that when playing the open rudimental style rolls the right hand strikes on the one, the "and," the 2, and "and,"

The seven, being a one-way roll starting with the left hand and written to end on the beat, would have to start on the "e" of the count.

As a matter of interpretation, all military or rudimental type solos, such as the *Downfall of Paris*, and *Connecticut Half-time*, should have the open rolls.

Clear Notation of Rolls

To take the guesswork out of the style of roll to be used modern writers are using the correct notation for the roll.

Just one more bit about the five and seven in rudimental type music. The seven was the rudimentalists' stock-in-trade. The drummer who could not do a good seven-stroke roll lost face. The five-stroke was very seldom used.

About marching and sticking Bruce says, "while marching bring down the left foot at the commencement of each bar, or measure, and raise it at the middle. At the beginning of a march, the last stroke of the first roll (pick up) must come down with the first note." That puts the right stick at the beginning of each measure. In analyzing rudimental solos and marches I find this to be true.

Due to the fast tempos used in concert band music the five-stroke rolls are more freely used than the sevens. Also, we play with a great deal more precision. Moeller, in his book says, "Many fine musicians, trying to play with a great deal of precision, are much irritated to have the drummer start off a couple of beats ahead of time." In concert drumming, the drummer must be able to start and stop his rolls exactly with the other musicians.

Five-Stroke Suggested

As a suggestion, when playing in the concert band and you come to the time figure

use five-stroke rolls. Stick the measure

If you have one roll in the measure and want to keep the sticking pattern of starting each measure with the right hand, play a seven, but start it exactly on the "and." Here a more closed type of roll is desired. Play a triplet for the first six notes of the roll (bounce each stick). The last, or seventh note of the roll will be the first note of the next measure.

The seven may also be used in the following measure:

Here the accent should be with the left stick on the first note of the roll:

In the following time figures, often found in the trio of many marches

either the five or the seven may be used. This would depend entirely upon the closeness of the roll desired, and the drummer's ability to play a clean roll.

The Thinking Drummer

Louis Bellson

THE MODERN PERCUSSIONIST is called upon to play many instruments and many styles of music. We are concerned here with helping the established concert percussionist make the transition from an already successful band or orchestra performance technique to an adequate dance band technique. Because of the nature of dance band drumming no school percussionist should be allowed to begin study on the dance band drum set until he has proved to be a successful rudimental drummer.

Must Understand Position

The job of handling a full set of drums can be a frustrating experience at first, and the transition is often a serious problem for the band as well as for the drummer. The drummer is in the "driver's seat," so to speak, and he must propel the beat (rhythm) so the rest of the organization can function properly. Thru the drummer the band is guided rhythmically. He is part of the "backbone" of the group. The first, and most important requirement is that the dance band drummer have such a well-developed sense of rhythm that he can keep a *rigidly* steady tempo without ever having to think about it.

The basic equipment for the dance band drummer is a small bass drum with a foot pedal, a snare drum, 14 inch hi-hat cymbals, 16, 18, and 20 inch suspended cymbals (commonly called ride cymbals), a small and large tom-tom, sticks, brushes, timpani sticks, and additional accessories as required. All equipment must be good quality and in good working order. Take good care of your drums and make sure they are tuned properly for the correct sound. The drum heads are of utmost importance and should be matched for best results. The snare drum must be tuned to a very "crisp" sound, the tom-toms should be tuned to medium tension, and the bass drum should be kept slightly loose for a good "thud" sound. The batter heads on all drums should be slightly less tight than the other side.

The bass drum should be muffled by placing a strip of felt inside the batter head. The felt should be three inches wide and run from rim to rim slightly off center. There should be a strip of felt one and one half inches wide inside the front of the drum. All cymbals should be medium heavy. Extra sticks, brushes, etc., should be kept within reach at all times.

Independence

After we understand the position of the drummer in the band the next step is to learn a basic beat. Here is where our title *The Thinking Drummer* comes in. Having to use both hands and both feet simultaneously requires concentration, all the while keeping a rigidly steady tempo. We must concentrate to the extent that we are able to let each hand and each foot work independently of the others.

In all the examples to follow the student must remember that traditionally the time signature for jazz is *alla breve* but that it is always played four beats to a measure.

The right foot is used to play the bass drum on every beat, except for special accents. The left foot is used to open and close the hi-hat cymbal. The following example shows the basic beat for the bass drum and the hi-hat cymbal. This must be practiced over and over in all tempos until it is mastered and the student can keep a steady beat.

The basic hi-hat beat is also used in all tempos. The pattern may be played on a suspended cymbal as well as the hi-hat. It is important that the cymbal be struck with the bead of the stick to produce a good sound. The student must remember that the dotted-eighth and sixteenth rhythm seen so often in jazz is played as a triplet figure. The hi-hat beat is written:

After the student has mastered the two patterns above he is ready to combine them, now using the right hand and both feet:

It is very important at this point to work for independence of the hands and feet, for to concentrate on one rhythm to the exclusion of the others will result in unevenness and lack of coordination. The drummer must both hear and feel the sound he wishes to produce. This rhythm will take much practice in all tempos before it is mastered, especially since the hi-hat is being played with the right hand while being opened and closed with the left foot.

Left Hand Added

After the above rhythm is mastered the student is ready to add the left hand and to practice variations in the rhythm. The left hand in the following examples is used to play on the snare drum.

The Brushes

In many arrangements or sections of arrangements the drummer will use the brushes rather than the sticks on the snare drum. The right hand usually plays the basic beat of Example 1 while the left hand moves in a continuous clockwise motion, never lifting the brush from the head of the drum. The left hand moves in such a manner that the brush passes the 12 o'clock position in the clockwise motion on the second and fourth beats. The following is an example of the brushes used in a fast or medium tempo, with the left hand playing the snare drum and the right hand playing the hi-hat cymbal:

In a slow number the left brush would make a complete circle every beat instead of every two beats. For the best clear *swish* with the brush use the tip; for accents use the lower handle against the rim of the snare drum.

Reading the Drum Part

The dance band drummer is essentially an *ad lib* player. The drum part in any arrangement is nothing more than a sketchy guide. Here is where the drummer must use his imagination and his concentration. For example, the part may be written:

But this would be very dull indeed, so the drummer would probably play something like the following with added fills at the ends of the phrases:

Important accents are written into the part and must be played as written. The good drummer listens carefully to every new arrangement and decides how he will play each section, which instruments he will use, and how he will accent the melody and rhythm of the band. He must be imaginative enough to add interest to the skeleton part and to enhance the parts played by the band. He must guide the band rhythmically and consider his solo work as secondary in importance. He must realize that the most simple beats can be the most effective. He will listen carefully to recorded and live performances to learn. He will practice intelligently with the band and alone. He will concentrate when playing. He will be a *thinking* drummer.

International Percussion Reference Library

The purpose of the International Percussion Reference Library is to bring copies of all compositions featuring percussion to one central location. Library facilities have recently been enlarged to include literature and texts for elementary and secondary schools, as well as university and professional chamber music. Anyone interested in learning of compositions that would fit their particular performance situation may contact the Library for information. For example, the best composition for a given situation might be available from a standard publisher's catalog, or from a generally obscure source. Inspection copies of scores are available on a short term loan basis. However, it is necessary to obtain performance copies from the regular source.

The Library facilities are now available for use, although the first complete listing will not be available until the Fall of 1962. Composers and performers are invited to inquire about submission of scores and inspection of compositions. Write Mervin Britton, International Percussion Reference Library, Arizona State University, Tempe, Arizona.

August 1962

Literature for Timpani

Mervin Britton

The solo material for timpani listed below is on file in the International Percussion Reference Library. Under the rules of the Library, scores are available on a short-term loan basis for study. Performance materials should be secured from the publisher.

While facilities of the Library are now available for use, a complete listing of all material will not be available for several months. Directors interested in learning of compositions that fit their particular performance situations are invited to contact the Library for information.

For further information concerning submitting scores or inspection of compositions please contact Mervin Britton, International Percussion Reference Library, Arizona State University, Tempe, Arizona.

Composer	Title	Publisher
Grade I		
Bach	March (Timp. & 3 Trpts.)	Marks
Noak	Andante (Piano acc.)	Glissano
Noak	Classical Timpani March	Music for Perc.
Grade II		
Britton	Solo Piece (Piano acc.)	Music for Perc.
Colgrass	Easy Timpani Solo No. 1	Music for Perc.
Harr	Cuckoo Quickstep	Cole
Harr	The Downfall of Paris	Cole
Harr	The Green Diamond	Cole
Harr	Newport	Cole
Harr	The 400	Cole
Kohs	Nightwatch: Dialogue for Flute, Horn, and 2 Timpani	Am. Comp. Alliance
Latimer	Andante for Flute & Timpani	Latimer
McKenzie	6 Graded Timpani Solos (Grades I & II)	Music for Perc.
Vito	Concerto (Piano acc.)	Boosey & Hawkes
Grade III		
Berryman	Beguine the Conga (22 parts)	Band Shed
Gardner	Variations on a Theme for Timpani (Band acc.)	Staff
Liest	Timpat (Band acc.)	Mills
McKenzie	Concertino (Piano acc.)	Music for Perc.
Noak	Dance Primitive (Piano acc.)	Music for Perc.
Noak	Rondo (Piano acc.)	Music for Perc.
Noak	Suite for Timpani (Piano acc.)	Music for Perc.
Rothmuller	Divertimento (Solo Trombone, Timpani, and String Orchestra)	Boosey & Hawkes
Schinstine	Tympendium (Piano or Band acc.)	Southern Music Co.
Schinstine	Tympolero (Piano or Band acc.)	Southern Music Co.
Tcherepnin	Sonatine for Timpani and Piano	Boosey & Hawkes
Tice	Four Pieces for Brass Quartet and Timpani	Univ. Mus. Press
Vito	Scherzo (Piano acc.)	Frank's Drum Shop
Waxman	Sinfonietta (Timp. & String Orch.)	Boosey & Hawkes
Weinberger	Concerto for Timpani (4 trpts, 4 trombones)	Boosey & Hawkes
Grade IV		
Bigot	Timpanian (Piano acc.)	Leduc
El-Dabh	Fantasia-Tahmeel for Timpani and Strings	Peters
McKenzie	Song for Trombone, Timpani, and Percussion	Music for Perc.
Noak	Fantasy-Scherzo (Piano acc.)	Music for Perc.
Price	12 Graded Timpani Solos for Contest (Grades I-IV)	Music for Perc.
Grade V		
Carter	Recitative and Improvisation for 4 Kettledrums	Associated
Colgrass	Concerto for Timpani and Brass	Interlochen Press
El-Dabh	Sonic No. 7 & 10 for Derabucca Drum (or Timp.)	Peters
Jones	Sonato for 3 Unaccompanied Kettledrums	Peters
Miller	Ngoma for Timpani & Orchestra	in manuscript
Parris	Concerto for 5 Kettledrums and Orchestra	Am. Comp. Alliance
Tanner	Concerto for Timpani and Brass Instruments	in manuscript
Thrarichen	Concert for Timpani & Orchestra	AMP

Big Bertha Booms Again

Harold B. Bachman

RECENT ACCOUNTS OF "BIG BERTHA" the giant exhibition bass drum now featured with the University of Texas Longhorn Band remind me of some of the interesting items in the early history of the drum as it was being featured with the University of Chicago Band on Stagg Field and other gridirons in the Big Ten Conference.

Big Bertha once boomed out for the University of Chicago Band, but after a long and silent retirement was moved to the University of Texas where the boom now is as lusty as ever.

When I became director of the University of Chicago Band in 1935 "Big Bertha" already had become a well-established part of the band and University traditions.

The drum had been presented to the University in 1922, along with a complete complement of band instruments, by Carl G. Greenleaf, then president of the C. G. Conn Band Instrument Company in Elkhart, Indiana. Mr. Greenleaf was an 1899 graduate of the University and had been a student in the days when William Rainey Harper, first president of the University, would take time off from his administrative duties to play cornet with the band. The director of the band when the drum was presented to the University was M. Emmett Wilson.

Mr. Greenleaf wanted to be sure the Chicago Drum would be larger than the famous Purdue University drum. Expert buyers were sent to the Chicago stockyards to search for animals from which the largest drum heads could be dressed. Actually the size of the heads determined the size of the drum. The diameter is 8 feet 3 inches on one side and 8 feet on the other, because two hides of exactly the same size could not be found. The drum is 44 inches in width and mounted on its carriage it stands over 10 feet high. It was reputed to be the largest drum ever constructed without the use of spliced or synthetic heads.

The name "Big Bertha" was taken from the giant long-range cannon with which the Germans had shelled Paris during World War I.

In a letter to the Chairman of the University of Chicago Council, dated October 13, 1922, Mr. Greenleaf stated that this was "just one foot larger than the Purdue drum. I do not think they will beat this very soon, because it takes absolutely the largest skins that can be obtained."

Original Heads Still There

It is a tribute to the canniness of the buyers as well as to the toughness of the beasts that the original heads are still on the drum. While it became necessary to replace the metal rods and accessories several times, the heads showed little sign of wear. Vincent DiNino, director of the University of Texas band says that when the drum was moved to Texas in 1955, the heads were removed, soaked in a swimming pool, remounted, relettered with the University of Texas insignia, and are still booming in support of the "Longhorns" of Texas with the same resilience and vigor that they once boomed in support of the "Maroons" of Chicago.

One story, which was delivered with the drum, was that when it was built no one had given thought to how it was to be gotten out of the shop where it was constructed. It was discovered too late that no door in the building was large enough to accommodate the drum and it became necessary to knock out a wall of the workshop before it could be removed. Because of this and other unforeseen complications the drum almost missed arriving at Stagg Field in time for its debut at a Chicago vs. Ohio State football game.

I cannot vouch for the story, but I can believe it, for I had numerous opportunities to be aware of the many problems involved in the transportation and storage of "Big Bertha." For example, the regular entrances to the driveways under the west stands at Stagg Field were not large enough and a special slot had to be cut in the entrance-way in order to get the drum into the hangar where it was stored.

When transported by truck it was necessary to figure out detours to avoid viaducts where the overhead clearance was not sufficient to allow the drum to pass. Many of our trips were made by rail and the drum would not go thru the doors of an an ordinary baggage car. The Illinois Central did have a special baggage car which would accommodate it and it was necessary to arrange for that particular car to be available when the band planned a trip by rail.

At Ann Arbor there was not a tunnel or entrance to the University of Michigan Stadium large enough to admit the drum. When the band accompanied the Chicago team to a game with Michigan, the drum was hoisted over the stadium wall and carried down the many rows of seats to the playing field by a crew of bandsmen.

Friendly Arguments Still Persist

I certainly agree with Howard Mort, who preceded me as director of the University of Chicago Band, when he said that "Big Bertha" was the most troublesome mascot in existence. For this reason, when designing a giant exhibition drum for the University of Florida Band, I took pains to insist on having one built which would give an equivalent, or better, sound but which would be more practical to store, transport and maneuver.

It has recently been reported that partisans of the University of Texas, not wishing to be outdone in any particular, have again raised the issue of the comparative sizes of giant exhibition drums in various institutions. In fact there have been suggestions of legal injunctions to restrain Purdue University and the University of Florida from making certain claims regarding the size and sound of the drums used by the bands in those institutions. At the risk of prolonging an argument, I venture the opinion that the Purdue drum is slightly wider, though not as large in diameter as "Big Bertha." Perhaps sometime the combined scientific resources of Purdue University and the University of Texas can be marshaled to determine precisely which of the two drums is the larger. In the meantime the University of Florida will rest its case on assurances given by William F. Ludwig, the manufacturer of the "Gator" Band drum, which is a mere 6 feet in diameter and 25½ inches in width, that ours is "the largest practical drum ever built." In a statement quoted in a Chicago newspaper in 1953 Mr. Ludwig described the University of Florida drum as "the world's largest drum that will boom properly." Let others dispute for the dubious distinction of having the largest drum in the world. The University of Florida merely claims to have "The Drum With The Biggest Boom In Dixie."

But Not for Toscanini

"Big Bertha's" tremendous size prevented it from realizing what could have been its most glorious moment in music. In the late nineteen thirties Arturo Toscanini was scheduled to conduct a performance of the Verdi *Requiem* in Carnegie Hall for a benefit for a musicians welfare fund. Participating were members of the NBC Symphony Orchestra, the New York Philharmonic, and a large chorus. The score of his work calls for a few very important notes by the bass drum, and the maestro apparently was not satisfied with the sound of the standard size drums available in New York City. An enterprising publicity man had seen the University of Chicago drum and described it to the great conductor, who asked to have it sent to New York for the special concert. In response to telegrams from New York we secured the special baggage car and sent the drum. After much difficulty it finally was unloaded, mounted on its carriage, and towed to Carnegie Hall. Upon its arrival it was found that while those who had made the request were aware of the dimensions of the drum, no one had thought to look into the dimensions of the several entrances to the stage! Much to the chagrin of the promoters of the event it was found that there were no entrances to the stage large enough to admit the drum. It was reported that Toscanini personally tested the tone of the drum and pronounced it ideal for his purpose. But "Big Bertha" could not reduce, even to please the great conductor. It was reloaded into its special car and shipped back to Chicago without the experience of having played under his inspired baton. Accounts of this fiasco were widely circulated by the New York and Chicago newspapers and we at the University were consoled by the thought that more publicity probably was realized because of the miscarriage of the plans than would have been forthcoming had the drum actually been used in performance.

Retired from Gridiron

I came to the University of Chicago during the twilight of its era as an athletic power in the Big Ten Conference. The University offered few courses for students who wished to prepare for careers as school band directors and the membership of the band consisted largely of students who were not majoring in music. This, of course, placed us at a distinct disadvantage as compared to some of the other bands in the Big Ten Conference which could rely on a solid nucleus of members whose primary academic objectives were the study of instrumental music and band techniques. Since our football band was the smallest in the Conference, with a very restricted rehearsal schedule, we relied heavily on "Big Bertha" as the center-piece and featured attraction of our gridiron presentations.

Two Texas Bandsmen test the BOOM of Big Bertha

The problems of maintaining enthusiasm among members of the football band in the face of diminishing interest in the team were tremendous. Some of my colleagues in the Big Ten credit me with having remarked at one time that while the Chicago Band did not have as many skilled musicians as other bands in the Conference, the I. Q. of our players was higher. While I do not confess to having made such a remark, I will say that even had there been reason to take pride in the superior intellectual attainments of students at the University of Chicago, this was small consolation to those of us who were interested in building a strong band program or developing winning athletic teams.

After several years of unequal struggle under the regime of President Robert Maynard Hutchins, the University of Chicago finally withdrew from athletic competition in the Big Ten Conference. While many predicted that this would mean the end of the Chicago band, it really marked the beginning of a highly successful period. We developed a concert band which represented the University with distinction until it was disbanded during World War II. During this time "Big Bertha" spent most of its time in the hangar under the stands at Stagg Field and was brought out only occasionally to serve as a background for the band in an outdoor concert.

Witness to History

As the clouds of World War II gathered "Big Bertha" became a mute witness to events which were to have a profound influence on the outcome of the war and in fact, were to change the entire course of human history. The modest quarters of the University of Chicago Band were in rooms under the grandstand on the west side of Stagg Field. At about the time the University gave up trying to compete with other Big Ten Universities on the gridiron a portion of this space was converted into a laboratory. Bandsmen frequently would observe Professors Compton, Fermi, and other distinguished scientists on the premises. As the demands for laboratory space increased the band was moved to other quarters on the campus. But there was no other space available for "Big Bertha" so the drum was sealed up in its hangar under the stands and the laboratory was built around it. Here originated the early experiments which led to the development of the atomic bomb. The first nuclear chain reaction took place in the runway under the stands just outside the drum's hangar.

The results of the experiments conducted in that laboratory are now a matter of history. After the war, when the laboratory was moved to more commodious facilities, the hangar was unsealed and the drum was found to be in first-class condition. Tests with a Geiger counter proved that it was free from any radioactive contamination and the giant of percussion instruments was pronounced fit for further active service.

Almost Retired as Museum Piece

Since the University of Chicago no longer maintained a band it was proposed to retire the drum honorably and return it to its original donors in Elkhart, Indiana, to be displayed as a museum piece. But enterprising emissaries from the University of Texas, searching for, as might be expected, "the biggest drum in the world", learned of the availability of "Big Bertha" and procured it for the Texas "Longhorn" Band, where it has been since 1955.

As one who was responsible for the care and management of "Big Bertha" during its last active service at the University of Chicago I am pleased to note that it is still performing the functions for which it was created; that it is again serving as a symbol of school spirit in a dynamic University where the manifestations of school spirit in support of an athletic team or a band are not considered to be uncultured or inconsistent with high standards of excellence in classrooms and laboratories. It seems entirely fitting that the noble voice of this titanic missile of the music world should boom forth across the plains of Texas as an instrument of the "Longhorn" Band; a band named for the animals from which the venerable, and seemingly imperishable, heads of this monstrous drum were fashioned.

September 1962

The Enchanted Third

Serge de Gastyne

TAKE A MAJOR THIRD, C5 and E5, held for eight beats—two whole notes tied—in an andante or an adagio movement.

What do you hear? Two flutes? A flute on top? A clarinet on the bottom? A flute on the bottom, a muted trumpet on top? First violins playing a tremolo C to E, pianissimo, and the second violins playing a tremolo E to C?

Do you hear two oboes? Do you hear two flutes, perhaps doubled at the octave below by two bassoons; or doubled again at the octave above by two piccolos; or doubled two octaves below by two trombones with a sforzando going to a pianissimo and perhaps followed with a crescendo?

Do you hear strings playing glissandos: C to E to C to E to C? Do you hear an organ? Do you hear two saxophones? Do you hear a wild mixture of single-reed instruments, double-reed instruments, flutes, and brass? Do you hear a shimmering sea of marimbas rolling the third over the complete four-octave range, perhaps set off by the strong accent of the vibraharp on the first beat, with tones sustained and sounding in waves of full, wide vibrato?

Do you hear a mixture of brass with assorted mutes from the cardboard mute to the wah-wah mute? What aural dimension are you going to give that third? How many overtones? How many undertones? Will you write the brass pianissimo? The low flutes around middle C, forte, the clarinets *mf*, the oboes *mp?* Will you have the family of mallet instruments playing with hard mallets, medium hard mallets, soft mallets and very-soft mallets?

The enchantment of this third will emerge according to which age and which era you are "hearing" in.

The third can be scored over two octaves in the chimes to evoke—or not to evoke—a pastoral scene, depending upon the context. This might be set off with the bright, sparkling sounds of the orchestra bells.

In this day and age, a knowledgeable composer or arranger with a large symphonic organization at his disposal could write (and should be able to write) an interesting three to five minutes of music on the *held third*, C and E. We will not delve into the rhythmic interest that is possible in such a piece based on one interval, but continue with the exploration of possibilities that can be achieved within the instrumentation alone.

What is Available?

And what is the *latest* dimension available to us in 1962? None of the woodwinds, none of the brass, and certainly none of the strings. There is the electronic music, the concrete music, of the tape machine, for example. (You can rattle some kitchen glasses and by judicious adjustment of the tape speed, make the pitch conform to the pitches of C and E.) But primarily, the added dimension will be found in the family of mallet instruments: orchestra bells, chimes, xylophone, marimba, and vibraharp. (And if you have the courage—the steel band.)

We have, then, two notes to work with: C and E. The timpani would give us three notes: the low E, one of the lowest notes of the timpani (and the lowest, really practical note), the C above that (an octave below middle C) and the E above. We could roll these, or tremolo them alternately. The two upper notes especially could be set off with a very sharp sforzando using hard sticks. They could also be trilled pianissimo with very soft sticks so that the sound would be more "felt" than "heard".

The marimbas can roll the notes throughout four octaves, although the C itself actually appears in five octaves. The orchestra bells will play that C an octave higher. The vibes are in the middle of the register of both of these instruments.

Reluctant Composers and Arrangers

There is an endless realm of possibilities. And yet, when you go to the concert hall to hear contemporary music, what do you hear? For all intents and purposes, a re-hashing of the orchestrations of almost a century ago. There is good reason for it. The serious composer dreads, above all, the possibility of being cheapened (he thinks) by the use of "popular devices" which, in his past associations, may have been of doubtful character. To the serious composer, the marimba evokes the exotic; vibes evoke a "night-club-combo" atmosphere; and orchestra bells—the Town Policemens' or Firemens' Concert Band! The xylophone is associated with the comical effects of compositions of 50 years ago: *Dem Bones, Dem Bones, Dem Dry Bones* and the macabre effects of Camille Saint Saëns' *Danse Macabre,* or at best, the satirical howling of Shostakovich's *Polka* from the *Golden Age Ballet.* And how often has the glorious sound of chimes been confined to a syrupy nocturne, a corny oratorio, or the finale of a country wedding scene?

Misconceptions Should be Corrected

But the *sound* of these instruments is only a matter of context. If an instrument is characterized as a novel instrument, it is because it has been so used, not because of what it is intrinsically. The triangle has been used in many sublime ways which have nothing to do with the "come-and-get-it" sound. Certainly when Beethoven used a triangle and a contrabassoon in the opening of the last movement of the Ninth Symphony, he was thinking of the so-called Turkish sound of the time, and for us, it is a sublime sound.

Frankly, it is up to us to use these marvelously versatile instruments such as the orchestra bells, the chimes (Sibelius' Fourth Symphony), the xylophone, the marimba, and the vibes in a way which will be sublime and will have nothing to do with previous misconceptions so often accepted as characteristic of these instruments.

A Beethoven of today may choose the marimba to open his Fifth Symphony. A Rachmaninoff of today may choose the vibes to state the theme of his Second Piano Concerto. A Johann Sebastian Bach of today may choose the xylophone to state the theme of his fugue.

Be it an enchanted third held for eight beats, or be it a beautiful theme that the whole world will sing, it is the responsibility of today's composer of integrity to state his material in a manner and with a sound in keeping with the feeling of today.

The new feeling—the new sound—is that of the revived wind and brass instruments such as the flügelhorn, the contra-alto clarinet, the alto clarinet, *etc.,* and the mallet percussion instruments which have waited too long to take their rightful place as bona fide, full-fledged instruments in the symphonic band and symphony orchestra.

The Marimba in the Concert Band

Gordon Peters

THE DIRECTOR IS RESPONSIBLE for developing percussionists in his band. The result of proper training will be a more enthusiastic and dynamic percussion section, with all students better prepared for future musical experiences, whether they be amateur or professional. In order to be both versatile and functional the school percussionist must have a knowledge of and facility on the keyboard percussions. Technical facility on the keyboard percussion instruments (marimba, xylophone, bells, and vibes) can best be developed thru study of the marimba.

The philosophy exists in some quarters of the band world that a standard instrumentation, that is, one that is fixed, is an ideal objective. However, this concept has too often restricted and, in some cases, even reduced the number of instrumental colors used in band compositions. It would seem that the concept of constantly seeking tonal color contrasts would provide more interest aesthetically, as well as aurally and visually. If standard instrumentation were to include the full gamut of percussion colors available there would, of course, be less cause for debate.

Advantages of the Marimba

We must give percussionists music including melody and harmony to play, not just rhythms. It becomes monotonous for the percussionist to function only in the role of accompanist and sound-effects man to the band. Adding a marimba to a band department will open the door to much fine chamber music for percussion ensemble; it is time we made musicians of our percussionists, not just drummers.

The use of the marimba in the band has many other advantages: some of the extra drummers and glockenspiel players needed for the marching band can be utilized during concert season; the elimination of some of the idle, noisy, bored, and discontented percussionists sitting around doing nothing; the cost is no more than any other large band instrument and can accommodate two players; marimba students will be able to participate in ensemble experience. Piano and accordion students who wish to play in the band can easily transfer their keyboard knowledge to the marimba. A student who has developed a good mallet grip plus a sense of pitch relationships is a natural candidate for playing the timpani.

The marimba is an easy instrument to teach: There are no bowings, no fingerings, no embouchure, no tonal or intonation problems. The fact that these instruments exist, and some composers and arrangers write specifically for them, further justifies a complete family of keyboard percussion instruments. To use substitute instruments for such parts (if it is financially feasible to have the instruments) is not only a musical effrontery but sheer carelessness and apathy.

The Marimba Part

In order to realize the preceding ideals, marimba parts need to be published with band arrangements. Below are some recommendations as to what should be included in published marimba parts:

1. Use double-staffed parts: top line, treble clef—bottom line, bass clef; avoid crossing of parts.
2. Score as much for the marimba as possible without interfering with the basic intentions of the desired tonal color. In tutti passages the marimba can always be used, because it blends well and will not predominate. In both solo and ensemble use it can lend a color contrast to the sonority of the wind instruments.
3. Incorporate double stops and octaves. Use four-mallet parts (per person) sparingly and then in an optional way.
4. Indicate clearly which notes are to be rolled (sustained) and which are not. Include phrasing and expression marks.
5. Indicate the type of mallets desired (and subsequent mallet changes): Rubber (Hard—H, or soft—S); Yarn (H or S).
6. The range of the marimba is usually 4 octaves, starting at C3, (one octave below middle C). (However, optional notes can be written down to A2, since this larger size instrument is available from some manufacturers.)

The use of the marimba in the band will serve both musical and educatonal ends. It is up to the band directors however, to request publishers to include marimba parts in their band publications. Your letters have a greater impact than you might surmise.

Emphasis, Punctuation, and Unusual Color

The School Percussion Section

Larry W. McCormick

PROBABLY THE MOST OBVIOUS function of the percussion section is to supply rhythm for the band or orchestra. Rhythm is a broad term. Used here it means that the section emphasizes pulsations, syncopations, adds cross-rhythms, and supplies punctuation to the band or orchestra. A primary assignment of the ensemble is emphasis of accents, dynamic changes, and phrases. In modern music the percussion section is receiving recognition for the colorful timbre it adds. Modern composers are striving for new sounds and are writing more extensive parts for the percussion section. Unusual effects, often termed musical colors, can be achieved by combining various percussion instruments, or using unusual techniques on the standard instruments. Two such effects are the timpani glissando and the swishing sound obtained by scraping a coin across the radius of a cymbal.

Other functions of the percussion section are to strengthen tonality through the use of the timpani on the tonic and dominant tones of a key, to reinforce climaxes, to aid in anticipating the director to lead the group thru tempo changes, and the carrying of the melody line by one of the mallet instruments. We must not overlook the job of holding the band together and keeping them in step, for this is the percussions' assignment using street beats when marching.

Avoiding Discipline Problems

We hear much about the selection of players for various instruments according to their physical and mental capacities. This is also an important factor in selecting percussion players. Of prime importance is to select mature and responsible people for the percussion section. Most of the time the percussion section is in the back of the group, they usually stand and can move about during a number, and also spend much of their time counting rests and waiting to play parts. These seem to be strong factors for inciting disipline problems. Added to this is the fact that drums appear easy to play and the average person believes that drumming does not require practice, and that the drummer merely plays along in rhythm with the band. We know that the expression "anyone can play a drum" is a misconception, but for these reasons many undesirable students are attracted to the drum. These are the people who think that rhythm instruments are all play and no work, and who often create discipline problems.

The physical requirements for becoming a good percussion player are more obvious. Natural rhythmic feeling, coordination, dexterity, and agility are all desirable traits in the beginning percussion player. Therefore, cautious initial selection of the player for the percussion section is of utmost importance.

Section of Six Ideal

The quantity of percussion players varies greatly from school to school and all too often we send our "cast offs" from other instruments into the percussion section, which causes an overlarge section. Ideally we should have six percussionists in the band: a snare drummer; a bass drummer; a cymbal player, who will be responsible for all cymbal parts including crash and suspended cymbals; a timpani player; a mallet instrument player, who will be responsible for all xylophone, vibes, and bell parts; and one person responsible for all the traps, who could double on snare drum when necessary.

Rhythm section instrumentalists should become proficient on all of the percussion instruments including the pitched instruments, such as bells and xylophone. Therefore, it is recommended that the players be rotated from number to number giving each person the experience of playing all percussion instruments.

Instruments Needed

The following is a minimum list of instruments a percussion section should include:

1. 2 concert snare drums.
2. 2 or 3 field drums.
3. 2 bass drums, one large concert drum and a scotch drum for marching.
4. 2 pair cymbals, one 20" pair for concert and one 16" pair for marching (medium weight). (Additional sizes and weights as available.)
5. Timpani, a set of 4 if at all possible and a stool for the player, who should be seated when playing.
6. Bell lyre, marimba or xylophone, and vibes.
7. Traps, including tambourine, triangle, castanets, wood block, cow bell, gourd, maracas, claves, and brushes.

Additional optional instruments to complete the section would include:

1. Chimes
2. Set of dance drums
3. Orchestra Bells
4. Traps; slapstick, whistles, temple blocks, etc.
5. Gong
6. Bongos

The ultimate goal of every band and orchestra should be to have sufficient players skilled enough to play any percussion part in any arrangement, and to have at their disposal any instrument for which the composer may write a part.

The Mallet Percussions

Wallace Barnett

THE EMPHASIS on mallet percussion instruments today is due in part to the excellent recordings currently being released. Even more significantly, the music educator who wishes to raise the musical standards of the percussion section emphasizes the importance of this family of instruments.

To fully utilize the mallet instruments already in the section and to justify the purchase of instruments necessary to complete the section, directors are asking for listings of band, orchestra, and ensemble materials which include vibes, marimba, xylophone, chimes, and bells parts.

Our purpose here is to present a sampling of an informative bibliography of such material. This extensive project—one year in preparation—has revealed some facts that will be valuable to publishers, manufacturers, composers, arrangers, and educators: (1) Names of the outstanding composers and arrangers who understand the tone color potential of the family of mallet instruments appear repeatedly in the bibliography. (2) Generally speaking, mallet instrument writing in the easier band, orchestra, and ensemble material leaves much to be desired. (3) Much wider use could be made of chimes, marimba, and vibraharp, in the area of specific writing for these instruments as well as in providing adequate and imaginitive cues—the composer-arranger is more familiar with bells and xylophone and therefore writes in a more articulate manner for these instruments. (4) Manufacturers could be of valuable help to the composer-arranger by making available charts showing the accepted standard ranges of mallet instruments.

The purpose of this bibliography has not been to provide an all inclusive list of material, but rather to indicate the amount of good music available which requires the use of mallet instruments. In some compositions the parts are not large, but they *are* important for adequate performance.

Instruments Necessary

Most instrumental music departments have a set of orchestra bells or a bell lyra. For this reason many compositions and arrangements have parts written for bells instead of vibes and chimes simply to make certain the part will be played. In other compositions an alternative is sometimes given, such as "bells *or* vibes." Good taste must be the guide when making substitutions. A triangle is *not* a substitute for chimes. On the other hand, what is a good substitute for chimes?

Since most marches include parts for bell lyra, they are not included in this listing unless they are unusual in some way, such as an effective use of chimes or other mallet instruments, or have been written in a different style, etc.

The code used to indicate mallet instruments required in the compositions is as follows:

B — Bells
Ch — Chimes
V — Vibes
Xy — Xylophone
Mba — Marimba

It should also be mentioned that much excellent music is included in Grades II and III and that such grading does not imply that more advanced groups should limit their performance to material in their particular grade listing.

Grateful acknowledgement and appreciation is given to:

The music publishers for their cooperation and generosity in making reference scores available.

Mervin Britton of the International Percussion Reference Library, Arizona State University at Tempe.

J. C. Deagan, Inc., Chicago, for invaluable assistance and for providing many scores for evaluation.

Editor's Note: A complete bibliography of recommended material incorporating the family of mallet percussion instruments will be sent without charge to school instrumental music directors submitting their request to J. C. Deagan, Inc., 1770 Berteau Avenue, Chicago, 13. The bibliography includes Band Books (Grades I, II, III), Band Compositions (Grades I-V), Orchestra Compositions (Grades I-V), Percussion Ensembles (Grades II-V), Stage Band Compositions (Grades II-V), Mallet Instrument method books (vibes, marimba, and xylophone), collections (solos and duets for vibes marimba, and xylophone), and solos (vibes, marimba, and xylophone). The bibliography contains more than 850 titles. Supplementary listings of new material will be added as new publications are released.

The following is a selected list taken from the complete bibliography of band compositions using mallet instruments. The grade level indicated is for the composition and not for the mallet instrument part.

Grade II

Title	Composer-Arranger	Pub	Mallet Insts Required
Adagio Pathetique	Godard-Vitto	CF	Ch.
America the Beautiful	Ward-Walters	Ru	Ch. B
Andante Cantabile	Tchaikovsky-Davis	BD	Ch
Autumn Silhouette	Walters	Ru	B or V
Back of the Moon	Kepner	So	B or V
Bells of St. Marys	Yoder	CG	Ch, V
Burlesk for Band	Washburn	BH	Xy, B
Ceremony for Winds	Cacavas	Bo	B
Chimes of Iron Mountain	Fillmore	CF	Ch
Chimes of Peace	Roberts	CF	Ch
Cinderella, minuet	Olivadoti	Mi	B or V
Civil War Suite	Waters	Ru	Ch
Cowboy in Cuba	Grundman	BH	Xy, B
Dance of the Toy Clowns	Parris	HE	V
Dance Toccata	Agay	Fo	B, Xy
Deep Purple	DeRose-Beeler	Ro	Ch
Design for Autumn	Dedrick	Ro	B or V
Die Meistersinger	Wagner-Osterling	Lu	Ch
Elegy	Mendelssohn-Erickson	Be	B
Estrellita	Ponce-Walters	Ru	B, V
Forest Splendor	Olivadoti	Ru	B or V
Glory and Honor	Rachmaninoff-Houseknecht	Kj	Ch, B
Guest Artist, solo bells	Bowles	Fs	B
Gypsy Baron	Strauss-Walters	Ru	B
Happy Christmas Holiday	Herfurth	Ro	B or Ch
Holiday in Paris, suite	Offenbach-Isaac	CF	Xy, Mba, B
Huldigungs March from Sigurd Jorsalfar	Grieg-Johnson	Ru	B

Title	Composer-Arranger	Pub	Mallet Insts Required
In a Clock Store	Orth-Vitto	CF	B
In the Cathedral	Pierne-Cheyette	GS	Ch, B
La Nuit	Cacavas	Wi	B or V
Legend, A	Tchaikovsky-Cheyette	Fo	Ch, B
Linda Mujer	Duchesne-Isaac	Ro	B
Londonderry Air	Dedrick	Kn	B or V
Londonderry Air	Walters	Ru	B or V
Mexican Overture	Isaac	CF	Xy, B
Midnight Bells	Heuberger-Mesang	Hn	B or V
Mission Festival	H. Johnson	Kj	Ch
Mission Valley	Barnes	Sc	Ch
Music Man, The	Willson-Reed	Fn	Ch, V or B
Night Piece	Klein	BH	B or V
Over the Rainbow	Arlen-Herfurth	Fe	B or V
Parade of the Icicles	Dedrick	Kn	B or V
Pavane	Ravel-C. Johnson	Ru	B
Pennsylvania Dutch Festival	Green	Ld	Xy, B
Percussion Espagnole	Prince	Ld	B, Ch, B or V, Xy
Pizzicato Polka	Strauss-Nutt	Kj	B
Pomp and Circumstance	Elgar-Walters	Ru	B, Ch
Portrait of This Old Man	Widdowson	Lu	B, Xy, Ch
Prayer of Thanksgiving	Kremser-Buys	Be	Ch
Prelude in C Minor	Rachmaninoff-Johnson	Ru	Ch
Praeludium for Band	Cacavas	Bo	Ch
Salvation is Created	Tschesnokoff-Houseknecht	Kj	Ch
Scarlet Ribbons	Danzig-Segal	Mi	B, Ch
Second American Folk Rhapsody	Grundman	BH	Xy
Skip to My Lou	Harr	Kj	Ch, B, Mba
Slavonic Folk Suite	Reed	Hn	Ch
Sunset Soliloquy	Walters	Ru	B, or V
Suite No. 1 for Band	Green	Ld	B, Ch
Take Me Along	Merrill-Reed	Hn	Ch, B or V
Tango Triste	Dedrick	Kn	B
Theme from Cornwall	Cacavas	Mi	B or V
Toy Symphony	L. Mozart-Gordon	CF	B
Two Pieces for Band	Dedrick	Kn	B or V
Under Paris Skies	Hubert-Walters	Ld	V or B
Unsinkable Molly Brown, The	Willson-Reed	Fn	Ch, B
Welsh Folk Suite	Davis	Lu	Ch, B

Grade III

Title	Composer-Arranger	Pub	Mallet Insts Required
Adeste Fideles	Gould	CG	Ch
Ado for Drummers	Vinter	BH	Xy, B, V
American Youth Concerto	Ward	Pr	Xy, B or V
Aschenbroedel, march	Herbert-Herfurth	Pr	B
Bright Eyes	Finlayson	BH	B
Calypso Man	Fenstock-Cacavas	Wi	B
Cambodian Suite	Varman-Cray	Lu	B, Xy
Carnival of Melody	Hawkins	Ro	B or V
Carol Festival, A	Ades	SH	B, Ch
Cathedral Canyon	Hanson	Lu	B, Ch
Chimes of Victory	Bergeim	BH	Ch
Cocoanut Dance	Herman-Yoder	BM	Xy
Cranberry Corners	Klein	BH	Xy
Deep South	Isaac & Lillya	CF	Mba
Die Meistersinger	Wagner-Osterling	Lu	Ch
Doll Dance	Brown-Beeler	Mr	B, Xy
Dollin' Up Dolly	Bueche	CF	Xy
Drummin' Thru' the Rye	Ostling	Be	B, or V
Easter Morning	Gould	CG	Ch, V
Einzugs March	Strauss-Barnes	Lu	B
Fields in Summer, The, from "Land of Wheat"	Gillis	Kj	V, B, Ch, Xy
Flamingo Ballet	Cacavas	Lu	B, Xy
Flash Harry	Binge-Hawkins	BT	B, Ch
Gigi	Loewe-Bennett	CG	Xy, B
Greenwillow	Loesser-Reed	Fn	Ch, B
Gypsy Life	Herbert-Isaac	Be	Xy, B, or V
Hi-Lili, Hi-Lo	Deutsch & Kaper–Hawkins	Ro	V, B
Hollywood Moods	Newman-Yoder	BT	B or V
In a French Music Hall	Green	Mi	Xy, B
Intermezzo for Band	Thompson	Bo	Xy, B
Jamaican Rhumba	Benjamin-Lang	BH	Xy
Jazz Pizzicato	Leroy Anderson-Lang	Mi	Xy
Land and the People from "Land of Wheat"	Gillis	Kj	B, Ch, V
Lincoln Overture	Long	Kj	B, Xy
Little Suite for Band	Grundman	BH	V, B
Malaga	Farnon-Cacavas	CG	Mba, B
March Carillon	Hanson-Leidzen	Pr	Ch
Marche Symphonique	Savino-Hawkins	BT	B
Meet the Band	Green	Ld	Ch, Xy, B
Midnight Matinee	Schaefer	Bo	Xy, B
Miniature Suite of Waltzes	Brahms-Mohaupt	Om	B or V
Musical Typist	Munro-Lang	Mi	Xy
Music Man, The	Willson-Lang	Fn	B or V
Musical Memories	Lang	Mi	B
Nola	Arndt-Huffnagle	Fo	Xy, B or V
Pastels	McRae	Su	V, B, Ch
Pentagon	Green	Ld	Xy, B
Prelude and Passacaglia	Purcell-Cailliet	HE	Ch, Xy
Prelude for Band	Saylor	Kn	B, Xy
Proud Heritage	Latham	Su	Ch
Reeds to the Front	Leonard	Ditson	Ch, Xy
Ring Those Christmas Bells	Fisher-Ades	SH	B
Round and Round (with Old Joe Clark)	McRae	Su	Xy, B
Russian Sailors Dance	Gliere-Isaac	CF	Xy
Sagamore Hill, march	Luckenbill	AM	Mba, B
Silent Night	Gould	CG	Ch
Spring Magic	Applebaum	Fo	Ch
Squeeze Play	Hallberg	SH	Xy
Studio One	Osser	Ld	V or B
Sussex Psalm	Howland	BH	Ch, B
Tribute to Romberg	Romberg-MacLean-Beeler	MP	Xy, B
United States Steel Suite	Green	Ld	Ch, B
Valzer Campestre, from "Suite Siciliana"	Marinuzzi-Harding	Ri	Xy, Cel or V
Vincent Youmans Fantasy	Youmans-Yoder	Mr	B or V
Washington Star	Howard-Gastyne	Lu	Ch, B
Where or When	Rodgers-Leidzen	CG	Ch
Whistling Boy	Davis	Kj	B
Whistling Shoemaker	Klein	BH	B, Xy
Yellowstone Suite	Klein	BH	B, Mba

Grades IV-V

Title	Composer-Arranger	Pub	Mallet Insts Required
American in Paris	Gershwin-Krance	NW	Xy, B
American Salute	Gould-Lang	Mi	B, Mba, Xy
Bagatelles For Band	Persichetti	EV	Xy
Ballade Bravura	Overgard	Kj	B, V, Xy
Burlesque	Shostakovich-Cailliet	Pr	Xy
Cafe Rio	Gould-Cacavas	GC	Mba, B or V
Celebration, from "Billy the Kid"	Copland-Lang	BH	Xy
Death Valley Suite	Grofé-Bennett	BT	B or V, Xy, Ch
Divertimento for Band	Persichetti	OD	Xy
Dixie Fantasia	Emmett-Dragon	Fo	Xy
Fanfare and Fable	Overgard	Fo	B, V, Xy
Fireworks from Symphony No. 2	de Gastyne	GL	B, Xy, Ch
First Noel	Gould	CG	Ch
Flute Cocktail	Simeone	SH	V, Xy, Ch
Golden Cockerel, The	Rimsky-Korsakov–Harding	Kj	Xy, B
Guaracha	Gould-Bennett	Mi	Xy
Halloween	Gould	CG	Xy
Harvest Celebration, from "Land of Wheat"	Gillis	Kj	Ch, B, Xy
Hurricane	Yoder	Kj	B, Xy, V
Jazz Suite, A	Mersey-Hunsberger	Fo	V
Jet Flight	Gilbert-Stevens	So	B
La Fiesta Mexicana	Reed	Mi	Ch, Mba
Lazy Days, from "Land of Wheat"	Gillis	Kj	V, Xy, B
Linnets Parade	Brewer-Brown	BH	Xy
March and Scherzo, from "Love of Three Oranges"	Prokofieff-Duthoit	BH	Xy, B
Meditation, from "Thais"	Massanet-Harding	Kj	Mba, B
Musica Simpatica	Rhodes	Su	Ch
Nightflight to Madrid	Leslie	Wo	Xy
Nocturne	Bucci-Bilik	Fh	B, V
Nocturne in a Modern Manner	Herman	Fi	Ch, Xy
Parade of the Cliche's	Gearhart	SH	B, Xy
Parisian Street Dance	Green	Mi	B or V, Xy
Perpetuum Mobile	Strauss-Winter	BH	B
Planting, The, from "Land of Wreat"	Gillis	Kj	Xy, B, Ch, Mba
Prelude & Theme	Mairs	Ld	B, Ch, V
Puppet	Langendoen	HE	Xy
Suite of Old American Dances	R. Bennett	CG	Xy, V, B
Symphony for Band	Persichetti	EV	Xy
Symphony in C minor	Williams	Colin	Mba
Thrashing Bee, from "Land of Wheat"	Gillis	Kj	Xy, Ch, B
Tsar's Bride	Rimsky-Korsakov–Harding	Kj	Mba
Twinkle Toes	Gillis	Mi	B, Mba, V
Variations on a Shaker Melody	Copland	BH	B, Xy
Whirligig	Sear	Ch	Xy
Windjammer	Gould-Yoder	CG	Ch, B
Whirlwind Polka	Cardew	BH	Xy

Key to Publishers

AM	Associated Music Pub.	Hn	Hansen
Be	Belwin, Inc.	Kj	Neil Kjos
BD	Byron-Douglas	Kn	Kendor
BH	Boosey & Hawkes	Ld	Leeds
BM	Broadcast Music	Lu	Ludwig
Bo	Bourne	MP	Music Pub. Holding Corp.
BT	Big Three	Mr	Miller
CF	Carl Fischer	NW	New World
CG	Chappell Group	OD	Oliver Ditson
Ch	John Church	Om	Omega
EV	Elkan-Vogel	Pr	Theodore Presser
Fe	Feist	Ri	G. Ricordi
Fh	Samuel French	Ro	Robbins
Fi	Fillmore	Ru	Rubank
Fn	Frank	Sc	Schmitt, Hall & McCreary
Fo	Sam Fox	SH	Shawnee
Fs	FitzSimons	So	Southern
GC	G & C Music	Wi	M. Witmark
GL	G. Leblanc Corp.	WO	B. F. Wood
HE	Henri Elkan		

Valid and Reliable Tuning References

INTONATION AND PERCUSSIONS

Ralph R. Pottle

WHAT AN UNUSUAL TITLE for an article on tuning! How can percussions possibly influence the technique or manner of achieving good intonation? What have they to do with it? Are they that important in the instrumental school music program?

Let's observe what is happening in the field of instrumental music by answering the last question first.

During the past five years percussions have experienced the greatest popularity growth in over forty years. Moreover, this growth is continuing. It is manifesting itself, first, thru composers who are treating the percussions far more liberally than in the past. It is evident, secondly, thru the publishers who are responding with vividly conceived arrangements which challenge the capabilities of performers. Thirdly, instrumental directors are training the finest percussionists this country has ever heard. Fourth, the manufacturers are bringing out the most beautiful percussions ever crafted. Fifth,—and what an important fifth—this whole movement is being accepted. The professionals are happy over the development, and the public simply loves it.

It is inevitable that such vigorous growth in percussions must be reckoned with. And when I speak of percussions I include three sets of instruments which might be classified roughly as rhythmic, harmonic, and melodic percussions. The rhythmic instruments include cymbals, triangle, tambourine, castanets, maracas, sandblock, and other non-tunable accessories. The harmonic percussions include the timpani and harp, tunable as to frequency, and the various drums, tunable as to tension only. In the melodic percussions we find what I term the pre-tuned (fixed-pitch) instruments such as the vibraharp, xylophone, marimba, orchestra bells, glockenspiel, chimes, piano, piano accordion, and the electronic organ. The last three could be considered harmonic in some respects, but they remain pre-tuned instruments.

Tuning Must Remain Constant

It is this group of melodic percussions or pre-tuned instruments, which concerns us momentarily, and which challenges every intonation precept we have developed. This group can spell next to disaster for us if we fail to achieve a very precise and steady tuning throughout a concert or rehearsal. But what a pronounced asset these melodic percussions become when we properly respect them.

The fact that these melodic percussions are pre-tuned at the factory to A-440, the same frequency to which all wind instruments are tuned by the manufacturers, should facilitate rather than impede accurate tuning. Too, the fact that their pitch is inflexible and unchangeable should also simplify close tuning. But it is precisely this factor which refutes some of our most traditional tuning techniques. Those techniques are evidently erroneous because, while pre-tuned melodic percussions remain constant or steady throughout a concert, we allow our wind instruments to fluctuate extensively in tuning frequency while being played, and this unsteadiness results in mistuning with the pre-tuned percussions. Consequently, if we propose to utilize to best advantage these popular fixed pitch instruments we must tune to their A-440 and stay tuned throughout our concerts and rehearsals.

Tuning References

To accomplish this demands, first, the use of valid and reliable tuning references. Where tuning bars are to be used as references there should be four, B♭, E♭, F, and A, so as to reach sensitive tuning notes on each instrument and to afford multiple checking on all winds. An ideal reference, where available, is a vibraharp, with vibrators off, which affords chromatic tuning.

Effective tuning demands the adoption of proper tuning techniques thru which the A-440 standard can be maintained once it is established. What are these techniques?

Warm-Up Important

The most important is a thorough pre-warming of wind instruments by the players' breaths prior to checking the A-440 tuning. This is because wind instruments are designed for optimum tuning at A-440 in temperature of 72°F. after warm-up, not while cold. The merits of **pre-warming wind instruments before checking tuning adjustments have been greatly underestimated by** many school music conductors. **But this must be stressed anew here, for thru this process of thorough warming, followed by careful tuning, we derive three distinct intonation advantages.**

Two advantages of pre-warming can be discerned by reviewing frequency measurements taken while representative wind instruments, unwarmed, were being played for five minutes in temperature of 70°F. They showed this wide disparity in average fluctuation:

Flutes	sharped	14.0	Cents[1]
B♭ Clarinets	"	10.2	"
E♭ Alto Saxophones ..	"	9.0	"
B♭Cornets	"	16.4	"
B♭ Trombones	"	6.3	"
F French horns	"	12.4	"
B♭ Euphoniums	"	8.0	"
BB♭ Sousaphones	"	7.8	"

A cent is 1/100th of a half-step.

Thus, if the director follows the traditional routine of tuning winds to A-440 while instruments are cold, or prior to thorough warm-up, during performance they will rapidly become sharp to the pre-tuned A-440 percussions by rather widely varying amounts, as indicated above. Such action (1) throws winds out of tune with one another, and (2) creates the illusion of flat sounding melodic percussions, an undesirable situation in any ensemble. On the other hand, by tuning after thorough warm-up we achieve steady intonation during performance and thereby avoid both problems.

Crowded Room Effects Tuning

The third advantage of the pre-warming manifests itself in the event of a radical increase in atmospheric temperature, for instance, from 70°F. to 80°F. Such increase in temperature is more likely to occur during a "standing room only" concert than at a rehearsal because of the added warmth of 98.6°F. radiating from the concert audience. But where the pre-warming has been thorough, a ten degree increase in temperature affects small instruments only slightly and all winds by diminished amounts. Note the measurements shown below taken while wind instruments were being played after warm-up. Figures represent the sharping which took place because of increase in temperature from 70° to 80°F.

Flutes	sharped	6.2	cents[1]
B♭ Clarinets	"	4.3	"
E♭ Alto Saxophone	"	7.1	"
B♭ Cornets	"	6.2	"
B♭ Trombones	"	6.9	"
F French horns	"	7.8	"
B♭ Euphoniums	"	9.1	"
BB♭ Sousaphones	"	14.2	"

Because of thorough pre-warming the small instruments sharped only slightly when room temperature rose and only the horns, baritones, and sousaphones necessitated anything more than minimal adjustment downward in order to maintain the level of the A-440 percussions.

An outstanding feature of the 1961 Mid-West Band Clinic in Chicago was the exciting brilliancy and sheen imparted to the Cass Technical High School Band of Detroit by both orchestra bells and chimes. They beautifully supported the organization, which started and ended its concert exactly on A-440. The instantaneous standing ovation accorded them, accompanied by prolonged applause and punctuated by innumerable shouts of "bravo" and "more," attested to unqualified approbation by the distinguished audience of 3500 directors.

Complete Warm-Up

The assiduous conductor, in all events, exercises meticulous care in achieving complete warm-up prior to intonation checks, whereupon his tuning (1) is close between all winds, (2) remains steady at the A-440 in normal temperature (so essential in successful use of fixed-pitch instruments), and (3) demands only minimal correction in rising temperature.

In conclusion, the winning director is always the one who strives to command the greatest number of potential assets and who exercises the alertness, patience, and diligence to convert them into prime assets. Inherent in the several fixed-pitch melodic percussions and other pre-tuned instruments enumerated above are assets in the form of unexplored musical possibilities barely at the threshold of realization. These instruments are firmly established and are gaining in popularity. They are coming into their own! Therefore, the patient and resourceful conductor will discern their manifold value to his organization and will devise the skills by which to utilize them to their full effectiveness.

1. Ralph R. Pottle, *Tuning the School Band and Orchestra*, published by the author.

December 1962

The Marching Band Percussion Section

Maxine Lefever

THE GOOD MARCHING BAND must leave its audience with both a visual and an auditory impact. No matter how well a band performs, it cannot be considered a truly fine band unless both aspects are developed fully.

The drum section, because it plays throughout the half-time show, and because of the physical motion involved in playing the various percussion instruments, can add to or detract from the performance more than any other section.

The director, therefore, should be very concerned with the development of this small but important section of the band.

The steps followed by the staff of Purdue University's Marching Band in developing a versatile section could be followed by any band with the necessary adjustments to fit each particular situation.

Planning for the football season should begin at the close of the previous school year. At this time the director should decide upon the instrumentation of the section for the coming season. This will allow ample time for purchase and repair of equipment during the summer months.

The Purdue Band, with 220 playing members, uses a twenty-man percussion section: eight 12″ x 15″ field drums, four 12″ x 17″ tenor drums, four 10″ x 28″ bass drums, and four 18″ medium weight cymbals. The section is aligned in two ranks of ten, with the cymbals at the ends of each rank. The eight snare drums fill out the first rank, and the four bass drums form the center of the second rank. The remaining four places in the second rank are filled by the tenor drums, two on each side of the bass drums.

Different Functions

Each type of drum has its particular function. Too often the tenor drum is used merely as a bass drum supplement. This can lead to a "tom-tom" effect and a monotonous, repetitious sound which is most undesirable as a steady fare. The tenor drum has a sound of its own and should be used as an independent voice in the percussion section. It is most often used to highlight accents and to "fill in." Correct usage of the tenor drum will create some extra work in writing special parts, both for cadences and for tunes, but the extra dividend in sound achieved makes this effort well worth-while.

The other drums are less often misunderstood. The snare drum provides the interest, the "melodic line" of the section. The bass drum gives a solid, basic beat. The cymbal contributes brilliance and augments climaxes. The cadence in Example 1 demonstrates a correct usage.

For occasional contrast, the snare drum and tenor drum can switch roles. Some marches lend themselves particularly well to this. The snare drum can play a steady rhythmic background—paradiddles, perhaps—and the tenor drum can assume the more "melodic" role. This use of the tenor drum has the added advantage of giving the snare drum section some relief from learning so many new parts for each show. This should not be employed, however, on more than one number in each show, because the tenor drum could become monotonous and over-balancing if so used too frequently.

The First Weeks

Following the theory that each member of the drum family has its special contribution, do not place all the best players on snare drum, but try to distribute them throughout the various sections. At least one or two good men in each section will form a nucleus that can be of great assistance in helping the weaker members.

Since, as said previously, the visual and auditory effects are both important, it is essential to select drummers who play and march well. If a choice must be made between the two abilities, it must be realized that a student can usually be taught to march well more quickly than he can be taught to play well—and the time is limited.

Now to begin serious work with the section—as individuals, as families within the unit, and with the section as a whole. Individual conferences will identify most quickly and remedy the specific problems of each student; this will ultimately help the "sound" of the section. Small sectional rehearsals (the snare drums as a unit, the bass drums, etc.) provide an opportunity to work on precision and marching routines, which will add to the visual effect. Rehearsals of the entire percussion section will reinforce previous instruction and will improve balance.

The drum section is now ready to march with the rest of the band, but must continue to receive a considerable amount of supervision. Here it is particularly important that they be observed from the spectators' vantage point in the stands. The sound of the section will undoubtedly be quite different from this distance, and adjustments must be made to achieve the proper balance. Also, flaws in the routines will be more readily discernible, and individual help may again be necessary for those who are not performing adequately. This type of assistance can often best be given by another member of the section who can demonstrate the correct technique.

Work is not yet finished at this point. It is difficult for the individual member of the section to get a correct over-all view of what is being (or not being) accomplished from his position on the field. The ideal solution is to make sound movies of a performance, by which the individual can spot his own errors, and which will motivate him towards constant improvement.

January 1963

A Likehand Grip For Holding Snare Drum Sticks

Neal Fluegel

MANY ARTICLES AND INSTRUCTION books have been published explaining how best to hold drum sticks in practicing and performing. Most of these have defined and discussed the traditional grip. This is the grip familiar to all band and orchestra directors and private teachers and has been considered the correct and accepted method. It has been used throughout the history of snare drum playing.

The traditional grip developed from earlier periods when most of the snare drum playing was in the military bands with the players wearing a sling. This sling caused the drum to slant extremely to the right, and the left stick had to be held differently than the right in order to strike the drum head properly. It was not necessary to make any change in this basic grip. There was only a limited amount of concert literature available and in concert playing, a concession was made to the field-trained drummer, and the drum was set on a stand at the same slant.

We have gradually come to a stage of musical development that demands more technical facility from all performers, and particularly from the percussionist. Compositions for percussion instruments only (percussion ensembles) have been written during the past few years. Contemporary composers are writing increasingly difficult percussion parts.

Although percussion music as a whole has advanced rapidly during the past thirty to forty years, techniques have not. We should be considering new techniques to meet the increasing demand for more virtuosity.

A different method of holding snare drum sticks is now in its experimental stages and may be one answer for improving the technique of percussion performance.

Many Names

The method under consideration has been called by many names—primitive, experimental, identical, new, basic, matched-hand. Only time will determine the ultimate terminology, but for our purposes here it will be referred to as the "like-hand" grip.

What is it? Stated simply, it is holding the left hand stick in the same manner as the right is held in the traditional grip. The right hand remains the same in either method. The advantages of this grip are many.

Utilize the natural position of the hands and arms. If an individual is asked to hold his hands and arms out straight, his natural response will be with the top of the hands and arms facing up. Or, give a child a pair of sticks and, because it is natural, he automatically will hold them both in the way the right-hand stick is held. It goes without saying that when something is done the most natural way, it usually is done more readily, more easily, and more competently.

Less tension will be encountered. Because of this natural position there will be no undue strain and pull on the arm muscles to cause tension. An extra pull on the muscles of the left arm is unavoidable in the traditional method, because of the arm's rolling movement. Most people are right-handed, so the abnormal positioning is an added burden on the less well developed arm. A drummer's tendency to pull his left arm in close to his mid-section creates even more tension. The like-hand grip eliminates these problems of tension and their obvious disadvantages.

Superior Sound

A more equal and unified sound will be obtained. When the sticks are held in the same manner with each hand, and the drum is struck using the same muscles of each hand, wrist, and arm, the sound produced will be the same with each stick. Therefore, the rudiments, including the long roll, will sound more unified and will develop faster.

It should be mentioned at this point, that the location of the drum in relation to the performer can be one of three positions. It can be completely level, angled slightly toward, or slightly away from the performer. The choice is essentially the performer's.

If he is performing on one drum in a concert position, it is recommended that the slight angle be away from the drummer to compensate for the slight body angle. However, if he is performing on a number of drums, or on the march, which requires a lot of movement, there should be a slight angle with the low part nearest the performer's mid-section, or no angle at all.

The important point to remember is that the drum should not be angled either to the right or left. The reason for this is quite obvious. Since we are striking the drum in the same manner with each stick, the drum should be situated in the same position so that each hand can obtain the desired "like" tone color, which is one of the advantages of using the "like-hand" grip. The sticks themselves, should form about a 30 degree angle rather than the traditional 90 degrees in relation to each other.

More flexibility can be achieved. Movement from one drum to another, as in dance drumming or performing a contemporary percussion composition or part, will be easier to achieve with greater accuracy and speed. This will become obvious immediately if the reader will experiment on his own.

It is quite difficult to reach a drum situated to the far left when the left stick is pointing directly to the right. When it is pointed straight ahead, however, as in the like-hand method, it can be reached more easily. Improved versatility is a consequent benefit.

Fundamental Grip

Easier transfer can be made to other instruments of the percussion family. All mallet instruments and timpani are played with a fundamental "like-hand" grip.

The transfer from snare drum, when using the traditional method, is usually quite a problem. The weak left hand must be drilled on a new technique before the student can learn the other instruments. This has been very discouraging to students during their study of percussion instruments. With the "like-hand" grip there is no real problem in transferring. Eliminating that hitch can save both the teacher and student time and torment.

The typical condition existing in our high schools, that of producing only snare drummers, would be partially eliminated with the adoption of the "like-hand" method. Students could then learn and perform simultaneously on all percussion instruments rather than just on the snare drum. This comprehensive approach to percussion teaching would seem to be basic.

Marching

One major criticism of the "like-hand" method is, "It will not work while marching." Now available on the market are certain pieces of equipment which hold the drum in the playing position mentioned earlier. As he marches the player does not have to contend with the drum flipping from side to side in front of him. It will remain in a fairly stationary position.

Another answer is to mount the percussion equipment on inexpensive carts which roll on the field. This has been done with complete success at Southern Illinois University and is well worth considering.

Such relatively simple adjustments would seem to invalidate any criticism of "like-hand" from the standpoint of field movement.

Gaining in Popularity

It was mentioned earlier that this method is in the experimental stage.

Jack McKenzie, percussion instructor at the University of Illinois, is teaching "like-hand" technique and is finding it to be quite successful. He has changed to this method in his own performance and is teaching it to more than 50% of his private and methods class students.

Mervin Britton, percussion instructor at Arizona State University, also has changed to the "like-hand" method after having studied and performed with the traditional grip. He is beginning to teach some of his students the new approach.

Donald Canedy, director of bands and percussion instructor at Southern Illinois University, has been teaching his students this method and has found it to be quite successful. Many high school band directors also have joined in teaching "like-hand" after observing its fine results.

This does not in any way represent a complete list of people experimenting with the like-hand grip, but it certainly hints at its increasing popularity among outstanding teachers in the field of percussion.

The author also has taught this method to high school students in northern Illinois and at the Arizona All-State Music Camp at Arizona State University. He has found it to be completely successful and rewarding and has converted to the "like-hand" method in his own playing.

In conclusion, let it be stated that the simple transition from the traditional grip to the "like-hand" grip solves many problems and lends increased flexibility. Whether such transition is accepted as universal practice will depend on the future teachers, performers, and students of percussion. The author would be pleased to hear from any readers about their experiences, successful or not, with the "like-hand" method of teaching snare drum.

February 1963

Suggestions for increasing interest in your—

Percussion Class

David A. Tobias

PERCUSSION IS A FASCINATING SUBject, and with a little extra planning percussion classes can be alive and meaningful. By incorporating ear training, rhythmic improvisation, composition techniques, and sight reading into your class activities, much of the dullness often encountered can be prevented. It is not necessary to play rhythms on practice pads week after week. While melodic and harmonic variety are not so readily apparent with percussion as with wind or string instruments, it is possible to teach correct techniques on all of the percussion instruments in a creative and informative way.

Bring many different percussion instruments into the class and demonstrate special techniques on each one. For added interest invite outstanding percussionists from the area to demonstrate technique.

Include Many Instruments

Throughout the year cover all of the instruments that band and orchestra music may call for, including timpani, xylophone, marimba, orchestra bells, chimes, hand cymbals, suspended cymbals, bass drum, tom-tom, triangle, woodblock, tambourine, castanets, the Latin-American instruments, and a complete dance band outfit. Use some of the more unusual and interesting traps as well, such as the ratchet, slide whistle, slapstick, etc.

Be sure that each person in the class gets a chance to play each instrument. Just because many of these instruments are played in grade-school rhythm bands does not mean that all students know how to handle them correctly without instruction.

Use Recordings

Make use of recordings to stimulate the class. Assign the drum parts to some of Sousa's marches: *The Washington Post March* (easy), *Belle of Chicago* (inter.), or *Semper Fidelis* (adv.) are possible choices, but many others are equally good. After one or two practice sessions, play along with a good recording. Have three students play the snare drum, the bass drum, and the cymbals as the rest of the class play on practice pads. Rotate so that everyone gets to play on the instruments.

When studying timpani, obtain the orchestra part to an easy symphony or overture. You can find the parts in a good timpani method book as standard repertoire, or you can borrow or rent the parts from a music store. Try to have several timpani parts available so that everyone can follow the music as one person plays along with a recording. Some excellent numbers, interesting and not too difficult, are Mozart's *Jupiter Symphony*, Weber's *Oberon Overture*, Rossini's *William Tell Overture*, and Dvorak's *New World Symphony* (4th Movement). These compositions present opportunities for learning proper choice of sticking, muffling techniques, dynamic control, how to change pitches while counting measures *(New World Symphony)*, abbreviated notations, etc. Playing with a recording is the next best thing to getting actual playing experience with an orchestra.

To make your class sparkle when things begin to lag just before vacation time, introduce the Latin-American percussion instruments—maracas, chocallo, gourd, claves, bongos, cowbell, etc. Demonstrate and have the class play along with a good recording which uses these instruments. Rotate the various instruments so that each person plays as many different ones as time permits.

Keep Lesson Moving

Keep your lesson moving at a quick pace. When concentrating on snare drum technique, have one student play on a drum while the rest play on practice pads. Students should take turns on the drum for each new exercise or solo, in some pre-arranged order. (If the class is standing in a semi-circle or straight line, have each person take his turn automatically in order from left to right so that the teacher does not have to call on students.) In this way, everyone gets a chance to play on the drum and feel the difference in rebound, and yet everyone is playing at all times. The teacher is able to look around the class constantly and check on the position and stroking of every student and still hear the one person at the drum easily above the others. (Sometimes, especially in the very early stages, it is good to use only practice pads.)

Read Literature

In addition to the usual exercises, read many solos and ensembles. The teacher should build a library of collections of drum music to use for sight reading in class. Set reasonable tempos and read thru one number after another in ensemble without stopping. Piano accompaniments will add interest. Work for and insist upon good sight reading habits so that students will never have to ad lib a band part for a tricky new march.

Teach Rudiments

Introduce and teach all of the standard drum rudiments. Have students take pride in playing them well. Rudiments are to the drummer what scales are to any other instrumentalist. All drummers should know how to play a paradiddle with facility, just as all wind and string players should know how to play a B♭ major scale. Remember that rudiments are used extensively in martial music, but must be used with discretion in orchestral music. Develop this discrimination in your students.

Include ear training and improvisation in your classes. Play a four-measure rhythm on the drum several times and have a student write it on the board. The rest of the class may write the rhythm on paper. Repeat the process until you have accumulated sixteen measures, preferably in 2/4 time. Then have the class play the rhythm on their practice pads while someone plays a 2/4 folk tune or march on the piano.

Also use folk tunes to teach how to improvise on, or to vary, a simple rhythm. Assign a rhythm from a song and have each person make up his variation of it by adding flams, ruffs, rolls, or syncopation. Each person then plays his variation while a pianist plays the tune or the class sings or whistles the tune. (Even if the teacher is a competent pianist, it is better to have someone play the piano who is not a member of the class and is free to come on days these activities are planned so that teacher and students both are free to concentrate on percussion.)

For a very rewarding experience for the students, have each person write his own composition for a percussion ensemble of four to ten persons using any of the instruments played in class. Be sure to bring in some good percussion ensemble music first for the class to play or hear. Discuss different combinations of instruments, special effects, notation of parts, and the use of musical form or structure. After the pupils write the parts the group should play the numbers and both teacher and students can make suggestions for improvement. After correcting and revising the parts and after several rehearsals, have a concert with the class playing its own compositions. Each person may conduct the ensemble for his own composition and also play a different instrument in each number. The values the student derives are (1) experience playing in an ensemble; (2) an understanding of modern percussion ensemble literature; (3) a better understanding of all percussion instruments with regard to sound, range, technique, mallets, sticks, etc.; and (4) an understanding of percussion notation and scoring.

Develop student pride by having good percussion equipment and taking proper care of it. Most drum companies will send free catalogs and literature for the class. Discuss how to reset a drum head, how to tune a snare drum, how to tie a square cymbal knot, etc. There are also many fascinating stories to be told about the history and the background of some of the instruments.

March 1963

With the proper raw material you can develop a timpani player in

Just Three Weeks

Kenneth Krause

If you need a timpani player in a hurry, you can have one in three weeks.

Of course, to turn out a good product in any field, you must start with the right raw materials. In this case, the necessary materials are these: (1) A set of good pedal timpani with plastic heads; (2) A snare drummer who can sing a major scale. (If your drummers are poor singers, at least try to find one who can *recognize* a major scale when he hears it.)

For a drummer who has never played timpani, the change in "feel" and technique can be a problem, although it should be less of a problem for a drummer than, say, a piano player. This is one reason for picking a drummer rather than another instrumentalist. Drummers invariably have better technique on timpani than someone who has had no previous percussion training.

Stick Grip

Timpani sticks are held like the right hand snare drum grip, except that the thumbs are on top. While I have seen a few timpanists use other grips, the majority of top-notch professionals use the thumb-on-top grip. Since the bounce is not used on timpani, one can get much more power and control with this grip.

Have the student hold the sticks in front of him, using his right hand snare grip, but with the thumbs on top; then lay the sticks on the drum parallel to each other, still using this grip. This should bring his knuckles close together. Now, if he will raise one stick at a time, using only wrist motion, until the stick points toward the ceiling, he will begin to get the proper action.

Single Stroke Roll

He should practice this faithfully, on different pitches each day, eventually working rudimentally into a single stroke roll (slow-fast-slow), keeping both hands the same volume, until he can do it smoothly. The single stroke roll is the only acceptable roll on timpani. Attempting to use bouncing double strokes will not produce a satisfactory roll. By practicing the roll on different pitches, the drummer should soon learn that he must speed up his roll on the higher-pitched notes to make it more smooth, and roll more slowly on the lower notes to obtain maximum tone. In general, timpani players should use single, alternating sticking except where it is necessary to double up with one hand to obtain a desired effect or to cross from one drum to the other.

Since a timpani head vibrates from the center out (the center thus being relatively motionless), the best beating spot is about half way between the center and the edge. Staccato can be obtained by moving nearer the center or nearer the edge. Near-center seems to work best for soft staccato, while near the edge is better for loud passages.

Teaching Tuning

You need not wait for the tyro timpanist to master the technique of the instrument before you begin to work on tuning; the two can be practiced simultaneously. The basic pair of drums should be tuned to B♭ and F. This is their basic pitch, without any pressure from the pedal, or with the pedal all the way "off." It will be the director's job at first to see that the basic pitch is correct at the beginning of the practice period, but with plastic heads this is no problem. Since plastic heads will usually maintain their pitch for a period of weeks if not tampered with, keeping them in tune for one practice period or one concert is merely a matter of leaving them alone once they are tuned.

Scale Practice

Beginning with the basic pitch on the large drum, the student should practice playing up the first five notes of an F scale, using the pedal. The notes obtainable on the large drum should be at least F, G, A, B♭ and C. It is not likely that notes above C will be practical on this drum. He should practice these notes going up the scale, down the scale, and then skipping around until he is thoroughly familiar with them and has memorized the pedal position for each note. This is akin to learning the correct finger placement on violin. With plastic heads the pedal positions are very reliable, and usually as accurate as using tuning gauges.

When the student has mastered the notes on the low drum he can practice the same routine on the high one, using the notes B♭, C, D, F♭ and F. It may be possible in some cases to get above this note on a 25″ kettle, but not always.

After achieving reasonable accuracy in hitting the notes of the F and B♭ scales, the student can tackle some easy band parts, and find that most of the notes are in his "vocabulary." In order to play notes which are not in these scales, it is easiest for the student to go a semi-tone up from the scale note just below by pushing the pedal approximately half the distance to the next scale tone. The director can help the student find the exact pedal position. It is better to go up from the lower note than to come down, since the head does not always release all the way, due to friction at the edge of the bowl. (This is why you often see timpanists pushing in the center of the head with their hand.)

After a few weeks of serious practice the student should have mastered the proper technique and the pedal positions of the complete chromatic scale within the playing range. Now he can make fast changes in tuning, and with experience become a proficient timpanist.

The heart of the band is
THE BASS DRUMMER

Betty Masoner

DO YOU DREAM OF HAVING AN ASsistant? You do? Well, stop dreaming, because you have one right in your own band. Where? Your bass drummer! Perhaps you are unaware of what your bass drummer can add to the overall performance of your band. John Philip Sousa, dean of all band directors, was just as fussy about the bass drummer's rendition of a composition as that of the first cornetist. And so, if you demand meticulous performance from the cumbersome object in the back of your band you will be aiding yourself and your band. Let us analyze the problem a bit!

Although a 30 inch drum is to be recommended the size has no effect upon how it is played. Separate tension should be specified when making a new purchase but any drum can be put in working order by using a little time and effort. Grease on the screw rods; soap and water on the heads; perhaps a little paint on the shell and hoops, and most drums will be ready to go into business. Give the heads a once over and even if they are not broken, if they are hard and dry and seem to have lost their elasticity it is time to replace them. Always demand that the drum be kept in spotless condition. And to facilitate easy up-keep, it is wise when purchasing an instrument to choose a plastic shell.

The stand is really very important. It should be very sturdy, and heavy enough that the drum will not slide when struck. A heavy wooden cradle is preferred if transferring it from storage to rehearsal area is not a problem. The stand should place the drum at a height which will require the performer to reach up to it slightly rather than being able to lay on it. The latter is a practice which should never be permitted.

Beater Important

The drummer should stand to the right of the drum with the music stand also on the right of the drum and in a direct line with the director. The stick is of utmost significance. It should be a double-end, short model lambs wool beater. The grip is in the center of the shaft, thus allowing a short controlled stroke. The drummer should also be supplied with a pair of timpani sticks with which to execute long rolls— single strokes on one side of the drum, a la timpani.

The drum should be tuned to an indefinite pitch on the loose order and then controlled by the left hand and right knee. The left hand is held against the left head and by means of changing the amount of pressure exerted on the head the tone can be controlled; the right knee on the head can be used in the same manner. If you use the cymbals attached to the base drum a commercial muffler may be used, but this device does not allow the desired variation in tone.

Remember that the bass drum is no more a monotone than any other music instrument. Various pitches and qualities of tone are readily obtainable— pitch by position of striking the head and quality by control of the pressure exerted on the heads with the left hand and right knee. Of course, loudness is determined by the force of the blow. The basic beat is accomplished by striking the drum with a glancing blow about mid-way between the center of the drum and the hoop with the thought of pulling something out of the drum rather than pounding the head thru it. A snapping wrist action is used rather than a forceful movement from the upper arm.

Plays All Nuances

The first duty of the bass drummer is to transfer the thought waves of you, the director, by way of the drum to the rest of the band. Secondly the drummer should add the filigree to the work of art. This is done by playing all nuances, including crescendos and accents wherever marked. The drummer must judge the composer's wishes and play each number in the character that the writer intended, not a thud for a waltz movement or a monotonous trip-hammer effect for a march. Demand that the bass drum be played musically, with feeling, as is every other instrument and you will begin to realize the possibilities of the true art of playing the large drum. The character of the composition should be studied painstakingly and interpreted with utmost care. Every minute desire of the director and the composer must be reflected in the playing of the drum.

If you desire special effects they may be obtained by using wooden beaters or Scotch drum sticks, although there is no limit to the variation possible with the conventional stick if it is handled properly.

Percussion Ensemble

If your bass drummer is bored with his lot in your band perhaps you should organize a percussion ensemble. Contemporary music calls for more than a boom-boom from the bass drum and the modern ensemble requires the highest degree of musical taste. There are a number of compositions available which have bass drum parts that would challenge the best players. Or if you prefer there are also a number of solos available.

For a valuable assistant, find yourself a true musician, put him on bass drum, and let him help you help your band. A band will follow the nuances of the bass drummer. O.K.?

May 1963

MALLET PERCUSSIONS

Can produce scintillating sounds and new sonorities

James D. Salmon

COMPOSERS AND ARRANGERS HAVE re-discovered the sounds of the mallet percussion instruments and have brought them into new focus and a more useful prominence in every type of music ensemble. We now hear these scintillating sounds generously sprinkled throughout the musical scores to movies, television shows, Broadway musicals, commercial announcements on radio and television, dance bands and combos, and on recordings that feature classical, symphonic, and popular music. In like manner, professional and non-professional percussion ensembles have been featured in concerts and have recorded successfully during the past few years. With the recent appearance of new recording techniques for high fidelity and stereophonic reproductions, we find that all percussions seem to have been given a new place of prominence on the family tree of music instruments.

This prominence is filtering down to our school bands and orchestras, possibly because of the alertness of our music educators. These educators realize the many possibilities available with the extensive use of bells, chimes, marimba, xylophone, and vibes in their modern ensembles. These instruments provide the educator with the essential equipment needed to attract, hold, and develop the more progressive type of students desired for the percussion sections of the bands and orchestras of today.

Percussionists find that more than a perfunctory crash, bang, or boom of their instruments is necessary for a musical performance. They must show more technical skill, musical depth, and artistic taste, all complemented with an understanding and use of all the mallet percussion instruments. In brief, percussionists now need the same musical and artistic standards required of the members of the reed, brass, and string choirs in their respective organizations.

Increased Interest

As often as is feasible and in good musical taste, the composer or arranger should include melody, counter-melody, and harmony parts for the mallet percussions in arrangements for band and orchestra. This could help to increase the interest of the young percussionists in their music ensemble activities. It could also become a genuine challenge and an extra opportunity for them to complement their playing abilities on the non-melodic percussions with those of the melodic, or mallet percussions.

Many of the current publications for school ensembles have special or optional parts for the mallet percussions. In most cases these special parts are scored for a specific percussion sound in the plan of the arranger. However, a suggested substitution usually is included in the conductor's score. For example, a melody scored for vibes could be played on bells; a xylophone solo might be played on the marimba (or vice versa); a single note for bells could be played on chimes.

With a little imagination in the study of the band and orchestra scores the director usually will be able to find appropriate sections where the mallet percussions can be included to add to the standard tonal colorings of the ensemble. A little experimentation with this technique will bring some very interesting results.

Trained Musician Learns Quickly

In a situation where the members of the percussion section do not have very much facility on the mallet percussions, or where they do not read very well in the treble clef, a good pianist, a proficient string instrumentalist (violin or guitar), or perhaps an accomplished accordionist could join the percussion section and play these parts with little difficulty. They will need a few lessons in the handling of the mallets, but their reading ability and knowledge of keys and chord progressions can help them play the percussion parts. This also might be a practical way for the music educator to indicate to his percussionists that perhaps they would be wise to increase their playing abilities on the mallet percussion instruments.

To assist the mallet percussion performer to place the written notations against the true sounding ranges of these instruments correctly, the following range information is included, with some performance suggestions for each of the instruments. The actual, over-all chromatic range of the mallet percussions extends from A2 to C8. (C4 is middle C.)

Bells (or Glockenspiel)

Case Bells: has 30 metal bars, G3 to C6; no resonators under bars; housed in a carrying case. The sound is two octaves higher than the written notation.

Bell Lyra (marching band bells): has 25 metal bars, A3 to A5; has no resonators under bars; built on a metal lyre-shaped frame for easy carrying with a leather shoulder strap. The sound is two octaves higher than the written notation.

Alto Bell Lyra (marching band bells): has 21 metal bars, A3 to F5; has small resonators under each bar; built on a metal lyre-shaped frame for easy carrying with a leather shoulder strap. The sound is one octave higher than the written notation.

Playing suggestions:

1. Use mallets with hard rubber, plastic, or brass tips for best sound.
2. The metal (brass) tipped mallets give an interesting bell-tinkling sound in solo melody sections.
3. Intervals of thirds, sixths, and octaves sound very good as harmonized "double stops" on the case bells.
4. Try bells on the melody of the march trio using metal tipped mallets.

Chimes

Plated tubes, 1¼ or 1½ inch in diameter, arranged chromatically on a floor rack; set contains 18 tubes with a range from C4 to F5. Chimes sound one octave higher than the written notation.

Playing suggestions:

1. Always play the chime mallet against the contact area (the striking cap at the very top of the tube) for the best sound.
2. A rawhide mallet (cabinet maker's hammer) is the most common striking device used in chime playing; however, bell and xylophone mallets may be used for special sound effects.
3. Because of the special tuning employed in building chimes, thirds, sixths, and octaves played as "double-stops" do not sound in tune. Chimes sound their best when played as single tones, or in a melodic passage. Fourths and fifths are effective "double-stops" in certain harmonizations.

Marimba

Four octave model has 49 rosewood bars; range C3 to C7.

Three-and-a-half octave model has 44 rosewood bars; range F3 to C7.

Three octave model has 37 rosewood bars; range F3 to F6.

Two-and-a-half octave model has 30 rosewood bars; range C4 to F6.

Special model has 52 rosewood bars; range A2 to C7.

All marimbas sound the actual written notation.

Playing suggestions:

1. Harp parts may be played on the larger marimbas. Use the softer yarn-wound mallets for the best effect here.
2. Try using four-mallet marimba accompaniments with choral units for an interesting change from the usual piano or organ accompaniments. Use the softer yarn-wound mallets for a more suitable blend of tones in this type of performance.
3. Marimbas adapt easily as solo instruments with piano, band, or orchestra accompaniment.

Vibraharp

Three octave model has 37 metal bars; range F3 to F6.

Two-and-a-half octave model has 30 metal bars; range C4 to F6.

These instruments sound the actual written notation.

Playing suggestions:

1. For playing purposes the vibes will have a softer, more legato tone quality when yarn-wound mallets are used, and a brittle, staccato tone quality when cord-wound mallets are used. The cord-wound mallets are more adaptable to use in combos and stage bands.
2. A good damper pedal technique is very important in the playing of the vibes. For the most satisfactory performance the damper bar should be level and must make posi-

tive contact with the under side of all the bars on the instrument. Allow about ¼ inch for the movement of the damper bar between the "on" and "off" positions. The least amount of pedal motion will result in the best mallet articulation, and allow the performer to obtain the best phrasing in all types of playing.

Xylophone

Four octave model has 49 rosewood bars; range C4 to C8.

Three-and-a-half model has 44 rosewood bars; range F4 to C8.

Three octave model has 37 rosewood bars; range C5 to C8.

All xylophones sound where notated on the staff. However, the range of the xylophones extends one octave higher in pitch than the marimba keyboard of comparable size.

Playing suggestions:

1. Hard rubber and plastic tipped mallets sound better on the xylophone keyboard than the softer rubber and yarn-wound mallets.

2. For an interesting effect at your next concert, try using the xylophone (or marimba) on the transposed-transcribed E♭ clarinet part of one of the standard marches for band.

3. The xylophone also adapts easily as a solo instrument with piano, band, or orchestra accompaniment.

4. The xylophone (as well as all other percussion keyboards) will stay in better playing condition for a longer length of time if the proper mallets are always used at each dynamic level. The mallet tips will produce the proper sound at all times if the performer and the ensemble director will agree mutually on what mallet will produce the best musical effect for the music being played.

Keep all percussion keyboard instruments in a storage room when they are not in use. Cover marimba, chimes, vibes, and xylophone when not in use. Have the factory retune the bars when necessary.

The mallet percussion instruments are legitimate music instruments in every way, shape, and form. As such they merit the same handling, study, performance, and respect that all the other music instruments receive. Much serious study and practice are necessary for the percussionist to master the many playing techniques needed in his chosen field of music.

June 1963

TAMBOURINE TECHNIQUE

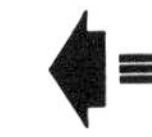

William Sebastian Hart

THE TAMBOURINE IS SUCH A WELL known instrument that it is believed to be extremely easy to play. Unfortunately, many conductors believe that this instrument, together with the triangle, can be entrusted to anyone. Many conductors are satisfied when the player enters at the correct time and somehow thwacks out the rhythm. To play the tambourine well requires careful study, an excellent sense of timing, and a remarkable degree of touch control.

Jingles

The main thing to remember about the tambourine is that the sound should be that of *jingles.* The jingles are the primary function of a tambourine. A good player should have several tambourines at hand in order to play the symphonic literature. To play all tambourine parts on the same instrument is the mark of an amateur. The tambourine sound must necessarily follow the character of the music. Jingles are high pitched, medium pitched, and low pitched. The diameter of the instrument has much to do with its tone. There are some tambourines so constructed as to have a double row of jingles. For example, the tambourine solo which occurs in the *Danse Arabe of* Tchaikovsky's *Nutcracker Suite* should be played on a tiny tambourine with extremely high-pitched jingles. On the other hand, the *Espana Rhapsody* of Chabrier requires a large tambourine of great depth and sonority. The *Carnival Overture* of Dvorak similarly requires one of the largest tambourines made, possibly one with double sets of jingles.

Whenever possible, the rhythm should be tapped out by the fingers or hand of the player on the wooden rim of the instrument. This necessitates turning the instrument upside down and holding it with the membrane at the bottom. The hand which is holding the instrument grasps it at the point where the little hole is to be found. The little hole formerly was constructed so that dancers might insert a finger here so as not to lose the instrument while twirling around the stage.

Played on Rim

The player, while holding the instrument in one hand, taps out the rhythmic pattern with the other hand on the rim of the instrument. Thus the sound comes forth with a clear jingle-like quality further reinforced by having the membrane of the instrument act as a sounding board. When two hands are necessary to play intricate rhythms *pianissimo,* the tambourine can be placed on the player's knee with the hands resting on the wooden rim balancing the instrument and allowing the fingers freedom to tap out the rhythm. Occasions do arise when good taste prompts the player to strike the head of the instrument. Good results follow if the player's hand or fingers strike near the wooden rim or actually on it, for the best jingle tone. It is in extremely loud passages that the player's fist is used on the head—striking it in the center. Then the quality is that of a shot and this may be just what the composer intended. The tambourine has a tendency to sound "behind the beat" to the conductor and to the audience unless struck on the rim—directly over the jingles.

It should be stressed again that a jingle-like quality should emanate from the tambourine. If the tambourine is played in a manner which produces a "drummy" sound (by concentrating too much on the head of the instrument) the good effect is lost.

Use of Fist and Knee

Finally, in this discussion, much must be made of extremely loud rhythmic passages which must be executed with rapidity and dispatch. Such a passage can be found in *Trepak* of the *Nutcracker Suite* by Tchaikovsky. Here a very large tambourine is to be used. The single beats in the opening of the work are to be played as "shot" tones, i.e., striking the head in the center with the fist. Later on, as the rhythmic patterns become more intricate, the player is to strike the head between two focal points. The knee is brought into a position to strike the membrane and the fist is also in a position to strike it. Between the two (knee and fist) the pattern is brought to life. The result is a continuous succession of heavily accented blows. Great care must be taken to try to make the blow of the knee match the sound which the fist makes on the instrument. This is impossible to do since the fist is striking with the bare skin of the hand of the player whereas the knee is covered by clothing. However, in this instance, the player must make the best of a bad situation.

Rarely is there any musical term to indicate how the tambourine passage is to be played—with the fingers, tambourine upside down, against the knee, with the fist, with snare drum sticks, etc. The method of execution is left to the player and to the consent of the conductor.

The Tambourine Roll

The roll on the tambourine may be played in two ways. The most common way is by gripping the instrument in the place where the hole occurs on the rim and shaking it rapidly in the air. The only dynamics possible with this method are *forte* to *fortissimo*. After the roll is produced, no matter how violently the instrument is shaken, it can produce a tone no louder than the one it gives off in the first encounter with top speed. A crescendo and diminuendo, therefore, is to be played in this manner: The player grips the instrument and begins a violent shaking of it, first putting it behind his back and then bringing it forward before his body and then returning it to the same point behind his body. The strength of the sound is the same but the effect to the listener is that of crescendo and diminuendo because of the positions behind and before the player's body.

Another method of producing a roll is by turning the tambourine upside down and placing the thumb against the rim, rubbing it over the edge of its diameter. The thumb used to press into the membrane and thus produce this roll should be moistened or rubbed with rosin in order to create friction. A sensible way to insure perfect results at all times is to glue strips of sand paper to the rim of the tambourine on its head. Then when the player rubs his thumb over this surface friction materializes and a roll results.

A general rule to follow is that loud rolls are played by shaking the instrument, whereas soft rolls are played by rubbing the rim to produce friction and cause the jingles to create sound.

A word about picking up and laying down of the tambourine: This must be done with great care so as not to "telegraph" the entrance before it actually appears in the score. The instrument should rest with its membrane on a chamois or handkerchief. This will provide a cushion when the player returns the instrument to the table after playing it.

August 1963

Instrument Care and Repair

Roy Markle

Maintaining Percussion Equipment

Ideally, all percussion hardware should be kept dry at all times; however, such equipment is used out of doors and is subjected to dampness. When it gets wet, all the moving parts—bolts, screws, and strainers—should be wiped dry and oiled lightly with a thin oil.

It is not difficult to tension a snare drum if the batter side is adjusted first. Draw the hoop down evenly by turning one screw until snug but not tight; continue around the drum tightening each screw about the same amount. During the process, keep testing the tension of the head with the forefinger. When the head is at playing tension this finger pressure should cause it to "give" just a little in the center. The snare side (if it is a double tension drum) may be tightened by using the same technique, but should be left with a little less tension than the batter side.

Under ordinary conditions, when the heads are adjusted to good playing tension they should need no further adjusting. The exception to this rule is damp weather, which necessitates tightening the tension in order to keep a good tone. After playing, the tension on the heads should be slackened back to normal so that the shrinkage during drying will not cause the heads to crack or break. When the drums are to be out of use for a week or more, the screws should be loosened about one turn.

Of the several types of snares in use the gut snares require the most care. They should be kept under tension at all times so that they do not stretch due to the atmospheric conditions. Some other types of snares tend to wear or cut the snare head at the edge. This can be prevented or repaired by placing a short strip of half inch adhesive tape under the point of contact.

Timpani heads are quite sensitive to weather conditions and occasionally shrink so much that they will not produce the low tones. When this occurs they can be re-stretched by removing the counter hoop and moistening the head thoroughly on both sides several times at about ten minute intervals. Replace the head and apply tension evenly all around until the counter hoop is drawn down about one-half inch. Place a slightly damp cloth over the entire head and leave it to dry completely (about two days). Ease of tuning may be maintained by treating the edge of the kettle with a little talcum powder or paraffin wax. Either, however, should be removed periodically and re-applied.

Since percussion instruments are often left out between rehearsals, they should be protected with cloth covers. Timpani heads should also have a rigid disk placed over them.

September 1963

TIMPANI TUNING
in Difficult Weather Conditions

Roland Kohloff

NO OTHER MUSIC INSTRUMENTS are affected quite so violently by weather and atmospheric conditions as are the timpani. When the air is clear and warm, with little or no moisture in it, the heads have a tendency to go sharp. Conversely, when the humidity is high the heads go flat. It is a rare day indeed when they seem to be stable and remain tuned.

When I used the word violent in the above paragraph I meant just that. I have seen days when a note would noticeably go flat shortly after beginning a roll. This sort of thing is not only distressing to the timpanist and detrimental to the music, but the player invariably will find himself the target of a glaring scowl from the podium. Every instrument has its unique problems, but in this one aspect none can compare with the timpani.

Controlling the Moisture

Let's examine this problem a little closer to see what can be done about it. To compensate for excessive moisture it is possible to install a device known as a "damp chaser" in the kettle. This is a circular metal tube which contains a heating filament. By using a toggle switch attached to the exterior of the drum the player can use a small amount of heat whenever he feels it necessary. I have installed a pair of these in the timpani I play with the San Francisco Symphony and Opera. They are especially helpful during opera performance, where we are in a pit. Not only have they proven to be highly satisfactory in helping to control the moisture inside the kettle but also in helping to prevent excess "collar" on the timpani head. This, of course, insures a fresher, more lively head for a longer time.

When the heads are going flat do not keep a lot of tension on them. Release the tension from the head, and re-tune the drum shortly before you have to play.

Extreme Dryness

During hot, dry weather the heads will go sharp. There are several things which can be done in this situation:

1. Keep tension on the head when not in use. During a long rest tune it to a high note, then bring it down to the note you need shortly before your entrance.

2. Another thing that can be done under extremely dry conditions is to cut up several long, thin pieces of sponge, soak them thoroughly in water, and insert one into each kettle thru the air hole in the bottom. This gets some moisture directly inside the kettle and often will solve the problem.

3. Sometimes even this is not sufficient. As a last resort, when all other measures have failed, apply moisture directly to the head. May I emphasize again that this should only be done when everything else has failed to correct the situation. Great care must be exercised to see that not too much water is applied to any one part of the head. There should not be any "bubbles" or "puddles" of any kind. Even one drop of water may destroy the head if it gets under the counter-hoop, so take extra care.

There are two ways to do this:

A. Using a damp, but not sopping sponge, gently caress the head in several places, using swift, light strokes. What we are trying to do here is to get the head to relax enough to give us the "collar" we need to obtain the necessary notes. We are not trying to re-set the head completely. In performance, this technique can be applied during some period of rest. It is best to keep slight tension on the head so that it will stretch just a bit. If the player will have 15 minutes or so before he will have to use his drums again he can take the sponge and rub the entire surface of the head, and apply pressure on it to bring back his collar.

B. Another method of dampening the head, preferred by some timpanists, is to have two or three handkerchiefs slightly moistened, and placed upon different areas of the head. It is important to keep rotating the position of the handkerchiefs so that no one area will become too wet. Once again great discretion must be used, as it always should be whenever you are applying water to the head.

Be Prepared

We were about to perform Richard Strauss's *Electra*. Leopold Ludwig, the famous German conductor, entered the pit of the auditorium and headed toward the podium. While the maestro was making his way, the trombone and tuba players were busy closing the doors over the stairs to the pit and placing their chairs and stands upon it.

We hadn't gone very far when it became evident there would be a severe problem of maintaining a collar on my timpani. With part of the brass section sitting on top of the only exit it also was obvious there would be no chance of obtaining any wet sponge. *Electra* presented an additional problem in that it is an opera without an intermission.

The atmospheric conditions proved to be so extreme that during each rest I began tuning my large kettle a third higher than its theoretical range. Then, shortly before each entrance, I would ease the head down to pitch. Still I found that I was losing some collar each time.

Approximately two-thirds of the way thru the opera there is an exposed. fortissimo timpani solo on low F. Realizing I was going to have some trouble obtaining this note I tuned the kettle a fourth higher than its normal playable note. Just before this important entrance I eased the head down to the F. I tapped the skin softly and breathed a sigh of relief as I heard it slide in on pitch. What I did not realize was that the head would continue to rise so that by the time I was to play the solo it was lying just on top of the rim of the kettle.

Maestro Ludwig gave a strong cue for me to start the solo. I roared in. and all sorts of things happened. The head rattled around on top of the kettle, sounding more like a cardboard box than a timpani. The Kappellmeister's head spun over in my direction as if he'd just received a roundhouse right to the jaw from Joe Louis. A bewildering look of amazement crossed his face. I guess he had never heard anything quite like that before. Neither had I! I vowed that I would never hear anything like it again.

Whenever you have the least bit of suspicion that you might have some trouble holding a collar, enter the stage armed with a couple of handfuls of wet sponge—some for possible insertion into the kettle and some in reserve for the heads themselves. The patrons may think you've made your entrance in order to take a sponge bath. You and I will know differently.

Editor's Note: With plastic timpani heads these problems are not so severe.

October 1963

Purposeful Practice for Drummers

Charles Perry

"PRACTICE" IS USUALLY A DREADED word among young people just beginning their musical careers. Even for the older, more mature musician, it is not the most exciting and stimulating form of musical expression, to say the least. No one, however, disputes the idea that practice is vital to proficiency. Musicians—in our case, drummers—must work to develop correct habits—functional techniques that become so ingrained, finally, that they are performed without conscious thought or premeditation.

Performance vs. Practice

Vast differences exist between performance and practice. Performance drum sticks are not abnormally heavy or oversized; practice sticks are. Performance drumming does not consist entirely of hand-to-hand sticking; most practice methods do. In performance, the bass drum and hi-hat always are used; in practice-reading, the bass drum foot sometimes is used, the hi-hat foot never.

At the advanced levels of performance drumming, drum-chart execution requires a variety of sticking, such as right or left hand alone. right or left hand lead, left hand independence, bass drum independence, combinations of rights and lefts—both single and double strokes, division of the notes between hands and feet involving the use of the entire set, right and left hand together (simultaneously), and hand-to-hand sticking. Moreover, today much drumming is spontaneous, an immediate response to a given stimulus. Obviously something more than the customary method of practice is needed to properly prepare the student drummer for performance drumming.

This is not to say that there is no longer a place for the traditional method book in the drummer's plan of practice. Traditional material is profitable, indeed, if presented in the proper context—as one of many types of reading in which the successful drummer must be proficient. But the fact remains that a good many of today's drummers are weakest in the area in which they should be strongest—the interpretation and execution of the modern drum-chart, which constitutes almost all of what is termed popular or jazz-type reading. What is needed, then, are materials and methods which will adequately prepare the drummer for performance of today's music and which will do so in a stimulating and purposeful manner.

Practice Suggestions

1. At first, use sticks on a drum pad. Next, try brushes, mallets, and sticks on the set.

2. Use a reading book that consists of jazz-type syncopated figures ranging from simple to complex. The practice tempo should be slow enough to allow accurate playing of the various rhythms, gradually becoming faster with proficiency. When accuracy is attained in a given tempo, introduce the desired shading, inflections. Fill in the open spots with simple "fills," as you would in performance playing. This kind of improvisation is vital to on-the-job playing. After playing a page from top to bottom, going from one exercise to the next, precede every four-

measure line with four measures of the ride-rhythm. This will result in eight-measure periods when working with the usual thirty-two-bar chorus.

3. Practice to recorded music. Playing with a musical accompaniment is quite unlike playing without it. First, the drummer's "time" must be flexible to coordinate perfectly with the recording. Secondly, his interpretation, both of the written part and of any amplifications or improvements thereof, will reflect a keen sensitivity to the recorded music—performance, style, etc. (One can also practice intricate sticking patterns with recorded music and make them "swing.") Especially good for drum-book practice are the rhythm section practice records of the Music Minus One series, consisting of simple rhythm section backgrounds (without other instruments). Such a drum-chart and record combination is the most realistic kind of practice.

Whether the drummer plays in a band, orchestra, dance band, or privately for his own amusement, he will find that practice with records (with other fine musicians) is an interesting and invaluable experience.

November 1963

Harnessing the Student Drummer

Nicholas Tawa

FORTUNATE IS THE BAND DIRECTOR who never has had any headaches from his percussion section. For, though musical crimes can be committed by any band member, the delinquency rate among drummers often seems disproportionately high.

Unnecessary delays result from the inadequate amount of time which drummers allow themselves to set up and adjust their extensive equipment. Unnecessary noises disrupt the rehearsal: a cymbal crashing to the floor in the midst of a Mozart Adagio; sleigh bells slipping during "Silent Night"; the bass drum vibrating a discordant solo in the midst of a soulful oboe passage.

In playing their parts, the percussionists seem to excel in rendering with extroverted loudness those passages requiring great delicacy, in coming in raggedly, or in completely missing entries. They neglect to practice their parts, adding insult to injury by improvising their own—an offense that sometimes gets by the conductor who uses a condensed score and has not had the time to know the percussion parts thoroughly. And often, through their disorderliness, forgetfulness, or irresponsibility, they prove themselves to be the "uncooperative individualists" that one well-qualified and experienced director has termed them.

Fortunately, there are several possible solutions to all these headaches—some in common use and others that often are overlooked. The equipment of the entire drum section can be set up first, either by having the drummers come in earlier in the day or, if the room should be used for a choral rehearsal just before the band meets, by having some reliable members of the choral group take out the equipment and put it in place at the end of their rehearsal.

A percussion table placed in front of, not behind, the drummers, and on which are placed the tambourine, claves, sleigh bells, and other smaller items, can prevent many accidents. Any sturdy table will do, with a pad or cloth covering to cut down the noise made in picking up or depositing these smaller percussive devices. Also, between numbers and during long rests, it often is wise to have unoccupied percussionists sit down in chairs, safely away from their equipment, in some stipulated rest position—for instance, with both feet on the floor, sticks under their left arms, and arms folded.

The best solution to the problem of the persistently loud player is to put him on a practice pad. He quickly will get the message and will be delighted to subdue his sound if only he can get his snare back.

Certainly, the director should take pains to know the drum parts thoroughly, clearly marking all entries on the reduced conductor's score. He also may find it advantageous, in the preliminary scale warmups to have the drummers go over their fundamentals at the same time.

It is amazing how many irritations begin to diminish the moment the director pays more attention to his drummers. Ignored and neglected, they lose interest, play poorly, shirk responsibility. But with considered attention from a director who will not let things slide but pays heed to every player in his band, the enthusiasm and group spirit of the drummers know no bounds. Fortunate, indeed, is the director of such a percussion section. Fortunate and wise.

DETACHED ROLLS IN SNARE DRUMMING

Mitchell Peters

ONE OF THE MOST IMPORTANT ASpects of percussion articulation—one that is grossly neglected in most percussion methods—is the playing of detached, or separated, rolls. As a result, the execution of detached rolls on the snare drum, particularly in concert work, is often misunderstood.

To avoid any confusion of terms, let us define a detached roll as a roll (regardless of its length) that is not tied to a stroke or another roll, but is either separated from the next stroke or roll or is followed by a rest.

It must be remembered that the roll is the drummer's method of sustaining sound. The problems of attack and release of a sustained tone are common to all instruments. The difference lies only in the means of producing the tone itself. A quarter note roll on a percussion instrument should give somewhat the same effect as a tongued quarter note on a trumpet. We will, therefore, examine three aspects of a tone: (1) its attack, (2) its prolongation, and (3) its release.

Attack

A good attack begins with an "ictus," that is, a rhythmical stress or accent. This is achieved on the snare drum by a slight accent or "bite" on the first stroke of the roll. The amount of accent on the attack will vary according to the style of the music being played. But generally speaking it should not be too heavy—only strong enough to help define the start of the tone more clearly. It should sound like a "taa" would on a trumpet.

Supporting the Sound

After the attack, the next step is to support the tone properly. This is done by maintaining the required level of volume for the note's duration with a steady, even repetition of strokes (generally double, sometimes single or multiple).

The height of the stroke is the major factor in volume control. One cannot support a *f* roll with the drumsticks raised only slightly above the drum. Conversely, one cannot play a *p* roll with the sticks raised a foot above the drum. A very common fault among drummers is the failure to support the sound to the end of the roll, thus creating an unintended forte-diminuendo effect.

Release

The third aspect of the drum roll—its release—is the most difficult. It is also the least understood by the drummer and will therefore need the most discussion.

The difficulty lies in the problem of sustaining the roll its full duration and then creating a slight separation before the next note. During the roll the wrist motion remains uniform, but instead of rolling directly into the next note (which would create a tied roll), the final wrist motion should turn into a light single stroke, rather than a double or multiple stroke. This gives the roll a good release from a fully sustained note value.

The light, single stroke, therefore, is the key to the whole release. It must be played at just the right volume to help lengthen the sound but not so loud that it is heard as a single beat. This stroke must blend in with the preceding strokes of the roll. It is best for the drummer to play the terminating single beat slightly softer than the dynamic level of the main part of the roll.

Some Drills

Below are some illustrations of the mechanics of roll release. At the tempo indicated, a good roll speed would be four wrist movements per quarter note. Here is the movement involved in playing two untied quarter notes:

As can be seen, the number of wrist movements is the same as though the roll were tied to the next downbeat, except that the last double stroke is left out.

At a slightly slower tempo, a good roll is achieved by using more wrist movements per quarter note. The basic rolling speed is about the same, however.

At a yet slower tempo the technique would look like this:

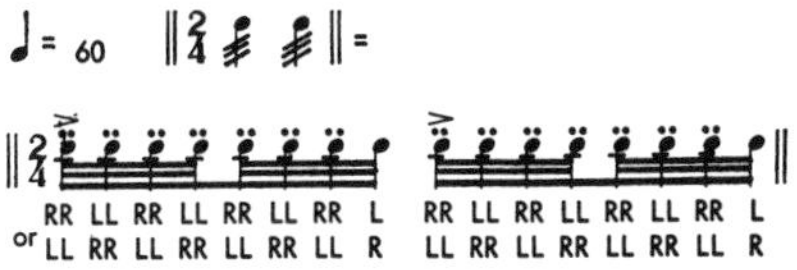

♩ = 60

RR LL RR LL RR LL RR L   RR LL RR LL RR LL RR L
or LL RR LL RR LL RR LL R   LL RR LL RR LL RR LL R

At a very fast tempo the roll would look like this:

♩ = 160

RR LL R   LL RR L
or LL RR L   RR LL R

So far only quarter note rolls have been illustrated. For rolls longer than a quarter note, the same principle applies in releasing the roll. The sustained part of the roll is, of course, longer. For example:

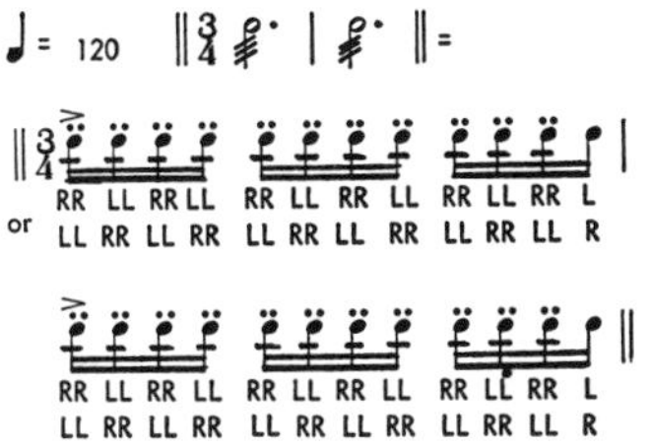

♩ = 120

RR LL RR LL   RR LL RR LL   RR LL RR L
or LL RR LL RR   LL RR LL RR   LL RR LL R

RR LL RR LL   RR LL RR LL   RR LL RR L
LL RR LL RR   LL RR LL RR   LL RR LL R

Here are some elementary exercises to help one get the feel of separated rolls.

Exercises 1 to 3 are good for providing correlated wrist movements in playing both tied and detached rolls. These exercises should be practiced at various tempos as well as with various dynamics and nuances to give the drummer the utmost control and flexibility.

1)

2)

3)

4)   5)

6)

A word of caution is in order before closing. The drummer must realize that composers do not always properly notate percussion parts; they may unwittingly indicate untied rolls when tied rolls are intended. Because of this, it is wise that the drummer sharpen his musical awareness. He must learn to listen to the rest of the orchestra or band and try to develop a good sense of ensemble. Close listening will help to solve many musical problems.

1964-1965

236	Ten Contest Tips for Percussionists	Maxine Lefever	January
238	A Tuning Indicator for the Kettledrum	Charles L. White	February
240	Mallet Percussion vs. Composers	Joel Leach	March
241	Our Responsibilities in Percussion	Gordon Peters	April
242	Organizing the School Percussion Section	Gordon Peters	May
243	Percussion Book Reviews		June
244	Equipping the Cymbalist	Sam Denov	June
245	Techniques of Cymbal Playing	Sam Denov	September
246	The Stage Band Drummer	Kenneth Krause	October
248	Tambourine Technic	Mitchell Peters	January
251	Equipment Recommendations	Gordon Peters	January
253	Care and Maintenance of Percussion Instruments	Gordon Peters	February
256	Tips on Contest Snare Drumming	Ron Fink	March
258	The Triangle: Don't Underestimate It	James J. Ross	April
259	Initiating a Percussion Ensemble Program	Gordon Peters	May
261	The Matched Grip vs. The Unmatched Grip	Jerry Carrico	June
262	Changes in Percussion Adjudication	Percussive Arts Society	August
266	Percussion Scoring	Hoyt F. LeCroy	September
268	Parts for Marching Bands	David Maker	October
270	Latin American Percussion	David A. Tobias	November
272	The Double Stroke in Mallet Technique	Mitchell Peters	December

Ten Contest Tips for Percussionists

Maxine Lefever

How can a school band director help prepare his percussion students for their solo and ensemble contest numbers? This question is often a perplexing one—particularly when the director is not a percussionist himself. The experienced percussion adjudicator knows that problems peculiar to each instrument consistently appear at every contest. These problems will not be exhibited by all contestants, nor will they appear in the same manner or degree; however, they can be expected to present themselves in a large percentage of cases.

It seems advisable for the director to be aware of some of the bad habits, the improper executions, and the incorrect types and tuning of instruments commonly observed and noted by the percussion adjudicator. By "pre-judging" the performance himself with some of these problems in mind, the band director should be able to offer suggestions which will serve as a guide toward gaining a higher contest rating for his students and, more important, toward improving their individual musicalness.

1. Snare Drum Position

Even before the student plays his first note, he is observed and perhaps pre-judged by the adjudicator. There is no absolute position for drummer and equipment; but if the player's position does not fall within the generally accepted norms, the judge may expect that some difficulties will be encountered in performance.

The snare drum should be slanted slightly downward to the player's right unless the matched grip is employed (in which case the instrument would be level). The drum should be just below the performer's waist, so that his arms will be in a natural and relaxed position. His elbows should be free from his body, in such a way that they are not cramped, and his shoulders and the entire arm should be relaxed at all times. The player should hold the sticks lightly, with the tips at right angles to each other.

Slight deviations from these positions are usually acceptable to judges and often are not commented upon provided they do not interfere with the player's maximum efficiency.

2. Drum and Size Tuning

The professional drummer employs different-sized drums in the performance of various types of literature, but it certainly is not expected that the student drummer have a great variety of equipment. However, he is expected to tune his instrument correctly. The best-executed solo can be marred seriously by a drum that is too loose or too tight. The drummer should spend some time before the contest day experimenting with his drum to find the proper tension for the best tone. Many students, upon questioning, admit to having given little or no thought to this subject. If, after lengthy efforts at tuning, the student fails to produce an acceptable sound on the drum, he should conduct further experiments with the types of snares available (wire, gut, or a combination of these) and with the two types of heads (plastic and calfskin). When proper attention is devoted to these details, even the oldest drum can be made to produce a satisfactory sound.

3. Stick Grip

A certain amount of leeway within the standard norms is acceptable to most adjudicators regarding the player's method of holding the snare drum sticks. He must hold the sticks at a point approximately three-and-one-half inches from the butt end in order to achieve a good balance. There are three widely accepted grips for the right hand, and few problems are found here. The left hand grip, however, rarely fails to evoke some criticism.

In the correct grip, the left stick is held primarily by the thumb. It rests on the middle joint of the player's ring finger, with the third and fourth fingers held close to his palm. His first and second fingers are curved around the stick but are not necessarily touching or guiding it in any particular way.

A very common fault in left hand position is the extension of all fingers out and away from the palm. This causes the player to lose much of his control of the stick and invariably hinders his performance.

4. Snare Drum Roll

A smooth roll can be obtained only through diligent practice; no "short-cut" method can be recommended. The most frequently encountered incorrect technique here is the employment of a "buzz" or "press" roll.

In order to master a good roll, the student must master the individual stroke—first with each hand separately and then together. His next step is to master the stroke and controlled rebound, again separately and then alternating. Those who have difficulty developing a smooth roll, particularly the press roll, should spend the first portion of each practice period playing a "slow closed roll"—that is, a double stroke roll played at the slowest speed possible. To do this, the player must raise the sticks about ten inches for each stroke, exaggerating arm and wrist movements. He should employ a strong upward motion in order to make both the first and the second tap of each stroke of equal volume. The student himself can readily observe any lack of evenness in sound and be aware of his progress. Once he masters this very controlled roll, he can gradually speed up his roll to the desired rate.

5. Bass Drum Stroke

Bass drum solos are actually performed in contests, but this author sees little merit in this literature—either for performer or for audience. The bass drummer, however, should be encouraged to participate in the percussion ensemble since he is an important member of this group.

Among the percussionist's most common problems in bass drum technique is mastering the quick upstroke necessary to produce the best tone. For this, he should make each stroke in the same manner: a snap of the wrist in a quick upward motion allowing the drum head to vibrate freely.

The point at which he strikes the drum has a decided effect upon the tone. Generally, the most pleasing tone is achieved by striking the drum in an area one third of the way between rim and center. Experiments should be made to determine the best spot for the desired sound.

Any variations of the preceding suggestions should be used sparingly and only for special effects called for in the literature, such as using two beaters, turning the drum on its side, and so forth. These indications should be observed carefully.

6. Cymbal Grip

An advertisement was once printed which depicted two garbage can lids being struck together; this is altogether reminiscent of the sound often produced by even a good pair of cymbals in the hands of an inexpert player. Because of the sometimes loud and often obvious nature of this instrument, it is vitally important that the cymbal player produce a musical sound rather than a "noise."

A good tone can be made on the cymbals if the performer uses a correct grip, one that gives him complete control of the instrument. Winding one's hand into the strap may be less tiring (and *may* be recommended for marching), but it does not afford a high degree of control.

The cymbal should be held with the thumb on top of the strap and the fingers beneath. By spreading his thumb and little finger out toward the edges of the cymbal, the player will attain a maximum degree of control. When the student masters this grip, he is ready to proceed to other techniques of cymbal playing. This writer would like to recommend a very recent book by Sam Denov called *The Art of Playing Cymbals* (Henry Adler, Inc., 1963) as a "must" for all cymbal players.

7. Tuning Timpani

The "average" high school timpanist has a fair technique (although his roll may not be too smooth), but he often is lacking in knowledge of timpani tuning.

The timpanist, like other players in the band or orchestra, needs a solid foundation in harmony and ear-training. He must be able to recognize and sing intervals and to match any given pitch. A serious timpanist should pursue such training with his band director or with a vocal instructor.

The timpanist must also be able to tune his instrument quietly (when the rest of the band is playing): he can best accomplish this by placing his ear close to the timpani head and flicking the head with his middle finger—not with the stick.

Needless to say, the drum must be in tune with itself before any attempt is made to tune it to any particular note. It is most advisable that the timpanist arrive at the performance early (with the harpist, who has a similar problem) to accomplish this.

8. Bells

Bell solos are rarely pleasing, and it is this author's recommendation that they not be played at all. The cost of a piccolo xylophone is actually less than the cost of a new set of bells; therefore, this instrument is recommended when a xylophone or marimba is not available. If bells must be used, orchestra bells are preferable to the glockenspiel. If a glockenspiel is the only instrument available (as is often the case in small schools), it should be placed flat on a table and played with *two* mallets.

Great care must be exercised in the selection of solo literature for this instrument. It was this author's questionable privilege to adjudicate a contestant who played "Trumpeter's Lullaby" with one mallet on an upright glockenspiel; the resulting sound was terrifyingly unmusical—as if all the bars had fallen off the frame and were being shaken around in a sack.

9. Ensemble Balance

As is the case with the wind player, good technique is to no avail to the percussionist if he cannot achieve proper ensemble balance in performance. Separate instrument tuning is the first prerequisite towards achieving this. It is absolutely essential that the percussionist tune similar instruments (as when multiple snare drums are used) as nearly alike as possible.

Once the instruments have been tuned, a good blend in performance must be kept foremost in the player's mind at all times. He should be urged to listen to the other parts in the piece and to blend with them both rhythmically and in tone quality and quantity. This can be best achieved if each player is provided with a full study score of the music. The director should attend several rehearsals of his group and check the overall balance by listening carefully from the back of the room.

10. Musicality

Percussionists must remember that they, too, are musicians and must give careful attention to all aspects of good musicianship. It is indeed unfortunate that so many technically well-executed percussion performances do not receive a high rating because the players completely fail to observe dynamics. True, dynamics sometimes are not indicated in percussion literature—particularly in the rudimental solos. When this is the case, the soloist and/or director should examine the selection carefully and enter such markings that seem most appropriate to the style of the music. This author often has wondered why percussionists, more than other instrumentalists, so often ignore dynamic indications. A logical explanation might be that many young drummers are well instructed in the development of technique via the rudiments—which because of this emphasis, become the end, rather than the means to the end of musical performance.

The goal of any player must lie beyond the mere execution of notes; he must possess, in addition to the ability to play well technically, the awareness, the sensitivity, and the versatility to present these notes in a meaningful and musical manner.

A Tuning Indicator for the Kettledrum

Its Design, Function, and Advantages

Charles L. White

ANYONE WITH THE SLIGHTEST knowledge of musical instruments can imagine how difficult it would be to play a one-string musical instrument even with the full use of the customary four fingers for making pitch changes. Restrict the player to the use of only one finger on such an instrument and the playing becomes even more difficult. If the fingerboard of the instrument were only five or six inches long, the difficulty would be compounded by the lack of gratifying musical results. Now, if the limitations were further increased so that the player had to use his *foot* to bring about pitch changes, the difficulty would indeed seem insurmountable. Yet, that is exactly what is asked of the modern timpanist! His foot must move a pedal an extremely small distance for pitch changes, in fact, only a few inches produces the full range of the instrument.

Fortunately, the music written for the kettledrums is not as a rule very complicated. But even small changes from one note to another are largely a matter of guesswork. A change in pitch of one tone usually requires but a small movement of the pedal, especially with a drumhead of substantial thickness. It is so slight that no matter how short a distance the player tries to move it, the pedal is likely to travel too far. He must trust his long years of tuning experience, and his well-trained ears, if he is to even approximate playing in tune, especially when pitch changes are made during the playing of a composition. The experienced timpanist will use his skill in establishing tuning cues to compare with the pitch of his drums while the other instruments are playing, if there is a remote possibility of doing so, but quite often there is little or no time in which to prepare the next note. Instead, he will make a thoughtful kick at the pedal and pray that the new pitch will be in tune. Some players, after many years of practice, are able to do this feat fairly well, but as a rule they are merely good guessers.

Tuning Demands

The timpanist, whether he is a seasoned performer or a rank novice, must do his utmost to accurately tune his instruments as indicated in the score. This requires balancing himself on one foot while, with the other, he tunes a drum on a tiny "fingerboard" on which a movement of but a small fraction of an inch may produce a full tone or more. At times, while the player is effecting a tuning change with one foot and balancing himself on the other, he is expected to play with both hands on yet another drum. To make matters even more difficult, many modern composers and arrangers write for kettledrums as if they were scoring for piano. They sometimes require complete tuning changes after a bar or two of rest. Although easy to do on the piano, this is a colossal undertaking for a young timpanist. Seemingly, some composers understand little about the tuning exploits they often ask of players, especially those in school orchestras or bands where the young timpanist is likely to have but two hard-to-tune drums at his disposal.

Some years ago, the writer attended a concert in which several school orchestras participated. Having played special concerts, for at least three decades, with the Los Angeles Philharmonic for the numerous schools in Southern California, I was interested in knowing if the incipient timpanists had gleaned anything from hearing our performances. I was pleasantly surprised to see and hear them do a good job of playing, both musically and with a certain display of style—that necessary adjunct of a good timpanist.

There was one thing, however, that was disturbing: the student player's inability to *tune* the drums. The orchestra leader had to walk back to the timpani and tune them between numbers on the program. This, of course, caused the young timpanists to appear inadequate, despite their ability to handle the sticks and read music.

I decided right then to do something about it. A *reliable* tuning indicator seemed to be the logical solution, so I set about to devise a means that would provide a foundation for the beginner to stand on while in the process of training his ear, and which also would give the experienced player valuable help in his tuning problems.

From Europe

My book (*Drums Through the Ages*, Sterling Press, 1150 Santee Street, Los Angeles 15, California) describes the principle involved in a reliable tuning indicator that has been used in Europe for generations. This simple, easily-made gadget has been used by many of the world's leading timpanists. As *Drums Through the Ages* fully describes the indicator for those who may wish to make them, space will not be given in this short article. However, it may be of interest to read about this type of gauge and learn what it will do.

It is largely due to early European tuning indicators that modern timpani parts are written with so many changes of pitch. When the first pedal drums were invented about a century ago by Pittrich, an adequate tuning indicator was incorporated in their mechanism. Modern timpani of American manufacture, while being the most practical in the world, are an incomplete instrument. They lack the simple keyboard that correlates the pedal of the drum to the pitch of its head. This is the reason why some timpani parts are playable without difficulty on instruments of the Dresden type and yet are almost impossible on our drums which have excellent pedals but which are not equipped with an indicator to show the player the position of the pedal in relation to the pitch of the instrument. This is one of the reasons why modern composers and arrangers write impossible things for inexperienced timpanists to play. Without realizing it, they are writing for drums that are almost non-existent in America.

The helpful European tuning gauge lacks one thing, however, as far as American players are concerned: it is not usable on American-type pedal timpani! The indicator attaches to a part of the instrument which has no counterpart in any of the American-type drums. It was my desire to design an indicator which uses the long-tried and universally accepted principle of the Dresden gauge in a form that would be readily adaptable to our fine American kettledrums, and which could easily be made by anyone with a slight knowledge of woodworking tools.

Simple Mechanism

The tuning indicator tells the exact and precise position of the pedal at all times. A very simple mechanism translates the vertical position of the pedal to a position on a horizontal "keyboard," which is plainly visible to the player. (See illustration.) A movable pointer marks a position on the keyboard which corresponds to the elevation or depression of the pedal. It cannot be other than accurate. *Its function is to register the location of the pedal.* This it does without fail. The player has but to glance at his keyboard to tell what notes his drums are tuned to, or it will tell him exactly how far he must move the pedals in order to tune the next notes written in his part.

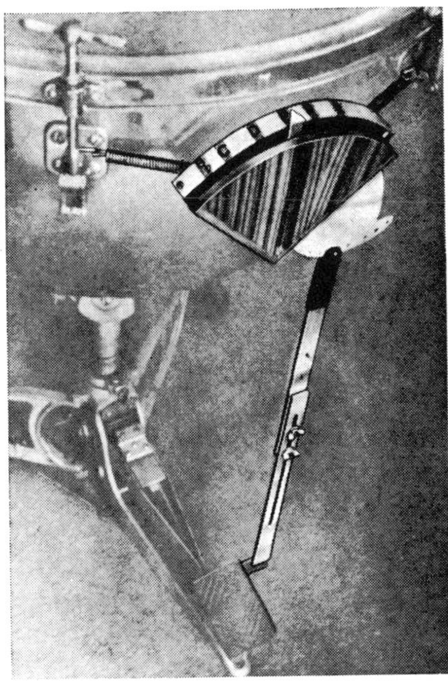

A close-up view of the tuning-indicator showing the rod connected from the foot pedal to the moving arm of the indicator. The initial tuning process of adjusting the indicator to match the drum pitches is described in Mr. White's article.

The tuning-gauge requires movable note-tabs that may be slid sideways on the track that forms the keyboard. After the intervals of the indicator are established, they may need very little attention as long as the same drumhead is used and like weather conditions prevail. Modern heads and pedals may need six or seven tabs for marking the names of the notes.

Initial Tuning Process

Tuning the head of a kettledrum is one of the most difficult assignments the timpanist will have. But the head must be exactly in tune with itself, so when it is struck there will be no waves nor vibratos in its tone—there will be a simple sound of bell-like clearness. There may be overtones, perhaps, especially with calfskin heads, but there should be no noticeable ripples or pulsations of sound. No "beats."

After tuning, the drum must be correlated to the keyboard of the instrument. If the drum is properly positioned tonally in relation to its range, a 28-inch drum should have a good low F at *almost* the highest elevation of the pedal. When this well-tuned F is located on the pedal —and the head forced down so it will not flat when struck—a note-tab is moved exactly opposite the pointer, F is written on it with a marking pencil, and low F is established at the lower end of the keyboard. The pedal is next fully depressed. The indicator will move to the right with the action of the pedal and it will point to a spot on the keyboard where the extreme top note of the drum is located. The note may be E♭ or perhaps E♮, depending on the characteristics of the head. (Thick heads have a longer range than thinner ones; but this feature is not always desirable, as there is too little space between notes.) A tab is located opposite the pointer, marked with the appropriate note, and the upper end of the range is fixed.

Next, tune the notes in between low F♮ and high E♭, or E♮. Release the pedal and tune the head *below* C. Press the head firmly to fully relax it and then tune *up* to C. Move the tab opposite the pointer and mark it C. A minor third is an interval easily tuned, so relax the pedal again, force the head down to stretch it fully, and then move *up* to A. Adjust the tab and mark it A. D can now easily be located and marked, then G and B. The "black" notes, which are not marked, are not quite halfway between the tabs for the "natural" notes. If preferred, the drum may be tuned with a piano or some other instrument. *It is important to remember to always press the drumhead down and tune up to the desired pitch.*

A 25-inch drum would be tuned and adjusted the same way, starting with B♭ at the bottom of the range and extending to high F♯ or G♮, depending on the head used and the placement of the pitch.

Drumhead Factors

Kettledrums, like other instruments, can get out of tune. Drumheads are extremely sensitive to atmospheric changes and to acoustical surroundings and are apt to go sharp or flat at the slightest provocation. This is not a great problem when Dresden-type timpani are used, for they have a "masterkey" which tunes the unison of the whole drum either up or down. The established keyboard of the tuning indicator remains constant, so the pitch of the head needs only to be raised or lowered until the tone of the drum matches the note pointed to on its keyboard. American-type kettledrums, however, having no masterkey, must be tuned very carefully, either up or down, by means of the individual tuning-screws until the pitch of the head and the note pointed to on the keyboard are in agreement.

Plastic timpani heads, while lacking in some respects, certainly make up for it in others. They are practically immune to changes in humidity, and once carefully tuned to a perfect unison they have a beautiful, clear tone, and once matched to the timpani keyboard they will remain surprisingly constant. Calfskin heads occasionally vary in thickness and texture at different places in their circumference. The unevenness will cause the head to react in different degrees to the conditions affecting it. Thin places will stretch or contract at a different rate from thick ones, and a carefully-tuned head may become so false from the maladjustment that it will have to be completely re-tuned.

Sometimes even the kettle must be turned, as a different spot on the head will produce the best tone. In such cases, the position of the tabs on the timpani keyboard may not exactly match the pointer. It will have to be learned from experience whether it is best to move the individual note-tabs slightly so they will again coincide with the pointer, to re-tune the head—providing, during performance, there is time to do so—or to simply adjust the arm that connects the pointer to the pedal of the drum. This arm changes the position of the pointer so it will indicate any note on the keyboard, but it should not be moved to such an extent that its range extends beyond the limits logically prescribed.

Doubtless Benefits

Timpani alone, of all of the instruments of variable pitch, have reached present-day musical life in America without the benefit of some kind of keyboard, an asset that has been deemed a necessity since the first day of the invention of pedal, or "machine," timpani. The few who are fortunate to possess or play drums of the Dresden variety know of the benefits connected with using a good tuning-indicator. There are others who are less enlightened, who believe the tuning-gauge to be a sort of crutch for incompetent players. Unfortunately, some of those who have tried to use a tuning device did not know how to use it, and they played out of tune in spite of the gauge. This unquestionably gave the tuning-gauge a bad reputation, but, if its purpose and function are understood, a reliable gauge will make the player's task of tuning much easier and faster, and it will provide the beginner with a basis upon which to train his ear. He will be able to both hear the note played on the drum and see its position on a keyboard, and before long he will be able to associate the pitch of his drum with a certain musical note. He is then ready to play the kettledrums as bona fide musical instruments.

March 1964

Mallet Percussion vs. Composers

Joel Leach

It is now known that the mallet percussions are capable of many colorful effects when used soloistically or as part of an ensemble. Although composers are now devoting increasingly more attention to their use in new scores, they seem to exhibit a lack of willingness to employ them more frequently. There is one problem in writing for mallet percussion which may provide the foundation for this reluctance: the instruments' variable ranges. The lack of understanding of the total available ranges of these instruments has resulted in solo and ensemble literature that makes use of only a portion of the available ranges. It is possible that composers would like to score for the extremes of the instruments' ranges but instead "play it safe" and limit themselves only to those ranges they know to be available.

Two Sizes of Instruments

The discrepancies existing in the matter of range can be found easily through random investigation of orchestration books; few of them agree about the advisable range of the common mallet instruments, and still fewer state accurately—or state at all—their acoustical properties (i.e., where they sound).

Most of this confusion has stemmed from the fact that the mallet percussion manufacturers produce at least two sizes of almost every instrument. This is justifiable, since most parents of beginning students often like to start "junior" on an "economy-sized" instrument with the intention of buying a larger one as he progresses. The small instrument serves this purpose well. However, it is safe to assume that the advanced student will have the larger instrument at his disposal. It is also true that schools and symphonic organizations generally purchase—and rightly so—the largest of each instrument for their use. Any literature, therefore, written either for the advanced soloist or for the mallet percussionist of a professional group may use the maximum ranges as shown below. The ranges are shown as *written ranges.*

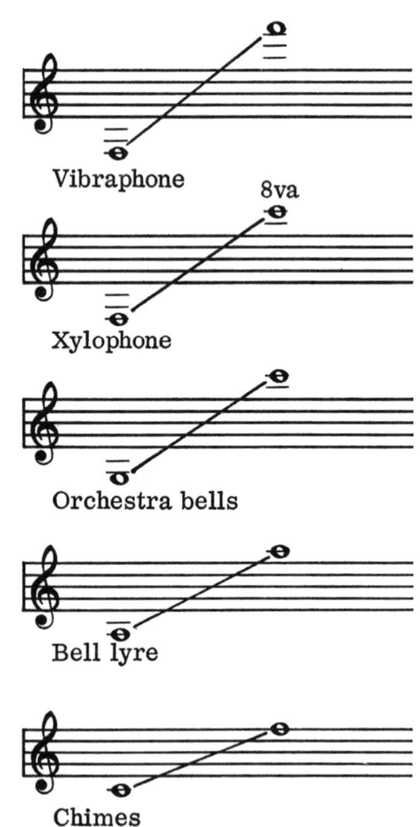

The marimba and vibraphone sound the actual written pitch. The xylophone sounds *one* octave higher than written pitch. The orchestra bells and bell lyre sound *two* octaves higher than written, and the chimes sound *one* octave higher than written pitch.

Because of the peculiar timbre of the transposing instruments, the composer should not take the transposition factors too seriously. That is, he should remember that the listener tends to hear the *type* of sound rather than the octave in which a tone is sounding. It is therefore most important that the composer and arranger become familiar with the timbres and acoustical phenomena of the mallet percussion instruments. He will score for them more effectively.

April 1964

Our Responsibilities in PERCUSSION

Gordon Peters

Editor's Note: With this issue, The Instrumentalist *takes pleasure in welcoming Gordon Peters to its staff of contributing editors. Mr. Peters's broad musical background, coupled with his characteristic thoroughness and conscientiousness in addressing the task at hand, cannot fail to provide readers with the very finest coverage of percussion topics.*

THE USE OF PERCUSSION INSTRUMENTS has increased tremendously in all areas of musical activity in the last two decades. Regrettably, however, this rapid growth has not been paralleled by comparably improved and expanded percussion instruction.

Many performers, music directors, and full-time percussion teachers are not aware of progressive tonal concepts and techniques involved in modern percussion playing and pedagogy. One reason for this is that institutions of higher learning have failed in meeting their responsibilities in percussion education. One has only to consider that of the approximately 550 institutions conferring music degrees in the United States only about 50 employ a trained percussion instructor.

Also, how many private "drum teachers" teach more than just the snare drum? Very few, unfortunately. As a result, it is too often falsely assumed by teachers, music directors, and ultimately by the students that mastering basic snare drum strokes and techniques is an open sesame to playing the timpani, the mallet-keyboard instruments, and the bass drum, cymbals, triangle, tambourine, and so forth.

These instruments all require individual techniques and must be given lesson time. For example, in the teaching of the techniques of instruments such as the triangle and tambourine, the factors of stance, height, grip, angles, articulation, strokes, rolls, beating areas, and many other aspects are involved and must be given due consideration.

To attempt to rectify our deficiencies in percussion knowledge, it will be this editor's intent to seek out the areas of percussion weakness and to suggest corrective measures. Generally, the associations which music educators have with percussion instruments can be found in the following list: (a) teaching students how to play them; (b) understanding the functions and sounds of percussion instruments in the band (concert and marching) and orchestra; (c) orchestrating for percussion instruments (orchestration classes and texts on the subject); (d) purchase, care, maintenance, and repair of percussion instruments; (e) percussion ensembles (literature, performance); (f) literary writings on percussion (books, articles, dissertations); (g) recordings; (h) percussion education (courses, method books, clinics); (i) percussion manufacturers and/or dealers (catalogues); and (j) contests.

Specifically, here is a partial list of proposed future article titles.

Administration of the Percussion Section

Helping Percussion Instrument Manufacturers to Help the School Music Director

The Basic Embellishments in Snare Drum Playing: Extension and Interpretation

Improving Rolls in Percussion Instrument Playing

The Art of Cymbal Playing

Realizing Maximum Tonal Response from the Timpani

The Concept of Singing Applied to Percussion

Latin-American Instruments and Rhythms

Percussion Clinicians: How to Help Them Help You

Artistry in the Percussionist

Extraneous Noises in the Percussion Section: What They Are and How to Avoid Them

Percussion Literature for School Use

Care of Percussion Instruments

Purchasing Percussion Instruments: Order and Specifications

Orchestration and Percussion

Chamber Music and Percussion

A Balanced Curriculum for Percussion Education at All Levels

Tonal Objectives with Percussion Instruments

Percussion: The Key to Variety in the Band

In pursuing these and other topics, qualified persons will be asked to write for this column. Questions, observations, debate, dissatisfactions, and suggestions for articles are encouraged from the reader. The measure of success of this endeavor is largely dependent upon participation and communication. Only with *your* good counsel through letters can this editor fully meet *your* needs.

Organizing the School Percussion Section

Gordon Peters

THE FIRST STEP IN IMPROVING A percussion section is to meet with your chief drummer. If you have not yet appointed one, you will find that doing so will benefit all concerned. Whether you choose him by seniority, ability (which includes versatility with all the percussion instruments[1]), rotation, or sectional vote is largely a personal matter. Democracy and equal opportunity are good guides in choosing a principal percussionist, but, practically speaking, the music director must make his choice on the basis of what is best for the entire organization. The timpani chair is a "section in itself," and putting the timpanist under another percussionist's jurisdiction, or having him in charge of the percussion section, is usually over-burdening and impractical.

The primary responsibility of the principal percussionist is to distribute parts and assign players to instruments. This should be done as soon as the music is put into the folders. After the principal percussionist has studied the music, he should make a chart listing the names of the pieces, the players on each instrument, and other necessary instructions. The chart should be left inside the folder with the music for the other players to peruse in advance of the first rehearsal. Each player should mark neatly in black pencil what he plays and when he is to move to another instrument. The director should decide whether a percussionist is assigned to a "home base" instrument to play throughout a program (author's preference, but use rotation from program to program), or whether the players are rotated among the various instruments for each separate piece.

SAMPLE ROUTINE CHART

TITLE	GORDON	JIM	SAM	AL
Concert Overture	Bells Chimes Vibraharp	Bass Drum Xylophone Triangle I (all except #7)	Pair of Cymbals Suspended Cymbal Temple Blocks	Field Drum Tambourine Triangle II (#7 only)
Symphony	Machine Castanets Castanets on Paddle Sleigh Bells	Bass Drum Small Tambourine	Cymbals(pair) Gong	Snare Drum Suspended Cym. Slapstick
NOTE: "Home Base" Instruments: Mallet-keyboards: Gordon; Bass Drum: Jim; Cymbals: Sam; Snare Drum: Al				

It is the principal percussionist's additional task to see to it that all the instruments needed are available and in good playing condition. He should inform the director if any instruments are missing or damaged or if any special-effect instruments are required. It is preferable and will help to minimize mistakes if only one person is on a part. If more percussion players are needed than are normally assigned to the section, this should be made known to the director. Each percussionist should have his instruments set up by rehearsal time. If having a class the preceding hour prevents him from doing this, he should work out an arrangement with a colleague.

Preparing for Concert

Once the concert program is determined, the physical set-up of the percussion instruments must be considered. During the course of an average program, it is often necessary to move both players and instruments. These movements must be kept to a minimum. There is nothing more distracting to an audience than noise and excessive movement. If there are duplicates of instruments, they should be put to use to minimize movement. This is particularly important in the performance routine of a percussion ensemble.

A common difficulty in public school bands or orchestras is that the drummers often become discipline problems. Many times this is due to their having nothing to play. The music director should help the percussionists by seeing to it that they are kept busy by assigning them to a percussion ensemble, sectional rehearsal, repair and cleaning project, or some other constructive musical activity.

If the parts to be played are few and the number of drummers many, two players can be assigned to a marimba, reading from a piano score marked by the conductor. If the music department does not own a marimba, the music director might well make this a priority on his instrument purchase list. There are numerous potential advantages to be derived from this instrument (see article in the October 1962 issue of *The Instrumentalist*: "The Use of the Marimba in the Band").

In Grammar School

Because the grammar school music director is confronted with a number of problems at the beginning of the school year, including giving attention to the other instruments of the band or orchestra, and because the music on this level contains inadequately printed percussion parts, the percussionist is usually relegated to a "sit and be quiet" role. When this situation is pro-

[1]The music director has the responsibility to encourage his percussionists to learn to play all the instruments in the percussion section. The lack of versatility many times prevents the percussion section from playing all the parts indicated in the music. Yet more important: a percussionist may wish to continue playing in college or even play professionally; without experience and training on all the major percussion instruments before college (ideally before high school), his competitive position is greatly weakened.

longed, the player's interest and love for music slowly withers, and the orchestra or band soon is without drummers.

This problem is often best resolved by not involving the drummers in the band or orchestra until they are technically developed enough to contribute to the ensemble. Formation of a percussion ensemble is an excellent vehicle to use as a primer to the band. The motivational benefits and musical progress achieved are well worth the little extra time necessary.

A growing number of publishers have fine materials for percussion ensembles at this level utilizing all combinations of instruments; these include:

Joseph Berryman, The Band Shed, Itta Bena, Mississippi; Kendor Music Publishers, Delevan, New York; Music for Percussion, Suite 611, 1841 Broadway New York, New York; and Southern Music Publishers, San Antonio, Texas.

If we only take time to understand some of the problems of the percussionist, we can improve discipline, interest, and musical results.

June 1964

Percussion Book Reviews

Guide to Teaching Percussion, Harry R. Bartlett, 1964, William C. Brown Company, 135 South Locust Street, Dubuque, Iowa, $4.00.

This text is the most comprehensive percussion instrument instruction method published to date. It is to be unqualifiedly recommended to all percussionists (students, teachers, and professionals), instrumental music directors, and students engaged in instrumental school music preparations at our colleges and universities. The author's genuine understanding and knowledge of practical percussion problems and techniques on all the percussion instruments, as well as the teaching of same, are well reflected in this text.

The specific content of the *Guide* is best reviewed by quoting from the second paragraph of the author's preface:

> . . . organized in ten chapters and an appendix, with each topic listed separately in the Table of Contents for easy reference. Chapter 1 contains introductory material which serves as orientation to the basic concepts of percussion playing and the author's pedagogical viewpoint. Chapter 2 consists of a comprehensive chart of 56 percussion instruments showing their physical and acoustical properties, methods of playing, and characteristic usages. Chapters 3 through 8 deal with the snare drum, bass drum and cymbals, mallet-played instruments, timpani, other percussion instruments, and Latin-American instruments, respectively. Dance band drumming is the subject of Chapter 9, and Chapter 10 treats the percussion section of the marching band. The Appendix contains varied material of a less technical, yet very useful, nature. Included are such topics as stage deportment for the percussion section, an annotated bibliography of percussion teaching materials, and a glossary of percussion terms.

The general format used is to list pertinent historical data, basic playing techniques, and teaching procedures and suggestions. The liberal use of diagrams and sequential photographs lends further clarity to text comprehension.

In summary, Mr. Bartlett is to be congratulated for this contribution toward elevating the arts of percussion playing and teaching.—G.P.

Handbook for the School Drummer, Jerry Kent, 1964, available through author, 7912 North Zuni Street, Denver, Colorado, $3.00.

This text is aimed primarily at the school drummer at all levels. The author indicates the following on the cover of the text: "Ideas to help the drum student get the best possible musical experience out of his band or orchestra." Matters of attitude, morale, percussion section routine, and many practical suggestions on improving one's playing in the band and orchestra are discussed.

Mr. Kent's style of illustration and humor is used cleverly to communicate with the school drummer in his (the student's) language. Most young drummers take private lessons to learn how to play their instruments. Seldom, however, do they have their teacher next to them in the band and orchestra rehearsal, saying: "No, not that way, try this . . . or this way." A bridge between private lessons and actual playing in the school music organization has long been needed. Some of the topics discussed in the *Handbook* are: "How to Follow the Conductor," "The Section Leader," "The Equipment Foreman," and "Reading Procedure in the Concert Band and Orchestra."

In summary, Mr. Kent's text will make a more functional percussionist and musician out of any drummer who takes the time to absorb these thoughtful pages. The only real weakness of the text is the lack of discussion of timpani and mallet-keyboard percussion instruments. A sequel to the present text rounding out the complete percussion instrument family would be most welcome.—G. P.

The Art of Cymbal Playing, Sam Denov, 1963, Henry Adler, Inc., New York, New York, $1.50.

This is the first and only text presently available dealing exclusively with concert cymbal playing. Included in the book is a knowledgeable background, a liberal use of pictorial sequences and photos, plus a complete explanation of playing techniques for various types of cymbals. Mr. Denov offers this book as his own personal beliefs and conclusions as opposed to any dogmatic approach. Inadequate cymbal playing and understanding, particularly in school situations, has plagued us for too long. This text is a fine vehicle with which to remedy the situation. Every percussionist should include this in his "basic text" library.—G.P.

Equipping the Cymbalist

Sam Denov

Although an articulate cymbalist is of indisputable importance to a concert organization, no knowledgeable person associated with instrumental music would proclaim that expert performance is possible with improperly selected cymbals and equipment. Yet, many music directors seem to be unconcerned with the quality of cymbal performance, the equipment, or both, in their performing groups. By giving some attention to these factors as well as to cymbal sound, techniques, and choice of player, music directors will improve the sound of their groups.

The director should select a prospective young cymbalist who has had some musical training. The cymbal's very large dynamic range and infinite variety of sounds demand a performer who is keenly aware of and sensitive to ensemble tone and color. When such a player is chosen, the director should next supply him with the proper cymbals and accessories. It is this subject which I will discuss in this article.

Choosing Cymbals

Since the finest Turkish-type cymbals are domestically produced and are available at moderate prices, the use of inferior equipment is inexcusable. However, the first consideration should be the acquisition of a good-sounding pair of hand cymbals.

Directors continue to ask what diameter cymbals they should purchase in relation to the size of their organization. It is a mistake to categorize cymbals in this way. Diameter alone is not the determining factor in the proper selection of cymbals. The tone quality of cymbals varies greatly with both diameter and thickness. Increasing the diameter or decreasing the thickness causes them to sound *higher* in pitch. The converse of this is also true.

Cymbal tone is enhanced in direct proportion to the amount of metal contained in the cymbal. Plurality of overtones and sustaining quality increase as the *quantity* of metal increases. Also, cymbals should not be forced to produce great volume. If sufficient volume cannot be produced by a moderate effort on the part of the performer, the cymbals are either too small in diameter or too light in weight.

It has always been my belief that the size and muscular development of the performer is a more important factor to consider than the size of the band or orchestra. In a school situation, where the players change periodically, there must, of course, be some compromise. Practically speaking, the grammar school instrumental groups would perhaps use a pair of cymbals about 15 inches or 16 inches in diameter, medium to thin in relative thickness. In high school, two pair of cymbals might be best: 16-inch, medium thickness, and 18-inch or 19-inch, medium thickness. The total use of the cymbals must also be borne in mind: for example, will the same pair have to be used for both concert and marching groups (a bad practice)? As a general rule, regarding both diameter and weight, cymbals should be only as large as can be handled comfortably by the performer.

The specific qualities to be sought in a fine pair of cymbals are: (1) speed of response, (2) comparative lack of fundamental pitch, (3) a balance of high and low overtones, and (4) resonance (long duration of vibration).

Irrespective of one's ultimate determination of diameter and weight, the hand cymbals to purchase are those that have been *paired* by the manufacturer. This important matter of matching cymbals is usually best left to the experts.

In summary, the music director must develop an aural concept of good cymbal tone and then pursue this objective with the aforementioned guides.

Pads and Straps

Hand cymbals should be outfitted properly with pads and straps. Soft, pliable rawhide straps which have been knotted under the dome of the cymbal are preferable. Pads should always be used, since they increase the performer's control of the instrument. Lambswool pads, however, should never be used in concert, as they restrict the cymbals' vibration, but they may be used in a marching organization, where comfort may be a more important consideration.

Wooden handles that are bolted to the cymbals should not be used under any circumstance. These contraptions exert pressures on the cymbals which may cause them to crack. They also mute the cymbals somewhat. There is available, however, a type of rawhide strap with a wooden grip attached that functions well for the marching cymbalist.

Suspended Cymbals

When the music calls for a suspended cymbal, the music director should not allow one player to hold a cymbal while the bass drummer rolls on it. Suspended cymbals require good solid stands as well as a variety of yarn-wound mallets. Snare drumsticks and even triangle beaters (used with discretion) are sometimes used. However, timpani sticks should not be used on cymbals, since the soft felt produces a tone less distinct than that resulting from the use of yarn mallets.

The player must also be careful that no extraneous sounds derive from the cymbal stand because of the lack of proper insulation around the top of the pole.

Generally, a suspended cymbal should be about 16 inches in diameter and on the medium-thin side. In high school and college, when the budget allows, a second suspended cymbal, perhaps 18 inches, thin to medium thickness, can be added.

After the director has acquired his basic equipment, he must next focus his attention on the player and the techniques involved in playing cymbals. These matters will be taken up in a subsequent article.

Techniques of Cymbal Playing

Sam Denov

THE MUSIC DIRECTOR, HAVING procured the basic equipment needed for cymbal playing and, hopefully, having chosen a musically-trained player (preferably a percussionist), is now ready to concentrate on the basic techniques involved in artistic cymbal playing. He must insist on the most artistic performance possible, since no other single instrumentalist can influence the collective tone color of a concert organization as can the cymbalist.

Body Position

The whole body is involved in the proper handling of the cymbals. The body should be held erect without being stiff, and the feet should be placed about fifteen inches apart with one foot a little ahead of the other. With the weight now well distributed and the cymbals held properly, we can next concentrate on how the cymbals are struck.

Holding the Hand Cymbals

The grip used to hold the cymbals is the same for both hands. The double strap (which has been folded over on itself and knotted under the bell of the cymbal) is grasped with an overhand grip, and the fingers are curled tightly underneath but *not* through it. The hand should be as close to the bell of the cymbal as possible. The thumb should be spread and its bottom placed against the pad, parallel to the cymbal. Control of the cymbal is accomplished by pulling the strap with the closed fingers while pushing against the pad with the thumb.

The cymbals are held directly in front the chest. They should be parallel to each other but not touching. The arms should be in a natural position, neither tucked in too close to the body nor stuck out at obtuse angles.

Striking the Hand Cymbals

To produce a good-sounding crash, both cymbals should be in motion to the same extent. All too often, one sees the cymbal in the left hand practically motionless while the cymbal in the right hand is struck against it.

One cymbal should be raised and the other lowered in preparing for

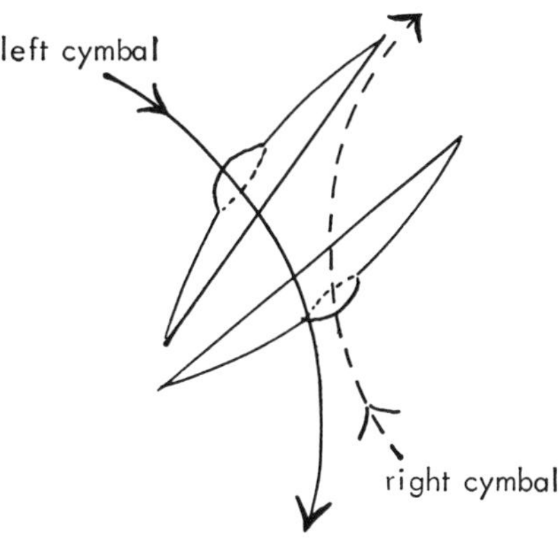

a crash. Both cymbals should then move to meet each other so that the entire circumferences do *not* contact each other at the same time. They must meet so that the edge of one cymbal first strikes the underside of the other cymbal about an inch or two from the edge at a small angle; otherwise, the air is forced out and a partial vacuum momentarily locks the cymbals together, resulting in a dull thud rather than a brilliant crash.

The up and down movement in which the cymbals meet and separate should be a continuous one. Tilting both cymbals will aid in their meeting properly as well as help in adjusting the volume obtained. The more horizontal they are at the moment of impact, the louder they can be played. Listened to closely, the sound emanating from them will be like two closely spaced syllables, "ka-RASH," like a quick grace-note.

If the cymbals are to be allowed to ring, the follow-through motions will bring them approximately to shoulder height with the undersides facing away from the performer with the edges of the cymbals about fifteen inches apart. When dampened, the "plates," as they sometimes are called, have their edges pulled up against the chest and shoulder sockets.

The Suspended Cymbal

The suspended cymbal generally is played with yarn-covered mallets, *not* timpani sticks. The yarn may be either wound or crocheted (evenly) over a hard rubber or composition core.

Single strokes all should be played with the same hand, leaving the other hand free to muffle the cymbal when necessary. The cymbal is struck close to the edge unless a rapid rhythmic figure is to be played. In this latter circumstance, the player would use two strikers somewhat closer to the center.

In a roll, the mallets are placed near the edge as before. The roll is produced by a rapid succession of alternating single strokes. The mallets should be placed one on each side of the cymbal near a line which runs through its center. This will prevent the cymbal from "riding" away from the performer. In cases where snare drum sticks are used for rolls, the player should use a double stroke closed roll.

When the suspended cymbal is to be struck with a wooden stick, the butt end of a snare drum stick should be used. The cymbal should be struck *on* its edge rather than on the top *near* the edge.

A variety of different mallets, such as triangle beaters and xylophone hammers, may be used from time to time. The performer must have all of these ready for use on short notice.

These are the basic techniques of playing the cymbals. Only through practice, including self-observation in front of a full-length mirror, can the movements and sounds involved in performing with the cymbals become graceful to the eye as well as accurate and dazzling to the ear.

October 1964

The Stage Band Drummer

Kenneth Krause

Of all instrumentalists, the drummer probably has the most difficult time in transferring from the concert organization to the stage band. The nature of the concert percussionist's job is so far removed from his function in the dance- or jazz-oriented group, that there is little in his concert training to prepare him for stage band membership.

In the concert band or orchestra the fundamental emphasis is on reading music and precision in the interpretation of rhythm patterns. The concert percussionist generally functions as an embellishing soloist; that is, a soloist because he rarely plays a part that is doubled by any other percussion instrument. Only on marches does the concert percussionist have the feeling of being an integral part of the whole; yet, he must possess enough technique on *all* the percussion instruments to execute the most difficult passages when they occur.

Quite different is the situation of the stage band drummer, who is immediately part of a section which is the foundation of the group—the rhythm section. His first job is to develop a steady sense of time or pulse (which may be inborn or have to be acquired). To achieve this he may have to do battle with one or more individuals or sections who habitually "rush" or "drag."

The stage band drummer must also evolve the proper "feel" when playing the jazz styles. This is achieved through a controlled relation, a coordination of many muscles, and a receptive aural awareness; but, it is also a matter of style, and the "feel" varies for different styles of jazz and dance music.

Proper interpretation of rhythm patterns in the jazz and dance styles is necessary knowledge for the stage band drummer, since these styles are not notated exactly as played. Concert training, therefore, tends to work against the percussionist in this respect. If he is aware of the interpretive differences between the exact notation and the jazz interpretation, the jump from concert to stage band drumming is not so great.

Another important requisite for the stage band drummer is the ability to improvise. He can contribute to the overall sound and feel of the band through tasty fill-ins, lead-ins, kicks and back-up figures which are seldom indicated in the music and must be improvised.

The basic equipment the drummer uses for this demanding task is the drum set, which, although it is comprised of a number of dissimilar instruments, must be played as a single entity. Mastery of the drum set as an integrated whole is something even the most talented professionals work hard to achieve, since performing on a drum set actually means doing several things at the same time. Perhaps Jim Chapin best described it by the term *coordinated independence.* The drummer uses his set for playing *time,* for fill-ins, and for solos. For solo work each item of playable equipment might be considered a *tone,* and the minimum number of tones is usually five: the snare drum (S.D.), the bass drum (B.D.), the sock cymbal or hi-hat (H.H.), the ride cymbal (R.C.), and tom-tom (T.T.). When playing *time,* however, each functions differently.

Training Routines for the Stage Band Drummer

The following exercises are divided into four categories: time, feel, interpretation, and improvisation. Some time should be spent each day practicing at least one exercise in each category, including playing at different dynamic levels for developing greater control.

I. *Time*

The importance of using records instead of a metronome to learn to keep steady time should be stressed. First of all, in practicing with the metronome, the drummer tends to follow the metronome instead of keeping time himself; he becomes dependent on the metronome rather than independent. (This is not to say that there is no good use for a metronome!) Second, and perhaps more important, he cannot learn *feel* by practicing with a metronome, but he can by playing along with records. A valuable feature of practicing with records is that other musicians on the records tend to play ahead or behind the beat, and the drummer gets used to keeping steady time against the "pull" of other sections. Furthermore, practicing with a metronome often results in a *stiff* beat rather than a relaxed *groove.*

A. Practice a straight four beats per measure, playing only with the right stick on the ride cymbal. Practice all the way through at least one record, choosing a different tempo (and record) each day, until the right hand can keep a steady beat at any tempo.

B. Practice the cymbal *ride* beat (right stick on cymbal) with records at various tempos. Note that regardless of how it is written, the ride beat is usually played in the triplet pattern. Again, be sure to choose different tempos, as this beat

Written

I

A.

B.

C.

D. Any of the above played at very slow tempos.

Played

(Played same as above, except at a very fast tempo, where it might be played as written.)

must be played steadily at any tempo from very slow to very fast.

C. Add bass drum (either 4 or 2 beats to the bar) and sock cymbal (on counts 2 & 4) to either of the above exercises.

II A. "Time" with Bass Drum 4-to-the-bar

B. "Time" with Bass Drum 2-to-the-bar

R.C.
B.D.
H.H.

Note: The bass drum is usually played very lightly in contemporary jazz, while the rock n' roll crowd uses a heavy style with frequent syncopated figures. (See *Interpretation:* item "C".)

D. Practice with right hand on the ride cymbal (with B.D. and H.H.) playing straight 8th notes or continuous triplets instead of the ride beat, as in current rock n' roll styles, with records.

E. Using the ride beat, add a left hand *kick* on the last note of the 4th beat, to coincide with the last note in the measure of the ride beat.

III A. "Time" with left hand "kick" beat

R.C.
L.H.
B.D.
H.H.

B. "Kick" beat on Bass Drum

R.C.
B.D.
H.H.

F. Practice playing the above *kick* beat with the bass drum or hi-hat instead of the left hand.

G. Practice with the brushes at any tempo. (The most common brush beat is to play the ride beat with the right hand while the left *swishes* back and forth.)

H. Since modern jazz is expanding into five, seven and other odd-beat groupings, the drummer should also practice time-keeping and other exercises similar to the above in these time signatures. (Use records as much as possible. Also, some new drum-set methods incorporate uncommon and mixed meter exercises.)

II. *Feel and Fill-ins*

A. *Feel* can best be acquired by imitating the time of drummers on records, provided the student has obtained records with drummers who play in a relaxed *groove.* The fill-ins must conform to the style to be effective.

B. Learn *one* or *two* good fill-ins, using any of the published books as sources or creating some of your own. It is important to learn only one or two at a time and to practice them until they come naturally. The drummer who tries to learn too many fill-ins at once usually finds that when actually playing on the job he cannot think of a single one.

C. Practice through the same record three times. First keep time only, while listening to the drummer on the record; second, play the fill-ins learned in "B" above at the same spots where the drummer on the record plays his; third, copy the fill-ins used by the drummer on the record. (To simplify copying, play LP records at 16 rpm.)

III. *Interpretation*

A. In order to interpret stage band music in correct style, the drummer must first have a thorough knowledge of syncopated rhythms. There are some good books of syncopated rhythms on the market, and the wise drummer will digest as many of these as he can. At first he should practice these rhythms in a *straight* or *legitimate* manner (some would call it *square*) until he can play them correctly.

B. After learning the syncopated rhythms, he should begin to play them with a jazz *feel.* The underlying basis of jazz syncopation is the triplet rhythm, and even though syncopation may be written in 8th notes, it

IV

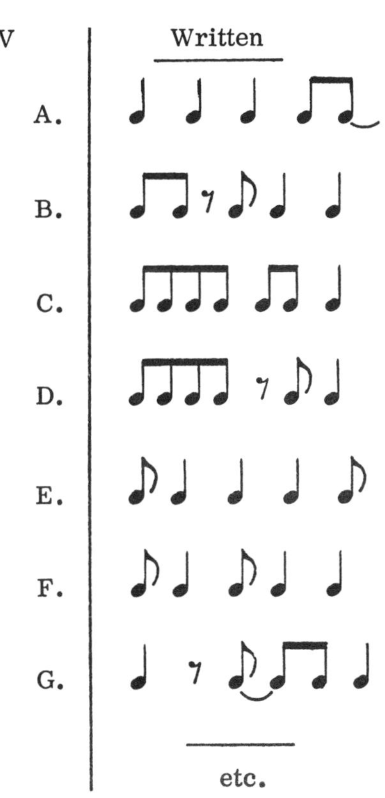

is usually played on the last *third* of the beat rather than the last half. Large groups of 8th notes (four or more) are usually played straight, but the syncopations almost always fall into the triplet pattern. The principal exceptions to this are the Latin-American and rock n' roll styles which frequently employ a steady 8th note pattern as the underlying pulse.

C. As soon as the student can play *time* using the ride cymbal, bass drum, and sock cymbal, he should begin practicing the syncopated rhythms against this with his left hand on the snare drum. When he can play one or two rhythms this way with the left hand, he should practice playing the rhythms on the bass drum while keeping time with the hands and left foot. In other words, he should learn to play all the syncopated rhythms on any *tone* of the drum set, while keeping time with the others. The ultimate sequel to this is to learn to play four different rhythms simultaneously, one with each hand and one with each foot.

IV. *Improvisation*

A. Fill-ins can be learned from books, copied off records or created by the student himself; but they should be learned only a few at a time (See section IIB). Two or more short fill-ins may be strung together to make longer solos or breaks.

B. Another good practice method is to play the rhythm of the melody line on the snare drum while keeping time, then fill in between the melodic accents, scattering the accents around on the different tones.

Practicing the snare drum, timpani, mallet instruments or concert *traps* does not give the stage band drummer the basic techniques he needs for his job, except for developing his hands and learning to read music. He must still learn to play the drum set as a unified whole and to function as a leader of the rhythm section, whose job it is to hold the band together rhythmically, even though others may be pulling it apart. He can contribute to the band's enthusiasm by his *feel* and he can contribute to the band's style with his fill-ins and solos. His contributions, however, must be made within the framework of steady *time*, developed to the point of being a matter of habit. Practicing with records develops a sense of style, feel and interpretation along with a steady sense of time, things which a metronome cannot do; and, after all, how else could one play with Count Basie, Woody Herman, Miles Davis and Gerry Mulligan (or Guy Lombardo, if you wish) all in the same night?

V

"Old MacDonald" (a very primitive example)

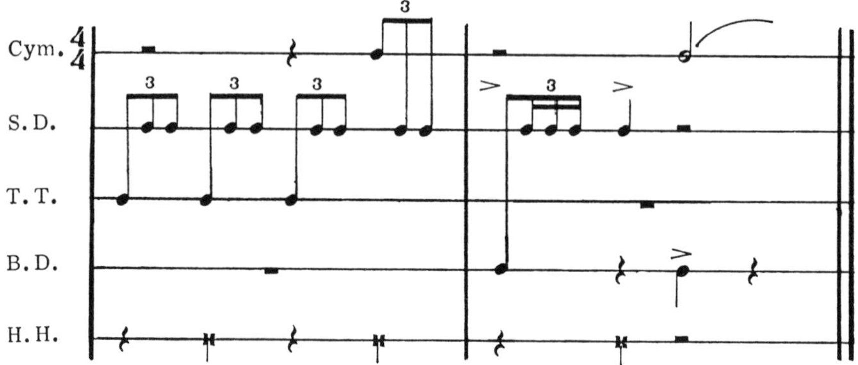

December 1964

Tambourine Technic

Mitchell Peters

The concept of all-around percussionists, rather than drummers, for our bands and orchestras is no longer an ideal but a necessity. Assuming the role of a percussionist implies having a performing knowledge of the accessory instruments (tambourine, castanets, triangle, etc.) in the percussion family as well as of the major instruments (snare drum, timpani, xylophone, etc.).

One of the most frequently used of the accessory instruments is the tambourine. The most common method of playing the tambourine is to hold it in one hand and strike it in the center of the head with the other hand. This method, though good for many passages, is wholly inadequate for other passages, because it is limited in speed, dynamic control, and tonal response.

Many drummers are not familiar with the other methods of playing the tambourine, which are not complex but do require some time and effort to master. Generally speaking, tambourine technique can be divided into three basic divisions: (1) single beat patterns, (2) roll patterns, and (3) combinations of single beats and rolls.

Single Beat Patterns

The means of articulating single beat patterns on the tambourine is usually determined by two factors: the volume, and the velocity of the passage being played. The most common method has already been touched upon, that of holding the tambourine in one hand and striking it with the other hand. The part of the hand used to strike the tambourine will depend on the dynamic level desired. For a full sound (mf-f-ff), the best results are achieved by striking the head with the flat surface of the fingers between the first and second joints of a loosely closed fist.

It is best to hold the tambourine about chest high or even higher and at an angle of approximately forty-five degrees, rather than horizontally or vertically. Holding the tambourine at an angle allows the jingles to be in their most responsive position, firm and crisp but not too stiff or rigid.

Some percussionists have a tendency to move the tambourine toward the free hand rather than keeping the hand holding the tambourine stationary and striking it with the free hand. This causes the jingles to give a slight grace note effect to the stroke, which is not desired.

Actually, it is the sound of the jingles that is most important, rather than the sound of the head. In loud playing the sound of the head reinforces the sound of the jingles; in softer playing the sound of the head is best avoided. The tone quality of the tambourine is determined by the quality of the jingles.

To illustrate the method cited above, the following example is provided (the same example will be used to illustrate the other methods, but the dynamics and tempo will differ):

♩ = 88 2/4

f

To play the above pattern at the same speed but softly will require a slight alteration of method. Instead of striking the tambourine in the center of the head, the player now must strike the edge of the head over the rim. Instead of striking with the closed fist, the hand is opened and the under tips of the fingers are used. The number of fingers used can vary from one to all, depending on the volume level desired. Either side of the tambourine can now be used, depending on whether or not the head sound is desired with the sound of the jingles. To avoid the head sound, one can lay the palm of the hand against the head while striking above the rim with the finger tips of the same hand, thus dampening the head sound. One can also muffle the head by placing the fingers of the hand holding the tambourine against the under part of the head. To avoid the head sound completely one can turn the tambourine over and strike only the rim.

Often it is necessary to combine the above methods to play a crescendo or diminuendo.

♩ = 88 2/4

ff — *p*

To play the above example one must start in the center of the head, striking with the closed fist, and then gradually shift the stroke toward the edge of the tambourine, at the same time gradually shifting the stroke from a closed fist to an open hand striking with the fingers or a finger. With sufficient practice the transition from one type of stroke to the other will be completely unnoticeable. For a crescendo the procedure is simply reversed.

For extremely loud strokes it is best to strike the tambourine with the closed fist, but the palm of the hand must be used as well as the flat surface of the fingers between the first and second joints, both striking the head at the same time. The palm provides the extra power and volume. There will, of course, be considerable head-slap sound resulting and proportionately less jingle sound.

The above methods can be used only as long as the rapidity of the rhythm can be executed with one hand. To execute a faster passage, the tambourine is still held with one hand, but it must be played between the free hand and the knee. It is best to use the upper part of the knee, for using the point of the knee can cause head breakage. Also, in playing in this manner, it is easier if the knee is slightly elevated, perhaps by resting the foot on a rung of a chair.

The tambourine is held with the head side facing the knee, and the free striking hand is placed above the opposite side of the head. Then the instrument is moved back and forth between these two points with the necessary wrist action. Strict alternation between the knee and the hand is not always the best procedure, however. One could compare the alternation to the use of single and double tonguing. The knee stroke would be used like the "tu" attack or on notes falling on the strong parts of the beat, and the hand stroke would be used like the

♩ = 132 2/4

f Tu TuKu Tu TuKu Tu Tu Tu Tu TuKuTuKu Tu Tu TuKuTuKu Tu

K = Knee K K H K K H K K K K K H K H K K K H K H K

H = Hand

"ku" attack or for notes falling in between those on the strong parts of the beat.

For more delicate fast passages that require a soft touch, the leg can again be used but this time merely as a resting place for the tambourine. The tambourine is placed on the leg above the knee either with the head up or down, depending on which sound is desired. Then both hands are placed on the instrument to hold it in place while the fingers of both hands execute the passage, playing on the rim above the jingle area.

The above are by no means the only ways to execute single beat patterns, though they are the most common. Perhaps it would be a good idea briefly to mention a few other possibilities.

For fast passages, some prefer to place the tambourine on a cushion or pillow and strike the instrument with a pair of timpani sticks or with the hands. However, this method does not really produce a very good tambourine tone.

Those with very strong and facile fingers will find that many quick soft passages can be executed with one hand using alternating fingers on the rim of the instrument.

For loud fast playing it is also possible to use two identical tambourines and play one on each knee in an alternating manner from a sitting position. This was more common with European orchestras of by-gone days and is hardly used today.

Roll Patterns

There are two basic rolls on the tambourine: the roll produced by shaking the tambourine, and the thumb roll.

The shake roll is the more common and is easier to execute and control. It is executed by merely shaking the tambourine with the turning of the wrist, thus causing the jingles to sway from side to side, creating the impression of a roll.

The volume of the roll is controlled by the length of the arc created by the movement of the tambourine. At the dynamic of mezzo-forte (*mf*) or louder, this roll can be executed very easily and has no time limitations as does the thumb roll. Going to the softer side dynamically, the shake roll requires a great deal more control.

In the above example begin shaking the tambourine on count one and stop just before count three. Commencing and terminating the shake roll should find the tambourine at its original forty-five degree angle. This will avoid extraneous jingle noise before and after the roll that results from the tambourine being in too vertical a position.

Many times the roll will be tied to another note.

This is played by shaking the tambourine for two beats, then striking the tambourine with the free hand on count three (lightly, unless an accent is desired). The shake must tie into the third beat.

Sometimes, depending on the passage, conductors prefer to have the beginning of the roll attacked for greater definition. For this a slight tap on the head is given with the free hand as one starts to shake the tambourine with the other hand.

The thumb roll is more difficult to execute; but it is good for rolls of a short duration and for soft rolls. It produces a much tighter and smooth sound than the shake roll.

The thumb roll is executed by sliding the thumb upward around the edge of the head on (or near) the rim. The friction between the thumb and the head causes the jingles to vibrate. While the thumb slides upward, the tambourine is turned downward (or pressed somewhat) against the thumb.

Because of the means of execution, the thumb roll is limited in the length of rolls it can produce. Once the thumb reaches the point where it can no longer continue around the head, the roll will cease.

The speed of sliding the thumb as well as the amount of pressure applied will control the dynamics of this roll. Because of this a softer roll can be held longer than a loud roll. Also, an extremely loud roll usually is best produced by shaking.

To execute the above example start the thumb sliding upwards on the first beat of the measure and lift the thumb off the head just before count three of the measure.

To execute the same roll tied to a single note (above example), the stroke on count three must be played with the same hand that is sliding the thumb for the roll. The stroke is executed with the palm of the hand. This enables the roll to continue into the third beat without a break. This, of course is to be done when an articulated beat is desired after the roll. If the rest of the ensemble does not articulate the tied note after the roll, the thumb roll should merely stop in rhythm *on* count three.

The thumb roll is very temperamental, and even the experienced professional can miss. To insure safety, many use artificial means, such as:

1) moistening of the thumb;
2) rubbing rosin or beeswax along the edge of the head;
3) gluing a strip of aloxite paper or fine sand paper around the edge of the tambourine;
4) shellacking the head, with fine sand ingrained;
5) spraying on "Ruff-Kote."

One final reminder: the commencement and conclusion of the roll must find the tambourine at forty-five or less degrees off the horizontal to avoid extraneous noises.

Combination of Single Beats and Rolls

This passage can be executed with either thumb rolls or shake rolls, depending on the individual's taste; and the single strokes are played in the normal one-handed fashion. If the shake roll is used, the half-note rolls should begin with an attack by the striking hand. This will make the basic rhythm of the phrase stronger. If the thumb roll is employed, the notes following the rolls are played in the normal way, rather than tying into the next note by playing it with the palm of the hand.

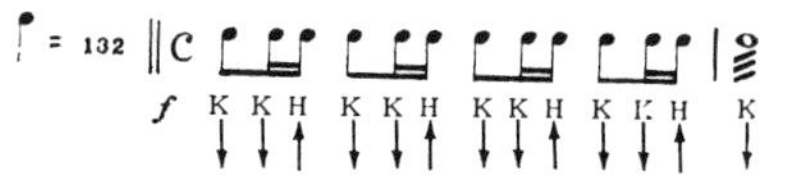

The rhythm in the first measure must be executed between the knee and the hand. It is also best to use a knee ictus on the shake roll in the second measure, for this will help to end clearly the rhythmic pattern started in the previous measure.

The thumb roll is especially good for short duration rolls such as the ones in the above example. The pianissimo single beats are best played with the tips of the fingers of one hand on the edge (head side) of the tambourine.

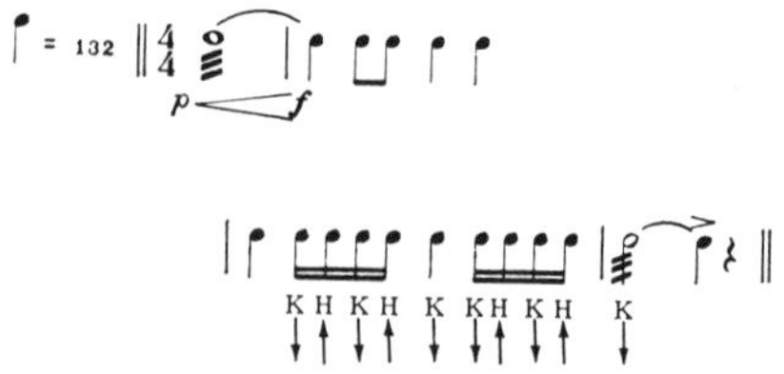

This example will require a little shifting. Crescendo and diminuendo rolls are generally easier to control by the shake method. The roll in the first measure is best played as a shake roll crescendoing into a solid stroke in the second measure. Often a crescendo roll is more effective if started with the tambourine below the waist and, as the volume increases, raised to its normal playing level. The reverse of this is also used, that is, to lower the tambourine on a diminuendo roll. The second measure is played with one hand playing very full, and the tambourine should be in a position with the head facing down to facilitate the knee and hand execution of the next measure. Between count one and count two of the third measure the player must shift to the hand and knee position to execute the sixteenth notes at the tempo of this passage. The shake roll in the fourth measure is best begun by a knee ictus and the stroke on count three is best played by the free hand.

This passage will also require a little shifting. The roll in the first measure would be best played as a thumb roll. During the quarter rest on count four, the player must shift the tambourine to rest on the leg to execute the rhythm of the second measure with the tips of the fingers of both hands playing on the rim (head side). Then the player must return to the thumb roll for the third measure and to the leg position for the fourth measure. (This is an instance in which, if the performer has strong fingers, the rhythmic figures can be executed by the alternating fingers of one hand, with the change of position of the tambourine thereby eliminated.)

January 1965

Equipment Recommendations

Gordon Peters

Music directors are becoming increasingly aware that today's compositions and arrangements call for an ever greater spectrum of percussion color. Hence, a periodic reassessment of just what percussion equipment our school instrumental music departments should have available to meet these growing needs is essential.

In the following outline guide an attempt has been made to list all of the instruments and equipment required to meet the present-day demands of the school percussion section. It is hoped that by comparing this guide-list to one's own inventory sheets, shortcomings can be quickly and accurately determined. Note while reading through this list that simply having "*a* snare drum" or "*a* tamborine" is no longer adequate. Many instruments must meet certain qualifications of construction, quality, and specifications to fulfill today's subtle and complex playing demands.

I. SNARE DRUMS

A. Concert-type
1. Metal shell
2. Dimensions: 6½" x 14" (5" x 14" for grammar school)
4. Snares, thin:
a. Nylon
b. Gut
c. Wire (particularly for grammar school) (no more than 14 snares in a set)
d. Combination of full gut and full wire (two wire to one gut)
(Note: The old-styled wire-wrapped silk should be discarded)

B. Marching-type
1. Separate tensioning on each head
2. Wooden shell with choice of finish (pearl, lacquer, etc.)
3. Dimensions: 12"x 15" (10" x 14" for grammar school)
4. Plastic heads
5. Snares: gut or nylon (thicker than for concert drums)

II. BASS DRUMS

A. Concert-type
1. Separate tensioning on each head
2. Dimensions: 16" x 36" (14" x 28" for grammar schools)
3. Calf skin heads

B. Marching-type (Scotch bass drums)
1. Separate tensioning on each head
2. Dimensions: 10" x 28" (8" x 26" or 10" x 28" for grammar schools)
3. Calf skin heads

III. TENOR DRUMS

A. Concert and/or Marching types
1. Separate tensioning on each head
2. Dimensions: 12" x 15" (10" x 15" for grammar schools)
3. Calf skin heads

IV. CYMBALS

A. Concert-type (pair)
1. Crash
a. Diameter: 17" or 18" if one pair (15" or 16" for grammar schools)
b. Diameter: 16" and 19" if two pairs
c. Thickness: medium
2. Suspended (two)
a. Diameter: 16" and 18" (15" or 16" for grammar schools)
b. Thickness: medium to medium-thin

B. Marching-type (one or two pairs as needed)
1. Diameter: 16" or 17" (14" or 15" for grammar schools)
2. Thickness: medium heavy

C. Straps and Pads
1. Leather or plastic varieties
2. Avoid lambswool for concert (OK for marching)
3. Avoid wooden handles completely

V. TIMPANI

A. Copper bowls (fiberglass for grammar schools, with smooth surfaces on inside and outside)
B. Pedal type, pedals on floor
C. Diameters
1. Basic pair: 26" and 29" (pre-

ferred) or 25″ and 28″
2. Third drum: 32″ (preferred) or 30″
3. Fourth drum: 23″

D. Plastic heads

E. Calf skin heads only for those situations where full knowledge of tipani mechanics, head care, and playing exist

VI. TRIANGLES

A. Size: 10″, two (8″ for grammar schools)

B. Holders (one for each instrument), wooden or metal clips with two separate loops of strong but thin plastic fish line leader

C. Beaters: one pair thin, one pair medium, and one pair heavy

VII. TAMBOURINES

A. Sizes:
1. One 10″, double row smooth, cupped jingles
2. One 8″, single row fluted edge jingles

B. Sandpaper (fine), rosin, or snare drum head roughening spray to apply to head for thumb rolls

VIII. CASTANETS

A. Two pairs plastic (or rosewood if budget allows) castanets mounted on paddles

B. One pair castanets mounted on block

IX. GONG (TAM-TAM)

A. Diameter: 30″ plus (no smaller for basic instrument); other smaller gongs as needed (24″ gong for grammar schools)

B. Beaters: one heavy beater (metal core and handle), covered well with either yarn or lambswool; one pair largest bass marimba yarn wound mallets for tremolos

X. BELL-LYRA

A. Pitched in "C" (if also used as a substitute for glockenspiel, it can be ordered in "B♭" to facilitate playing from solo trumpet parts)

B. Aluminum bars

C. Range: is standard on all instruments

XI. GLOCKENSPIEL (ORCHESTRA BELLS)

A. Steel bars (aluminum is adequate for grammar schools)

B. Range: 2½ octaves

XII. XYLOPHONE

A. Range: 3 octaves, "C" to "C"

B. Model: preferably on wheels: if in a case, remove when using and put on top of an ordinary restaurant tray stand

XIII. CHIMES

A. Diameter of tubes: 1½″ or 1¼″

B. Foot pedal damper as opposed to manual control

XIV. VIBRAPHONE

A. Range: 3 octaves, "F" to "F" (standard range)

B. Variable speed motor optional

XV. MARIMBA

Range: 4 octaves, "C" to "C" (larger range: optional)

XVI. AUXILIARY INSTRUMENTS

A. Two wood blocks (each with two different pitches)

B. Five temple blocks, all in *one* row

C. Sleigh bells

D. Slapstick (the larger, the better)

E. Sand paper blocks

F. Rachet

G. Finger cymbals

H. Other miscellaneous instruments and sound effects as needed

XVII. LATIN-AMERICAN INSTRUMENTS

A. Maracas, at least one pair (wooden)

B. Claves, rosewood, one pair

C. Gourd (guiro)

D. Bongos, tuneable (plastic or calf skin heads)

E. Timbales, calf skin heads

F. Conga drum, tuneable, pig or goat skin head

G. Cow bells, two different sizes

XVIII. ACCESSORIES

A. Bass drum stand (well-padded to prevent rattles and marring of bass drum finish)

B. Two portable trap tables (can be made by using: 1) ordinary restaurant tray stand, and 2) rectangular plywood top, well padded)

C. Suspended cymbal stands, two

D. Sturdy snare drum stands, as many as needed

E. Bongo stand (with attachment on bongos)

F. Timbales' stand

G. Conga drum stand

H. Sturdy gong stand

I. Wood block and/or cow bell holder(s)

J. Fibre cases and *thick* cloth covers as needed

XIX. MALLETS AND STICKS

(those marked "*" should be supplied by players)

*A. Snare drum sticks
1. 2A or 2B for general concert work
2. 1S or 2S for general marching work

*B. Brushes, two pairs

*C. Timpani sticks (at least three pairs of varying degrees of hardness, plus one wooden-headed pair). Specifications:
1. Round wooden core
2. No seam on covering of felt
3. Good quality felt, tightly drawn
4. Non-flexible shaft

D. Bass drum sticks
1. One lambswool two headed beater (not for playing tremolos)
2. One pair felt or lambswool heads, slightly smaller than the regular beater (for playing tremolos)

E. Suspended cymbal mallets
1. One pair medium hard yarn mallets
2. One pair snare drum sticks (2A or 2B)

F. Bells and Xylophone mallets
1. Two pairs brass (to be used only on steel bells)
2. Two pairs hard plastic
3. Two pairs medium hard rubber

G. Vibraphone mallets
1. Two pairs medium hard yarn
2. Two pairs medium soft yarn

H. Chime hammers
1. One pair large rawhide
2. Two pieces of chamois to cover one end of each hammer for soft playing

I. Marimba mallets
1. Two pairs soft rubber
2. Two pairs next harder rubber
3. Two pairs medium yarn

Chrome on all metal finishes, both on instruments and accessories, is recommended. This author's feelings on plastic versus calf skin heads for educational situations are these: *plastic:* timpani, snare drums, and bongos; *calf skin:* bass drums, tenor drums, timbales, and bongos; timpani only if a full knowledge timpani mechanics, head care, and playing is available. Information as to storage cabinets and stage band percussion equipment can easily be ascertained from most percussion instrument catalogues.

To insure accurate service when purchasing percussion instruments, it is recommended that the music director acquire the latest catalogues and educational aids from the percussion instrument manufacturers and makes out his own purchase order list, complete with full description of color, sizes, model and catalogue numbers, price, etc. With the usual bunching of orders for instruments during the summer, these matters might best be taken care of now.

In general the manufacturers of percussion instruments have contributed qualitative and imaginative products and continue to attempt to improve their instruments. However, if you have any recommendations or suggestions for improvement, they may only become a reality if you personally write to the manufacturers requesting their consideration of these ideas.

The names and addresses of percussion manufacturers of mallet-keyboard instruments, drums and general percussion equipment, plus accessories can be obtained from the annual (July-August) issue of the INSTRUMENTALIST or from any large music dealer.

This author stands ready to assist in advising any readers concerning their percussion problems. Next month's Percussion Clinic will go into the subject of care and repair of percussion instruments.

February 1965 (Original, not shown)
May 1975 (With adaptations, printed here)

Care and Maintenance of Percussion Instruments

Gordon Peters

With the ever-increasing interest in percussion shown by composers, conductors, and players, school music directors are regularly adding more equipment to their already-large percussion inventories. Obviously more funds will be available for the purchase of necessary new equipment if the repair budget for existing instruments can be kept as low as possible.

A conscientious program of care and maintenance can add considerably to the life and playing efficiency of percussion instruments. In general, I recommend that you follow the manufacturer's written instructions on care and repair, but do not hesitate to seek personal assistance from them on specific problems. Also, a professional percussionist living in your area can be very helpful as a consultant. Here are some other suggestions:

1. Appoint a percussion section leader to supervise storage and care of instruments and to report necessary repair to you.

2. Keep instruments away from radiators, windows, and air vents.

3. Adequate storage and protective cases and covers should be made available.

4. All instrumentalists (including the drummers) should be reminded that the percussion section is not a place for intermission entertainment! Unauthorized personnel should not be allowed to handle percussion instruments.

5. A lecture to the members of the percussion section on the care (and perhaps repair as well) of percussion instruments might save dollars in the future.

6. The concept of utilization of "traps" tables for the purpose of laying down instruments will aid in avoiding accidental dropping of instruments.

7. The manual training, wood and metal shop teachers, and the local hardware store can often be of assistance to the percussion section in resolving repair problems or in evolving custom made equipment.

8. Music stands, screws and nuts controlling height and angle should always be checked before uncovering instruments for use. Many heads on timpani, snare drums, and tambourines have been broken by the tops of stands falling on them.

9. In ordering instruments and parts from manufacturers *complete* descriptions (size, color, catalogue number, price, etc.) should be included.

10. All cracked, warped, and broken sticks should be discarded. All worn out mallets and timpani sticks should be recovered.

11. An annual "Percussion Equipment Day" should be designated whereby all percussionists get together with the music director for general purposes of repair, adjustment, and reappraisal of needs and problems.

12. Keep equipment dusted, cleaned, and polished.

Snare Drum

Stands

1. Tighten height and angle screws fully.

2. In putting the drum on the stand, see that the three supporting arms on the stand are in their proper positions, particularly the adjustable one which should be fully extended until the drum is set and then pushed into position.

3. The third adjustable arm may be bent down, in which case the snares of the drum and even the head might be resting on the center of the stand; this is a common cause of damage and head breakage.

4. Use only sturdy snare drum stands.

Heads

1. To prevent breakage and insure a maximum tonal response, *all* heads should be evenly tensioned; that is, they should have the same pitch opposite each tension rod.

2. Use plastic heads for minimum care and economy.

Snares

1. Keep tension on the snares when the drum is not in use.

2. Bent wire snares should be straightened if possible, removed if not, or a completely new set installed.

3. Gut snares are influenced by humidity and must be adjusted periodically to maintain the same tension throughout the set.

Sticks

1. See that the tips of the sticks are smooth (use sandpaper if necessary).

2. Size of sticks should be matched to drum size to avoid head breakage.

3. Players should have their drums adjusted to such a height and angle so that their sticks are just clearing the rim of the drum and the angle of the sticks with the drum is not acute.

4. In playing rim shots lay one stick on the drum touching the drum head and rim simultaneously while the other stick strikes the first stick. If the struck stick is held at an acute angle on the drum head and struck too hard with the other stick, a broken head might result.

5. Taping cracked sticks is a malpractice: these sticks should be discarded.

Lugs

Keep the screws holding the lugs to the drum well tightened (from the inside of the drum shell; merely remove the top head to get at the screws).

Tension rods

1. They should be cleaned and lubricated periodically.

2. Stripped threads can cause head breakage because of uneven tensioning: such rods should be replaced.

Cases

1. Fiber cases are recommended for maximum protection. Cloth covers and cases are second best but better than no cases. If a cloth case is used, additional protection can be gained by cutting thick cardboard disks the size of the drum heads and keeping them in the cloth case.

2. Head breakage is more apt to occur when we grow careless and pack other percussion instruments with the snare drum without adequate protection to the heads.

Articulation

1. Avoid playing in the exact center of the head (a physically weak spot).

2. By conceiving of drawing the tone *out* of the drum rather than pounding it *into* the drum, less head breakage will result. The stroke-articulation should be: "Strike and lift (the stick or mallet)," *not* a high lift *before* the stroke.

Timpani

Check the height and angle, tightening screws on music stand(s) before uncovering the heads.

Instrument base (or standard)

1. See that all screws, nuts, and reinforcement rods and legs are in their proper position and secure.

2. Tension springs should be properly lubricated and adjusted.

3. In adjusting pedals or removable kettles from bases, care must be taken in relieving the head and pedal tension to avoid a snapping of the pedal and other metal parts.

Heads

1. Use plastic heads for most educational situations and for all outdoor playing. Calf skin heads should only be used where an understanding of timpani mechanics and proper head exists.

2. For even tensioning the same pitch must prevail opposite each tension rod.

3. When cleaning the heads, leave them on the drum. For calf skin heads use only lukewarm water. For plastic heads a little mild soap can be mixed with the water. In any event, water should be kept away from the edge of the heads so that it does not get into the flesh hoop area.

Sticks

1. The angle of the sticks with the drum head should be minimized to avoid head breakage.

2. The balls of the sticks should strike the timpani three or four inches from the rim. If they strike closer, at an acute angle and *forte* or more, the possibility of head breakage is very high.

3. The balls of the sticks should be protected with plastic covers secured with a rubber band when not in use: this keeps felt wear at a minimum.

Tension rods

1. Replace any rods having stripped threads.

2. Keep them lubricated and clean (excessive grease easily accumulates and spots clothes).

3. Straighten or replace bent rods.

Covers

1. When timpani are not in use, they should be covered with both cardboard or fibreboard disks as well as cloth-skirted covers for maximum protection.

2. When traveling, fiber trunks and/or thick movers' covers should be used.

Bowls

Dents can be removed by removing heads (keep foot on pedal!) and carefully hammering them out with a hard rubber hammer.

Marimba, Xylophone

Mallets

They should be appropriate to the instrument: avoid hard plastic and very hard rubber mallets on the marimba (and, needless to say, do not use brass-headed mallets on wooden bars).

Bars ("Keys")

1. Clean and wax them periodically.

2. Cracked bars should be sent to the manufacturer to insure correct replacement bar and octave. Otherwise, be sure to indicate exact length, thickness, width, pitch, manufacturer, model number, and color of key to be replaced.

3. Tuning (the same on all bar instruments) is best left to the manufacturers. Instruments should be checked annually for intonation; the upper octaves are the first to show need of tuning. Any self-tuning should be done slowly with an abrasive wheel and checked with a stroboscope for accuracy. To sharpen, remove material from the end. To flatten, remove material from the under side, center. The recommended functional pitch standard is A - 441 for marimbas or A - 442 for xylophones, glockenspiels, vibraphones, and chimes.

Cases and covers

1. Keep instruments covered when not in use.

2. Avoid setting other instruments on top of mallet instruments unless a cloth cover is set down first.

3. When traveling use fiber cases or adequate blankets. It is best to dismantle the instrument when traveling.

4. When moving the instrument intact (within a building, up and down stairs, etc.), adequate manpower should be used both in number and competence. Accidents can be avoided by paying serious attention to proper gripping of the instrument and matters of balance. The instruments must be kept horizontal at all times when being moved.

Resonators

1. Simple caution, proper handling, and adequate case protection are the best remedies to avoid denting and marring.

2. Dust and dirt should be blown out annually with an air hose.

3. They should be placed below the bars at a point of maximum resonance. There are usually two or three alternate level slots at the left ends of the marimbas for this. As the temperature increases, the resonators should be raised closer (higher) to the bars.

Parts

1. Cords should be tightly secured, old cords replaced.

2. Guide posts are easily bent against keys causing restricted vibration of bars. Missing posts should be replaced.

3. Insulators on posts dry out and need replacement after several years.

4. The frames eventually become knicked. Proper paint for touch-up should be used (best to consult manufacturer for type).

Glockenspiel (Orchestra Bells)

1. Use any good metal polish for cleaning bars.

2. Avoid the use of brass-headed mallets on aluminum keyboards.

3. Keep screw-posts on bell-lyras tightened.

4. Insulation on guide posts should be checked. Bent posts should be straightened.

Vibraphone ("Vibes")

1. Avoid the use of metal mallets on this keyboard (which is made of aluminum alloy).

2. The motor must be oiled periodically as recommended by manufacturers.

3. All moving parts should be lubricated.

4. All screws and nuts should be tightened before using.

5. When plugging in the cord, be sure that a proper connection is made for AC or DC current. Also, be sure the cord and end connections are secure and not worn.

6. See that the cords are not worn and that the bars are seated properly before playing.

7. Motor belts stretch and fray through normal use: replace as needed.

8. See that the damper mechanism fully dampens all the bars.

Chimes

1. Use rawhide and wooden mallets only, no metal.

2. Suspension cords should be checked periodically for fraying.

3. Never strike chime tubes other than at the top.

4. The damper mechanism should be checked periodically.

5. Use metal polish for cleaning as recommended by the manufacturers.

Cymbals

1. For salvaging cracked cymbals, see the sheet put out by the Avedis Zildjian Co., P.O. Box 198, Accord, Mass. 02018.

2. Remove grease and accumulated dirt by washing the cymbal in a mild solution of oxalic acid and scrubbing with a soft bristle brush which is used in a motion paralleling the striations of the instrument. Rinse and dry. Follow this process with an application of a low abrasive-type cleaner. Rinse again and dry with a soft cloth. Avoid buffing cymbals: maintain and protect the striations on the cymbals as long as possible for maximum tonal response.

3. Check cymbal straps for wear and replace as needed.

4. Insulation of rubber sleeves and felt pads on cymbal stands should be checked periodically.

5. Avoid wooden handles on cymbals to avoid cracking.

Tambourine

1. Check security of tacks, holding head and jingles.

2. Avoid the use of knuckles in playing. A fist can be simulated by bunching up the fingers; this practice saves many broken heads.

3. When the instrument is not in use, some system should be evolved to protect the head.

Wood Block

1. Do not use triangle beaters as strikers.

2. Do not play with sticks below the angle of the horizontal: this will prevent chipping and cracking.

Gourds and Maracas

1. Because of their comparative brittleness, extra caution must be taken in storing.

2. For educational situations, these instruments are best purchased in more durable materials.

Gong (Tam-tam)

1. Check suspension material for wear.

2. Use only a sturdy standard.

Bass Drum

1. Lugs get loose quite easily because of the high degree of vibrations: check twice a year (must remove one head).

2. Separate tension bass drums cost less to maintain because of individual control.

3. Dirty heads (calf or plastic) can be cleaned with a mild soap and a soft brush. Avoid using water around flesh hoops.

4. Tension screws should be lubricated and cleaned periodically. Bent screws should be straightened or replaced.

Tips on Contest Snare Drumming

Ron Fink

My experiences as precussion clinician and adjudicator have prompted me to write an article, which, I hope, will be brought to the attention of snare drum students preparing for contests. The following check list contains general items which a student may work on before contest, and, if observed, should make for better performance and rating:

Choice of Music

Existing solos are often unmusical, unimaginative, unchallenging, and are predominantly of the "8 bar cadence-rudimental type." To spend much time memorizing this type of solo limits musical development. Granted, the rudiments contain fundamentals which students need to acquire, but most of the rudimental-styled training is not applicable to the important phases of drumming encountered in current concert music.

It is my opinion that we need more solos which demonstrate the many styles and techniques which the modern percussionist needs to play in order to meet the demands of all types of music. Presently, lists exist from which the contestant *must* choose his solo. Because of this restriction, is it not important to have solos included which demand real musicianship? Solos, for example, that are multi-metrical, or that have "odd" time signatures; solos which call for multiple drums, traps, or effects like muffling, dampening, use of different types of sticks, mallets, or brushes, use of rim shots, playing on the rim, near the edge, having irregular note groupings, hand independence, effective dynamic and expression markings, etc. What can the student soloist do about this? In addition to picking a demanding solo, I would also keep the remarks made above in mind in making the final selection. If allowed, I would also recommend that the contestant write in his own dynamics, nuances, ritards, etc. into the music.

Style

Depending on your choice of music, you must determine which of the basic two styles to play: military (open) or concert (closed). As discussed above, most solos are of the military style and dictate open playing. Both styles are consolidated in the playing of rudiments, with " 'open' to 'closed' to 'open' " interpretation.

Size and Condition of Drum

This is directly related to the style in which the student plays. The parade (field) drum, depth: 10-12 x diameter: 14-16, is analogous to the military style. The student who owns or plays exclusively on this drum has no alternative except to play the military (open) style because of the size of the drum and batter head. The smaller concert drum, depth: 5-8 x diameter: 14, is adaptable for either style. It is probably the more popular because of the ease in playing, the superior sound for the top-line models, and the flexibility in angling with a drum stand. Caution should be taken to make sure that the drum is in good condition (all hardware tight on the inside and out, threads lubricated, etc.) and that you don't play on a drum which is an extreme size, such as the "combo" drum (3 x 14). There are also some poor sounding parade drums, usually due to disproportionate size or inferior construction.

Size and Condition of Sticks

Sticks should be directly related to the size of the drum and the thickness of the batter head: the bigger the drum—the thicker the head—the bigger the sticks; the smaller the drum—the thinner the head—the smaller the sticks. In other words, the parade drums take larger sticks to get the maximum response and "feel," whereas the concert drum with more sensitive heads takes the lighter weight sticks. Of course, stick size also should be proportionate to hand size. Avoid pencil models at one extreme, or clubby, extra large sticks at the other. Sticks which are generally satisfactory are in the proximity of 2A, 3A, 5A, 2B, etc. It is also best to have an extra pair handy, since sticks will sometimes chip or splinter around the beads.

Be particular when buying your sticks. Check to see that the sticks match in weight, balance, and pitch by switching sticks from hand to hand seeking to find that pair which best balances in the hands. Closer scrutiny is not always possible since manufacturers currently are matching and packaging their sticks. Dealers and manufacturers get truly "bugged" (and rightly so) if you insist on opening all their stick packages. For the most part, we'll have to trust them.

Tone Production

This item is as important to snare drum sound as it is to any other instrument. The drum heads *must* be tensioned evenly to produce a good sound and to get the proper "feel." Check the following when trying to improve the tone: (a) Condition of the head. Often an old head replaced by a new one is the answer. The student should familiarize himself with the thicknesses and the grades (professional, standard, economy) available. Manuacturers have different names for these grades and thicknesses, so inquire; *but* buy the top line. (b) If the heads are all right, tension the drum until the sound improves from tightening or loosening the batter and/or snare head. The batter (playing) head should be tighter than the snare (bottom) head. (c) Excessive ring in a drum is annoying and can be remedied by using your internal muffler or improving the fine tension of the heads or snares. The same pitch, hence tension, should be evident opposite each tension screw. Some models have no mufflers, so you must resort to felt, tape, moleskin, etc. This type of muffling is sometimes overdone, and consequently the tone gets worse instead of improving. (d) Check your wire or gut snares to see that they are intact and can be "drawn-up" securely and with even tension. (e) Check the playing area. To produce like sounds, the sticks must strike near enough to one another and must strike the area which produces the best sound and "feel." The heads often respond better, as do many instruments of the percussion family, if they are struck "off center." Dead center often sounds hard, and the sticks respond awkwardly because of acoustical considerations. The conscientious player may play in different places on the drum head when observing the dynamics and should not be restricted to the middle-area of the drum head. However, he should attempt to continue to play above the snare bed (that is, the area on the top head directly over where the snares run across the bottom head). On this important item of tone production, I would suggest taking the drum to a professional or a drum shop to be tuned correctly.

Height-Angles

I like to see a player using his sticks at right angles to each other and his arms and elbows "free" from the body (2 or 3 inches). The height of the drum should not restrict the player but should be at the level which allows maximum freedom of horizontal arm motion in playing. Preferably, the drum should be low enough to give the performer the required distance for "stick action" in accents and "forte" playing. When the player must play sensitive "pianissimo" passages, requiring great control, he merely arches his body over and gets nearer the drum. It seems more feasible to have the drum low for better body flexibility than too high where free arm action is hampered. I am not particularly critical of a student's placement of feet; however, I can play better myself by having one foot in *front* of the other for reasons of balance. I prefer to see a performer adapt to whatever position is necessary rather than stand with a rigid, motionless, "at-attention" stance.

The angle of the drum, depending upon which grip or drum is used, is important. If the player plays with the *matched* grip, the drum can be horizontal. When the *traditional* grip is used, a slight angle is all right, as long as it is not so extreme that it causes the left hand to be extremely higher than the right. When a drastic angle is used, the sticks do not rebound readily but ricochet off to the side.

Tempo

Tempo has many implications, the most important one being an asset which every drummer must have: *Steady Time* or *Pulse!* Playing "steady time" means the ability to avoid rushing, dragging, or the combination of both. The beat must not fluctuate from its intended marking and must be as solid as a rock. Another facet of tempo is to determine just how fast to play a solo which may have no markings or indication at all. The rudimental-military style is often abused. It is not intended to be played extremely fast (unless marked), but you hear it interpreted from "MM♩: 132" on up. This loses the characteristic style and intent of the solo, and it becomes a gaudy display of technique.

Appearance

In most contests the contestant receives a rating on his appearance. This is one seemingly small but important segment of the over-all rating which should not be overlooked. Usually a student needs no prompting on this subject, because his own common sense should dictate a well-groomed appearance. If I might make some rather obvious suggestions, however, I would include some of the following: Wear your best suit and tie, have your shoes polished, preferably wear dark and not white socks for boys and hose for the girls, leave the gum and candy outside, leave your letter sweater at home with all of your medals, be on time, and, if possible, get in some practice time. Contests have been known to run behind schedule, so patiently wait for the judge to finish his paper work before running to him with your music before or after your performance. Be careful of bad habits like foot-tapping, fancy stick twirling, and head twitches or facial expressions that distract from your playing. Some excellent practice suggestions at this point would be helpful. For example: practice in front of a mirror, use a tape recorder, use a metronome, and as often as possible, play for an audience, to gain valuable experience.

If you are nervous, avoid displaying it, because judges well realize that there is pressure on each performer. Keep your mind on what you are doing, and be serious and attentive to the judge at all times. To be courteous is a virtue but over-familiarity or emotional outbursts (by the student or the student's *mother*) before, during, or after the contest is undesirable. Accept your rating graciously and try harder the following year to improve on your weak points. Don't blame the judge, your private teacher, or your band director at home for your mistakes.

In closing, I might mention that adjudication procedures, rules, etc. are in a state of change and improvement; hence, the potential contestants and teachers should each year, acquaint themselves with the prevailing rules.

The Triangle: Don't Underestimate It

James J. Ross

The triangle is one of the most important instruments in the percussion section and perhaps the most abused. The greatest composers have utilized its beautiful tonal qualities in some of the major works of the repertory. For some unknown reason it is overlooked by many conductors, and therefore most anything can happen and often does. If played well, it can be a most beautiful and effective asset to a band or orchestra, and by the same token, it can be just the opposite if *not* played well.

First, and perhaps most important, is the choice of triangle. A poor instrument cannot possibly sound well no matter how correctly it is played. A rather thick steel triangle 10 inches per side and one-half inch in diameter is the best all around choice. Aluminum triangles should be avoided because they produce an inferior tonal response.

Second in importance are the beaters which should also be made of steel and should be purchased in pairs, preferably a pair of very thin, a pair of medium, and a thick pair. One beater will *not* do the job properly. The reason for having pairs is that some passages are too fast and difficult to execute correctly with one beater; therefore, the triangle must be clipped to the music stand leaving both hands free to play the part. Incidentally, the medium and heavy beaters are readily available. However, the thin ones must be made, and the best material to use is drill rod cut up in 9 inch lengths. It is available at large hardware stores.

Third in importance is the triangle holder. By far the best is the wooden clip-type which *cannot* be purchased but can be made very easily. Purchase a long wooden music clip (as used in outdoor playing), remove the metal extension, then saw off the extra wooden part so that the front ends are even. After that, drill two small holes just large enough for two thin cords (preferably nylon harp or nylon fishing line) to pass through. The holes should be about in the middle of the bottom of the clip approximately an inch apart. The cord that actually holds the triangle should be as short as possible to avoid side-sway, and the second cord should be a little longer. The purpose of the longer cord is to prevent the triangle from falling in the event the holding cord should break during a performance. Once you have tried this type of holder, you will never go back to the clumsy metal type or holding it by a piece of string, etc.

As far as the actual playing of the triangle is concerned, here are some basic points and suggestions. Hold the triangle in the left hand with the open end to your left (for *left*-hand players the opposite position is recommended). Place the thumb between the wide opening of the holder, rest the forefinger on top of the forward end and place the middle finger on the underside. Flex the wrist so that the triangle hangs freely in a natural position making sure that no part of the clip or hand touches the triangle. The instrument should be held high, at least at eye level.

Generally speaking the triangle should be struck on the base about half way between the middle and the right hand corner at about a 45 degree angle.

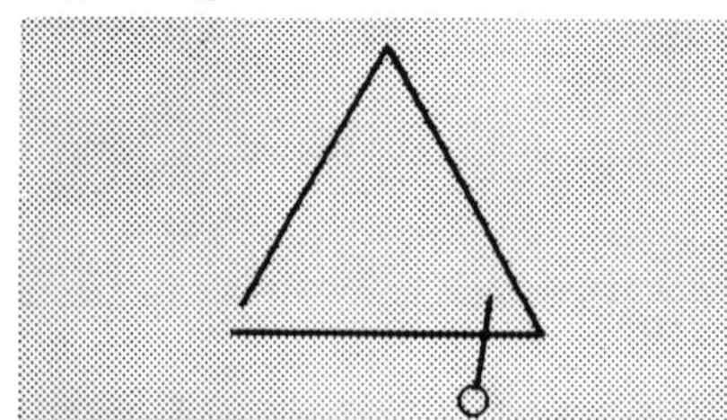

Figure 1

For those who prefer, it may also be struck near the top of the right side.

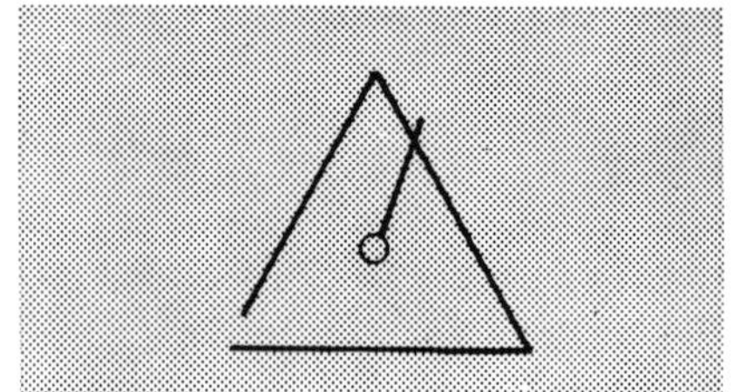

Figure 2

The tonal response on the bottom of the triangle amplifies the lower overtones, the upper side, the higher overtones. Some players play the lighter passages on the outside and the stronger ones on the bottom.

The tremolo or roll is made by a rapid shake of the beater in the inside right-hand corner. For soft rolls the beater should be kept close to the right-hand corner.

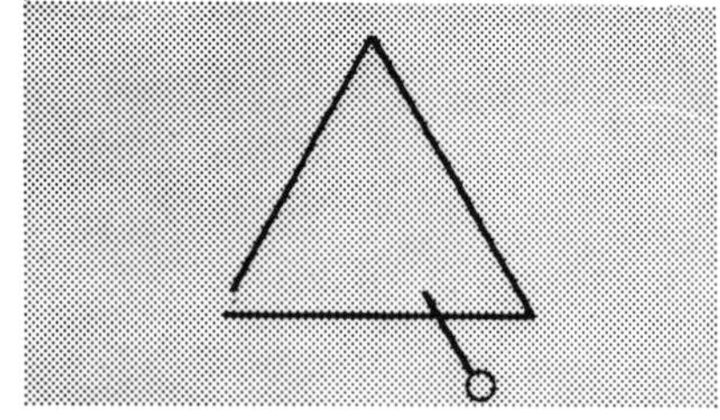

Figure 3

For louder rolls one can move farther away from the corner. When using two beaters, the base should be struck in the middle with a downward direct blow.

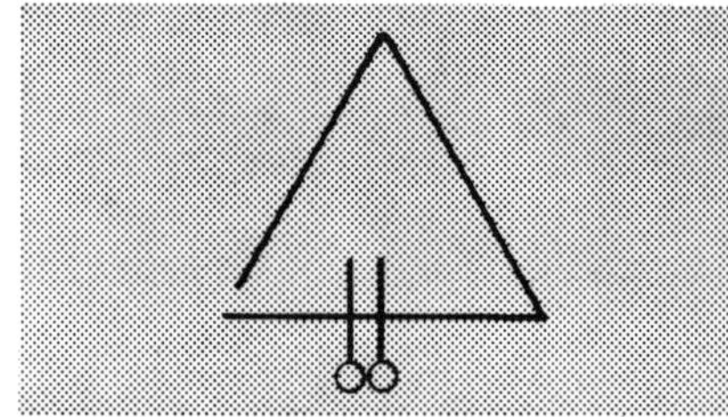

Figure 4

Also, two beater playing can be articulated around the top corner of the triangle.

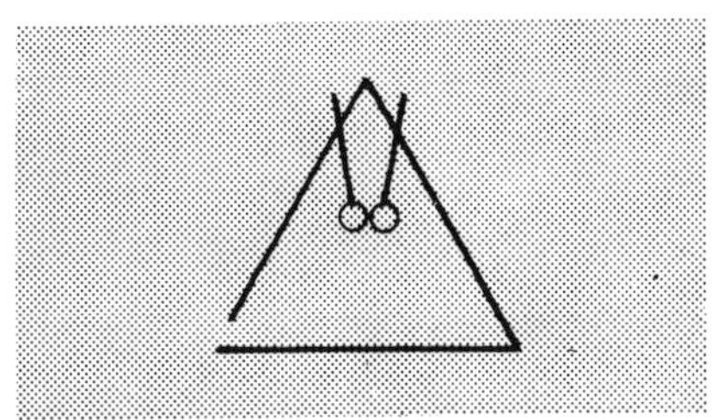

Figure 5

As a general rule the triangle should be held up when possible, the only exceptions being when two beaters are required to play certain intricate passages and also if there is a quick change from triangle to another instrument. Experience is the best guide in these situations. When finished playing a passage, it is recommended that the triangle is either rested on a padded table or clipped to the music stand. Avoid laying it on stools, chairs, bass drum, bells, xylophone, or on the floor.

For single or delicate sounds, hold the beater with the thumb and forefinger in a relaxed grip using a glancing blow and for loud and technical passages, hold the beater a little firmer using all the fingers and striking with a *direct* blow. Never use a wooden beater unless indicated so by the composer (which is very rare).

In summary, music directors and players should treat the triangle as a most valued member of the percussion family such as the great composers of the past and present have.

Don't underestimate or belittle the triangle: *RESPECT IT!*

May 1965

Initiating a Percussion Ensemble Program

Gordon Peters

Music directors find that giving their students small ensemble experience provides them with a more subtle vehicle through which to develop an awareness of phrasing, balance, expression, etc. which in turn will be reflected in the larger musical organization. Ensemble programs, however, often have been grounded on the argument that the "curriculum allows no further scheduling of new activities." This is often merely a defensive excuse for some other reason: it is a common human behavior axiom that there can always be room made for something good and beneficial.

Percussion students should be privileged with a chamber music program just as are other instrumentalists. Besides giving the percussionists a more subtle musical experience, it gives them an opportunity to develop techniques on a greater variety of instruments than is possible in the larger musical organization. For instance, the director can "break in" a prospective timpanist by having him play timpani in the ensemble. Also, the exposure of comparative playing abilities of the players on different instruments develops a healthy competitive environment. [Note: see *The Instrumentalist*, April, 1962: "Why Percussion Ensembles" by Gordon Peters: objectives of having a percussion ensemble.]

The primary hurdle to a formal percussion ensemble program coming into existence on the college level is sometimes the school administration. Administrators must be indoctrinated as to the background and importance of this program educationally.

First of all they must be impressed with the value that such a program would have in the overall instrumental ensemble program. To accomplish this one might arrange for a live performance of a percussion ensemble witnessed by administrators, be it a voluntary group from the school involved, a visiting percussion ensemble from another school, or a professional group. Many college percussion ensembles have annual tours and are delighted to find new locations to play. A school assembly program of such a group, particularly one where the players demonstrate the instruments, are superb educational vehicles for *all* students. The impact of personal observation of such a fascinating group plus some background in the objectives and resultants of such a program often is sufficiently convincing to administrators. Also, use of recordings, pictures, percussion ensemble programs, and printed reviews of works performed elsewhere will help in selling the idea. Student expressions in favor of such a program are also difficult to ignore.

The administrator must then be made to realize that to pursue such a program means an expansion in the budget allowed for the percussion department, for additional instruments may well have to be purchased, old instruments may have to be repaired and brought into use again, and percussion ensemble music will have to be purchased. This music is no more expensive (in many cases less expensive) than music for other instruments.

At the outset a program outside of regular school hours is better than none at all. In high schools the music director's time seems to have more and more demands made upon it. If he is unable to spend sufficient time with such a program, a student conductor or an advanced student might be used at first. Perhaps the director already has a faculty assistant that could carry on this work. Another alternative is to have a percussion specialist visit the school regularly to coach percussion ensembles and perhaps also give private percussion lessons.

Finding someone who has the time to coach a percussion ensemble program is another consideration, for these reasons: 1) many music directors are not qualified to perform such a task due to their percussion education being inadequate (many times through no fault of their own), 2) some percussion instructors themselves are inadequate when it comes to this new task because of no prior experience with percussion ensembles, and 3) the necessity of performing a certain amount of interpretive and conducting duties (as well as administrative) finds some instructors lacking in background. If at all possible percussion ensemble programs on the college level should be made formally a part of the curriculum, that is "with credit."

The physical facilities for a percussion ensemble program must also be considered. Designating a rehearsal room that is close to where the percussion instruments are kept will save many rehearsal minutes. The problem of possibly disturbing others with rehearsals of the group must certainly be considered: acoustics and percussion are not always compatible. Ensemble rehearsal can be scheduled during the band and orchestra rehearsal whenever the director is rehearsing works or sections where the percussion section (or part of same) is not needed. However, percussion ensemble rehearsals should never take the percussionist out of the band or orchestra rehearsal when he is needed nor should regular *sectional* rehearsal be supplanted by them. At the grammar school level a beginning percussion class can eventually include simple ensemble playing, first with the practice pads and drums and later with the addition of the accessory instruments.

There may be some initial reticence on the part of the percussion students who have never participated in ensembles. This would stem mainly from the student's fear that he would not have enough time to prepare his other studies adequately. However, once the student has participated in such a program and realizes the benefits to be derived, his motivation is so enhanced as to carry over into his other studies and even results in some students asking for more ensemble practice!

Matters relating to the staging of percussion ensembles requires "planning ahead," as there is a different arrangement of instruments necessary for each piece. The drawing of charts indicating the placement of instruments for each piece will soon facilitate moving instruments between pieces. To save time it is best to request of the players that they are set up for the piece(s) to be rehearsed *before* the appointed hour of rehearsal.

Finding repertory to accommodate a specific number of players from semester to semester is another consideration. Today there is a sufficient abundance of music to choose from, and in some cases parts can be doubled or divided up between players. If there are not enough percussion players to cover all the parts, other instrumentalists can be recruited.

In the choice of repertory the conductor-coach of an ensemble must be very discerning. Much ensemble music is of inferior musical worth due principally to the comparative newness of the medium of percussion chamber music. At the outset of the evolution of this repertory many percussionists without composition training and/or talent were attracted by publication offers as were many young composition students who wished to become famous "overnight" and have works published. However, more serious composition talents have now been attracted to this medium of expression, and, as each year passes, finer works are being evolved at all levels of difficulty. Some works, of course, even if of questionable musical worth do serve certain laboratory needs through offering technical challenges to the players. Most publishers are now including percussion ensemble music in their catalogues.

There is one other type of percussion ensemble in existence today whose objectives are not primarily to teach people how to play percussion instruments, but rather to teach young people of early school age (and sometimes adults) the basic elements of music and to appreciate musical art works through the use of percussion instruments.

Carl Orff[1], more known today as a prominent German composer, has evolved a set of seven books called *Music for Children* in which he basically gets the children to translate speech patterns from nursery tunes and such into rhythmical patterns which are "experienced" on specially built percussion instruments.

Charles Bavin[2] of England has evolved a system whereby young and old alike get acquainted with the best musical literature by playing along with great music (either in live performance or with recordings) on a percussion instrument of some kind.

Satis Coleman[3] of the United States has also evolved some practical educational schemes for young children in learning about music through activity with percussion instruments.

The Jacques-Dalcroze School of Eurhythmics[4] has for years integrated percussion, rhythm, music, and movement in its course of study for both young children and adults.

Whatever obstacles or problems may exist in connection with a percussion ensemble program, regardless of age or academic level, this ensemble activity pays rich rewards in developing motivation and musical development. It is particularly a necessary adjunct to the development of the serious percussion student.

---

1. Orff, Carl and Gunild Keetman. *Music For Children* (Orff-Schulwerk), in seven volumes. English adaptation by Doreen Hall and Arnold Walter. New York, 1950. Assoc. Music Publ. (G. Schirmer).
2. Bavin, Charles. *The Percussion Band from A to Z.*
3. Coleman, Satis N. *Creative Music for Children.* New York, n.d.
4. Rosenstrauch, Henny. *Percussion, Rhythm, Music, Movement.* Availability: Miss Henny Rosenstrauch, 5628 Forbes St., Pittsburgh, Pa.

The Matched Grip vs. the Unmatched Grip

Jerry Carrico

In the drumming world today, the stick grip of drummers has become a very controversial issue. There are two schools of thought concerning this matter, the first being called the unmatched or traditional grip. This grip consists of holding the right hand stick as a pool cue is held with the right wrist moving up and down. The left hand stick is held with the palm turned in a vertical position with the wrist turning sideways. This grip had its beginnings with the military fife and drum corps when drums were carried on slings over the shoulder in the same manner as today's drum corps and marching bands. It was used because it adapted itself especially well to the position of the field drum. Being on the left leg, the drum tilted downward toward the right and the grip of the left hand allowed the stick to be raised higher to make up for the height difference, while the right hand could play lower.

Even before this unmatched grip had its beginnings, the second type of grip, called the matched grip, was being used by timpanists in all the European orchestras. This grip consists of holding both the left hand and right hand sticks as a pool cue would be held. These instruments are horizontal when in playing position and thus no raised left hand was needed to make up for a difference in height.

Both of these grips served a useful and logical purpose in their development, but today, with more and more demands being placed on the percussionist, the argument has arisen—which is more practical? I believe that from the standpoint of an all-around percussionist the matched grip is the most practical. By an all-around percussionist, I mean a person who is capable of playing all the percussion instruments not only the snare drum.

Now, to understand my reasoning, the instruments which a percussionist uses must first be examined in relation to the stick grip used. Most of the instruments are played with the matched grip, including: timpani, temple blocks, timbales, bongos, concert tom-toms, bass drum, chimes, marimba, vibes, bells, and xylophone. The only exceptions are the snare drum and drum set, on which the unmatched grip is used. This means that the good percussionist will spend about 90% of his time using the matched grip and about 10% of his time using the unmatched grip, which in itself makes the latter rather impractical.

A second factor is that the matched grip is better suited for the percussion player. Many times during the course of a work, three or four different instruments may be used by one man. If he first has to play the timpani and concert tom-toms, which use the matched grip, and then switch to the snare drum, it is again impractical to change the stick grip, as well as time consuming.

Also upholding the matched grip is the increased easiness for developing technique. The right hand grip is by far the easiest in which to develop technique, not only because most drummers are right handed, but also because the wrist action used is natural to the hand. The left hand is in an unnatural position in the unmatched grip, and thus it takes a much longer time to develop. I know this through my own experience and through that of other drum instructors.

These reasons show why the matched stick grip is more practical; however, drum corps drummers would most likely refute this argument on the grounds of tradition and the drum position while marching. Fighting this argument on the grounds of their tilted drum positions and need for special unmatched left hand grip is really quite illogical. In drum corps, there are three kinds of drummers: bass, tenor, and snare. Since drum corps started using tenors, which was about fifteen years ago, these tenor drummers have always used the matched grip. Yet their fellow snare drummers are still using the unmatched grip! Also, the drums could easily be made horizontal by using two slings.

What this argument really boils down to is whether or not tradition is going to stand in the way of progress, but even this is declining. Some jazz drummers have for many years been using the matched grip. The University of Illinois Football Band has also used it. As for everyday use, however, the answer still seems to be "Don't use it—not yet."*

*Jack McKenzie, "The Matched Grip," *Ludwig Drummer*, p. 30, Vol. 3, No. 2.

Changes In Percussion Adjudication

one of the first projects completed by the Percussive Arts Society is this report on new adjudication procedures for the percussion solo and ensemble contest at the high school level.

The Percussive Arts Society was formed principally to elevate all facets of percussion knowledge. It was formed in 1963 largely through the efforts of Donald G. Canedy and today boasts a board of directors representative of the entire percussion field to assist in the direction of its activities. A quarterly journal called the *Percussionist* is issued by the Society and contains articles and studies covering diverse areas of percussion activities and knowledge.

One of the early projects of the PAS was to delve into the inadequacies of percussion solo and ensemble contests at the high school level. To quote from the first paragraph of Volume 1, No. 2 of the *Percussionist*:

> It seems that one of the best ways to make immediate progress toward raising the standards of percussion performance is to undertake a project which affects at once the student and the teacher in the public and private schools across the country.

Based on an article on the subject by Gordon Peters appearing in the *Ludwig Drummer* (Spring 1963, Vol. 3, No. 1) Mr. Peters was asked to form a committee to study this subject. The recommendations resulting from this project appear below. It is hoped that music directors will take the time to study these proposals and bring them to the attention of their students and state adjudicating committees.

The following rules and evaluation sheet for the percussionist at the high school music contest were prepared and are recommended by the Percussive Arts Society Committee: Gordon Peters, chairman; Ramon E. Meyer; Laverne R. Reimer; and James D. Salmon.

Rules for Solo Event

1. At least ten minutes shall be allowed per event.
2. Solos shall be performed only on the following percussion instruments: snare drum, timpani, marimba, xylophone, and vibraphone. The following instruments shall not be acceptable for solo performance by themselves: bass drum, bell-lyra, glockenspiel (concert bells), chimes, and dance-drum set.
3. The choice of solo(s) should be made on the basis of the musical merits of a work plus its compatibility with the performer's technical resources.
4. The duration of the solo should be between two and five minutes. The judge should stop the contestant beyond this maximum time to allow for the other categories on the evaluation sheet to be tested.
5. A contestant will be permitted to play solos on two major percussion instruments with the permission of his music director. However, these shall be regarded as separate events. In no case shall the same contestant be permitted to perform in more than two solo events, however.
6. Each contestant shall supply the judge with a copy of the solo (or score if accompaniment is involved) with the measures numbered. Student compositions will be allowed only if they have strong musical qualities and include sufficient technical material.
7. All snare drum rudiments shall be played at the contestant's maximum controlled speed with the sticking indicated on the evaluation sheet in this manner: *forte* . . . a diminuendo to *piano* . . . returning through a crescendo to *forte*. The total duration of this procedure shall be between seven and fifteen seconds.
8. All abstract rolls (those not appearing in solos) on instruments other than the snare drum shall be played both *forte* and *piano* unless otherwise indicated.
9. The choice of scales and arpeggios shall be made by the judge, but only those with not more than four sharps or flats shall be considered.
10. Any anatomically correct grip of sticks and mallets shall be acceptable, including the matched grip on the snare drum.
11. The snare drum may be rested on a snare drum stand or hung from a sling. Either wire, gut, or a combination of the two types of snares will be acceptable. Plastic and calf-skin heads are both acceptable and may be used in combination. The angle of the drum should be consistent with the grip used: tilted for the traditional grip and flat for the matched grip.
12. Each contestant shall perform a solo in one of the three major areas (snare drum, timpani, or mallet instrument) or a multiple instrument solo including any one or

more of the major instruments and any number of auxiliary instruments. He shall also perform the minimal requirements indicated in SECTION III of the evaluation sheet in the two areas not including his major solo instrument. In addition the contestant should be prepared to perform the techniques indicated in SECTION IV; the judge may choose any one of the areas listed, depending on time restrictions.

13. The judge shall use the Evaluation Sheet as follows:

a. SECTION I: All solo events.

b. SECTION II: Only that division pertaining to the contestant's solo instrument.

c. SECTION III: Only the two non-solo instrument divisions.

d. SECTION IV: Choose one of the divisions if time allows. The judge may either use music or merely have the contestant demonstrate single beats and roll techniques.

e. The judge shall indicate a check opposite those factors he finds unsatisfactory. Upon totaling these checks the judge must then determine the various rating categories. Contestants with the least number of checks will rank highest.

f. Any further written comments will be helpful to the contestant and should be included within the limits of time.

g. The judge should hold the following as being his fundamental objective and criteria: to determine the comparative degrees of musical and technical development and the contestants' abilities to play several percussion instruments.

14. The following rules regarding sight reading shall prevail:

a. The materials used shall be from any standard percussion method book; no manuscript-type notation shall be used.

b. The level of difficulty shall be between elementary and intermediate.

c. The length shall be eight to sixteen measures.

d. Similar materials shall be used for all the contestants.

e. The tempo will be set by the judge.

f. Any meters common to the literature being performed by high school bands and orchestras shall be considered suitable.

15. The only pitch that a timpani contestant will be allowed from the piano shall be an "A" or "B♭". This same rule shall apply to SECTION III (timpani).

16. Each music director should be thoroughly acquainted with the evaluation sheet and rules, and he should provide each percussion contestant with a copy of same at least three months in advance of the contest. The rules and evaluation sheet should act as a guide to the student in preparing for his contest appearance.

17. All music directors shall use the evaluation sheet as a guide for a proficiency examination of all prospective contestants prior to their enrollment in contests to see that they are qualified to compete.

18. The host school of the contest shall be responsible for furnishing the following percussion instruments: piano, timpani (at least two with pedals, preferably four), chimes, marimba or xylophone, vibraphone, orchestra bells, bass drum, snare drum (on stand), a pair of cymbals, one suspended cymbal, triangle, tambourine, plus at least ten music stands for ensembles).

Evaluation Sheet

SECTION I: SOLO INSTRUMENT CRITERIA (all contestants)

Technique

Left Hand	Right Hand
......	...... Grip
......	...... Up and down stroke
......	...... Arm
......	...... Wrist
......	...... Equal height of sticks or mallets

Accuracy (Memorization)

...... Number of stops
...... Correct rhythm and/or pitches
...... Steadiness of tempo
...... Avoidance of extraneous noises

Interpretation

...... Appropriate tempo
...... General volume
...... Accents
...... Dynamics and other nuance
...... Expression
...... Phrasing
...... Character
...... Rhythmic clarity, precision

General Effect

...... Conviction
...... Stage presence
...... Posture
...... Grace of movement
...... Appearance (neatness)

Appropriateness of Solo

...... Musical content
...... Sufficient display of techniques
...... Appropriateness to instrument
...... Appropriateness to player's musical and technical resources

Accompaniment

...... Accuracy
...... Ensemble
...... Balance

Sight Reading

...... Accuracy
...... Consistency of tempo
...... Dynamics and other nuance

SECTION II: SOLO INSTRUMENT CRITERIA (all contestants, solo instruments only)

A. SNARE DRUM

Tone

Head Tension
...... Batter (top)
...... Snare (bottom)
...... Snare adjustment
...... General sound

Sticks

...... Tips equidistant from rim and snare bed
...... Appropriateness to size of drum
...... Angle with drum (above rim)
...... Angle with arms (almost straight)
...... Angle with each other (90 degrees)

Rolls

...... Evenness
...... Attacks
...... Releases

B. MALLET INSTRUMENTS

Tone

...... Striking center (or extreme ends) of bars

...... Degree of mallet hardness (for instrument)
...... Mallet appropriateness to solo

Rolls (except vibraphone)

...... Evenness
...... Legato technique
...... Attacks
...... Releases

Muffling (vibraphone)

...... With pedal
...... With mallets

Mallet Versatility

...... Use of both two and four mallets

C. TIMPANI

Tone

...... Correct playing area (approximately three inches from rim *both* sticks)
...... Quality of sticks
...... Stick appropriateness
...... Stick angle with head (above rim: minimize)
...... Avoidance of clicking rim and/or "T"-screws with stick shafts

Rolls

...... Speed in lower register
...... Speed in upper register
...... Attacks
...... Releases

Tuning

...... In tune with self (balanced head)
...... Intervallic intonation (pedaling)

Muffling

...... On time
...... Quietly
...... Completely

SECTION III: BASIC TECHNIQUES (all contestants, other than solo instruments)

A. SNARE DRUM Rudiments (ask for no more than two in each section)

Rolls

...... Single stroke
...... Double stroke, open
...... Double stroke, closed

Flams

...... LR LR LR LR etc.
...... RL RL RL RL etc.
...... Alternating

Drags

...... LLR LLR LLR LLR etc.
...... RRL RRL RRL RRL etc.
...... Alternating

Four-stroke ruffs

...... LRLR LRLR LRLR etc.
...... RLRL RLRL RLRL etc.
...... Alternating

B. MALLET INSTRUMENTS Scales And Arpeggios (ask for any two in each section)

Scales (two octaves) (up and down)

...... Major
...... Minor (harmonic form)
...... Chromatic (start on any pitch)
...... Whole-tone (either one, start on any pitch)

Arpeggios (two octaves) (up and down)

...... Major
...... Minor
...... Diminished
...... Augmented

Four-mallet chords, closed position (one octave) (up and down)

...... Major
...... Minor
...... Diminished
...... Augmented

C. TIMPANI

Tuning and Technique (any two pitches; ask for two)

...... Perfect fifth
...... Major third
...... Perfect fourth
...... Major sixth
...... Roll evenness
...... Correct playing area (equidistant from rim, about three inches)

SECTION IV: AUXILIARY INSTRUMENT AND TECHNIQUES (all contestants if time allows, judge choosing one area)

A. CYMBALS

Technique

...... Stance (one foot in advance)
...... Grip of straps (thumb nails parallel to cymbal)
...... Height of cymbals (chest)
...... Preparatory stroke (both cymbals moving)
...... Follow-through stroke

Articulation

...... *Forte* crashes
...... *Piano* crashes
...... Use of entire cymbals
...... No "cupping" (vacuum)

Suspended Cymbal

...... Beating spot (edge)
...... Roll (two yarn mallets, opposite edges)

B. TRIANGLE

Technique

...... Height of instrument (shoulder)

Striking points

...... Side (opposite open end, ¼ of distance from corner)
...... Bottom (¼ of distance from closed corner)
...... Tip of beater
...... 90 degree angle, beater and triangle

Roll

...... Evenness
...... Equidistant (from corner) striking of sides
...... Grip of holder
...... Muffling

C. TAMBOURINE

Technique

Roll:

...... Shake
...... Thumb
...... Near horizontal place at commencement and termination of roll
...... Thumb or fingers muffling head sufficiently

Articulation

...... Knee-fist (loud, fast passages)
...... Fingers (soft, slow or fast passages)
...... Predominance of jingles (sound over head's sound)

SUMMARY OF POINTS LOST

...... SECTION I
...... SECTION II
...... SECTION III
...... SECTION IV
...... TOTAL

RECOMMENDED FOR...............

(Division I, II, III, IV, V)

SIGNATURE OF JUDGE:

Rules Ensemble Event

1. A maximum of ten (10) minutes shall be allowed for each event. This must include time for setting and breaking the stage as well as performing the music.
2. The ensemble will be judged on the basis of the musical merits of the work plus its compatibility with the performers' technical resources.
3. Each director or principal percussionist shall supply the judge with a copy of the score with the measures numbered.
4. The names of all instruments used must be placed in the diagonal blanks at the top of the evaluation sheet prior to submitting this sheet to the judge.
5. Memorization of ensemble music is not required.
6. The judge will use the evaluation sheet as follows:

a. Checks will be placed opposite those factors found unsatisfactory. Upon totaling these checks the judge will then determine the various rating categories. Ensembles with the least number of checks will rank highest.

b. Written comments will be made on the back of the sheet. The judge will make as many pertinent comments as possible within the alloted time.

7. The judge will hold the following as being his fundamental objective and criteria: to determine the degree of musical and technical attainment of each ensemble as a unit.

Percussion Ensemble Evaluation Sheet

I. *Technique** as related to:

1. position of sticks and/or instrument
2. playing area
3. rolls
4. muffling
5. tuning of drums (timpani only)

II. *Tone** as related to:

1. stick choice
2. head tension
3. playing area
4. articulation
5. instrument and stick position

III. *Ensemble*

1. balance
2. clarity and accuracy of rhythm and pitch
3. steadiness of tempo
4. avoidance of extraneous noises

IV. *Interpretation*

1. appropriateness of tempo(s)
2. character
3. choice of sticks and mallets
4. dynamic contrasts
5. phrasing
6. accentuation

V. *General Effect*

1. conviction
2. stage presence
3. posture
4. grace of movement
5. appearance (neatness)

VI. *Appropriateness of Selection*

1. musical content
2. sufficient display of technique
3. appropriateness of player's musical and technical resources

(Division I, II, III, IV, V)

SIGNATURE OF JUDGE:

*All the instruments for which the composition is scored are listed after Technique and Tone Sections.

Supplementary Observations And Suggestions

1. Ideally, more than ten minutes per event should be allowed to test more broadly the contestant's qualifications. The judge would then be permitted to make more meaningful written comments, making the contest a more profitable experience for the contestant. Additional percussion judges might be engaged where economically possible.

2. Restrictive lists of solo and ensemble literature should be discarded to make way for new and better literature (see rule No. 3.)

3. Some persons are of the opinion that bell-lyra and orchestra bells (glockenspiel) solos should be included as solo instruments. This committee takes this stand: the criteria for inclusion in the solo group should be the instrument's potential value as a vehicle for solo *musical* performance, not just the availability of the instrument and/or literature for it or the excuse that a music department only owns a set of bells in the mallet department!

4. Jazz traps-set solos might be considered in the future, with the stipulation however, that the contestant also perform rudiments or a "legit" solo on another major percussion instrument.

5. Securing the services of capable percussion judges for this proposed program may pose some problems. It is the moral responsibility of contest officials to seek out only competent judges. How else can percussion standards be elevated?

6. When possible, the judge might hold a session of summary and allow for questions and answers. All contestants should attend such concluding sessions as well as other events in the percussion category.

7. The excuse of school budgets not allowing for purchase of pedal timpani and mallet instruments may not always be a valid argument. It is the music director that determines *where* the money goes. These instruments are necessities in today's music-making and should rate an equal priority with other instruments. As to the host school supplying all the indicated instruments, if it does not own them it should either rent or borrow them from another institution(s). It is regrettable that most of our music-teacher institutions have so grossly neglected percussion education: this is the root of the limited concepts of percussion prevalent today.

8. More solo and ensemble workshops between two or more schools should be encouraged. This, plus clinics, usually benefit the students more than do competitions.

9. Adaptation of these rules and adjudication criteria can easily be evolved from the foregoing to fit local situations, including grammar school levels.

10. The overall objectives that guided the formulation of these suggested rules and adjudication sheets were:

a. To promote the concept that percussion embodies *all* the percussion instruments, not any one to the exclusion of the others.

b. To test competitively the factors of musicality, technical control, *and* versatility with *several* instruments.

c. To elevate the art of percussion playing and understanding among music directors and young percussionists by providing an outline-guide of basic percussion concepts and techniques.

11. The proposed contest rules were derived from a cross-section of thinking representative of all phases of contest procedures and problems.

Percussion Scoring

HOYT F. LECROY

Band directors continually are writing more and better arrangements for their marching organizations. Most of these arrangements sound very good and are very well written, except for the scoring of the percussion section. Seemingly, most arrangers have the attitude of writing an arrangement, and then saying to themselves, "Well, now what do I give the drums?"

Actually, as almost everyone will agree, the percussion section is one of the most important elements of the marching band. Why, then, should arrangers not give more attention to scoring for this section of the band? Usually, arrangers merely permit the percussion to grunt out the time-worn, over-used "oom-pa, oom-pa" cliche which becomes boring to both listeners and performers. Since the subject under discussion involves marching, it seems that a rhythmical phrase, such as the following, repeated underneath the music, would give a more secure "feel" for marching:

Ex. A:

However, it is obvious that it would become boring to repeat continuously such a rhythm as that given in example above, thus, variations must be found.

First of all, let us examine what tones and what instruments we have at our command. The top "voice" of the section is the snare drum, with the tenor and bass drums acting as the middle and bottom "voices," respectively. The cymbals add "spice" (and hence used sparingly) to these three voices.

Perhaps the easiest way to vary the example would be something similar to the following:

Ex. B:

As it will be noted, both of these examples merely involve giving the tenor drum the reverse of the snare drum part. The bass drum fills in the gap at the end of the phrase, while the tenor and snare drums "breathe." (Also, the cymbals may be used alternately with the bass drum, to fill in this gap.)

In another way of scoring the tenor drum might be given a completely different rhythm from that of the snare drum:

Ex. D:

SNARE
TENOR
BASS

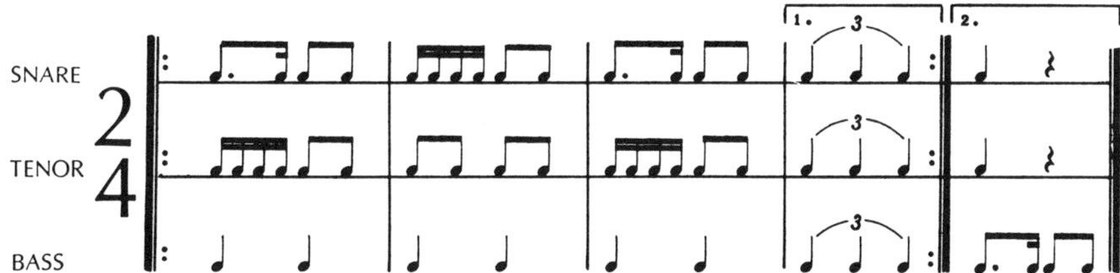

In yet another style the tenor and bass drums might merely follow the accents of the snare drum part:

Ex. E:

SNARE
TENOR
BASS

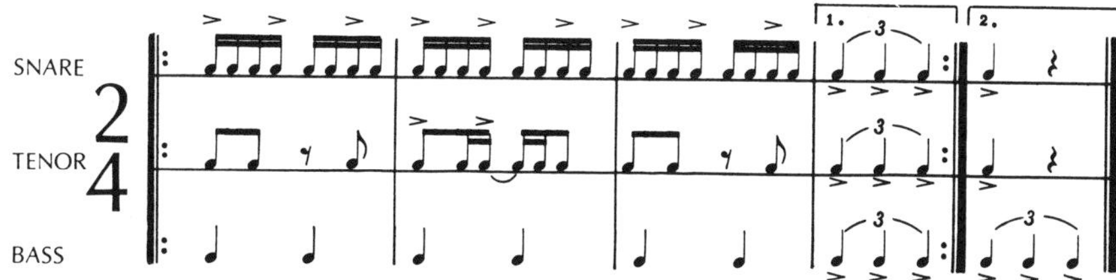

For an arrangement in six-eight time, the following rhythm could be used:

Ex. F:

SNARE
TENOR
BASS
(cym.)

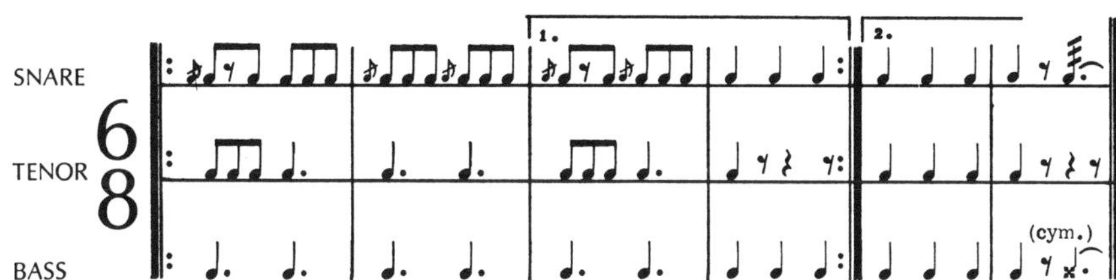

However, the rhythms that seem to be the most popular with drummers everywhere are those of the "cross accent" type:

Ex. G:

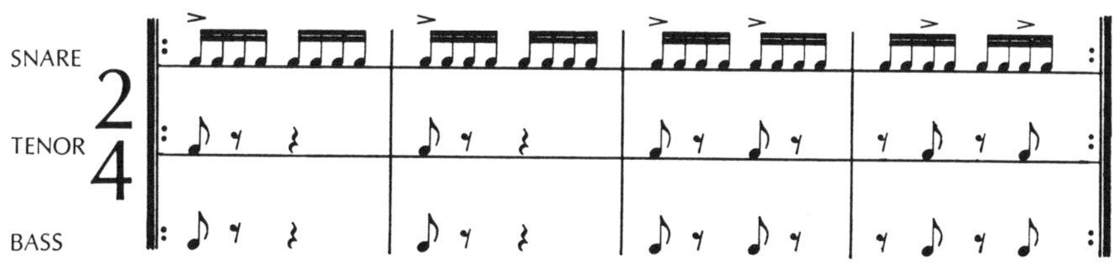

SNARE
TENOR
BASS

Ex. H:

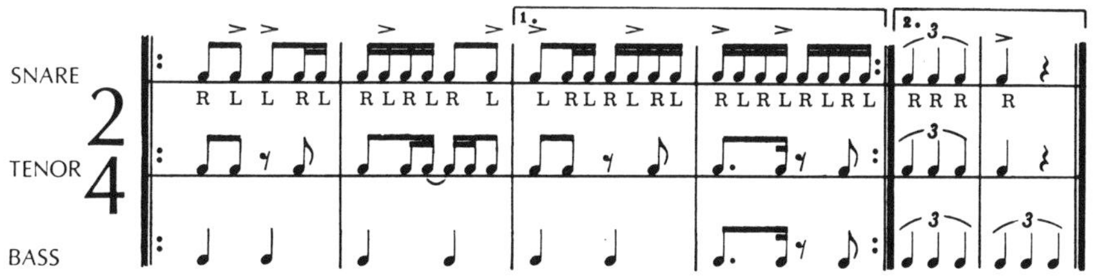

SNARE
R L L RL
RLRLR L
L RLRL RL
RLRLRLRL
RRR
R
TENOR
BASS

For these drum sections having greater technical facility, the part might look something like the following:
Ex. I:

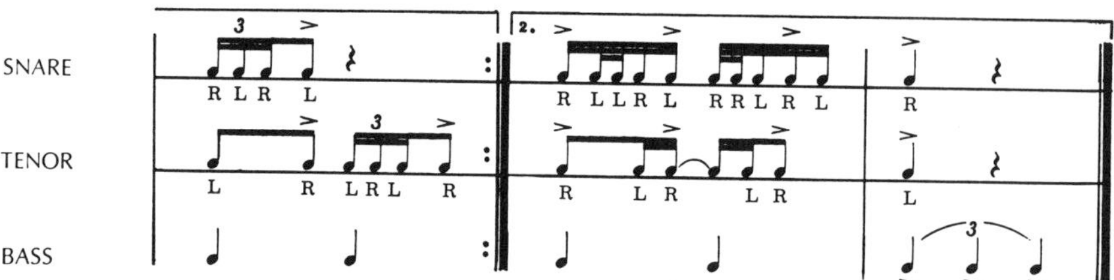

These are only a few of the possible rhythm combinations which may be used to construct better percussion parts. The individual arranger will probably be able to concoct many new ideas from those already given.

In closing, it might be mentioned that this method of scoring may be used in writing many effective street cadences. It will be found that these cadences, with only minor alterations, will fit well behind many new arrangements, thus saving the arranger much valuable time in writing percussion parts.

Ed. note—For purposes of ensemble, beginning upbeats, particularly rolls, are best avoided. Also, embellishments (flams, drags, ruffs) are omitted at fast tempos for purposes of definition, technical facility, and rhythmic strength.

October 1965

Parts for Marching Bands

DAVID MAKER

Marching bands are changing, evolving, in many quarters actually growing artistically, at a faster rate than ever before. The direction of change seems to be away from the traditional military marching band and its music. Perhaps some day, if football-type marching bands are able to achieve artistic integrity, they and military bands will be entirely separate organizations. This trend, however, does not justify ignoring the teaching of such drum rudiments to our percussionists. These are somewhat the basic strokes of *all* styles of snare drumming and must be learned.

The present day function of the drums is to provide a *very strong* metric and rhythmic foundation for the rest of the marching band. In earlier days a metric foundation was provided by what may be called the "oom-pah" style: bass drum and sousaphone played on the beat, and snare drum and French horn played on the afterbeat. This style has been abandoned in today's marching band arrangements. The sousaphone and the French horn can be used to better advantage as harmonic or melodic instruments, since the drums are more than loud enough to establish the meter by themselves.

The drums, also, dropped the "oom-pah" style for a number of reasons. As arrangements have become faster and faster, afterbeats have become harder and harder to play evenly. Furthermore, "oompah" has too little rhythmic vitality for modern arrangements. Most schools of composition throughout history have acknowledged that one may increase rhythmic vitality by using shorter note values. That is, by replacing

with

For drums it has become a matter of replacing

with

or some similar pattern. To make reading easier, such parts are often written *alla breve*:

Following is a sample drum part in this new style. The part accompanies the first line of "I Could Have Danced All Night," a song from Lerner and Loewe's *My Fair Lady*.

Notice how the distribution of eighth notes enhances the shape of the melody. This is the key to musical writing in this style. How much better this is, than a repetitive pattern which has nothing to do with the music it accompanies! Furthermore, memorization of this kind of writing is better musical training for the drummers.

Notice that an important function of the drums is to provide continuity while the rest of the band is breathing. These are "drum breaks" on a small and frequent scale.

Notice that the bass drum is still confined mainly to keeping the beat. The need for this is obvious. However, the bass drum may occasionally give "that extra kick" to a strong syncopation (meas. 14-15), drop a few "bombs" off the beat, or indulge in counterpoint with the snares (meas. 9-13). Tenor drum and cymbals generally double the bass drum in this style (but see Maxine Lefever in the December '62 *Instrumentalist*).

Notice the snare drum sticking (along with perfect memorization synchronized sticking should be *rock bottom basic*). It is written out here for purposes of demonstration. The basis of the system is alternation of hands as opposed to a double stroke or bounce with the same hand. Paradiddles of all kinds are out. Why? Again it is a question of rhythmic vitality. At high speeds, paradiddles

R L R R L R L L

degenerate to

R L R R L R L L

which is scarcely better than

R L

For clarity of rhythmic figures, all flams, drags, and ruffs, as such, are also omitted.

Although it is not a necessity, our example follows the stipulation that every measure begin with the right hand. This rule—a modified Straight system—explains the doublings in measures 3 and 7. When this rule is used, strong rhythmic patterns can constitute an exception, as in measure 15. Measures 9, 11, and 13 show the customary sticking for a short type of syncopation.

R L L R L

R L R R L

The above style of percussion writing accommodates "up-tempo" or simple-time music. A second style is needed to accommodate "swing tempo" or compound-time music. The basic pattern of this style is the familiar ride beat of jazz:

Following is a short passage in this style.

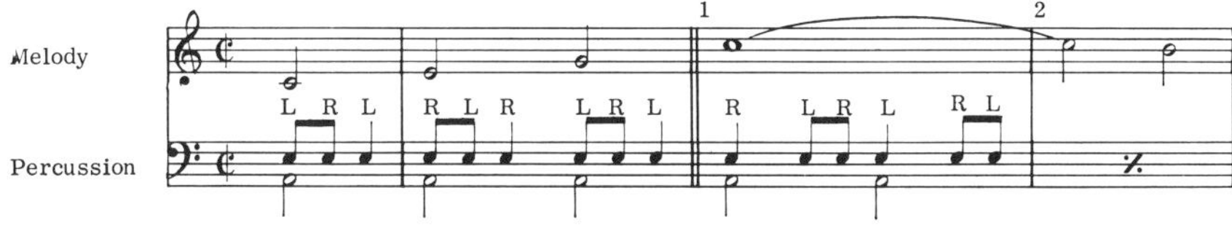

By equating "swing tempo" with "compound time," we accommodate 6/8 meter under this heading; we also imply that a strict interpretation of the dotted eighth and sixteenth is *not* to be desired.

The basic sticking rule for the swing tempo style is that the right hand begin the first beat; the left, the second; the right, the third; the left, the fourth. The simple syncopation sticking mentioned before, and triplet eighth notes, will always work out with no need of extra doubling.

In this style, and in some other instances, a single suspended cymbal, played with a stick, can be used effectively. To facilitate the switch from two cymbals to one, the cymbal player can wear a snare drum sling with the plain hook end free. Thus he can hang the unused cymbal at his side.

The up-tempo and swing tempo styles, then, can account for all regular music at marching tempos. It is assumed that the director will create variety in his shows by using slower tempos and rhythms occasionally, as in fanfares, big intros and endings, and concert numbers. These are the places for dramatic use of rolls, rests, and other percussion techniques from the concert band repertoire.

November 1965

Latin-American Percussion

David A. Tobias

Latin-American numbers are becoming more and more a part of the band and orchestra's repertoire. Almost every modern high school concert program includes a rhumba, beguine, samba, mambo, or cha-cha-cha; and the percussion section is vital to the effective performance of these compositions. Many times the composer or conductor is satisfied with using just a few of the more common Latin-American percussion instruments such as the maracas and claves. There are many additional ones, however, that are relatively inexpensive and can add considerable aural and visual color to one's program.

If there are not enough members in the percussion section, one can recruit a clarinet or trumpet player who needs an extra spark or challenge. The students must learn the correct names of these instruments and the proper way to hold and play them. A demonstration and explanation of these instruments by the percussion section provides interesting and educational material for a school assembly program.

First, the claves can start to play softly, with the addition of each available instrument, one at a time, every two or four measures. When all the percussion instruments are playing the band finally enters and proceeds to play the selected Latin number. If this procedure is followed, the regular introduction of the piece may be omitted.

The players must be rehearsed until they can play in a relaxed manner, achieve dynamic balance, and evolve perfect rhythmic ensemble. One of the most difficult things will be to get the players to pace themselves for climaxes and to follow the general dynamic levels of the band.

The claves are a pair of rosewood sticks about one inch in diameter and one has a lower pitched sound than the other. The lower pitched clave should be held in the left hand. The lower sounding clave should be marked so that the student can easily tell one from the other. Cup the upturned left hand to produce a hollow "tone chamber" and place the clave against the base of the thumb with the fingertips lightly holding it in position. Hold the higher pitched clave in the right hand between the thumb and first two fingers and strike the left clave over the "tone chamber" to produce a resonant click.

The clave beat is the foundation of Latin-American rhythm and practically all of the other instruments are guided by this beat. Great care should be taken in choosing a student to play the claves who has a good sense of syncopation.

Clave rhythm: ♩. ♪ 𝄽 ♩ | 𝄽 ♩ ♩ 𝄽 :‖

The maracas are two oval or round dried gourd shells (sometimes wood or plastic) mounted on a handle with dried peas, beads, fine gravel, or "shot" inside. One maraca should have a lower sound than the other, and this one is held in the left hand. Grasp the handles tightly with the thumb on top and fingers underneath. Alternately, use a sharp forward motion of the wrists so that all the pellets strike the shell at the same time.

The rhythm of the maracas is a constantly pulsating one. The sixteenth notes can both be played with the left hand or the player may alternate left to right. If the student is very inexperienced the rhythm can be simplified by playing all eighth notes.

Maraca r.h.
rhythm: l.h.

For "rolls", the maracas can be swirled in a circular motion. For loud playing two maracas can be held in each hand in hour glass fashion.

The chocallo, also called a kameso or "shaker," is a long cylinder-shaped wooden or metal shell containing beads, dried peas, or "shot," and it reinforces the maraca sound. Grasp it at each end and play with a back and forth rocking motion of the forearm and wrist. Like the maracas, push forward with a sharp motion so that the beads hit against the wall with a solid click.

Chocallo rhythm:

The guiro, or gourd, is a large cucumber-shaped dried squash or gourd with the seeds removed. The top side has ridges or grooves cut in it. Hold the gourd in the left hand with the thumb through the hole underneath. Scrape a wire prong or a thin wooden dowel across the notched top. The rounded corner of a wire coat hanger also gives good results.

For the quarter notes in the guiro rhythm, scrape the entire length of the ridging. For eighth notes, scrape up or down halfway, similar to the principle of violin bowing. Also, one can apply "on the string" and "off the string" violin techniques to guiro playing.

Guiro rhythm:

The cowbell, or "cencerro," plays a straight beat and controls the tempo for the other instruments playing more difficult rhythms, just like the bass drum does in the dance band. It is important to buy a good quality cowbell whose tone color fits appropriately in the Latin sound colors. Hold the cowbell flatly in the palm of the left hand to muffle the ringing overtones. It can even be muffled further by putting adhesive tape around the inside of the bell. Try to get a dry, metallic sound.

Use a thick dowel or the butt end of a drum stick to strike the cowbell. Strike the lip or edge of the bell for the low sound and hit the stick flatly against the side of the bell to get the high sound.

Cowbell rhythm:

bell
lip

The cabaza is a large round gourd covered with rows of strung beads. It has a bulb-shaped handle which is held in the right hand. There is a different movement for each beat. On the first beat slap the gourd against the open palm of the left hand. On the next beat slap the gourd against the extended fingers of the left hand. On the third beat, which is accented, rotate the cabaza by quickly turning the right wrist back and forth. On the fourth beat turn the wrist back to its original position. The sound is produced by the beads hitting and sliding against the gourd shell.

Cabaza rhythm:

The quijada, or "jawbone of an ass," adds a very unique color to the ensemble. It may be difficult to find the instrument, but most percussion instruments' manufacturers have them listed in their catalogues. Hold it in the left hand at the closed end of the jawbone with the open end pointing up. Make a fist with the right hand and strike the flat side of the jawbone to make the loose teeth rattle. Since this is an unusual instrument both in appearance and sound, choose a player with showmanship. The jawbone should be held high and struck on every fourth beat.

Quijada rhythm:

The conga drum is a large barrel-shaped drum which should rest on a floor stand. It can also be held by a shoulder strap or, if it is not too large, placed between the player's knees. For the higher pitched notes the fingertips should strike the head near the edge. For the lower sounds slap the flat palm of the hand in the center of the drum.

For accompaniment purposes the conga rhythm accents the rhythm of the bass instruments in the band. For solos the conga drum player may improvise more intricate rhythms.

Conga drum rhythm:

edge
center

The bongo drums are very popular but are often played incorrectly. They can be made with wooden or metal shells. The heads may be tacked on or attached to tension screws for tuning. The latter type is preferable to keep the heads tight for proper resonance and the desirable high crisp sound; otherwise, the heads must be held over heat to shrink them when they become loose and dull sounding.

The bongos are gripped between the knees or may be mounted on a stand with the larger one on the right. This is opposite from the standard timpani placement. Keep extended fingers straight but relaxed. The middle three fingers are used, with the first and second fingers doing most of the playing. Strike the fingertips near the edge with a snapping wrist movement. Also, the right thumb is often used on the larger drum for contrast.

The first rhythm given follows the clave rhythm closely and is effective for most Latin music. The second rhythm is another possibility and may be preferable. After these basic beats are mastered the more advanced percussionist may create various beats of his own.

1st. Bongo rhythm:

2nd. Bongo rhythm:

The timbales are a pair of tom-toms with brass or copper shells attached to a floor stand. Like the bongos, they are open at the bottom and have heads only on the top end. The larger one is placed on the left, the same as timpani are placed. The timbales are played with special timbale sticks which are thin wooden dowels. Regular snare drum sticks are generally too heavy. Both sticks are gripped the same way as timpani sticks (as if shaking hands with the stick).

The left hand plays on the second and fourth beats, striking the timbale heads halfway between the center and the edge. (This is for the basic beat presented here. Regular timbale technique also involves playing rim shots and striking near the edge and in the center of the head for various solo effects.)

The right hand plays a "paila" rhythm by tapping against the shell of the timbale. The accents of the "paila" rhythm follow the clave beat.

Timbale rhythm:

shell
high
low

These foregoing suggested rhythms are only basic and should be adapted to the composition with appropriate modification. The players may also wish to ad-lib at the ends of phrases or at break strains. The conductor, however, must be sure that it is always done in good taste.

The Double Stroke in Mallet Technique

Mitchell Peters

Technique on mallet instruments (xylophone, marimba, vibraphone, and bells) is about 90% based on the use of alternating single strokes as the means of manipulating the mallets. This is as it should be, for the single stroke provides the most rhythmic and least complicated method of moving over the instrument. Single-stroke technique must be thoroughly mastered as a basis for performing on the mallet-played instruments.

However, the use of the double stroke—or two strokes in a row with the same hand—is also a very important technique to the mallet player. The use of a double stroke in the logical place can facilitate the execution of a passage which would be awkward if played using alternating strokes exclusively. It basically minimizes time and motion in getting to the next pitch.

One should not confuse the term "double stroke" with the expression "rebound stroke." The double stroke uses two distinctly executed wrist strokes with the same hand, both the first and second notes identical in attack and in method of execution. The rebound stroke uses one basic wrist motion, with the second stroke being a rebound of the first and not identical with the first in attack or in method of execution. Although the rebound can be controlled with the use of the fingers and can be executed faster than the double stroke, it is of little value to the mallet player, since it does not have the clarity and consistancy of volume of the double stroke.

The above example is from a transcription of the Bach *Sonata No. VI for Unaccompanied Violin* and provides an excellent example of how using only alternted strokes would tie the player's hands in a knot. Regardless of which hand starts the passage, the player's hands, if completely alternated, would have to cross each other in such a way as to make the passage unplayable. The only sensible way to play this section is to insert double strokes at key points, as illustrated.

The example is only one instance, but there are many in which the use of a good double stroke can be employed. To have a good double stroke when needed the student must practice it. The following are a few possible technique studies for developing this stroke.

The above exercise is to be repeated numerous times: play first with single strokes, then on the repeat with double strokes, then on the next repeat with single strokes again, *etc.* It is a good exercise in that it gives one a chance to match the sound of the single and double strokes. The exercise should be practiced slowly until the strokes match in all respects. Then it should be practiced at faster tempos, but always with the goal of achieving perfectly matched in sound and height strokes. Accenting the second stroke is another way of strengthening it.

One of the best ways to develop a good double stroke is to work on a good triple stroke.

The above exercises are good for developing facility and control with various intervals by use of the double stroke. Again, the student must practice for clarity, not speed, and must use a double stroke, not a rebound stroke.

All the above exercises can be transposed into all major and minor keys. The student should use as much variation as possible, practicing at various tempos, with various dynamics, various "touches," *etc.* In other words, he should become flexible.

The following are a few points to remember regarding the use of the double stroke:
1) If possible, select small intervals for the use of this stroke.
2) Be sure to use a real double stroke and not a rebound stroke.
3) Most important, do not use the double stroke unnecessarily.

The above examples are only a few exercises that will be useful to the student in developing the double stroke. The number of exercises is infinite. *Mallet Control,* by George Stone, is one good source of exercises. The student also should be taught to invent his own exercises. However, he must always work for clearness and not speed. He must develop a sensitive ear and become his own most severe critic. Consistency in volume avoidance of the node of the bar: these matters can best be checked through the use of a tape recorder assisting the ear to discriminate more acutely.

1966-1967

277	The Marimba in the Band	Gordon Peters	January
278	Concert Bass Drumming	Gordon Peters	February
282	Care and Maintenance	John H. Beck	March
284	Ear Training and the Timpanist	Gordon Peters	April
286	Tune Up Those Drums	Joel T. Leach	May
290	Outline Guide to Percussion Orchestration	Gordon Peters	June
292	Improving Your Marching Band Drum Section	Larry W. McCormick	September
296	The Beginning Percussion Class	Jesse Pearl	October
297	Common Faults of School Percussionists	Paula Culp	November
298	Teach Your Drummers to Sing	Gordon Peters	December
299	Percussion Ensemble Floor Plans	Ramon Meyer	January
302	A Revised Percussion Contest in Wisconsin	Jay Collins	February
307	Teaching Mallet Percussion	Bob Tilles	March
308	Factors in Percussion Tone Quality	Mitchell Peters	April
310	More Latin Rhythms: Samba, Baion, Bossa Nova	Thomas Brown	May
312	Camp Duty	Lewis Harlow	June
315	Marching Band Percussion	James Salmon	September
320	The Percussive Arts Society	Gordon Peters	October
322	Effective Use of Cymbals	Larry McCormick	October
323	Forget the Music, Drummers — Just Try to Follow!	Alyn Heim	November
325	The Notation and Interpretation of Rolls	Ramon Meyer	December

The Marimba in the Band

Gordon Peters

Educationally, the band director has a responsibility for developing versatile and musical percussionists. One way to achieve this is to insist that all drummers learn to play the mallet keyboard instruments. The by-products of improved sight-reading and musicianship are certainly worth the effort. The results will be a more enthusiastic and dynamic percussion section. The individual student will be better prepared for future musical experiences, whether amateur, professional, or collegiate. More and more college-level institutions will not accept percussion majors unless they can demonstrate a reasonable keyboard percussion technique.

The percussionist's technical skill at the keyboard percussion instruments can be developed best through his study of marimba techniques, inasmuch as the marimba is the *primary* keyboard percussion instrument.

Here are a few guides relative to the fundamental playing knowledge of the marimba for those who may not have the benefits of a percussion keyboard teacher.

GRIP—Turn the hand until the palm faces the ceiling. Then lay the mallet shaft diagonally across the fingers, crossing the last finger at its third joint and the first finger at its first joint. Make a fist and turn the hand over so that the top of the hand is parallel to the ceiling. The basic grasp of the mallet shaft can be achieved in one of three ways: thumb and first finger, thumb and second finger, or thumb and both fingers. The center of the thumb cushion should be in a position extended along the shaft but not any further forward than the first finger. Also, it should be in a concave posture rather than "goose-necked." Whether the player chooses to hold the shaft at the end or somewhat nearer the center is largely a personal matter.

STROKE—The mallet head must operate in a strict vertical plane for controlled accuracy. To insure this, three physical postures must be maintained:

1. the wrist must bend in a strict perpendicular plane to the playing surface (top of the wrist parallel to ceiling);
2. the last two or three fingers grasp the shaft loosely to prevent it from moving uncontrollably from side to side;
3. as to the pivotal function between the thumb and the fingers, the shaft is allowed less freedom here than with the snare or timpani stick. The forearm should not be allowed to work in a pump-handle fashion from the elbow: the wrist alone does the majority of the work.

TECHNIQUE—The bars should be struck in the middle wherever possible. When a passage moves rather quickly and/or awkwardly, the upper keyboard (the "black keys") should be struck at the end of the bars. The nodes (where the cords go through the bars) should be avoided except for special effects where less resonance is desired.

Facility can be gained best by maximizing fast *and accurate* horizontal movement (in other words do not raise the mallet heads any higher than necessary).

Conventional exercises of scales and arpeggios can be applied easily to the marimba. Alternate malleting is recommended wherever possible (R L R L etc.). However, as long as consistent dynamic levels and rhythmic clarity are maintained, double sticking (R R or L L) is permissible to avoid physical awkwardness.

The philosophy exists in some quarters of the band world that a standard instrumentation, that is, fixed, is an ideal objective; however, it would seem that the concept of constantly seeking tonal color contrasts would provide more interest esthetically, aurally, and visually. If standard instrumentation were to include the full gamut of percussion colors in existence, there would be no cause for debate.

We must give percussionists music (including melody and harmony) to play, not just rhythms assigned to different instruments. It becomes monotonous for the percussionist to function only in the role of accompanist and sound effects man. Adding a marimba to a band department will open the door to complete musicality for the percussionist. Much fine chamber music will be made possible—a very important part of every musician's development.

The use of the marimba in the band has many other advantages.

a. Some of the extra drummers and bell-lyra players needed for the marching band can be utilized in the concert band.
b. It costs no more than any other large band instrument and can accommodate two players.
c. Marimba students would thus be given an opportunity to participate in an ensemble experience.
d. Piano and accordion students who wish to play in the band could easily transfer their keyboard knowledge to the marimba.
e. A student who has developed a good mallet grip plus a sense of pitch relationships is a natural candidate for playing the timpani.
f. The teaching of the marimba is perhaps the easiest instrument for a music educator to teach: no bowings, no fingerings, no embouchure, no tonal nor intonation problems.

The fact that keyboard percussion instruments exist and some composers and arrangers write specifically for them further justifies a complete family of these instruments (marimba, xylophone, glockenspiel, vibraphone, chimes) if it is financially possible.

In order to fully realize the preceding ideals, marimba parts would have to be published with band arrangements. Below are some recommendations as to what should be included in marimba parts to band arrangements.

Use double-staffed parts: top line, treble clef; bottom line, bass clef; avoid crossing of parts.

Score as much for the marimba as possible without interfering with the basic intentions of the desired tonal color in a phrase. In tuttis the marimba can always be used, because it blends well and will not predominate. Its use soloistically and in thin orchestration lends a fine color contrast to the wind instruments' sonority. Melodic, bass, and/or accompaniment parts can be scored for the marimba.

Incorporate double stops and octaves; use four-mallet parts (per person) only sparingly and usually in an optional way unless advanced players are available.

Indicate which notes are to be rolled (sustained) and which are not. Also, include as much in the way of phrasing and expression marks as is possible without losing clarity.

Indicate the type of mallets desired (and subsequent mallet changes): Rubber: hard ("H"), soft ("S"); Yarn: "H" or "S".

The range of the marimba is usually four octaves, starting on *C* below middle *C*. However, optional notes can be written down to the *A* a minor third below, as some manufacturers have this larger instrument.

Until such a time as music publishers may be convinced to provide marimba parts with band works, the music director can make available a condensed score to his players. He can mark these sections of the score to be played on the marimba or trust his players to evolve their own parts. Ideally, of course, each player should have his own separate part.

Educationally, musically, and artistically the marimba offers great potentials for players, organization, and audience.

February 1966

Concert Bass Drumming

Gordon Peters

In choosing a bass drummer for the school band or orchestra, a common practice is to select the poorest snare drummer of those available, or to choose the student who has been taking drum lessons the shortest time. The director holding musical aptitude as the basic criteria for choosing a bass drummer will reap greater dividends. Some form of ensemble experience, even if in another instrument family, would be a helpful qualification in selecting a bass drummer. Also, a pianist who has shown high musical aptitude and awareness to pulse will prove more competent than a second or third rate snare drum student.

Attitudes

The position of bass drummer has come to enjoy comparatively low prestige because of various factors. First of all, the techniques of playing the bass drum certainly are not nearly as involved as the snare drum, marimba, or timpani. The sheer numbers of notes played is probably less than the snare drum or timpani: therefore, playing the bass drum is not as much "fun" for the percussion student as playing the other percussion instruments. He regards bass drumming as a menial chore that is far beneath his musical and technical abilities. It is no wonder, then, that we look askance at the position of the bass drummer.

Let us look objectively at the position. The matters of tuning and stick choice truly require imagination and musicianship. The fact that *all* percussionists are "solo" as opposed to "tutti" players immediately imposes an important responsibility on the bass drummer. When it comes to playing martial music the bass drummer could well be considered the most important musician in the band. A weak bass drummer in a parade situation would cause disaster. The bass drummer is expected to be no less a musician than anyone else when it comes to the refinements of music making: dynamics, phrasing, nuance, attacks, and releases, etc. Why then saddle a band or orchestra with a low calibre talent? It is the music director's responsibility to "sell" his selected candidate on playing the bass drum in the organization and make him aware of the responsibilities and importance of this position.

Training

The form of training to be pursued is, of course, dependent on the student's musical background. Presumably, there has been some prior musical training (probably another percussion instrument). Percussion sectionals on the music being played or a laboratory pre-band (or supplementary to) percussion ensemble situation would be one manner of teaching the musical considerations of ensemble playing not learned at the private lesson. Dance band drumming provides a fine experience in conditioning a player to setting and maintaining a steady beat (pulse).

Specific tonal concepts and how to achieve them must be taught. Matters of coordination of eyes and ears with the music and conductor must be explained. Appropriate studies involving combinations of single beats and rolls plus various musical problems of notation, nuance, tempo, and pulse changes should be used (snare drum method books can be used minus embellishments if suitable bass drum training materials cannot be found). Here are some basic exercises that may prove helpful (try to get not only tonal but character contrast as well):

Use lambswool beater.

Alla Marcia ♩ = 116

f p f

B.D. & cym. B.D. only Tog.

Use lambswool or felt pair of beaters

Use medium hard pair of beaters.

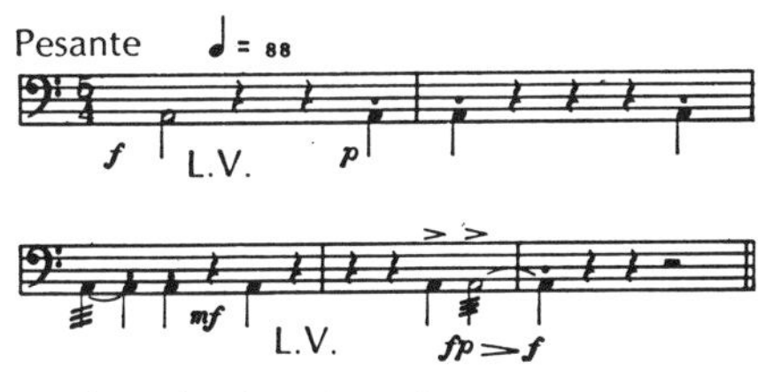

Use large hard stick on first part.
Use gong beater on second part.

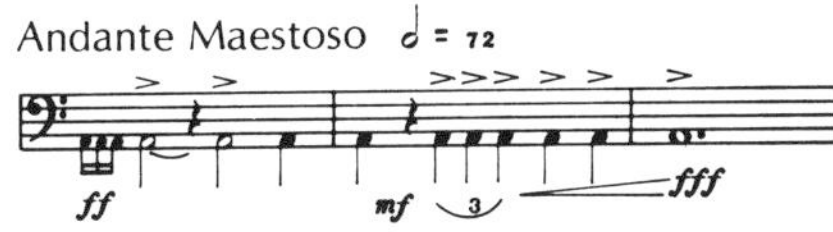

There are far too many situations today where instrumentalists are allowed to "sign for band" and *then* start taking lessons! These school situations are improved immediately if the beginning percussionists are kept in a separate class until after the first of January, because their techniques are so different from that of the other instruments. In disciplined music programs prospective band or orchestra players have at least a year of either class and/or private lessons.

Generally, the first position provides the best response to the ears of the audience. The third position should be used only for very intricate passages requiring two beaters. "How it sounds to the audience" should be the criteria for all music making: *not* how it sounds to the player, near the player, or on the podium. Because of the many intangibles involved in acoustics, experiments with position are recommended. Of course, for general playing, the first position is traditionally used.

Indoor and outdoor situations may require different sticks and beating spots. Again, experimentation (including comparative volumes) is recommended to try to achieve the desired sound in any given environment.

The hole(s) in the shell of the drum is present to relieve the pressure between the heads when one of them is struck. The use of this hole as a target for ice cream sticks, paper clips, chewing gum, etc. should not be tolerated.

Tensioning

The basic tonal objective of a bass drum is a deep resonance. To achieve this the head being struck should be tensioned low enough so that *no* definite pitch can be heard, yet high enough to give body to the tone when struck a "fortissimo" blow. The other head should be tensioned slightly looser than the playing head. The tension rods should be turned only half a turn at a time. In most school situations the author has visited it was found that both bass drum heads were extremely taught. For marching a somewhat tighter than concert tensioning is advised, however.

Positioning

In most large musical organizations the bass drum is best placed near the center rear and ideally near the bass brasses and/or strings. The cymbal player is generally to the right of the bass drummer (unless the latter is left-handed). The same player should not play bass drum and cymbals with one cymbal attached to the bass drum and the other in the free hand, unless specifically directed in the music. Also, wherever possible, the bass drummer and cymbal player (*all* percussionists for that matter) should read from separate parts (this will help minimize errors and improve "playing on time," the music being placed in direct line with the conductor).

Music Stand

The bass drummer should be taught to adjust his music stand to a height where he can see both conductor and music in a straight line and with a minimum of eye motion between the two. Any height and angle screw adjustments that may be on the stand should be checked for security before playing. Avoiding falling music stands is one less rehearsal distraction out of the way.

Acoustics

There are some basic acoustical factors that should be understood about the bass drum. The directional nature of the heads' response must be understood in order to project maximum tonal response to the audience. Three basic positions can be considered:

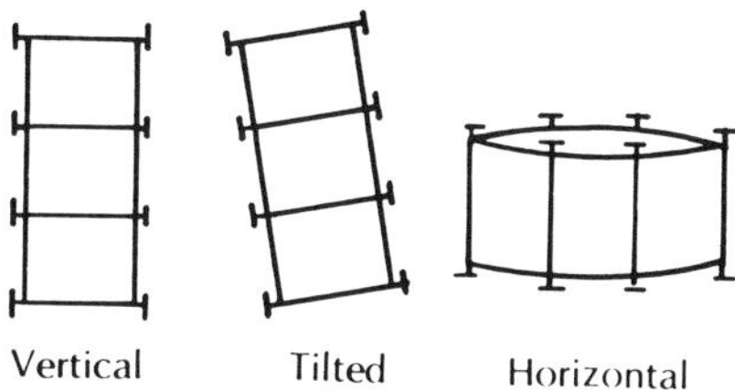

A further refinement necessary is the balancing of the heads, that is, obtaining the same tension opposite each tension screw on both heads. It is not the relative tightness of one screw to another which determines balance but the relative elasticity of the head opposite each tension screw. Ideally, we would "tune" the head as we do a timpani, but the low frequencies are next to impossible to differentiate.

Head Collar

On calfskin heads the collar (that portion of the head stretching between the flesh hoop and the rim of the drum) must be maintained to allow flexibility in tensioning. If there is not enough collar, low tones may not be obtainable in dry weather; therefore, the head must be dampened with a cloth (until the head begins to get wavy) and the tension screws drawn down a turn or two. (Care must be exercised not to allow water to seep into the flesh hoop; positioning the drum horizontally during this process will help.) Repeated stretchings will eventually build an adequate collar. In order to maintain a collar, the heads should be tensioned about a turn and a half each after every rehearsal and then loosened before the next rehearsal.

Should there be *too much* collar, the head may have to be retucked on the flesh hoop or put temporarily in a dry place to absorb the over-collar. Flesh hoops or counterhoops that warp out of shape can sometimes be readjusted on the drum shell by releasing the tension screws and repositioning the hoops to attempt to achieve a more concentric fit. Plastic heads, of course, come with set collars and the influence of humidity on them is almost nil.

During the course of a concert the heads may have to be retensioned, depending on the degree of humidity change. On such occasions a periodic cracking sound often occurs as the tension of the heads changes. By squeezing the heads together now and then (at convenient applause or "forte" moments), the audibility of this cracking sound can be dispersed unoffensively.

Playing Area

Once we have an understanding and control of the drum heads, matters of articulation should be considered. The following pictorialization will help to clarify the alternative beating areas and their results:

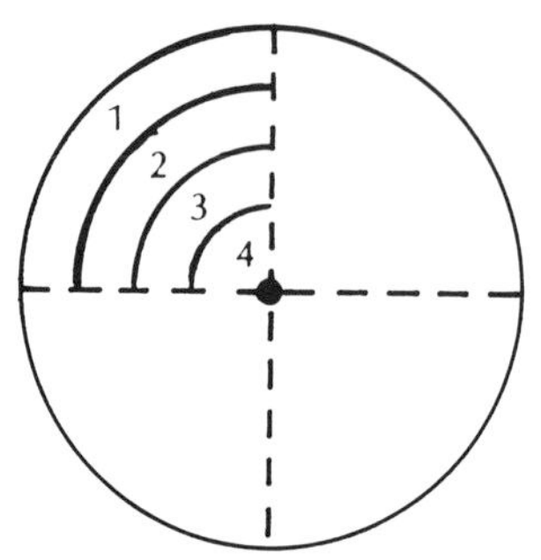

1. Less articulate and resonant, higher pitched, "thinner tone"
2. Maximum resonance and depth, best tone quality
3. Less resonant, more articulate, "hard tone"
4. The nodal area (center) is used seldom and then only for harsh, non resonant percussive effects.

Player Position and Stroke

The feet of the player should be placed to the rear right (for right-handed players) of the bass drum with the right foot extended a half-step forward far enough so that the knee when moved a few inches toward the head will touch it about a quarter of the distance of the diameter from the rim. The shaft of the beater is usually grasped about a third of the way up the shaft similar to the snare drum stick in actual grip except that there should be no pivotal action (except in the roll) and the thumb nail should be facing upwards.

The direction of the blow with the beater on the head has been much discussed. Tonally, this author advocates a direct blow (perpendicular to the head with a slight elipse) for concert music rather than a glancing blow (almost parallel to the head and more conducive to martial playing), the latter producing somewhat of a superficial response. If the distance from the head to the beater is less in the preparatory stroke than after the head is struck, the player shall derive greater success in playing on time (not behind the beat) and also a better tonal response (drawing the tone *out* of the drum rather than pounding it in).

The Roll

In the matter of the roll, it should be executed with a matched pair of large-headed medium soft beaters (using the traditional snare drum grip when the drum is in a vertical position). Using one beater which has two different sized heads cannot produce an even roll and should not be used.

Muffling and Muting

Curiously enough one's legs have their role in playing the bass drum. Normally, the player stands closer to the head being struck with the side of the knee of the leg closest to that head acting as a mute or muffler as needed. ("To mute" means to partially inhibit the vibrations altering the tonal derivative; "to muffle" means to stop the vibrations completely as quickly and quietly as possible.) Both hands (one on one head, one on the other) are used, of course, to assist in muffling as well. The left hand muffles with the palm and the right with the fingers not involved in grasping the beater. Particularly in jazz-styled concert works, where minimum resonance is sought, the bass drummer must learn to effectively mute his heads. This can be achieved by using the palm of the left hand and the right knee pressing against the heads with a medium hard beater striking lightly near the center of the head. Muting and muffling are very important bass drum techniques and should not be glossed over. Considerable time should be spent on this aspect of the bass drum instruction.

Notation

The matter of controlled resonance is an important consideration that is too often unclear in the printed part. Most composers ignore the fact that many percussion instruments continue to produce an audible sound for some time after they are struck. They do occasionally indicate "L.V." or a slur-type sign to indicate that the instrument should be allowed to vibrate freely after being struck. Either the player or the conductor should make certain that every bass drum (as well as other resonating percussion instruments) note in the music being played is clearly marked and understood by the player relative to resonance duration: (1) "L.V. (let vibrate, indefinitely); (2) muffle at a specific spot; (3) muffle immediately, staccato ("//").

The decision of whether or not to muffle (or how much) is usually decided by what the other instruments of the band or orchestra are playing. In general, the bass drum should be muffled at the rest following the note played. Quarter, eighths, and shorter valued notes (staccato) are muffled as quickly as possible (usually) except for marches. Because of the vagaries of duration indication, however, it is best to edit percussion parts to utilize the maximum tonal potential of the bass drum (as well as all the other percussion instruments) and to control duration. Editing of accents and dynamics in marches is particularly effective in the bass drum and cymbal parts.

Equipment

For high school concert band or orchestra, a bass drum shell diameter of 36″ and a width of 16″ or 18″ are recommended. For elementary school a smaller size (28-30″ diameter; 14″ in width) is more appropriate. An important factor is width of the shell: the wider the shell, the more the depth and resonance of the drum. Some schools use narrow bass drums (Scotch bass drums) used during marching season for their concert playing. In this situation budgetary allotment should be made immediately for purchase of an appropriately sized concert bass drum. The choice of finish of the shell is a personal matter.

When talking about types of heads, the perennial question of "plastic or calfskin?" must be discussed. As a generality I would recommend plastic heads for most educational drum head needs (snare drum, timpani, etc.). Why? Plastic heads need less care, primarily because of their resistance to changing moisture conditions. However, for the bass drum (which has a large head, tensioned rather loose), calfskin serves one's needs better: greater depth of tone can be achieved. But as plastic heads continue to be improved the day may not be far off when plastic will equate calfskin response in the lower frequencies. There are, of course, different tonal *qualities* of response between calf and plastic. One should choose what is felt best meets one's conception of bass drum tone. With the smaller bass drums (30″ and under), plastic suffices.

Bass drums having single tension (tightening screws only on one side used to tension both heads simultaneously) should be discarded in favor of double (separate) tension tuning rods for each head. The latter are more expensive but necessary. Also, chrome hardware is a better investment than nickel in the long run.

The most important consideration in caring for the bass drum (other than the heads) is prevention of extraneous sounds. Probably the most common extraneous noise connected with the bass drum is a metallic rattle which results when the lugs (housings to which are attached the tension screws) become loose through repeated vibration. To tighten them, one of the heads must be removed (preferably the head opposite the playing side) and the loose screws tightened from within the shell.

The tension screws themselves sometimes cause rattles. If the humidity is very low and the heads have little or no collar, the clamps (pulling down on the counterhoops) attached to the tension screws may be so loose that some rattle. Also, the top of the "T" on the tension screws sometimes becomes loose from the rod proper, in which case replacement is necessary. (Most percussion instrument manufacturers now have individual parts to all their instruments listed in their catalogues. When ordering from your dealer, complete description and catalogue information, including approximate year of purchase, should be given.) If a tension screw turns hard, one of three things is probably wrong: (1) stripped threads (should be replaced); (2) lack of lubrication (vaseline or grease can be used); or (3) a bent rod (should be replaced) or a rod that is not exactly perpendicular to the flesh hoop.

Metallic parts can be shined up periodically with any good metal polish. A good plan is to instill a sense of responsibility in young percussion players by having one or two "care and repair" sessions per year with them in which all the percussion equipment is checked and cleaned.

When cleaning the heads, an art gum eraser should be tried first. If dirt still remains, a natural bristle brush with mildly soapy water (sparingly used) can be applied (with the bass drum in a horizontal position). The soapy solution should be removed with a wet cloth as soon as possible. Usually, finger marks and dust are the only things to be removed from the shell of the drum: a damp cloth will serve adequately.

When replacing a head, be sure to order the correct size (measure the diameter of the shell, outside surfaces). Also, be sure to stipulate the type of head you desire: plastic or calfskin. This same procedure should be used in ordering any drum heads. The heads come mounted on flesh hoops, but in the case of calfskin, a collar usually has to be evolved.

There are different types of bass drum stands and cradles. Some are made of wood, but the majority are of metal and usually have an adjustable height. Any loose metallic parts or improperly insulated cross-supports (where the bass drum touches the stand) will cause extraneous sounds and should be properly insulated. One manufacturer presently has a bass drum support on wheels, which allows the bass drum to be tipped to any playing angle desired.

Most bass drum beaters have a wooden shaft and a wooden or felt core covered with lambswool. When greater depth and resonance are desired, a gong beater can be used on the bass drum. This type of beater generally has a greater weight in both handle and core. On bass drum beaters having large and small ends, the smaller end can be used for special effects but should not be used with the big end for rolls.

In the author's opinion most commercially sold bass drum beaters are too light in weight to draw out the full potential depth and resonance inherent in a bass drum. Sticks with various sized heads and degrees of hardness and weight can be obtained through a little astute shopping in catalogues and drum shops. The bass drummer should minimally have a lambswool double-ended beater, a pair of the largest timpani or like-pair for rolls, and a hard stick for staccato notes. Also, the previous recommendation of a gong beater for certain passages might well be considered.

Other covers besides lambswool can be used on bass drum beaters for special effects: felt and yarn are two such alternatives. In addition to an adequate weight, a sufficiently large size of head should be used. Timpani sticks often are both too light and too small for the bass drum (in spite of such occasional directions from composers). Various medium to large sized yarn marimba mallets can be used on the bass drum for special staccato effects and even some softer roll situations. This stick should have more usage than it does, as the conventional lambswool beater does not provide a clear articulation because of its texture softness. A wooden head is rarely used in concert; however, it is common in marching bands.

When a beater needs recovering, one can purchase a strip of lambswool from a large drum shop or merely purchase a new beater. The latter plan is more expedient and not that costly. Beaters should be kept clean. Dirt induces excessive wear of the beater head and drum head.

One of the major offenses that the student concert bass drummer commits is to habitually use the top of the bass drum or music stand on which to lay beaters. He should be taught to rest the beaters on a trap table instead. It not only looks better, but extraneous noises of dropping sticks will be minimized.

Conclusion

The bass drum along with the snare drum and cymbals is one of the basic percussion instruments of the concert and marching band. We should see that young percussionists understand them fully before going on to the more sophisticated members of the percussion family.

Traditionally, we have given drummers a fundamentally rudimental styled snare drum education and called them "percussionists," falsely (unconsciously perhaps) presuming they would just "pick up" the rest of the percussion instruments and styles themselves. The art of percussion playing today requires versatile players and teachers who understand and can demonstrate the techniques of playing *all* the instruments of percussion.

March 1966

Care and Maintenance

John H. Beck

Nothing is more disturbing to a professional percussionist than seeing percussion instruments treated in a slovenly manner. I have seen examples of mistreatment in many of our public schools. Whether done out of neglect or ignorance by either students or band director, this treatment is inexcusable. There is a correct way to care for percussion instruments: in some instances common sense is all that is required; in others specific knowledge is necessary. Knowing that an instrument in good condition will sound much better than one in need of repair justifies this article. Much has been written on how to play the various percussion instruments, but it is of little value if there is no knowledge of how to keep the instruments in condition for playing.

Drums

The drum's construction is simple and requires mostly common sense to keep it in good repair. "Drum" refers to all snare drums (field, orchestra, dance, and concert), bass drum, tom-tom, and tenor. The main body of the drum is called the shell and can be either wood or metal. Most wooden shells are covered with a pearl finish which requires only that it be kept free of dust and fingerprints. This can be done with a wet or dry cloth, depending on how dirty the pearl has become. If the shell is lacquered and has become marred in several places, it can be refinished in the same manner as one would refinish a table top. A metal-shelled drum should be kept free of fingerprints and dirt—a dry cloth will suffice. The better drums have chrome hardware (tension rods, lugs, and snare strainers) and will not tarnish; however, if fingerprints appear they should be wiped off with a dry cloth. Nickel hardware will tarnish and requires some kind of metal cleaner to retain its luster.

If a tension rod, lug, or any of the snares or snare strainer should break they must be replaced immediately. Since oil is very messy, vaseline is a good lubricant for the threads on the tension rods. I have tuned some snare drums in high schools and found that turning the key on the tension rod was impossible. A small amount of vaseline on the threads was all that was needed. Many students feel that the one or two tension rods that turn hard are not to be turned at all; thus, the drum head becomes lopsided.

Trying to produce a good sound from a drum with a lopsided head is practically impossible. Likewise, trying to produce a good sound from a drum with a worn out or mistreated head is impossible. A worn out head can be detected by the size of the collar—the distance the head has stretched down along the shell. If the collar is so large that the top of the rim is level with the edge of the shell, the head is worn out. Another check would be to try a rim shot—if it is impossible to play, the head needs to be replaced. Most likely this would not occur with plastic heads; however, it is a good idea to change plastic heads every couple years if they are used continuously. It is also a good idea to remove the heads from the shell every year and wipe off the accumulation of dust on the edge of the shell and around the flesh hoop. Cloth or fiber covers offer necessary head protection when storing or transporting the drums.

Following these simple suggestions will insure not only good sounding drums but good looking drums.

Timpani

More than common sense is required to keep timpani in good condition. Although their construction is similar to that of the snare drum, some specific knowledge is required. The bowl of a timpano is copper and requires polishing with an appropriate cleaner to keep its luster. Fiberglass bowls are now being made which do not need polishing; however, the copper bowl is the most common. If the bowl receives a dent, it must be pounded out. This can be done by first removing the head. Then, from the inside of the bowl, gently tap with a chime mallet or rubber hammer until the dent is removed. A dent in the bowl will interfere with the quality of sound produced by the drum. I have seen timpani in some schools that had dents so large that the pitch produced was practically unrecognizable. The hardware on the timpani is chrome and should be kept free of fingerprints by wiping with a cloth. The pedal mechanism is precision tooled and must be kept lubricated—household oil (used sparingly) is suitable.

Removing a timpani head requires more knowledge than removing a snare drum head. The most common type of pedal mechanism is the spring tension. Ratchet or friction pedals are also used, but these require only that the tension is off the pedal when removing a head. When removing a timpani head from a spring tension pedal, *always keep your foot on the pedal.* As you loosen the tension rods, you change the balance on the spring and at one point it will "let go." If the pedal is not under the control of your foot, the force with which it flies forward is enough to break the pedal in half. When the spring "lets go," ease the pedal forward and remove your foot. Once the head is removed, all attention should be focused on the edge of the bowl. This is the part over which the head is constantly moving and where all the head squeaks occur. Rubbing your finger around the edge of the bowl will quickly detect any nicks or scratches: rubbing fine emery paper around the edge will quickly eliminate them and the chance of their cutting into the head and breaking it.

Graphite sprinkled onto a cloth and rubbed around the edge of the bowl is an excellent lubricant and will eliminate all head squeaks. Putting on a plastic head requires only that it be placed on the bowl and the rim placed over it. A calf head requires wetting before placing it on the bowl. This assures that there will be a sufficient collar with which to tune. A damp cloth rubbed over both sides of the head will give enough moisture to assure a good collar—3/8″ to 1/2″. After placing the head (whether plastic or calf) on the bowl, careful attention must be paid to the number of turns given each tension rod. If each tension rod is turned evenly, there is a good chance that the head will be in tune with itself when the proper playing range is reached. A final check for pitch at each tension rod, however, is recommended. A calf head must be allowed to dry for twenty-four hours before it can be played upon—plastic heads can be played upon immediately. Good quality heads, properly tuned and taken care of are a must for the timpani. A timpani head should be changed when the quality of sound becomes inferior. This will be determined by the use or abuse it receives and by personal judgement.

Timpani with plastic heads should be left at mid-range *A* and *D* when not in use (25″-28″ or 26″-29″ diameter timpani). Timpani with calf heads should be left on high or low pitches depending on the existing weather conditions. In extremely dry weather they should be left on high notes *C* and *F*. In extremely damp weather they should be left on low notes *F* and *B♭*. *D* and *A* are recommended the majority of the time. Covers of a hard texture (masonite), one side covered with cloth (felt), placed over the timpani heads are a necessary insurance for longer life for the heads.

Mallet & Keyboards

Keyboard percussion instruments, like drums, require only a minimum amount of attention to keep them in good condition. Considering first the instruments with wooden bars (marimba and xylophone), the Honduras rosewood bars should be kept free of dust. This can be achieved by cleaning with a dry cloth and by always covering the bars with a large cloth when not in use. (Always cover *all* keyboard instruments when not in use.) Never put furniture polish on the bars. A common furniture wax suffices to maintain key luster. If the finish becomes worn, the bars can be sent to the factory to be refinished.

The orchestra bells, which are housed in their own case, have bars of steel or aluminum. These bars should be kept free of dust and fingerprints. If they should go out of tune, they can be re-tuned at the factory. The peg holding each bar in place must be kept perpendicular to the bar; otherwise, the bar will not vibrate freely. A light tap with a hammer will straighten it.

The vibraphone has aluminum bars and should be kept free of dust and fingerprints. The resonators are metal and likewise need to be dusted. The motor on the vibraphone must be kept lubricated and in good working order. Oil holes appear over the rod which turns the "butterfly" inside the resonator, and these places must be kept lubricated—household oil is sufficient.

Chimes are made of brass and are subject to fingerprints. An occasional cleaning with a cloth will help to maintain a bright luster. A periodic check on the material holding the chimes in place will insure a free sound and avoid possible accidents. A cloth cover placed over the chimes will help to keep them clean.

Cymbals

The statement "cymbals improve with age" is true, with reservation—it depends upon how quickly they have aged. This instrument is probably the most widely mistreated instrument of the percussion family. Most of the mistreatment comes from improper playing. Yes, dropping a cymbal will tend to ruin it. If it doesn't destroy the quality of sound, it may cause the cymbal to crack. If the crack occurs along the edge of the cymbal, it can be cut out without affecting the sound. If the crack runs from the edge to the center or occurs at the center, the cymbal must be replaced.

Keeping cymbals clean is no longer a problem as there are several cymbal cleaners on the market which are excellent. When not in use cymbals should be stored in a specific place, preferably wrapped in a cloth rather than lying around a rehearsal hall. A cymbal case is excellent protection when storing or transporting the cymbals.

Traps

Triangles, castanets, and tambourines are the three most important accessory instruments and the ones usually in need of repair. To keep a triangle in good condition means only to keep it clean. Yet, I have seen triangles in some schools that surely must have spent a winter on the football field. Triangles should never be held with anything but a piece of thin gut. Just recently I visited a school and the triangle was being held with a Christmas ribbon. The triangle clip is a worthwhile investment.

Keeping castanets in good condition means to keep the gut which holds the castanets to the wooden handle at the proper tension. If the gut should break, rope or string is not an adequate substitue. Gut can be purchased from most music stores. If one of the castanets should crack, it must be replaced. A cracked castanet will not resound when it strikes the wooden handle.

Tambourines are like drums in that they have a head which must be kept in good condition. Jingles (disks of metal) give the tambourine its characteristic sound and these must be kept free of dents. Jingles will respond with dents in them, but the dents tend to decrease the quality of their sound. Dented jingles should be removed and replaced. When humid weather causes the tambourine head to become loose, there is very little one can do. Heat will tighten the head; however, many tambourine heads have gone up in smoke from a match held too closely. A coating of shellac on a taut head will help to keep the moisture out. The new tambourine with a plastic head is eliminating the weather problem, though it produces a much different tonal quality.

Storage

An important point to consider which will help in keeping all percussion instruments in good condition is a storeroom or storage area. Nothing is going to damage the instruments more quickly than letting them lie around a rehearsal hall for every amateur drummer to try out his skill. Trumpets, clarinets, violins, etc., are not left lying around and neither should percussion equipment. Because of their size, timpani and keyboard instruments must be left in the rehearsal hall, but if they are properly covered, nothing will happen to them. The smaller instruments must be put away.

Following this simple yet necessary care and maintenance procedure will insure good sounding equipment, good looking equipment, a sense of pride from the percussionists, and a sense of respect for percussion from everyone else.

April 1966

Ear Training and the Timpanist

Gordon Peters

In many instances seniority or snare drum proficiency have been the criteria used in selecting a timpanist. And what has been the result? Timpani are often played out of tune--used solely as rhythmic *percussive* instruments rather than as *pitched* instruments.

It is only fair that the members of the percussion section be given the first opportunity to fill a timpani vacancy when one occurs, but the basis of selection should be aural: does the player have the potential of developing good aural discrimination? Can he match pitches and intervals with his voice? Many pupils declare that they cannot sing. Chances are that their reluctance to sing is based on shyness, embarrassment, and/or a lack of pitch training rather than sheer inability.

Once the drummers' fraternity uses the standard of pitch criteria in selecting a timpanist a whole new respect and interest will arise for the timpani. Should a percussionist not be found with the necessary aural equipment, a talented vocalist from the chorus might be considered. Singers have some background with both pitch and ensemble experience. With this background in music, intervallic training usually comes easy or is unnecessary. Learning to grip the sticks and other coordinative and mechanical matters involved in timpani playing are comparatively simple, compared to the demands of tuning and coordination with counting.

Ranges of the Drums

Once a timpanist has been selected he should be given a basic functional knowledge of the instruments. The first thing to be done is to determine the diameters of the timpani available. Most schools have at least two timpani. These usually measure 28″ and 25″ in diameter (of the timpani bowl) or 29″ and 26″. A third timpano will usually be 30″ or 32″, and a fourth, 23″. The normal playing ranges of these drums are:

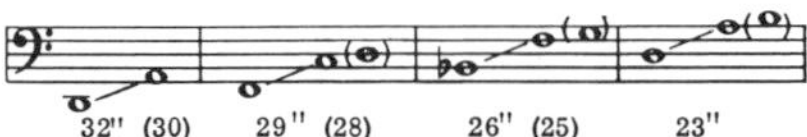

With plastic heads the upper pitches indicated can be raised a whole step (in brackets).

Next, the low basic pitches indicated above on each timpano should be set. To do this place the pedal in the position of least tension. Adjust the "T" handle tension screws (if necessary) to achieve the desired pitches, turning each screw equally, a half turn at a time. The pedal should then be pressed to maximum tension. If it does not hold at both the highest and lowest pitches on any particular timpano, the tension screw may have to be adjusted (usually found immediately above the pedal): tighten it if the toe does not depress completely, and vice versa. (Some timpani do not have a tension spring screw adjustment; in these cases the spring tension mechanism is so constructed as to be self-adjusting in the internal mechanism.)

Balancing Heads

Next, the heads need to be balanced. Depress the pedal to about one-quarter of maximum tension. Tap the drum head with a finger one-third the distance from the rim and center of head (radius), tapping opposite each tension screw to see that the same pitch prevails at each screw. The head should be tapped strongly enough for the ear to hear the fundamental pitch, as opposed to a "surfacey" tone distorted by many inharmonic overtones. Also, the head should be completely muffled between each strike. The ear should listen to the pitch of the *strike tone* (the sound heard a fraction of a second after the head is struck) rather than the *hum of duration tone*. Periodically, the head can be depressed gently in the center with the palm to insure the head fully reacting to the turning of the tension handles.

In order to hear the fundamental pitch at each tension post more clearly, one can place a mute in the center of the head (a handkerchief will suffice). Another aid to discerning an accurate pitch is to place one's ear *close* to the head and in the *same plane* with the head when tuning (that is, right *next* to the bowl [A] as opposed to above the head [B]).

The heads should be balanced before every rehearsal, particularly when more than one timpanist is involved. However, players should try both methods to see which permits them to hear differences in pitch most clearly. One then should check the basic pitches of the drums to see that the lowest pitch of each timpano is still present and make any necessary adjustments. When using calfskin heads this also should be done periodically during the rehearsal or concert. (Some players advocate balancing the head first and *then* getting the low note of the range. This procedure is foolhardy because one's balancing efforts can be completely ruined if, when the pedal is moved to the position of least tension, the head becomes wrinkly from a lack of adequate "T"-screw tension.)

Tuning

We are now ready to tune the drums to the first pitches we need for the music to be played. The timpanist can get a starting pitch from the tuning note of the orchestra *(A)* or band *(B♭)*. It is here that the timpanist must possess a facile knowledge of intervallic relationships. He determines the pitches intervallically from the tuning note (usually by softly tapping a finger or stick on the head) and sets his pedals accordingly. A method to double check and refine one's tuning is to hum the correct pitch (in tune!) into the timpani head about four inches from the rim, moving the pedal slowly back and forth, stopping at the point of maximum sonority of sympathetic vibration (when the head speaks back the loudest to the "hummer"). One must develop a "vocal tenacity" in order not to alter one's humming pitch to conform with the pitch deriving from the timpano! Until the ear (and voice) is sufficiently developed, a pitch pipe is a handy tool to check one's tuning.

To develop an acute intervallic discrimination, various aural conditioning procedures can be used. First of all, the timpanist must acquire some basic fundamentals of music theory. This should include the ability to read in the bass clef, understand scales (major, minors, chromatic, whole-tone) and arpeggios, key signatures, and interval identification. Intervallic exercises within the scales and arpeggios studied should be practiced. The mistake often made at this point is that "study" is usually interpreted only as a mental and written process. Everything learned and written on paper in the course of learning music essentials should be practiced by playing at the piano (or some mallet-percussion keyboard instrument or at least a pitch pipe) and by singing. All of one's faculties must be used in this process: visual-mental, aural, and vocal.

Once a solid aural structure has evolved, abstract intervals (disassociated from keys, both up *and down* from a given pitch) should be practiced. By "practiced" we mean sung correctly and then tuned on the timpani, changes in pitch being checked each time with some master tuner (piano, marimba, bells, pitch-pipe, etc.). Here is a suggested order of difficulty of abstract intervals to be pursued: unisons and octaves; fourths and fifths (perfect); thirds and sixths (major and minor); seconds, sevenths, and ninths; and tritones. The ultimate aural objective might be stated thus: to identify the interval, sing it, and tune the timpani to any interval while the band or orchestra is playing in any key, without losing one's place.

A further aural exercise should include abstract interval sequences: give a pitch, have the student sing it, then name a few intervals (mixed, both up and down, alternating), checking the student's pitch as soon as he gets out of tune. For example:

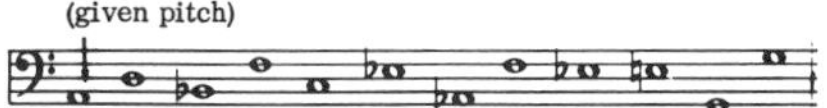

(This can, of course, be sung an octave higher with female students and young male players.)

An aural training exercise that has proved particularly rewarding appears below:

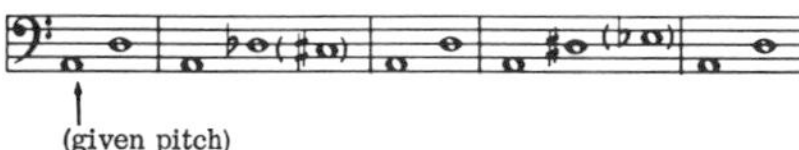

The interval of a fourth (any interval can be used)

These should not only be sung but also tuned on the timpani and checked with a master pitch source. The basic objective here is to focus the ear to a clear differentiation between half and whole steps. By purposely singing and tuning a half step sharp or flat we condition our ear to a clear difference in sound and distance between the right pitch and the "wrong" one. This pattern should be applied to every interval. Also, practice should be given in thinking of intervals above and below a given pitch. For some reason most of us tend to think of intervals only in an upward direction.

The general tendency of timpani students is to sing flat. This is usually caused by improper breath support, a closed mouth, and use of the throat as the focal point of sound instead of the head cavities (sinuses).

Practice

All during this period of basic music study, the teacher should supplement the student's practice with two drum exercises without tuning changes. There are several timpani method books available with such materials. However, the teacher should see that the student tunes the timpani to the pitches indicated (and helps if necessary), rather than using just *any* pitches. If availability of timpani is a problem at the outset, two snare or field drums can be used. At home, two pillows set on a table suffices. Matters of grip, articulation, rolling, muffling, muting, stick changes, etc. can be taught while the student is developing his ear. (These matters will be covered in subsequent articles.)

Once the teacher is satisfied that the timpani student has acquired a minimal theoretical understanding and aural ability, exercises at the timpani, including tuning changes, should be incorporated. In any case, "playing in tune" should be the constant objective and each lesson and practice session should have attention focused on aural practice. One more hurdle remains: the problem of counting measures rest while tuning.

Tuning While Counting

To keep track of numbers of measures rest while simultaneously tuning involves a concentration and mental coordination. It should be practiced with a metronome and at lessons with the teacher conducting. The ultimate objectives to be realized here are accuracy, speed, and *quiet* tuning, plus entering on time after the measures rest.

Many timpani exercise books do not demand adequate tuning practice. This can be remedied by inserting tuning changes at different points of any exercise with varying lengths of measures rest and different interval combinations.

The Lesson

Ideally, a weekly hour lesson should be considered a minimal lesson duration time during the integral aural training period. Here is an outline of what a timpani lesson might consist of, once initial musical and aural understanding are gained. The instructor might have the student do the following:

1. Release the tension of the pedals fully and see to it that the proper low basic pitch is set on each drum to be used. (Care should be taken to see that a pitch-tension of the head is maintained while moving the pedal to the position of least tension by tightening the tension rods so that the air seal between the head and the bowl is maintained, insuring maximum tonal clarity.)
2. Balance one head per lesson (no more than one-sixth of the total lesson time on this item).
3. Strike *A* (or *B*♭), tune drums to the pitches needed for the "etude(s) of the day" (no tuning outside of initial pitches needed until student is sufficiently advanced).
4. Aural practice:
A. Sing intervals.
B. Tune timpani (stick or finger tuning) to various intervals (check each interval against a master pitch source).
5. Eventually include etudes with tuning changes with specific numbers of measures rest. (At first use only single drum tuning changes, pitch changes on *all* drums being used during a single group of rest measures after the pupil proves that he can tune one drum consistently.)

Once the pitches are set on the timpani, they must be checked during measures rest and adjusted immediately if not absolutely in tune. There are times when quick changes of pitch occur on more than one drum, not allowing for a tuning check. In this case it is necessary for the timpanist to sit on a stool with his feet on the pedals so that he can adjust the pitches if his "pitch guess" is wrong. Calf skin heads, of course, need closer attention to tuning than do plastic heads because of the influence of humidity.

The matter of assignment of pitches to specific drums should be determined on these bases: (1) On which timpano will the pitch sound best? The best aural response is generally derived in the middle and upper registers of the timpani; hence, the pitches should be assigned accordingly, if possible. (2) Avoid awkward sticking and distance situations by assigning pitches to adjacent timpani wherever possible.

Conclusion

Just as we develop a verbal vocabulary, so must we condition ourselves to an aural vocabulary. We learn to string words together in different order producing sentences; in the study of the timpani the student must learn to string intervals together in different combinations with equal facility. It is unfortunate that our early training in music does not stress ear training: it would elevate the art of music making and appreciation of same to a much higher plane. Regardless of the type of "musical education of others" we are involved in, whether it be children or adults, music majors or amateurs, we must stress the training and awareness of the ear far more than we do: after all, *music is an aural art.*

May 1966

Tune Up Those Drums

Joel T. Leach

Many public school teachers assign the responsibility of tuning the drums to their first chair drummer. The young drummer, never having had proper instruction in the tuning of drums, generally makes numerous adjustments to suit his personal concept of a "good drum sound"—although he probably has an entirely erroneous concept of what that actually is!

Secondly, young drummers often employ various methods of damping the drum's vibrations which generally only takes them further away from a good drum sound.

It is the purpose of this article to describe the best approach to the proper tuning of drums, and to qualify the use of damping techniques and devices.

The Equipment

First, it must be understood that the two physical factors which most significantly affect the drum's tone (disregarding the shell itself) are the tension and quality of heads and, on snare drums, the snares. Use of cheap and inappropriate equipment or improper tuning of the very best equipment will result in a poor drum sound. With well chosen and well adjusted heads and snares, most drums can be tuned to produce an excellent or at least very satisfactory sound. Because of the demands made of public school drum equipment, it is suggested that plastic heads be used. These heads are all but impervious to humidity and temperature changes encountered both indoors and outdoors, and will therefore relieve the director of numerous problems relating to head care.

The Snare Drum

Most drum manufacturers designate their batter heads as "field" or "concert" which means they are of different thicknesses. At least one company sells heads in three thicknesses, with the thickest being designated for field drums and the others for both concert and dance drums. The thickness of the batter head not only affects stick rebound, but also the drum's tone.

As with batter heads, snare heads are also available in two or three thicknesses. The thickness of the snare head will have a tremendous effect on the general tone of the drum as well as on snare response. It will cause the drum to project more or less, to sound thin and weak, or full bodied. A medium snare head for the field drum and a thin or medium snare head for concert drum will suit most tastes.

Tensioning the Snare Drum

The snare drum's batter head should be very taut so as to give full rebound to the stick's stroke. The amount of tension necessary will obviously be affected somewhat by the size of the sticks being used; slightly more tension will be required on the field drum batter head to give proper rebound to the heavier sticks. If the head is too loose or too tight, both sound and rebound will be affected. When the batter head is properly adjusted to the "feel," it will likely be very close to proper adjustment for production of the best tone as well.

The tone of the snare drum is produced when, following a blow on the batter head, the air inside the drum forces the snare head downward, in turn forcing the snares downward. The tension of the snare head brings it back immediately; the snares follow and slap against the head, producing the typical snare drum sound. Therefore, if the snare head is too tight, it cannot move sufficiently to throw the snares away. If it is too loose, it will not respond to the force of the air from within. The snare head should be slightly less firm than the batter head.

Snares

Wire snares respond readily at low dynamic levels but may distort at extremely high levels. Gut snares respond poorly at low dynamic levels, but sound clean and full at high levels. Combination snares (half gut and half wire) combine the best qualities of each. For the type of work demanded of the concert snare drum, wire snares or combination wire and gut (or nylon) are most practical.

Because the field drum is the rhythmic backbone of the marching band and needs both power and clarity, the features offered by gut snares are more practical for that instrument. These may be installed dry on any snare drum as done in the factory, or they may be soaked in lukewarm water prior to installation, thus insuring a perfect form-fit when they dry. As with the concert drum, some drummers use combination snares on their field drums to their complete satisfaction.

Adjusting the Snares

All concert drum snares should be adjusted so as to allow a ***slight*** after-ring which, contrary to some common belief, is most desirable for it gives body and resonance to the snare drum's sound (the same qualities are insisted upon for all other instruments). The most common error is to stretch the snares too tightly, thus hampering their movement and resulting in a "choked" sound. Slightly less common is the drum whose snares hang too loosely, thus producing a lengthy, annoying after-buzz.

Gut snares for the field drum, however, are generally thicker and therefore begin to respond only at moderately heavy blows. For maximum clarity at the louder dynamic levels, gut snares should be stretched tightly across the head.

The Tenor Drum

A snare drum without snares cannot substitute for a tenor drum, as some people believe, for the tenor drum must be 1″ to 2″ larger in diameter than the matching snare drum to allow for proper tonal balance within the section. A converted snare drum will not allow for sufficient adjustment.

Secondly, it is important that all tenor drums, regardless of whether they are played horizontally or vertically (marching band), be equipped with two batter heads for maximum tone production.

Tensioning the Tenor Drum

The most common error in respect to tensioning of the tenor drum is that of applying too much tension. A tight tenor drum will actually begin to produce a definite pitch which will obviously be undesirable when mixed with the band's varying harmonies. Therefore, the tenor drum should be only moderately tight. Most important, it should balance equally between the sounds of the snare drum and bass drum, without being too near either one.

With the vertically mounted tenor drum (played on top head only), it is relatively easy to get the desired sound, for adjustment of tension on either head will affect the picth level of the drum. Therefore, once the proper "feel" is obtained on the batter head, it is still possible to raise or lower the drum's pitch somewhat by adjusting the bottom head accordingly.

The horizontally mounted tenor drum (played on both heads) is more difficult to tune, for it is absolutely necessary that both heads have the same pitch. Therefore, any pitch adjustment made with one head must be matched with the other in order to maintain the proper balance.

The Field Bass Drum

It is this author's belief that with

one exception, the extremely thin bass drums (6″ thru 10″) which have captured the public school market do not musically fulfill the needs of most marching bands. The exception involves the elementary or junior high school marching band which must use this drum size because of the occasional necessity of having to assign the instrument to a very small boy. However, the high school marching band director can generally be more selective in choosing his bass drummer, and will therefore have no need for the slim bass drum which produces such a thin, weak sound. Most of our fine college bands use no less than a 14″ bass drum on the marching field for this reason.

It must be realized that a bigger bass drum does not mean that it is automatically louder. Volume is determined by the player and *not* the instrument. Rather, the larger size drum will give a deeper, richer sound that will strengthen the low instruments and supply a solid foundation for all rhythmic structures.

Tensioning the Field Bass Drum

It is important that the drummer remember the name of the instrument *(bass)* when tensioning the drum. It should not be too tight, or it will lose the bass characteristic and become an annoying tenor throb.

The Concert Bass Drum

A marching bass drum can never substitute successfully for a larger, more resonant concert model. The importance of a good concert bass drum is often minimized, although it is interesting to note that most major symphony orchestras make use of no less than two, and often three, bass drums to best suit the character of any selection they may perform. This is obviously not the answer for the public schools, but it does point to the fact that the school should own one fine concert-size bass drum.

Tensioning the Concert Bass Drum

Various authorities have said they prefer tuning their bass drums to G (bottom line bass clef) or the *F* below that, etc., while in truth they are saying the most desirable sound results when they have lowered the bass drum's pitch to that general area. In other words, one must be seeking a particular *type* of sound and not a definite pitch when tuning the bass drum.

Damping Devices and Techniques

Most damping techniques employed on drums are musically as objectionable as the technique of tonguing both the beginning and end of every note on a brass instrument. Because dampers cancel nearly all intermittent vibrations, the intervals between stick taps and bounces (as in a roll) become "dead spots." The natural ring of a drum without a damper will smoothly fill in these minute pauses and give the roll a much smoother sound. This natural resonance also gives life and body to the drum's tone but does not directly affect volume.

The various damping methods found to be most acceptable for drums are discussed here so that the music educator and serious drum student may better understand the pros and cons of each.

Concert Snare Drum

A well tuned concert snare drum which has quality heads and snares, as mentioned previously, should not make use of any damping device. Many prominent drummers in all idioms order their drums to be delivered without tone controls; the drummers who do make use of tone controls carefully position them to touch only very lightly against the heads. Students often turn the tone control on to the extreme, which causes a bulge in the head. In reality, they have not just removed excess vibrations, but they have stretched the head in that spot and exerted uneven tension which may cause the head to break. Whether the head breaks or not, such an adjustment will certainly harm the drum's tone.

Admittedly, there are some cases when a damped sound is quite desirable. However, since these are definitely in the minority, a temporary damping device should be utilized, the simplest of which is a folded handkerchief placed on the far side of the batter head. Different degrees of damping can be achieved with the manner in which the handkerchief is folded and its exact placement on the head's surface.

It is unwise to install any other type of internal or external damping device, for these will only be further away from a good concert drum sound.*

Field Drum

The field drumming style generally relates closely to the rudimental idiom, where it is desirable that one be able to hear each individual stroke and bounce (as in an open styled roll). In order to make these all distinguishable, an effective damping device must be used.

The tone control often cannot withstand the punishment dealt it on the field drum, and it will break or work loose from its mountings. Even if this does not happen, its small contact area on the head will do little good in this case.

The most effective damper here is a strip of cloth roughly the consistency of bed linen and about 1½″ wide which may be stretched across the shell (off center) before the batter head is installed. If stretched tightly, it will maintain perfect contact with the head, being held in place by friction between the flesh hoop and shell. When this type of damper is installed, it is wise to remove the tone control from the drum altogether to avoid maintenance problems with that mechanism and with the head in the event the control should be improperly adjusted by a student. A moleskin strip also works effectively.

Tenor Drum

The tenor drum needs only minimal damping. Therefore, the use of ordinary ¾″ adhesive tape installed on the inside of each head will generally be sufficient. Because the tape can be seen through the head, it may be installed in a design—possibly the shape of the school's letter. This type of damper will allow for both adequate resonance and clarity.

A cloth strip such as discussed previously for use on the field snare drum may also be used on the tenor drum if the adhesive tape

---

* *A carefully and properly tuned drum which still has a lengthy after-ring is generally in need of better heads (of proper thickness), snares, or both.*

proves insufficient. Do not use both devices simultaneously, however.

Concert Bass Drum

In the concert idiom, a "round sound" is demanded of the low brasses, so the bass drum should match this type of sound. One exception might be in a march where many directors want a well-punctuated beat which can be achieved as mentioned below.

It is not recommended to install *any* type of damping device on or in the concert bass drum. In this respect, one should follow the example set by the orchestral bass drummer who uses the drum for full, resonant, single note effects (undamped) but can immediately use the finger tips or palm of the free hand pressed against the head for slight damping. When further damping is needed to separate strokes which follow in rapid succession, the knee may be placed against the head lightly to absorb excess vibrations. This type of damping enables the drum to serve both functions (damped/undamped) equally well, whereas the drum which contains cloth strips, paper, or feathers is limited to one particular sound.

Remember that damping doesn't necessarily decrease volume. Volume is determined by the manner in which the drum is struck, and should therefore be controlled by altering the force of the blow and/or the striking spot.

Field Bass Drum

The field bass drum usually needs no damping device. If one is desired, however, the best method is to install a strip of cloth roughly 3″ wide on the underside of each batter head (off center) as previously discussed for the field snare drum.

Other damping methods are used primarily by drum and bugle corps which demand a different type of sound. These include the use of shredded paper or feathers partially filling the drum to even further damp the drum's vibrations. These methods are *not* recommended for marching band or concert band use, however.

Again, many people use various combinations of these devices in an attempt to soften the bass drum's sound when all that is necessary is a firm word to the player. For practical purposes, the player serves as the volume control and the damper as the tone control. Be careful not to confuse these functions.

Conclusion

In addition to tuning and damping devices, many other factors greatly affect a drum's tone. Some of these are briefly discussed below.

1. When tensioning all drum heads, be sure they are properly balanced; there should be no great pitch variance at any spot on the head. If such a variance exists, adjust the rod or rods nearest that area to bring the head into balance.
2. The exact spot where the drum is struck will alter the sound considerably:
a. The concert snare drum should be played slightly off-center in most cases.
b. The field snare drum is generally played in the center or very near to the center for maximum clarity of each stroke and bounce.
c. Both the field bass drum and tenor drum are generally struck in the center to obtain a solid, pulsating beat.
d. The concert bass drum is struck off-center except for special effects.
3. The type of stick being used will also affect the sound:
a. Concert snare drumming generally calls for 2B or 5B sticks with "S" sticks being used only for compositions of a martial nature (and then on a field drum), and "A" sticks being used for special delicate passages.
b. Field snare drumming on the high school and college levels calls for 3S or 2S sticks which will give maximum rebound and aid in cleaner playing in this style.
c. Tenor drum sticks should be of one-piece solid felt with wooden handles for best service; rawhide thongs properly laced through the fingers will allow for twirling and prevent dropping of the sticks.
d. Field drum sticks should be of one piece solid felt, medium in size with wooden handles; rawhide thongs will also prove useful here.
4. The "touch" used by the player is an intangible but very real part of drumming technique. A well trained drummer will get an entirely different sound from a given snare drum than will a novice under the same conditions. Touch is unfortunately something which must be demonstrated to be best understood.
5. The building or areas in which the drums are played always affects tone and volume. This is understandably noticeable in concert halls, but often forgotten in regard to football stadiums. In the latter, drum sections are sometimes criticized for playing too loudly at marching competition when the stadium is empty and the sound of even a single drum resounds as though amplified. This should be taken into consideration by the drum section, band director, and judges. More than once a strong negative comment about this has caused a director to wrongly employ various damping devices the following year as his solution.

It is the author's wish that this article regarding adjusting of drums for tonal improvement will generate serious thought when tuning the drums or considering the employment of damping devices. As most music educators realize, the drum section is of fundamental importance to all performing organizations, and requires the same serious attention given technique, tone, and timing on all other instruments.

June 1966

Outline Guide to Percussion Orchestration

Gordon Peters

I. *Snare Drum*

A. Embellishments

1. Flags:
2. Drags:
3. Ruffs:

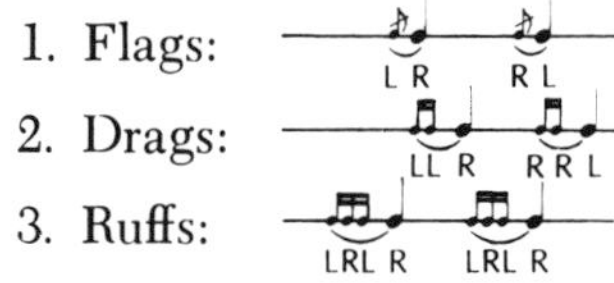

Embellishments are used in conjunction with single beats for purposes of ornamentation, emphasis, and/or contrast. Type and speed of drags used depends on style and tempo: martial type passages are played with more space between the beats

B. Colors available

1. With snares (can be muffled with a handkerchief, minimizing resonance)
2. Without snares (can be muffled)
3. Rim shot (stick across drum head and rim: struck with other stick)
4. On the rim
5. Brushes
6. With felt stick (s)
7. Head struck in center: near rim

II. *Timpani*

A. Functional Ranges and Sizes:

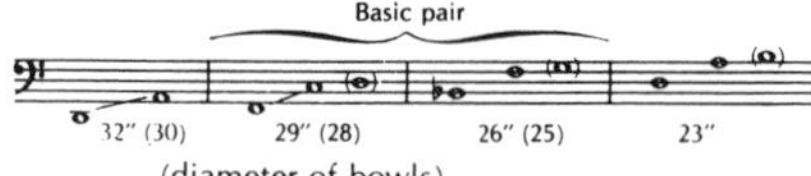

(diameter of bowls)

(Notes in brackets indicate possible tones on plastic heads and calf-skin heads where the humidity is low.)

B. Never include other percussion parts in the timpani part.

C. Most timpani have pedals today; however, allow sufficient time (5 seconds minimum) for changes in tuning.

III. *Mallet-keyboard Percussion*

A. Usual Ranges (actual sound)

1. Marimba (wooden keyboard): sounds where written
2. Xylophone (wooden keyboard): written *one* octave below sound
3. Vibraphone (aluminum keyboard): sounds where written
4. Bell lyra (aluminum keyboard): written *one* octave below sound
5. Orchestra bells (steel keyboard, usually): written *two* octaves below sound
6. Chimes (brass tubes): sounds where written

B. Mallet types:

1. Indicate degree of hardness: hard, medium, soft (H, M, S) where pertinent

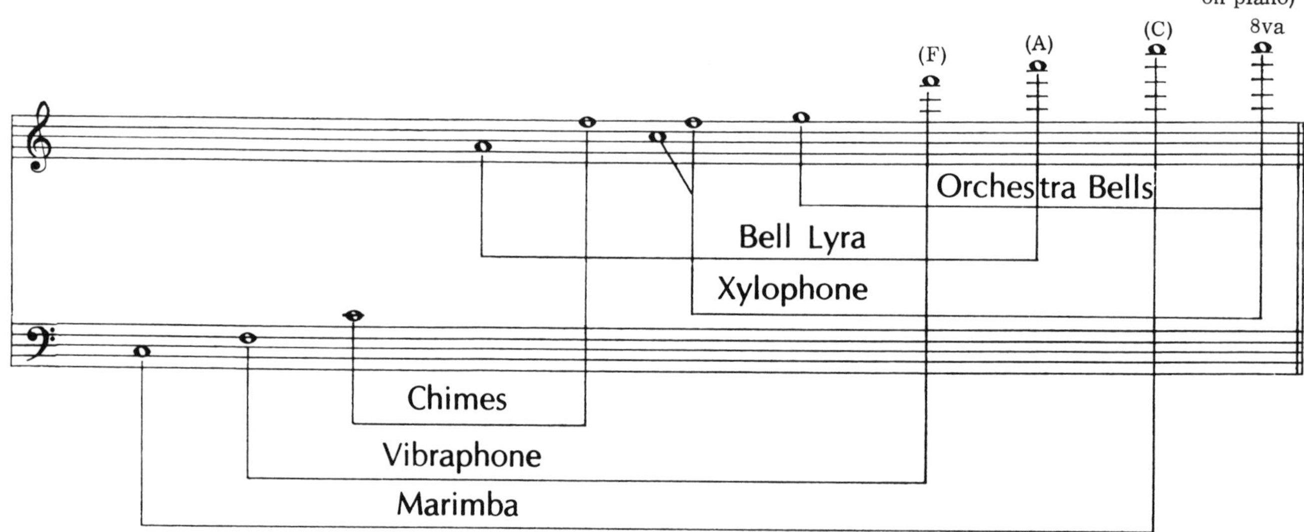

Mallet Types	Marimba	Xylophone	Vibraharp	Bell Lyra	Orchestra Bells		Chimes
					Steel	Aluminum	
Vulcanized Rubber	x	x	(x)	x	x	x	
Yarn-wound Rubber	x	(x)	x				
Metal					x		
Rawhide				x	x	x	x
Felt	x		x				
Wood	(x)	x		(x)	(x)	(x)	x
Plastic (hard)		x		x	x	x	x

2. Two, three, and four mallets can be used by one player

C. Chimes are struck with large rawhide hammer-shaped beaters.

D. Damper Pedals: found on "Vibes" and Chimes (work similar to piano damper pedal); indication should be made as to their use.

E. Indicate "motor on" (vibrato) or "motor off" when scoring for "Vibes."

G. "Use of the Marimba in the Band" by Gordon Peters, can be found in *The Instrumentalist* (December, 1965, pages 61-62).

H. Primary differences between the marimba and xylophone:

1. Marimba primarily a *solo* instrument; xylophone primarily an *orchestral* instrument.
2. Marimba bars are thinner and larger than xylophone bars.
3. Range of marimba is lower than xylophone.
4. Marimba bars are tuned to octave (2nd partial); xylophone to 5th (3rd partial).
5. Tone quality of marimba is very sonorous, akin to an organ when sustained; the xylophone is brittle and brillant.
6. Softer mallets are usually used on the marimba.
7. Marimba always have resonators; xylophones often do, but need not have them (as the European (strohfiedel").
8. The bars of both are made from Honduras rosewood.

IV. *Accessory Percussion Instruments*

A. Cymbals

1. Indicate "pair" or "suspended," "large" or "small."
2. If suspended, indicate "yarn mallet" or "wood stick" or triangle beater.
3. Sock cymbals (hi-hat), with pedal, can be used for jazz effects in concert; this effect can be achieved with a single cymbal by holding a stick under it while striking it, alternately muffling the cymbal.

B. Tambourine

1. Indicate "large" or "small."
2. Indicate "with thumb" or "shake" for rolls; thumb rolls are limited in duration, perhaps three seconds.

C. Other accessory percussion instruments

1. Field drum (large drum, with snares) (deeper than snare drum)
2. Tenor drum (large drum, no snares)
3. "Tambour de Provence" (deep drum, no snares)
4. Tom-tom ("any" drum, no snares)
5. Bass drum
6. Antique cymbals (pitched)
7. Finger cymbals (non-pitched)
8. Triangle
9. (Chinese cymbals, not commonly available)
10. Tam-tam (gong-like, no definite pitch; indicate "high" or "low")
11. Wood block, high or low
12. Castanets (two types: on paddles, and on block)
13. Metal castanets (finger cymbals, mounted on a spring handle); not common
14. Temple blocks (5 in a set, no pitch, ranged "low" to "high")
15. Ratchet
16. Sandpaper Blocks
17. Sleighbells
18. Slapstick
19. Anvil
20. Auto horn (s)
21. Siren
22. Wind machine
23. Thunder sheet
24. Steel plate
25. Brake drum (automobile)
26. Horse's hooves (coconut shells)
27. Bird whistles
28. Police whistle
29. Pop gun
30. Lion's roar (string drum)
31. Dog's bark (string friction drum)
32. Jingles or jingle clogs
33. Jingling Johnny (bell tree, Schellenbaum), not common
34. Bell tree (graduated metal cups on short mounted pole)
35. Ship's bell
36. Train whistle
37. Wind chimes (metal, wood, bamboo, glass)
38. Chains
39. Slide whistle
40. Pistol (shots)
41. Steam Board whistle
42. Nightingale (record: *Pines of Rome*—Respighi)
43. Flexitone, not common
44. Cuckoo
45. Typewriter
46. Typewriter bell
47. Baby Cry

V. *Latin-American Instruments*

A. Maracas (gourds with gravel, also, plastic and wooden)

B. Claves (rosewood cylinders)

C. Guiro or gourd (rasper, scratcher, guaracha, reco-reco); also, of plastic, animal horn, wood

D. Jawbone (Quijada)

E. Shaker (Chocalho, Chucala) metallic cylinder filled with gravel

F. Casaba (gourd with beads on outside)

G. Bongos (hand drums)

H. Timbales (stick drums)

I. Conga Drum (deep hand drum, sometimes in pairs)

J. Cowbell (Concerro)

K. Dome of Cymbal

(Note: for further information on Latin-American instruments and rhythms see: Latin-American Instruments *by Humberto Morales, Adler.)*

VI. *Notation*

A. *Percussion score versus individual parts*:

Percussion parts in score form *are recommended* and very functional insofar as the case of distributing parts is concerned among the players. However, when *too many* instruments are represented in one part, it often becomes too cumbersome and makes page turning almost impossible.

In evolving separate single instrument parts for the percussion section or parts for small groups of percussion instruments, the following combinations are most functional:

1. Primary Percussion Parts:
   a. Bass drum and cymbals (written on the same part, but a separate part for each player);
   b. Keyboard percussions (all on the same part but duplicate copies for each keyboard instrument used);
   d. Timpani;
2. Secondary Percussion Parts:
   a. If a second keyboard instrument or a second snare drum is used simultaneously with the first part, it can be scored on the first part on a separate

staff, and duplicate parts used.

b. As to triangle, tambourine, castanets, etc., these instruments should be inserted in the primary percussion parts into which they best fit. Cross-cuing, however, is very helpful. As a rule, all of one part (such as *all* the triangle notes) should be fitted into the part where all of it can be played by one man. However, the part can be divided if necessary. If only a little percussion playing is involved, but requiring two players, all these instruments should be put on one part; however, each player should have his own copy.

B. Each player should have a part for himself.

C. When scoring, time must be allowed for the percussionist to change from one instrument to another (quietly).

D. Do not write "Tacet" in the percussion part for a portion of a movement and then expect to have the player come in with his part on time. This is common in older editions particularly and is point of great distraction to the percussionist.

E. If cues of other instruments are indicated in the percussion part, they should be of those instruments predominating as opposed to some less prominent voice that might be difficult to hear. These cues are very helpful to the percussionist when there there are literally hundreds of measures to count.

F. Relative to terminology of instruments, use *English*, not a foreign language.

G. Indications of style and character are helpful to the percussionist whose very role is one of heightening the character and mood of a work.

H. The composer-arranger must realize that the percussionist has available (in most cases) a great diversity of instruments and mallets; hence, the more he can provide in the way of directions to the percussionist, the greater control he can exert in the ultimate resultant color evolved by the percussionist.

I. Indicate complete dynamics and nuance. Indicate "tops" and "bottoms" of "*crescendo* and *diminuendo*, e.g.

p < *mf* > *pp*

J. Be explicit as to how long those instruments of percussion that continue to vibrate after being struck should be allowed to do so (i.e. cymbals, triangle, chimes, bells, timpani, etc.).

K. Rolls: Use three lines thru a stem to indicate rolls rather than *tr* ~~~~ indicate the termination of rolls by using the "tie" ; the single note at the end of a roll to which the roll is tied should be construed as being the final note of the roll, unaccented.

L. Indicate phrasing to assist percussionist in interpreting together with other instruments.

VIII. *Supplementary References*

A. Bartlett, Harry. *Guide to Teaching Percussion* (Wm. Brown & Sons, Dubuque, Iowa)

B. Kennan, Kent. *Technique of Orchestration*, pp. 194-228.

C. *The Percussionist* (official journal of the Percussive Arts Society)

September 1966

Improving Your Marching Band Drum Section

LARRY W. McCORMICK

Perhaps from time to time, you have seen drum sections that you thought were exceptional in their contribution to the marching band. You may look at your own band and say: "Why doesn't my percussion section sound like that?" It is the purpose of this article to examine some of the factors that make a percussion section truly outstanding. We shall explore the following points: precision technique, instrumentation and size of drum section, drum parts and arranging for the drum section, and showmanship.

Precision Technique—If you have ever watched a really top drum section you will see what precision in a drum section can mean. Precision technique will give your drum section and band solidarity as well as power. It seems logical that three drummers all striking the drum at the same precise instant will produce more volume than three drummers who appear to be striking together but in reality are just a fraction apart. This may sound like a minor point, but check your drummers. Ask them to play a succession of quarter notes and see how often they all strike the drum *precisely* together.

The type of training we give our beginning drummers for band or orchestra performance is not specific enough for developing a *precise technique*. We are often satisfied with developing basic reading skills and an ability to play only a few easy rudiments of drumming such as the buzz roll and the flam. To be honest, for the *average* drum part they do not need much more, but this does not justify our teaching only the essentials. It is our job to develop a student's musicianship and technique to its highest possible level.

If we want true precision in a drum section we must teach precision technique. First, we must teach the basic stick motions and positions of drumming and show the student how they apply to all figurations and rudiments that we perform. Once the basic positions are mastered by the student, he will have a strong foundation from which all rudiments of drumming can be developed. Any rudiment or rhythmic configuration can be broken down note by note and placed into a logical system of stick positions and motions. I label this system *Precision Drumming*. Although the system is based on common sense and is quite simple to understand, I wonder how many drum teachers and band directors utilize it.

I will present a condensed version of my system. There are three basic positions of drumming: the stroke, the tap, and the grace note. Each position requires a different striking technique or motion. The first position, or stroke, is a loud beat with a full arm motion. The strike should commence from approximately 18 inches above the drum. The second, or tap, position is *only* a wrist motion struck six inches above the drum. Care must be taken not to put too much effort into striking the tap. It requires only a snap of the wrist. The third position is the grace note position. The grace note is an extremely soft beat played by using a finger tip motion with the stick about one inch above the drum head. It is so soft and delicate that it requires only the weight of the stick to make the sound. No force should be applied when playing a single grace note in a figure. The grace note position is used only on single grace note rudiments which include any of the flam family. When performing rudiments from the double grace note family we use the tap position for the grace notes. This would include any of the drag rudiments. The reason for this is that we interpret the double grace notes as 32nd note taps when learning the rudiments. Technically, grace notes have no rhythmic value; but, when teaching rudiments *per se* as a part of technique, we should teach *control* of the double grace notes so that they are heard distinctly and not allow the beats to become crushed and uneven.

Now let us examine a few rudiments and see how the system applies. The first rudiment a student should learn is the single beat roll. We begin by showing him the first position and explain the stroke motion. We tell him that when he plays any beats he should be very exacting in his positions and that his sticks should always return to the very same place before striking a new beat. We teach him that in learning the rudiments he must "run down" the rudiments. In other words start very slowly with the beats spaced, gradually increasing their speed hence closing the spaces between them. When peak speed is reached, reverse the process and return to the slow starting speed. Make a strong point that the student should never accelerate to the speed point of loosing control, as this will only develop careless habits. Learning to run down a rudiment properly teaches coordination, control, and listening abilities (concentration and discrimination). A mirror is most helpful at these beginning stages.

Perhaps the next rudiment we should teach is the triplet, as it incorporates the stroke and the tap

the triplet 3 3 R L R L R L stroke tap tap stroke tap tap

position, demand that the student prepare each beat prior to striking it by putting the sticks at the proper height and position.

The next rudiment I would take up is the open roll. This is the roll that we use for marching and outside performance (not to be confused with the concert roll which produces a buzz sound). This open roll, when performed properly, sounds like a succession of fast 32nd notes. The open roll is made up of two beats in succession from hand to hand, equally spaced and equal in volume. At no time should the beats in an open roll be squeezed down to resemble the buzz roll. All beats in the open roll should be played from the first or stroke position.

The next rudiment to teach is the flam. It incorporates both the stroke and the grace note position.

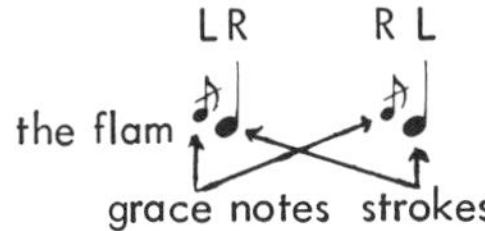

Have the student play grace notes properly, only about an inch from the head. No force should be applied to a grace note and do not allow the student to pick up the stick just prior to the grace note. The sound of all flams should be consistent and similar in sound to saying the word "flam." The natural tendency is to play the grace note too hard achieving a sound that we call a flat flam, caused from striking the beats at the exact same time.

Using the above four rudiments, we have covered the fundamental motions and positions of Precision Drumming. Now it is possible to take any rudiment and break it down into its component parts for our system. Let's look at one more rudiment to make sure we understand this breakdown concept. This is one of the more advanced rudiments:

Using this precision system to teach drum technique to beginners will result in a much more uniform drum section. You will automatically develop tonal and visual uniformity, power, and a solid beat in your section.

Size and Instrumentation—The average marching percussion section for a band of 65 or 70 pieces should include a minimum of three snare drums, three tenor drums, two bass drums, and one pair of cymbals. For a band of 70 to 100 pieces I recommend adding another snare and tenor, as well as another bass and pair of cymbals. The snare drums should be field drums and preferably 12″ by 15″ (diameter) sizes. The tenor drums can be the same size as the snares. Tune the tenor drums approximately a fifth below the snares in pitch to allow for tonal contrast. I prefer to use bass drums of different sizes. In my own group, I use three pitched bass drums. I tune the largest drum to the tonic of the key we play in most while on the field, the middle drum is pitched a fifth above that to the dominant, and the high drum I pitch to the octave of the low drum. With these pitched drums I can do a great deal to reinforce low brass figures and almost do the job of timpani. In choosing cymbals I like the larger variety between 17″ and 20″ for those climactic crashes; but why limit yourself to one size: use several sizes for a variety of effects.

Effective Parts and Arranging—This is an area where most bands need help. The majority of percussion parts for bands are written by composers without a percussion background. Their percussion parts are very basic in nature and lack imagination. Perhaps as a band director you arrange your own music for marching, and perhaps you, too, experience difficulty in writing for the percussion section due to a weak background in percussion training. If this is the case, you are one of the majority.

How can you utilize your percussion section to better enhance your music? First, let us look at the voicing in the percussion section and compare it to a choir. We use snare drums as the soprano or lead voicing, tenor drums as the tenor voice (which supply counter-rhythmic and re-enforcing parts to the alto and tenor voices in the band), and the bass drums which supply the bass voicings. Personally, I prefer to use two types of bass drums in my group: pitched and rudimental. I use smaller drums (10″ x 24″) to play rudimental bass drums, meaning that they play complex figures using two beaters and a variety of rudiments and patterns. By using rudimental bass drums it is possible to play sustaining patterns which really give depth and support to the underlying voices. For example the rudimental basses might accompany the trombones in a syncopated figuration such as,

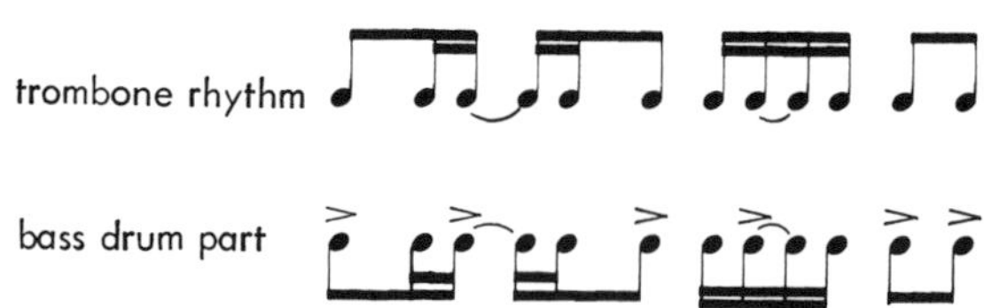

or they could fill in and help sustain a low brass chord,

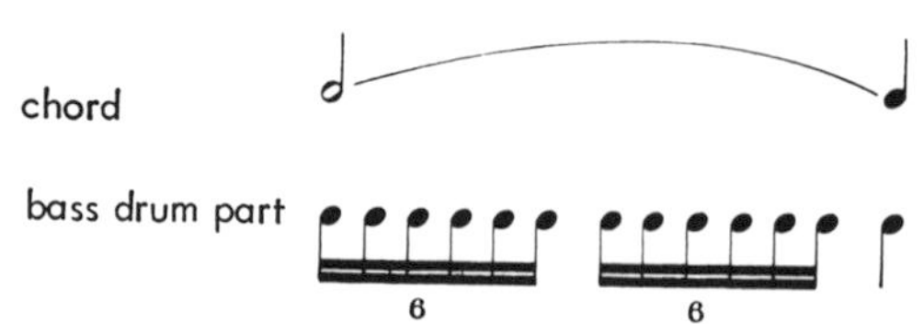

and they can give movement to a long line of slow moving tones to add motion.

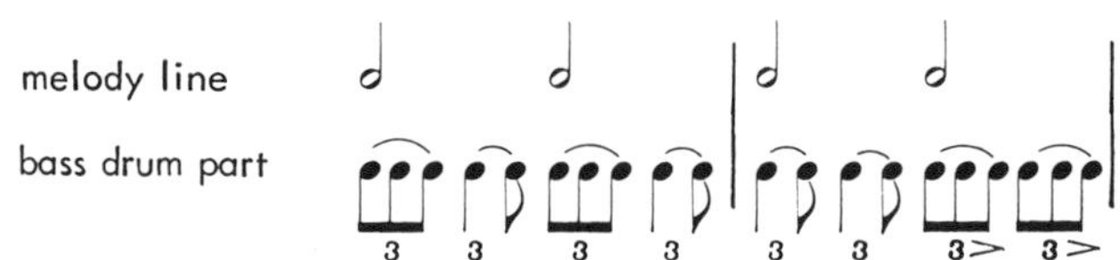

Think also of using the bass durms in a melodic sense as well as rhythmical. By using two or more bass drums in the marching band much can be done to add new flavor to the overall band sound.

When writing snare and tenor drum parts, keep in mind that they should supply the styling and mood for the musical arrangement. Whether you want swing, Latin, march, two beat, or a waltz styling, it is the job of the percussion section to establish the mood. Generally, the snare drums will supply the lead with a counterpart for the tenor, although interesting sounds come from giving the tenor voice the dominant part occasionally. The following are a couple of typical measures for the percussion section in the various styles. The top line is snare drum, the middle line tenor drum, and the bottom line bass drum.

Easy Swing

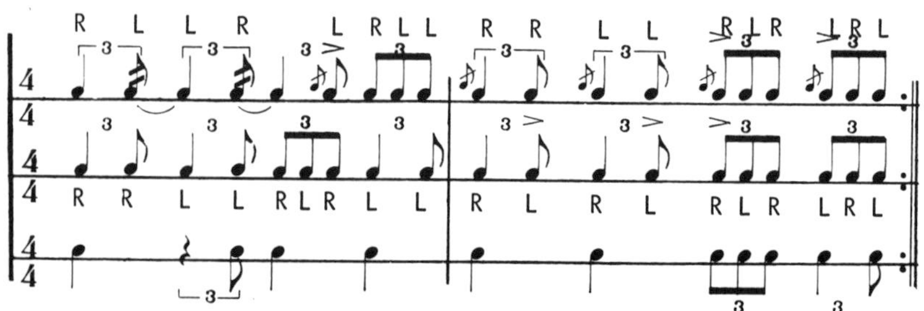

Beguine

R R R L (rim shots) R R L L R L R L L

R L L R R R RL R L R

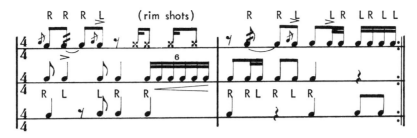

Driving up-beat

Jazz Waltz

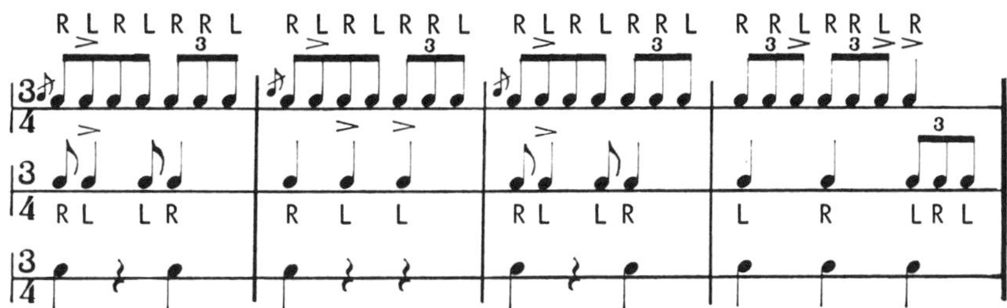

Percussion parts in the marching band usually suffer from lack of imagination, again as a result of the director's weak background in percussion. I hear one drum part after another composed of the same old clichés, making the drum section and the musical arrangements sound trite. To avoid this, one must seek assistance in finding new ideas and reference materials and professional help.

Showmanship—Certainly the percussion section can add more showmanship to the marching show than any other section in the band. This is simply because of the visual aspects of drum sticks in motion. Capitalize on this visual motion in presenting your routines. Don't hide your drum section: put them out in front where they can be seen. Have your drummers work out intricate sticking figures. Use sticks that are easily visable. Add some of the newer ideas in visual appeal that are fairly simple to master, such as "back sticking," or teach your rudimental bass drummers the style of armswing that comes over the head. This old style is very impressive when used by two or more bass drummers together. Try using a tune to feature the visual aspects of the percussion section, or feature the drums in an extended drum solo in front while the rest of the band performs some intricate manuevers, which would give them freedom to concentrate on the drill and rest their lips. But remember, of prime importance in attaining maximum visual appeal is insisting on *precision* and *uniformity*.

Now, let us sum up the important points for improving your drum section's effectiveness. First is precision in technique which leads to uniformity; second is size of section and effective instrumentation: don't limit yourself to traditional thinking; third is effective percussion writing: stay away from trite drum parts; and last is showmanship: feature your drum section and let them work for you visually. *Most of all, use your imagination!!*

The Beginning Percussion Class

Jesse Pearl

It has been said that it is very difficult to teach percussion instruments in a mixed instrumental class. There are several reasons for this type of thinking on the part of instructors:

1. The percussion instruments were not included in their preparation for the profession.
2. Classes are integrated, mixed instruments, and it is difficult to devote time to the percussion instruments.
3. Improper screening is given to prospective students.
4. Instructors depend on private teachers to prepare members of the section.

Having a *separate* class in percussion would negate the above reasons.

General Aims of Percussion Class

If it can be agreed upon that percussion instruments are necessary to bands and orchestras, that they present individual problems, and that they deserve time and attention, then there is valid justification to conduct a separate class of percussionists that will have an equal opportunity to learn their instruments. By virtue of concentrated training on all instruments of the percussion family for a time allocation equal to that of other instrumental classes, much can be accomplished. The performance groups they later enter will be greatly enhanced.

Organization and Requirements of Class

At the time that students are advised on the proper selection of an instrument, a large number usually indicates a preference for the drum. Where the desire is not too strong, other instruments are tried, and the number of would-be drummers is reduced considerably.

Those who are selected for the class must pass a "quickie" rhythm test by successfully imitating rhythm patterns tapped on the legs by the teacher. This is not a foolproof method of selection; but acceptance is on a trial basis so that talent, desire, and coordination can be appraised during the progress of the class.

The majority of students are started in the summer, during our six weeks summer program. Scheduling is very flexible then, and there are no conflicts with other recreational programs going on.

The beginning percussionists are asked to provide a beginning drum method, a pair of large sticks, and a drum pad. The pad is held with the student's own stand, or he may place the pad on a music stand. This is the basic equipment which is used for the entire summer.

A new, second group of drummers, much smaller than the original, is added to this group in September. Very little conflict in progress occurs. The summer group enjoys a review of the work covered, and the new group must make hasty decisions as to continuing in a drum class, while catching up to the others.

Dropouts happen during the summer and a few drop out after the first two weeks of September. The reasons for the student dropouts are usually:

1. the realization that better coordination is required than the student possesses;
2. the realization that the student had an entirely different concept of what work was entailed in the training of players of these instruments;
3. boredom brought about by practice and repetition; and
4. the realization that the student made a bad choice of instrument and would like to try a different instrument.

The number of participants is usually pared down to below 20, and it is with this group that we train in earnest. With this number, the director will have an ample number of students from which to select for his concert and intermediate groups the following year. If any of the students are in the 9th grade, their training is such that, by audition, they may qualify for the marching, concert, dance, and/or orchestral groups in the high school.

The other classes that I teach on this schedule are the advanced, reserve, intermediate, and beginning bands. The percussion class makes up the fifth teaching hour with a one-hour planning period on the schedule. The students from the previous year's percussion class are assigned to the above classes according to need and ability.

Very rarely do students repeat the percussion class. Students should qualify for one of the above groups or be advised to drop, in favor of something else. This is not to say that they should be performing artists at the end of one year's training in this class. Rather, this experience should qualify them to become functioning members of instrumental classes. The class provides them with a knowledge of reading and rudiment recognition so that they will be of assistance to the director and be able to accept corrections in a quicker and more musicianly fashion. The training they receive does much to remove the ulcer-making aggravations caused by drummers who are expected to perform without "equal time" training.

Course Content and Method

For the entire first semester work is concentrated on the snare drum, the percussionist's basic instrument. The pad, rather than the drum, is utilized. This, plus fat (not heavy) sticks (2B to 2S) are intended to give strength and control to the wrists. The practice pad being the practice instrument of the professionals, should be good enough reason for the student to prefer this to the drum. In addition it saves wear and tear on the ears of the listeners and exposes mistakes better.

Initial training is devoted to hand position, sticking patterns (alternating), and reading. Fundamental rhythm patterns are practiced and reinforced by means of review materials.

When the values of the quarter, eighth, and sixteenth notes and rests are firmly established, rudimental work is introduced. Each rudiment, from its fundamental rhythmic aspects to its final form, the way it might appear in written music, should then be introduced in context materials.

The lesson is now divided up into three phases: (1) warm-up exercises for the fingers and wrists; (2) rudimental practice; and (3) reading exercises. It takes about a full semester to introduce all of the rudiments to the class.

When progress is observable on these rudiments, a record of the playing of the rudiments is introduced. The students are asked to play along with these rudiments, from the open to the closed position. When the speed of the record exceeds that of the student he drops out temporarily, and picks it up again when the rudiment opens up to the point where he left off. Daily improvement can be seen by using the record.

In the second semester, further work is done on the snare drum rudiments and work is begun on the real instrument. Thinner sticks are substituted for the thick ones and the difference in playing duly noted. The other instruments of the family of drums are introduced, studied, and practiced upon (cymbals, bass drum, triangle, tambourine, etc.). Ensemble and solo work is started and literature of varying kinds and degrees of difficulty is introduced. The keyboard instruments are introduced to the class and all partake in the reading of music in both clefs. Once a reading knowledge of the marimba is accomplished and the basics of notation learned, the timpani can be introduced.

Experts from the ranks of professional percussionists are invited to observe, comment, demonstrate, and add to the experience of the students.

The students are constantly evaluating their progress in the group by means of challenges and tests. By the time promotion or selection is upon them, they know pretty well who will advance to the more preferred performing groups. The very best students are recommended to study privately.

Conclusions

I have shown to my superiors and to myself that the inclusion of a percussion class is a worthwhile and necessary adjunct to the instrumental music curriculum. While this report was not intended to be a syllabus of the course, it was the desire of the writer to show the elementary or junior high instrumental music teacher that inclusion of this course in the curriculum would take care of many problems in building a true percussion section that can enjoy music in the same manner that other instrumentalists do. The results are worth the trouble and effort.

November 1966

Common Faults of School Percussionists

Paula Culp

At a recent high school band and orchestra concert I found myself making notes about the percussion section on the back of my program. I listed the faults that seemed most common to percussion sections in general and I would like to repeat them in the hopes that repetition will stimulate correction.

Extraneous Noise (or Improvised Sounds)

This problem is so typical of percussion sections that it definitely deserves first mention. Any accidental intrusion into the music is pure carelessness on the part of the player. Of course, for those who prefer the psychological approach, there is always the explanation that percussionists tend to be insecure and crave attention. They subconsciously plot to drop a cymbal during a rest, conveniently forget to oil a squeaky timpani pedal, purposely leave rattling snares on, and accidentally brush a gong with the buttons on their coat sleeve. (Don't forget the ingenious timpanist who props a triangle beater neatly behind his right ear and later bends over to tune!)

The solution to this problem is to place all sticks, mallets, beaters, and small traps in a secure, accessible place. If a regular trap table is not available, build or improvise one. A small table can be mounted on the bottom half of a practice pad stand. It can be lined with any soft material—sponge, foam rubber, rug material, or toweling. A restaurant tray stand can be purchased and a covered board rested on it. Whatever you do, do not allow small traps or sticks to be left on the floor where they can be stepped on or left dangerously on stands, chairs, or the tops of bass drums.

General Stage Appearance

Of all sections, percussionists must work the hardest to achieve satisfactory stage presence. Since the percussionists usually stand and move around during the course of a concert, they become the focal point for audience attention. Therefore, chewing gum must go, the collar must be closed, and the sleeves unrolled. Once located behind the proper instrument it is desirable to remain stationary until the end of a selection. Percussionists too often distract attention by bobbing up and down, running back and forth, or conversing with each other during the music.

Care of Instruments

It takes only a few minutes a day to care for instruments properly. Don't throw all small items into a "miscellaneous chest." Sort and match sticks and mallets. Make a mallet bag with separate compartments for pairs of sticks. These bags, tied to the timpani handles, can be useful when changing sticks several times during one piece. Some players identify matching mallets by marking them with dots of colored ink, paint, or tape.

Label instruments and their corresponding cases for quick packing. It is also a good idea to label timpani covers. Sometimes it is difficult to tell which cover belongs where. Keep instruments covered when not in use and place them in a safe place where they will not be knocked over or tampered with.

Keep tambourine heads repaired. It is not difficult to change a head. Timpani sticks, bass drum beaters, gong beaters, yarn marimba mallets, etc. should be recovered or replaced when they wear thin. Keep all equipment well oiled and greased and correctly tuned and tensioned. If you cannot do these things yourself, seek the aid of an experienced percussionist.

Choice of Sticks, Mallets, Beaters

Would you play a $5000 cello with a $1 bow? Of course not. Why then, do we see performers using huge field drum sticks on small concert drums or pencil-thin sticks on large marching drums? A good player selects his beaters carefully. He uses his ear, experiments with sounds, and learns how to produce the best possible results on each instrument. He knows that yarn-wrapped mallets sound better on a suspended cymbal than large, fluffy timpani sticks. He knows that a triangle sounds best when it is strung with gut, held high, and struck with the proper sized beater, rather than when it is suspended with a shoestring, mounted on a music stand, and hit with a nail.

In a final observation, we note that a good percussionist is a tireless worker and one who must have a sense of organization. His development as a player is somewhat similar to crossing the "hump" in the long stroke roll. It is not until he has become aware of, and sensitive to, the fine points of performing on his many instruments and has become genuinely involved in his art that he becomes a true musician.

December 1966

Teach Your Drummers to Sing

Mervin Britton

A snare drum, as with all instruments, is capable of producing different sounds but not that aesthetic quality called music. Only those sounds put into it by the performer are amplified as the characteristic tonal quality of any instrument. How does the student of snare drum learn about the variety of musical sounds possible on the instrument? What effect does it have on his technique?

First, he may be made aware of the numerous sounds by vocalizing syllables on a one pitch rhythm. Such syllables will vary with each person. However, they must fit the style of the music. A fast staccato passage might be sung with the following syllables:

A slow marcato section might use these syllables:

Although the rhythmic pattern is the same and may use similar sticking, it is obvious that these two examples will sound completely different when sung in each fashion.

This by no means should be interpreted as a method of rote learning. The student must have a solid basis of reading as well as a knowledge of rudimental phrases before he begins to use these syllables. Only after he has learned to count divisions of the beat such as "1 e & d" is he ready to use syllables.

Any student with the capacity to learn the technique of an instrument can learn to sing in the previously described fashion. Of course, he must adopt a set of syllables and manner of singing which works best for him. Such singing must produce or represent grace notes, embellishments, staccato, marcato, and legato phrasing as well as open and closed rolls. The sounds "plu-t" or "p-lum" may represent an open grace note, while the sound "fl-t" a closed grace note.

Open rolls may be produced by a flutter tongue, while closed rolls with a buzzing "Z." If a student is unable to produce a flutter tongue, the sound "Zuu" would indicate a more open sound that pure "Z."

Once he becomes aware of the infinite varieties possible on one pitch, the student can begin to work on control. Control is necessary to sing or perform on the drum several tones with like quality; to produce successive matched embellishments; to produce staccato, marcato, and legato sounds; to phrase and emphasize cadence points.

A phrase, for example, ends on count two with the following eighth note being a pick-up into the next phrase. The performer should place vocal emphasis on the 3rd eighth note in the 2nd measure stopping the tone:

Taking a breath, he should then sing the 4th eighth note as leading into the next phrase. If he should happen to carry the phrase through the 4th eighth note and take a breath prior to the 1st count of the following measure both phrases are greatly altered. The sensitive snare drummer must decide which way is correct and impart his interpretation to anyone listening.

Having learned to discriminate vocally, the student should sing while performing. He should concentrate on making the drum tone match whatever he is singing—not sing whatever happens to come out of the drum. In this manner, he should develop the knowledge that it is the mind that controls the arms and resulting tones, instead of the too common belief that the arms work independently without need of musical thought.

Through the use of a purely technical approach to drumming, the student is likely to assume that only physical practice is necessary to obtain his goal. The choice of goals may even be in question. Too often such a goal is only to play louder and faster than anyone else. The student assumes that hours of diligent practice on patterns and embellishments will eventually prepare him to handle all performance problems. Once a certain technical level has been reached, it is falsely assumed that musicianship will be automatic or absorbed by osmosis.

Repetitious practice of technical problems for muscle development and control is of course necessary. However, it should take place only after a musical concept has been established, permitting the musical mind to be in control of the necessary muscles. In this manner musicianship and technique work with each other in development.

Singing the part concentrates technical muscle control in the lips, tongue, throat, and stomach muscles. This not only forces the student to "make music" from within, but frees his arms, wrists, and fingers from unnecessary tension. They are permitted to freely follow or imitate the controlled tongue, throat, and stomach muscles. It does take practice to develop control in these parts of the body.

Students are often embarrassed when asked to sing. Such embarrassment can be lessened when it is made clear that a pure vocal tone is not at all necessary. It is the articulation that is important. This may be obvious when the percussion teacher demonstrates the singing. Whenever the teacher injects humor and sings along with the student, such natural embarrassment is soon overcome. Fortunately, the student can usually notice improvement in his performance soon enough to be encouraged to continue vocalizing music for his performance medium. It goes without saying that this vocal concept should be applied to *all* the percussion instruments. We must make our ears, mind, and heart guide us in our playing, not only our eyes!

January 1967

Percussion Ensemble Floor Plans

Ramon Meyer

Percussionists are the physical fitness experts of the musical world. Who could fail to be in top shape after regularly carrying such bulky equipment hither and yon! This problem of portage and placement of instruments takes on enormous proportions in the percussion ensemble since no other musical en-

	PERCUSSION ENSEMBLE FLOOR PLAN
Title	
Composer	
Instrumentation	
Figure 1	CONDUCTOR

Titles			PERCUSSION ENSEMBLE COMPOSITE PLAN
Insts.	Mallets	Props	
			CONDUCTOR

semble has such a high equipment-to-player ratio. There are no easy ways out of the necessity for carrying equipment. There are, however, certain procedures which will substantially reduce the distracting and time-consuming movement of instruments between numbers in a percussion ensemble rehearsal and concert.

A mimeographed form on which the proper placement for instruments, props, and stands is charted will take the guesswork out of setting up each rehearsal and concert (Figure 1).

Floor plans used for concerts are composite arrangements of all of the works to be performed on a given segment of the program, i.e., all the numbers to be played before intermission are arranged on one floor plan and those played after intermission are arranged on a second plan.

Since compositions are rarely rehearsed in the same sequence in which they are performed, the floor plans used for rehearsal are arranged with only one composition on each chart. This will allow the conductor maximum flexibility in planning his rehearsals.

The use of floor plans will make it possible for the property manager to accurately set the stage for each rehearsal. If more than one work is to be rehearsed, the first one can be set up in its entirety and succeeding works can be arranged by the players, under the supervision of the property manager, between numbers.

All floor plans are drawn with symbols. A set of symbols can be developed to represent all the necessary instruments and props. Figure 2 lists a few appropriate symbols.

To develop rehearsal floor plans two steps must be followed:

1. Arrange all equipment needed by each player in one place so that the most rapid changes called for in the score can be easily manipulated. This procedure calls for a careful study of each part so that the problems of rapid instrument-change are recognized and solved in advance of the rehearsals.
2. If two or more players must share an instrument, the set-ups for these players must be adjacent (Figure 3).

If careful floor plans have been prepared all the conductor needs to do for an efficient use of his rehearsal time is to give the property manager charts for each number to be rehearsed.

For concerts the proper use of composite floor plans can make or break the program. Forcing an audience to sit through pauses which frequently approach the length of the pieces themselves while instruments are moved for the next number is obviously unwise. An equally ill-advised aspect of such a maneuver is the unreasonable demands made on the performer. He is forced to carry heavy equipment from place to place and then, panting and perspiring, he is expected to take up his sticks and play like an artist! Without the use of composite floor plans to check his work, the property manager runs the risk of overlooking the proper placement of an instrument, or of coming to the frustrating realization that an important instrument is not even in the concert hall!

Developing a composite floor plan can be accomplished most successfully if the following suggestions are followed.

1. The first composition to be charted should be the one which uses the most instruments per player (Figure 4).
2. Add next the composition requiring the second highest number of instruments per player (Figure 5).

If two or more instruments needed by separate players in the first composition are used by one player in the second composition, the chart must be adjusted to place these instruments adjacent to one another. Figure 6 shows an adjustment of the first chart (Figure 4) to allow player two access to both bass drum and tam tam for the second composition (see Figure 5).

Figure 7 illustrates the completed plan for the first and second compositions.

3. Keep adding new works and adjusting previously charted ones until the only movement necessary is a movement of *players,* not instruments.
4. Cases will arise where it will be more expedient to use duplicates of some instruments rather than moving these instruments between numbers. Figure 8 shows the addition of an extra pair of cymbals for the third composition in preference to moving the existing pair to the side of the bass drum between numbers.
5. To check the accuracy of the plans as well as to show every player's responsibility for each number, assign a color to every composition and circle all the instruments used by each player for that composition (Figure 9).

The composite floor plan will, of necessity, be different from the rehearsal plans, therefore it should be used for the last few rehearsals to give the performers and conductor time to accommodate themselvse to the new arrangement and to check the accuracy of the chart so the property manager can have everything in readiness for the concert.

The inventory of equipment used in a percussion ensemble concert is enormous and the placement of this equipment so crucial that it is wise to have a walk-through with the players before each performance. In a walk-through the players take their places behind their instruments for the first number, checking to be sure that each piece of equipment is ready, each drum is tuned, each stand tightened, and each stick in place. This procedure is followed in sequence for each number on the program.

By using carefully developed floor plans the conductor can save hours of time and effort as well as insuring a smooth operation of his ensemble at all times.

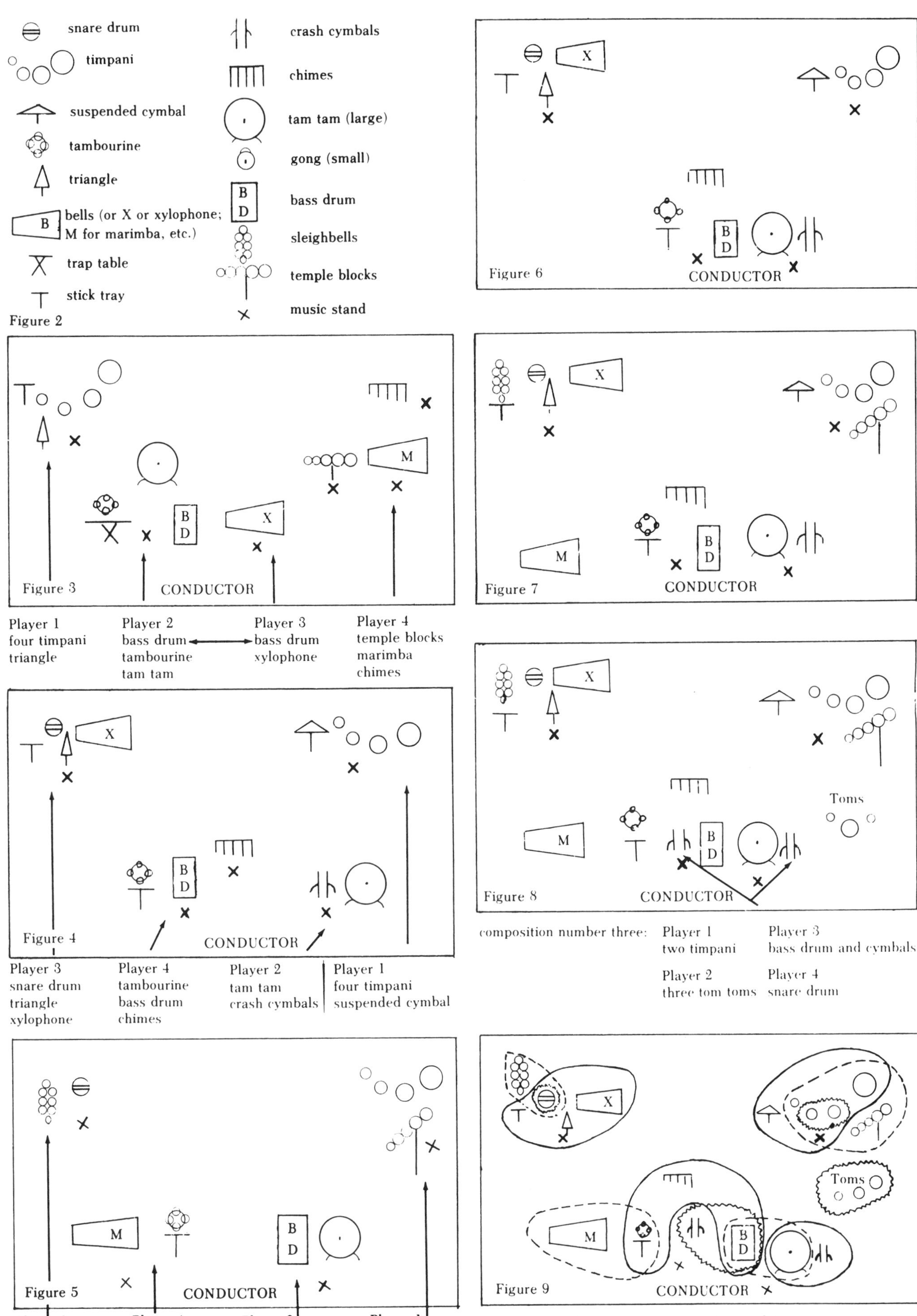
snare drum
timpani
suspended cymbal
tambourine
triangle
B
bells (or X or xylophone; M for marimba, etc.)
trap table
stick tray
Figure 2
crash cymbals
chimes
tam tam (large)
gong (small)
B D
bass drum
sleighbells
temple blocks
music stand
X
B D
Figure 6
CONDUCTOR
M
B D
X
Figure 3
CONDUCTOR
Player 1
four timpani
triangle
Player 2
bass drum
tambourine
tam tam
Player 3
bass drum
xylophone
Player 4
temple blocks
marimba
chimes
X
M
B D
Figure 7
CONDUCTOR
X
B D
Figure 4
CONDUCTOR
Player 3
snare drum
triangle
xylophone
Player 4
tambourine
bass drum
chimes
Player 2
tam tam
crash cymbals
Player 1
four timpani
suspended cymbal
X
Toms
M
B D
Figure 8
CONDUCTOR
composition number three:
Player 1
two timpani
Player 2
three tom toms
Player 3
bass drum and cymbals
Player 4
snare drum
M
B D
Figure 5
CONDUCTOR
Player 3
sleigh bells
snare drum
Player 4
marimba
tambourine
Player 2
bass drum
tam tam
Player 1
temple blocks
four timpani
X
Toms
M
B D
Figure 9
CONDUCTOR
color code: first composition red ( )
second composition blue ( )
third composition green ( )

A Revised Percussion Contest in Wisconsin

Jay Collins

In an article about percussion contest adjudication which appeared in *The Ludwig Drummer* (Spring, 1963, Vol. 3, No. 1), Gordon Peters voiced the concern of many percussionists that our school competitions in percussion were not serving the purposes for which they are intended. By no means were the contests giving consideration to the percussionist as an all-around performer on even the basic percussion instruments. It was due to this concern that the Percussive Arts Society asked Mr. Peters to form a committee to study this area and submit recommendations for improvement. A set of rules and evaluation sheets were proposed by Mr. Peters which appeared in Volume 1, No. 2, of the *Percussionist*, quarterly journal of the Percussive Arts Society. The committee which he selected was comprised of Ramon E. Meyer, Laverne R. Reimer, and James D. Salmon. Mr. Peters was chairman. Their recommendations were reported in the August, 1965 issue of *The Instrumentalist* (Vol. XX, No. 1).

As is probably the case with many music directors, percussionists, contest adjudicators, and students in other geographical areas, there was considerable concern about the percussion contest in Wisconsin. Luckily, the concern was from those in a position to do something about it. This, unfortunately, has not been the case in some other states. It is sincerely hoped that other contest committees will take the time to re-evaluate their present procedures and make alterations where necessary. These alterations, however, should be based on that which will be of practical benefit to the student and his performance organization, regardless of traditional practices or personal prejudices which might seem to conflict.

The festival rules committee of the Wisconsin School Music Association organized a committee in June of 1964 with the charge to "improve and update the percussion area of the WSMA music contest." The committee consisted of Willis Buettner, Ohskosh, Wis., chairman; Harvard Erdman, Wautoma, Wis.; and Arthur Hayek, Menomonee Falls, Wis.; with Jay Collins, Whitewater, Wis. as advisor. Richard G. Gaarder, executive secretary of the WSMA, was an ex-officio member of the committee.

There are many variations of contest outlines among the various states, but in Wisconsin each contest event is divided into three classes—A, B, and C—with Class A comprising the most difficult selections. In addition a rule exists in Wisconsin which prevents contestants from performing selections which are not included in the "Required Music List." If the music committee is unable to list approximately 30 selections for a solo event (about ten per class), "Permission All Classes" appears in the music list heading for that particular event; "No Exceptions" appears in the heading when the appropriate number of selections is listed. In the latter case it is not usually possible for a contestant to perform any music other than the particular selection, edition, or arrangement specified in the WSMA Music List. It was this realization which became an immediate source of difficulty for the percussion committee since any event which might be a departure from the usual solo or ensemble event would necessarily pose problems in music selection. With much debate and hard work seeking solutions to these problems, this committee was able to change the percussion contest in Wisconsin from a contest of two solo and three ensemble events to a contest containing five solo percussion and six percussion ensemble events—an increase of six categories.

Percussion Contest Categories

The percussion contest categories from which a contestant may choose are divided into two main groups: Solo Events and Ensemble Events. Under the present contest rules a student may enter a combined total of four events but only once in each percussion category. The list of percussion contest events is as follows:

Percussion Solo Events

Snare Drum Solo (concert drum or parade drum)
Marimba or Xylophone Solo
Vibraphone Solo
Timpani Solo
Multiple Percussion Solo (multiple percussion and/or drum set)

Percussion Ensemble Events

Drum Duets (Drum duets may consist of any combination of drums and/or drum sets.)
Keyboard Mallet Duets (Keyboard mallet duets may consist of any combination of keyboard mallet percussion instruments.)
Drum Trios (Drum trios may consist of any combination of drums, drums and hand cymbals, and/or drum sets.)
Keyboard Mallet Ensembles (trios and above)
(Keyboard mallet ensembles may consist of any combination of keyboard mallet percussion instruments for three or more players.)
Drum Ensembles (quartets and above)
(Drum ensembles may consist of any combination of drums, drums and hand cymbals, and/or drum sets for four or more players.)
Miscellaneous Percussion Ensembles (three to 18 members)
(Miscellaneous percussion ensembles may consist of any combination of drums, keyboard mallet percussion instruments, and/or miscellaneous percussion instruments from three to 18 members. String bass, guitar, piano(s), and celesta may be used and will be considered in the adjudication of the general effect of the ensemble, but the

players of these instruments will not be counted in numbering the members of the ensemble.)

It was decided that each solo performance should consist of a solo selection; a set group of required rudiments or fundamental techniques; and appropriate sightreading. For this to be possible the contest regulation allowing six minutes for solos and eight minutes for ensembles had to be revised for the percussion events. A compromise was reached by changing the rule as it applies to percussion events to allow eight minutes for solos and six minutes for ensembles. This was a most important consideration financially since the number of entries in a contest has considerable bearing on keeping the festival chairman from operating in the "red." It was necessary to make this time change since only the percussion solo events require the display of both fundamental techniques and sightreading in addition to the prepared solo selection.

A rule preventing piano accompaniment for snare drum solos was replaced with a provision allowing accompaniment. It was decided that percussion solos having written accompaniments which are essential to the successful performance of the selection should be accompanied. Other solos in which the omission of the accompaniment does not impair performance should be performed without accompaniment.

A statement to festival managers concerning equipment which must be provided included the following instructions:

1. One piano tuned to A-440 so as not to cause intonation problems for keyboard mallet percussion instruments.
2. One pair of pedal timpani of either 25″ and 28″ or 26″ and 29″ combinations.
3. One concert bass drum on stand.
4. Electrical outlet close to performance area for use with vibraphone.
5. Music stand for each member of the largest percussion ensemble.

Effecting the Change

For the contest to be an educational experience for the student, providing him with incentive, criticism, and award, it was necessary that it become a more realistic and practical experience for the percussionist. The committee agreed that the contest should contain standards and requirements in each event which would present the student with individual goals for achievement. It has since been observed that many students have begun personal drill and practice in areas which had previously been almost, if not entirely, untouched. For example, many are having their friends drill them on pitches and intervals which are required as part of the fundamental techniques for the timpani solo event. Many have started timpani practice who had never been interested in timpani before. Numerous students throughout Wisconsin have turned to the keyboard mallet percussion instruments in order to complete the needs of certain ensemble events and to provide themselves with additional solo event categories. This expansion of competitive opportunities has created much incentive among the student percussionists of the state and has kindled the percussion interests of their directors and teachers. The contest changes have already benefitted the contestants individually and will eventually benefit the instrumental directors by helping them to have better percussionists in their various organizations.

A special problem confronted the committee and the WSMA executive secretary in effecting the many percussion changes. Qualified adjudicators had to be found who could judge this new percussion contest. It was not possible to obtain all percussion specialists to serve as adjudicators. After much consideration it was decided that the committee should publish a percussion regulations handbook for the contest and make it available to adjudicators and anyone interested or involved in the percussion contest. In October of 1965 the *Percussion Contest Regulations Handbook* was issued by the WSMA. Copies of this handbook are available at the office of the Executive Secretary of the Wisconsin School Music Association, 115 West Main Street, Madison, Wisconsin 53703.

Two of the most radical changes in the contest which are outlined in the handbook pertain to the manner of performing the snare drum rudiments and the long roll. The contestant is required to play all of the rudiments or fundamental techniques which are listed in his class for each solo event. For the snare drum solo event this amounts to six rudiments per class. The snare drum event also requires that the contestant (in Classes A and B) play the long roll in two styles representing parade and concert style. These rolls are referred to as single rebound and multiple rebound rolls respectively. As explained in the handbook:

> The single rebound roll is the conventional long roll or "da-da-ma-ma" roll. This roll is *not* to be played as an open-close-open rudiment as indicated on the N.A.R.D.* rudiment sheet. Instead, the contestant will start the roll at his maximum controlled speed and will vary the dynamics keeping the speed constant. The starting volume is to be mf, crescendo to ff, diminuendo to pp, crescendo to mf, and then stopped.
>
> The multiple rebound roll is the concert style roll used in concert band and orchestra drumming. Essentially this roll is the roll produced by closing the long roll beyond the single rebound style. This roll is commonly referred to as the "buzz" roll. The contestant will start the roll at his maximum controlled speed and will vary the dynamics keeping the speed constant. The starting volume is to be mf, crescendo to ff, diminuendo to pp, crescendo to mf, and then stopped.

*National Association of Rudimental Drummers

In *The Ludwig Drummer* (spring, 1966, Vol. 6, No. 1) Wm. F. Ludwig, Jr., secretary-treasurer of the National Association of Rudimental Drummers, wrote of the Wisconsin percussion contest in the N.A.R.D. Bulletin No. 116. Mr. Ludwig expressed an appreciation for the requirement that the contestant be tested on roll dynamics and added: "the Wisconsin requirements deserve special commendation by all of us, especially the very fine specifications set forth for the size, number, and groups of percussion ensembles and also in the testing of the various drum set rhythms." He objects, however, to the performance of the single rebound roll at the contestant's maximum controlled speed without starting slowly and building up to that speed and then slowing it down again.

Mr. Ludwig expressed his view that there "is still plenty of reason to start the roll open and gradually close it to its maximum playing speed and then open again and that this tradition should be continued in contest."

It should not be assumed though that students in Wisconsin will no longer be taught the traditional open-closed-open sequence of the single rebound roll. Mr. Ludwig's cautionary remark, in which he states, "Learning the roll strictly as a rebound rudiment causes some distortion in that the first beat often sounds louder than the second," is one which should be emphasized.

It seems important to emphasize at this point that in the revised WSMA percussion contest the contestant is made to realize and display the fact that there are two styles of playing the long roll—as a single rebound roll (two sounds per stick) and as a multiple rebound roll (multiple sounds per stick). In an effort to test the student on his ability to perform both types of the long roll immediately, as he would be required to play them in band, orchestra, etc., the committee adjusted the requirement to fit this more practical method of displaying actual performance ability.

Since it was anticipated that the performance of the long roll in two playing styles would be a matter of concern to Wisconsin students and directors, an article on "Snare Drumming Styles" was prepared for *The Wisconsin School Musician* (October, 1965, Vol. 35, No. 1, p. 28), official magazine of the WSMA and the Wisconsin Music Educators Conference. This article has been reprinted in *Percussive Notes* (Vol. IV, No. 4, June, 1966 p. 7) which is published by James L. Moore, 5075 Henderson Hts., Columbus, Ohio 43221. In this article the single rebound and multiple rebound styles of playing the long roll are discussed in detail. In further implementing the contest changes in Wisconsin, the Southern Wisconsin Educators Association presented a percussion clinic demonstration of the new contest in the instrumental music section of the annual meeting in Madison, Wisconsin in February of 1966.

Percussion Event Requirements

The committee that had been established by the WSMA felt that rudiments and fundamental techniques should be required for all solo events. It was decided that both the student and the adjudicator would benefit by knowing exactly what the student should be required to perform in addition to his solo selection. Since so many contestants in the past had appeared with inappropriate equipment, it was decided that equipment requirements be included. The committee also noted that rote learning has been present among percussion players in the past to a considerable degree and decided to require sightreading for each solo percussion event. In each case the tempo is set by the adjudicator. The contest requirements for the percussion solo and percussion ensemble events are as follows:

PERCUSSION SOLO EVENTS
Order of Events

The order in which the percussion solo events should be performed is as follows:

1. Solo selection
2. Required rudiments or fundamental techniques
3. Sightreading

Contest #500 Snare Drum Solo

Equipment

This event includes solos for the concert snare drum or the parade drum. The type of snare drum to be used for each solo is indicated on the music list. The concert snare drum is meant to be the size 8″ by 15″ or smaller. The parade drum is meant to be the size 10″ by 14″ or larger. Stick sizes 3A, 5A, and 1B are to be used for solos performed on the concert snare drum. Stick sizes 2B, 1S, 2S, and 3S are to be used for solos performed on the parade drum. The use of a sling for the parade drum is optional. The contestant should indicate on the adjudication card, 500 Concert or 500 Parade, corresponding to the type of solo entered.

Required Rudiments

The contestant will be required to play *all* the rudiments in his class.

Class C

N.A.R.D.
#1 Long roll
(single rebound)
#2 Five stroke roll
#8 Ruff
#21 Single paradiddle
#5 Flam Accent #1
Flam Accent #2

Class B

N.A.R.D.
#1 Long roll
(single rebound)
#1 Long roll
(multiple rebound)
#3 Seven stroke roll
#6 Flam paradiddle
#11 Double paradiddle
(with single accent)
#13 Triple ratamacue

Class A

N.A.R.D.
#1 Long roll
(single rebound)
#1 Long roll
(multiple rebound)
#7 Flamacue
#10 Double drag
#20 Flam tap
#14 Single stroke roll

All the rudiments, *except the rolls,* should be started at a moderate speed and increased to the contestant's fastest controlled speed and then stopped. Variations in volume are not a requirement for these rudiments.

Sightreading

The tempo is to be set by the adjudictor. The required sightreading will include the following:

Class C—1 time signature in one selection

Class B—2 time signatures in one selection

Class A—2 time signatures in one selection

Contest #501
(Marimba or Xylophone)

Equipment

Each contestant must furnish his own instrument for this event. The number placed after each selection on the music list indicates the maximum number of mallets required for performance.

Generally, two mallet melodic selections in the marimba contest should be performed with soft rubber, medium-hard rubber, or hard rubber mallets or their equivalent. Mallet marimba selections which are chiefly harmonic in style as well as three and four mallet selections should be performed with soft yarn, medium-hard yarn, hard yarn, or any of the various yarn mallets in any combinations the contestant deems appropriate to the selection being performed. Any hard commercially produced xylophone mallet is acceptable for use in the xylophone contest.

The contestant should indicate on the adjudication card, 501 Marimba or 501 Xylophone, corresponding to the type of solo entered.

Required Fundamental Techniques

The contestant will be required to play all the fundamental techniques in his class. The techniques include 2 mallet techniques, 4 mallet techniques, and the roll.

Class C

Two Mallet Techniques:

1. Scales and arpeggios for two octaves, ascending and descending in the keys of *C* major and *A* harmonic minor as eighth notes with the recommended minimum required speed: ♩ = 120 M.M.
2. Alternated single stroke roll varying the volume by starting at pp, crescendo to ff, diminuendo to pp, and then stopped. This roll is to be played on 3 successive *F* naturals, each one octave higher than the last.

Four Mallet Techniques:

1. The chords are to be rolled and played ascending from root position to first inversion, to second inversion, to the octave above and then descending to root position in the keys of *C* major and *A* minor.

Class B

Two Mallet Techniques:

1. Scales and arpeggios for two octaves, ascending and descending in the keys of *F* and *G* major and *D* and *E* harmonic minor as eighth notes with the recommended minimum required speed: ♩ = 144 M.M.
2. The single stroke roll as described in Class C.

Four Mallet Techniques:

1. Same as Class C but in the keys of *F* and *G* major and *D* and *E* minor.

Class A

Two Mallet Techniques:

1. Scales and arpeggios for two octaves, ascending and descending in the keys of *B♭* and *D* major and G and *B* harmonic minor as sixteenth notes with the recommended minimum required speed: ♩ = 96 M.M.
2. The single stroke roll as described in Class C.

Four Mallet Techniques:

1. Same as Class C but in the keys of *B♭* and *D* major and *G* and *B* minor.

Sightreading

The tempo will be set by the adjudicator. The required sightreading will include the following:

All Classes

1. A two mallet melodic selection without rolls.
2. A four mallet harmonic selection rolling all notes.

Contest #502 (Vibraphone)

Equipment

Each contestant must furnish his own instrument for this event. The number placed after each selection on the music list indicates the maximum number of mallets required for performance.

Generally, two mallet melodic selections should be performed with soft, medium, or hard cord-wound vibraphone mallets. Two mallet selections which are chiefly harmonic in style as well as three and four mallet selections should be performed with soft yarn marimba mallets, or soft to medium hard cord-wound vibraphone mallets.

Required Fundamental Techniques

The contestant will be required to perform the same fundamental techniques as required in all corresponding classes of contest #501 with the following variations:

1. When performing two mallet techniques the damper pedal should not be depressed, since the notes should not be sustained.
2. When performing four mallet techniques the contestant will sustain the chords by use of the damper pedal rather than by playing rolls.

Sightreading

The tempo will be set by the adjudicator. The required sight reading will include the following:

All Classes

1. A two mallet melodic selection without use of rolls or damper pedal.
2. A four mallet harmonic selection using damper pedal to sustain and render proper value to all notes.

Contest #503 (Timpani)

Equipment

The host school will provide one pair of either 25″ and 28″ or 26″ and 29″ timpani. If additional timpani are required it is the contestant's responsibility to provide them. The contestant should use the type of mallet indicated on the selection. If one is not indicated, the solo should be performed with the soft piano-felt mallets used for general playing. The soft piano-felt mallets should be used in performing required techniques and sightreading. *Automatic tuners cannot be used during the contest.* The number of timpani necessary for performance has been indicated after each selection on the music list.

Required Fundamental Techniques

Class C

1. The contestant will be requested to perform the alternated single-stroke roll varying the volume from ppp, crescendo to fff, and diminuendo to ppp. The roll should be performed on the *F* pitch on the large timpani and also on the high *F* pitch on the small timpani.
2. The contestant will be required to tune both timpani to any pair of pitches requested by the adjudicator, using the interval of a perfect fourth. A pitch pipe or any other device can be used to tune the large timpani but the small timpani must be tuned by ear.

Class B

1. The single-stroke roll as described in Class C.
2. Same as Class C but using the intervals of a perfect fourth and a perfect fifth.

Class A

1. The single-stroke roll as described in Class C.
2. Same as Class C but using the intervals of a major third, perfect fourth, and perfect fifth.

Sightreading

The tempo will be set by the adjudicator. The required sight reading will include the following:

Class C—A selection with no pitch changes.

Class B—A selection with a pitch change of a whole step on one drum. The pitch change is to be made while the rests are being counted in tempo.

Class A—A selection with pitch

changes on two drums. The pitch changes are to be made while the rests are being counted in tempo.

Contest #504 (Multiple Percussion Solo)

Equipment

Each contestant must furnish his own instruments for this event. The music list will indicate the combination of instruments required for performance after each selection.

Contestants who are performing selections which are primarily drum set solos must be equipped with a complete drum set regardless of the outfit needed for performing the selection. This regulation must be strictly complied with since the complete set will be needed for performing the fundamental techniques and/or sightreading.

A complete drum set includes the following equipment:

1. 1–20″ or 22″ bass drum with spurs and a foot pedal.
2. 1–5½″ by 15″ or smaller snare drum on a stand.
3. 1–8″ by 12″ or 9″ by 13″ tom-tom mounted on bass drum on player's left or similarly placed if on a drum stand.
4. 1–14″ by 14″ or 16″ by 16″ floor tom-tom. (A conventional parade or tenor drum on a stand may be substituted if snares are released enough so as not to vibrate during the performance.)
5. 1–set of hi-hat cymbals on hi-hat stand with foot pedal. (Cymbal sizes to suit contestant's preference. Sizes in pairs from 13″ to 15″ are suggested.)
6. 1–ride cymbal mounted on bass drum on player's right or similarly placed if floor cymbal stand is used.
7. 1–pair of snare drum brushes.
8. 1–pair of drum sticks. (Stick sizes to suit contestant's preference. Sizes should be selected from 8A through 11A or their equivalent.)
9. Any additional equipment required in the solo selection.

Required Fundamental Techniques

Fundamental techniques for all multiple percussion solos, except solos which are primarily drum set solos, will be selected from any of the previous lists from their corresponding classes at the adjudicator's discretion, depending upon the combination of instruments being used. Preferably, representative required techniques should be selected from each major percussion category (snare drum, keyboard mallet percussion, and timpani) being employed.

The drum set fundamental techniques are the same in all classes. All six rhythm patterns are to be performed at the tempos indicated. Each measure is to be played four times. The adjudicator will judge the accuracy of performance and the contestant's ability to maintain a steady tempo and rhythmic consistency.

Drum Set Notation
Drum Set Rhythms (Sticks)
Drum Set Rhythms (Brushes)

Percussion Clef

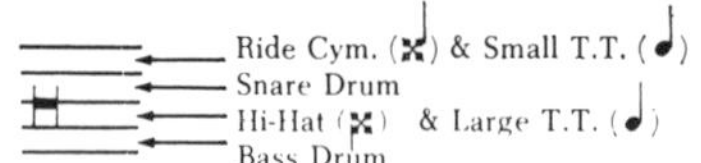

No. 4, No. 5, No. 6—the rhythms are the same as No. 1, No. 2, and No. 3 but with the right hand using a brush on the snare drum playing the ride cymbal rhythm and the left hand using a brush in a continuous sweep (circular, stirring motion) over the top of the drum head instead of playing on the second and fourth beats as required above.

Sightreading

Sightreading for all multiple percussion solos, except solos which are primarily drum set solos, will be selected from any of the required sightreading of the four other solo events listed from their corresponding classes at the adjudicator's discretion, depending upon the combinations of instruments being used. Preferably, portions of representative required sightreading should be selected from each major percussion category (snare drum, keyboard mallet percussion, and timpani) being employed.

Drum set solo sightreading will consist of the conventional use of the bass drum and hi-hat pedals plus notated parts involving left hand rhythms on the snare drum. In Classes B and A, combinations of snare drum and tom-tom rhythms will also be used. The rhythms may be syncopated in Class A only.

PERCUSSION ENSEMBLE EVENTS

Equipment

The type of snare drum to be used for ensembles in contests #520, #530, #540, and #561 is indicated on the music list. The concert drum is meant to be the size 8″ by 15″ or smaller. The parade drum is meant to be the size 10″ by 14″ or larger. Stick sizes 3A, 5A, and 1B are to be used with performances on the concert snare drum. Stick sizes 2B, 1S, 2S, and 3S are to be used with performances on the parade drum. The use of a sling for the parade drum is optional.

Two mallet melodic selections performed on the marimba in contests #521, #531, and #561, should be performed with soft rubber, medium-hard rubber, or hard rubber mallets or their equivalent. Two mallet marimba selections which are chiefly in block-chordal style, as well as three and four mallet marimba selections, should be performed with soft yarn, medium-hard yarn, hard yarn, or any of the various yarn mallets in any combination the contestants deem appropriate to the ensemble being performed. Any hard, commercially produced xylophone mallet is acceptable for use on the xylophone.

Generally, two mallet melodic selections performed on the vibraphone in contests #521, #531, and #561 should be performed with soft, medium, or hard cord-wound vibraphone mallets. Two mallet selections which are chiefly harmonic in style as well as three and four mallet selections should be performed with soft yarn marimba mallets, or soft to medium hard core-wound vibraphone mallets.

If orchestra bells are used, one of the following types of mallets should be used, depending upon the character of the selection: (1) brass mallets; (2) hard plastic mallets; (3) hard rubber marimba mallets; (4) wooden bell mallets.

Percussion Editor's Note: It is the editor's hope that in presenting this comprehensive report on one state's awareness of the need of modernization of percussion events at school contests that others will be inspired to re-evaluation. The governing principle, however, goes much deeper; we must train our percussionists to become conversant in playing all the instruments of percussion and provide them with the basic essentials of music theory so that they may continue in music as a profession if they so desire.

March 1967

Teaching Mallet Percussion

Bob Tilles

The percussion keyboard instruments have become increasingly popular and common in the past five years. More and more percussion music is being published each year featuring the marimba, vibes, xylophone, orchestra bells, and chimes. Contemporary composers and arrangers are utilizing the percussion keyboards in their writing and correspondingly the need for mallet players is increasing. New music for percussion ensembles is needed and the keyboards appear destined for more featured roles in the future.

The manufacturers of mallet instruments are struggling to produce enough keyboards to match the demand. In a recent interview, Mr. R. J. Richardson, president of Musser Marimbas, reported that they have recently built a new modern, enlarged factory. Despite modernization and increased production, the demand for instruments still exceeds the supply and there is a waiting period for new vibes and marimbas. Musical organizations, from the elementary school to the college level, are rehearsing more percussion ensembles each year and the demand for mallet players and instruments is increasing in direct proportion.

Unfortunately, there is a serious problem in percussion instruction and study. Specifically, mallet teachers are relatively scarce and in many areas adequate instructors are completely lacking. One of the reasons for this shortage is that while there has always been an abundance of drummers everywhere, there has also been a famine in mallet players. This shortage continues on with the teachers of the percussion instruments; we have many drum teachers and very few mallet teachers.

Another problem is that the aspiring mallet player usually comes from the snare drum ranks. Now, while a well trained drum student will have proper wrist and finger technique, he usually lacks a sound background in the fundamentals of music theory and harmony. This drum student may make the transition to a marimba or other keyboard from a technique standpoint, but his probable lack of theory or harmony presents a serious obstacle to beginning study on the keyboard. Since the keyboard percussionist requires training comparable to that of a pianist, our student must now acquaint himself with scales, chords, and harmony, as well as sight reading, solfege, etc.

If a percussion student cannot find a qualified mallet instructor in his home city, then he should consider the following alternatives: (1) Class or private study in harmony, theory, and music fundamentals; (2) Private study in piano; (3) Travel to another city for competent instruction in mallet playing, or piano, or harmony.

The student should definitely further his *musical* knowledge and master basic harmony principles. This is imperative to successful mallet playing.

Informed and interested groups, like the Percussive Arts Society*, are striving to upgrade the level of percussion instruction. Major percussion manufacturers spend considerable sums of money on clinics and free educational publications and service.

The Ludwig Drummer magazine, for example, enjoys a circulation of over 150,000 copies and contains expert percussion articles and studies. *The Instrumentalist* for over 20 years has included timely and informative articles on percussion. The Rogers, Slingerland, and Gretsch drum companies, in addition to Ludwig, sponsor many percussion clinics and offer free services to students. Each year there is some progress in expanding mallet education and the optimistic hope is to eventually have competent instructors located in every music center.

As to the specific study and practice habits relating to the keyboard

*Readers interested in joining the PAS can write to: Mr. Gordon Peters, School of Music, Northwestern University, Evanston, Illinois.

instruments, the following steps should be perfected:

The student should familiarize himself with the keyboard by playing chromatic scales. Care should be taken to avoid striking the bar over the nodes (drilled area) and good wrist action should be practiced.

The next step is playing major and minor scales in every key, to be followed by arpeggios using the major triad, the minor triad, and the dominant 7th chord. It is desirable to also practice the augmented 5th and diminished 7th chords.

When the scales and basic chords have been played in every major key, then the student should add four mallets to his study.

The beginner should practice four part harmony in prime (root) positions using basic chord voicings, and the intermediate student should practice inversions and simple chord alterations such as major 6th's, minor 7th's, etc.

At this stage of progress, the student can travel two different routes: (1) he can start on sight reading and eventual repertoire, or (2) he can continue along modern lines, playing tunes, improvising, etc. In either case, the ground work has been established and the student has a good background in scales, chords, and transposition.

Continuing on to advanced study the beginning mallet player should work on sightreading both classical and jazz studies, and should improve his chord voicings. He then should begin work on modern improvisation.

In teaching mallet players I have found a need for written material containing modern improvising and harmony as applied to the keyboards. To help alleviate this situation I have written a book for teaching mallet students and other instrumentalists. Its title is: *Practical Improvising* by Bob Tilles, edited by Sandy Feldstein and published by Henry Adler Music Company (1966).

This text is a modern harmony course containing both writing and playing exercises of scales, chords, and intervals. There are also examples of improvising exercises, chord and progression alterations and substitutions, introductions, turn arounds, modulations, blues, and other typical progressions, as well as other harmony exercises.

With both a classical and modern background, our mallet student should now be well prepared for any musical situation, whether it be concert band, symphony orchestra, percussion ensemble, or modern combo.

April 1967

Factors in Percussion Tone Quality

Mitchell Peters

Music being an aural art, it stands to reason that the quality of sound (tone quality) produced is of the utmost importance. Tone quality is a facet of playing that has long been stressed for woodwinds, brass, and string instruments; but in percussion technique and pedagogy it has been much neglected. Over the past years there has been an improvement in the conductor's and performer's concern for the quality of percussion performance and sound, but there is still a great deal of room for betterment.

Actually, the first step is the most important step: that of becoming aware that tone quality is as important to the percussionist as it is to the violinist, flutist, or any other instrumentalist. Due to the staccato quality of sound and the lack of definite pitch, in the case of most percussion instruments, many conductors and percussionists seem to forget—or perhaps never realized —that tone quality is very important to the percussionist. To play with a concept of tone is just as important as playing the correct rhythm. The conductor should speak to the percussion section about tone quality just as he does to the brass, string, or wind sections.

There are many factors that combine to affect the tone quality produced by percussion instruments. If any one factor is neglected, the optimum result cannot be achieved.

Quality of the Instrument

The importance of having good quality instruments cannot be overstressed. One will not get a high quality sound from a low quality instrument. A cheap single tension snare drum with bad snares will never sound like a double tension snare drum with good snares, no matter who plays it. A triangle with an inherently bad tone cannot be coaxed into producing a beautiful tone.

I've known many instances where band directors have spent great amounts purchasing good brass and wind instruments. Then, having spent the biggest part of their budget, they purchase cheaper quality percussion instruments. These same directors then wonder why their percussion section sounds bad. If one wants the best possible tone, one must use the best quality instruments.

Condition of the Instrument

Good instruments in bad condition will sound like bad instruments. A good set of timpani with bad heads will have a poor tone, just as a good snare drum with good heads, but with bad or poorly adjusted snares, will have a poor tone.

To get the best possible tone, all heads must be in good condition and be properly tensioned (evenly and with the ideal degree of overall tension), all moving parts must be well lubricated, and all internal screws should be tight to avoid rattles.

Not only must the instruments be in good condition, but so must the stands and holders. A good suspended cymbal sound can be ruined if a floor cymbal stand is being used and someone hasn't taken the care to insert a good piece of rubber tubing to keep the cymbal from vibrating against the metal of the stand.

Having your mallet instruments (bells, xylophone, etc.) in tune is another important point to consider. They do get out of tune; and, when they are out of tune, obviously they will not sound good. Perhaps you didn't realize that they can be retuned? Well, they can, and it makes a big difference in the sound. (The bars need only be gathered, properly packed and insured, and shipped to the manufacturer, stipulating what master pitch you desire, e.g. A = 440, A = 441, A = 442.)

These things may all sound obvious, but have you checked over the condition of your instruments lately? Keeping your percussion instruments in good condition is essential to good tone production.

Tone Color of the Instrument

To the percussionist, tone quality also refers to the color of sound that is produced by a particular instrument. For example, the color of sound produced from two triangles, which are both good triangles, can be very different. One may have a bright, small tone, the other a darker, fuller tone. In a particular musical passage the small triangle would provide a better tone quality; in another musical passage, the larger triangle may work better.

A 5″ x 14″ snare drum with wire snares will have a different color than a 6½″ x 14″ snare drum with gut snares. Both are good instruments, yet with a completely different tone color. Each drum in its proper musical environment would provide the appropriate tone color; e.g., the 5″ x 14″ wire snare drum in a lighter piece, the 6½″ x 14″ gut snare drum in a heavier or military type composition.

A common error is for a conductor to tell the cymbal player to play "louder" and "bigger" to get more sound. If the player is using a pair of 16″ cymbals to achieve the sound that the conductor is after, he cannot fulfill the conductor's wishes; larger cymbals would be required. Yet, for many other passages, the 16″ cymbals would provide the best tone color.

The well-equipped percussionist or percussion section must have more than just one of each instrument at hand in order to convey a refined sense of tone coloring, and this is one of the important functions of percussion in orchestral and band literature. There are different tambourines with different jingles, different sizes and weights of cymbals, different sizes and sounding triangles, different sounding wood blocks, etc. The more good, quality instruments with varying timbre that are available, the better the percussionist will be able to provide the best tone coloring. Again, to reiterate, one good quality instrument would still be better than three bad ones.

Quality and Type of Stick

Have you ever seen a high school band with a new set of timpani with good heads that are well adjusted; and then the timpanist proceeds to play with a set of "fluffy baseball bats." A good set of timpani with good heads will have a bad tone if poor sticks are used.

In most percussion instruments the vibrating body is set in motion by means of a stick or mallet, so it stands to reason that the selection of a good stick will be very important in the production of good tone.

The type of stick will also play an important part in the color of sound produced. For example, a suspended cymbal can be played with a wooden stick, a metal stick, a soft felt stick, or a hard felt stick, only to name the more common possibilities. There are endless possibilities of timbre that can be achieved by the use of different type sticks. The well-equipped percussionist has a great many different types of stocks and mallets available that will enable him to provide the many shades of tone and color he is called on to produce.

The Manner in Which the Instrument Is Struck

How the instrument is struck is also a very important factor in tone production. The development of a musical sounding stroke is imperative to the development of good tone quality.

For a basic approach to the best means of striking percussion instruments, much can be learned by studying the hammer action inside the piano. As one presses the key, the hammer strikes the string and immediately pulls back to its original position. This idea of pulling the stroke out rather than pushing or digging in is perhaps the most important fundamental idea in striking (articulating) percussion instruments. This method will enable the player to get the clearest, most distinct sound.

By making alterations in grip and strokes it is possible to get different quality sounds. By using a firmer hand grip one will get a more staccato and less resonant sound out of the instrument. A more legato sound can be achieved with a more relaxed grip. This is particularly true on instruments that have resonance such as timpani, cymbals, and bells. A sharper sound can be achieved by using more wrist snap as the stick is being drawn away from the instrument.

When one gets involved in the field of tone and color, there is a significant factor of personal taste involved. In many cases it is impossible to dictate what is right or wrong. The important point is for the individual to be aware of tone and color and to perform with as much regard for the proper timbre as for the right rhythm. Each player should constantly be asking himself, "How does it sound?"

It is only when the percussionist develops a feel and awareness for percussion tone (through listening and concentration) that he becomes a fine percussionist.

More Latin Rhythms: Samba, Baion, Bossa Nova

Thomas Brown

The popular Latin-American Rhumbas, Sambas, Boleros, even Bossa Novas may easily be augmented by the knowlegeable director with rich and colorful percussive effects not designated by the composer. Parts written for an average of three or four percussionists could attractively be transformed into an authentic Latin-American percussion sound by using three or four more players in the section.

The "Rhumba," most familiar of the Latin-American dances, is most easily augmented with claves, cowbell, maracas, guiro, bongo drums, Conga drum, and timbales (or snare drum with snares off as a substitute). This was discussed in The *Instrumentalist,* October, 1964. The less familiar dances, however, are those "in two," also very important though seldom properly augmented with the correct Latin rhythm instruments. Familiarity with the Latin rhythms and instruments may prove to be the deciding factor in creating the authentic and exciting element—often the final touch so important in Latin arrangements.

Samba

The most popular dance with the feeling of duple meter is the Samba. This Brazilian national dance was first introduced in New York City during the late 30's and soon this shuffling step became the most popular. First used as a carnival dance, the typical Samba is usually written in the major key with the melodies strongly influenced by the Portuguese.

The rural dances are fast and furious while the city styles, such as the "Samba Carioca," popular in Rio de Janiero, are slower and more sophisticated. Countless variations to the Samba depend on the area of the country in which it is played.

The rhythms and instruments are basically African in origin. Instruments used in the Samba are cowbell, chocallo, guiro, Conga drum, timbale, cabaza, and tambourine.

Cowbell

The cowbell lends a very strong element to the percussion section if percussion is being featured. In the Samba it is actually a substitute for the "adja," a conic metal bell, or an iron slab called the Agogo. The bell should be held in the left hand with the open end facing away from the performer. It is struck near the open end and in the middle of the flat surface to produce a low and high pitch variance. The cowbell should not be used on the slower, more melodious compositions.

The rhythm is free flowing and light:

Example 1

o o x x   o o x x

Example 2

o o o   x x o

o = open end (lower pitch)
x = flat surface near closed end (higher pitch)

Chocallo

The chocallo's role in the Samba is very similar to the role the maracas play in the Rhumba. Since maracas are not used in the Samba, this metallic cylinder, filled with beads, seeds, pebbles, or shot, adds a most important shuffling sound to the dance rhythm which in itself is a shuffle.

The tube is about 12″ to 15″ in length, sealed at both ends, and produces a crisp yet hollow swish. It is held firmly, with one hand at each end, and shaken up and down; this action causes the beads to strike the top and bottom of the chamber. Both the forearm and wrist should be used, forcing the beads to fall in a uniform manner. The rhythm is:

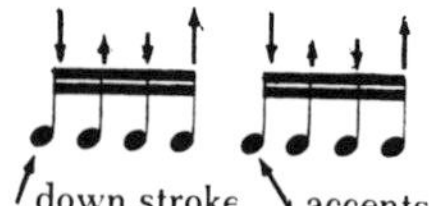

A strong, firm stroke is used on the heavy down stroke arrows. By stressing the second beat an added lilt or swing will be produced, so essential to this dance.

A substitution may be made for the chocallo by using two maracas held in one hand, handles parallel and the gourds extended from each side of the hand. Although the maracas' sound is higher in pitch, the basic shuffle rhythm is simulated.

The Kameso, a wood shaker, originally called "Amele" in Brazil where it originated, may be even more effective as a chocallo substitute since it produces a louder and more rolling sound. Its shape is similar to the chocallo and it is played in the same manner.

Guiro

The shuffling scrape of the guiro, rasper, or guachara, is a natural addition to the full rhythm section and could utilize the same rhythm as the cowbell. Do not attempt to utilize the full scraping surface on fast tempos. The guiro should be played with careful attention to balance since it must fit dynamically into the entire percussion sound. To help *blend* with the other rhythm instruments, the following playing elements must be observed: (1) the material of your guiro (the cow or goat horns are higher pitched than the wooden or dried vegetable shells), (2) size of the guiro, (3) the size of the scraper in relation to the width of the etched corrugated surface, (4) pressure of the scrape, and (5) speed of the scrape. The rhythm may be:

Conga Drum

The Conga drum assumes the same role in the Samba as in the Rhumba—the bass sound of the drum family. Producing a simple, uncluttered rhythm, the Conga drum adds a strong accent to the beat. Because it is the low voice playing the basic beat, it would be wise to deviate very little from the initial rhythm.

(1) R L R R L R

(2) R L R L R L R L

(3) R L R L R L R L

o = open head slap

[second beat of the measure (in two) receives the accent on the open head slap]

Remember the Conga drum, although not tuned to a specific pitch, should be tuned lower in pitch than the larger timbale head. Two strokes are used: (1) the press stroke where the hand remains on the head for a muffled sound, and (2) the open head tone, allowing the head to vibrate freely after striking it with a sharp wrist snap.

The fingers of the left hand are raised and lowered for a strike while the base of the thumb remains on the head. The right hand slaps near the rim for a strong, crisp snap. This technique could be applied to all notes except the all important second beat of the measure which requires an open head slap for a lower and more resonant sound.

Snare Drum

This instrument adds a busy and involved shuffling sound, complete with varied muffled drum tones, by using a brush in the left hand and a stick in the right. The Samba sounds involved and complicated due to countless variations. However, once the simple basic technique is learned, the variations will fall into place with ease.

Basic beat:

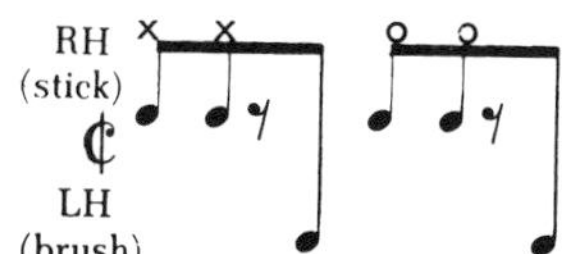

x = near rim or slight rim shot

o = near center of head

The brush is held with the right hand in a basic snare grip (between thumb and first finger) except the hand is face down on the head and the fingers are resting over the brush. The wrist motion is directly up and down, producing a muffled effect.

The right hand interchanges between the rim, or edge of the drum head, to the head center. Notice how the open head tone, produced by playing near the center, is on the second beat, similar to the Conga drum.

Other variations are:

RH

LH

RH

LH

The freedom in the Samba will allow for variations in head pitch and rhythm. The rim may be hit or missed without hurting the feeling of abandon and freedom.

Cabaza

Another final touch and one step closer to the true Samba feel is the use of a cabaza.

This least familiar of all the Brazilian instruments is a large, naturally round gourd with a handle placed at the tapered base. It is like a giant maraca, only with the beads outside instead of inside, enveloping the surface loosely in a thin, net-like fashion. The sound is produced by striking the surface with open palm, then slapping it with the fingers of the same hand. The cabaza is then turned rapidly from side to side with the left hand, causing the beads to scrape effectively over the surface.

The four varied movements are utilized in the following rhythm pattern:

palm fingers surface scrape

Claves and bongos are not used in the Samba. Bongos maybe substituted for Conga drum, much the same as maracas can similate a chocallo sound.

A tambourine may be added for still more color. The tambourine is played by placing the hand on the head and using the fingers near the rim to get the jingles to sound on this basic rhythm:

(1)

or (2)

or (3)

Remember, after combining all the instruments, there may be a tendency to rush the beat. The two beats per measure must have a relaxed feeling. Each instrument should keep a steady tempo within an even balance and provide an accent on the second beat of each measure.

Baion

The Baion rhythm is very closely related to the Samba and is varied only in a more staccato playing of the rhythms. Of the various rhythm examples for each instrument, pick the rhythm more closely related to:

The Baion melody is often smoother in style, while the Samba is more staccato in character. The staccato playing of the rhythms will be a contrast to the smooth melody.

Bossa Nova

The most recent arrival on the Latin-American scene is the Bossa Nova. It was first believed to be conceived in 1953 as a jazz form of the Samba. Since the Samba did not contain as many syncopations as the Cuban dances, the Bossa Nova was the answer to the needs of Brazilian jazz. The instruments are more delicate and subdued in effect, quite similar to the Samba shuffle beat.

There are three basic elements in the complete Bossa Nova beat.

Rhythm 1

Brushes on snare drum head playing single stroke taps
Brushes swishing sideways for softer legato effect
Brushes on cymbal for soft effect
Stick on cymbal or hi-hat for louder effect
Sandpaper blocks
Chocallo or cabaza
Tambourine for jingle effect
Guiro for broader, legato sound
Maracas
Triangle held with cord, allowing fingers to stop the ring for all staccato notes:

Rhythm 2

(Triplet feel may also be used)

Snare drum with hand holding stick while resting flat on snare drum head, palm down, with butt of stick overlapping rim for a muffled rim-"pop" sound
Wood block for higher click sound
Temple block for lower pitched sound
Claves
Cowbell (well muffled) played with a soft rubber, cord, or yarn-wound mallet

Variations are limitless depending upon the melodic and accompanying rhythms.

Rhythm 3

(1) (2)

Conga drum
Bongo drum
Timbales
Tom Tom
(String bass also plays this rhythm)

Keep the beat simple. The suggested instruments are not to be played simultaneously. Proper selection of the above listed percussion instruments for each rhythm is essential depending upon the dynamics, character of the selection, and size of the organization. Other percussion instruments can also be used as substitues. Many a ballad style band composition might easily be transferred into a Bossa Nova as a different approach to a familiar arrangement.

Band, orchestra, and stage band arrangements can be transformed from average to exciting by means of the proper selection of instruments and good balance of an augmented Latin percussion section. This transformation requires extra thought, effort, and practice, as well as tasteful handling, but the result enhances the color of the entire musical picture. In his concern about intonation, balance, section entrances, and solo passages, the director can easily overlook his percussion section. Once the *full* Latin-American rhythm section is utilized, though, its absence and potential will never again go unnoticed!

June 1967

Camp Duty

Lewis Harlow

The date was May 30, 1892. The place was the historic Boston Common. The occasion was a Memorial Day parade, and the Common was well populated by paraders and their music escorts who had fallen out at the end of a long and hot march. My father, 19 years old at the time and teacher-leader-principal-drummer of the Silver Fife & Drum Corps, was sitting on his drum under an elm tree. The S. F. & D. C. had played another job for pay. There was always a pay job for the Grand Army of the Republic on Memorial Day.

A veteran slumped to the ground: maybe heat prostration, maybe a heart attack. My father observed, jumped up, hooked on his drum, and played "Surgeon's Call."

The elapsed time of playing would have been about 32 seconds, because my father was a purist in matters like repeat marks. By the time "Surgeon's Call" was completed, there were three doctors attending the stricken veteran. It is noteworthy that even in 1892 three doctors would have identified the drum call for their services.

The first formal battle of the American Revolution was begun by a dummer, William Dinman. Aided by a fifer unidentified in history, he sounded the call "To Arms" and the fight was on. The British of course heard the call, and knew exactly what it meant because they had been using the same drum and fife signalling system for their own infantry and artillery movements since the days of Shakespeare and good Queen Bess. Back of this, history is not too clear, though there is an occasional reference to the drums and fifes of the Swiss. Drums alone were used to command the foot soldiers on the crusades of the Middle Ages. Bugles, trumpets, and horns existed through the whole period, but because of their portability, they were reserved for the more aristocratic signalling of the cavalry.

In America at least, the technical and artistic detail of drumming and fifing was passed down from generation to generation by word of mouth until the 1830's. Then Ashworth's *Rudimentary School* appeared. This is a work long out of print which would have been irrevocably lost except for the fact that the two great drum authorities of the 1860's each acknowledged their debt to Ashworth and claimed to have copied his earlier work exactly. This claim is not quite valid, since their publications, rare but still existant, are not quite identical.

The Drummers' and Fifers' Guide by George B. Bruce (drummer) and Dan D. Emmett (fifer) was first published by Firth, Pond & Co. in 1862, and republished in 1885. Mr. Bruce lists his qualifications as Drum Major and Principal Instructor of the Drum and Fife at the School of Practice on Bedloe's and Governor's Islands, where his success won for him the approbation of Lieutenant General Scott, General Wood, Adjutant Generals Jones and Thomas, and other officers of rank. He also states that his long acquaintance with the leading fifers in the United States enables him to avail himself of their experience, and he is specially fortunate in securing the aid of Mr. Dan D. Emmett, late principal fifer in the 6th U.S. Infantry, whose name is a sufficient guarantee for the correctness of the fife department of this work.

The parallel authority is Strube's *Drum and Fife Instructor*, published in 1869-1870 by Gardiner A. Strube, Drum Major 12th Infantry, N. G. S. N. Y., formerly drummer in Company A, 5th Regiment N. Y. V. Durea's Zouaves. To add even more authenticity, this work was commissioned by the federal government, to be published privately and distributed by the War Department to those studying and playing drum and fife for the U. S. Army. As a result, the Strube book did not enjoy the wide circulation of the commercially-published Bruce & Emmett book. In 1925, there were estimated to be only four copies of the Strube book still in existance. (This did not include a copy owned by my father, and if the person who borrowed my father's Strube book happens to read this, no questions will be asked if he chooses to return it.)

The Strube and the Bruce & Emmett manuals both begin with the classic 25 rudiments of snare drum playing. Both also include the *Camp Duty*, the official drum and fife music used by the U.S. Army for signalling, ceremony, and prescribed parading. Beyond these points in common, the books go their separate ways into non-official quicksteps and such dance music as can appropriately be rendered by drum and fife.

Here are the rudiments, in the order of the Strube presentation. You may want to compare the list with what you find in drum manuals of more recent times:

The long roll; the 5, 7, 9, 10, 11, 13, and 15-stroke rolls; and flam; the ruff; the single and double drags; the single, double, and triple ratamacues; the flam accent; the flamacue; the flam tap; the single and double paradiddles; the flam paradiddle; the flam paradiddle-diddle; the drag paradiddle number 1; the drag paradiddle number 2; the quick Scotch.

Contemporary drum methods usually include a 26th rudiment, the single-stroke or timpani-type roll. There could also be, of course, an infinite number of rhythmic variants of the basic 25, but this gets out of the rudiment category and into rhythmic variety for its own sake. The traditional rudiments cover as much technique as can be applied to the head of a snare drum by a drummer equipped with two hands and a stick in each.

Here is the start of *Camp Duty* as presented by Bruce & Emmett. It is far more than the succession of fast 2/4 and 6/8 quicksteps usually associated with drum and fife. There is some 3/4, and much of the 2/4 is paced from 60 to 90 steps to the minute—each piece at the tempo that will strain the virtuosity of the drummer to its limit.

Reveille begins with "Three Caps" or "Points of War." Then the "Slow Scotch," then the "Austrian," then the "Hessian," then the "Prussian," then the "Dutch" (in 3/4 time), and finally the "Quick Scotch." These pieces are separated from one another by prescribed rolls and pauses.

Fatigue is a single piece, the "Pioneer's Call." For routine fatigue duty, it is played by drums alone, but when used to drum disorderly women out of camp, fifes are added

Fifteeen minutes before breakfast, the "Drummer's Call" is beaten at the guard house, and this is followed by the "Breakfast Call" or "Peas Upon a Trencher" with fifes.

And so on and on through the day until the time for *Tattoo*, prescribed at 9:00 P.M. Tattoo begins with the "Doublings," then the quickstep "New Tatter Jack," "Doubling," "Slow Tattoo March," "Doubling," "Downfall of Paris," "Doublings," "My Lodging's on the Cold Ground," "Doublings," "Troop" or "Trust to Luck," "Doublings," "Tattoo Quickstep," "Three Cheers," "Doubling," then a pause of 15 minutes, and finally "Taps,"—literally three taps on the drum as the signal for putting out lights.

The irregular duties of wartime demand signalling rather than ceremonial from drum and fife. There are specific calls for all personnel above the rank of Private, and there are obviously useful calls like "Advance," "Retreat," "Halt," "Double Quick," "Commence Firing," "Cease Firing," and "Parley with the Enemy." ("Parley" is also used as "Church Call.") Personnel calls are usually for drum and fife while the calls for military action are for drums alone.

The authoritative Bruce & Emmett differs from the authoritative Strube in three ways.

1. Dan Emmett's fife parts tend occasionally toward the florid and ornamental. Both Emmett and Strube acknowledge Ashworth as their source, and as no one seems to have seen Ashworth recently, you will have to decide the right and wrong of this for yourself.

2. The drum parts of Bruce and Strube are surprisingly alike, or rather they *can be played* surprisingly alike. In the very few points of actual difference, the Strube version demands a slightly greater degree of virtuosity. Again the decision of authenticity must be yours.

3. There is major difference in the manner of putting the drum music on paper. In the rudiments, both authorities hold to the unconfusable practice of stemming left-hand notes upward and right-hand downward. Strube continues this practice throughout his book, but Bruce, in the *Camp Duty* and the miscellaneous quicksteps which follow, stems all grace notes and other ornamentation upward and all "big" notes downward.

Bruce's apparent disregard for niceties of left and right stroking is not as completely confusing as it may seem. Just as the first violins in a symphony orchestra will for the most part bow alike by taste, logic, and tradition, so a group of schooled drummers will distinguish similarly between right and left by the same imponderables of musicianship. There are exceptions, though, in both groups. Occasionally the concertmaster must settle a bowing argument, and occasionally the drummers are confronted by, say, a group of four unadorned notes to the marching beat. Should they be played hand to hand or should they be played as a paradiddle? Only reference to Strube will solve this—or at least reference to someone who remembers how Strube had written it.

After Bruce and Strube, the military history of drum and fife begins to eclipse. For ceremony and orderly troop movement, the band comes into its own, and for signalling, the bugle takes over most of the infantry duty. A few drummer's calls still persist—if there is a band present with a drummer qualified in the skills and repertoire.

Outside the military, though, a phenomenon was taking place. Civilian drummers discovered the smouldering torch by the side of the road, picked it up, and nursed its flame back to brightness. A precious art form was saved from extinction, not so much by intent as by the instinct that makes any good musician respect and want to perpetuate anything and everything that is good about music.

At first, there were living authorities who had played or at least heard the military drumming of the 1860's. A century has now passed, though. The line of music heredity fades badly at the grandson level, and suddenly there exists an all-new generation of musicians who again owe everything to teachers, books, and curiosity.

Here is the kind of thing that is going on today. A surgeon, a postal inspector, and a jazz drummer get together, on the first Wednesday evening of every month to play through, severally and collectively, the *Camp Duty*. Might this be called a jam session? Anything but! These men have no specific name for their objective, but subconsciously it is a shared craving for orderly perfection

On one of their Wednesday evenings, they are joined by a stranger, who somehow has heard of them and who has come, say, a thousand miles to sit in. He is welcomed, there are introductions all round, and then a general unlimbering of drums. For warm up, each man plays the "Three Caps" solo.

The surgeon, the postal inspector and the jazz drummer listen very intently to the stranger's "Second Camp." The explosive taps which finish his ten-stroke rolls are right. This man has proved himself, and there is no need for explanation of ground rules or other delay. *Camp Duty* begins.

Four left sticks come up in unison, and four rights. There is no leader and there are no followers. No group of Rockettes ever performed with greater precision or negotiated an evolution of greater complexity. Occasionally there is a mistake, discovered and acknowledged by its perpetrator, and a repeat of something extremely well done for the sheer joy of repeating.

When "Dinner Call" or "Roast Beef" is reached, the stranger is asked to take it alone. He understands why, and takes it alone. The double drags in "Dinner Call" permit two interpretations, neither of which (like the rhythm of the Viennese waltz) can be indicated accurately on paper with conventional music notation. The trio joins in on the repeat, using the stranger's interpretation, which may or may not have been their own. This is the kind of *esprit* and mutual respect which a get-together for *Camp Duty* inspires.

Suppose you are not a drummer and that you have never heard *Camp Duty* performed. (For greatest impact, you should hear it taken "solo.") Your first impression of its more complex beats is that you are listening to two drums, one a background drum that seems to be supplying a more or less continuous roll, the other a rhythm drum generating a pattern fantastically fast and complex. Then you realize that all this is coming from one drum, and respect is born.

Camp Duty is not for utilitarian marching service in the football stadium where the band must be brought on, moved in evolution, and removed in the limited span allotted to the halftime spectacle. As previously mentioned, most elements of *Camp Duty* which could be marched to if played faster can't be played faster because of many-too-many notes to the beat. The modern simpler drum beats are the only possible answer, and there is no quarrel with their effectiveness at the speed at which they must be played. Selected bits of *Camp Duty* could be used, though, for entertainment value, and if the inspired creators of halftime programs think well of the idea, they can take it from here.

In this and any other generation, a fair percentage of those who drum is hardly more than along for the ride. The principal reason for lack of technique is that elementary tone production on the drum is too easy. The beginning drummer knows none of the physical pain of learning to blow a trumpet and none of the awkward frustration of applying the left hand to the violin. There is no reason for the beginning drummer to respect technique, his own or any other. If he graduates to combos or the like, his group will often be as undisciplined as he is, and he can just enjoy himself with the little he knows. The cymbals and other accessories keep him from getting bored with his ignorance. If he has been lucky enough in school to have played under an inspired leader, he will have acquired a degree of musicianship (not to be confused with technique). If this inspired leader develops in this drummer a potential of musicianship that is above average, the pupil can go all the way to a lesser symphony orchestra with hardly more rudimental technique than a good tight roll.

This beginner should not be blamed severely. In the ordinary course of music, there is very little incentive to practice drumming, and there is very little drum music to be practiced that offers (1) complete frustration at the start, (2) evidence of some accomplishment after a lot of hard work, and (3) eventual recognizable triumph.

Camp Duty, quite alone in available drum music, satisfies all three of these conditions. It is frightfully difficult. It is all so logical and right that the learner is aware of and inspired by every step in his progress. And once attained, the reward is the respect of people who really know rudimental drumming—as well as his own self-respect.

Camp Duty is by no means out of print. Several good drum methods include it, usually as the final lesson in the book. Wherever you find it, it will be presented with fair authenticity, but you should shop around for an edition that employs maximum symbolism to distinguish right from left. Once learned with fair proficiency, it is then worth while to consult the venerable Bruce & Emmett, and possibly even the Strube, in the rare book archives of a good library. A single glance will probably clear up any uncertainty.

September 1967

Marching Band Percussion

James Salmon

Most marching band, gridiron shows, are basically theatrical in nature and might best be treated as such in their preparation and presentation. The melodic and rhythmic lines of the music must be clearly defined, steadily played, strongly projected, and appropriate to the theme and action of the show.

The percussion section can contribute most effectively in the development of this solidity, style, and stabilization of the music if it will *develop* and *wisely use* a variety of practical rhythmic patterns designed to fit the many styles and moods of music used in the shows.

The drummers in our Michigan Marching Band follow such procedures, and in doing so they are only following routines that have been successfully initiated and used through the years by most professional show drummers. This system, when it is used carefully, will allow any percussion section to maintain more clearly defined rhythmic lines, keep a steadier tempo, and give greater support to the melodic lines of the music, without becoming so involved as to cause the section to "lose the beat," or confuse the ensemble.

Basically, all of our drummers in the Michigan Band are rudimentally oriented in their snare drumming performance techniques, and they usually have had some combo, or stage band experience

EX. I "Song of India," rhythm style

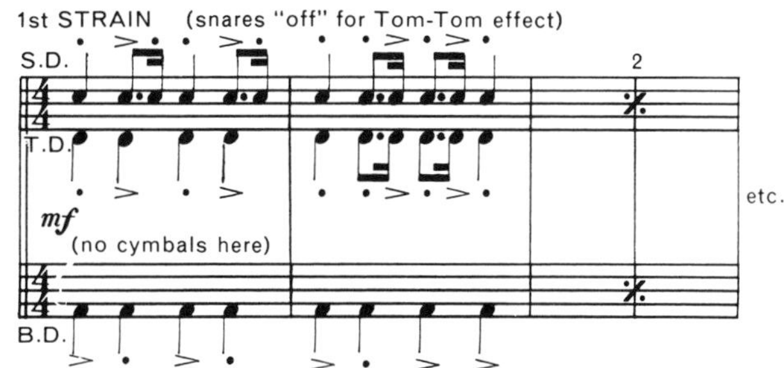

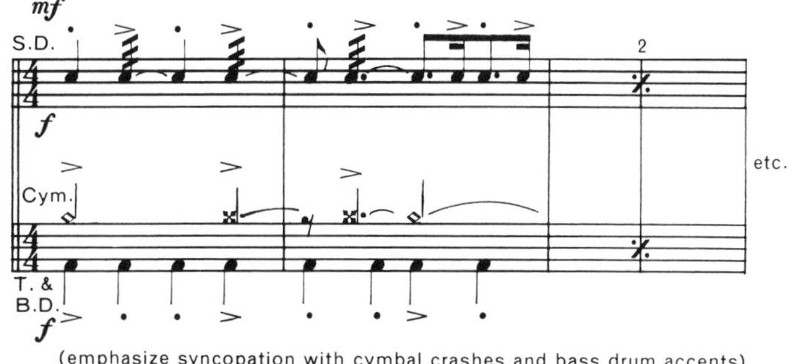

EX. II "String of Pearls," rhythm style

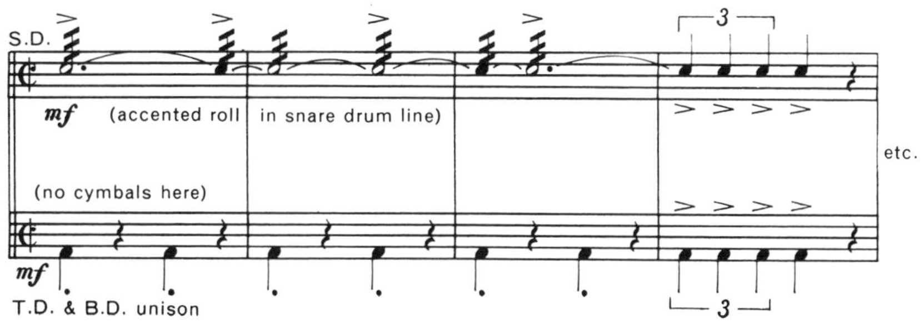

EX. III "Bugle Call Rag," rhythm style

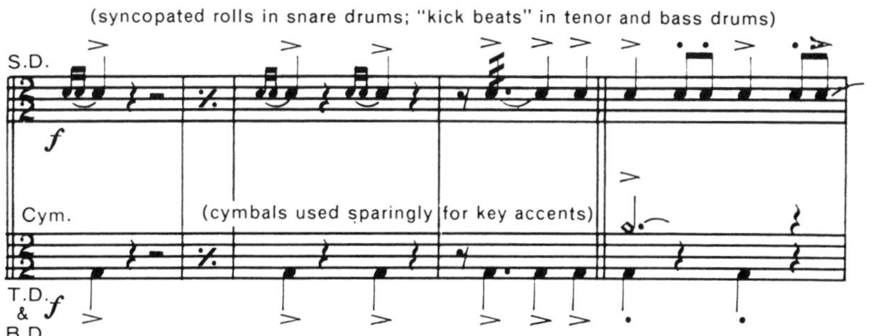

during their high school years. This means that they can read their part and make it come out, even with the brass licks and riffs in our arrangements. The primary consideration here is to let the concept of musical style predominate throughout the interpretation of the percussion parts of our arrangements.

The following examples of percussion notation will show how some of our field routines are scored:

A rule of thumb in the use of *flams* and *ruffs** in this type of music can be set up as follows:

a. Use them in loud passages.

b. Don't use them in soft passages.

c. Flams and ruffs are thickening devices for the snare drummer and can "muddy-up" a rhythmic line quickly if they are not used carefully.

d. Single notes correctly played and spaced properly, plus careful attention to accents and "kick beats," will help the marching band more than any other technique.

Fill-ins For Standard Arrangements:

When music is of the "up-tempo" speed it is more practical for the field drummers to omit rolls, excepting the last measure of the arrangement, or last ending of a strain, with a fermata.

Use of Rolls in Music

All rolls will usually be played more rhythmically and sound fuller if they are conceived and played from measured patterns, rather than by strokes alone. A suggested rule of thumb is as follows: 1. Use open stroke rolls in loud dynamics; 2. Use closed rolls in softer dynamics; 3. Use hand-to-hand rhythmical patterns that fit the tempo and meter signature of the music. See Example VII.

Try using the triplet roll when performing The Star Spangled Banner. Use heavy sticks and play open style. Don't crush the blows of each stick against the drum head; keep a steady hand-to-hand triplet feeling throughout. See Example VIII.

**Editorial Footnote: Snare drum embellishments were originally conceived for marching at much slower tempi than are usually used on the gridiron today.*

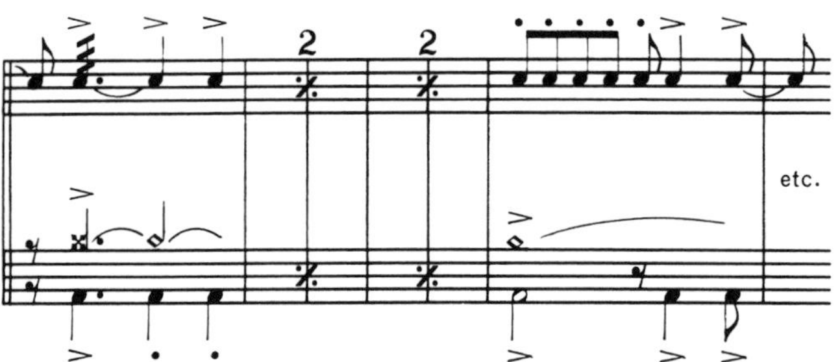

EX. IV "Sing, Sing, Sing," rhythm style

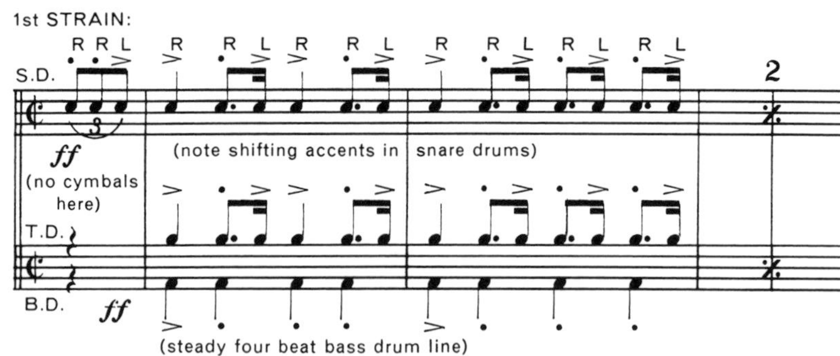

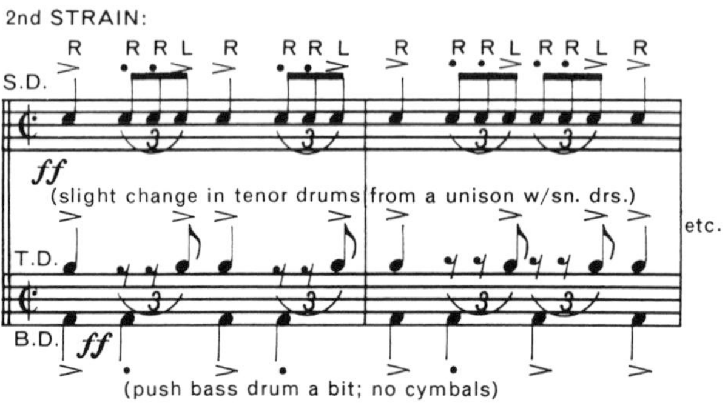

EX. V "Temptation," rhythm style

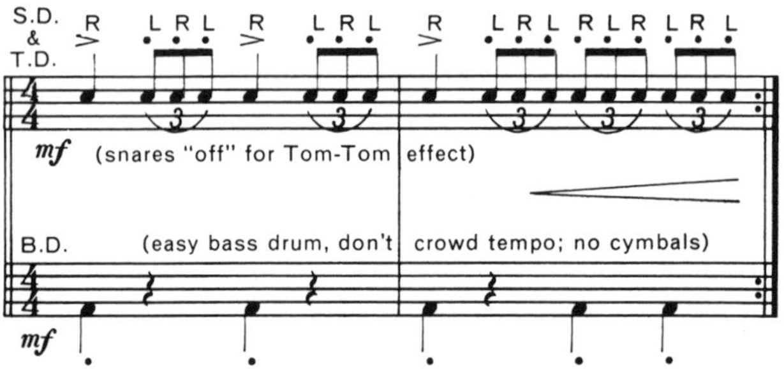

EX. VI

EX. VI A "Fill-In's"

Very Fast Tempo (no rolls)

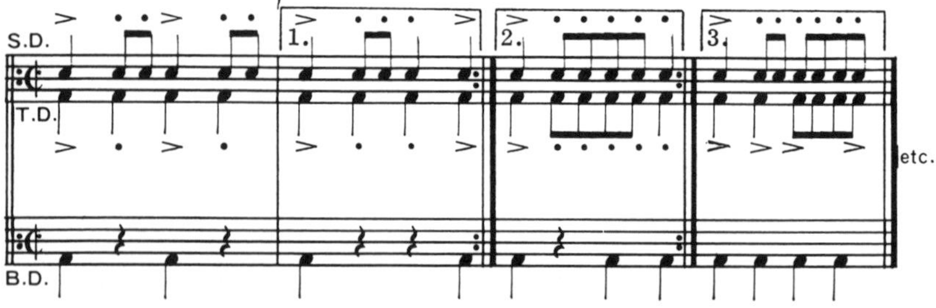

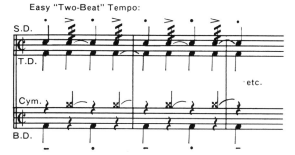

EX. VI B

EX. VI C

EX. VI D **EX. VI D.D.**

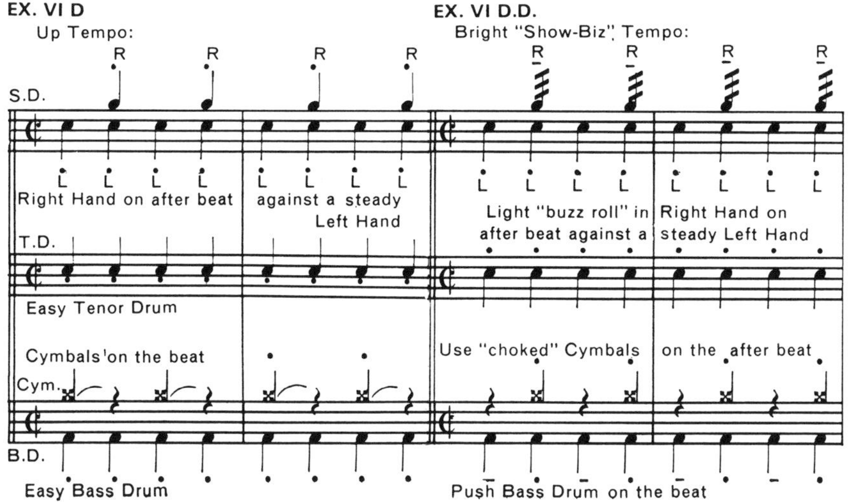

EX. VII Measured Rolls

Written notation:

EX. VII-A
(Moderato Tempo)

EX. VII-B
(Slower Tempo)

EX. VII-C
(Brisk March Tempo)

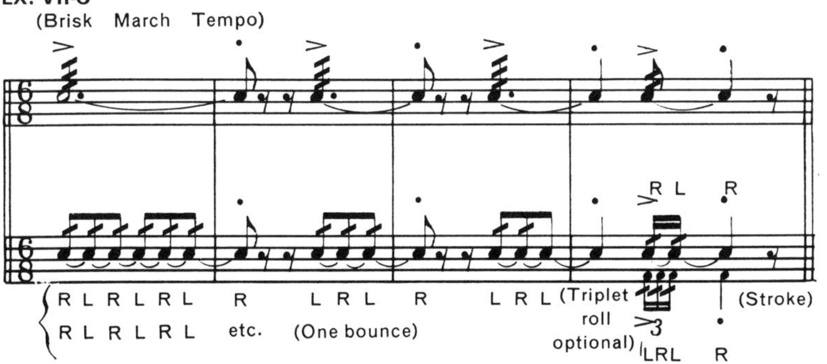

Some Suggestions For Marching Cadences and Street Beats

Examples based upon three standard rudiments of drumming; A. *The single drag*; B. *The double drag:* and C. *The ratamacue.* See Example IX. (Pages 107, 108.)

The sticking is a *constant factor* in rudimental snare drum performance techniques, while the notation *can be the variable factor*; therefore, it is possible to use the traditional rudimental sticking on other than the traditional 2/4, and 6/8 meter signatures in use in the older military music styles. See Example X. (Page 109.)

Miscellaneous Suggestions

To get a solid sounding drum section, the following should be meticulously observed by every drummer in the rank:

a. All *field drums* should be tensioned alike so that the entire line of drums sounds like one drum. Each drum must match the other drums through proper head tension and snare adjustment.

b. All *tenor drums* should be tensioned alike; and for better use in the line, they should carry a pitch that is about half way between that of the field drums and the bass drum(s). If your tenor drummers play them in a vertical-held style (like bass drums), make certain that *both* heads carry the same pitch-sound, otherwise all of their playing will not have a solid quality.

c. Most marching bands use the smaller depth bass drums; this is more practical for the player, as it allows more freedom of movement throughout all field maneuvers on the gridiron. Be sure that *both bass drum heads* are *tensioned* to sound *alike* when both heads are to be played upon by the drummer.

When more than one bass drum is to be used in the band, make certain they all sound alike (for obvious reasons).

d. All the players on one particular instrument should use the *same model of drum sticks* (i.e. field drummers, tenor drummers, and bass drummers).

e. All drummers should *memorize all music* used, and *employ the same sticking* throughout all selections played during the entire marching band season.

f. All performances, rehearsals, and supervision of the percussion rank should be under the direction of a *selected section leader;* he is responsible to the band director(s) for the performance of his line at all times.

g. All percussion equipment should be in the *best of operational condition for every performance.* This means cymbals polished brightly (inside, and out); batter heads on all drums free of dirt, smudges, etc.; drum slings freshly laundered; all drum shells polished and as free of surface scratches as possible; decent looking drum sticks and mallets throughout the complete rank.

h. *Proper storage cases should be available to house all equipment safely when not in use,* or when the band may be on tour.

Percussion sectional rehearsals are very important at Michigan, as they help to decrease lost time in full ensemble practice, when some players may not have their music in the proper degree of performing readiness. To ease this problem a bit, our drummers normally arrive *one hour before* the scheduled band rehearsal time so

EX. VIII National Anthem

The use of the triplet roll for long passages can be very useful when adapted to a National Anthem, or song of similar type, such as the Alma Mater of any school.

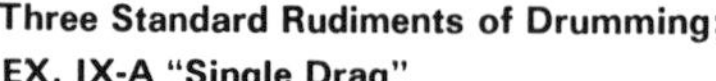
Three Standard Rudiments of Drumming;
EX. IX-A "Single Drag"

EX. IX-B "Double Drag"

EX. IX-C "Ratamacue"

Variations on the Three Standard Rudiments per EX. IX-A-B-C (above)
EX. IX-AA Using "Single Drag" Sticking

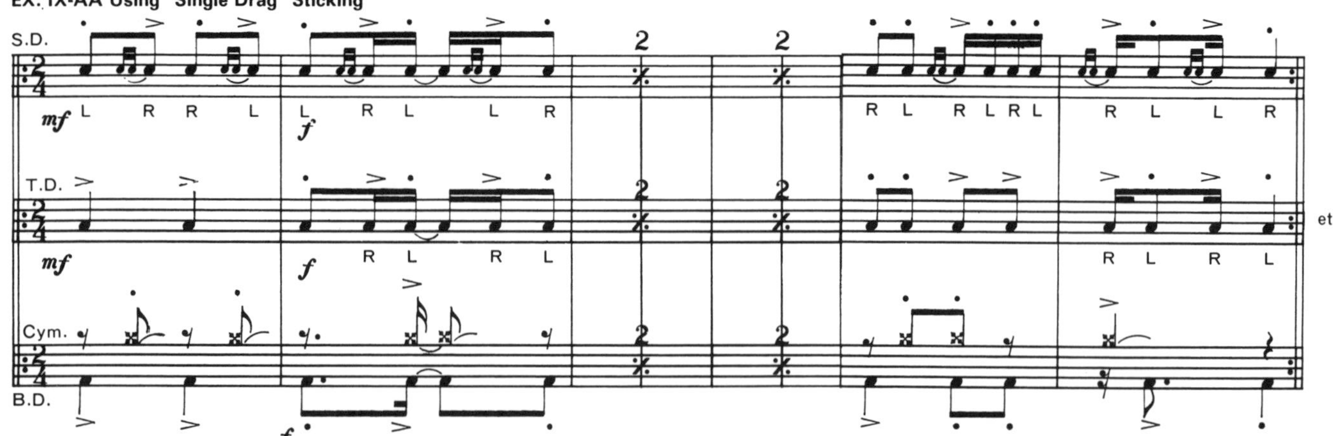

EX. IX-BB Using "Double Drag" Sticking

that they can be better prepared to work with the whole band at regular rehearsal hours. This rehearsal is under the direction of the section leader, who methodically checks on: (1) all cadences to be used, (2) the music for the current week's show, (3) all sticking and rolling patterns to be used in all music, (4) care and upkeep of all equipment, and (5) any individual problems that may come up, especially among the newer members of the section.

Generally speaking, the percussion rank usually has their music memorized by the Wednesday before each game. This includes the alternate members of the rank also. Since it is next to impossible to use any kind of a music folder on the field during a performance, this has to be a very rigid requirement within the rank—it is merely self-preservation!

I have presented some ideas, performance practices, and related suggestions as to how our percussion problems are handled within our marching band at Michigan. I hope that this material will be of interest and value to you in your situation.

EX. IX-CC Using "Ratamacue" Sticking

EX. X-A Standard 6/8 Marching Cadence

(Standard printed notation for percussion music).

EX. X-B Suggested Variation on the 6/8 Cadence

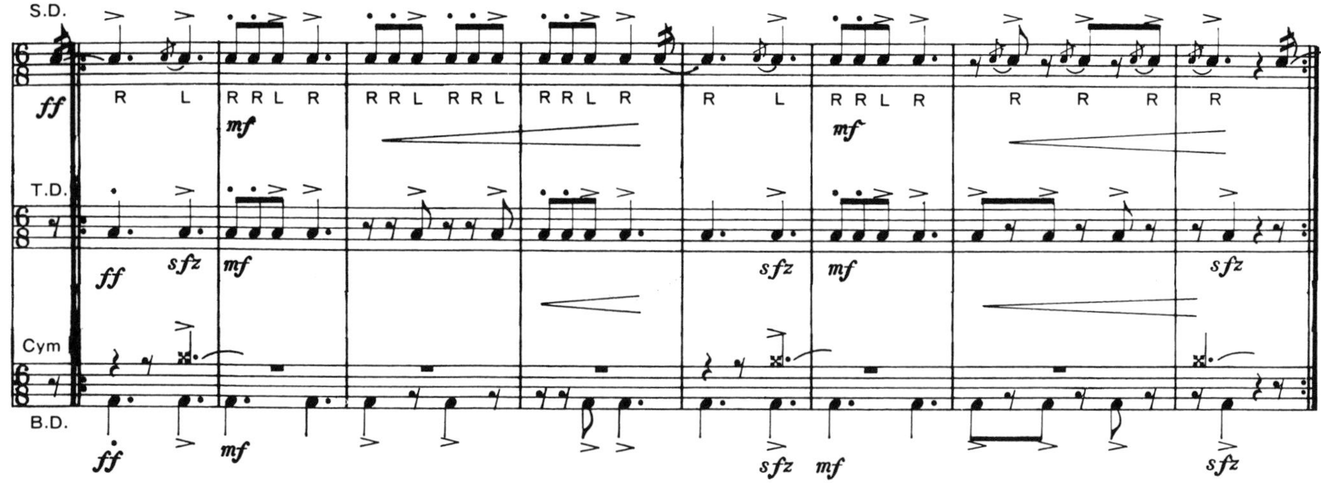

October 1967

THE PERCUSSIVE ARTS SOCIETY

Gordon Peters

Percussion instruments are the oldest of the musical instruments, having been used in primitive rituals, dances, and festive occasions, as well as in military engagements throughout history. Yet, paradoxically, they were the last major instrument family to develop in Western music. Today, just how much *is* percussion involved in our musical culture? We find percussion instruments being used in school concert bands and orchestras, football bands, stage bands, combos, drum and bugle corps, military and community bands, symphony orchestras, and percussion chamber ensembles. The significance of percussion in music today, both culturally and commercially, is great indeed.

The increased use of percussion has come so swiftly in the last two or three decades that many "vacuums" exist in performance practice, education, and research. The only means available for the exchange of information on percussion activities and ideas have been single percussion articles in more generally oriented music journals and personal correspondence. Some focal point was needed *just* for percussion.

To meet this need a group of professional players, educators, and manufacturers met in 1960 and conceived the idea of the Percussive Arts Society (PAS). By 1963 a board of directors had been established and a constitution and a proposed program of future activities were adopted. The PAS also issued this statement of purpose:

> To raise the level of musical percussion performance and teaching; to expand understanding of the needs and responsibilities of the percussion students, teachers, and performers; and to promote a greater communication between all areas of the percussion arts.

Donald Canedy was elected executive secretary and I was elected president. During the early period of the development of PAS Mr. Canedy, then instructor of percussion and director of bands at Southern Illinois University, initiated a quarterly journal, *The Percussionist,* and he continued as its editor until his resignation in 1966. At that time Neal Fluegel was elected to fill the vacancy. A second publication, *Percussive Notes,* is published tri-annually (starting with the 1967-68 academic year), and this periodical is less formal in content and format. Its founder and editor is James Moore.

Why is the PAS unique? There are many reasons. The principal one is that all major facets of the percussion profession are equally represented on its board of directors: professional players; collegiate, secondary, and primary school educators; professional teachers; marching percussionists; instrument specialists (dealers); publishers; manufacturers; and members at large. The current board of directors is composed of the following members: Frank Arsenault, Remo Belli, Mervin Britton, Barbara Buehlman, Saul (Sandy) Feldstein, Frederick Fennell, Neal Fluegel, John Galm, Roy Knapp, Ronald LoPresti, Maurie Lishon, Larry McCormick, Thomas McMillan, James Moore, John Noonan, Gordon Peters, Richard Schory, Robert Tilles, Robert Yeager, and Robert Zildjian. The editorial staff consists of editors Neal Fluegel and James Moore and assistant editor Al Payson. There are no salaries paid and membership dues are used solely to defray the costs of publications, projects, and administrative expenses.

Through research projects, the formation of state, regional, and foreign PAS chapters, and a concerted effort to gain not only more PAS members but greater participation in project committees, more articles on pertinent topics, and an increased exchange of members' activities, percussion "information technology" has emerged as a reality—to everyone's mutual benefit.

Several committees have been established to investigate specific areas of interest and a brief summary of these committees and their projects follows:

1. Percussion Contest Adjudication Procedures. Chairman: Gordon Peters, 1337 Ashland Ave., Wilmette, Illinois 60091.

This committee has prepared a complete study on adjudication procedures, involving suggested adjudication rules and evaluation sheets for the secondary level. This is the first project pursued by the PAS, and reports of the study have appeared in numerous periodicals and individual copies have been sent to over 600 persons across the country. Many states have already altered their concepts of percussion contest format as a result of this study. Currently, an extension of this project is being evolved, relating to stage band and multiple percussion instruments.

2. Percussion Contest Materials (Elementary and Secondary). Chairman: Jay Collins, 216 Freemont, Whitewater, Wisconsin 53190.

This committee's primary task is to explore currently available percussion literature in all categories of contest percussion performance and to make recommendations as to works that might be included in recommended lists of literature for contest use.

3. Elementary Percussion Education. Chairman: Al Payson, 2130 Glenview, Park Ridge, Illinois 60068.

This committee is concerned with the aims and methods of teaching and inadequacies and needs in the field of elementary percussion education. Reports of this committee's activities have appeared in *The Percussionist* and will continue to appear until a composite committee report has evolved.

4. Acoustics of Percussion Instruments. Chairman: James Moore, 5085 Henderson Heights, Columbus, Ohio 43221.

The science of acoustics as applied to percussion has had comparatively little attention. Mr. Moore is writing his doctoral dissertation on this subject and an initial article extracted from this work appeared in a recent issue of *Percussive Notes.*

5. Stage Band Percussion. Co-chairmen: Bob Tilles, 6153 North Claremont, Chicago, Illinois 60645, and Ed Shaughnessy, 325 West End Avenue, New York, New York 10023.

The primary function of this committee is to explore and recommend improvements in stage band drumming and vibraphone technique, pedagogy, and materials. Initial articles on this subject have appeared in *The Percussionist.*

6. Percussion Curriculum and Materials, College Level. Chairman: Ronald Fink, School of Music, North Texas State University, Denton, Texas 76203.

A comprehensive questionnaire has been evolved by this committee to determine the scope of percussion education in existence at the higher institutions of learning and to recommend improvements. The study will have far reaching influence not only on existing percussion curriculums, but particularly at those institutions where percussion is not taught as yet. In time, this study will be extended to the secondary level also. Over 300 of these questionnaires have thus far been circulated to colleges and universities across the country. Included is a request for listing of unpublished graduate essays and dissertations on percussion.

7. Percussion Notation and Terminology. Chairman: Wallace Barnett, 5 Ridge Court, Decatur, Illinois 62522.

The results of two initial studies which I made were published in *The Percussionist.* Mr. Barnett will carry on the work in this important area, where inconsistency in practice has been a problem to everyone. This study will continue in two stages: first, to recommend a basic uniform approach to notation, terminology, and format (this has been requested by a publishers' association); thereafter, a more sophisticated report will be made, based not only on these matters but on future trends.

8. Avant-garde Percussion Music. Chairman: Jack McKenzie, School of Music, University of Illinois, Urbana, Illinois 61801.

The chief function of this committee is to explore and explain various aspects of this new music. Articles on the subject by Max Neuhaus and George O'Connor have already appeared in *The Percussionist.*

9. Percussion in Musicology and Ethnomusicology. Chairman: Rey Longyear, College of Arts and Sciences, University of Kentucky, Lexington, Kentucky 40506.

This newly formed committee will be concerned with activities and articles dealing with the historical and inter-cultural aspects of percussion. Their writings will appear in future issues issues of *The Percussionist.*

10. Promotion and Membership. Chairman: John Galm, School of Music, University of Colorado, Boulder, Colorado 80302.

11. State, Regional, and Foreign Chapter Formation. Chairman: Sandy Feldstein, Dept. of Music, State University College, Potsdam, New York 13676.

Such sub-organizations are necessary in implementing the overall program of the PAS and in strengthening percussion activities at the local level.

In addition to its own committees, PAS cooperates fully with the International Percussion Reference Library (Mervin Britton, IPRL, Dept. of Music, Arizona State University, Tempe, Arizona 85281), by encouraging composers and publishers to send two copies of works dealing with percussion to the Library. Through this affiliation conductors and percussionists are made aware of the latest percussion publications.

Many directors may ask at this point: "Why should *I* have an interest in the Percussive Arts Society?" Fundamentally, there are two reasons: (1) to keep abreast of current concepts and activities (particularly if your own training did not embody a formalized percussion techniques class) and (2) to bring the PAS to the attention of all students of percussion instruments.

PAS annual membership dues are as follows:

Student and Library	$ 2.50
Regular	5.00
Publisher, Dealer	25.00
Manufacturer	250.00

Membership includes four issues of *The Percussionist*

and three issues of *Percussive Notes,* yearly. Presently, there are over 800 members of PAS, including ten manufacturers, and 80 libraries. It is largely through the commercial members and special gifts that the low student membership rate and project development are possible. Prospective members should send their name, address, and membership dues to:

Mr. Neal Fluegel, Exec. Secr.
Percussive Arts Society
R. R. #7, Box 506
Terre Haute, Indiana 47805

The PAS is eager to hear from music educators and to be of assistance in any way possible. Formal application forms can be obtained in quantity from the above address.

Only through research and the dissemination of existing knowledge can there be measurable progress in improving percussion teaching and playing. The music director has a pivotal and vital position in a young drummer's education in music and percussion techniques. It is the earnest hope of the PAS and its many devoted members that the readers of this article will bring the Percussive Arts Society to the attention of their students and other music directors, as well as considering membership for themselves.

October 1967

Effective Use of Cymbals

Larry McCormick

Aside from being a band director, I have the privilege of teaching the percussion section of the "Cavaliers" Drum and Bugle Corps of Chicago, present national champions. It is my job as percussion writer and teacher to make their percussion show as musically and visually effective as possible in order to achieve top scores in competition.

In this year's show we decided to demonstrate the merits of cymbals and worked to emphasize their value in our marching show. In the "Cavaliers" we use three sets of cymbals which may or may not be practical for the average high school marching band; certainly, I think it would be possible to use two sets in almost any band.

My idea was to use different sized sets of cymbals for different musical effects. Most good bands have more than one set of cymbals and all trained percussion players know that a variety of cymbal sounds are called for in the modern band repertoire. I acquired three sets of cymbals including a very fine set of 26″ Avedis Zildjian cymbals. The other two sizes were 17″ and 20″. Now, you are probably saying to yourself, "26″ cymbals! How can they possibly play them?" Well, I selected a good strong boy to carry them and of course we don't play an overabundance of crashes with these cymbals because of their weight and great dynamic volume. Using the giant cymbals has proven to be one of the best things we have done this year, both musically and visually. We do a few feature spots in our marching show where the cymbal player comes forward in front of the group and the crowd reaction is great.

The corps also plays a portion of *Les Preludes,* by Liszt, and the spectacular cymbal crashes make the number musically complete as well as supplying visual impact. I use the two smaller sets of cymbals in more traditional ways, emphasizing syncopations and accents. I have written some sequence parts using the three cymbal sounds in a melodic fashion. The smaller cymbals also do a great deal of visual work through the use of twirling and spinning.

Now, how specifically can you use your cymbals more effectively in the marching show?"

A. *Plan* your cymbal parts. *Don't* just hand the cymbals to the oboe player you can't use for marching, and let her crash away.

B. Try a set of *big* cymbals. You will be amazed at the positive reaction they have musically and upon the audience; the 26″ size is magnificent.

C. Use your cymbals *visually* as well as musically. Feature your big cymbals in the show. Let your players work out twirling routines. Twirling is quite easy with a little practice.

D. *Write your own cymbal music.* Emphasize the cymbals by writing crashes to *lead* into syncopations by the brass, or *during* sustained fortissimo tones by the entire band. Use the cymbals *with* the strong syncopations by the band, and try some *solo* crashes in outstanding places.

E. Use leather straps only on your cymbals. The best tone is achieved when a cymbal is free to vibrate. Handles of wood or metal tend to restrict the tone. The use of wood or metal handles also can cause cymbals to crack.

F. Select your cymbal players wisely. Choose someone who is a musician first and a showman second. Someone who has a good ear and sense of rhythm will add a great deal; but, also, a person with imagination is needed to work out the visual aspects of the cymbal performance. As I stated before, don't just pick any "weak stick" in the band and put him on cymbals because there is no other place for him to be used.

G. Cymbals can be used for other musical effects than crashes. Cymbals can be used on the field for suspended cymbal rolls by having the cymbal player hold one of the cymbals out while a tenor or snare drummer plays a roll with soft mallets. A "hi-hat" sound can be attained by having the cymbal player hold the cymbals horizontally and closing them together on the 2nd and 4th beats of the measure

open close open close

4/4 ... etc.

while the snare drummer plays a typical cymbal ride beat on the same cymbals.

H. Select your cymbals wisely and personally if possible. Cymbals vary in tone a great deal and the sound that *you* like may not be the same sound that *I* like. Cymbal sounds also vary greatly with different brands of cymbals. As a percussionist I would recommend staying with the leading name brands in purchasing new cymbals; select them *personally* if at all possible. For marching band, the heavier weights of cymbals (marching band weight) are the most practical.

November 1967

Forget the Music, Drummers — Just Try to Follow!

Alyn Heim

Many skills are involved as the performer plays his part, follows the conductor, and blends his line with the other voices. Physically, his eyes read directly from the music while his peripheral vision makes him aware of the director's motions. Musically, his ear listens and is guided by the sound of the ensemble. Still a director will say to the bass drummer, ". . . forget the music, look at me, and try to follow my beat." Out of desperation, he is insisting that the drummer perform unmusically!

Anyone who has ever conducted an ensemble knows that sight alone will not control the group. We know, too well, that helpless feeling when the group takes off without us. Our motions at a time like this can do nothing to save the situation. As we flail and beat the air, the group goes firmly on, usually in an accelerating tempo that begins to sound like a race. Only a dramatic foot-stamping or baton-beating on the stand will attract the ear of the group and regain for us the control we should never have lost.

A *sound* is needed to end the race as a sound must always be heeded in a group performance. Sound and sight together can bring us security of control. The bass drummer, therefore, should be told to *read and listen,* while he follows our baton.

Sound and sight: the ears and the eyes; but still a third element is needed in a group performance —the words and figures: the letters, lines, and abbreviations on a page of music. These are the signals that a musician must heed. Before the music slows down we are signaled, ritard; then we *hear* it happening as we *see* the broadening, slowing motions of the director. If we miss the signal, we still might catch the sound or sight of a ritard but we are not as secure in our position. So we need this third element, the words and signs around the notes, to warn us of what is to come. Sound, sight, signals—we need all three for a musical performance.

But all of this we know! As musicians, performers, and conductors, we realize that the ear, the eyes, and the intellect are all needed for an artistic ensemble performance. However, as teachers our job is to pass on what we know to our students, and it seems there is one section of our band or orchestra that is not being passed its full share.

Why does the percussion section so often give forth the most unmusical performance? Is the individual who chooses to study drums, by his very nature, an unmusical person or might he not be as musical as the next child? Perhaps the reason why drummers often turn into less musical performers can be found in the materials that they study or in the way these materials are taught.

If the materials do not encourage musical judgement, the student's innate ability will be buried under a heavy cover of rudimental exercises and complicated rhythmic gymnastics. After such a preparation, it is not surprising that a young student cannot make sense out of the band or orchestra part that must to him seem like a wasteland of rests, dotted with outbursts of rhythm. Since much percussion music is by its nature somewhat "less musical" (i.e., lack of pitch in many cases), it demands that the performer be musician enough to sense the music that his part is complementing.

We must, therefore, arm the percussionist with experience in the refined elements of musical performance: dynamics, tempo control, ensemble finesse, and, of course, the vocabulary used to represent these refinements.

A noble statement . . . but how shall we begin? Let's start with sight.

Sight

Inasmuch as the dramatic sounds produced by the percussion section can so easily upset an ensemble, conductors seem to be unnerved by the sight of a percussionist intently reading his part, seemingly ignoring the director. Even at the professional level, percussionists choose to look up at the conductor in crucial passages, and most often this is done for the conductor's sake, not for the percussionist's.

We realize, of course, that it is possible to look at the music while we sense the motions of the director from the periphery of our vision. However, we often do not realize that our students also need to know this fact. Unfortunately, it is not enough to say "watch me from the corner of your eye," or "keep one eye on me and one on the music." We need a graphic demonstration to capture the students' attention.

Have each musician look at his music stand, insisting that every eye be focused on the stand and not on you. Now move your hands as you might if directing. The students will realize, with perhaps a reminder to keep all eyes focused on the stand, that they can sense your motions and see the music at the same time. To show they can follow, choose an initial tempo and rhythm, and with all eyes still focused on the stand, have the rhythm performed to your directions as you start, stop, and vary tempo and dynamics.

A simple, and to us obvious, demonstration; yet when it is first used, we always see a look of discovery on many faces in the group. Some extra advice might very well be given to the drummers in reference to positioning their rather awkward instruments (as well as optional music stand positioning and height) so that sight lines are good.

Sound

The ear is the next to be considered as we teach the "read and follow" techniques, for without attention to sound, group performance would be impossible.

The bass drummer does not really lead the marching band but follows along with everyone else. A runaway cornet section or some lagging trombones are as often as not the culprits who cause a marching tempo to disintegrate. Unless the entire group is feeling and hearing a tempo together, it will not remain secure. True, due to its pointed and dramatic sound, the bass drum can occasionally save the day; but we hesitate to depend on him alone (and, therefore, should not blame him alone when a tempo is upset). We must teach our percussionists, as well as other musicians, to listen if they are to perform musically.

One time tested but, in the case of percussionists, seldom used way of developing the "group ear" is through chamber ensemble performance. The ensemble part demands more of the individual since his instrument receives a larger portion of the responsibility, and to perform without a conductor demands that the ear be more attentive. For the percussionist, since the band or orchestra parts often demand so little of him, it is an exciting experience to be challenged in this way; and like everyone else, they will grow up to the demands made of them or will languish if left unchallenged.

Too often, though, as busy directors we become discouraged at the prospect of trying to add a percussion ensemble to our schedule; and, because we do not have the time to develop a regularly rehearsed ensemble, we give up. This is sad, for no matter how seldom or how simple the attention we give to our percussionists, it will show itself in their interest and improved musical performance. We have all noticed them stand a little straighter and prouder when they finally get a good part to play. They will be even more proud after a little special attention from the director in a percussion class or ensemble. But do not let this attention take the form of a novelty tune put into the concert for a change of pace; but, rather, let the attention be a sincere interest shown in them and in relation to their performance as musicians.

Signals

Unless the young players understand and observe all of the markings around the notes their effectiveness will be limited. The words and symbols used to represent tempo and dynamic levels are too often not taught to the percussionists by the method books, which rely mostly on the teaching of rhythms and rudiments. Therefore, the teacher must take the time to explain these markings if they are to be understood. Building up the music vocabulary in this way will save much time, since the printed page will communicate more to the performers without having the details explained each time they appear.

But let us realize that it is not enough to say to a percussion section, "Forte means loud, piano means soft, and crescendo means to grow louder." If this has not been a part of their training on the instrument it will not penetrate. They must work with tempo and dynamic control if they are to comprehend the technique. They should be warned of the dangers: accelerating with crescendo, ritarding with diminuendo. They should know that, although natural, these pitfalls must be avoided. It is not practical to say, "This is a clarinet—play it!," anymore than it is practical to say, "These are dynamic markings—observe them." In both cases the student needs more guidance.

There are materials available, books and ensemble pieces, that include experience relating to the sound, sight, and signals we have considered. If we include these principles of musicianship in our percussion instruction we will find the percussionists proving themselves to be as musical and as sensitive as their fellow performers.*

**Editor's Note: I would like to add an extension to the author's "Sound" category. To listen to other players (exterior) for purposes of ensemble is one thing; to "feel" tempo and expression (interior) we must have* concept *and* concentration. *The best way to achieve this (and this applies to conductor and player alike) is through the performer's singing the part to himself, inaudibly. This insures the factors of concept (forethought of expression) and concentration (extension of span of attention). The European concept of* solfeggio *is merely being applied here. In the case of non-pitched percussion instruments, any syllable (nonsense syllables included) can be used for the rhythms. The young percussion student should, of course, study a mallet percussion instrument (preferably marimba or xylophone) as early in his percussion studies as possible, together with basic music theory for reasons of developing musicianship.* Gordon Peters

The Notation and Interpretation of Rolls

Ramon Meyer

Two kinds of roll notation are used in percussion parts for orchestra, band, and ensemble. A majority of editions of the standard orchestral literature employs the trill sign to denote a roll. Most band and ensemble literature employs cross hatches. Although percussionists would prefer to see the latter method universally adopted since it is the more accurate of the two, both performers and conductors need to be able to interpret either method.

Cross hatches were devised as a short-hand method of notation which would relieve the composer or copyist of the time-consuming task of writing long series of repeated notes. Up to a certain point the use of this system is equally applicable to all instruments of the orchestra. Each cross hatch is equal to a beam or flag: one cross hatch, beam, or flag indicates eighth notes; two indicate sixteenth notes; three, thirty-second notes, etc.

One cross hatch above a whole note or through the stem of a half or quarter note indicates that eighth notes should be played for the duration of that note.

Example 1

Two cross hatches (or a combination of one cross hatch and one flag or beam) indicate that sixteenth notes should be played for the duration of the given note.

Example 2

For all instruments except percussion and strings, three cross hatches would indicate thirty-second notes just as do three flags or three beams. For percussion, however, the use of three cross hatches denotes a roll. For strings this notation denotes unmeasured tremolo.

Example 3

Inconsistency in the application of this theory of notation has created many instances where the composer has used only two cross hatches, but a close study of the score will reveal that he intended a roll.

Use of the trill sign for rolls on melodic percussion instruments is obviously impractical. Since these instruments can actually trill, the performer would not know whether a trill or a roll was intended. Even when restricted to non-melodic instruments the exact duration of the roll is frequently difficult to determine.

Example 4

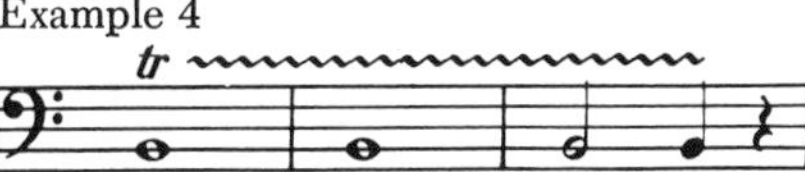

Such notation as found in Example 4—common though it is—does not clearly indicate whether the roll is to stop after the half note or is to continue through the quarter note. Other examples, equally as confusing, leave the performer in doubt about whether he should connect or separate long rolls.

Example 5

In Example 5, taken from Brahms' *Symphony No. 4,* the continuous trill sign implies that all the notes are connected into one long roll.

Example 6

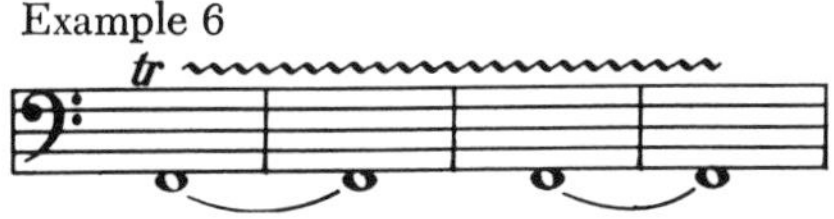

Such is not the case in Example 6 from Beethoven's *Sixth Symphony.* Here, in spite of the continuous trill sign, the roll should be broken between the second and third measures. Other orchestral timpani parts include passages similar to Example 7 from Rossini's *La Gazza Ladra* overture which would seem to indicate a separation between each roll.

Example 7

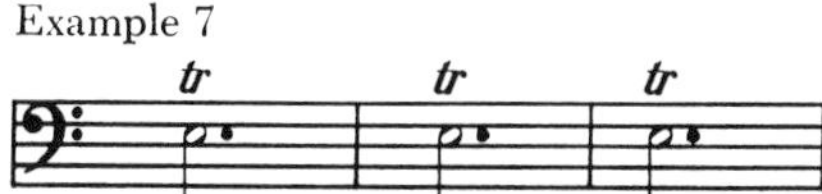

A close look at the score, however, will reveal that all of the rolls should be tied.

From the confusion which surrounds roll notation and interpretation, some guidelines should be drawn for the composer, conductor, and performer.

The composer and arranger should employ three cross hatches to indicate rolls and should scrupulously avoid the confusing trill sign. Ties should be clearly marked in all instances where they are intended.

The conductor must not take an accurate notation of percussion parts for granted. He should compare these parts carefully with the wind and brass parts to determine exactly how long rolls should last and whether they should be tied or separated.

The performer, however, should assume that the notation of his part is accurate. He should make no attempt to adjust the part unless the conductor asks him to do so. If he cannot tell whether a roll is to be tied or separated or how long it should last, he should ask the conductor to make the decision. Notational procedures for percussion can never be stabilized if each percussionist is allowed to adjust all roll notation he encounters.

1968-1969

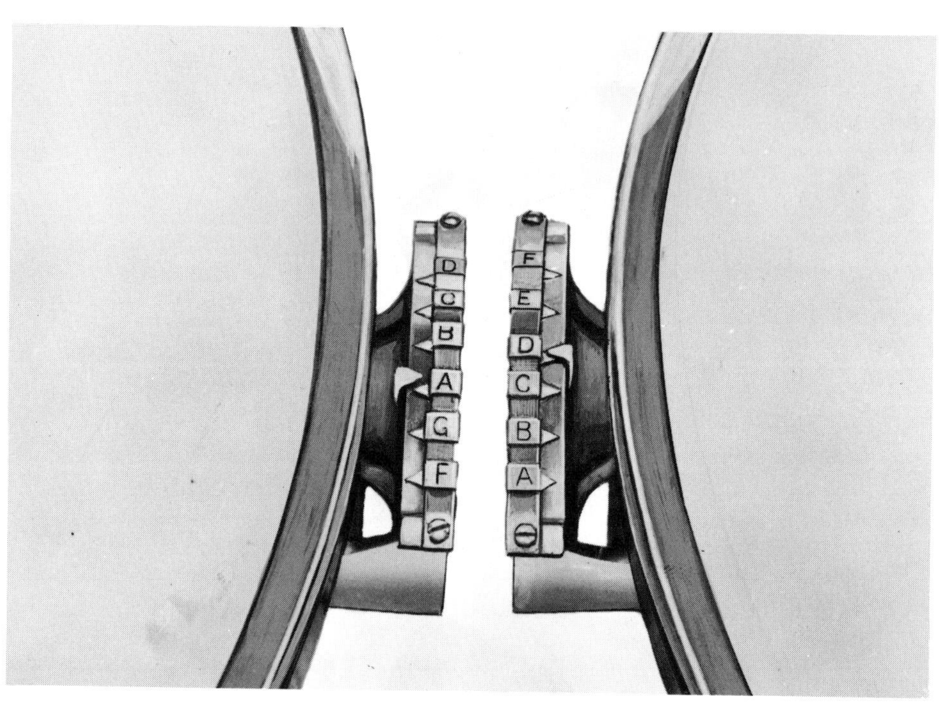
D
C
B
A
G
F
F
E
D
C
B
A

New Ideas for Clinics

John Galm

In February of this year, the University of Colorado hosted a clinic for clarinet, French horn, and percussion for high school intermediate and advanced players of the Rocky Mountain area. Since the percussion clinic was held at the same time as the other two clinics, we all adopted the same general procedure. This was as follows:
1. A concert by each of the performing organizations of the University. (Percussion Ensemble, Horn Ensemble, and Clarinet Choir.)
2. A class lesson in the various instruments of the clinic, taught by the university instructors and their students.
3. A rehearsal to develop a performing ensemble of the high school students.
4. A concert of the three high school student groups. (Percussion Ensemble, Horn Ensemble, and Clarinet Choir)

Steps 1 and 2 were relatively easy to arrange but steps 3 and 4 presented quite a quandary. Namely, what do you perform with a possible ensemble of 50 players of varying abilities with only a two-hour rehearsal in which to prepare for a "concert"? The first answer that came to mind was possibly doing the "Dies Irae" timpani excerpt from the Berlioz *Requiem* or maybe 50 snare drums playing the *Downfall of Paris.* Both Dr. William Kearns and Dr. Jerry Smith, who were directing the French horn and clarinet clinics respectively, were planning to use four and five part compositions which could have many players on each part and not disturb the musical intent. In searching the percussion literature for music of this type, I found Carl Orff's *Musik für Kinder.** This is a system of music instruction for the primary grades used extensively in Germany, England, and recently in the United States. Since this system makes use of compositions written for many percussion instruments and the degree of difficulty ranges from simple hand clapping to three-mallet keyboard percussion parts, it suited the needs of the clinic. With the music for the large ensemble selected, we turned to the other aspects of the clinic and developed some other interesting approaches. Perhaps I can best illustrate by relating the events of the day.

Clinic Procedure

The three clinics were held simultaneously in order to attract more instrumental instructors and to have an audience for the other performing groups. In spite of a snowy, windy morning, 70 clarinets, 40 French horns, and 30 percussionists managed literally to blow into Boulder. The percussionists were asked to bring a snare drum and stand, a triangle, and timpani and keyboard percussion mallets. The objectives were to show them how to tune a snare drum, play a triangle, and improve their technique on timpani and keyboard percussion. Also, we hoped to stimulate purchases, if they were needed, on the part of the percussionists as well as the instrumental directors.

In the opening concert, the University Percussion Ensemble performed in three areas of the percussion literature in order to present an historic perspective. To illustrate the Baroque style of writing for percussion, we performed the *March for Two Pairs of Kettledrums* by Jacque and André Philidor written for the carrousel of King Louis XIV in 1683. Next, since the state solo and ensemble contest were a few months away, we played several tunes from the Bruce & Emmett, *A Drummers and Fifers Guide.* The Ensemble showed how these tunes sounded in their original context of the Civil War era with the fifes and deep drums reaching the upper limits of the sound capacity of our 500-seat Music Hall. Finally, to illustrate the 20th century's concern with timbre and unusual sounds, we performed two duets from *Six Allegro Duets for Two Snare Drums* by Michael Colgrass. These use timpani sticks, brushes, fingers, different playing spots on the head, and other devices to demonstrate some of the tonal possibilities of the snare drum.

Our class lesson in percussion consisted of five lessons, each 20 minutes long. Our aim was to present as much of the variety of percussion techniques as possible and to have the students play as much as possible in order to help them with difficulties they might be having. Two university students were in charge of each area and they compiled an outline of their lesson for the student. The areas chosen were snare drum, keyboard percussion, timpani, sit-down drums (dance drums), and a trap lesson (triangle, bass drum, and cymbals). The scope of the lessons was:

Snare Drum—Tuning the drum; selecting sticks for straightness, pitch, and balance; comparison of matched grip with the traditional; individual work on various rudiments such as rolls, flams, and ruffs.

Keyboard Percussion—Demonstration of the various instruments and stick types; the staccato and legato strokes; various technical exercises to develop evenness and speed.

Timpani—Tuning the head to itself and tuning to various pitches; stick types; staccato and legato strokes; roll exercises to work for evenness and good tone.

Sit-down Drums—Bass drum techniques; hi-hat techniques; left hand fills; use of rudiments such as flam, paradiddle, and flam accent in drum breaks; four measure solos and extended solos.

Triangle, bass drum, and cymbals—Proper holding and suspension of triangle; where to strike;

how to roll; bass drum tuning; stick types; dampening; suspended cymbal stick types; rolling; plate crashes; use of flam for good sound.

Admittedly, to cover these points and work on individual problems was a difficult, if not impossible, task. However, the students were divided into five small groups and moved to a different lesson every 20 minutes. This gave the college student-instructors the advantage of concentrating on one area and becoming familiar with the problems encountered in that specific area. Also, as stated before, the students had an outline of the class lesson with space left for notes and questions. The success of this class lesson period was quite evident later when the students were questioned concerning their lessons. Some said they had never played a keyboard percussion instrument, some had never tuned a timpani, and others had never been shown how to play a cymbal crash. At the same time the university students had the experience of teaching a percussion class while demonstrating their technical abilities.

After lunch the rehearsal period was first given over to answering questions resulting from the individual class lessons. Then some unaccompanied solo percussion literature was heard with a performance of Benson's *Three Dances for Solo Snare Drum, Three Preludes for Vibraphone* by Serge de Gastyne, and *March of the Antarctic Penquins,* which I wrote and also performed.

The first composition rehearsed from the Orff *Musik für Kinder* was a rondo (Vol. I, p. 81) for body percussion. This involved the use of hand claps, finger snaps, knee slaps, and foot stamps. Since these body sounds are written on four lines played by one performer, this gave good practice in multi-percussion score reading. As nearly everyone brought a snare drum, we next rehearsed a piece for recorder and hand drum (Vol. IV, p. 32). The recorder part was performed on the xylophone by one player and the rest turned their snare drums into hand drums. Again this gave practice in score reading, as both parts are on the same page. The hand drum part is divided into playing at the edge of the drum and in the center. Sticking is indicated in an unusual manner by the direction of the stems of the notes (up for right, down for left). Delicacy and balance were important since 30 snare drums were accompanying one xylophone played with soft mallets.

Next, two dance pieces were played (Vol. IV, p. 22 and Vol. II, p. 22) which are written for six keyboard percussion parts, timpani, snare drums, tambourines, triangles, bass drums, cymbals, wood blocks, and hand clappers. Again, score parts were used so that the players could get used to reading this type of music and would be able to follow the other parts. The Orff *Musik für Kinder* is very carefully marked with dynamics, phrases, and articulation indications; these were fully explained and rehearsed.

The concert was well executed and for the most part quite musical. Those who are familiar with Orff's *Carmina Burand* and *Antigone* know how well he uses the percussion instruments. The same musical use of percussion is found in these compositions for children; therefore, they are highly recommended for developing musicianship in percussion ensembles.

The success of our clinic resulted from the fact that we were able to give individual attention to the students and at the same time present them with new techniques and ideas. Also, we developed performance techniques by being able to combine the students into an ensemble.

We were very pleased with the results of our clinic. It is our hope that, in presenting our format and ideas in *The Instrumentalist,* similar clinics might be conducted by other colleges and universities or by PAS state chapters, or even by groups of interested high school teachers.

It is hoped that through such clinics a broader understanding of the entire field of percussion can be gained and we can look forward to the day when we have more musicians in the percussion section and fewer "head-pounders."

If anyone would like further information concerning our clinic, please contact me at the College of Music, University of Colorado, Boulder, Colorado.

**Carl Orff-Gunild Keetman,* Musik für Kinder, *Mainz: R. Schott's Söhne, 1956-1961. 5 Volumes.*

February 1968

TRIANGLE TECHNIQUE

Mitchell Peters

The triangle is a very beautiful and colorful instrument when played musically and artistically. It can be delicate at soft dynamics and brilliant at loud dynamics. It is also one of the most used of the many accessory instruments in the percussion family, and therefore warrants serious attention on the part of the student, teacher, and conductor.

Triangles come in various sizes, which all have different relative pitches and timbres. (The word pitch is not used in a sense of definite pitch, for triangles are not tuned. Rather, the term is used in a sense of the comparative highness and lowness of the pitch produced by various triangles.) Most drum companies list 6", 8", and 10" as standard sizes for triangles. This does not mean that triangles can be only those sizes: a triangle can be of any size. The size of the triangle refers to the length of one side of the triangle. Most triangles are constructed as equilateral triangles, but some are also constructed as isosceles triangles. It should be mentioned that one corner of the triangle is always open.

For most purposes a good heavy smaller triangle, about 6", will prove to be the best sounding triangle. It will produce the higher pitch and overtones which are usually associated with the triangle. The larger triangles tend to sound too "gongy" for general use.

However, you should have more than one triangle, for occasions may arise when you will prefer the color of a larger triangle. Also, some modern band, orchestra, and percussion ensemble music calls for more than one triangle at a time, with the object that the triangles must contrast in pitch; therefore, there must be different sizes to adequately provide the pitch differences desired.

The theory that a larger triangle is needed to play louder is not accurate. A good 6" triangle can be played sufficiently loud for any occasion that will arise in band or orchestra performance. In fact, the higher pitch of the smaller triangle will project through an orchestra or band with much less effort and a more musical sound than will the sound of the large triangle.

It must be said that many triaangles made by drum companies today are somewhat inadequate in regard to tone quality. One of the best available triangles on the market today is a 6" symphonic triangle made by Alan Abel, a percussionist with the Philadelphia Orchestra. This triangle sells for $15.00. Having a good triangle is essential to producing a good triangle sound.

Another extremely important item is having a good triangle holder. There are two types of holders generally in use: the loop holder, and the clamp holder.

The loop holder is merely a piece of thin gut or a similar material, tied in an approximate 2" loop. The loop is then placed on the first finger of the hand that will hold the triangle. The triangle is then placed through the loop. Have the loop as close as possible to the palm of the hand. This will keep the hand in a good position to act as a damper. The open end of the triangle should be to the left if it is held in the left hand and to the right if held in the right hand.

The clamp holder is probably the more common of the two. It can be held in the hand or placed on a music stand so that the triangle can be played with two beaters for rapid passages. The clamp holder is merely a clothespin or similar object with two small holes drilled about an inch apart on the bottom. Thin gut or a similar material is threaded through the holes to form a loop and is knotted at both ends.

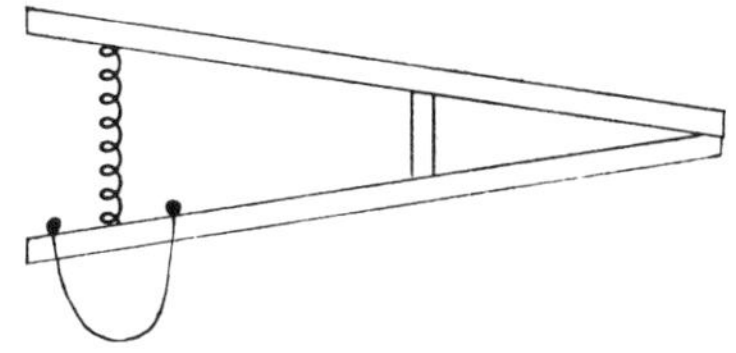

To hold the clamp holder in the hand, the closed end of the holder is put between the second and third finger with the thumb resting under the other side of the holder. The bottom part of the hand is then in position to act as a damper when needed.

Muffling the triangle when it is held in the hand is achieved merely by placing the three bottom fingers around the triangle when you desire to stop it from ringing. A dotted note would be dampened immediately. Normally when a note is written thus, ♩, it is not meant to be muffled. Muffling is a technique that the player must know, but it is not used except in particular instances, for the normal sound of the triangle is intended to ring whether it is written as a quarter note, half note, or whole note.

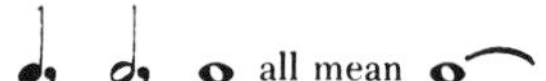

If the triangle is attached to the music stand and two beaters are being used, the triangle is muffled by using the free fingers of one hand to stop the vibrations.

In addition to a good triangle and holder, some good beaters will be necessary. Triangle beaters are merely rods made of steel. Sometimes even extremely large nails can be used. However it is best to use special beaters made for striking the triangle; these can be purchased at most music stores. Drill rods can also be used and have many advantages in that they are available in infinite diameters and can be cut to length to suit individual players. It is a good idea to have numerous pairs of beaters of various sizes and weights for various tonal colors. It is necessary to have two of each size for executing rapid passages. It must be stated that even though it is good to have more than one pair of beaters, "99% of the time" a good pair of solid, heavy beaters will prove to be best. They will produce a tone with more body, which for even piano passages is superior to the weak sound of thin triangle beaters.

Wherever possible, the triangle should be played with one beater. This will allow the triangle to be held in the other hand rather than having it clamped to the music stand, thus enabling the performer to have better control over the triangle. Also, the triangle will have a much freer, resonant sound when it is not attached to the stand. Holding the triangle will enable one to position the triangle so that one can see the triangle, the music, and the conductor in a straight line, and at the same time the sound will project more clearly.

Normally the triangle is struck in one of two places. One spot is outside the upper right leg of the triangle, the other spot is the right side of the lower leg.

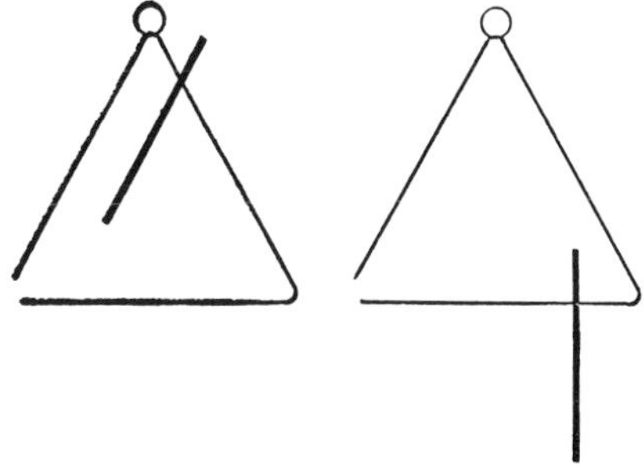

It must be stated that triangles vary and the player must determine by experimentation which playing spot produces the best sound for that particular triangle and musical passage. There are no rules to prevent one from striking the triangle on any particular spot as long as it produces a good tone.

Striking the triangle with the beater perpendicular will produce a more diffuse sound with more overtones—a very useful sound:

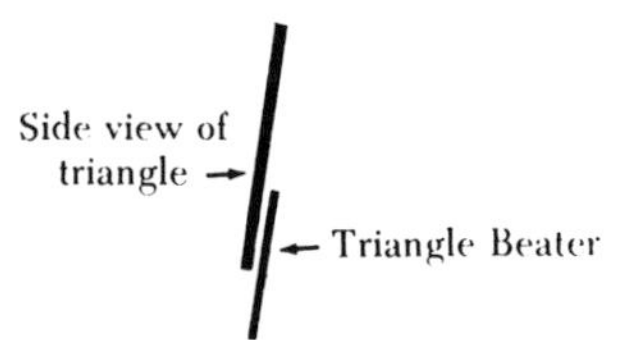

Rolls are indicated by the signs

The tremelo or roll with one beater is played at either closed end of the triangle. It is played by rapidly moving the beater between two sides. The softer the roll, the closer to the corner one must play.

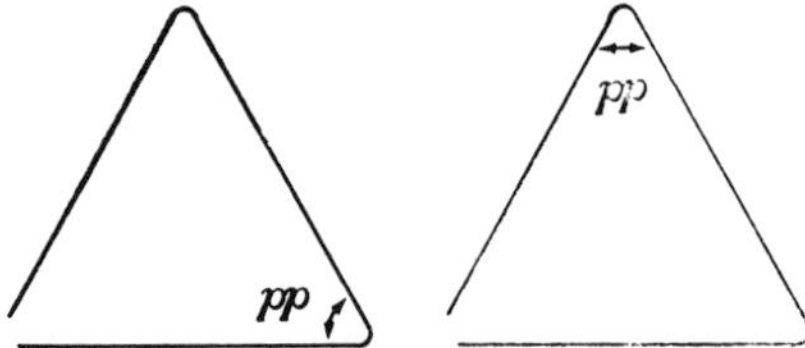

As a louder roll is desired, move further away from the corner.

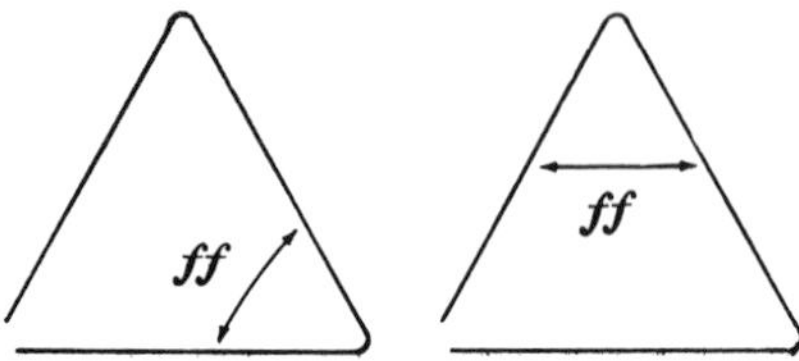

Sometimes it is easier to get a clear end to a loud roll

if the roll is played between the two upper sides of the triangle

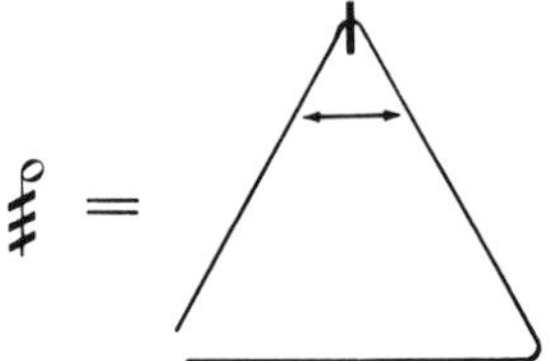

then for the end, use a downward stroke striking the bottom of the triangle.

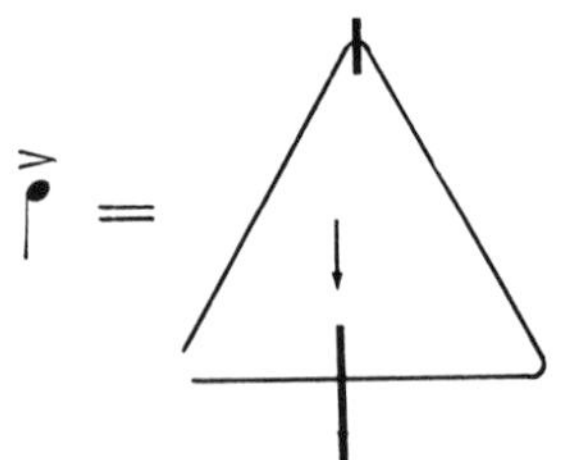

Many passages will have patterns that are too fast to be played with one beater. In such cases the triangle must be clamped to the music stand and played with two beaters of identical length, weight and size. When using two beaters, the triangle can be played in one of two spots.

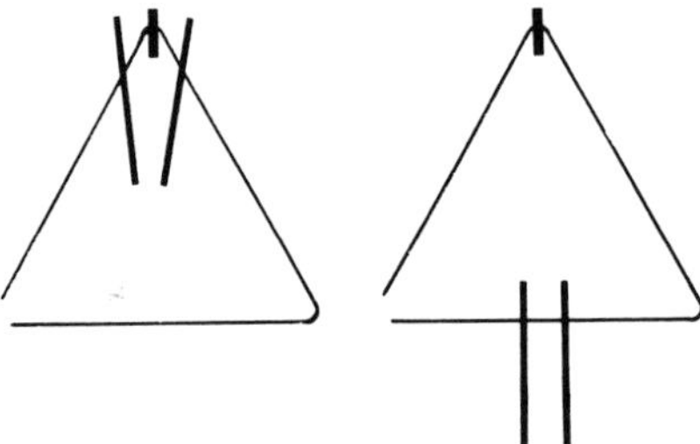

Sometimes, when two beaters are used, the triangle will have a tendency to move about too much. In such a case the triangle can be suspended with two clip holders from a music stand. However, this does kill the tone quality a great deal, and is not recommended unless a partially muted triangle sound is desired.

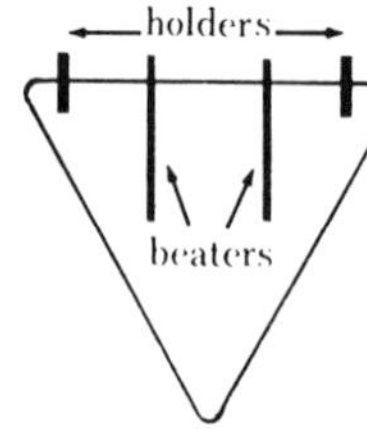

A roll can also be executed with two beaters playing a rapid single stroke either at the bottom or on the upper sides of the triangle.

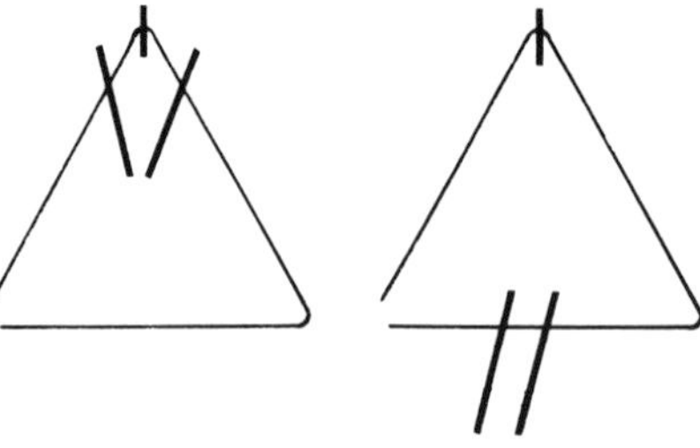

For very light playing the triangle should be struck with the tip of the beater.

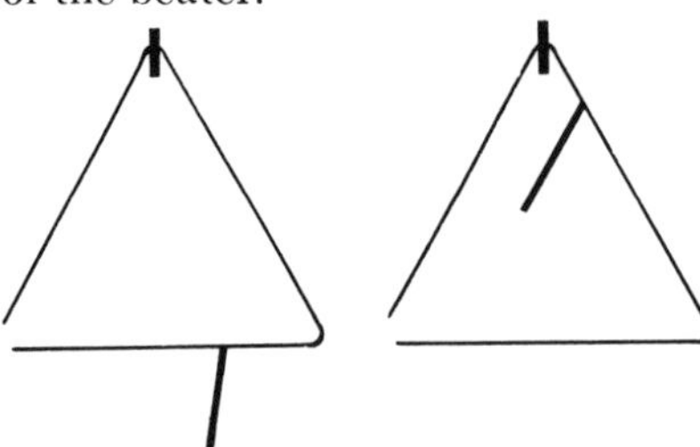

When a fuller tone is desired, move further in on the beater.

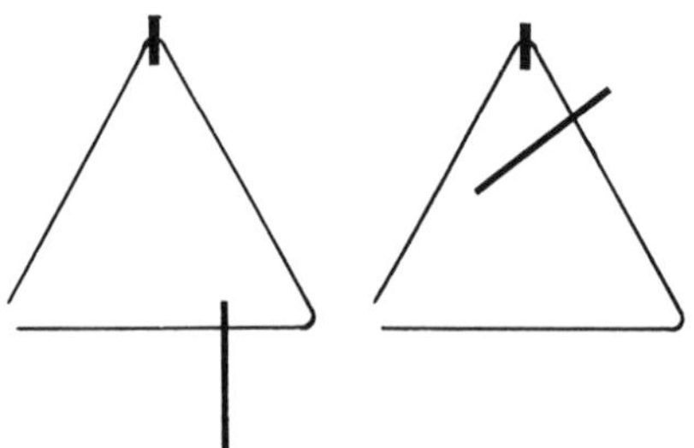

Some quick rhythmic figures can be executed by using one beater against two sides of the triangle, much the same way a roll is executed, but in a rhythmic pattern.

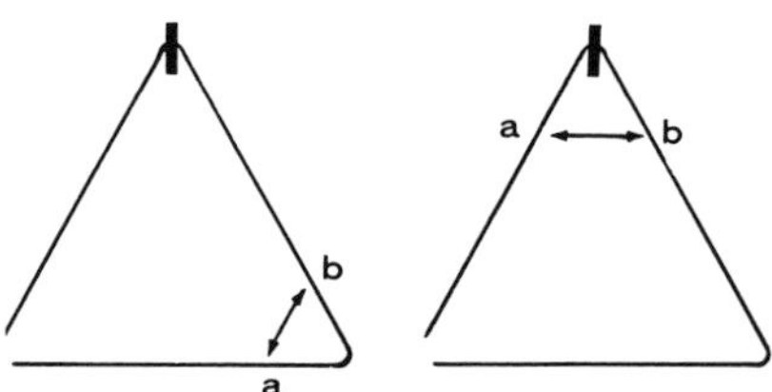

When this technique is used, do not use strict alternation. Strike the "a" side for notes on the stronger beats such as eighths and quarters; and strike the "b" side for notes in-between. This process is similar to the use of single and double tonguing. The "a" side being the *tu* syllable and the "b" side being the *ku* syllable.

When only single notes are used, the triangle should be held around chin height, so that a clear line of vision between the triangle, the music, and the conductor can be maintained. If rolls are employed, the triangle will have to be held slightly lower to enable execution with ease.

The tone of the triangle must be drawn out. The striking action must be like the hammer action of the piano. The beater strikes the triangle and comes right off. A wrist motion is used to manipulate the beater. The beater can be held like the right hand snare drum stick with the wrist flat, or it can be held like the right hand timpani grip with the wrist vertical and the thumb up. Actually the player may find that both grips will be useful, depending on the passage being executed.

On rare occasions the triangle is indicated to be struck with a wooden stick. This is a very particular effect and does not produce a characteristic triangle sound, but it is not intended to.

At times the triangle can be used effectively in a Latin American rhythm section. One good effect is to play straight eighth notes on the triangle and vary the sound of the triangle by dampening and opening the sound of the triangle.

This pattern could be used effectively in certain bossa novas or rhumbas, if this color were desired. The triangle can also be used in sambas.

These are by no means the only ways a triangle can be employed in a Latin sound, but are two possibilities to give an idea of the usefulness of this color in Latin music.

As with all of the percussion instruments, the triangle can be played musically and sound like a musical instrument or it can be clanked and sound like a noise maker. It can sound like a beautiful metallic instrument with a tone, or it can sound like a trolley-car bell. It is hoped that this article will help to make it sound like a musical instrument.

March 1968

THE MULTIPLE BOUNCE ROLL

William Schinstine

Much misunderstanding has developed over the years since Fred Hoey and I first introduced the term *multiple bounce roll* in our basic drum method book in 1960. This roll is not really anything new or mysterious; most professional players have used it for many years. It has been called both a *press* and *buzz* roll. Very simply, it is a roll played with more than two strokes or taps per hand.

What is new, however, is teaching it to beginning drum students. We discovered in our respective teaching practices that the use of the *multiple bounce roll* instead of the traditional *da-da-ma-ma* approach eliminated or greatly reduced many of the difficulties students encountered in producing their first rolls.

First of all, the hand movement of a multiple bounce roll stroke is similar to a single tap. No double movement, which is necessary in the start of the traditional double stroke roll, is needed. In effect, we are starting with a closed roll. Our system allows a student to produce a usable roll in a matter of weeks rather than the many months required to develop a usable controlled stroke and single bounce roll. Granted, it is not always very even, but for the beginner who is usually in grade school, it is no worse than the long tones produced by his contemporaries on other instruments.

Secondly, we emphasize the *rhythmic* approach to learning the so called "stroke" rolls. We avoid calling them by numbers because a *multiple bounce roll* does not have a definite number of strokes. Also, when young students attach numbers to rolls, they often lack the understanding of the rhythmic fundamental which is necessary in order to perform them correctly. For greater understanding we substitute rhythmic comparison. After all, the rhythmic fundamental changes for a given note depend on the tempo of the music.

Third, the use of these multiple bounce strokes in the shorter varieties of rolls gives a more saturated, sustained sound. The roll, remember, is the drummer's long tone.

We do not fail to recognize the eventual need for developing the traditional double stroke roll (stroke and single bounce). About half-way through our intermediate method book we introduce this type of roll, along with all of the numbered stroke rolls. By this time most students have developed enough stick control to be ready to cope with the double stroke roll and have little difficulty.

The traditional method of teaching the roll, from open to controlled bounce, nearly always caused students to arrive at a definite break between the two. For many students, crossing this barrier was a major difficulty. With our method of first using multiple bounce strokes for at least a year, very few students encounter this trouble. In fact, since I changed over to this system 15 years ago, not a single case involving this problem has developed. After having played all manner and length of rolls by the multiple bounce system, most students can be taught all of the uneven and even stroke rolls in a single lesson with complete success.

Before approaching the traditional open roll we also acquaint our pupils with the various different rhythmic fundamentals possible to use on a given notation of a roll for different tempi. This is most necessary in the correct interpretation of 3/4, 6/8, and other less common meters.

Almost immediately after arriving at the point where we introduce the traditional roll, we suggest using the two techniques side by side for comparison. This eventually leads us to the future development of all types of saturation of rolls. The really expert drummer must be capable of playing almost any degree of saturation of his roll from one to five per hand.

It is our belief that a drum roll should be saturated by this means rather than by making the arms and wrists move faster. Saturation of a roll by multiples of the basic stroke permits more relaxation because less wrist speed is necessary to produce the same relative sound.

Let us be practical and admit that all of our students are not going to be professional musicians. A great majority play to become part of a school music group. At the beginning they need rapid success in order to develop the desire to attain greater success: they need to *enjoy* playing the drums. How can they enjoy it when they must struggle with a roll for a year before achieving even a reasonable amount of success?

If you are still teaching rolls in the traditional way, try this system on a few beginners and observe the improvements yourself. The chances are you will never go back to the rigid old way again, with its frustrations, drop-outs, and lack of consistent success.

April 1968

ORGANIZING THE PERCUSSION SECTION

I. INTRODUCTION

H. Owen Reed and Joel Leach

Imagine a small symphony orchestra whose woodwind section is composed of all woodwind specialists. Although the clarinetist is most proficient on the clarinets, he can also play the piccolo, flute, oboe, English horn, bassoon, and contrabassoon. This ability to play *all* of the woodwind instruments is evident throughout the section.

Imagine, too, that on the score the composer wrote the woodwinds on only three staffs. Although the flute and piccolo would primarily occupy the top staff, other woodwind instruments might also be written there. The second and third staffs would likewise serve for the notation of any woodwind instrument. In fact, one of the staffs might, for example, be used for oboe I and English horn playing simultaneously (stems up and down) and, after a few measures, each would change to clarinet and bassoon, respectively.

Imagine, then, that the music is passed out to the members of the orchestra. (Each woodwind player would have a part—in the form of a woodwind score.) The conductor enters, and the first rehearsal is about to start:

Maestro: All right orchestra . . . from the beginning.

Any Woodwind Player: Maestro, if you please, we haven't yet decided how to divide up our playing responsibilities.

M.: Please hurry, then.

W.P.: Yes, Maestro.

M. Now may we please begin?

W.P.: Maestro, the music is written so that we must have *two B♭* Clarinets. Since both are sounding at once, we'll have to rush out and get another clarinet.

M.: Please hurry!

W.P.: While we are waiting, Maestro, will you please check at measure 19. I have to change from English horn to bassoon in only two measures!

M.: Two measures is correct. If you can't move the bassoon closer and make the change, see if you can't get one of the other performers to cover the bassoon at that spot.

W.P.: I can, if someone else can cover the piccolo part at measure 25.

M.: Well, try to work it out among yourselves somehow. Now that we have two clarinets, can we begin?

W.P.: One more minute, Maestro. The composer wrote a low *B* for the flute, and my model only goes down to *C*.

M.: Then play an octave higher. No one will notice it anyway. Now please let's . . .

W.P.: Maestro! One more question before we get started. The composer calls for a Heckelphone. We don't own a Heckelphone, and the only one I know of is on rental at Maurie's Woodwind Shop in Chicago.

M.: There's neither time nor money for rental. Stuff a sock in the bell of the contrabassoon and play it on that. And now . . .

W.P.: Maestro: I *am* sorry, but do you know if the composer plans for the piccolo to sound as written or an octave higher? He doesn't say on the part.

M.: Well, it's rather difficult to tell the exact octave on a piccolo, but no doubt since he is an American composer, he wants it to sound an octave higher. After all we are *not* in Mozambique! Now if we may . . .

W.P.: Maestro: At measure 79 the composer has written a glissando on the flute from low *C* to the *G* above my highest *C*. Obviously I can't play that high *G* except on the piccolo, and it would be almost impossible to change without a rather noticeable break!

M.: Naturally: Then change the *G* to an octave lower and play it all on the flute! And, by the way, why don't you write the composer about this? He would no doubt appreciate it, and you might suggest that he use the traditional note heads. Music is difficult enough to read without using x-headed notes for the double reeds and diamond-headed for the single reeds. Now can we *please* start rehearsing? The percussion section is getting restless!

W.P.: Just one more question, Maestro. I specialize primarily on the flute and piccolo, but the composer asks me to change to bossoon for a rather difficult solo at measure 50. Wouldn't it be better if we had another copy of the woodwind score duplicated so that Pierre could play this?

M.: By all means—if we ever do play it! And now, gentlemen, ***if we may!***

M.: (after a few measures of rehearsal) Now where was the clarinet at measure 20?

W.P.: Maestro, the composer has allowed us so little time to change from one instrument to another that we will need to make a placement chart.

M.: (Screaming) Manager! Librarian! Please collect the parts and score and return them immediately to the composer. Tell him that due to unforseen circumstances we will have to postpone the performance of his work until a later date. And now, gentlemen, please put up *Eine kleine Nachtmusik!*

Rather chaotic, isn't it? This couldn't really happen? No? But it does—time after time—*in the percussion section!*

Editors Note:
The preceding is taken from the Introduction to a new book, Scoring for Percussion, *by H. Owen Reed and Joel T. Leach, soon to be published by Prentice-Hall, Inc. Used by permission.*

II. THE SECTION LEADER—KEY TO ORGANIZATION

Michael Combs

Major strides have been made in the advancement of percussion education and many new concepts and philosophies have been developed in this area. No matter what methods are used in percussion education, no matter what sticks are used, or how the techniques are taught, the *ultimate test of training is performance.*

Instances are not rare in which the music teacher or teachers have made a serious attempt to give their young percussion students excellent training, selecting the best method books, carefully planning the class lessons, and establishing sound objectives; yet, when the band or orchestra performs, the percussion section is one of the poorest.

One serious consideration of percussion training which should be at the top of the list is too often overlooked—organization in the section. No matter how highly trained the percussionists, lack of organization will cause poor performance.

The percussion section encounters problems and faces situations unlike any other in the musical organization. Only in the percussion section are the players required to perform on several instruments, frequently in the same composition; only in the percussion section must instruments constantly be picked up and put down.

The following suggestions are given to help eliminate many of the problems caused by lack of organization.

Select A Section Leader

Whether the group is a professional orchestra or a grade school band, one member of its percussion section must be selected to "run" the section. This is a real "must." Not only does a section leader instill unity in the section, but he will also save the director hours of extra work, both during and outside of rehearsals.

When selecting the section leader keep in mind that the best player may not always be the best leader. Making the first chair player automatically section leader may cause problems, especially when the best player is not an especially strong leader or mature individual. For student groups, the most successful way to select a leader is by a vote of the entire section. Students will be more likely to follow a leader they have selected themselves rather than one appointed by the director or selected on the basis of technical ability.

The section leader will be even more effective if the director gives him support by making the leader's position clear to the section and by giving him the responsibility of his position. Directors should allow the student leader to do as much of the organizing, rehearsing, etc., as he can handle. Students will not maintain respect for a student leader unless the director demonstrates *his* respect for that leader.

Some of the section leader's duties are:

1. Assign parts to be played. This can involve much time spent in drawing charts, making lists, or marking music. This time spent outside of rehearsal can save double that amount of time in rehearsal.
2. See that the proper instruments are available at the rehearsal and put away after the rehearsal. (An efficient section leader will delegate duties to other members of the section by making sure they take care of particular instruments.)
3. Make sure instruments are in good playing condition. Repair and maintenance of percussion instruments can take much of the director's time when it should be the responsibility of the percussionists.
4. Suggest the purchase of needed drum heads, triangle beaters, and other expendables. It is a major job to keep track of the large supply of percussion equipment which tends to get mislaid or broken.
5. Conduct sectional rehearsals. In many cases, when percussion parts need to be "woodsheded," the section leader can lead the rehearsal, allowing the director to work with other groups.
6. Act as a liaison between the section and the director. The section leader is the one to officially voice student complaints and suggestions to the director and, likewise, to clear up problems in the section at the director's request.

Organize The Rehearsal

It is difficult for the percussion section to have the proper equipment ready when it is given only a few moments notice of what piece will be played. Posting a list of the pieces to be rehearsed well in advance of the rehearsal allows the students an opportunity to prepare the needed instruments and get the music in order. This is a small consideration, often overlooked, that can save much rehearsal time.

Percussionists must learn to sit quietly when not playing. Boisterousness in the percussion section seems to be an ever-present problem in poorly trained or unorganized sections. Several music magazines or even copies of the scores might be made available in the section for students who do not play for an extended period of time. When some or all of the percussionists are not needed for a portion of the rehearsal, they should be kept busy sorting music, working with uniforms, clearing and/or repairing percussion instruments, assigning parts for the next piece, or with any of a number of constructive activities. For an especially large section, practice pads may be used for some of the extra students to play along.

One chair or stool for each player should be provided in a convenient location for rehearsals and performances. However, unnecessary movement in standing and sitting should be avoided during a performance.

Plan The Section

Each director has his own seating arrangement, and the placement of the percussion section varies from organization to organization, depending frequently on the size of the stage or rehearsal room. As a rule, the timpani should be placed on the inside of the section, as close to the center as possible. Moving outward, the bass drum and cymbals would come next, followed by the snare drum or drums, with the traps and mallet instruments on the outside. This basic arrangement, whether on the left or right side of the ensemble, will eliminate many problems and enhance organization. If at all possible, avoid separating the timpani from the rest of the section.

Instrument cases and percussion cabinets should be located close to the percussion section to facilitate a minimum amount of movement. Padded trap tables are essential to all percussion sections. A cymbal box, at a convenient height, is most valuable. All instruments must be kept neat and orderly in areas where they are readily available.

Ideally, a percussion section should carry six players. Although more or less are found in many sections, caution should be exercised to avoid overloading the section. The six players, who may change instruments from piece to piece, cover the following areas:

1. Timpani
2. Bass drum
3. Cymbals
4. Snare drum
5. Keyboard mallet instruments
6. Traps

These general assignments by category will cover a large amount of band or orchestra literature. Some college or professional sections have success in assigning one player to each area for a semester or year. One player would play all the snare drum parts, one would cover all the mallet parts, etc.

Problems in the section frequently stem from the fact that the music is disorganized. Some sections may have only one or two folders marked "drums" or "traps." Much time can be wasted looking through folders for the needed parts. The music can be organized best if each area has one folder (i.e., one timpani folder, one mallet folder, etc.).

Summary

Keeping these suggestions in mind will eliminate many embarrassing moments. Any director who has ever cued a solo cymbal crash only to find his section scrapping over who is to play snare drum or any director who has had to hold up his concert while the percussion section searches for the triangle beater or bell part, knows well the importance of organization in the percussion section. It takes only a little effort to have a well organized section and this small amount of effort can make the difference between a fine performance and an exhibition of embarrassing incidents.

Editor's Note: For a further discussion on this subject, see the Percussion Clinic in the May 1964 issue of The Instrumentalist.

May 1968

ENHANCING PERFORMANCE THROUGH IMAGERY

Sherman Hong

Every movement that a musician makes during a performance should be expressive of the music. Broadly speaking, every expression, every gesture, and every posture used in performance elicits some association of musical meaning.[1] Just as a dancer conveys meaning and associations through his body movements, so, too, does the percussionist express his music. The properly trained percussionist uses the psychology of mental and motor imagery* and the laws of acoustics.

One of the fundamentals taught the percussionist is to "draw or pull" the sound from the instrument. The words "draw" or "pull" infer that the student lift the tip of the stick or beater immediately after impact with the sounding surface. If the stick were not "pulled" there would be a tendency for the percussionist to "push" or force the tip of the stick into the surface. This forcing destroys or mutes some overtones; hence, the true quality of the instrument is not realized.

Closely associated with the mental imagery of "pulling" the

*Mental imagery may be defined as the ability to not only hear but to "feel" an image in the "mind's ear" when listening to music, responding to the rendition presented with a sensitivity to the persons, instruments, and the total situation. Motor imagery is the capacity of noting relationships and fixing them in memory so that when a situation is anticipated or recalled the image presents it in accurate and vivid detail. (Carl E. Seashore, *Psychology of Music.* New York: McGraw-Hill Book Co. Inc. 1938) sound out is motor imagery. The rate of speed of the stick movement away from the struck surface depends on musical tempo and stylistic markings. In playing staccato, for example, the percussionist thinks staccato style and grasps the stick with very firm pressure and pulls the tip of the stick away from the instrument in a precise, quick movement. The resulting sound will be staccato—the end product of mental and motor imagery used in conjunction in working toward a common goal. By varying the grip and wrist tension, and by varying the speed, the same procedure can be used in producing legato, marcato, scherzo, and other styles.

Many percussion teachers advocate a vocal approach to phrasing percussion lines; i.e., to play the lines as a singer would sing them. Although many percussion instruments are unable to produce melodies, musical inflection is just as important to the percussionist as it is to other performers. The percussionist must know and have mental and motor images of time, pivot notes, phrase markings, interpretation of symbols, metronomic markings, and musical terminology. In essence, the musical ideas and intentions of the music must precede the appearance of the music itself.[2]

The vocal approach incorporates the actual singing of the rhythms and/or melodies of the percussion part. Britton advocates the syllabification of rhythms to facilitate the proper rhythmic reproduction. Using syllables and the same basic rhythm, Britton gave two examples:[3]

Fit - ta - ta - ta zut

the first example played in a slower tempo and different style might become:

plum -du-du-du ta - ka tu

The *ta* sound is shorter than the *du* sound (this fact corresponds to tonguing syllables used on wind instruments). The percussionist should concentrate on making the percussion sound match what is produced vocally. For example, two staccato eighth notes would require a tighter grip and a quicker stroke than would be required for two legato quarter notes, which require a more relaxed grip and slower stroke movement. By singing the rhythms, the percussionist: . . .

> should develop the knowledge that it is the mind that controls the arms and resulting tones, instead of the too common belief that the arms work independently without the need of musical thought.[4]

Physically speaking, singing activates muscle control in lips, throat, tongue, and stomach. The vocal approach stimulates the student to make music *from within* and frees his playing muscles from unecessary tension.[5] An absence of tension facilitates better motor production response to mental and motor imagery.

Singing rhythms will make the percussionist more conscious of agogic accents and nuances not notated in the music. A piece of drum music may simply be noted:

Utilizing the vocal approach and coordinating mental and motor imagery, the example might sound:

du du du ta ta du du du dah dah

The syllables used will depend upon the tempo and style.

In addition to using mental and motor imagery, the percussionist should utilize the physical properties of his instrument. Melodies on the marimba should be phrased and tapered at the ends of those phrases. To aid himself in tapering a phrase, the percussionist should move his mallets closer to the ropes (nodal points of the bars) and elevate the handle slightly.

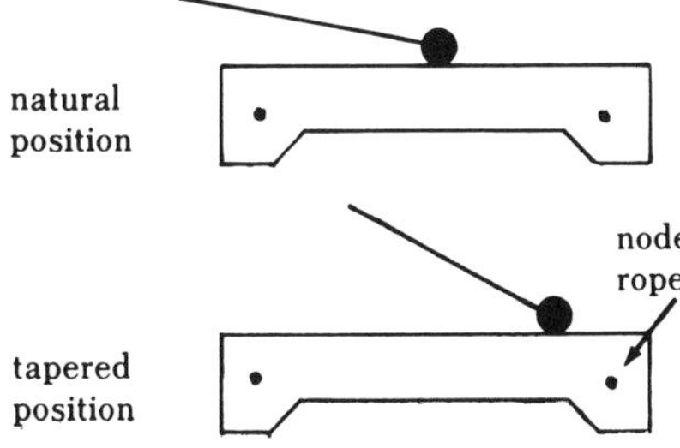

Moreover, if the mallet player were to sing *in his mind* and *breathe* the phrases the same way as a vocalist, the actual sound produced would be much better.

The percussionist generally has a more limited control over sound duration than other instrumentalists; therefore, he must use every physical aid possible. Primarily, the percussionist varies sounds by (1) playing on different areas of the instrument; (2) using different sizes and materials of sticks and mallets; (3) striking the instrument with different grip and stroke action; and (4) using discriminate sticking.[6] The fourth point must be elaborated. A simple rhythm can be sticked in various ways; for example:

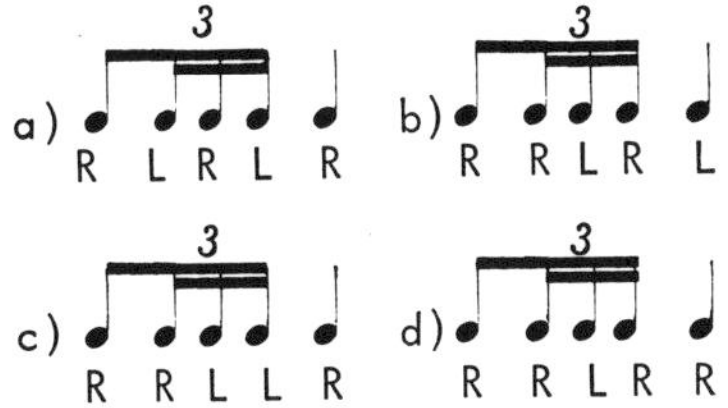

All those variations will produce different phrase sounds. The pattern chosen in performance will depend on what the other instrumentalists are playing. Is the rhythm an upbeat into a new phrase? Is it the end of a phrase? What is the articulation used by others? Or, if the percussionist is playing a solo, what is the pattern of the general phraseology of this composition?

The mental singing of intervals must not be neglected. It should be the primary goal of timpanists and mallet keyboard players to sing intervals and melodies mentally. The ability to produce mental intervals is of paramount necessity for the timpanist, who must often change pitches while the rest of the performing group continues to play, many times in a key foreign to the desired tonality of the timpani. Mental singing helps the mallet keyboard player phrase and articulate more musically.

The outstanding example in the use of mental, visual, auditory, and motor imagery in performance is the playing of the tambourine. Psychologists have noted that man hears not only with his ears, but with his *eyes*. Combining this psychological fact with imagery and the laws of acoustics, the tambourine player is able to utilize the shake (hand) roll and give the *illusion* of changing the dynamics of the roll. The tambourinist can *not* roll softer by using less and slower wrist action because the jingles would cease to vibrate properly. Using these facts: (1) that people hear with their eyes; (2) that people associate dynamics with position; and (3) that absorbent or porous materials in front of the sound waves of a vibrating surface will absorb much of the produced sound, we can say that the percussionist really *does* produce dynamic changes in a shake roll. Beginning the roll in the natural playing position (about shoulder height) the percussionist produces decrescendi by lowering his arm to his side or behind his body. The resultant sound is softer, not because he is playing softer, but by using the three points just discussed, he gives the *illusion* or imagery of playing softer. The procedure is reversed in the production of crescendi. This same procedure can be applied to playing maracas, castanets, and other instruments.

Another example of illusion can be found in the playing of hand cymbals. The actual body movements and even the facial expression of the performer can change the sound produced for the hearer. A cymbal player who grimaces or plays a forte crash in an aggressive, choppy motion will produce a different sound than that produced by a player who uses the same dynamics and speed of clashing motion, but with fluidity. Physically there is some difference (tension in wrists, amount of arm tension and motion), but the majority of the difference in sound will be perceived by the hearer's *eyes.* This example, along with the prior examples, should point out the need for correct playing procedures and stage presence for the percussionist.

Percussion performance involves a multiple of elements: the psychology of mental imagery, the psychology of aural imagery, the psychology of visual imagery, and the resulting element produced by compounding the first three: motor imagery. Having a conscientious awareness of those facts should motivate the percussion teacher and the percussionist himself to become better teachers and/or performers. There can be no good music without good interpretations:

> . . . even if the most complex disposition of the musical deviations are presented in a piece of music, they function only as necessary causes for the particular connotative experience aroused.[7]

The percussionist must utilize all the psychological, aural, and motor imagery possible to interpret percussion parts musically. With proper conditioning in imagery, the percussionist can become a fine musician.

---

[1]J. L. Marcuse, *Areas of Psychology* (New York: Harper and Brothers, 1954), p. 511.

[2]James Sewry, "Musical Performance and the Percussionist," *The School Musician,* XXV, No. 3 (November. 1963), 14, 16.

[3]Mervin Britton, "Teach Your Drummers to Sing," *Instrumentalist,* XXI, No. 5 (December, 1966), p. 80.

[4]*Ibid.*, pp. 80-81.

[5]*Ibid.*, p. 81.

[6]Al Payson and Jack McKenzie, *Music Educators' Guide to Teaching Percussion* (Long Island: Belwin, Inc., 1966), 90.

[7]Leonard B. Meyer, *Emotion and Meaning in Music.* (Chicago: Univ. of Chicago Press, 1956) p. 264.

June 1968

FEAR NOT THE KETTLE DRUM

Mervin Britton

The timpani, or kettle drums, may well be an enigma for the instrumental director as well as the student performer. While each kettle appears to be a large, simply designed instrument, directors often find themselves faced with common yet apparently complex problems. Such difficulties as an immovable pedal, a pedal which flies up, a pedal which flies down, a pedal that won't hold pitch, a head which will not produce the correct basic pitch or range, a terrible noise each time tension is put on the head—all of these may be daily headaches in the school instrumental program. Most of these problems can be avoided or corrected quickly if those involved with the drums understand the delicate balance principal and the simple mechanism which maintains this balance.

People often believe that there is some sort of complicated mechanism inside the frame that may be severely damaged if they try to adjust any part. This is not the case, although some part may be broken if extreme external force is applied. Maintaining a kettle in correct playing condition is no more complicated than maintaining any other instrument. It is merely different.

There are two main types of kettle design. The original and simplest design is the hand tuned kettle. Each tension rod, or tuning post, must be turned separately, by hand, to change head tension. Such tension is maintained by tension rods. (See illustration below.) All machine drums have some central means of changing head tension at all the posts. While details of design differ, the most common machine drums use some type of pedal mechanism. Such drums are built on the principal of balanced tension between the head and some other force—often a master spring. For the purpose of explanation, the design of the balanced pedal timpani will be used. The clutch design will also be illustrated.

The illustrations below show the main parts of the timpani.

Correct collar size is the one most important aspects of a properly adjusted drum. If the collar is too little or too extreme, there will be a dire effect on the balance between head tension and pedal mechanism. Each kettle has a basic pitch at minimum head tension. At this point, the collar for a calfskin head should average between ½" to ¾". This seems to place the head in its maximum, flexible tension range. Such tension is comparable to a strong spring. A strong spring completely contracted requires a great deal of force before it is stretched. A spring which is pulled to its maximum stretching point looses strength and flexibility.

Inadequate collar indicates the head is so contracted that extreme force is necessary to stretch the head. The head is less flexible and may break if such force is applied. Excessive collar indicates the head is stretched to such a point that its tension is weak. If this condition remains, the head will loose its elasticity. It is, therefore, of prime importance to maintain a correct collar. *If the collar is not correct, it is the first item to correct before any other adjustment is made.*

Plastic heads have the collar set at the factory and will not expand or contract in response to humidity changes. However, it is just as necessary to set the head at the correct basic pitch and to maintain correct balance between the head and kettle mechanism with plastic heads as it is with calfskin heads.

To set an even collar when mounting a wet calf skin head, all tension rods must be adjusted to equal length. Once the head has dried, it may be necessary to make some further minor adjustment in order to obtain an equal pitch at each tuning post. This equal tuning is more important than a completely even collar. If the pitch is the same at each tuning post, do not be concerned if the collar is a little uneven. If the collar becomes too uneven it will not be possible to maintain equal pitch or good resonance of tone. The head should then be removed, moistened until the collar line is soft, and put back on the kettle as an original mounting.

Each kettle size has a specific fundamental pitch. This fundamental is the lowest note of good resonance that can be expected of the head and kettle. Lower tones will be unclear. It is all right to set the original post tension so that the lowest possible pitch is as much as a half step below the fundamental. This furnishes a safety margin in case the organization should go flat, the head doesn't release completely from a higher pitch, or the calf head contracts during performance.

Normal playing range for each kettle is a perfect fifth above each fundamental. Extension of this range depends on many variables such as type of head (calf or plastic), condition of the head, and humidity. It is generally expected that a plastic head will have a higher range than a calf head and that the very lowest notes will sound better on calf heads than on plastic. The standard fundamental pitches and the normal range of each kettle size are listed below.

In order for the pedal to work properly, the tension of the master spring must balance the tension of the head. When it does, the pedal will hold at all positions within the normal playing range of a perfect 5th to major 6th. Trouble results when these forces do not balance.

Calf skin collars tend to become excessive on timpani played and stored in areas of high humidity. Humidity causes a skin head to relax. Therefore, to obtain the basic pitch and keep the balance, it is necessary to tighten the tuning posts. Such procedure results in excessive collar. However, if the tension posts are loosened so that the head is loose at even maximum tension, high humidity will not stretch the head. It will only be

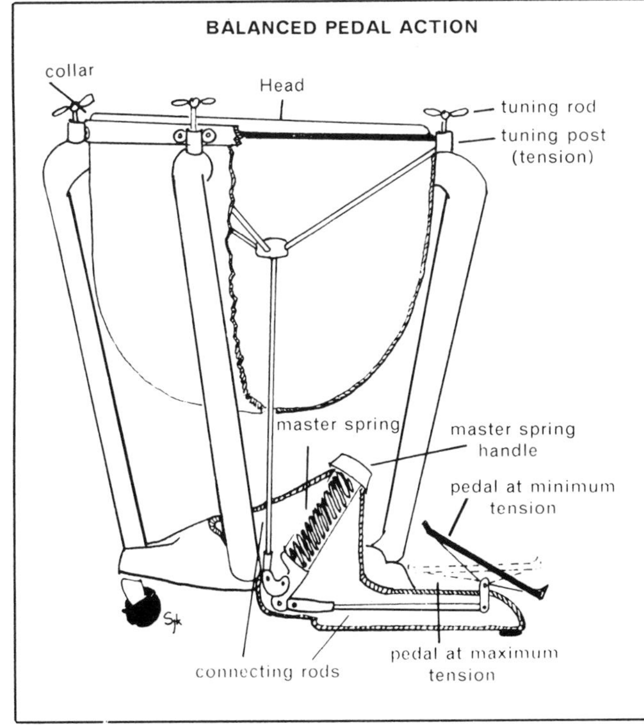

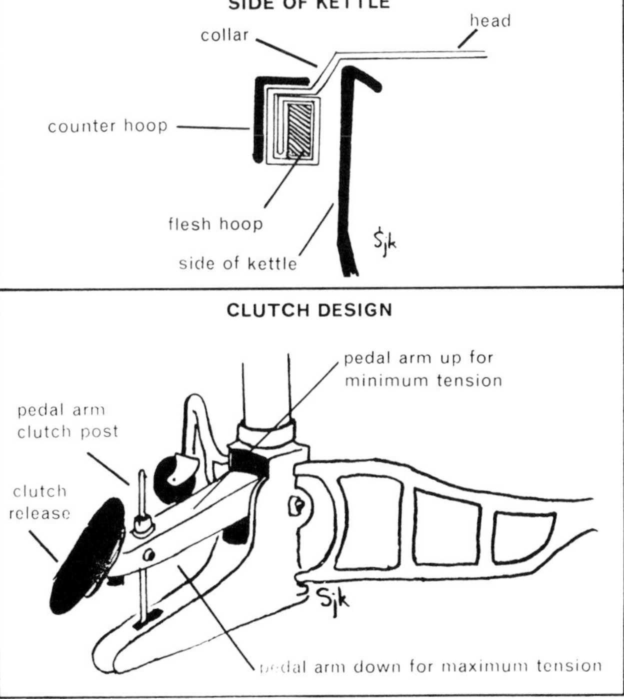

necessary to tighten the posts, bringing the head up to basic pitch at the next session. Such action will prevent or at least delay the development of an excessive collar.

In an area or period of low humidity the problem and procedure are reversed. It is necessary to loosen the screws for each session and to tighten them afterward. Between sessions the head should be left tight so that the lowest note is above basic pitch. Should the head be left in a relaxed state during periods of low humidity, it will contract, starting a process which will result in lost collar. The following rule will help avoid collar problems. *Extreme adjustments applied to tension rods prior to or during a performance should be undone after each session.*

Once the collar has been lost or stretched for several days, a more time consuming procedure is necessary. The head must be removed from the kettle. As the tension is rapidly released from the head, the pedal may suddenly snap up (toe down). The head tension no longer equals the spring tension. This sudden snap can be avoided by firmly holding a foot on the pedal, permitting the pedal to move slowly.

A wet sponge or towel should be rubbed over both sides of the head until it is soft and pliable and the rim crease is eliminated. Do not let water run under the flesh hoop. Water inside this flesh hoop may cause the head to pull off the hoop. Place the wet head on the kettle, adjusting the tension screws so that a ¾″ collar will be left after the head dries.

The head should be allowed 24 hours to dry in moderate humidity. If, after drying, the lowest pitch is much higher than the basic pitch, it may be necessary to rub additional moisture into the mounted head. When the head relaxes the pitch will drop. A little more collar may be added at this time. This collar will put just a little extra stretch on the head. If the head again contracts above basic pitch, this extra collar can be loosened, lowering the drum to the basic pitch without too much loss of adequate collar.

Summary—Problems and Solutions

The following section is a summary the most common problems and their solutions. These must be understood in order to keep the timpani in playing condition.

1. Problem: The pedal slides flat in the middle range.
Cause: The head has reasonable collar and is tuned to the correct basic pitch, but the master spring is not balancing the head tension.
Solution: Turn the spring handle to the right until the pedal holds at any place within the normal range.

2. Problem: The pedal slides sharp on low notes.
Cause: While the collar and basic pitch is correct, the master spring is too tight to balance the head tension.
Solution: Loosen the master spring by turning the handle to the left.

3. Problem: Although the balance was fine yesterday, the pedal now slides sharp in the low register.
Cause: The humidity is much higher today. The head has not been brought up to the basic pitch.
Solution: Tighten the head to the basic pitch. Remember to loosen it after the session.

4. Problem: Although the balance was fine yesterday, the pedal is frozen and will not respond to foot pressure.
Cause: The humidity is much lower. The lowest pitch on the kettle is above the required basic pitch.
Solution: Loosen the head until it produces the correct basic pitch. If the head continues to tighten during the session, rub a damp cloth over it to add moisture. Leave the head tight after the session to avoid losing the collar.

5. Problem: The collar is quite excessive and the pedal creeps sharp. There is not time to soak the head before the next session.
Cause: Excessive collar indicates weakened head tension. The head tension is not balancing the spring tension.
Solution: Loosen the master spring to balance with the head tension. Correct the collar as soon as possible, remembering to readjust the spring.

6. Problem: There is not enough collar at the correct basic pitch. The pedal will not hold in the higher range. There is no time to soak the head before the next session.
Cause: The head has contracted to the point that its tension is much greater than the master spring.
Solution: Never force the pedal. Rub a slight amount of moisture into the head so that the collar may be increased at the basic pitch. Do not make the head soggy. It may be necessary to add slight tension to the master spring. Soak the head as soon as possible.

7. Problem: A loud noise is produced whenever tension is increased on the head.
Cause: Dirt has accumulated between the head and rim or there is no lubrication at this friction point.
Solution: Clean the dirt from the rim of the kettle and the crease in the head. Lubricate the rim lightly with paraffin or candle wax or lanolin. *Never use Vaseline or oil.*

8. Problem: A buzz is produced when the head is struck.
Cause: Excessive wax has become dry and is vibrating against the head, or dirt under the head is vibrating.
Solution: Remove the head and clean the wax or dirt from the head.

9. Problem: A new head, or one that has been put on a kettle that is lubricated with Vaseline or lanolin produces a dead tone.
Cause: Vaseline or other excessive similar lubrication will deaden the head if it extends even a fraction of an inch onto the head from the rim.
Solution: Such material must be completely cleaned from the head.

10. Problem: A friction squeak is produced even though the rim is clean and lubricated.
Cause: The squeak is in the moving parts of one or more of the tuning posts.
Solution: Use light oil to lubricate these moving parts.

11. Problem: A metal vibration is produced when certain pitches are played.
Cause: There is a loose nut or washer.
Solution: Tighten all nuts and bolts on the kettle and its base. Whenever the head is removed, it is a good policy to check all nuts inside the kettle.

The importance of correct head adjustment should now be quite apparent. Such adjustment is just as necessary for clutch, ratchet, or hand tuned drums as for the balanced pedal design. Ratchet or clutch drums lock the pedal in place instead of balancing the tension. The lever arm makes it possible to counter the head force when adding tension. Whenever the pedal is released, the normal contracting force of the head pulls on the lever, lowering the pitch.

As stated in the above material, correct timpani maintenance is not complicated, but *is* just as necessary as the daily care given any other instrument.

September 1968

A Beginning Percussion Class

Rees Olson

Finding the best way to include percussion students in a beginning instrumental program is often a problem. First of all, there is the matter of numbers. No matter how convincingly the director sells the needs and opportunities for other instruments, drums will always attract more students than can possibly be admitted into a beginning band or orchestra. This fact provides the justification and actual necessity for careful screening of drum students. However, if students who are rhythmically responsive and intellectually alert are selected as beginning drummers, the problem of maintaining their interest is made even more difficult because they do have such ability and talent.

The percussion parts in beginning method books are not challenging to students of high capability when compared with the much more intricate and varied learnings involved in playing a wind or string instrument on the same level of difficulty. Talented students can progress much more rapidly in the reading and playing of rhythms than is provided for in a band class method. The learning challenge can be increased if a drum method is used, but that instruction is concentrated so exclusively on exercises for the development of snare drum technique that the student's need for an aesthetically satisfying musical experience is often neglected. The materials do not provide satisfactory opportunities to apply these techniques in a *musical* ensemble as they are acquired.

There is no reason why instruction should be limited to the snare drum only when so much more variety and interest can be maintained by having the children play several percussion instruments from the beginning, including the mallet instruments. In an attempt to reduce the frustrations of beginning percussion students and the instrumental teacher, classes in the Centralia (Calif.) School District were conducted in several elementary schools in which traditional drum instruction was replaced with an exploratory percussion class.

Although the primary motivation for organizing the class was to train percussion players for the instrumental program, an attempt was made to broaden the musical experience beyond that embodied in the process of learning to play the percussion instruments. The range of experiences, in addition to that of learning drum technique, which were envisioned for the class included the following:

1. Reading both rhythms and melodies.
2. Making up rhythm patterns and playing them.
3. Hearing rhythm patterns played by another person, "writing" them, and playing them.
4. Combining rhythms to make percussion ensemble compositions.
5. Participating from the outset in a percussion ensemble composed of a variety of percussion instruments.

Since one objective of the class was to use rhythm patterns created by the students, a graded sequence of rhythms was not pre-determined. A structure, however, was provided by working at each stage within a specific meter or combination of meters and with a limited number of note and rest values within the meter. No limitation was placed on the complexity or irregularity of the rhythms employed, other than the children's readiness to understand and perform them.

The procedure which was developed to achieve these goals was suggested, not by instrumental methods and materials, but rather by techniques of the Orff *Schulwerk* and by experiments in employing the discovery method to the teaching of music. It was apparent that what we wished to do could not be accomplished by following any published material—at least none of which we were aware. This lack of suitable music turned out to be fortunate, however, because it motivated us to *create* rhythm patterns and percussion music as the class proceeded and to find a way to efficiently involve the students in this creative process.

Selecting the Students

A maximum number of 10 students was set for the class in each of the schools which participated, and we attempted to accept only those who demonstrated a high potential in regard to rhythmic ability. As a first step in screening these children, we asked each teacher in grades 5 and 6 to recommend three children who appeared to possess the following characteristics:

1. A great interest in percussion instruments is important; children with drum or piano experience can be included but this should not be the determining factor.
2. The child should demonstrate good work habits and perseverance.
3. The child should show quick reactions, rhythmic responsiveness, and physical coordination.

The average number of students who were thus recommended was about 25 students per school, and a three-step evaluation was then administered to them:

1. Each child was interviewed briefly to determine his music background and interest in percussion

instruments. Children who were not enthusiastic about playing percussion instruments were eliminated for this reason.

2. The students were given the Drake Rhythm Test, Part A. This test measures the student's ability to maintain a steady tempo.

3. Each child was given an individual, teacher-made test which was designed to measure the student's ability to perceive and reproduce rhythmic figures. It consisted of the teacher tapping a series of one measure rhythm patterns in 4/4 after which the child would tap back the rhythm pattern as he heard it.

Introducing notation by the Rhythm Pattern Builder

So that children could discover note relationships and construct rhythm patterns through their own experimentation, a Rhythm Pattern Builder was devised. A variety of notes and combinations of notes were written on strips of tagboard, each of which was cut to a length which corresponded exactly with the duration of the note it represented. These note and rhythm pattern cards were assembled by placing them in a pocket chart holder which was a standard supply item in our schools. We felt that the pocket holder would permit the children to line up the notes more evenly and quickly than if a flannel board had been used. A measure card of colored tagboard was cut to correspond to the width of four quarter note cards placed side by side, and this served as a background to show how many notes and rests could be combined to make a 4/4 measure of music. Any combination of note and rest cards which could be assembled to correspond in width with the measure card would result in a properly notated measure of music. We first tried using 12″ as the size of a 4/4 measure but found that by reducing this to 10″ it was possible to "write" three measures of rhythm across one line of the chart which we used. The widths of the cards were as follows:

4/4 and ¢ measures = 10''

3/4 and 6/8 measures = 7½''

2/4 measures = 5''

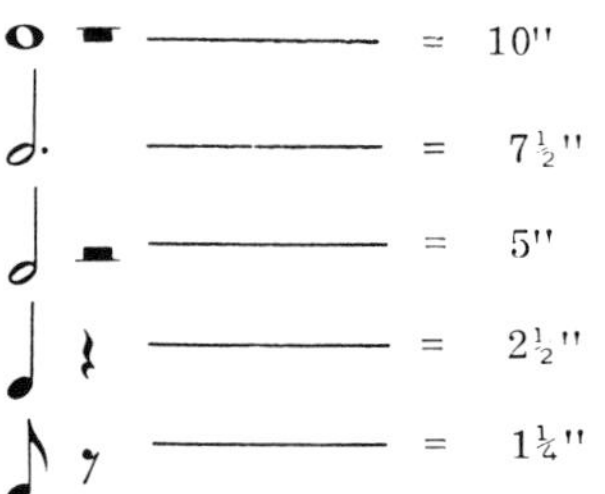

We found that according to the scale which we used, sixteenth notes would become too small and crowded together to be readable, and so the chart was not used for notes of shorter duration than eighth notes. Other strips of tagboard were folded over to show the method of counting the rhythms and for symbols which occur beneath the notes such as accents, slurs, and dynamic variations. These symbols could be moved readily to any position in the measure. It was through this shifting use of the accent sign that the concept of syncopation was first introduced.

The Rhythm Pattern Builder was used as an aid in carrying on several different types of activities pertaining to basic rhythm patterns. First of all, the students learned the relative value of the notes and rests by matching, for example, two eighth note cards with one quarter note and discovering that they were the same width. The quarter and eighth note cards were then assembled in many combinations to construct rhythm patterns of one measure. The children were assured that regardless of the sequence of notes, the pattern would be a properly notated measure if it lined up with the measure card at both beginning and end. Syncopated patterns were accepted and performed whenever they occured without suggesting to the children that they were difficult or unnatural. As soon as a rhythm pattern was assembled on the chart it was performed immediately with snare drum sticks and on other percussion instruments.

The process was also reversed so that a child would be asked to think of and play a rhythm pattern in the established meter using only the notes agreed upon. Another child would then "write" the rhythm on the chart by re-arranging the note cards to represent the rhythm which he heard. So that all children would have an experience with the rhythm pattern, the sequence for this activity was as follows: One child play—all children play—one child "write"—all children play again.

The advantage of using note cards in this way, rather than having the children write the notation on the chalk board, is that the child's response was not slowed down by concern for drawing the notes properly. Even by using this system, the child could not assemble the notes as quickly as he could make the correct choice. To further help the child speed up the process of showing the notation, rhythm patterns of one measure were made and then the student would merely have to select the correct measure from several possibilities available to him.

Snare Drum technique

Although the development of rudimentary snare drum technique was not the sole goal and activity of the class, it was not neglected. A portion of each class was spent in playing single stroke and double stroke rhythms at various speeds for the purpose of developing stick control and preparation for the long roll and other rudiments. The echo technique was also used—the teacher would play a rhythm pattern and the students would play it back, using a variety of sticking sequences.

Playing the Bells

After the students had become familiar with reading rhythms, the playing of melodies on the resonator bells and alto xylophone was introduced. The playing of rote and improvised ostinato patterns helped the students gain confidence and facility on the instrument and provided a means of including the bells in the ensemble before the ability to read melodies was mastered. At the same time, the reading of melodies was started through the use of the bells part in an easy band ensemble book.

Ensemble Playing

From the beginning of the class, students used a variety of percussion instruments including bass drum, snare drum, cymbals, bells, alto xylophone, tambourine, wood block, triangle, and maracas. All students were expected to become proficient on all the instruments, including the bells, and the same rhythms were performed on many of these instruments. The first original ensemble selections created during the class were put together in a cumulative form in which one type of instrument would begin a rhythm pattern and continue playing it as an ostinato while other instruments would begin in turn with other patterns, until all instruments were playing different patterns at the same time. Each instrument would then drop out, one at a time, until the selection ended the same way it began. Ensemble selections in canon and rondo form were also constructed using the rhythm patterns which the children had invented. Besides playing original ensembles created by the class, the students also performed the percussion parts from an easy ensemble book for band which was scored for bells, snare drum, bass drum, cymbals, triangle, and wood block.

Although one purpose of the class was to train percussion players for the band and orchestra, the procedures employed were controlled by more general objectives. An attempt was made to provide an experience which would be complete and aesthetically satisfying in itself. It is not expected that all of the students in the classes will become drummers in the school instrumental organizations. Those whose interests develop in a different musical direction can apply the acquired musicianship in playing other instruments or in playing percussion instruments with other types of music groups. Students who qualify, however, will be able to assume a position in the beginning band and orchestra, not only with a good introduction to drum technique and the reading of rhythms, but also with an experience covering a wide range of musical effects using percussion instruments. The achievement and response of the students have been excellent, and the Percussion Ensemble Class will be established as a regular feature of the beginning instrumental music program in our schools whenever feasible.

1. Student building a 4/4 measure using quarter notes and quarter rests. (**Note:** The measure card in these pictures does not show enough contrast to be easily visible.)

2. Student building a 4/4 measure using quarter notes and eighth notes.

3. Measures of 4/4 rhythm.

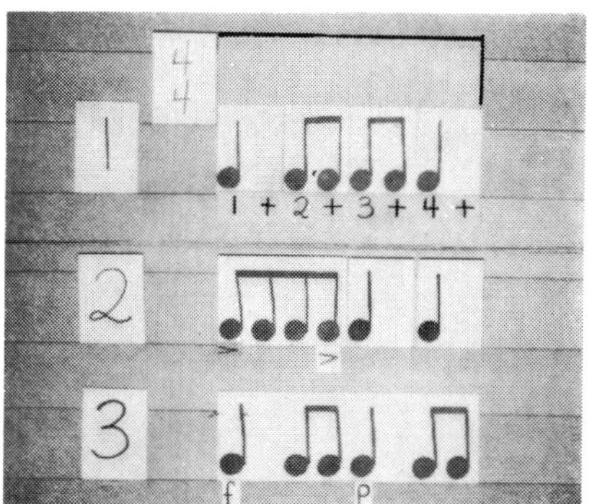

Line 1 shows a measure built from quarter note cards and double eighth note cards. The counting card, which hooks on below the notes is also shown.

Line 2 is built with a card showing a four note grouping of eighth notes and quarter note cards. The accent sign, which can be shifted to any position in the measure, is also shown.

Line 3 is a complete measure card to which forte and piano signs have been added.

4. 4/4 measures which introduce the tie and dotted quarter note.

Rondo For Percussion Ensemble A B A C A (ABC) A

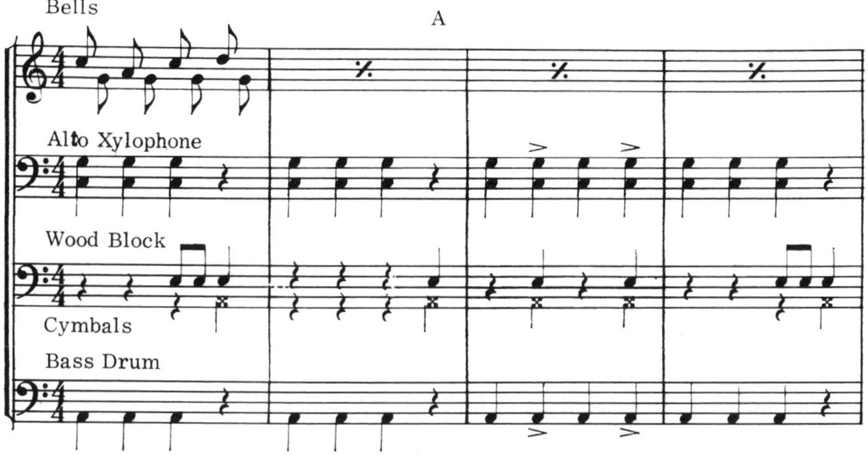

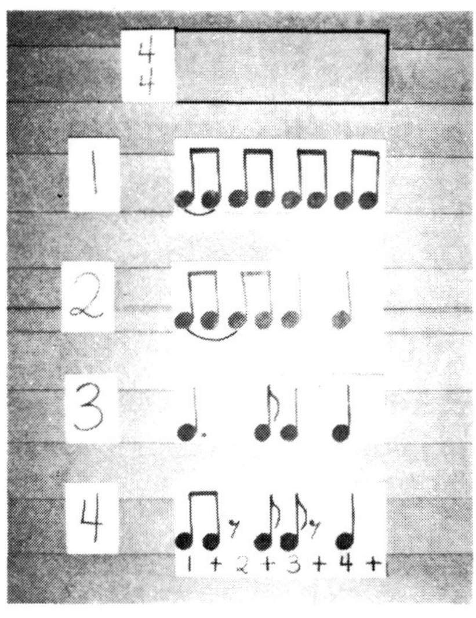

5. Six 4/4 measure cards placed so that they may be played in sequence as a single rhythmic selection.

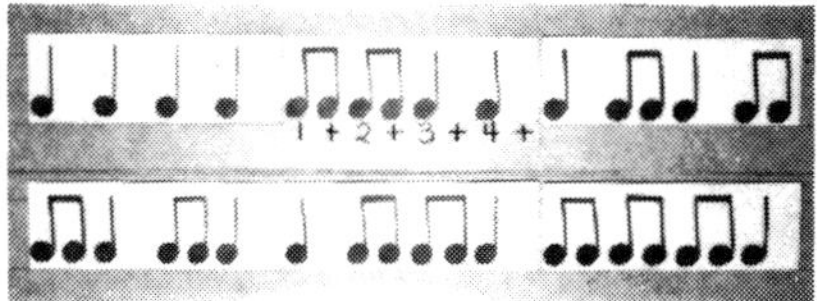

6. Measures in ¢ and 3/4.

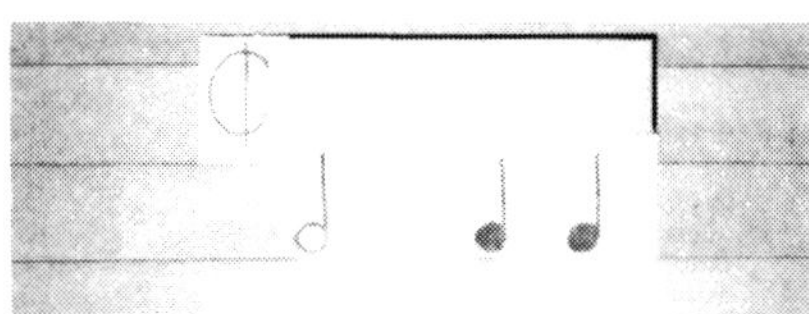

7. Measures in 6/8 showing methods for counting in a slow tempo and in a fast tempo.

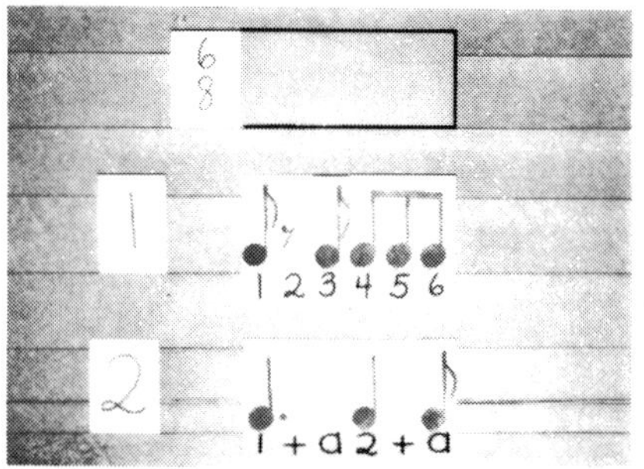

October 1968

Multiple Percussion Playing

Saul Feldstein

The term multiple percussion is often misinterpreted as meaning one player having the ability to perform on all of the percussion instruments. Although today's percussionist must be able to do this, rather than merely being able to play snare drum, timpani, or keyboard, multiple percussion has a more specific meaning. It involves the technique of one player playing more than one instrument simultaneously.

Many compositions in orchestral and band literature, as well as solo and percussion ensemble literature, require the performer to read music involving two, three, or more instruments. The notation may appear on a five line staff with a key indicating which line or space designates each instrument.

Example 1.

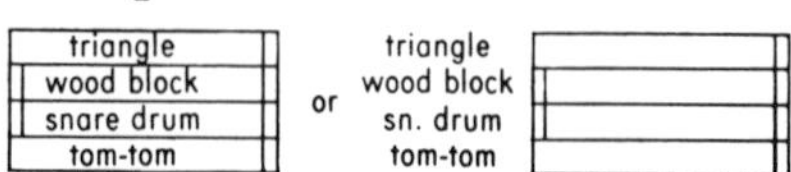

It may also be written on a staff where each instrument has its own line. Example 2.

A part involving three instruments would have a three line staff and a part involving four instruments would have a four line staff. (Stravinsky's *L'Histoire du Soldat*, which uses 13 percussion instruments, uses 13 lines.)

The percussionist has primarily learned the problems of multiple percussion techniques through trial and error when being faced with literature that demanded knowledge of this type of playing. This approach to learning made the sightreading of multiple percussion parts virtually impossible. It also limited the development of these techniques to the advanced player who was confronted with this type of music more often than the beginning player. As music has advanced, the role of percussion in young performing groups has increased to the point where the young percussionist, too, is being confronted with multiple percussion parts. More music educators and private teachers are feeling the need for developing percussionists. The accessory instruments, as well as keyboard and timpani, are being taught. The student who studies only "drums" until his sophomore year in high school, and then, if he shows promise, is given the opportunity to experiment with the other percussion instruments, is gradually disappearing. It is heartening for percussion specialists to see this long-needed growth and development. Multiple percussion playing, combining the knowledge and technique of playing each of these instruments simultaneously, involves specific problems which must also be studied systematically, not merely through the literature.

The movement from one instrument to another necessitates analysis of the motion involved in playing. Although different concepts and theories exist related to this subject, if one would experiment to find out how the three main joints of the arm (wrist, elbow and shoulder) function, certain basic concepts would be very readily seen. The wrist most naturally works in an up and down motion. The elbow can motivate the forearm in an up and down, as well as side to side motion. The shoulder can motivate the entire arm in a forward and backward motion. For the multiple percussionist, this implies that the strokes of playing any instrument should be motivated by the wrist, leaving the elbow free to motivate the forearm along a horizontal plane and leaving the shoulder free to motivate the arm forward and backward. If the forearm is used to play each stroke, it will not be free to facilitate movement from one instrument to another. For development of multiple percussion technique therefore, it is a necessity that the student be able to motivate the stick, mallet, or beater with the wrist and fingers alone. This concept of motion is applicable to keyboard percussion, timpani, and the drum set, as well as multiple percussion playing. On the keyboard, for example, the wrist would motivate the mallet to strike each note, and the elbow would be used to play different pitches on the natural notes (white keys), and the shoulder would be used to play the chromatic tones (black notes). If this approach is followed, the technique of moving around the instrument in fast passages (or in slow passages, which are rolled and meant to be played legato) would be limited only by the speed at which the performer could play alternating strokes motivated by wrist and fingers and coordinate them with elbow and shoulder motion.

The student who has never been exposed to multiple percussion techniques will find movement from the center of the snare drum to the rim to be a challenge. This movement, which is short in distance, is a good place to start developing multiple percussion techniques. In most cases, a two line staff has proven to be less confusing to the beginning student of multiple percussion playing, and will therefore be used in the examples below. (Example 3)

After the student has developed a relaxed motion between the snare drum and the rim, he is ready to add a second instrument to his study. This instrument may be a woodblock, triangle, or another drum, such as a tom tom. The movement from one instrument to another will thus be expanded. Here it must be pointed out that the set up of the instruments is very important. A proper set up will facilitate playing where an improper one can make an easy part virtually impossible. The music should be carefully studied before devising the proper set up. In beginning materials this set up should be indicated for the student. For ease of performance, a trap bar, a stand adjustable in height from which accessories can be suspended, would be advantageous. A woodblock holder and triangle clip are also important. Tonal quality and pitch relationship must constantly be stressed so that the percussionist will develop musically as well as technically. The music used for multiple percussion students should evolve and grow from the student's background, taking full advantage of his knowledge of rhythm, rudiments, etc. (Example 4)

The tonal variety of two instruments can be greatly enhanced by a change of mallet, stick, or beater. The student should experiment with different beaters to find the one most applicable for the specific study or composition. Often the player is required to switch types of beaters within the course of a composition. This technique must also be developed. To make the change quickly and quietly while counting measures rest involves practice. (Example 5)

Changing one beater while playing with another is also a technique which needs development. The student must again switch quietly, but this time while concentrating on playing a short section with one hand.
(Example 6)

A trap table, a table covered with a soft material, will aid this technique. After developing the ability to play two instruments simultaneously, to change beaters during rests, and to change one beater while the other continues playing, the student is ready to proceed by adding a third tonal color. In the beginning of this stage the use of the center, the edge, and

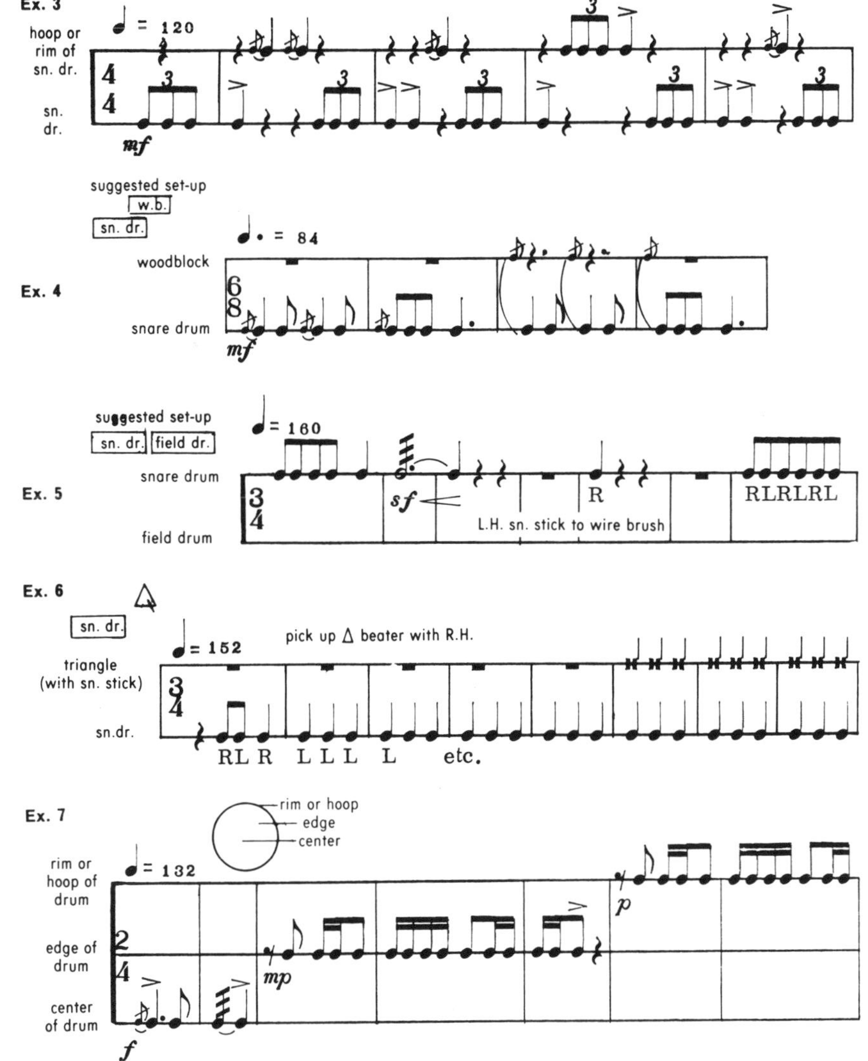

the rim of the snare drum can be very advantageous in spreading the student's eye perception to the three line staff.
(Example 7)
The techniques involved in this discussion can very easily be applied to the drum set. This instrument is, by its own nature, a multiple percussion instrument involving the feet, as well as the hands.

The tonal variations and technical and musical demands are never ending. The challenge to the performer musically, as well as technically, opens new and heretofore unpursued avenues to percussionists at all levels of development, rather than just to those who have obtained a substantial amount of facility with the instruments.

Author's note: The examples used in this article are from "Percussionist Solo Series," a collection of soloistic studies of various levels of difficulty designed to introduce the drummer to multiple percussion playing with percussion. All examples have been used with the permission of the publisher, Belwin Inc., Rockville Centre, Long Island, New York.

November 1968

Questions, Answers, and Suggestions for Mallet Instruments

Joel Leach

Q: I intend to purchase a mallet instrument. What size should I buy?
A: Mallet instruments for school use should be of the following sizes: Marimba: 4 octaves; Xylophone: 3½ octaves; Vibraphone: 3 octaves; Chimes: 1½ octaves.
Q: Can I save money by buying a smaller instrument?
A: Yes, you can save money by buying a smaller instrument. However, the size limitation will severely hamper effective use of the instrument in many cases, due to the extensive demands being made upon the mallet instruments by contemporary composers.
Q: Does this mean that the smaller instruments have no purpose?
A: Not at all! They were designed mainly to save the beginning student money. As we all know, the beginner sometimes gives up on an instrument shortly after commencing study. The smaller instrument allows for the beginner to try it out without excessive financial risk.

Smaller instruments are acceptable if the financial belt must be tightened. The marimba size may be trimmed to 3½ octaves, and smaller xylophones (usually without resonators, and mounted in fold-up cases) are usable. However, it should be understood that in both cases some difficulties will arise due to the abbreviated range. And in the case of the xylophone, the tone will be somewhat inferior due to the lack of resonators.
Q: How about small kits which contain the glockenspiel and drum pad?
A: Tremendous idea! The kit (which generally contains a glockenspiel, drum pad, sticks and mallets) sells for about $70.00 and has the advantage of allowing the beginning drummer to carry on the melodic studies along with his drum lesson each week. Although this particular type of glockenspiel is not suitable for use in your band or orchestra, it is an excellent training instrument for the beginner.
Q: My budget allows for the purchase of one mallet instrument only. Which one should I buy first?
A: A glockenspiel. This instrument is used more than the other mallet instruments in both band and orchestra literature, and its presence will still allow for training for the percussionists in the area of melodic performance.
Q: If I can afford another one, should I buy the xylophone next?
A: No. It is not surprising that this instrument usually comes to mind immediately when we think of mallet instruments. However, its tone color (brittle and glassy) limits its use to only those parts written especially for it. Admittedly, it can be used for mallet training, but it is not the most versatile of the mallet instruments.
Q: Then which one should I buy next?
A: A marimba. It can be used as a solo instrument, for its smooth and fluid tone quality blends well in nearly any ensemble. Without transposition, it can reinforce or replace a missing oboe, flute, or violin. With simple sight-transposition, it can assist weak 2nd and 3rd clarinets, tenor saxophone, or treble clef baritone. With a little more transposition effort, the marimba can assist or substitute for the English horn, alto saxophone, French horn, alto flute, or numerous other instruments found in the band and orchestra. In short, the marimba is a very flexible and versatile instrument with both solo and ensemble capabilities. Two players can play it simultaneously using a piano score—an excellent training ground for sightreading and ensemble.
Q: If I own a marimba, what can I do when a xylophone part appears in the music?
A: Use a harder marimba mallet and transpose the part up one octave. It will closely approximate the xylophone sound. Thus, one can see that the marimba is capable of substituting rather well for the xylophone, while the opposite is not true.
Q: How about purchasing a used

instrument?
A: Surprisingly enough, chances of locating an old marimba are very good—even in small towns. The marimba has been with us a long time, and its vaudeville popularity some time ago led many people to buy them. Many of these instruments have been stashed away in attics or basements for years, and are still in excellent condition. This author has never had difficulty in locating a used marimba for a student or school. If your school allows for the purchase of used instruments (with justification), it is suggested that you run an ad in the local paper for a length of time. And, try the nearest large city. Chances are that you will turn up a suitable instrument for $300 or less.

Q: How do I know if the used instrument I find is a good buy?
A: First, you should know whether it is a marimba or xylophone, for many people innocently offer these two instruments for sale under the wrong name. If it is a 4-octave instrument, check to see if the next-to-lowest *C* sounds as middle *C*. If it is 3½ octaves, or less, the lowest *C* should sound as middle *C*. If so, it is most likely a marimba. And, the front set of resonators will most likely be shaped symmetrically rather than tapered upwards. This is not *always* true, however.

Keep is mind that the frame can be repaired and refinished. Therefore, one's main concern is the condition of the bars. If they have not suffered from extreme abuse, and if they still produce a rather good scale, they may be sent back to the manufacturer who will retune or replace bars for a very reasonable fee. This is usually in the area of $60.00 unless a large number of bars need to be replaced. And, when they return the bars, they will have been refinished so as to look like new.

Q: I understand that the bar widths vary. Should I purchase a marimba with narrow or wide bars? . . . . or does it matter?
A: Wide bars allow for greater accuracy at high speeds. The price difference between two instruments of identical type but with different bar widths will be slight. However, if this difference will prohibit the purchase of the more expensive instrument with the wide bars, by all means, buy the one with narrow bars! That is far better than having none at all!

Q: My marimba (or xylophone, or vibe) has a *dead* bar on it. What should I do?
A: Remove the bar and send it to the manufacturer. He will retune or replace it for approximately $10.00 (depending upon size of the bar), and refinish it to match those already on your instrument. It will be as good as new once again.

Q: A few bars on my marimba (or xylophone, or vibe) have gone out of tune. What should I do?
A: Again, remove the defective bars and send them to the manufacturer. Severe humidity changes can cause a few bars (or an entire instrument) to go out of tune. This can often be corrected at the factory without replacing the bars. Keep in mind that they are able to both raise or lower the pitch of any bar by shaving wood from different areas on each bar. So, this can often be remedied without costly repair bills.

(Editor's note: Specify what master pitch should be used: A = 440 or A = 442. When tuning the entire keyboard, A = 442 is recommended for all except the marimba, which should be set at A = 441 [a necessary compromise to the piano and other instruments].)

Q: Which mallets should I use for these instruments.
A: The following list is by no means complete. However, it should enable you to choose mallets to suit most of your needs.

Marimba:
Musser #1—Good for practice and general playing.
Musser #6—Good clarity in upper register.
Musser #7—Less bite than the #6 mallets.
Musser #8—Good for soft, legato playing. Excellent in low and middle register.
Musser #10—Designed for use in low register.
Deagan #2014—(Equivalent to Musser #6) Good for approximation of xylophone sound in upper register.
Deagan #2016—Good for soloistic playing on entire instrument.

Xylophone:
Musser #5—Plastic mallets which are excellent for general playing.
Wooden mallets—(Available through several manufacturers) Close approximation of plastic, but with a little less bite.
Deagan #2014—Less bite to sound than the plastic mallets.
Deagan #2015½—Less bite than the #2014 mallets.
Deagan #2016—Smoother sounding; good for legato playing at lower dynamic levels.

Vibes:
Musser #8—Good for general playing at piano-forte dynamic levels.
Musser #7—More bite than Musser #8. Greater clarity; good for solos.
Musser #6—More attack than Musser #7. Good for solo playing.
Deagan #2016—Excellent for soloistic work.
Deagan #2015½—More bite than the Deagan #2016 mallets.
Deagan #2014—Sharp, metallic sound. Equivalent to Musser #6.

Q: What book should I use for teaching the mallet instruments?
A: The music educator will find it quite easy to introduce the mallet percussion instruments through use of "Modern School for Marimba" by Morris Goldenberg (Chappell Pub. Co.). This sh[illegible]d be supplemented with additional materials as soon as the student has achieved some degree of success on the instrument. "Keyboard Technic" by Tom McMillan (Pro Art Pub. Co.) offers excellent supplementary material. Also good for any instrument is: "Rhythmic Articulation" by Pasquale Bona (Publ. by Carl Fischer).

Q: Where can I locate solo materials?
A: The Musser Company has a booklet available for one dollar ("Solo and Ensemble Literature for Mallet Percussion Instruments", by James Dutton, 505 E. Shawmut, LaGrange, Ill. 60525) which indexes a tremendous amount of solo material. The Earl Hatch Publishing Company (5140 Vineland Avenue, North Hollywood, California 91601) handles excellent mallet instrument material. Mr. Hatch has a catalog available which grades and describes each selection.

Don't forget also that violin, oboe, and some flute literature transcribes very well for the mallet instruments. The Handel violin sonatas are an excellent example.

Rules for Mallet Players
Marimba and Xylophone

1. Stand with your heels about 9" to 12" apart; weight evenly distributed.
2. Mallets are held with matched grip (like right hand snare drum grip).
3. Backs of hands should be up; elbows 4" to 6" away from body.
4. Mallet handle should pass through first joint of first finger and should be held there firmly by the thumb. First finger should curve about the handle at this point rather than protrude straight beyond the stick.
5. Approximately 1½" of mallet handle should protrude from back of hand.
6. In playing position, mallets should form an inverted "V" in front of body.
7. When both mallets are playing on a single bar (as in a roll), the left mallet should be farthest from the body.
8. Strike center of all bars. (*Advanced students* may strike nearest edge of sharp bars, but only when necessitated by speed.
9. Rapidly moving rolls also may be executed at the ends of the sharp bars, providing proper playing position is maintained. (Be sure that both mallets straddle the rope, and that rule #7 is observed.)
10. Move body to middle of range in which you are playing; move to new area (rather than reach) if there is a register change.
11. Always slide feet to new position; don't cross-step.
12. Mallet action should be up and down–not oblique or circular.
13. Beginning students should play at a *forte* dynamic level in order to develop proper fundamental technique. This is very important!
14. Use proper mallets (see attached listing). Plastic, wood, and metal mallets seriously damage marimba bars.

Vibe:

1. All the rules above, except #8, 9, and 14 apply to vibes also.
2. The vibe damping bar mechanism is mounted in such a manner as to make the ends of the sharp bars poor targets even at high speeds as their tones will decay much too rapidly. It is wise, therefore, for the vibist to strike the center of *all* bars.
3. Legato playing is best executed by damping the previous note (with finger) just prior to striking of a new pitch. Slurring requires that the previous note be damped at the *exact instant* the new pitch is struck.
4. Metal mallets may damage vibe bars. Mallets of plastic and wood are not recommended unless called for by the composer.

Chimes:

1. Hold the mallet handle in a horizontal position to the floor. This will protect the knuckles when playing the sharps.
2. Strike directly at the tube caps from the side, glancing off in an upwardly direction after impact.
3. When traveling to a contest, it is both practical and logical to remove a single tube rather than transporting the entire instrument. A small wooden rack may be built to handle three or four tubes, thus saving a great deal of transport labor.
4. The commercial rawhide mallet may be softened by wrapping a single thickness chamois around the mallet head. A leather disc may also be glued to one side of the double-headed chime mallet, thus assuring the chime player of at least two different mallet hardnesses.

December 1968

Sightreading In Percussion Contests? Yes!

Maxine Lefever

The percussionist, like the wind player, must develop competencies in the several facets of *total* musicianship. The musician's ultimate aim is to so interpret the printed notes that the end result is a musical performance. Implied in this process are (1) the ability to read the notes, (2) the technique to perform the notes, and (3) the knowledge and sensitivity to render these notes in a musical style.

Let us, for the purpose of this discussion, limit ourselves to the snare drummer–realizing, of course, that our remarks may be similarly applied to those who perform on all instruments of the percussion family, as, indeed, to all wind and string instrumentalists.

The pros and cons of the rudimental approach to snare drum instruction have been debated throughout the years. The pendulum of thought swings from one argument to another, with no universal and firm consensus emerging. This is an important consideration, but irrelevant to our discussion, for all agree that some form of training in the "rudiments" (and the term "rudiments" is used in its broadest sense) or "fundamentals" of technique is essential. Let us, then, answer that our hypothetical snare drummer under discussion has indeed acquired, via some route, a technical facility. He can peform single strokes and double strokes in all of the mathematically infinite combinations. Hopefully, he can also perform the multiple bounce roll.

Is our drummer now a musician? No, for it still remains for him to interpret the printed notes in order to produce a *musical* performance. This involves considerably more than the mere technical ability to play groups of notes in various prescribed "patterns." He must transform the composer's notations into the intended musical result.

The ability to render a musical

performance involves familiarity with the language of music—the notes, the rests, the dynamic markings, the tempo markings, the many musical terms.

The learning process is as old as the history of man. Here, too, various methods of learning have had their proponents and their periods of dominance: learning by rote, by memorization, by drill, by experience, by practice in meaningful situations, etc. No matter what particular approach may be advocated by the teacher, surely all must agree that some form of "practice" is essential. In music, this necessarily involves the reading of increasingly more complex patterns of notes. Thus, our student must have material to read to further develop this phase of his musical competency.

Our music contests pay great attention to the technical phase of the snare drummer's development. Many states require the actual performance of some of the 13 or 26 standard rudiments and this performance has a definite bearing upon the rating received by the students. Several of the categories for grading concern themselves primarily with the technical mechanics of performance. And this is as it should be, for without the essentials of technique our student cannot aspire to attain greater heights of musicianship.

We might well ask whether the performance of the solo indicates the student's other qualities of musicianship. Unfortunately, the answer is often a most emphatic "no." The great majority of our snare drum contestants play rudimental solos. Often, these solos do not contain *any* tempo, dynamic, or expression markings, with the possible exception of accent marks. The adjudicator may be well convinced of the student's technical mastery of some or all of the 26 rudiments, but he is provided with no opportunity to observe the student's facility in the other facets of musicianship.

Many auditioners will remark about the snare drummer who presented a beautifully prepared solo but who was subsequently discovered to be unable to read a simple part. Such a student may have flawless technical ability and may have learned to perform that particular pattern of notes by some means, but he is totally lacking in other essential musical qualifications.

One possible solution to this this problem would be to ban the performance of rudimental solos, arguing that wind instrumentalists do not present solos of mere simple combinations of the various scales and arpeggios *per se*. However, realizing that the rudimental solo is an integral part of our percussion literature and that it can serve a place in the development of the percussionist, this would not appear to be a good solution.

It would thus seem essential that we add a category to the requirements in contest for the percussionist—that of sightreading. In addition to serving the rather obvious function of presenting the adjudicator with further information on which to base his opinion and rating, it also provides our contestant with another area of performance. It is to be hoped, then, that our student will prepare himself in this area just as he prepares himself for the presentation of his solo and of the rudiments.

It must be pointed out that the time element is not a factor to be considered in the discussion of adding sightreading to our contests. Snare drum solos are notoriously short—often of less than a minute's duration. The adjudicator can hear the solo and the presentation of the separate rudiments and still have more than half of the allotted time to write his comments. An additional minute allowed for sightreading will not cause him to fall behind in his schedule.

Sightreading material should ideally be prepared by a contest official or by the adjudicator himself just prior to the contest. This will insure that it is truly sightreading material for all of the students. It should contain selections of different tempi and should employ a variety of musical terms.

The following is suggested:

Tempo marking have intentionally been omitted. The adjudicator may suggest that the student select his own tempo or the adjudicator may establish the tempo.

In many years of auditioning students for all-star organizations, clinic bands, camp bands, and placement in high school and university bands, I have found a very high degree of correlation between performance of the above materials and actual performance by the student within the organization. Other auditioning materials have been utilized but none have been found to be so effective.

Many of our progressive states are adding a sightreading category to the contest requirements for the percussionist. It is to be hoped that those states which have not already done so will give it serious consideration for the future. Let us give our percussionist further incentive to develop and exhibit the full scope of his musicianship.

Preparation for the Collegiate Percussion Audition

Terry Applebaum

The high school senior seeking admission to a college or university as a percussion major, with the intent to pursue a career in music, faces many questions concerning his collegiate future. Perhaps the most perplexing of these relates to his percussion audition. The college or university's expectations in terms of the percussion instruments to be utilized, the literature to be performed, and quality of performance expected remain virtual areas of darkness to the student. Although specific audition standards and procedures do differ among the various institutions, some common denominators do exist nevertheless, to offer guidance.

The past four decades, being a period of rapid development of percussion music, have created great challenges for the percussionist. Today he must be able to perform well on *all* the percussion instruments, individually and in combination. He must be able to play timpani, plus *all* of the various drums, mallet instruments, and traps. Many colleges and universities have, for the most part, met this challenge.

The necessary relationship of these performance demands to the percussion audition is apparent if one realizes that it is not uncommon to observe *every* percussionist in a percussion ensemble, orchestra, or symphonic band actively meeting these demands. Indeed, versatility should be a primary consideration in the selection of prepared audition pieces. As many of the following areas as possible are recommended:

I. Snare drum
  A. Solo pieces
    1. Rudimental style (integrating flams, drags, ruffs, and rolls)
    2. Orchestral style (integrating flams, drags, ruffs, rolls, and mixed meters)
  B. Rudiments
  C. Orchestral and/or band excerpts
  D. Sightreading

II. Mallet instruments
  A. Solo piece(s)
    1. 2 mallets (integrating meters)
    2. 3 or 4 mallets (integrating legato technique)
  B. Orchestral and/or band excerpts
  C. Scales (major, minor, chromatic) and arpeggios (major, minor, augmented, diminished)
  D. Sightreading

III. Timpani
  A. Solo piece integrating tuning changes, rolls, muffling, *fp* rolls)
  B. Identification and singing of melodic intervals
  C. Orchestral and/or band excerpts
  D. Sightreading

IV. Multiple percussion solo and/or chamber music piece (a tape is usually sufficient)

V. Orchestral and/or band excerpts on other percussion instruments (triangle, tambourine, etc.)

VI. Dance drums
  A. Solo
  B. Various jazz and show styles
  C. Various Latin rhythms

Although percussion music is primarily a product of 20th century composition, the audition literature should represent as many of the style periods as possible. Music selected for audition purposes should not be so far above the student's level of ability that he is unable to cope with the challenge. The audition is the opportunity to convey one's capabilities, not deficiencies.

The level of collegiate performance today, musically and technically, is incredibly high. The outstanding percussionist is no longer narrowly associated with an outstanding technique alone. Rather, he is considered to be an accomplished *musician*, utilizing his technical proficiency in the various percussion areas as one of several means to an aesthetically satisfying end. The collegiate percussionist must be able to communicate his sensitivity for form, phrase structure, and embellishing nuance. This discussion is relevant for the auditioning student, for while technical proficiency is the easiest attribute to achieve and convey, none of the musical qualities of a performance should be sacrificed in favor of a technical display. Choice of tempo is the most common offense, velocity apparently being of more importance than the other factors mentioned. If there were an absolute hierarchy of performance factors and their relative importance, speed would surely rank low. Any given audition piece should be performed only as fast as it can be performed *well!*

This discussion could leave the impression that evaluations of specific performances at a single audition are the only factors affecting collegiate admission. This is not entirely the case. An audition is judged on the basis of present musical ability and potential achievement. The auditioner's appraisals, combined with high school grade transcripts, college board examination scores, and personal interview commentaries provide the college or university with a comprehensive dossier upon which to base predictions concerning the probable success or failure an applicant will experience as a student and alumnus.

It should be apparent that a percussion audition for college admission requires special preparation. The musical responsibilities placed upon an entering freshman are great. The percussion audition must be prepared to demonstrate clearly the student's ability to meet these responsibilities.

Training Today's Percussionist

Donald Stanley

Those of us familiar with the trends exhibited by contemporary composers of band and orchestra music are well aware of the increasing musical and technical demands made on the members of a percussion section within such an organization. The growth and prosperity of the percussion ensemble as a serious means of musical expression likewise creates a need for newer and more demanding skills from the percussionists. Serious solo repertoire, while still lacking in quality, requires a mature musical understanding and technical proficiency equal to, and, in many cases, beyond that of any other music medium. All of these factors indicate a need for a well-planned method of instruction and training of young percussion students.

Unfortunately, most of today's beginning percussionists are exposed to the same methods and procedures that have been employed for the past 30 years. These methods and procedures, outdated as they are, do little more than teach a student some of the basic fundamentals of rhythmic structure and how to play some of the snare drum rudiments. Even if a student were to master his method books and rudiments, he would still be prepared to play only 5% or 10% of the literature written for percussion instruments. Little, if any, attention is given to the mallet instruments and timpani even though performance in these areas is highly important and essential in the modern percussion section. It is obvious that if we are to prepare our students to cope with these musical and technical problems we must adapt our teaching procedures and materials to these needs. The following ideas are presented as a means of preparing the percussionist to meet the challenges he will be exposed to in serious music performance.

1. It would seem advisable to require *all* beginning percussion students to study piano concurrently. One can hardly expect a youngster playing drums to gain the same experience and musical understanding as the beginning clarinetist who is not only reading rhythms and learning how to hold and finger the instrument, but is also exposed to the problems of pitch, phrasing, and becoming acquainted with the melodic and harmonic structure of music. Recently, some percussion instrument manufacturers have been promoting a percussion kit with both bells and snare drum. While this is certainly better than omitting melodic instruments altogether, the study of piano along with the snare drum would seem to offer greater value in terms of carry-over as the student begins his study of other percussion instruments. This type of requirement might also help to alleviate the frequent problem of an overabundance of beginning percussionists. Those students and their parents who are less serious about the study of instrumental music might be made to realize the complexity and diversity involved in becoming a percussionist.

2. The study of mallet percussion and timpani should be introduced early in the student's study of the percussion family. The handholds and basic playing characteristics of all percussion instruments have a considerable degree of similarity and do not present any insurmountable problems even to a beginner. By introducing the study of these instruments early, the student will become aware from the very beginning of the various instruments on which he must be able to perform. The study of the mallet percussion instruments, along with his piano study, will expose him to the same kinds of musical problems encountered by other beginning instrumentalists. His work on timpani will require the same intense kind of ear training necessary for the trombonist or string player. This more expanded kind of percussion training will make demands on the number of percussion instruments needed, but this should not prevent its implementation. We would not think of asking a beginner on tuba to stand in the back of the room for two years and clap out rhythms until an instrument was available. It has already been mentioned that percussion kits including bells are available and beginning percussionists and their parents should understand that they must provide their own instrument just as the beginning trumpet player does. If the school owns two or three pair of timpani, these can afford the young beginner adequate opportunities to gain experience in this area of performance.

3. The percussionists in an ensemble section should work on a rotating basis. All of the students should be exposed to performance on each instrument in the section in various compositions. Too often we tend to think of one student as the snare drummer, another the timpanist, and another as the cymbal player. If we are really training a *well rounded* percussionist, he must be able to play *all* of the instruments in the family. I once taught at a college where a freshman enrolled as a percussion major. I was astounded to find that his only experience in the percussion area was that of playing bass drum in his junior and senior high school bands. If a student received instruction on all percussion instruments at an early age, he would not only be able to cover any type of percussion part completely, but would welcome the diversity provided by this kind of experience.

It should be noted here that some students frequently become more proficient on one instrument than another. However, if the conductors of organizations will examine carefully the degree of difficulty of each percussion part, they can make assignments accordingly. If, for instance, a composition calls for frequent and rapid changes on the timpani, a more proficient player should be assigned that part. The student whose technique and ear training is more limited could play timpani on a less demanding number. Remember, however, that students must work especially hard to improve their facility on the weak instruments so that they do not always rely on someone else to play the difficult parts.

4. Organize and promote a percussion ensemble as part of the instrumental music program in your school. The value of and the need for small ensemble participation to augment the larger organizational training is well known. For the percussion section this type of training is probably more essential than for most other sections. The percussion ensemble must be more than the old idea of two snare drums, bass drum, and cymbals. A reasonably good repertoire of serious literature has been developed for various combinations of percussion instruments with various numbers of players required. This training and experience as an independent unit not only acquaints the student with new and different performance practices and problems but does much to create pride and high morale. The percussion ensemble also affords the teacher an opportunity for class instruction in techniques that are unique to the percussion instruments.

5. As much as possible, avoid the practice of placing just anyone in the percussion section. Like any other young musician, the percussionist needs to feel that what he is doing is important, and indeed it should be. There are few things more demoralizing to a section than the practice of substituting various other members of the band or orchestra in the percussion situation for special occasions. If this practice is necessary during marching band or for some other rare occasion, be certain that the person you add to the section receives some instruction on the instrument they are to play. It is difficult for the regular members of the percussion section to gain the respect of their fellow musicians if the impression exists that anyone can play percussion instruments.

6. As a conductor of an organization, treat the percussion section with the same respect and understanding as other sections. Study the score and know what to expect from the percussion section in a particular composition. If a percussion part is not included in your score, check the individual parts and write integral parts and entrances in the score. Do not permit the section to "fake" their way through a composition. Take time to rehearse difficult parts and be demanding in correct execution of the part. Try to avoid using unmusical terms when rehearsing the section. If, for instance, you want an accent, then ask for an accent instead of telling the percussionist to "really bang that" or "whack it harder." If we want our players to think in terms of musical sounds, then we should not ask for noises.

7. It would be a serious omission not to mention the need for teacher training institutions to revise their curriculums to include a more thorough program of percussion instruction for future instrumental teachers. It is indeed regrettable that so many music schools do not have a percussion specialist on their staff. We do not expect to take trombone lessons from a string player or piano lessons from a clarinetist at the college level. Likewise, future instrumental music teachers should not be expected to study percussion with a flute teacher who probably received his percussion instruction from another non-percussionist. To remain cognizant of the trends and materials in any one instrumental area is a full time job. Those teachers who are themselves percussionists are best equipped to train our future teachers in the area of percussion teaching and materials. To offer these future teachers less is, in most cases, defeating the purposes of instrumental music training. This is not to deny that there are a few individuals, though not percussion players themselves, who do a very adequate job of relating essential facts about the percussion instruments and their playing characteristics and techniques. However, it is an almost impossible task to keep up with recent trends and materials, and it appears that it will be even more difficult in the future.

The type of percussion instruction program outlined above can better meet the aims and goals of our instrumental music program, because it is based on developing a *musician* rather than a drummer. The end product of instrumental music instruction, is not so much a great trumpet player, a superb clarinetist, or a fantastic percussionist. We are, and should be, more concerned with developing a sensitive and intelligent musician who, through his instrumental music experiences, has gained a greater understanding and appreciation of music which will manifest itself in a desire for continued musical experiences. Such an objective will be of value to the student who pursues music as a career, to the student who continues his participation in the community band or orchestra, and to the student who becomes a consumer of music and supports the music activities of his community.

Questions and Answers About Timpani

Joel Leach

Q: Two-drum sets come in 25″-28″ and 26″-29″ sizes. What's the difference?
A: First, it must be understood that the ranges for both sets are the same. There is a small price difference. Most important, however, is the fact that professional timpanists generally agree that the 26″-29″ set will produe a better tone quality.
Q: What's the difference between fiberglass and copper kettles?
A: The copper kettle drum produces a better tone. There is, admittedly, about a $160 price difference between a two-kettle set of copper and a two-kettle set of fiberglass, with the copper set being more expensive.
Q: Would you then suggest that I disregard the fiberglass timpani?
A: I would suggest that you purchase the copper kettle timpani if at all possible. They will definitely serve your purposes much better. However, if the price difference is absolutely critical, then the fiberglass kettles will do satisfactorily.
Q: Fiberglass kettles don't dent like copper, right?
A: Right! However, they are not impervious to damage either. This author has seen fiberglass kettles which were bumped very hard, and had "structurally shattered" much the same as heavy cardboard will do if subjected to a sharp impact.
Q: I own two timpani at this time, and intend to add a third drum. Which one should I add next?
A: There is a wide difference of opinion in this area. However, I believe that the smaller drum (23″) will satisfy your needs more effectively than the larger (30″) drum *for public school use.* This is not necessarily true in all instances, however.

Q: What are the fundamental notes and approximate ranges for the timpani?

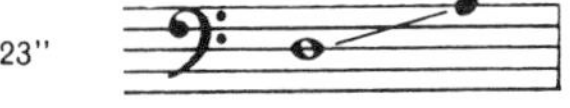

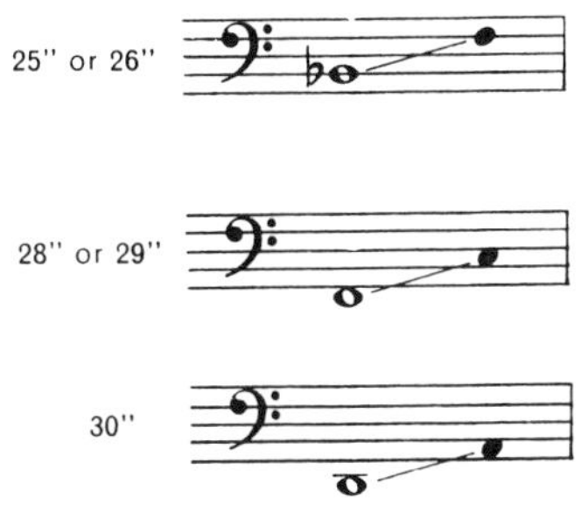

A: The fundamental tuning note for each drum is shown as a whole note; the black note designates the probable range extension for that particular drum. (Most timpani can go at least a whole step beyond the note shown here).
Q: What type of sticks should my timpanist use?
A: Basically, the timpanist should have a minimum of three pairs of sticks, designated soft, medium, and hard. Timpani sticks appear in all drum catalogues. However, it is recommended that the timpanist investigate the professional model timpani sticks which are available for only a slightly higher price. Such sticks are made by Saul Goodman (New York Philharmonic), Al Payson (Chicago Symphony), Vic Firth (Boston Symphony), and several others. Write directly to one of these persons (address letter to him in care of "Symphony Hall" in that city) and he will ship directly to you or see that one of your local music stores stocks a supply of sticks for you.
Q: Where do wooden sticks fit in?
A: Never use wooden sticks unless: (1) specified by the composer; (2) called for by the conductor.
Q: How will my timpanist know which sticks to use?
A: Some contemporary literature is specific in stick designation. However, if no specifications are given, it is a wise timpanist who uses sticks "one degree harder" than what might sound good to him standing so close to the timpani.
Q: What book should I use for teaching beginners?
A: I highly recommend the "Timpani Technic" book by Tom McMillan (Pub. by Pro Art). "Modern Method for Timpani" by Saul Goodman (Pub. by Mills) is also quite popular. "Timpani Method" by Alfred Friese (Pub. by Adler/Belwin) is an excellent text which contains extensive aural exercises along with the written material. "Modern Method for Timpani" by Carl Gardner (Pub. by Carl Fischer) is also widely used. All of these books will serve your purpose well.
Q: How are the timpani sticks held?
A: The German grip is exactly the same as the marimba stick grip and the right hand snare drum grip: back of the hand is up. The French grip is very similar but for the fact that the thumbs are held on top, and that there is more finger control involved. Professional timpanists often use both, depending upon the dynamic level indicated. I suggest, however, that the music educator teach the German grip, as it is both easier to teach as well as easier for the student to comprehend immediately. There is a great deal of immediate transfer between this and the marimba and snare drum grips.
Q: Where do you strike the head?
A: About 3″ to 5″ from the rim, depending upon the relative size of the drum. (Another formula would be: ⅙th the diameter from the rim.)
Q: Should the timpanist stand or sit?
A: The fact is that he must be at the proper height in order to have his hands at the correct angle to the drums. A tall timpanist will generally use a stool in order to achieve this angle. However, it must be understood that the timpanist never "sits" on the stool—he leans against it. Fast tuning changes may further necessitate the use of a stool.
Q: What is the best approach to

teaching the roll?

A: Remember that it must be a single stroke roll, first of all! A bounced roll is never used on the timpani. The best approach is to have the student play eight beats worth of quarter notes, sixteenth notes, and thirty-second notes and back again to the beginning. During this exercise, he should make certain that both stick heights are the same, that there is no angular motion, and that the sound is perfectly consistent. The use of a mirror for self observation is ideal.

Q: My timpanist has difficulty tuning. What should I do?

A: If he thoroughly understands the mechanics of the drums, and the fact that roughly five steps are available on each drum, he will then automatically be a little more accurate through the use of some logic regarding pedal movement. Of course, he should always tune carefully with a pitch pipe (*F* to *F*). It is wise to make the student prepare melodies using at least two drums. This will develop pitch awareness in the low register. A recent publication dealing with Timpani Tuning (by Mervin Britton, pub. by Adler/Belwin) will also be of assistance. Music theory and intervallic training are "musts" for the timpanist.

Q: How should I teach cross-sticking?

A: On a very limited basis! Although young timpanists dream of the day when they will be able to do some cross-sticking, it happens to be only a secondary approach to most timpani parts. In other words, it is best to *avoid* cross-sticking if at all possible, because there are many variables which cause the resulting sound to be inconsistent. In fact, most passages can be played *without* cross-sticking—and they will sound much better. This is not to say that cross-sticking should not be taught; it definitely should be included in timpani studies, and it does appear in every text. However, be sure that your timpanist uses it in good taste.

Q: One of my timpani heads sounds very bad. What can I do to improve it?

A: If this is an old calfskin head, there is a possibility that the natural oils have evaporated, leaving a lifeless hide. In that case, it can only be replaced. If it is a plastic head of late 1950 vintage, it may also be somewhat inferior, for plastic heads were rather new at that time, and a lot of improvements were to go into them before they were to hold their own on the market. It might be wise to replace such old plastic heads also. There is still another possibility: that of bad dents in the kettle. Such dents destroy the acoustical construction of the kettle, and may tend to reinforce otherwise subtle harmonics; such timpani are often hard to tune accurately. These dents should be removed carefully. In most cases of bad sounding heads it is probable that the same pitch does not exist opposite each tension screw. This process of equalizing the pitch is called "balancing the head."

Q: How do you balance the Ludwig pedal mechanism?

A: Follow these three simple steps: (1) place the foot pedal in "heel position" by force if necessary; (2) *now* tune the head to its proper fundamental pitch; and (3) check to see if the pedal mechanism operates properly. If not, it will react in one of three ways:

(a) If the pedal then refuses to hold upper pitches within its proper range, turn the spring tension knob (located at base of drum) in a clockwise direction, two or three half-turns. Make additional small adjustments if necessary.

(b) If the pedal has a tendency to flop partially or totally to a "toe down" position, turn the spring tension knob (located at base of drum) in a counter-clockwise direction two or three half-turns. Make additional small adjustments if necessary.

(c) If, after making these adjustments, the pedal still does not function properly, seek the assistance of a competent repairman (or write to the manufacturer), for there is nothing more you can do.

Q: The pedal of my Slingerland/Leedy timpani slips on the vertical rod. Can this be repaired?

A: This is usually caused by some lubricant which has been smeared along the rod. Clean the rod with something that will cut the grease.

Q: My timpani squeak!

A: Remove the head and apply paraffin to the edge of the kettle. This will probably stop the squeak. (This is for calfskin.) If not, it may be necessary to lubricate the pedal itself. For plastic heads one should use a minimal amount of vaseline. Never use an oil base lubricant on calfskin heads.

Q: My plastic heads have dents in them. What can be done about that?

A: It is best to ignore them. If a head sounds bad even after it has been finely tuned, it should be replaced.

Abbreviated Playing and Teaching Techniques

1. Arrange drums in a semi-circle so that the proper playing spots will be readily accessible as the timpanist rotates in the direction of each drum.
2. Use a stool, if necessary, in order to be in a better playing position. This will eliminate bending over the drums, and will facilitate proper use of the arms, thus resulting in a more relaxed performance.
3. Stick positions should form an inverted *V* with both sticks falling on the line of an imaginary circle located 3" to 5" in from the rim (depending upon the relative size of the drum).
4. Strike the exact same area of the drums at all times.
5. Be careful to avoid angular or circular motions in roll execution.
6. Roll height must be consistent with both hands.
7. Be sure to strike the proper playing area on each drum as you move from one to another.
8. Practice playing melodies on two drums (25" and 28", or 26" and 29") and later bring the other drums into play in the same manner. This develops familiarity with the pedal mechanism and results in a smoother and easier approach to tuning.
9. Use a pitch pipe for all basic tuning, and learn to tune by intervallic relationships from that point.
10. After hearing the desired pitch, sing it to yourself before trying to tune the drum. This will be a tremendous help.

The Place of the Marimba in the School Music Program

Carolyn Reid Sisney

Does a marimba belong in the school band or orchestra? My answer is *yes*!

Let's follow a marimba player through his or her school days. This could be a school in a rural area with a band enrollment of 15-30 or a big city or consolidated school situation of 65-200 players.

1. Find a marimba. Almost every town has one or more owned by someone. Beg, borrow, rent, or buy it.

2. Almost any music teacher can teach a student the fundamentals of the mallet technique, if the instructor follows the method book picture guides for holding the mallets and stresses a relaxed grip.

3. The marimba (if it has been kept in a reasonably constant room temperature) always stays in tune. This is perhaps the only instrument that does. What a help this is to the school music teacher who is working in sectional classes of beginners! Let the marimba player play with any group of instruments—flutes, clarinets, double reeds, saxophones, or any of the strings. Such sectional practices are easy because group instruction series have the parts transposed for ensemble instruction. What better, easier way to build band and orchestra intonation than to have an example to help students correct intonation flaws?

4. The marimba can support, double, or substitute where instrutation is weak or non-existant. The marimba player (who often starts out as a pianist) can read bass and treble clefs. Give the marimba student bass clef baritone, trombone, bassoon, cello, or bass parts, or treble clef flute, oboe, or violin parts—or even a conductor's score.

5. The marimba can supply the brittle quality of a xylophone by using hard marimba mallets or xylophone mallets. For still more authentic xylophone tone, remove the resonators. (A word of caution: xylophone mallets will cause small pit marks on the bars. This will not damage the tone, however.)

6. The marimba player can double on any instrument in the percussion section except possibly the snare drum.

7. The marimba player who plays musically and correctly can enter the school contest and bring home a creditable rating, because competition is almost non-existent.

8. A marimba soloist will highlight a concert with a minimum of rehearsal time. Such evergreens as "Flight of th Bumble Bee" (in *C* for orchestra, *B♭* for band), "Nola," "Minute Waltz" by Chopin, "Clarinet Polka," "12th Street Rag," "Xylophone Rag," and "Stars and Stripes Forever" are easily adapted. Some are already published with marimba solo parts. Others can be arranged by giving the marimba the melody and dividing the second and third parts among the whole section. For example: "12th Street Rag" has the solo part in the trumpet section. Divide the harmony (second and third parts) among all the trumpet players. The marimba part could be transposed from the first trumpet part, or better still, use the melody line from the piano solo. It is already in the correct key and has some interesting variations.

If the marimba player is outstanding musically and technically, and the orchestra is fine, consider "Rondo Capriccioso" for violin and orchestra by Saint-Saëns. The orchestra parts are not difficult, except in the tuttis, and the marimbist can easily play the violin part. A good suggestion for band accompaniment is the "Symphonie Espagnole" for violin and orchestra by Édouard Lalo. This was adapted some years ago for violin and band by band director/composer Lawrence Fogelberg of Pekin, Illinois High School. The violin part is difficult but adapts readily to the marimba.

Any violin, flute, or oboe concerto by Bach, Handel, or Mozart can be transcribed for marimba solo and the orchestra parts are of reasonable difficulty. The "Concertino" written originally for marimba and orchestra by Paul Creston is a good work of the contemporary repertoire.

9. Many excellent percussion ensemble selections are being written today with considerable emphasis on the instruments of defined tone. From one to three mallet performers are needed to play these, because they are scored for marimba, vibes, xylophone, glockenspiel, chimes, and timpani.

10. The school music system that has a planned adaptability and training program could well use a combination of the marimba-percussion method of Carl Orff, along with Kodály's. Add the ever faithful song flute and you can build fine musical awareness and understanding. A period of time spent using these music training programs before beginning the band and orchestra classes would make the initial instrumental training much easier and help lower the drop-out rate in the early years.

Changing Concepts in Percussion

Donald Gilbert

Since the end of World War II, music education in the public schools has grown at a tremendous rate. For a number of reasons, musical opportunities exist in our public schools today which were not available a few years ago. This is particularly true in the field of percussion. The young percussionist in the course of his public school career may be asked at one time or another to perform in any of the following performing groups: symphony orchestra, chamber orchestra, concert band, stage band, marching band, percussion ensemble, small ensemble, or solo performance.

The young percussionist today must acquire a number of diverse skills in order to fulfill the responsibilities required of him. The day is past when the student will get by if he is "a drummer." Today it is essential that he be *a percussionist.* Very often the student must rely on his band director for the necessary percussion instruction. It is important, therefore, that the school music director view percussion performance in its proper perspective. The band director who looks on percussion playing only as "drumming" sees only a part of the art, a very important part but still only a part. Time and again, for example, the school band or orchestra director has faced the dilemma of being confronted with a very essential xylophone part in a particular score and having no one capable of playing it. In most situations this problem could be avoided if the director's approach to teaching percussion were not so limited, particularly at the elementary level.

In many elementary schools throughout the country, children in the primary grades begin their music education through the use of percussion instruments. It is not surprising to find children in kindergarten or first grade classrooms using rhythm band instruments and Orff instruments in their daily music classes. In far too many cases, however, one could return several years later and see these same students in the fourth or fifth grade beginning "drum" classes. In the music room one would see a number of students each with a drum pad, a pair of sticks, and a "drum" book. For the next several years the student seldom parts company with his pad, sticks, or book. What happened to the Orff keyboard instruments that he used in first grade or the cymbals, triangle, tambourine, etc., that he used in the rhythm bands? Since many students are familiar with percussion instruments at a very early age, why shouldn't the knowledge gained through these early experiences with such instruments be transferred to the student's instruction in applied percussion from the outset? The percussionist, if he is to be successful, cannot spend many years studying one instrument. He must learn to perform on *all* the percussion instruments. In most music organizations, there is no room for a percussionist specializing in snare drum, cymbals, or xylophone, etc. It seems essential, therefore, that from his first lessons the young student should be trained to become a *percussionist* and not just a "drummer."

At his very first percussion lesson the young student should "get his hands dirty" from all the percussion instruments. He should have an opportunity to experience the sound and feel not only of the snare drum, but also the bass drum, cymbals, and bells. Within the time period of his first few lessons, he should have had the opportunity to perform on most of the standard percussion instruments. This initial experience with all the instruments will help to establish the *percussion* concept in the mind of the young student. From the very beginning, he must realize that there is more to being a percussionist than meets the eye.

One aspect of a percussionist's abilities that is very often neglected entirely (unless he happens to study privately with a professional percussionist) is his facility and technique on the mallet instruments, i.e., marimba, bells, xylophone, vibraphone. Thus, with the exception of timpani playing, the student's reading ability develops only on the horizontal plane. This problem could be eliminated if the student's instruction on mallet instruments paralleled that on the snare drum. A set of orchestra bells is a good instrument upon which a child in the fourth or fifth grade can begin mallet instruction. Most school music departments have at least one set which is easily transportable. The use of orchestra bells solves not only the problem of transporting a keyboard instrument to those elementary schools which do not own one, but also that of finding an instrument which is compatible with the physical size and reach of the child in the fourth or fifth grade. The transition from bells to xylophone or marimba at a later date will then be relatively easy.

As a result of the ear training and music reading activities being carried on in the primary grades in many of our elementary schools, the aural training which is necessary in order to play the timpani should not entail a repetition of aural abilities already learned. However, such repetition is often necessary due to the time gap between the student's early exposure to aural training and his first experiences with the timpani. This problem could be avoided if aural training continued, beginning with the first percussion lesson. Thus, although the elementary percussion student may not be able to master the technical aspects of timpani playing because of physical limitations, he can continue to develop those all important aural skills. By the time he is capable of handling the necessary motor skills, the aural aspects of timpani performance should be highly developed.

It is my opinion that each elementary school should own at least one each of the following percussion instruments:

1. One bass drum, with cradle and beater
2. One pair of lightweight qual-

ity cymbals
3. One tambourine
4. One triangle, with appropriate holder and beater
5. One set of claves
6. One set of maracas

With the above instruments, plus one or more snare drums and at least one mallet instrument, each elementary school would have the minimum basic equipment that is needed for adequate percussion instruction. If other instruments such as castanets, suspended cymbal, and tam-tam can be added to the inventory of basic percussion instruments, so much the better.

The prospective percussion instructor in the elementary school might well ask what printed text material he should use for such a heterogeneous percussion class. Unfortunately, there is a dearth of material available at present. The nearest professional percussionist or college percussion instructor would be able to advise the school music director on this matter. The present lack of such material, however, does provide both the elementary instrumental teacher and the students with a number of creative alternatives. Elementary percussion ensemble compositions now exist in great numbers. Young students would gain valuable insight into the nature of both percussion notation and the limitless sonorities which could be obtained from various combinations of percussion instruments by the use of such ensembles. In addition to percussion ensembles, both teacher and students could engage in the composition of multiple percussion solos, i.e., the composition of percussion solos using two or more instruments both simultaneously and juxtaposed. Students should be encouraged to use their creative imaginations as much as possible.

In summary, if we as music teachers are to be expected to supply the music organizations mentioned in the first paragraph of this article with competent and qualified percussionists, it may well be necessary for us to change our concept of the elementary percussion class. With a little imagination we could make the elementary percussion class an exciting musical experience for its participants. Through a variety of percussion activities, the beginning student can familiarize himself with the many facets of percussion performance. With this type of beginning instruction, perhaps we can at last begin to educate versatile percussionists instead of one-instrument "drummers."

June 1969

School Directors and Their Percussion Sections

Anthony Cirone

An instrumentalist's most vulnerable period of development occurs during grade and high school. Not only does he develop technically, but his attitudes towards music in general are also shaped. The majority of these students are dependent on the music director for guidance in both areas; a minority of students take private lessons and are influenced by this more intimate relationship.

A director naturally has a greater knowledge in one area of instruments (e.g., woodwinds, or strings, or brass) than others because he has probably studied one instrument much longer and usually is very proficient on that instrument. This director can therefore be more helpful in that area of instruction and more valuable to the students studying that particular instrument. The problem for the student percussionist is that the majority of directors are wind or string players; therefore their knowledge of percussion is limited, since they usually cannot speak from first-hand experience.

The percussion family covers a very large number of instruments, each one requiring special techniques of some kind to make it easy to handle and to produce the proper sound. I feel, in many cases, students are left to use their own common sense when performing. This will not prove to be satisfactory. For the timpani, snare drum, and mallet instruments, a certain amount of basic technique is necessary for even the simplest part, but with the smaller instruments such as cymbals, tambourine, bass drum, etc., any instrumentalist can pick up the appropriate beater and strike the instrument. However, this is not the same as *playing* the instrument.

For a director to have a complete knowledge of all the techniques required may be asking a lot, but it is necessary for the students to be aware that they are handling musical instruments and not toys!

I feel the primary reason school directors do not have a more thorough knowledge of the family of percussion instruments is because of the published teaching material available. The majority of all beginning drum books deal with the rudimental approach to drumming. This would be fine if the music program consisted of a year-round marching band or drum corp, with no concert band or orchestra. If a student is trained to play strictly rudimentally for the football season and then continues to play in this manner on orchestral parts, he will be playing the percussion parts incorrectly. The whole idea of rudimental drumming has been tremendously overrated; it is a skill that is limited largely to amateur performing groups, such as a drum corps, and has no place in the field of professional music. There are no professional bands to which a performer can turn to make a livelihood. The point is not to think every student *will* eventually become a professional, but to train him as though he were so he will develop to his highest potential. This training will also produce a more qualified future educator.

Rudimental drumming should not be confused with a student practicing rudiments. There are basic drum patterns called rudiments that a student must practice in order to develop technique. However, these patterns are not necessarily used when reading music. For example, a student practices paradiddles, which are combinations of single and double sticking; however, a student should never use this paradiddle sticking when playing notes written on a page unless the composer specifically asks for it. Generally, if a composer writes four sixteenth notes, he wants them played as evenly as possible. A snare drummer should use one stick if the tempo is slow enough; at a fast tempo, alternating each hand would produce the more even and consistent sound. For a student to play this figure with a combination of single and double sticking (paradiddle) would be as wrong as a wind player adding phrasing (two slurred and two tongued, for example) when none is written.

The problem is mainly one of awareness. Since most of the method books require the students to play rudimentally, the students think this is the only way it should be done and generally nothing is said to contradict this idea. One obvious difference in rudimental and orchestral playing is that a rudimental roll is measured and a concert roll is not measured. When a composer writes a sustained sound (roll) for snare drum, he does not want a feeling of rhythm throughout the roll, but one continuous sound from beginning to end. Most of the beginning methods teach a student to use a 5 or 7 or 9-stroke roll when reading quarter notes or half-note rolls; this really is playing incorrectly. The student should be taught to play a sustained sound from one point to another. At fast tempos it is possible to use a 5, 7, or 9-stroke *closed* roll for certain figures, but this should be taught later, after the concept of a sustained sound is introduced.

The majority of drum students that are able to take private lessons generally only study snare drum and no instruction is offered on xylophone or the smaller percussion instruments (cymbals, bass drum, triangle, tambourine, etc.). As I mentioned earlier, these instruments each require a special technique and the students should be made aware of them. There are some excellent percussion manuals on the market that explain the techniques required in detail.

One of the most important concepts a director must convey to his drum students is that each and every one of them must be able to play the mallet instruments and timpani. It is very unfair to have a pianist or other instrumentalist play mallet and timpani parts because they can read treble and bass clef and are able to tune timpani. If any of the snare drummers would decide to enter college as a music major, he would find the competition very stiff; and without knowledge of mallet instruments and timpani, he would be very limited as a percussionist. Also, for a student to begin to learn those instruments as late as high school and try to enter college (as a music major) is a very difficult task.

I feel very strongly that students should be made to realize that orchestral music is the backbone of the history of music. The professional orchestras around the world play music that has lasted through centuries and has made the symphonic orchestras the strongest music force in existence. Other musical groups such as concert bands, rock groups, drum corps, jazz bands, and the many small instrumental ensembles are very important to music and musicians; but, to devote all the training to any one group is missing the point as to what music is all about. This is even truer for the person who wishes to have a career as a professional musician. As a person develops, he may find himself leaning towards one type of music—this is fine since he will probably perform best in that area. However, in the same sense that a pianist should not only study jazz, a drummer should not study only rudiments.

September 1969

Mambo Rhythms

Jerome Mouton

No doubt many concert or stage band directors are not familiar with the Cuban, (i.e., Caribbean or "Latin" American) rhythms of the musical mambo, as well as the proper execution of these rhythms. There are band directors who shy away from performing music

which utilizes mambo rhythms simply because of a lack of sufficient knowledge in this area. The proper performance of these rhythms will make a significant didactical contribution to the percussion players of a band.

The following article will try to expose a music field heretofore inadequately explored and misunderstood by many. An acquaintance with the exciting and stimulating rhythms of the mambo could well motivate band directors and composers of band music to investigate further the tremendous musical potential that exists in the music and rhythms of all of Caribbean "Latin" America.

Some composers, in their "Latin" flavored band music, compose a rhythmic pattern that is not compatible with the melodic rhythm. In addition, these rhythm patterns (played by the percussion section) are usually diluted or distorted versions of a "Latin" beat. In order to rectify this situation, the composer or band director must first ask two questions: (1) What are mambo rhythms? (2) How does one determine whether or not a melody is adaptable to mambo rhythms? The answers to these questions lie in the study of the mambo music as performed in the Caribbean area. Parenthetically, a person who studies all aspects of mambo music both visually and aurally can further develop his rhythmic instinct and also increase his skill in reading syncopated rhythms. The following musical examples are representative of typical mambo melodic rhythms.

We should next extend our investigation into mambo rhythms and the role of percussion instruments in their performance by describing the function of two very inportant drums associated with the mambo, namely, the *bongos* and *congas.* These two instruments come in pairs and in both cases one drum is larger than the other. The following execution chart (and subsequent charts appearing in this article) are designed for right-handed players. Left-handed players should reverse the process.

The Bongos

Placing the bongo pair between your knees, execute the following rhythmic pattern thus:

Example 1.

♩ = 120

S S S S S S L S
X O O X X O O X

Repeated pattern

R1 L2 R3 LTB R1 L2 R3 LTB

Execution Chart

RI—index finger of right hand
R_3—index, heart, and ring finger of right hand
L_2—index and heart finger of left hand
LTB—left hand thumb base
L_3—index, heart, and ring finger of left hand
L—large drum
S—small drum
O—indicates that the player strike near the center of the drum
X—indicates that the player strike near the rim of the drum

(This basic eighth note pattern may be also executed in a similiar manner on the conga drums, except where RI and L_2 are indicated, R_3 and L_3 should be substituted in order to achieve greater sound projection.) From a starting position, LTB is resting on its strike area with L_2 elevated and poised for a strike. RI strikes a hard downward, (i.e., glancing) blow. L_2 follow by striking near the center. However, once L_2 have struck they should immediately slide back towards the rim into the area initially occupied by LTB. Obviously, this action must be executed within the time segment of an eighth note. Elevating the LTB by bending the wrist will facilitate the backward sliding of L_2. Although the proper playing procedure involves the use of bare hands only, drum sticks may be effectively used if necessary. In this case, the bongos may be placed upon a stand, but without covering the open ends. The disadvantage of playing with sticks is that no subtle coloristic effects are possible. In addition, sticks tend to produce an excessively brittle and percussive sound.

A concert or stage band should possess a set of timbales. The basic set for mambo playing consists of the timbales (two drums, also of different sizes), a small cow bell (attached between the timbales), and a "ride" cymbal (suspended cymbal on a separate stand). Throughout the performance of a typical mambo, the timbale player will execute essentially three rhythmic patterns (using the specifically designed timbale sticks)—usually in this sequence:

Example 2.

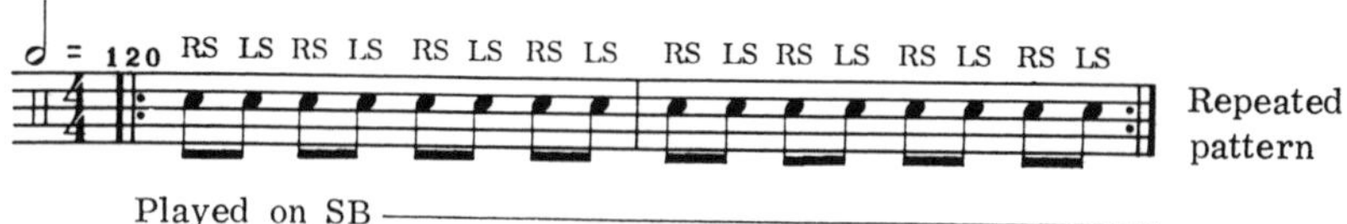

Execution Chart
RC—ride cymbal
RS—right hand with stick
SB—side body shell of timbales
SD—smaller drum
CB—cow bell
LD—larger drum
LS—left hand with stick

At the beginning of the musical selection the basic eighth note pattern will be employed. Later, at the discretion of the band director, the rhythm pattern may be changed to produce a more excitable or *mas caliente* ("hotter") mambo.

Example 3.

The SD pattern may be executed on RC or CB using the timbale sticks. The LD pattern is executed with all fingers of the left hand.

An indispensable instrument for the mambo is a large cow bell called a *cencerro.* This instrument is laid flat and held firmly in the hand with the narrow closed end nearest to the player. A rounded piece of wood, approximately 7" long and 1" in diameter should be used in striking the cencerro. No special playing technique is required except to strike in the center near both ends in such a manner as will produce an optimum resonance in sound. Of course, if the stick is too short or held too firmly, a resonant sound will not result. The following three music examples will help to clarify its function:

Example 4.

Example 5.

Example 6.

Example 6 is excellent for a <u>mas caliente</u> section

Execution Chart
LE—large open end
SE—small closed end
In examples 5 and 6, above, notice the two bar rhythm pattern that is so prevalent in Caribbean "Latin" American Music.

The use of *claves* in the mambo serves to define the rhythmic and melodic stresses. The clave rhythm is based upon a rhythmic isochronism of two measures. The first measure is antecedent, strong, and the second is consequent, weak. The rhythmic pattern is as follows:

Example 7.

A melody will not always commence with an accented measure. In the following music example, the first measure is actually an anacrusis to the second measure which is the measure with the melodic stress:

Example 8.

The clave rhythm may be varied as follows:

Example 9.

Important rhythm patterns can also be supplied by the string bass, tuba, or trombone. The following example is a *sine qua non* for the basic mambo rhythmic pulse:

Example 10.

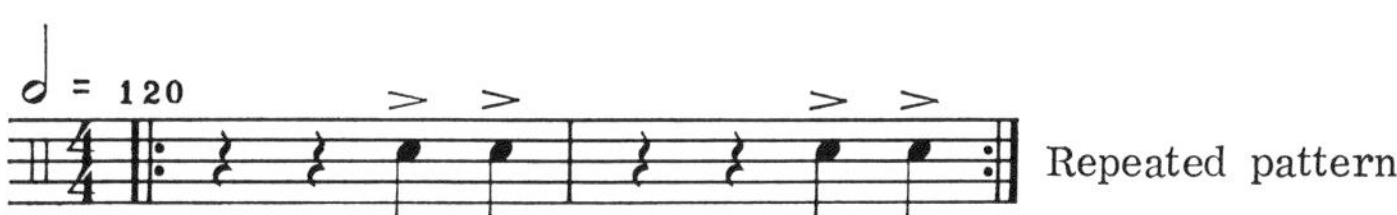

Beats three and four of a mambo receive special emphasis.

Interesting ostinato patterns may be created as long as the basic pulse is maintained. One of the following patterns may be employed in a *mas caliente* section or all of them simultaneously:

Example 13.

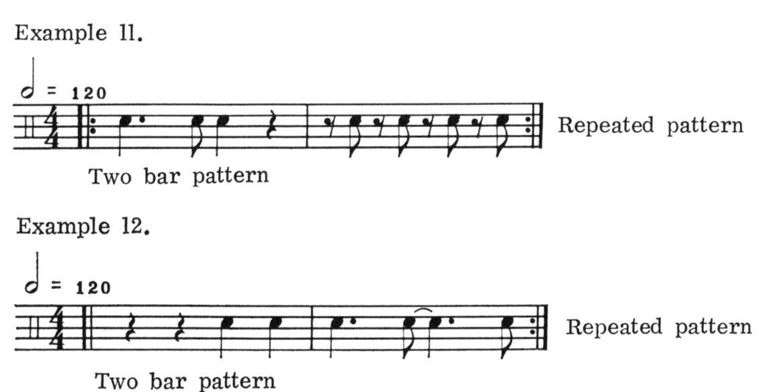

Example 14.

One bar pattern

This pattern is highly compatible with melodic rhythm examples A., B., and C.

The inherent rhythmic characteristics of a melody, along with the melodic stresses, will determine any additional ostinato patterns to be employed. The harmonic scheme of the melody should aid in determining the melodic intervals of the ostinato patterns.

Orchestrated below are melodic rhythmic examples 'F' and 'G'. Example 'F' represents the beginning of the piece and example 'G' represents a typical *mas caliente* section.

Orchestration of Melodic Example F:

Orchestration of Melodic Example G:

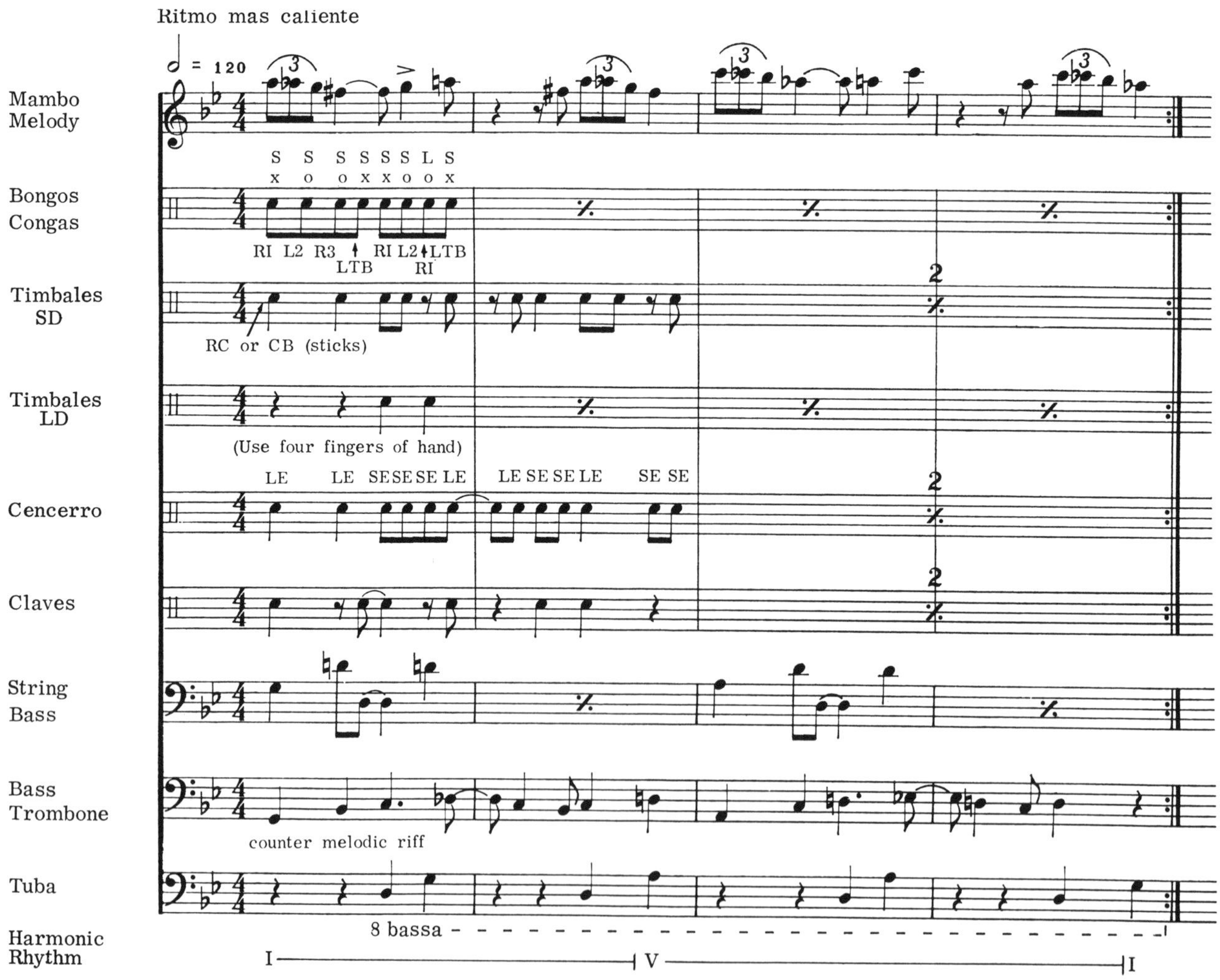

Ritmo mas caliente

= 120

Mambo Melody

S S S S S S L S
x o o x x o o x

Bongos Congas

RI L2 R3 LTB RI L2 LTB RI

Timbales SD

RC or CB (sticks)

2

Timbales LD

(Use four fingers of hand)

LE LE SE SE SE LE LE SE SE LE SE SE

Cencerro

2

Claves

2

String Bass

Bass Trombone

counter melodic riff

Tuba

8 bassa

Harmonic Rhythm

I V I

October 1969

The Second Annual International Percussion Symposium

More than 150 student percussionists, band directors, and professional musicians from throughout the United States and from Canada and Sweden met in August at the Evanston (Illinois) campus of Northwestern University to participate in the Second Annual International Percussion Symposium. For two weeks they studied and performed with the nation's outstanding teachers and professionals. Co-sponsored by the University and the Ludwig Drum Company, the Symposium covered every aspect of technique—rudimental, rock, stage, jazz, and concert—as well as instruction in mallet instruments and timpani. Attention was also given to the newest developments in literature, methods, and materials. Classes were held daily from 9:00 A.M. to 6:00 P.M., and, through arrangements with Northwestern, the Symposium was offered as an accredited course of study.

Among those who directed the discussions and classes were: Terry Applebaum, percussion instructor at Northwestern; Al Payson; Gordon Peters (principal percussionist with the Chicago Symphony Orchestra and editor of the Percussion Clinic in *The Instrumentalist*); Frederick Fennell, conductor of the University of Miami Wind Ensemble; Donald Koss, timpanist of the Chicago Symphony; Mitch Markovich, rudimentary percussion specialist; James Coffin, director of the University of Northern Iowa's marching band; Gary Olmstead, percussion instructor at Indiana University (Pennsylvania); John Welsh, Orff presentation specialist and educational director of the Kitching Educational Division of Ludwig Industries; Saul Feldstein, president of the Percussive Arts Society and percussion teacher in the New York State college system; Allen Swain, noted piano instructor; Roy Knapp, dean of Chicago percussionists; Isaac "Red" Holt of Holt, Young Unlimited; Rick Powell; and John Rodriquez, famous Latin percussionist.

Representing the world of jazz were: Gary Burton, *Down Beat* magazine's 1969 "Jazz Man of the Year" and No. 1 vibist in the polls of jazz critics; Joe Morello; Bobby Christian; Edmund Thigpen, and Roy Haynes.

Dick Schory, vice president of marketing for Ludwig and conductor of the famed Percussion Pops Orchestra, was in charge of the Symposium's College Workshop. The Band Director's Workshop was led by James Sewrey, educational director of Ludwig Industries. The High School Workshop was under the direction of three percussion authorities: Duane Thamm, Ludwig clinician and well-known Chicago performer; Robert Tilles, head of the percussion department at DePaul University in Chicago and author of numerous percussion works; and John Baldwin, percussion instructor at Wisconsin State University at Oshkosh.

In addition to the daily class and workshop sessions several evening demonstrations, recitals, and concerts were offered. These were open to the public at no admission charge and were well attended by those in Evanston and the nearby Chicago area. The first program, on August 6, was a demonstration of marching percussion by the Vanguard Drum and Bugle Corps under the direction of John Thirion. On the following evening the faculty of the Symposium presented a recital. The last two evenings of the two-week meeting were highlighted with concerts by the student participants. The High School Ensemble performed on Wednesday, August 13, and the College Ensemble on Thursday, August 14. A Guest Artist program was also a part of the Thursday evening concert and this featured several of the noted performing artists who had taken part in the Symposium.

December 1969

Organizing the Percussion Section

Donald Gilbert

If the percussion section of the band or orchestra is going to be a musical asset to the organization, the director must carefully consider the physical organization of the section.

Instrument and Player Placement

The first concern is the placement of the percussion section within the group and the placement of each percussionist within the section. In the marching band, the percussion section can be best utilized if it is placed in the middle of the band as it appears in block formation. The determining factor in considering the placement of the players within the section is the number of players in the section and the instrumentation of the section. If two bass drummers and/or two cymbal players are used, it is better if they are placed as close together as possible within the section in order to preserve the rhythmic stability.

The usual placement of the percussion section in the concert band is at the rear of the band and to the conductor's left as he faces the ensemble. The timpani are normally placed on the outside and to the right of the section. The most common position of the percussion section in the orchestra is to the rear of the ensemble, behind or beside the brass, with the timpani again on the outside of the section. * [Editor's note: most professional orchestras have the timpani in the center of the orchestra in the last row or in front of the percussion section, the latter being to rear right or rear left.]

The placement of the percussion instruments other than the timpani within the section in the concert band or orchestra will depend for the most part on the nature of the music being played and the number of players available. Those portable instruments which are used very little or only in one composition should be placed in such a way that they can be moved out of the playing area when they are not needed. If they are too large to be moved, they should be conveniently placed so as not to clutter the playing area when they are not in use. If one player is required to play two or more parts in the same piece of music, the instruments needed should be within easy reach. Mistakes can be avoided if the travel time and movement of the players in the section is kept to a minimum. A trap table to hold sticks, beaters, and small percussion instruments such as tambourine, triangle, castanets, etc. should be a part of every concert percussion section and should be easily accessible to everyone in the section.

Assignment of Parts

The assignment of parts to each performer in the percussion section is a very important point which is so often overlooked by the director. The director can very easily do this himself, since he knows the musical and technical capabilities of all his students. After briefly studying the score, he can assign the proper parts to the proper person. He can, however, save himself time by appointing a section leader and delegating this responsibility to him. The creation of the position of section leader or first percussionist can be an incentive to the members of the section. It may impress upon the players the importance of good organization and the responsibilities connected with being a section leader. Furthermore, the section leader, however, should always remain under the careful supervision of the director.

Regardless of who assumes the responsibility of assigning parts in school ensembles, it would be more advantageous to have the assignments vary from one composition to another. Such a rotation system would provide musical and technical experience in the many facets of percussion performance for all members of the section. It is wise, however, to have the assignments fixed for each particular composition. Once the assignments are set, they should be posted in advance for each member of the section; thus avoiding much confusion. * [Editor's note: One important additional point might be made in the name of percussion section efficiency: each player should have his own piece of music.]

Equipment

Equipping and maintaining the school percussion section poses certain problems. The amount of commercially available percussion equipment is so vast that it is sometimes difficult to know when to stop buying (assuming that funds are available). Financially speaking, equipping the percussion section is no small task, particularly in a school system which has several types of musical organizations. If a school has a marching band and a concert band, for example, the purchase of additional equipment is necessary. Besides the field, tenor, and bass drums in the marching band, the director will have to purchase another bass drum and one or more snare drums which can be used in the concert organization. In addition, the cymbals which are used in the marching band are not suitable for the concert group. Unfortunately, much of the equipment is used during only a small part of the school year. If the concert percussion section must be equipped from nothing, the author has found it expedient to devise a basic minimum list of equipment which can be purchased in any one year. If this list is not complete, or funds are not available to acquire all of the necessary equipment in one year, the director should set aside a portion of each year's instrument budget for the purchase of percussion instruments. Even if the purchase of other instruments takes priority over percussion instruments, a nominal amount of money will purchase castanets, or a set of maracas, etc. The guideline for deciding which percussion instruments should be purchased at any one time should be based on which instruments are used the most. If, for example, enough money is available to purchase a set of orchestra bells or a set of Latin timbales but not both, it would be wiser to invest the money in the orchestra bells since they would be used more.

As in the case of any purchase, you get exactly what you pay for. In the long run, the music director will be money ahead if he buys his equipment from the established manufacturers of percussion instruments. The nearest college percussion instructor or symphony percussionist can advise the school music director on the craftsmanship and the reputation of the leading companies that manufacture percussion equipment. As with other instruments, several models of the same percussion instrument (timpani for example) may be available from the same company. Again, if the director himself knows little about percussion equipment, he should consult the nearest experienced percussionist.

Player Ownership

There are several practical ways in which the music director can save his money for his school system. One way is by insisting that each school percussionist purchase his own set of small instruments. As a minimum, this should include one pair of snare drum sticks, one pair of timpani sticks, one triangle with beater and holder, and one tambourine. Compared to the investment of other students who are required to buy clarinets, cornets, etc., this is a small investment indeed. It is this small equipment that is most often lost or broken through neglect or carelessness. If each percussionist were required to buy his own set of small instruments, the equipment would probably last a great deal longer.

Custom Accessories

Some percussion equipment can be constructed in the school workshop. Such items as trap tables and cymbal racks, both for crash and suspended cymbals, can be designed and built to fit any special needs. One can also build a castanet machine by using hand castanets and a scrap piece of sonorous lumber. Triangle holders can be constructed from metal photo clips or by adapting an outdoor music clip. With a little ingenuity and imagination, the band or orchestra director will be able to think of many other ways to improvise in the acquisition of percussion equipment without sacrificing sound quality.

Storage

Storage and maintenance of equipment play an important role in the well-organized percussion section. Perhaps the most important piece of equipment in any percussion section is the storage cabinet. Such a cabinet is available commercially or can be built to serve the needs of any particular organization. A well-designed storage cabinet can serve a number of purposes. It should have enough drawer space to hold all of the small pieces of equipment such as beaters of all types (triangle, bass drum, tam-tam, etc.), triangles, tambourines, maracas, etc. If it is mounted on wheels and constructed in the proper way, it can double as a trap table or a table for orchestra bells.

Adequate storage facilities will be of little value, however, if the music director does not insist on their use. Each percussionist in the section must assume the responsibility of putting away every piece of equipment where it belongs. If this procedure is not firmly established, the percussion storage area eventually becomes a junk pile. The section leader should check the percussion area of the rehearsal room at the end of each rehearsal to see that all equipment is returned to its proper place. The section leader should keep track of all percussion equipment and its condition and report to the director any equipment that needs to be repaired or replaced.

Inventory

At the end of every school year the music director should take an inventory of his percussion equipment. This is also the time to check on the condition of the equipment. Are the drum heads worn and do they need to be replaced? How many beaters and mallets have been lost or broken through the course of the year? Are the bowls on the timpani in good shape or have they been dented through misuse? Throughout the year, and particularly at contest time, it would be wise for the music director to have certain spare pieces of equipment on hand. Such spare parts should include at least one set of snare drum sticks, one set of heads (batter and snare) for the concert snare drums, one set of heads for the field drum, and one or more triangle beaters and holders. At the end of the school year, such equipment can be used for replacement and new spare parts ordered for the following year.

Summary

This article has been written to provide the non-percussionist music director with a number of practical hints for the organization of his percussion section. In itself, each point discussed may seem relatively unimportant, but collectively, the suggestions can mean the difference between a good or a poor percussion section. A poor percussion section can only adversely influence the entire ensemble, while a good one will certainly enhance it. Thus, the organization of the percussion section is vital not only for its own success, but also for the success of the ensemble at large.

1970 - 1971

February 1970

It's Contest Time Again

Al Payson

Twelve-year-old Johnny Smith, a clarinetist, is standing in a hall at the Riverdale Junior High School. He is a solo contestant in the annual inter-city spring music contest, and he is awaiting his turn to perform. His throat is dry and his palms are damp with perspiration because he is nervous. His nervousness is due not only to the ordinary pressures of competition and playing before a judge, but is also due to the extremely unusual conditions to which his band director is subjecting him. First, he has only his clarinet mouthpiece. The clarinet itself is being supplied by the host school so that he does not have to "go to the trouble" of bringing his own instrument. Secondly, the clarinet that he will use is also being used by all the other contestants; thus it will not be available to him in advance to try out, to warm up on, or to run through his solo. He can only tootle on his mouthpiece.

Apprehensions keep popping up in Johnny's mind. His music director said that the host school promised to provide an instrument that was in good working order. But what if it isn't? Or what if it feels different—or sounds different? He thinks to himself, "If I could only run through my solo a couple of times in a practice room. Let's see, how does the middle section start?" His nervousness increases.

Finally it is his turn. He walks into room and picks up the clarinet. His heart jumps. It is a different brand than his own! He slips on the mouthpiece and fingers the keys. Some of them work a little stiffer than his own, and (panicsville) two of them are placed a little differently on the instrument. The judge motions him to start. He summons his courage, plunges in bravely, and for a while things go pretty well. But then the strange instrument starts to work against him and his fingers stiffen, his mind is drawn away from the notes, he skips a line or two of music, and things deteriorate rapidly. Somehow, he makes it to the end.

Johnny walks out of the room dejected and thinks to himself, "I guess I just don't have what it takes to be a musician."

Do you, as a school music director, let this situation occur with your students at the spring music contest? "Of course not!" you say. Ah, but you *do*! Not with your clarinetists, to be sure, or your trumpeters, or saxophonists, or flutists or bassoonists. *But you do with your timpanist.* It is standard practice for the host school to provide timpani so that other participating schools do not "have to bother" to bring them.

Think about it. Your timpani contestant goes into the contest room with only his own mallets. The drums are strange, often of different manufacture, often with different pedal mechanism. (It is very difficult for even experienced timpanists to adjust to a different pedal "feel" to tune.) If the *T* handles are in a different place, it is more than likely that he will inadvertently strike them a few times. Since the drums are used by everyone they must remain in the contest room, so he cannot warm up on them or run through his solo. It is not unusual for the drums to be out of adjustment, in a sad state mechanically, and/or to have poor heads. It was my experience, as a judge at one high school level contest, that the mechanism of the timpani was completely inoperable, forcing the contestants to perform without tuning.

How can the timpani contestant be expected to perform creditably under these conditions? Is it fair to him? Is this a sound educational concept? Is this inconsistency in treatment (of the timpanist as opposed to all the other instrumentalists) instilling the proper attitude in the student, and providing him conditions for a rewarding musical experience? Is it *really* that much trouble to bring your own school's timpani?

May 1970

A Good Snare Drum Grip and Seven Deadly Errors

Mervin Britton

After many years of working with elementary and secondary school snare drum performers, the author has found that serious technical limitations of any student can invariably be traced to one or more of seven specific faults. These errors are related to grip or approach to it. A correct grip is just as important as an embouchure or bow arm. It is also likely to be just as difficult to correct after bad habits are formed. These seven errors range from muscles which are tightly jammed, twisted out of normal position, to grips that are so oose the student is really not sure where he is holding the stick.

A correct grip is one that is firm, yet relaxed and which permits the joints and muscles of the fingers, wrists, and arms to move in their most normal position. Since the easiest way to correct traditional left hand problems is to use the matched grip, this article deals only with that grip which is traditional for the *right* hand.

The stick should be held at a point from four to six inches from the butt, in the first joint of the index finger with the fleshy pad of the inside of the thumb. An imaginary pin through the center of the thumb nail should pass through the center of the stick and into the joint of the index finger. The stick tends to be toward the side of the finger which is nearest the thumb. (See illustration.)

The tip of the finger curls under the stick and is responsible for a great proportion of the stick motion and control. While the second finger tip also touches the stick, assisting the motion of the index finger, it does not grip. The third and fourth fingers should be curved around the stick in a relaxed manner without clasping it. These two may later come into use with more advanced finger control. Between the thumb and hand is an open space which allows stick resonance. Even more important, this space permits the necessary motion of the joints of the thumb and index finger for stick control. If such a good grip goes bad, it is usually because the student is forced to play material that is too complicated before the grip becomes routined.

The First Error

Perhaps the most common fault is placing the stick in the second instead of the first joint of the index finger. In this position, the use of finger tip control by either of the first two fingers is reduced to a minimum and then only with maximum exertion and concentrated practice. This also requires twisting the first finger to get the tip farther back on the stick as well as straining the muscles in the back of the hand in order to use the second finger. Much worse, the natural spring and manipulation function is lost in the three joints on both the thumb and first finger. Therefore, most of the stick control is forced upon the wrist. Without the natural help of the fingers, the wrist is not capable of working the stick with the speed and finesse necessary for modern drumming. When the stick is in the second joint, the length of the thumb is also more likely to rest against the side of the finger and palm. Such a position chokes the stick. This choking can be heard each time the stick strikes the drum.

The Second Error

A second error is holding the stick in the correct first joint, but destroying all the natural advantages by keeping the tip of the finger straight instead of curved under the stick. Without this curve, the stick has a natural tendency to fall from the hand. In order to prevent this, the student makes one of two incorrect adjustments. He either squeezes the stick in a vise like grip between the finger and thumb, again forcing all the action upon the wrist. Or, he curls the second finger around the stick so that the actual grip is between that finger and the thumb. However, their points of force may be an inch or more apart down the stick, presenting a weak arrangement for adequate finger control. The first finger has little if any control of the stick.

The Third Error

A low thumb, or one that appears to be holding the stick with side or full length, is a third common error. When the thumb is low, the natural action of the stick is to slide up from the first to the second joint of the index finger. Again, the thumb closes against the finger and palm, forcing all the action upon the wrist.

The Fourth Error

Four other common errors in the approach to the stick or drum pad prove just as troublesome as an incorrect grip between thumb and fingers. One of these comprises a wrist and forearm turned so that the back of the hand is perpendicular to the floor with the thumb on top of the stick. The wrist is forced to pivot in its narrow side arc. This position also involves jerky forearm motion. Emphasis should be placed on keeping the back of the hand parallel to the floor for maximum free motion in the wrist. It should be acknowledged here that a compromise between the parallel and perpendicular position is necessary for advanced performance. However, the more perpendicular position should be avoided until the performer is ready to use it for a specific purpose.

The Fifth Error

If the butt of the stick is allowed to rest under the fingers out beyond the palm, the shaft assumes a position that is parallel to the front of the performer. One of two bad habits result from this position. The palm is twisted out away from the forearm at the palm. Unnecessary stress on the wrist muscles is the result of such a position. If the palm remains straight with the stick in this parallel position, the wrist and forearm must rotate in order to work the stick rather than using the natural wrist and finger pivot motion. The butt of the stick should tend to rest near the crease of the thumb at the back center of the palm. While the stick may work forward somewhat, depending on the individual, it should never be allowed to reach a position beyond the palm.

The Sixth Error

A drum which is too low for the player forces the wrists to be bent upward from downward-projecting forearms. Such a position not only cramps the wrists in an upward position, but limits their motion to less than one-fourth their normal potential.

The Seventh Error

A drum which is too high cramps the forearms because of the smaller angle at the elbows. While this position may not be as bad as a drum that is too low, the normal potential and reserve motion of the wrists are again greatly reduced. The smaller angle and high forearms may also hinder the regular relaxed motion of the fingers.

The correct height for the drum would permit the angle at the elbow to be an approximate range of 125 degrees. Naturally, the exact angle will vary with each individual. In this range, the wrist's normal position is in the center of its up and down arc. This central position permits the wrist to have maximum motion either up or down. (Editor's note: with the matched grip the drum head should be parallel to the ground, not at an angle.)

Conclusions

A firm yet relaxed grip between the thumb and first joint of the finger is not difficult to teach or maintain, providing the teacher catches the above errors as soon as they start to develop. While it is not hard for a beginning student to assume the correct grip, it does take time to develop the muscles involved of the thumb, fingers, and hand. Such necessary control takes reasonable practice time and appropriate progressive material.

A sudden push into extremely rapid note passages or rudimental combinations is a prime factor that causes the grip to slip into bad habits. On the other hand, a student should not be kept on dull, slow moving material using notes of long duration. In addition to the obvious motivation factor, sticks and hands must work often enough to develop necessary muscle strength. A practical compromise between use and strain must be maintained here as with any muscle developing activity.

In closing, it is important to stress that the extra time used to establish a good grip, avoiding the seven errors, listed above, will be well spent. The teacher should not be concerned about the apparent delay in more advanced technical development. With a secure, relaxed foundation upon which to build, the student will obtain higher long range goals in a shorter total period of time.

June 1970

JOIN THE PERCUSSIVE ARTS SOCIETY

Gordon Peters

Purposes of the PAS

To raise the level of musical percussion performance and teaching; to expand understanding of the needs and responsibilities of the percussion student, teacher, and performer; and to promote a greater communication between all areas of the percussion arts.

Officer Representation Categories

Professional, College Education, High School, Elementary School, Private Teacher, Composer, Drum Corps, Dealer, Publisher, Manufacturer, Distributor, and Members at Large.

Publications

All members receive the journal *Percussionist* (four issues per academic year) and the magazine *Percussive Notes* (three issues per academic year). These publications contain articles and research studies of importance to all in the percussion field, and serve to keep all members informed of current news, trends, programs, and happenings of interest.

Memberships

Professional $8.00 (Percussionist)
Individual $5.00 (Music Educator: non-percussionist)
Student $5.00 (Any full-time student at any educational level)
Library $5.00

Note: All memberships are based on a fiscal year, September 1st through August 31st, and are automatically continued with annual billing unless cancelled by member. Please report changes of address promptly.

Specific Projects under Study

Acoustics of Percussion Instruments; Avant-grade Percussion Music; College and University Percussion Curriculum and Materials; Elementary Percussion Education; Improvement of Percussion Solo and Ensemble Contest Adjudication Standards, Procedures, and Materials; Musicology and Ethnomusicology as Related to Percussion; Percussion Literature Improvement; Methods, Solos, Ensembles, Percussion Parts to Band, Orchestra, and Stage Band Music; Stage Band Drumming; Standardization of Terminology and Notation of Percussion Instruments.

Special Note to Students

All students with an interest in percussion should take advantage of this excellent opportunity to join PAS. Student membership in this organization along with private lessons from a fine teacher should be the goal of every aspiring percussionist.

Write and send remittance to:
Percussive Arts Society
130 Carol Drive
Terre Haute, Indiana 47805

A Percussion Perspective: 1970

Gordon Peters

In order to gain a view of the state of the Art of Percussion, it might help to look at various aspects of the medium individually. It would seem that the categories of Performance and Teaching, Literature, Instruments, Communication, and Problems would accommodate most of what there is to be said.

Performance and Teaching

One area that has made great strides in the last 10 or 20 years is the percussion ensemble. This "new" outlet (beyond the bass drum-cymbal-snare drum area of literature) has shown percussionists that they must be able to move from one instrument to another, and play in many different styles. The ensemble experience (unavailable in sufficient quantities elsewhere) is very valuable; however, the literature is, for the most part, musically inferior.

The "Marimba Masters" (a marimba ensemble of seven players which I formed in 1954) proved to be a musically rewarding experience in chamber music for the players, a great hit with the public, and remunerative. Other groups have had the same experience. Percussion instructors who are opposed to musical transcriptions for the marimba ensemble are restricting their students' (and their own) development. After all, percussionists must learn to phrase — to play melodies and harmonies — not just the rhythms to which most percussion ensemble literature is limited. Playing baroque, classic, romantic, 20th century, and pops music on mallet instruments — with a great deal of finesse — is essential for today's professional percussionist. Also, don't overlook the musical experience of playing chamber music with instruments other than just percussion.

The various levels of percussion teaching should be examined to gain a better perspective of our art. The first is the rhythm band exposure to the very young (ages 5-10), in which general music teachers often employ the systems of Carl Orff and Zoltan Kodály involving membranic, wooden, and metallic percussion instruments, including the keyboards. It is curious to find in the next stage of percussion education (taught by instrumental specialists) that instruction is generally limited to the snare drum!

In the last several years, many music education departments at our universities have included percussion classes and even private lessons for their non-percussion students, helping to raise the level of percussion understanding and teaching of our future music directors. Some basic questions to be raised by the percussion student who is considering a private teacher are these:

1. Is the teacher qualified by training and experience to teach the area of percussion the student wishes to study?
2. Is the teacher aware of current percussion literature available?
3. Has the teacher produced capable players in the recent past?
4. Is the student's development of greater concern to the teacher than the collection of his fee?

Admittedly, the answers to the above are difficult to ascertain initially. Some teachers may feel that it is impertinent for a student to raise these questions. However, during my early student percussion days, I could have chosen some of my teachers more wisely had someone suggested such inquiries to me. Also, my own choice of teachers has always been those who have had practical playing experience.

One-Teacher Limits

There is a further relationship which needs mentioning: the student who is "married" to one teacher. The limitations of perspective here are obvious. No student should stay too long with one teacher, with the possible exception of the qualified university percussion instructor who, with today's varied demands, *can* keep an industrious and talented pupil involved in creative study for four or five school years. Weekly one-hour lessons should be the minimum diet for the student who may have professional aspirations. Perhaps the most honest and functional insurance for a valid student-teacher relationship is to have a good chat about goals and course of study. A lesson environment should be developed where questions can be asked and ideas exchanged freely.

The matter of "course of study" (curriculum) is extremely important to the pupil at all levels. It is obvious that the needs and goals of pupils vary, but too often we find the unimaginative teacher adhering to a stereotyped study plan with little or no variation from one pupil to the next.

The matter of contests, particularly at the secondary school level, has improved in the last five years, largely as a result of the urging of the Percussive Arts Society (PAS). Basically, I think we can all agree that the demands made by percussion music should be tested in the contest situation. The matter of versatility, sight reading, tuning, multiple percussion facility, etc. should serve as goals, as well as testing areas, for the percussionists. How else can we advance our art if the goals and standards during the formative period are antiquated?

The perpetuation of the percussion art is largely in the hands of teachers. We must all work toward a more imaginative, self-disciplined, and communicative approach if our art is to flourish and grow.

Literature

The volume of percussion literature that has appeared in the last 20 years is staggering. I think it is fair to estimate that the percentage of valid, meaningful percussion method books and performance literature is probably about the same. The teacher must plow through all of these materials and choose what he feels is consistent with his musical concepts and will best fit into his teaching plans.

There are three basic sources of printed music: the publishers themselves (write directly to them for catalogs, music on approval); large music stores and drum shops; and the International Percussion Reference Library, Music Department, Arizona State University, Tempe, Arizona 85281, where over 1100 titles are available (with full scores) on a two week loan basis.

Publishers have some fine works on a rental basis only. Because of high costs, this may discourage potential performances. However, publishers have indicated that as the demand for these works increases, more will be made available for sale.

The performance literature known as "multiple percussion" (playing several percussion instruments simultaneously and in rapid succession) is filling a previous gap in preparing our young percussionists to fulfill demands made upon them in bands, orchestras, and stage band drumming.

Films and Papers

Another comparatively new type of "literature" for percussion are the many films now on the market on how to play and teach percussion instruments. They are particularly valuable to those persons in areas where a competent percussion teacher is not available. Many of these are in color, and, though they may appear costly to some, with repeated use they are a fine institutional investment.

Graduate papers on percussion in the form of essays, theses, and dissertations have gradually increased as percussion has been recognized by music schools as a degree instrument. In fact, there are now a few institutions offering the Doctor of Musical Arts degree in percussion.

The literature for percussion ensemble has grown by leaps and bounds in the last two decades. There are works available for virtually every combination of instruments and numbers of players. Most of our publishers have at last been convinced that there is a real market for percussion music. Many times the emphasis is still on membranic and rhythmic percussion to the near-exclusion of the pitched and exotic instruments. It has been my personal choice for 10 years, at both the Eastman School of Music and at Northwestern University, to program percussion ensemble works on the first half and marimba ensemble on the second. I can trace part of my own musical growth to this dual experience.

Instruments

The development of percussion instruments in the past 15 years has been nothing short of spectacular. I feel that this growth has been motivated not only by the dollar-incentive which businessmen must consider, but also by genuine educational motives, and competition between manufacturers. Further, refinements demanded by some percussionists (not forthcoming from established firms) have spawned many excellent custom-made products, which have ultimately led manufacturers to produce both modifications and new products.

Generally, instrument quality has improved greatly. There are those occasions, of course, where quality control breaks down. This is understandable when mass production techniques are used. The only recourse is to write directly to the manufacturer (send a copy to the dealer) stating the problem encountered and requesting that an adjustment be made.

The advent of the plastic age has had considerable influence on percussion. This, along with electronics, will continue to play a major role in the development of new and modified instruments. Plastic drum heads have certainly been a valid answer to the problems of humidity. Also, plastic shafted mallets have eliminated the problem of warping.

Perhaps one reason why percussion manufacturers have been able to sustain a great growth trend in business is that, in addition to the general expansion in school music, drums have been a part of every new "fad:" the drum and bugle corps of the '20's, the swing era of the '30's, the accordion rage of the '40's, the percussion ensemble explosion of the '50's, and the guitar and electronic music of the '60's. All of these have required percussion instruments in one form or another.

Problems

I see some weaknesses which demand attention. Since each topic could be expanded into a full article, I will mention only "germ motives:"

1. The influence of easier money, greater leisure time, less parental discipline, and less teacher discipline, in many cases, and the availability of many percussion teachers who are not really qualified above a certain level — all of these factors have had their impact on percussion education.

2. In instrumental music education, elements of basic music theory, including sight reading of rhythms, are usually ignored.

3. Teachers often do not teach enough about routine and organization to their students. Percussion players especially need to come early enough to assemble equipment, decide upon the most efficient instrument set-up, note changes of instruments necessary, and mark parts accordingly. This ability to plan ahead is of far greater importance to percussionists than for other instrumentalists.

4. There is a general lack of versatility amongst players, i.e., not being able to play *all* the percussion instruments.

5. Students should be taught to do more thoughtful practice *before* going to the instrument. They should know what the piece will sound like. Phrasing, tempo, and sticking should all be considered well in advance of the first reading with the actual equipment.

Communication

As an art, industry, or activity grows, there is a strong motivation among those involved to know what others are doing in the field. In the early 1960's, the Percussive Arts Society (PAS) was formed to attempt to fulfill this need. Among the projects accomplished to date are: contest percussion adjudication procedures; university percussion curriculums; percussion notation; bibliographies, including graduate theses and chronological listings of periodical percussion articles. Many other projects are in progress or under consideration.

All PAS efforts are volunteer. In addition to members' dues, support comes from manufacturers, wholesalers, drum shops, and publishers. The communication of ideas among these diverse interests in percussion is marvelous. Perhaps the greatest step forward in percussion in this century has been the formation of this organization.* As with the ecological problems confronting us today, we have started something for our art, but we all can do much more.

*Readers interested in joining the Percussive Arts Society should refer to the June, 1970 issue of *The Instrumentalist* or write directly to PAS at: 130 Carol Drive, Terre Haute, Indiana 47805.

September 1970

Percussion Contests—Time for Change?

Donald K. Gilbert

Another school year has come, which means for many junior and senior high school percussionists that another year of solo and ensemble contests is ahead. After both adjudicating and listening to many percussionists in this area, the thought occurred to me that percussion contests and the criteria for judging them are many years behind the times. I should like to reflect on my experiences of the past year and suggest some much-needed changes if we as percussionists and music educators are going to provide school percussionists with meaningful and valuable musical experiences. I have the feeling that the problems that I have encountered are not unique, but are problems that many other percussion adjudicators have also found.

Drummers Everywhere

The status of percussion performance in the public schools at the present time is such that it has not significantly progressed much beyond the stage of rudimental drumming. This fact was forcefully brought home to me when I recently spent one entire day listening to percussionists in solo and ensemble contests. It would be more accurate to say that I spent the day listening to "drummers," since out of over fifty entries for that day, only one person played a mallet solo.

Of all the ensembles, less than five were of mixed percussion instruments. All the rest were snare drum duets, trios and quartets, sometimes with an added bass drum. Most of my time was spent listening to the *Downfall of Paris*, *Connecticut Halftime*, etc. (excellent compositions, but, like good wine, should be enjoyed in small quantities). To make matters worse, some of the entries were so poorly prepared that the compositions became totally unrecognizable.

Where Are The Mallets?

On another occasion I was asked to judge candidates in percussion who had applied for membership in a specific music organization consisting of the best school musicians in the area. An adjudication sheet was passed out to all applicants prior to the day of audition, specifying performance on snare drum, timpani, mallets, and traps. The statistics concerning this event are again, most revealing. Not one applicant was capable of performing in all four areas. Indeed, not one person was able to play on any of the mallet instruments. Some applicants did not even know how to hold the triangle.

I Have the Rudiments

To my knowledge this was the first time they had been exposed to this type of audition. I am sure many of them were disappointed in not being asked to demonstrate the first thirteen rudiments and play a rudimental drum solo. Indeed, at least one music director voiced his disapproval directly to me.

I came away from those auditions with great misgivings and a profound feeling that somewhere along the way these students had been cheated out of a competent and valuable percussion education.

If these students represented the best in the area, then the rest, through no fault of their own, are certainly not receiving their money's-worth out of the music education programs in their respective public schools.

Where does the fault lie? Many of these students are not fortunate enough to have private teachers whose major instrument is percussion, and must rely on the instruction that their music directors can give them. I suspect that in many instances such help is very minimal since non-percussion-major music directors themselves have not had an adequate percussion education — in some cases only a single semester of a percussion methods class. This is barely enough time to cover the basic fundamentals of the snare drum, let alone the myriad of other percussion instruments. To be sure, if many music directors can glean enough out of such classes to adequately prepare their percussion sections for the marching season, they can consider themselves lucky. It is illogical for us to expect a high level of performance from high school percussionists if we cannot supply our students with the resources necessary for attaining a high level. Ideally, two full semesters of class percussion methods (instead of one) in the teacher-training curriculum would help.

Time in itself, however, is not the only factor involved. The second aspect to consider is the *quality* of percussion methods classes. At the present time, teachers of such classes must decide whether the subject material should be presented in breadth or depth. There is no time for both. Traditionally, depth in one instrument (usually the snare drum) has been emphasized, with a large part of the subject material (particularly instruction on mallet instruments) left untouched, or, at best, treated superficially. Such a limited education sets off a chain reaction, and produces high school students who go to contests and auditions in the condition which I have described above. Even within the time limits of one college semester, emphasis should be placed on covering the gamut of percussion instruments now used freely by many composers. Methods classes should be provided with as much bibliographical material as possible, including listings of the most important percussion method books, textbooks, solos and ensembles, plus the most important publishers and manufacturers in the percussion field. The least that should be done for the non-percussionist is to provide him with the necessary tools which will enable him to continue his percussion education on his own.

In addition to *The Instrumentalist,* school music teachers should be aware of such source materials as *Percussionist* and *Percussive Notes* (published by the Percussive Arts Society), which strive to present current trends and the latest thoughts in the field of percussion. The non-percussionist music teacher might do well to become an active member of the Percussive Arts Society . . . and certainly encourage his percussion players to join . . . since this organization could probably be his largest single source of percussion information.

Percussion teachers and adjudicators may have to force the necessary quality changes in the percussion curriculum into the public schools by taking every opportunity to upgrade percussion contest and audition requirements. This should be done realistically, however, keeping in mind the final objective we wish to accomplish, namely the development of well-rounded high school percussionists who feel at ease playing on any of the many percussion instruments and in any of the percussion media.

In my opinion, general contest requirements should include performance demonstrations on snare drum, timpani, at least one mallet instrument (either xylophone, marimba, or bells) and a variety of the standard traps. A simple audition that has proved very adequate for my uses is as follows:

A Simple Audition

1. A solo in any one category (snare drum, timpani, or mallet instrument).
2. Sight-reading of a short passage from the standard orchestral repertoire in the two categories not covered by the prepared solo.
3. Demonstration of ability to tune the timpani in fourths, fifths, and sixths from any given note (two drums only).
4. Play major scales (to three sharps and three flats) in quarter notes, two octaves, at a reasonable tempo, on one of the mallet instruments.
5. Demonstrate ability on a number of the standard trap instruments (crash cymbals, suspended cymbal, bass drum, triangle, tambourine, etc.) selected by the auditioner. The evaluation is based on three criteria: (1) rhythmic accuracy, (2) melodic accuracy, and (3) general musicality, including interpretation, dynamic levels, tone quality and, in the case of timpani, intonation. The audition includes all of the basic percussion techniques I feel a student should have mastered by the time he reaches the ninth grade.

These are minimum requirements for that age level. Naturally, a greater competency is expected from those students in the higher grades. Since this type of audition has a great amount of flexibility, those responsible for designing contest and audition requirements can vary the materials to suit their own particular purposes. What should remain constant, however, are the four general categories in which the percussionist is expected to display his skills.

I have discussed what I consider to be necessary changes in the school percussion contest; however, if requirements are to be upgraded, a change in philosophy is also required. The school percussionist must be thought of as an integral part of the music organization in which he is participating, with both his teachers and his peers seeing him as a *percussionist,* rather than just a "drummer" who can play the snare, bass, and cymbals. In order to perform the very demanding scores in common use today, the percussionist must be recognized for what he really is: a *musician* — just as much as any other member of the organization.

October 1970

Snares Alive, Where Are You?

William Hertel

How do you hold the interest of beginning percussion students? A desire to practice must be instilled — the student must have some incentive, a set of goals, some way he can be rewarded for his efforts not only at the *end* of the school year, but just as soon as possible — *now*!

Soon after the clarinet student begins studying his instrument, he can play simple, familiar melodies such as *Mary Had a Little Lamb,* or *Twinkle, Twinkle Little Star.* Before he completes his first six weeks of lessons he is more than likely performing these simple melodies for his parents, relatives, neighbors, and friends, and is given almost immediate recognition for his achievements through *positive* comments made by his audience – this "early audience" will almost always be sympathetic. But what kind of a response will the beginning percussion student receive when he asks his parents to listen to the fine technique he has acquired learning to play half notes and quarter notes correctly on his snare drum?

Some of you say, "My percussion students do not have this problem — all of them purchased a small set of bells when they started and they *can* play simple melodies very early in their studies." Fine, but now that you have them practicing melodies on the bells, how do you get them to develop good snare drumming technique? Are they going to want to practice typical exercises found in most beginning snare drum method books (play-rest, rest-play, etc.)?

When I begin teaching rhythms to my beginning students I try to include the playing techniques of other percussion instruments in addition to the snare drum. This eventually involves all of the Latin American instruments that my school owns (timpani, bells, chimes, vibraphone, marimba, cymbals) as well as hand clapping, foot stomping, and finger snapping. The desired percussion ensemble sound is built almost from the very first lesson. Many variations are possible; for example, the claves, cowbell, and tambourine play four measures, immediately followed by the snare drum, bass drum, and cymbals playing the next four measures.

My students seem to enjoy my ability to ad lib simple tunes on the piano as they perform an exercise on practice pads, snare drums, or one of the other instruments. They feel that what they are doing is actually enhancing or improving the melody so that it will be more enjoyable to the listeners' ears.

Encouraging Home Practice

Now, if these students are enjoying their class lessons (and I have every reason to believe that they are), why do they come to each lesson somehow not quite as prepared as one would expect them to be? What is missing at home? No place to practice? Poor scheduling of time? Lack of encouragement from parents?

At home, there is no melodic line, nothing to enhance.

But with the aid of a cassette tape recorder, it is possible to record simple melodies which the student could take home and accompany on a snare drum, practice pad or whatever. Certainly, progressive studies could be written which would help the student develop vital techniques at the same time that he is "making the music sound better." Not only would he be more motivated to practice on his own, but he would probably receive more parental encouragement, especially if the tune that "Johnny" accompanies is familiar to them.

Needless to say, not everyone has a cassette tape recorder, but there are many records available of marches and children's tunes to which many snare drum exercises can be adapted. I highly recommend a series of records which includes written etudes and tunes for snare drum and bell accompaniment (produced by *Sounds for Success,* 1201 No. Torino Ave., Tucson, Arizona 85716).

Too many times I have observed that the drum section is far below the musical ability of the other sections in the band. This need not be so. If the percussion students are given a good start, their performance ability can be just as refined as that of any other section.

A concentrated effort by all teachers is needed to help the student to first realize and then hear the relationship of his part to whatever else is sounding around him. Why not encourage this melodic-harmonic concept from the start and let it grow? Snares alive, I do not want to hear tap-tap-tap — I want to hear a melodic phrase, harmonic phrase, imitation, and more. Encourage those beginning, intermediate, and advanced percussion students to develop a musical ear — not a mathematical one . . . and let them have fun doing it!

October 1970

Care and Repair of Percussion Instruments

Donald F. Knaack

I. Snare Drum

A. Heads

1. Plastic heads are advisable. They are better economically and they do not require as much care as a calf head.

2. To get maximum tonal response and prevent breakage, the head should be evenly tensioned (the same pitch should be present opposite each tension rod).

3. If plastic head becomes dirty, remove from drum—scrub with mild abrasive—rinse—dry—remount on drum.

4. Play on head only with the proper sticks or mallets.

5. When putting a new head on a drum, put a thin coat of paraffin or cork grease on the shell rim to ease the friction between the head and the rim.

B. Snares

1. Keep under tension when not in use.

2. Wire snares are recommended for high school use. Wire, gut, nylon or combinations (such as two wire to one gut) are preferred for college and professional use.

C. Sticks

1. Tips should always have a smooth finish (it is possible to sandpaper-off minor damage to the tips).

2. Do not use taped, cracked, or warped sticks.

3. Sticks commonly used on snare drum.

a. Snare drum sticks.
b. Brushes.
c. Timpani mallets (felt).
d. Yarn mallets.

D. Shell

1. Keep clean. Wax occasionally

with a thin coat of fine wax.

2. Keep all working parts (such as screws and lugs) secure.

3. Keep all working parts (such as screws, snare strainer) lubricated.

4. Replace any worn or stripped parts.

E. Stands

1. Keep all nuts, bolts, screws, and working parts lubricated. Replace any part that becomes stripped or worn.

2. Use only sturdy stands.

3. When folding for packing, always fold correctly (never force parts).

4. When drum is on the stand: always make sure that all screws, nuts and bolts on the stand are secure.

5. Make sure the legs of the stand are positioned properly on the floor to assure maximum balance.

6. When placing the drum on the stand: always make sure that the three support arms are in their proper positions—the adjustable arm being fully expanded until the drum is in place. The arm should then be pushed into place and tightened.

F. Cases

1. Fibre cases are preferable.

2. Cloth cases are a good second choice. Use cardboard discs (the diameter of the drum) to protect the heads from breakage.

3. Never pack sticks or stands with a drum in a case.

4. Never store drums in extreme hot or cold.

II. Xylophone-Marimba

A. Mallets

1. Only use xylophone or marimba mallets (no snare drum sticks, triangle beaters, etc.).

2. The mallet should be appropriate to the instrument. Never use hard plastic or extra-hard rubber mallets on the marimba. Avoid using brass mallets on any wooden keyboard.

B. Bars

1. Clean and wax (thin coat of fine paste wax) periodically.

2. Cleaning and waxing should be determined according to the amount of usage.

3. Cracked or damaged bars should be replaced. Send damaged bars to their maker to insure correct replacement bar and octave; or indicate exact length, width, thickness, pitch, manufacturer, and model number of the key to be replaced.

4. Always cover instruments when not in use with something such as a quilted blanket.

5. Suggested pitch standards.

a. Marimba and vibes: A-440 or 441.

b. Xylophone and glockenspiel: A-442.

6. Do not set anything on top of a mallet keyboard.

C. Resonators

1. Occasional waxing with a thin coat of fine wax helps to retain the finish.

2. Resonators dent easily. Be cautious when packing and handling.

D. Parts

1. Cords for the bars should be tight. Old cords should be replaced.

2. Bent or missing guide posts should be replaced.

3. Insulators on the guide posts dry out and need replacing after several years.

4. The framework should be cleaned and waxed occasionally. Any nicks should be touched up with paint (consult manufacturer for type).

E. Cases

1. Fibre or wooden cases are preferred.

2. When traveling, always dismantle the instrument.

3. Always make sure the bars are wrapped up well when traveling (to avoid dents and marks that can affect intonation).

4. When moving the instrument intact (such as from one room to another) be careful not to jar or pull loose any parts. Always make sure there is adequate manpower present when lifting.

5. Be especially careful to lock the music stand securely. Many timpani heads have been split open following a blow from a music stand which slipped.

III. Other Keyboard Percussion

A. Glockenspiel

1. Clean periodically with any good silver polish.

2. Avoid using brass-headed mallets on an aluminum keyboard.

3. All bent and missing guide posts should be replaced.

4. All guide post insulators should be replaced after they have dried out.

5. Never place anything on the keyboard.

6. Always use a sturdy stand to support the instrument, such as a regular glockenspiel stand or a very sturdy restaurant stand.

B. Vibraharp (Vibes)

1. Avoid using plastic, hard rubber or brass-headed mallets on the aluminum alloy keyboard.

2. Motor must be checked and oiled periodically as recommended by the manufacturer.

3. Keep all working parts lubricated.

4. Replace cords if they are worn.

5. Make sure all nuts and screws are tight before using.

6. Check electrical cord and end connection periodically.

7. Make sure proper electrical connection for A.C. or D.C. is made.

8. Damper pedal should be handled with care and checked periodically for malfunctions.

9. Instrument should be covered with quilted blanket when not in use.

10. Cases (See Marimba & Xylophone.)

C. Chimes

1. Use rawhide or wooden mallets only (no metal).

2. Strike chimes only on crown (cap) at the top of the tube.

3. Suspension cords should be checked periodically for wear.

4. Damper pedal and mechanism should be checked periodically.

5. Use a thick "drop-cover" for protection.

6. Care should be taken when moving so as not to dent the tubes or harm the pedal mechanism.

VI. Timpani

A. Base

1. When adjusting pedal, keep your foot on the pedal when releasing all of the tension so the pedal does not snap against the base and crack. *(Keep your hands out from under the pedal!)*

2. The tension spring should be adjusted and lubricated periodically.

3. Make sure all screws, nuts and tension rods are secure, clean, and well-lubricated. Replace any worn or stripped parts.

4. If drums are too low for the performer, they can be raised by placing blocks of wood under the base legs.

5. Check base periodically for security.

B. Heads

1. Plastic heads are recommended for educational institutions.

2. To clean heads.

a. Plastic—mild soap and warm water, keeping the water away from the hoop.

b. Calf skin—only lukewarm water, keeping it away from the flesh hoop.

3. Heads should be evenly tensioned (the same pitch should be present opposite each tension rod).

4. Keep heads covered with fibreboard discs (the diameter of the head) when not in use.

5. When reheading a drum: steel wool the rim—clean—dry—apply a thin coat of lanolin or paraffin around the rim—and put on the head.

6. When not in use, leave tensioned in dry climate or during the winter. In damp climate or during the summer, they should be left loose.

C. Sticks

1. Always make sure the balls are free from foreign materials (excessive thread build-up, etc.) that could cause damage to the head.

2. Use only timpani sticks. No triangle beaters, snare drum sticks, etc.

D. Bowls

1. Periodically, remove the head and beat dents out with a hard rubber hammer. On the inside of the bowl, work from the edges to the center of each individual dent.

E. Covers

1. When not in use, in addition to the fibre head protectors, there should be cloth drop-covers that cover the entire drum to insure maximum protection (quilted blanket material is excellent).

2. Traveling: mover's covers and fibre or wooden trunks should be employed for maximum protection.

VII. Smaller Percussion Instruments

A. Bass drum

1. Periodically check all lugs (lubricate and replace any that are worn or stripped).

2. Plastic heads are preferable (see snare drum).

3. Use only bass drum mallets.

4. Always use a sturdy stand.

5. Always use cases or covers when transporting.

B. Cymbals

1. Should be cleaned periodically: wash with a mild solution of oxalic acid and scrub with a soft bristle brush (scrubbing motion parallel to grooves). Rinse and dry. Then apply "2nd." Rinse and dry with a soft cloth.

2. Never buff or use a strong cleanser (wet) on the instrument. It will hamper maximum tonal response.

3. Cymbal stands should be checked periodically for worn or warped parts and bad insulation.

4. On hand cymbals, check leather straps for wear. Replace if necessary.

5. If a cymbal becomes cracked, consult a professional or write to the manufacturer for information concerning the salvaging of the cracked cymbal(s).

6. Avoid putting the cymbals under pressure when storing (such as "cramming" them into close quarters causing the cymbals to bend). Always store in a cymbal pouch, trap case or a shelf where they would be out of contact with other articles.

C. Tambourine

1. The head can be treated with string bass rosin or a strip of light sandpaper to aid thumb rolls.

2. Check jingles, head, and tacks periodically.

3. Avoid the use of knuckles. Use four fingers in a "bunched-up" position to strike the instrument.

4. When storing the instrument, make sure the head is covered. It is possible to make a small case for the tambourine, out of wood. This type of care will prolong the instrument's life considerably.

5. If a calf head breaks, consult a professional and check the possibilities of re-heading the instrument.

6. The wood shell is preferred over the metal shells. Also, a double row of jingles is preferred over a single row.

D. Triangle

1. Always use a metal triangle beater. No snare drum sticks, etc.

2. Suspend instrument with a piece of nylon or gut string (old harp or bass string). Connect string to a triangle clip (available commercially or one can be made from a clothespin).

3. Have a specific drawer or use trap case to store the triangle and its beaters (the beaters can be misplaced very easily).

E. Wood Block

1. Do *not* use brass mallets or triangle beaters.

2. Apply a thin coat of fine furniture wax periodically.

3. Store in a trap case or some safe place.

4. Preferred sticks are snare drum sticks or xylophone mallets.

F. Temple Blocks

1. Use only soft mallets (marimba), to avoid denting the wood.

2. Wax periodically (fine furniture wax).

3. Make sure the stand is secure.

4. When storing or transporting, make sure the individual blocks are packed securely.

G. Tam-Tam (Gong)

1. Check stand for sturdiness.

2. Check suspension material for wear. Nylon rope is good suspension material.

H. Gourds and Maracas

Store in a safe place because of the fragileness of the instruments.

Summary

1. All percussion instruments should be checked, cleaned, and the working parts lubricated periodically.

2. Each instrument should be stored in a safe manner and in a safe place (away from extreme heat or cold).

3. Unauthorized personnel should not be allowed to handle the percussion instruments.

4. A lecture to the percussion section on care and repair might be a big help.

5. Always follow the manufacturer's suggestions and instructions on care and repair.

The Improvisation — A Creative Experience

Terry Applebaum

Until the recent surge of interest in the percussion section and ensemble as a medium of artistic performance, the percussionist was generally limited to such duties as maintaining the pulse and embellishing the apex of a phrase. Much of the newer literature has presented the percussionist with added musical and technical challenges. However, percussion music based on the concept of creative teaching and learning is in short supply, causing a serious deficiency in the training and development of the truly *musical* percussionist. Although there have been some significant additions to the literature, it would appear as though a more permanent solution to the problem would have to include the discovery of additional means of expression — new approaches which effectively apply the *creativity concept* to percussion education.

Spontaneous Creation

One of the more exciting directions worthy of consideration is the avant-garde improvisation. Since an "improvisation" is a piece of music which is spontaneously created by its performers, it certainly fills the *creative* requirement. However, improvisations may not always produce music which is aesthetically and educationally sound. For this reason, the teacher is included as an integral member of the performance group, in order to aid in the creation of a valid musical endeavor. The teacher-performer has a very difficult function in that he must help give the improvisation musical direction in terms of form, motivic development, and dynamic contrast, but must never stifle the creative expression of the other performers. While an improvisation is in progress, the teacher utilizes various conducting gestures to achieve his goals.

Preparation prior to an improvisation should include discussions concerning form, motivic development, ostinatos, tension and release, texture variation, and dynamic contrast. A selected listening list of representative works is strongly recommended. In this way, the students at least will have the basic tools with which to build a rational piece. When this academic knowledge is blended with the elements of emotional spontaneity and considerable patience, a truly creative and meaningful composition often results.

One of the most difficult problems associated with improvisations is the tendency for a student to play too much, too loud, too soon! To avoid this tendency (which leads to the creation of very little real music), a rehearsal for an improvisation might include the following types of etudes to be applied individually or in combination:

1. A 15 second piece in which each performer is allowed to play one note.
2. A 15 second piece based on a given rhythmic or melodic motive.
3. A 15 second piece to be performed at a consistent level of *pp*.
4. A 30 second piece involving crescendo and diminuendo.
5. A 30 second piece based on ABA form.
6. A 60 second piece utilizing only metal instruments of indefinite pitch.

These represent, of course, only a few examples of the types of pieces that are suitable for improvisation rehearsals. The possibilities are only as limited as the musical needs of the students.

Elaborate Equipment Unnecessary

There is not any minimum or maximum amount of equipment needed, although the use of more instruments will usually add to available color combinations. A lack of percussion gear should not be allowed to act as a deterrent to such experimentation.

The reaction of students is generally mixed after the first attempts at improvisation. Some react positively — often as a result of the opportunity to play fast and loud. Those who react negatively usually do so because early efforts at improvisation generally do not yield music of outstanding merit. However, after improvisational ability develops, there is almost invariably a positive reaction, since results then clearly demonstrate that an aesthetically satisfying musical entity has been created... spontaneously... by the living, breathing people who are there!

Avant-garde improvisations can be an extremely valuable supplement to the present elementary, junior high, high school, or collegiate percussion curriculum. Because major emphasis is placed upon musical development through self-expression and creativity, it can also be a most exciting mode of teaching and learning.

2B or Not 2B?

Paul T. Mazzacano

In far too many music rooms and private studios across this nation, identical statements made to student drummers by non-percussionist instrumental directors will go unchallenged . . . "Get a pair of 2B sticks and start practicing." And, numerous enthusiastic young students will obey this directive only to find themselves facing serious musical and technical problems.

Why a 2B stick? Why not one of the many personally endorsed models? Or a model identified solely by letter? Will the sticks be plain or nylon tipped? round, oval squared or tapered bead? . . . *ad infinitum.* If it has to be a 2B stick, which manufacturer's. product shall the student choose? The difference is more than just a name brand! *(See chart # 1)*

Drum sticks, like mouthpieces, are manufactured to specific weights and measurements supposedly for the expressed purpose of meeting the performance demands of the individual percussionist. It is an accepted fact that accomplished drummers will use several different sizes of sticks as their work demands. This practice is the result of experimentation and experience. Our main concern at this point is the beginning drum student.

Only Tradition Says 2B

What criteria dictates that a drum stick approximately 15 7/8 inches long and 5/8 of an inch in diameter is the correct size for any beginning student's hand? Are we so tradition bound (in this case, tradition representing a bad habit well-learned) that we can justify a poor musical beginning for our percussion students because of our lack of knowledge and concern?

The first step towards the selection of proper drum stick size is for the instructor to have a large selection of sticks available for the student to try. The same rhythmic pattern should be played when testing each pair of sticks. *(See chart # 2)*

Several basic points of concern should be given special attention during the selection of drum sticks.

The circumference of the stick should be such that the student can comfortably support and sustain the stick between the index finger and the thumb of the right hand — or the opposite, if the student is left-handed. The necessity of muscular exertion for the thumb and index finger to sustain, support and balance the stick would indicate that this particular stick size is not correct. The larger the circumference of the stick, the greater the problem of controlling the stick with the thumb and index finger. It is primarily this factor which drives drummers to use a hammer-like grip. The more fingers on the stick to aid in supporting the stick, the less control and flexibility the player will realize. There is also a serious impairment of tone quality with the above grip. More than likely, this full hammer-like grip will produce a buzz rather than one clear stroke.

Band directors have perpetuated a myth. . .the belief that the larger the drum stick, the greater the sound. True, there is greater volume (possibly) resulting from the use of these "miniature logs," but this is due largely to the fact that being extreme in size, these "logs" are held in a hammer-like grip *and used exactly like hammers to pound the drum!* Volume, yes — but at the expense of good tone quality and technical proficiency!

Just as important as the production of good tone quality is the avoidance of the restriction of fluent, speedy technique induced by a hammer-like grip. When the stick is held in a hammer-like grip, with all fingers around it, rebounds are virtually impossible, as well as effective technique at dynamic levels of *mp* and lower. The "S" model sticks are highly impractical, and in a majority of cases, detrimental even to a developed drummer's technical proficiency. 7A, 9A, lightweight pencil and pee-wee models satisfy the demands of particular styles of music, but only in the hands of an accomplished percussionist.

The length of the stick is also of great importance. If the stick is too

Chart #2 Warm-Up Exercises

Chart #1

Table of Weights and Measurements
Selected 2B Snare Drum Sticks

Co.	Length	Weight	Body Diameter	Tip Diameter & Shape
A	40.4 cm	64.2 gram	16.5 mm	10.6 mm
	40.3 cm	54.9 gram	16.89 mm	10.27 mm
B	40.4 cm	63.2 gram	15.63 mm	11.0 mm
C	40.5 cm	50.8 gram	14.68 mm	9.63 mm
D	40.0 cm	58.9 gram	16.15 mm	10.51 mm

long, the player will have to grip the stick closer to the center, thus creating a balance problem. The stick must be slightly overbalanced to the front if it is to rebound correctly. Holding the stick at the exact point of balance or its near proximity would necessitate the percussionist's need to use wrist action to move the stick *to* and *from* the drum head. In this situation there would be little or no possibility of the stick rebounding; therefore a serious impairment of the player's technique . . mainly *no roll*! There would also be a surplus length of stick extending beyond the right wrist, (or left), causing the player to hold his hand downward, creating an uncomfortable and restricting severe angle at the wrist. A stick that is too short for the player's hands will create the adverse situation. That is, the student will need to grip the sticks so close to the butt end that he will drastically reduce the ability of the stick to rebound. The left hand, (or right hand for left-hand players), would need to be turned counterclockwise at more than a 45 degree angle to raise the stick from the drum. As a result, the left elbow would be forced from its natural position, in towards the side of the player. To compensate for this unnatural position and its added discomfort, the player would undoubtedly grip the stick with as many fingers as possible to regain control and support of the stick.

Stick Selection — Constant Quest

The quest for the correct drum stick size should be constant. To insure the student's use of the correct size sticks to accomodate his technical progress and physical growth, he should repeat the process of stick selection periodically.

At present, the manufacturers of percussion instruments, fully aware of the advantage and necessity of correct stick size, are meeting the demands of student and professional percussionists by producing xylophone, marimba, field drum and timpani mallets of varied shapes, weights, lengths and materials as well as the array of drum sticks listed below. *(See chart #3)*

2B OR NOT 2B . . . The answer is in your hands!

Table of Drum Stick Sizes, Weights, and Lengths

Chart #3	Model No.	(Length (inches)	Weight (ounces)	Bead
COMPANY A	1A	16 3/4	9/16	A
	2A	15 3/4	5/8	O
	3A	15 5/8	9/16	SB
	4A	15 7/8	9/16	Caps.
	5A	16	9/16	MO
	6A	15 1/2	3/8	SO
	7A	15 1/4	1/2	MO
	8A	15 7/8	3/8	A
	9A	15 3/4	5/8	MLO
	10A	15 7/8	1/2	MLO
	11A	15 5/8	1/2	MLO
	12A	14 3/4	9/16	A
	13A	15 1/2	9/16	MO
	18A	15 3/4	*	A
	19A	15 3/4	*	O
	21A	16	*	O
	1B	16 3/8	5/8	MLB
	2B	15 7/8	5/8	MO
	5B	16	9/16	MLO
	7B	16	1/2	No Bead
	1S	16 7/8	5/8	LO
	2S	17	11/16	LB
	3S	16 7/8	3/4	VLB
	4S	16 7/8	3/4	LB
	1H	16 7/8	*	LA
COMPANY B	2A	15 3/4	*	A
	3A	15 1/2	*	A
	5A	15 7/8	*	O
	6A	14 3/4	*	A
	7A	15 1/8	*	LO
	8A	15 3/4	*	A
	2B	15 7/8	*	A
	5B	16	*	A
	1S	16 7/8	*	LO
	2S	16 7/8	*	A
	3S	16 7/8	*	LO
COMPANY C	1A	16 3/4	*	A
	2A	16	*	O
	3A	15 1/2	*	B
	5A	16 1/8	*	SO
	6A	15	*	O
	7A	15 1/4	*	*
	9A	15 1/4	*	Taper
	11A	15 5/8	*	O Tpr.
	1B	16 3/8	*	*
	2B	15 7/8	*	SB
	5B	16 1/8	*	Taper
	1S	16 7/8	*	LO
	2S	17	*	LB
	3S	17	*	LB
COMPANY D	A	16 5/8	3	*
	B	14 3/4	3 1/2	*
	C	15 3/4	3 1/2	*
	D	15 5/8	4 1/4	*
	E	16	2 3/4	*
	F	16 1/2	3	*
	G	16 1/2	4	*
	H	16 1/2	5	*
	L	15	2 1/2	*
	P	15 1/2	3	*
	S	15	2	*

KEY:

A — Acorn	*Caps. — Capsule*	*L — Large*
B — Ball	*S — Small*	*VL — Very Large*
O — Olive	*M — Medium*	** — Not Available*

A Director Looks at His Percussion Section

Gene A. Braught

What do you expect from the percussion section? As you "mold" the band into a performing organization, will you be as demanding of your percussion players as you are of those who play melody instruments?

If you are uncertain about the techniques of percussion, perhaps this article will be of some assistance.

I have no desire to compare the merits of band versus orchestra drumming in this article, but we are all aware that in marching and concert bands of today, we use from two to eight (or more) snare drummers, whereas the symphony orchestra will use only one snare drummer most of the time. The approach is different—*soloists* in the symphony; *section players* in the band.

Since there are so many percussion instruments, I will confine my discussion to snare, tenor, bass, cymbals, and timpani.

Equipment

What percussion instrumentation do you use? Perhaps most university bands are larger than the average public school band; therefore, the percussion section would likewise be larger. However, the balance would be approximately the same. At the University of Oklahoma we use 8-10 field drums, 4 tenor drums, 2 bass drums, 4 pairs of cymbals, and 2 bell lyres in the marching band. Others may desire a different balance, but this particular distribution works well for us.

Field Drum: Most directors use field drums (I have heard of those who do not). I would suggest a drum 12" x 15" with metal hoops and "gut" snares. It is also important that a *1S*, *2S* or *3S* stick be used with such a drum. This is as important as using the proper mouthpiece for a given instrument. The S stick was manufactured to produce the proper field drum sound, and the "gut" snares produce the desired deep-rich resonance expected by the percussionist. I am informed that the manufacturers produce field drums with wire snares because band directors insist on such. The reason is no doubt a lack of knowledge as to the proper sound. Many directors are of the opinion that the field drum should produce a high, crisp sound as does the concert snare. This is not the case. The tone should be deep, rich and full, with no snare rattle to distort the actual sound of the drum. I often hear so much rattle in the drum sound that it is impossible to detect the roll or rhythm separation. If your field drums do not have *tone control felts*, you should use a cloth *under the batter head*. Stretch the cloth from side to side, across the drum, replace the head and the cloth will remain taut. This will eliminate the "ring" of the drum and cause the rhythmic figures to speak clearly. Plastic heads seem to be the most practical, and a good sound can be produced. The one great advantage of the plastic head is that humidity will not affect its tautness, thus the drum will retain the desired sound.

Concert Snare: The most common sizes are 5" x 14" or 6½" x 14" with wire or gut snares, and I suggest the use of a *2B* stick. The small *A* series stick is difficult for most drummers to control, and it is possible to play very softly with a *2B* stick and maintain good control. The *A* series stick could be used for dance band and orchestral drumming. One might like to try the field drum (gut snares) with one concert snare on martial music and on much of the contemporary literature. A concert snare with gut snares will also give a different and often desired sound to the concert band.

Bass Drum: A 10" x 28" bass drum with plastic heads is satisfactory for the marching band. The concert drum could vary from 36" to 42" (we use a 42" drum with calf heads for the University Symphonic Band). Since the band bass drummer generally plays on every beat, the "ring" often desired for orchestral bass drumming (much less playing) is somewhat distasteful for band music. Some type of muffling is then required for a band bass drum. Possibilities are: (1) feathers in the drum; (2) a felt strip across the inside of one or both heads; (3) long shreds of newspaper about one-eighth or one-quarter of an inch in width; or (4) cloth (an old sheet works fine), double thickness and about four inches in width, stretched across the drum, same as for the field drum. You must be careful not to make the drum too dead in sound.

Many players have a tendency to "pound" the drum and, all too often, this instrument is much too loud for good musical taste and balance. Make the tone blend with the bass section. I suggest a Ludwig Bass Drum stick #330 for use with the marching band. Should you desire a more prominent sound during cadence work, use a regular marching felt or wood stick. Do become more sound conscious and make the percussion instruments blend with the rest of the organization. The stick for concert work should be the double end lamb's wool model. In addition, each bass drummer should be required to have a medium soft pair of timpani sticks for rolls. The left hand and right knee should be employed for dampening the sound of the bass drum in concert work.

Cymbals: For marching band a pair of 16-inch cymbals are most satisfactory. They can be carried easily, without tiring the player, and they produce a good sound. For concert use, a larger pair is desired (we use 20" symphony weight Zildjians). The big problem in selecting a pair of cymbals is that those classified as "band weight" are usually too heavy and do not produce a satisfactory sound. Select either what is known as "symphony" or "medium" weight cymbals, with leather straps. May I suggest you see a good percussion teacher for additional help?

Tenor Drums: Recommended size is 12"x 17". It is possible to use the same beater as for the marching bass drum. The Ludwig #330 beater does not produce a prominent tone quality from the tenor drum, but it does produce what we desire at Oklahoma. When special parts are written for tenor drum (either in cadence form or when the band is playing), a felt or wood beater may be used.

Timpani: Most original works for band require three or four kettles, but as a basic pair, one should have either the 25" and 28" or the 26" and 29". Three kettles would include one of the above sets plus a 30" or 32" kettle, and the fourth would be the 23", this followed by the piccolo timpani. There are good solos written for three, four and five kettles, and your timpani player should be exposed to this literature. There are certainly weather (humidity) advantages to the plastic heads, but we prefer the tone quality produced with calf heads. If your timpanist does not study with a competent instructor and make his own sticks, I would recommend he use professional model sticks. Encourage your timpani player to have at least a *soft*, *medium* and *hard* pair of mallets. Become acquainted with both the French and German handhold. I would recommend the Saul Goodman *Modern Method for Timpani.* This method very adequately explains the handhold, the position of the sticks in both *pp* and *ff* playing, the *sfz* attack, cross-sticking, melodic playing, scale and interval study, etc. Great care should be given to the selection and training of the timpanist.

Rolls and Understanding Them

Again, I repeat the basic difference between the marching or concert bands and the symphony orchestra is the fact that in band work we use a *section* of performers (two or more) whereas in the orchestra there is usually only one performer on snare drum.

The often heard adage "a rudimental drummer is flashy but very unmusical" is not a correct statement. No section in any music organization can sound better by having each member play his own way and in his own style—and the band conductor should not accept such a performance from his percussion section (especially the snare drummers).

Regardless of what sound the conductor might desire in a snare drum roll, drummers should be playing the same number of taps. I would like to present two basic rules for snare drum rolls:

(1) To determine the length of the roll, divide the roll note into 16th notes (played single stroke); double this, then add one if the roll is tied, or subtract one if the roll is untied. In any roll, the single stroked 16th notes are what we term the "basic roll beat." Should the roll sound be either too open or too closed for your personal taste, use rule number two:

(2) If the roll, as determined in rule number one, produces a sound too *open* for your taste, use a greater number of strokes per beat as the "basic roll beat;" and, if the roll, as determined in rule number one, produces a sound too *closed* for your taste, use a lesser number of strokes per beat as the "basic roll beat." (*see examples*)

As in "enbouchure teaching" by outstanding instructors, there are various thoughts on the "handhold" of drum sticks, on the method of playing rolls, etc. May I suggest to those directors who feel an uncertainty in the teaching of percussion instruments that you contact a recognized teacher in your area for individual instruction or for a percussion clinic. All percussionists should be well-informed in both schools of thought concerning snare drum rolls: (1) the measured roll, and (2) the multiple bounce roll. I believe that the sticking of both rolls should remain constant, but the control is different and thus produces a different style and sound. Your band will sound cleaner if the percussion section develops a togetherness and a clean precise style of performance.

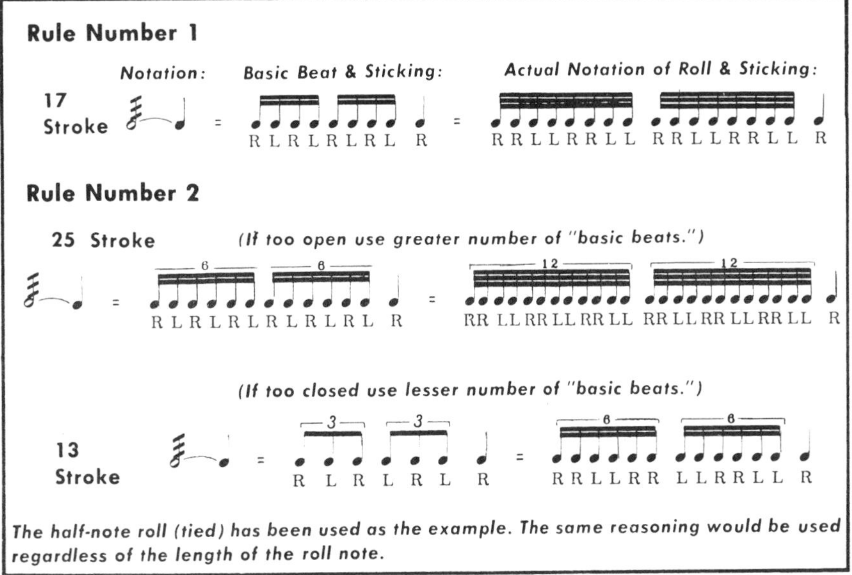

Sight-Reading on the Snare Drum

Sherman Hong

Many snare drummers can play practiced music very well, but the same people are weak sight-readers. There are several reasons: (1) inadequate rhythmic training, (2) failure to comprehend rhythmic patterns and phrases, and (3) lack of systematic sticking procedures.

Inadequate Rhythmic Training

Several studies have proven that, as a group, percussion students are almost the poorest achievers in rhythmic understanding. *How can this be?* I feel that when a student chooses, or is chosen to play drums, it is because he possesses a "feel" for rhythm; but having this "feel" is *not* the same as *knowing* and *understanding* rhythm. It appears that many instrumental teachers give more help to non-drummers, but drummers must be taught the concepts of rhythm even more thoroughly.

Failure to Comprehend Rhythm Patterns as a Whole

It is obvious that isolating rhythm patterns for practice is functional, but the eyes of the student must be trained to see *whole* patterns and phrases, not just the components.

Students should be required to *sing* the rhythms alone and then play and sing the rhythms simultaneously. Although most percussion instruments are unable to produce melodies, musical inflection is just as important to the percussionists as it is to other performers. Percussionists must know and have mental and motor images of time, pivot notes, phrase markings, interpretation of symbols, metronomic markings and musical terminology. The vocal approach stimulates the student to make music from *within* and frees his muscles from unnecessary tensions.

Lack of Systematic Sticking

This third weakness is one which causes even the more talented drummers to stumble through sight-reading. Many drummers have been trained rudimentally or by a closely-related method. Rudimental training has its place; that is, to teach stick control and clean playing. Following this concept, many teachers advocate the playing of nearly all rhythmic patterns hand-to-hand (alternated). To apply this concept to all rhythmic patterns is to invite awkward sticking and limited phraseology.

Problems Not Serious

My experiences have proven that use of the right-lead (straight) system facilitates students' sight-reading performances. The system, which is recommended for intermediate and advanced students, will present a few problems to those already rudimentally trained, but the problems should be easily resolved.

Every Pulsation Is Right

Simply explained, the student will use the right hand on every pulsation; that is, on the beat and on the up-beat in duple meters and on every 8th note pulsation in triple meters (duple: [two eighth notes, R R]; triple: [two groups of three eighth notes, R R R R R R]). The right-lead system can accomplish two things:

1. It divides the basic beat into two or three equal parts (depending on whether the meter is duple or triple). By dividing a basic beat into smaller equal units, the performer should have a more thorough comprehension of time and have less tendency to waver from the set tempo.

2. It should improve the performer's abilities to play evenly and expressively. Instead of playing all rhythmic patterns hand to hand, which often results in uneven sound production, the performer can use only one hand to insure more evenness of sound. Drummers often have a weak left hand; hence, the sound produced by stroking with the left hand will usually be slightly weaker than that produced by the right hand. The resultant uneven stroking can ruin any drummer's ability to play musically and with finesse.

When working with the right-lead system, there are basically only two patterns to remember and almost any other rhythmic pattern can be played from this basic system:

Duple	*Triple*
[quarter note] R	[dotted quarter note] R
[two eighth notes] R R	[three eighth notes] R R R

Remember that in duple meter (2/4, 2/8, 4/4, 8/8, etc.) the right stick strikes *on* the beat and *on* the *up-beat*. Whatever notes come between the down-beat and up-beat are sticked with the left. Examples of duple sticking:

[4/4 example] R RR R RL RL R | RLRL RL LR R | R

[2/4 example] R RR | R LR RL | RL R | R

Notice the sticking for the [dotted-eighth–sixteenth pattern, R L L] pattern in the 4/4 example. The reason for use of two left strokes can be understood if it is remembered where the downbeat and up-beat occur. Visual explanations may be helpful:

1. Draw arrows on the beat and on the up-beat.

2. Remember that whatever notes come between those pulsations are played with the left stick. Example:

[example] R R R RLR L | RLRR R | R

Patterns with triplets call for more discretion. The sticking for patterns as [triplet patterns] require the performer to consider whether the triplet is at the end of a phrase or leading into another section of the phrase. Such patterns can be sticked R RLR L RLR or R LRL RLRL, depending on the phraseology.

Embellishments should also be viewed in light of the right-lead system. In concert work, flams and drags are best played one way.

Example:

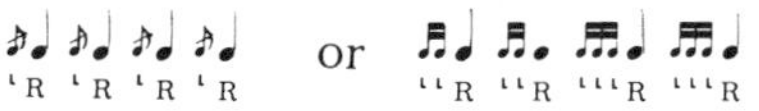

'R 'R 'R 'R or ''R ''R '''R '''R

Triple Pulse Patterns

Triple-pulse use of the system requires discrimination in regards to the tempo at which such sticking is feasible. Fast tempos will normally require alternate sticking, but slow to moderately fast tempos can utilize the right-lead system. Remember that in triple pulse patterns the right stick strikes on every basic 8th note pulsation and the left stick strikes other notes. Examples of triple pulse sticking:

R R R R RLRL R LRRL R R R R R

R R R R R RLRLRL R R R LR R

Embellishments are best played one way.

'R 'R 'R 'R R 'R 'RLRLRL

'R 'R ''R ''R ''R

The right-lead system is not fail-safe, but when used conscientiously it can help the drummer to sight-read better and to improve the drummer's capabilities to play musically. Snare drummers can improve their sight-reading abilities if they are (1) given adequate rhythmic training, (2) given basic concepts about rhythmic patterns and phrases, and (3) use a systematic sticking procedure.

Mervin Britton, "Teach Your Drummers to Sing," **The Instrumentalist** XXI, No. 5 (December, 1966), p. 81.

April 1971

Rudimental Families

Mervin W. Britton

Snare drum rudiments are necessary for modern practice and performance . . . but not the standard 26!

Over the past years, many non-percussion specialists who teach percussionists may have found themselves questioning the apparently divergent views they hear and read. Clinics and articles have given the impression that: (1) it is still necessary to study 26 original rudiments . . . or those rudiments aren't used in modern study — there are only two real rudiments; (2) there are academic reasons for studying the rudiments . . . or there are academic reasons for not studying the rudiments.

But the demands of literature are such that all modern performers and teachers probably use rudiments in a similar fashion in actual performance.

A realistic approach to rudiments can make learning snare drum technique easier and faster. It is beneficial to the student for whatever area he may later concentrate upon, be it drum corps, legitimate concert, jazz or rock.

A student covering standard literature is called upon to execute certain patterns and phrases. Many of these patterns are some form of what have been traditionally called rudiments. But the "Standard 26" charts present patterns as separate unrelated items, when in reality many are closely-related patterns, or variations of certain basic rhythm patterns. Recognizing these facts can save a great deal of time and energy.

As important as they may be, rudiments should not be taught in the first few weeks of snare drum study. This would be like teaching embellishments to other instrumental students in their first lessons. Instead, rudiments should be approached only after the student has good control of his grip and can play basic rhythmic patterns in different sticking combinations with relaxed facility. This is why the paradiddle family is the first one suggested for teaching.

Eight Families

Standard rudiments now generally used in all styles of music can be grouped into eight families. They are listed and discussed here in their suggested order of study.

Paradiddles

Single		Double	
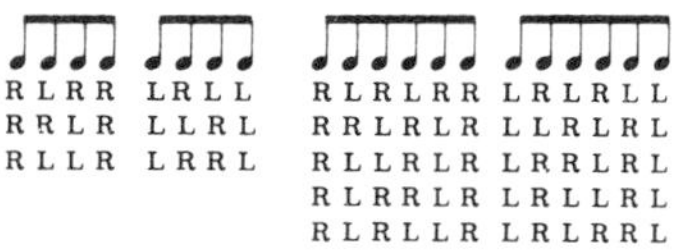 RLRR	LRLL	RLRLRR	LRLRLL
RRLR	LLRL	RRLRLR	LLRLRL
RLLR	LRRL	RLLRLR	LRRLRL
		RLRRLR	LRLLRL
		RLRLLR	LRLRRL

Double sticking of the paradiddles tends to produce a phrase of two slurred sounds combined with single articulations. For practical use, the performer should be able to play all variations equally well. These variations set up many sound patterns when used on just the head of the drum, different parts of the drum and more than one drum — such as a full set. The double paradiddle should be taught later than the single, but it is still part of the family.

Rolls

single stroke **double or bounce**

RLRL RLRL

All rolls are produced in similar fashion. It is necessary to have rapid control of a series of alternate strokes for both single and "double" or "multiple bounce" rolls. The latter requires control of sounds between the strokes. However, technical production is the same for all bounce rolls listed as 3, 5, 7, 9, 10 and 13. They differ only in their length or, supposedly in the number of sounds. It should also be pointed out that none contains the number of strokes commonly stated. For example, a seven stroke roll contains only four strokes.

strokes

Flam

A flam is a single grace note with a main rhythmic note. The grace note is produced primarily with wrist and fingers while the main note uses more arm and wrist. The time between the two should be controlled to fit the style of performance.

Flam Taps

Flam taps are one or more single notes following the flam, but within the same rhythmic or phrase pattern. Some performers prefer to alternate each grouping, while others play them all starting with the same hand. There are also two common schools on sticking for the flam and one tap. The flamacue is merely a variation of the flam taps.

Drag

A drag is two grace notes before the main note but close together like a bounce. Otherwise, the production is the same as for a flam.

Drag Taps

LLR L RRL R | LLR L R RRL R L | LLR L R L RRLR L R

Drag taps are performed exactly like flam taps, but with a drag in place of the flam. Any rhythmic variation of the taps within a phrase grouping does not change this basic rudiment.

Ruffs

3 stroke	4 stroke	5 stroke
RLR LRL	LRLR RLRL	RLRLR LRLRL

Ruff embellishments differ completely from the sound of the drag. Ruffs are alternating embellishments with a more articulate sound. For [drag figure] there is often a question whether to play a ruff or drag. The final criteria is to determine which sounds better for the particular style of performance. If other instruments are playing modent-type sounds, the snare drum should probably match with a ruff. A drag is generally used in a military march or any rudimental style, while a ceremonial march may well sound better with 3 stroke ruffs. Old notation of rudimental music often shows the 5 stroke roll — written out. This looks like a 5 stroke ruff, (see above) but should be played as a roll.

Ruff Taps

3 and 5 stroke ruffs may also be used.

All ruff taps are played like flam and drag taps. The student has only to concern himself with production of the ruff. By this time, the tap sticking should be part of the old routine.

If rudimental families are introduced when the student is ready to handle them, they will present comparatively few problems for him, and both quality of performance and rate of progress will be greater.

May 1971

How to Organize a High School Percussion Ensemble

Donald Knaack

In order to add a percussion ensemble to an existing instrumental music program, one must have the interest of several prospective players as well as the support of the administration. Most of the preparation should begin at least a year in advance in order to insure a smooth-running, interesting, and productive program.

A live concert by a professional ensemble is an ideal way to gain the interest of both the prospective players and the administration. Nearby college percussion ensembles are often available. The use of recordings (see below) or presentation of a lecture/demonstration by a local percussionist can also be effective.

Administrators must be convinced that the percussion ensemble is of great value to the students, is essential to a well-rounded instrumental music program, and will not interfere with normal schedules.

Securing the Instruments

A percussion ensemble can be organized using only the "standard" equipment already in use in most schools: two timpani, one snare drum, one field drum, two tom toms, triangle, tambourine, bass drum, suspended cymbal, crash cymbals.

The use of mallet instruments is essential to the training of student percussionists and to the development of the complete ensemble. Marimba, xylophone, etc. should be purchased as soon as possible.

Securing the Players

A group of four players is large enough for ensemble experience (learning to listen and play with others). Starting with this size will eliminate many problems common to very large groups.

A repertoire sheet for the audition should be announced well in advance. This will not only allow time for preparation, but will also stimulate more interest. Auditions should be "closed door" (players unknown to judges), with at least one professional percussionist on the judging panel. Once chosen, each student should agree to be a "member in good standing" (attend all rehearsals, be punctual, and attend all performances).

As with other teaching areas, if the instructor is weak in percussion, it would be advisable for him to seek the assistance of someone with more knowledge.

Securing the Music

The program can be initiated with the purchase of about ten dollars worth of music. As with any instrumental ensemble, the ability, number, and taste of the players should be considered when choosing the repertoire. Compositions within the current performance capability of the ensemble (yet still a challenge) should offer a variety in instrumentation, style (marches, popular, Latin American, avant garde, etc.) and form (rondo, sonata, minuet, etc.).

Most major publishers offer catalogs that include the number of players needed and the degree of difficulty of their percussion compositions.

If he has the ability, the instructor can write original compositions which can be "tailor-made" for the technique and musical ability of each player. When each part is a challenge and good rehearsal techniques prevail, progress will be made.

The Rehearsal Plan

Rehearsing once or twice a week immediately after school in a sound-isolated place (near the percussion equipment storage area) seems to work best. I have found the following rehearsal plan to be most effective:

1. Brief history of the instruments to be used at the rehearsal.
2. Discussion of composition(s) to be rehearsed (type, form, etc.).
3. Verbal run-through, noting dynamics, rhythm, repeats, fermatas, etc.
4. Work on difficult sections. (Make sure the students remain aware of what is going on around them. Teach them to listen to each other: teach them to make music).

Recommended Recordings

Edgar Varèse — Complete Works. Vol. 1 — EMS401. Frederich Waldman, conductor, Juilliard Percussion Ensemble.

A 25-year Retrospective Concert of the Music of John Cage — Avakian: KO8P-1493 to 8.

Sound Adventure — Period: SPL-743. Paul Price, conductor, Manhattan Percussion Ensemble.

Antheil — Ballet Mecanique — Urania: UR134. Robert Craft, conductor, Los Angeles Contemporary Music Ensemble; Paul Price, conductor, Manhattan Percussion Ensemble.

Varèse — Ionisation — Urania: UR106. Paul Price, conductor, American Percussion Society.

Concert Percussion for Orchestra — Time: 58000. John Cage conductor, Paul Price, conductor, Manhattan Percussion Ensemble.

Evolution — Boston: B207. Harold Farberman, conductor, Boston Percussion Group.

Alberto Ginastera — Columbia: ML5347. Henri Temianka, conductor, Los Angeles Percussion Ensemble.

June 1971

Playing Percussion Musically

E.L. Masoner

Recently, I heard a director say to the drummers, "You played technically correct; now play musically." In order to discover what he meant, let us analyze some of the facets of a musical performance in regard to the percussion instruments.

Pitch

The clarinet, for example, changes its pitch by player manipulation of the numerous keys. The drummer changes pitch (with few exceptions) by changing instruments. Even though drums are not tuned to a definite pitch, it is very important that the pitch and tone quality complement the ensemble and enhance the composition being played. For example, the piccolo snare drum can be used to great advantage for some modern symphonic compositions where the punctuating rhythms of the percussion instruments must cut through the strong dissonances of the strings and winds; the orchestra snare drum should be chosen for the classical works, while the street drum, equipped with gut snares, is preferred for the standard march.

Tone quality, closely related to pitch, may be defined as the property of sound waves which depends on the number of harmonics (partials) and their prominence. The percussion instruments have been sometimes labeled as non-musical because their partials are inharmonic and create to some ears, at least, an unmusical timbre.

Although the drums have some leeway in determining their given pitch by adjusting the tension on the heads, it must be remembered that such instruments as cymbals, triangles, wood blocks, etc. have not. Therefore, it is necessary to have access to an assortment of these instruments in order to have the desired pitch and tone quality available when needed. An important factor not to be overlooked in control of tone quality of percussion instruments is the beater, which must match the instrument.

Phrasing and Articulation

Phrasing on percussion instruments is no different than on any other instrument. Articulation does present a minor problem, as means of sustaining a tone are limited to using either the roll or an intensification of the stroke. Legato passages are interpreted by means of the roll; staccato notes by stopping the vibrating media. During rapid passages where stopping by hand is impractical, the instruments may be struck on the nodes — center of a drum or point of suspension of a bar — to shorten the period of audible sound.

Dynamics

There is no limit to dynamic possibilities on percussion instruments. Anything from the quietest whisper to the loudest *ffz* may be produced. The only problem is to have the proper size equipment for the job. Increasing the size of the cymbal to be used when more sound is desired is especially important.

Finesse

Is it possible to play percussion instruments musically and with finesse? Of course, but both director and player must always *listen*! One cannot strike percussion instruments the same when the woodwinds have the melody as when the brass have *a fortissimo*. The bass drum should either blend with the ensemble, or stand out when need be. Cymbals played *pianissimo* are a thrilling sound when added to a legato march strain. Try different types of drums — i.e., street drums with gut snares, concert drums with wire snares, and the new piccolo drum. The style and tempo of the march should determine what equipment to use. How does one decide? *Listen*! In concert music there is no limit to the colors of the spectrum that can be derived from the percussion section. Always ask the two questions: does the sound fit the character of the music, and does the sound embellish the composition — if not, try something else. Remember to listen before striking, during striking, and after striking any percussion instrument. Never stop listening.

Yes, drums can be played musically. The approach is a little different, but with the proper tools, technique, and a fine musical ear, the product will be music in the true sense of the word.

September 1971

A Marching Band Percussion Audition

George Frock

Each year many instrumental directors are faced with designing a percussion audition which will help in assigning students to the various music organizations the school sponsors. The type of audition varies, depending mostly on the materials available and the experience of the director, but also on the type of music organization for which the student is auditioning.

The Marching Section

Because of the nature of the marching band percussion section, the student will need to demonstrate the basic rudimental techniques, including open rolls, flams, flam taps, and paradiddles. Each student selected should approach the drum with a uniform hand position and stroke motion. Without this, the percussion section cannot be uniform in appearance. This may seem like a small point to many, but compare this to the importance of a uniform step: it would be inconceivable for a band to march with several different types of steps or strides, yet many percussion sections pay little or no attention to uniformity (other than playing the notes together).

The exercises which appear here can be used to help the director select his section. Each exercise may be played individually, in pairs, or by the entire section.

Many teachers may not agree with the particular sticking given here; however, the markings will help to indicate which students are able to adapt and play with a uniform sticking.

Since many bands are employing the use of marching timbales, some exercises in pitch reading

MARCHING BAND PERCUSSION AUDITION CHART

Snare Drum

are included (see Tom Tom or Timbales).

There is no attempt to trick students with difficult and complex exercises. With the simplicity of these exercises, the student should be able to relax and demonstrate his reading and technical facility.

No mention will be made at this time as to stroke *motion* (concepts vary from one teacher to another); the important element is finding a degree of uniformity amongst those auditioning which can then be refined — hopefully into a section with sparkling precision.

Tenor Drum and Bass Drum

Tom Toms or Timbales

October 1971

Developing the Rudimental Snare Drum Grip

Joe M. Pullis

For the young percussionist desiring to become a sound rudimental drummer, no other aspect of his training is so important as that of developing the proper rudimental grip. Often overlooked by many a young drummer is the fact that this grip evolves through stages and is not assumed during his first lesson or even his first year of drumming. This is to say that the proper grip for the rudimental drummer is relative to his experience and ability and is not an absolute.

It is unfortunate that many young drummers, in their efforts to imitate more experienced percussionists, regress to a double rabbit ear grip with their left hand. Such a grip enables the student who has not developed his wrist to produce a type of "buzz" roll which is anything but clean and crisp.

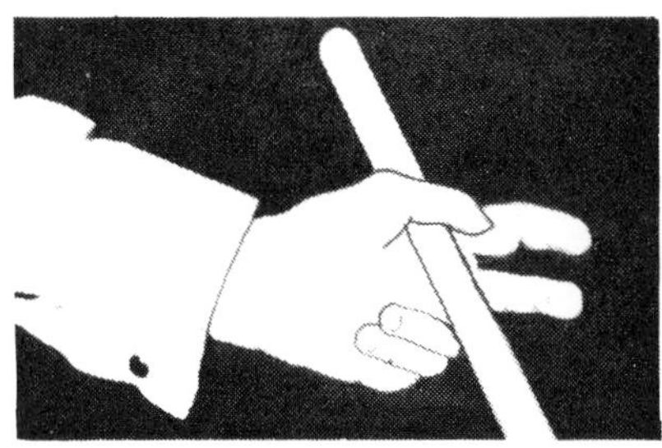

Double Rabbit Ear Grip

While the double rabbit ear is the worst of all possible grips, another almost as damaging to the beginning drummer is the single rabbit ear. The single rabbit ear grip is in some respects confusing, especially since several method books offer as a prescribed grip one which may look similar to it; and no doubt many a drummer develops a second-rate grip in an earnest effort to follow proper form.

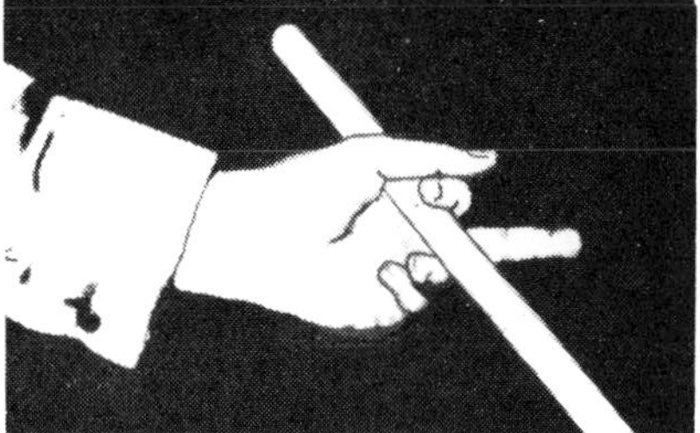

Single Rabbit Ear Grip

The basic problem produced by the single rabbit ear grip is that the young drummer has not developed his wrist before he attempts to use the grip, and he thus permits the stick to bounce in an uncontrolled state.

If the beginner does not use, from the first day he picks up a pair of drum sticks, a grip that will foster and promote proper wrist action and wrist control, he has little chance of developing the art of drumming to any appreciable degree.

The beginning rudimental grip is one that depends very little upon the bounce of the sticks and focuses upon the rapid movement of the wrists for stick action.

Notice that the index, second, and third fingers of the left hand are *on* the stick, and effort should be made to see that "daylight" never shows between these three fingers and the stick.

Beginning Rudimental Grip

With the right hand, effort should also be made to keep the thumb and all four fingers on the stick. Notice that the stick protrudes out from the hand and not down the arm.

It should be noted that if the student is not observed closely he will "discover" that by bringing the index or second finger of the left hand and the second, third, and fourth fingers of the right hand off the stick, he can produce a "roll." This is indeed tragic and results in one of the rabbit ear grips previously mentioned.

In the beginning stages of drumming — the first two to three years — the index and second fingers of the left hand should *both* remain on the stick. If "daylight" shows between the stick and the second or third fingers of the left hand, the wrist is not developing to its fullest capacity. All fingers of the right hand should likewise grasp the stick in order to cause the wrist to become responsible for the movement of the stick. This does not mean, of course, that the sticks are held so rigidly that the wrist muscles are in an inflexible state, for it is these muscles that must be used for proper stick control.

After, and only after, the drummer has developed his wrists to the extent that he can open and close the rudiments effortlessly by "wrist control" with all fingers firmly on the sticks should he venture into the practice of controlled bounces and press rolls. After the drummer has developed to this state of proficiency, the only finger on his left hand which should ever be lifted from the stick is his second finger. At this stage, the drummer should think of the stick not as bouncing but as rebounding. With this idea of rebounding in mind, the drummer should always have the feeling that he has complete control of the sticks at all times.

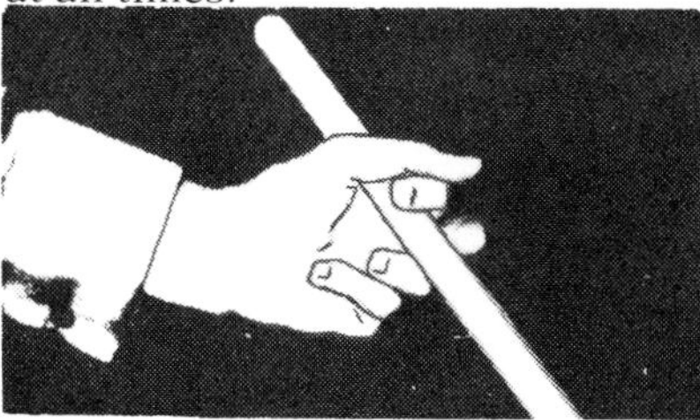

Advanced Rudimental Grip

Placing the accent on the second beats of the long roll is an excellent deterrent to developing improper grips. When the student opens and closes this roll, he should try to carry the accent as far into the roll as possible. He will soon learn that without the proper grip and wrist control, this cannot be accomplished. However, by the time he is able to maintain this accent far into the roll, his wrists are so well developed that he will have complete control of the sticks, and he may relax the second finger of the left hand and third and fourth fingers of the right hand.

During the first few years of training, only sticks large enough to be used in field drum work should be used. This is not to imply that the field drum itself should be employed. Young drummers should spend much time in an isolated practice room, playing on practice pads of the proper height, drilling intensely on rudimental exercises. Rudiments are the heart of drumming and should be executed correctly with proper stick and wrist control — control that must be developed from the beginning.

The rudimental drummer who has developed proper wrist control can adapt quite easily to the press roll required of the orchestra drummer; but if the beginner tries to mimic such rolls without first developing his wrists, he will find it impossible to ever correctly execute a crisp, closed press roll or a clean, open rudimental roll.

November 1971

Developing a Good Snare Drum Roll

Mervin W. Britton

The roll, be it single stroke or some kind of double combination, is probably the most difficult snare drum technique. A single stroke roll is a rapid, smooth alternation of single sounds or pulses. While a stroke is generally considered to be an arm motion, a fast or closed single stroke roll is produced primarily with finger and wrist motion. A bounce roll involves some type of doubling sound with each hand. While the single stroke roll is important and used to some extent in the bounce roll, it is the latter type of roll that will be discussed in this article.

In order to understand the bounce roll, we need to know what goes into its production. Every roll has two main parts. The first of these is the stroke or pulse. This impetus is produced primarily by arm motion and travels on through the wrist and fingers. Alone, it is an open single stroke roll. However, it is also the skeleton of a bounce roll. Without a good relaxed skeleton, the body of such a roll cannot properly develop.

The second part of a roll is the body or "filler." It may be comprised of one or several sounds and is produced primarily with finger and wrist control. It is the type of filler which determines the style of roll produced.

There are two basic styles of rolls. One of these is commonly called *rudimental, military* or *double bounce* roll. The other is known by the terms *buzz, press, multiple bounce* and occasionally *jazz* or *orchestra* roll.

The rudimental roll theoretically has one sound doubling or bouncing from the main stroke. This doubled note, called a tap, is produced by wrist motion. It should be equal in volume and equidistant to the strokes. It is generally considered to be more "open" (to have more space between its sounds) than the multiple bounce roll.

Rudimental Roll

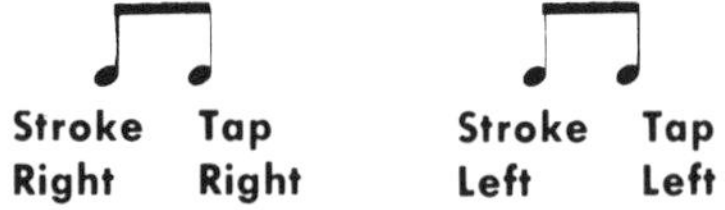

The multiple bounce roll, as the name indicates, is a series of bounces which come directly out of the stroke pulse. Encouraging this series of bounces requires more finger than wrist action. The volume diminishes throughout each series.

Multiple Bounce Roll

A fine flexible snare drum roll is a combination of both these types. In addition, styles of music dictate that at certain times a performer's roll should lean toward one or the other. Therefore, both of these types (in the proper order and combination) should be used in developing the roll.

From the first lessons, the student can practice making individual bounces with either stick. However, extensive use of this technique in series should come only after he has a secure grip and can play simple rhythmic patterns such as 16th and 8th notes with reasonable control.

One of the best ways to begin roll study is to review previously worked exercises. In slower more relaxed tempos, 16ths or 8ths become the stroke skeleton. Let the stick bounce several times for each note. It is extremely important to keep the tempo and stroke skeleton steady and secure. Variance in number and volume of bounces may be improved with time, providing the skeleton is relaxed and steady. For example, the following exercise

can be reviewed bouncing either the 8ths or 16ths, depending upon the student's technique. Sticking should be flexible so that either hand is used to begin and end the bounce patterns. The tempo may be gradually increased as the student gains more control.

There are several advantages to using this bounce technique early and regularly, so that the student develops the habit of building each roll upon a regular skeleton of strokes. A common misconception is that the roll is produced by extremely fast alternate "crushed" bounces. Such a spastic roll is not only offensive to the ears, but also damaging to good technical improvement. The bounce technique may be used with any rhythm patterns such as two, three, four or six that the student can perform. Flexibility with such patterns helps him learn how to fill the proper duration of a roll completely — so that there will be consistency in performance. The sound produced by this technique is smooth and a reasonable facsimile of a good roll. It blends well with the music of other instruments in class work and is psychologically pleasing to the student.

The finished product of this roll technique should not be dictated by the old rudimental numbers 5, 7, 9, etc. Such numbers work only for a certain degree of open style at a set tempo. Students who have practiced these specific lengths out of context often have difficulty trying to fit them into actual performance. Also, a seven stroke roll actually uses only four strokes — another inconsistency with that approach.

Open to Closed — Avoid

Before going on to the rudimental roll, it might be well to discuss an old roll technique which should be avoided, or at least delayed, until the student has reasonable control of both the rudimental and bounce rolls. This is the practice technique of starting a roll with the open rudimental doubling and closing the roll into a multiple bounce.

The most obvious deficiency with this technique is bridging the gap between the rudimental and multiple bounce roll. Such bridging involves a major problem of switching from *arm and wrist* to *fingers and wrist.* Without good finger control, the wrist can only produce a plodding, weak-sounding closed roll. Students commonly try to change their grip in order to bridge this gap. The problem is much like that of the register break on clarinet or perhaps more like the sound barrier for airplanes. The grip and muscle control are shaken when they are not ready for the strain.

Another deficiency is the constantly changing tempo with the resulting muscle strain. Such tension does not permit muscles to develop strength and control like the *constant tempo* method. The *open-to-closed* technique also does not help a student develop a sense of steady tempo.

The student is ready for the rudimental roll whenever he can approach it through multiple bounce control and whenever he is ready for the required slow and disciplined practice. It is difficult to give the proper control to both arm and wrist when the roll is at a medium closed position. Also, as the roll is closed, more and more finger control becomes necessary. Most beginning students are not able to use this type of finger control even if they are aware that it is necessary. However, it can be approached through the multiple bounce roll by limiting the bounces to only one per stroke. This single bounce can then be worked into a tap which is even with the strokes. The same type of review exercise with the basic skeletons can also be used for this rudimental roll development.

Another special exercise may be used to develop speed and equality between the strokes and taps. At a steady tempo, play a short series of strokes alternated with a short series of strokes to which the taps have been added. When the tap series can be played in a relaxed manner, it should be slightly extended. After it has been extended two or three times, the whole exercise should be repeated at a little faster tempo. Five or ten minutes a day with two or three tempos will, over a period of weeks, produce considerable roll improvement.

A well-developed, professional-sounding roll is a combination of both the multiple bounce and the rudimental techniques. The sound of the multiple bounce is *attack-decay, attack-decay,* while the rudimental roll may sound too mechanical and open. Both of these techniques played closed require a great deal of fine finger control. The well-polished roll needs the *evenness* of the rudimental and the *filling* of the multiple bounce. To obtain such a roll, the arms, wrists and fingers work toward producing a rudimental roll as closed as possible. The fingers encourage extra bounces beyond the single tap. In the style of other visual diagrams (above) this roll would look something like this:

When done correctly, the sound is a full and even flow from hand to hand.

Reviews of Percussion Materials

F. Michael Combs

The Art of Snare Drumming. William D. Werner. Percussion Publishing Co. 72 pages. $3.00 paper.

A "refreshing, practical approach" describes *The Art of Snare Drumming*. The author, William D. Werner, has written this book because his own teaching experience has revealed a definite need for a high quality, comprehensive beginning method.

Although the technical patterns are limited to the basic rudiments (rolls, strokes, flams, ruffs, and a few others), the reading exercises advance quite rapidly. Dynamics are introduced in the second page, eighth notes on the third, and sixteenth notes by page 13. The book is especially applicable for fast learners and transfer students. Also included in this 72-page publication are a few duets and trios and a three page explanation of the performance techniques of bass drum, cymbals, triangle, and tambourine.

The printing of the text is of inferior quality; the notation, however, is clear and accurate.

The Slingerland Elementary Method for Orchestra Bells and Bell Lyra. John Tatgenhorst. Slingerland Drum Company, Niles, Illinois.

This method for bells is directed primarily toward a melodic approach. Following a brief introductory explanation of basic techniques and notation, melodic material (usually familiar tunes) occupies 34 of the 48 pages of the book. Although the melodic material is limited to the keys of C, F, B♭, E♭, A♭, and G, scales ranging through six flats and five sharps are listed on the last page. The notation and clarity of printing are of especially good quality.

Quite a bit of space is devoted to the lines of Slingerland orchestra bells, bell lyras, and mallets.

Elementary Drum Method. Earl Erickson. E.J. Erickson Co., St. Peter, Minnesota. $2.50.

The author of this new publication claims several innovative features. A new clef sign, which is yet to be seen in percussion literature, is supposed to make the multiple bounce roll easier. A "new notation" of the flam (double notes) occupies one page of the book and is accompanied by a very brief introduction. Vertical count (simply writing the count under the notes) is another feature of this 52-page publication.

Through the entire book, the right hand is notated on the top space and the left hand on the third space — another feature of which composers have yet to take advantage.

At the end of the book, six to eight measure phrases plus short introductory explanations are included for bongos, maracas, claves, and guiro.

The book contains no pictures or illustrations and lacks any explanations of grips, parts of the drum, or tuning and adjustment of the drum.

The Percussion (Second Edition). Charles L. Spohn and John J. Tatgenhorst. Allyn and Bacon, Inc., Boston. $7.95.

This publication is an excellent basic manual on the percussion instruments. The book opens with an introductory chapter covering some 15 different points relevant to school situations in particular. The rest of the first half of the book covers the basic techniques and specifications of the snare (and tenor) drum, the keyboard mallet instruments, timpani, and the secondary percussion instruments. The final chapter of this first section entitled "Percussion and Some of Its Uses," includes information about the marching band, stage band, the percussion ensemble, and history of percussion.

The second half of the book contains exercises and excerpts for snare drum, keyboard mallet instruments, timpani, and accessories. A very brief presentation of percussion books, periodicals, method books, solos, and ensembles is also included.

Guide to Teaching Percussion. Holloway-Bartlett (2nd Edition), Wm. C. Brown Company. 172 pages. $4.50.

This new edition, containing a large amount of practical and theoretical material, is designed for the pre-service and in-service training of instrumental music teachers. It covers playing techniques and teaching procedures of over 50 instruments. Especially noteworthy are the practical sections on marching band, and on the drum set. Numerous pictures, illustrations, and charts add clarity and understanding to this comprehensive volume. An annotated bibliography of percussion method and refence books, plus a glossary of percussion terms are both of particular interest to public school teachers.

Let's Play Percussion (Level one) from the Learning Unlimited Audio-Visual Band Series. Charles E. Merrill Pub. Co. Percussion Packet (tape and book) $9.95.

This innovation in teaching percussion (and other band instruments) consists of a cassette tape and a nearly 50-page book. When used together, the tape and book present the fundamentals of playing snare drum and "bar percussion" (bells, xylophone, vibes, etc.) so clearly and simply that any young student should be able to learn with only minimum assistance from a teacher. The exercises, usually familiar tunes, can be played on snare drum and/or a bar percussion instrument. Not only are the tunes themselves on the tape, but there is also interesting combo accompaniment which varies from just guitar and rhythm to a large ensemble.

The snare drum technique includes strokes, flams, and some introductory material on the roll. The melodic material stays within the range of a ninth and includes keys of C, F, and G.

Music reading, including time signatures, notes and rests up to 16th notes and quarter rests, dynamics, tied and dotted notes, etc., are presented with unusual clarity and accuracy. As suggested by the publisher, the student can rewind the tape and review any material as many times as necessary. The advantages of this type of programmed learning have already been proven.

Mallet Repair. Arthur Press. Belwin-Mills Publishing Corp., New York. $3.00.

This book fills a real need in the area of percussion mallet making. Condensed into 24 pages are over 100 photos and drawings illustrating the techniques of making or recovering timpani and yarn covered mallets. Also included are hints regarding chime mallets, brushes, and felt tipped drum sticks.

Techniques of Playing Bass Drum, Cymbals, and Accessories. Al Payson. Payson Percussion Products, 2130 Glenview Avenue, Park Ridge, Illinois 60068. 65 pages. $3.50

Filling a real need in the area of percussion, this new publication covers those instruments often regarded by students as too unimportant and too simple to play to merit any formal study. Actually, as pointed out by author Payson, percussionist with the Chicago Symphony, these instruments are extremely important in the concert percussion section. Although they may not be as difficult to play as the snare drum, timpani, and xylophone, they all have specific techniques which must be mastered.

A great deal of space is devoted to tambourine, castanets, triangle, bass drum, and cymbals. Clear explanations are presented for each instrument along with illustrations and several excerpts. Explanations also cover finger cymbals, antique cymbals, tam-tam and gong. A table of foreign terminology is found at the end of the book.

A Practical Workbook for the Modern Drummer. Richard DiCenso. 15 Kiley Dr., Randolph, Mass. 02368. $4.00.

The title of this new publication is very appropriate. Written primarily for the drum set, this 70-page book makes no pretense of being a snare drum or drum set method book. There are, however, a few pages devoted to music fundamentals such as tied and dotted notes and triplets. The author suggests in the forward that "the workbook can be opened to any page that will serve the individual's particular needs."

The book simply contains the rudiments of drumming and a collection of contemporary and ethnic rhythms for the drum set that are used in jazz, rock, Latin American, and commercial music.

Explanations of patterns and beats are not detailed, but are limited to a few concise sentences. Specific instruction is left to the teacher, or to a supplementary instruction book.

1972 - 1973

397	The Beat	Richard Hochrainer	February
400	Chamber Percussion: Approach to Musicality	John Bircher, Jr.	March
401	Keyboard Percussion in the School Music Program	F. Michael Combs	April
402	Percussion Materials Review		April
403	The Super Soft Roll and How to Develop It	Roy Burns	May
404	Which Marching Band Drumming Style Do You Prefer?	Geary Larrick	June
406	Organize Your Marching Band Drum Section Early	F. Michael Combs	September
407	Editing the Marching Band Percussion Part	Bill Kreutzer	October
409	Three Way Flams	William J. Schinstine	November
411	Three Multi-Timpani Works Before Berlioz	David Whitwell & Ronald Johnson	December
412	Selecting a Snare Drum Method Book	F. Michael Combs	December
413	Survey of Percussion Specialists	F. Michael Combs	January
414	The Evolution of Early Jazz Drumming	Theodore D. Brown	February
416	Percussionists and the Contest/Festival	F. Michael Combs	March
417	The Set Drummer — Advice from the Pros	F. Michael Combs	April
418	A Guide to Foreign Percussion Terms	Tennessee Chapter of the Percussive Arts Society	May
419	How to Apply Drum Rudiments to $\frac{6}{8}$ Meter	Haskell W. Harr	June
421	Marching Tonal Percussion	Larry B. Snider	September
423	Percussion Ensemble Literature	F. Michael Combs	October
427	Percussion Students' "Inventions"	LaVerne R. Reimer	October
429	Some Remarks About Multiple Timpani and Berlioz	C.B. Wilson	November
431	University Marching Band Drum Cadences, Part I	F. Michael Combs	November
433	University Marching Band Drum Cadences, Part II	F. Michael Combs	December

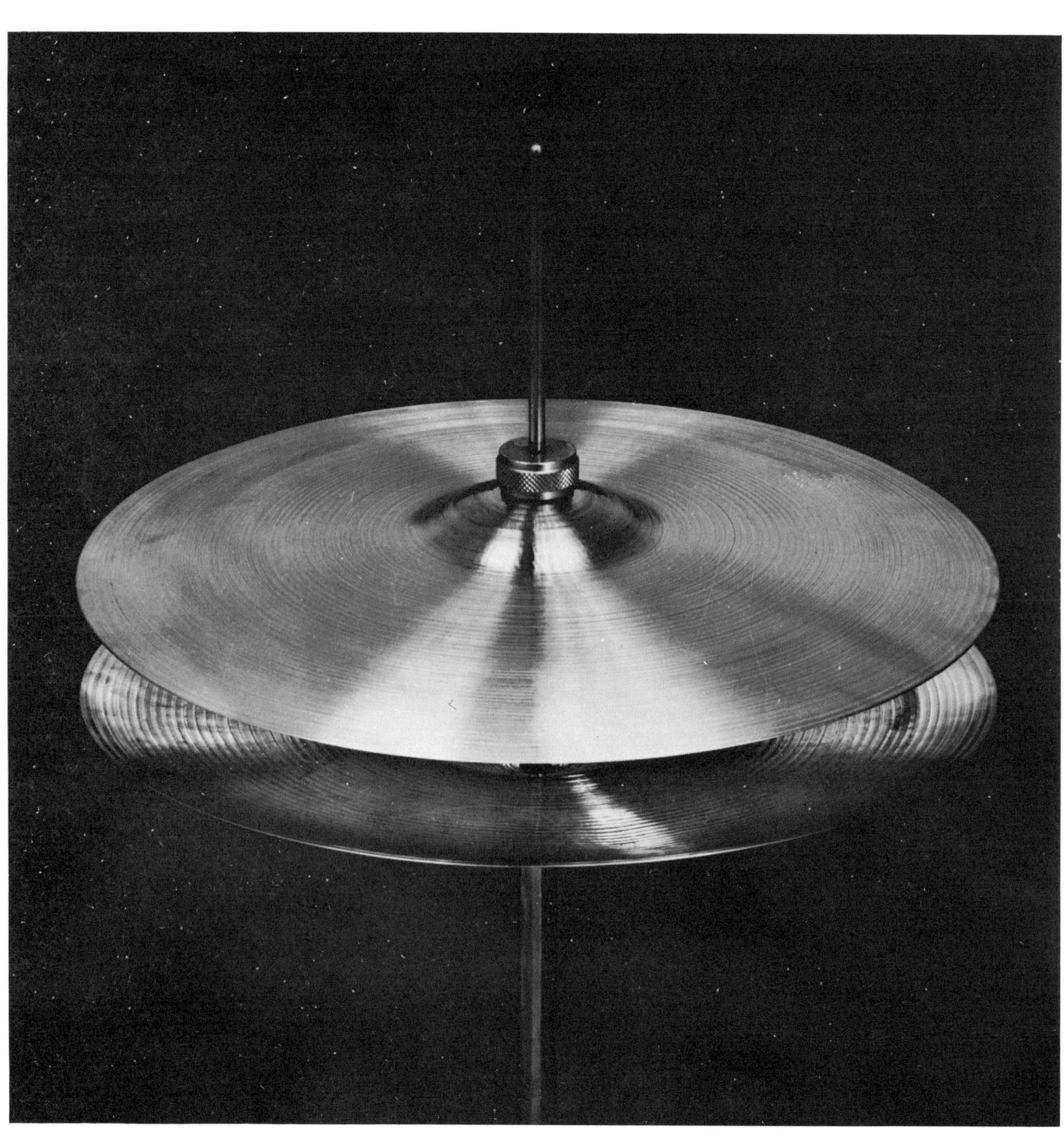

The Beat

Richard Hochrainer, translated by Harrison Powley

This article first appeared in German in "Das Orchester — Zeitschrift für deutsche Orchesterkultur und Rundfunk — Chorwesen, Organ der Deutschen Orchestervereinigung" 16 Jg. Heft 9/1968 and has been translated at the request of Prof. Hochrainer. Permission for publication of this English translation has been obtained from B. Schott's Söhne.

The translator has tried to obtain an equitable balance between the many subtleties of Prof. Hochrainer's idiomatic Viennese style and idiomatic English.

A string player draws his bow over the string, for example, the length of a half note, a wind player must blow just as long. What does the percussionist do? He "strikes just once" and allows his cymbals, drums, triangle, or timpani to ring and then he accordingly muffles the sound at the end of the half note. This view is false! Experienced percussionists generally allow the tone of their instruments to ring much longer than the note value indicates and usually at least a little longer. For string players the note value is controlled by the duration of the bow stroke, for wind players it is the duration of the air stream, but for the percussionist it is controlled by the beat and not by the duration of the sound. No good percussionist would simply strike when he sees a note in front of him. No, he must carefully consider that his beats ought to express the appropriate note value quite exactly so that instead of mere striking the result may be true performing. A simple experiment on the piano, also a percussion instrument, can easily show us the correct way. One counts in *andante* — one, two, three, four — a full chord notated as a sixteenth note will be struck on the next downbeat.

(a)

The exact attack of the fingers and hands should be noticed in this experiment. In the next experiment in *andante* — one, two, three, four — a full chord notated as a quarter note will be struck on the next downbeat.

(b)

The third experiment in *andante* — one, two, three, four — a full chord notated as a whole note will be struck on the next downbeat.

(c)

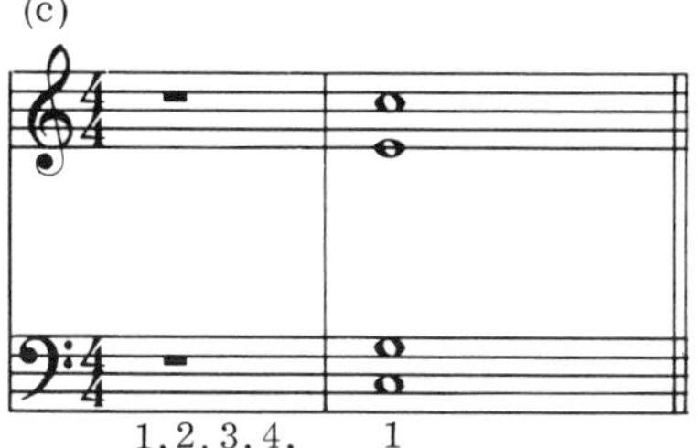

With the larger note values the movement of the fingers and hands is slower, therefore, the player is obliged to take more breath for these chords. This is self-evident to the wind player, and even the string player will lift more with his bow for an entrance of a whole note than, for example, a quarter note. Moreover, there is, in our good and long-tested notational system, a very interesting, but difficult to explain parallel. (A whole note is rarely written immediately after the bar line, but a single sixteenth note almost certainly is.)[1] To the percussionist the nature of his entrance and his beat is an important part of his musicianship — of his function in the orchestra. Although many believe that the roll is the most important technique on the timpani, snare drum, or other various percussion instruments, it should be realized that the *most important factor is merely the beat*. The roll, a means of prolonging sound, which is analogous to a string tremolo, is, therefore, not so typical of the instrument as the simple beat.

What then is beating? Do we *pound* with a stick on the skin? Is it a *chopping* motion or do we *knock* the tone out of the skin with the stick? Do we make the skin vibrate with a *push* or do we *throw* the head of the stick on the skin? Do we *press* the mallet on the bells? Do we *pound* our two sticks on the timpani and *sling* the two cymbals against each other? Do we allow the beater to *fall* on the triangle? Of all the above similar actions, however, none is a genuine *beating*! Certainly everyone has heard something about free fall, but what about a beat? Nevertheless, each one who has driven a nail at one time carefully distinguishes whether it is a large nail or a tack. Where is there a beat in this technique? Yet, only when one takes a hammer or a similar tool in his hand and strikes a nail or another solid object is one careful not to hold the hammer so stiffly that it hurts the hand. On the piano an almost similar action

Richard Hochrainer demonstrates on the timpani

is clearly seen in the hammer action which strikes from underneath. Conversely our hands can only work from above. Every percussionist should remember this when he picks up a stick.

Beating is lifting, accelerating, and relaxing. Lifting is the power which is in the hand and arm that brings the stick to a vertex from which it will be able to be accelerated. It is impossible to make a good beat from a distance of a yard, for example, without lifting.
The stick must be accelerated so that the small mass of the head of the stick can bring into vibration with an essential strong impulse another mass — skin, wood, or metal. Relaxing after the beat is, perhaps, the most important step for the reason that the first vibration can freely expand, because the rebound is not hindered and the sound, therefore, will not be stopped. Our wrists move much slower than the vibrations of a sound producing body. Certainly in *staccato* playing this "slower" movement has its proper function because in this case the sticks will be tightly held and thus the first vibrations already will be stopped.

How the sticks will be held is also important for the quality of a beat. On this point experienced timpanists know anatomically as well as mechanically two correct ways — the position of the hands in soft and loud timpani playing. In playing softly the sticks are held between the first joint of the index finger and the thumb, while the third and fourth fingers lie underneath in order to assist the playing.

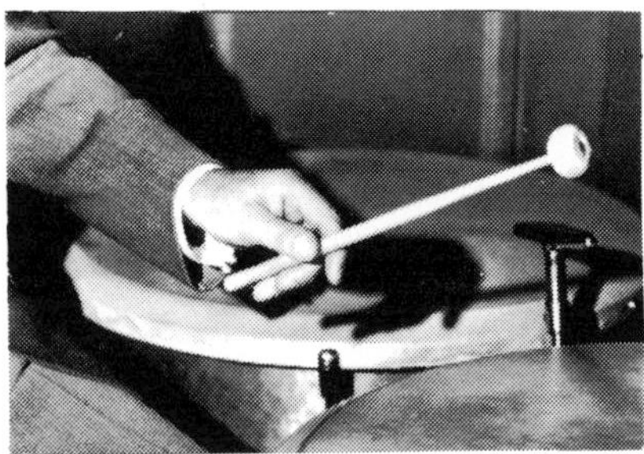

Hand position for soft playing — timpani

The true nature of the beat which forms our style uses first the finger and only afterwards the hands and arms. In playing loudly it is better to hold the rotation axis (fulcrum) of the stick between the thumb and the last joint of the third finger whereby the third, fourth, and fifth fingers can assist the playing by moving the stick. The sticks are allowed to swing freely.

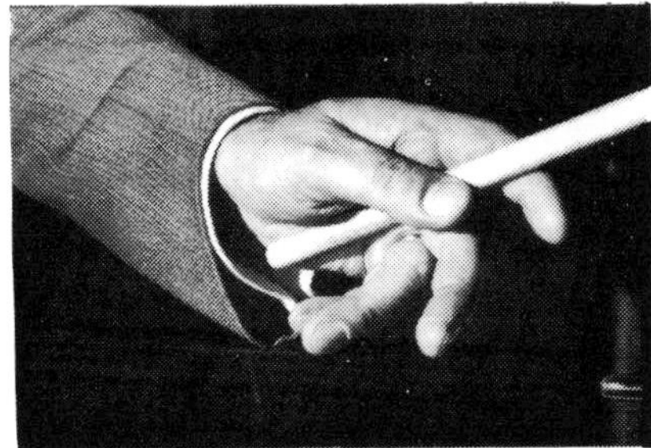

Hand position for loud playing — timpani

For loud playing, sticks never should be held between the thumb and the second joint of the index finger, because their freedom of movement would be too limited. We play the snare drum (always slanted so that the tone does not echo against the floor) with one hand in a different position. The thumb and the third finger of the right hand form a support and the other fingers move the stick as in timpani playing,

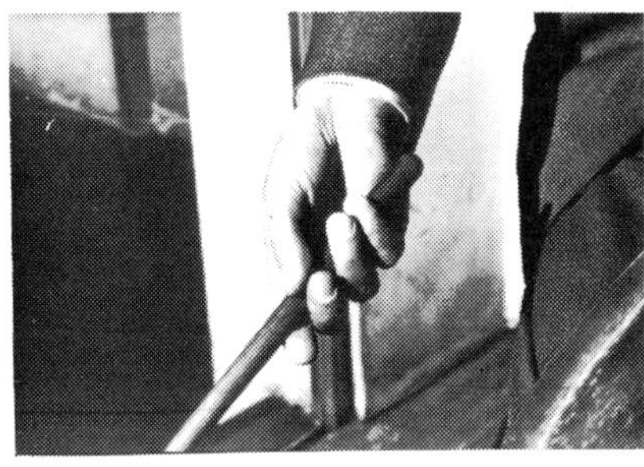

Right hand position — snare drum

whereas in the left hand the stick moves freely between the thumb and index finger.

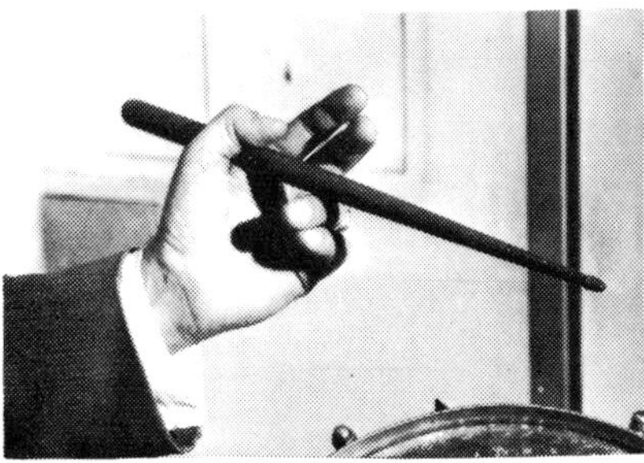

Left hand position — snare drum

In this case the movement of the stick is controlled by the motion of the bent fourth finger against the tip of the thumb. In order that a ringing beat may be produced, the sticks must always make more movement than the hands and arms. Many a percussionist could play much better if he would only exchange his tightly held sticks for deliberate control. In the last century, as history records, the timpanist could distinguish exactly among a half, a quarter or an eighth note beat.[3]

Because the strong entrance of a large body of sound, for example, on a sustained chord, is always somewhat sluggish, composers do not write, in such instances, a whole note for the percussion instruments, but only a quarter or even an eighth as, for example, Anton Bruckner in his *Symphony No. 8.* In the "Adagio" movement he notates only an eighth note for a *fortississimo* cymbal crash although all the winds sustain it.

Anton Bruckner VIII Symphonie C- moll[4], *p. 100, m. 239.*

Certainly he wrote each note and chord with great care so that in a totally foreign chord it was not beyond him to write something other than the usual notation for a cymbal crash. In passing, Bruckner notated the high piercing ring of the cymbals as B♭ in the treble clef of an E♭ major chord (see example above), and later as an E♭ of a C♭ major chord.

Anton Bruckner, VIII Symphonie C- moll[4], *p. 101, m. 243.*

However, one often reads that percussion instruments were notated in smaller values because their sound does not last any longer. The usual notation for bass drum and cymbals in martial music shows that this cannot be completely true.

In this example no percussionist would dampen the notes because it would be technically too difficult. Often for this reason people say that the method of notation is wrong and that each measure has to be notated with two half notes.

No! Perhaps a composer would write a triumphal march in this way if it were determined more by brilliant music, corpulent steps, and a certain repose. The quarter notes plus quarter rests are better suited and correct for strict inspiring march music and also would be performed accordingly by the drummer. Many similar examples for the bass drum, tam-tam, and especially the triangle could be noted. It should be mentioned that the German name for the triangle is *der Triangle* (nominative masculine singular) because of its masculine, steel-like sound. This is affirmed by all my professional colleagues as well as the Duden dictionary. The neuter use of the word triangle (*triangulum* has little pertinent connection and no one says that he would like to play *"das Dreieck"* — a three-cornered piece of steel).

If the note indicates to us the type of beat, how long may the struck tone ring? Before any answer to this question can be suggested, we should mention that about 50 years ago many composers tried to notate the length of sound of percussion instruments. But soon it was evident that by this means the orchestral sound became too weak and also somewhat sluggish, and the brilliance of the entrance was lacking. Today this is no longer done.

Therefore, how long may our tone sound? The first rule reads: "As long as the harmony lasts, that is to say, does not change." This means that if the orchestra plays a single quarter note, the bass drum, for example, may not ring any longer. Consequently, it must be dampened according to rule one and its corollary, "when dampening, damp in time and not earlier." Unfortunately, premature dampening is heard all too often and this always produces an ugly sound. The second rule, which was established by experienced percussionists as was the first, reads: "The tone is controlled according to the good taste of the percussionist." It will sometimes be correct to adopt these statements to the character of the music — one beat being quickly dampened, another allowed to ring with special effect over the orchestra. For example, a loud unmuffled timpani tone can be very effective if played on a short orchestral chord.

In order to remember the different ways of playing the notes, experienced percussionists write a free tie [♩⁀] for the notes which are to ring indefinitely and an apostrophe [♩'] for the notes which are to be dampened.

Exact attention to the conductor's movements, an acute sense of concentration, and a thorough knowledge of the composition are requisite to the percussionist's profession. The ringing beat which is a very diverse, an extremely interesting, difficult and a splendid art, should generate from the play of the fingers and hands; from *beating* should come *performing*.

Ludwig van Beethoven, Overture No. 3 zu Leonore, *op. 72a, p. 180, mm. 628-633.*[5]

etc.

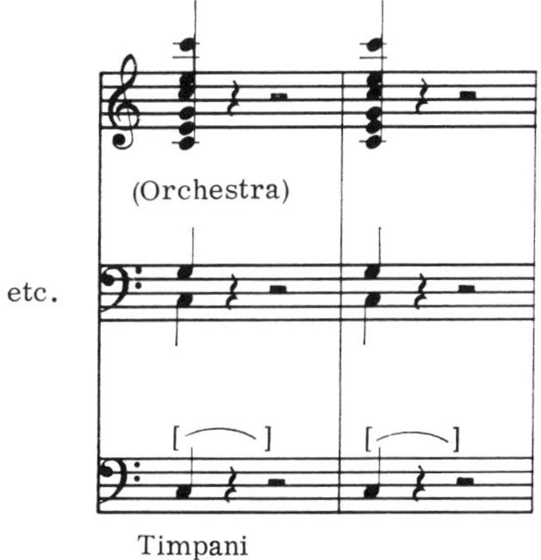

Translator's Notes

1. The reader is referred especially to the musical autographs of Mozart as reproduced in Emanuel Winternitz *Musical Autographs from Monteverdi to Hindemith* (New York: Dover Publications, Inc., 1965), II, 60-80. The whole notes, it will be observed, are written clearly in the middle of the measures and not next to the bar lines. Professor Hochrainer believes that this notational tradition is extremely important to the correct interpretation of timpani and percussion parts during the classical and romantic periods.

2. The pictures of Professor Hochrainer demonstrating on the several percussion instruments were taken under my direction in the orchestra pit of the *Staatsoper*, Vienna, Austria in the spring of 1966.

3. Johann Ernst Altenburg, *Versuch einer Anleitung zur heroizch=musikalischen Trompeter=und Pauken=Kunst* (Halle: Joh. Christ. Hendel, 1795), pp. 129-130. My translation of the section on the timpani, now ready for publication, clearly explains the tradition of timpani playing referred to by Professor Hochrainer.

4. Anton Bruckner, *VII Symphonie C-moll*, ed. Dr. L. Novak (Vienna: Musikwissenschaftlicher Verlag der internationalen Bruckner-Gesellschaft, 1955).

5. Ludwig van Beethoven, *Fidelio*, edition with the Leonore Overtures and introduction by Wilhelm Altmann (Leipzig: Peters).

Chamber Percussion: Approach to Musicality

John Bircher, Jr.

The world of percussion is swamped with attitudes, arguments, methods, and materials which seem to be aimed in the direction of perpetuating the *technically* proficient drummer, but *musical* consideration is often the last to be given the aspiring percussionist.

Through the "chamber method," musicality may be developed and enhanced through all levels of instruction and proficiency. The interaction, subtlety, and awareness which can be cultivated by this means is essential to the formulation of a musical concept.

The concept of chamber music (small group, flexible instrumentation, one player for each part, unity of ensemble, lack of solo emphasis) may be applied to the percussion ensemble or to any small ensemble utilizing percussion and various other instruments. The chamber method recognizes the *independence* of each part from another as well as the *dependence* of each player on the entire group. However, this term must not be thought to include *all* "percussion ensemble" literature, since pieces of novel character, and those based solely on showmanship do not necessarily exhibit chamber qualities.

The small size of a chamber group allows for much flexibility in scheduling, and does not rely on a large percussion inventory. Both factors contribute to this being a workable approach for the secondary school program.

To develop musicianship, the percussionist must take a decisive role in the making of music. The traditional "go practice" (in an isolated practice room) often develops more bad attitudes than it does musical understanding. On the other hand, a chamber ensemble — homogeneous in nature — utilizing 2-10 players, allows a feasible basis for learning musical skills. Since the basic technical considerations are transferrable from instrument to instrument, a practical approach to teaching may be put into effect. But even more important are the *musical* values which may be transmitted. For instance, the manipulation of tone color is possible simply by changing a mallet; dynamics may be controlled by merely striking a different area of an instrument. Thus a wealth of learning may take place without advanced technical skill. Within this group can be developed a sense of tonal and coloristic subtlety hard to achieve in other ensembles.

Through lack of time (but also sometimes because of limited ability of the director) the percussion section in a large organization is sometimes all but forgotten. Directors almost always *expect* precision, perception, and vast technical knowledge, but in some cases they do not *teach* it. Through chamber playing, however, the percussionist gains an understanding of music which is transferrable to any musical situation.

Contemporary band/orchestra literature demands a "total percussion" approach — not simply snare drum, bells, or timpani alone. By organizing the high school percussion section into a chamber unit, all instruments may be studied and applied seriously.

Most college music departments require that students entering their percussion program display playing proficiency in at least two areas of percussion, to be chosen from (1) snare drum, (2) mallet instruments, (3) timpani, and (4) accessory instruments.

Control of Sound

The contemporary chamber ensemble as a unit was begun through the compositional pioneering of Stravinsky (*L'Histoire du soldat*, 1918), Varèse (*Ionization*, 1931), and Bartók (*Music for Strings, Percussion, and Celeste* and *Sonata for Two Pianos and Percussion*) to name a few. These compositions have in common the inherent contrast and color capabilities of percussion. To understand and play compositions for percussion, the technique of sound and tone color control must be mastered. To achieve the perfect control of nuance and subtlety required of chamber performance, each striking area of every instrument must be precisely chosen. A smooth scale on the xylophone or marimba requires not only that the right bars be struck but that these bars be struck in the proper areas. To execute smooth rapid rhythms on any drum requires that the sticks be held with equal tension and that they strike the same approximate area of the head.

Sound and color may be varied to vast degrees by choice of beater. On each sounding surface, every substance has a characteristic sound variant. Using wooden sticks to strike a suspended cymbal creates quite a different sound from that achieved with soft mallets. A metal nail or a coin will bring about yet another variation. Every percussion instrument has the potential to elicit as many sounds as there are striking agents. By working with percussion through a chamber ensemble, the percussionist has the opportunity to explore all of these sound possibilities.

Some Rehearsal Techniques

The percussive arts can be strengthened most effectively by applying teaching techniques which have the development of *musicianship* as their aim. Techniques which strengthen and sharpen the senses can be applied to the chamber percussion rehearsal. Exercises which I have used as a warm-up drill have helped to develop the concept of "listening." Such exercises require judgement by each player regarding balance of sound, dynamic contrast, and tone color.

The first exercise uses the long roll. All members of the ensemble sustain a sound on the instrument to which they are assigned. Basic sound capabilities of each instrument are discussed. It is important to recognize, for example, that the snare drum has the type of tone which will cut through the total ensemble sound; that a bass drum roll requires a slower roll motion in softer dynamic levels than in loud playing; that it is difficult to sustain a low dynamic level with the suspended cymbal, but that it can become overpowering quite quickly. All of these unique qualities must be considered by the players.

During this sustained roll, each player in turn is asked to change dynamic levels, following the lead player. This requires accurate adjustment of sound — *by ear*: there is no sight contact with a conductor. The exercise is complete when each player has led the dynamic level of the group at least twice. This "follow-the-leader" exercise is based on total aural perception and concentration, and the absence of physical cues.

The second rehearsal technique is improvisation. For this study, instruments are divided into basic categories of *pitched* and *non-pitched*, with the former subdivided into *high, medium*, and *low* sounds. Players are assigned to a category of instruments. Each person, in turn, chooses the character and mood of improvisation by selecting from the instrumental sounds at his disposal, and playing for a short period of time. The remainder of the ensemble is to follow the character of the first idea as closely as possible. Pedantic evaluation as to whether a certain player is "right" or "wrong" is not important. The main value is in the discussion which follows, when opinions of the appropriateness of sounds and rhythms used by each player are expressed.

Improvisation of this type stimulates judgement and growth in perceiving and utilizing tone color and texture. It serves as a useful tool for the teaching of expression, without the worry of technical means. Suppose a lead player starts sporadically swishing on the large suspended cymbal with a brush. An appropriate accompaniment may be found in using the fingers to strike the bass drum, but random 16th notes at a loud dynamic level would not be fitting in this texture.

Notation Problems

Perhaps no other instrumental area is plagued by the lack of standardized notation common to percussion writing. In some scores a rhythmic pattern for multiple drums may be shown on two or three independent staves, while in another score it may be condensed into one staff. The triangle, cymbal, and other accessory instruments are often notated by stars, diamond-shaped notes, or various other devices. The job of interpreting the notation of each composer is left to the percussionist. In chamber percussion study, an infinite number of interpretation problems may be seen, worked with, and mastered.

The standardization of terminology and notation would be a help to the confused composer, arranger, and percussionist in their mutual search for communication. Several clarifying books have been published (like Owen Read and Joel T. Leach: *Scoring for Percussion;* New York: Prentice-Hall, 1969).

The Artist-Percussionist

The unique musical situations and opportunities found in the study of percussion should be used as a basis for developing percussion as an art, and most important, for developing the artist-percussionist. The chamber percussion ensemble is an organization through which concrete musical learning may take place. Aural perception may be strengthened by the emphasis on listening which is required in chamber playing, and the diversity of sound, style, texture, and color to be found in chamber literature opens the realm of interpretation.

April 1972

Keyboard Percussion in the School Music Program

F. Michael Combs

Not too many years ago, the public school music director could perform a large percentage of the standard band and orchestral literature and find very few parts written for any of the keyboard mallet percussion instruments. Until recently, the extent of keyboard mallet training in most ensembles was limited to a marimba played by one or two piano-transfers doubling flute, oboe, or violin parts.

Times have certainly changed. With the new concern for tone color, contemporary composers have taken advantage of the great variety of timbre available in the percussion section and have shown a particular interest in the keyboard percussion instruments. If a director wants to present a varied program and expose his students to literature being written today, it will be necessary not only to have several keyboard instruments but also to have skilled players to perform on these instruments.

Based on today's band and orchestra literature playable at the public school level, the director should be familiar with the following instruments:

Orchestra Bells

Mandatory in any percussion section, the orchestra bells (or glockenspiel) not only can play designated bell parts but also may double high wind parts or substitute for vibraphone or chimes. The marching band bells or bell lyra which is most effectively used with a marching unit, may be used as a satisfactory substitute for the orchestra bells despite the fact that the bars of the marching bell lyra are constructed of a lighter weight metal alloy. Mallets for the orchestra bells should be brass or hard plastic.

Xylophone

Running a close second in priority to the orchestra bells, xylophone parts appear quite frequently in contemporary literature, even at the elementary and junior high level. The thick, dense xylophone bars, when struck with hard rubber or plastic mallets, produce bright, penetrating sounds. The xylophone sounds an octave higher than written and is usually tuned to an A=442 vibrations per second. A three octave instrument is adequate. Resonators are optional.

Chimes

The cost of a first line set of chimes may seem prohibitive. The depreciation, however, is negligible, and the color of the chimes (usually simulating cathedral bells) can hardly be duplicated by any other instrument. Wound rawhide hammers are used to strike the chimes directly on the edge of the caps. A damper pedal may be found on some models.

Marimba

A mellow, blending sound is characteristic of the marimba. Because of this fact the instrument may be used effectively to double other instruments in a large ensemble. The thin wooden keys with resonators lack the piercing sound of the xylophone. The larger range of the marimba, however, makes it suitable for adaptations or arrangements of solo literature written for many other instruments. Soft rubber mallets and cord or yarn wound mallets are most commonly used.

Vibraphone

The vibraphone is characteristically a solo instrument and is often used in a small jazz ensemble. Limited to a three octave range, the "vibes" are used only occasionally in a concert band or symphony orchestra. Rotating fans positioned in the resonators under the metal bars of the instrument produce a vibrato. Also, because of the slow decay, a damper pedal is necessary. Mallets used on the vibraphone are usually cord or yarn-wound, although there are a number of special effect mallets available.

Percussion Materials Review

Drum set books have flooded the market during the past few years. Two publications from Creative Music are, however, substantial contributions to this area. Marvin Dahlgren's *Drum Set Control* is probably worth the rather high price of $5.50. It is well printed, and is generally a clear and practical approach to gaining technical skills for the drum set. The main emphasis, according to the author, is to explore the possibilities of using the rudiments in conjunction with the bass drum. Beginning with single strokes and going through all the double stroke and flam rudiments, this approach is certainly made clear throughout the book's 80 pages.

Latin American Rhythms for the Drum Set by Ron Fink contains 25 of the most frequently played Latin American dance rhythms, with numerous variations. Also, contained within the 48 pages, are brief explanations regarding technique and interpretation. The selling price is $4.00.

The two volumes of *Professional Drum Studies* are appropriately titled. The author, Rufus Jones, has admirable credentials, including time with Lionel Hampton, Maynard Ferguson, Count Basie, and Duke Ellington. These new publications by Gwyn Publishing Company (Box 5900, Sherman Oaks, California 91413) are well-printed, clear, and contain only a few, brief explanations. The music, which almost fills the 25 pages of each volume, are more than contemporary exercises; they are ideas that can be developed in a practical situation — backing a combo or big band. Each book sells for $2.50.

Gwyn should also do well with *Drums: Jazz and Rock*. John Guerin, the young Hollywood drummer who wrote the 24-page publication, uses the space almost entirely for beats applicable to what's happening in today's rock and jazz music. For $3.50, the buyer receives a good dose of Afro bossa nova, boogooloo, fills, cross time, shuffle, and rock patterns.

The title is the only thing really new about *A Funky Primer for the Rock Drummer*. Gwyn took a more conservative approach in this 45-page publication. The first 30 exercises, which involve only single strokes, would probably encourage any young student to take up the kazoo. Nine line look-a-like exercises are in 4/4 and note values are eighths, sixteenths, or triplets. The author, Charles Dawd, is a West Coast drummer who studies with Antonio Cirone of the San Francisco Symphony. His book sells for $3.00.

Twenty four pages of scale patterns, which are to be practiced in all keys, are written out in a book entitled *Keyboard Mastery for the Mallet Percussion*. (Fred Wickstrom, University of Miami Music Publications — sole agent: Sam Fox). According to the author, the exercises contained in the book, when practiced diligently, will result in a degree of keyboard mastery applicable to the vibraphone, marimba, xylophone, and bells. The investment of $2.50 for the book may be worthwhile for the student who would benefit by having basic scale studies written out for him.

The Super Soft Roll and How to Develop It

Roy Burns

The buzz roll, often referred to as the concert, multiple bounce or press roll, is perhaps the most controversial of all drum rudiments and techniques. It can be a nightmare to the percussionist who encounters a super soft buzz roll solo while reading a new piece of music. It can also be a frustrating problem to the student who can't master the control and technique necessary to develop this essential drum sound.

The buzz roll might be more properly referred to as the "universal roll." It is understood throughout the world that all rolls will be played as buzz rolls unless the music specifies otherwise. However, the double stroke roll has been traditionally over-emphasized for three reasons: (1) the misconception that double strokes when played quite rapidly will produce the closed-buzz roll sound; (2) the misconception that double strokes are technically more difficult than the buzz roll; and (3) the misconception that practicing double strokes will aid in the development of the buzz roll. In actuality, it is only the practice of the buzz roll that will lead to its eventual perfection.

For these reasons, most directors do not realize that the buzz roll is not only a legitimate technique, but a prerequisite for becoming a musical percussionist. And, as any percussionist will tell you, a truly musical buzz roll requires control, practice, sensitivity, and dedication.

Sound

A well-played roll should create the illusion of a perfectly sustained sound; much like tearing a sheet, rubbing sand paper evenly over a piece of wood, or pouring sand or fine pebbles onto a piece of board.

As in all music, the conception of the "type" of roll sound achieved (in regard to texture) varies with individual players and the style of music. For example, traditionally, concert players have generally preferred a coarser or more grain-like texture in the buzz roll, while drum-set players seem to prefer the finer, smoother, silky type of buzz roll sound. These are generalizations; but taken as such, they do have validity.

Variables That Affect the Sound of the Buzz Roll

1. The weight and model of the drumstick used.
2. The way the drum is tensioned and tuned.
3. The way the snares are adjusted — tight or loose.
4. The type of snares on the drum — wire, gut or nylon.
5. The size of the drum — 3", 5", 6½" deep, etc.
6. The volume of the roll played.
7. The style of music performed.

Considering all of these variables, it is no wonder that there are differences of opinion as to the "ideal" sound for the buzz roll. However, all agree that it should be an even, sustained sound and that it takes patience, consistent practice, and sensitivity to achieve a musical "buzz" roll.

Method of Practice

The "grip" (method of holding the drumsticks) is as critical as a trumpet player's embouchure. The Rogers Elementary Drum Method gives detailed information on what I consider to be the correct grip.

When attempting to develop the buzz roll, it is best to select a stick with a certain amount of weight. Extremely light sticks can be a handicap because they do not have the rigidity which is necessary to produce a good roll sound. It is difficult to designate the ideal stick for practicing the buzz roll (specifications and design vary, depending on the manufacturer), however, as a general rule, the stick should not be much lighter than a 2B to a 5A for practicing the buzz roll.

The buzz roll should never be practiced on a rubber practice pad, because the rebound response of rubber is actually slower than the rebound response of a drum head. If a snare drum is not available or practical, the Remo Tunable Practice Pad is the most musical and practical alternative. Its plastic head can be tensioned and is much closer to the actual drum "feel" than any rubber pad.

After selecting an appropriate stick, with the aid of a qualified teacher if possible, you can now begin to practice the soft "buzz" roll. With the right hand, from a height of no more than two inches, press the stick lightly against the head by lowering the hand. As soon as the stick makes contact with the head, relax the hand and allow the stick to bounce freely. Note that the stick bounces from a slower to a faster speed until it stops, just as a golf ball would if dropped onto the floor and allowed to continue bouncing until it stopped. Once the feeling of a free, relaxed bounce is achieved, repeat the same process with the left hand.

At the end of each "buzz," you will notice a sort of "smudging" of the buzz sound. To eliminate this, lower the stick, not too rapidly, and allow the stick to buzz, and raise (pick up) the stick just before the "buzz" would stop. This eliminates the "smudging" effect.

Be certain that the sticks move straight up and down. If allowed to make a circular pattern, an undesirable scraping effect will result.

Now, using both hands alternate the sticks slowly and lightly, and gradually increase the speed until the buzz with each stick connects with the other. You should now be playing a soft buzz roll. Now, try to play the buzz roll from a height of no more than one inch.

In order to play an extremely soft buzz roll *(ppp)* the pressure at the *fulcrum* (the actual gripping point) must be firm. Using very little downward pressure against the head, this firm grip tends to lighten the front of the stick so that you can play softer than the weight of the stick would normally allow. It is possible to play the buzz roll at a height of about ¼ inch and still produce a long enough buzz to alternate the sticks at a moderately slow rate of speed. It is best not to move the hands too rapidly when playing the soft buzz roll because this will require more downward pressure with the sticks against the head and increase the possibility of an uneven sound. Do not "dig" the sticks into the head for any reason.

The sticks should be kept as nearly parallel to the head as possible when playing the soft buzz roll. Also, both sticks should form exactly the same angle in relation to the drum head. The correct position is easiest to achieve when the drum head is somewhere near the level of the belt buckle; however, when playing matched grip, it may be comfortable to have the snare drum a little lower than when using the traditional left-hand grip.

Buzz Roll Dynamic Principle

The height of the sticks is directly proportional to the volume of the roll. As the height increases, the sticks meet the head with greater force, producing a buzz of shorter duration. This requires that the rate of alternation between sticks also increase in order to produce a sustained roll sound.

The SOFTER the buzz roll, the CLOSER the sticks are to the head and the SLOWER the speed of alternation between sticks.

The LOUDER the buzz roll, the FARTHER the sticks are from the head and the FASTER the speed of alternation between sticks.

To illustrate this principle, try the following exercise, allowing at least one minute for the complete dynamic range.

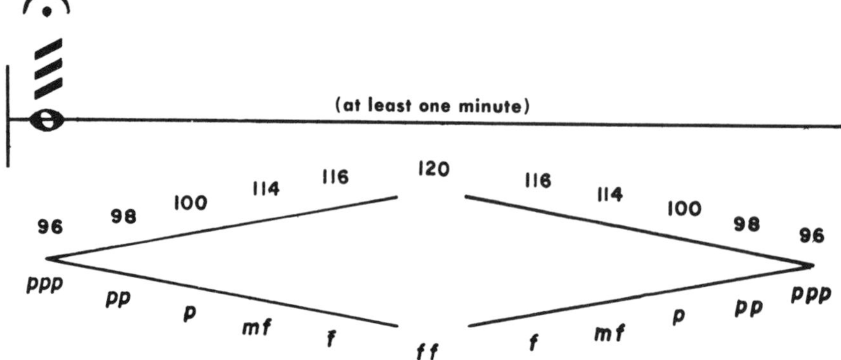

Note that the metronome indications are approximate, intended to be used only as a guide. Some drummers play with a faster or slower rate of alternation depending upon their technique and control, and the type of roll sound desired.

Metronome markings are in quarter notes, but the rates of alternation of the sticks are in sixteenth notes. For example, if the tempo is marked 96, the alternation pattern is R L R L at ♩= 96.

The daily practice routine should also include a buzz roll at a selected alternation speed for at least five minutes — without stopping and without changing the alternation rate of the sticks. Select a different alternation speed (96, 98, 100, 114, etc.) for practice each day.

Roll Texture Principle

The fineness or coarseness of the soft buzz roll is determined by the firmness of the fulcrum (actual gripping point on the stick) and the amount of downward pressure of the stick against the head.

Moderate downward pressure, combined with a relaxed grip, produces the fine, smooth, silky soft roll sound usually preferred by most drum set players.

Very little downward pressure, combined with the tight grip, produces the sandy or grain-like textured soft roll sound preferred by most concert players.

This description does not imply that one is better than the other, and certainly not that one is more even sounding than the other. The choice — based upon the music being performed — is left to the player.

All players agree that nothing is more beautiful or compelling than a sensitively and artistically executed super soft roll, but do not expect to play a perfect roll the first time you attempt it with this method. However, I know you will find that the rate of improvement in the roll which can be accomplished in a relatively short time with this approach is nothing short of amazing.

June 1972

Which Marching Band Drumming Style Do You Prefer?

Geary Larrick

Most directors are well aware of a general difference in style between concert drumming and marching band drumming, but different marching band drumming styles? — Who cares?! Apparently the majority of directors copy the style of their college marching band and let it go at that.

Listening to marching band drum sections in different parts of the country, many different styles are evident; but, four very specific styles seem to have the most influence. As might be expected, most marching band drum sections combine two or more styles. Perhaps many marching bands could be improved if the director realized the different techniques and equipment used in connection with the four basic styles.

Scottish Drumming

When hearing a Scottish bagpipe-and-drum band, a very distinct style of drumming is evident.

Equipment. Snare drums in a Scottish drum line are tuned to get a very tight, crisp sound; usually there are snares on both the top and bottom heads. "Scotch" bass drums are usually not very wide (ca. 6" x 28") and are often dampened by placing a thin strip of cloth under the heads. Snare drum sticks are similar to our "A" classification (e.g. 5A, 7A) in size and weight, with a spherical bead on the striking end. Bass drum beaters are often leather-covered wooden beaters.

Technique. Snare drum rolls are very "tight" and closed — not open as in rudimental drumming; snare drum parts are intricate and complicated — quite suited to the usual tempo of the band (ca. M.M. 90 - 100). The following example typifies the Scottish snare drum part:

Since there are only two main voices in the Scottish band, the drums play a role nearly equal to the pipes — they accompany, or embellish, as the bagpipes play, and perform soloistically when the pipes are silent.

Drum and Bugle Corps Drumming

Unlike Scottish drumming — which has a tradition that is centuries old — drum and bugle corps drumming is currently going through an evolution from military-style drumming to a very exciting, polyphonic style, apparently influenced by the 20th-century artistic emphasis on contrasting timbres.

Equipment. The modern drum and bugle corps percussion section consists of several kinds of drums, ranging from various sizes of snare, tenor, and bass drums, to timpani that are carried. Latin instruments are sometimes added. The most common size of bass drum is the Scotch bass drum (6" x 28").

Snare drum sticks are usually in the "S" category (e.g. 1S, 2S), and drums are often dampened (especially snare and bass drums) with cloth placed under the heads, or by other means. Bass drum beaters are usually wood or hard felt.

Technique. Snare drum rolls are open as in rudimental drumming, and many of the standard drum rudiments are used in the snare drum parts. Most parts (including bass drums) are intricate and complicated — suitable for the standard marching tempo (i.e. M.M. 110). Following is a typical part written for the drum section of a drum and bugle corps:

The drum section of a drum and bugle corps accounts for approximately one-half the timbre potential of the entire group (as in the Scottish band); therefore, the drum section is treated soloistically, trading solos between snares, tenors, timpani, etc.

Military Drumming

Most of us are familiar with the sound of a drum section in a military-type band. The drum section adds rhythm and drive to the band in performance; it does not serve as a separate, solo section, as in the Scottish band and the drum and bugle corps. Therefore, the bass drums are comparatively large (often 14" x 28") and are not dampened; this allows the drum to add impetus and a rhythmic "bass" to the band.

Open rolls are used by snare drums, with little soloistic work performed by the drum section, compared to the drum and bugle corps drum section.

Fast-Step Drumming

For want of a better term, "fast-step" refers to the traditional marching band that usually marches at a fast tempo (ca. M.M. 160, 180. etc.). Many marching bands throughout the Midwest march in this style.

The drum section of a "fast-step" band serves approximately the same function as the drum section in a military-type band — it adds rhythm and drive to the band. The drum section thus serves a subordinate — although very important — function, and does not often play extended solos. Accents are of utmost importance to the drum section of a fast-step band. Uniformity, rather than contrast, is the rule — the drum section acts as a unit in playing accents, etc.; there is not the complex interplay of sounds as in the drum and bugle corps drum section.

The drums are not dampened, and bass drums are usually comparatively large (e.g. 14" x 28"); bass drum beaters are usually hard felt or lamb's wool. Open rolls are used on snare drums, but snare drum parts are comparatively simple, in contrast to the complex drumming of the Scottish band or drum and bugle corps sections. (This is not to say that the snare drum parts are any easier to perform — unison 16th notes at ♩= 200 are not at all easy to attain!) Following is an example of a typical drum part written for a fast-step band:

Bass drum and cymbals add accents — not complicated solos as in the drum and bugle corps. The purpose is to enhance the overall performance of the band — not to serve as a soloistic voice.

"How Does This Relate To Your Band?"

1) If a school song is played at

a fast tempo and the drum section sounds like an undisciplined firing line, perhaps the drummers are trying to play parts that are too complicated. The same applies to drum cadences — they should be uncomplicated if played at a fast tempo, with emphasis placed on accents, not a lot of notes.

2) If bass drums are dampened, one should be sure that the resulting sound meets his preference (e.g. working toward more complicated bass drum parts, rather than primarily accents).

These are only two considerations — there could be many more. It may be best to confine a drum section to playing in one style — or perhaps advantages might occur in combining styles (e.g. one style for street marching and another style for playing the school song, etc.). Whatever your choice, a consideration of the different drumming styles may be of assistance.

September 1972

Organize Your Marching Band Drum Section Early

F. Michael Combs

Now is the time! By following a few simple steps early this year, many of the problems which often occur throughout marching season can be minimized. The secret is to organize early.

Section Leader

Step number one should be to establish a student section leader. How this is done will depend on the maturity of the section; however, an election will probably have the best results. Students will be more likely to follow a student they have elected, rather than one who has been selected by the director.

This student section leader — or "drum captain" — can save the director many hours. Duties include:

1. Selecting, organizing, and even writing cadences and patterns
2. Calling cadences and patterns during rehearsals and performances
3. Rehearsing the section
4. Maintaining equipment (replacing heads, buying sticks, etc.)
5. Acting as a liaison between the students and director

The director should always back the decisions of the section leader, but may find it necessary to counsel him in private.

Establish Patterns

At the very first rehearsal of the full band, the drum section will have to play an interesting part that fits the music and is within the technical range of the section. If the printed drum parts work well, fine — but, too often, the printed part is too simple, too difficult, or will not sound effective outdoors. Many marching units use special arrangements that might not have any written parts for the drum section.

After reviewing the type and style of music that will be used most often during the year, an assortment of appropriate patterns should be established (see examples).

Patterns should be memorized and labeled with a number, letter, or name. During rehearsal, the director or section leader can simply tell the section to play "Pattern A," or "Pattern One," or "The Bulldog Pattern." This method of identification is far superior to singing rhythms to the section or writing out patterns for each tune.

At any time when the printed drum parts are not satisfactory, the section should have an assortment of patterns which can be used at a moment's notice. As the section develops throughout the season, or from year to year, a larger repertoire of patterns will be developed.

Establish Cadences

Drum cadences should be written or selected carefully, considering the technical range of the drum section and the style and needs of

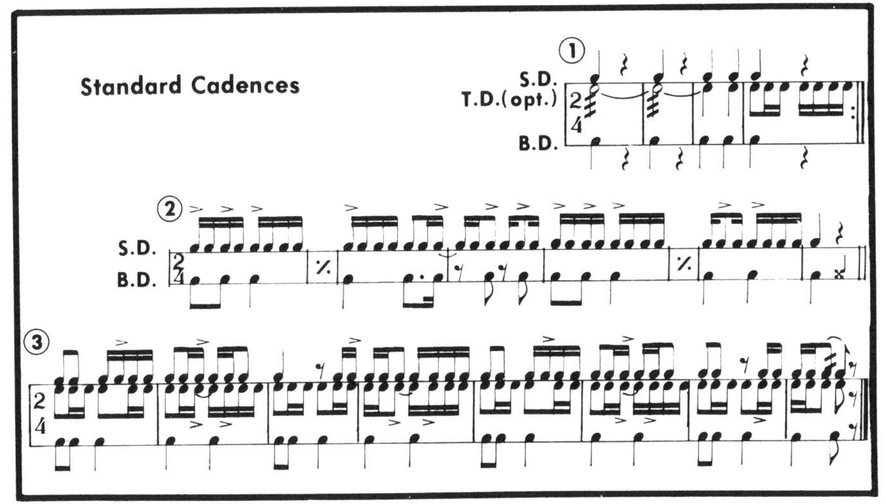

the marching unit. As with the patterns, the cadences should be memorized and named, enabling the director or drum captain to quickly and accurately signal the section as to which cadence to play.

The first cadence established should be technically and musically quite simple. Such a cadence would be most useful during rehearsals and on long parades when the band is not in a featured position (see cadence #1).

For entering the field, moving between formations, etc., a more complex cadence is necessary. A tenor drum part may be added by actually adding tenor drums to the section, or by having half of the field drum section play the tenor drum part with snares released (see cadences #2, #3).

The creation of additional cadences is limited only by the ability and creativity of the section. Although there are several published collections of cadences available on the market, I feel that directors should create a learning situation by having the students compose the cadences themselves.

Ensemble

When the band marches on the football field, many problems are present that do not exist in the band room or auditorium. Because of the spacing of the players and frequent sound lag, it becomes a problem to follow the conductor and most difficult to keep together by *listening* to each other.

But even when the section is separated in a formation, they can keep perfectly together by *visual* contact — watching the hands or feet of the bass drummer, or even the feet of the players close to him.

If two bass drums are used, they will not be able to hear each other (unless placed side by side) and will have difficulty staying together by *listening*. One bass drummer should be selected as the leader (#1), and given the major responsibility of following the conductor and keeping the beat steady. The other bass drummer (#2) should *visually* follow #1, as described earlier. In the event of a formation shift where #2 may have his back to #1, it may be necessary for #1 to follow #2 temporarily.

Conclusion

The organization that has been suggested does not have to involve many lengthy sessions of preliminary preparation. In many cases, it will be sufficient to meet with the drum section for only a few hours prior to the first band rehearsal of the season. At that time, (1) the section leader should be chosen, (2) a few patterns and cadences should be learned with corresponding numbers, letters, or names, and (3) the section should be taught how to watch each other for good ensemble playing. Although section rehearsals may be necessary throughout the season to learn new cadences and patterns and to work out special problems, early organization — in advance of the first full rehearsal — will greatly increase the efficiency of the rehearsals and allow the director to devote more of his time to the total program.

October 1972

Editing the Marching Band Percussion Part

Bill Kreutzer

Good marching band percussion music should be as simple as possible without losing the full, rich sound needed for rhythmic drive. Some published drum parts must be edited — strengthened with minor embellishments (flams, short rolls), or simplified in order to clean up messy sounding figures (ruffs, other unnecessarily intricate patterns). Even a competent drummer, marching at a tempo of 140 or more, will find it difficult to execute complicated figures on a drum head surface that is constantly swinging about. Thus, the following guide lines — for the snare drummer in particular — should help in rearranging your published parts so that *coherence* instead of *confusion* may reign in your percussion section.*

Most standard military marches contain an excessive number of afterbeats, usually written as a

* See Fred Hoey, *Let's March on the Field* (Southern Music Co.) for a more fundamental approach to the problem of steady marching performance through basic band percussion know-how. The set includes a director's manual and partbooks for the various marching percussion instruments.

single stroke (see example 1). This figure is likely to hinder precision and accuracy to a noticeable degree.

Ex. 1

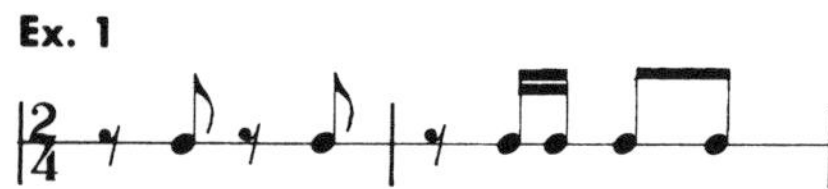

An excellent remedy for this is the use of the *flam tap*. In this figure the "gaps" on the beat are filled in by a single stroke while the more important afterbeat is emphasized by a flam (see example 2). This fig-

Ex. 2

ure eliminates the problem of counting, or feeling, the eighth-note rests of the original version. In addition, the flam tap tends to make the part much richer and more coherent.

Rolls, especially odd-numbered ones, are equally messy sounding if not executed accurately and with rhythmic precision (see example 3). Rolls are often written in the same rhythm as the melodic phrase, as in the "probable original" of example 3. I have found, however, that eliminating these figures and using a set pattern, such as that in the revised version of example 3, will serve the music equally as well and produce a more precise ensemble sound.

A good general rule on the march is to use rolls only for introductions and phrase beginnings and endings. Since drummers do not use music when marching (and rightly so), they can protect themselves by starting *all* marches with a long roll (see example 4). The clean, accented attack of the roll does far more to give the band a good solid start than the printed version of example 4, which causes the age-old problem of each drummer coming in with various accompaniments to the melodic rhythm of the introduction. This also tends to set the director's ulcer at ease — he doesn't have to wonder whether his drummers will remember the particular rhythmic pattern for the introduction to this or that march, or whether they will come in at all because they don't know which march is up. It is no wonder that experienced marching band drummers have coined the phrase, "When in doubt — *roll*."

With the advent of the rock era, the music publishing industry has dumped a vast amount of the "latest sounds" on the market. Most rock tunes lend themselves nicely to a smooth, clean rhythmic figure. Unfortunately, most arrangers leave the drum section with an unnecesarily complex, impossible-to-play-together part. Just as in the standard march, only a simple, cohesive pattern need be used in a 2, 4, 6, or 8 bar phrase pattern in order to achieve the desired sound (see example 5). The use of two bass drums can provide an even better "rock" feel for the more competent drum section. One can play straight beats to emphasize the metric pulse (using a standard lamb's wool beater), while the other

Ex. 3 (Melody)

Original

Revised

Ex. 4 (Melody)

Original

Revised

Ex. 5 (Melody)

Original

Revised

improvises on a pattern similar to the one written in example 5, using hard wooden beaters. The part could also be played on tenor drum if more readily available than a second bass drum.

Nearly everyone recognizes that the percussion section can almost make or break a good Latin American arrangement, but many directors are neglecting a vital source of sound available to them in the percussion section. With the new marching percussion equipment available, the opportunity to embellish these arrangements is virtually unlimited. Example 6 shows a simple Latin pattern with some "extra" parts which could be played by "overflow" members.

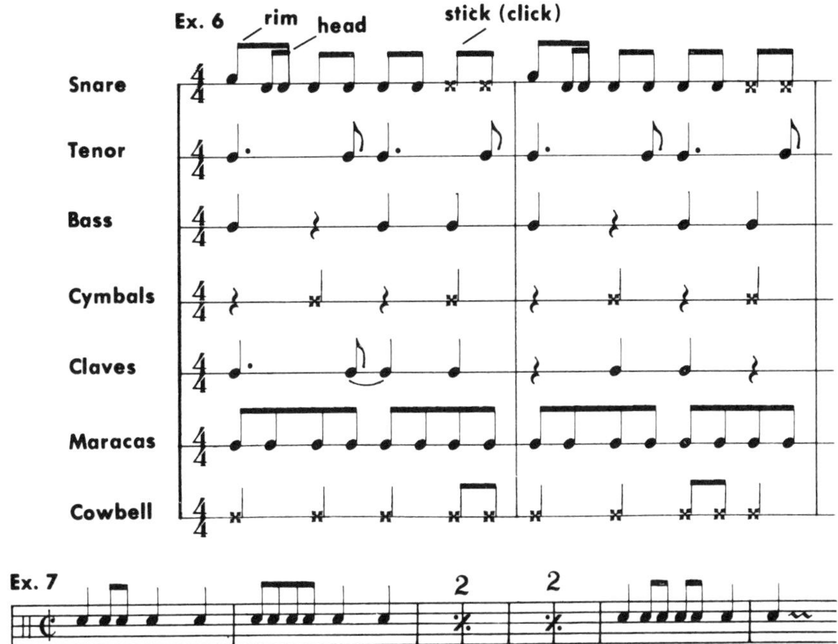

For many pop tunes, it is possible to extract a rhythmic pattern from the published part and use it repetitively, adding rolls at the beginnings of phrases and using running sixteenth-notes for phrase endings, cadence points, etc. The rhythm must enhance the melodic and harmonic rhythm of the tune. Once an effective pattern is discovered, stick to it.

November 1972

Three Way Flams

William J. Schinstine

Most drum methods describe the flam technique in only one way: starting with one hand high and the other hand low, the low hand strikes the grace note and the high hand strikes the main note. When completed, the low hand is high and the high hand is low, and this places the player in the correct position to play the next alternate flam. This can be described as a Direct Follow Through flam (see Ex. 1). It is used whenever playing alternate flams or the first flam of a flamacue.

In order to understand the other ways of playing flams, an understanding of the four basic stick movements is desirable.

1. *High to High* — Start high, strike drum, and rebound back to the high position.
2. *High to Low* — Start high, strike drum, then catch the rebound just above the drum head.
3. *Low to Low* — Start low, strike

Ex. 1 FLAMS

Direct Follow Through (D.F.T.)

This process includes two different types of strokes.

1. The low hand strikes quickly and rebounds to a high position.
2. The high hand strikes just after the low hand and the rebound is kept low.

This is called the *Direct Follow Through* flam. Each flam prepares for the next alternate flam.

Left Flam

Right Flam

the drum, and catch the rebound just above the drum head.

4. *Low to High* — Start low, strike the drum, and rebound to the high position.

The Direct Follow Through method of playing flams is totally inadequate. This becomes evident to the student when he attempts to apply it to the full range of rhythms in which it is used. For example, most professional percussionists perform consecutive flams with the same hand in order to produce a more consistent sound. To do this, the Direct Follow Through flam must be replaced by a Reverse Follow Through flam (see Ex. 2).

A third flam technique is used whenever flams are followed by fast single note(s). Using either of the previous follow-through techniques will result in an unbalanced and awkward feeling. Therefore very little follow-through should be used. This technique can be described as the No Follow Through flam (see Ex. 3). The low hand stays low (low to low) and the high hand stays low (high to low).

Acquainting students with these 3 types of flam technique helps increase their ability to perform flams in any musical situation. When flams cause problems for any drummer, it is usually because of faulty application of one of the 3 techniques.

The reader should note that these same techniques (direct follow through, reverse follow through, and no follow through) also apply to the execution of ruffs ♫. in drumming.

Art work by Robert Kingsley, Pottstown, Penna. See Schinstine-Hoey. *Basic Drum Method*. San Antonio, Texas: Southern Music Co., 1972 for additional information on various aspects of drumming.

Ex. 2 FLAMS

Reverse Follow Through (R.F.T.)

Reverse Follow Through is used when you find it necessary to repeat a flam starting with the same hand. Start with one hand high and the other low. The low hand strikes first and remains low. The high hand follows but rebounds back to the high position.

Left Flam
Reverse Follow Through

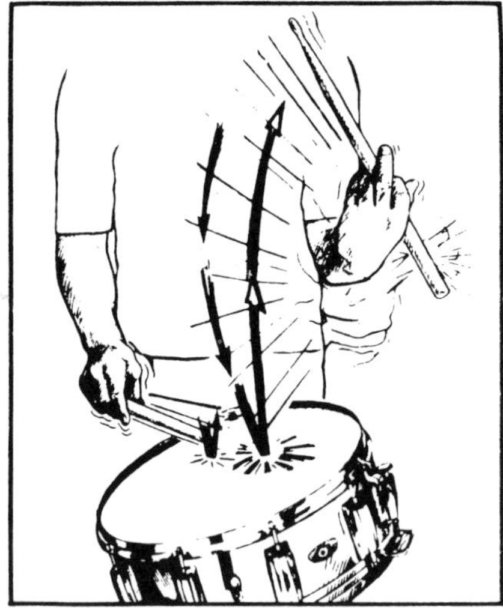

Right Flam
Reverse Follow Through

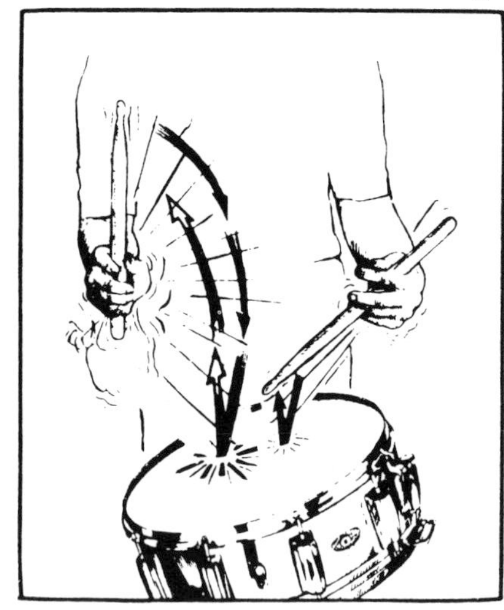

Ex. 3 FLAMS

No Follow Through (N.F.T.)

The no follow through or little follow through flams require little or no rebound.
The low hand strikes first and stays low.
The high hand follows and the rebound is kept low.

Left Flam
No Follow Through

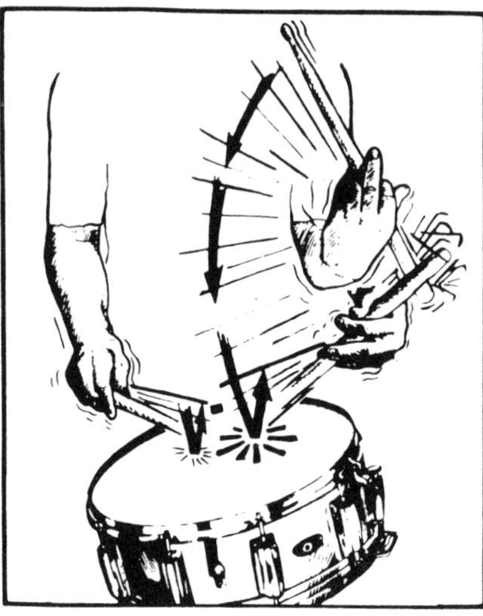

Right Flam
No Follow Through

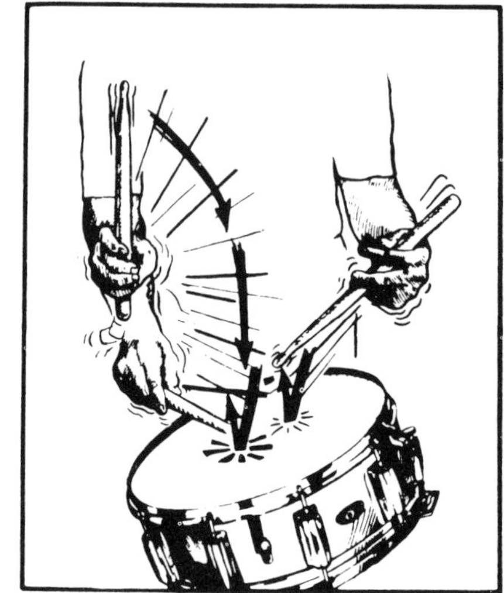

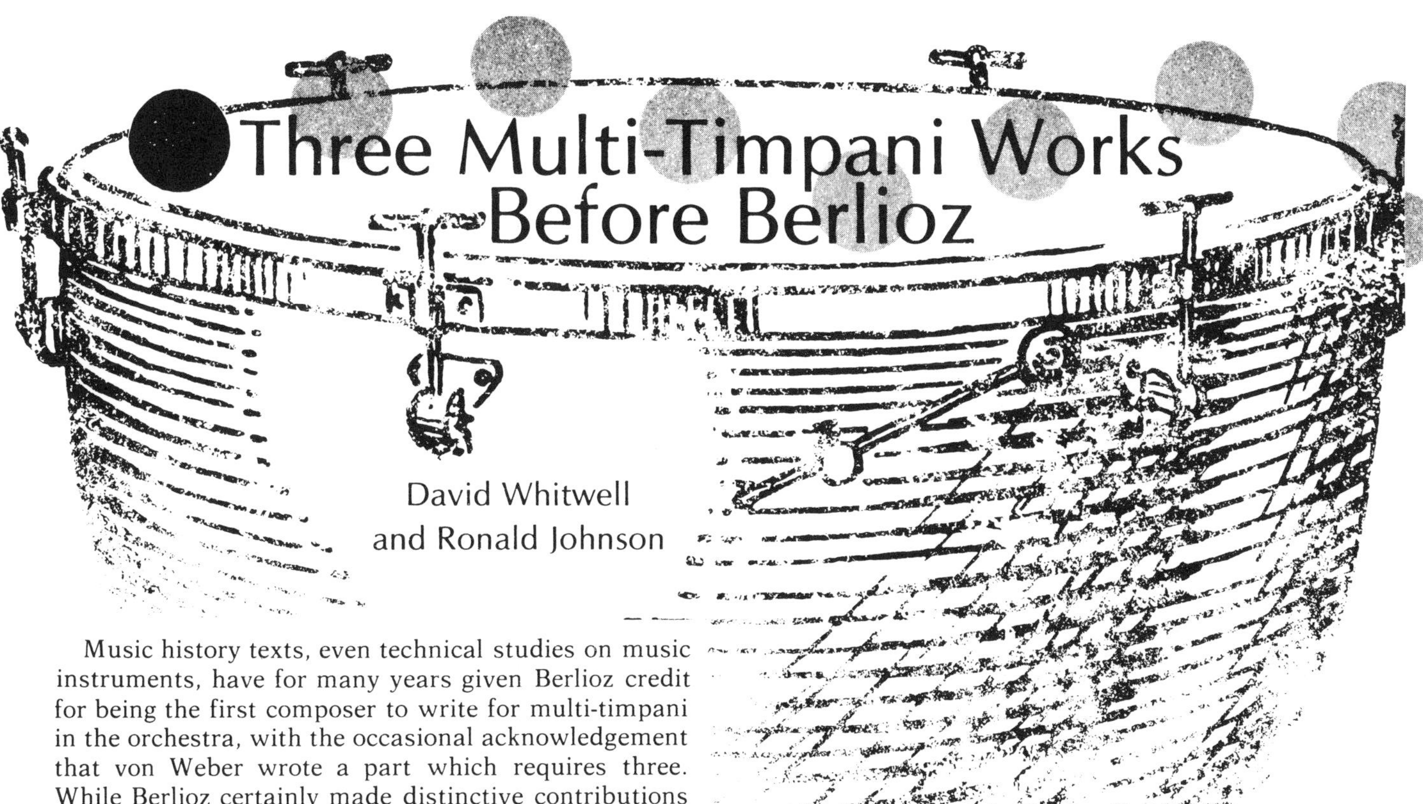

Three Multi-Timpani Works Before Berlioz

David Whitwell
and Ronald Johnson

Music history texts, even technical studies on music instruments, have for many years given Berlioz credit for being the first composer to write for multi-timpani in the orchestra, with the occasional acknowledgement that von Weber wrote a part which requires three. While Berlioz certainly made distinctive contributions in the colors and effects he drew from his multi-timpani, he does seem to have had a predecessor in Georg Druschetzky (1745-1819).

We have recently uncovered four extraordinary works for timpani and orchestra by this composer in the National Library, Budapest. First there is a *Concerto*, in two versions, for six timpani with orchestra accompaniment. We date this work between 1794 and 1806; it is probably the earliest real timpani concerto, with orchestra, yet discovered. Next is a solo *Partita* for six timpani and orchestra. Finally there is a solo work for violin and orchestra which employs seven timpani and is dated by the composer as being prepared for a festival in 1799.

The earliest reference to this Czech composer is 1760 when he was conducting a military band. He soon resigned and moved to Linz, in Austria, where he developed a reputation as a good timpani player. He entered the service of Count Grassalkovitch about 1787, staying until the Count's death in 1794. Sporadic dates on his manuscripts reveal that by the turn of the century he was in Budapest where he gradually rose to the important position of Director of Music to the Archduke, Elector of Hungary, Josef Anton Johan. This would have made him the most influential musician in this, one of the three great cities of the Austro-Hungarian Empire. He composed in all forms from opera down to the necessary military marches. He seems to have had a wide reputation as a composer of wind music, particularly *Harmoniemusik*. We find the following reference to Druschetzky in the famous *Encyclopedia* (1790), by Gerber:

> **Druschektz,** George . . . has for the past 10 years composed a great number of excellent Partien for wind instruments, namely 2 oboes, 2 clarinets, 2 horns, and 2 bassoons. These are not only for the whole Kaiserly army, but have received merit and invigorated all Germany. He has composed many concerti, especially for oboe and other wind instruments, but also for violin, although all are only in manuscript. But all prove his good taste and his fertile talent in composition. It is said that he has gone to Linz as a timpanist. But he should distinguish himself also in this art.

A survey of Druschetzky's extant wind music includes two large collections, 24 partitas for sextet and 17 partitas for 2 oboes, English horn, basset horn, and bassoon, as well as many fine octets both for the concert hall and for the military. In addition there is a very interesting group of original works for SATB soli accompanied by octet, on texts of Schiller. Finally there is a very curious *Partita*, a comic partita, for octet during the course of which the members put down their instruments and take up various toy instruments. By the end of the work all eight players are playing toys!

In general, these solo timpani works of Druschetzky far surpass the usual technical requirements of the late-Haydn and early-Beethoven period. Beethoven, in particular, is often given much credit for such things as the simultaneous playing of two timpani in the *Ninth Symphony* and for his use of the roll or tremolo. Such technical devices lose all significance when compared to Druschetzky's far more musical employment of the same ideas.

Even though there are six instruments, in the two solo works, ranging diatonically from low G to E, it is evident by the set-up diagram, found on the cover of the *Partita* in Druschetzky's own hand, that the timpani were still thought of in pairs. They are arranged from left to right: E, B, D, A, C, G. Inasmuch as the solo part contains many running diatonic passages, even a non-timpanist can visualize the difficulty resultant in this distribution of the instruments.

It is interesting to find Druschetzky's own sticking on the manuscript solo parts, the right hand notated above the staff and the left below in a tradition still observed in Europe.

The final general note is that while the timpani was thought of as a transposing instrument during this period, and is so used in Druschetzky's other compositions, here in the works for solo timpani exact pitches are of necessity used.

For the concerto both the score and an early set of parts exist in Budapest. As mentioned above there also exists an abbreviated version of the first movement, apparently intended as an optional possibility complete in itself. A later hand has added a cimbalom to the solo part, making this the earliest known concerto for multi-instrument percussion — although Druschetzky's intention was clearly for timpani alone.

The concerto is in the normal three movement form, fast-slow-fast. The final movement ("Allegro") is a theme and variations form presenting an obvious showcase for the soloist. We know the percussionists will be curious to have at least a glimpse of the solo material:

Another point of considerable interest with regard to the concerto is the opportunity for a cadenza in the first movement. Altogether we have three different cadenzas among the material in Budapest, no doubt the original work of three different players. Taken together they offer an exceptional perspective of the player of this day. They employ a considerable dynamic range, a wide variety of articulation marks, and two end with a double trill!

The *Partita* is in a four movement form, consisting of an Allegro, Minuet and Trio, Adagio, and Rondo. The order of movement comes not from the symphony form, but from the divertimento form of the previous generation. Again it is a solo work for six timpani and in general requires a higher level of technique than the *Concerto*. In addition it is more expressive, especially in the slow movement which explores a much wider range of dynamic markings in the solo voice. On the whole it seems more musical than the *Concerto*.

The remaining work, *Ungaria*, is for solo violin and orchestra. The timpani part requires seven instruments (now the high F is added) and has solo and tutti passages of considerable difficulty. *Ungaria* is a one-movement work, existing in the autograph score dated May 26, 1799.

For the modern player these works do not present any special problems, providing one sets up the instruments after the custom today and not in the manner Druschetzky practiced. This is not, however, to deny the extraordinary contribution these works represent for the literature. In addition, for the historian these works demand a new consideration of the state of the percussive art before Berlioz.

December 1972

Selecting a Snare Drum Method Book

F. Michael Combs

One task most instrumental teachers must face is the selection of a beginning snare drum method book.

It wasn't too long ago that only one or two snare drum method books dominated the field; but today it is a completely different story. The band director who has one "tried and true" method book (the one he may have used himself as a student) might be surprised to find out that now there are dozens of books from which to select.

It is easy for a teacher to continue using the book he has memorized — one which he may think contains all the answers; but it is the responsibility of every educator to take time periodically to re-examine his choice of method books in relation to the materials currently available.

The following five considerations are suggested as a basis for examining a beginning snare drum method book.

Objectives

Before selecting a book, it is essential that the teacher carefully examine his objectives. Is the student being prepared for the marching band? Is he being groomed for the stage band? Is the orchestra the ensemble for which he is being trained? Or is your objective to educate a versatile percussionist who is capable of meeting every challenge from any style?

One snare drum method book may possibly prepare a student to do nothing more than play in the marching band or perform rudimental snare drum solos. Does that book follow your objectives? Another book may avoid rudimental technique but stress rock and jazz beats. How does that book underline the goals you have set for your students?

Price

Is the cost of the book completely justifiable, or is a similar publication available at a lower price? If you, as a teacher, do not ask this question, you can count on it being asked by parents. Compare the cost of the book you now use with others of similar size, style, and number of pages. It will not take long to notice quite a range in prices.

Physical Characteristics

Is the music legible? Are illustrations clear and accurate? Is the paper of adequate weight? Is the binding sufficient? No matter how valuable the content of the book may be, it is useless as a method if pages begin to fall out after only a few weeks of use. I have found that some method books contain vague or misleading illustrations, as well as numerous printing errors.

Interest

A successful method book should contain pictures, solos, duets, tests, accompanying recordings, or the like to sustain the student's interest. An 8-measure phrase entitled "Solo Number 1" is much more interesting to a youngster than a line of music labelled "1" or "A."

Pace

Technical skills and fundamentals should be introduced simultaneously in a logical order. Would a method book that introduces rudiments in rapid fire order or all note values in a few pages be suitable for most young beginning students? It makes more sense for a book to begin with the elementary techniques or basic skills and build one level at a time. Exercises should be numerous, containing the new skills or techniques combined with previously introduced material.

Ideally, the balance between the introduction of new concepts and the reinforcement of old material should set a pace which will neither confuse nor bore the average student.

Conclusion

Price, physical characteristics, pace, and interest are all important considerations in selecting a beginning snare drum method book. The most important, however, is whether the book underlines carefully and realistically the objectives established by the teacher.

Having found a book which seems to satisfy the established criteria, the successful teacher must continue to re-evaluate his objectives in the light of the changing world of percussion; and, he must be prepared to someday abandon the book he has spent so much time selecting in favor of one which then proves to be superior.

January 1973

Survey of Percussion Specialists

F. Michael Combs

The growing popularity of percussion instruments and the ever-increasing challenges and opportunities for players have resulted in the development of a large number of skilled percussion players in the public schools — and many of these students are considering a career in some area of the percussion field. A recent survey has provided information which could be useful to seniors interested in advanced percussion study.

The Survey

Questionnaires concerning salary, degrees, and other information important to the professional percussionist were sent to all members of the Percussive Arts Society. Over 600 were returned, but those completed by full-time students, graduate assistants, or non-percussionists were eliminated from the final tabulation. The occupations of those counted fell into 3 main areas: college teachers, professional performers and public school teachers. Since all are PAS members, it is assumed that they are all percussion specialists.

College Teachers

Of the 87 college teachers who returned questionnaires, only 11 indicated holding a doctorate, but 26 felt that this degree is necessary in order to be successful in their profession. It is also interesting to note that 32 are currently working toward an advanced degree (26 toward a doctorate and 6 toward a masters). The majority (all except 9) have at least a masters degree and 1 has an artists diploma.

Of those who reported, 14 have an annual salary of over $18,000 and only 5 make less than $7,000 — the average salary being between $7,000 and $12,000. Although well over half (48) of those included in the sample felt that they were not receiving an adequate remuneration, only 8 failed to recommend that a young person enter the field.

In addition to the 87 full-time college teachers, 17 others reported that their occupation was evenly divided between college teaching and professional playing. Only one of the 17 did not recommend that young people pursue this occupation, and one other indicated he would rather be in another field. The degrees in this category included 10 masters and 5 bachelors; 3 are without degrees and 1 has a certificate.

Professional Performers

Professional performers returned 167 questionnaires. Degrees included 60 bachelors, 34 masters, 2 doctorates, 13 "others," and 37 with no degree. Those presently working on a degree numbered 41. The average salary is about $13,500. A majority of the group strongly recommended that young students begin their study at a music conservatory.

Others reported their occupation to be equally divided between professional performance and another occupation (10 in public school teaching and 9 in other work). Of this group, 5 have no degree, 10 hold the bachelors, and 3 have earned a masters.

Public School Teachers

The largest group responding to the questionnaires reported their primary occupation to be public school teaching. Out of 215 reporting, 104 have at least a masters degree; 74 are working toward a degree; and only 5 felt that no degree is necessary for success in their occupation. Although there were 4 who made no response to the question, none reported having less than a bachelors degree. Six indicated an income exceeding $18,000; with 7 earning less than $7,000, leaving the majority (103) of public school teachers in the $7,000-$12,000 bracket.

Almost half of the sample recommended a small college or university as the place for a young person to begin his study, while the others recommended a large college or university. Only 14 endorsed a music conservatory and 46 suggested other means.

A sense of satisfaction seems to be evidenced by the 151 public school teachers who stated that they would not want to be in any other occupation and by the 211 (all but 4) who recommended that a young person pursue the occupation of public school teaching.

Other Occupations

A diverse number of occupations ranging from music store owner to railroad clerk was given on 66 questionnaires. Very little correlation seems to exist between salary and degree. Of the 16 with no degree, 4 reported a salary of over $18,000. Seven with a bachelors degree are making over $15,000; but 7 with masters degrees or higher are making less than $12,000.

Relationship of Salary to Occupation and Degree

Although satisfaction in an occupation cannot be determined by salary alone, a study of the relationship of salary to occupation and degree may be helpful to young students surveying the field (see chart).

Relationship of Salary to Occupation and Degree	over $18,000	$15,000-$18,000	$12,000-$14,999	$7,000-$11,999	under $7,000
Occupation					
College Teacher (86)	14	11	21	35	5
Professional Performer (167)	36	19	16	49	47
Public School Teacher (213)	7	27	70	103	6
Other (often a combination of categories) (97)	19	9	9	33	27
Degree					
Bachelor (213)	15	13	29	109	47
Master (191)	30	37	61	50	13
Doctor (17)	9	1	5	2	
Other (18)	4	2	2	6	4
None (55)	9	7	8	9	22

This article is based on a research project sponsored by the University of Tennessee Bureau of Educational Research and Service. A complete report of the tabulation of the project may be obtained from the author at the Department of Music, University of Tennessee, Knoxville 37916.

February 1973

The Evolution of Early Jazz Drumming

Theodore D. Brown

At the beginning of the twentieth century, early jazz flourished in the dance halls and cabarets of the Storyville district in New Orleans. Jazz moved off the streets and the funeral parades into a more comfortable position in the night life of the Crescent City. Musicians too made the transition. They brought their instruments, usually left-overs from the military bands of the Civil War, into the night clubs to play from 8 p.m. to 4 a.m. for wages of $1.50 to $2.00 plus tips.[1] The music they played consisted mainly of dance steps which included mazurkas, waltzes, polkas, schottisches, and the quadrille, a medley of popular tunes played in 2/4 or 6/8 meter. Later these dances were replaced by the two-step, slow-drag, ragtime one-step, and the fox trot. The instrumentation of the early jazz band varied, but included several melodic instruments plus a banjo, piano, and drums for the rhythm section. The drummer's main purpose was to supply the rhythmic foundation for the various dance steps. When the time came to play an improvised blues songs, the drummer played a concoction of military beats plus his own rhythmic inventions.

The interweaving melodic line improvised by the other instruments presented a problem to the rigid, strict playing style of the military oriented drummer. He could no longer serve as the metronome within the group; instead he had to bend his rhythmic patterns to fit the rhythm and melody of the song. It became the drummer's duty to supplement the ensemble textures and accent the speech-like cadences played by the other instruments. This was quite a task for the drummer whose only techniques consisted of an assortment of rolls, flams, ruffs and other military rudiments.

As the drummer was called upon to provide support for the changing texture of the jazz ensemble, he began to experiment with different percussive sounds, paving the way for the subsequent growth of the drum set to include a wide variety of whackable accessories. Drummers began to use woodblocks, cowbells, Chinese tom-toms, gongs, cymbals, triangles, anvils, castanets, Chinese temple blocks, and similar exotic paraphernalia.

In order to break the monotony of his playing, the early jazz drummer used contrasting rhythmic figures for different musical strains. Warren "Baby" Dodds, probably the most influential of all the New Orleans drummers, illustrates this technique in "Manhattan Stomp" recorded with pianist Don Elwell in 1946. On this recording, Dodds plays the following roll pattern for the first chorus:

Since this is a moderately fast tempo blues, Dodds used five stroke rolls. For the second chorus, Dodds used this pattern:

This figure was commonly played by early jazz drummers and is the exact reverse of the ride cymbal beat used by all modern jazz drummers today:

We might not be able to attribute the evolution of this figure to Baby Dodds but we can say that he was a key figure in the process.

Early jazz drummers served a melodic as well as rhythmic function. As the ensemble played the melody, the drummer tried to tie the phrases together and fill in the gaps left by the other instruments. This was often done by rolling at the end of one phrase into the beginning of the next.

It is obvious that the roll was the basis for the technique of the early jazz drummer. With it, he was able to create a wide variety of nuances to fit the music he played. For example, the five-stroke roll was used for fast tempos, the seven-stroke roll for medium tempos, and for slow blues, the nine-stroke roll. Often a variety of rolls would be used within the same number, using perhaps a series of five-stroke rolls for the first chorus and switching to nine-stroke rolls for the second chorus.

Unfortunately the playing technique of the early jazz drummers is not well documented on records. The early recording sessions prohibited the use of either the snare drum or the bass drum, because it was feared that these loud instruments would drown out the melodic instruments. Consequently, most of the playing of which there is evidence, was done on the snare drum rims, bass drum shells and woodblocks. On the recordings made during the 1920's, most of the drumming is covered up by either the piano or banjo.

The early jazz drummer often did not play solos, since his main function was to provide rhythmic support for the ensemble. When he did play a solo, it sounded more like the drum part to "Stars and Stripes Forever" than improvised rhythmic expression. Baby Dodds illustrates this solo technique during his solo "Rudiments with Drumstick Nervebeats." (This recording was made in 1951 by Folkways Records and Service Company in an attempt to provide information about the early jazz styles.) The solo begins with a two bar introduction followed by a street-beat-like cadence played on the snare drum. The following example shows the eight measure rhythmic scheme which is the primary pattern of the solo.

The "nervebeat" section of the solo occurs twice, both times at the end of the eight bar theme. "Nervebeats" were played by holding both drum sticks loosely in one hand and making them rattle by tightening the forearm muscles and shaking the sticks violently.[2]

Another solo style is demonstrated by Dodds on "Spooky Drums I." The rhythmic foundation for this solo consists of two patterns: and Dodds repeats these patterns over and over in various sequences using the different tonal sounds of his drum set. The following illustration shows the wide variety of sounds available to the early jazz drummer.

1 cymbal
2 snare drum rim
3 cowbell
4 woodblock
5 bass drum rim

Equally as important as the evolution of playing styles was the development of the drummers' equipment.

Originally, two drummers were used in the early jazz bands, a snare drummer and bass drummer. This was a direct carry-over from the funeral parade bands which influenced the beginnings of jazz. Credit is given "Dee-Dee" Chandler for the invention of the bass drum pedal around 1894-95 which enabled one drummer to play both instruments.[3]

As was true of most instruments used in the early jazz bands of the 1900's, the drums were descendants from the post Civil War military bands. Bass drums came in an assortment of sizes, but the most popular drum was 28 inches in diameter. The snare drum used during this period was very good even by today's standards. This was an all metal drum with double tension rods which enabled the player to tune each head separately. However, this type of snare drum was often quite large, sometimes exceeding six inches in depth.

When the role of the drummer changed within the jazz group, he began to experiment with new sounds and ideas. He borrowed cymbals from his classical counterpart in the orchestra and hung them on his crude drum set. Drummers would use these cymbals to reinforce the melodic accents in the melody as well as for novelty effects. Two types of cymbals were used: Zildjian cymbals from Turkey and Chinese cymbals. Both were made of thick metal and were very heavy. The chinese cymbal had turned-up edges with a one inch raised cup in the middle. Very often rivets were placed on the cymbal much like the "sizzle" cymbal of today.

One of the most important parts of the drummers' equipment was the woodblock. They came in various shapes and sizes and were primarily used for rhythmic accompaniment during soft melodic passages played by the piano. Drummers often used more than one woodblock with their drum set.

Cowbells served more of a melodic function than rhythmic. Dodds, for instance, used four tuned cowbells to play melodic solos.

With the addition of the tom-tom, drummers came closer to realizing their melodic potential. Often drummers would tune their tom-toms to specific intervals such as fourths and fifths. The most popular tom-tom used during this period was the "Chee-foo" tom-tom. It ranged in size from very large, which were placed on timpani stands, to a smaller type, which could be attached to the bass drum. The heads of these tom-toms were made of tough pig-skin. Strung through the middle of the smaller drums were several wires which gave this drum a characteristic buzz when struck. Like the bass drums used at this time, tom-toms had pictures painted on the drum head.

Generally speaking, most of the equipment used by the early jazz drummers was used for novelty effects rather than for percussive sound. Tom-toms could be found in a variety of sizes and were hung around the drum set in the most convenient places. The chee-foo drum was often placed in a stand similar to those used to hold gongs today. The head of the drum was horizontal, thus enabling the drummer to play the tom-tom like a marching bass drum. These stands were placed high behind the drummer either to the right or left and, when the drummer wanted to play this drum, he swung his arm over his shoulder, striking the tom-tom with his stick. This must have looked quite flashy; however, complex rhythmic patterns would be almost impossible to play.[4]

The playing style of the early jazz drummer has been highly influential in the progress of jazz drumming to this day. Very few of our modern drummers have not been affected by the legacy of our early jazz musicians.

1. Samuel B. Charters, *Jazz; New Orleans 1885-1963* (New York: Oak Publications, 1963), p. 18.
2. Bruce King, "The Gigantic Baby Dodds," *The Jazz Review*, Volume 3, Number 7 (August, 1960), p. 14.
3. Charters, p. 6.
4. James Salmon, from an interview November 21, 1966.

March 1973

Percussionists and the Contest/Festival

F. Michael Combs

Many percussion experts have raised serious questions about the treatment of percussionists in the contests/festivals of many states. For example, there is no justification for requiring a snare drum soloist to play with the drum suspended from a marching shoulder sling. If the position of the drum is detrimental to the performance, the adjudicator may want to adjust the rating; but the method of holding or suspending the drum should be a minor factor in evaluating the performance. Also, snare drum rudiments are of value only if the student is able to apply them in the music; there is no need for them to be performed out of context for the adjudicator.

Although there are two basic grips, matched and traditional, it is not necessary to set up rigid requirements and exacting specifications on how to hold the sticks. Also, published sticking indications should be taken as suggestions — not as mandatory rules for playing the solo. However, stick selection is an important consideration and should be criticized with regard to (1) size of player's hands, (2) type and size of the instrument, and (3) style of composition.

The main criteria for the evaluation of a snare drum solo is sound; all other considerations are secondary. When the sound is inferior, it should be the responsibility of the adjudicator to suggest ways to improve.

Contest/Festival problems are numerous for percussionists. As an aid to those who desire improvements, I offer the following brief comments.

Timpani

The timpanist's ability to tune without the use of gauges or other mechanical devices and the capability to produce a fine tone are the most important qualities to be judged. Type of mallet or grip (French, German, or variation), sticking, or striking area are all secondary.

Keyboard Mallet Instruments

The tremendous increase in the use of keyboard mallet instruments by composers should warrant a serious interest in this medium by educators. Both contestant and adjudicator should have a complete understanding of the physical characteristics of the three basic solo instruments — marimba, vibraphone, and xylophone. (Solo literature for orchestra bells is very limited and, for chimes, almost non-existent.)

Special skills to be evaluated are pedal technique (for vibraphone), tone production (bar striking area), mallet selection, grips, and rolls.

The performance of arrangements, transcriptions, or adaptations of literature from other media is considered acceptable practice by most authorities and should not be discouraged at the music contest.

Multiple Percussion

Performing on more than one percussion instrument during a single contest appearance creates unique problems for the student (or judge) who has had most of his training and experience with reading one rhythmic line and playing one instrument. The major concern is simply playing the proper instrument at the proper time! Other problems involve extraneous noise, instrument arrangement, continuity of line, timbre, body movement, and accuracy.

Percussion Ensemble

The percussion ensemble runs the gamut from a snare drum duet to works with hundreds of instruments and dozens of players; but most of the standard literature at the high school level usually involves no more than a dozen players and only the basic instruments found in the percussion section of a band or orchestra. Even so, it is only with an accurate knowledge of the standards of all the percussion instruments that an adjudicator can effectively contribute to the musical growth of a young percussion contestant.

Sight-reading

Too often, music contest participants spend many hours perfecting one solo and are evaluated on their ability to perform only that one piece — not necessarily on their ability to play the instrument. Required sight-reading will help to identify the student who has truly mastered the basic skills of the instrument.

Versatility

Whenever possible, the contestant should display his ability to perform on as many percussion instruments as possible. The following requirements are now in use by some state organizations and are being considered for adoption by others:

1. *Proficiency Examination.* Contestants take a proficiency examination, for their particular grade level, which covers the techniques of all standard percussion instruments.
2. *Scales.* All solo contestants must perform one or more prescribed scales on a keyboard mallet instrument.
3. *Sight-reading.* Each contestant must sight-read a short passage on snare drum, timpani, marimba, triangle, bass drum, and cymbals.
4. *Multiple Entries.* A contestant is permitted (or required) to play a solo on two major percussion instruments.

Conclusion

The following suggestions are based on information provided by 34 state music festivals or contests.

1. Festival manuals and rule books should be complete and clear in regard to what is expected of the percussion contestant.
2. Contests should be structured by educators who are knowledgeable in the area of percussion instruments and who will encourage study of several percussion instruments and styles.
3. Contest officials should select an experienced adjudicator who has specialized training in percussion.
4. The objectives of the music festival should be stated clearly, and the rating system should be made clear to both the performer and the adjudicator.
5. The rating forms used for percussion solos and ensembles should be in keeping with the purposes of the festival.

April 1973

The Set Drummer

Advice from the Pros

F. Michael Combs

Ed Shaughnessy, Al Dawson, Roy Burns, and Bobby Rosengarden are all successful professional musicians whose instrument is the drum set ("trap set," "dance drums"). Each man has vast knowledge and experience in this field (Burns, for example, is the author of a dozen or so books on the subject). While the questions asked and the answers given represent only a very small percentage of their expertise, readers should find considerable food for thought in their comments.

Ed Shaughnessy is the drummer for the NBC Johnny Carson Tonight Show. He has wide experience in the big-time entertainment field and presents educational percussion clinics.

Combs: At what age should a young student begin playing the trap set?
Shaughnessy: The earlier the better. Students around 12 years of age seem physically able to play the pedals, etc. with good facility — when younger it is possible but a bit more difficult.
Combs: Should a young student begin his training with a complete drum set or build as he progresses?
Shaughnessy: It is *imperative* for future drum set players to start in with *at least* the bass drum and hi-hat, together with snare drum — so as to get good early coordination between hands and feet. In today's music, this is more urgent than ever since the feet are busier.

Al Dawson, drummer with Dave Brubeck, is an instructor at the Berklee School of Music.

Combs: Should a student whose primary interest is in playing drum set also learn to play keyboard mallets, timpani, and other percussion instruments?
Dawson: I think all the percussion instruments are helpful in developing an approach to the drum set, and the mallet instruments are particularly helpful in developing a much needed melody sense. The degree of importance would vary depending on the field the student is entering. However, I would definitely schedule the other instruments in such a way as to afford sufficient time on the drum set (2 hours per day on set).
Combs: How important is technique as compared to other profes-

sional requirements (such as knowledge of tunes and styles, flexibility, etc.)?

Dawson: Technique is very important simply because it is a means to an end. A person should develop his ability to execute, so that he can forget about it when he plays and concentrate on the music, form, etc. If the drummer has practiced enough, the technique will make itself adapt automatically. Incidentally, I have heard students say "Elvin Jones has technique," or "Roy Hanes has technique." I feel that these players have more than adequate technique to execute within their field and style. Let's face it! There's a different technique required for playing fast tempos for 45 minutes than for playing Ravel's *Bolero.*

Roy Burns has played drums with nearly everyone in the business — Benny Goodman, Charlie Mingus, NBC Orchestra, etc. — fulfilling their diverse professional requirements. He is presently Staff Artist for Rogers Drums.

Combs: How important is it for a trap set student to use methods or exercise books?

Burns: Depending on the books, it is vital, especially for younger students; but every student needs good reading material for the set. A book to be used in combination with a recording allows students to practice with pros . . . and this is extremely valuable.

Combs: What sort of practice routine should a student develop (i.e., time, frequency, etc.)?

Burns: 20 minute warm-up — playing around the set; 1 hour working on the lesson for that week; 1 hour playing with records with earphones. (Hour sessions could be 45 minutes.) With whatever time is left, the student should practice improvising, work on solos, and experiment.

Bobby Rosengarden, a drummer with many years of experience on the road and in the studio, is music director for the Dick Cavett TV show.

Combs: Is it essential that a trap set player be able to read music?

Rosengarden: There are two answers to that question. The first is short — *Yes*!! The second answer is a little longer. There are drummers and there are musicians who play the drums. Both require talent but the second of the two also requires a great deal of work. The rewards — both musical and financial — are commensurate with the amount of work devoted to it. As in any field where physical technique is required, coordination is most essential. Not only are muscles involved but also total mental attention is important. Learning to read music while learning the basic rudiments of drumming are so much a part of each other, it is impossible to consider yourself a musician if you cannot read music. I can hear a few comments being made already, i.e., "What about Buddy Rich?" or "How about blind musicians?" or "What's wrong with Erroll Garner?" Without going into too many details, I think it is sufficient to say if Buddy Rich (a good friend of mine) could read music, it wouldn't do anything but *help* his total musicianship — and I know he would be the first to admit it. I don't know of any exceptions to the rule nor have I ever heard of any. Every professional player I have ever worked with in forty years of experience agrees.

Combs: How important is a college degree(s) in getting a job as a professional performer?

Rosengarden: This question also requires two answers. The first answer is a qualified "not very." The real or second answer for now, is not as simple. In years gone by there was a tremendous amount of work available "on the road" under all kinds of maturing conditions. Unfortunately for the young player and arranger of today, the only place to get this kind of *most important* experience is in colleges and universities.

In the final analysis only one thing is important to a musician. The time or moment of truth comes when someone in charge says "Shut up and play!"

You had better be ready! You may not get a second chance.

May 1973

A Guide to Foreign Percussion Terms

Tennessee Chapter of the Percussive Arts Society

Today's percussionists come in contact with a great deal of specialized terminology. The situation is complicated by the fact that they are about as likely to see these words in French (F), Italian (I), or German (G) as in English. Since many of the terms cannot be found in most music dictionaries, this brief (but representative) list has been compiled.

Amboss (G) *Anvil*
Am Rand (G) *At the edge*
Antiken Zimbeln (G) *Antique cymbals*
Au bord (F) *At the edge*
Avec timbres (F) *With snares*
Bachette (I) *Sticks*
Bachette di feltro (I) *Felt sticks*
Bachette di legno (I) *Wood sticks*
Bachette di spugna (I) *Sponge sticks*
Baguettes (F) *Sticks*
Baguettes de bois (F) *Wood sticks*
Baguettes d'eponge (F) *Sponge sticks*
Baguettes douce (F) *Soft sticks*
Becken (G) *Cymbal*
Becken Tamburin (G) *Tambourine*
Besen (G) *Brush*
Bloc de bois (F) *Wood block*
Bloc de metal (F) *Metal block*
Blocs a papier de verre (F) *Sandpaper blocks*
Blocs chinois (F) *Chinese blocks*
Bois (F) *Wood*
Bolte a clous (F) *Maracas*
Brosse (F) *Brush*
Bubboli (I) *Jingles*
Caisse claire (F) *Snare drum*
Caisse roulante (F) *Tenor drum*
Campane (I) *Chimes*
Campanelli (I) *Bells*

Campanello di vacca (I) *Cow bell*
Casse di legno (I) *Wood blocks*
Casse di metallo (I) *Metal blocks*
Castagnetta (I) *Castanets*
Castagnettes (F) *Castanets*
Catene (I) *Chains*
Ceppi cinesi (I) *Chinese blocks*
Ceppi di carta vetra (I) *Sandpaper blocks*
Chinesischen Blöcke (G) *Chinese blocks*
Cinelli (I) *Cymbals*
Cloches (F) *Orchestra bells*
Cloches tubulaires (F) *Chimes*
Con corde (I) *With snares*
Crecelle (F) *Ratchet*
Crotales (F) *Antique cymbals*
Crotalo (I) *Antique cymbal*
Cymbales (F) *Cymbals*
Cymbales antiques (F) *Antique cymbals*
Drahtbürste (G) *Brush*
Enclume (F) *Anvil*
Filzschlägel (G) *Felt stick*
Fouet (F) *Slapstick*
Frusta (I) *Slapstick*
Glocken (G) *Chimes*
Glockenspiel (G) *Orchestra bells*
Gran cassa (I) *Bass drum*
Grelots (F) *Sleigh bells*
Grelots de vaches (F) *Cow bells*
Grosse caisse (F) *Bass drum*
Handratsche (G) *Ratchet*
Heerdenglocken (G) *Cow bells*
Holz (G) *Wood*
Holzharmonika (G) *Xylophone*
Incudine (I) *Anvil*
Jeu de timbres (F) *Bells*
Kastagnetten (G) *Castanets*
Ketten (G) *Chains*
Kleine Trommel (G) *Snare drum*
Krotalen (G) *Antique cymbals*
Kuhglocken (G) *Cow bells*
Löwengebrüll (G) *String drum*
Macchina a venti (I) *Wind machine*
Macchina di tuono (I) *Thunder sheet*
Machine a vent (F) *Wind machine*
Machine de tonnerre(F) *Thunder sheet*
Mailloches (F) *Drum stick*
Marache (I) *Maracas*
Metallkasten (G) *Metal block*
Militär-Trommel (G) *Field drum*
Mit Schnarren (G) *With snares*
Mugghio di leone (I) *String drum*
Ohne Schnarren (G) *Without snares*
Pauken (G) *Timpani*
Peitsche (G) *Slapstick*
Percussione (I) *Percussion*
Piatti (I) *Cymbals*
Raganella (I) *Ratchet*
Râpe (F) *Gourd*
Raspa (I) *Gourd*
Raspel (G) *Gourd*
Ratsche (G) *Ratchet*
Ruhrtrommel (G) *Tenor drum*
Ruten (G) *Brushes*
Sans timbres (F) *Without snares*
Schellen (G) *Sleighbells, Jingles*
Schellentrommel (G) *Tambourine*
Schlägel (G) *Sticks*
Schlagzeug (G) *Percussion*
Senza corde (I) *Without snares*
Silofono (I) *Xylophone*
Sirena (I) *Siren*
Sirene (G) *Siren*
Sirène (F) *Siren*
Sonagli (I) *Sleighbells*
Strohfidel (G) *Xylophone*
Sul bordo (I) *At the edge*
Tambour de basque (F) *Tambourine*
Tambourin provençal (F) *Tenor drum*
Tambour-militaire (F) *Field drum*
Tamburello (I) *Tenor drum*
Tamburin (G) *Tambourine*
Tamburo basco (I) *Tambourine*
Tamburo grande (I) *Bass drum*
Tamburo militare (I) *Field drum*
Tamburo piccolo (I) *Snare drum*
Tamburo rullante (I) *Tenor drum*
Timbale (F) *Timpani*
Timbres (F) *Jingles*
Triangolo (I) *Triangle*
Verges (F) *Switches*
Verghe (I) *Brushes*
Vibrafono (I) *Vibraphone*
Vibraphon (G) *Vibraphone*
Vibraphone (F) *Vibraphone*
Wirbeltrommel (G) *Tenor drum*

June 1973

How to Apply Drum Rudiments to $\frac{6}{8}$ Meter

Haskell Harr

Since my retirement, I have had the opportunity to visit many drum solo contests and have been very surprised at the number of soloists who have selected march-type solos in 6/8 time, but are totally unprepared to play them. Actually, a very simple method of playing this rhythm may be worked out by changing a few drum rudiments from 2/4 to 6/8 meter.

When played at march tempo (at least 120 counts per minute), 6/8 time is a two count meter, with three eighth notes per beat. The sticking of the rudimental *Flam Accent No. 1* will fit one measure exactly (omit the grace notes).

Count: 1 - - 2 - -

R L R L R L

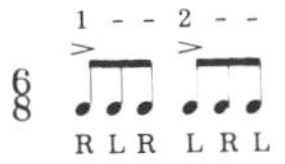

The sticking of the rudimental *Flam Accent No. 2* gives a nice swing to a march (omit the second and fifth notes).

Count: 1 - - 2 - -

R R L L

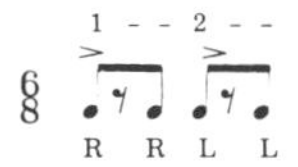

Always count and stick these measures the same.

Many easy and medium drum solos contain only these two time figures, combinations of the two, and a few rolls.

Rolls in 6/8 Time

Applying rolls to 6/8 time seems to be the biggest problem. 2/4 rolls will not fit into a 6/8 march if left in their original rudimental form. They must be notated differently and accented differently. For example, a five stroke roll has three fundamental hand movements, regardless of the time signature. It is played hand-to-hand (r-l-r, then l-r-l). The first two movements are bounced; the third is played with a single stroke.

RR LL R   RR LL R

Remember that if a roll ends on an accented note, the last beat must be accented. But this is not always the case. Sometimes a roll starts on an accented note, and so the first beat of the roll must be accented, not the last one. Many drummers automatically accent the *last* note; they must also be taught to accent the *first* note, as well as to start and stop a roll with *no* accent.

Use of the Five Stroke Roll in 6/8 Time (♩.=120)

Count: 1 - - 2 - -

Written: 6/8

Played: 6/8

RR LL R LL RR L

accent

In 6/8 march time this roll will be more open than a five stroke roll in 2/4 time. If more finesse is desired, a multiple stroke roll (one with more rebounds) should be used. But do not change the hand movements, and be sure to keep them in rhythm.

Use of the Seven Stroke Roll in 6/8 Time (♩.=120)

Count: 1 - - 2 - -

Written: 6/8

Played: 6/8

RR LL RR L

A seven stroke roll has four fundamental hand movements — the first three are bounced, the fourth is a single stroke. In 6/8 time, start the roll with the right stick if it starts on the accented first beat of a measure.

6/8

RR LL RR L R

If it starts on the second beat, start with the left hand and end on the right, which will be the first accented beat of the next measure.

6/8

R L R LL RR LL R

The Eleven Stroke Roll in 6/8 Time (♩.=120)

Count: 1 - - 2 - -

Written: 6/8

Played: 6/8

RR LL RR LL RR L

The eleven stroke roll has six fundamental hand movements, the first five are bounced, the sixth played with a single stroke. In rudimental drumming, the eleven stroke roll is a one-way roll — starting with the left stick and ending with the right stick, but it should be learned both ways for use when the right stick is free.

Editor's Note: *The following short solo for snare drum was composed by Haskell Harr especially for the purpose of illustrating the points made in his article. The 32-measure solo contains multiple examples of each of the rudiments discussed:*

① **Flam Accent No. 1**

② **Flam Accent No. 2**

③ **5-Stroke Roll**

④A **7-Stroke Roll (accented)**

④B **7-Stroke Roll (unaccented)**

⑤ **11-Stroke Roll**

⑥ **13-Stroke Roll**

⑦A **Fast 5-Stroke Roll (end w/acc. beat)**

⑦B **Fast 5- Stroke Roll (end w/unacc. beat)**

For proper sticking of the rudiments, see the appropriate paragraph in the article above. Other sticking is indicated on the music.

The Thirteen Stroke Roll in 6/8 Time (♩. =120)

Count: 1 - - 2 - -

Written: 6/8

Played: 6/8

RR LL RR LL RR LL R

The dotted half note tied to an eighth note is equal to seven eighth notes. The thirteen stroke roll, with its seven fundamental beats, fits perfectly in this situation. As this roll starts on the accented first beat of the measure, it will start with an accent, and, as it ends on the first beat of the following measure, it will also end with an accent.

The Fast Five Stroke Roll

One other roll that often occurs in 6/8 time is the short roll of two eighth notes tied together. This is the regular five stroke roll, but it is played rapidly.

September 1973

Marching Tonal Percussion

Larry B. Snider

Since the invention and evolution of timp-toms, marching timpani and tuned bass drums, each marching season brings more groups onto the field with new instruments in their percussion sections. While adding excitement, interest, aggressiveness, and color to the entire marching unit, these new percussion instruments are not always used to their full tonal and musical advantage. And a number of problems involving the balance, the marching drill, the percussion score, and the musicians performing on the new instruments are created for the director. With a knowledge of pitched drumming, a total understanding of each instrument, and a familiarity with composition techniques, however, any tonal drum section can definitely become an asset to a marching organization.

Instrumentation

The selection of types and numbers of instruments depends on three major points.

1. With a correct selection of pitched drums, it is possible for a complete drum section to encompass approximately three and one-half octaves. Thus, to get the maximum number of pitches possible in a drum section, it would be wise not to duplicate pitches. For example, if the tenor timp-toms are pitched to A, C, and E, there would be very little use in tuning the tenor drum to the same C.

Instrument Ranges	
Snare Drum (12x15)	E5-A5
Tenor Drum (12x15)	B♭4-E♭5
*Tenor Timp-Toms	B♭3-E♭5
*Baritone Timp-Toms	E♭3-A♭4
*Bass Timp-Toms	A♭2-B3
**Timpani	F2-E♭4
**Bass Drums	D♭2-G3

*Depending on depth and diameter
**Depending on size

2. Balance should be a major consideration in a pitched drum section. Naturally, the more pitches encompassed within the line, the larger the drum line will be, and careful balance will be necessary to bring out each pitch. (In the now-outdated monophonic drum section — using only snare, tenor, and bass drums, plus cymbals — the snare drum dominates, but with a tonal percussion section, each part is equally important to the sound of the section.)

The basic instrumentation listed below is balanced within the section. Even though some pitches are left out, a wide range of tones is available. A director may expand the section to his taste, but any additions must be made according to the size of the wind section. Obviously, the drum section should neither overpower nor be smothered by the remainder of the organization.

Basic Instrumentation

3 snare drums (12x15)
3 tenor drums (12x15)
2 baritone timp-toms (22-20-18)
2 marching timpani (23″ and 26″)
3 bass drums
(14x22, 14x26, 14x30)
3 cymbals (17″, 19″, 21″)

3. Since the individual players must be responsible for their own parts in a tonal percussion section, each person must be completely compatible with his instrument — physically and musically. For example, a small girl would probably not be able to carry a 26″ timpano even though she may be an excellent timpanist; but it would also be impractical to select a large boy if he cannot hear timpani tunings.

Tunings

Correct pitch and intonation are of major importance to the tonal drum section. Tuning should start with finding the desired pitch of the lowest drum and then working up through the snare drum. The most practical pitches are based upon a definite chord structure of thirds, fourths, fifths, or sometimes seconds. Pitch should be checked regularly.

Mallets and Sticks

Many interesting timbres can be produced through creative selection of mallets and sticks. One very interesting combination of sounds is produced when the small bass drum is played with a wooden mallet, the middle bass drum is played with a small hard felt beater, and a large felt beater is used on the large bass drum. Timp-tom or timpani players can carry both felt and wooden mallets on the field and use them interchangeably according to the desired sound. Using the same size and brand of snare drum and tenor drum sticks will help different players produce a consistent sound.

Marching Problems

The size and construction of timp-toms, duo-tenor drums, and marching timpani cause marching and maneuvering problems. Fast foot pivoting and the maintenance of an interval or dress consistent with the other performers — vital to the execution of most precision drills — is next to impossible to achieve. Also, a bulky drum may very well distract from the effectiveness of a picture creation in a pageantry show.

To eliminate these problems, the drum section is often treated as a band within a band, with its drill limited to the center of the field. In this way, the drum section can use its own space intervals without being closely compared to the remainder of the organization. The central location helps to eliminate sound phasing problems created when the rhythm section is too far away from the rest of the band.

Composing and Scoring

Sadly, it would seem that the unwritten philosophy of the marching drum composer has been, "louder and more difficult = better." Happily, there is now more interest in making the section sound musical. As a result, the good composers and arrangers are considering all moving parts in the wind score when composing for the drum line, instead of simply following the melody — a practice of so many who have written for the monophonic drum section. The person who writes for a tonal drum section must know the techniques of each percussion instrument.

Individual Instruments

Snare Drum. This instrument probably has more facility for difficulty than any other drum, but (like the tenor drum and bass drum) it is less definite in pitch and thus, less melodic. Techniques such as back sticking, stick flips, and Swiss rudiments can be used, but care should be taken to write in correct stickings for the entire snare line. Uniform sticking not only looks good, but also aids in the smoothness and phrasing of each statement. Compare the two versions of the phrase at the top of this page.

Tenor Drums. The tenor drum may be used as a supplement to another drum, as a rhythmic reinforcement adding a different tone color,

or with its own independent function.

Except in a very advanced section, the tenor parts are usually free of flams, rolls, grace note patterns, and other technically difficult requirements.

Timp-Toms and Duo-Tom. These instruments have the same basic sound characteristics as the tenor drum. Double sticking and cross sticking from one drum to another should be avoided in fast passages.

Timpani. Although the marching timpani are probably the least mobile instruments of the drum section, they may complement the wind instruments more than any other drum. Many timpani parts follow the low brass or tuba, providing much reinforcement and depth in that tonal area.

The addition of more timpani increases this reinforcement and is especially helpful when changing chords or modulating to a different key. Timpani parts should generally be written in slow rhythm. Because of the acoustical qualities of the instrument, fast passages played on the timpani are not distinct. The one major exception to this is the roll.

Bass Drums. Since the bass drum is of less definite pitch, its primary function is to provide *metrical* rather than *tonal* reinforcement. So never sacrifice meter for a rhythmic pattern that may be difficult for the performer to execute properly. A less experienced group may want to complete each rhythmic motive on the beat (see the "resolved" version in the example below). In this way, a steadier meter can be maintained. Later, the director may want to eliminate the "resolving" beat.

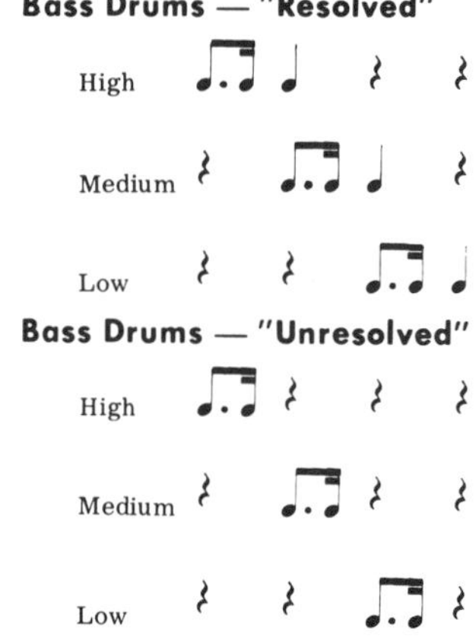

Cymbals. It is neither necessary nor desirable for the cymbals to be played *all* of the time. In fact, before deciding how the cymbals can best enhance the sound of the ensemble, many writers wait until the rest of the percussion score is written. Some even delay the decision until after the wind and percussion sections have played their parts together.

A New Era

In the past five years, marching percussion has changed drastically, and many people are not aware of the advances. The tonal percussion sections used in today's marching bands are much more interesting, exciting, and musical than the monophonic drum sections of the past. Along with this expansion of opportunity has come greater responsibility for each individual marching percussionist. In spite of and because of the greater challenges presented by these expanded percussion sections, they may well become a part of every marching unit. So it is incumbent upon marching band directors to learn as much as possible about the current techniques as well as the potential capabilities of *marching tonal percussion.*

Tonal Marching Percussion — Sample Score

October 1973

Percussion Ensemble Literature

F. Michael Combs

In response to numerous requests about percussion ensemble literature, here are some general guidelines for the school instrumental music teacher interested in selecting percussion ensemble music for training purposes. This is not a comprehensive list, and the works mentioned are only examples of what is available.

Level of Difficulty

Although percussion ensemble compositions are quite varied in style, instrumentation, and difficulty, most works tend to fall into general categories. For this discussion, the easy level of difficulty refers to the elementary works appropriate for students in their first two years of study. Medium level literature is designed for junior high students and difficult works for late high school or early college. Using these standards, the difficulty level noted here may differ from that given by the publisher or composer. All works mentioned, however, are within the technical and musical range of student percussion groups through the twelfth grade.

Style

A good portion of existing literature, particularly works written prior to the last decade, tends to be of a military style, more commonly (and misleadingly) referred to as rudimental. Today's demands on the school percussionist are quite a bit different than those of 15 or 20 years ago, and the more recent solo and ensemble literature tends to emphasize total percussion, multiple percussion, and the melodic percussion instruments. Some have interpreted this as a turning away from military performance, but it might be better to say that, while the emphasis on military percussion ensemble music has risen only slightly, the interest in the other areas of percussion has greatly increased. In any event, it is the task of the school music teacher to first determine what he wants to train his students to do and then select the percussion ensemble music that most closely underlines his objectives.

Easy Percussion Ensembles

Once a group of beginning percussion students has learned some of the basic fundamentals of playing snare drum, easy percussion ensembles can be used effectively not only to motivate learning but also to provide a means of gaining experience on some additional percussion instruments (such as bass drum, cymbals, triangle, etc.). Snare drum duets, trios, and ensembles for 4 or 5 players may be adjusted to accomodate larger groups by doubling some of the parts. The following works involve no more instruments than snare drum (or field or tenor drum), bass drum, and cymbals and are well suited as training pieces for a very young group.

Brown. *Drum Fun* (quartets on pp. 13, 14, 20). Kendor.
Hartzell. *Chi-Chi's Cha-Cha* (snare drum trio). Swing Lane.
Hartzell. *Two of a Kind* (snare drum duet). Swing Lane.
Schinstine. *Three's a Crowd* (snare drum trio). Southern.
Schinstine. *Wallflower Waltz* (snare drum duet). Southern.
Thamm. *Rudimental Rock and Rolls* (quintet). Creative.

It is advisable to introduce timpani (and even keyboard mallet instruments) at an early level. The following easy percussion ensembles involve simple instrumentation as above, along with two timpani and/or a few standard accessories.

Benson. *Scherzino* (quartet — triangle, milk bottle, wood block, snare drum, tom tom). G. Schirmer.
Brown. *Drum Fun* (quartets, some with timpani). Kendor.
Buggert. *Short Overture* (quartet — snare drum, bongos, tambourine, triangle, timpani). M.M. Cole.
Erickson. *The Firecracker* (3 snare drums, tenor drum, timpani). Erickson.
Feldstein. *Breeze-Easy Percussion Ensembles* (quartets — snare drum, bass drum, cymbal, accessories). M. Witmark.
Gould. *Parade for Percussion Ensemble* (3 snare drums, tom tom, cymbal, 2 bass drums, marching machine). Chappell.
Raab. *March for Percussion* (6 snare drums, bass drum, cymbal, triangle, tambourine, timpani). Music for Percussion.
Whaley. *Etude* (quartet — snare drum, triangle, tom tom, maracas, bass drum, gourd, cymbal, tambourine). Kendor.

Percussion ensemble works that include parts for bell, xylophone, or other keyboard mallet instruments may be too difficult for the students or call for instruments that the school does not own However, there are a few works available that have melody lines simple enough to be played on almost any melodic percussion instrument.

Brown. *Drum Fun* (quartets on pp. 10, 16 — basic set with bells). Kendor.
Christian. *A Roman Holiday* (5 or more players — bells, triangle, tambourine, snare drum, 2 timpani, cymbal, bass drum). Creative.
Christian. *Teen-Tam-Tum* (5 or more players — bells, triangle, castanets, snare drum, 2 timpani, cymbal, bass drum). Creative.
Peterson. *Percussion Piece* (6 drums, 2 timpani, bells, xylophone). Kendor.
Schory. *Baja* (quintet — bells, tambourine, snare drum, güiro, cowbell, 2 timpani, bass drum, cymbal). Creative.
Ward. *Impact* (quintet — standard set with 1 bell part). Pro-Art.

Medium Percussion Ensembles

The majority of percussion ensemble literature falls into the medium level. To give more complete information, the instrumentation as well as the number of players needed has been indicated. In addition, the works have been grouped into military and non-military categories.

Military

Grant. *Uncle Gus* (2 snare drums, timpani, bass drum). Mercury.
Lefever. *Mesa Verdi* (5 players — 2 snare drums, field drum, bass drum, cymbal). Kendor.
Lefever. *San Luis* (4 players — 2 snare drums, bass drum, cymbal). Kendor.
Lefever. *Shiprock* (5 players — 3 snare drums, bass drum, cymbal). Kendor.
Lefever. *Summit* (snare drum duet). Kendor.
Peters. *March of the Eagles* (2 timpani, snare drum, 2 tom toms, cymbal, bass drum). KSM.
Schinstine. *Overlap* (snare drum trio). Southern.

Non-Military

Abel. *Alegre Muchacho* (sextet — bells, marimba, xylophone, tambourine, chimes, timpani, drums). Ludwig.
Anslinger. *Percussion on the Prowl* (sextet — basic drums, 5 timpani, chimes). Pro-Art.

Benson. *Trio for Percussion* (trio — tom toms, triangle, wood block, cymbal, maracas, gong, bass drum). Music for Percussion.
Brown. *Percussion Trajectories* (quartet — triangle, pop bottle, 2 snare drums, bells, 2 parade drums, tambourine, cowbell, bass drum, cymbal, timpani). Kendor.
Brown. *Three by Three* (trio — snare drum, timpani, bass drum). Ludwig.
Brown & Musser. *Percussion Studies* (quartet collection — snare drum, timpani, bass drum, accessories). Kendor.
Buggert. *Introduction and Fugue* (11 players — marimba, piano, snare drum, 2 tom toms, bongos, xylophone, wood block, maracas, tenor drum, triangle, cymbal, 4 timpani, chimes, bass drum, gong). Music for Percussion.
Charkovsky. *Pentatonic Clock* (nonet — piano, xylophone, marimba, bells, chimes, cymbal, triangle, 2 wood blocks, tenor blocks, 4 tom toms, ratchet). Creative.
Chavez. *Toccata* (sextet — basic drums, 3 timpani, bells, xylophone, chimes). Mills.
Colgrass. *Six Allegro Duets* (duet — 2 drums each). G. Schirmer.
Colgrass. *Three Brothers* (nonet — bongos, snare drum, 4 timpani, cowbell, maracas, tambourine, cymbal, 3 timp toms). Music for Percussion.
Davis. *El Races de la Camptown* (octet — vibes, marimba, bells, xylophone, whip, güiro, siren, set, tenor blocks, bongos, maracas, timbales, bass). Creative.
Davis. *Latin Resume* (sextet — drums, 2 timpani, melody instrument). Creative.
Davis. *Mau Mau Suite* (octet — vibes (or marimba), xylophone (or bells), 2 timpani, tenor blocks, bongos, 4 tom toms, güiro). Creative.
Davis. *Oriental Mambo* (octet — vibes, xylophone, claves, marimba, tam tam, hi hat, bass drum, cowbell, tom tom, güiro, timpani, bongos). Creative.
Davis. *A Taste of Brahms* (octet — castanets, marimba, xylophone, whip, güiro, siren, set, tenor blocks, bongos, maracas, timbales, bass). Creative.
Davis. *Waltz for Swingers* (sextet — snare drum, tambourine, wood block, cymbal, 3 timpani, melody instrument). Creative.
Fink. *Ritmo* (septet — bongos, conga drum, set, maracas, claves, jawbone, cowbell, gong, güiro, shaker). Associated.
Frock. *Three Asiatic Dances* (sextet — basic instruments plus brake drums and vibes). Southern.
Heim. *Fanfare for Percussion* (quintet — snare drum, tom tom, timpani, bass drum, tambourine). Music for Percussion.
Hovhaness. *October Mountain* (sextet — marimba, glockenspiel, 3 timpani, bass drum, gong, tam tam). Peters.
Kraft. *Scherzo a Due* (duet — snare drum, field drum, bass drum). Try.
Latimer. *Motif for Percussion* (septet — triangle, cymbal, wood block, tenor blocks, snare drum, 4 drums, 4 timpani). M.M. Cole.
Leonard. *Circus* (quintet — standard drums plus chimes, 3 timpani). Volkwein.
Masoner. *Trio for Percussion* (trio — tambourine, bongos, bells). Kendor.
McKenzie. *Nonet* (nonet — bongos, 2 conga drums, gourd, bass drum, cowbell, tam tam, cymbal, maracas, claves, 5 tom toms, marimbula or tenor blocks). Music for Percussion.
Moore. *Scherzoid II* (trio — xylophone, timpani, snare drum, tom tom). Ludwig.
O'Reilly. *Three Episodes* (quintet — standard drums, non-pitched). G. Schirmer.
Ostling. *Suite for Percussion* (quartet — snare drum, triangle, field drum, wood block, cymbals, bass drum, timpani, tenor blocks, bells). Belwin Mills.
Peters. *A La Nanigo* (quintet — assorted non-pitched instruments, 3 timpani). KSM.
Peters. *A La Samba* (sextet — xylophone, bells, gourd, marimba, triangle, cowbell, 4 timpani, bongos, maracas). Mitchell Peters.
Planchart. *Divertimento* (trio — timpani, snare drum, tom tom, tenor blocks, gong, triangle, cymbal). Music for Percussion.
Schinstine. *Woodland Drive* (septet — tambourine, snare drum, field drum, cymbal, bass drum, 2 timpani). Southern.
Tilles. *Big Jinks* (octet — vibes, marimba, xylophone, chimes or bells, set, conga drum, 2 timpani, bass guitar). Down Beat Magazine.

Udow. *African Welcome Piece* (12 players — 6 drummers and 6 bull-roarer players who also play rattle. Also includes African chant). University of Miami Press; Sam Fox.

Von Klein. *Hay, Jay!* (trio — vibes, timpani, trap set). Southern.

Difficult Percussion Ensembles

The difficult ensembles listed below are within the scope of many mature high school students but may call for instruments that a school does not have.

Military

Collins. *Chief Judge* (snare drum, tenor drum, bass drum, cymbal). Creative.

Grant. *Double Bubble* (2 snare drums). Mercury.

Markovich. *Just Two* (2 snare drums). Creative.

Morey. *Bunker and San Juan Hills* (2 drums and cowbell). Kendor.

Non-Military

Bellson. *Four Stories* (4 drum sets). Try.

Colgrass. *Percussion Music* (4 tenor blocks, 4 toy drums, 4 hi toms, 4 deep toms). Edwin Morris.

Davis. *Greensleeves* (sextet — vibes, marimba, bells, set, accessories, bass). Creative.

Firth. *Encore in Jazz* (septet — 4 timpani, 3 drums, vibes, marimba, indian drum, cowbell, bongos, conga drum, set). Carl Fischer.

Gilbert. *Soliloquy for Percussion* (quintet — tom toms, marimba, timpani, snare drum, cymbal, chimes, bass drum). Southern.

Harrison. *Song of Quetzalcoatl* (quartet — 5 each of dragon's mouths, wood blocks, tenor blocks, cowbells, brake drums, tom toms, and bass drum, plus maracas, rattle, güiro, wind chimes, snare drum, triangle, gong). Music for Percussion.

Hopkins. *Duo for Percussion* (many instruments plus xylophone, marimba, bells). M.M. Cole.

Kraft. *Suite for Percussion* (quartet — assorted drums, flexatone, glockenspiel, vibes, tenor bells, tuned gongs; gongs, flexatone and pitched instruments are used in only 2 of the 5 movements). Mills.

Ott. *Ricercare for Percussion* (trio — timpani, piano, cymbal, bass drum, gong). Claude Benny Press.

Parchman. *Symphony for Percussion* (septet — set, cowbell, maracas, bass drum, chimes, slap stick, bongos, triangle, cup bells, gong, vibes, claves, cymbal, glockenspiel, tambourine, tenor blocks, bass drum, castanets, güiro, snare drum, gonza, 4 timpani). Elkan-Vogel.

Peters. *Swords of Moda-Ling* (octet — bells, xylophone, chimes, piano, 4 timpani, wood block, tenor blocks, triangle, bass drum, gong, cymbal, optional vibes and marimba). Franks Drum Shop.

Roldan. *Ritmica No. 5 and No. 6* (11 players — güiro, timbales, bongos, jawbone, bass drum, bass, 3 cowbells, 2 pairs claves, tenor blocks). Southern.

Strang. *Percussion Music* (trio — assorted non-pitched instruments). Presser.

Tilles. *Blue Percussion* (sextet — vibes or marimba, xylophone or marimba, bells, 2 timpani, set, bongos).

Weiner. *Cataphonics* (10 players — xylophone, triangle, cowbell, bells, vibes, gong, marimba, bass drum, tambourine, tom toms, cymbal, tenor blocks, bongos, snare drum). University of Miami Press; Sam Fox.

Other Areas

Because of the physical considerations, mallet ensembles are usually limited to colleges and conservatories. But if a school owns only one or two mallet instruments, a whole new world of literature is available to the students. Almost any duet, trio, etc., of like instruments can be adapted to the keyboard mallet instruments. Although a "purist" may object to arranging a violin duet for xylophone and bells, the music educator must remember that he has the duty to train *all* his students (even the drummers) in the areas of melody and harmony as well as rhythm. A few sources of keyboard mallet ensemble literature, both original and transcribed, are: (1) Black River Folk Co., Rt. 2, Woodview Dr., Onalaska, Wis. 54650; (2) William Dorn, 401 13th Avenue, Belmar, N.J. 17719; (3) Ron Fink, North Texas State University, Denton, Texas

76203; (4) Marimbas Unlimited, 5140 Vineland Avenue, North Hollywood, Calif. 91601; (5) James Moore, 5085 Henderson Hts., Columbus, Ohio 43220; and (6) Percussion Arts, 410 Michigan Avenue, Chicago, Ill. 60604.

Whether you like it or not, avant garde music is here to stay. If you want to give your students the exposure they need to graphic notation, electronic pieces, and aleatoric works, you might look to some of the following sources: (1) Theodore Presser (Music for Young Players — a series of easy graphic works); (2) C.F. Peters Corp. (especially works by John Cage and Lou Harrison); and (3) Media Press, Box 895, Champaign, Illinois 61820.

Conclusion

Now, after having made a very broad sweep over the area of percussion ensemble literature, I'm sure many readers will be most concerned that I did not mention "Paradiddle Piddle Pot" or some similar piece. Since I have not attempted to provide a complete listing, there are certainly many excellent publications that have not been mentioned. But I do hope that the general guidelines and direction that I have tried to develop will encourage readers to acquaint themselves with a great variety of the available percussion ensemble literature.

October 1973

Percussion Students' "Inventions"

L.R. (Verne) Reimer

Photos by Jack Witmer

Whenever the student drummers at York Community High School feel a need for storage facilities or special equipment, we discuss the problem and usually come up with a solution. One of our first efforts was a practice pad fastened to the bottom of a music stand (see photo 1). Then we tried a cymbal storage box mounted on a stand (see

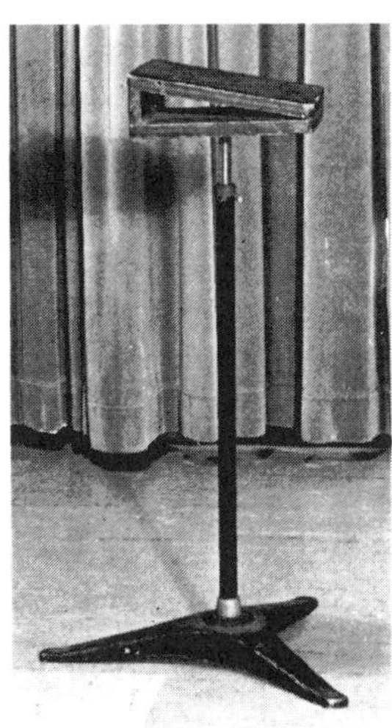

1 — Practice Pad

2 — Cymbal Holder

3 — Trap Table

4 — Tall Drummer Stand

5 — Original Storage Unit

6 — Stick and Trap Storage Cabinet (fits into large unit)

photo 2). As our percussion section grew and became more versatile, the students found a need for small portable trap tables. Again, their answer was "use the bottom of a broken music stand" (see photo 3).

A few years ago, two of our very tall drummers became quite uncomfortable since they had to bend over so far in order to play the snare drum. After quite a bit of thought and a thorough search of our storage room, they came up with a stand for the tall drummer (see photo 4).

Many years ago most band rooms were merely converted classrooms — with no storage areas. The room used by the York Band was typical of the period. In order to get the instruments off the floor we had shelves built and fastened to the wall. At the same time one of our percussion students measured the drums and drew up a sketch for a drum storage unit (see photo 5). Recently we decided that our modern band room needed a new storage unit Perry Deutsch, one of our drummers who had decided to major in architecture, drew the plans (see photos 6 and 7). Perry also constructed a set of pipes (called for in one of our percussion ensemble pieces) from material he had picked up in a junk yard.

7 — New Storage Unit

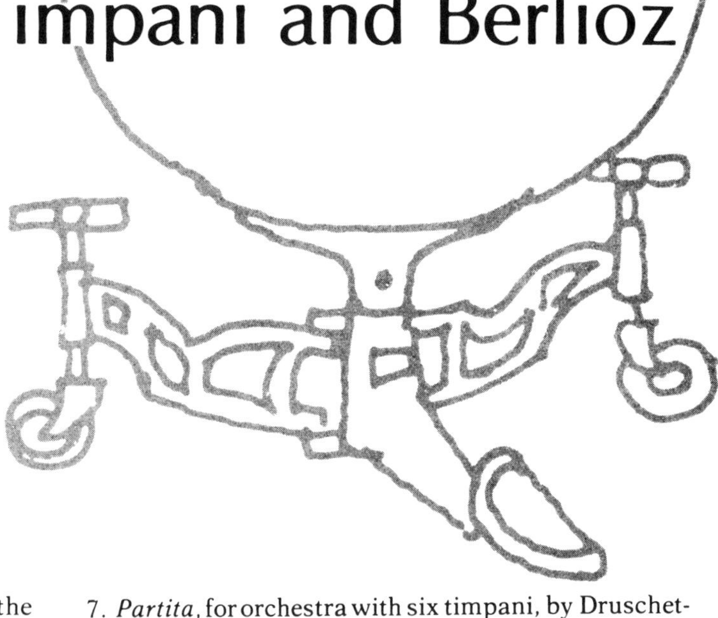

Some Remarks About Multiple Timpani and Berlioz

C.B. Wilson

Hector Berlioz made numerous contributions to the art and craft of instrumentation, not the least of which was his imaginative use of multiple (i.e., more than two) timpani. As is often true in many such "innovative" situations, however, one can cite conceptual precedents which may have led directly or indirectly to later practices.

A well-known example of a multiple timpani work by Berlioz is the *Requiem, Grande Messe des Morts,* completed in 1837, in which a maximum of sixteen drums is required. Prior to that time, a number of composers had utilized more than the standard pair of timpani, as illustrated by the following works:

1. *Sinfonia,* by J.W. Hertel (1727-1789), composed about 1748. This work requires eight timpani (the part is designated *obbligato*) and includes a timpani cadenza.
2. *Sinfonia No.* 99, by J.M. Molter (1695-1765), composed about 1750. Five timpani are required.
3. *Divertimento,* K. 187, originally attributed to Mozart, dating from 1773. This ten-movement work, written for two flutes, five trumpets (3 in C, 2 in D), and four timpani, is now thought to have been composed in part by Josef Starzer (1726-1787), in part by Gluck, and copied or arranged partially by Mozart but mostly by his father. In the most recent Köchel catalog it is identified as K. 159c.
4. *Divertimento,* K. 188 (new K. 240b), by Mozart, composed in 1776. This work, like K. 187, is for two flutes, five trumpets, and four timpani.
5. *Concerto,* by Georg Druschetzky (1745-1819), composed about 1795(?). This work requires six timpani, and includes a timpani cadenza in the first movement.
6. *Ungaria,* for solo violin and orchestra, by Druschetzky, composed in 1799. Seven timpani are required.
7. *Partita,* for orchestra with six timpani, by Druschetzky, composed about 1800(?).
8. Overture to *Peter Schmoll,* from an opera composed by Weber in 1801 using three timpani.
9. Overture, *Der Beherrscher der Geister* (*Ruler of the Spirits*), composed by Weber in 1811 using three timpani. This is a revision of the overture to the opera *Rübezahl,* composed in 1804.
10. *Sapho,* opera composed by Anton Reicha (1770-1836) in 1822. Three timpani are used.
11. *Masaniello,* opera composed by Auber in 1828. Three timpani are used.
12. *Robert le Diable,* opera composed by Meyerbeer in 1831. Four timpani are used.
13. *Calvary,* oratorio by Spohr, composed in 1833. Six timpani are used.
14. *St. Paul,* oratorio by Mendelssohn, composed in 1836. Three timpani are required.

All of these multiple timpani works, with one exception, may be performed by a single player. The exception, the Spohr oratorio, utilizes two players, each responsible for three drums. In this instance, the piece might be described as a "double multiple timpani" work, because each player is required to perform on more than a basic pair.

In all the works discussed thus far, one player has been required to play three or more timpani. The first composition in which Berlioz required this of a single player was *Les Troyens,* completed in 1858. Prior to *Les Troyens,* Berlioz had written a number of works for 3 or more timpani, but in these instances he consistently requested more than one player for more than two timpani. With the obvious exceptions of sounding chords of three or more notes and executing simultaneous rolls (both of which necessitate more than two hands), the general effect of Berlioz' practice was no doubt similar to that of the others who wrote for multiple timpani. From the performance point of view, however, the demands upon the players might be quite different. Druschetzky's parts, for example, especially in the *Concerto*, were probably conceived for a virtuoso performer, possibly the composer himself. Berlioz, on the other hand, was no doubt thinking more orchestrally than soloistically, and he probably considered the practical general level of ability of contemporary orchestral players as well. At the same time, he of course realized that the additional players would allow for the use of such things as three-note chords and simultaneous rolls.

Berlioz' own thoughts on the subject appeared in both editions of his *Treatise* (1843 and 1855).

> *For many years composers complained about the impossibility of using the kettledrums in chords in which neither of their two tones appeared, because of the lack of a third tone. They had never asked themselves whether one kettledrummer might not be able to manipulate three kettledrums. At last, one fine day they ventured to introduce this bold innovation after the kettledrummer of the Paris Opera had shown that this was not difficult at all. Since then composers writing for the Opera have three kettledrum notes at their disposal. It took seventy years to reach this point! It would obviously be still better to have two pairs of kettledrums and two drummers: this is indeed the scoring used in several modern symphonies* [*no doubt a reference to his own* Symphonie Fantastique]. *But in theaters progress is not so rapid, and there it will probably take another score of years . . . . One may employ as many kettledrummers as there are kettledrums in the orchestra, so as to produce at will rolls, rhythms and simple chords in two, three or four parts, according to the number of drums.*

It should also be noted that in most of his works that require timpani, Berlioz used only two drums. As he mentioned in the *Treatise*, most of the orchestras of the day *had* only two drums. However, in the same document he described his concept of the ideal concert orchestra, which would include four timpani and four players, as well as the ideal festival orchestra, which should have sixteen timpani and ten players. (It is perhaps noteworthy that at one time Reicha, Berlioz' teacher, had recommended an ideal festival orchestra with twelve timpani.)

The works in which Berlioz required more than two timpani include the following:

1. "Resurrexit" from *Mass of 1825* (autograph 1824) uses four timpani, four players.

2. *Huit Scènes de Faust*, Op. 1 (autograph 1828), seventh movement. Four timpani and four players are used. This work was later incorporated into *La Damnation de Faust*.

3. *Hymn des Marseillais* (arranged by Berlioz; autograph 1830) uses six timpani, three players.

4. *Symphonie Fantastique*, Op. 14 (autograph 1830). The third movement uses four timpani, four players; the fourth uses four timpani, two and later three players; and the fifth uses four timpani and two players (with the third and fourth players assigned to bass drum).

5. *Lélio*, Op. 14 [bis] (autograph *ca.* 1831-1832). The third movement (from 1828) and sixth movement (from 1830) use four timpani and two players.

6. *Requiem, Grande Messe des Morts*, Op. 5 (autograph 1837). The "Tuba miram," "Rex tremendae," and "Agnus Dei," use sixteen timpani and ten players, while the "Lacrymosa" uses sixteen timpani and eight players.

7. *Benvenuto Cellini* (autograph 1838) uses a maximum of three timpani with two or three players at various times.

8. *Roméo et Juliette*, Op. 17 (autograph 1839) uses a maximum of four timpani, with at least two players.

9. *Hymne à la France*, Op. 20, No. 2 (autograph 1844) uses four timpani and two players.

10. *March Marocaine*, composed by Leopold de Meyer and arranged by Berlioz (autograph *ca.* 1845-46), using four timpani and two players.

11. *La Damnation de Faust*, Op. 24 (autograph 1846) uses a maximum of four timpani, played at various times by two, three, or four players.

12. *La Menaçe des Francs*, Op. 20, No. 1 (autograph *ca.* 1850) uses four timpani and two players.

13. *L'Impériale*, Op. 26 (autograph 1854). There are six timpani and three players. In this work, the three pairs of drums are each tuned to the same pitches.

14. *Les Troyens* (autograph 1858). There are two instances of three-note chords for which three players are requested. Most of the work, however, requires two or three timpani played by one performer. As noted above, this was exceptional for Berlioz.

Clearly, Berlioz cannot be credited with the introduction of multiple timpani, since a rather large group of both well-known and lesser-known composers preceded him in that practice. It should be remembered, however, that in contrast to Berlioz' works, the earlier multiple timpani compositions generally involved one player for three or more drums. Berlioz' real contribution, then (in addition to his experiments with different types of sticks, muffling the sound, striking one timpani with both sticks simultaneously, and other matters not touched on here), was to exploit and expand the possibilities of the mechanically-limited multiple timpani by requiring multiple performers as well.

University Marching Band Drum Cadences

F. Michael Combs

Part I

A good drum cadence can add so much to a halftime show or street parade. In addition to raising the spirits of the band members and the listeners, a really exciting cadence can provide the percussion players with additional technical and musical challenges.

The cadences which follow have been collected from various university bands. Others will be printed in future issues.

University of Iowa

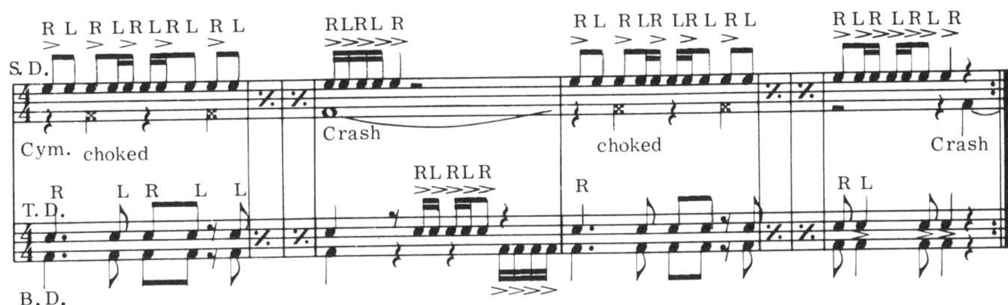

Utah State University

Penn State University

University of Tennessee

Indiana University

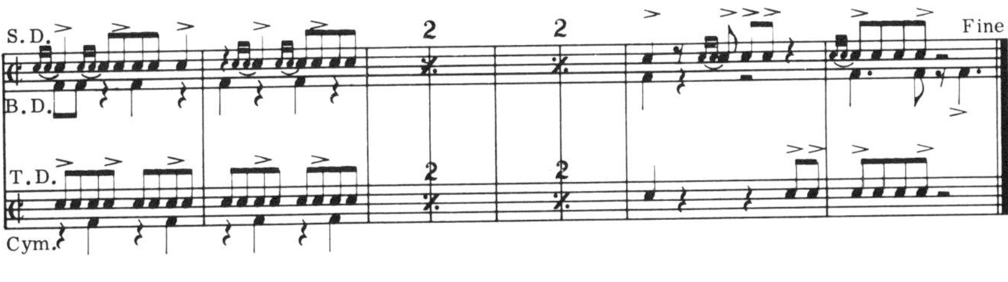

University of Arkansas

University of Michigan

University of Washington

Part II

University of South Carolina

University of Kansas

North Dakota State University

Michigan State University

University of Kentucky

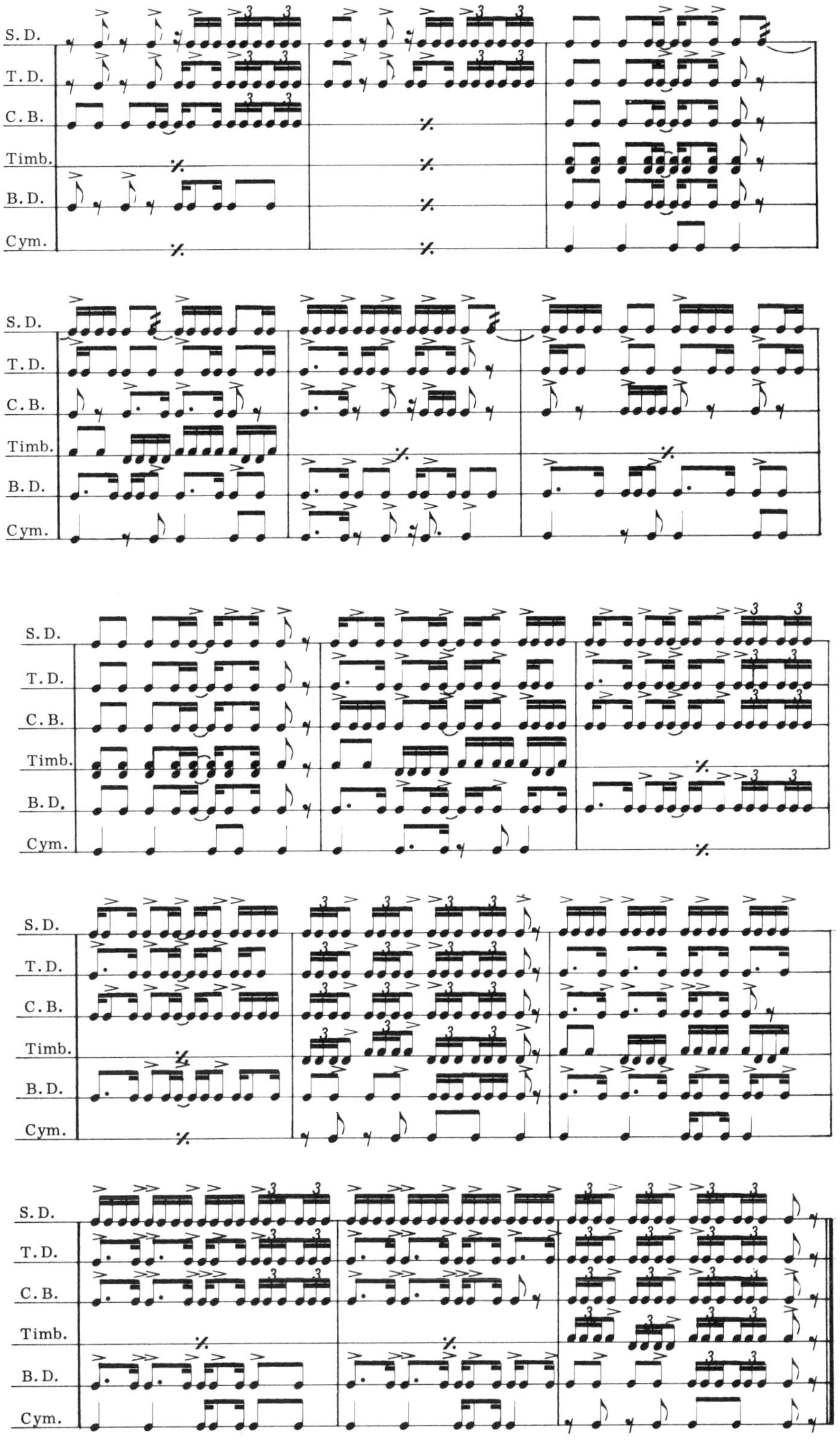

S. D.
T. D.
C. B.
Timb.
B. D.
Cym.

S. D.
T. D.
C. B.
Timb.
B. D.
Cym.

S. D.
T. D.
C. B.
Timb.
B. D.
Cym.

S. D.
T. D.
C. B.
Timb.
B. D.
Cym.

S. D.
T. D.
C. B.
Timb.
B. D.
Cym.

Purdue University

1974-1975

439	Techniques of Tambourine Playing	Donald F. Knaack	January
440	Careers in Percussion, Part I	Ron Fink	February
441	Careers in Percussion, Part II	Ron Fink	March
443	What's Next for Mallets	Thomas A. Brown	April
444	Cymbal and Gong Techniques	Dennis E. Kahle	May
445	An Interview with Fred Sanford	Ron Fink	May
447	University Marching Band Drum Cadences, Part III	F. Michael Combs	June
450	Snare Drum Method Books	F. Michael Combs	September
451	Performing a Musical Show	James R. Beckham	October
454	Selecting Suspended Cymbals	Lynn Glassock	November
455	Concepts for the Inexperienced Mallet Player	Larry Snider	December
457	Flams, Ruffs, and Rolls	Terry Applebaum	January
459	The Conga Drum	Ron Delp	February
461	Marching Percussion – An Interview with Larry McCormick	Ron Fink	March
463	Developing Keyboard Mallet Technique	Karen Ervin	April
465	Today's Field Percussion	Fred Sanford	June
468	Notational Standards for Percussion	Frank McCarty	June
470	Percussion Notation	Vaclav Nelhybel	June
471	A Band Director's Guide to Percussion Texts	Jim McKinney	June
474	The Percussionist/Band Director: An Interview with Robert Winslow	Ron Fink	September
475	Fundamental Techniques for the Marching Drum Section	Sherman Hong	October
477	The Buzz Roll	Lynn Glassock	November
478	What to Tell Your Stage Band Drummers	Ron Fink	December

Techniques of Tambourine Playing

Donald F. Knaack

The simple structure of the tambourine may lead some to believe that students can learn to play it "on their own." On the contrary, tambourine playing techniques are not easy, and competent instructors are a necessity if students are to be expected to perform the tambourine parts in the orchestral and ensemble repertoire. Since even the most fundamental techniques — such as proper positions and sound production — are often neglected in percussion instruction, these will be emphasized here.

The tambourine is normally held with the left hand and struck with the right. The left arm, wrist and thumb form a straight line — with the thumb placed on the head of the instrument and the fingers wrapped around the shell forming a C.

Producing Unsustained Sounds (Single Strokes)

The basic loud single stroke is produced by striking the instrument with the inside portion of the right fist (with the thumb in its natural position — to the side of the fingers), making contact at a point on the head between the center and the edge. The exact point of contact should be determined by the timbre desired. If a softer stroke is needed, the head can be muffled by placing the second finger of the left hand on the bottom side of the head. A more dry-staccato sound can be produced by a quick release of the left arm (at impact) in the direction of the stroke. This sudden release prevents excess jingle rattling, and a dry-detached sound results. The arm, wrist and thumb should maintain their "straight line" during this movement.

Loud-rapid single strokes, too rapid to execute with one hand, can be played in the following manner: prop the right leg up on a foot-stool or chair; turn the tambourine upside down; and alternate strokes between the fist on the inside of the tambourine head and the knee on the normal playing surface of the head.

Soft-rapid strokes can be executed by placing the tambourine upside down on the knee (using a foot-stool), placing the lower arms and wrists on top of the rim to balance the tambourine, and playing the rhythms on the rim with the ball of the index and second fingers of both hands. Another technique for soft-rapid playing is to place the tambourine (head up) on a pillow or pad and play the head with soft timpani sticks.

Producing Sustained Sounds (Rolls)

There are two basic roll techniques for the tambourine: the shake roll and the thumb roll. The shake roll (used for moderate to very loud rolls) is produced by a rapid side-to-side (agitator-type) movement of the tambourine using the wrist as a pivot. Beginning the roll with a tap on the head (using the fingers of the right hand) will give a definite attack to the shake roll. Also, a terminating note can be achieved by stopping the roll with a tap. The taps must always be the same dynamic level as the rolls. In general, dynamics are determined by the intensity of the shake and the position of the instrument with respect to the performer's body. For example, if the instrument is held at eye level, the sound will carry more than if it is held closer to the floor.[1]

The thumb roll (used for softer dynamic levels) is executed by moving the ball of the right thumb along the head (near the edge). The thumb must be in a straight position with just enough pressure to keep it from bending. Many times the thumb fails to grip the head enough to cause the necessary vibrations. Several solutions to this "slipping of the thumb" are: (a) wet the thumb prior to the roll, (b) rub rosin on the head prior to the roll, or (c) treat the head with Ludwig "Ruff-Kote." Thumb rolls can be sustained for long periods of time by moving the thumb in a figure 8 pattern over the right half of the head.[2]

Some Special Techniques

In addition to the standard techniques discussed above, some composers have called for various special techniques. In Respighi's *Pines of Rome*, for instance, two tambourines are taped together (the unheaded sides), set on a pillow, and played with timpani mallets. Jingles are rolled and slapped in Daniel Pinkham's *Signs of the Zodiac*. And the tambourine is used without the head (often mounted on the hi-hat) in rock music. One special technique, referred to as the Brazilian tambourine, is often associated with the playing of samba rhythms. The technique involves the production of a variety of percussive sounds on the tambourine by using different parts of the hands and fingers independently. In the following example, the instrument is struck successively by the side of the right thumb (T), the second finger of the right hand (F), and the heel of the right hand (H) — sometimes in conjunction with a muffling effect produced by placing the second finger of the left hand on the underside of the head (M).

A Final Note

This article has approached

1. Shake rolls, as well as single strokes, can be heard in *Roman Carnival Overture* by Berlioz.

2. Stravinsky calls for thumb rolls in *Petrouchka*.

tambourine technique from a "right-handed" point of view. If a player is left handed, all directions should be reversed. The important factor (ignored by many) is that the same hand should hold the tambourine at all times while the other hand plays the strokes. Switching the instrument from hand to hand for various strokes will only result in additional problems.

Always remember that the tambourine is a very sensitive instrument. Any excess noise from the instrument (due to picking it up too quickly, setting it down carelessly, or turning it over) will cause a distraction in a rehearsal or performance.

The techniques of tambourine playing require much thought, hard work and — just as important — a good instructor.

February 1974

Careers in Percussion

Ron Fink

The material which follows was selected from a tape recording of a panel discussion presented for students in the percussion department at North Texas State University. Panel members were:

David C. McGuire — professor of music and coordinator of graduate music education at NTSU, graduate degrees from the University of Michigan and Indiana University, organizer of the first percussion ensemble at NTSU in 1963.
Gerald Unger — principal percussionist with the Dallas Symphony Orchestra, degrees from Indiana University and hours toward a DMA at NTSU.
Ed Soph — professional drum set performer with teaching experience on the part time faculty at NTSU, former drummer with the 1:00 o'clock lab band and Woody Herman Band.
Leon Breeden — professor of music and administrator of the lab (dance) band program at NTSU, conductor of 1:00 o'clock lab band, coordinator of the program of jazz studies.
Ron Fink — associate professor of music and coordinator of the percussion department at NTSU, degrees from the University of Illinois, teaching experience in schools and colleges since 1961, part time professional musician with orchestras and local shows.

Fink: Dr. McGuire, how do you perceive the future of a young student who wants to get into the field of percussion?
McGuire: I think you're all aware of the surplus of teachers in the public schools nowadays. Within the next five years or so, we'll probably put out something like 30,000 beginning teachers, and they're not leaving the field that fast. I'd really like to see it as an advantage. . . maybe for the first time in the history of the U.S. you might be able to do something about raising the quality of teaching in the public schools, and I'm not just talking about music but all areas.

If you are a band director, or if you are shooting in that direction, then I think there will be jobs available for some time. We haven't had any trouble yet placing people in band directing positions. Probably with a major emphasis in percussion, though, you may find yourself in a job such as assistant band director or maybe working with two or three band directors and their percussion sections. In the state of Texas we see a lot of team teaching. You might have a junior high school responsibility and teach percussion all through a town. This may be exactly where you have to start, to get your foot in the door in the profession. That doesn't mean you have to stay there all your life, but it might be the first rung on the ladder. But what has been exciting to me is to witness just within the past ten years, the increased demand for percussion at the college level. . . and we're still seeing more of that, so that's still a possibility.
Fink: Mr. Unger, what about jobs in the symphony profession?
Unger: I believe that if a person is willing to "pay his dues" and put in the practice that is going to make him a virtuoso on *every* instrument in the percussion section then it doesn't matter — I think there will be a job open for him. Now, we all know that there are a limited number of professional orchestras in the country, between 27-30, and all of them are not top-paying organizations. Each year there are approximately four or five jobs open, with about 20 people auditioning for each one. The majority of the people auditioning are *not* very good and there *is* room at the top. You might not make a whole lot the first couple of years unless you also do some teaching. But there is room at the top for those who are willing — and I'm very serious — to put in four or five hours of practice each day, and just really "work up their chops."
Fink: What do you think of the future of the symphony orchestra?
Unger: I think the orchestras are going to stay around. You know the financial squeeze and the economic situation. I don't think it's going to eliminate the

orchestra. There are enough interested people with money to help sustain orchestras, and besides that, the government is putting out more and more all the time to fill in the gap that the orchestras cannot raise themselves. Take Europe as a prime example. Orchestras in Europe are almost entirely supported by the government.

Fink: Mr. Soph, what is the situation in professional playing?

Soph: Well, I'm going to concentrate mainly on jazz because that's all I really know about. Basically, the situation is going to be about the same as what you have here at school — and not much different from the situation in the symphonic field.

First, there's going to be a lot of competition and secondly, there's always going to be room at the top. Here at school, there are maybe four or five drummers who are at the peak, and then there is a big gap and it drops down. It's the same way in the professional field. Now, in preparing for professional drum set playing, you're really at a disadvantage, because there is really no repertoire to study. All you can do is study styles, get your Latin down, your rock, etc. But you also need a uniqueness in your approach, you have to build your own style and play musically. Now, the question is, how do you attain this musicality in your drumming? All you can do in school is build your technique — get your "chops" together. But, in actual playing, don't rely on your technique to pull you through, because it's not the technique that's going to do it. If Buddy Rich didn't have any musicality and just played technique — so what? But Buddy Rich has tremendous musicality and a very unique, personal approach that comes from building his technique around his ideas rather than taking technique and trying to build his ideas out of that. The *idea* must come first.

Breeden: I would disagree with Ed Soph that all he knows is jazz drumming. The first time I ever laid eyes on him, he was playing in the All-City Houston Orchestra and one of the Houston area schools, and doing a fantastic job. I think this background is one of the reasons he has that natural insight that makes the difference between a tub-beater (I mean a musician) drummer and just a timekeeper. And speaking of *musicians,* there's also the very versatile Dee Barton — well known as a writer as well as a drummer. I've often thought of the consternation of drummers all over the country when this *trombone* player in Stan Kenton's band went over and started playing drums — playing well enough that he kept the job! I think Dee's ability to write (Dee has often said this) has helped his drumming tremendously because he really knows the charts. If you know your number that deeply, I think you'll be by far a better, more stylistically creative player.

March 1974

Part II

Fink: Mr. Breeden, what about the role of jazz education in developing musicians and in career preparation? NTSU has such a large jazz band department with so many majors who are primarily drummers — not all of these people are going to go out and succeed as a drummer and make it professionally, we know that. What other outlets are there? Do you recommend additional education so that they can teach a school jazz band? Where would you advise them to go?

Breeden: I don't know . . . it's a very difficult thing. The young man who wants to be strictly a professional performer is facing tremendous odds, unless he's also prepared to do something else. I hear from dealers in music, men who have been in music all their lives selling instruments and so forth, and they say, "How can you encourage these guys to go on?" But how do you discourage someone who someday may be the next Louis Bellson? You just don't know. We've seen students here that were fairly weak to start with; and they get exposed, they start seeing the challenge, they start working, listening, they realize they've got a lot to learn. And it's amazing how far they've come within three or four years. You just can't believe it's the same player! But I would not encourage anyone to say it's a bright future.

Fink: Well, I think we should encourage everybody, regardless of the instrument, to become as proficient as they can and do what they can, but they must realize that it's not going to be so rosy.

McGuire: I think the student is here to specialize in his music, to put in the hours that Ed Soph talked about, to see if he really can live up to his expectations. Unfortunately, there are many frustrated guys in the world who don't make it and have not taken into consideration some alternative. I think both possibilities need to be on the outside of your thinking even though right now you're going to give it everything you can to become the best possible percussionist. I think you'll open more opportunities for yourself if you do this.

Breeden: Attitude is the big important thing. It's terrible to have a disgruntled teacher in a field unhappy because he failed at something else he wanted to do, and forcing his unhappiness on his students.

McGuire: Well, if you really do *not* intend to be an assistant in a high school band in charge of percussion and stage band, and nevertheless that's the job you have, that you signed a contract to take, it's up to you to do the best job possible.

Unger: I'd like to tie in some of the statements that have been made by everybody here. In the first place you know when I became principal percussionist with the DSO I didn't start out with any big aspiring goals to play professionally. I started out with the idea of going into a high school teaching music. When I was an undergraduate I got two degrees a music ed. degree and a straight applied degree. I went out and taught everything in a public school for five years from the fifth grade up strings included. During the summers I got my masters degree in music education and then was lucky enough to get a college job. When you're in college the head of the department is always going to say, "When are you going to start working on your doctorate?" So, I started to work on my doctorate . . . and also started looking for a principal percussionist job. The only one I auditioned for was the Dallas job, a one-in-a-thousand shot, but I was lucky enough to get it. The point I'm making is, you don't know what you're going to be doing five years from now. You have absolutely no idea. So the best thing that you could do is to think in as broad a category as possible. For example, most of the available teaching jobs demand a broad background. I belong to a teacher placement service and have been getting job notices for the past five years. I picked out a couple of the cards. These are the kinds of college jobs that are available:

> Masters degree required. Percussion instructor with good background in all percussion instruments. Must be able to teach class in music theory, orchestration, form and analysis, and composition. Rank of instructor to assistant prof. to begin. Salary varying from $9,000 to $9,500 for 9 months.

Here's another one:

> Teach percussion, percussion techniques, literature and ensemble, assist with stage band and complete with a normal load of theory or music literature and history. History of black music. Rank and salary open.

And one more:

> To direct marching band, teach private and class percussion, percussion ensemble and teach class piano and class in arranging. A Masters minimum with more education welcomed.

So you have to be a master of all trades if you're going to get a college job. And for each one of these jobs, I'll bet that they have 50 guys applying for them.

Next year I'm going to be teaching on a part time basis. The department head showed me some of the applications that he had for the band director position. It was amazing the number of highly qualified people applying for that one job who didn't get it because of the rough competition.

Fink: When I went through school at the University of Illinois I felt much like young people still feel today — that playing was going to be my whole life, even though I was in music education. There weren't many concert percussionists making a living at that time, and I felt that at least there was security in music education. As it turned out, education was the thing I really wanted to do. I feel that I am happier doing something in the daytime — not having to go out and play dance jobs every night. Still in my position as an educator, I play as much as I want to, whether it be symphonic opera dance jobs or shows. There is an outlet for playing even though you are in the teaching profession, and the practicing that I did on the drum set and other instruments and the experiences I have had playing I wouldn't trade for anything. It helps in my teaching.

It's true, you *don't* always know what you'll be doing in five years — your goals change, the job situation changes, you change. But whether you want to prepare yourself for a specific kind of position or whether you want the versatility that will allow you to compete in several areas, a brief description of the requirements for the various job opportunities for percussionists may be helpful.

College Teacher. Teaches percussion and anything else which the specific position may require. Usually a masters or doctorate is required.

Public School Teacher (bands and/or orchestra). The requirement for full time employment here is at least a bachelors degree in music education. There are percussion teachers who do not have degrees who teach in school systems part time, giving private lessons to the percussion students.

Private Studio Teacher. This does not require a degree and the teacher may teach in conjunction with a music store that provides the room and instruments, or he may teach in his own home.

Drum Corps Teacher. This person must be proficient in writing and drilling in this idiom. A degree is not essential.

Business. This could be an involvment with a manufacturer as his representative. A knowledge of business may be required, but many of the people in these positions were former professionals and teachers, and still function in that capacity to a certain extent.

Author, Composer, Arranger. Does not require a degree.

Professional Percussionist. A player who makes his living performing with or without a degree.

Dance Drummer. A drum set specialist who performs with bands.

Show Drummer. A drummer who can read music and handle other percussion instruments when necessary.

Studio Drummer/Percussionist. The most difficult of all positions to obtain. It involves work with recordings TV, films and requires extreme proficiency and experience.

What's Next for Mallets

Thomas A. Brown

Changes on the percussion scene are so frequent today that it is difficult for the instrumental music director and percussion teacher to remain well-informed about this important area. Percussion catalogs from the manufacturers are an excellent source of the latest information; in fact, they are considered to be the best current "reference books" available — not only for equipment, but also for new trends in methodology.

New Marimbas and Xylophones

Marimbas and xylophones have undergone a revolutionary new change — the bars for both instruments may now be obtained in a man-made wood which gives greater tonal projection. The xylophone can project like never before with a brighter tone, while the marimba's tone has increased resonance requiring a special resonance control attachment. The material is more durable than wood and can be struck with the hardest mallet (even on a marimba keyboard) without denting or cracking. Pitch remains steady even under extreme humidity and temperature changes.

New Concepts in Vibes

Using electronic aids, stage band or jazz/rock ensemble vibe players are now able to produce a tone as large as the ensemble itself. Some vibes are "purely electronic," *i.e.* the unit is struck with mallets but, instead of resonating tubes to aid in tone production, there are electronic pickups directly beneath each bar. Since the bars are thinner and the sound production is electronic, striking a thick vibrating substance is no longer a necessary part of the tone projection.

Special pickups can be fastened on the board beneath the bars of standard vibes quite easily. A standard jack is attached to the pickup and may be utilized by plugging into either a bass or guitar amp. The pure and natural vibe bar with ordinary tube resonation is merely amplified for extra sound power. Fuzz tone, reverb, and all the amplified attachments are available with both types of electronic vibes. These new effects create completely fresh sounds which can add a great deal to rock arrangements. Parts can be extracted from guitar parts, condensed scores, or piano parts.

Another excellent reason to use this attachment on a standard set is that it enables the vibes to be used independently without the pickup. If you intend to use the instrument in a percussion ensemble, band, or orchestra *sans* amp, it is not dependent upon the amplification. This is very practical, indeed.

Remember, too, there are special attachable rheostats for the electronic vibe motor enabling the performer to govern the vibrato speed.

Selecting the Correct Mallet

Tonal color is greatly dependent on the correct size and hardness of the mallet. On steel bell bars, brass mallets are especially effective for producing a clear response with great projection. Wood mallets produce a softer attack, yet can still project. Xylophone mallets made of plastic and rubber (available in various degrees of hardness) are also good for producing a particular tone and dynamic level.

To render a brighter, crisper sound, special vibe mallets made with tightly woven cord can be used. If an extremely large, mellow tone is desired, mallets with a single wire shaft and extra large head are effective on the wider vibe bars.

Chimes are often completely misunderstood. They are capable of a deep, round tone with great grandeur, but too often the percussionist picks up a small "half chewed" chime mallet producing dull, thudding sounds — as if each tube had a serious nasal problem.

Remember to select a chime mallet consistent with the tube size, *e.g.* a small mallet is not large enough to draw the full tone from a 1 1/2" tube. There are many types of chime mallets available in raw hide (the most popular), rubber, plastic, nylon, or fiber. The new "interchangeable" chime mallet is outstanding for its versatility since a variety of tips can be used.

The marimba is also the victim of improper mallet choice. Mallets for this instrument are available in various head sizes and degrees of firmness. Larger mallet heads can draw a deeper and more resonant tone from the lower bars. Remember, too, that rubber mallets are often more desirable for producing a crisp attack in the upper register.

Make certain that a full selection of mallets is available. Finding the right mallet for the production of a particular tone is extremely important for the percussionist. And remember that the most expensive instrument can sound only as good as the mallet used to strike it. The catalogs will aid greatly in obtaining mallets to fit your purpose. Each company carefully labels materials (rubber, plastic, yarn, cord, etc.) as well as firmness (soft, medium, and hard). Select your mallet as carefully as the instrument.

Accessory Products for Mallets

As a visiting clinician I find it necessary to mention basic points regarding simple maintenance — things which add to the life of the instruments and, more importantly, help to instill a feeling of student responsibilty for equipment which they use daily.

There are many excellent products which will assist in maintenance and long life of the mallet instruments. Special heavy duty covers for every keyboard instrument are available — and chimes should be no exception. Even though chime tubes are extremely vulnerable to damage and especially costly to repair, they often seem to be left without a cover. Covers are so necessary for long instrument life, and young percussionists should be trained in correct maintenance techniques along with correct playing techniques.

New mallet cases and bags are available that will keep mallets in order and safe from damage. More important, they will be safe from loss, the greatest problem in school percussion sections. There are also mallet holders that fasten onto the instrument and provide an alternative to placing spare mallets between the playing bars. Too often those bottom two bars appear to be constructed for the sole purpose of holding mallets. Let's liberate the entire keyboard for playing use.

Percussion Kits

Percussion kits that include a 2 1/2 octave bell set and practice pad may well be the answer to a well rounded and highly successful percussion section. Students will develop both melodically and rhythmically by learning to read bell music along with the standard drum pad training.

The complete early training offered by these percussion kits will provide students with basic mallet experience that may lead to more intensified study of xylophone, marimba, bells, vibes, and chimes in later years. Timpani training will also develop much more rapidly because of the already acquired knowledge of pitch relationships learned through the mallet instruments. If the option is taken not to continue the mallet study in later school years, it should be the individual's decision. Unfortunately, many potentially excellent players are being deprived of the opportunity to even make such a decision due to the absence of percussion kits offering basic mallet training.

Whether reappraisal is necessary regarding maintenance, mallets, new equipment, or early training, it will be a personally satisfying feeling to know that by exploring and expanding your mallet percussion spectrum, *you* made the direct difference in developing complete percussionists.

May 1974

Percussion: Cymbal and Gong Techniques

Dennis E. Kahle

There are a great many new percussion techniques which are quite familiar to percussionists specializing in contemporary music. Unfortunately these are less commonly known to most students and educators. Since these techniques are so varied, I will focus only on those special playing techniques associated with cymbals and tam-tams (gongs).

Cymbals

Cymbal Tremolo

Use rather light, brilliant cymbals, up to about 18", with dominant upper partials. One hand holds the stick or mallet, while the other hand is cupped, palm down, and poised just above the crown. The cymbal is struck *forte*, and the cupped hand moves in a rapid up-and-down motion from just above the crown to an excursion of about two inches. The sound produced is similar to that of a fly-swatter moving rapidly back and forth through the air.

Cymbal Vibrato

Use very thin, light cymbals, about 12" to 16". This technique consists essentially of playing a roll with one hand while raising and lowering the pitch of the cymbal with the other. The suspended cymbal is grasped with one hand at the far edge while the inner edge is pressed into the player's waist (damping the cymbal). Using the waist as a fulcrum, the player bends the cymbal into a bowed shape and then gradually releases it to its original shape. Meanwhile, the other hand is playing a single-stroke roll. One may use two rather hard xylophone mallets (one on top and the other on the bottom), striking the cymbal alternately top-bottom-top, etc. Or, one may use a snare drum stick grasped in the middle and held palm-down on top of the cymbal. Rapidly rolling the arm will cause the tip and butt of the stick to strike alternately, producing a single-stroke roll. An interesting variation of this technique consists of occasionally releasing the holding hand for a split second while still rolling. The resulting brief explosion of sound will permit effective intensity contrast.

Producing Strong Cymbal Fundamentals

Any cymbal will do, but heavier ones are most effective. Lay one hand lightly on the plate about halfway between the crown and the edge. With moderate force strike the edge of the cymbal with the shoulder of a wooden stick. The stroke should "chop" at the edge of the cymbal (a glancing blow). This technique will produce a dull clang, rather like a church bell. It might be mentioned that the same results can be produced by placing a block of felt or strips of masking tape onto the cymbal, thus leaving both hands free to play. This method, however, will restrict the use of the cymbal as one must remove the material for other types of playing. I find that damping with the hand is not only much more convenient but, with practice, can be done very quickly and precisely.

Producing the Effect of a Glissando

For best results use medium-size, relatively light cymbals, about 16" to 20". Remove the cymbal from the holder and place it crown down on the head of a pedal timpani. Hold it in place (edges off the head) by pressing the fingers against the inside of the crown. Using soft or hard sticks, strike or roll lightly on the cymbal while simultaneously moving the pedal up and down. Actually, the timpani is being used as a resonator, but the effect is that of the cymbal changing pitch. This technique offers a great variety of sounds but I have found that it requires some amount of experimentation with different types of sticks, a selection of instruments, and a variety of striking points. For this reason I do not recommend a particular type of stick or a certain striking point, but rather encourage the percussionist to seek his own preferences.

Tam-tams

Tam-tams or gongs should be considered as large cymbals — the bass voice in a choir of cymbals. However, due in part to their relative bulk and to the fact that they are suspended vertically rather than horizontally, none of the previously described techniques are as effective. The following are effective tam-tam techniques.

Water Gong

This will work with any tam-tam, but a smaller one is obviously easier to handle. Strike a tam-tam with near maximum force, and while it is still ringing, lower it into a tub filled with water. It is also possible to execute the roll as the instrument is being lowered into and raised from the water. This technique will both raise and lower the pitch of the tam-tam and simultaneously change its timbre.

Bowed Tam-tam

Using a well rosined bow (I have found a bass bow to be most effective), slowly draw the hair across the edge of (and perpendicular to) the tam-tam surface. The resulting sound is similar to that of a power saw cutting through hard wood. Various pitches and complex sounds may be produced by changing bow speed, duration, pressure, area and so on. Using the other hand to touch various places on the edge or surface will increase sonic possibilities. This technique is also effective on the larger cymbals.

Producing Strong Tam-tam Fundamentals

One may use any tam-tam, but larger instruments work best. Rubbing a *superball* across the surface of a tam-tam in a to-and-fro motion will produce only the fundamental with no audible partials. A *superball stick* may be constructed to make this and other similar techniques easier. Drill a hole slightly smaller than a rattan handle about halfway through a superball. Dip the handle in white glue and force it into the hole.

Other Percussion Instruments

Once a student has perfected the above techniques, he should be encouraged to experiment with them on other percussion instruments. The possibilities are limited only by the availability of sound sources. The following examples offer only a few such possibilities. Tremolo is equally effective on orchestra bells, vibraphone and almglocken. Vibraphones, cowbells, musical saws and even electronic heat sinks can be bowed. Drums of various sizes may be used as resonators. Water effects need not be limited to only cymbals and tam-tams. Superballs and other objects may be rubbed on drums, the floor, walls or used as conventional mallets.

"... the need for aural training must be obvious."

Although I have not stressed the necessity for optimum quality equipment and mallets, this factor cannot be dismissed lightly — since none of these techniques will work well with sub-standard equipment. Also, the need for early aural training must be obvious. Perfection of all of these techniques requires a sensitive ear. Finally, students must be put in touch with the existing literature which uses these techniques (Stockhausen, Crumb, etc.) — so that they may be brought into practice and realized in real musical situations.

May 1974

An Interview with Fred Sanford

Fred Sanford has served as a high school band director and also as percussion instructor and arranger for the Santa Clara (California) Vanguard Drum & Bugle Corps, the 1973 Drum Corps International (DCI) Champions. He is one of an increasing number of musicians who are involved in the two formerly separate (sometimes even hostile) fields.

What is the current state of "field percussion"?

It is undergoing a tremendous surge of growth and development. The percussion sections of today's drum and bugle corps, as well as those of many high school and college marching bands, are rapidly expanding with the advent of many new percussion instruments. The traditional tenor drum has been replaced with multiple tom-tom devices (known as *timp-toms* because of their timpani-like resonance). Bass drums in different sizes provide additional pitches. Marching timpani have become very popular, as have a number of "percussion effect" instruments such as bongos, timbales, and conga drums. Further expansion is possible with the use of tambourines, cow bells, wood blocks, antique cymbals — the list of trap instruments is really limitless. And now mallet instruments have also found their place in the marching percussion section. The addition of piccolo xylophones and orchestra bells (both carried horizontally) has made it possible for the entire percussion section to function as a self-contained musical entity.

What instruments are used in a typical field percussion section today?

Instrumentation is, of course, a personal preference but you might consider the following: 3-5 (or more) snare drums; 3 sets of timptoms (or other multiple tenor device); 3 or 4 bass drums (usually of different sizes for better tonal separation); and 3 or 4 pairs of cymbals (cymbal sounds and colors vary greatly depending on size and weight). Additions to this might include 2 or 4 marching timpani, marching mallet instruments, or any of the Latin effect instruments. The various trap instruments can be played by all members of the percussion section.

How do you score for these new percussion instruments?

I'm glad you asked that question, because I am sure that you, along with many high school and college band directors, find that the percussion parts supplied with most of today's marching band arrangements are totally inadequate. By scoring your own, the percussion section can contribute substantially to the success of the arrangement. To illustrate, let's assume you have arranged Gustav Holst's "March" from his *First Suite in E♭* (for military band) for field use. The snare drum part can follow the melodic line;

a timp-tom part might adapt as follows;

four tuned bass drums could contribute additional sounds;

and cymbals could be used to highlight the rhythm.

This scoring might seem rather elementary, but because of the various tonal colors of the timptom and bass drums, the result is a percussion ensemble blend that is full and rich — and yet the scoring is simple and straightforward enough to be well defined.

If timpani were added, I would suggest using the original timpani part as Holst conceived it, as this part could be converted easily to marching timpani. Trap instruments such as tambourines and triangles could also be used effectively. The degree of difficulty written into your percussion arrangements should relate of course to the proficiency level of your students. Challenging your drum section with better and more difficult material is good and will stimulate growth and interest, but all directors should realize that it will take a long time to develop a well balanced percussion section — just as it takes time to develop a fine brass, woodwind, or string section. And I mean time that is measured in seasons and years, not in days and weeks.

Is it difficult to find players for all of these additional percussion instruments?

Many band directors have found additional members for the percussion section by utilizing those students who normally play instruments not designed for outdoor use. A student pianist, for example, can usually adapt quite easily to a marching xylophone, and with some instruction in basic percussion techniques, other students have proven themselves to be quite adept at filling out the tonal spectrum of the expanded drum lines. Needless to say, this idea not only gives more students the chance to participate, but also enhances their complete musical awareness by giving them the opportunity to experiment in another family of musical instruments.

What are some of the more important things which directors need to teach their percussion students?

Correct tuning is extremely important. For a drum to perform at its optimum potential, it must be tuned as carefully as, say, a violin. The idea here is to tune each drum within the playing range that sounds and projects the best, without interfering with the sound colors of the other percussion instruments. Equal tension on each lug is essential as is having good quality drum heads. Muffling of any drum should be used with discretion. The bass drums, for example, will require a small amount of muffling; a small linen square of three to four inches taped to the inside of the head is usually sufficient. But don't forget that the "ring" inherent in every drum is its key to sound projection — and if it is eliminated, the drum will lose a large part of its projecting ability.

Mallet selection is another very important consideration. Playing a bass drum with a tenor drum mallet is as incorrect as playing a string bass with a violin bow. The general rule to remember is that the size of the mallet should correspond to the size of the drum. Mallets made of different materials (wood, felt, plastic, etc.) can produce quite an array of sound colors. All one has to do is experiment a little. Try a pair of soft lamb's wool mallets on the timptom for a smooth and mellow sound, or lightly scrape a triangle beater across the top of a cymbal for an eerie swish.

We hear many arguments about rudimental drumming — pro and con. How do you feel about this controversial subject?

You're right. Opinions differ. I've heard some people say that "rudimental drumming" is really an evil theory that transforms good, solid percussion students into nonmusical robots capable of playing a long roll for days at a time without food or water. I hardly think so.

In my adolescent days, I was given a book that contained what my teacher called "rudiments." There were 26 of them and most looked like they were quite difficult. I considered them as exercises to be mastered, like learning scales in order to play the piano. Later, a percussionist friend of mind in college told me that rudimental drumming was nothing more than a militaristic style of playing that Generals use to march their troops to and from breakfast — simplified to the extent that everyone can stay in step with the drummer's beat. It is nonmusical, monotonous, etc., etc. I don't buy that definition, either.

I prefer to think of rudimental drumming as a style — open with precise rhythmic subdivisions. For example, an open roll is played with the hands moving at 16th-note speed with a bounce on each stroke, producing an even series of 32nd notes. This kind of exact time division makes it possible for an entire section to play a rhythmic pattern simultaneously and to produce a volume level that is much louder than one drummer could play alone — an ideal approach for outdoors where a very large sound is needed. I also think rudiments are helpful as a means of developing physical coordination, technique, and finesse when studying any percussion instrument.

What is the best way to integrate the percussion section into the marching show?

I would suggest that the section be kept together (excluding timpani) as much as possible and not be involved in intricate drill patterns. I'm not advocating that the drum line remain stationary for the entire show; but due to the fact that many of these instruments are rather bulky and hard to maneuver, I prefer to keep the drum line drill patterns separate from the main body. However, if the percussion section can be worked into a feature drill without an excess amount of maneuvering then, by all means, it should be done.

Well, it sounds like percussion sections are in the midst of an exciting and expanding era.

Yes, I think these expanded percussion sections are largely the result of society today being more aware of the various sound colors inherent in percussion instruments. As a result musical arrangements for field use are going in new directions and investigating innovative styles in every conceivable musical idiom. Also, percussion solos or features are becoming increasingly popular in today's field shows and have truly added a whole new dimension to the concept of "musical pageantry." It should be obvious to almost everyone by this time that a drum section can no longer march with only a bass drum, field drum and a pair of cymbals.

June 1974

University Marching Band Drum Cadences

(Part III)

The cadences which follow have been collected from various university bands. Others were printed in the November and December 1973 issues.

University of Illinois

North Texas State (Soul Rock)

Dickinson (N.D.) State College

North Texas State (Bossa-Rock)

North Texas State (Soul Rock)

Baylor University

University of Northern Iowa

Snare Drum Method Books

F. Michael Combs

Recently a number of new beginning snare drum method books have appeared on the market that seem to be of particular significance.

Bill Schinstine and Fred Hoey, both successful teachers with many outstanding students to their credit, have worked together on *Basic Drum Book* (available from Southern Music Company for $3.75). In 84 pages, the book covers the basic fundamentals of music as well as snare drum techniques. Illustrations of the snare drum, hand positions (matched and traditional are both explained), and flam executions are hand drawn but clear enough for a student to comprehend. While keeping a well-organized approach to the fundamentals and techniques, interest is maintained through imaginative titles of each of the exercises — including solos, duets, and quartets. Although the book is primarily concerned with snare drum techniques, seven pages are devoted to bass drum and cymbals. Forty flash cards of musical symbols have also been included as an aid to students.

Al Payson, Chicago Symphony Percussionist, has written a *Beginning Snare Drum Method* (61 pp.) which comes with a play-along record. The book contains the basic fundamentals of rhythmic notation along with exercises of graduated difficulty — including single stroke exercises, the buzz roll, flam techniques, and the "open" or "military" roll. There are also a number of exercises which incorporate melody lines. The play-along record contains 11 of these melodies performed first by snare drum and piano, then repeated with piano alone. The publication lists for $3.50 (record included) and is published by Payson Percussion Products, 2130 Glenview Avenue, Park Ridge, Illinois.

The Performing Percussionist by James Coffin (formerly University of Northern Iowa, now educational service manager for a major drum company) is an excellent, fresh approach to the snare drum *and* other areas such as triangle, cymbals, bass drum, multiple percussion, and bells. The 58-page Barnhouse publication is filled with attention-keeping devices: various styles and types of print are used for emphasis; and all new material is set off in boxes for easy study. The numerous photos, used to show performance techniques, grips, etc., are of particularly good quality.

The Boston Music Company (Frank Distributing Corp.) has published a revised and enlarged edition of Thomas McMillan's *Contemporary Method for the Snare Drum* (originally published in 1962). Standard techniques and musical principles are introduced in a rather rapid fire manner and, even though one of the stated purposes of the book is to "provide the student with abundant musical exercises . . .", each lesson is limited to about 10 lines of music. Specific sticking is noted in almost all lessons and the book concludes with a list of basic snare drum rudiments. The 51-page publication is priced at $3.95.

Mervin Britton, percussion teacher at Arizona State University and established author of several articles and books, has taken a major step forward with *Creative Approach to the Snare Drum* (Byron-Douglas). Unlike most similar books, Mr. Britton begins his exercises with 16th notes in 1/4 time. Almost all exercises are in duet form in order to develop independence, a sense of ensemble performance, and avoid unintentional rote learning. The technique of singing the rhythm and sounds is introduced as an aid to development of student musicianship. One significant feature of this method book is the fact that it contains 71 clearly-printed pages and lists for only $2.50.

Saul Feldstein, in collaboration with Fred Weber, has authored a particularly interesting elementary level drum method entitled *Drum Student* (Belwin-Mills, 40 pp., $1.25). New items, lesson titles, and other important points are printed in red for special emphasis. The interesting titles for the exercises and solos will help keep the student's interest. Three correlating supplementary books and an ensemble book for the percussion section are also available.

Here's the Drum by Emil Sholle has been on the market for a few years, but it is still one of the best buys in a straight-forward snare drum method book. The pace is rather slow with new rhythms and techniques introduced gradually and limited to only the basic principles of sticking and notation. The 38-page publication lists for $1.50 and is available from Brook Publishing Company, 3602 Cedarbrook Rd., Cleveland Hts., Ohio 44118.

Although printed in Austria, Richard Hochrainers *Übungen für Klein Trommel* (Exercises for Snare Drum) is quite practical and applicable to the demands of standard band and orchestral snare drum literature. The book consists of 104 exercises (48 pp.), each containing a particular notational or technical challenge. There is no accompanying explanatory material. It is published by Verlag Doblinger and is available in this country through Associated Music Publishers for about $3.50.

For the student who has just transferred to the snare drum from another instrument and needs special attention in technique, *Developing Dexterity* by Mitchell Peters may be the answer. With all emphasis on technique, the 48-page publication contains numerous short exercises covering single strokes, rolls, flams, paradiddles, rebound strokes, finger strokes, and other aspects of snare drum technique. The exercises are not presented in sequence according to difficulty but are catagorized in groups pertaining to various phases of technique. This collection of stick exercises and patterns is available from the author at 3231 Benda Place, Los Angeles, California 90028.

Musical Studies for the Intermediate Snare Drummer by Garwood Whaley is especially appropriate for students who need to develop reading and other musical skills. The first half of the book contains no rolls or embellishments (allowing the student to become completely familiar with dynamics and accents), while the second half makes extensive use of flams, drags, and rolls of varying duration. Published by JR Publications, 3 Sheridan Square, New York, N.Y. 10014, this 32-page book lists for $2.00.

Since most drum students could use practice in reading music, Bob Tilles's *Reading Exercises for the Snare Drum* (Vol. 1) should be a welcomed addition to the list of snare drum books. The 31 pages are clearly printed and emphasize notational problems in an orderly, sensible manner. Despite the title of the book, technique does have an important place and the performance of flams and ruffs is explained. Specific sticking is indicated in many exercises and the book concludes with a list of the 26 standard rudiments. Volume 1 is available from GIA Publications (2115 West 63rd Street, Chicago, Illinois 60636) for $1.50.

October 1974

Performing a Musical Show

James R. Beckham

As the quality of the musicians in our high schools and colleges improves, more and more schools have begun producing Broadway musicals as well as other types of musical theatre. This has provided many new learning experiences for the students involved — especially for the percussionists, who not only have to learn new playing techniques but must also develop new organizational methods in order to cover all of the parts.

Most musical shows have a large pit orchestra which includes 2-3 percussionists or more — one assigned to the dance set while the others cover mallet instruments, timpani, and accessories. For a variety of reasons, most schools restrict the size of the pit orchestra and necessarily reduce the number of percussionists, so that one student percussionist must attempt to cover parts that in a professional situation were performed by several players. In this situation, the most difficult task for the young percussionist is determining how to set up his instruments so that he can reach everything with a minimum of effort and without moving a great distance. It should be remembered that in percussion performance *distance is time*... it takes a certain amount of time to move several feet from one instrument to another and the closer the instruments, the less time required to make the change. So the percussionist must not only be able to condense the amount of space his instruments cover but also determine the best physical lay-out for the particular show being played.

The first step in determining the physical lay-out is to make up an inventory which lists all of the percussion instruments needed for a particular musical show.

This can be accomplished by listing the instruments needed in each number, then condensing the list to the total list of instruments needed. After comparing the instrumentation with the available space in the pit and the logistics of reaching each item to be played, a decision can be reached on possible substitutions that must be made (see Table).

Instrument — Substitute

Timpani — floor tom-tom, other tom-toms when multiple pitches needed

Xylophone — orchestra bells, marimba

Temple blocks — wood block(s)

Chimes — one chime tube hung singly on a rack, or orchestra bells

Vibes — orchestra bells

Marimba — xylophone

It is important for the student percussionist to learn that he should use the types of sticks and mallets called for and substitute only when a change of beaters is impractical (due to a lack of time) or when the conductor determines that another type of beater or stick would best serve to complement the action on stage.

At this point the percussionist should make a drawing of a possible set-up which would allow him to reach all of the instruments easily. Ideally he would never have his back to the conductor. There are times, however, when placing an instrument behind the normal set-up is unavoidable (e.g., a large mallet instrument or timpani). If this is the case, the player should choose the instrument that is played least often, then memorize the part, so that he can watch the conductor over his shoulder without having to read music at the same time.

The drum set is usually the center of activity, so it should naturally be placed in the center of the set-up, facing the conductor. Around this central core of instruments, arrange the other instruments so that they can be reached easily, with those instruments used most often in the most convenient locations.

By analyzing each of the instruments needed to perform the musical and determining the best methods of mounting, hanging, laying, or holding them, the percussionist can save himself much time and effort and assure a smoother performance. Triangles, for instance, must be hung in order to sound, while wood blocks and cowbells can be held in the hand, laid on a padded table, or mounted on a stand, table, or bass drum rim with commercially manufactured mounts. For most percussionists who play musicals, mounting these is most expeditious since it frees the holding hand to play something else. Also, when an instrument is mounted or fixed, it has less chance of accidentally falling onto the floor in the middle of a performance.

Trap tables, ordinary small tables, typewriter tables, and music stands all make acceptable areas on which to lay small instruments such as tambourines, castanets, claves, maracas, etc. Cover any surfaces on which instruments are laid with padding so that no noise results when instruments are put down. Ordinary bath towels (a double thickness) work well for covering trap tables or stands. Thick felt, carpeting, carpet padding and sheets of foam rubber are also excellent padding materials. Since foam rubber can be obtained in a variety of sizes and thicknesses, it is often the best choice for large tables. A 2' x 1 1/2' rectangle of 3/4" foam rubber can be laid over the bars on the orchestra bells when they are not in use and light-weight instruments laid on this.

I have found that music stands with the desks tilted horizontally often provide the best place on which to lay small instruments and mallets . . . a triangle can even be hung from a stand. Most stands are quite sturdy, can be varied in height, have a "ledge" to prevent small objects from rolling off, and they take up very little floor space. A music stand can be placed in a tight area where even a small table will not fit.

One consideration in choosing a trap table or stand is the height; it should be low enough to be on the same level as the player's hands when he is sitting on the drum throne, so that he does not have to stand in order to reach instruments or mallets laying on the table. The same consideration should be given to a stand or table for the orchestra bells. (Typewriter tables are sometimes a good choice.) Other mallet instruments present a real height problem since their built-in stands cannot be lowered and one must usually stand to play them as in the case of timpani, vibes, xylophones, etc. For this reason, as well as space problems, it is sometimes desirable to substitute orchestra bells for xylophone or vibes . . . especially if they are needed for only a few measures. Obviously the best sound will result from using the instrument indicated in the score, but sometimes that is just not feasible. Before making a major substitution, however, the percussionist should consult the conductor.

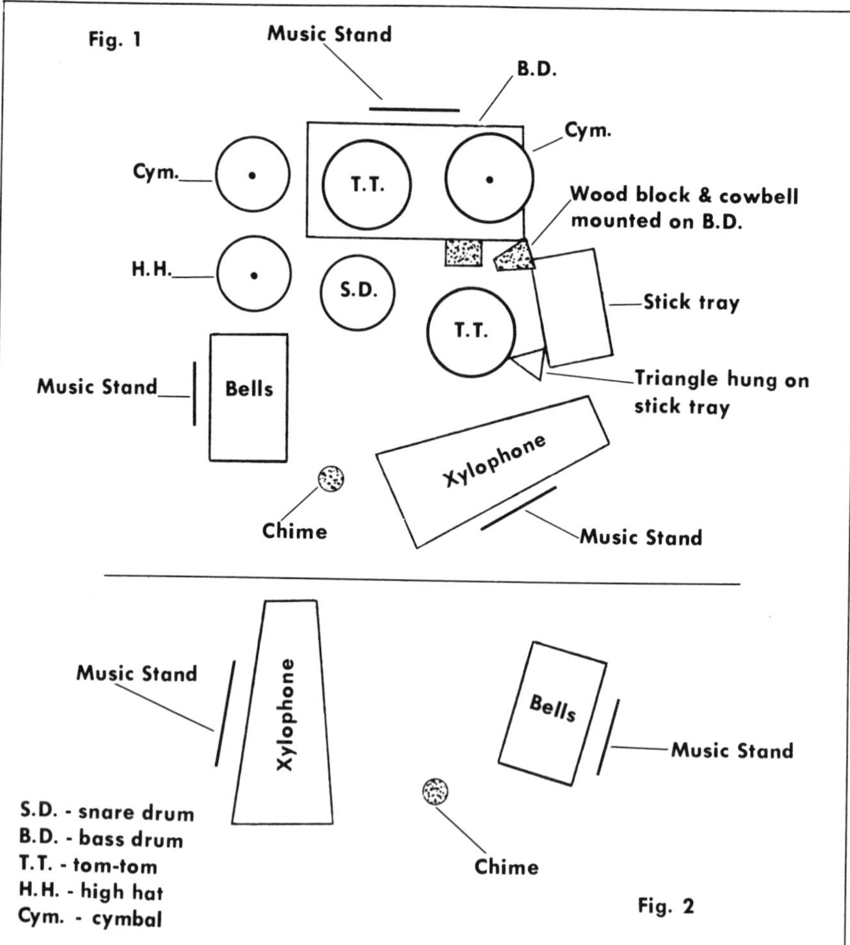

Percussionists are sometimes of the opinion that the more drums and cymbals they have in their drum set the better they will play, but this is neither necessary nor practical in the musical show. The more drums and cymbals used, the more of a problem it becomes to place instruments other than the drum set in the allotted space, so it should be emphasized to percussionists that they should have only the minimum number of drums and cymbals needed to perform the show adequately.

A Typical Show

Let us take a hypothetical musical and go through the steps of setting up the percussion section. Our inventory shows the instrumentation needed includes: dance set, wood block, triangle, tambourine, cowbell, chimes, xylophone, bells, and timpani. After completing the inventory, we review the space allotment in the pit. Finding space somewhat limited, we might eliminate the timpani since they take up a great amount of space and we find in looking at the score that the timpani parts can be played on the tom-toms. Obviously this is not an ideal substitution, but we have to do the best we can within the available space. Now drawings can be made of possible arrangements including music stands, tables, and instruments.

One possible arrangement is that outlined in Figure 1. Here, all of the instruments are within easy reach, but the sticks and mallets may pose a problem — it's just too easy to grab the wrong pair from the stand on which the mallets and sticks are laid. At this point we should go back to the inventory list, add an extra column for the mallets and sticks used, analyze when and where they are used (making substitutions if possible), determine the best placement for each pair, then add this information to the drawing.

Sticks and Mallets

Let us assume that the stick-mallet inventory includes the following: snare drum sticks, brushes, hard bell mallets, hard xylophone mallets, timpani mallets, and soft yarn mallets for suspended cymbal. Since we did not have room to include timpani in our set-up, there is no real need for timpani mallets (soft yarn mallets can be used on the tom-toms). If there are rapid changes from bells to xylophone, it may be best to use the same pair of mallets for both instruments. Remember, however, that metal bell beaters should *never* be used on any wooden bar instruments such as xylophone or marimba or on any other instrument made of wood. Mallets which have snare drum sticks on one end and timpani mallets on the other can be useful in making rapid changes. However, they should not be used to substitute for soft yarn mallets, since playing cymbals with timpani mallets tends to pack the felt in the mallet heads, creating hard spots in normally soft mallets. With the list we have compiled, any further substitutions of sticks or mallets would not be possible — we must have drum sticks (including an extra pair in case of breakage or loss of a stick) and nothing will substitute for brushes.

In some cases it may be best to choose a general purpose mallet for each instrument and leave them on the instrument. In this way a pair of mallets is waiting on the instrument when it comes time to play the part. This solves the problem of having to sort out the proper pair of mallets from several pair lying together on the stick tray. We find in rehearsing our hypothetical musical that it works best to leave one pair of hard mallets on the bells and one pair on the xylophone.

The schematic drawing is now complete, showing arrangement of the instruments and mallet placement. This set-up seems quite feasible — until we arrange the instruments and begin to practice. The fast switches from dance set to bells and back are presenting problems. Perhaps we could play some of the bell parts with one hand to free the other hand for dance set work. If the right hand is the stronger, the bells should be moved to the right side.

After some rehearsal using this set-up and seeing that it works well, we move our instruments to the pit for rehearsals and find that the chimes will not fit in the available space. We can substitute bells for chime notes but there is one particularly important solo chime note. This problem can be solved easily by hanging that one important chime tube on a metal rack (similar to a coat rack) which is narrow enough to be used in the pit.

Mark Your Place

Once everything is properly arranged and the percussionist can play each part and reach each instrument, the floor should be marked with tape to indicate where each instrument belongs. In this way if the percussion instruments must be moved for other rehearsals or if the instruments are moved when the pit is cleaned, it will not be necessary to go through the process of arranging the instruments again. A difference of less than an inch can prevent the percussionist from being able to reach an instrument in time to play a critical part, so when the set-up is right, *mark it*! Outline music stands, drums, tables, mallet instruments — anything that has legs or feet — and label each piece of tape, so you won't forget what goes where. This also solves the problem of other instrumentalists complaining that the drummer is taking up more and more space in the pit each night!

Finally, here are some helpful hints that might make playing a musical a little bit easier for the percussionist. It is sometimes useful to have a triangle hanging on each music stand, so that there is always a triangle within easy reach. The same rule applies to other small instruments — it may be easier to use two small instruments in different locations than to reach several feet to play one single instrument. Finger cymbals can also be hung from triangle slips and played with a triangle beater or hard bell mallet if necessary.

A triangle beater carried in the breast pocket of a coat or shirt may mean the difference in playing a crucial triangle part and *not* playing it; it is also wise to leave a triangle beater on the stick tray within easy reach. If the güiro scratcher keeps disappearing or rolling away when needed, tie it to the güiro with a two-foot long piece of string . . . this way if the güiro can be found, so can the scratcher! Chime mallets can be placed on top of the "natural" tubes (on a set of chimes) or hung from the rack with a leather thong when using single tubes on a fabricated rack.

Occasionally it becomes necessary to play the snare drum with bell mallets prior to a quick change to bells. This works well, but playing bells with snare sticks is not a good option. Snare drum sticks are not hard enough to produce a bright, piercing sound on bells. In the same way, yarn marimba or vibe mallets can be used on timpani if there is no time to switch to timpani mallets, but timpani mallets do not work well on marimba or vibes. It is also possible to hold snare drum sticks and, at the same time, have a triangle beater or any type of mallet inserted between the fingers of one hand. Though cumbersome, this allows the percussionist to make a rapid switch of instruments easily. If a siren or police whistle is called for, it can be hung around the player's neck; this solves the problem of locating the whistle, picking it up, then laying it down again.

Another possibility is to make temporary use of some of the non-percussionist orchestra members. For example, multiple latin instruments, such as maracas, claves, güiro, etc., can be played by members of the orchestra who have rests during that portion of the show. This will fill out the percussion section, producing the complete sound as indicated by the composer.

These are only some of the possible playing arrangements and performance techniques that percussionists involved in musicals use daily. Both students and professionals should work out the organizational plan that best serves their playing abilities. Of course, the type of set-up and overall organization used by a percussionist will vary from musical to musical and even from one orchestra pit to another. There are no absolutes, and the player must experiment to find what works best for him. But whatever the situation, the percussionist will not be successful unless, in addition to being a fine player, he is well organized and inventive in finding easier, faster, and more musical ways to meet the demands placed on him by the music and the action onstage.

November 1974

Selecting Suspended Cymbals

Lynn Glassock

Cymbals are available in a variety of sizes and weights (thicknesses). Those used most commonly as suspended cymbals in bands and orchestras vary in size from 14-20 inches (18" is perhaps most prevalent). The weight is usually thin, medium-thin, or medium. Heavier cymbals (medium-heavy and heavy) are used as the "ride" cymbal for the drum set, because they tend to have a higher pitch and more distinct "ping" sound that is better suited for the jazz style of playing.

Although probably no two cymbals will ever sound exactly alike, the relationship of size and weight is very important in determining how a cymbal will react. Thicker cymbals have more sustaining power, vibrating longer than a thinner cymbal of equal diameter, but the thinner cymbal will have a quicker response than a heavier one. This means that a 16" thin will usually speak faster and die away sooner than a 16" medium-heavy. The heavier cymbal also has more potential power and can produce a larger, fuller sound without the possibility of overplaying. A cymbal that is overplayed will not produce a good sound and continual overplaying will often result in early breakage.

Larger cymbals have approximately the same relationship to smaller ones that heavier cymbals have to those that are lighter: the larger cymbal has more potential power; it has a slower response; and it will vibrate longer. Thus, a 20" medium cymbal will have a slower response than a 16" medium cymbal, but will ring longer and can produce more volume without being overplayed.

Because the larger and heavier cymbals vibrate longer, muffling can sometimes be a problem after a loud crash. One hand is usually not enough to stop the sound instantly and completely, and since the other hand is holding the mallet or stick, it is not very efficient in muffling. Also, when muffling with both hands, care must be taken to avoid letting the shaft of the stick or mallet come in contact with the cymbal, as this will cause extraneous noise.

A cymbal that would be excellent in one situation might not be a good choice in another. For example, a 19" medium weight cymbal would be very good for producing a sustained fortissimo roll while the entire band or orchestra was also playing at a loud volume. However, if the music called for a series of rapid staccato forte crashes with the trumpet section, the 19" cymbal would be too large and heavy to produce the desired effect. It would be difficult to control, and muffling with the hand would not stop the sound immediately. A 15" thin cymbal would be much more appropriate. It would speak quickly and, just as important, it could be muffled between crashes so that the sound was really staccato. However, the smaller, lighter cymbal would not be as good a choice for the fortissimo roll in the first example.

It is certainly not necessary for the typical band or orchestra to have twenty cymbals to cover all needed effects. The important thing is to choose the cymbal best suited for the situation when two or more cymbals are available. In actually selecting cymbals for your organization, it is important to remember that the needs of one group can vary considerably from those of another. A small junior high school band could probably operate reasonably well using just one suspended cymbal — 16", thin to medium-thin. A large high school or college band should probably have three suspended cymbals: one should be fairly large (19" or more) and of medium-thin to medium weight; another should be of medium size (about 18") and of medium-thin weight; and the third cymbal should be a smaller size (14"-16") and of thin weight.

Because the size and the quality of the organization have so much bearing on the type of cymbals that the group should have, it is necessary for the director to know how different cymbals react so that the right choice can be made — both in the purchasing and in the playing.

Concepts for the Inexperienced Mallet Player

Larry Snider

When teaching mallet instruments to grade school, high school, or even college percussionists, many teachers initially become more involved in teaching note reading than technique. This provides the student with the ability to read melodies, but fails to give him the technique to play musically and accurately. This situation can be easily remedied by avoiding overemphasis on notation and concentrating on the following techniques and concepts from the very start.

Mallet Grip

For best control, the thumb and index finger should be placed on the mallet at an equilibrium point, the rest of the fingers falling loosely around the mallet. Emphasis should be placed on keeping the back of the hand parallel to the floor; this will help insure better control and a cleaner stroke. If a student is having difficulty, place a quarter on the back of his hand, and tell him it must stay there while he plays. This exaggerates the palm-down position but is effective in giving the student a good idea of the correct position.

The Strokes

The most commonly used stroke on any mallet instrument is done by snapping the wrist immediately after the mallet strikes the bar. This produces a very distinct articulation as well as a good tone. In explaining this type of stroke to a student, the analogy of touching a hot stove can be effective (the wrist must be snapped back immediately to avoid getting burned).

Accented notes should be played in the same way — but with more stress. However, young mallet players tend to push the stick into the bar to produce an accent instead of making the necessary snap of the wrist. The result is a very dull unmusical sound.

The *staccato stroke* is not generally used as much in the primary stages, but if learned at the start, the technique will eventually become almost automatic. To get a staccato sound, the student should use a much firmer grip and a quicker snap of the wrist. Staccato effects can be enhanced by the extension of the index finger over the mallet (if used with care) and the use of harder mallets.

The *legato stroke* is done with a loose, relaxed grip and with the mallets quite close to the bars. Many players use a slight downward motion to prepare for the initial stroke. Softer mallets will enhance legato effects.

The Roll

Begin with a single stroke roll, again stressing the importance of snapping the wrist. This technique should be practiced every day and during every lesson until a clean even roll is produced (see Ex. 1).

Ex. 1.

Legato rolls should also be studied in the initial stages. The student should lean into every note without creating any sort of accent — attempting to create a smooth continuous sound. This can be practiced by playing a legato roll on scale degrees (see Ex. 2).

Ex. 2.

Certain warm-up exercises (Ex. 3) will help the student develop staccato, legato, and marcato strokes, as well as the roll.

Ex. 3.
(Use any major or minor scale.)

Reading Music

One of the most common problems among beginning mallet students is keeping the eyes on the music. Students tend to look at the keyboard rather than the music. As a result, reading ability may deteriorate or fail to develop, and of course the student may continually lose his place in the music. To avoid problems in this area, students must learn to use peripheral vision, concentrating on the relationship between the keys on the upper and lower keyboards.

Unfortunately, many bell kits on the market and many older xylophones and marimbas have the note names engraved on each bar, encouraging the student to look for the engraved note name rather than depending on peripheral vision. In such cases, it may be necessary to place masking tape over the note names. The tape causes only a slight deterioration in tone quality and can be removed as soon as the student has learned to use peripheral vision.

Foot Work and Body Motion

Although beginning mallet playing is generally confined to a one- or two-octave area, it is important for students to learn foot coordination in preparation for the large leaps that occur in more advanced music.

Students playing music within a limited range have a tendency to put most of their weight on one foot. Then, if an extended jump is necessary, the student is likely to go through an uncoordinated shift which may cause a break in the melodic line. If, on the other hand, the student had learned to stand with an even distribution of weight on each foot, he would be able to shift smoothly either up or down the keyboard. A good analogy would be the football linebacker — who is prepared to go either left or right when the play starts. Most beginning material does not require large leaps, but by using two- or three-octave arpeggios and scales in each lesson, the student can begin to learn the basic techniques of foot and body manipulation.

Three and Four Mallet Studies

As soon as a student is able to manipulate two mallets and read simple melodies, he should be introduced to 3 and then 4 mallet techniques. Since simple whole- and half-note melodies must be used at first, students who wait too long will feel as though they are regressing and may have difficulty maintaining sufficient interest to really succeed in mastering these techniques. A beginner should probably use the cross stick grip (the mallets are easier to handle), rather than the more advanced Musser grip. Some teachers advocate using the 4 mallet grip while playing 2 mallet exercises in order to give students the "feel" of 4 mallets before actually playing with all four. Although there are many books devoted to 3 and 4 mallet techniques, *My Marimba and I* by Earl Hatch is one of the best, and it will appeal to both young and older students.

Each of the preceding mallet concepts can be used to facilitate the development of technique in the initial stages of mallet instruction. With emphasis on these concepts in warm-ups and lessons, the inexperienced mallet player will soon develop more control of his instru-

ment as well as the technical precision and sight-reading ability that form an essentail basis for more advanced stages of performance.

The exercises shown in Ex. 4 can be used as a general introduction to 3 mallet playing, which, in my opinion, must precede 4 mallet studies. The student uses 2 mallets in the right hand and one in the left, and then the reverse. In this way, the problem of using 2 mallets in one hand is approached "one-hand-at-a-time."

January 1975

Flams, Ruffs, and Rolls

Terry Applebaum

A solid and dependable snare drum technique, including flams, ruffs, and rolls, is considered essential to the student percussionist today. Many hours have been devoted to these basic techniques and much has been written about their execution, yet mediocre playing persists. The dilemma may be attributed to four broad areas about which students have little or no understanding: (1) the function of flams, ruffs, and rolls; (2) the performance principles associated with embellishments and rolls; (3) various roll types; and (4) the meaning of "even" playing.

Flams

A flam is comprised of one grace note that precedes one principal note (notated  LR RL). Its function is to produce a sound that is wider or thicker than one made by a single stroke. Flams may be played *closed* (only a fraction of a second between taps) or *open* (slightly more time between taps); the choice is largely subjective, with the musical style always considered. Open flams are more often associated with music that is martial in nature and closed flams with concert-style music. A special type of flam, in which both the grace and the principal notes are played at the same volume, is written as one note with two stems (). In any case, the characteristic sound of a flam is a combination of two taps used to create a single entity — not two unrelated notes.

It is important to remember that a flam is an *embellishment*, not a new rhythmic figure, nor an accent; and it does not sound as a double stop. The principal note should sound at the same volume as the unembellished notes which surround it, but the grace note, which falls just prior to the main note, should be softer. Thus, when performing a passage at a constant dynamic, the player must actually control two volume levels: one for principal (or unembellished) notes, and another for grace notes. This is an important point. If the grace note is not softer than the principal note, every flam will tend to sound accented.

In order to execute flams successfully, I recommend thinking in terms of *preparation, attack,* and *follow-through* positions. In the preparation position, the stick that is to play the grace note is placed low, very close to the head, with the stick that is to play the principal note in a normal position. When feasible, the hands should be moved to the preparation position in rhythm, on the upbeat before the attack. One suggestion frequently offered to help students play flams is to have them imitate the sound of the word "flam" with the sticks. Sometimes asking a student to think of both sticks falling to the head simultaneously is also helpful — the sticks will arrive slightly separated, because the preparation position places them at different heights.

Immediately after the grace note is played, the stick begins the follow-through by moving upward and assuming the preparation position for the principal note of the next flam. Once the principal note has been played, that stick moves upward and assumes the preparation position for the next grace note. The basic idea is that the sticks are not in the same plane except during the split second they pass in the air. A properly executed flam should give the visual impression of a pulley.

The preparation, attack, and follow-through sequence, as discussed above, assumes the application of alternate sticking. However, when playing a series of flams that are not executed hand-to hand, the follow-through is altered so as to allow each stick to return to its previous preparation position. In either situation, the performance principle remains constant — the sticks are kept in different planes.

Ruffs

A second category of snare drum embellishments includes ruffs or drags. The three-stroke ruff (LLR RRL) is the most common, although the four-stroke ruff (LRLR RLRL) is seen with some frequency. The function and principles of execution for ruffs are the same as those for flams. Also similar is the open-closed style option. It should be understood, however, that the characteristic sound of a closed ruff is still a pre-determined number of attacks, generally three or four in rapid succession, and not a one-handed buzz roll.

Rolls

If a percussion student or teacher is asked to enumerate those technical problems which are most persistent, the inability to play an even snare drum roll will surely appear high on the list.

Uneven rolls have been a source of frustration to students and teachers for years, yet few subjects associated with percussion pedagogy have been given more lines of print in professional journals or received more hours of rehearsal, clinic, and lesson time. While there are many reasons why the realization of an even snare drum roll has become a pedagogic enigma, I believe a significant factor has been that many students do not thoroughly understand how a roll is articulated, the differences and similarities between basic roll styles, and perhaps most important, what it means to play *even* rolls.

The function of a snare drum roll is to sustain the drum's tone by means of reiterated attacks in rapid succession. These taps essentially result from a series of wrist strokes played with alternate sticking (RLRL or LRLR). Following each wrist stroke, the stick is allowed to bounce one or more times. The number of wrist strokes played in a given length of time is a variable directly affected by tempo. In Example 1, the beamed groups of notes written above the rolls represent the probable number of *wrist strokes.* Observe that the same musical passage requires a different number of wrist motions for each of the three tempos.

Example 1

Further, note that in all three tempos the wrist strokes are equidistant and specific rhythmic values have been assigned. Although this wrist stroke rhythm is frequently referred to as the "underlying pulse" of a roll, it is important to understand that, ultimately, the rhythm is to be more *felt* than actually heard.

There are basically two types of snare drum rolls: (1) the measured roll, frequently referred to as rudimental or military style; and (2) the multi-bounce roll, also called a concert style roll. Decisions concerning which roll-type to use must depend upon the style of the music being performed. And percussionists must be able to execute both types of rolls in order to accurately perform music of various styles. The technical difference between the two types involves the number of bounces following each wrist stroke. Measured rolls are open-styled, requiring only one bounce, and multi-bounce rolls are more closed since they utilize several bounces. But measured and multi-bounce rolls share some important characteristics. Example 2 demonstrates how, in both cases, the same rhythmic value can be applied to the wrist motions. Another common characteristic is that all taps are equidistant. In the case of the measured roll, the single bounces in combination with the wrist stroke rhythm pattern yield a predetermined *total roll rhythm* that is twice the speed of the wrist motion (Ex. 2b). When playing a multi-bounce roll, the total number of taps is not predetermined, since the number of bounces following each wrist stroke is described only as being "several." Although two or three bounces are frequently articulated, this number should not be construed as a consistent performance practice. The only rule concerning the number of bounces in a given multi-bounce roll is that the same number should follow each wrist stroke. Note also that for all standard snare drum rolls, the final tap is a single wrist stroke that should not be accented unless indicated.

Example 2a. Written

Example 2b. Measured Roll

Example 2c. Multi-Bounce Roll

wavy line = several bounces

Many students do not thoroughly comprehend the distinction between wrist strokes and bounces. Often, students associate the fast successive attacks of a roll with rapid wrist movement in a 1:1 ratio. A basic principle demonstrated in the above examples is that although the roll consists of many fast notes, the wrists move at a rather moderate speed. An awareness of a given underlying pulse has the added advantage of supplying a rhythmic structure that the student can use as a basis for counting.

In order to decide upon the number of wrist motions required for a given roll, the exact duration of that roll must be known. Unfortunately, composers have not always notated rolls with precision or consistency. Most difficult to interpret are rolls that have no tie indicating where the final attack occurs. Such notational ambiguities and some probable solutions are shown in Example 3. None of these solutions should be considered inherently superior. Any one could be chosen, depending on the musical context.

Example 3.

Even Rolls

Once a student understands the different roll types and how they are played, the teaching emphasis can move toward the development of an *even* roll. But, what does "even" mean? Do our students have a real understanding of the word? Can they identify basic elements of evenness? Unfortunately, many students have only vague ideas about this basic concept of percussion performance.

Evenness simply means that both hands sound identical. The grip (neither too tight nor too loose) is extremely important in accomplishing this sameness. The following basic elements must also be present:

1. *Matched Sticks.* Finding a perfectly matched pair of sticks is

all but impossible, but the essential characteristics (length, weight, thickness, etc.) must be the same.

2. *Matched Volume.* If both sticks travel the same distance (both stroke and bounce) and strike the head with equal force, the volume produced will be the same.

3. *Matched Timbre.* For consistent sound, both sticks must strike the drum head as close to the same spot as possible Moving the sticks straight up and down will help to hit a very small and restricted area.

4. *Matched Articulation.* Exactly the same number of taps should be played in each hand, with all taps spaced precisely the same distance apart.

Note that such physical elements as stance and wrist/arm/elbow position must be correct in order to provide the necessary control of the sticks. Only when students really understand these basic elements can they begin to practice efficiently.

I am convinced that a significant amount of time devoted to practicing snare drum rolls is wasted, because many students are unable to clearly identify what is wrong with their playing. They spend hours playing roll exercises over and over, with the hope that somehow the repetition will improve their roll. Sometimes the roll does sound better. But rarely does it improve to a significant degree, because thoughtless repetition tends to reinforce rather than correct bad habits.

The problems that percussion students experience with flams, ruffs and rolls are not necessarily associated with the degree of their inherent musical talent. These difficulties generally result from not understanding the basic mechanics of playing embellishments and rolls, and an inability to first identify specific technical problems and then to work efficiently toward their solution. Fortunately, the quality of percussion teaching has been steadily improving. As a result, we can look forward to hearing our students give quality performances of all sorts of music — whether it involves complex structures or just the basic flams, ruffs, and rolls.

February 1975

The Conga Drum

Ron Delp

One of the most important percussion instruments used in modern jazz and rock music is the conga drum. Though primarily a Latin American instrument (via Africa) and for a long time confined to music of that idiom, the conga has firmly established itself as a jazz/rock instrument, one which can add a modern touch to the school stage band.

The playing technique is quite simple but requires practice, since the physical technique has next-to-nothing in common with snare drum, timpani, etc. And, if improperly played (or tuned), the conga drums will sound muddy or sloppy instead of providing sharp, articulate rhythms.

Choosing the Drum(s)

In traditional Latin music, each player usually performs on only one drum. Today, one performer playing two, three, or four drums is not uncommon. But due to finances, most stage bands are limited to only one drum, so knowing how to pick the best drum is extremely important.

Congas are available with wood and fiberglass shells. Fiberglass is generally a little more expensive, but the sound tends to "cut" better. However, the most important considerations when choosing a drum are the size (head diameter) and quality of the head.

Conga drums come in three basic sizes (which may vary slightly between manufacturers): quinto (9-10" head), conga (10-11" head), and tumba (11-12½" head). If only one drum is to be used, the conga size is preferable. The usual order of purchase is conga, tumba, then quinto (the solo instrument).

Heads are made of a variety of materials, including mule skin, kip hide, cowhide, and plastic. Mule skin is traditional, but its thickness makes it more difficult for inexperienced players to obtain the proper sounds. Thin muleskin (less than 1/8") or kip hide is much easier to play, especially on the conga and quinto sizes. Cowhide is less desirable, because it is too thin to produce a good solid sound and, in my opinion, plastic heads should be avoided entirely.

Both tunable and non-tunable models are available. The tunable models are provided with various types of clamps or bolts which may be tightened with an end wrench or similar tool. Models using tension rods which are operated with a drum key (similar to a snare drum) should be avoided, as the player can badly bruise or cut his hands on the rods (and this type of drum usually comes with plastic heads).

With non-tunable drums, the head is tacked directly onto the shell. The major disadvantage here is that there is no way to alter the tension on the head if it should stretch or contract due to atmospheric conditions. (It is possible to tighten the head by holding it over a can of Sterno which will dry out the moisture.)

One final item to keep in mind when purchasing a conga drum is a stand (usually tripod-shaped). These are available for all models and can be very useful, since the traditional method of balancing the drum between the legs is quite difficult for the beginner.

Tuning the Drum

The tautness of the conga head is extremely important. If the head is too loose, "open" tones will sound dull and "slaps" may not work at all. On the other hand, if the head is too tight, slaps will be easier, but open notes will be too high-pitched. Tuning the drum extremely tight or loose to make certain sounds easier to obtain is *never* a substitute for good technique. Once a certain amount of technique is learned, experimentation will usually result in a well-tuned drum. Listening to recordings by professional conga players will certainly aid in finding the right sound.

Drum and Hand Position

The most important consideration when beginning the study of the conga is to remember that the drums are played from the wrists *only;* arm movement should be kept to a minimum.

Begin without the drum. Sit with your back straight on a chair or stool and, with elbows about two inches from your sides, hold your forearms out in front of you parallel to the floor. Extend your fingers, palms facing the floor, with the fingers together and the thumbs firmly alongside the index fingers. Cup the hands slightly (see Fig. 1).

Fig. 1

Now, completely relaxing the wrists, allow the hands to drop loosely toward the floor, keeping the fingers and thumbs together. Then bend the wrists quickly in the opposite direction so that the fingers point upward. Repeat this up-down procedure about fifty times working up speed as you go. You should do this warm-up exercise with both hands moving together, then alternating (one hand up, the other down). As you do the exercise, make sure that the fingers and thumbs are together, that the forearms do not move . . . and relax!

If a stand is not used, the drum must be balanced between the player's legs. With the bottom of the drum resting on the floor, the head should come up approximately to the player's navel. Using an adjustable drum stool rather than a chair will make it easier to position the head at the proper playing height.

Sitting on the edge of the stool, place the feet flat on the floor, approximately 14" apart, with the left heel (for right handed players) 4-6 inches in front of the right. Place the drum on the floor between the legs and tip it so that it rests against the inside of the right thigh, just above the knee. Move the left leg in so that it rests against the other side of the drum. Now, adjust the left foot so that the drum can be held firmly (with the head at a comfortable playing angle) without using the hands.

If a conga stand is used, the leg position is arbitrary, and the head angle is easier to control. The player may even stand if desired.

Striking the Drum

There are three basic sounds produced on the conga: the open tone, the closed tone (sometimes called muffled or bass tone), and the slap. All three are equally important.

Open Tone

The open tone is produced by striking the rim of the drum with the palm (under the knuckles that connect the fingers with the palm), and allowing the fingers to slap on the head. Once the fingers strike the head, bend the wrist back snapping the fingers off. The resulting sound should be a ringing pop (see Fig. 2).

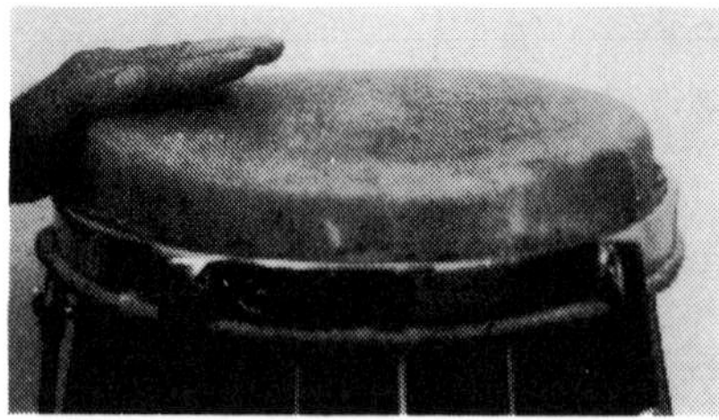

Fig. 2

Be sure to keep the fingers and thumb together and the wrist relaxed. When using the technique with both hands, try to get the same sound from each. Remember that the drum is actually struck only by the palm against the rim; the fingers just fall on the head as a result of the strike. Rolls on the conga drum are rapidly played open tones.

Closed Tone

The closed tone uses an altogether different technique, and is usually played with only the left hand (for right-handed players). The basic hand/arm position is the same as for the open tone, except that the fingers, instead of pointing straight out in a slightly cupped position, are bent upwards. The fingers should still be together (see Fig. 3).

Fig. 3

The drum is struck in the center or just off-center, with the same portion of the palm used in producing the open tone (under the knuckles that connect the fingers to the palm). Some arm motion is necessary, but keep it to a minimum. Unlike the open tone, the hand is not drawn away from the head immediately, but lingers a split-second to insure a fully muffled "thud" (see Fig. 4).

Fig. 4

The Slap

Sharp accents on conga are performed with the slap tone, which produces a loud, sharp, pop resembling the crack of a whip. It is definitely the most difficult tone to produce and requires much practice. Slap tones are generally produced with the right hand (in right-handed players), but it is often necessary to use the left as well especially for heavily syncopated rhythmic figures.

The hand/arm position for the slap is the same as for the open tone, but the manner in which the drum is struck is different. Here, the *center* of the palm (closer to the heel) strikes the rim, causing the fingers to be slapped onto the head, and the fingers remain on the head for a split-second to kill the ring. As the fingers strike the head, a small "grabbing" motion with the fingertips will help obtain a good, sharp slap. Also, if the stroke is slanted outward (instead of straight down) the tone will be sharper (see Fig. 5).

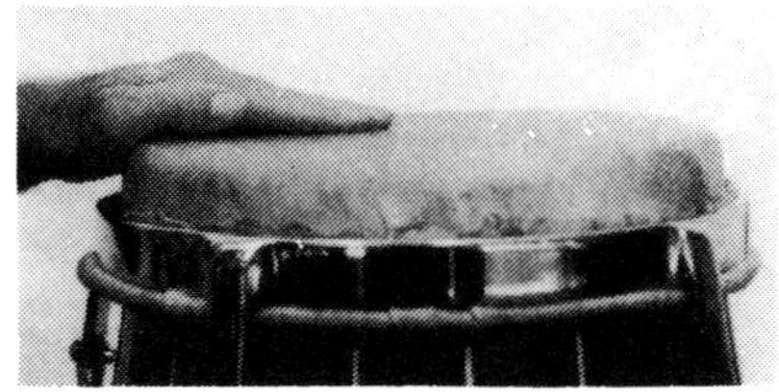

Fig. 5

The slap tone is difficult to produce on a thick head or on a loose one. You might try tightening the head a little to get the feel for the slap, then loosen it gradually back to normal as you get better at it. But even when you do get the feel of it, it is hard to produce 100% of the time.

Combination Strokes

Some interesting sounds can be obtained by combining strokes. A muffled slap can be attained by producing a closed tone with the left hand, then a slap with the right while the left muffles the drum. A softer open tone can be produced by striking a closed tone with the left hand and an *open* tone with the right. Very loud accents may be accomplished by playing a "flam" with slap tones in both hands (one as the grace note). Different pitches can be obtained by pressing the left elbow into the head with varying pressure while striking open tones with the right. Interesting glisses may be produced by rubbing the tip of an index or middle finger across the diameter of the head; moistening the fingertip first will help. Striking an open tone with the other hand at the same time will provide more volume.

Striking the conga drum, with any of the above techniques, can bruise the hands, causing some degree of discomfort. Professional, full-time conga players build up a layer of callouses which protect them. But for beginners and/or part-time players, it is a good idea to cover the knuckles with a layer or two of adhesive tape to help eliminate any painful bruises that might interfere with technical development.

March 1975

Marching Percussion — An Interview with Larry McCormick

Ron Fink

Larry, I know that you have gained quite a reputation in the marching percussion field and are in demand for clinics and workshops. I'm interested in your over-all concept of the marching band, especially as it relates to the percussion section.

I think the marching band's purpose is primarily promotional — I mean that its job is to sell music through the presentation of a pleasing and entertaining audio/visual program for as large an audience as possible.

For the marching band show to be most effective, it must be performed with a very high degree of precision; unfortunately, this is seldom achieved by the typical high school or college band. I think the failure to reach the level of professionalism and excellence that today's standards demand is largely due to the belief that there must be a totally *new* show for each appearance. I believe that a basic show structure can be designed that allows the group to use some elements over and over (perfecting them as the season progresses) while still presenting something new and fresh at each performance. Also, I believe that the drill must grow out of the music (not the other way around) — otherwise, you are not directing a band, but simply a musically-accompanied drill team.

For over-all band precision it is mandatory that the percussion section provide a solid tempo. Obviously, they can do this job best if they are in the center of the band, so I treat the percussion section as a separate entity — not as a part of the standard ranks and files — and I do not require them to perform rapid movements, high-stepping or any other maneuvers that will hamper their primary purpose — *to produce a steady tempo and a solid sound.* This is not to say that the visual aspects are not important; there are plenty of movements (juggling the sticks, spinning the cymbals) that can add eye interest without taking away from the sound and the precision.

What size percussion section do you recommend for the marching band?

I like an eight-member section for bands with up to a total of about 75 pieces, and I would assign them to 3 snare drums, 2 different size bass drums, 2 timp-tom trios, and 1 cymbal.

Let's assume that you are directing a marching band, have an unlimited budget (!) and wish to buy a complete set of percussion instruments. What would you get?

I would buy 12" x 15" field drums, with gut snares, and probably with the chrome finish (they are the most popular today). That size drum requires a heavy stick, so I would choose an S1, a 3S or 2S, but certainly not the 2B that so many groups use (I find the pointed bead to be most unattractive for field drumming). I would probably choose a black sling (rather than the more traditional white), simply because they don't show the dirt. Also, I would get a multi-angled carrier — a device that can be hooked onto the sling; it's used to level the drum, reducing the severe angle that requires the left hand to be held so uncomfortably high. All drums should have mounted leg rests, so the instrument does not bounce around and the player has a predictable target.

I would not purchase tenor drums for today's band. Marching timp-tom trios provide a much broader and more musical spectrum. It is also an exciting instrument visually. My first choice would be the 10" depth by 14", 16", and 18" diameters. For the second set, some directors like the slightly larger 12" depth by 16", 18", and 20" diameters; but I prefer two identical sets, because this provides a cleaner, less cluttered sound. Most current methods of carrying these instruments are inadequate, although some special carriers are now being made available.

When choosing bass drums, I recommend creating a section made up of various sizes. My first choice is the 14" x 28", then the 14" x 22" or 24". If I could add a third drum, it would be a 14" x 32" or a 16" x 34" in order to provide an even bigger and deeper quality to this section. The beaters should be chosen for the size of the drums — hard felt for the small and medium size, and fur-covered (less articulate) for the large bass drum. The new padded bass drum carrier is probably the most comfortable method now available of carrying the drum.

I would buy medium-heavy weight cymbals for field durability. At least 16" for the first pair, then 18", followed by 20" and 22" (medium weight is best for these). The high luster finish is most dramatic for field show use. The smaller cymbals could be equipped with the spinning cymbal handles, but the larger ones should have leather straps with pads.

I would add a pair of marching timpani (26" and 23") and, if possible, even a third (29"). The most practical way for a band member to carry these drums on the field is with a special carrier, but I'm not opposed to the wheeled devices — they avoid having to actually carry all that weight.

The marching xylophone, orchestra bells, and bell lyra will add some interesting tone colors to the section; and I recommend using them. The bell lyra should be held horizontally, with a special carrier, so that the player can use *both* hands for playing the instrument in the new two-mallet style.

Bags should be attached to the drums in order to have other instruments readily available on the field — I mean such things as tambourines, cow bells, gongs, wood blocks, plus an assortment of sticks and beaters in various sizes and weights.

How about tuning, adjusting the proper head tension. What do you do?

The best way to tune the percussion section is to take the group out on the field, stand back where most of the audience will be, and listen. Then experiment with the tension until you get the most pleasing sounds. I find that the typical high school section gets a poor sound mostly because they use too little tension. I recommend that snare drums be very tight — to get a clean, crisp, dry sound. The timp-tom trio should be tuned to either a minor or a diminished triad, but not in a key commonly used by the band (a B♭ chord is *not* the best choice).

What style of drum cadence do you prefer?

I like those that use the full instrumentation of the section — including the new melodic possibilities — and are visually exciting at the same time. A good cadence will instill pride in the members of the section, as well as motivate them to improve their level of technique and musical mastery of the percussion instruments.

Are you optimistic about the future of the percussion section in the school marching band?

Absolutely. The marching percussion section can be the strongest addition to the marching band *if the players are challenged*; but up until just recently, demands upon the percussionist have not been great enough to encourage them to achieve a higher degree of excellence in their performances. The band director must provide the challenge for the many capable and talented young percussionists in the school systems today. Fortunately, there are an increasing number of specialists in this field who can give the directors the kind of expert help they may need.

Developing Keyboard Mallet Technique

Karen Ervin

Two-Mallet Technique

The mallet should be held firmly (but not too tight) about a third of the way up the handle, with the thumb and forefinger opposite each other. The other fingers should be curved around the mallet, touching it lightly. (The little finger does not necessarily touch the mallet at all.) The fingers should be tight enough to control the mallet but loose enough so that there is some motion of the mallet handle within the hand.

The basic motion of the mallet is from the wrist. A good stroke is produced by striking the bar with a relaxed hand and wrist and immediately lifting the mallet back to its original position. It should feel as if the mallet "bounces" off the bar. At the same time, be sure that the "white" keys of the instrument are struck in the center and the raised keys in the center or on the edge nearest the player. Be careful not to strike on the nodes; these are "dead" spots where the string runs through the bar.

Many studies are available for developing two-mallet technique. Some of my favorites include: Vic Firth's *Mallet Technique* (Carl Fischer); Garwood Whaley, *Fundamental Studies for Mallets* (JR Publications, 3 Sheridan Sq., New York, N.Y. 10014) for beginners; Wohlfahrt, *Sixty Studies for Violin* (G. Schirmer) for intermediate players; and, for advanced players, Dale Anderson's *The Well-Tempered Mallet Player* (TRY Publications, Professional Drum Shop, 854 N. Vine St., Hollywood, Calif. 90028).

Sight-reading is also important in developing mallet technique — and it is essential in many student and professional situations. Students should sight-read daily from the very beginning. Choose a suitable book, easy enough to read the first time without too many mistakes, and have the student play through each page or piece once (without repeating unless the first try was disastrous). If possible, students should read duets with other players (mallets or otherwise). This will prevent stopping whenever a mistake is made, a common fault of many students when sight-reading.

Two-Mallet Technique — Common Problems

- Fingers are too tight — the mallet is not "giving" in the hand.
- Thumb and first finger are not opposite each other; first finger is loose and straightening out along the mallet.
- One or both mallets are held too far up or back.
- Too much use of the arm in producing the stroke.

Four-Mallet Grips — Common Problems

- Too much pressure from thumb and first, third and fourth finger — or both. Too much pressure in one part of the hand results in lack of control (mallets tend to fly apart or together); and if both parts of the hand are too tight, the hand and the sound will be stiff.
- Sticks are held too high or low on the handle.
- Sticks are too high in the air; the mallet approaches the bar at a bad angle.
- Mallets are not bouncing off the bar.
- Too tight an arm or too much arm motion (especially common in rolls), resulting in a hard, stiff sound.

Four-Mallet Technique

My students begin three- and four-mallet technique as soon as they have a working knowledge of the keyboard — usually by the third or fourth lesson at the latest. It takes a while to be comfortable with four mallets, so an early start really helps.

Cross Grip A is the most common four-mallet grip. The handle of the inner mallet is crossed over the handle of the outer mallet, with about an inch of mallet below the crossing point (see Fig. 1). To hold the mallets, the third and fourth fingers should be placed at the crossing point and the thumb and first finger between the mallets, with the outside mallet touching the thumb at the base of the thumb nail. Both thumb and first finger should be bent for the smaller positions and straightened out as the interval between the mallets widens. The second finger rests against the outside of the outer mallet. Four-mallet control seems to be achieved by balancing pressures. The thumb and first finger exert a little pressure to keep the two mallets apart. The other fingers, especially the third and fourth, exert pressure to keep the mallets together. If there is too much pressure the hand will be tight and stiff, and if there is too little pressure the mallets will be uncontrolled.

Fig. 1. Cross Grip A in closed position (2 views).

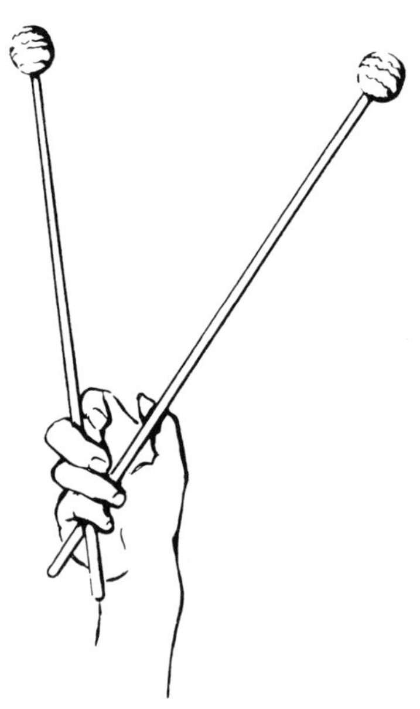

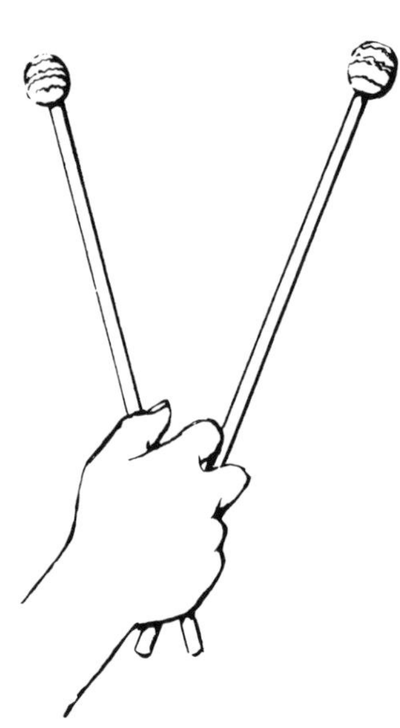

Cross Grip B is the same grip as Cross Grip A, but the outer mallet-handles are crossed over the inner.

Burton Grip is a variation of Cross Grip B. For a complete explanation, see Gary Burton's *Four-Mallet Studies* (Creative Music), pp. 3-5.

Musser Grip is different from the others in that the mallets are not crossed; thus, they can act with a certain amount of independence. In this grip the outer mallet is held by the third and fourth fingers, the inner by the thumb and first finger. The second finger aids the first finger in controlling the inner mallet.

As in two-mallet playing, it is extremely important that the mallets lift or "bounce" rapidly off the bar — no matter which grip is being used.

Elements of Four-Mallet Technique

Since most music for marimba or vibraphone uses a combination of techniques at all times, dividing the techniques into different elements is useful in teaching, in divising exercises, and to make sure that no single area is being slighted in the student's practice.

1. All four mallets together. The student may begin with two mallets in one hand, then two in the other. In a typical first lesson for control of two mallets in a single hand, the student should work with one hand at a time. An exercise, such as Example 1, might

Ex. 1. Right hand alone, then left hand alone.

be practiced in a number of keys or extended in range. Then add similar exercises with jumps instead of stepwise motion. A series of exercises of this type is Earl Hatch's *Mallet Manipulation* (Earl Hatch Publications, 5140 Vineland Ave., North Hollywood, Calif. 91601). Once these initial exercises have been mastered, the student can begin working on chordal exercises (Ex. 2). Much material of

Ex. 2. Play each chord, no roll; roll each chord; then roll each chord, connecting smoothly.

this type is available. Among the best exercises are *Graded Reading Exercises for Four Mallets* by Max Neuhaus (Music for Percussion) and Earl Hatch's *My Marimba and I* (Earl Hatch Publications).

2. Independence of two hands. This type of technique is really a variation of the type discussed above. One hand may play two

Ex. 3

simultaneous notes alone; the other may play one or two notes (Ex. 3). The exercises in the Neuhaus book are especially good for developing this technique.

3. Pivot. The pivot is the use of the two mallets of one hand independently. With Cross Grips A and B and the Burton Grip, a rocking motion of the hand is necessary. In the Musser Grip, the pivot is achieved through the independent use of the fingers. An exercise,

Ex. 4

such as Example 4 (played in several keys), can be used to develop the various pivot techniques. For more advanced pivot exercises, I use the chordal studies in the Neuhaus book, repeating them several times with variations, as shown in Example 5.

Ex. 5.

4. One-mallet melodic playing. Exercises for this type of technique are easy to find. First, play scales, arpeggios or any melodic line with each mallet — while holding two in one hand. (The exercises in Burton's *Four-Mallet Technique*, pp. 21-24, are especially good.) Then play a melodic line with two mallets in one hand, using a combination of pivot and single-mallet techniques.

Today's Field Percussion

Fred Sanford

The area of field percussion is undergoing a tremendous surge of growth and development. The percussion sections of today's drum and bugle corps, as well as those of many high school and college marching bands, are rapidly expanding with the advent of many new percussion instruments. The traditional tenor drum has been replaced with multiple tom-tom devices (known as timp-toms because of their timpani-like resonance). Bass drums in various sizes are providing additional pitches. Marching timpani have become very popular as have a number of "percussion effect" instruments such as bongos, timbales, and conga drums. Further expansion is possible with the use of tambourines, cowbells, wood blocks, antique cymbals — the list of trap instruments is really limitless. And now mallet instruments have also found their place in the marching percussion section. The addition of piccolo xylophones and orchestra bells (both carried horizontally) has made it possible for the entire drum line to function as a self-contained musical entity, providing melody, harmony and rhythm.

Adapted from "New Developments for Today's Field Percussion," *Remo Percussion Topics* No. 1, 1974. The original publication is available from Remo, Inc., 12804 Raymer St., North Hollywood, California 91605.

Instrumentation and Personnel

Instrumentation is, of course, a personal preference but you might consider the following: 3-5 (or more) snare drums; 3 sets of timp-toms; 3 or 4 bass drums (usually of different sizes for better tonal separation); and 3 or 4 pairs of cymbals. Additions to this might include 2 to 4 marching timpani, marching mallet instruments, or any of the Latin effect instruments. The various trap instruments can be

played by all members of the percussion section.

Many band directors have found additional members for the percussion section by utilizing those students who normally play instruments not designed for outdoor use. A student pianist, for example, can usually adapt quite easily to a marching xylophone, and, with some instruction in basic percussion technique, other students have proven themselves to be quite adept at filling out the tonal spectrum of the expanded drum lines. Needless to say, this idea gives more students the chance to participate and enhances their complete musical awareness by giving them the opportunity to experiment with another family of musical instruments.

Selecting Instruments

Snare drums

The most popular size for marching use is the 12″ x 15″ snare drum (*i.e.*, drum shell depth x head diameter). I prefer using gut snares for a dry, crisp sound and, for head selection, a batter head with transparent center piece applied to the smooth white film — in combination with a regular, medium weight bottom snare head — will produce a clean, well-defined quality of sound.

Timp-toms

Timp-toms are available in a variety of drum combinations and sizes. Compared to the larger models, tenor timp-toms (10″ x 14″, 16″, 18″) are relatively easy to carry and do not interfere with the lower pitched percussion instruments such as bass drums or timpani.

Bass drums

Selecting bass drums is at times a problem due to the number of sizes available. The most popular sizes for pitched bass drum use are 12″ x 28″, 14″ x 26″, 14″ x 28″, 16″ x 34″. To insure a full resonant tone quality from any bass drum, the depth of the drum should measure at least half the diameter of the drum. The term "pitched bass drum" indicates only that the sound of the drum falls into a certain tonal area (high, low, medium, etc.) in relation to other bass drums of different sizes — it does not refer to a specific pitch to which the drum must be tuned.

Cymbals

Cymbal sounds and colors vary greatly depending on the size and weight. For practical purposes, most marching groups use the heavier weight cymbals in sizes varying from 16″ to 26″. I have had good success using four pairs of cymbals — 18″, 20″ and 22″ in heavyweight and 26″ in the medium weight. The 26″ cymbals should be used sparingly as the size and weight make them rather hard to manipulate, and the very large sound generated by these cymbals should be reserved for strong accents and emphasizing musical climaxes.

Timpani

Marching timpani come in three standard sizes — 23″, 26″, and 29″. A typical section of four marching timpani would include 1 - 23″, 2 - 26″, and 1 - 29″.

Mallet Selection

Selecting the correct mallets for these various percussion instruments is extremely important. Playing a bass drum with a tenor drum mallet is as incorrect as playing a string bass with a violin bow. The

general rule is that the size of the mallet should correspond to the size of the drum.

A 3S stick is preferred for a field snare drum for a full sound and adequate projection. The timp-toms respond well to various types of mallets. A hard mallet is excellent for medium to loud dynamic levels; it also produces a good staccato sound. For a mellow, more legato quality on timp-toms, try a pair of soft felt or lambswool mallets. Bass drums respond best to a hard felt mallet.

Mallets made of different materials (wood, felt, plastic, etc.) can produce quite an array of sound colors. A little experimentation will help you determine which mallet is most appropriate in any given situation.

Instrument Condition and Adjustments

The first consideration is to have good quality drum heads. Severe dents or "played out" heads can greatly affect the sound of any drum. If necessary, the heads should be replaced. Tuning is also an essential factor in the sound of the ensemble and should be checked outdoors while standing at least 25 feet from the drum. When checking the tuning, remember that the sound changes according to the angle from which it is heard — especially on bass drums. The fullest, most resonant sound will be heard only when the bass drum head faces the listener.

Periodically, it will be necessary to check snare drum heads for evenness of tension by lightly tapping 1″-2″ from each lug to match up the sound. If a discrepancy in tension arises, make the necessary corrective adjustment by starting with the lowest pitch first and matching it with the highest. The batter head can and should hold a fairly high tension, but the snare head is usually much thinner and not as much tension is required.

It is also essential that all snares be of uniform tension. You will find this to be an arduous task, but for the snare drum to deliver a good, solid, crisp tone, the snare strainer must be adjusted properly. However, snare tension should be moderate; if the snares are too tight, the drum will sound choked and there will be no response at soft playing levels. As with any object under tension, snares are apt to stretch, slip out, or be knocked out of proper adjustment through mishandling and will need occasional readjustment.

Most smaller drums, including the snare drums and timp-toms, should not require muffling. The tone control adjustment on the snare drum should be enough to eliminate the more pronounced ring. In the case of the timp-toms, muffling only serves to impair sound projection as well as produce an inferior tone quality. The only drums that I recommend be muffled would be the bass drums — and even then with extreme discretion. With too much muffling, the drum will begin to sound like a cardboard box.

The Percussion Section in the Field Show

Integrating the percussion section into the marching maneuver provides some unique problems. In general, try to keep the percussion section together (excluding timpani) as much as possible and avoid involving them in intricate drill patterns. I am not advocating that the drum line remain stationary for the entire show but, due to the fact that many field percussion instruments are rather bulky and hard to maneuver, I would suggest that "floating" (*i.e.*, keeping the drum line drill patterns separate from the main body) will produce the best results. However, if the percussion section can be worked into a feature drill without an excessive amount of maneuvering — then it should be done.

Scoring and Arranging for Field Percussion

Many high school and college band directors find that the percussion parts supplied with most of today's marching band arrangements are totally inadequate. In order for the percussion section to contribute substantially to the success of the arrangement, it may be necessary for the director to score the parts himself. For instance, with a transcription for field use of Gustav Holst's "March" from his *First Suite in E♭* (for military band), the percussion parts might be scored as follows.

The snare drum part can follow the melodic line:

etc.

A timp-tom part might adapt as follows:

Four tuned bass drums could contribute additional sounds:

And cymbals could be used to highlight the rhythm:

etc.

Timpani could also be added to this field arrangement, and I would suggest using Holst's original timpani part, as it could be converted easily to marching timpani. Trap instruments such as tambourines and triangles could also be used effectively.

This arrangement might seem rather elementary, but the various tonal colors of the timp-toms and bass drum will produce a percussion ensemble blend that is full and rich and yet straightforward enough to be well defined

The degree of difficulty written into your percussion arrangements should relate of course to the proficiency of your students. Challenging your drum section with better and more difficult material will stimulate growth and interest. But all directors should realize that it takes much time and patience to develop a well balanced percussion section, just as it takes time to develop a fine brass, woodwind, or string section. And I mean time that is measured in seasons and years, not in days and weeks.

The area of field percussion is truly in the midst of an exciting and expanding era. The expanded percussion sections and the increased popularity of percussion solos and features in today's field show have truly added a whole new dimension to the concept of musical pageantry.

Notational Standards for Percussion

A Report on the Ghent Conference

Frank McCarty

Musical notation, the link between composer and performer, is facing its strongest test in this century. Many composers have begun to exploit expressive resources such as tone color, speech sounds and physical gesture; there is a tendency to specify more subtle and demanding passage work and some composers use notation to evoke special improvisatory situations rather than to specify distinct pitches or rhythms. As new notational formats appear, performers are placed in strange and complex surroundings. This is especially true for percussionists, who suffer the fate of having to play a wide variety of instruments in many different ways.

At present, the percussionist is often faced with compositions using different notations to stand for the same sound, instrument, or performance technique. In some cases, the staff may be augmented or replaced by written instructions or graphic symbology. One characteristic of a large percentage of recently composed music is the appearance of a "legend" to describe or define unfamiliar signs and special notational practices. Among other things, the composer has become a cartographer, and performers have had to become logicians and cryptologists!

The Index of New Musical Notation of the New York Public Library at Lincoln Center, through the efforts of Kurt Stone and Gerald Warfield, has collected and examined many examples of contemporary musical notation. They have also sent a large, detailed questionnaire to composers and performers in all parts of the world. These activities climaxed in October, 1974 with an International Conference on New Musical Notation (held in Belgium at the University of Ghent), where the results of the previous research on notational practice were presented in the form of suggested notational standards which the delegates could either accept, modify or reject.[1] This plan was intelligently tempered by a desire to codify without imposing restrictive absolutes. The scope of the notational considerations was generally limited to some of the newer aspects of *staff notation*. Other notational systems were, for the most part, avoided.

Of those invited to the conference, the performers (such as the American violinist Paul Zukofsky and the German percussionist Christoph Caskel) made some of the most significant and practical contributions. I believe that it was Zukofsky who reminded us that sight-reading must somehow be preserved. On the other hand, composers like Roger Reynolds and Earle Brown as well as the German composer/scholar Erhard Karkoschka, upheld the concept of *notational context*. We were thus prevented from the pitfall of simply selecting isolated symbols without considering the environment in which they would be used. These two issues — practicality and consistency — permeated the deliberations. At the end of the four-day Congress, many issues had been solved. But the composers, performers, publishers, and scholars participating in the conference found that even within the limited areas of concentration, many problems and controversies still existed.

As one of the American delegates, I was asked to prepare proposals for notational standards and to chair group sessions in percussion and electronics. These were the only areas in which the New York Index had not done major research. The notational problems found in percussion and electronic music are actually quite similar; in both cases one must first define the "instrument" before considering the notation of specific performance gestures. The ballot sheets submitted to the percussion group session included names of some sixty different instruments and about thirty different types of beaters. In electronic music, it is possible to "design" an infinite number of "instruments" depending upon the way in which modules are connected and how controls are set. While the percussion group spent about 75% of its time dealing with symbols to be used for instruments and beaters, the electronic music group devoted its entire time to the definition of "instruments."

In notating for percussion, it is usually necessary to keep instrumentation instructions as separate as possible from the music itself. It is indeed possible to write "snare drum" in the margin of a piece of music, but it becomes notationally complex when a percussionist is asked to play that snare drum with a variety of beaters in a variety of ways. And it becomes even more complex when the percussionist is asked to use several instruments, each calling for a variety of beaters and performance techniques. Written instructions, or even abbreviations, are often too cumbersome to be of value, especially when they are also used to describe special performance techniques, expressions, gesture, theater, etc. Furthermore, notation should be as universal as possible. In addition to his van full of instruments and cases of mallets, it is hardly practical to ask an Italian percussionist to carry musical dictionaries in English, French, German, Russian, Polish, etc., simply to know which instrument to use.

Following the lead of many significant composers as well as many percussionists and writers (such as Reginald Brindle-Smith),[2] we agreed to recommend the adoption of symbology for instrumentation. The

1. Information about the conference is beginning to appear (see the *Contemporary Music Newsletter*, Jan.-Feb. 1975); a forthcoming issue of *Interface* (published by the University of Ghent) will contain preliminary reports from the Conference.

2. R. Brindle-Smith, *Contemporary Percussion* (London: Oxford University Press, 1970).

Fig. 1. Representative Pictograms.
a. Suspended Cymbal
b. Whip
c. Xylophone
d. Snare Drum
e. TamTam
f. Snare Drum Stick
g. Soft Rubber Mallet
h. Medium String- or Yarn-Wound Mallet
i. Hard Timpani Mallet
j. Metal Hammer

suggested symbols are in the form of pictograms, simple line-drawings used to represent the most common percussion instruments and beaters (Fig. 1). The content of the list of pictograms presented to the conference was drawn from the results of a questionnaire which I circulated among American percussionists prior to the meeting in Belgium. (This preliminary survey was jointly sponsored by the Index of New Musical Notation and the Percussive Arts Society.) The symbols originally suggested were not newly invented. Rather, they were taken from many existing scores and various other sets of symbology. While pictograms are of extreme value in a composition using a large number of instruments and beaters, they are of little significance in simpler musical situations. Thus, we did not recommend that they be used in all cases.

Since the staff is the most widely accepted means of communicating pitch configurations, its application in the notation of pitched percussion is uncontestable. Yet certain factors, such as the printed format of manuscript paper and publishers' score layouts, have determined that most non-pitched percussion parts also appeared on the five-line staff. Some newer notational approaches place non-pitched percussion instruments on single lines rather than on the staff. This not only saves space, but it is of conceptual significance and allows for greater ease in reading solo multiple-percussion parts. Compositions such as *Circles* by Luciano Berio incorporate special "percussion scores" in which the set of instruments played by a percussionist appear on a line-score "system" following a logic of high to low ordering. In contrast, Brindle-Smith suggests the use of single lines for multiple percussion parts, accompanied by pictograms to indicate instrument changes.

The percussion group at the Conference felt that each of the above mentioned scoring techniques had value. The composer should make scoring decisions based upon the piece itself: the number of instruments and players used; the amount and speed of instrument changes required; the type of notation used for other instruments; etc. To aid these determinations, we suggested several general guidelines for percussion scoring. First, we proposed a percussion "score order" which may be applied in solo multiple percussion parts as well as in orchestral scores where the assignment of players to instruments is generally left up to the percussion section itself. This "suggested score order" accounts for the normal manner in which the percussionist sets up his instruments. In this way, the percussionist is able to read in the same high to low order in which his instruments are normally configured (Fig. 2).

Fig. 2. "Score Order" for Percussion.
A. Glass, Metal and other "Hanging Objects"
B. Non-pitched Woods
C. Keyboard Instruments
D. Non-pitched Skins
E. Effects/Novelty Instruments
F. Timpani

Within this basic outline, members of sub-families should be notated by pitch or size from high to low.

It was further recommended that multiple percussion scores incorporate single lines for single, non-pitched instruments. These should be spaced in such a way that the reader's eye can easily differentiate between members of families; the single instrument lines should not be equidistant. The five-line staff should only be used for instruments capable of playing melodically. And finally, within this suggested system, "relatively-pitched" multiples of the same instrument (five temple blocks, three tom toms, two cymbals, etc.) can be grouped around abbreviated staves. One line can accomodate up to three instruments, two lines up to five, three lines up to seven and so on (Fig. 3). Following the concepts of this

Fig. 3. Notational Examples on Abbreviated Staff/Systems.
a. Two Woodblocks
b. Three Tom toms
c. Five Temple Blocks

suggested system of scoring, Figure 4 shows how a solo multiple percussion part, or the percussion section of a large ensemble score, might appear. Some notations for specific performance techniques were also recommended. The most significant of those

Fig. 4. Example of Scoring for percussion.

appear below (Figs. 5, 6 and 7).

Fig. 5. Snare Drum "normale" and Rim Shots.

Fig. 6. Snare Drum playing on Head, Rim, and Shell.

Fig. 7. High Hat Cymbal, changes in pedal.

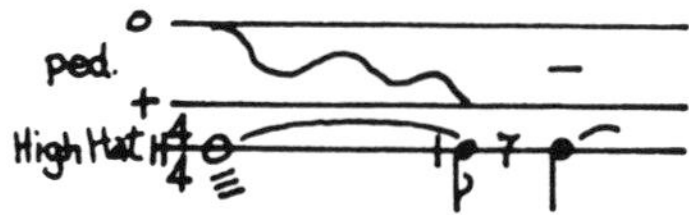

It was the hope of just about everyone at the conference that the deliberations and suggestions would be accepted in a positive way by the musical community. The goal was not to restrict the notational creativity of composers but to help composers and performers by suggesting flexible but viable notational techniques. If some kind of standardization is achieved, then the problem of "decoding time" will be eliminated for performers, making them more effective in reading and ultimately in performance.

June 1975

Percussion Notation

Vaclav Nelhybel

Right now we are witnessing the emergence of percussion as an equal partner to the mighty trinity of woodwinds, brass and strings. The percussion section has become more important in many symphonic and band works and the percussion ensemble has become a standard performing group in the music departments of most American universities.

In many of the works that I have composed for band and orchestra, percussion are used extensively, as an equal partner with winds and strings. Since I have conducted these compositions with many junior high and high school bands and orchestras, I have come to know the players and their ability to reproduce the printed page of my compositions. In the process, I have learned (and continue to learn) how to notate the percussion parts so that young players will produce the sounds as I had originally conceived them.

Choice of Mallets or Sticks

Young players tend to use sticks with which they feel most comfortable in all situations — whether they are appropriate or not. To avoid any problems here, I often ask the bass drum and timpani players to show me their sticks and, if necessary I ask them to get a more suitable stick, explaining why this is necessary. Composers should provide the inexperienced player with more specific instructions. While the string player has in his part such indications as *arco, pizz., con* or *senza sordini*, the percussion player generally has only indications of rhythm, dynamics and (sometimes) pitch.

To make my intentions somewhat clearer to the percussion player, I indicate the degree of hardness of the stick or mallet to be used for all mallet instruments as well as for timpani, bass drum, tenor drum, tom-toms, gong and suspended cymbals. It is, of course, important to avoid confusing these indications with dynamics, so I place them inside parentheses and use a relative scale which is somewhat different from that of conventional dynamic indications.

ss — very soft
s — soft
m — medium
h — hard
hh — very hard

Although the system is relative (a very hard mallet on the xylophone is certainly not the same as on bells, etc.), it has been effective in suggesting to the player the kind of sound the composer intended. Of course, these indications will only begin to make sense to the young player when he develops an awareness of the variety of sounds that can be achieved by the same instrument with different sticks or mallets.

Duration of Notes

Some percussion instruments, such as cymbals and gong, have a rather long fading-out time. The player knows from his part when to initiate the sound, but he is free to stop it (or not) at any time. To remedy this situation, I have begun to indicate the exact overall duration of these notes (sometimes two or more measures long); and to my great pleasure I have found that the players do observe the indicated duration. I have even notated the diminuendo of the fading sound, especially in gong parts *(sffz)*, and the results are most encouraging.

In timpani and sometimes bass drum parts, one often sees a quarter note ♩‿ , or "let ring" or even both. It seems to me that doubling the note value would be a notational simplification of the part. For instance, if a timpanist has two half notes in a 4/4 measure, he will certainly let the notes ring for two beats each. On the other hand, if an eighth or sixteenth were notated, then the note would be stopped. The choice of the actual durational symbol would, of course, depend on the tempo of the music and the intention of the composer.

Rolls

When a roll functions as a sustained over-all subpedal below the pitch structure of the band or orchestra, then I expect the drums to achieve a maximum of "continuity" of sound — as many notes as possible should be played evenly. If, however, the roll is the final diminution of different simultaneous layers of rhythms, then it has the function of a basic micropulsation and it should have an exact number of strokes per beat according to the time division used in that particular segment of the composition. To indicate exactly what kind of roll I want, I have considered using the sign *tr* for the saturated roll (as in Stravinsky, Bartok, Honegger, etc. — but I have heard arguments against the use of *tr* and have not yet begun to use it) and the sign ≡ for the measured roll.

The notation of percussive sounds is a complex matter. And it becomes even more complex as the music for percussion becomes more and more sophisticated. Because of a lack of a standard notation, the composer may find it necessary to verbalize his instructions in whole sentences, which clutter the performer's part. On the other hand, if the composer does not provide instructions, then the conductor will have to "clutter" the rehearsal time with lengthy explanations.

It is clear that the standardization of notation for percussion instruments is a very urgent matter. Exciting things are happening, not only at the university level, but in many high schools. By clarifying the notation and by using it on all levels, we would help the band and orchestra director to develop a more musical percussion section.

June 1975

A Band Director's Guide to Percussion Texts

Jim McKinney

Band directors who are not percussion specialists are often interested in finding better texts and methods for their percussion students — but many don't know where to look for them. To help directors overcome this problem, I have compiled a graded list of percussion texts that I have actually used. The list is by no means comprehensive, but it does include some of the best books available among both recent and older publications. Though the list does not contain any individual solos, there are many good solos within almost all of these books.

The books are listed by category and in order of my evaluation of their difficulty. Thus, the first book listed under each category is the easiest in that group, each succeeding entry is progressively more difficult, and the last is the most difficult in that particular category.

The list is divided into eleven categories, which can be described as follows:

Snare Drum Rhythm. These books could be used by any instrument. They consist almost entirely of rhythms, with very little use of rolls, flams or ruffs.

Snare Drum Rudimental. All books use forms of rudiments, with double stroke rolls. Sticking is given for nearly every note.

Snare Drum Technical. No rudiments are given, and sticking is not specified. Concert buzz rolls should be used.

Timpani Methods. Four drums are required by nearly all books.

Xylophone and Marimba. Most of these books require at least a 3½-octave instrument. Some four-mallet technique is needed.

Vibraphone. Most books require four-mallet technique.

Trap Set. All types of styles are covered in these books, including rock, swing, etc.

Multiple Percussion. One person plays two or more instruments.

Cymbals, Triangle, Tambourine, Castanets, Bass Drum and Accessories. These books are generally the "how-to-play" type.

Orchestral Technique and Excerpts. These books are devoted to percussion section excerpts from the orchestral literature.

Special. This is a miscellaneous listing, including books that do not fit into any of the above categories.

Snare Drum Rhythm

1. *Progressive Steps to Syncopation,* Ted Reed (Ted Reed Publ.).
2. *Teaching Rhythm,* J. Rothman (J. Rothman Publ.).
3. *Modern Reading Text in 4/4,* Louis Bellson (Henry Adler, Inc.).
4. *Reading Can Be Odd,* J. Rothman (J. Rothman Publ.).
5. *Multi-Pitch Rhythm Studies,* Ron Delp (Berklee Press).
6. *Rhythmic Patterns of Contemporary Music,* Whaley & Mooney (J.R. Publ.).

Snare Drum Rudimental

1. *Snare Drum Method,* Swanson (Swanson).
2. *Drum Method* Book I, Haskell Harr (M.M. Cole).

3. *The Drummers Heritage,* Frederick Fennell (Carl Fischer).
4. *Futuristic Drum Solos,* William Schinstine (Southern Music Co.).
5. *Drum Method* Book II, Haskell Harr (M.M Cole).
6. *America's NARD Drum Solos* (Ludwig Drum Co.).
7. *American Drummer,* E.B. Straight (Franks Drum Shop).
8. *Ancient Rudimental Snare and Bass Drum Solos,* J.S. Pratt (Belwin-Mills).
9. *The All-American Drummer,* Charles Wilcoxon (Charles Wilcoxon Publ.).
10. *Adventures in Solo Drumming,* William Schinstine (Southern Music Co.).
11. *Modern Rudimental Swing Solos for the Advanced Drummer,* Charles Wilcoxon (Charles Wilcoxon Publ.).
12. *14 Modern Contest Solos,* J.S. Pratt (Belwin-Mills).

Snare Drum Technical

1. *Basic Drum Book,* Schinstine-Hoey (Southern Music Co.).
2. *Musical Studies for the Intermediate Snare Drummer,* Garwood Whaley (J.R. Publ.).
3. *Reading and Rolling in Cut Time,* J. Rothman (J.R. Publ.).
4. *Intermediate Duets for Snare Drum,* G. Shaley (J.R. Publ.).
5. *Modern Drum Studies,* Simon Sternberg (Alfred).
6. *Snare Drum Method* Book II, Vic Firth (Carl Fischer).
7. *The Gardner Modern Method,* Gardner (Carl Fischer).
8. *17 Plus 1 Percussion Pieces,* William Schinstine (Southern Music Co.).
9. *Standard Snare Drum Method,* B. Podemski (Mills Music).
10. *Variations of Drumming,* R.C. Pace (R.C. Pace Publ.).
11. *Modern School for Snare Drum,* M. Goldenberg (Chappell).
12. *Six Allegro Duets for Percussion,* M. Colgrass (G. Schirmer).
13. *Six Unaccompanied Solos for Snare Drum,* M. Colgrass (G. Schirmer).
14. *Advanced Snare Drum Studies,* M. Peters (M. Peters Publ.).
15. *Percussion Studio* Book V — The Roll, Siegfried Fink (N. Simrock — London).
16. *Contemporary Studies for the Snare Drum,* Fred Albright (H. Adler, Inc.).
17. *Portraits in Rhythm,* Anthony Cirone (Belwin-Mills).
18. *Works for Percussion Battere* ("Percussion Duos") Regner, Schingerlin & Stadler (Schott).
19. *Douze Etudes pour Caise-Claire,* Jacques Delecluse (Alphonse Leduc).
20. *Concert Etudes for Snare Drum,* Al Payson & J. Lane (Payson Percussion).
21. *The Solo Snare Drummer,* Vic Firth (Carl Fischer).

Xylophone and Marimba

1. *Music for Marimba* Book I, Art Jolliff (Rubank).
2. *Elementary Method for the Bell Lyra,* H.S. Whistler (Rubank).
3. *Fundamental Studies for Mallets,* Garwood Whaley (J.R. Publ.).
4. *Music for Marimba* Book II, Art Jolliff (Rubank).
5. *78 Solos for Marimba,* Art Jolliff (Belwin-Mills).
6. *Music for Marimba* Book III, Art Jolliff (Rubank).
7. *Soloist Folio,* J. Quick (Rubank).
8. *Percussion Keyboard Technique,* T. McMillian (Pro Art).
9. *Mallet Student* Level III, Saul Feldstein (Belwin-Mills).
10. *Studies & Melodious Etudes for Mallets* Level III, Saul Feldstein (Belwin-Mills).
11. *Bach, Beethoven, Brahms Duets for Mallet Instruments* II, H. Faberman (Belwin-Mills).
12. *Selected Duets for the F Horn,* H. Voxman (Rubank).
13. *Bach for Bars* Book II, Faulmann (UMMP — Sam Fox).
14. *21 for Four-Mallet Marimba,* Paul Yoder (Kjos).
15. *Contemporary Marimba Solos* Book II, Bobby Christian (Creative).
16. *The Gardner Modern Method for the Drums, Cymbals, & Accessories,* C. Gardner (Carl Fischer).
17. *Masterpieces for Marimba,* T. McMillan (Pro Art).
18. *15 Bach Inventions,* Morris Lang.
19. *Method per Silofono & Marimba,* Torrebruno (Ricordi).
20. *Contemporary Marimba Solos* Book III, Bobby Christian (Creative).
21. *Rhythm Articulation,* Bona (G. Schirmer).
22. *Billy Dorn's Reading and Technical Studies,* B. Dorn (H. Adler, Inc.).
23. *305 Selected Melodious Studies for French Horn,* Pottag & Andraud (Southern Music Co.).
24. *Modern School for Xylophone, Marimba, Vibraphone,* Morris Goldenberg (Chappell).
25. *Master Works for Marimba,* C.O. Musser (Forster).
26. *Portraits in Melody,* A. J. Cirone (Belwin-Mills).

Vibraphone

1. *Bach, Chopin, Tchaikovsky, Beethoven, Schubert for the Guitar,* arr. Leon Block (Edward Marks).
2. *Vibraphone Folio,* Lionel Hampton (Leo Feist).
3. *Mallets in Mind,* Tom Brown (Kendor).
4. *Four Part Chorales* Book I, Bach (Kalmus).
5. *All Alone by the Vibraphone,* Feldman (Gwyn).
6. *Solos for the Vibraphone Player,* Ian Finkel (G. Schirmer).
7. *Six Unaccompanied Solos for Vibes,* Gary Burton (Creative).
8. *Bach Sonatas and Partitas,* Hermann (G. Schirmer).

Timpani

1. *Basic Timpani Technique,* T. McMillan (Pro Art).
2. *Fundamental Studies for Timpani,* Garwood Whaley (J.R. Publ.).
3. *Timpani Tunes,* William Schinstine (Southern Music Co.).
4. *Timpani Method,* Friese-Lepak (H. Adler, Inc.).
5. *Musical Studies for the Intermediate Timpanist,* Garwood Whaley (J. R. Publ.).
6. *Etuden für Timpani,* R. Hochrainer (Verlag Doblinger).
7. *Modern Method for Timpani,* S. Goodman (Mills Music).
8. *The Solo Timpanist: 26 Etudes,* Vic Firth (Carl Fischer).
9. *Eight Pieces for 4 Timpani,* E.C. Carter (Associated).

Trap Set

1. *Progressive Steps to Syncopation,* Ted Reed (Ted Reed Publ.).
2. *Rudimental Patterns for the Modern Drummer,* Joe Cusatis (Belwin-Mills).
3. *Recipes with Singles Around the Drums,* J. Rothman (J.R. Publ.).
4. *Recipes with Doubles Around the Drums,* J. Rothman (J.R. Publ.).
5. *Show Drumming,* Irv Green (J. Rothman Publ.).
6. *A Manual for the Modern Drummer,* Dawson & DeMichael (Berklee Press).
7. *Independent Thinking,* J. Rothman (J. R. Publ.).
8. *Double Bass,* J. Rothman (J. Rothman Publ.).
9. *67 Backbeats,* P. J. Ritter (Swing House).
10. *Advanced Techniques for the Modern Drummer,* Jim Chapin (Jim Chapin).

Multiple Percussion

1. *Elementary Percussion Solos,* Burns & Feldstein (H. Adler, Inc.).
2. *Intermediate Percussion Solos,* Burns & Feldstein (H. Adler, Inc.).
3. *Advanced Percussion Solos,* Burns & Feldstein (H. Adler, Inc.).
4. *Multiple Percussion Music,* Feldstein (Alfred).
5. *Studies in Solo Percussion,* M. Goldenberg (Chappell).

Accessories

1. *The Art of Playing Cymbals,* Denov (H. Adler, Inc.).
2. *Triangle, Tambourine, and Castanets,* P. Price (Music for Percussion).
3. *Castanet Playing,* L.A. Elkington (Elton).

4. *Techniques of Playing Bass Drum, Cymbals, and Accessories,* Al Payson (Payson Percussion).

Special

1. *Mallet Technique* (38 Studies), Vic Firth (Carl Fischer).
2. *Andersen 18 Studies for Flute,* revised by Cavally (Southern Music Co.).
3. *Practical Duets,* Amsden (Barnhouse).
4. *Solos for the Percussion Player,* John O'Reilly (G. Schirmer).
5. *Stick Control,* G.L. Stone (G.L. Stone).
6. *Developing Sight Reading,* G.D. Peter (C. Colin).
7. *101 Street Beats Cadences and Exercises for Percussion,* Samuel A. Floyd Jr. (Hansen).
8. *128 Rudimental Street Beats Modern Rolloffs and Modern March Beats,* John S. Pratt (Belwin-Mills).
9. *Roto-tom Solos for the Melodic Drummer,* William Schinstine (Try Publ.).
10. *For the Vibist Only,* Shelly Elias (Music Minus One).
11. *Good Vibrations,* Shelly Elias (Music Minus One).
12. *Mallet Repair,* A. Press (Belwin-Mills).
13. *Basic Jazz Improvisation,* J. Levey (Shawnee).
14. *Improvising Jazz,* Jerry Coker (Prentice-Hall).

Orchestral Studies

1. *20th Century Orchestral Studies for Percussion,* A. Abel (G. Schirmer).
2. *20th Century Orchestral Studies for Timpani,* A. Abel (G. Schirmer).
3. *Romantic Symphonies for Timpani,* compiled by M. Goldenberg (Chappell).
4. *Classic Overtures for Timpani,* compiled by M. Goldenberg (Chappell). Al Payson (Payson Percussion).
5. *The Snare Drum in the Concert Hall,* Al Payson, (Payson Percussion).
6. *20th Century Orchestral Snare Drum Studies,* T. McMillan (Creative).

List of Publishers

Adler, Henry — 136 West 46th St., New York, New York.
Alfred Music — 75 Channel Dr., Port Washington, New York 11050.
Alphonse Leduc — Editions Musicales, 175 Rue Saint Honorè, Paris.
Associated Music Publishers — 866 Third Ave., New York, New York 10022.
Barnhouse — 110 B Ave. E., Oskaloosa, Iowa 52577.
Belwin-Mills — 25 Deshon Dr., Melville, New York 11746.
Berklee Press Publications — 1140 Boylston St., Boston, Mass. 02215.
Chapin, Jim — 50 Morningside Dr., New York, New York.
Chappell — 609 Fifth Ave., New York, New York 10017.
Cole, M.M. — 251 E. Grand Ave., Chicago, Ill. 60611.
Colin, Charles — 315 W. 53rd St., New York, New York 10019.
Creative (Ludwig Drum Co.) — 1728 N. Damen Ave., Chicago, Ill. 60647.
Elton — 323 E. 34th St., New York, New York.
Fischer, Carl — 62 Cooper Square, New York 10003.
Forster — Chicago, Ill.
Franks Drum Shop, Inc. — 226 S. Wabash Ave., Chicago, Ill. 60604.
Gwyn — P.O. Box 5900, Sherman Oaks, Calif. 91413.
Hansen — 1860 Broadway, New York, New York 10023.
J.R. Publications — 3 Sheridan Sq., New York, New York 10014.
Kalmus — New York, New York.
Kendor — Main & Grove Sts., Delevan, New York 14042.
Kjos — 525 Busse Highway, Park Ridge, Ill. 60068.
Leo Feist — 1540 Broadway, New York, New York.
Ludwig Drum Co. — 1728 N. Damen Ave., Chicago, Ill. 60647.
Marks Music Corp. — 136 West 52nd St., New York, New York 10019.
Mills Music — 1619 Broadway, New York, New York.
Music for Percussion — 1108 S. Lincoln Ave., Urbana, Ill. 61801.
Music Minus One — 43 W. 61st St., New York, New York 10023.
Payson Percussion Products — 2130 Glenview Ave., Park Ridge, Ill. 60068.
Peters, Mitchell — 3231 Benda Place, Los Angeles, Calif. 90068.
Prentice-Hall — Englewood Cliffs, New Jersey.
Pro Art — 469 Union Ave., Box 234, Westbury, Long Island, New York 11590.
R.C. Pace — 975 N. Broadway, White Plains, New York.
Reed, Ted — Clearwater, Florida.
Ricordi (c/o Belwin-Mills).
Rubank — 16215 N.W. 15th Ave., Miami, Florida 33159.
Schott Music Corp. (c/o Belwin-Mills).
Shirmer, G. (Associated Music Publishers) — 866 Third Ave., New York, New York 10022.
Southern Music Co. — P.O. Box 329, 1100 Broadway, San Antonio, Tex. 78292.
Simrock — Hamburg and London.
Stone, G.L. — 27 School St., Boston, Mass. 02108.
Swanson, Ken — Springfield, Missouri.
Swing House — 18412 Gault St., Reseda, Calif. 91335.
Try Publishing (Professional Drum Shop, Inc.) — 854 Vine St., Hollywood, Calif.
UMMP (Sam Fox) — 62 Cooper Sq., New York, New York 10003.
Verlag Doblinger — Vienna and Munich.
Wilcoxon, C.S. — 349 The Arcade, Cleveland, Ohio.

The Percussionist/Band Director

an interview with
Robert Winslow by Ron Fink

The tremendous growth in the percussion area in our band and orchestra programs across the country has greatly influenced composition, teaching, musicianship and careers for students, teachers, professionals, authors and manufacturers. From this "percussion-emergence" has come Robert A. Winslow, a successful percussionist whose career is now devoted primarily to college band directing.

Why are there so many more brass and wind players than percussionists in the band conducting field? Are more percussionists now trying to get conducting jobs?

It is not surprising that fewer percussion performers are conductors since we achieved full status as "musicians" later than any other instrumental performers. It wasn't until the period immediately following the First World War that Igor Stravinsky and Edgar Varèse employed the percussionist in a manner which demanded virtuoso and innovative performance techniques. It has taken approximately fifty years for the knowledge of these techniques to become common within the percussion community. But now, because there are many more well-qualified musicians with a major performance emphasis on the percussion instruments, it seems fair to assume that a more representative number will gravitate toward conducting.

What advice would you give to the band director whose knowledge of percussion is rather limited?

The average conductor, whether with a high school band or a major symphony orchestra, experiences some anxiety when confronted with the large percussion resources called for in most contemporary compositions. The problem is more acute within the wind instrument medium because so much of the music written for winds uses greater percussion assets.

The primary problem arises from the fact that many musicians are not inclined to apply the same musical criteria to the performance techniques of the percussion instruments as they would to any other family of instruments. The same concepts of timbre, intonation, dynamic variation, articulation, style, etc., can be applied to all music and musical instruments, but the manner in which these concepts are achieved varies more among the nearly infinite number of percussion instruments than it does among the various members of any other instrument family. The conductor can deal with this lack of standardization of either performance techniques or notation if he has an open mind and is willing to experiment, relying on his basic musical judgments. In general, considerable discussion and experimentation — involving both the conductor and the percussionists — must precede a satisfactory performance. Most percussion parts call for "routining," the process of outlining the physical movement of the performer from one instrument to another. In addition, a design must be formulated whereby all of the necessary instruments for each performer are easily accessible. This process includes identifying the style and type of mallets which are to be employed at specific moments throughout the composition. Very often, completely original performance techniques or equipment must be created.

I know that you are interested in recent innovations on the marching field — in the percussion section and elsewhere in the band. What do you consider to be the most important changes?

Marching bands have changed the least over many generations in the area of orchestration, the combination of sounds. Composers, arrangers, and orchestrators have been very limited by the nature of a medium which demands that all instruments be portable. But the advent of electronically produced sounds and the improvement in the construction of many percussion instruments now offers greater potential for change than at any time in the past several hundred years.

All of the instruments of the orchestral percussion family are now available for marching use. The membranophones have plastic heads and lighter and stronger construction. The idiophones, particularly the xylophone, have also been adapted for use on the field.

The use of electronically amplified instruments dates back to the 1950's but it has only become practical recently with the development of more portable equipment. In 1970, a major manufacturer produced a prototype self-contained amplifier and speaker system which could be used with either electric bass or guitar. This unit was and is quite effective because of the advancements in the art of electronics and the fact that it was mounted on wheels for increased maneuverability. An organ and a synthesizer were later additions to this portable system.

Do you have any closing comments on the relationship of the percussion section to directors, composers, and students?

An accurate rendition of a score demands extraordinary musical and intellectual sensitivity to the inanimate object — the printed page. Directors and performers must not be reticent to follow their intuition and training when realizing a performance, particularly of a new, untried score. Composers who want to use extensive percussion resources in their works might follow the example of Igor Stravinsky when he composed *L'Histoire du Soldat*. Since his percussion writing was extremely innovative, he acquired the necessary instruments, arranged them in his apartment and determined the feasibility of his unique notation and performance techniques. It is also essential that a conductor study all instruments so that he can become familiar with their capabilities and limitations — and the resulting problems that may confront performers.

October 1975

Fundamental Techniques for the Marching Drum Section

Sherman Hong

The best marching percussion sections display impressive technical skills, original sounds, and a sharp appearance of the drum line. The following simple exercises will help improve precision. In working on the exercises, two to four students should practice together in front of a mirror large enough so they can see themselves simultaneously (a full-length dressing mirror will easily accommodate two persons).

Grip

Use the strongest and most controllable grip possible. I prefer the one most similar to the grip used for concert work, in which finger-hand-wrist control in the right hand is stressed. This grip can be strengthened through stressing hand-wrist control and by holding the stick with a very firm grip. The finger(s) are used only for more technical rhythm patterns and the forearm only for loud playing.

The traditional left hand grip, with the control point in the crotch of the hand between the thumb and index finger and the index and middle fingers curved over but not touching the stick, is practical for concert drumming but not strong enough for good field drumming. For a stronger grip, merely lay the index finger on the stick. This simple act automatically produces a louder and heavier sound from the drum. Maintain the same ball-and-socket forearm-wrist movement used with the concert grip: the forearm pivots at the elbow, and the up-and-down movement of the forearm is minimized except in loud playing.

Strokes

Each drummer must understand the following basic strokes and how they are used:

1. Arm stroke — use of the forearm-hand as one unit. The forearm moves up and down from the elbow, with the tip of the stick always moving first.

2. Full stroke — primarily wrist-hand motion. Minimize arm movement up and down. Beads of the sticks go straight up and down into the head, beginning and ending approximately twelve inches above the head. All movements should be precisely executed.

3. Half stroke — primarily wrist-hand-finger movement. Forearms do not consciously move up or down. Beads of sticks begin and end approximately six inches above the drum head.

4. Tap — primarily wrist-hand-finger movement. Forearms do not consciously move up and down. Beads of sticks begin and end approximately three to four inches above the drum head. Most general drumming is done with this stroke.

5. Grace note — primarily hand-finger movement. Beads of sticks begin and end approximately one inch above the drum head. The same concept applies to double grace notes (drags).

6. Accented strokes. One stroke usually begins and ends above the stroke used for unaccented notes.

All strokes can be made louder and harsher by playing them as accents. Accents are produced by increasing the speed and pressure on the downward strokes — not necessarily by increasing the distance the stick moves. Remind your students that different dynamic levels are generally associated with the different strokes

1. Arm stroke = *ff*
2. Full stroke = *f*
3. Half stroke = *mf* to *f*
4. Tap = *mp* to *mf*
5. Grace notes = *pp* to *mp*

Control Exercises

When working on the exercises, always mark time, play unaccented notes as taps (*mf* to *f*), and play accented notes only *one* stroke above. Once good control has been achieved, change the stroking: unaccented strokes as half strokes, accented ones as full strokes, etc. Repeat exercises until precise and even, and always check the height of the sticks. To establish ensemble time, drummers should mark time for several measures before beginning to play. All exercises can be applied to all drums.

1. Single Hand Exercises

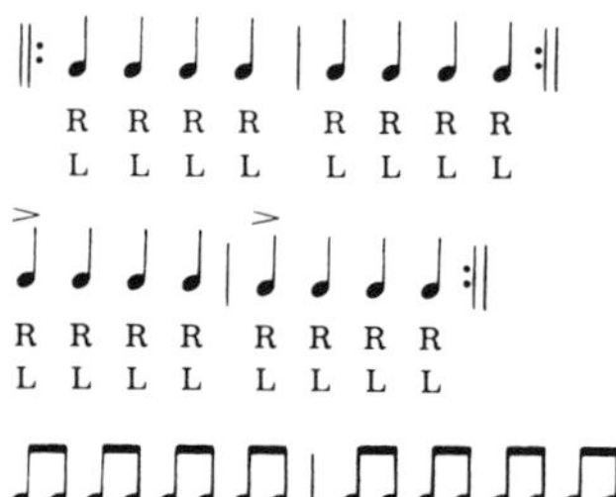

R R R R R R R R
L L L L L L L L

R R R R R R R R
L L L L L L L L

R R RR RR RR R R R RR RR RR
LL LL LL LL LLL LL LL LL

Do *not* use rebound! No accents!

2. Alternate Hand Exercises

R L R L

Check for evenness of sound.

No accents!

RL RL RL RL

RL RL RL RL RL RL RL RL

RL RL RL RL RL RL RL RL

Use second measure to check tempo.

RL RL RL RL

3. Added Grace Notes. Add single grace notes to accented notes in the previous exercises. Remember that for grace notes the beads of the sticks begin and end approximately one inch above the head.

4. Sixteenth Notes (Alternated). Play unaccented notes initially as taps; beware of false accents.

R L R L R L R L

R L R L R L R L simile

RL RL RLRL simile

Do not rush! Reverse the pattern.

5. Double Stroked Rolls. Rolls must be even and rhythmically in time (tempo).

R R R R R R R R simile
L L L L L L L L simile

R R simile RLRL simile
L L simile LRLR simile

R L R L - - - - - RRLLRR L L simile
L R L R - - - - - LLRRLL R R simile

Notice that the hand beginning *on* the beat is also on the *upbeat*.

6. Five Stroke Rolls

Basic rhythm:

R LR L RL or RL R RL L

Rolls:

R LLRR L RRLL or RRLL R LLRR L

7. Seven Stroke Rolls

Basic rhythm:

R L R L R L R L or R L R L R L R L

Rolls:

R LLRRLL R LLRRLL

8. Other Roll Patterns:

Nine stroke:

R L R L R RRLLRRLL R
L R L R L LLRR LLRR L

Thirteen stroke:

RLRLRL R RRLL RRLL RRLL R
LRLRLR L LLRR LLRR LLRR L

9. Triplets

RL RL R L simile

Vary dynamic levels.
No false accents!

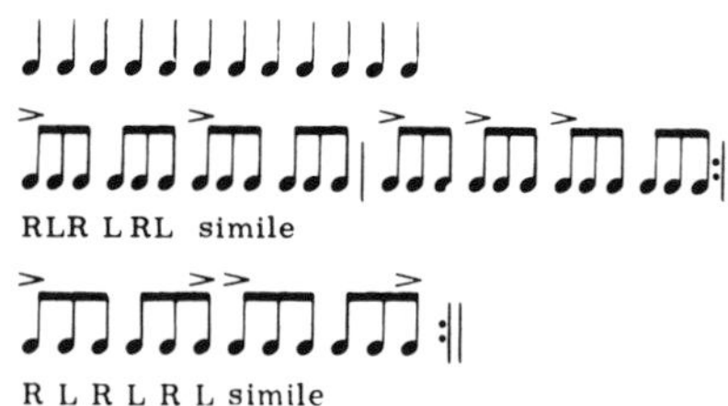

RLR L RL simile

R L R L R L simile

RLR LRL etc.

fpp — *ff*

Also reverse the dynamics (*ff* to *pp*)

10. Sextuplets (double time all triplet exercises).

Vary dynamic levels.

11. Triplet Roll

R L R L R L etc. RRLLRR RRLLRR etc.

12. Rudiments Combining Single and Double Strokes

Paradiddles consist of two alternating single taps and a double tap. Use RLRR LRLL sticking with the exercises listed above under #4. Then practice dragadiddles — by putting a double tap in place of the first note in the paradiddle pattern

RRL R R LLR L L

Triplets. With the exercises given above in #9, use one double plus single taps: RLL, RLL or LRR, LRR; RRL, RRL or LLR, LLR.

Drags. Play double grace notes the same way they are executed in a double stroke roll at a *pp-mp* level.

LLR RRL

Be sure that the grace notes are not as loud as the main stroke.

These simple exercises, if done well, can lead to more precise executions of any rudiments and patterns the students will need to use. Execution, precision, and time are the keys to good drumming.

November 1975

The Buzz Roll

Lynn Glassock

Many percussionists have difficulty playing a smooth, evenly sustained buzz roll on the snare drum — in spite of the fact that they are called upon to perform it frequently. Young students often try to solve the uneven sound by playing the buzzes as fast as they can in an attempt to fill in the gaps with more buzzes. But the player inevitably uses too much downward pressure, making the individual buzzes too short and preventing the head from vibrating freely. The gaps may not be as long but they are still there — and there are more of them. Add to this the fact that the dominant hand is almost always considerably louder than the other hand and the resulting sound is neither smooth nor even.

The best way to overcome this problem is by first learning to play a good buzz stroke. If you begin by simply dropping the stick on the head and allowing it to rebound freely, you will notice that (1) the rebounds will get increasingly faster (the first few being too far apart) and (2) the volume will decrease with each rebound. With a small amount of pressure the rebounds can be made to sound fairly even in both speed and volume. To determine the exact amount of downward pressure needed, isolate the stroke first, then learn to make a series of such strokes that will produce a good sustained sound. The following sample exercises will help the student isolate the stroke, allowing him to concentrate on making each buzz the same in both length and volume. Buzz strokes (notated by a wavy line) should be as long as possible without hearing any individual rebounds; the sticking should be alternated.

Ex. 1

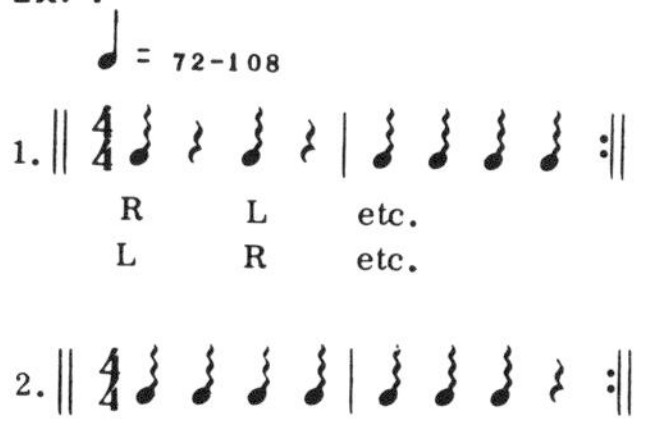

♩ = 72-108

1.

R L etc.
L R etc.

2.

3.

4.

5.

Once adequate individual buzzes can be produced, they should be combined into smooth sounding rolls. This may not be as easy as it would seem at first. Even players who have mastered the individual buzzes have a tendency to resort to the short forced buzzes when faced with roll notation. But this problem can be avoided by learning to play a certain number of buzzes per beat according to the tempo.

One system that allows an easy and gradual way to learn the number of buzzes to be played at various tempos is shown in the following examples. Each example is divided into three parts showing (A) the number of strokes that should be played, (B) which of the single taps will become buzzes, and (C) how the example would be written in normal snare drum notation.

Ex. 2

♩ = 88-108

A

B

C

Version A will provide the feel of the hand motions required, and B transforms the appropriate taps into buzzes. Then, while playing B the student should look at Version C to become accustomed to roll notation.

When the number of buzzes per beat is an even number (as in Ex. 2 and 3), simply use half that number of buzzes for a roll that must last for half a beat. If there is an uneven number (Ex. 4 and 5), divide in half and round off to the next higher whole number to determine the number of buzzes for each half beat. It is also important to understand that in a time signature such as 6/8, it is still the *tempo* that determines how many buzzes are needed.

Normally the student will find it easiest to begin by playing the "measured" rolls using four buzzes per beat in 4/4 at a tempo of approximately 96. Other tempos and meters can be used after this one becomes comfortable, but it is really not necessary to have practice

Ex. 3

♩ = 58-72

A

B

C

Ex. 4

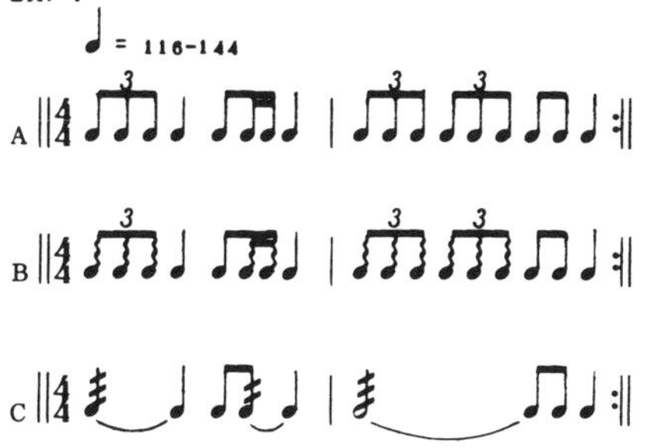

♩ = 116-144

A

B

C

Ex. 5

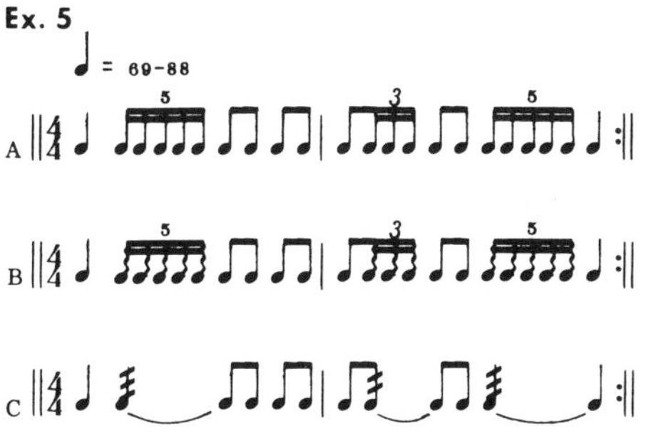

♩ = 69-88

A

B

C

exercises using all the possible combinations. Although measuring rolls can be a useful tool, especially at first, it usually works best for rolls of short duration. Those lasting for several beats can often be played more easily when they are not measured. For example, it is easy enough to play three buzzes for one beat at the tempo of 160, but it is not as comfortable to play several beats in this manner. Thus, if the first roll in Ex. 7 were played at a comfortable rate of speed, it would probably have 10 rather than 12 buzzes; the second roll would have 3 buzzes.

Whether or not to measure the longer rolls can best be determined by the student's ability and the individual situation. In fact, it is a decision that the student can easily make himself — once he has learned to play good buzzes and to combine them into smooth, even sounding rolls.

December 1975

What to Tell Your Stage Band Drummers

Ron Fink

Stage band directors don't need to know how to play the drum set. But listening to the drummer's performance, making constructive comments, and obtaining guidance from some experts can all help make the difference between a lackluster band and a fiery band with real spirit and drive. Remember that your drummer is a critical "time keeper" for the band, so give his playing special attention.

Equipment

Buy or recommend only top line or near top line equipment by a major reputable company — it will provide you with the best service over the longest period of time. (Consult a local professional player or a clinician for brand names.) And don't let anyone talk you into purchasing superfluous equipment. You probably won't need a double bass drum outfit with more than two or three tom toms, for example. These sets may look flashy, but they're not necessary for most stage bands. A minimum basic outfit should include the following:

1. *Bass Drum.* Useful accessories include telescopic spurs, which prevent the drum from sliding or tilting, and an anchor, consisting of two sharp prongs which fit on the front of the drum to prevent forward slippage. For a good sound, you'll need felt strips running down both drum heads (since a player can't muffle a dance bass drum) and possibly moleskin (*e.g.*, Dr. Scholl's) or black patch placed where the ball of the bass drum pedal strikes. I suggest using both heads on the bass drum rather than just the one. One-headed drums work well enough for some rock music, recording, or when a microphone is used in the drum. When you tune the heads, allow some "give" to the head on the playing side. I like a loose bass drum head, but not so loose that it puckers. The bass drum pedal is one of the most important items of equipment. Buy a durable one with good action.

2. *Snare Drum.* The same snare drum used in the concert band can double in the stage band.

3. *Cymbals.* Get started with a ride cymbal and two cymbals on the sock pedal. Eventually you will need to add other cymbals for effects such as fast responding crashes. To get a bigger sound from the sock cymbals, choose a heavier cymbal for the bottom, so that the light cymbal on the top can move without too heavy an action from the foot. Since the ride cymbal should not have much ring to it, select a cymbal that is heavier in weight and about 20 or 21 inches in diameter. Add tape to a cymbal if it is ringing too much. For crash cymbals that respond quickly, choose 18″ medium or thin weight cymbals. The cymbal set will be complete with a heavy-duty cymbal stand and small stand attachments ("Zil-snaps") which eliminate the trouble of unscrewing the wing nut every time you put on or remove a cymbal.

4. *Stool.* Don't skimp on a good stool. It is essential to buy one that is very comfortable and strong.

5. *Sticks, Brusnes, Mallets.* With such a wide variety of sticks available, it's difficult to recommend a particular model. Experiment with plastic and all-wood tips to see which you prefer on the cymbals and drums. For brush work, get brushes with the wire loop end so you can play "zings" on the cymbals. When you bend the loop over, the end of the brush (the loop) fits well in your hand. Mallets can be used for playing rolls on cymbals and low tom toms. The yarn mallets used on marimbas are especially good for these rolls.

Musicianship

The most important areas in the development of all-around good drummers are time, taste, and technique — in that order. First, to develop the time sense, directors should encourage the drummer to concentrate on maintaining a steady tempo and listening to his beat in conjunction with the entire rhythm section. Playing along with records helps develop steadiness and awareness of other musicians.

Second, good taste in drumming is knowing how to use technique — sensing how not to overplay fills, the bass drum, or solos. Listening to records is a helpful way to learn from good examples. Too many young drummers play the same rhythmic patterns for all occasions, resulting in unimaginative solos that often sound trite and dated. Urge your drummer to embellish the drum part, rather than just playing straight what was meant as a basic outline or sketch. Arrangers assume that a good drummer will know how to interpret a drum part, so they tend to keep it pretty simple, but the young drummer often needs prodding to experiment with some interpretation.

Third, the drummer's most important technical job is to achieve a good feel on his ride cymbal pattern and a solid "chuck" sound to his sock cymbal. Technique should also include the ability to read and play all styles of music. This skill comes mainly from experience but can be supplemented with the use of certain books as study guides (see below).

Styles

The good drummer should be able to handle any style, especially if he wants to be eligible for a variety of professional jobs. Encourage your drummer to explore diverse styles such as the following:

- Shuffle — for basic rhythm
- Straight 8th's — used in rock or Latin music
- Triplet feel — on the ride cymbal; found in spirituals
- Jazz waltz — usually in "one"
- Swing or Jazz — the typical ride beat with a jazz conception
- Dixieland — emphasizing loud afterbeats
- Rock — a very familiar style to most drummers
- Latin — rhythms vary according to different dances (mambo, rhumba, samba, bossa nova, merengue, tango, etc.)
- Country Western — some includes much shuffle-type playing
- Blues, Rhythm and Blues — 12-bar blues structure
- Show drumming — a combination of any of the above styles; need to handle any type of music event from rodeo to musicals
- Commercial — usually called "2 beat" or "society" style of drumming; includes playing many old standards.

Books

Here is a list of some of the best study guides for dance drumming. Most of them are a bit too advanced for beginning drummers, but they can be very helpful for more advanced players.

1. Independence and Coordination

Advanced Techniques for the Modern Drummer, Jim Chapin.

Coordination Patterns with Hi Hat and Bass Drum, Joel Rothman.

Independent Thinking, Joel Rothman.

2. Rock Drumming Technique

Beyond the Rockin' Bass Drum, John Lombardo.

Rockin' Bass Drum, John Lombardo and Charles Perry.

3. Technique Around the Drums

Around the Drums with Open Rolls, Paul Capozzoli.

Around the Drums with Rhythm, Paul Capozzoli.

Around the Drums with Triplets, Paul Capozzoli.

Rhythmic Patterns for the Modern Drummer, Joe Cusatis.

4. Reading for the Drum Set

Drum Set Artistry (with LP), Roy Burns.

Drum Set Music, Roy Burns.

Drum Set Reading, Ron Fink.

Practice Kit (book and LP of Dick Grove Big Band), Roy Burns.

5. Styles

Beats and Variations, Joel Rothman.

Latin American Rhythms for the Drum Set, Ron Fink.

Latin Percussion Techniques . . . for Rock, Pop, and Jazz, Fred Wickstrom.

1976 - 1977

483	Repairing the Tambourine	Michael W. Udow	January
484	Playing Flam Patterns	Mark Johnson	February
485	Guide to the Private Percussion Lesson	Garwood Whaley	March
487	Tips on Timpani	Vic Firth	April
489	Acoustics of Percussion Instruments, Part I	Thomas D. Rossing	May
491	Acoustics of Percussion Instruments, Part II	Thomas D. Rossing	June
494	Timpani Tone – The Untapped Potential	Ronald F. vernon	September
495	Acoustics of Tuned Bars	Thomas D. Rossing	October
499	Understanding Ruffs and Drags	Paul Lawrence	November
501	Concert Preparations for the Timpanist	Larry D. Snider	December
503	Play a Multiple Percussion Solo	James R. McKinney	January
505	Repertoire for Percussionists	Merrill Brown	February
508	How and When to Teach Rolls	Donald K. Gilbert	March
509	Multiple Percussion Techniques, Part I	Donald R. Baker	April
511	Multiple Percussion Techniques, Part II	Donald R. Baker	May
514	Height Adjustment and Placement of Percussion Instruments	Hoyt F. LeCroy	June
515	A Beginning Percussion Curriculum Based on Comprehensive Musicianship	Jeffrey M. Dire	September
517	Percussion Instrument Recommendations for the Schools, Part I	Frederick Fairchild	October
521	Percussion Instrument Recommendations for the Schools, Part II	Frederick Fairchild	November
524	Latin American Instruments and Rhythms	Hugh W. Soebbing	December

Repairing the Tambourine

Michael W. Udow

Too often I have observed the sad plight of the broken tambourine — we either use it as though it were in perfect condition or we throw it away. If a string broke on a cello or if the cello had a bad crack, would you throw the instrument away? Repairing a tambourine is an easy and enjoyable process which can not only save you money but can also help you create precisely the type of sound you desire. Teachers and their students might work together on the project and should carefully follow these suggestions.

Repairing a cracked shell (A cracked shell will greatly affect the sound of the tambourine because the vibrations will be interrupted at the crack.)

Materials needed: white glue, small rags or cloths, clamp, sandpaper.

1. Force white glue into the crack by rubbing across the cracked area.
2. Place two small cloths over the area where the jaws of the clamp will tighten against the tambourine shell. Tighten the clamp.
3. Wait until the glue is completely dry (24 hours), remove the clamp and carefully sand off the excess glue.
4. If the cracked area is large, you will have to remove the jingles with pliers and use more than one clamp to insure a secure repair job.

Replacing a membrane

Materials needed: hammer, tacks (must be shorter than the thickness of the wooden shell), damp cloth, membrane (may be purchased through a percussion specialty shop — specify 5 cm larger than the diameter of the shell), ink pen, three large rubber bands, pencil, exacto knife, support (to be placed under area that will be hammered — see diagram #2) scissors, sandpaper (light or smooth).

1. Place the shell on top of the membrane making sure that an extra 5 cm of membrane extends beyond the edge of the shell.

Diagram #1.

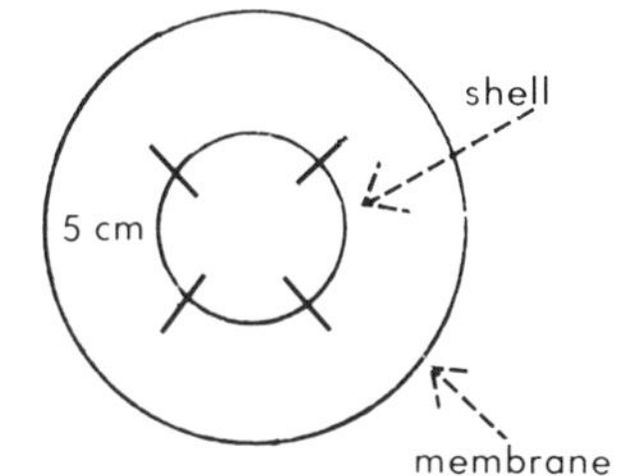

Diagram #2.

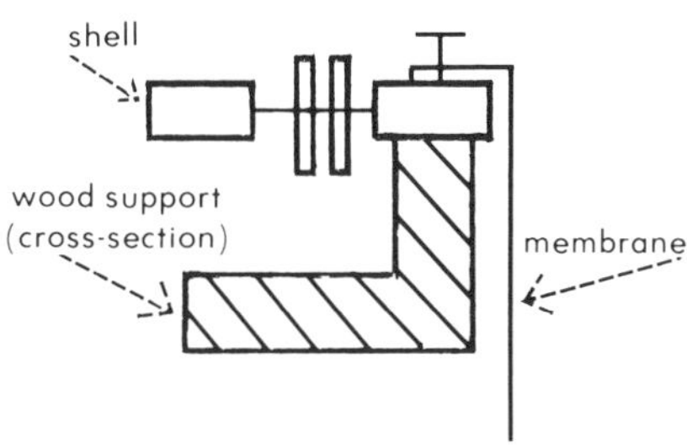

2. With a scissors, cut out the membrane — 5 cm or larger than the diameter of the shell (see diagram #1.)
3. Soak the membrane in lukewarm water for approximately 10 minutes or until easily pliable.
4. While the membrane is soaking, use fine sandpaper to smooth the area of the shell where the membrane will be tacked, making sure that there are no rough or sharp edges.
5. Spread a thin layer of white glue over the area of the shell that will come into contact with the membrane.
6. Optional (I have been able to eliminate this step). Stretch the membrane (rough surface up) across the shell and hammer in the first tack. Make sure that the support is under the shell when hammering or the shell may split. Continue to pull membrane tightly while hammering in tacks following a clock-like sequence, 12-6-9-3-10-4-2-8-11-5-1-7.
while hammering in tacks.
7. Place rubber bands around the tambourine shell (and over the tacks) to secure the membrane.
8. Place a small, damp cloth on the center of the membrane to keep the area moist until the rim is completely dry.
9. Remove the cloth, and allow the center to dry completely.
10. Remove the rubber bands. At first you may be tempted to leave the rubber bands around the shell for added security; however, imagine the sound the rubber bands would make as they burst loose against the jingles during a pianissimo oboe solo in *Scheherazade.*
11. Carefully trim excess membrane with the exacto knife, approximately 1 cm below the tacks or just above the jingles.
12. With the ink pen, write the date that you replaced the head on the inside (smooth) surface of the membrane for future reference.
13. Optional. Shellac the rough and smooth sides of the membrane. Pick a dry day to help the area to dry more quickly. Shellac playing (rough) surface of the membrane once again. When shellac becomes sticky, press your thumb on the edge of the playing surface around the circumference of the instrument. This will rough up the membrane and enable the performer to execute thumb rolls. At a performance, I prefer to have several tambourines, one or two of which are prepared for passages which call for extensive use of the thumb roll. If the passage is rather short, I either discretely wet my thumb with saliva or use rosin on my thumb to aid in producing friction between the membrane and the thumb. ■

Some of the material in this article appeared in *Percussive Notes*, Volume 14, No. 1 in the "Fix It-Build It Corner" and has been used with permission.

Playing Flam Patterns

Mark Johnson

To the eye and the ear, flam patterns can seem deceptively simple, but any snare drummer knows how troublesome they can be. When learning to play flam patterns, the student is likely to encounter one or more of the following problems:

1. Making the wrong kind of flam sound (either too "open" or too "closed")
2. Getting the sticking turned around (especially when playing all the flams with the same hand)
3. Developing awkward or excessive arm motions (either pushing the sticks back and forth or swinging them from side to side)

These problems develop because flam patterns are often poorly taught. Many teachers and writers of method books seem to have no logical system for introducing them, nor do they seem to understand how the patterns work or have any appreciation for their hidden difficulties. There is no way to make flam patterns simple, but if they are properly taught they need not be the stumbling blocks they often are.

The Solution

All flam patterns have one thing in common: they use double sticking (i.e. the playing of two or more consecutive sounds with the same hand). It is logical, therefore, to first learn the common flam sticking patterns in a rhythmically even context. I have all my students play the following set of exercises (Ex. 1) smoothly before they are introduced to flam patterns. Practice each pattern 10-20 times, beginning slowly and evenly, and gradually increasing the speed.

Once this set of exercises is learned, take each pattern, grad-

Ex. 1

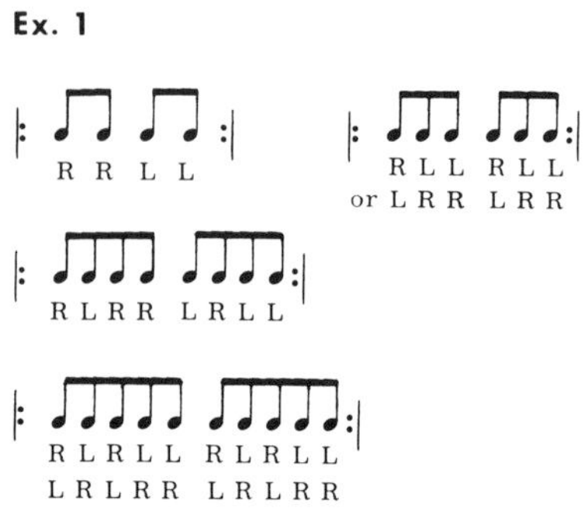

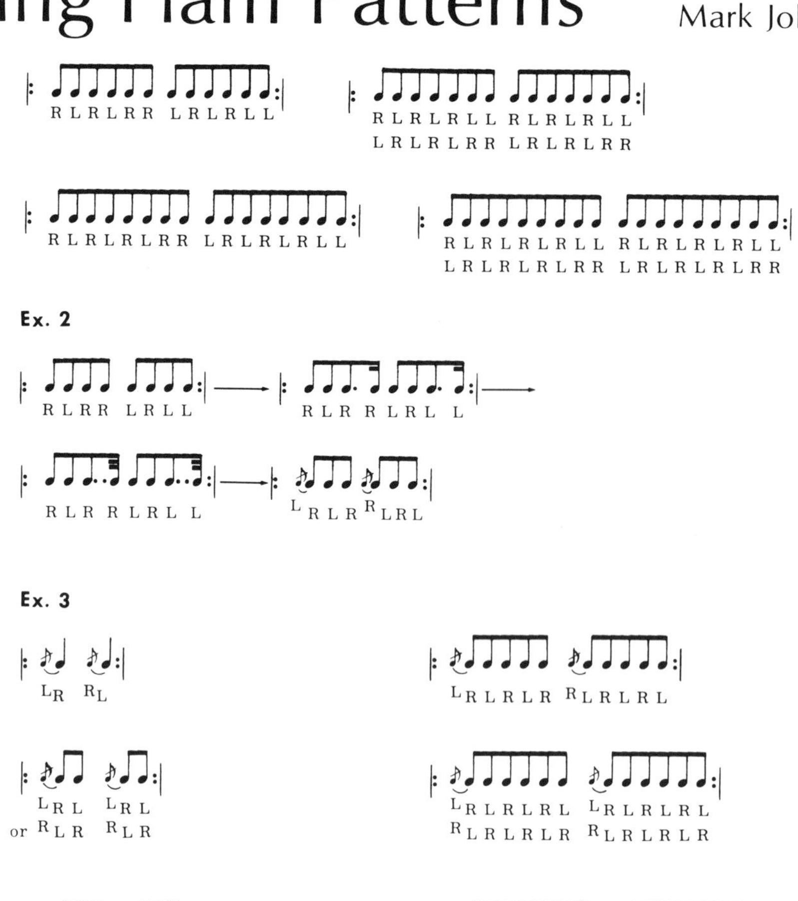

Ex. 4

Ex. 5

Ex. 6

Ex. 7

R L R L L R L R L L L R L R L L R L R L L R

Bounce Strokes

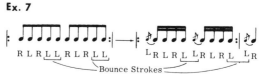

ually alter it, and turn it into the flam pattern to which it is related. (See Ex. 2). (For younger students who might be confused by the rhythmic notation, this process is best taught by rote imitation.)

These flam patterns, created by rhythmically altering the preceding set of double stick exercises, should each be played 10-20 times, beginning slowly and keeping the flam sound consistent as the tempo is increased. (See Ex. 3.)

The Flam Sound

In snare drum music, the flam which functions as the agogic accent (i.e. accent of duration), is perceived as a single broad sound, made up of two separate sounds — the "grace" note and the main note. Although the exact spacing of these two sounds will vary slightly depending on the player's personal preference, the context in which the flam appears, the dynamic level, or the style of the music; it should always sound "FLAM", not "FA-LAM" or "FLAM"! By learning patterns in the manner described above, the student is always approaching the ideal flam sound from the "too open" side rather than just taking a stab at it. I never teach the flam as an isolated sound — any student who can play a good flam sound in the context of moving rhythms can play an isolated flam with no difficulty.

Sticking Rules

These are two rules for sticking which will work in nearly every situation in which flams occur. In rhythmically even passages, where each beat or succession of beats is subdivided into notes of equal value, the "grace note" of the flam is always played by the same stick which played the preceding main note. (See Ex. 4.)

In figures which are rhythmically irregular, the sticking pattern for the main notes in the pattern is always the same as it would be if there were no flams present; and, as one would expect, the "grace note" of the flam is always played by the opposite stick from that used for the succeeding main note. (See Ex. 5.)

The Rebound

Since all flam patterns involve double sticking, the student must go through one more step before being able to play them rapidly.

Rudimental Flam Patterns

Rudimental flam patterns, such as the flam-top and the flamadiddle, are frequently encountered in snare drum solos and marching music. They are harder to play than the basic flam patterns because they involve using the same stick three times in succession and should not be attempted until the basic flam patterns are learned. When the student is ready, follow the same process discussed earlier: learn the sticking pattern in even rhythm, then alter it to produce the desired flam pattern. (Ex. 6.)

Any double stick combination can be played with a rebound or bounce stroke but the student must have a well-controlled double rebound roll to try it. The related sticking pattern is first learned in even rhythms and then rebound strokes are substituted. (Ex. 7.)

Summary

This system of teaching flam patterns has several advantages:

1. The exercises do not depend on the player's ability to read rhythms. They can be used as soon as the student has sufficient control of the basics of grip and single stroke motion.
2. It emphasizes the sticking patterns before the flam sound, so the student is less likely to lose sight of one objective while he is struggling with another.
3. The ideal flam sound is approached gradually from one direction — it is then more likely to develop correctly and consistently.
4. It is adaptable to all styles of snare drumming.
5. Because the first step involves playing rhythmically-even stick patterns, the problem of excessive or awkward arm motion is less likely to develop.
6. It helps the student to understand (to hear, to see and to feel) how flam patterns really work.

March 1976

Guide to the Private Percussion Lesson

Garwood Whaley

The versatility necessary to perform today's music makes it extremely important for teachers to develop well-rounded performers. This is a difficult job (especially when one considers the number and diversity of percussion instruments), but not an impossible task if the teacher has a progressive plan in mind. Snare drum, the basic member of the percussion family, is generally the first instrument to be studied. Snare drum lessons should be divided between reading (covering compound time, syncopation, rolls, rudimental solos, etc.) and developing technique. To accelerate the reading process, several books dealing with a variety of reading exercises should be used simultaneously.

After the first six to nine months of study, when most students have developed basic reading and performing techniques, the drum set should be introduced. Learning how to play the "set" helps the student develop a good sense of time and prepares him for multiple percussion studies. Also, the set will give him status with his peers. A drum set method book should be used in combination with dance rhythms (bossa nova, cha-cha, rock, etc.) written out by the teacher. To expand awareness of style and consistency of tempo, the student should be encouraged to listen to and play along with recordings.

Accessories

The study of percussion accessories should begin when the student has reached the intermediate level and is spending much time in concentrated practice. It might be wise to start by devoting several lessons to Latin percussion instruments, since many of them require only an elementary technique. Study of the triangle, tambourine, cymbals, castanets and bass drum should follow. Have the student develop the necessary technique on each instrument (use a beginning snare drum method book for reading). Then apply this technique to the standard band and orchestral repertoire.

The Mallets

Mallet percussion studies should be introduced when the student has developed a satisfactory technique on the accessories. Beginning mallet studies should stress reading, memorizing, and improving technique. Learning to read is a difficult and often frustrating task for the keyboard percussion player. The student must become so accustomed to the keyboard that he can play without looking at the instrument, and then develop a "sixth sense" which will enable him to read the music, follow the conductor, and play at the same time. In addition to using a graduated method book, excellent supplementary reading studies can be found in the violin, flute and guitar literature.

Timpani

By the time the student has a strong foundation on the snare drum, the drum set, various accessories, and reaches an intermediate level on mallet instruments, preliminary timpani exercises should be included in each lesson. But first, he should become acquainted with bass clef and learn to recognize and sing all intervals (ascending and descending) within the octave. When teaching timpani, it is necessary to stress roll studies, and in many cases, to compose short exercises which cover the attack, the speed of the roll, and dynamics. A portion of each lesson should be devoted to tuning and the student should be encouraged to memorize the "A" 440 ("B♭" for band).

Teaching Materials

Most instrumental music instructors prefer a variety of books, materials and teaching aids, most of which are readily accessible. The recent onslaught of new method books, ensemble and solo literature makes it necessary to take an objective look at the materials and select works which will improve the techniques of percussion instruction. The following is an annotated listing of new and old materials which I have found most effective in developing versatile, well-rounded percussionists. Also included is a list of books that contain excerpts from the repertoire for various percussion instruments. The Percussive Arts Society's publications, *Percussive Notes* and the *Percussionist*, are excellent sources for listings and reviews of new percussion materials.

SNARE DRUM

Beginning

Rothman, Joel. *Reading & Rolling in 6/8 time.* New York: Alfred Music Co., Inc., 1967.

A comprehensive foundation study in 6/8 time.

Rothman, Joel. *Rolls, Rolls, Rolls.* New York: JR Publications, 1967.

An absolute necessity for developing an understanding of the snare drum roll.

Rothman, Joel. *Teaching Rhythm.* New York: JR Publications, 1967.

Provides a fine rhythmic foundation for all instruments.

Sholle, Emil. *Here's The Drum.* Cleveland Heights, Ohio: Brook Publishing Co., 1959.

A fine graduated beginning method.

Whaley, Garwood. *Fundamental Studies for Snare Drum.* New York: JR Publications, 1973.

A graduated method which contains many duets and odd meter signatures.

Intermediate

Podemski, Benjamin. *Standard Snare Drum Method.* New York: Mills Music, Inc., 1940.

Good reading studies.

Schinstine, William J. *Southern Special.* San Antonio, Texas: Southern Music Co., 1955.

A good collection of intermediate solos. Rudimentally oriented.

Whaley, Garwood. *Intermediate Duets for Snare Drum.* New York: JR Publications, 1973.

Duets contain changing meters, contrasting dynamics, flams, rolls, etc.

Whaley, Garwood. *Musical Studies for the Intermediate Snare Drummer.* New York: JR Publications, 1971.

Each page is a musical study with written comments. Contains a wide variety of dynamics.

Advanced

Cirone, Anthony. *Portraits in Rhythm.* New York: Belwin-Mills, Inc., 1966.

Perhaps the best, most musical advanced method book on the market.

Goldenberg, Morris. *Modern School for Snare Drum.* New York: Chappell & Co., Inc., 1955.

Contains extensive excerpts from the standard repertoire. Also, instructions on playing tambourine, triangle, etc. and a glossary of percussion terms in four languages.

Payson, Al. *The Snare Drum in The Concert Hall.* Illinois: Al Payson, 1970.

A publication of merit. Contains many excerpts.

Mooney, Joseph M. and Whaley, Garwood. *The Rhythmic Patterns of Contemporary Music.* New York: JR Publications, 1973.

An advanced work which exploits mixed meter, metric modulation, and artificial rhythmic groups.

DRUM SET

Burns, Roy. *Advanced Rock and Roll Drumming.* New York: Belwin-Mills, Inc., 1968.

A comprehensive rock book.

Chapin, Jim. *Advanced Techniques for the Modern Drummer.* New York: Jim Chapin, 1948.

The standard book for developing independence for jazz drumming.

Cusatis, Joe. *Rhythmic Patterns for the Modern Drummer.* New York: Henry Adler, Inc., 1963.

Excellent for developing speed around the drum set.

DeMichael, Don and Dawson, Alan. *A Manual for the Modern Drummer.* Boston: Berklee Press Publications, 1962.

Good overall coverage of basic beats. Also contains pertinent information on style, solos, etc.

Rothman, Joel. *The Complete Jazz Drummer.* New York: JR Publications, 1974.

A comprehensive collection of materials relating to jazz drumming. Over 500 pages.

Rothman, Joel. *The Complete Rock*

Drummer. New York: JR Publications, 1973.
A virtual encyclopedia of rock drumming covering every imaginable aspect.

MALLETS

Beginning

Feldstein, Saul. *The Mallet Student: Elementary Method-Level I.* New York: Belwin-Mills, Inc., 1969.
A fine method for the beginning student with no musical background. This book moves at a relaxed pace while motivating the student.

Feldstein, Saul. *Studies and Melodious Etudes for Mallets: Elementary.* New York: Belwin-Mills, Inc., 1969.
Provides an assortment of interesting and musical material for beginning students.

Intermediate

McMillan, Thomas. *Percussion Keyboard Technic.* New York: Pro Art Publications, Inc., 1962.
Contains excellent reading studies based on the works of Bach, Mozart, Beethoven, etc.

Whaley, Garwood. *Fundamental Studies for Mallets.* New York: JR Publications, Inc., 1974.

This text integrates reading, technique, and memorization of familiar tunes. All basic keys are used, and the student is prepared for ensemble performance.

Advanced

Goldenberg, Morris. *Modern School for Xylophone, Marimba, and Vibraphone.* New York: Chappell & Co., Inc., 1948.
Excellent reading studies plus extensive excerpts from the standard repertoire.

McMillan, Thomas. *Masterpieces for Marimba.* New York: Pro Art Publications, Inc., 1971.
Contains movements from Baroque and Classical concerti and sonatas arranged for mallets.

Moore, James L. *Bach for Marimba.* Delevan, New York: Kendor Music, Inc., 1974.
Arrangements of a variety of Bach's works for two, three, and four mallets.

Whaley, Garwood. *4 Mallet Technical Studies for Xylophone, Marimba, Vibes.* New York: JR Publications, 1975.
Contains many studies for the development of flexible four mallet technique.

TIMPANI

Intermediate

Goodman, Saul. *Modern Method for Tympani.* New York: Mills Music, Inc., 1948.
The standard tympani method. Contains a variety of excerpts.

Whaley, Garwood. *Fundamental Studies for Timpani.* New York: JR Publications, 1973.
A beginning method covering all the essential techniques and including many studies in musicianship.

Whaley, Garwood. *Musical Studies for the Intermediate Timpanist.* New York: JR Publications, 1972.
Each study in this book contains an abundance of musical elements such as frequent dynamic changes, musical expressions, glissandi, tuning changes, and changes of meter.

Advanced

Firth, Vic. *The Solo Timpanist.* New York: Carl Fischer, Inc., 1963.
Excellent musically conceived solos for timpani.

BOOKS

Able, Alan. *20th Century Orchestra Studies for Percussion.* New York: G. Schirmer, Inc., 1970.
Excerpts from contemporary literature. A must for the serious student.

Abel, Alan. *20th Century Orchestra Studies for Timpani.* New York: G. Schirmer, Inc., 1970.
Excerpts from contemporary literature. A must for the serious student.

Gardner, Carl E. *The Gardner Modern Method for the Bells, Xylophone, Marimba & Chimes.* New York: Carl Fischer, Inc., 1919.
Mallet excerpts.

Goldenberg, Morris, compiler. *Classic Overtures for Timpani.* New York: Chappell & Co., Inc., 1961.
Timpani parts to a variety of classical overtures.

Goldenberg, Morris, compiler. *Classic Symphonies for Timpani.* New York: Chappell & Co., Inc., 1963.
Symphonies of Haydn, Mozart, and Beethoven.

Goldenberg, Morris, compiler. *Romantic Symphonies for Timpani.* New York: Chappell & Co., Inc., 1964.
Symphonies of Dvorak, Schumann, et. al.

Goldenberg, Morris, compiler. *Standard Concertos for Timpani.* New York: Chappell & Co., Inc., 1969.
Concertos of Mendelssohn, Tchaikovsky, et. al.

Leavitt, Joseph. *The Rhythms of Contemporary Music.* New York: Henry Adler, Inc., 1963.
Several hard to find excerpts.

April 1976

Tips on Timpani

Vic Firth

A successful timpanist must not only have well-developed musical and technical skills, but must acquire a great deal of knowledge about his instrument. Without knowing how to tune, how to select the mallets, and how to adjust the head, his performance will suffer.

Sticks

Because the plastic heads now used have a harder and less flexible surface than calfskin, choosing mallets carefully and caring for them properly has become increasingly important. Regardless of the brand you select, try to use the softer sticks whenever possible — a hard stick tends to accentuate that annoying "contact" sound. Keeping the felt head of your sticks free of dust and dirt will also help eliminate the "contact" sound, especially when playing rolls.

Playing Area

Be careful to observe where on the head you strike the drum, especially when playing on four drums or in a cross-sticking passage. The best sound is produced at a distance of not less than two and not more than five inches from the lip of the bowl. This three inch-wide area enables you to play all the light and dark shadings called for in the repertoire. If you play too close to the rim, the sound becomes very nasal, and when striking the head beyond that five inch limit, the sound becomes "tubby" and the pitch tends to blur.

Tuning

Producing a good sound in the low register has always been a problem, whether you use the harder, plastic head or the more flexible calfskin head. Whenever possible, tune lower notes on the next larger drum. For example, a C on the 25 inch drum could be played on the 28 inch, and an E natural on the 23 inch will always sound good, but will probably be more powerful on the 25 inch drum. By the same token, a low G on the 28 inch drum would have more definition on the 30 or 32 inch drum. Try to avoid a low F on the 28 inch, a B♭ on the 25 inch, or a D on the 23 inch drum. These notes are simply too low for the drum size and the tension on the head is too loose to give a satisfactory sound with a strong pitch definition. Sometimes peculiar tunings cannot be avoided, so try not to over-play these passages.

For some unkown reason, when adjusting plastic heads, players have a tendency to tune sharp. Or perhaps it is because when tuning softly and discreetly, (during a performance, for example) one tends to hear the lower partials more prominently. A head tuned this way will cause a subsequent forte entrance to sound sharp. The note may not sound terribly out of tune, but it will lack good sonority and blend poorly with other instruments. As a result, it will just sound too loud. Playing loudly, particularly in the low register of any drum, puts additional pressure on the head and increases the tension, thus raising the pitch.

After playing the timpani for a short while in a rehearsal or concert, its pitch goes down slightly as the stage temperature goes up. The warmth of lights and bodies softens the mylar, causing it to stretch slightly. Once the head adjusts to the temperature change, the stretching ceases. Converselv, when playing on a cool stage (60 to 70 degrees), the heads appear somethat brittle and do not vibrate as freely; rolls tend to display beats more obviously, and the player has to work harder to achieve results. Heat and cold seem to affect the drum in both high and low registers.

Moving Instruments

Instruments that are constantly moved create headaches. No matter how carefully they are handled, someone always manages to pull on the rods, release the pedal, or do something to disturb the head in its set position on the lip of the bowl. If the head should move sideways on the bowl, you'll have to re-center it and check the pitch very carefully at each rod, several times around. Make adjustments only when absolutely necessary. When you listen — *strain* — and do this in absolute privacy and quiet.

Applying the Head

It is terribly important that the head properly fit the body of the instrument on which it will be played. If it is not put on correctly, the low register will "slap," the pitch will be false, and the sound, in all but the highest register, will be unsatisfactory. If the head does not vibrate freely, it will be impossible to produce a beautiful, sustained legato sound.

Step 1. Remove the old head. With American-type timpani make sure that the pedal does not snap forward when the rods are unscrewed. This can be done by placing a block of wood under the pedal while it is in an upright position, and tuning the drum to its lowest note. With a German-type instrument, the rocker arm must be blocked, the pedal must be in an upright position, and of course, the instrument must be tuned to its lowest note. If the rocker arm is not blocked, the mechanism will drop from the base when the tension rods are unscrewed.

Step 2. Thoroughly clean the lip of the bowl removing all grit, grease, wax and dirt. Use a fine double "0" steel wool, literally polish the lip, and then apply a thin layer of paraffin.

Step 3. Check the new head to see there are no wrinkles in the artificial collar (if there are, reject it immediately). Apply a thin coating of paraffin, about two inches wide, along the area where the lip of the bowl makes contact with the head.

Step 4. Place the head inside the hoop and then on to the drum. Be sure that the head is centered on the bowl so that the area between the lip of the bowl and the counterhoop is the same for the entire circumference.

Step 5. Apply the tension rods and be particularly careful — each rod must exert the same amount of pressure at each point on the head.

With German-type timpani, turn the rods with your fingers so that you can feel the resistance to the increasing tension, and check each rod several times (by feel). Take your stick and tap each point as you check with the tuning key to be sure that an even pitch has been achieved. Again, I stress, try to do as little adjusting as possible.

Step 6. Take up some tension on the main screw, depress the pedal into the middle register of each drum (30 inch — G; 28 inch — A; 25 inch — D; and 23 inch — E), and remove the block of wood from under the rocker arm. Again, check the pitch. Make any adjustments that are necessary and then tune the drum to its high register (30 inch — A; 28 inch — C; 25 inch — F; and 23 inch — G) and let the drum stand overnight, preferably in a warm room (70 to 80 degrees). The following day, tune the head back to its middle register, adjust the main screw, if necessary, and check the pitch at every rod.

Follow the same procedures (Steps 5 and 6) for an American-type drum. If you can't turn the rods with your fingers, use the key. Because the key gives additional leverage, try to be especially sensitive to tension as you turn the rods. Many players move the rods by "counting" the number of turns. This is a reasonably successful approach if you can be absolutely sure that the rod makes contact with the bearing at exactly the same point at each spot on the head. If it doesn't, then a half turn more or less on one rod can either make a head sound great or destroy all your careful efforts — that's why the last tuning check in the middle register is crucial.

Keep the "fine-fussing" to a minimum for the first few days. I've found that a head tends to improve after several days of playing. If the head sounds good when you first put it on, it will always sound good and probably improve. If it sounds poor or only fair at first, although it will improve slightly, it will never be totally satisfactory in all ranges. So save your time and frustration and discard it.

Once the head is properly adjusted and the instrument is correctly tuned, a precise and musical performance depends on you.

May 1976

Acoustics of Percussion Instruments

Part I

Thomas D. Rossing

Percussion instruments, man's oldest musical instruments (with the exception of the human voice), have recently witnessed a surge of interest and popularity. What is often termed the "contemporary sound" makes extensive use of percussion instruments. Many novel percussion instruments have been developed recently, and more are in the experimental stage. Yet, in several years of teaching courses in musical acoustics, I have found that very little material has been published on the acoustics of percussion instruments, in contrast to the very extensive literature on string instruments and the recent interest in the acoustics of wind instruments.[1] Perhaps a discussion of the basic acoustical principles will aid in your understanding of percussion instruments.

Behavior of Vibrating Systems

All musical sound is generated by a vibrating system, whether it is a string on a violin, the air column of a trumpet, the head of a drum, or the voice coil of a loudspeaker. Often the vibrating system consists of two or more simple vibrators which work together, such as the reed and the air column of a clarinet, the strings and the sounding board of a piano, or the strings and body of a violin. Percussion instruments generally employ one or more of the following basic types of vibrators: strings, bars, membranes, plates, air columns, or air chambers. The first four are mechanical, and the latter two pneumatic. The string and the air column tend to produce harmonic overtones; the others, in general, do not.

All vibrators must have mass and also a force that restores the mass toward its rest position when it becomes displaced from this position. The non-existent "simple" vibrating string has no stiffness of its own, depending entirely upon tension to provide the necessary restoring force when it is plucked or bowed. It can vibrate in one of many different modes which are harmonic; that is, their frequencies are simple multiples of a fundamental frequency. The first 8 modes (harmonics) of such a vibrating string are shown in Figure 1. The second harmonic is an octave above the fundamental, the third harmonic a twelfth, etc. Because of the regular harmonic spacing of the overtones, string instruments generally sound well in ensembles.

Those real strings used on musical instruments have some stiffness of their own, which adds to the restoring force supplied by the string tension. The effect of stiffness becomes most noticeable in the higher overtones (partials), where the string bends more sharply. The overtones of a real string, therefore, are not quite harmonics of the fundamental, because the spacing between successive overtones is a little too large. Ordinarily, this departure from the harmonic sequence of the overtones alters the timbre of a string slightly, but is not objectionable. To minimize the effect, however, the heavier strings on pianos, violins and guitars consist of a solid core with a spiral wrapping, since a wrapped string is more flexible than a solid string with the same mass.

Fig. 1

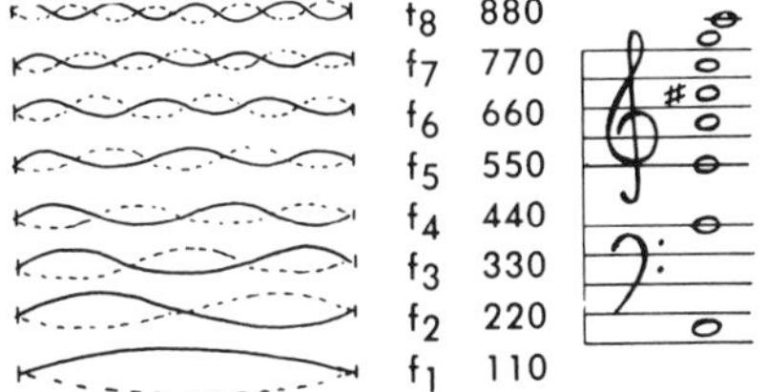

The first 8 modes of a vibrating string tuned to A_3 (f=110 Hz). The modes are harmonic — that is, the frequencies are multiples of 110 Hz.

The greater-than-harmonic spacing of the overtones of real strings is the principal (though not the only) reason that pianos are "stretch tuned," that is, tuned with stretched intervals. To have the overtones of the strings near the lower end of the keyboard more nearly match the corresponding notes at the higher end, the intervals are tuned slightly larger than normal, especially at the upper end of the keyboard.

Simple pipes have modes of vibration which are harmonics of the fundamental mode. The addition of a mouthpiece, tone holes, etc., change this so that the bore may be tapered or a bell added in order to make a wind instrument sound overtones which are harmonic.[2, 3, 4]

Bars, membranes and plates are 3 classes of vibrators whose modes of vibration are *not* related harmonically. Thus the overtones they sound will not be harmonics of the fundamental tone. The inharmonic overtones of these complex vibrators give percussion instruments their distinctive timbres, quite unlike those of the string and wind families.

A membrane may be thought of as a two-dimensional string, in that its restoring force is due to tension applied at the edge rather than being due to its own stiffness. Thus a membrane, like a string, can be tuned by changing the tension. A membrane, being two-dimensional, can vibrate in many ways. Some modes, for example, describe circular patterns, some do not. A real drum head, like a real string, has a little stiffness of its own, but for the most part it behaves like a simple membrane.

Bars and plates, on the other hand, are stiff vibrators which require no outside tension from without. Bars are essentially one-dimensional, while plates are two-dimensional. Percussion instruments using tuned bars include marimbas, xylophones, chimes, vibes, triangles, etc. Cymbals, gongs, tamtams, and even carillon bells are essentially vibrating plates.

Vibrations of Bars

Now that we have described a bar as a one-dimensional stiff vibrator, let us discuss in more detail how it vibrates.

A bar (or rod or tube) can vibrate either longitudinally (by expanding and contracting in length) or transversely (by bending at right angles to its length). Percussion instruments nearly always use the transverse modes of vibration (one exception being the aluminum "stroke rods" which are excited longitudinally when stroked by a rosined cloth or gloves). Longitudinal vibrations are much higher in frequency than transverse vibrations, and the various longitudinal modes are related harmonically. The frequency of vibration depends upon the length of the rod and upon the elasticity of the material from which it is fabricated, but it is independent of the thickness, surprisingly enough. In fact, the frequency of vibration of a longitudinal rod is expressed by the simple formula $f_n = nv/2L$, where v is the velocity of sound in the rod, L is its length, and n = 1, 2, 3,. . . denotes the number of the harmonic (beginning with n = 1 for the fundamental frequency).

When a bar vibrates longitudinally, its motion is almost identical to the movement of the air in a pipe which is open at both ends (as in a flute, for example). Maximum movement occurs at the ends of the bar or air column (called anti-nodes), and one or more points in between have a minimum of movement (called nodes), as illustrated in Fig. 2. For the fundamental mode, there is one node, and that occurs at the center. For the first overtone (the second harmonic), there are two nodes with another anti-node at the center. One can selectively excite any desired mode of vibration in a bar by clamping it at the location of one of the nodes for that particular mode. If the fundamental mode is desired, the bar should be supported at the center only.

Table I

Formulas for vibration frequencies of strings and bars

String	
transverse vibration:	v = velocity of waves in the string = $\sqrt{T/m}$
$f_n = n(v \div 2L)$	L = length of the string
	n = 1, 2, 3,. . .
	T = tension
	m = mass per unit length
longitudinal vibration:	v_L = velocity of sound in the string = $\sqrt{Y/p}$ (does not change with tension)
$f_n = n(v_L \div 2L)$	Y = Young's modulus of elasticity
	p = density of string
Bar with free ends	
transverse vibration:	v = velocity of sound = $\sqrt{Y/p}$
$f_n = (vK \div L^2)m^2$	Y = Young's modulus of elasticity
	p = density
	L = length
	m = 3.0112, 5, 7. . . (2n+1)
	K = "radius of gyration"
	$K = t/\sqrt{12}$ for a rectangular bar
	t = thickness
	$K = \frac{1}{2}\sqrt{a^2+b^2}$ for a tube
	a = inner radius
	b = outer radius
longitudinal vibration:	v = velocity of sound = $\sqrt{Y/p}$
$f_n = n(v \div 2L)$	L = length
	n = 1, 2, 3. . .

Transverse vibrations in a bar are a little more complicated. First of all, there are three possible end conditions for the bar: clamped end, free end, or pinned end. However, nearly all percussion instruments employ bars with free ends, so only the free bar will be considered. (One exception is the electronic carillon which sometimes employs bars or rods which are free at one end and clamped at the other.)

Fig. 2

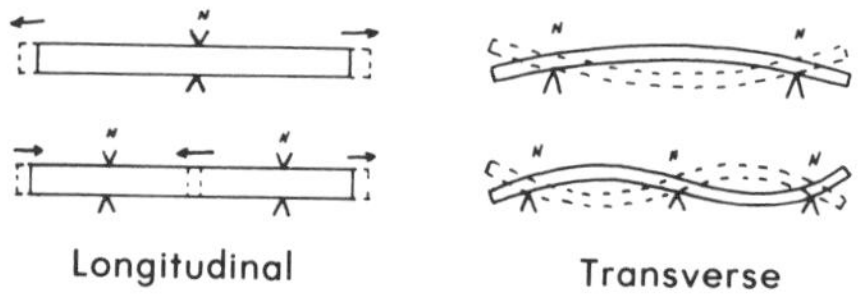

Longitudinal   Transverse

Longitudinal and transverse vibrations of a bar with free ends. Note that in longitudinal vibration the bar has n nodes, whereas in transverse vibration it has n+1 nodes, where n is the mode number beginning with 1 for the fundamental.

Once again, we expect the frequency (pitch) of a bar in transverse vibration to depend upon the length, the elasticity, etc., but in transverse vibration the frequency depends upon the thickness of the bar as well. The frequency of transverse vibrations in a free bar is given by the formula: $f_n = (vk \div L^2)m^2$ where v is the velocity of sound, L is length, and K is related to the size and shape of the bar. (For a flat bar, K is thickness divided by 3.46; values for other shapes are given in Table I.) Note the following differences from the longitudinally-vibrating bar: (1) the frequency depends upon L^2 rather than L; (2) the modes are not harmonic, but increase as m^2; (3) the frequency depends upon the shape of the bar through the factor K. The frequencies of the modes are proportional to the squares of the odd integers — almost. m begins at the value 3.0112 and then continues with the simple values 5, 7, 9. . .(2n+1).

The frequencies of the modes of vibration of a uniform bar thus have the ratios 1 : 2.76 : 5.40 : 8.93, etc., which is anything but harmonic and in fact match no intervals on the musical scale. They give a distinctive timbre to instruments such as chimes, orchestra bells, and triangles, which employ nearly-uniform bars. (The bars of marimbas, xylophones and related instruments are not uniform; they have been cut to have quite a different set of mode frequency ratios and thus have a different timbre).

Pitch of Complex Tones

When a tone composed of partials with harmonically-related frequencies is sounded, the lowest common multiple of these frequencies, the fundamental, is heard. The ear will identify the pitch of the fundamental mode even if the fundamental is very weak or missing altogether. For example, if presented with a tone having partials with frequencies of 600, 800, 1000, 1200 Hz, the pitch will nearly always be identified as that of a 200 Hz tone, the "missing fundamental." The ear's ability to pick up the fundamental makes it possible for the undersized loudspeaker of a table radio to produce bass tones and also forms the acoustical basis for certain mixture stops on a pipe organ.

When the ear is confronted with an inharmonic series of partial tones, however, the determination of the pitch is more subtle. Various theories of pitch perception predict similar but not identical behavior. One theory which explains this behavior is the "residue theory" formulated by Schouten and colleagues[5] about 20 years ago. According to this theory, the ear picks out a series of nearly-harmonic partials somewhere near the center of the audible range (300-500 Hz, near the center of the piano keyboard), and determines the pitch to be the largest near-common factor in the series. For example, if frequencies of 630, 830 and 1030 Hz were presented, the perceived pitch would correspond to approximately 208 Hz (since $630 \div 3 = 210$, $830 \div 4 = 208$ and $1030 \div 5 = 206$), rather than 200 Hz, which is the "difference" tone. Of course, the exact pitch heard depends upon the loudness of the partial tones. For a comprehensive discussion of modern theories of pitch perception, a recent article by Wightman and Green[6] is recommended. *(To be continued)*

1. T.D. Rossing, "Resource Letter MA-1: Musical Acoustics," *American Journal of Physics* 43 (1975): 944-53.
2. A.H. Benade, "On the Tone Color of Wind Instruments," *Selmer Bandwagon* 59 (1969): 17.
3. A.H. Benade, "The Physics of Brasses," *Scientific American* 229 (1973): 24.
4. J. Backus, "Resonance Frequencies of the Clarinet," *Journal of the Acoustical Society of America* 43 (1968): 1272.
5. J.F. Schouten, R.J. Ritsma, and B.L. Cardozo, "Pitch of the Residue," *Journal of the Acoustical Society of America* 34 (1962): 1418.
6. F.L. Wightman and D.L. Green, "The Perception of Pitch," *American Scientist* 62 (1974): 208.

June 1976

(Part II)

Chimes

One of the interesting characteristics of chimes is that there is no mode of vibration with a frequency at, or even near, the pitch of the strike tone one hears. The frequencies excited when a chime is struck are very nearly those of a free bar described earlier. Modes 4, 5, and 6 appear to determine the strike tone. This can be understood by noting that these modes for a free bar have frequencies nearly in the ratio $9^2 : 11^2 : 13^2$ or $81 : 121 : 169$, which are close enough to the ratio $2 : 3 : 4$ for the ear to consider them nearly harmonic, and use them as a basis for establishing a pitch. The largest "near-common factor" in the numbers 81, 121 and 169 is about 41.

Figure 3 is a plot of the frequencies of a G and a C♯ chime as functions of n, along with those predicted by the free bar theory described so elegantly by Lord Rayleigh[7], a hundred years ago. The strike tone frequencies, which lie one octave below the 4th modes, are also shown. The first modes of the C♯-chime are shown on a musical staff (which is the musician's equivalent of logarithmic graph paper!).

Fig. 3

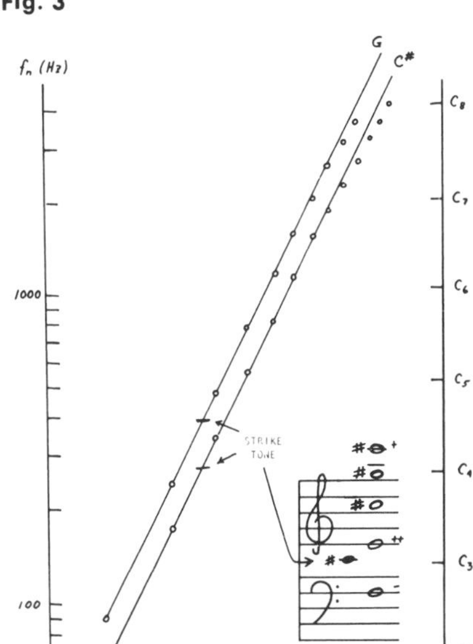

Modes of vibration (partials) of two chimes along with the frequencies predicted by Rayleigh's theory for a thin bar. Horizontal and vertical scales are logarithmic. The first modes of the C♯ chime are shown on a musical staff, which is the musician's version of logarithmic graph paper. Note the position of the strike tone.

The modes of vibrations of chimes do not have quite the frequencies of a free bar, as can be noted in Figure 3. For one thing, they are usually fitted with a plug, which lowers the frequencies of the lower modes by increasing the mass that vibrates. Secondly, the frequencies of the higher modes of a thick bar or tube are slightly lower than those of a thin bar due to secondary mechanical effects (rotational inertia and shear stress). In addition to lowering the frequencies of all the modes, these secondary effects also change the ratios of the modes, although the changes are predictable. In Figure 4, the frequencies of a G-chime with and without the plug are compared with the theory for a thin bar (Rayleigh) and with the more detailed theory for a thick bar (Flugge).[8] The plug has little effect above the first few modes.

Fig. 4

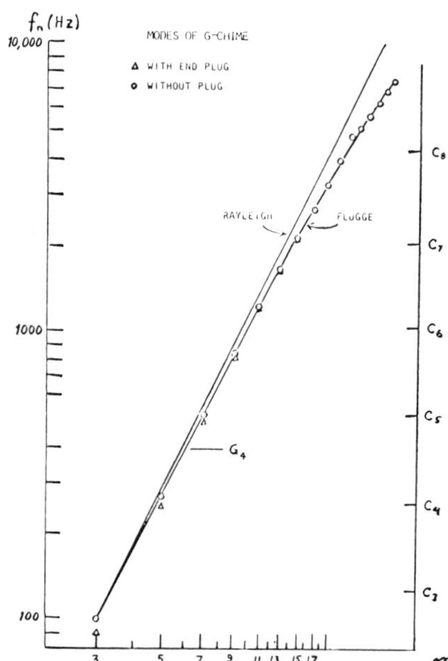

Modes of a G-chime with and without the end plug compared to the theory of Rayleigh and the more exact theory of Flugge for a thick pipe.

The ratios of the modal frequencies of a chime tube with and without a load at one end are shown in Table II. The ratios considered desirable for a tuned carillon bell are also given. Note the similarity between the partials of a chime and those of a carillon bell. Adding a load to one end of a chime lowers the frequencies of the lower modes more than the higher ones (see Fig. 4), and thus "stretches" the modes into a more favorable ratio. The end plug also adds to the durability of the chime, and helps to damp out the very high modes.

The well-known bell-like quality of chimes has been utilized in many compositions for band and orchestra (Tchaikovsky's 1812 Overture, for example). This bell-like timbre can be maximized by selecting the optimum size of end plug for each chime. For the G-chime in Table II, the 193-gram plug, with which the chime was originally fitted, is probably near the optimum. Most chime makers use the same size plug throughout the entire set of chimes, but the timbre changes in the course of the scale, typically being optimum near the center. We feel that a set of chimes "scaled" to have the same timbre throughout would be advantageous.

A well-tuned chime not only has its overtones tuned to resemble those of a carillon bell, but it is also free of "beats" between modes with nearly, but not quite, the same frequencies of vibration. These beating modes occur when the chime tube is not perfectly round or its wall thickness is not perfectly uniform. As a result, the transverse vibrations will have slightly different frequencies in two different transverse directions, and beats will result when both modes are excited. These undesired beats can be eliminated by squeezing the chime in a vise or thinning the wall slightly on one side to bring the modes into tune.

Vibrations of Plates

Before discussing bells and gongs, which can be considered stiff plates with special shapes, we will briefly describe the vibrations of flat plates. Plates have many modes of vibration, some exhibiting great complexity. Although the edges may be clamped, free edges are the norm in percussion instruments such as gongs, cymbals, tamtams, etc.

One time-honored method for studying the modes of vibration of thin plates is by creating Chladni patterns in fine sand or salt sprinkled on the plate.[9,10] Vibrations may be excited in the plate by bowing it, by driving it mechanically with a vibrator, by acoustic excitation with a loudspeaker, etc. The sand or salt is agitated by the vibrating plate, and tends to settle at the *nodes* or regions of minimum vibration. The resulting Chladni pattern is a map of the nodal lines which result from a particular mode of vibration.

Figure 5 shows some Chladni patterns obtained by vibrating a thin circular plate. The nodal lines include diameters and concentric circles. The formula for predicting the frequencies of the various modes of vibration is complicated, although a few simple relationships can be noted. The frequencies of the modes with only nodal diameters are proportional to n^2, where n is the number of nodal diameters.

Needless to say, the overtones of uniform plates are not harmonic, and the timbre of such plates is not particularly musical. However, plates with special shapes, like gongs, cymbals, and bells are frequently used in musical performance. Perhaps it is stretching the imagination a bit far to think of a bell as being a plate, but the general principles of its vibrational behavior are similar in that the circular edge is free and that each mode of vibration gives rise to circular and radial modes.

Tuned Bells

Although bronze bells were known to have been cast in China as early as 1,000 B.C., the art of tuning the overtones of bells probably began in Europe during the fourteenth century, and the technique of tuning was perfected during the seventeenth century by Dutch bell founders, especially the Hemony brothers. The Hemonys are said to have done for bell-making what the Cremona makers did for the violin. Unfortunately, the "secrets" of their tuning techniques

Table II

Ratios of mode frequencies for loaded and unloaded chime tube (compared to strike tone)

n	Thin Rod	Tube	Loaded with 193g	435g	666g	tuned bell
1	0.22	0.24	0.23	0.22	?	0.5 or 0.6
2	0.61	0.64	0.63	0.62	0.61	1
3	1.21	1.23	1.22	1.22	1.22	1.2
						(1.5)
4	2	2	2	2	2	2
						(2.5)
5	2.99	2.91	2.93	2.95	2.94	3
6	4.17	3.96	4.01	4.04	4.03	4
7	5.56	5.12	5.21	5.21	5.18	5.33
8	7.14	6.37	6.50	6.43	6.37	6.67
strike tone		416 Hz	393 Hz	383 Hz	381 Hz	

(Diameter of tube is 1.37% of length; strike tone is G_4 with f=393 Hz. All modes are compared to nominal strike tone.)

were lost for centuries.

Although the mathematical description of the vibrations of a bell are understandably complex, the principal modes can be described by specifying the number of circular nodes, which run horizontally around the bell, and meridian nodes, which run from the crown to the lip. The lowest node of vibration, called the hum tone, is generally agreed to have four meridian nodes, so that alternate quarters of the bell move inward and outward.

Fig. 5 *

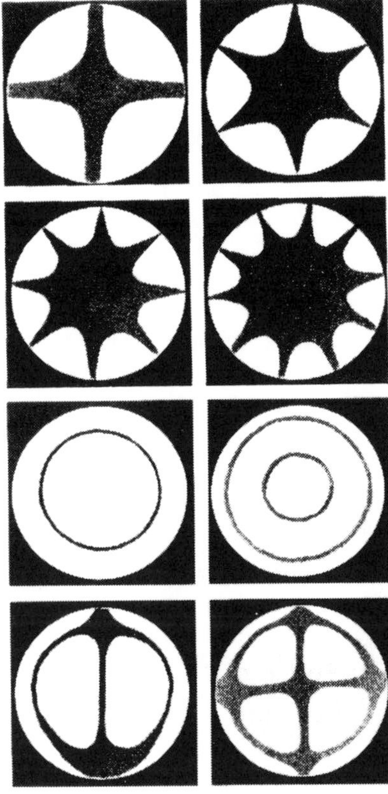

Chladni patterns showing vibrations of a circular aluminum plate. The first four have nodal diameters only, the next two have nodal circles only, and the last two have both nodal circles and nodal diameters.

* Reprinted from *Acustica* 29 (1973): 14. S. Hirzel Verlag, Stuttgart. Used with permission.

In the Flemish tuning of a carillon bell the mode called the third is tuned a minor third above the strike tone, whereas the upper third is a major third above the octave. The strike tone is determinded by the octave, the twelfth and the upper octave, whose frequencies have the ratios 4 : 3 : 2, like the chimes described earlier. Unlike chimes, however, carillon bells have a mode called the prime or fundamental with a frequency tuned to the strike tone. Careful studies have shown however, that the pitch of the strike tone is determined by the 3 modes mentioned above rather than by the prime.[11] The character of the vibrations in the principal bell modes are shown in Figure 6, which is adapted from a paper by Grützmacher, et al.[12]

Fig. 6

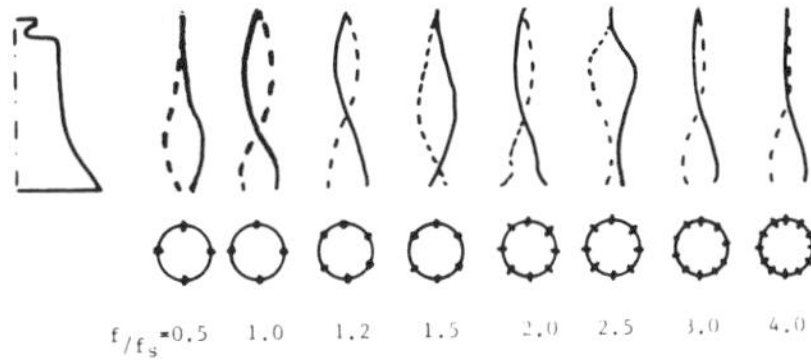

First 8 modes of vibration of a tuned bell (after Grützmacher, et al.). These modes have from 4 to 12 nodal meridians running the length of the bell; some of them have a nodal circle around the bell, some do not. The frequencies with respect to the strike tone are given.

The so-called English tuning of bells is quite similar to the Flemish tuning, except that the hum note is tuned a sixth below the strike tone rather than an octave. English bells, usually designed for sequential "change" ringing rather than playing in harmony, are not as carefully tuned as Flemish bells.

One of the most complete discussions of bell acoustics and also an account of tuning technique is given in a dissertation by E.W. Van Heuven.[13] Bells are usually cast thicker than required to allow for tuning, and then tuned by removing metal from the inside of the bell. In order to tune the different overtones, the vibration pattern must be known exactly, for thinning the bell at any particular place will have varying effect on the different overtones. Many tuned carillons are in existence, although a number of fine bells were destroyed during World War II. The world's largest carillon is the 72-bell Rockefeller Memorial Carillon in New York cast by the English firm of Gillett and Johnston, with the largest bell weighing over 18 tons.

Because of the high cost of casting and tuning bronze bells, most carillons in recent years have employed electromechanical bells, with tuned metal bars or rods, carefully shaped to vibrate with bell-like overtones. A suitable pick-up device converts these vibrations to electrical signals which can be amplified and used to drive large loudspeakers, perhaps filtering out a few undesired overtones along the way.

7. Rayleigh, *The Theory of Sound.* (New York: Dover Press, 1945).
8. W. Flugge, *Statik und Dynamik der Schalen*, (New York: Springer-Verlag, 1962).
9. E.F.F. Chladni, "Entdeckungen über die Theorie des Klanges," trans. by T.B. Lindsay, in *Acoustics: Historical and Philosophical Development*, (Dowden, Hutchinson and Ross, 1973) p. 155.
10. M.D. Waller, *Chladni Figures, a Study in Symmetry*, New York: Bell and Sons, 1961).
11. J. Pfunder, "Uber den Schlagton der Glocken." *Acustica* 12 (1962): 153.
12. M. Grutzmacher, W. Kallenbach, and E. Nellessen, "Akustiche Untersuchen an Kirchenglocken," *Acustica* 16 (1965/66): 34.
13. E.W. Van Heuven, *Acoustical Measurements on Church-Bells and Carillons.* The Hague: De Gebroeders van Cleef, 1949).

Mr. Rossing would like to acknowledge the following people for their help in preparing this article: Calvin Rose, Randy Culver, Tim Martin, and Hera Leighton. Some of the experimental studies in this paper were made possible by a grant from the Research Corporation.

Timpani Tone – The Untapped Potential

Ronald F. Vernon

Many conductors underestimate the tonal potential of the timpani in their ensembles. The timpani can contribute more than just the dynamic and rhythmic elements of music, and conductors of any ensemble should expect more than just accurate pitch and rhythm from their timpanists. Sensitivity of style and beauty of tone are both possible and desirable.

Although a beautiful sound on the timpani is no easier to attain than on any other instrument, there are only a few factors which contribute to good timpani tone. These points are readily apparent to players and conductors and are relatively simple to understand even by non-specialists. They may be successfully taught by anyone who takes the time and interest to discuss them.

Striking the Proper Spot

One of the simplest and most obvious factors affecting tone is which spot is struck on the drum head. Almost everyone knows that the center of the drum produces a dull thud. But a more common error is striking the drum too near the rim, which produces an excessive amount of overtones rather than a clearly focused pitch. The director should first experiment with each drum to find the ideal striking spot, and then tell the timpanist to concentrate on striking the same place each time. The size of the striking spot on each drum will vary according to the pitch being played. With plastic heads, there is no harm in marking the striking area with pencil until good playing habits are firmly established.

Choice of Sticks

Any timpanist who expects to meet more than the simplest musical demands in band and orchestra will need several pairs of sticks. The pairs should differ not only in hardness but also in size and weight. School-owned sticks are rarely a good solution. Fine timpani sticks cost between $12 and $15 a pair, and school ownership almost invariably results in abuse and neglect which quickly destroys the felt heads. Since other instrumentalists are expected to purchase or rent instruments costing several hundred dollars, it is fair to ask timpanists to purchase their own sticks. At the high school and even junior high levels, it is worthwhile to obtain professional quality sticks (usually manufactured under the name of a symphonic percussionist). Fine sticks are required to produce a fine sound.

Timpani sticks usually fall into four basic categories:

1. *General Purpose*. These sticks are a compromise between a moderately firm head for good articulation and the greater size and weight which produce a darker sustained sound (with fewer overtones). These sticks may be used satisfactorily for many different types of music.

2. *Staccato*. The heads of these sticks are of hard felt and are usually small in size for clean, distinct articulation. The small size, hard head, and relatively light weight tend to produce a sound with a strong attack and a sustained tone relatively strong in overtones (which most listeners describe as a "bright" sound). Although these sticks do not produce a true staccato sound, the pronounced attack is suitable for the rhythmic figures and percussive sounds so prominent in much contemporary music.

3. *Legato*. These sticks are somewhat softer and usually heavier than the general purpose sticks. They are suitable for parts in which rolls predominate or for parts which require a rich tone but lack rhythmic interest. The softer head reduces the attack sound to a minimum, and the heavier weight produces a tone strong in the second partial (the note we hear as the pitch) and relatively weak in the higher partials. This is especially noticeable at loud dynamic levels. These mallets should allow loud rolls without producing a harsh or distorted tone. (At softer dynamic levels, legato tones may be produced more easily with general purpose mallets.)

4. *Wood*. These sticks should be used only when specified by the composer. The sound of wood striking the drum head produces a unique attack tone which is not really characteristic of timpani tone. Wood sticks are not the ultimate stick heads for articulation, but they can work well as a special effect.

Considerations such as stick length and composition of shaft, type of head construction, and weight distribution are matters of personal preference. There are many types of mallets which produce satisfactory results, and a little experimentation will determine which type is best for a particular timpanist.

Choice of Drum for Particular Notes

The traditional pitch ranges for the two most common sizes of timpani are:

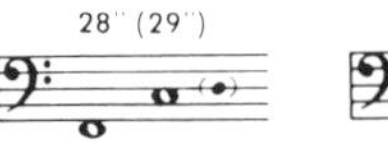

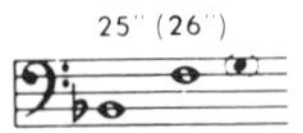

It should not be assumed, however, that each note within these traditional ranges sounds equally good. The graph below represents the relationship of head tension to tone quality:

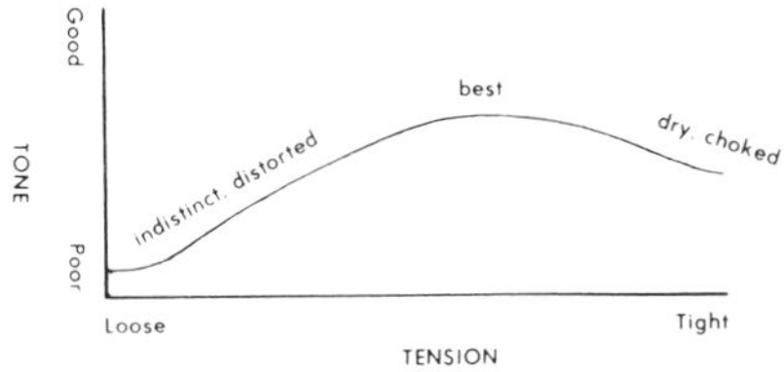

This graph illustrates the importance of having smaller and larger sizes of drums available for use, particularly the larger sizes. The following set of ranges gives the extended and ideal ranges for each drum size, but even these ranges are approximate.

o Extended Range

• Best Tone

Every drum is different. Both conductor and player must first experiment with each drum to find out which notes sound best and then plan drum changes so that each note is played on the drum that will sound best.

Stroke Technique

There are many different approaches to stroke technique, grip, and hand position. Each system has its merits, and this article will not attempt to cover these matters in detail. Nevertheless, there are some observations which can apply to almost any approach to stroke technique.

First of all, remember that the timpani should produce a sustained sound. To attain this sound, the head must be free to vibrate, which requires a quick, lifting stroke that does not allow the stick to remain on the head for very long.

A simple exercise for developing this sustained type of stroke is to practice single strokes beginning with the stick three or four inches above the drum head and finishing about eight inches above the head. Finishing the stroke relatively high helps to emphasize the stick lift. In addition, the student must be cautioned to avoid pressing on the drum head with the sticks during a stroke, which deadens the tone and produces a distorted sound with poorly defined pitch.

The lifting approach to stroke technique is particularly important for rolls. Each time the stick comes in contact with the head, the tone will be muffled in both loud and soft rolls if there is any downward pressure. Practicing soft rolls with an exaggerated stick lift can help to counteract a tendency to use excessive downward pressure.

More and more timpanists are beginning to play rolls with the stick heads separated by six or eight inches. They find that this technique produces a smoother, more resonant and sustained sound than when the stick heads are played close together.

Balancing the Heads

A final factor essential for good sound is "balancing" the heads. Any drum head should have equal tension all around, but the proper tension is much more significant for timpani than for other drums. Each tension post may be thought of as an individual instrument. If six clarinets play the same note but at slightly different pitch levels, the resulting sound will be unfocused, unsteady, and simply annoying. The same is true of the timpani with poorly adjusted tension posts.

Since striking the drum head at any dynamic level will distort the head, it is best to balance the head without using sticks. If the drum is tuned to any note, and if that note is hummed or sung about four or six inches from the rim, the drum will resonate that note distinctly. The same is true of the perfect fifth above the note to which the drum is tuned. If the head is balanced properly, both of these tones will resonate *freely* and *steadily* at each tension post. If these tones sound weak or wavering, the post should be adjusted until the head is properly tuned.* It may be helpful to use an electronic tuner or tuning fork to make sure the reference tone is constant.

It is important to remember that a major adjustment affects the tension all around the drum head, but especially the area directly across the head from the tension post. Using a tone near the midpoint of each drum's range may make it easier to balance the head.

Since no pedal mechanism operates perfectly, normal play on the drum will result in the gradual unbalancing of the head. Fortunately, frequent maintenance can eliminate the need for a major overhaul.

Although none of these points is exotic or complicated, each does require thought, care, perseverance, and some practice. Attaining mastery over the various factors must come from the determined belief of the conductor and the timpanist that the drums must make a beautiful sound as they contribute the expected dynamic and rhythmic elements.

October 1976

Acoustics of Tuned Bars

Thomas D. Rossing

In "Acoustics of Percussion Instruments" (*The Instrumentalist*, Parts I and II, May and June 1976) where the behavior of various vibrating systems was described, we learned that the simplest vibrators, such as strings and air columns, have modes of vibration which are harmonics of the fundamental mode (see Fig. 1 in Part I). Thus when set into vibration the vibrators radiate sound with harmonic overtones, which blends well with the sounds of other musical instruments. Bars, membranes, and plates, however, vibrate in more complex modes which are not, in general, harmonic. The inharmonic overtones of these vibrators give percussion instruments their distinctive timbre.

Very little experimental research on the acoustics of bar percussion instruments has been done. (One notable exception was the unpublished doctoral research of James Moore at Ohio State University about seven years ago.[1]) Thus we find many incorrect and misleading statements in textbooks and articles, especially regarding the modes of vibration and the overtones of the bars. Perhaps the information in this article (first reported in a paper read to the Acoustical Society of America in 1975[2]) can help clear up some misconceptions.

Rectangular Bars: The Glockenspiel

Glockenspiel or orchestra bells employ rectangular steel bars 1 inch to 1-1/4 inches wide and 3/8 inches to 5/16 inches thick. Their range is customarily from G_5 (f=784 Hz) to C_8 (f=4186 Hz), although they are scored two octaves lower than they sound.

written range

The glockenspiel is usually played with brass or hard plastic mallets. The bell lyra is a portable version which uses aluminum bars and usually covers the range A_5 to A_7.

When struck with a hard mallet, a glockenspiel bar produces a crisp, metallic sound which quickly gives way to a clear ring at the designated pitch. Because the overtones have very high frequencies and die out quickly, they are of relatively less importance in determining the timbre of the glockenspiel than are the overtones of the marimba or xylophone, for example. For this reason, no effort is made to bring the enharmonic overtones of a glockenspiel into a harmonic relationship through overtone tuning.

The frequencies for the transverse vibrations in a thin bar with free ends have these ratios: 1.00 : 2.76 : 5.40 : 8.93 : 13.34, etc.[3] These frequencies are anything but harmonic. (The ratio 2.76, for example, represents an interval slightly over an octave plus a fourth, an augmented eleventh.) However, even for the lowest note on the glockenspiel, this overtone has a frequency of 2160 Hz, which is getting into the range where the pitch discrimination of human listeners is diminished. (This will not be the case for other bar percussion instruments, however, as we shall soon see.)

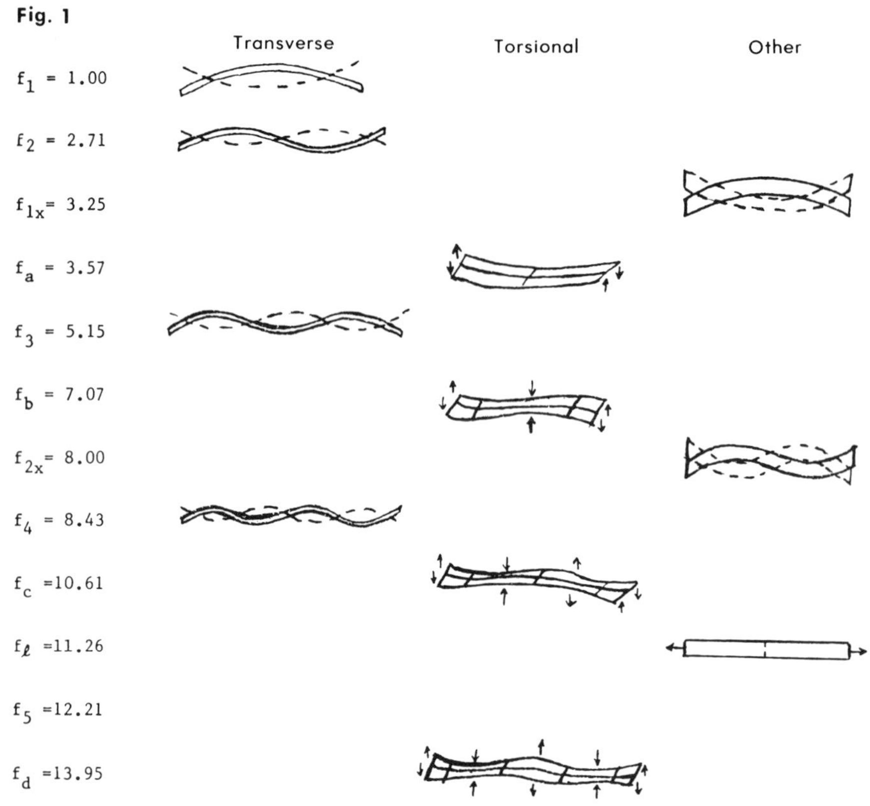

Modes of C_6 glockenspiel bar, which lie within the audible range of frequency. The transverse modes are labeled 1, 2, 3, 4, and 5; a, b, c and d are torsional modes; ℓ is a longitudinal mode and 1x and 2x are transverse modes excited edgewise. Mode frequencies are given as ratios to the fundamental. The sound spectrum at the bottom shows the relative amplitudes of the partials associated with these modes.

We can play an educational game, however, by exciting a glockenspiel bar in as many modes as possible. Calvin Rose did this in our laboratory by passing an electric current from an audio amplifier through a C_6 glockenspiel bar with a magnet placed nearby. He identified 12 modes of vibration within the audible range, 5 of which are the modes of transverse vibrations we have already mentioned, and assigned the numbers 1 through 5 (see Figs. 1 and 2). There are also two modes of transverse vibration edgewise, which we call 1x and 2x. Four modes, which we label a, b, c, and d, were found to represent a torsional or "twisting" motion of the bar. The remaining one represents longitudinal vibration, and we call this mode "ℓ."[4] Of course, if Rose had chosen to go above the audible range of frequency, many more modes could have been observed. Fig. 1 lists the frequencies of the modes along with sketches of the vibrations they represent. Other bars show similar behavior, although one or two of the modes may change places. For example, in the E_6 bar, Rose found that modes a and 1x changed places.

Fig. 2

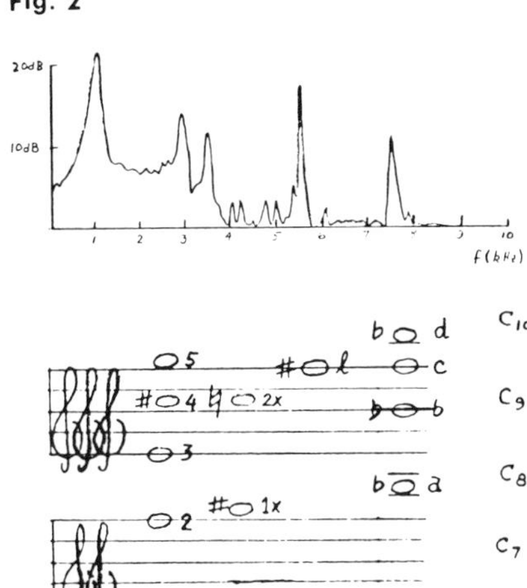

Sound spectrum of a C6 glockenspiel bar, together with a representation of the lowest 12 modes of vibration on musical staffs. To avoid the use of many ledger lines, we have invented 2 new clefs, a "super treble" clef (ST) two octaves above the treble and a "supra-super treble" clef (SST) four octaves above the treble. We apologize to any musicians who might be offended by our shenanigans.

Note that the transverse modes are spaced a little closer together than predicted by the simple theory of thin bars. This pattern is similar to the behavior of chimes noted in my earlier article (see Fig. 4 in Part II), and is easily explained by applying a more sophisticated theory for thick bars.

What can be learned from this little game of mode identification? Not very much that is directly applicable to the sound of a glockenspiel. However, an understanding of this relatively simple case of vibrations in a rectangular bar may help us to understand the more complicated vibrators in the percussion family.

The Marimba

The marimba typically includes 3 to 4-1/3 octaves of tuned rosewood or Kelon bars, graduated in width from about 1-3/4 inches to 2-1/2 inches. Beneath each bar is a tubular resonator tuned to the fundamental frequency of that bar. The marimba is played with soft mallets, producing a rich, mellow tone. The playing range of a large concert marimba is A2 to C7 (f= 110-2093 Hz), although bass marimbas extend down to C2.

A deep arch is cut in the underside of marimba bars, particularly in the low register. This arch serves two useful purposes: it reduces the length of the bar required to reach the low pitches, and it allows tuning of the overtones (the first overtone is nominally tuned two octaves above the fundamental). Fig. 3 shows a scale drawing of a marimba bar and indicates the positions of the nodes and the ratios of the frequencies for each of the first seven modes of vibration.

Fig. 3

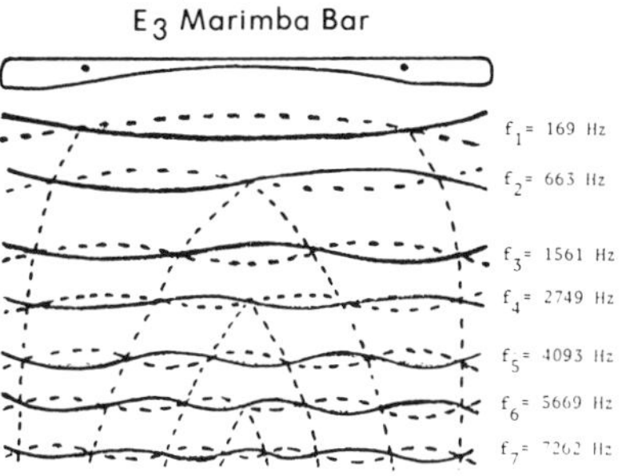

A scale drawing of a marimba bar tuned to E3 (f=165 Hz). The sketches locate the nodes observed for the first 7 modes.

(This figure may be compared to Fig. 1 which shows the nodes of a glockenspiel bar without a cut arch, and also to Fig. 1 in Part I of this article, which shows the modes of a vibrating string.) Note that the second partial (first overtone) of this bar has a frequency 3.9 times that of the fundamental and is close to a two-octave interval (ratio of 4.0).

The sound spectrum of the E3 marimba bar (see Fig. 4), along with the partials on musical staves, indicates the presence of a strong 3rd partial, which is about three octaves plus a minor third above the fundamental. The relative strengths of the partials depends on where the bar is struck and the type of mallet used. To emphasize one partial, the bar should be struck at a point of maximum amplitude for that mode (see Fig. 3).

Fig. 4

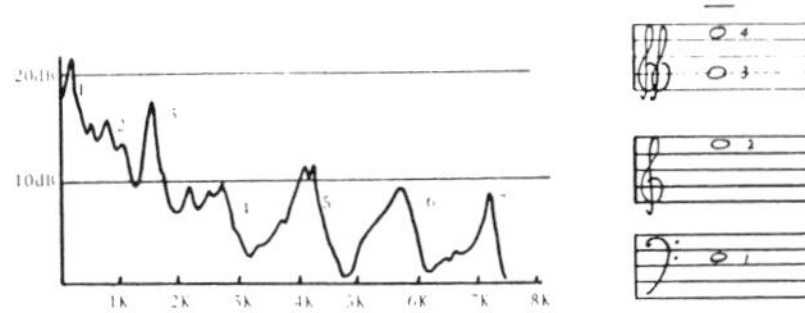

Sound spectrum for E3 marimba bar in Fig. 3. The partials are also indicated on music staves which include a super-treble clef.

Marimba resonators are cylindrical pipes tuned to the fundamental mode of the corresponding bars. A pipe with one closed end and one open end resonates when its acoustical length is half of a wavelength of the sound.[5] The purpose of the tubular resonators is to increase the volume which is done at the expense of shortening the decay time of the sound. We have measured the decay time (60 dB) of a rosewood bar in the low register (E3) and found it to be 1.5 seconds with the resonator and 3.2 seconds without it. Decay times in the upper register are generally shorter; we recorded 0.4 seconds and 0.5 seconds for an E6 bar with and without the resonator. The corresponding decay times for Kelon bars are somewhat longer.

Although the first overtone of marimba bars in the low register appears to be carefully tuned to the double octave of the fundamental, considerably less care is exercised in cutting arches in bars in the upper register. We studied four marimbas in the Northern Illinois University music department and found that the tuning of the first overtone extends to about 1-1/2 to 2-1/2 octaves below the top note. Apparently careful overtone tuning is not deemed necessary in the upper register because of the shorter decay time and the diminished pitch sensitivity of the ear (even though overtone frequencies of 2000 - 4000 Hz are still within range of sensitive hearing).[6]

It is not difficult to test the overtone tuning of your own marimba (or other bar percussion instruments) by noting the positions of the nodes in Fig. 3. To suppress the fundamental mode and emphasize the first overtone, one should touch the bar firmly at the center and strike the bar at one end or else at a point about one-third of the way from the center to either end.

I have contemplated building a marimba using bars with several overtones carefully tuned, possibly with additional sets of resonators that can be opened and closed to vary the timbre in the manner of organ stops. I know that marimbas have been constructed with two sets of resonators, but I have never heard one played.

The Xylophone

The xylophone is a close cousin

to the marimba (or perhaps "uncle" is a better term, since the xylophone apparently has a longer history). Xylophones typically cover a range of 3 to 3-1/2 octaves extending from F4 or C5 to C8 (349-4186 Hz), and may have bars of Kelon or rosewood. Modern xylophones are nearly always equipped with tubular resonators to increase the loudness of the tone.

Table of Measurements on Modes of Bars*

	Frequencies	Ratios
Marimba (Musser)		
A2	110.1, 444**, 1109**, 1971	[1 : 4.03 : 10.1 : 17.9]
A3	221, 887**, 2211, 3725, (5558)	[1 : 4.01 : 10.0 : 16.9 : 25.1]
A4	440.7, 1780**, 4026**	[1 : 4.04 : 9.1]
A5	883.1, 2928, 5675	[1 : 3.3 : 6.4]
Xylophone (Musser)		
A4	444.5, 1338, 2798	[1 : 3.01 : 6.3]
A5	880.0, 2590, 4765	[1 : 2.94 : 5.4]
Vibes (Musser)		
A3	220.2, 883**, 2324, 3815, 5045	[1 : 4:01 : 10.6 : 17.3 : 22.9]
A4	440.2, 1768**, 4010, 6109, 8840**	[1 : 4.02 : 9.1 : 13.9 : 20.1]
A5	881.9, 3340, 6527, 10,193	[1 : 3.79 : 7.4 : 11.6]
Orchestra Bells		
A5	885.3, 2410, 4679, 7651**, 11224**	[1 : 2.72 : 5.3 : 8.6 : 12.7]
A6	1771.1, 4782, 9072, 14,661**	[1 : 2.70 : 5.1 : 8.3]
A7	3552.3, 9299, 17,438**	[1 : 2.62 : 4.9]

* Reprinted from James L. Moore's unpublished doctoral dissertation, "Acoustics of Bar Percussion Instruments," University Microfilms, Ann Arbor, Michigan.

** "very strong" modes.

Xylophone bars are also cut with an arch on the underside, but the arch is not as deep as the one on the marimba, since the first overtone is tuned to a twelfth above the fundamental (three times the frequency of the fundamental). Since a pipe closed at one end can also resonate at three times its fundamental resonant frequency, the twelfth is also reinforced by the resonator. This overtone boost, plus the hard mallets used to play it, gives the xylophone a much crisper, brighter sound than the marimba. We have found that careful overtone tuning is ignored in the upper register, as in the case of the marimba.

Vibes

A very popular bar percussion instrument is the vibraphone or vibraharp (popularly called "vibes"), which has aluminum bars tuned over a three-octave range from F3 to F6 (175-1370 Hz). The bars are deeply arched so that the first overtone is the double octave, as in the marimba. The aluminum bars tend to have a much longer decay time than the wood or synthetic bars of the marimba or xylophone, and so vibes are equipped with pedal-operated dampers.

The most distinctive feature of vibes, however, is the vibrato introduced by means of motor-driven discs at the top of the resonators which alternately open and close the tubes. The vibrato produced by these rotating discs or pulsators consists of a rather substantial fluctuation in amplitude ("intensity vibrato") and a small fluctuation in phase, but no detectable change in frequency ("pitch vibrato"). The speed of rotation of the discs may be adjusted to produce a "slow vibe" or a "fast vibe." If the motor is turned off, vibes may be played without vibrato. They are usually played with soft mallets or beaters, which produce a mellow tone, although some passages call for harder beaters.

Fig. 5 illustrates the mode frequencies for three vibe bars tuned to F3, G4, and G5. Also shown is the sound spectrum for the F3 bar.

Fig. 5

	f	f_n/f_1	f	f_n/f_1	f	f_n/f_1
f_1	175	1	394	1	784	1
f_2	700	4.0	1578	4.0	2994	3.8
f_3	1708	9.7	3480	8.9	5995	7.6
f_4	3192	18.3	5972	15.2	9400	12.0
f_5	4105	23.5	8007	20.2	14014	17.9
f_6	6173	35.4	11119	35	18796	24.0
f_7	8080	46.3			21302	27.2

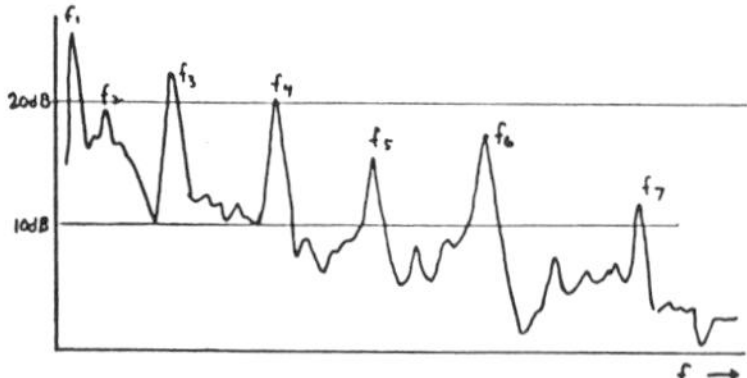

Mode frequencies of vibe bars tuned to F3, G4 and G5; the ratios to the fundamental are also given. The sound spectrum is that of the F3 bar.

Just as in the cases of the marimba and xylophone, we observe careful tuning of the first overtone only in the low register (up to D5 or G5 for different instruments). (Our figures agree with those in Moore's dissertation, the only other measurements which we have found that record the mode frequencies of tuned bars. His data, which also indicate careful tuning of the first overtone in the lower registers only, are summarized in the Table of Measurements on Modes of Bars.)

Because vibraphone bars have a much longer decay time than marimba and xylophone bars, the effect of the tubular resonators on decay time is more dramatic. At 220 Hz (A3), for example, we measure a decay time (60 dB) of 40 seconds without the resonator, and 9 seconds with the tube full open.[7] For A5, we measure 24 seconds without the resonator and 8 seconds with it.[8] In the recording of sound level (see Fig. 6), the intensity modulation may be clearly seen, as well as the slow decay of the sound.

Fig. 6

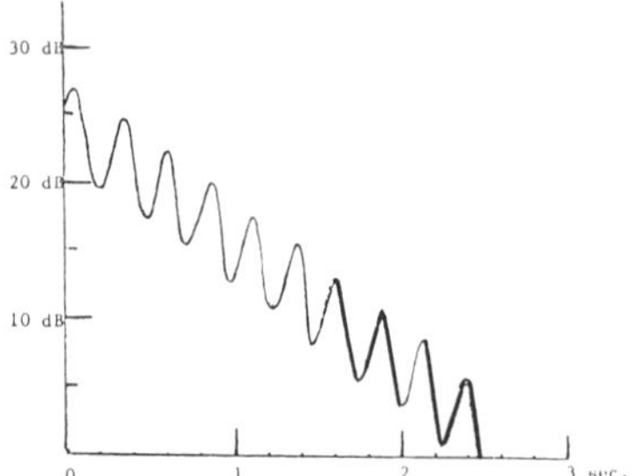

Sound level recording for A3 bar (f=440 Hz) with a vibe rate of about 4 Hz. The intensity level fluctuates about 6 dB, and the decay time (60 dB) is 7 sec.

Mr. Rossing would like to acknowledge Alan O'Connor, Garry Kvistad, and the N.I.U. Music Department for the loan of several instruments. Special thanks go to Calvin Rose, who gathered much of the data in this article. Some of the work was supported by a grant from the Research Corporation.

1. J.L. Moore, "Acoustics of Bar Percussion Instruments," (1970) University Microfilms, Ann Arbor, Michigan.

2. C. Rose, and T.D. Rossing, "Modes of Vibration of Tuned Bars in Percussion Instruments," *Journal of the Acoustical Society of America* 58 (1975): 5131.

3. The formula was given in "Acoustics of Percussion Instruments" (Part I) as: $f_n=(vK/L^2)m^2$ where m=(3.0112), 5, 7 . . . (2n+1). K is 0.346 times the thickness of the bar.

4. The formula for frequencies of longitudinal modes, also given in "Acoustics" (Part I), is: $f_n = nv/2L$. Note that the relative positions of the longitudinal and transverse modes depends upon the length, since the transverse frequencies vary with $1/L^2$ but the longitudinal frequencies vary only as 1/L.

5. The acoustical length of a pipe turns out to be slightly greater than its actual length, because the sound reflects slightly beyond the open end of a pipe. The acoustical length L′ is given by the actual length, L, plus 0.6 times the radius, r. Thus the length of a marimba pipe should be 4v/f - 0.6r, where v is the velocity of sound and f is the desired resonance frequency.

6. It is a little amusing to note that at least one of the manufacturers of the marimbas tested advertises "fundamental and octave harmonic tuned to ±.001 semitone tolerance."

7. The decay time can be shortened still further to 4 seconds by turning the disc so that it slightly constricts the resonator tube.

8. The resonator tube changes the effective radiation impedance of the bar, a concept not easy to explain in easy terms. From a simple consideration of energy, however, it is easy to understand why increasing the loudness decreases the decay time of the sound.

November 1976

Understanding Ruffs and Drags

Paul Lawrence

The correct rudimental interpretation of ruffs and drags in snare drum literature is a problem for many young drummers. This article presents a detailed rhythmic analysis, with a series of practical, playable exercises to demonstrate the correct interpretation. The material is designed to be useful to music teachers who are not percussion specialists.

Flams and ruffs must be treated as grace notes for the drum part, just as grace notes embellish any musical phrase. The most common fault is to play the grace notes too "open," — that is, too separated, — or too detached from the main note. A "flam" should be played in the same way the one-syllable word "flam" is spoken: as a short, quick grace note barely separated from the main note; don't play it as if you were saying "fa-lam" or "kerplop." The word "ruff" is also one syllable, although it takes a little longer to say. Perform the ruff the way it is pronounced; never let it become "chick-a-boom."

The Ruff (Rudiment #8)

In playing the ruff in rudimental style, it is best to start very slowly, thinking of it as notated in 6/8 time:

Ex. 1

Begin playing with the metronome set at ♩=60. Be sure that the proper stick positions are used. Start Ex. 1 with the left stick low and the right stick high. The left stick will play two taps and then go up as the right stick goes down. After the right stick plays its first note from "high" position, it will remain low, ready for the next two sixteenth-notes. The left stick is already up, in position for its accented note. The right stick plays two taps from "low" position on count six, the left plays an accented note on count one, and the procedure continues.

Gradually increase the tempo, but keep the rhythm and the ratio of the time values the same. As the speed increases, the two sixteenth-note taps will become a controlled bounce, rather than two separate notes. This bounce is the proper way to execute the ruff at performance tempos. The student should continue to increase the tempo to maximum speed, then slow down, returning to the original tempo without changing the rhythm.

The Single Drag, the Double Drag, and Lesson 25 (Rudiments #9, #10, and #25)

Apply the fundamentals of the ruff discussed above when it is used as part of a larger rhythm pattern such as the single drag, double drag, or Lesson 25.

It is helpful to consider the drag grace notes as two thirty-second-notes, i.e. 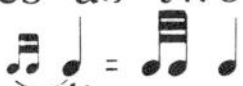, or as a segment of a rudimental roll played at a moderate tempo.

Begin by playing the five stroke roll in rudimental style: open — closed — open. Start very slowly, then gradually and evenly increase the speed until it is as fast as comfortable. Take an equal amount of time to return gradually to the beginning tempo. Begin the five stroke roll again very slowly. When it is at a speed of about 𝅗𝅥=120 leave out the fourth note (see Ex. 2).

Ex. 2

Five stroke roll

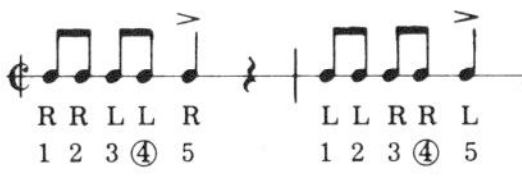

becomes

Single Drag

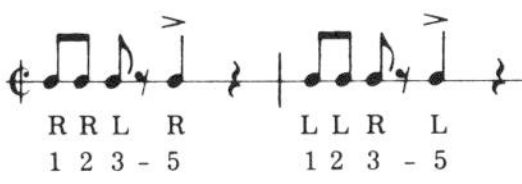

Gradually increase the tempo, but be sure to keep the rhythm and time values constant. As the speed increases, the first two notes will become a controlled bounce, just as they do in a five stroke roll. In Ex. 3, play the exercises in Steps 1-4 (left column) first, noticing that the accented notes fall *after* the beat. Then play those in the right column, where the examples have been shifted so that the accented notes come *on* the beat.

The double drag may be learned in the same manner as the single drag, but it should be approached through the phrasing of the nine stroke roll. When the roll reaches the speed 𝅗𝅥=132, leave out the fourth and eighth notes. As the speed increases, notes 1, 2, 5, and 6 will become controlled bounces form- the drags (Ex. 4).

Ex. 3

Exercises for the Single Drag

First time through, accented notes after the beat

Step 1: Five stroke roll as written

RR LL

Step 2: Five stroke roll as played

Step 3: Fourth note omitted

Step 4: Notation (and sound) changed from thirty-second-notes to grace notes: basis of single drag

RRLR LLRL

Second time through, accented notes on the beat

Step 1: Five stroke roll as written

& 1 & 2 & 3 & 4 &

R R LL R

Step 2: Five stroke roll as played

Step 3: Fourth note omitted

Step 4: Notation (and sound) changed from thirty-second-notes to grace notes: final form of single drag

& 1 & 2 & 3 & 4 &

RRL R LLRL RRL

Ex. 4

Exercises for the Double Drag

Step 1: Nine stroke roll as played

Step 2: Fourth and eighth notes omitted

Step 3: Figure moved so that it occurs one half beat earlier

Step 4: Thirty-second notes changed to grace notes ahead of the beat

RR L RRL R LL R LLR L

Lesson 25 may be approached through the phrasing of the seven stroke roll. Use the same procedure as before, but omit the fourth and sixth notes. To put the accent on the beat, move the rhythms to the left one-half count (Ex. 5).

Ex. 5

Exercises for Lesson 25

Step 1: Seven stroke roll as played

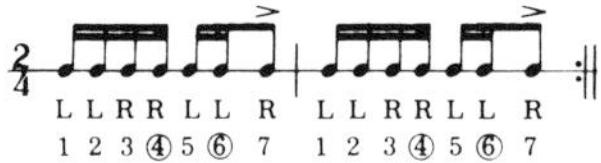

Step 2: Fourth and sixth notes omitted

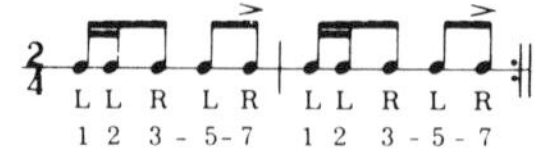

Step 3: Figure moved so that it occurs one half beat earlier

Step 4: Thirty-second notes changed to grace notes

LL R L R LL R L R

Drag Paradiddles Nos. 1 and 2 (Rudiments #22 and #23)

Before undertaking a study of the drag paradiddles, it would be wise for the student to review the ruff and all the paradiddle rudiments, particularly the single paradiddle. Be sure that the sticking and stick motion are correct and that the rudiment can be played reasonably well at all speeds (open — closed — open).

Think of drag paradiddle No. 1 as being written in 3/4 time with the ruff notated as two thirty-second-notes (see Ex. 6).

Ex. 6

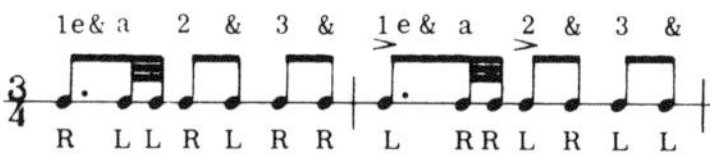

Begin playing quite slowly (♩=72 or less). Be sure that the two thirty-second-notes are exactly in rhythm. As the tempo increases, these grace notes will become a controlled bounce. This is the correct style and interpretation for most performance tempos.

Drag paradiddle No. 2 should be considered in the same way, but in 4/4 time (see Ex. 7).

Ex. 7

Single, Double and Triple Ratamacues (Rudiments #12, #26, and #13)

The grace notes of the ruffs in ratamacues are traditionally played slightly more open (separated) than they are in the other rudiments. Ratamacues are seldom seen in orchestral notation, but they are a standard part of drum corps literature. They each contain a triplet figure and are most easily interpreted in 6/8, 9/8, or 12/8 time.

The single ratamacue should be played first in 6/8 time, ♩=72. (see Ex. 8).

Ex. 8

6 & 1 2 3 4 5 6 & 1 2 3 4 5

LL R L R L RR L R L R

Gradually increase the tempo, but keep the ratio of the rhythms constant so that the interpretation is correct even at very fast tempos.

Notation in 9/8 time gives each note of the double ratamacue its proper place (see Ex. 9).

Ex. 9

This rudiment has a strong feeling of 3/4 time when played faster. The accent on the third count gives it a nice "lift" or swing feeling. However, if this execution is troublesome to the young player, the notation may be moved to the right so the accent falls on "one." Putting the accent on a strong beat may make it easier to play (see Ex. 10).

Ex. 10

The thirty-second-notes may then be changed to grace notes (see Ex. 11).

Ex. 11

Similarly, the triple ratamacue may be notated in 12/8 time (see Ex. 12).

Ex. 12

As the tempo increases, there is a strong feeling of 4/4 time, with the accent on count 4. This accented weak beat forms a syncopation that most players find interesting. If the young player finds the syncopation troublesome, the figure may be shifted so it occurs one count later (see Ex. 13).

Ex. 13

The thirty-second-notes may be changed to grace notes (see Ex. 14).

Ex. 14

Hints to Students and Teachers

Exercises at various tempos have been suggested for all of the common drag and ruff rudiments. The information here is only a beginning for the student; once mastered, he should then learn to play the rudiments at all speeds. In a contest, presentation of the rudiments is done open — closed — open, or slow — fast — slow. The rhythm must not change - only the tempo may change, and it changes very gradually.

The serious student should listen to good percussionists as often as possible. He should be sure that the interpretation he adopts is the correct one. It is important to remember that the open style of drumming is correct for drum corps but is not correct for orchestral or symphonic band playing. The orchestral style is tighter and more concise; here, the individual strokes are not as important as the total musical sound or phrase.

December 1976

Concert Preparations for the Timpanist

Larry D. Snider

The concert timpanist must not only be a critical, technical, and musical performer, but he must also be a very organized musician. His great importance in any large music organization, and the sensitivity he must bring to it, require that the timpanist plan ahead in his preparation for concerts so that he can add effectively to the color and excitement of the rest of the group. The following pre-concert suggestions, if used properly, will definitely help him perform a more *musical* concert.

Timpani Location and Arrangement

Whenever possible, the timpani should be placed as close as possible to the center and rear of the orchestra or band. This placement enables the timpanist to evaluate accurately the intonation of his instrument and its relationship to the rest of the ensemble. Since the rhythms of the bass drum coincide closely with the timpani part in many compositions, the timpani set-up should be very near the bass drum. This arrangement makes unison articulations and balance in ensemble playing much easier and more musical. It is also wise to place the timpani as close to the low brass as possible so that the timpani part can support the rhythm and chordal performance of the low brass — a vital consideration in most contemporary band and orchestra literature.

Preferably, the timpanist should use a high stool on which to lean (not sit). This enables him to move quickly and easily when tuning, playing *glissandi*, and so forth. A high stool properly positions the player so that he can use the correct playing area of the head as well as correct stick placement and arm movement.

The music stand should be placed between the two timpani being used the most (usually the 25″ and 28″ drums). The stand should be adjusted to allow a direct line of sight over it to the conductor's baton

Composers, arrangers, and performers are generally aware today of the importance of timpani timbre to composition and recognize that timbre can be changed readily by using different sticks and mallets. Since many pairs of sticks may be needed in a single performance, it is helpful to keep a variety of stick types on a trap tray next to the player (Figs. 1 and 2).

Fig. 1

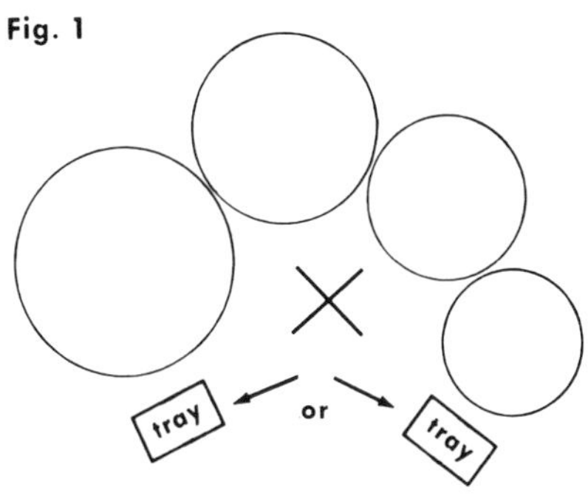

Fig. 2

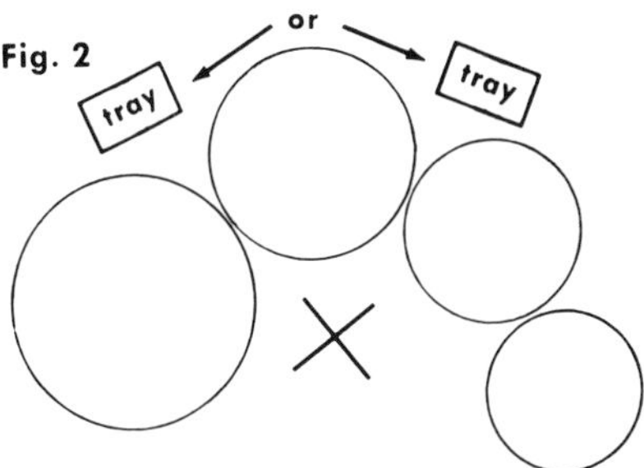

Players who find a trap table too cumbersome to work around sometimes adjust a sturdy music stand to a horizontal position and use it for a table (Fig. 3). This seems to be the perfect size for three or four sets of mallets without too much extra space. To avoid extraneous noises caused by sticks on the metal stand, place a towel over the music stand.

Fig. 3

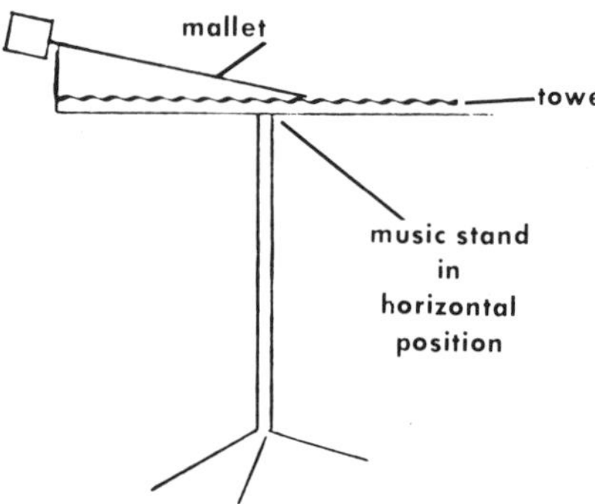

Timpanists may also consider the use of colored tape on stick handles to insure correct and fast identification of mallet softness or hardness. This is especially important since many manufacturers have made it visually difficult to tell how hard or soft a stick is because all models look alike. A somewhat standard color code is:

yellow or white — soft
blue — medium
red — hard

Pre-Concert Tuning

It is imperative that the timpanist arrive at the place of performance well before concert time. He should first check each drum to be sure that its tuning lugs are set so that the same pitch sounds at each lug. Even though tuning should occur during rehearsal at regular intervals, moving the drums may cause slipping and a different performance site may create a predominance of different pitches. If calf heads are used, considerable time should be allotted for this tuning procedure to make tuning with the concert ensemble easier and more accurate. Pitch pipes may be used, although a tuning fork produces a more accurate tuning. The final tuning *must* be done with the entire ensemble during the performance.

The timpanist should use some of his pre-concert preparation time to listen and get used to the sound of the concert hall while keeping in mind the acoustics of the timpani. A different hardness of sticks, for example, might be necessary to give the best overall sound in the hall. If the hall is acoustically very alive and the timpanist has a very articulate, fast passage to perform, he may need to use a harder stick than he used during rehearsals so that the articulation will sound clear to the audience. Similarly, in a very dead hall, the same articulate passage might necessitate softer sticks than those used in rehearsal so that the tone of the instrument rather than just a "tom-tom effect" reaches the listener.

Muting the drum may also help to create a more articulate sound. The timpani may be muted by placing a round piece of felt about 5 inches in diameter on the head (the size of the mute depends on the size of the drum). A slight change in articulation can be achieved if the mute is placed directly in the center of the head. As the timpanist moves the mute slowly toward the timpani rim, the sound becomes progressively drier until about 3 or 4 inches from the rim where it deadens the head (see Fig. 4). Care must be taken so that the mute of each timpani is not placed where the player may accidentally strike it with his mallet, thus producing an uncharacteristic sound.

Fig. 4

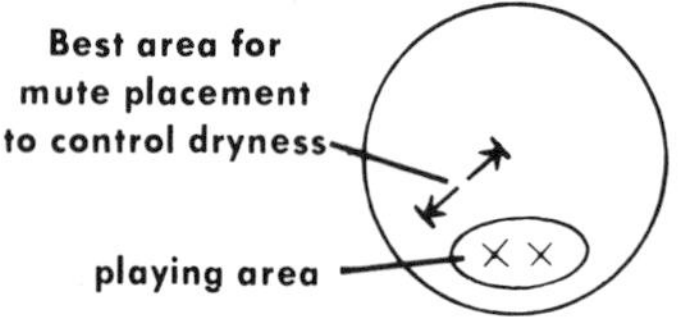

Sometimes the timpanist has a long passage in which only two or three of the four drums are used. In this case, it is wise to put mutes about four inches from the rims on the drums that are not being played. This prevents the sound produced by the resonating drum head from causing sympathetic vibrations in the other drums.

Effective mutes may be made easily at home.

1. Cut 2 circles of 5-inch diameter felt.
2. Cut a 2-inch diameter piece of felt.
3. Place the 2-inch diameter piece of felt in the center between the 5-inch pieces (this is for purposes of weight).
4. Sew the 5-inch pieces together.
5. (Optional) Sew an end of cord approximately 2 feet long to the edge of each mute. By tying the other end around the timpani lug, the mute is easily accessible during a performance. Lightweight yarn may be used because it will not cause a "buzz" sound when the head is struck (Fig. 5).

Fig. 5

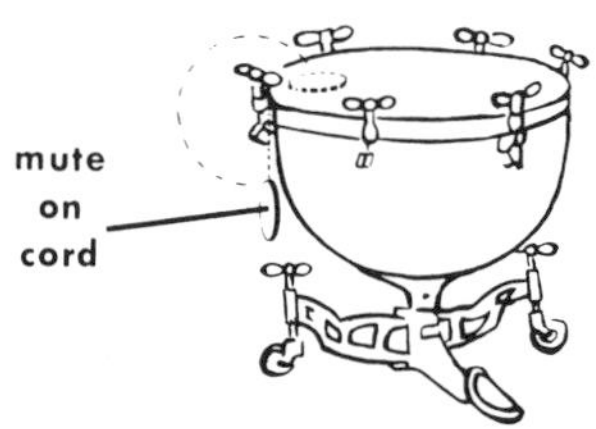

It is important that the timpanist as well as the conductor experiment with various combinations of stick hardnesses and mutes to create the best sound in a given acoustical surrounding.

Music Marking

Music marking should take place during rehearsals. It is wise to use pencil only (never ink). Many timpanists find coding with colored pencils very helpful. For example, one might circle all tuning changes in red and also possibly write in the interval of pitch change to make quick tunings much faster ("A↗B♭ - half step"). Conducting changes should also be written in the music ("in 2"). After several rehearsals, the timpanist must mark in the stick changes and difficult technical stickings throughout the piece. If he is playing other instruments beside the timpani, he should remind himself of instrument changes ("to triangle" or "to △"). Pictorial diagrams of instruments are being used more and more for these changes. One should never trust his memory for these preparations.

Musical Preparation

Besides working out rhythmic, technical, and sticking problems, it is wise for the timpanist to listen to many performances of the composition. He may discover some different interpretations as well as other timpanists' choices regarding hardness or softness of sticks. With these ideas in mind, it is important that the timpanist use some of his own musical imagination and experiment with mallets and stickings. After all, the interpretation he hears on a recording of the piece may not be the best one!

Tunings must also be worked out in advance. Not only during full rehearsal, but also during individual practice, the timpanist should work with a metronome to accomplish tunings in the allotted time. Many times, it is helpful if a pianist plays some of the parts of the full score (in concert pitch) or even the chord changes around difficult tuning places so that the timpanist can better prepare his ear and gauge the speed of tuning for these changes. Playing along with a recording can also be useful.

Visual Aspects During Performance

For many concertgoers, one of the most exciting aspects of the percussion section is visual. Excessive movement lessens the visual excitement of the necessary moves of the percussionist. At the same time, added motion may be considered if it enhances the musical style and is done with good taste. Long rest-counting passages give the timpanist an excellent opportunity to prepare himself by mentally going through the composition and performing his next entrance. He should therefore remain seated during tacets and long rests. Indecision will not be present to mar the musically aggressive appearance of the performers if the stick and pitch changes and performance-helps are well marked and rehearsed.

A timpanist at any age level can be a fine musician and technician, but he may ruin his and his ensemble's performance unless many small but important preparations are made before and during the performance. Method books and excerpt studies are only a part of becoming an expert timpanist. Planning ahead for a performance is a vital part of the timpanist's musical performance.

January 1977

Play a Multiple Percussion Solo

James R. McKinney

Learning a multiple percussion solo can benefit you or your students in several ways. First, since it is a solo composition involving more than one type of percussion instrument, it gives the percussionist experience in reading notation for more than one instrument simultaneously: vertically as well as horizontally. Percussionists who have learned to play mallet instruments or timpani may already read vertically, but for many "drummers" the multiple solo is a new experience in reading notes on more than one line at a time. Second, good hand independence is also developed in playing most of these solos. If the student has a weak left or right hand, playing a multiple percussion solo will probably help him strengthen it. And third, it helps a student become a more complete percussionist, by broadening his repertoire and allowing him to master more instruments than just the already familiar snare and bass drums.

Performance Suggestions

The following 10 points should be helpful in performing multiple percussion solos.

1. *Arrange the instruments in order of pitch, from high on your right to low on your left.* This high/right to low/left set-up corresponds to the familiar arrangement of timpani and keyboard percussion instruments. A semi-circular arrangement is usually best, since it allows you to reach the outside instruments easily.

Most solos are printed with this high-to-low idea in mind. For example, in James Moore's *Sonata No. 1* the following set-up and legend is given:

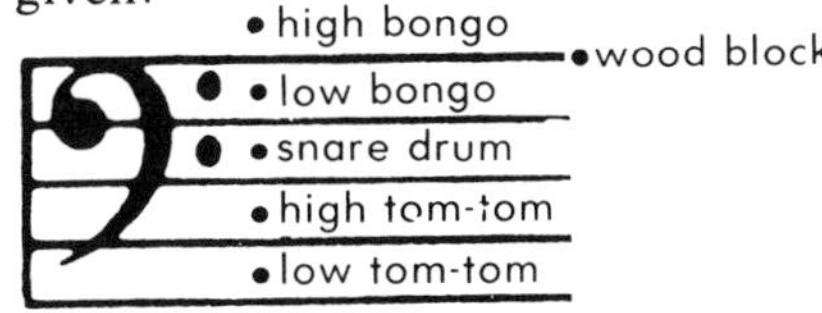

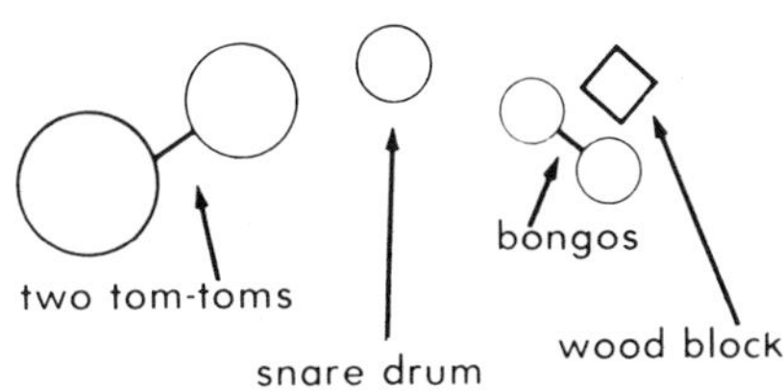

This set-up is a good basic arrangement to follow if the composer doesn't suggest any set-up or if you find his set-up awkward.

2. *Use the matched grip for multiple solos.* Use of the matched grip on all instruments (including the snare drum) permits smoother movement between the instruments. It is even essential for some pieces, such as the "Sarabande" in William Kraft's *French Suite* which calls for the use of four yarn mallets, two in each hand. An adequate matched grip technique can be developed in a relatively short time by a student who has a good traditional grip technique.

3. *Use a stick/mallet tray for quiet stick changes.* You can make a good stick tray from a music stand by covering the music desk portion with a rug remnant, soft cloth, or foam rubber and adjusting it to a horizontal position. Find a convenient place for the tray. (Occasionally the composer will suggest a spot for the tray, but you should feel free to use whatever set-up is most comfortable for you.) During fast changes in a performance, be sure that the mallets or sticks do not roll off the tray.

4. *Place small accessory instruments on foam rubber pads or*

rug remnants to absorb unwanted sounds.

5. *If you have no time to change sticks, choose an all-purpose stick or mallet.* For example, you may need to play the timpani and/or other drums with a yarn-wound mallet as in Jared Spears' *Prologue and Jubilo*. In Thomas L. Davis' *Spanish Dance*, four instruments — timpani, suspended cymbal, snare drum, and castanets — are all played with medium rubber mallets!

6. *Use custom-made mallets for some quick changes.* When you don't have time to change sticks or mallets, you may wish to use "reversible" ones with different heads on each end. Then you can play a variety of instruments simply by flipping the sticks over. Snare drum sticks with strips of adhesive moleskin wrapped around the butt ends make a versatile combination. Some works specify this type of double-duty mallet, as in Darius Milhaud's *Concerto for Percussion and Small Orchestra* (Universal) which calls for a mallet with felt timpani balls on one end and hard xylophone balls on the other. Do not be afraid to experiment on your own — the results can be very rewarding.

7. *Study the legend and symbols in addition to the sticks and mallets used before you attempt to play the solo.* Unfortunately, composers do not use standardized symbols or legends, so each multiple solo will have different notation. It is very helpful to become familiar with a pamphlet called *Standardization of Percussion Notation* published by the Percussive Arts Society. It can be ordered for $1 from PAS, 130 Carol Dr., Terre Haute, Ind. 47805.

8. *Strive for a balance between all of the instruments.* Smaller accessory instruments (wood blocks, temple blocks, castanets, tambourines, etc.) must usually be played harder to balance the larger drums and cymbals. Don't just strike the instruments — listen to the overall sound and adjust each instrument accordingly.

9. *When playing two or more instruments at once (or two notes on the same instrument), strike the instruments simultaneously.* Be careful not to play a flam, unless notated.

10. *Try not to substitute instruments called for in the score, but if you must, keep the substitution as close as possible to the original.* Here are some possible substitutions:

Original	Substitute
marimba	xylophone (play part down one octave)
tom toms	snare drums (without snares), bongos, timbales
timbales	snare drums (without snares and with loosened heads)
congas	low tom toms
temple blocks	various pitched wood blocks
vibraphone	bells (in the lowest register possible)
anvil	small length of pipe or muffled cow bell

Selected Multiple Percussion Solos

The following graded list of selected multiple percussion solos is divided into solos and collections for three levels (junior high, high school and advanced high school or college).

Abbreviations

ant. cym. - antique cymbal
anv - anvil
B.D. - bass drum
cast - castanets
Fld. D. - field drum
mar - marimba
sus. cym. - suspended cymbal
S.D. - snare drum
tamb - tambourine
T.B. - temple block
T.D. - tenor drum
timb - timbales
timp - timpani
T.T. - tom tom
tri - triangle
vib - vibraphone
W.B. - wood block
xyl - xylophone

Gradings

Grade		Level
I	very easy	junior high
II	easy	junior high
III	medium	high school
IV	advanced	high school
V	difficult	college and professional
VI	very difficult	college and professional

Publishers

Adler	Henry Adler, c/o Belwin-Mills, 25 Deshon Dr., Melville, N.Y. 11746
Berklee	Berklee Press, 1140 Boylston St., Boston, Mass. 02115
Byron-Douglas	Byron-Douglas, c/o Belwin Mills (see Adler)
Chappell	Chappell and Co., Inc., 609 5th Ave., New York, N.Y. 10016
Creative	Creative Music Co., c/o Ludwig Drum Co., 1728 North Damen Ave., Chicago, Ill. 60647
Leduc	Alphonse Leduc, Editions Musicals, 175 Rue Saint-Honoré, Paris, France
Peters	C.F. Peters, 373 Park Ave. So., New York, N.Y. 10016
Southern	Southern Music Co., San Antonio, Tex. 78206
Western	Western International Music, 2859 Holt Ave., Los Angeles, Calif. 90034
Wingert-Jones	Wingert-Jones, 2026 Broadway, P.O. Box 1878, Kansas City, Mo. 64141
Wolf-Mills	Wolf-Mills Music/WIM, 2859 Holt Ave., Los Angeles, Calif. 90034

Junior High Level Solos

Composer	Title with Instruments and Grading	Publisher
Britton, Mervin	*Play Ball!; First Hit; Home Run; Safe at Third; Batter Up* All use tri, sus. cym., S.D., T.T. OR any 4 contrasting instruments (I)	Byron-Douglas
McClaren, Court	*Piece No. 1* sus. cym., S.D., T.D. (II)	Wingert-Jones

Junior High Level Solo Collections

Burns, Roy, and Feldstein, Saul	*Elementary Percussion Solos* 7 solos using S.D., tri, W.B., T.T., sus. cym., Fld. D. — no solo uses more of the above instruments (II)	Adler

High School Level Solos

Schinstine, W.J.	*Scherzo for a Skinflint* S.D., T.T. (III)	Southern

————.	*Etude for Membranophones* S.D., Fld. D., 4 T.T. (III+)	Southern
Davis, Thomas L.	*Spanish Dance* 2 timp (28"), cast, sus. cym., S.D., tamb, xyl (or bells) (IV)	Creative
Payson, Al	*Die Zwitschermaschine* S.D., guiro, low T.B., W.B., cow bell, tri, small anv (or small length of pipe), xyl (or bells) (IV+)	Creative
Moore, James L.	*Sonata No. 1* 2 T.T., S.D., 2 bongos, W.B., sus. cym., 4 T.B., vib (or bells) (IV)	Ludwig
Kraft, William	*Morris Dance* S.D., Fld. D., B.D. (IV)	Western
Spears, Jared	*Prologue and Jubilo* 2 timp (28" and 25"), bells, sus. cym., 4 tuned T.T. (III)	Southern

High School Level Solo Collections

Burns, Roy, and Feldstein, Saul	*Intermediate Percussion Solos* 6 solos using S.D., 2 T.T., 2 sus. cym., W.B. — no solo uses more than 5 of the above instruments (III)	Adler
————.	*Advanced Percussion Solos* 6 solos using S.D., 3 T.T., 2 sus. cym., tamb, W.B., tri (IV)	Adler
Delp, Ron	*Multi-Pitch Rhythm Studies* any combination of instruments (I, II, III, IV)	Berklee

College and Professional Level Solos

Russell, Armand	*Facets* 2 timb (or 2 T.T. or 2 bongos), 2 sus. cym. (different sizes), 5 T.B., tri, S.D. (V)	Schirmer
Feldman, Morton	*The King of Denmark* bell-like sounds, many skin instruments, cym, gong, timp, tri, vib, ant. cym. (V+)	Peters
Desportes, Yvonne	*Thème et Variations* 4 timp (standard sizes), B.D., cym, cast, W.B., tri, bells, cow bell, vib, xyl, piano acc. (V)	Leduc
Johnson, Warren	*Five Words* 4 sus. cym. (different sizes), mar, 4 T.T. (or 4 bon), W.B., 4 T.B., tri (V)	Southern
Kraft, William	*French Suite* in four movements Third movement ("Sarabande") uses 2 sus. cym., 2 bongos, 2 S.D., Fld. D., T.D. (V+)	Wolf-Mills

College and Professional Level Solo Collections

Goldenberg, Morris, edited by Ralph Satz	*Studies in Solo Percussion* 26 pieces using from 2 to 13 instruments including tri, sus. cym., bell tree, 5 T.B., W.B., and others (II, III, IV, V, VI)	Chappell

February 1977

Repertoire for Percussionists

Merrill Brown

This is one in a series of articles concerning repertoire most often performed by college wind and percussion students. "Repertoire for Brass Soloists" appeared in the December 1976 and January 1977 issues of *The Instrumentalist*. The articles are based on material published by the writer and are used with permission.

The selection of appropriate music literature is one of the most important responsibilities facing every performer and teacher. Many "recommended" solo and ensemble lists have been published. These lists are often of value and interest but they understandably reflect the bias and personal taste of their compilers. In addition, there are many books, catalogs, and lists that contain information about the availability of materials; while these compilations are useful to those wishing to order music, the biggest task facing the performer and teacher is knowing *what* to order. Since no one can hope to be familiar with all the literature available, the following compilation may help provide you with a means for selecting repertoire. It is the result of a survey designed to determine what music is being performed in college wind and percussion student recitals. The results seem to indicate that a basic repertoire for most instruments has become established.

About the Survey

To collect the information for this survey, 701 leading college and university music departments in the United States were contacted for programs of all student recitals performed during the 1971-72 school year. An estimated 4,500 programs were received from 273 schools representing music departments in 48 states and the District of Columbia. A total of 15,607 performances were tabulated from these programs — 10,995 solos and 4,612 ensembles. This article reports some of the findings concerning repertoire used for percussion solos and ensembles.

Findings

Of the 921 percussion solo performances catalogued, mallet instruments accounted for the largest number (43 per cent), followed by multiple percussion (22.5 per cent), timpani (21 per cent), and snare drum (13 per cent). But of these 921 performances only 394 different compositions were used, representing only 237 composers.

In addition, 634 percussion ensemble performances were compiled (requiring from 2 to 13 players), which represent 356 different compositions and 247 different composers. Percussion ensembles using wind instruments received 130 performances, and there were 15 performances of percussion ensembles with voice.

The compositions listed below represent the most frequently performed works appearing on the recital programs received from the schools. But just because the music has the endorsement of a number of college teachers does not mean it is appropriate for junior or senior high school students or even all college students. Most of the selections listed below are grade IV to VI, with the most difficult pieces appearing on the senior and graduate recitals. Nonetheless, most teachers, especially those new in the field, will find some frequently performed literature in the lists below with which they are unfamiliar. While these lists should not serve to maintain the status quo, these compositions do deserve investigation for possible use in developing an expanding repertoire for performance and teaching. Many excellent compositions that received few performances warrant more attention. Also, new compositions are continually being published which deserve consideration.

Repertoire Listing

Compositions are listed in order of frequency of performance. The following information concerning each solo is recorded:

1. Total number of performances.
2. Number of performances on "general" recitals (programs which gave no indication of being either a "senior" or "graduate" recital).
3. Number of performances on recitals specified as a "senior" recital.
4. Number of performances on recitals specified as a "graduate" recital. These included both masters and doctoral recitals.

Multiple-Percussion Solos

A total of 208 performances were tabulated, in which only 84 different compositions were played, written by 54 different composers.

Composition	Total Perf.	Gen	Sen	Grad
Kraft, *French Suite*	15	7	5	3
Milhaud, *Concerto for Percussion and Small Orchestra* (piano)	13	5	7	1
Feldman, *King of Denmark*	10	5	3	2
Russell, *Sonata for Percussion and Piano*	8	3	4	1
Stern, *Adventures for One*	7	2	5	-
Stockhausen, *Zyklus No. 9*	7	3	2	2
Kraft, *Morris Dance*	6	2	4	-
Tagawa, *Inspirations Diabolique*	6	3	-	3
Tomasi, *Concert Asiatique for Percussion and Piano*	6	3	3	-
Davis, *Spanish Dance*	5	3	2	-
Desportes, *Thème et Variations*	5	1	4	-
Morello, *Shortnin' Bread*	5	4	1	-
Peters, M., *Rondo for Four Tom Toms*	5	2	2	1

Mallet Solos

A total of 397 performances were tabulated, in which 178 different compositions were played, written by 107 different composers.

Composition	Total Perf.	Gen	Sen	Grad
Creston, *Concertino for Marimba*, Op. 21	30	19	10	1
Bach, J.S., *Concerto in A Minor for Violin*	15	12	1	2
Tanner, *Sonata for Marimba and Piano*	12	8	3	1
Peters, M., *Sonata-Allegro* (marimba and piano)	11	8	2	1
deGastyne, *Preludes*, Op. 37, Nos. 1-7 (vibes)	9	4	3	2
Frazeur, *Rondo for Marimba and Piano*	8	6	2	-
Milhaud, *Concerto for Marimba and Vibraphone*	8	2	4	2
Musser, C., *Etude for Marimba*	8	2	3	3
Diemer, *Toccata for Marimba*	7	5	1	1
Khachaturian, *Sabre Dance*	7	5	2	-
Chopin, *Valse No. 7*, Op. 64, No. 2 (marimba)	6	4	2	-
Fissinger, *Suite for Marimba*	6	2	2	2
Handel, *Sonata No. 3 in F Major* (marimba)	6	3	3	-
Bach, J.S., *Partita No. 1 for Solo Violin* (marimba)	5	1	2	2
Bach, J.S., *Partita No. 3* from "Six Unaccompanied Violin Sonatas and Partitas"	5	3	2	-
Brahms, *Hungarian Dances Nos. 1 & 5*	5	3	2	-
Dinicu, *Hora Staccato* (marimba and piano)	5	4	1	-
Frock, *Concertino for Marimba*	5	3	2	-
Russell, *Two Archaic Dances* (marimba)	5	4	1	-
Steiner, *Four Bagatelles for Vibes*	5	2	2	1

Snare Drum Solos

A total of 122 performances were tabulated, in which 71 different compositions were played, written by 38 different composers.

Composition	Total Perf.	Gen	Sen	Grad
Colgrass, *Six Unaccompanied Solos for Snare Drum* (selections)	12	9	3	-

Benson, *Three Dances for Solo Snare Drum*	10	7	3	-
(traditional), *Connecticut Halftime*	6	4	2	-
Harr, *Three Camps*	5	5	-	-

Timpani Solos

A total of 191 performances were tabulated, in which only 58 different compositions were played, written by 35 different composers.

Composition				
Carter, *Eight Pieces for Four Timpani* (Of the 34 performances, 12 were for "Recitative and Improvisations," a part of *Eight Pieces* which is also published separately.)	34	14	17	3
Beck, *Sonata for Tympani*	11	10	1	-
Tcherepnin, *Sonatina for Timpani and Piano*	11	6	5	-
Bergamo, *Four Pieces for Timpani*	9	5	2	2
Colgrass, *Concertino for Tympani and Brass*	9	5	2	2
Jones, *Sonata for Three Unaccompanied Kettle Drums*	9	5	3	1
Firth, *26 Solo Etudes for Tympani* (selections)	8	7	1	-
Ramey, *Sonata for Three Unaccompanied Timpani*	8	6	2	-
Goodman, *Ballad for the Dance*	5	2	3	-
Graeffe, *Scherzo for Four Timpani and Piano*	6	5	1	-
Tharichen, *Concerto for Timpani and Orchestra*	5	3	1	1

Ensembles

A total of 634 performances were tabulated, in which only 356 different compositions were played, written by 247 different composers.

Composition	Total Perf.	Number of Performers Needed
Chavez, *Toccata for Percussion Instruments*	12	6
Colgrass, *Three Brothers*	11	9
Benson, *Streams*	10	7
Hovhaness, *October Mountain*	9	6
Colgrass, *Duets for Percussion*	8	2
Peters, G., *The Swords of Moda-Ling*	8	8
Volz, *Prelude and Allegro*	8	5
Bach, Jan, *Woodwork*	7	4
Leonard, *Symphony for Percussion*	7	9
Bartok, *Sonata for Two Pianos and Percussion*	6	4-5
Schiffman, *Musica Battuta*	6	7
Strang, *Percussion Music for Three Players*	6	3
Benson, *Trio for Percussion*	5	3
Bergamo, *Interactions*	5	
Erb, *Four Movements for Percussion (4 for Percussion)*	5	4
Firth, *Encore in Jazz*	5	7
Heim, *Fanfare for Percussion*	5	5
Iverson, *Contrarhythmic Ostinato*	5	6
Kelly, *Toccata for Marimba and Percussion Ensemble*	5	7-8
Khachaturian, *Sabre Dance*	5	4
McKenzie, *Three Dances*	5	3
Varese, *Ionization*	5	13
Zonn, *Spice Island*	5	

Percussion with Winds

(Does not include brass ensembles using timpani)

A total of 130 performances were tabulated in which 62 different compositions were played, written by 56 different composers.

Composition	Total Perf.
Tanner, *Diversions for Flute and Marimba*	10
McKenzie, *Pastorale for Flute and Percussion*	9
Russell, *Pas de Deux for B♭ Clarinet and Percussion*	9
Dahl, *Duettino Concertante for Flute and Percussion*	6
Hovhaness, *The Burning House Overture for Flute and Percussion* (3 percussionists)	5

Percussion with Voice

A total of 15 performances were tabulated in which 9 different compositions were played, written by 7 different composers.

Composition	
Udow, *African Welcome Piece* (percussion ensemble of 13+ performers and optional voices)	6

How and When to Teach Rolls

Donald K. Gilbert

One of the most difficult areas of snare drum technique is the development of good rolls. We all know what type of sound we want our student percussionists to develop, but teachers are often uncertain how to achieve that sound, when to begin teaching rolls, and what type of roll (rudimental or multiple bounce) to teach first.

The achievement of the smooth, even sound of the roll takes many years of persistent effort and practice time. The question as to when a student should begin learning rolls can therefore be answered quite easily: as soon as possible. The snare drum student, regardless of his age, is ready to begin roll study after his fourth or fifth lesson.

Of the two roll types, multiple bounce and rudimental, the multiple bounce roll is perhaps the better type of roll to teach first for the following reasons: 1) it may be the easier of the two types to learn because the student does not have to worry about controlling the number of bounces each time the stick contacts the head of the drum; and 2) it is the roll that is most often used.

It is a good idea when working with a new student to concentrate on one hand at a time. If you choose the left hand, you should have the student raise the stick as high as possible (using only the wrist, not the arm) and let it fall to the drum head, bouncing until it comes to a complete stop by itself. The student should not be concerned with how many times the stick strikes the head, nor should he try to control the stick in any way. His wrist and forearm must be perfectly relaxed so that he can take advantage of the natural rebound of the stick. By attempting to control the stick he may inadvertently tighten his grip on it, thereby causing the wrist muscles to become rigid. This stiffening in turn will produce a crushed roll with very few bounces.

Constantly check the student's hand positions and insist that they be correct. Very often, while attempting to relax the wrist muscles, students allow one or several of the fingers to drop from the stick. (This is especially true of the left hand when the traditional grip is used.) Allowing the wrist to cave in, another common left hand error in traditional grip, also causes tension in the wrist muscles. The student should imagine a straight line extending from the elbow through the wrist to the palm of the hand, with the stick as an extension of the hand. After one stroke is completed and he has made all of the corrections you suggest, he should repeat the process. At the early stages of roll development, this process should be repeated carefully with the same hand perhaps a dozen times before working with the opposite hand. Between strokes be sure to point out errors and make corrections. Your comments may take up extra minutes, but in the long run they can save your student hours of having to unlearn bad habits and relearn correct ones.

After working with the left hand the same procedures can be applied to the right hand. Several hand position problems tend to occur when applying the multiple bounce technique to the right hand. Perhaps the most common problems are the tendency to drop the thumb or the fourth and fifth fingers from the stick. The thumb and both of these fingers must remain around the stick at all times, but they should not be clenched. Allow just enough room for the stick to move. The fingers, wrist, and forearm must be relaxed, and the motion of the stick should result solely from the use of the wrist. One method you can use to check the tension in the wrists and hands is to ask the student to freeze his motion. Then try to remove the stick from the student's hand. If you have to use an appreciable amount of force to withdraw the stick, he is squeezing the stick too much. The idea of stopping for corrections after every stroke, especially at the initial stages of roll development, cannot be overemphasized. As with the left hand, the process should be repeated a number of times after the necessary corrections have been made.

The third step in the overall procedure should be to repeat the entire process using alternate hands beginning with either the left or the right hand. Students, particularly young ones, often attempt to roll too fast too soon. Care must be taken to avoid this tendency because the wrist muscles have not yet fully developed. Otherwise, the end result may be a crushed roll with very few bounces. Another factor to remember is that the roll will sound uneven at first with accents occurring with every other stroke. This is due to the fact that one hand (usually the right hand) is probably stronger than the other. To correct this situation extra effort and practice time should be spent working with the weaker hand alone. Be sure to stress to your student that the process of working with each hand separately and then alternating hands will be a part of each lesson and should be included in every practice period. If the above procedure is followed, a good, even, clean-sounding roll should gradually develop.

Band directors often complain about the quality of the rolls performed by their snare drummers. Perhaps they fail to realize that the roll is probably the most difficult percussion technique to master and cannot be achieved quickly. Even after a good roll is produced consistently, the conscientious percussionist must work diligently to maintain it. But with proper instruction at the early levels of roll development and constant, patient application, the student percussionist can develop very acceptable rolls.

April 1977

Multiple Percussion Techniques

Part I

Donald R. Baker

This article is a companion to James R. McKinney's article, "Learn a Multiple Percussion Solo" (January 1977 issue).

Compositions using multiple percussion are being played in an increasing number of band and orchestra festivals as well as in solo and ensemble competitions. In fact, a specified multiple percussion etude is now part of the required repertoire in the snare drum/percussion division in the state competition of the Michigan School Band and Orchestra Association. Other festivals in Ohio and Illinois and the Mid-Western States Festival of the Percussive Arts Society also have divisions for multiple percussion proficiency. Certainly, opportunities to perform multiple percussion solos are available to the student — but is he prepared to face the challenge?

Approaching the Solo and Selecting Instruments

When you begin study on a solo, start by reading the music without any attempt to perform it. Approach the score intellectually. As you read through the work, hearing it mentally, be thinking about what instruments you might choose and how you could arrange them to create one homogenous sound. If the composer calls for a tom tom, ask yourself which size would be most suitable. If he asks for three temple blocks, you may have to decide whether to use the top three or the bottom three of a set of five — or maybe every other one. What size cymbal is "high," "medium," or "low"? What you have in stock usually determines the answer, but try to use your best musical judgment. Try to hear mentally the sound of each instrument *in relation to each other, not as a separate entity*. You are making an instrument from instruments.

If the set-up calls for two snares and several tom toms you probably will find that it is better to use drums of widely contrasting pitch rather than those whose pitches differ by only a step or two. For example: if the two snares are scored above the two tom toms, use a piccolo snare and a 5″ x 14″ snare, and tom toms which graduate in size from 6½″ or 9″ x 14″ to 12″ x 14″. If the snare drums are on the bottom, try a parade snare drum, a 6½″ x 14″ snare drum, and a pair of timbales on top. Two field and two concert snare drums — one of each pair having the snares off and the other with snares on would not be a wise choice unless you think the composer intended a duet effect. Usually there is no "right" or "wrong" way; but the instrumentation should enhance the music and be technically practical.

Another important consideration is the selection of bass drums. Many young performers seem to forget that bass drums come in different sizes and respond differently. In Goldenberg's *Studies in Solo Percussion*, several works call for bass drum. The diagrams are often misleading, making the performer think that a large 16″ x 36″ drum is required. Make it a habit to discuss thoroughly with students the advantages and disadvantages that various sizes have on the set-up and musical clarity. In most cases, students voluntarily switch drums at the next session for a more homogeneous sound. Large bass drums do not speak rhythmically well unless they are muted properly (which changes the tone). They also can make physical placement very difficult and sometimes drop the "melodic pitch line" too far, disrupting the melodic flow. But there are times, even in a very dense and crowded set-up that you might not give up that huge instrument; the beauty of its low pitch may be necessary to the music.

The great variety of tone colors available on cymbals and accessories should be considered carefully when you choose other instruments and mallets. When striking a cymbal, you must listen not only to the relative pitch and tone (is it far too high, just a little too high, or totally in the wrong range?), but also to the length of the envelope (decay pattern). If the sound dies away too soon, it may result in a very chopped phrase ending, but if it rings too long, it may interfere with a continuing melodic passage. Accessories such as wood blocks come in many different pitches, colors, and sizes, so choose them judiciously.

Stick selection (like instrumentation choices) requires musical considerations. Some composers are specific, indicating model numbers and brands; some supply general descriptions such as soft or hard; others include no stick indications at all. Even if certain mallets are specified, the performer still must use his musical judgment so that the mallets he uses are suited to his instruments and concert hall. The performer should understand that when a composer refers to a hard, medium, or soft mallet, beater, etc., he is not comparing soft timpani mallets to hard brass bell mallets but is differentiating within choices on one instrument. (A soft bell mallet is harder than a soft timpani mallet.) If there is no time to change mallets during a composition, the only choice is to use the mallet that works best for all the instruments. A medium rubber beater, for example, would sound fine on the temple blocks but would give a dull clunk on the cymbal. Use a medium hard yarn mallet for both. The inside hardness gives clarity to the temple block, but the yarn maintains the softer sound needed on the cymbal.

The relation of stick sizes to drums is also an important consideration. Small sticks should not be used on the large tom toms or bass drum because they do not bring out the lower pitches. When using a relatively low set of drums, use a stick with a fairly large bead. Use smaller sticks on smaller drums. When the large bass drum is mixed with several tom toms try to find a large-beaded stick that has a light response.

When playing several instruments incorporated in a single melodic line, maintain the same color and style on all of them. Do not strike one cymbal with a yarn mallet and all others with a wood stick unless you are trying to achieve a special effect. If the bass drum is treated as the lowest pitch in a series of drums, it should probably not be the only instrument struck with a big soft beater. Always keep in mind the musical line(s) and try to maintain a sense of unity throughout the multiple percussion instrument.

Remember to keep your mind and ears open. Sometimes considerable searching is needed before the instrument and mallet combination that captures the desired effect is found. But never give up too soon. And don't be afraid to change instruments or mallets if doing so will help you achieve the sound that best describes what you believe the composer wanted. When working on the third movement of the *French Suite* by William Kraft, I remember going through every cymbal at the university and some 20 pairs of rattan mallets before I felt I had captured the particular "buzz" effect called for at the end of the piece — achieved by placing the rattan end of a yarn mallet on an already-vibrating cymbal. If the composer has indicated specific stick sizes or models, you should generally concur provided they seem to give the proper results. But when the composer leaves the decision to the performer, use your best musical judgment to help you select the right instruments.

Planning Set-Ups

The set-up (physical arrangement of the instruments and equipment) affects playing technique more directly than it influences the final musical effect. But I have never met an accomplished multiple percussionist who has not had a well-defined, creatively-designed set-up. Set-ups can be very large, but it is best to begin with a very simple one. A new student cannot suddenly comprehend a massive set-up as one melodic structure. He should be allowed to progress from a single melodic-line "floor-mat" to the more complex polyphonic compositions that require large set-ups.

Think about possible set-ups during your first mental reading of the piece. Use the published set-ups as a starting point and proceed from there. Published diagrams are intended as suggestions, not mandates, from the composer. The rare exception is when a composer is striving for a theatrical or spatial effect. I use many different set-ups and constantly change them, keeping collections of diagrams on file for the more complicated works. The following concepts and diagrams may be helpful in planning set-ups. Remember that what works for someone else may not work for you.

Multiple percussion compositions can be thought of in small units and layers of instruments.* In most score diagrams the drums are in the middle layer, the accessories are on the top, and the larger instruments are on the bottom or side. The layers overlap to some extent especially when they are vertically aligned (see Fig. 1). When they are horizontally aligned, the layers usually are separated or only slightly interrelated.

*Rather complicated layering concepts have been set forth for the advanced performer by Ronald George in *The Percussionist*, Vol. 12, No. 3 (1975), pp. 110-131.

Fig. 1

Vertically

Side view

Top view

Horizontally

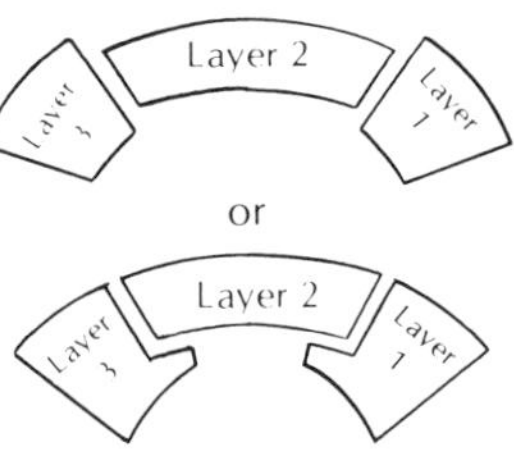

Switching layers around may have its advantages also. A good example is having the timpani out in front of the tom toms instead of behind them. It is a little easier to reach the tom toms this way, but it makes the timpani pedals less accessible (see Fig. 2).

Fig. 2

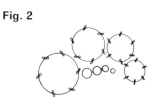

Another common set-up is to build the instruments around a central mallet/keyboard area. Place the keyboard in Layer 2 and place the other instruments in Layer 3. The drums work out best as an extension at the small end of the marimba or as a block section of Layer 3 (see Fig. 3).

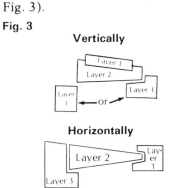

Fig. 3

Vertically

Horizontally

Timpani are usually arranged low to high (left to right) as the player views them. If tuning changes are needed and if there is no time to dampen the drums, consider using mutes. In most cases, when one timpano is used, numerous gliss effects are required (or no special pedaling at all). When glissandos are used, place the timpano at the immediate end of Layer 2 or behind you (see Fig. 4).

Fig. 5

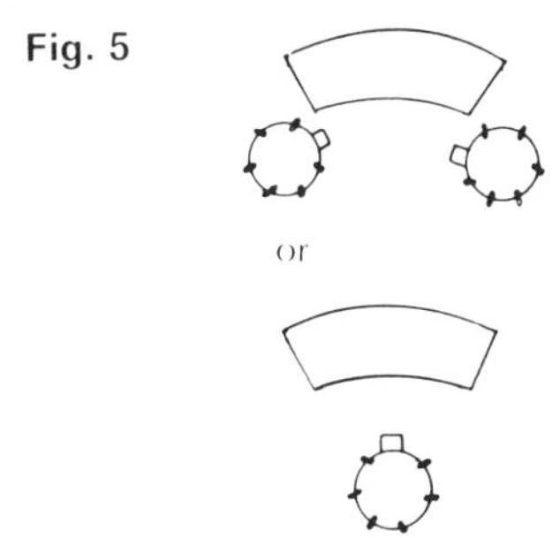

When struck alone the timpano can be placed rather remotely in Layer 3. Just give it enough space to be struck properly, and don't worry — it is rather a large target.

Keyboards are best located centrally with the rest of the instruments around them as in Fig. 3. Sometimes they can be placed to the side of the other instruments (see Fig. 5). Try to put the narrow end closest to the other instruments so you can always reach over them to the accidentals. If you will be using the lower notes the most, then move it up.

Fig. 4

As a general rule, the low to high (left to right) arrangement is practical for drums, but many times a part can be played more easily if the drums are set up differently. If a part has a challenging tempo, try one of the set-ups in Fig. 6. The highest drum is number 1.

Fig. 6

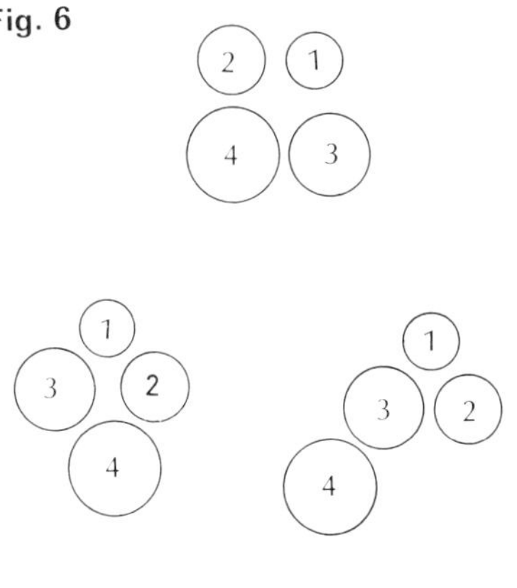

When a single snare drum is combined with a series of tom toms, analyze in which hand or in what part of the melodic line it most often occurs. If the snare and tom tom parts are not interrelated, consider one of the arrangements in Fig. 7.

Fig. 7

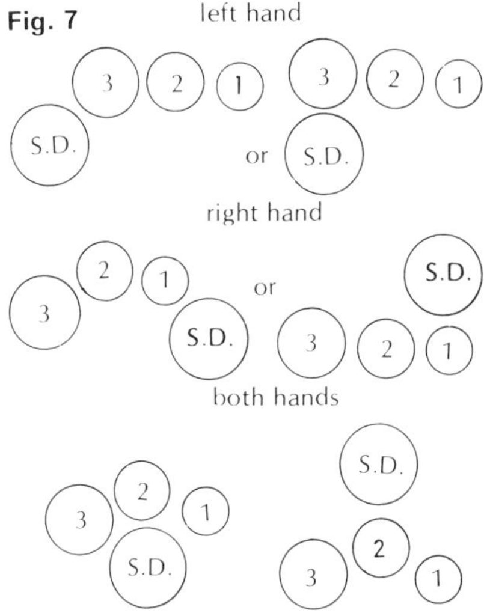

Remember that it is generally easier to pull the arm back or sideways when you have to double a stoke than it is to push it out, so arrange the instruments accordingly.

Multiple Percussion Techniques

Part II

Donald R. Baker

Cymbals are best set up on straight poles which can be squeezed into narrow spaces. When placing cymbals, consider accessibility, which hand strikes them the most, and whether the cymbal part is an integral part of the musical line or independent. Fig. 8 includes several possible cymbal placements.

Fig. 8

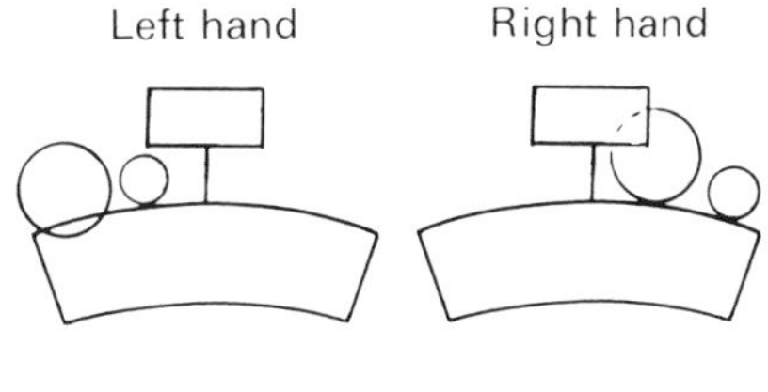

Both hands

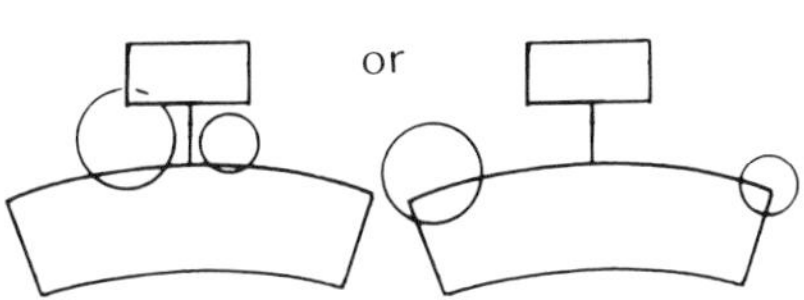

Be sure that you understand what kind of tone color best fits the work you are performing. For example, long dark cymbal sounds are produced by striking the cymbal on its edge. If many of these sounds are needed, the cymbal should be placed well above the other instruments so that there is room for the hand, arm, and cymbal to move freely. If the bell sound is used frequently, do not place a music stand/triangle above the instrument or overlap the cymbals. Additional space and unobstructed playing surfaces are needed for rolls.

When several suspended cymbals are needed, try overlapping them in a staircase fashion or hanging them in a series on knotted rope (see Fig. 9).

Fig. 9

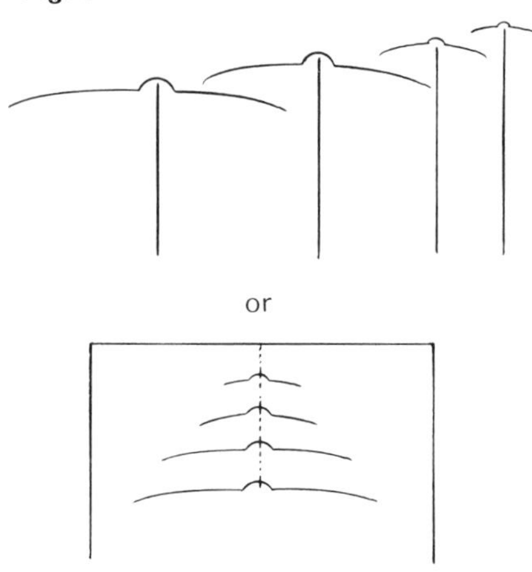

Crash cymbals often have to be handled quickly and quietly. A vertical cymbal holder within easy reach provides a good place to put them during a performance. A padded table or stand at the edge of your set-up or behind you may also be used.

Gongs and tam tams may be kept behind the performer but are best placed at either side and mounted on a high hoop stand. Be sure the instrument has enough "sway area" after it has been struck. Muting may be achieved by placing tape across the surface or clamping cloth on the edges with triangle clips. Muting helps the decay pattern, but it also dulls the tone.

When arranging accessories in the set-up, it is very important to be innovative. Use special stands, multi-mounts, hose clamps, pipe clamps, boxes, mike stands, padding, etc. Accessories should be placed where they can be reached quickly and easily as their correct target areas are usually very small. Triangles can be hung two ways:

narrow end up with one clip △ ;

or wide end up with two clips ▽ .

Hanging the triangle with one clip allows more freedom on both sides to strike down and out while the other hand is busy on other drums. Always try to strike the instrument where the preferred tone will sound. Tambourines are best mounted on a suspended cymbal stand (through the hole on the shell) or laid flat on a very well-padded table. Woodblocks work best on woodblock mounts attached to cymbal stands or to heavy-based music stands. Temple blocks can be mounted in any order. If your temple block stand does not go high enough (a common problem), you may place the base of the stand on a raised platform. The disadvantage is that the stand cannot be very close to you if it is on a platform. When several accessories are called for in the music, try to keep them in score order, either horizontally or vertically. Layering the accessories is very helpful in performances. Some accessories (springs, gongs, bells, pipe, etc.) are more accessible if they are hung on large frames built out of pipe or wood.

Holding devices for your sticks and mallets are essential to a complete set-up. If the instrument set-up is relatively simple, you may use part of a trap tray or a covered music stand for your sticks. The location should be determined by when you need a stick or release one stick for another. Keep three things in mind: 1) how fast you need to change sticks, 2) what instrument you just left and where are you going next, and 3) whether your arms will cross or be in the way of each other. Remember to keep your tray area clear for "landing" and "take off." Unless you need space to approach the trap table from above, it might fit in a little niche between a suspended cymbal and a drum. If the tray area is used a lot, the sticks should be kept in a meaningful order. If you have to throw them down in a hurry, consider attaching a padded wicker basket or wide-mouth cloth bag to convenient instruments so you can just drop what you don't need. Keep a duplicate pair of sticks on the tray ready for the next entrance. Above all, don't make a show out of picking up and putting down sticks and mallets.

Whenever possible, the set-up should be visually attractive to the audience. Lines of sight between the performer and audience should be kept open, not blocked by gongs or by music stands at awkward heights. Keep in mind that percussion playing is often appreciated as a visual as well as an aural art, so consideration should be given to the overall appearance of the equipment and its arrangement, even though accessibility may have to be the prime concern.

Grip Considerations

The only grip suited to multiple percussion is the matched grip. Countless alterations to the matched grip are possible — a key factor in choosing it for multiple percussion compositions. The traditional practice of using only downward strokes does not apply to these works, which may call for many accessories, besides layered instruments demanding numerous roll techniques. The performer must learn to use controlled levels of power at all the rotational positions of the forearm in combination with the wrist. He must also learn to hold more than one mallet at a time and to work with mallets of various diameters and weights in the same hand. The stroke action will mature with daily practice, but often performers forget to consider using more than one type of mallet at a time. The Musser four-mallet grip is extremely helpful in multiple percussion playing. It allows mallet independence and freedom for a rebounding snare drum stick. The cross grip has limitations in certain positions, and overlapping different-sized sticks can become difficult. Further description of the grips may be found in an article by Lynn Glassock in *The Percussionist*, Vol. II, No. 1 (1964), pp. 2-11.

When using four mallets the performer may find it helpful to use the middle two mallets or sticks in combination and the outside mallets or beaters in opposing fashion. A good example is in Stockhausen's *Nr. 9, Zyklus*, where the performer carries snare drum sticks in positions two and three, a triangle beater in position one, and a yarn mallet in position four. Other combinations of yarn mallets, plastic and/or rubber mallets, and snare drum sticks are common. Experiment with the double-ended mallets used for many years in pit orchestras. Some works call for specially-made mallets which give you a chance to be very creative. Mallets can be double-sided as well as double-ended, and can be equipped with special shafts for playing even more instruments.

Your feet don't really fit into the "grip" category, but they will probably be used increasingly in multiple percussion compositions. Feet have been used for a long time on drum sets and now composers are writing for percussion consoles which require pedaled gongs and drums.

Rehearsal Suggestions

In most rehearsal situations at schools, instruments are used by more than one performer, so time must always be allowed for setting up equipment before practice can begin. After completing the set-up, mentally combine the individual instruments into one set and think about the music and what you want to accomplish. Play through the work, quickly analyzing the problem areas. Then divide the work into musical sections and rehearse one section at a time. Select the most suitable sticking and stay with it. (It is important to get accustomed to a "feel.") But don't be afraid to change sticking if it is obvious that the change would be a significant improvement. Sticking is determined by tempo and by the musical groupings. (Triplets might sound better if thev are struck RLL or LRR than if they are alternated.)

Practice the melody alone by separating it from all contrapuntal or accompanying parts. Play it slowly and accurately. Then work on the ostinato patterns, contrary motion, and accompanying lines by themselves. They may be very simple; and once you understand them, you may not have to read all the parts literally all the time.

Combine the different musical parts or lines for the total sound. If coordination problems occur, stop to analyze them. Usually the problem is more mental than physical. If coordination problems do exist, isolate the problem and work on that passage slowly and deliberately. Try playing the rhythm on only one instrument if necessary.

New set-up designs require learning new physical motions all the time. Always set up long enough before rehearsal to allow time to practice the physical movements needed for certain passages over and over until they become natural. Then place the particular physical motions in context. Relax so that you give an impression of floating around to various instruments, not darting frantically from one to the other.

As soon as possible, begin to apply musical values to the work. Interrelate lines when necessary, separate colors or dynamics, and project contrapuntal lines beyond the edge of your equipment. After the necessary technical control is achieved and the musicianship is thoroughly understood, start to work on tempo. Throughout your practice sessions, keep relative note values and tempos accurate. Do not rush during easy passages — you might do that in the final performance.

Practicing heightens one's ability to communicate a work of art to a listening audience, but musicianship is the most important goal. If you play a few wrong notes but still succeed in conveying the musical content of the work to the audience, you have achieved your goal.

The Final Performance

Rarely do performances reach the apex of perfection one so often imagines. Although minds can splice together all those "great" moments from the practice room, they seldom peak at performance. But that is what you should strive for.

Before the performance, personally check that all stands are firmly secured and that mallets are in place. If the set-up is very complicated, the instruments should be set up in advance. If it is necessary to make physical changes during the concert, draw a diagram for the stage crew so they may bring the instruments to the correct general location. It is most important that *you* make the final adjustments and microscopic decisions on angel, distance, or light reflection. Sticks and mallets should also be adjusted so they can be picked up easily, and extra mallets (needed in case of breaks or drops) should be convenient.

Before beginning to play, mentally picture the set-up. Pause and take a deep breath, let the noise subside in the audience, and then sing the first few phrases to yourself. In other words, get involved before you strike anything. Accept the audience's gratitude before and after each piece, and also acknowledge your accompanist or fellow performers after each work.

Multiple percussion compositions provide the greatest challenge for the percussionist, whose success will depend as much on certain preliminary steps — such as choosing instruments, planning a set-up, and evaluating the music — as it does on his regular practice and performance. With a comprehensive approach, paying careful attention to all these important aspects, the percussionist may find the greatest musical satisfaction in multiple percussion solos.

Height Adjustment and Placement of Percussion Instruments

Hoyt F. LeCroy

Directors often insist that their brass, woodwind, and string players use correct playing positions and that straps and stands be adjusted correctly. However, many of the same directors neglect similar requirements in the percussion section. Although the following suggestions may appear to be very basic they can help solve important technical and musical problems.

To begin, let's consider snare drum height adjustment. The height and angle of the drum are largely personal matters, but in general the drum should be adjusted at about waist height. It is the length and proportion of the upper arm and forearm (rather than the person's overall height) that determine the proper height. The most common adjustment error is to place the drum too low. In addition the drum is sometimes slanted inward toward the player instead of being slanted out and away from the player or with the high side to the left for use with the traditional grip. In this grip the direction and degree of angle is determined by the slant of the left hand stick; if a matched grip is used there should be no slant of the drum.

The timpani also are subject to problems of height adjustment. It is obvious that not everyone will be able to fit his physique to timpani of unadjustable height. Until the major manufacturers pay closer attention to the problem other measures can be taken. If the timpani are too low, you can build a small platform for them (to be used by players who prefer to stand while playing) or you can use stools for players who prefer to sit. When players are being rotated in the section, it is best to use stools of various heights because the platforms are noisy and time-consuming to adjust for each player. The major point is that the height of a set of timpani does not meet the needs of *every* player any more than would one unadjustable snare drum stand.

Height is also an issue for the xylophone and marimba, and very few players realize that they might improve their playing simply by raising the instrument. (In some commercial catalogs, height adjustment wheels designed by keyboard manufacturers may be found to replace the standard wheel and socket.) Blocks of wood can be placed under each wheel to serve the purpose nicely. This adjustment will improve the player's posture and also, most likely, his sight-reading ability. The music stand should be as low as possible to allow the performer to see the music and the keyboard at the same time.

Orchestra bells are frequently placed on a table that is much too low. The table should be raised to fit the physique of the player. A double-layered kitchen tray stand, which is readily available at restaurant supply stores, serves this purpose well.

The triangle and tambourine are generally held too low. The player should hold these instruments near eye level to project the sound, to give the player a better view of the conductor, and to improve the visual aspect of performance. (Of course, very technical triangle and tambourine parts might be more effectively played when held lower, but whenever possible, hold the small instruments high.)

Placement

If the snare drum is to produce a very cutting, sharp sound and play rhythmic figurations with the trumpet section, you might want to place the snare drum near the trumpet section, but not near the outer edges of the ensemble. Because the bass drum is a very directional instrument, it is unwise to position it with either head turned toward the audience. From the podium the sound may seem acceptable when the drum is turned sideways; but the audience (at a greater distance) would "enjoy" a very heavy dose of bass drum solo accompanied by the band or orchestra. Room acoustics and stage placement will determine how the cymbal player should face the audience and how open his cymbals should be.

Keyboard percussion instruments generally have difficulty projecting from the back of a group and should be placed near the edges of the ensemble. Loud chime parts will project without difficulty; but when a soft sound is scored, it might be worthwhile to move the chimes closer to the audience.

The timpani are bass line instruments as well as powerful rhythmic instruments. For this reason they should be placed near the bass instruments of the band but not at the very edges of the ensemble. A location near the low brass will be valuable in helping to achieve good intonation. If the timpani are placed too near the bass drum, some undesirable sympathetic vibration may result.

Attention to the neglected areas of percussion height adjustment and instrument placement will produce better results with very little effort. Proper height adjustment will give the players improved posture, relaxed muscles, and a better view of the conductor. Often the improvement of physical conditions will help students perform with more confidence and accuracy.

A Beginning Percussion Curriculum Based on Comprehensive Musicianship

Jeffrey M. Dire

The first several months of instruction are of great importance to the future of young percussionists. Concepts and instruments should be presented in proper sequence and all instruction should be based on the principle of comprehensive musicianship. Through study of areas in addition to performance (theory, listening, etc.) students learn to become total musicians, and through study of various percussion instruments in addition to the snare drum, students learn to become total percussionists. When teachers integrate these two overall instructional areas in their lessons, their students can develop into performers who are proficient both technically and musically.

Basic Instruction

The first instrument that should be introduced is the snare drum. Although total percussion education for students must remain the overall aim of the percussion teacher, it is best if the student can firmly establish a strong technique on the snare drum at the outset. In fact, the first six to eight months of study should be spent on the snare drum because it is here that all basic physical movements including types of strokes, articulation, and hand positions are learned. Dealing immediately with many instruments, although seemingly in conformity with the philosophy of total percussion teaching, does not provide a sufficiently solid performance basis. By emphasizing to the student that the majority of the techniques used in playing the snare drum apply to all other percussion instruments, the teacher can help make the student aware that his basic study is really the first step in his development toward becoming a total percussionist.

From the very beginning the student should use the matched grip in his snare drum playing. As the matched grip is used on all mallet instruments and timpani, learning to use it on the snare drum will help the student feel at ease when he approaches other instruments later on, and will again allow him to think in terms of being a total percussionist from the first day of instruction.

Students should early understand that practice sessions ought to be divided among three areas: technical exercises, solos or etudes, and sight-reading. The first portion of each session is best spent on developing technique. The teacher should constantly emphasize to his students that technique is not an end in itself, but only a means toward the ability to express themselves musically. Young students like to compare themselves with their peers on such skills as the speed of their hands, and must be discouraged from placing so much importance on isolated techniques.

Approaching Rhythm Correctly

After the instrument and its fundamental techniques have been introduced, the student should learn the basics of rhythm reading. Measures and time signatures should be explained carefully. Time signatures are usually approached through $\frac{4}{4}$ meter, when the student learns that there are four beats per measure and that each quarter note receives one count. But this explanation merely introduces the student to one type of time signature without providing him with an understanding of the significance of each number. After acquainting his students with the meaning of both numbers, the teacher should ask what $\frac{6}{8}$, $\frac{9}{8}$, $\frac{12}{8}$, and $\frac{9}{16}$ mean. He might even ask what a hypothetical time signature like $\frac{108}{93}$ would mean. Even though the student may not be able to play rhythms in these time signatures, he will understand the function of the time signatures. And time signatures such as $\frac{7}{4}$ and $\frac{5}{4}$ should be used very soon so the student becomes aware that such music actually exists.

Articulation, Dynamics, and Phrasing

The student should be introduced next to the variety of articulations possible. There are four areas on the drum head that affect articulation: 1) the center (for dry, short, staccato playing); 2) off center (for general playing); 3) about ½″ from the rim (for soft playing); and 4) at the very edge (for extremely soft passages). The student should use many different articulations during his daily practice.

When students have acquired some proficiency in counting and playing quarter notes, dynamics and phrasing may be explained. While studying exercises using quarter notes and rests, the student should stop to identify phrases and add dynamics. Each student should be able to perform in class his interpretation of the assigned exercise and to explain his choice of phrasing for all types of rhythm studies. Each week students should compose a study using the rhythms learned that week. They should mark each phrase, indicate the correct counting over each figure, and be prepared to perform their pieces for the class. The class should then criticize each student's technique, and a discussion of the musical elements used in the composition should follow.

Accessory Instruments and Ensemble Compositions

Approximately every two weeks during the student's snare drum study a new accessory instrument may be introduced (the triangle, suspended cymbal, cymbals, bass drum, temple blocks, wood block, tambourine, and gong or tam-tam). The student should then be encouraged to compose multiple percussion solos to be performed for the class. The solos should use many of the instruments and musical ideas he has learned about. Students may also compose a percussion ensemble to be played by the whole class, and should conduct their own pieces. This project provides an opportunity for each student to learn the basics of conducting, score writing, and combining musical elements.

Mallet Instruments

Although it is unrealistic to expect every student to be equally proficient on all instruments, I believe that every attempt should be made to make mallet percussion the student's most proficient area. The techniques needed on snare drum accessories and timpani may be learned at a later time, but those necessary to mallet percussion playing must be well established early in the performer's experience.

Mallet instrument instruction provides an excellent opportunity for comprehensive music study. If a method book is used that contains music of many different historic periods, the elements and styles of those periods may easily be discussed. Through mallet instrument study, students can become thoroughly familiar with all chords, scales, and arpeggios. The teacher should point out these elements in the structure of various compositions so that the student will understand the value of learning them. Students should be encouraged to analyze the elements of the music they are playing — no matter how simple it may be. They should recognize the scales and arpeggios used, give suggestions for correct sticking, and identify the phrases and cadences. Analysis of the music being performed should be an integral part of each student's musical experience.

Mallet ensembles provide additional opportunities for music study. There is a shortage of ensemble literature for mallet instruments, but string ensemble music works well. The string bass parts can provide experience in bass clef reading, and the cello and viola parts may be transposed easily to treble clef. The number of instruments needed will vary according to class size, but two sets of orchestra bells, a xylophone, and a marimba are usually enough (and two students can play both the xylophone and marimba). The form and structure of the music performed in the ensemble should always be discussed. At first, the music teacher can present various examples of form types. Later on, students should attempt to identify form types on their own. Students should be required to compose mallet ensemble pieces in different keys and forms, and should be able to conduct their compositions, explaining the musical elements used.

Timpani

After basic snare drum technique has been firmly established and the student has some experience in mallet playing, the timpani may be introduced. Learning to tune the timpani correctly presents a greater challenge than learning the necessary playing techniques, so instruction should focus on tuning. The best approach is through basic sight-singing and ear training.

The student should first learn to sing and identify intervals and major scales. Instruction and practice should take place *away* from the timpani on a mallet instrument or the piano. The etudes used in mallet instrument study may include simple melodies whose intervals the student can readily identify. After students have learned the basic intervals, each student should be assigned specific intervals to tune on the timpani. The other class members should evaluate the correctness of the pitches. Students may also be asked to play simple tunes that are basically scale-like. (The teacher should sound only the first pitch of the interval or song.)

Listening

Periodically, the teacher should choose percussion recordings for listening. After listening to the music the students should be asked questions like these:

1) What instruments are being used?

2) What performance techniques are being employed?

3) What types of mallets are being used on the various instruments?

4) How does the percussion enhance other musical elements within the composition?

5) Are the various percussion parts well played?

The following compositions provide interesting percussion for study: *Hary Janos Suite* by Kodaly; *Symphonic Metamorphosis* by Hindemith; *The Love for Three Oranges* ("March" and "Scherzo") by Prokofiev; *La Fiesta Mexicana* by H. Owen Reed; and *Carmina Burana* by Orff.

Improvisation

Improvisation can be an effective means for exploring many different musical effects, percussion techniques, and percussive colors. Every session of improvisation should be used to teach one or more of the elements of music. The following are examples of instructional techniques for improvisation:

1) Students build their own percussion instruments and use them within an improvisation.

2) Students, given rhythmic patterns, apply these patterns on various instruments using different dynamic levels.

3) Given a particular form, students improvise within this form.

4) Students improvise a pointillistic composition.

5) Students listen to and evaluate improvisations by professional performers.

The extent to which comprehensive musicianship can be applied in percussion teaching may vary depending on the limitations of the teaching environment, but the elements of comprehensive musicianship (composition, analysis, performance, listening, and evaluation) should become an integral part of the learning experience regardless of time limitations. Through comprehensive study, students can become better musicians and better percussionists. ■

October, 1977

Percussion Instrument Recommendations for the Schools

Part I

Frederick Fairchild

The following lists present suggestions for percussion instruments, sticks, and related equipment that will meet the minimum requirements of the band, orchestra, and percussion ensemble music played by elementary, junior high, and high school groups. Composers choose from hundreds of percussion instruments for their pieces, so it is impossible for any school to own the instruments needed for every situation — but the instruments recommended here should cover most music that the school director will encounter.

There are separate lists for the elementary, junior high, and high school levels. Each of the lists is organized so that after snare drum, mallet-keyboard instruments, and timpani (which are considered of equal importance), the remaining instruments are given in suggested order of purchase. When two or more levels share the same instruments, the school should purchase the items needed by the more advanced performing group. If the younger players find that the bigger bass drums and cymbals are too large to handle, then "in-between" sizes should be purchased.

Most drums can be equipped with plastic heads. But concert bass drums, tambourines, and congas should have skin heads, since the available plastic membranes cannot produce an adequate tone. Even in these cases plastic will probably work in elementary and junior high schools where the immature wind or string sound seldom demands the higher drum dynamics. But calf skin heads are essential for the mature high school band and orchestra.*

Cases are recommended for all drums and mallet-keyboard instruments for protection during travel and storage; fabric covers are sufficient for day to day protection. A percussion cabinet is indispensable for everyday storage of cymbals, drums, small instruments, stands, and sticks.

Drum sizes given in the lists are presented in standard form: shell depth first and head diameter second (thus, 5½" x 14" specifies a drum that is 5½" deep and 14" in diameter). A list of stick and mallet recommendations appears at the end of the article.

* * * * * *

*I make this recommendation in spite of the fact that there are some special problems associated with skin heads: they must be ordered from percussion specialty shops; they are expensive; and they often require adjustment as they become too loose on days when there is high humidity and too tight on days of low humidity.

Elementary School (Beginning Band)

Item	
For Organizations:	
1 or 2 snare drums	5½″ x 14″ or 5″ x 14″. Wire snares.
1 or 2 snare drum stands	Heavy duty. Adjustable to standing height.
Bells	2½ octaves. Steel bars.
Bass drum	14″ x 28″. Plastic heads.
Bass drum stand	Folding style.
Pair of cymbals	16″ diameter. Medium.
2 trap tables (one for cymbals, one for small instruments and sticks)	24″ x 30″ plywood boards covered with carpeting.

Junior High School

Item	**Specifications**
1 or 2 snare drums	5½″ x 14″ or 5″ x 14″. Wire snares.
1 or 2 snare drum stands	Heavy duty. Adjustable to standing height.
Bells	2½ octaves. Steel bars.
Pair of timpani	28″ and 25″ or 29″ and 26″.
Timpani stool	Padded director's stool. Adjustable.
Xylophone*	2½ or 3 octaves. On wheels or in case for placing on tray stand. Synthetic bars.
Bass drum	16″ x 30″. Plastic or calf heads.
3 tray stands	Restaurant tray stands.
Triangle	8″. Steel.
Triangle holder	Spring clip type.
Tambourine	10″. Single row of jingles.
Woodblock	
Suspended cymbal	16″ or 17″ medium thin.
Cymbal stand	Heavy duty.
For Class or Individual Lessons:	
Percussion "kits"	Practice pad, bells, stand, snare drum sticks, bell sticks, and case are included in each kit.
Bass drum stand	Folding style or tilting style.
Pair of cymbals	17″ or 18″. Medium.
Suspended cymbal	17″ or 18″. Medium-thin.

*Contributing Editor's Note: I recommend a 3½ to 4 octave marimba (rosewood or synthetic bar) for the study of solo mallet/keyboard literature. Certain ensemble works do require a marimba for their performance.

Cymbal stand	Heavy duty.
2 trap tables (one for cymbals, one for small instruments and sticks)	24" x 30" plywood boards covered with carpeting.
3 tray stands (one for bells, two for trap tables). (One additional stand is needed if the xylophone has no legs.)	Restaurant tray stands.
Triangle	8". Steel.
Triangle holder	Spring clip type.
Tambourine	10". Single row of jingles. Calf head.
Woodblock	
Pair of maracas	
Pair of claves	
Güiro	
Cowbell	At least 5" long. Latin style.
1 single pair of castanets mounted on handle	

High School Marching Band

The following recommendations are for the standard contemporary marching band. All drums should be equipped with parade weight plastic heads.

Item	Specifications
Parade drums (and slings)	12" x 15". Gut snares. Lug bracket for adjusting playing angle. Swivel leg rest.
Bass drums (and slings or carriers)	General purpose size: 14" x 28". Additional sizes if "pitched" effects desired: 14" x 26", 14" x 30", 14" x 24".
Pairs of cymbals (with straps and pads)	General purpose size: 18" heavy-marching. Additional sizes if "pitched" effect desired: 16" heavy-marching, 14" heavy-marching, 20" heavy-marching.
Timp-tom trios (and straps or carriers)	Each set should have the same combination of different drum sizes: 10" x 14", 10" x 16", and 10" x 18".
Marching bells (not bell lyre) with horizontal carrier	
Marching xylophone with horizontal carrier	

Several combinations of bongos, timbales, and congas are available with appropriate carrying devices. In addition, cowbells, tambourines, maracas, whistles, sirens, etc. may be carried by individual members of the section. Some bands use timpani.

Stick and Mallet Recommendations

(These refer to all levels and are not listed in order of purchase.)

Instrument	Stick(s) or Mallet(s)
The following sticks or mallets should be owned by the student.	
Snare drum	Depends on player's hand size, but larger drums usually require larger sticks. Suggested model numbers are 3A (or equivalent) wood tip for small sticks, 2A for medium and 2B or 5B for large. Set players often prefer smaller sticks; many prefer a nylon tip because it produces a more definite "ping" on a ride cymbal. Brushes are sometimes required.
Timpani	Junior high: one pair medium (general purpose), and one pair firm (staccato). High school: 3 pairs — soft, medium (general purpose), and firm (staccato). Wood sticks may be required.
Marimba	Soft, medium and hard rubber. Soft, medium and hard yarn or cord.
Xylophone	Plastic is best for loud passages (but may split some of the newer rosewood xylophone bars which are often made of improperly seasoned wood) and very hard rubber for softer passages. Rosewood mallets produce a good, brittle sound.
Vibraphone	Soft, medium, or hard cord for soft, medium, and hard attack sounds.
Bells	Brass headed mallets. Hard rubber for softer effects.
Timbales	Timbales sticks (can be made from dowel rod).
Triangle	Make beaters from steel rod stock. Elementary and junior high require 1 pair (⅛" x 8"). High schools need 2 pairs (⅛" x 8" and 3/16 x 8").
Tenor drum (concert)	Heavy snare drum sticks. Felt sticks are required by some scores.
Parade drum (concert)	Heavy snare drum sticks.
Bongos	Light snare drum sticks or timbale sticks. (Playing with the hands will not produce a loud enough sound for bands and orchestras, and many bongo parts specify "with sticks.")
Concert tom toms	Snare drum sticks or felt sticks as appropriate. Stick size generally varies with the size of the drum(s).
Cow bell	Butt of large snare drum stick.
Wood block	Hard rubber xylophone mallet. Snare drum sticks for "soft shoe" effect.

Temple blocks	Medium to medium-hard rubber marimba mallets. (Snare drum sticks or plastic mallets may split the blocks.)
Suspended cymbal	Medium yarn marimba mallets. Snare drum sticks when required, brushes, triangle beaters, etc. for special effects.

The following sticks should be owned by the school:

Chimes	Rawhide or composition mallets. Do not use wood.
Bass drum	Heavy weight with piano felt or fur covering. The larger the drum, the larger the beater. Elementary: 1 general purpose. Junior high and high school: 1 general purpose and 1 pair roll sticks (smaller than general purpose).
Güiro	Thin wood scraper or dowel rod. A scraper made of two or three pieces of stiff wire embedded in a flat handle is also useful.
Tam tam	Heavy beater designed for tam tams made of wool covered hard felt or yarn covered rubber.

Marching band (only parade drum sticks should be student owned):

Parade drum	"S" model sticks (all drummers should use the same size for uniform sound).
Timp-toms	Double ended felt and wood sticks.
Bass drums	Hard felt with large heads. The larger the drum, the larger the mallet.
Bells and xylophone	Plastic sticks.
Bongos and timbales	Timbales sticks or light snare drum sticks.
Timpani	Double ended hard felt and soft felt sticks. ■

November, 1977

Percussion Instrument Recommendations for the Schools Part II

Frederick Fairchild

High School

Item	**Specifications**
For Bands and Percussion Ensembles:	
Snare drum(s)	6½" x 14". Wire-gut combination or wire snares. Metal shell. A second drum for use in lighter music should be 5½" x 14" or 5" x 14" with wire snares and metal shell.

Snare drum stand(s)	Heavy duty.
Bells	2½ octaves. Steel bars.
Xylophone	3½ octaves. On wheels. Synthetic bars.
4 timpani	In addition to the basic pair of 28″ and 25″ (or 29″ and 26″), the following sizes are mandatory (listed in order of purchase): 32″ (or 30″) and 23″.
Timpani stool	Padded director's stool. Adjustable.
Marimba	4 to 4½ octaves. Rosewood or synthetic bars.
Bass drum	16″ x 36″. Calf heads.
Bass drum stand	Tilting style.
Pair(s) of cymbals	Large groups: 20″ medium or medium-heavy. Smaller groups: 18″ medium or medium-heavy. Ideally, organizations should own a large and a small pair.
Suspended cymbals(s)	18″ medium thin. 16″ thin cymbal.
Cymbal stand(s)	Heavy duty.
3 trap tables (one for cymbals, two for small instruments and sticks)	24″ x 30″ plywood boards covered with carpeting.
4 tray stands (one for bells, three for trap tables)	Restaurant tray stands.
Triangle(s)	8″ steel. An additional triangle (10″ steel) will add another color.
Triangle holder(s)	Spring clip type.
Tambourines	10″, with single row of jingles and calf head. 10″, with double row of jingles and calf head.
2 woodblocks	One higher in pitch than the other.
Pair of maracas	
Pair of claves	
Güiro	
Cowbell	At least 5″ long. Latin style.
Castanet machine	
2 single pairs of castanets on handles	
Sleigh bells	25 bells on handle.
Ratchet	Cog made of wood.
Pair of finger cymbals	Heavy metal.
Tam tam on stand	At least 26″ in diameter.
5 temple blocks on stand	"In line" stand.
Bongos on stand	Stand adjustable to standing height. Adjustable heads.

Chimes	1½″ diameter tubes.
Vibraphone	3 octaves. Adjustable motor speed. Wide bars.
Timbales on stand	
Afuché	Medium.
Metal tube shaker	
Vibra-slap	
Set of 4 concert tom-toms on stands (graduated in size)	Sizes: 9″ x 13″, 10″ x 14″, 12″ x 15″, 14″ x 16″. Stands adjustable to playing height.
Conga drum	11″ to 12¼″ head diameter. Barrel shaped body. Wrench or key tunable skin head.
Conga stand	Ring base type.
Tenor drum*	12″ x 15″. Wood shell.
Tenor drum stand	Snare drum stand. Adjustable to standing height.
Parade drum*	12″ x 15″. Metal shell. Gut snares.
Parade drum stand	Snare drum stand. Adjustable to standing height.

*The reason that the tenor drum and parade drum are listed last is that most schools already own them as part of their marching band inventory. It is best, however, to have drums specifically designated for concert use.

For Jazz Band:

Drum set:

Snare drum	5½″ x 14″ or 5″ x 14″. Wire snares.
Snare drum stand	Heavy duty.
Bass drum	14″ x 22″.
Bass drum pedal	
Bass drum spurs	
Hi-hat	Direct pull.
2 hi-hat cymbals	14″ or 15″ medium-thin hi-hat.
Ride cymbal	20″ to 22″ medium ride.
Crash cymbal	18″ medium-thin crash.
2 cymbal stands	Heavy duty.
Throne	Padded. Heavy duty. Wide seat.
2 mounted tom toms	8″ x 12″ and 9″ x 13″.
Dual tom tom mount (for mounting on bass drum)	
Floor tom tom	16″ x 16″. Equipped with legs.

Cowbell and holder	Cowbell at least 5″ long. Latin style.
Rug (for placing under set to prevent bass drum and hi-hat from sliding)	6′ x 6′ rug.
Other Jazz Band Instruments:	
Vibraphone	3 octaves. Wide bars. Variable speed motor.
Tambourine	Headless rock or folk tambourine. 10″. Single row of jingles.
Maracas	
Claves	
Güiro	
Afuché	Medium size.
Metal tube shaker	
Vibra-slap	
Conga	11″ to 12¼″ head diameter. Barrel shaped body. Wrench or key tunable skin head.
Conga stand	Ring base type.
Triangle	10″.
Triangle holder	Spring clip type. ■

December, 1977

Latin American Instruments and Rhythms

Hugh W. Soebbing

Each Latin American instrument has a distinctive sound and a characteristic rhythm pattern, but unless individual percussionists know how to play these instruments properly, it will be impossible to produce the authentic texture of a Latin rhythm section. Because the subject is too-often neglected in the education of percussionists, the following brief explanations are offered as an elementary foundation for performance on the more common Latin American instruments.

Claves

Claves are two hardwood sticks (usually ebony, snakewood, or redwood), about one inch in diameter and eight inches in length. They are played by resting the left stick against the cupped left hand then striking the right stick against the left. The sound should be hollow and penetrating. There are two basic rhythmic patterns generally played by the claves, but one is simply an inversion of the other (examples 1-2). Because these rhythms underlie many of the most common Latin American rhythms, it is absolutely essential to master them.

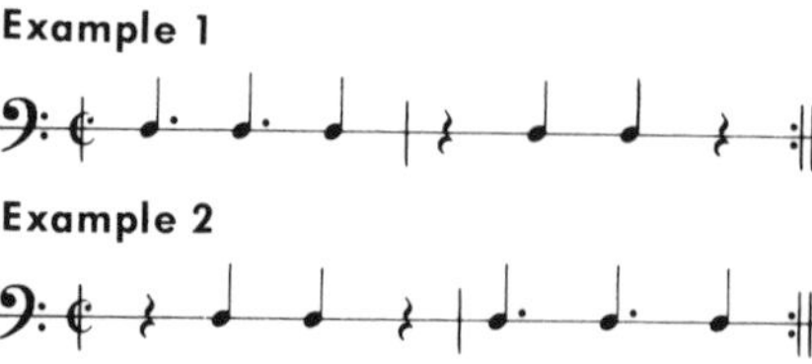

Timbales

Timbales are a pair of shallow, one-headed tom-toms. Sizes of the two drums vary, but in all cases a pair consists of two different sizes. One or two cowbells are often attached to the drums. Sticks consist of two untapered 12" or 14" lengths of 3/8" dowel. Each stick is held in the same manner as the right hand in standard snare drumming (matched grip).

The basic timbale rhythm is termed *motivo*. When playing the motivo, the left hand rim note should be played by striking the rim with the shoulder of the stick while the left hand holds the butt in the center of the head. The three fingers should be extended to control the muffling of the drum. The butt end of the stick should remain in contact with the head at all times, providing a point of leverage for the stick. The basic motivo rhythm is shown in example 3; examples 4 and 5 show slight variations. Stems up indi- left hand. ♩ indicates notes to be played on the drum and 𝅘𝅥 (x) notes played on the rim.

Example 3

Example 4

Example 5

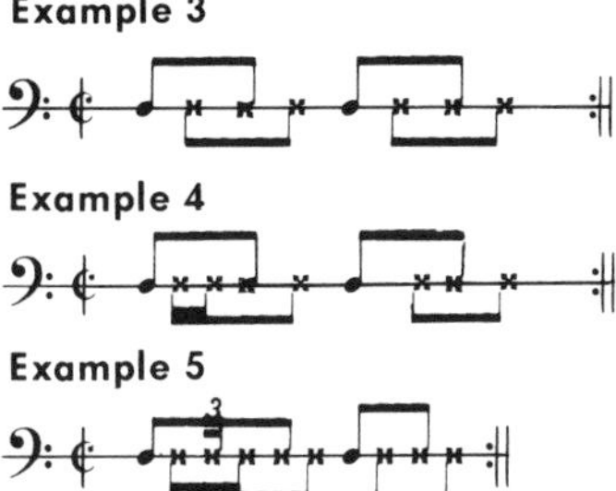

When cowbells are added, they take over the right hand rhythm of the motivo and may introduce a number of rhythmic variations (examples 6-10). However, in improvising new cowbell patterns one should be careful to make the beat consistent with the rhythm of the claves and the straight eighth-note pattern of the motivo. The cowbell can be incorporated into the motivo pattern as shown in example 6.

Example 6

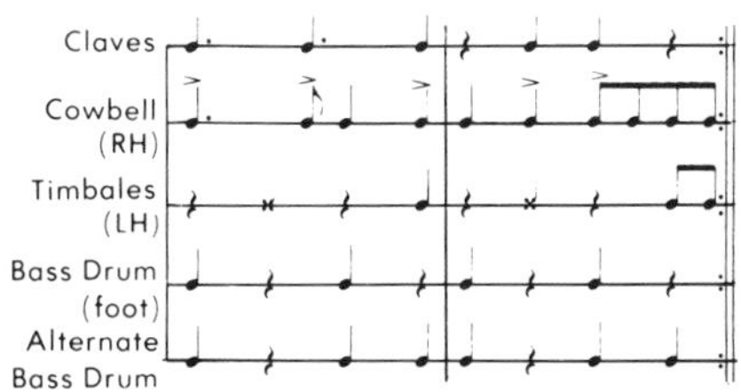

Examples 7-10 show some of the variations possible in the cowbell rhythm. In each of these the right hand may be played on the outside of the shell (paila) for a softer sound.

Example 7

Example 8

Example 9

Example 10

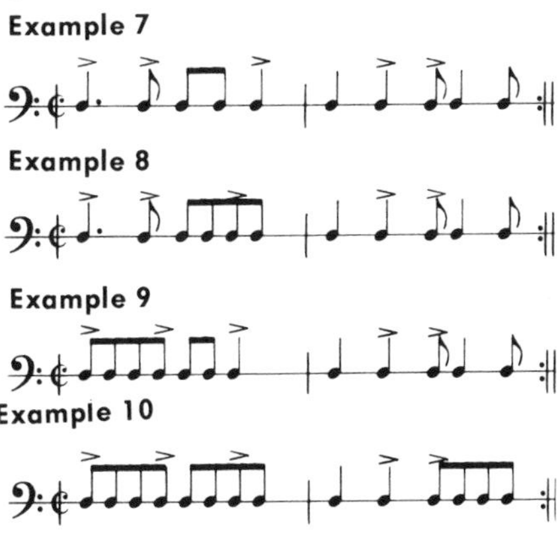

When it is time to break the motivo, the following patterns can be used as a transition to a new rhythmic pattern. (In these examples, all notes are open rim shots.)

Example 11

Example 12

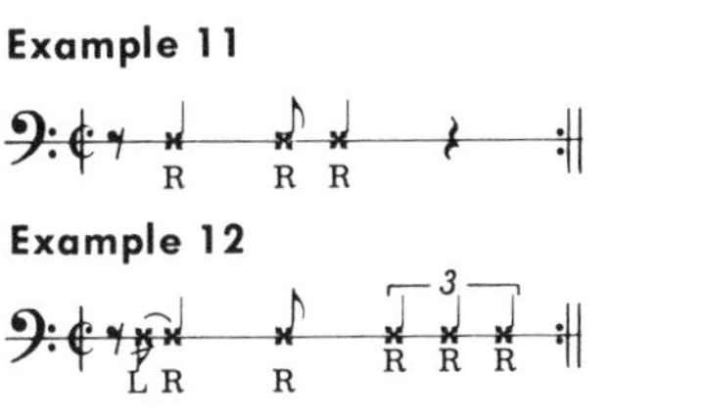

Example 13

Example 14

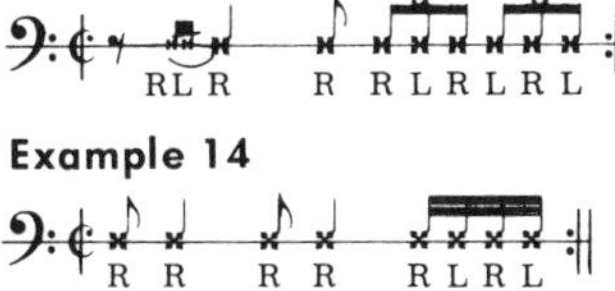

Within the basic framework of the motivo, a variety of accent patterns may be obtained by retaining the straight eighth-note pattern but altering the sticking. The sticking in examples 15-16 produces an accent pattern consistent with the rhythm of the claves (♩♩.♩).

Example 15

Example 16

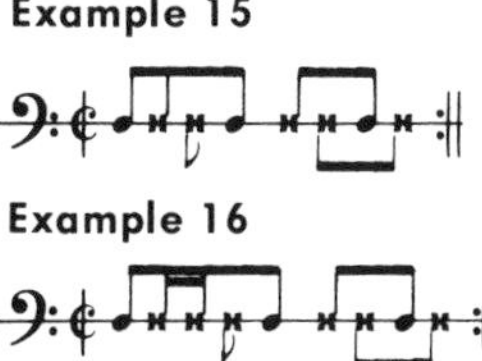

Some additional ways to vary the sound of the basic motivo pattern include the following: (1) playing count 4 on the small timbale or alternating between the large and and the small; (2) playing all or some of the right hand rim notes as rim shots (rim and head played together); (3) doubling various eighth notes as in example 4 but with the sticking used in example 16.

The cowbell itself can produce a variety of sounds if different parts of it are struck with different parts of the stick. In this manner four basic sounds are easily obtained, two loud and two soft. The two louder sounds can be produced by using the shoulder of the stick on the open and closed ends of the cowbell. The softer sounds result by using the tip of the stick on these same areas. These sounds can be used in a number of ways to alter the sound of the motivo rhythm, but the most authentic is to change on the 1st and 2nd beats of the measure.

Another important timbale rhythm is the *paila* rhythm, a commonly used accompaniment for boleros and rumbas. This pattern is played on the sides of the timbales with both sticks. The tip of the stick is used for soft and the shoulder for loud. Generally the paila rhythm is used for soft to medium loud playing. At slow and moderate tempi, the paila rhythm should be played as in example 17. L is left hand; R is right hand; and B is both hands together.

Example 17

Example 18 shows the sticking for paila rhythms at medium and fast tempi.

Example 18

(Med.) R L R L R L R L R L R L R L R L
(Fast) R L L R L L R L R L R L R L R L

The timbales are often used to play short breaks and fill-ins, ranging in length from one to four bars. For short breaks (one measure or less) the patterns of examples 11-14 will suffice. For longer solos and breaks a combination of motivo and cowbell rhythms are effective. Other possible and often-used solo effects include triplets (usually eighth-or quarter-note triplets) and single stroke rolls.

Maracas

Maracas are two hollow gourd shells (with attached handles) filled with seeds. In a matched pair of maracas the right hand maraca should be higher in pitch.

The proper tight, crisp sound of the maracas is obtained with a tight wrist or arm motion, controlling the seeds so that they strike the shell together and make a tight, clicking sound. Practice getting the correct sound by playing on the knee with short quick strokes. For extremely soft playing tap the top of each maraca lightly with the index finger of the holding hand. (Note: the seeds should not strike the top of the shells.)

In most cases, the maracas' rhythm consists of straight eighth notes accented on the beat (example 19), but slight rhythmic variations are acceptable (examples 20-21).

It is possible to play a roll on the maracas by moving them in a large circle. This will cause the seeds to roll around on the inside of the shell, producing a continuous swishing sound.

Guiro

The guiro is a long, dried gourd with ridges cut across one side, and two finger holes and a sounding slot cut into the other. It is held by the thumb and first finger, with the sounding slot facing forward; and it is played by scraping the corrugated surface with a wire or wood scraper. The sound is varied through changes in the speed and direction of the scrapes. A wood scraper will produce a subdued sound while a wire one will result in a cutting, coarse sound.

The basic guiro rhythm is straight eighth notes with an accent pattern like the claves (example 22). The accents are played by moving the scraper faster over the corrugations. The guiro pattern can be altered by varying the note lengths, but the accent pattern remains the same (examples 23-24). D indicates downstroke and U is upstroke.

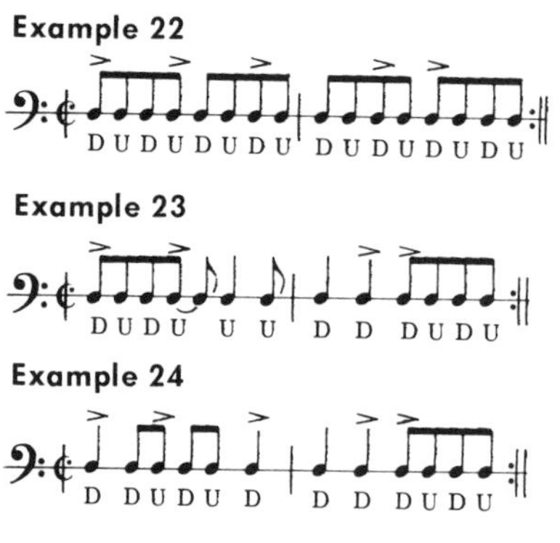

Because all of these patterns are based on straight eighth-note rhythms and follow the accents of the claves, they are applicable to timbales as cowbell or paila rhythms, and the cowbell rhythms (examples 25-27) are applicable to the guiro.

Cowbell (Cencerro)

The cowbell is held in the palm of the left hand (to muffle the sound) and struck on the top with one clave stick, producing a deep, metallic thump. Its function in the Latin rhythm section is to establish and hold the basic tempo in montunos, rumbas, congas, or other compositions in which a syncopated rhythm predominates (it should not be used in boleros or other smooth, lyrical pieces). For this reason it is the only instrument in the section other than the claves to hold a steady rhythm throughout.

The basic cowbell rhythm is a simple series of quarter notes. It is best to begin with this pattern with more complex rhythms being introduced later on.

Example 25

The basic rhythm is especially good in mambos, but it is often altered in the naningo (example 26) or in dances with much syncopation (as in the conga, example 27). In these cases the altered rhythm is maintained throughout the number.

Example 26

Example 27

Conga Drum

The term conga refers not to one drum but to a whole family of drums ranging in size from the small quinto to the extremely large tumbadora. The most often used of the conga family, the tumba is medium in size — about three feet in length — with a head diameter of 8 to 11 inches. The other frequently used congas include the llamador (about the size of the tumba but higher in pitch) and the quinto (about 2 feet long with a head diameter of 6 to 8 inches).*

It is extremely important to keep the bottom of the drum off the floor, as this gives the drum its low pitch. Therefore, the conga is generally held between the knees with the base balanced on the feet several inches above the floor. Other common methods of holding the drum involve the use of adjustable conga stands or hanging the drum from the shoulder by means of a leather strap (though this restricts the hand motion somewhat and should not be used unless necessary).

In general, the drum is played by striking the head with the full hand or fingers, but variations in the way this is done can produce a wide range of sounds. Because these sounds are an integral part of the characteristic conga patterns, it is necessary to have them under control before attempting any of the basic rhythms.

1. *Open rim shot.* Strike the head and the rim of the drum at the same time using all the fingers above the middle finger joint. The sound produced should be open, ringing, and high-pitched. This should be practiced as single strokes using both hands and striving for evenness of sound.

2. *Open boom sound.* This sound may be produced in two different ways: by cupping the hand and playing in the center of the head, or by striking the rim of the drum with the palm of the hand allowing the fingers to snap over onto the head. The rim sound will not be heard because the rim is struck

*Contributing Editor's Note: Most commercial congas now available consist of a set of two or three drums, all generally longer in depth and larger in diameter.

with the fleshy part of the hand — only the finger sound will be heard. In both of the above methods, any sound of the hand or the fingers striking the head should be avoided in favor of the low-pitched boom of the drum.

3. *Thud Sound.* The right hand strikes the rim and head, while the left hand lies flat on the opposite side to muffle the head. A softer version of this sound can be produced with the left hand by raising the fingers and letting them fall onto the head. The heel of the hand remains on the drum to muffle the head.

4. *Slap sound.* The right hand slaps the head and the rim while the left hand presses the head producing a higher pitched, ringing tone than the thud sound.

As with most of the Latin instruments, the basic pattern for the conga is the straight eighth-note rhythm. The numbers refer to the different conga sounds listed above.

Example 28

The quinto or the small conga uses the same rhythm pattern but with the accent pattern of the claves.

Example 29

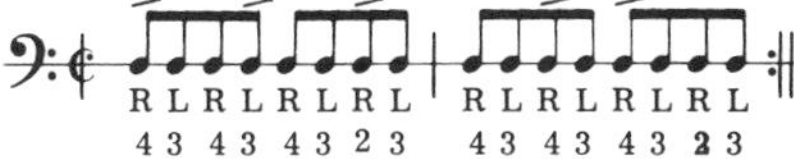

Several other basic conga sounds are often used by the conga drummer: the one-finger rimshot effect; the low thud of a clenched fist in the center of the head; pitch variation, obtained by varying pressures of the left fingers, hand, or elbow in the center of the head while the right hand plays on the head; and the conga roll, a single stroke roll played by using any of the conga sounds.

Bongos

Bongos consist of two wooden shells bound together; each one has either a tacked or tensionable head. Bongos come in many sizes, but the average pair has heads with a diameter of 6 and 8 inches. To obtain the desired high-pitched sound, it is often necessary to tighten the heads with dry heat (a light bulb or canned heat, not steam).

The bongos are held between the knees, small drum on the left, and are played with the index fingers of both hands. Although the drums are generally struck with only one finger at a time, all the fingers should be extended.

Because of the large range in dynamics and timbres of the bongos they have become the virtuoso instruments of the section. The bongos do have a basic pattern, but players often improvise freely around the rhythm of the claves and fill in around the patterns of the other instruments.

There are two basic bongo beats. One is the traditional Cuban beat (martilo), the other is an imitation originating in the United States. Both methods employ the same rhythm, fingering and distribution of notes between the two drums, so the actual sound of the two beats is similar.

It is advisable to learn the United States beat first because it is easier to learn, provides an entirely acceptable sound for most purposes, and is much easier to play loudly to cut through big groups. To play this beat (example 30), there are three basic sounds:

Finger stroke. This is produced by striking the tip of the index finger of either hand on or near the rim with a bouncing motion. The sound obtained should be merely a tapping sound. This is used for all unaccented eighth notes.

Rim shot. The rim shot is the loudest sound produced on the bongos. It can be played on either drum, but in the U.S. bongo beat it is played only on the small bongo with the right hand on count two. To make the rim shot, the hand must stop sharply, allowing the fingers to snap the head and immediately bounce away in a whip-snap motion (the same effect is possible using the thumb).

The open, low drum. This sound is produced by striking the large drum with either the whole index finger or thumb. The sound should be ringing and unmuffled. Experimenting with striking different head areas with different parts of the finger or thumb will produce the best sound.

Example 30

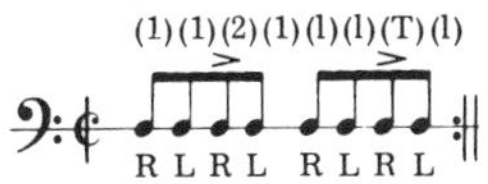

The martilo is played by alternating various fingers and the thumb on recurring eighth notes. A greater variety of sounds is possible with this method, and once the technique is mastered, it also gives the player greater speed.

The sounds of the U.S. style can also be applied to the martilo. However, in playing the basic beat, the right hand plays once with the index finger and once with the second finger in an alternating pattern. By indicating the index finger as (1) and the second finger as (2), we can notate the right hand pattern as (1) (2) (1) (2). The left hand finger stroke is made by alternating the left hand thumb and second finger (but the left thumb does not play a thumb-stroke, rim shot). By indicating the thumb note as (T) and the second finger as (2), we can notate the left hand pattern as (T) (2) (T) (2). Then, the martilo beat should be played as in example 31.

Example 31

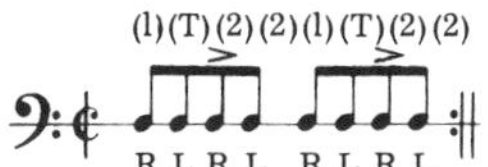

After the basic technique is understood, the student should attempt to achieve the proper open sound on the large drum (with the second finger) on count 4 and the proper rim shot effect on count 2. To aid in making this rim shot, the fingering may be altered slightly, placing a right hand rim shot (thumb) on 2.

The bongo roll is produced by fast alternation of single strokes using any of the sounds previously mastered. Most easily learned, however, is the index finger roll.

Bongo and Conga Solos

Soloists must maintain a relationship to the rhythm of the claves. To accomplish this while playing interesting combinations of the various sounds is not easy and requires much practice. Greater facility can be gained, however, by avoiding extremely complex rhythms and concentrating on fitting solo ideas into the basic patterns.

Other Instruments

Jawbone (quijada). The jawbone functions much like the cowbell in two respects: it is used only on numbers featuring the rhythm instruments, and it plays a very simple pattern. The jawbone is held in the left hand and gently struck with the right fist causing the teeth to rattle. Generally, the jawbone plays on the first and second beats in slow tempos and on the 2nd of two beats in fast numbers.

Cabasa. The cabasa is a large, round gourd covered with rows of strung beads. It is of Brazilian origin and used chiefly for sambas. The cabasa is played by slapping with the right hand and turning it with the left (the holding hand). It plays on each of the four beats of the measure in the following manner: (beat 1) slap the gourd with the open palm of the right hand; (beat 2) strike the beads with the fingers of the right hand; (beat 3) rotate cabasa by turning left wrist clockwise; (beat 4) rotate the cabasa in reverse to original position. The sound produced can be notated as in example 32. Note the accent on the third beat.

Example 32

Chocahlo. The chocahlo, a long metal cylinder filled with beads, is also used for sambas. It plays straight eighth notes with a motion as shown in example 33 (D indicates down, U indicates up).

Example 33

Tambora. The tambora is a two-headed drum from the Dominican Republic. It is struck with a stick held in the right hand, and the fingers and palm of the left hand. The stick strikes either the head or rim. The main use of the tambora is for the merengue, but since the tambora is often unavailable in the U.S., its merengue rhythms are generally played by snare drum (snares off) or timbales.

The director who wants to fill out arrangements with authentic instruments and sounds can use this material as a reference for instructing students. Try arranging master classes around three or four Latin instruments per meeting closing each class with an improvisation of all instruments studied up to that point. Some students may be inspired to compose or arrange music for a small percussion ensemble.

Using Latin American instruments and rhythms can augment any ensemble (concert band, orchestra, marching band, and jazz/rock ensemble) and the proper playing of them can produce the exciting texture of an authentic Latin rhythm section. ■

1978-1979

531	Percussion Instruction Methods by Computer	G. David Peters	January
534	How to Select Cymbals	Frank Shaffer, Jr.	January
536	Solo and Study Materials for Percussion	Don R. Baker	February
538	Drummer Confidence	Ed Soph	February
539	Choreography in Multiple Percussion Playing	Karen Ervin	March
541	The Creative Show Percussionist	Jerrold Michaelson	April
542	Multiple Percussion on the March	Bob Houston	May
545	Drum Tension and Muffling Techniques	David Levine	June
548	Cymbal Playing Technique	Larry C. Jones	August
550	Percussion Concerts: Impact and How to Achieve It	Russell Peck	September
551	Using Timp-toms Effectively	Mark Petty	October
554	Administering the Marching Percussion Section	Jay A. Wanamaker	November
555	Un-contestable Advice for Timpani and Marimba Players	Gordon B. Peters	December
557	The Snare Drum Roll: One Lump or Two?	Patrick Crowley	January
558	The Concert Bass Drum	Lynn Glassock	January
559	Teaching the Long Roll	Charles Holmes	February
560	Cymbal Acoustics, Selection, and Care	Larry C. Jones	March
563	Percussion Maintenance: Tips for the Band Director	Brian K. Shepard	April
566	Drum Head Selection	David Levine	May
568	Do Your Drummers Belong?	Raymond Willard	June
570	Updating a Percussion Program	Martin Zykowski	July
571	Meet the Steelpan	Wayne E. Charles	August
572	The New Marching Percussion Line	Robert Buck	September
573	The Bass Drum	Doug Howard	October
575	Drum Set Basics	James Piekarczyk	November
577	Big Band Drumming Basics	Ed Soph	December
579	Percussion Solos and Studies	Don R. Baker	December

January, 1978

Percussion Instruction Methods by Computer

G. David Peters

As the student begins a lesson on the PLATO computer, information is displayed on the terminal screen. The student, using a typewriter-like "keyset," can request information from the computer, select instructional lessons, leave messages for his teacher, and comment on the quality of a question or lesson. The use of "computer-graphics" allows for easy displaying of music notation, line-drawings for illustrations, and unique types and sizes of alpha-numeric symbols.

Editor's note: The idea of computer-assisted instruction (CAI) is not new to the field of education or music education. What may be new to you is the level of sophistication of CAI and the number of evaluated programs available in the instrumental music area. The following article covers one such program in percussion methods instruction used at the University of Illinois through the computer-assisted system known as PLATO.

The computer that prints the student's semester schedule in most school districts is also capable of instruction. As reported by Buloski and Korotkin (1976),[1] 58% of the secondary schools in the United States used computers in 1975 with 26% of the secondary schools using some form of computer-assisted instruction that same year. With over half of the schools using computers the availability of CAI to the instrumental music teacher is not a remote dream but a real possibility.

The purpose for using CAI in teaching is economy of time. Because of CAI's individualized instruction approach the student can study or review material at his own rate of speed. The PLATO program also saves time because a large amount of summarized material can be presented, thereby combining part of the classroom teacher presentations with the student study time. An example of this economy is the percussion methods program developed from nearly twenty different texts and resources.

The CAI approach is not a substitute for the classroom teacher; a computer cannot correct a student's hand position while he is learning to play the snare drum, but the computer can be used to teach the student an awareness of hand position through the use of slides and other graphic presentations. The CAI lessons described here are recommended for college students in an education program to be used as review and study materials after some hands-on experience with the instruments.

Lesson Structure and Content

Following the design of an earlier series of CAI lessons written for woodwind and brass instruments, the percussion pedagogy series was developed as a tutor program. In other words, the student was presented information and reference materials on a specific instrument and then asked questions assessing his knowledge of the information. If the student could not answer the questions, he could review the information before proceeding.

Each lesson (or session) with the computer is constructed for a 45- to 50-minute completion time with the actual time spent by students varying from 20 minutes to well over an hour per lesson. Students can sign-in and select a lesson from the areas listed by topic:

- snare drum pedagogy
- timpani pedagogy
- traps identification
- mallet instrument techniques (chimes, bells, marimba, vibraphone, xylophone)
- bass drum and cymbal techniques
- drum set techniques
- marching percussion organization
- functional concert percussion section

The PLATO lesson on Snare Drum Pedagogy covers three areas of common student problems: producing a tone, playing a series of notes, and developing a controlled sound.

The first section, producing a tone, reviews hitting the drum with good hand and stick position. The content includes questions (and answers) on hand position, stick position, choice of drum sticks, head adjustment, tonal playing areas, and sticking. Color slides on traditional and matched-stick grip are displayed on the computer as information is supplied to the student on applying each style of playing. After this graphic presentation students are shown slides of poor hand and stick position and asked to analyze the problems. Additional questions cover drum stand height and angle.

In presenting the second section, playing a series of notes, sticking was approached as combinations of two basic motions, the stroke and the tap. Four principal rudiments, the tap, stroke, flam, and roll (Ludwig, 1936),[2] are discussed with suggested references to other percussion texts. The Payson-McKenzie (1966)[3] listing of the two basic motions with four hand positions (low/low, low/high, high/high, high/low) are presented before a discussion and question section on types of sticking: alternating sticking, hand-to-hand sticking, professional expediency (Buggert, 1960),[4] and right-hand lead sticking.

Questions include marking the sticking for music examples displayed on the PLATO terminal for both right-hand lead and hand-to-hand sticking. Rudimental drumming is discussed, but students are not asked to read through the 26 rudiments at the computer terminal. This is one area better left to classroom presentation through performance and demonstration.

A final section, developing a controlled sound on snare drum, includes equipment discussions on gut, wire, and nylon snares; batter and snare head selection; drumstick selection; and tonal playing areas of the drum. Slides show sticks, snare drum size, and various types of snares, as well as listing checkpoints for teachers on ways to improve a student's sound through control and consistent playing.

After completing the materials in this lesson students are given their total score earned on the questions. They can then choose to return to the snare drum lesson for additional review, select another instrument for study, or stop working at the computer. In any case the student's records are stored by computer until he returns, and if he has to stop in the middle of a lesson, the next time he signs in, the computer will automatically take him to the point in the lesson where he had previously stopped.

A different approach to lesson structure is used in the presentation of the traps sessions to students. Color photographs of percussion instruments were prepared for this lesson. Because a great deal of time is required to review these instruments in class, time in reviewing names and spellings of the instruments is diminished by using the computer.

The lesson is structured as a simple drill. Each time a student signs in the computer randomly selects 50 instruments for the student to identify at sight. The student can request to study the instruments by viewing the slides with labels before being drilled on their identification. Correct spelling is required for continuation in the program; however, if the student is not able to identify the instrument with the correct spelling, he can ask the computer for the answer. The computer will give the student the correct answer, judge the student incorrect for that instrument, and the incorrectly identified instrument will be presented to the student later in the lesson.

The random-drill design of this lesson allows a large group of students to use the same program repeatedly without seeing the same instruments in the same order. Each time the student uses the lesson a new order and group of instruments are presented.

Another example of the extensiveness of the program can be seen in the outline of the material from the bass drum and cymbal lesson. It is also designed as a tutor lesson and includes slides as part of the lesson presentation.

Bass Drum and Cymbals

Cymbals

suspended cymbals, tam-tams, and gongs
sticks and mallets
chart of cymbal weights and usage
cymbal crashes

Bass Drum

placement and position

muffling

stroke patterns

rolls (tremolo)

mallet grip and posture

proper playing areas

Equipment Selection

Size and usage

The complete scope of percussion lesson programs available to students through CAI emphasizes the advantages of using these materials. In addition to comprehensively covering a subject CAI can be used on an open schedule, and it enables students to work individually at their own rate of speed.

Evaluation

The programs developed in percussion methods were evaluated for their scope, content, and effectiveness by collecting four types of information: lesson content evaluation, computer-collected data, student opinionnaires, and a pre-test/post-test evaluation of student progress.

The lesson content evaluation was started even as the programs were being written. Music faculty members helped in developing the lessons, and lesson content was checked repeatedly with all source materials to assure validity of information cited in answers to any questions. Graduate percussion students and faculty members reviewed the lessons before undergraduate students began to use the materials.

Students were encouraged to comment on the lesson content as they worked at the computer. The content of the lessons did stimulate student discussions both with the instructor and among themselves. Although impossible to measure, this stimulated study is a positive result noted by the instructor from semester to semester.

The second area of evaluation reviewed the student data collected by the computer as each student worked at the computer terminal. Information was collected on the number of correct answers the student made, the number of wrong answers, the number of times the student requested assistance from the computer, plus the amount of time the student spent on each question. This item by item data collection allowed for easy analysis of program faults and strengths, and an indication of the advantages of individualized instruction were verified.

To further determine the effectiveness of the programs a pre-test/post-test examination was given to students enrolled in the instrumental music methods classes. The effectiveness of the CAI lessons was judged on a number of factors related to the students' improvement in test scores from the pre-test to the post-test, including student percussion experience, study time, supplementary instrument experience and PLATO usage. In brief, students spending more time on-line with the PLATO system did improve their scores significantly (students with lower pre-test scores improved more than students with high initial scores, which is to be expected with a regression toward the mean in pre-test/post-test situations). This improvement in test scores is significant when one considers that the CAI program saved 25% of the in-class hours normally used in the presentation of this material and student study time was shorter when using PLATO than before the programs were available.

The fourth means of evaluation was an assessment of student reaction to using the computer. A questionnaire was given to the classes at the end of the semester evaluating the course and the PLATO materials. A majority of the students requested that additional lessons be made available.

The conclusions that can be drawn from the evaluations of the percussion lessons are positive. Individual differences in study patterns were noted with speed and variation between student completion of lessons being a strong argument for the continued use and development of CAI in this field. Also, there is a continuous up-dating process of the lessons taking place based on the evaluation results.

CAI Availability

The availability of CAI is, to a large extent, a measure of its value. The high school band director in Maine may see little value for his students of having a CAI network in southern California. Although it may be difficult for a person in Maine to afford to use a California computer, the rapid development and availability of CAI in the last five years has made other means of access possible.

The first approach is to use one large computer to serve hundreds of students. The PLATO computer, centered at the University of Illinois, serves students in elementary, high schools, and colleges in 36 states including Hawaii. Over 200 music lessons are available in music fundamentals, music theory, music appreciation, and the instrumental music areas.

The second approach to CAI is to use mini-computers which serve from one to thirty students. The smaller computer approach has been used successfully in elementary and high schools and does not require expensive telephone connections to one central computer. Several school districts in northern Illinois are experimenting with the mini-computer approach to CAI.

Variations in solving the CAI availability problem include using available computers and adapting them for instructional uses. Most school districts now use some computer time in student scheduling and budgeting and these computers are capable of being adapted for instructional use.

Projections

In looking to future successful applications the secondary school use of computer-assisted instruction is projected to grow to a 51% level in the next five to seven years as school computer use grows to the 100% level. The percussion pedagogy lessons described in this article are seen as part of a growing catalog of CAI materials available for students and teachers. To date the percussion lessons supplement the classroom instruction in the methods area with similar lessons being written for younger students as well as teachers.

The newly-formed National Consortium on Computer-Based Music Instruction is attempting to resolve questions of transferring lessons and making them available to a larger population. Over 100 NCCBMI members are working to share information, programs, and computer development with the profession.

Does the computer replace the teacher? The answer is no, but the computer is playing a larger role in individualizing instruction and utilizing time efficiently for students and teachers in the field of music. ■

1. William J. Bulokski and Arthur Korotkin, "Computing Activities in Secondary Education," *Educational Technology*, January 1976, pp. 9-23.

2. William F. Ludwig, *The Ludwig Drum and Bugle Manual.* Ludwig and Ludwig Inc. 1936.

3. Al Payson and Jack McKenzie, *Music Educators' Guide to Percussion.* Belwin, Inc. 1966.

4. Robert Buggert, *Teaching Technics for the Percussions.* Belwin, Inc. 1960.

The PLATO system is a computer-based system developed at the University of Illinois that is available world-wide from four computer centers, University of Illinois, Control Data Corporation at Arden Hills, Minnesota, University of Quebec, Canada, and Florida State University at Tallahassee.

Approximately 1,000 terminals are supported by the central computer system at the University of Illinois including 26 sites on the campus, 9 elementary schools, 2 high schools, 6 community colleges, 20 government installations, 27 medical sites, 30 colleges and universities, and 20 business-industrial installations. Terminals are scattered from San Diego to Boston, and from Madison to Wichita Falls, Kansas.

For further information about PLATO contact Donald Bitzer, Director of the Computer-Based Educational Research Lab, University of Illinois, Urbana, Illinois 61801. For more information concerning the music programs available on PLATO contact the author at College of Fine and Applied Arts, Office of the Associate Dean, 114 Architecture Bldg., University of Illinois, Urbana, Illinois 61801.

January, 1978

How to Select Cymbals

Frank Shaffer, Jr.

Are you getting the sound you want from your present complement of cymbals? If not, you might consider the possibility that your cymbals were improperly chosen for their uses. This article can help you select the right cymbals for your needs, whether for concert band or orchestra, marching band, or stage band.

Concert Cymbals

Suspended Cymbals. A suspended cymbal should "splash" or "crash" quickly when it is struck, maintaining a stable resonant sound afterwards and decaying very slowly. You can test these properties by striking the top edge of the cymbal (see figure 1) with a snare drum stick. Hold the stick loosely in your hand, striking the cymbal with the middle of the stick, not the tip, imagining that the cymbal is a piece of paper you want to cut with a knife. A good cymbal should give a splash or crash effect — a quick spread of both high and low overtones. The pitch will drop as the higher overtones tend to diminish quickly allowing the lower sustaining partials to become more predominant. The sound should ring for at least eight to ten seconds. The longer a cymbal rings at the volume level achieved at the moment of striking, the better it is.

Figure 1

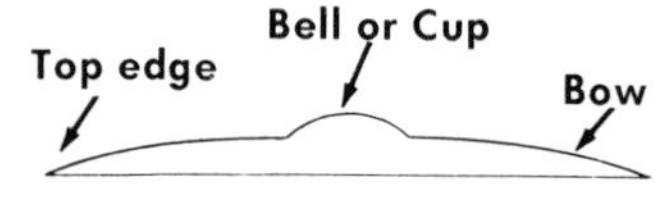

Next, strike the top edge of the cymbal and then strike it again near the center just below the bell or cup. Listen for a primary pitch at both places. There should be a pitch difference of at least a major 2nd and preferably a minor or major 3rd. If the cymbal's ringing makes the pitch differences hard to hear, choke the sound after striking the first blow.

Manufacturers designate cymbals not only by type but also by weight. The cymbal is stamped with markings such as "medium-thin," "medium," "medium-heavy," and "heavy." When you select a suspended cymbal you should generally ask for one that is either medium or medium-thin. Medium-heavy or heavy cymbals tend to respond too slowly for suspended cymbal work although your ear should be the final judge, not the weight designation. If you are testing several cymbals of the same weight, the pitch of any two or more may be decidedly different. If one or another possess about the same sustaining and resonating properties, select the one with higher pitch as it will cut through the ensemble easier. However, if the lower one sustains longer and has more resonance, it should be chosen. This highly individualistic pitch property of each cymbal will sometimes result in a heavier cymbal being higher pitched than a lighter one, and vice versa. Usually, three or four inches difference in diameter will assure a substantial enough pitch difference. If one suspended cymbal is all you can afford, purchase an 18-inch, medium-thin cymbal. If you can purchase two, a 16-inch medium-thin cymbal and an 18- or 20-inch medium-thin or medium cymbal will satisfy most of your needs. The smaller suspended cymbal will be good for fast crescendos with a quick, agile response at soft to loud dynamic levels, and the larger cymbal will possess the power and depth for finale crescendos and climaxes.

Crash Cymbals. There are only a few additional characteristics to look for in a pair of crash cymbals. Select a medium or medium-heavy cymbal for your test. (Some are designated as "band," "concert band," or "symphonic band.") Although medium-thin symphonic cymbals have a good sound and quick response, they are easily broken, cracked, or turned inside out by inexperienced players. Perform the same tests on each cymbal as you did with the suspended cymbal. If you try both symphonic and concert cymbals, realize that concert cymbals tend to be slightly heavier than symphonic cymbals and their response may be slower due to the increased weight. Also, if the cymbals come with pads as well as straps, remove the pads for the test because they have a tendency to dampen the general sound and filter out the higher overtones. After you have tested each cymbal separately strike one on the top edge and then the other to test for at least an interval of a major 2nd and preferably a major or minor 3rd between the two cymbals. This sound relationship between the two cymbals is commonly known as the "marriage" so necessary for a good crash sound. Finally, clash them together at soft to very loud dynamic levels to see how they speak throughout the dynamic range. Expect a crash effect that lasts for 8 to 10 seconds in the louder dynamic range. If you can afford only one pair, a 16-inch medium pair for junior high and an 18-inch medium pair for senior high would be the best choices. A larger size tends to be too cumbersome and is not as effective for soft playing. As a general rule, rather than buying cymbals larger than 20 inches, it is better to buy smaller cymbals and concentrate on playing techniques to produce a bigger sound. When you can afford more cymbals, a 16-inch medium or medium-thin pair for quick crescendos and a 20-inch medium pair for loud crashes are good additions.

Marching Band

Marching band cymbals usually suffer much more abuse so that cymbals of medium-heavy or heavy weight will be good choices. A 16- or 17-inch medium-heavy set would be the ideal single pair for either junior high or high school. Since the tendency in modern marching lines is to have multiple sets of hand cymbals, an 18- or 19-inch medium-heavy or heavy pair would be a good second choice with a 15-inch pair of the same weight being a good third set. You could create wide pitch variations with a set of three pairs in adjacent sizes (15, 16, 17 or 16, 17, 18).

Many times budget considerations make using separate sets of marching and concert band cymbals impossible. The general recommendations for concert band cymbals should then be followed. Avoid heavy-weight cymbals in this case. They tend to be less useful for concert band because of their slower speaking properties. Also, while pads seem a necessity for marching band, it would be better to take them off for concert season because they muffle the sound.

Stage Band

New criteria have to be met when selecting cymbals for stage band. Different sounds are needed in a minimum of three categories of cymbals: ride, crash, and hi-hat.

Ride Cymbals. These should have a dry quality without much ring and overtone. The term "ride" is the general category designation for many types of cymbals going under the different model names of ride, flat top, bebop, bounce, ping, top, or rock cymbals. The latest addition in this category are ride cymbals with smaller cups or no cup at all, creating a very high pitched sound with virtually no overtone buildup. As a beginning purchase I would recommend a bebop or ping ride cymbal, 18 to 20 inches in diameter in either medium or medium-heavy weight. To test the cymbal place it on a stand or hold it on one finger and tap various places on it from just below the bell to the edge. Then play a rock rhythm or jazz (ride) rhythm fairly loudly about halfway or three-quarters of the way up the cymbal from the edge. Listen to make sure the stick rhythm can be heard easily and distinctly. Ask someone else to play the same rhythm while you step away and hear how well it projects. If the ring is overpowering the stick rhythm, this is an indication of a poor ride cymbal. Try several of the different models to find which cymbal projects the best and rings without overpowering the stick sound.

Crash Cymbals. Test these cymbals the same as concert suspended cymbals. They both have the same function. I would recommend a 15- to 18-inch size of medium-thin weight.

A crash-ride cymbal combination is also possible although both categories suffer to some extent. These cymbals will ring more than a bop or ping cymbal but can be used to play some sustained rhythmic figures while getting a fairly good crash sound as well.

Various multiples of crash cymbals are used with drum sets and further investigation would depend on your taste and the tonal complement to your basic three categories.

Hi-hat. The "chick" or "chip" sound on afterbeats that is provided by the hi-hat cymbal is now being used for more rhythmic and special effects that were begun by rock and disco drumming. Testing hi-hat cymbals on a stand with the bottom cymbal properly tilted is the only way to discover a particular set's characteristics. I recommend a 14- or 15-inch set with a strong, powerful "chip" sound, a quick response when playing sixteenth notes on the top cymbal as you move the pedal up and down to open and closed positions, and a good distinctive cutting sound with rock and jazz rhythms in a tight, closed position.

Purchase only factory mated or blended hi-hat cymbals. A new line called the new beat or heavy hi-hat cymbals may suit your purposes if you have a group that uses a great deal of electronic amplification. These cymbals create a more responsive and powerful sound by having a heavy-weight cymbal on the bottom and a medium-weight cymbal on the top or a complementary pair of heavy-weight cymbals.

After purchasing the basic cymbal set-up, you may want to add particular color cymbals. According to your needs, sizzle, splash, or Chinese cymbals would be good choices. To produce a sizzle cymbal, holes are drilled and rivets are installed, to give a "sizzling" effect. Splash cymbals are small, thin cymbals used for fast crash sounds that are choked very quickly. They are particularly useful in ragtime, dixieland, and Broadway show music. Chinese cymbals with model names of swish or pang have turned-up edges giving them a quick, dissipating "pie pan" sound with rivets sometimes installed for more sustaining power.

If you are unable to test cymbals before purchase, be sure to check what the dealer's procedure is for return and replacement. It might be worth your while to visit a large city where there are many drum stores to make your tests; then you will have a much better idea of the variation of quality in cymbals. With a few simple tests and a little experimenting, you will be able to distinguish the characteristics of a good cymbal and will be able to find the best buys for your money. ■

Solo and Study Materials for Percussion

Don R. Baker

During the past year, publishers of percussion music seem to have concentrated on beginning materials and advanced solos, giving much less attention to literature at the intermediate level.

The advanced solos are significantly superior in quality, with the majority of them being written for timpani and mallet (keyboard). Much of this interest may be due to the influence of highly qualified solo performers who have been performing difficult and challenging works at conferences over the past few years. Music published for the intermediate player is limited in quantity, but certainly an asset to this level.

A collection that includes all the percussion instruments is *Master Solos Intermediate Level — Percussion* (Hal Leonard) by Peter Magadini. Not only does it have solos for snare drum, mallet percussion, and timpani, but preparatory exercises and additional training materials on other instruments are also included. The collection is not difficult and has the unique feature of an accompanying cassette tape that includes a performance of the solo followed immediately by the accompaniment at the same tempo.

No beginning timpani solos or methods were submitted for review, except the materials found in the Magadini collection. Only a few good publications are now available. Most methods accelerate too fast and are not practical for a young student who has not had training in rhythms. Part of this problem has developed because of professional disagreement over when a student should begin to learn timpani.

One work with a misleading title is Jim Hamilton's *Ten Contest Solos for the Marching Percussion Section* (Band Shed). The "solos" are really just street beats, at the most only 21 measures long. The manuscript is poor and the binding actually cuts through some of the music. The content does not outweigh the book's many problems.

Snare Drum

12 Progressive Solos for Snare Drum is a collection of Morris Goldenberg's solos from the mid 1960s. Divided into easy, intermediate, and difficult levels, they are all in his traditional style of composing with several of the difficult works written in odd and mixed meters. Wally Barnett's very easy solos with piano accompaniment use different stick and rim techniques to augment the color effect. They have been written in correlation with the book, *Band Today* by James Ployhar (Belwin Mills). *Readin', Ritin', and Rudiments* (Studio PR) by John W. McMahan is a fundamental reading book using the rudimental techniques approach. It is intended as a supplement to any snare drum text and accomplishes its purpose.

Timpani

Advanced high school students would do well to look at William Schinstine's *Sonata No. 2* and *Sonata No. 3* (Southern). *Sonata No. 3* requires five timpani, with the extra drum being 25 or 26 inches. Both works are in three contrasting movements and use mixed meters. Each one is appropriate as contest or recital music.

Two solos by Richard Kashanki, published by HaMaR Percussion Publications, are set in attractive functional music styles of jazz-waltz and rock. *A Semi-Straight Jazz Waltz* requires tuning changes to play the melodic line, and a cadenza is part of the finale. *Rock* looks stylistically better and more attractive from a fun point of view. Also, in this piece there is just one very easy tuning change at the end.

Theme and Variations (Studio 4 Publications) by John M. Floyd is a very challenging work and should be considered only by the advanced high school student. To achieve the total musical value of this work, a performer should have insight into modern phrasing and rhythms and good experience with contemporary music.

The only timpani study book reviewed was Anthony J. Cirone's *Portraits for Timpani* (Belwin Mills). This collection of 50 studies is a sequel to his very fine snare drum book, *Portraits in Rhythm*. The best use of this material is as a virtuoso technique builder, therefore, it is not a practical collection for the school timpanist.

Mallet-Keyboard

Contemporary Band Course (Belwin Mills) is a good collection of easy beginning literature of mallet solos with accompaniment. For intermediate and advanced students there is *Recital Pieces for Mallets* (JR Publications) by Garwood Whaley. The pieces have been transcribed for keyboard instruments and range from early 16th-century to 19th-century works. A short biography of each composer is included and a glossary briefly describes the many forms used in the compositions. Two-, three-, and four-mallet playing is required in the more advanced works. This is a fine collection of music which will expose the player to musical styles that are generally not available to a percussionist.

New works from Studio 4 Productions are very advanced and many require special techniques that very few students have at this time. One piece within the capabilities of an advanced high school marimba player is *Monograph IV* by Richard Gipson. Four mallets is a must for this piece and experience in independent use of these mallets is necessary before beginning the work.

Drum Set

Several of the drum set method books offer snare drum studies which also include drum set technique. These include *Rudiments to Rock* (Warner Brothers) by Carmine Appice, *Complete Instruction in Jazz Ensemble Drumming* (Studio PR) by Jake Jerger, *Gamut* (Chappell Music Co.) by Randy May, and *Drum Styles* (Amsco Music Publishing Co.). *Rudiments to Rock* is a good basic snare drum technique book which proceeds from basic snare drum rhythms to a beginning rock style. Unfortunately, only rudimental rolls are taught and there is nothing on flams. *Complete Instruction* is primarily a drum set book with emphasis on materials at the fundamental and intermediate levels, but it does include some advanced music. *Drum Styles* and *Drum Techniques*, both by Norman Grossman, are excellent books for the high school set player. Not only do they present basic techniques, but more importantly, they place a practical emphasis on chart reading and stylized playing. This is a definite aid in creating a diversified drum set player who will be able to play the many styles encountered in jazz/rock ensembles. In addition, the texts give sample rhythm patterns and suggestions on how to interpret the typical chart. Many styles of playing are covered in the jazz and rock idioms as well as the more traditional styles from mambos to Greek folk music.

For pure technique building, Joel Rothman's books will be helpful. For example, *Take A Break* (JR Publications) has some useful fills for accent figures that place hi-hat beats on top of snare and bass drum beats. This creates many different overlays allowing a drummer to compose hundreds of different rock patterns.

Flitation (Southern Music Co.) written by Dennis G. Rogers, fulfills the title's name with a fast moving, energetic flow from beginning to end. Because the hi-hat is found only in six measures, there may be a printing error in the score. The piece is a possible contest solo for the high school student.

Many of the solos and studies mentioned here are published by small companies whose material is sometimes hard for the instrumental director to find. Studio 4 Productions published several fine yet very difficult works for marimba and timpani as well as reprints of Clair Omar Musser's works in clearer editions. Another new company, Permus Publications, has printed quality marimba solos for intermediate and advanced players. Music for Percussion, HaMaR Percussion Publications, JR Publications, Award Music Co., and Paul Price Publications are all companies listing a variety of works that should be of interest to educators.

The most complete and up-to-date listing of solo and ensemble music for percussion (no method books) is available from the Percussive Arts Society. Published in 1977, *Solo and Ensemble Literature for Percussion* shows the number of required players and the level of difficulty.■

Drummer Confidence

Ed Soph

Very often a school stage band director will rehearse the reeds and brass down to the finest detail and merely give his drummer a cryptic command like "swing." The young fellow is probably already confused by the frightening array of drums and cymbals his parents gave him last Christmas and being told to "swing" doesn't help matters. Rather than make a mistake, he retires to a low-profile, feeling more at ease allowing the director to assume responsibilities that really belong to the drummer. The more he is directed, the more he withdraws, and a timid drummer does nothing to enhance the ensemble. But, there are ways to give your drummer self-confidence even if you yourself cannot sit behind the drums and "swing." It is mostly a matter of using the same teaching techniques with the drummer that you now use so naturally with the wind instrument players.

Reading Notation

First, you can teach your drummer how to read rhythmic notation. As simple and obvious as this sounds, it is too seldom accomplished. You can sing the figures and have the drummer sing them back. Then have him play them, always relating the sounds to the notes on the chart and helping him hear rhythmic patterns. When the mechanics of counting are absorbed into the total technique of hearing, memory and confidence will emerge. After a few playings with repeated associations of notes and rhythms within the framework of the ensemble the drum part should be removed; the chart must not be allowed to become a visual crutch that prohibits full concentration on the music and delays the development of confidence. Neither can the director stifle the growth of the drummer or the ensemble by conducting the group through every measure. The director is there only to count off the chart and give crucial cues and cutoffs.

Listening and Interpretation

After a drummer trusts himself and no longer needs the security of the chart or the director, he will then be ready to learn the important skills of listening and interpretation. The drummer must give the music his undivided attention by listening to himself in relation to the ensemble in order to interpret the music. He must listen in order to make musical use of rhythm, melody, dynamics, phrasing, and the accents and articulations within these areas. He must listen to learn his own technical limitations and be able to play within them. The director can show the drummer what to listen for and teach him how to interpret what he hears just as he taught him how to associate the notes on the chart with sounds and patterns in the ensemble.

One of the first aspects of interpretation that should be taught is dynamic range. After the young drummer has found his confidence, his only dynamic level is probably *fff*. The director can change that by asking him to play as softly as possible, then asking him to play even softer. Have him play a pattern in mid-range dynamics, then execute the same figure loudly. In essence make him aware of the tremendous dynamic spectrum he is capable of playing on the drum set and show him how important it is to use dynamic contrast. Again, the director should vocalize his requests. From a whisper to a shout he can relate this new musical language to the language already familiar to the drummer.

Undoubtedly, there will be a problem with lagging tempo when the drummer plays softly. This can be corrected by simplifying the beat pattern down to the basic beats of the measure. The same is true for loud passages which are usually rushed. In either case the director should not resort to nebulous commands like "keep on top of it" or "lay back."

Phrasing, another important aspect of interpretation, is making either long or short sounds on the drums and cymbals to complement or contrast what is happening in the ensemble. A director should not assume that the drummer knows that his right-hand man is the lead trumpet player, because more than likely he doesn't. Why not give the first trumpet part to the drummer? Ask him to become familiar with all the horn articulations and be able to reproduce them with the sounds available on his set. Again, vocalization by the director and the student can be used. For example, you might have the drummer sing a "doit" and then have him reproduce it on the drums.

The drummer must be made aware of the tonal possibilities of his set in order to relate to a melodic line. He should know the four basic voices: soprano (snare), alto (small toms), tenor (floor toms), and bass (bass drum). He should be shown how those voices can either complement or contrast with the basic ensemble voices. The same approach is necessary to demonstrate rhythmic interpretation or styles. A director can vocalize or clap a rhythm demonstrating how it will enhance the ensemble. This certainly does not require a detailed technical knowledge of the drums; it simply means taking a musical approach to teaching your drummer how to play in an ensemble.

Most young drummers have little difficulty interpreting straight eighth-note rhythms because we have all heard them so much in recorded pop music. Often this is where their knowledge stops. The director can expand this knowledge through the same medium. If it's a jazz band you want, then expose the students to recorded jazz music. Perhaps one period a week should be set aside for listening and discussing. The Smithsonian Collection of Classic Jazz is a good set of records to start with. Begin with early jazz and bring the students up to the present discussing musical roots and showing why jazz is played as it is. You will find that the more the students understand about the music, the more confident they will be when playing it.

Using Basic Books

A good private teacher can be helpful in dealing with technical problems which a director may not have the expertise to solve; but, unfortunately, one is not always available. If this is a problem, use some good basic books, coupled with an intensive listening program, to help the student and yourself. This is by no means a complete list, but it is a helpful beginning: *Drum Set Sight-Reading* and *Latin Rhythms for the Drum Set* by Ron Fink (Alfred Music); *Get Your Fills Together* by Sonny Igoe (Sonny Igoe), and *Stage Band Drummers Guide* by John Pickering (Mel Bay).

Any director can help his drummer become a confident, competent musician. You don't need a detailed technical knowledge of the drums, but you do need to use the teaching techniques with your drummer that you use with the rest of your ensemble. The same principles of musicality apply regardless of the instrument or the style of music being played. ■

March, 1978

Choreography in Multiple Percussion Playing

Karen Ervin

In multiple percussion performance there is the necessity for graceful, relaxed motion in order to create facility and good sound. It is important, particularly in difficult multiple percussion pieces, to plan specific sequences of motion, involving not only the hands and arms, but the torso, legs, and feet, At all times the player should aim for efficiency and freedom of movement. Choreography is the art of planning body movements; it is a necessary concept for the multiple percussion performer.

Multiple percussion music, strictly speaking is any music written for one person playing more than one percussion instrument. It falls into three broad categories. Beginning and many intermediate pieces are usually for two or more drums, with or without accessories (cymbals, woodblock, etc.). Another large group of intermediate to advanced pieces comes from the Paris Conservatory School. These pieces usually require timpani, one or more keyboard instruments, snare drum, and a collection of drums and accessories. Finally, there is a broad category of "setup" pieces which may require any grouping of instruments, up to and including the vast array needed for Stockhausen's *Zyklus* or Etler's *XL Plus One*.

The problems are the same in all types of multiple percussion: moving smoothly, often rapidly, from one instrument to another; producing a good sound on a variety of instruments.

The Setup

Instruments should be set up as close together as possible, without touching. Drums should be at the same height, either in a level position or slightly tilted toward the player. Cymbals and accessories can often overlap the drums slightly.

There are usually a number of different possibilities in setting up. The following simple four-drum line can be played equally well using three different arrangements of drums:

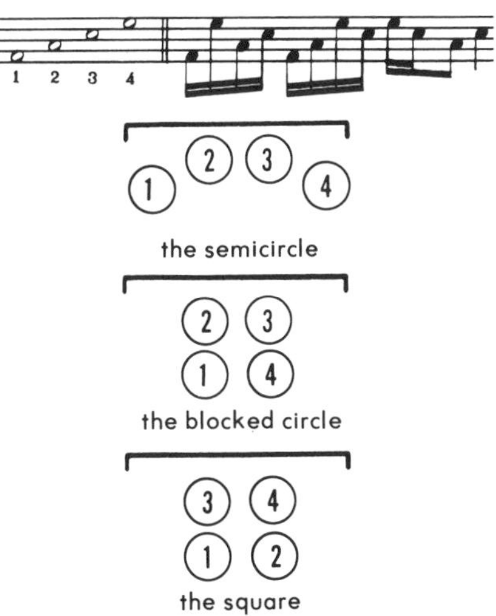

One setup which is undesirable because the two outside drums are too far from the player to be convenient, is often seen in stylized diagrams: (1) (2) (3) (4)

It might be a good idea for a student to experiment with these basic drum setups. Most players seem to prefer the semicircle, because it conforms to the American arrangement of timpani, but certain pieces will work better using the blocked circle or the square.

It is a good idea for each player to determine the correct size of the semicircle for his own height and arm length. He should stand in the middle of the semicircle, then move both hands from drum to drum. He can then place the drums so that they are at the point where the sticks fall naturally. In some cases it is wise for the percussionist to determine the length of his swing and set up an instrument at that point. For example, in a setup using a large number of instruments, the music may require a leap across many instruments from a tom-tom to cowbell; the player should practice a free arm swing from the tom-tom, discover where his stick will end up, and set up the cowbell at that point.

Of course, the more complex the piece, the greater the possibilities (and the limitations) in the setup. The performer will find that as he begins to learn a piece he will make certain changes. As the piece approaches performance, he will continually refine his setup as he learns more and more about the choreography required.

Relaxation

Relaxation is the absolute prerequisite to good motion. The hand must be relaxed, the fingers neither pinching the stick nor holding it too tightly against the palm.

Arm and shoulder muscles must be relaxed so the arm can move freely; the back should be erect but relaxed for free follow-through motion; knees should be slightly bent, feet slightly apart with the weight evenly distributed. All in all, the picture should be one of the confident athlete, muscles toned but never tensed.

The Arc

In order to produce a good sound on almost any percussion instrument, the stick must bounce upward from the head (or bar or metal). In playing a single drum or in a small range on a keyboard instrument, it is desirable that the stick should rebound straight upward.

However, in moving from one instrument to another the shortest possible distance should be covered, without losing the good sound resulting from an upward bounce. The ideal form of motion, therefore, is an arc from one instrument to another:

The stick bounces off the drum at a slightly oblique angle, and moves smoothly and without hesitation to the next instrument. This would seem self-evident. However, one of the most common faults seen in beginning or intermediate students is the pattern of motion seen below:

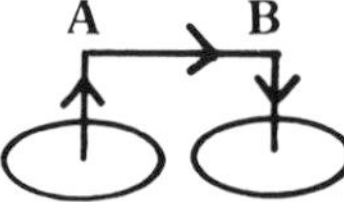

The stick, hand, and arm rise directly to point A, pause slightly, move to point B, and then turn downward to the next instrument. Not only has a greater distance been covered than in the arc, but there have been two pauses, or tiny jerks, in what should be a single smooth motion.

It may seem elementary, but the two approaches will differentiate between the smooth, facile, musical player and the stiff, inhibited performer. This is true not only in multiple percussion but in playing timpani and in advanced keyboard mallet techniques involving large leaps.

A simple exercise in establishing the arc would be to set up drums in the semicircle arrangement and move back and forth between drums 1-2, 1-3, and 1-4, with each hand separately. This should be practiced until the motion feels smooth and natural. Practice should be in slow motion at first, in front of a mirror if possible.

The Swivel of the Wrist

Over a small distance (two adjacent bongo drums, for instance) and particularly at the softer dynamics, a full arc involving the motion of wrist and arm is unnecessary. Instead, a technique considered unorthodox in traditional percussion playing may be used to good effect: the wrist is simply swiveled, with scarcely any horizontal motion of the arm, from one drum to another. When striking the right-most drum with the right hand, the thumb will be up.

This technique is often used by set drummers when moving from cymbal to snare or tom. The swivel should also be practiced between drums with each hand, first in slow motion, then increasing to a fast tempo. It should also be practiced from cymbal to snare, between woodblocks, etc.

Body Follow-through and Anticipation

Percussion players often think only of their hands and forearms as being involved in playing. In fact, correct use of the body itself will improve all types of percussion playing and is essential to good multiple percussion choreography.

This is a difficult area to define, because the line between relaxed follow-through with the body and unnecessary (hence inefficient) motion is a fine one. Loosely described, the percussionist/choreographer, standing with the weight evenly distributed, in a relaxed but athletic posture, allows the motion of the hands and arms to be followed by the body, with some bending of the knees or hips or turning of the torso.

Not only is body follow-through necessary for smooth playing, but there are many instances in which body anticipation can help smooth out a difficult change of instruments. The percussionist should shift his weight, and in some cases take a step toward the next instrument to be played, while his hands and arms remain in their original position. Then the hands and arms will follow the movement of the body toward their destination:

It is difficult for the performer to get a clear picture of his own body motion. Videotaping is the answer; practicing in front of a mirror may help. Percussionists who are not naturally supple and graceful might consider some type of movement-training; tai-chi, yoga, and some types of dance have all been tried with excellent results.

Planned Motion

Detailed planning of motion is usually unnecessary for the beginning multiple percussion soloist, because the player can reach all the instruments simply by moving his wrists and forearms. However, planned motion is often needed in orchestra and concert band playing at any level and the beginner should try to move around the percussion section with efficiency.

Planned motion is absolutely essential in many intermediate pieces. Music from the Paris Conservatory School often requires movement from one group of instruments to another and the number of steps and the time allowed to make the move must be calculated.

It is in advanced setup pieces that motion must be most carefully planned, and slow-motion practice is an excellent way of doing this. The hands, arms, and body perform the required movements like a slow-motion film, following an arc from instrument to instrument exactly as in final tempos. Some analysis of the actual motion required at more rapid tempos will be necessary for this to work: if there is time for only one step, practicing two steps can be fatal.

Another way of practicing choreography is in rapid motion with pauses for orientation: A note is struck on instrument A; the hand, with body follow-through moves rapidly to instrument B, pauses above the instrument for mental catch-up, then strikes B, departs toward C, etc.

Both of the above methods may be used successfully on keyboard instruments when practicing large leaps.

Blind Practice

Practicing arm swings and reaches without watching the instrument to be struck is often important, because during performance it may be impossible to rotate the head rapidly enough to watch all the instruments being used. Both slow-motion and rapid-motion movement with pauses may be used. After a little preliminary checking, leaps should be made, deliberately not looking at the instrument, even though there is time to do so at practice tempos.

Unorthodox Postures

There are times when unorthodox physical postures may be a good solution to a problem. If it is necessary to strike two instruments which are some distance apart, bending both knees may provide the extra arm length needed.

Another position useful in achieving extra distance is one in which one knee is bent forward, rather like a dancer's warm-up exercise. The right knee is bent if the right arm is being extended.

Bends, steps, and arm swings must be worked out in practice; in fact, they should be considered while setting up the piece, if at all possible. Planned motion is the essence of good choreography.

Appropriate Motion on Stage

The mature percussionist will also plan the appropriateness of his motion at all times he is on stage. If the player dashes onto the stage and then begins to play a slow, quiet opening, the audience will be disconcerted. Rapid, jerky stick changes, when unnecessary, may detract from the total performance picture. The performance should be a complete aural and visual experience.

Choreography is a subject which has barely been approached by even the most expert percussionists. Hopefully, the future of our art will include some type of movement training for the percussion player. In the meantime all percussionists should consider and constantly try to improve the quality of their motion in order to gain in technique, improved sound, musicality, and visual effectiveness. ■

April, 1978

The Creative Show Percussionist

Jerrold M. Michaelson

After several years of playing road shows from Broadway musicals to rock "happenings," I have noticed that competent percussion performance is possible only if the percussionist uses a little logic and a lot of creative thinking. It is not enough to possess a fine playing technique and hope that the conductor will supply any necessary musical advice to make the show come alive. You must often take the initiative by using common sense.

Here are a few practical suggestions:

1. Know the instrumentation in advance. A knowledge of basic show instrumentation will enable one to provide beforehand all but the most obscure instruments. The most common instruments needed are orchestral bells, timpani (2), xylophone, tambourine, triangle and maracas/cabasa.

2. Use a logical set-up arrangement. With a quick glance through the music the percussionist can determine the most predominent instrument or instruments in the book, and can arrange the set-up to provide the most efficient playing area.

For example, when timpani is the

major instrument scored, center the drums (usually two) in the front of the entire set-up. In a similar manner center one or more mallet instruments in the front of the set-up when they predominate. In addition all other instruments must be within easy reach. Below are diagrams of two common battery set-ups:

Timpani Predominance

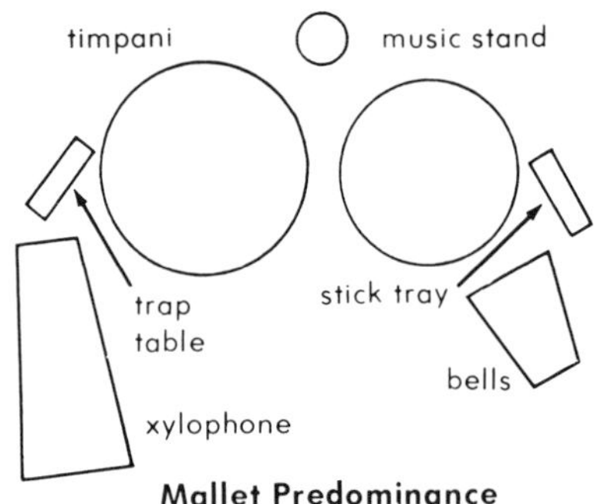

Mallet Predominance

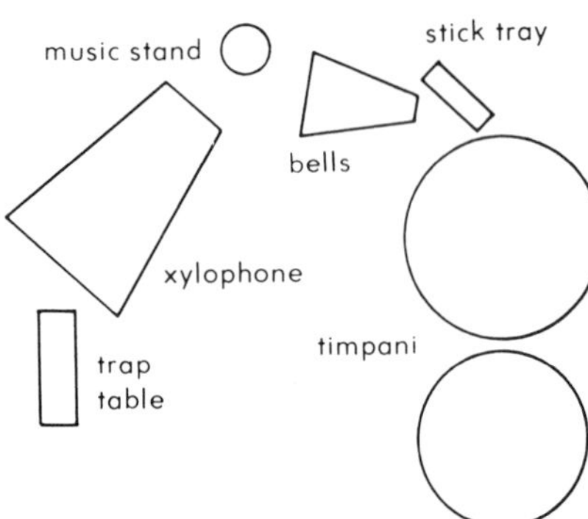

3. Select appropriate mallets. Mallets should be chosen to enable each instrument to project and provide the listener with the best tonal quality possible. For timpani performance wooden and staccato mallets (hard felt) provide the necessary definition of tone for sfz and fp markings. These markings are quite frequent in show books. Softer passages can be accomplished with medium hard mallets. In general, show performance requires one dynamic volume greater than that of symphonic playing.

The use of mallets which provide maximum projection and quality of tone is also important on the xylophone and orchestral bells. Hard plastic mallets are excellent for both, while brass mallets are useful for extreme dynamic requirements on orchestral bells. Wooden mallets on xylophone provide excellent tonal quality, but should be avoided in louder dynamic passages.

4. Have all instruments fine tuned and in position before the rehearsal starts. Many conductors are outraged, and rightly so, when they must wait for the percussionist to finish his set-up or to tune.

5. Always bring a pencil. Conductors may list changes which should be noted or helpful comments can be jotted down, enabling the percussionist to avoid embarrassing mistakes in the performance.

6. Know what to leave out. Many books have been arranged by musicians unaware of basic percussion problems, i.e. rapid passages of double stops or unrealistic instrument changes. Extremely rapid passages are handled by playing only at cadence points or by augmenting the basic figures. If instrument changes are problematic the percussionist should enter at the next phrase, not in the middle.

7. Contemporary show material requires that the timpanist tune with the precision and speed of the symphonic player while experiencing much louder music about him. He must, therefore, note pitch changes carefully and take every occasion to check for accuracy.

8. Timpani muffling is also a technique which should not be taken lightly. As in symphonic performance no sound must last longer than written. In show playing when percussion instruments are often electronically amplified, proper muffling can be critically important. ■

May, 1978

Multiple Percussion on the March

Bob Houston

Many directors want to incorporate multiple percussion into their programs, but are understandably bewildered by the numerous products that are available, and are frankly not sure just how to incorporate the section into their band. For many years a traditional percussion section consisted of one bass drum, snare drums, cymbals and perhaps a bell lyre. Later, for added color, the tenor drum was employed. The section was primarily a functional one; its main purpose was to keep time and aid marchers. The snare drums provided most of the rhythmic interest and the tenor drums provided support with a contrasting, usually simpler rhythmic pattern. In essence this kind of percussion section is a multiple percussion section, but the term (as used today) has much wider ramifications than just a wide assortment of percussion instruments.

Multiple percussion sections perform many different musical lines at the same time, sharing the interest between families of tuned instruments. The single bass drum has been replaced by several, each of a different size and of a different pitch. The tenor drum is all but obsolete; in its place are multiple-pitched double and triple timp-toms. Bells, xylophone, and chimes have been added and function as an independent melodic cell. Timpani are incorporated to provide additional harmonic support, and all of this sonority is combined with color provided by different sets of cymbals and percussion accessories that include cow bells, tambourines, woodblocks and shakers, to mention a few. In the traditional percussion section the main importance is placed upon a single rhythmic and textural line; the multiple percussion section creates a contrapuntal texture. This is not to imply that the snare drum's importance has been diminished, for it still constitutes the backbone of the section.

The Snare Drum

The standard marching snare drum still remains 12″x 15″, but manufacturers in the last few years have upgraded the quality of this drum size considerably. To accomodate the increased tension placed upon the plastic drum head, it became necessary to make the shell thicker. Many marching snare drums are now fabricated from five-ply plywood with heavy-duty lug casings to withstand the tremendous pressures resulting from tightly-tuned heads. The preferred choice for snares is still gut. Such snares should be treated with shellac once a year to help resist stretching from excessive moisture. Plastic batter heads for marching snares need to be at least 13 mil. thick and should be tuned extremely tight. The snare head should be just slightly looser than the batter head to allow for greater snare response. The gut snare should be tight but not so tight as to produce a tom-tom-like sound when the drum is played softly. The snare should be tight enough, however, so that the resultant sound at forte will be crisp and sharp. Use very little drum muffling, relying instead on the reinforced batter head with circles of plastic affixed to the center of the head to absorb any undesirable ring. If additional muffling is required, a felt strip no wider than two inches can be run under the batter head on one side of the drum.

Snare Drum Tuning

An inadequate tuning procedure is the single greatest problem of most marching band drum sections. The snare drums are often tuned too loosely, with the result that precision and clarity suffer. The drum must be in tune with itself. Each lug must have equal tension on it, such that a stick struck on the head approximately one inch from the tension rod will produce the same pitch all around the drum. It is vital that all of the 12" x 15" drums be tuned exactly the same in order to achieve a unified sound. The only time it might be advisable to tune snare drums differently is when two different sized drums are used. For example, a fresh sound can be achieved by using a smaller marching snare (12" x 14") with wire snares in conjunction with 12" x 15" drums equipped with gut snares. A ratio of two wire snare drums to three or four gut drums would be practical, giving the depth and power of gut combined with the high bright sound of wire snares. The combining of these two drum sizes can provide economical advantages because you may be able to get by with existing equipment and add only a few new snare drums rather than make a costly move at one time for all new snare drums.

Most snare drummers use a stick that approximates the diameter of a 3S. Some may wish to add weight and shift balance by adding tape to the stick, but the basic stick needs to be the same for each player. If your snare drum line consists of three or more drummers, and if your drums are in good condition, there will be no need for excessive force to produce enough volume to balance the band. Today's snare drum is capable of projecting far more sound with much less energy. With excessive force you lose precision and control without improving musical sound.

The Bass Drum

For many years the scotch bass drum was useful for most marching conditions. The 26" or 28" head attached to a 10" shell provided an adequate bottom for the band. With the advent of pitched bass drums, it has become necessary to widen the shell to provide more depth to the sound. Different sized drum diameters have been developed to produce a wide pitch range. It is not unusual to see a large corps perform with four different bass drums, each with an independent musical part. If your percussion section contains more than twelve players, you might consider using three bass drums tuned approximately a fifth apart in the following sizes: 34" or 32", 28", and 24".

Since the purpose of the wider shell for bass drums is to provide for a more resonant tone and greater depth to the sound quality, don't waste your money and proceed to fill the bass drum with newspapers, chicken feathers or felt strips. The least amount of muffling is the best. The most effective way to control excessive ring is to affix small square patches on the outside of each head. For such patches, use a mole skin or foam pad backed with adhesive. These pads should be a maximum of 4" x 6" for the 32" or 34" bass drum and a minimum of 2" x 3" for the 24" bass drum. These pads should be placed about three inches from the rim in the upper quadrant of the drum closest to the performer's body. It is important that bass drum head tension be uniform and both heads should be of the same pitch.

Bass Drum Tuning, Beaters

Always tune bass drums and all percussion used outdoors from a distance (at least twenty-five yards) and preferably in a setting similar to the intended performance site. Bass drums should be tuned approximately a fifth apart with the largest drum producing as low but as full a sound as possible. Do not strive to produce a tone that is a identifiable pitch, as it will distract from the tonality being played by the rest of the band. Most corps prefer transparent plastic bass drum heads with no reinforcement in the center.

The choice of beaters can vary, but one must remember that the larger the drum, the larger the beater head. Wooden mallets are not desirable because the pitch is obscured by the impact sound. Felt mallets at least 2" across provide the best sound for today's marching percussion. Each player needs two mallets.

Mutliple bass drums can represent a considerable expense, and there are alternatives to all new equipment which may be considered. If you have a small section and have customarily used a single bass drum, retune the drum to the specifications discussed above and use a drum-set bass drum as the second marching bass. The 20" or 22" bass drum will have a shallow sound, but it will serve as a compromise until your budget allows for the purchase of another marching bass.

Drum Shells

One must remember that although chrome-clad shells may have visual appeal over pearl shells, there are several liabilities. The chrome drums are considerably heavier, which might be of great concern to your younger players. They are also easily dented and scratched and are much more difficult to keep clean. Also, in most instances they are also more expensive. Pearl shells on the other hand are lighter, less expensive and easier to maintain. Perhaps a combination of chrome snare drums with pearl bass drums and timp-toms would give you the best combination of assets and liabilities. When you are building the inventory of your multiple percussion equipment, think carefully about the whole picture of what your eventual needs will be, and even though you may need to purchase your drum equipment over several years, careful planning will save you a great deal of expense.

The Timp-Tom Unit

Probably the most distinguishing mark that separates a traditional drum section from a multiple percussion section is the timp-tom unit. Available in double or triple combinations, the timp-tom is basically a glorified section of tenor drums with tonal capabilities. The most popular arrangement is to incorporate three timp-tom units, each unit consisting of a 14", 16" and 18" drum. The drums are mounted with the 18" drum on the player's left, the 16" drum on the player's right and the 14" drum in the middle. This arrangement provides for relatively equal physical balance. The drums are usually tuned to major or minor triads, Although most manufacturers offer different sized combinations of triple timp-toms the tenor timp-tom unit is the most popular, and it contains the sizes listed above. If you have funds for multiple sets of timp-tom units it is advisable to purchase the same sized units and use them in unison.

Tuning timp-toms requires extra care because the smaller drums are less resonant. Be sure that equal tension is placed on each lug and that the head when struck lightly close to the rod, produces the same pitch all around the drum.

It is recommended that the timp-tom players have a variety of sticks to effect different tonal qualities. Stick bags are designed for this purpose and can easily be carried on the drum or on a belt. Three sets should be sufficient: hard felt for general playing, soft felt for rolls, and wooden for articulate sections (not snare drum sticks).

If your budget does not permit the purchase of timp-toms, you can make a fairly satisfactory substitution by converting tenor drums. It is a relatively simple procedure to remove the bottom heads and mount two drums on a carrier. Although the two drums do not have the tonal depth of the commercial products, they will provide tonal contrast to the snare line.

Marching Timpani

The last membranophones that make up the marching percussion section are timpani, which can provide considerable harmonic support in outside settings. The number depends on the size of the section, but if timpani are used at all, you should have at least two, one 28" or 29" and the other 25" or 26". The timpani should be tuned by a crank mechanism which allows one person to play and tune at the same time. Because of the fact that the timpani are carried by shoulder harnesses, one edge of the drum is close to the body. The most effective playing area is three or four inches from the rim on the far side of the drum. As with timp-toms it is a good idea to have stick choices to produce different timbres.

Keyboard Percussion

With the addition of marching xylophone, bells, and (with increasing frequency) chimes, the percussion section has become a complete musical entity capable of playing harmonic and melodic structures. The addition of these last-mentioned instruments is optional, although more and more percussion sections include them. For the most part, the xylophone and bells should be used to highlight woodwind lines. Only when the percussion section is in solo cadence or in a percussion feature should they be scored independently. Multiple percussion should be used to enhance your band, and care should be taken to score for the section with good musical taste.

Percussion Color Group

The color group includes cymbals, tambourines, woodblocks, cow bells, vibra slaps, and shakers. When employing more than one set of cymbals, it is advisable they be of different sizes so that contrast is evident. For a large section of sixteen drummers, perhaps three cymbal sets would be practical. The most popular sizes include 18", 20" and 22" (heavy weight). Some groups use 26" cymbals, but these large plates should be used sparingly, being reserved for loud accents. If you have players for two sets of cymbals, one cymbal can function as a hi-hat playing off-beats while the other is used for emphasizing musical climaxes.

Most of the accessories can be handled by players of other percussion instruments simply by mounting them on the drums. For example, a cow bell and woodblock can easily be mounted on the snare drum, and tambourines can be carried by timp-tom players or keyboard performers. Shakers are also easily handled by keyboard players as both hands are usually free.

Field Placement

Where are you going to put all of this percussion equipment on the field and how are you going to incorporate it into your show? It is vital that a multiple percussion section stay together on the field. To do this, the most effective placement is to assign them as a floating unit which works primarily at mid-field between the hash lines. The bass drums are placed at the back of the section, and while on the march the heads are pointed at the audience. This insures that the maximum sound reaches the listener. Cymbals can be placed with the bass drums, providing a single rank.

The snare drum line is most effective when placed in a single rank in front of the bass drum. The timp-toms and timpani can be placed at an angle opposite each other and a little forward of the snare line. The keyboard instruments should be together, perhaps behind the timpani, so that they might be of tuning assistance if necessary. For important keyboard passages, they can be brought into position in front of the snare drums, or in front of the entire band.

As long as it is together, the floating unit can do simple drills and function effectively within about a five yard radius. Remember that much of the equipment is bulky and hard to maneuver, therefore it is best to leave intricate drill steps to other sections of the band, allowing the percussion to maintain a solid rhythmic line. If your show calls for a percussion feature, have the percussion section move forward, in front of the hash mark while the rest of the band executes a marching drill.

Corps-Style Scoring

In writing for the percussion section remember that the bigger the drum, the fewer the notes. Although the drum line should be contrapuntal, avoid the excessive use of several pitched drum parts sounding at once; keep the contrapuntal lines rhythmically restrained. It is not advisable to split the section into many separate and non-matching rhythmic parts. When possible, substitute triplet and sextuplet patterns for rolls in the snare drums to achieve greater precision. Try to develop two, four, and eight measure sections which can be adapted to several different tunes. This saves time and improves the prospect of good precision.

If you have weak snare drummers in your line, try to avoid writing those rudiments or patterns which leave them vulnerable. Simplify the snare line and dispense with rhythmic complexity. A series of consecutive eighth notes played precisely will be far more acceptable than three different concepts of a multiple bounce roll. Write snare drum lines that enhance the strong points in your section.

Finally, and most importantly, develop the multiple percussion section as a musical unit within the band whose primary responsibility is to enhance the total musical concept. Use the complete section only when it fits musically, to enhance rather than distract from the music being played. Simplicity and precision are the building blocks for a fine percussion section. ■

Suggested Multiple Percussion Dispersion

No. of Players	SD	BD	TT	Timp.	Bells	Xyl.	Cym.
1	1						
2	1	1					
3	2	1					
4	2	1					1
5	2	1	1				1
6	2	2	1				1
7	3	2	1				1
8	3	2	2				1
9	3	2	2				2
10	3	2	2	2			1
11	3	2	2	2	1		1
12	3	2	2	2	1		2
13	3	3	2	2	1		2
14	3	3	2	2	1	1	2
15	4	3	2	2	1	1	2
16	4	3	3	2	1	1	2
17	4	3	3	2	1	1	3
18	4	3	3	3	1	1	3
19	5	3	3	3	1	1	3
20	6	3	3	3	1	1	3

Drum Tension and Muffling Techniques

David Levine

In attempts to alter the sound of drums to suit diverse musical styles, some manufacturers have designed new drums and developed new construction materials. But rather than having a different drum for each style, it makes more sense to change what is easiest to change on any drum: the tuning, including tension and muffling. Drums sound differently according to the size and shape of the room in which they are played. Rock drums shouldn't be expected to sound like orchestral ones, and drums will often sound different to the audience than they do to the player. The point is that the drummer must know enough about his instrument to be able to cope with diverse playing situations. Attack and decay (initial contact and duration of tone), projection (the ability of the sound to carry or cut through), relative pitch, and stick response can all be controlled by careful tuning.

There are two major areas to be concerned with in the tuning of a drum: tension and muffling. Tension adjustment includes how high or low the drum should be within its tonal range, how tight the head needs to be for the desired response, and what the relationship should be between the two heads of a double-headed drum. Muffling includes the type and amount of muffling or muting needed to achieve the desired decay time, clarity of attack and desired filtering of overtones.

Tuning: Individual Head Tension

The most important step in tuning the drum head is to be certain it is mounted so that it is evenly tensioned, or "level." Leveling off the head and setting the collar (the portion of the head between the edge of the drum and the counterhoop) will insure the best musical sound and longest, most productive life from the head.

To level the head, tighten each tension screw the same number of turns, so that all tension points are the same in pitch. Check each pair of opposing lugs and then check each individual lug, going around the drum clockwise. For drums with an odd number of tension screws first check every other one before going around the drum. When this is correctly done the drum will be in tune with itself.

Relative Head Tension (Tom-Toms and Bass Drums)

On any two-headed drum you have a beating head and a vibrating head. The relative difference in tension and pitch between the two heads will determine not only the timbre that the drum will produce, but also its resonance. When the beating head is tighter in relation to the vibrating head, the drum will have more attack sound, less resonance, better rhythmic clarity, and the sound of the top head will dominate. When the vibrating head is tighter than the beating head, there will be less attack sound, more resonance, better projection, and the sound of the bottom head will dominate.

Relative Head Tension (Snare Drums)

Relative head tension on snare drums comes under separate rules because it has two heads of different thicknesses which have different functions than the heads on bass drums or tom-toms. When the top head is struck, the bottom head will cause the snares to vibrate. Thus it is generally more advisable to use a thinner head on the bottom for better response. I feel the best way to attain a crisp snare sound is to have the bottom head tighter than the top.

There is no firm rule as to what the tension relationship between the two heads should be; the player should decide how much that difference must be in order to achieve the sound he wants. For a less bright sound the snare head may be loosened so that it is even looser than the top head (though in general I do not recommend this). If the snares vibrate excessively when other drums or instruments are played the sympathetic vibrations that cause this reaction may be controlled by changing the relative difference of the two heads so that the drum is less resonant. Unwanted vibration may also be controlled by proper muffling (see section on muffling).

Tightening or loosening the snares themselves is another way to alter the crispness of the snare drum sound. When the proper snare tension is achieved, the most effective way of changing the overall sound of the snare drum is to adjust the tension of both heads by the same amount.

Drumset and Section Tuning

In all families of musical instruments there are high, middle, and low voices. The bass drum, tom-tom, and snare drum are the corresponding voices of the drum section. This order should be maintained for the fullest musical sound from the drums. Within these three voices some variation is common. The important concept, both musically and percussively, is to keep the lowest voice low, the highest voice high, and the middle voice in the middle. In this way the overall set or section will cover as much of the tonal spectrum as possible, while also providing the rhythmic foundation that is essential to each musical style.

Tuning the drums to specific pitches, or maintaining certain intervallic relationships around the drums are two ways to make sure that these ideas are carried out. But, since it is the sound rather than the means of achieving that sound that is important I prefer to leave the choice of method to the discretion of the person tuning, playing, or directing the drums.

Muffling the Drums

Drums, like other instruments, have a fundamental pitch and a related series of overtones. Different types of heads and methods of tensioning modify the sound of the drum by making the fundamental pitch and certain partials prominent. In general a prominence of low overtones can be heard over long distances and a prominence of high overtones adds a brighter sound which cuts through the thickest musical scoring. Anything that comes in contact with the drum head will muffle it and alter the overtones that are projected. Muffling may consist of an internal muffler, tape, cloth, a brushed surface coating, a laminated patch, or a hole cut in the head. Drum heads with varying degrees of muffling built into them are also available. In general, drums used in the field, concert, and for general playing will require the least muffling; popular drums, more; and those used in studio recording situations, the most. Muffling can be done on either the beating head, vibrating head, or both. Muffling the beating head affects the quality of the sound; muffling the vibrating head affects the quantity or resonance of the sound.

Internal Muffling

Internal tone controls supplied on most drums are effective in situations where minimal muffling is required. Since they work only in one small area and push opposite to the direction of the head as it is being struck, other methods are often more desirable. Felt or cloth strips placed under the head and stretched across the drum reduce head vibration significantly and are generally recommended for medium-size bass drums and large tom-toms. Newspaper, foam rubber, blankets, and pillows placed inside these drums may absorb sound without necessarily coming in contact with the head.

External Muffling

External tone controls that clip onto the drum hoop are commercially available. They alleviate the problem of opposing the motion of the head but they still affect only one small area of the head. Felt, leather, or cloth pads work in much the same way as external tone controls, although they usually provide a larger muffling area. Tape (adhesive, cloth, duct or masking) is the most versatile means available for muffling because the amount, size, shape, color, and design is left up to the player. Tape can also be easily altered for changing situations. The tape may be applied at only a few places around the edge of the drum head or around the entire edge of the head; it may also be used at the center of the head or in strips going from the center to the edge.

Other Muffling Methods

One of the most popular methods of muffling consists of using paper or cloth toweling, cut to form square or rectangular patches, then taped to the inside or outside of the drum head. They are placed between the center and edge of the head depending on the amount of muffling required. The closer such patches are placed to the center, the greater the muffling effect will be. One or more patches may be used on each drum. Obviously, if the patch is on the inside of the head it will not get in the way of your sticks; it will, however, be less accessible for modification or removal.

Cutting out a part of the head reduces its vibration. The larger the area cut out, the less the head will vibrate. Using a compass or pot lid, trace a circle on the nonbeating head, then use scissors (not a razor blade) to cut out the circle. This technique is most useful on bass drums but can also be used on tom-toms. This method is the least flexible and most final of all muffling procedures: once a portion of the drum head is removed, it cannot be replaced again. Remember, you can always increase the size of the hole if the sound is not satisfactory, so start small and enlarge the hole as necessary.

Another form of muffling and one that is often overlooked is to reduce resonance by loosening the head to the point where it hardly vibrates. This is often successful if carried out on the nonbeating head. Still another method is to loosen one or two tension points on the top head.

Like all musicians, percussionists must deal with a variety of musical styles. Proper muffling and tension techniques are among the most useful ways to modify the percussion sound to enhance the musical effect. ■

Drum Tension/Muffling

KEY
RHT = Relative Head Tension
BHT = Beating Head Tighter
SH = Snare Head
VH = Vibrating Head
BH = Batter or Beating Head
ITC = Internal Tone Control
E = Both Heads Equal
BHL = Beating Head Looser

DRUM USE/SIZE	Use	TUNING TENSION	RANGE	RHT	MUFFLING TECHNIQUE	EFFECT
FIELD & PARADE: Marching Band (MB), Drum Corps (DC), Pipe Band (PB)						
Snare (10 x 14 or 12 x 15)	MB:	Med	Mid	BHT	Internal tone control, cloth strip.	Deep, moderately crisp snare sound.
	DC,PB:	Tight	High	BHT	Remove ITC, use cloth patch of equal size taped to underside of head.	Crisp, dry sound; brighter than MB.
Tom-tom: Tenor (12 x 15 or 17)	MB:	Med	Mid	BHL	Cloth strips	Dull thud.
Timp-toms (various combinations 9-16 x 13-28, Dual or Tri)	DC,PE:	Med-Tight	Mid-High	E	Little to no muffling.	Clean sound with a more prominent pitch center.
Bass Drum: 14 x 22-30	MB:	Med	Mid	E	Cloth strips	Deep, semi-dry sound.
10 x 26, 14 x 22-30, 16 x 30 or 32	DC:	Med-Low	Mid-Low	E	Cloth patch taped to underside of head 1/4 of way from bottom to top	Well-defined tonal center with full resonance and power.
6-10 x 26 or 28	PB:	Med-High	Mid-High	E	Cloth strips	Short, dull sound.
CONCERT: Symphony Orchestra (SO), Concert Band (CB), Percussion Ensemble (PE), Solo, Chamber Music (CM)						
Snare (3-7 x 14, 12 x 15)		Tight	High	BHL	ITC, tape. To muffle entire surface of head evenly place a circle of tape around drum at edge.	Brittle, very crisp sound.
Tom-tom: Single head (5 x 6, 5 x 8, 6 x 10)		Med-Tight	Mid-High		Little to no muffling	
Single or double head (8 x 12, 9 x 13, 10 x 14, 12 x 15, 14 x 16)		Med	Mid	E or BHT	ITC, tape, or cloth patch; depending on amount needed.	Good rhythmic clarity, fair resonance. Should sound rich, full, and deep.
Double head (16 x 16, 16 x 18, 18 x 20)		Med-Low	Mid-Low	E or BHT	As above	More muffling will be needed with the larger drums to equal the resonance of the smaller ones.
Bass drum: 14 x 28-30, 16 x 32-36, 18 x 36-40	CB,SO:	Low	Low	BHL	Hand or knee against head	Carrying power and sustaining ability are important to the orchestral sound. In solo, chamber, and ensemble music more rhythmic precision is called for and the beating head should be tighter.
14 x 24-30, 16 x 32-36	PE:	Med-Low	Mid-Low	BHL/BHT	As above, cloth pads	
14 x 22-28	Solo,CM:	Med	Mid	BHT	Cloth pads, cloth patches	
POPULAR: Heavy Rock (HR), Light Rock (LR), Latin Band (LB), Casual/Pop (C), Big Band (BB), Jazz Combo (JC)						
Snare (5 or 6 x 14)	HR:	Loose	Low	BHL	Tape, pads, or patches (BH or SH)	There are many possible tunings. For rock, a dead sound is desirable. Removing heads, using lots of tape, and loose tensioning is called for. Because a more resonant sound is required for big band and combo work, use more tension and less muffling, and have the vibrating head tighter. Conga drums, timbales and bongos are tuned tightly so that they can cut through the other Latin instruments and the rest of the ensemble.
	LR,C,LB:	Low-Med	Low-Mid	BHL	Less, but as above.	
	BB:	Med	Mid	BHL	Still less as above, ITC.	
	JC:	Med-Tight	Mid-High	BHL	Least muffling, ITC.	
Tom-tom sizes same as "Concert"	HR:	Loose	Low	BHT	Tape, pads, patches, remove bottom head.	
	LB,C,LR:	Low-Med	Low-Mid	BHT		
	BB:	Med	Mid	E/BHL	Light tape, ITC.	
	JC:	Med-Tight	Mid-High	BHL	ITC, no muffling.	
Bass drum: 14 x 22-26	HR:	Loose	Low	BHT	Remove head, cut head, foam rubber, pillow, blanket, tape.	
14 x 20-24	LB,C,LR:	Loose	Low	BHT		
14 x 18-24	BB:	Med	Mid	BHT/E BHL	Cut head, felt strips, tape.	
14 x 18-22	JC:	Med-Tight	Mid-High	E/BHL	Little muffling, felt, tape.	

Cymbal Playing Technique

Larry C. Jones

Figure 1 How to Attach the Cymbal Strap

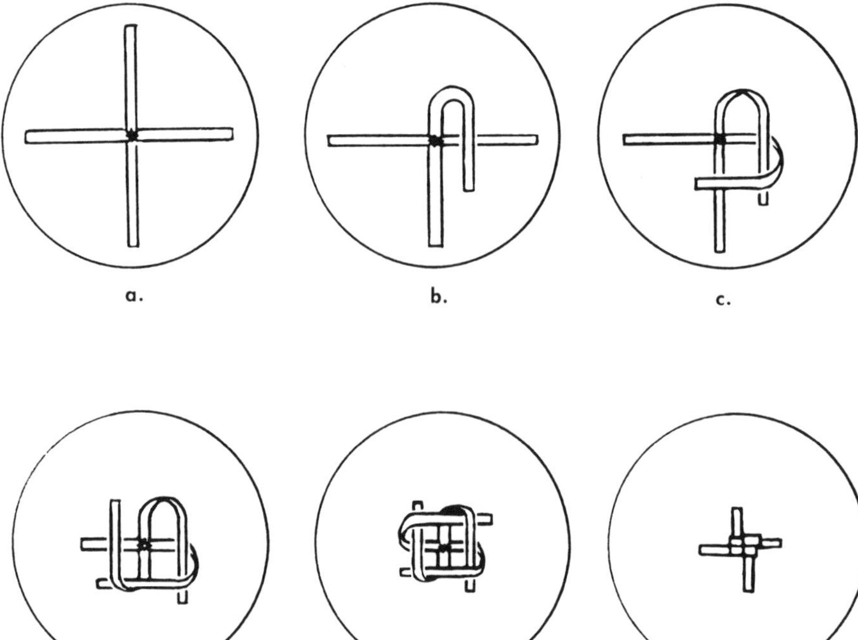

Figure 2 Grip

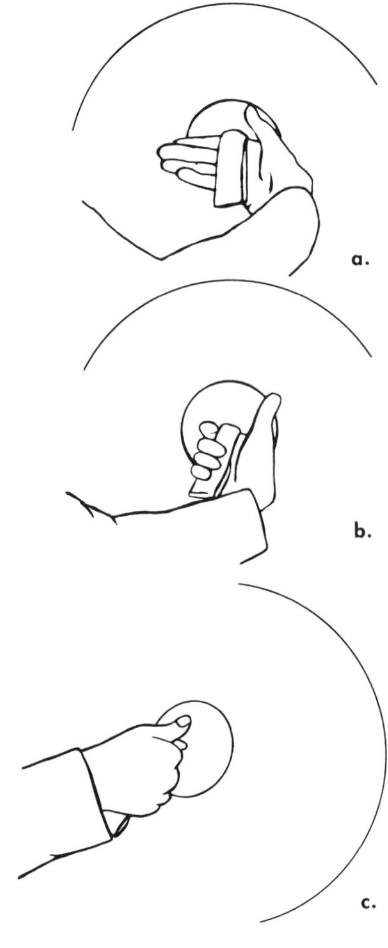

Young percussionists often are not taught the proper techniques of playing cymbals. This can result in poor musical interpretation of percussion parts and possible damage to the instruments. The cymbals must be practiced as any other musical instrument until the student is able to produce a desirable tone and interpret cymbal parts correctly. Only then will the student percussionist be an asset to the ensemble.

Holding the Cymbals

Many cymbal holders are available to the percussionist, but the best type is a rawhide strap which is tied with a cymbal knot (see figure 1); it permits a pair of cymbals to produce maximum vibration because there is very little contact between the strap and the cymbal's surface. A three-inch leather or plastic pad may be used on larger cymbals to give the player a more comfortable, stable grip. However, such pads should not be used on small cymbals because they will muffle the vibrations slightly. Soft lamb's wool pads should not be used as they will reduce the cymbal's resonance and deaden the sound. Nor should wooden handles and rigid twirling devices be used; they will eventually produce a crack in the bell and ruin the cymbals.

A player should place the strap across the palm of his hand and curl his fingers around it. His thumb should be pressed either into the cymbal or into the pad when it is used, giving him control of the instrument (see figure 2). His hand should not be placed through the loop of the strap because he would not be able to change quickly to another percussion instrument if the music demanded it.

The right cymbal is held slightly below the left with both cymbals forming a 45-degree angle to the floor. The left cymbal is held stationary while the right cymbal is struck against it. The top edge of the right cymbal should strike the top of the left to prevent a vacuum of air between the cymbals that will cause a choked sound. After the full crash, the cymbals should immediately be drawn apart. The follow-

Illustrations from: Payson, A. *Techniques of Playing Bass Drum, Cymbals, and Accessories.* Park Ridge, Illinois: Payson, 1971, p. 37. Reprinted with permission.

through stroke is important because it projects the sound toward the audience. As the stroke ends, the inside surface of both cymbals should be turned, pointed forward, and held in this position for the full value of the note.

Cymbal-isms

In general cymbal crashes should ring the full value of the written note. The cymbals are dampened at the end of the note's duration and on rests by bringing the edges against the player's chest or upper arms. A note marked *Lasciar Vibrare, L. V.*, or *Let Vibrate* indicates that the tone should ring and decay naturally without any dampening of the sound. *Secco* or short notes require the player to quickly muffle both cymbals after the stroke. The cymbals should not be dampened by pressing and holding them together unless you want the special sound effect of imitating the hi-hat cymbal.

A double cymbal roll is produced by holding the cymbals loosely together and rotating one against the other in a circular motion. If this effect is to be used, the composer will make a conventional roll notation preceded by the *a*2 sign, or the instructions may be written out for the player.

The swish or *Zischen* is described by Payson as a, "very delicate color. . . [that is] usually scored at a soft dynamic level. It is performed by lacing the edge of the right cymbal on the inside face of the left cymbal, near the bell, and sliding it upward across the grooves of the left cymbal. . . . Ordinarily, the swish is started before the printed note, and is timed so that the cymbals separate at the beginning of the note value."[1]

Some composers score in such a way that the bass drum and cymbals must be played by the same person. When this occurs a cymbal mount is attached to the bass drum and a cymbal is placed on it, playing side up. The player can then strike the mounted cymbal with another cymbal held in the left hand while holding the bass drum beater with his right hand. Although some composers, including Gustav Mahler, occasionally scored for this technique, it is seldom used today. In addition to the inferior tone quality of the cymbals caused by their being mounted on the bass drum, it is difficult for the player to dampen all three instruments quickly. The biggest drawback to this mounting is that it requires the player to move the cymbal a short distance with his left hand while the right hand moves a bass drum beater of a different weight a much greater distance. This makes a simultaneous stroke at the proper dynamic level a very difficult technique to master.

Suspended or Hanging Cymbals

The suspended cymbal is another percussion instrument which is often played incorrectly. This is partially due to the fact that composers seldom provide any instruction concerning the type of sound that should be played. The size and weight of the cymbal as well as the type of mallet to be used will affect the sound; none of this information is notated on the percussion part. The conductor and the percussionist must be aware of the suspended cymbal's many tonal characteristics and decide how the part will best enhance and blend with the ensemble.

Suspending a cymbal. There are two methods of suspending a cymbal. One is to attach a strap to the cymbal and hang it from the strap on a "gooseneck" stand. The other method is to place the cymbal on a pole-type floor stand. Some percussionists claim that the gooseneck stand is the superior method of suspension because the cymbal is allowed to vibrate more freely. However, the stand takes up a great deal of space in the percussion section and makes the cymbal more difficult to control. The difference in tone quality between the two methods is so small that the space problems presented by the gooseneck stand outweigh its tonal advantages.

In using a pole stand, the cymbal rests on a metal disc and felt pad. A wing nut is threaded on top of the stand to prevent the metal disc and felt pad from falling off when the cymbal is not being used. The wing nut must not be so tight that the cymbal is clamped to the felt pad and prevented from vibrating freely. Permanently attached T-shaped snaps can be purchased to replace the wing nut. These are threaded onto the top of the stand and the horizontal bar of the "T" swivels to allow the cymbal to be removed or locked in place. The cymbal snaps serve the same function as the wing nut but they do not have to be removed from the stand in order to remove the cymbal.

The stem of the pole stand passes through the hole of the cymbal. A soft rubber covering around the stem will protect the cymbal hole from damage and will eliminate rattles that sometimes occur when the cymbal is set into vibration.

Suspended cymbals can be played with wood snare drum sticks; a pair of matched triangle beaters; a pair of firm wire brushes; and soft, medium, and hard yarn marimba mallets. Even though suspended cymbal parts will occasionally call for timpani sticks, they should rarely be used. Due to their contact with the hard and often dirty surface of the cymbal, the covering of the timpani sticks wears out quickly. Thus few percussionists will use their expensive timpani sticks on the cymbal even when the part calls for it.

Playing areas. Each suspended cymbal has three playing areas: the bell, the bow, and the edge. The bell is the raised area in the center of the cymbal that is used to produce cowbell effects and bell-like tones. This is the most articulate and the least resonant area of the cymbal. The bow is the area which curves away from the bell and extends to the edge of the cymbal. Most playing is done on the bow in an area one-third of the distance from the cymbal's edge. The sound produced in the bow area is less articulate than that in the bell area but it has more resonance. Percussionists will sometimes move the playing area closer to the bell when a more precise articulation is desired. The edge of the cymbal is the most resonant portion. This makes it possible to play a loud, single note at the edge but not a complex rhythmic pattern. The pitch of the cymbal is lowest at the edge and becomes higher as you play nearer the bell.

Suspended cymbal techniques. The cymbal roll or tremolo is notated either 𝅝 or *tr* 𝅝 and is played with two mallets striking on opposite sides of the cymbal bow. The player should always use a matched grip on the sticks when playing the suspended cymbal roll. If snare drum sticks are used to produce a cymbal roll, a bounce stroke is usually best.

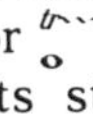

A composition may call for a scraped sound to be produced with a metal object. For this effect a triangle beater is drawn across the ridges of the cymbal usually from the bell to the edge. The player must be careful not to damage the cymbal by scratching the metal with too much force. A coin or large nail will produce the same effect in the absence of a triangle beater.

A sizzle sound can be made by holding a metal object such as a triangle beater on the cymbal while striking the cymbal with a yarn mallet or drum stick. A cymbal can be made permanently into a sizzle cymbal by drilling holes in the bow and inserting steel rivets. There are dangers in making your own sizzle cymbals. Drilling at too fast a rate will overheat the cymbal and cause a crack or split at the point of drilling. The heat can also cause a sonically dead spot that ruins the tone of the instrument. A better solution would be to order cymbals with rivets installed at the factory.

Contemporary Techniques

Many new techniques have been developed for altering the natural sounds of cymbals. It is possible to produce a vibrato on a thin suspended cymbal by playing a roll with one hand while changing the pitch with the other. The cymbal is grasped with one hand at the far edge while the inner edge is pressed into the player's waist. The player bends the cymbal into a bowed shape and gradually returns it to its original shape. At the same time the other hand plays a roll using one mallet on top and another mallet on the bottom of the cymbal.[2]

A cymbal can also be played with a cello or bass bow. The bow is drawn across the edge of the cymbal. Varying the bow pressure and speed will change the resulting sound, and a player can change the harmonics by placing his fingers in different areas of the cymbal while he is bowing.

To produce a unique color effect, place a cymbal upside down on a timpani and put one hand inside the cymbal bell to stabilize it; the other hand strikes the cymbal with a mallet while the foot moves the pedal of the timpani up or down. The effect is that of the cymbal changing pitch.[3]

A cymbal tremolo (not the same as a roll) is produced on a thin cymbal when one hand is cupped, palm down, directly above the bell. The cymbal is struck with a mallet or drum stick and the cupped hand moves rapidly up and down. This technique is rather subtle and will not be effective with heavy instrumentation.

Percussionists are now exposed to many contemporary compositions that require new ways of using cymbals. Experimentation with new techniques, some of which have been described here, will expand the number of tone colors available to performers and composers. ■

1. Payson, A., *Techniques of Playing Bass Drum, Cymbals, and Accessories*, 1971, p. 39.
2. Kahle, Dennis, "Percussion: Cymbal and Gong Techniques," *The Instrumentalist*, May, 1974, P. 34.
3. *Ibid.*, P. 35

September, 1978

Percussion Concerts: Impact and How to Achieve It

Russell Peck

One way to achieve impact is to hit someone over the head. This means doing something obvious and sensational. Consider *Mikrophonie* by Stockhausen, a piece using a gigantic amplified tam-tam. Visually, of course, there is tremendous effect. But such an obvious ploy for recognition stresses superficial impact over a more subtle level of communication. Impact of the sensational type requires more courage than craft. Not that this kind of impact has no value; we need more people with courage.

But there are other ways to achieve impact. Although they are not radical, they too require courage. Performers must accept full responsibility for the concert experience and realize that the concert is their creation exactly as the music is the creation of the composer. The goal of the concert, like the composition, is to project musical thought. If the communication of these thoughts is poor, then there can be no impact.

How can the performer communicate? He must immerse the audience in the concert experience. As soon as members of the audience say, "Hmmm, I'm at a concert, the seats are OK, my shoes are tight, it will be over at 10:30." — you have lost them. They are not in touch, they are bored.

Strategies for Impact

What are specific things that can be done to achieve impact? The first and most important is that ample time must be reserved for the consideration of all technical problems, with every aspect rehearsed until there is precision and reliability in the stage arrangement. Even if you wish to do nothing particularly imaginative with regard to staging, the necessary practical actions should be smooth, dignified, and efficient. This requires the same discipline and attention to detail that are inherent in the preparation of the music.

Consider equipment set-up, a

boring part of many percussion concerts. Can you really expect an audience to devote 15 minutes to watching performers move equipment around a stage, lay out various mallets, and adjust the height of music stands? One basic way to solve the set-up and rearrangement problem is to have multiple set-ups so that the performers move between compositions while the instruments themselves remain stationary. This method has one disadvantage: the idle set-ups are distracting. To correct this, use lighting to focus on one area at a time. Curtains or screens could cover 'all but the instruments in use. Naturally the details of how this is done must be carefully rehearsed, and the smooth movement from one set-up to another must be perfected. My point is that whether or not setting-up and tearing down can be within the definition of music, the art of performance includes everything the audience sees and hears.

There are an infinite number of lighting ideas that are useful to establish atmosphere and enhance the impact a piece has on an audience. Spotlights can be focused on chimes, cymbals, or metal of all sorts. In a darkened space, the ceiling reflections of light focused on vibraphone bars are beautiful, especially when the vibe is being played and the bars are in subtle motion. An inexpensive and very effective technique is to perform with stand lights only. The darkness brings the tactile sound of percussion closer to the listener, the shadows are dramatic, and it is a marvelous relief from relentless full lighting. There are any number of ways to make a provocative array of the instruments and just as many ways to light them. In fact, it is possible to think of the percussion concert with its beautiful and exotic instruments and its visually active performance as an experience in theater as well as music.

Theater includes movement as well as lighting and props. It is not dance motions I am talking about, it is the idea that a person makes designs and patterns in his movements. Percussion players will make a visual design, move and interact with other designs made by other players.

Percussion playing not only has large rhythmical movements in common with dance, but also stage blocking. Players move about the stage, congregating, separating, commanding space. All this can be planned as part of the performance, and its influence can be subtle but effective. A particular playing action might be made more interesting if the player is seen in profile. Or two active but widely separated players can split the focus of the audience and weaken an overall effect, not just visually but musically as well.

When can these techniques be taken to extremes? Whenever you think so. There is no absolute model of "correct" taste. You should be your own judge. Today's audiences respond to a performance that has a strong visual component. If independent percussion performance is to grow, it will do so by realizing more of its visual potential.

Although no analogy can be perfect, I think there is an undeniable similarity between musical pieces and paintings, between concerts and museums. The pictures in a museum have frames, they are not left raw at the edges. Similarly the music compositions should be framed by the concert experience itself. For example, the most crucial time in a concert is before a piece begins because the attention of the audience must be focused on the piece that is about to start. Otherwise the audience will see the mechanics of producing the piece and not hear the music.

All the elements I've mentioned, — set-up, lighting, and visual impact — take time to consider, but they are worth the extra time necessary to be sure the concert is done right. By this I mean not only checking the details of how every eighth note should be played, but also asking yourself if the piece is in the right visual context that will deliver it at full strength to the audience. This may require a look at other arts that share the common ground of visual presentations: theater, dance, design, painting, and sculpture. There is no guarantee of communication in any performance, no surefire method of reaching your audience. But by using impact-ideas to enhance the presentation, chances are good that you will not lose any member of the audience to boredom or indifference. ■

October, 1978

Using Timp-toms Effectively

Mark Petty

The marching timp-tom was introduced by percussion manufacturers in the late 1960s in response to the desires of competitive drum and bugle corps. As soon as these instruments appeared, many traditional marching bands began to purchase them to replace conventional tenor drums. Timp-toms are available in tenor, baritone, and bass ranges. Most successful users feel that only the tenor voice is practical because it does not interfere with the harmonic structure of the wind instrument part of the musical arrangement. The tenor timp-toms function much like the tom-toms of a drum set, as a relative pitch not harmonically related to the wind instruments. The baritone and bass timp-toms have such a clear pitch that they do in fact interfere harmonically. Timpani are superior in sound to baritone timp-toms, and the conventional two-headed bass drum (slightly muffled) has proven to be a more effective instrument than the timp-tom in the bass range.

Timp-tom Sizes

At one time timp-tom sizes were standardized at a 10-inch depth by 14-, 16- and 18-inch diameters. Although this size is useable and time-tested, three innovative variations have recently been made available: 1) scalloped shells (those with the back lengthened and the front shortened), 2) sound projectors (plastic quarter-spheres which fasten to the open end of the drum) and 3) deeper shells (generally only 1 inch less than the head diameter). The first two ideas provide a timbre which increases sound projection. The deeper shells provide greater shell strength for high tension and more resonance for high volume output. Timp-toms are now being offered with smaller head diameters to provide further tonal separation from other pitched instruments and to allow for easier maneuverability. Some groups are also experimenting with more than three drums per player in order to achieve a greater variety of pitches and patterns. The proven 10x14, 10x16, and 10x18 timp-tom is a safe buy and shouldn't be discarded. However, when the time comes to buy a first set of timp-toms or to replace old equipment, the smart purchaser will want to examine the new offerings.

The Carrying Brace

One other proven equipment idea is the carrying brace. Originally timp-toms were carried by slings. This method did not hold the drums steady, and caused awkward marching problems. Today's carrying brace is a definite advantage and should be considered as a necessary part of the instrument and not as an optional accessory.

Tuning Hints

Tuning timp-toms can be a time-consuming task, but it is as necessary as tuning any other band instrument. Timp-toms in fact act much like temple-blocks, taking on the sound of the intervals they are accompanying. Two concepts must be kept in mind when tuning timp-toms: first, each head must be in tune with itself, that is, the head must have the same tension at each tuning rod. This method is exactly like tuning timpani to have a clear, full tone. The second concept is that all heads of the same size must be tuned the same. For example, the 14-inch drum of one set of timp-toms must be in tune with the 14-inch drum of every other set.

In the past, groups experimented with several timp-tom sets, each tuned differently. This practice has been discarded because of the increased sound clutter between each set and the lack of projection of having one set on a part. Most groups now use at least two sets and preferably three or four. Generally, the drums are tuned to minor or major thirds. These intervals are similar to those used by rock drummers with many toms or the symphony player with a multi-tom part. However, marching timp-toms are tuned considerably higher than the drums in either of the preceding examples because of the overall density of rhythms and because the number of players in the ensemble is much greater. Timp-toms should not be dampened because this will reduce their characteristic resonant tone quality. The drums are small enough so that complex musical passages can be articulated without any additional muffling. For the same reason, patch or dot heads are not necessary.

Timp-toms must be re-tuned at the start of every rehearsal and every few hours during a long rehearsal. When several sets of timp-toms are used together, the poor tone quality that often results is actually caused by poor intonation. Because the head loosens while playing, more care is needed to keep timp-toms properly tuned than is necessary for any other marching percussion instrument.

Timp-tom Technique

Timp-tom technique is similar to that used on the snare drum but includes the added factor of moving from drum to drum. In general when several people are playing any unison percussion part, the less movement (arms and stick height) there is, the easier it is to play together. On the other hand outdoor playing with 50 to 200 wind instruments requires substantial volume. To maintain the proper balance under these conditions means that the position of the instruments on the drill field must be selected very carefully. The current trend in marching percussion is to play with only wrist movement, allowing a large number of players to achieve precision. This all-wrist style is particularly appropriate for timp-toms because of the tendency of their sound to distort at high volume levels. In order to maintain a consistent tone quality and minimize drum-to-drum mallet movement, specific playing positions (as shown in figure 1) should be designated. These positions also help maintain a visual uniformity among the players.

Figure 1. Timp-Tom Playing Positions

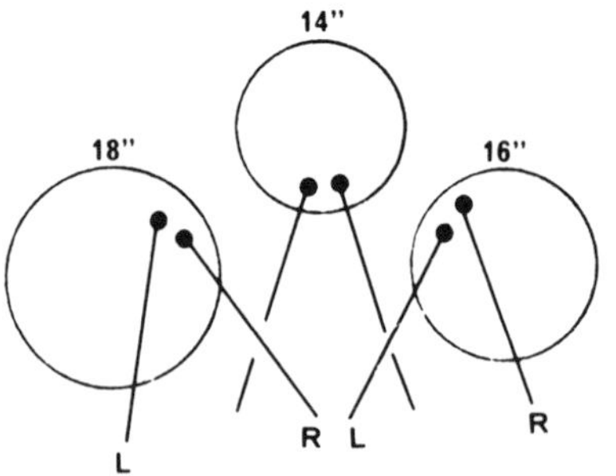

Arranging the Music

In arranging for timp-toms (or evaluating published parts), ask the following questions: 1) is the part playable (i.e., does it lay well or does it require awkward sticking) 2) does the part use tone colors as well as rhythmic effects and 3) does the part make sense within the total percussion ensemble (does it have clashing rhythm patterns or drum parts which are tonally overwritten)?

The basic building blocks for timp-tom music are the common eighth note/sixteenth note patterns (see figure 2). These patterns can be spread across several drums using three techniques: pattern change, accent highlight, and melodic use. Pattern change consists of having each rhythmic fragment played on a different drum (as in figure 3) to add variety of tone color. Accent highlight consists of accents within a rhythmic figure played on another drum and brought out by the tonal change (see figure 4). A special case of combining pattern change and accent highlight is the run-on drum-to-drum pattern where the pattern is dense and the rhythmic effect is achieved through tonal change (see figure 5). Melodic use is having almost every successive note played on a different drum to create a melodic effect (see figure 6). The previous examples are seldom seen in their pure form for any extended length of time, but are used in combination to create a musical statement. An example of a combination of techniques is given in figure 7.

Figure 2. Common Timp-tom Rhythms

a)

b)

c)

d)

e)

f)

g)

h)

i)

Figure 3. Pattern Change

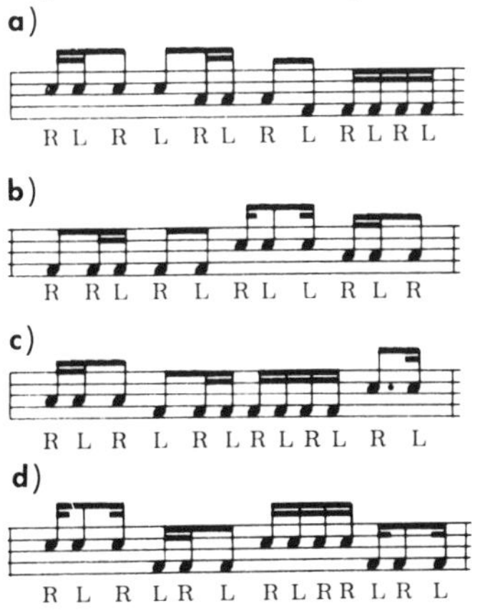

a)

RL R L RL R L RLRL

b)

R RL R L RL L RLR

c)

R L R L R LRLRL R L

d)

R L R LR L RLRR LR L

Figure 4. Accent Highlight

a)

R LR L R LR L RLRL R

b)

RLRL RL R L LR R L

c)

d)

Figure 5. Pattern Change/Accent Highlight

a)

RLRRLRLL RLRL RLRR L

b)

RLRL RLRL RLRL RLRL R

c)

RLRL RLRL RLRL R

d)

RLRL RLRL RLRL RLR

Figure 6. Melodic Use

a)

LRLR L RL R L R L

b)

RLRL RLRL RLRL R

c)

L LR LRLR RLR L

d)

RLRL RL R RL RLRL R

Figure 7. Combination of Techniques

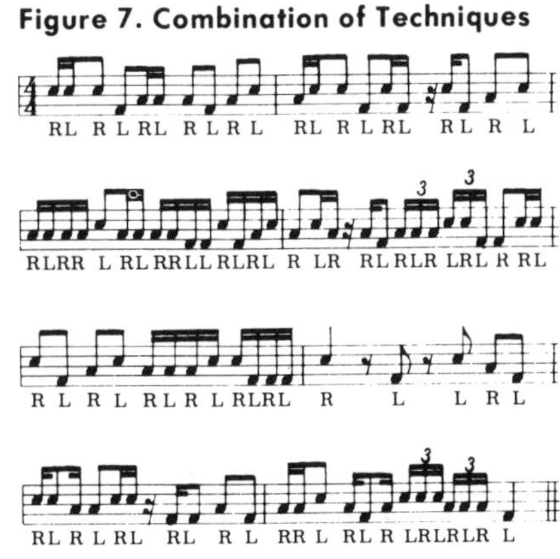

Style, Phrasing, Voicing

Writing for timp-toms must be considered in the context of writing for the entire marching percussion section. The major elements of marching percussion arranging are using the appropriate musical style, phrasing and accenting (for reinforcement, support and interest), and voicing for clarity. For example, timp-toms can be very effective in a legato passage if the part itself is a flowing one (i.e. if it has a constant density of rhythm) and if the instrument is played with soft mallets. In contrast the timp-tom can be very exciting in a driving syncopated situation. It can also function as a Latin-type instrument or as rock tom-toms. Phrasing must make sense within the rest of the arrangement, although phrases can overlap as they sometimes do in the wind parts. Accenting should be similar to the other percussion voices and all parts should follow the general contour of a melody or countermelody line (but usually not both). Rhythmic use can duplicate or expand on the wind line or can create a stylistic background such as Latin, rock, or disco.

Two rules that make life easier for the arranger and band director are to check the overall playability and flow of the part and to write in the sticking for each note. The extra time required for these two steps will be repaid by shorter rehearsal time and cleaner performances.

Some marching band directors become numb and are oblivious to the sound of their percussion section, concentrating only on the wind sound. A band director once justified his loudly pounding, distorted percussion section by saying, "It may not be musical, but it's the only way we can stay together." To this, I would counter "If it's not musical, who cares?" Always step back and listen objectively to the final product and be sure it is not destroyed by unmusical percussion noise. ■

Administering the Marching Percussion Section

Jay A. Wanamaker

Today's marching percussion section has grown considerably from the five-man — snare, tenor and bass drums, cymbal, and bells — section of the past. As the size and importance of the percussion section has increased, so have the responsibilities of the director. Here are some ideas to help the band director save time and money, avoid frustration, and produce a more organized and effective marching percussion section.

Responsibility

Few students will ever take the cost of percussion instruments as seriously as the band director who has to fit these costs into his budget. Two ways that students can be made to feel more personally accountable for their instruments are: 1) Have the school system carry an insurance policy on all instruments with the students paying a rental fee or deposit. 2) Have the school system provide arrangements for a student group policy where the students pay a deposit (premium) for their share of the insurance. The amount would vary according to the instrument's value. At the end of the season all instruments should be inspected and appropriate adjustments made to the deposit, depending on the instrument's condition.

I have found the check-out sheet shown here useful in keeping track of instruments and equipment.

Maintenance

Because of the high cost of equipping the percussion section, instruments should be treated with care to prolong their service to the band. To insure that the instruments are in good condition before being stored at the end of the season, schedule a work day for all percussionists during which some of the necessary repairs can be made. All moving parts — lugs, snare strainers, and marching timpani tuning mechanisms — should be oiled. Adhesive tape used to hold the felt patch inside the tuned bass drum should be changed each season. Drum heads in poor condition should be replaced (before reseating a drum head, make sure that no sharp objects protrude from the rim). Clean drum heads with soap and water or with a commercial window cleaner. Use furniture polish on wooden drum shells; use metal polish on chrome shells. Cymbals should be cleaned with a special polish available from the major cymbal manufacturers. Wooden bass drum rims should be checked each year and repainted if necessary.

Storage

Set aside a specific storage space with large locking cabinets for percussion instruments. Return each instrument to its cabinet after each performance. The storage area should not be located near a source of heat or moisture. Stencil the name of the organization and an identification number on every instrument and case.

Home Remedies

Percussionists can sometimes

Band Department Equipment Check-Out

Instrument Snare Drum **Value** $200.00

Description Chrome - 12" by 15", Ser. # - 1234567

Accessories Case <u>X</u> Sling <u>X</u> Harness

	Date Out	Storage	Property Master	Date In	Property Master
Student's Name	9/1/78			12/5/78	

Address

I have received the equipment described above and acccept responsibility for its care while in my possession.

Phone

Signature

make their own specialty equipment. Most standard mallets — including yarn, rubber, wooden, and timpani — can be made inexpensively. Techniques for wrapping mallets are presented in Arthur Press's book, *Mallet Repair* (Belwin Mills, 1971). Ambitious directors can design their own harnesses for timp-tom trios, clusters, marching timpani, and bass drums. These can be made at a fraction of their retail price. Music racks and stick bags that attach to drums can also be made.

Officers

Appoint a strong student leader to be "drum sergeant." This person can help run sectional rehearsals, teach parts, and call cadences. He can also appoint other students to assist in the administration of the section.

Another helpful assistant is an equipment manager who can take care of assigning and maintaining percussion equipment. This person would also make sure that enough extra slings, sticks, mallets, and drum heads are available.

Other Guidelines

Stress these guidelines with your percussionists each season:

- Always set the drum down on a flat, clean surface.
- Never put sharp objects in the bottom of the drum case.
- Never sit on any drum.
- Always dry the drum off as soon as possible after exposure to rain.
- Marching timpanists should carry a tuning fork or a pitch pipe.
- Like-instruments should always use the same size sticks or mallets.

With good administration and the assistance of student leadership, today's expanded percussion section can be as simple to administer as as the five-man section of yesteryear. ■

December, 1978

Un-contestable Advice for Timpani and Marimba Players

Gordon B. Peters

The Un-Contest is gaining greater acceptance in percussion education as a constructive device for improving a student's performance, especially in the early stages of his development. Its goal of increased communication between teachers and students will lead to drummers becoming percussionists and percussionists becoming musicians.

G.P.

I recently participated in an Un-Contest held at Northwestern University, sponsored by the Percussive Arts Society. There were eight performance categories ranging from snare drum and multi-percussion to mallet percussion, timpani, drum set, and various ensembles. Each student received a mini-lesson from a professional percussionist, and each performance and mini-lesson was recorded on a cassette tape which the student furnished. The students were all in high school.

As I listened to the marimba and timpani players, I began to notice certain common faults, such as foot tapping, poor wrist positions, improper standing positions, and improper mallet grips. If your students have some of the same kinds of problems, you may find the following suggestions useful.

Advice for the Timpanist

Foot placement. Place the feet flat on the floor about two feet apart and centered in the area being used, whether there are two, three, or four timpani. To allow free arm movement a player should not stand too close to the instruments. Foot tapping must be avoided.

Stick choice. Choose a stick that has (1) a ball or rounded disk (not a flat disk) with a wooden core; (2) good quality piano damper felt that is tightly and evenly drawn with no seam or ridges; (3) a hardness that is appropriate for the passages to be played. The shaft can be wood or metal, or any other material of a player's choice. I would not use felt or flat-surfaced, cartwheel-shaped cores; they tend to produce a "slap" sound.

Stick grip. I prefer the German grip, palms facing downward (this, to me, is a more natural grip than the French grip which has the thumbs up). Ideally, the grasp of the two sticks should be identical to produce the same sound with each hand. The thumb should be placed exactly parallel to the shaft handle. Opposite the thumb should be the first finger, the second finger, or a combination of the two, with the remaining fingers touching the stick.

Rolls. Pivot the stick between the thumb and the first and second fingers, or a combination of the two, and slightly agitate the stick with the remaining fingers. Both sticks should be raised to the same height.

Single strokes. There should be no pivot action when playing single strokes.

Articulation. Begin with the sticks close to the instrument. Strike the surface, then lift the sticks. Never lift before striking; this pounds the tone into the instrument. Lifting after striking the surface will draw the tone out. Use only the wrist to play soft dynamic levels; as you increase the volume, add the strength of the forearm (you may need to use the strength of the arm from the shoulder for playing at the fortissimo level).

Stick angle. The angle formed between the sticks should be 60-90 degrees. The angle to the head should be slight, and the same for both sticks.

Striking the head. The heads should be struck in the area closest to the player, about 1/3 the radius of the drum with each stick equidistant from the rim. Avoid striking the head too close to the rim.

Tuning. If a player does not have perfect pitch, he should use the tuning note of the band or orchestra, a pitch pipe, or a mallet-percussion instrument. Thereafter pitches must be found by being able to hear the proper interval. Once he knows the correct pitch, the player should hum it into the drum slightly raising and lowering the pitch of the drum with the pedal to find the point where the head "hums" back the loudest, producing the maximum sympathetic vibration. Plastic heads normally have a range of about an octave, but the player should tune the head within the fifth that is in the middle of the octave and not at either extreme end of the octave. The following are accepted as the basic ranges of a normal four-drum set:

Bowl diameter:

32″	29″	26″	23″
D2 – A2	F2 – C3	B♭2 – F3	D3 – A3

Subsequently, each head must be balanced or put in tune with itself with the same pitch at each tension screw. Putting a mute in the center of a head will help eliminate overtones as the player tests the pitch opposite each tension screw. To avoid sympathetic vibrations from the other drums, place mutes on them in the maximum muffling position midway between the center and the rim. Tap the head with one finger or the shaft of a timpani stick. Listen to the impact tone, not the duration or hum tone, muffling the head quickly and completely between each tap. The impact tone can best be heard by kneeling and putting one's ear on the same plane as the drum head. After the head is balanced, double-check the range, and be sure the pedal tension is still properly adjusted.

Musical expression. We teach our students good technique and an understanding of notes and notation, but we do not teach them how to analyze a piece of music and edit a work in light of this analysis. I advised the players to study the music away from their instruments, taking it to their instrument only when they can either sing it or have a mental impression of what it sounds like. Pitch, rhythms, dynamics, phrase markings and their alternative high points, sticking, and tempo are all aspects of the music that must be learned in advance.

It is also important to have students use cassettes to listen to themselves. After all, they are really working toward the goal of becoming their own teachers one day; now is a good time to start that process.

Advice for the Marimba Player

Foot placement. Determine the highest and lowest pitches of the work at hand, then place the feet about two feet apart in the center of this range. If it is possible, avoid moving the feet; if you need to move, keep one foot in place and move the other in the direction of the reach. Do not tap out the rhythm with your foot.

Grip. The grip is essentially the same as that of the timpanist. The only difference is that in performing a roll on the marimba, there should be no pivot.

Rolls. In a work having both single strokes and rolls, I suggest that the rolls be played *forte-piano* style, otherwise they will sound louder than the single strokes (which sound *fp* because of the decay).

Tempo. The speed of a work must not be too fast for the music or for the player's present technical control, and rushing adds to the problem. Rhythms with the same consecutive note value are especially easy to rush. Using the metronome will expose the problem.

Wrong notes. There are two fundamental reasons why players strike the wrong bar: position and grip. If the wrist is not moving straight up and down, the stroke will move toward the bar at an angle, likely hitting the wrong note. Have the student turn his wrist inward with the thumb nail perpendicular to the floor and the wrist downward (the German grip). The mallet should be held with enough tension to keep it completely under control. The third, fourth, and fifth fingers should be in contact with the shaft.

Editions. One student gave an inferior performance of a Bach violin concerto transcription because of the publisher's errors in notes, trills, and dynamics. I advised the player to buy an original violin version with piano accompaniment and make his own edition with the help of his teacher and a recording by an accepted violin soloist.

The Un-Contest was an opportunity for me to see the most common mistakes of high school timpani and marimba players. I feel that if students and teachers would pay more attention to the areas discussed here, the students would learn the basic techniques needed to play their instruments correctly, and would be on their way to becoming better musicians. ■

Guide to Notation

Pitches are referred to by the letter name plus the number of the octave. A (440), which appears in the 4th octave, is called A4.

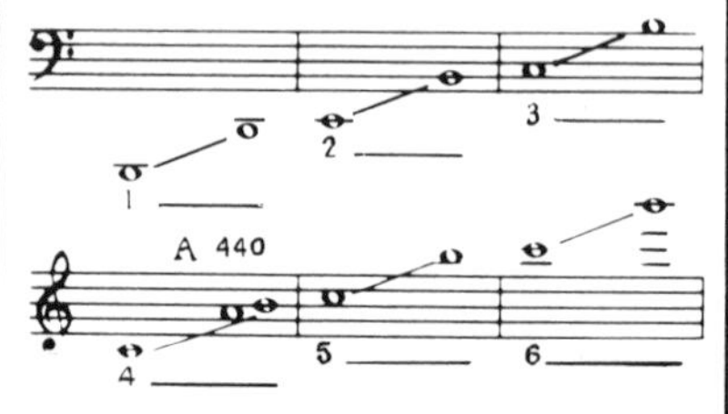

The Snare Drum Roll: One Lump or Two?

Patrick Crowley

There are two basic ways to sustain a sound on a snare drum: the open and closed rolls. Young percussionists are often confused as to which style should be used in a particular performing situation. A beautifully executed roll of the wrong style does nothing to enhance the musical quality of the band's performance.

The open, or rudimental style roll, is a rapid succession of single rebounded strokes. After each initial stroke, the stick is allowed to bounce only one time. The rhythmic quality and volume capabilities make the rudimental roll well suited for the marching band. The rudimental roll is a metered roll, containing a definite number of taps per beat, the number being determined by the tempo. The most common note value for each tap is the 32nd note. An open roll at 116 beats per minute would have exactly eight taps per beat (see example 1).

Example 1
mm=116

R L R L R L R L

R R L L R R L L R R L L R R L L

The open roll is sometimes called the "double-stroke" roll because the rebound stroke ideally should sound the same as the initial stroke. This is accomplished by slightly forcing the stick down with a snap on its rebound. Because the forced rebound sounds nearly the same as the initial stroke, and there are only two taps per hand, this roll can be played very loudly. Another advantage of the open roll for the marching band is the uniformity of sticking resulting from the metered quality. All players will start and end the roll with identical sticking. Thus, by using the rudimental roll, the drummer's main purpose — supplying the beat — can be maintained without destroying the impression of a sustained sound.

The rhythmic quality and loud volume that are favorable to the marching band are seldom desirable in concert band. The properly executed closed roll produces a smoother, non-metered sound for concert ensembles. The closed, or orchestral style roll, is produced by a rapid succession of multiple-rebounded strokes. Each stroke is made to rebound two or more times, producing a "buzz" sound. The number of strokes in the roll depends entirely upon the tempo, duration, and volume indicated by the music. The number of rebounds should be the same in each hand. Proper co-ordination of the hand speed, and the number or duration of the rebounds produces the smooth roll. This roll is the appropriate style to be used in concert band, wind and percussion ensembles, and orchestral performances. The only exception would be when playing a piece marked in a march style, or playing on a field or tenor drum.

There are many exercises which can be used to improve the execution of the roll. Both types of rolls can be improved by cleaning up the single stroke technique. A relaxed motion, clear tone, and good control of each single stroke will add to the smooth lines of a sustained roll. Start slowly with repeated single strokes (see example 2). Gradually increase the speed until the strokes are no longer clearly defined. For control, gradually slow down and stop. Repeat.

Example 2

R R R R L L L L

R R R R L L L L R R R R

This exercise will increase speed, endurance, evenness, and perception of rebound duration. The example should not imply that a closed roll has four taps per hand. The number just has to be more than one rebound per stroke, alternating the strokes at a speed that will produce a sustained sound. The application of a rhythmic base can produce a cleaner, more precise orchestral roll. To find the rhythmic base, the player must find the note value which produces a smooth sound with the hands alternately playing multiple bounces. The tempo determines the choice of the rhythmic base.

A comparison of the different rolls can be made with the exercise shown in example 3. Note that 16th notes are the rhythmic base for the closed roll in this example.

Example 3

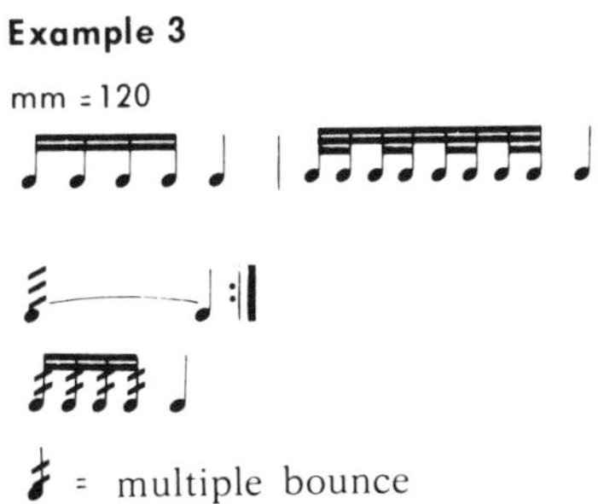

Many times one can hear "lumps" in the roll, interrupting the smooth, sustained sound. These flaws are caused by uneven hand speed, or by unequal rebound duration. The variable-speed tape recorder is an excellent tool for isolating the problem. By recording the roll at high speed, then playing it back at a slower speed, one can count the actual number of rebounds per hand, and then work toward making the strokes and rebounds more alike. ■

January, 1979

The Concert Bass Drum

Lynn Glassock

Most bass drums now have plastic heads and this is probably the best choice, especially in locations where the temperature and humidity vary greatly. Although the use of plastic heads is a practical necessity, under the right conditions (and with proper care) a bass drum with calfskin heads will produce a superior sound.

The Stand

The folding bass drum stand is by far the most common stand in use today. It should be free from rattles; none of the metal parts of the stand should touch the bass drum. The suspension bass drum stand is a definite improvement on the folding type in that it allows the drum to vibrate more freely. (It is surprising how much this stand affects the overall sound.) However, the suspension stand is considerably more expensive and its purchase may not be a possibility in many schools.

The Beaters

Bass drum beaters are not only important, but, as with the timpani, no one beater can cover all of the types of sounds that the music might call for. The mallet that should be used in most situations is a large, fairly heavy beater with a soft covering. It gives a big, full sound at a variety of dynamic levels. A pair of matched beaters (smaller than the one above but larger than timpani mallets) are needed when rolls are called for. One of these "roller mallets" can also be used when slightly more definition of impact is needed. A third type of beater is needed for the more pointed accents that are sometimes called for; this should be of medium size and weight and should have a harder covering or a solid felt head.

The concert bass drum, like the triangle and tambourine, is a relatively simple instrument that is often played far below its musical potential. It can produce a beautiful, full, deep resonant sound or a thin, dull thud. It is an instrument that has a gamut of musical (or amusical) possibilities. In an effort to obtain a desirable sound from the bass drum, four main areas should be considered: 1. the instrument itself, 2. the stand, 3. the beaters, and 4. the performer and playing techniques.

The Instrument

The size of the bass drum is, of course, an important factor. Most of the public school bass drums are 32-36 inches in diameter. The 16" x 36" drum is a good choice for a large high school band or orchestra. With every decrease in the size of the drum, there is also a decrease in some of its musical potential. Bass drums smaller than 16" x 36" ideally should not be used in these larger and more mature organizations.

It would be impossible for even the most experienced professional to get a good sound from a bass drum that is not in proper condition. Many junior high and high school bass drums are tuned too tightly. They should be tuned to a low indefinite pitch; a very important factor to the overall sound. The head should be tensioned equally for maximum tone quality and length of vibration. This can be accomplished by playing close to the rim at each T-handle with a timpani mallet and then adjusting the handle until the same pitch is heard at each point.

The Performer

Many students play too close to the rim. The full, deep, long ringing sound can best be obtained by playing 1/3 - 1/2 the distance from the center of the head. Playing close to the rim produces a thinner, higher pitched sound and should only be used for special effects. Playing in the direct center of the head will result in a shorter ring and more definition of the impact of the beater. Although this is not the sound that is normally desired, playing in the center can be used in certain situations, such as giving definition to a rapid series of notes so that the effect will not be that of a roll.

The stroke used for most dynamics is made with the forearm. The motion should be a direct stroke rather than a glancing one, and the beater should be allowed to rebound freely off the head. For softer dynamics the stroke is made by the wrist, with more arm and shoulder motion needed for the fortissimos.

Muffling Techniques

Proper muffling probably requires a more demanding technique than the actual production of the sound itself. There should be no muffling materials of any kind on the inside of the drum. Normally all of the muffling should be done by the performer. The bass drum can give its best musical quality when it is allowed to ring. Many players keep their hand on the non-playing side regardless of whether they are playing long or short notes. In many cases, both heads should be free to ring until it is time to muffle, then both heads should be muffled at the same time. This is especially true of long notes. Assuming that the drum is played on the right side, the left head will be muffled with the left hand and the right side with the right hand or the right knee, or both. For many isolated short notes, the left hand and right knee should muffle at the same time — immediately after the note is played, not before. Although the note will be of short duration, the deep, full quality will be heard. When there is a series of notes, or a single note is extremely short, one or both heads have to be partially muffled while playing. While this will not produce the best quality of sound, it is necessary to produce the desired effect. ■

February, 1979

Teaching the Long Roll

Charles Holmes

When you have a passage in a band composition that calls for a long roll, do you cringe at the sound your drummers produce, like a bowling ball rolling down a flight of stairs? If so, you have a problem faced by many band directors: — the inability of their drummers to execute a roll correctly. Nine times out of ten if a drummer's roll is poor, his playing technique in general is poor.

The long roll has two parts — the single stroke and the rebound. The rebound ("bounce") may be either single or multiple. The open roll (rudimental style) is a combination of the single stroke and the single bounce rebound. The buzz roll (concert style) is a combination of the single stroke followed by a series of rebounded strokes.

Students can develop a concert (buzz) roll by playing a transition passage starting with the single strokes, moving then to the rebound strokes and finally to the multiple bounce strokes. This generates a pattern similar to that shown in example 1.

The student should be able to go from one stage of the roll to another in a smooth and precise manner. There are two factors involved in making a smooth transition from single strokes to open rebound strokes: speed and distance. Have the student determine the slowest speed at which he can play a good clean-sounding roll, then have him play his single strikes up to exactly that speed before converting to the open roll. Also, have him notice how far the tips of his drum sticks rise above the surface of the drum head while he is playing an open roll at its slowest speed. When he plays the single stroke portion of the roll, be sure the sticks are at that same height. By paying attention to these two factors, the transition can be made smoothly.

Students can improve their roll execution by using three simple exercises. Stress the point that the student should first practice one hand at a time. This will allow him to concentrate only on the movement of the hand involved, and to make the necessary corrections.

In the "bounce" exercise, the student bounces his sticks over and over again. Have him start with the right hand and when it tires, switch to the left hand, (see example 2). The bounce exercise should be done in conjunction with the "accent" exercise, shown in example 3, which helps to develop the secondary beat of the bounce, normally weak in young players. However, an accent is not to be the end result. Strengthening the usually weaker second beat helps the student to achieve consistent strokes and rebounds of equal strength.

The third exercise, the "buzz" (see example 4), should be practiced like the bounce. The right stick should be "buzzed" over and over again. Exercise the left hand when the right hand tires.

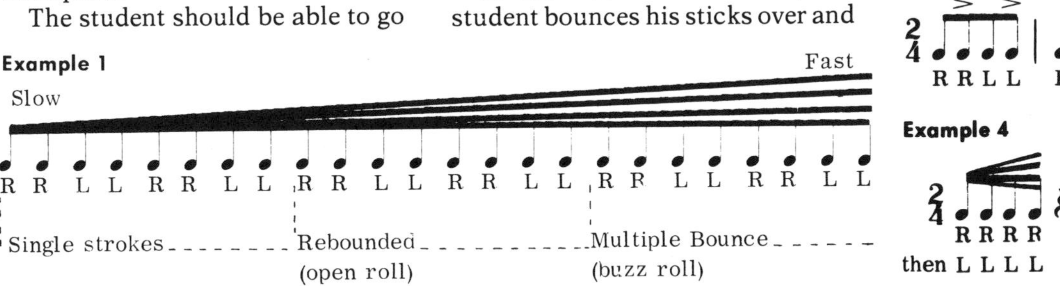

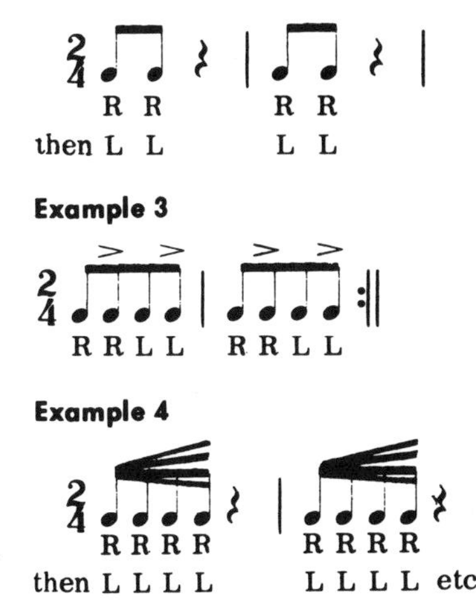

The student should be encouraged to play with a light touch while practicing these exercises. He should feel as if he is playing off of the drumhead rather than pounding or digging into it. Once a student develops a light playing touch, it stays with him and becomes a permanent part of his technique; it can also add speed to his playing. When practicing these exercises, the student should start slowly. Speed comes only with time, practice, and relaxation. Tension can be one cause of an uneven roll, and it does not add speed.

Stick selection is important, especially to elementary and junior high school students. These students usually have small hands and sometimes sticks that are too long or too heavy can add to the stick control problems they already have. I recommend an orchestral or "A" model stick for young students. The stick should be light to medium in weight, and short to medium in length, and have a gradual taper from the middle of the stick to the tip. The more taper the shaft of a stick has the easier it is to bounce the stick. Young students usually have a problem controlling sticks that are too long, such as a 1A. I recommend that they experiment with different sticks until they find one that is comfortable for them.

I believe elementary students should stay away from a stick such as a 2B which is thick with a very short taper. They sometimes have a problem getting these sticks to bounce correctly because the shaft has such a short taper.

Helping your students to learn the correct stick grip is very important. Whether you teach rudimental or matched grip, students should gain full control of the sticks and let them do as much work as possible. When using matched grip, only the thumb and the index finger should actually grip the stick. The others should be placed loosely around the stick to help control it. If the other three fingers actually grip the stick, you will restrict the bounce.

With the rudimental grip, the right hand functions as it does when using the matched grip. The left hand is quite a bit different. The muscles between the thumb and the index finger do the actual gripping of the stick, not the fingers. The thumb should be straight and not bent over the stick. Also, only the index finger should be placed over the stick, not the middle finger. This helps to ensure the maximum rebound ability of the stick.

Make sure that the student has the drum or practice pad adjusted to a height which is comfortable for him. Ideally, the top rim of the drum or top of the practice pad should be about even with the student's waistline. If the playing surface is too low, the student will dig into the playing surface rather than play off of it. Encourage your students to keep the tips of their sticks close to the playing surface. This will help to increase their speed by eliminating wasted motion.

The long roll is one of the most important tools a drummer has. By helping our drummers to improve their rolls, we are helping them to improve their playing technique as a whole. ■

March, 1979

Cymbal Acoustics, Selection, and Care

Larry C. Jones

Cymbal Acoustics

A cymbal vibrates somewhat like ripples in a pool of water. When a stone is tossed into the water, the ripples appear to be moving slowly further and further out until they fade into calm water. Actually, the ripples go out only a short distance, roll back to the spot at which the stone was dropped and roll back out a bit further. They continue to roll out further and further, each time returning to the starting point. A cymbal vibrates in much the same manner. The vibrating "ripples" roll into the center of the cup which receives the vibrations. The cup then throws the vibrations to the edge, the edge catches them, and again sends them back to the cup. The sound waves become more faint as the vibrations lose their sustaining power. This acoustical effect is known as decay and is an important quality of cymbals.

Every musical instrument produces its own distinct timbre or tone color. Pitched musical instruments have one identifiable fundamental frequency and an overtone series which allows the listener to discriminate both pitch and timbre. The cymbal's sound is comprised of many fundamental frequencies with partials sounding so close to one another that it seems non-pitched. However, it sounds that way to the listener not because it has no pitch but because it has so many fundamental frequencies that the resultant overtones are too dissonant for the listener to mentally organize and perceive any fundamental tone.

The inability of the listener to discriminate a single pitch is very important to the musical purpose of cymbals in an ensemble. If a cymbal were to have a well-defined pitch, it would become part of the harmony of the composition and thus lose the ability to give dynamic and rhythmic emphasis to the music.

When percussionists refer to the pitch of cymbals, they are talking about the characteristic tessitura of each individual cymbal. The tessitura of a cymbal is determined by a dominating tonal element. A high sounding cymbal will possess a full tonal scale, but the high frequencies will dominate. It is important for a cymbal to have a dominating tessitura, but not a dominating pitch. If a cymbal had an overtone series built on one particular pitch, it would lose its usefulness to the ensemble. This is because a cymbal reacts by sympathetic vibration to the fundamental root pitch and the harmonics of a chord being played by an ensemble. Because the cymbal has a large number of frequencies and harmonics, the sympathetic vibrations of any chord will send it into vibration. This is a characteristic of a high quality cymbal; when struck, such a cymbal will not destroy, or in any way alter, the harmonic content of the music.

Cymbal Selection

Musical style determines which type of cymbal to use, and a fine percussionist will attempt to choose cymbals that best interpret the music and produce the sound the composer intended. To achieve this goal, a wide assortment of cymbals should be made available in any performing organization.

Most school groups use cymbals which are vaguely defined as general purpose cymbals. A pair of general purpose crash cymbals may be 16 to 20 inches in diameter and of medium weight. However, it should be clear that no one type of cymbal will suit every musical need. Directors of school bands and orchestras should be encouraged to purchase at least two additional pairs of cymbals in order to meet most musical demands and to properly train young percussionists.

Choosing cymbals intelligently requires an understanding of how size (6 to 30 inches in diameter), weight (thin, medium thin, medium, medium heavy, and heavy), and type (crash, suspended, hi-hat, etc.) determine cymbal tone. Four aspects of cymbal tone should be considered when selecting a cymbal: response, sustaining power, actual power, and pitch.

Response. This is the amount of time it takes for the cymbal to reach full vibration after it is struck. The small and thin cymbals are the fastest to reach full vibration and are therefore the most responsive. Large and heavy cymbals are the slowest to reach full vibration and are the least responsive.

Response is usually the first consideration in the selection process because the percussionist must decide what type of sound is most appropriate for the music being played. Unfortunately, the various physical and acoustical properties interact with each other. For example, the percussionist must usually weigh relative importance of response to actual power (intensity of sound). If a fast response at loud dynamic levels is desired, a small and thin cymbal may not be the best choice because this cymbal can be overplayed easily. Such a cymbal would have to be struck so hard to create the desired loudness that it would produce an undesirable sound or cause damage to the instrument. In this case a compromise between the two needs must be worked out in relation to the cymbal's intended use. If a powerful cymbal with fast response is needed, the best choice would be an 18 to 20-inch medium thin cymbal. This is often the cymbal used as the crash cymbal on a drum set. It is also a common choice for French orchestral music where fast response and maintenance of proper ensemble are essential.

The very large diameter pairs of cymbals, which range from 22 to 26 inches in diameter, are known as "Wagnerian" cymbals. They produce the dark "clang" sound characteristic of German Romantic music.

Smaller diameter (18 to 21 inch) heavy weight cymbals will be slightly faster to respond than the Wagnerian variety. These are most often used by marching bands and drum corps because they will withstand constant hard use. In this case, a good tone is not as important and is compromised for durability. The sound of this type of cymbal is not usually desirable for concert band or orchestra.

Sustaining Power. This refers to the length of time a cymbal will vibrate after being struck. As a general rule, cymbals that respond slowly will have more sustaining power. Therefore, large, heavy weight cymbals (which respond most slowly) will have the most sustaining power. This type of cymbal, for example, would be the best choice if you need a cymbal crash that will ring or vibrate for a long duration after the attack.

To test sustaining power, strike a cymbal with a yarn mallet at various dynamic levels listening each time for the length of duration. If you find two cymbals of equal size and weight, the one with the most sustaining power would generally be the most desirable.

Actual Power. This is the intensity a cymbal is capable of producing. The actual power of a cymbal is dependent on the metals in its alloy, the responsiveness of the processed alloy, its molecular pattern ("grain" direction) and its size and shape.

The size of the ensemble and the type of playing to be done with the cymbal will determine how important actual power is in the selection process. Cymbals used in a marching band or drum corps may need the quality of actual power even to the point of giving up some of the other qualities. However, those cymbals used in chamber groups and small ensembles do not usually need a great deal of actual power, and in this case the qualities of response and sustaining power will be more important to the percussionist.

Pitch. As stated previously, cymbal pitch actually refers to whether a cymbal has a high, medium, or low tessitura. When a heavy tonal color is desired, a lower pitched cymbal is the best choice. These cymbals will also have a great deal of actual power and feature a slow response with a slow decay. If a light tone is needed, a high pitched cymbal is the obvious choice. These cymbals will also have a fast response and a fast decay.

You should hear a fundamental pitch difference of approximately a minor third between each disc when you are selecting a pair of crash cymbals. This difference will enhance the total sound because of the dual blend of overtones. A poor quality cymbal may have a definite pitch or obvious fundamental frequency, whereas a good quality instrument will have a balance of overtones.

Suspended cymbals have some unique qualities which should be discussed separately. Selecting cymbals for suspension is often difficult because of the variety in size, thickness, and tonal quality.

The response and tonal duration of a cymbal can be observed by hitting the cymbal with a yarn mallet and using the same tests as those for other cymbals. You can test the pitch of the cymbal by blowing a stream of air across the edge toward the bell. The light, soft sounds that you hear are the overtones. The higher the overtones, the brighter the sound will be when the cymbal is struck.

If you are choosing cymbals for a drum set, you will want a ride cymbal that can sustain a rhythmic pattern. A medium or medium heavy cymbal 16 to 18 inches in diameter is the usual choice. (However, many drummers prefer larger ride cymbals. Ed Schaughnessy and Shelly Manne both use 22-inch ride cymbals).

The drum set ride cymbal should have a high pitch and a relatively slow response so that it should never reach full vibration if it is played with the tip of a drum stick. If the ride cymbal should ever reach full vibration, the cymbal rhythm would be lost. It is also important to consider if the drummer will use plastic or nylon tipped drumsticks. These sticks will give the ride cymbal a more articulated sound and bring out the high cymbal sounds better than wooden tipped sticks.

The crash cymbal on a drum set, used for accents and climactic points in the music, should have a fast response and a fast decay. Drum set crash cymbals are usually thin or medium thin cymbals ranging from 14 to 18 inches in diameter.

Hi-hat cymbals should consist of a medium thin top cymbal and a medium or medium heavy bottom cymbal. This is beause most playing is done on the top cymbal and the medium thin weight will respond faster to a drum stick. The size of hi-hat cymbals range from 13 to 16 inches, depending on how much volume is needed. Hi-hat cymbals can be purchased in matched pairs that are designed by the manufacturer.

Care and Repair

Cymbals are composed of highly tempered alloys which make them brittle and susceptible to cracking, splitting, and warping.

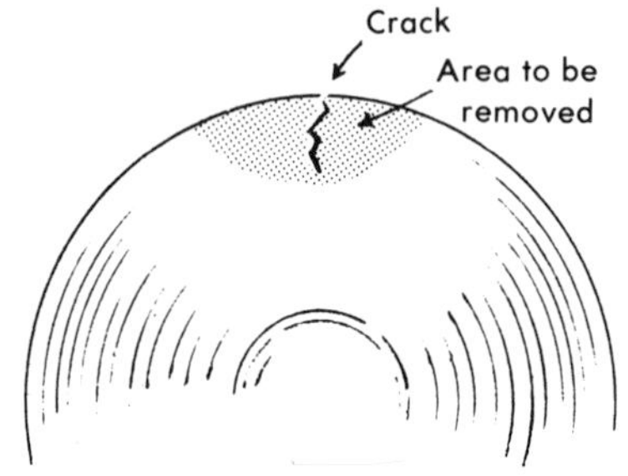

A crack or nick in a cymbal begins at the edge and spreads toward the bell; they usually result from dropping the cymbal or hitting it on the edge. Remember, all nicks and small cracks will eventually develop into large cracks. Cracks up to a half inch in length can be removed with a grinding wheel.

Cracks longer than 1/2 inch can be temporarily repaired by drilling a hole through the cymbal at the edge of the crack. A crack can also be removed by grinding a "V" into the cymbal as large as the length of the crack. When you are doing these repairs, drill or grind as slowly as possible to avoid heat build-up. Excessive heat can leave dead spots which ruin the tone and also make the cymbal even more brittle and susceptible to more cracking.

Another method of salvaging a cracked cymbal is to cut the cymbal down to a size which avoids the crack. The problem with this method is that the natural taper of thickness from the bell to the edge is changed.

Splitting can occur along a lathe cut within the bow of the cymbal. If this happens, the splitting can be retarded by drilling a small hole at each end of the split. This is effective only if the split is not too long. If a crack or split occurs in the bell, the cymbal is ruined; there is no effective repair.

The following list of suggestions should be considered when you are making any type of cymbal repair:

• Always leave smooth edges after any cutting or grinding. A sharp corner will soon produce a new crack.

• De-burring is necessary after grinding or drilling because the rough edge may produce a new crack. De-burr edges with a smooth file, and drill holes with a countersink.

• Pouring water slowly onto a drill bit will help keep it from overheating and destroying the temper of the alloy.

• Extend the repair slightly beyond all cracks. The material within the cymbal that is invisible to the naked eye may be cracked.

• Support the bottom of a cymbal with a piece of wood when you are drilling and use as little pressure on the drill as possible.

Remember that any repair is temporary. A repaired cymbal may last from only a few minutes to more than a year depending on the nature of the crack and the quality of the repair.

Warping can be avoided by proper storage and packing. Cymbals should be stored horizontally on a flat surface in a warm place. They should not be exposed to extreme temperature changes. If you move cymbals from warm to cold surroundings, pack them in good quality leather or vinyl storage bags and allow them to cool gradually.

Cleaning. Dirty cymbals neither look nor sound good. Unnecessary touching results in skin oils being worked into the lathe cuts and muffling the cymbal's overtones. There are many commercial cymbal cleaners available, most of which are expensive and do not work well. Metal polishes and cymbal rouges should not be used. Polishes may get into the lathe cuts and deaden the overtones. Rouges are usually too abrasive and scratch the surface of the cymbal. Electric buffers should not be used because the heat build-up from the friction of the buffing will damage the cymbal.

The following method works well for cleaning cymbals and involves both a minimum amount of abrasion and little chance of damage. First, soak the cymbal overnight in a tub or large sink with water and and dish washing detergent. This loosens most surface dirt and reduces the scrubbing time. Then, clean the cymbal with a cleanser that is not too abrasive. Rub with the lathe cuts. Afterwards, polish the cymbal with Brasso by gently rubbing the Brasso on with a clean cloth in the direction of the lathe cuts. Remove the Brasso and further polish the cymbal with window cleaner and a clean, dry cloth. The window cleaner removes any Brasso in the lathe cuts and leaves a protective film on the surface. You can continue polishing the cymbal if you want more shine or if any dirt still remains.

Cymbals can be kept clean longer if the players avoid handling the surface, picking them up by the edges like phonograph records. Daily cleaning with window cleaner will remove dust and fingerprints from cymbals that must be handled often. A cymbal's color changes with age and can never be returned completely to its original shine, but regular cleaning will keep cymbals looking and sounding their best. ■

April, 1979

Percussion Maintenance: Tips for the Band Director

Brian K. Shepard

Band directors often find their percussion instruments in bad shape, and yet don't know how to repair them. As a result the instruments are simply ignored and allowed to deteriorate. But percussion instruments require the same careful treatment a violin or oboe receives. This step-by-step guide should help you maintain the percussion instruments; proper care will improve the sound, and make playing more enjoyable for percussionists. Remember, no one likes to play on a broken-down instrument.

Timpani

Timpani require careful and frequent maintenance. To examine the instrument first remove the head. If the drum is a balanced action drum, like some Ludwig models (the pedal has no ratchet or braking system, but is kept in place by a heavy spring), hold the pedal firmly in the lowest note position with your foot while removing the head. When the head is off, slowly allow the spring to pull the pedal all the way up. Do not let it jerk. Now with the head removed, examine the rim of the drum, where the head rests (figure 1). Is it round, smooth and an even height all the way around? If the rim is not round use a rubber hammer to bend it back out. However if the height of the rim is not even or there are rough or jagged spots on the rim you will have to consult a professional repairman.

Figure 1. View of timpani with head removed showing rim, tension rods, and mounting hardware.

Without the proper equipment it is impossible to repair these problems correctly.

Next examine the counterhoop which puts tension on the head. If it is not round or level it must be replaced. Replace a dented, pitted, or sagging head. For timpani with a spring tension pedal, check that it remains in position no matter how hard the head is struck. If it does not, the spring is out of adjustment (a head not in its proper range may also cause the same symptom). When the pedal is hard to move up or slips down, turn the knob above the pedal clockwise, increasing the counter-tension. If the pedal is difficult to move down or if it slips up, the countertension is too tight; turn the knob counterclockwise until the pedal moves freely and remains on pitch. Remember, releasing the spring tension too much can cause the pedal to become disengaged, and a professional will have to repair the drum. Timpani with ratchet pedals should be checked to see if the notches are worn. If they are and there is slippage, the notched bar will have to be replaced.

Before replacing the head, spreȧd a little lubricant, such as cork grease, around the circumference of the rim. This allows the head to move more freely when tuning, and helps to eliminate squeaks. Place the head across the rim so that there is an even overhang of head around the rim. Clean the counterhoop with a damp cloth and place it on the head. Before inserting the tension screws, clean and oil them with one of the lug lubricants produced by the drum manufacturers. Do not use a regular oil or grease, as these will collect dirt and will foul the mechanism. Then lubricate the mounting holes on the counterhoop. The spring tension timpani pedal should now be returned to the lowest note position. Then adjust head tension to tune the drum.

For rattles and squeaks, check and tighten all mounting hardware and wheels and lubricate the moving parts. If a squeak occurs because the head moves over the bowl edge, start all over by removing the head and replacing it.

Timpani should be covered when not in use and be sure to keep them from banging against each other.

Mallet Instruments

Mallet instruments are usually fairly easy to maintain. Once they get in bad shape, however, they are difficult or impossible to restore. Be sure to keep them covered when not in use. Wipe off the bars with a glass cleaner, and clean out the resonators. Check that the pegs between the bars do not pinch the bars; if they do, gently bend them. When the cord running through the bars is loose, tighten it, and replace frayed cords. If the instrument rattles when played check the wheels and the resonator. There may be some foreign object in the resonator that vibrates with the sound.

Wooden bars on marimbas and xylophones should be replaced if splintered or cracked and the bars should also be checked for pitch. Wood bars are now kiln dried, so the wood dries out faster than normal causing the wood to settle unnaturally. Consequently, a wood barred instrument may go out of tune in a matter of weeks. The pitch of a wood bar can also be affected by the humidity in the instrument storage room, but in schools it's hard to control humidity levels. Also check that each bar is in tune with itself by placing a finger on the middle of the bar and striking the bar on the node (where the cord runs through the bar) with a mallet. On a marimba an overtone two octaves up from the fundamental pitch of the bar should sound; on a xylophone the overtone will be a twelfth up. A strobe tuner will help in determining the correct pitch. If a bar appears to be out of tune, first check it without its resonator, then with. If the coupling between the bar and the resonator is improperly matched it will sound out of tune. But tuning bars is a delicate and complicated procedure, so if the bars are out of tune the best thing to do is to send them to a reputable tuner of mallet instruments. However, you can tune a resonator by changing the length of the pipe. To do this, gently tap on the cap at the bottom of the resonator until it has reached the correct length. To reach the cap from above, tap on a dowel placed inside the resonator. Slight adjustments are usually adequate so be very careful and constantly check for resonance. When the tube resonates the correct pitch, replace the bar over the resonator and try it. The tone of the bar should now resonate.

On bells, chimes, and vibraphones examine the felt on the damper bar and on the carriage. If worn it may start to rattle so replace it. Examine the damper pedals and the motor and pulleys on the vibraphone for squeaks and apply a few drops of machine oil to eliminate any squeaks. Be sure that chimes are tied tightly to the frame so that when the tubes are struck they do not hit the back of the frame. A broken or worn cord should be replaced. Also check the striking cap at the top of the chimes; the cap is screwed on and may come loose, causing a rattle (figure 2). To eliminate the rattle, use a large pipe wrench to tighten the cap, being careful not to damage the tube itself.

Figure 2. Top of three chimes showing the striking cap. Note the chimes are tied tightly to prevent contact with the frame when struck.

Drums

Drums make up the majority of the percussion instruments in most bands, and are probably the easiest to maintain. Yet these instruments are often in the worst shape of all band instruments.

To prepare snare drums for use, remove the batter head (top head), and examine the rim, counterhoop, and head. Bad heads must be replaced, or the drums will have a dead sound. Be sure that all the hardware for the drum is present and secure; replace any that is missing. Clean the hardware with a dry or slightly damp cloth, and oil with a lug lubricant.

After inspecting and repairing the drum, reassemble and tune it. To mount the head, place it on the rim of the drum, put the counterhoop on top of it, and tension the screws for proper tuning. After tuning adjust the snares to produce a good sound at all dynamic levels. The snare mechanism must be able to bring the snares all the way on and turn them all the way off. If the snares are individually adjustable, all should be adjusted to the same tension. Any snares that are falling out should be removed with wire clippers.

Tenor drums, tom-toms, bass drums, and marching drums should recieve the same general maintenance as snare drums. Bass drum stands have a tendency to rattle, so isolate the noise and lubricate or pad to eliminate the rattle. Sometimes the stand will rattle against the floor; to solve this problem, set the drum on a rug or remove the wheels. Marching drum heads need to be replaced more often than other drum heads, and the drums must be frequently cleaned. Also tighten all nuts and bolts on carrying devices and replace worn straps.

Accessories

Often directors find they cannot locate the source of a problem with their percussion instruments, when a simple adjustment of a stand or some other accessory is all that is needed. Examine drum stands to see if any part of the stand touches the drum head or causes the snares to touch the head when turned off. If so, bend the arms of the stand upward until the snares hang freely and do not touch the head. Check that the suspended cymbal stands have rubber sleeves over the threads and felt pads under the bell of the cymbal (figure 3), otherwise the cymbal will rattle when played.

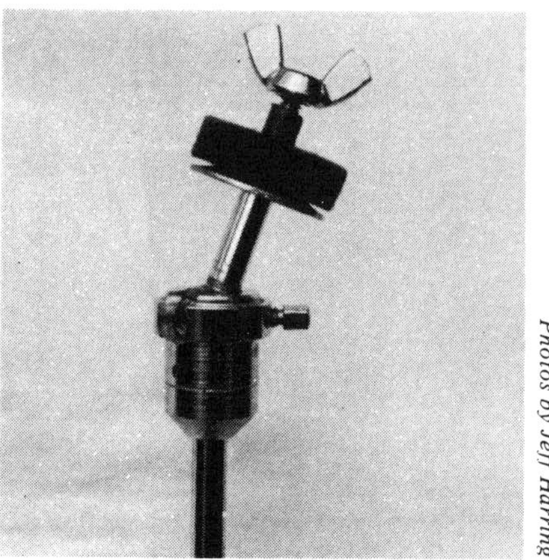

Photos by Jeff Harring

Figure 3. The top of a suspended cymbal stand showing the rubber sleeve over the threads and the felt pad that goes under the bell of the cymbal.

Triangles should be held from a holder and the cord that attaches the triangle to the holder should be shortened so it is barely larger than the diameter of the instrument. Also, an extra safety loop is recommended. All instruments that are not on stands should be placed on a padded table so the instruments can be set down without making any noise.

The troubleshooting guide on the following page should help band directors maintain their percussion instruments. Like any fine instrument, percussion instruments sound best when given proper care and maintenance. ■

TROUBLESHOOTING GUIDE FOR PERCUSSION INSTRUMENTS

	PROBLEM	PROBABLE CAUSE	SOLUTION
TIMPANI	Rattles.	Loose hardware. Loose wheels.	Tighten.
	Squeaks.	Head creaking on rim. Tuning mechanism sticking.	Put cork grease on rim. Oil.
	Pedal slips.	Countertension out of adjustment.	Adjust, clockwise to increase, counter-clockwise to decrease.
	"Dead" sound.	Bad heads. Heads out of adjustment.	Replace. Adjust tension evenly across head.
MALLET INSTRUMENTS	Bars muffled.	Pegs pinching bar.	Bend peg away from bar.
	Rattles.	Cracked bar. Loose wheel. Foreign object in resonator.	Replace. Tighten wheel casings. Clean out.
	No resonance.	Resonator out of tune.	Adjust effective length of resonator.
VIBRAPHONE CHIMES	Squeaks.	Pedal creaking. Motor or pulleys creaking.	Oil.
MARIMBA XYLOPHONE	"Dead" or out of tune	Bars out of tune with themselves.	Send to professional tuner.
CHIMES	Rattles.	Striking caps loose. Cords loose.	Tighten with a pipe wrench. Tighten.
DRUMS	"Dead" sound.	Bad heads. Heads out of adjustment.	Replace. Adjust evenly to proper pitch for instrument.
	Weak or thin sound.	Muffler too tight. Heads not tuned to same pitch.	Loosen so it just touches head. Tune.
SNARE DRUM	Bad snare sound.	Snares out of adjustment.	Adjust so a good crisp sound is produced at all dynamics.
	Snares rattle when turned off.	Snare mechanism not adjusted. Stand touching head.	Adjust so snares turn all the way off. Bend arms of stand upward.
CYMBALS	Rattles.	Cracked.	Drill hole at each end of crack or replace.
SUSPENDED CYMBAL	Rattles.	Rubber sleeve or felt pad missing.	Replace sleeve over threads or felt pad under bell of cymbal.
TAMBOURINE	Dark ringing sound.	Head too loose.	Hold over light bulb to allow heat to shrink head.

Drum Head Selection

David Levine

Until recently selecting a replacement for a worn-out or broken drum head was a simple matter. You would replace a calf head with one of the few plastic heads on the market. As synthetic heads have become more widely accepted, manufacturers have developed different kinds for varying purposes. The full-time professional drummer may be able to experiment with different heads, but most school directors don't have the time or the funds to do so. Therefore, when and what to change becomes important in order to make the best selection.

First, determine if you need new drum heads. A change of heads is due if you answer yes to the following questions. Is the collar excessively stretched? Are there dents in the playing surface? When the tension is relaxed does the head become wrinkled and uneven? When playing, is the drum head fatigued, causing slow stick response? Does a drum that once sounded bright and crisp now sound dull and mushy?

The heads supplied as standard equipment on new drums are those the manufacturer has determined to be best for the intended purposes of the drum. You should replace the old head with the same make if you are satisfied with the sound and performance of the drum. If you are not satisfied with the drum head, you will want to consider how the weight and type of drum head affect tone, response, and durability in making a suitable selection.

The appropriate drum sound for a music group is the primary consideration in selecting a head. A thin head is best suited for lighter playing situations where quick response and a bright, crisp sound is required. Such a head is useful for orchestra and concert band. For heavier playing a thicker head is more desirable because it will be more durable, deeper sounding, and have better sustaining capabilities. Marching bands and rock groups need to use heavier heads.

Smooth heads have an open, unmuffled sound while coated heads provide a brush surface. Fiberglass has a darker, more mellow sound than plastic. A laminated patch in the center of a head reinforces the head and increases the prominence of the fundamental tone while reducing the over-ring. Oil or fiberglass between the layers of a double-ply head give the drum a deeper, but muffled tone.

There are five drum head manufacturers in the United States. Specific information on sizes and colors of drum heads is available through the individual companies at the following addresses: Canasonic, distributed by Latin Percussion, Inc., Box 88, Palisades Park, New Jersey; Evans Products, Inc., Box 58, Dodge City, Kansas; Duraline, 11581 Federal Drive, El Monte, California; Ludwig Drum Co., 1728 N. Damen Ave., Chicago, Illinois; Remo, Inc., 12804 Raymer St., North Hollywood, California. Canasonic makes their heads in a one-piece construction of fiberglass cloth, impregnated with resin in a flexible fiberglass hoop. Duraline drum heads are a one-piece construction of woven fiberglass head and fiber hoop. Evans All-Weather uses a plastic film that is integrally molded to a polyester and fiberglass hoop in a one-piece construction. Ludwig has a thermolene plastic that is mechanically sealed in an aluminum hoop. Remo Weather King heads are made of Mylar plastic anchored in an epoxy channel in a rigid aluminum hoop.

The chart on page 58 lists the available drum heads by type, thickness, characteristics, and recommended use. Selecting the proper head is a fundamental, yet often overlooked, way of improving and enhancing the sound of your drum section. ■

Drum Head Selection

Recommended Use	Type	Thickness*	Brand Name	Characteristics
BRUSH SURFACE (COATED)				
Symphony Orchestra Concert Band	SD	.005	Evans Orchestra Batter Ludwig Thin (GR, EN) Remo Diplomat M5	Crisp, brittle sound.
School Band/Orch., Perc. Ens., Jazz Combo, Symphony Orchestra, Concert Band	SD/TT	.0075	Evans Orchestra Batter Ludwig Medium (RO, GR, EN) Remo Diplomat	Good stick and brush response; crisp sound.
Student, Big Band Casual, Light Rock	SD/TT/BD	.010	Ludwig Heavy (RO, GR, EN) Remo Ambassador	Most versatile of all heads; standard on many new drums.
Heavy Rock, Marching Band, Drum Corps	SD/TT/BD	.015 D	Remo Emperor	Durable head with a brush surface.
BRUSH SURFACE (FIBERGLASS)				
Symphony Orchestra, Concert Band Jazz Combo, Perc. Ens.	SD/TT/BD	.0075	Canasonic Thin Duraline Concert Remo Fiberskyn Thin	Good brush response; warm, dark sound close to calf. Excellent for live and recording work.
Big Band, Casual Light Rock	SD/TT/BD	.010	Canasonic Medium Remo Fiberskyn Medium	Canasonic and Duraline are made completely of fiberglass. Remo Fiberskyn is a plastic head with a fiberglass coating.
Heavy Rock, Studio Recording	SD/TT/BD	.015	Canasonic Heavy Duraline Studio	
BRUSH SURFACE (SPECIAL)				
Percussion Ensemble, Big Band, Casual	SD	.010 P	Remo CS	Reduced ring, more present fundamental tone.
Light Rock, Casual, Big Band, Heavy Rock	SD	.010 M	Canasonic No-Overtone	Fiberglass with coated edge; reduced ring.
	SD/TT/BD	.010	Canasonic Color Dot Sound Center	Fiberglass with coated center; reduced ring.
Heavy Rock Drum Corps	SD	.014 D .014 DO	Evans Rock Evans Hydraulic	
SMOOTH (OPAQUE)				
Symphony Orchestra, Concert Band Percussion Ensemble	SD/TT	.0075	Evans Tom-tom Ludwig Medium (GR, EN) Remo Diplomat	Unmuffled tone.
School Band/Orch., Student, Light Rock, Casual	SD/TT/BD	.010	Evans Parade Batter Ludwig Heavy (RO, GR, ST, EN) Remo Ambassador	Live, open, sound.
Heavy Rock, Marching Band, Drum Corps, Pipe Band	SD/TT/BD	.014 D .014 D .014 .015 D .015 D	Evans Looking Glass Evans Eldorado Ludwig Extra-Heavy (RO, ST) Evans Drum Corps Remo Emperor	Durable heads with punch and power.
SMOOTH (TRANSPARENT/ TRANSLUCENT)				
Symphony Orch., Concert Band, Percussion Ens.	SD/TT	.0075	Ludwig Medium (GR, EN) Remo Diplomat	Pure, clear, tone.
School Band/Orch., Student, Light Rock, Casual, Jazz Combo, Big Band	SD/TT/BD	.010	Ludwig Heavy (RO,GR,ST,EN) Remo Ambassador	Maximum amount of attack and decay.
Heavy Rock, Marching Band Drum Corps	SD/TT/BD	.014 D .015 D	Evans Blue-X Evans Red Head Evans Rock Glass Remo Emperor	Thick heads with a dull, pop, sound.
SMOOTH (SPECIAL)				
Light Rock, Casual, Perc. Ens., Heavy Rock, Marching Band, Drum Corps, Pipe Band	SD/TT/BD	.010 P	Ludwig Silver Dot (RO,ST,EN) Remo CS	Reinforced center reduces unwanted ring and brings out fundamental tone of the drum.
Heavy Rock, Marching Band Drum Corps, Studio Recording	SD/TT/BD	.014 DO .014 P .015 DM .015 DMP	Evans Hydraulic Ludwig White Dot (RO, ST) Remo Pinstripe Remo CS/Pinstripe	Oil muffles the tone. (see above) Fiber coating at edge acts as a muffler. (see above)
SNARE SIDE HEADS				
Symphony Orch., Concert Band	SD-S	.002	Remo Diplomat Snare	Brittle snare sound.
School Band/Orch., Student Perc. Ens., Jazz Combo, Light Rock, Casual, Big Band, Heavy Rock	SD-S	.004 .004 .003 .003 .003	Canasonic Snare Duraline Snare Evans Orchestra Snare Ludwig X-Thin (RO,GR,ST,EN) Remo Ambassador Snare	Best general purpose snare head
Heavy Rock, Marching Band, Drum Corps	SD-S	.005	Evans Parade Snare Remo Emperor Snare	Heavy-duty snare head.

KEY

RO = Rockers
GR = Groovers
ST = Striders
EN = Ensemble

SD-S = Snare Drum; Snare Side
SD = Snare Drum; Batter Side
TT = Tom-toms, Tenor Drums, Timp-toms, Concert Toms, Roto-toms
BD = Bass Drums

D = Double Ply
P = Laminated patch in center
O = Oil filled
M = Muffling coat of fiberglass around edge
*Given in millimeters

Do Your Drummers Belong?

Raymond D. Willard, Jr.

During my first year of teaching, the warm-up portion of my band rehearsal dealt primarily with the balance, volume, and intonation of the band, but left the drummers idle. This practice produced discipline problems, interfered with rehearsals, and most important, gave the drummers a feeling of being second class band members. Time and experience have given me insight into solving this problem, especially with elementary and junior high school students. Some of the following ideas may help you and your percussionists to be on the same wave length and in the same band.

As soon as I know how many percussionists I will have in each of my bands, I begin writing warm-ups. In this way the drummers can participate in warm-ups from the first rehearsal. I often begin rehearsal with a concert A♭ or B♭ scale, ascending and descending in whole notes. I write an eight-measure warm-up for the percussion section with a repeat and have the band repeat the top note of the scale before descending (see examples 1 and 2). When composing percussion warm-ups, consider the following suggestions:

Whenever possible, use as many different instruments as you have players. I have found that because many young percussionists prefer to play snare drum, the bass drum and crash cymbal parts are left to less advanced students. To avoid this situation, rotate parts each time you use a particular warm-up. This practice will also produce a better balance of volume within the section.

Avoid rolls of long duration. Younger players often play rolls too loudly and unevenly. I use mostly timpani, suspended cymbal, or snare drum for rolls. If using the rudimental approach, snare drum rolls should be specific as to the number of strokes needed, for example . In concert style, snare drum rolls will have no specific pulse; therefore, multiple stroke rolls should be used. When using suspended cymbal rolls, be sure to indicate softer dynamic levels so the roll does not overpower the ensemble. I have found that four-beat rolls work well in 4/4 time, for example  or 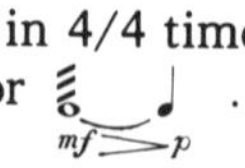 . Balance between the percussion warm-up and the instrumental scale is important so you can hear intonation problems or poor balance in the band while the percussionists are also playing. Using fewer rolls and rolls of shorter duration will aid you in this goal.

Keep the rhythmic difficulty less than what your players are capable of playing. I have found that complex rhythms often confuse younger players, and, in their confusion, volume has a tendency to increase. This defeats the purpose of any warm-up. Strive for rhythmic simplicity, and place the major emphasis of your warm-up on counting and timbre. To insure that the students are actually counting and not just following the strongest player, I often compose several warm-ups in a soloistic style: that is, no more than two people playing similar rhythms at the same time. This practice also keeps volume down so the entire band can hear the interaction between the scale and the percussion parts.

Concentrate on timbre. Have the percussionists listen to the quality of their sound during warm-ups much as wind players work at tuning. In writing the percussion parts, be very specific as to the sound you desire. Indicate exactly where to play on the instrument to achieve this sound, and specify the type of mallet to be used. On the suspended cymbal part, for example, you might choose one of the following: use coin on edge of cymbal, use soft mallets on edge of cymbal, use hard sticks on bell of cymbal, use suspended cymbal inverted on timpani head and play as pedal is moved up or down, roll with hard or soft mallets, or use hand on cymbal as it is played. Be careful to keep dynamic levels around *mf* or less. Stress musicality, timbre, and balance in your percussion parts as opposed to volume and difficulty.

Stress that your players are "percussionists" not just "drummers." By using all of the instruments you have available and trying to avoid excessive use of the crash cymbals, bass, and snare drums, you can instill in your students the broader concept of "percussionist." Basic piano, bell, and timpani parts can be included and composed to fit any scale so that even the novice player can become familiar with these instruments. Students need to know only one or two notes and the proper way to hold the mallets in order to play these instruments during warm-ups.

Write a musical warm-up so it will be most beneficial. Notes on a page can keep your students occupied physically, but you must keep their minds in motion too. Be creative in your writing as to your choice of timbre and use of instruments. Students are often amazed at the variety of items that can be used as percussion instruments.

You may be surprised at the change in your percussion section as the students begin to enjoy all the new and exciting sounds and instruments to which they have been introduced. Your innovations may help prevent possible discipline problems and also enable your "drummers" to feel like first class band members. ■

Example 1. Elementary Level Warm-Up*

Example 2. Jr. High School Level Warm-Up*

*Any combination of instruments may be used.

Updating a Percussion Program

Martin Zyskowski

Three major factors affecting percussion playing and teaching in the schools today are (1) the growth of professional level percussion and mallet-keyboard ensembles; (2) the popularity of jazz bands and the introduction of non-Western instruments and rhythms into them; and, (3) the use of corps concepts in marching bands.

Armed with only one college percussion instrument techniques course, a public school music teacher is usually unable to initiate a percussion program that will satisfy the needs of today's students. My conversations with music directors confirm that they have a common feeling of helplessness, inadequacy, and even a fear of percussion. Many directors are searching for help while others have temporarily solved the problem by ignoring the percussion section altogether. Judging from the number of poorly prepared student percussionists at solo contests and the confused look of directors when dealing with their percussion sections, help is definitely needed.

Individual circumstances will vary from one school to another, but the following ideas for improving a percussion program may have practical applications for many directors.

• Encourage students to study privately with a percussion specialist.

• Ask your more advanced players to share their expertise with less experienced students.

• Begin a percussion ensemble in your school. Ask a local college percussion instructor or professional symphonic performer to lay the groundwork for the group.

• Invite nearby college percussion ensembles to perform for your class; or, take your percussion section to an on-campus percussion ensemble concert or rehearsal. Hearing the variety of sounds possible in an ensemble can be a most stimulating experience for your young percussionists.

• Encourage students to join a drum and bugle corps.

• If there is a symphony in your area, ask its percussionists for clinics and performances with your groups. Often symphony percussionists form professional percussion ensembles designed specifically for public school performances and clinics.

• Encourage your school library and all percussion students to join the *Percussive Arts Society*, c/o 130 Carol Drive, Terre Haute, Indiana. Their publication presents trends in percussion, including new publications, educational records and tapes, performance and teaching techniques, and equipment.

• Make special arrangements for practice time on all larger percussion instruments.

• Reserve a practice room or area especially for percussionists. If the students don't need to spend half their time moving instruments to and from a practice room, they'll be more likely to schedule practice time.

• Purchase instructional recordings that give the student insight into stylistic interpretations.

• Invite respected jazz-rock drummers to present clinics or perform as guest soloists with your jazz ensemble. These players are often available through clinic programs sponsored by leading drum set manufacturers and will usually talk with the students and encourage them to read music and become acquainted with as many different percussion instruments as possible. They will also stress the importance of musicality in a performance.

• Promote interest and pride in how your percussion section looks. Storage cabinets, mallet racks (inexpensive ones built by your school workshop), and up-dated equipment are essential. Designate exact areas of percussion equipment storage and the location of each percussion instrument in each ensemble set-up. Appoint a section leader to assign and monitor the responsibility of taking care of the equipment. Establish a consistent routine of set-up and pack-up for every rehearsal and performance.

• Post the next day's repertoire and part assignments so your section will have adequate set-up time. If you simply let your percussionists know what is expected of them, many of the performance problems related to the percussion section will be eliminated.

• Meet with leading percussion teachers and performers in your area for their ideas and suggestions on teaching technique.

Percussion products, techniques, and music are changing faster than they can be included in one college methods course. The only way to stay on top of new trends is to establish and use a pipeline of information from the many sources available. ■

Meet the Steelpan

Wayne E. Charles

Editor's note: The steelpan was once only a curiosity, a unique sound created by islanders making use of discarded oil drums. However, in the hands of gifted performers it has become an instrument capable of great beauty, and well worth investigating as a possible addition to the school percussion program.

The steelpan, a musical instrument created from discarded oil drums, was first created by Winston Simon in the 1930s. The home of the steelpan is Port-of-Spain, the capital of Trinidad the most southern island of the Caribbean.

The transformation of industrial waste, a discarded oil drum, into a musical instrument is done by a tuner who starts by beating the end surfaces of the drum into a concave shape using a five pound sledge hammer. This thins out the steel so one must take care not to burst the surfaces of the drum.

Next the tuner marks out the location of individual notes with a piece of chalk and chisels grooves around the markings. Each area is raised slightly by hammering from below.

Some of the pans are then cut and burned at up to 300 degrees Farenheit for 30 to 40 minutes. Oil or water is then poured on the surface to temper the steel. After the preliminary work is completed, the exact pitches are tuned by delicately hammering each grooved area, using a harmonica as a guide. The tuning for pans is not standardized leaving the range of the instruments up to the individual tuner.

With some imagination pans can be incorporated into a school band. For an entire steel band five types of pans are needed: tenor, second, guitar, cello, and bass.

The tenor pan, also called the ping-pong, or soprano pan, is made from one oil drum top and usually has 20 to 25 notes on its surface. This pan is used primarily for playing the melody. The lowest note measures 5 to 6 inches square on the outer edge of the playing surface. The outer edge has from 10 to 12 notes; the inner circle can have as many as 5 to 10 notes. The note with the highest pitch is in the center. The single tenor is about 3 to 9 inches tall. Tenors are classified as "high or low" depending on which scale the pan was tuned to. Integrating the single tenor into a concert or jazz band is a popular technique. Barbara Streisand's hit tune *Gauva Jelly* used the distinctive sound of a tenor pan. When amplified, the tenor pan sounds somewhat like an electric guitar.

The second pan is a set of twin instruments which offers the player a range of 30 to 33 notes. The second is 12 to 14 inches high and has a range that corresponds to an orchestra's violas.

The guitar pans are also twin instruments, but about twice the height of the second and have 18 to 22 notes. Their ranges correspond to the horns and trombones.

Finally the steelband has the large cello and bass pans. Cellos have three playing surfaces, each made from three-quarters of an oil drum. They have a 20-note range and are used to play arpeggios or "running chords." The basses are made from the entire steel drum and come in sets of 4,5,6, or even 7 drums. A set of four oil drums is called a tenor or "high" bass. The bass pans can have between 18 to 25 notes.

In a steelband the higher instruments usually have the most players. If you choose to have a small band, four players in the tenor and double sections, three each on double seconds and guitars and two players on cello and bass would suffice.

All the pans are played with rubber mallets. The bass sticks have sponge balls, 1-2 inches in diameter. Sometimes a peeled golf ball is used. The stick length is determined by the individual player. For tenors, seconds, guitar, and cello pans stick ends are wrapped with rubber from bicycle tubes, handles from hockey sticks, innertubes of footballs, or wide rubber bands.

Pan playing is not difficult. With practice one develops style and technique. The unique sound of steelpans can enhance almost any instrumental music program. ■

The New Marching Percussion Line

Robert Buck

Editor's Note: This article contains material from the book, *Precision Marching Percussion* by Robert Buck, copyright 1978 by Alfred Publishing Company, Inc. Used with permission.

No longer can a drum section march with only a bass drum, a field drum, and a pair of heavy marching cymbals. The drum lines of today's drum and bugle corps and marching bands are expanding using additional bass drums, concert cymbals, timpani, bongos, timbales, and timp-toms. When and where possible, the percussion rank is further expanded with maracas, claves, guiros, cowbells, castanets, triangles, tambourines, and percussion effect instruments. In the marching band, the students assigned to these additional instruments are normally taken from concert band sections such as the double reeds, string bass, and lower single reed sections, because these instruments are not usually played on the march.

The demand for greater variety has led directors, composers, and arrangers to explore the many sound colors of the percussion family. The desire for sound color in percussion instruments is the all important force behind the new direction in marching percussion.

Directors and students need to be familiar with the equipment, terms, and playing techniques used in today's marching percussion lines.

• Timp-toms, also called tri-toms, are three single-headed drums carried by one member of the marching percussion section. Common tenor voice sizes are 10 inches in depth by 14, 16, and 18 inches in diameter.

• Marching machine timpani have fiberglass bowls and are suitable for carrying one drum per percussionist.

• Snare drums are most commonly 12 inches deep by 15 inches in diameter. They should be equipped with leg rests and gut snares.

• Bass drums in marching bands range in size from a width of 14 to 16 inches and a diameter of 24 inches to 34 and occasionally 36 inches.

• A segment is defined as like types of instruments. For example, all snare drums are a segment; all bass drums are a segment.

• Implements are devices used to strike an instrument.

• Height of rise is the vertical, horizontal, or combination swing or movement of sticks or implements within a segment in relation to the instrument while playing.

• Execution is playing beats simultaneously within a segment unless there is an obvious pattern that requires players to enter in an alternation fashion. The beats should be executed exactly together so the result sounds like one drum and the sound is uniform and precise.

• Line or drumline is the entire percussion section.

• Matched grip means that performers hold the sticks in the same manner with both hands, with the palms down facing the ground or the drum head.

• In the traditional grip the right hand is the same as the matched grip, the palm facing down. The left hand grip is quite different: the thumb is on top and the flat of the hand is almost perpendicular to the ground.

• Ring is the common term for the high-pitched sound that occurs in most unmuffled drums due to natural overtones.

• Muffle is the internal method of eliminating the ring in a drum, such as applying the tone control device of the snare drum or attaching a patch or strip of cloth to the inside surface of the head.

• Damping is the temporary muffling of a drum by external means, such as placing the hand or other object on the head to eliminate the ring.

Precision and uniformity is the goal at all times. Performing in segments must be done in a uniform manner. The instruments should be carried in the same position by each player and the players should grip the implements uniformly within each segment. The sticking should be notated in all scores to insure uniformity. The players should decide how to hold the implements while not playing.

Height system. In order to insure the same height of rise of each student's implement, a system has been established which trains the player in the proper approach to rudimental sticking. The following heights are assigned to each sound: grace note — 2 inches, tap — 4 inches, stroke — 6 inches, accented stroke — 9 inches.

The heights are important to the technical development of the performer but more important is knowing when to raise the stick for the upstroke and to what approximate height.

The following examples give the sticking of some rudiments and the desired heights.

Single Paradiddle

	R	L	R	R	L	R	L	L
From*	9	4	4	4	9	4	4	4
To**	4	9	4	4	4	9	4	4

Double Paradiddle

	R	L	R	L	R	R	L	R	L	R	L	L
From	9	4	4	4	4	4	9	4	4	4	4	4
To	4	4	4	9	4	4	4	4	4	9	4	4

Flam Paradiddle

	L	R	L	R	R	R	L	R	L	L
From	2	9	4	4	4	2	9	4	4	4
To	4	4	9	4	2	4	4	9	4	2

Flam

	L	R	R	L
From	2	6	2	6
To	6	2	6	2

Flam Tap

	L	R	R	R	L	L
From	2	6	4	2	6	4
To	6	4	2	6	4	2

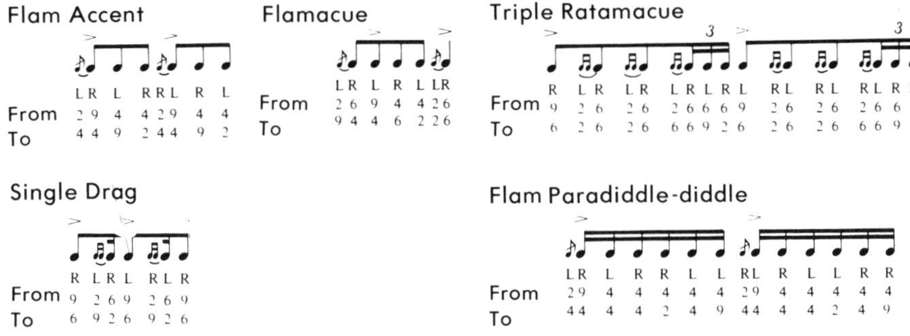

*Height in inches of stick before use.
**Height in inches of stick after use in preparation for next use (arrow shows next use).

Once the grip is mastered within reason and the rudiments can be performed with the proper heights, stop positioning, and upstroke placement, the basic techniques of wrist, arm, and finger control should be isolated and exercised separately.■

October, 1979

The Bass Drum

Doug Howard

The bass drum is one of the most misused and abused percussion instruments. Few directors realize that the bass drum, when properly tuned and played, can do more to enhance the overall sound of the band or orchestra than almost any other percussion instrument. The bass drum adds fullness to the sound of the other bass instruments in the ensemble.

Drum Size

A standard 16x36-inch shell produces acceptable results for concert band or orchestra use; anything smaller is incapable of producing the very low frequencies necessary for a full sound. If the diameter is increased from 36 inches to 40 inches, the sound becomes too difficult to control. The drum used by the Dallas Symphony Orchestra measures 18x36 inches, two inches deeper than the standard size. This drum has an added fullness or bottom to the sound that is difficult to achieve with a 16-inch depth.

Head Choice and Tuning

Plastic heads have not proven as successful on bass drums as they have on snare drums or timpani. The problem is tuning. To achieve the proper sound, bass drum heads are tuned to a very low, indefinite pitch. When a plastic bass drum head is tuned as loosely as it should be, an ugly flapping sound results. If the head is tightened enough to eliminate the flapping, the pitch is too high and the characteristic bass drum sound is lost.

Most professional symphony percussionists still prefer and use calfskin bass drum heads because of their superior sound quality even though they are more expensive and difficult to obtain than plastic heads. Also, calfskin heads require more frequent maintenance and adjustment because they are affected by changes in the weather, particularly changes in humidity. (In damp weather the heads become too loose and have to be tightened, and in dry weather they become too tight and have to be loosened.) While these adjustments are not difficult, they need to be done daily to keep the drum in proper playing condition. When younger students are involved plastic heads may be the logical choice. However, older students can learn to make the necessary adjustments if they are instructed properly.

Alan Abel of the Philadelphia Orchestra has developed a bass drum humidifier that supplies enough moisture inside the drum to keep the heads in playing range and to maintain a large enough collar. The humidifier, made from ivalon or polyurethane sponges sewn around a 5/16-inch threaded metal rod, is inserted into the drum through two holes on opposite sides of the shell. In dry weather the sponges are moistened with warm water and inserted into the drum.

A possible compromise in the plastic-versus-calfskin dilemma is to use one calfskin and one plastic head on the bass drum. Experiments done in the Dallas Symphony Orchestra showed good results can be achieved by using calfskin on the batter (playing) side and plastic on the resonating side because the playing side is more critical to the production of a good sound.

In the last few years a suspension stand has begun to replace the folding or cradle stand. With this type stand the bass drum is suspended from a steel ring by large rubber bands. The drum vibrates freely, resulting in greater resonance and depth of sound. A simple experiment can show why this is true. First, play a bass drum resting on a folding stand in the normal manner. Then while a person on each side lifts the drum off the stand so that it is suspended in the air, play the drum and you should hear considerable improvement in the sound. The use of a suspended-type stand achieves the maximum potential of the instrument. Because suspending the drum tends to amplify the pitch, the drum should be tuned to a very low, indefinite pitch.

Choice of Mallets

Avoid using a lightweight bass drum mallet. Because of the large size of the bass drum it takes a heavy mallet to bring out the low tones. The playing surface of the mallet should feel firm to the touch, and the covering should be sewn snugly. Avoid mallets that are soft and mushy. This is especially important when playing at *piano* or *pianissimo* dynamic levels where a soft but firm sound is called for. A mallet with a large head or playing surface is appropriate for most general playing. When clean articulation of repeated notes is needed, use a mallet with a slightly smaller head. The player should also have a matched pair of mallets for playing rolls; much lighter than the general playing mallet.

Playing Technique

The player should stand directly behind the drum, not off to the right side, to have the proper angle of attack between the mallet and the drum head. Hold the mallet in the right hand with a firm but relaxed grip. Place the thumb alongside the mallet shaft rather than on top of the shaft as in a snare drum grip. Make the basic stroke with the forearm and a slight breaking of the wrist just before impact. The stroke should be straight into the head with the follow-through straight back. Don't use a glancing or circular stroke; it reduces the force and weight needed to bring out the bottom of the sound.

The best playing area is approximately one-half to two-thirds of the distance from the rim to the center of the head. Moving closer to the center of the head provides better articulation but a less attractive sound. Avoid the center except for such special effects as cannon shots and articulation of rapid notes. The area close to the rim produces a thinner sound of a higher, more definite pitch, and should not be used.

Some modern bass drum stands are designed so the drum can be rotated from a vertical to a horizontal position. The horizontal position is useful for playing rolls. The sound of the drum is altered in this position because the bottom head is close to the floor. Therefore, for general playing, the drum should be in a vertical position. Rolls may also be played with the drum in the upright position by using the traditional snare drum grip in the left hand. The one-mallet bass drum roll should not be used.

Many students make the mistake of rolling too fast on the bass drum. Because bass drum heads vibrate at a much slower speed than smaller drums, the roll speed must also be slower. The player should feel the proper roll speed in response to the vibration of the head.

Muffling

No muffling materials should be placed inside the drum, nor should any permanent exterior muffling be used; all the necessary muffling should be done by the player. If the drum is tuned properly, almost all the muffling can be done on the playing side, using a combination of the left hand and the right knee. (It is helpful to have a small foot rest to raise the knee into the best position for muffling.)

The real purpose of the bottom head is to provide resonance, and this is nullified if it is muffled. If the bottom head must be muffled, the non-playing hand (generally the left hand) should be used.

Knowing when and how much to muffle is important. For instance, a group of successive quarter notes in a Sousa march may need to be muffled to sound distinct. The head may even need to be partially muffled throughout the entire passage. On the other hand, a single quarter note accompanying a whole-note chord may be allowed to decay naturally with no muffling at all.

The concert bass drum can be an asset to any musical organization. Good results are not difficult to achieve with a combination of good equipment and a musically alert performer. ■

Drum Set Basics

James Pierkarczyk

As the popularity of high school and college stage bands increases, the responsibility and importance of the drum set player also grows. Here are some drum set basics to help you hone the skills of your experienced performers and start your inexperienced players.

Setting up the Equipment

One elementary aspect of learning to perform well on drum set is to set up the equipment properly. A too high seat, for instance, may cause the player discomfort because it places the drummer's weight too far forward. Students should try several different seat heights and experiment by sitting at the edge of the seat and in the center. Have your drummer find a comfortable sitting position in which he can relax the upper leg muscles. This gives him control of the high-hat and bass drum pedals.

Similarly, students should place the tom-toms to get a relaxed feeling in their arms as they play. The tone quality of the tom-toms is also affected by their angle and height.

The main concern in bass drum placement is making the stroke. The beater should return to the starting position immediately after making contact with the bass drum head, thus increasing the player's speed and control.

Have your drummers experiment with the tension screws on the pedal to adjust the reflex action and try different distances that the beater comes to rest away from the bass drum head. If the beater's stroke is too short, the bass drum volume will be too soft. Correct length of the bass drum stroke produces the best tone quality in addition to enhancing the drummer's pedal-playing speed.

Adjusting the hi-hat cymbal stand properly lets the drummer produce the best sound with this important portion of the drum set. The spring in the hi-hat stand controls the tension required to compress the foot pedal and close the cymbals. It also controls the speed with which the pedal springs back. Some hi-hat stands now have adjustable tension springs so the amount of tension can be controlled. Whenever possible have your drum set player adjust the hi-hat pedal tension for his foot's most comfortable playing position. Different amounts of foot pressure on the pedal will create a variety of cymbal sounds.

The best height and angle of the other cymbals depends on the player's size and the type of playing. Don't have students set up cymbals in a certain way only because their favorite drummer uses a similar set-up. To help your drummer find the best cymbal set-up, let him experiment with a low set-up first. The cymbals should be fairly loose so they vibrate freely. This is equally useful in big band playing, show drumming, and general combo playing.

A high cymbal set-up means playing the cymbals at about a 45-degree angle on their stands; each cymbal has to be screwed tightly to its cymbal tilter. This set-up produces a dry, pinging sound. Some players prefer this sound for small progressive jazz groups and light trio playing. Your drummer's size, style of playing, and the group with which he is performing determine the best cymbal set-up.

Exercises

Incorrect drum set notation can confuse both beginners and experienced players. Here is the standard notation for a four-piece drum set.

There are several exercises drum set players can use as a daily warm up and to increase dexterity over a period of time. Your drummers can also experiment with different set-ups as they play these exercises in example 1.

Example 1 Bass Drum Hi-Hat

♩ = 60-100

3 3 3 3

Bass Drum and Hi-Hat in Combination

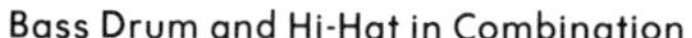

R L R R L R L L R L R R L R L L

Melodic Coordination:

Stage Band Drumming and Interpretation

The stage band drummer has more creative freedom than any other band member. The arranger's practice of writing drum set music as a guide instead of a precise part enhances the player's interpretive freedom, and if the drum chart were written too specifically, most players would have difficulty reading it.

The dotted-eighth-sixteenth-note cymbal beat, one of the most important elements in stage band drumming, should be interpreted four different ways, depending on the tempo.

1. Very Slowly

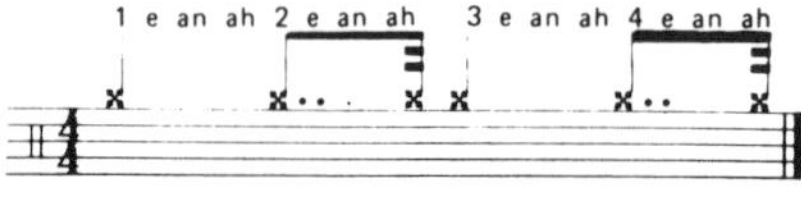

2. Medium

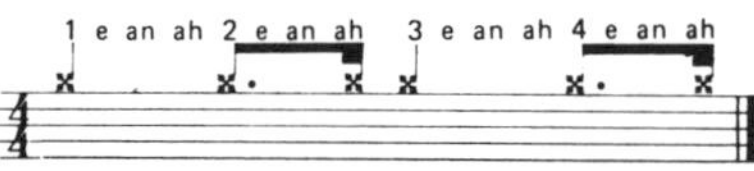

3. Medium Fast

4. Very Fast

Interpretating in drum set performance is most often a swing feeling. But at slow tempos, is over-exaggerated as in , and the emphasis is playing with a relaxed beat and not rushing.

Another fundamental aspect of interpreting the drum set chart is to play fills tastefully. The student can become proficient at playing fills if he anticipates how the figure will sound and sets it up tastefully.

Show the student how the figures look in the music, then add the set-up and have him sing each one as it will be played (see example 2).

Two books, Ted Reed's *Syncopation* and John Pickering's *Stage Band Drummers Guide*, provide additional practice material. In addition to performing and practicing, the best way to learn drum set basics is listening to exemplary recordings and live performances to imitate the drum set players' styles. ■

Example 2

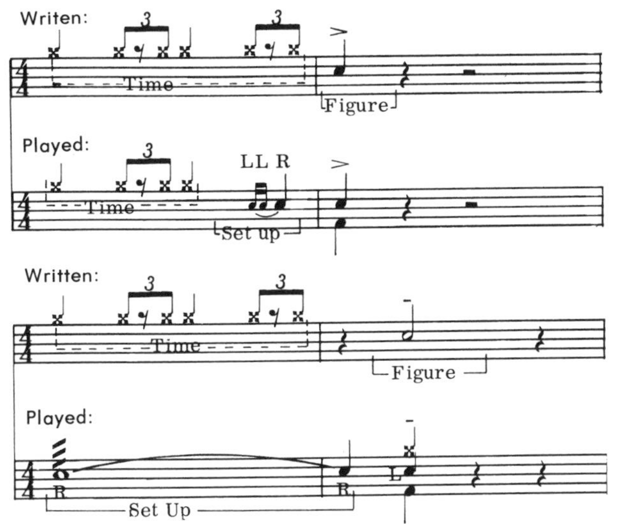

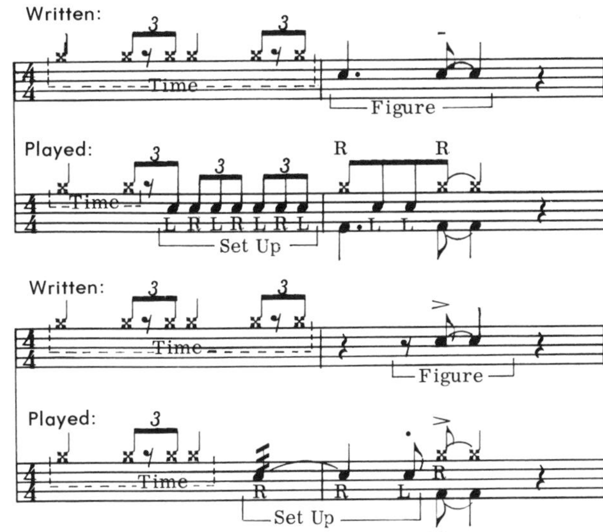

December, 1979

Big Band Drumming Basics

Ed Soph

We've all heard that the drummer's role in a band is to keep time. That's right, but he must also interpret the time by listening to the rest of the ensemble and complementing the music rhythmically, stylistically, dynamically, and tonally.

It's surprising how many aspiring players do not know how a big band becomes a cohesive ensemble. An average band has five saxes, four trombones, five trumpets, and three rhythm players. Each one of the horn sections has a lead player, and the other players in their specific sections listen to their lead player who sets the intonation, phrasing, dynamics, and tempo in his section. In the same fashion all of the lead players listen to each other to establish the intonation, phrasing, dynamics, and tempo of the band. There's only one way they can lead their sections, and that's by listening.

The drummer must listen to the other players in the rhythm section, the pianist or guitarist and bass player, and complement the bass line. For example, if the bassist or pianist plays a line like this:

the drummer should complement the line and play something like this:

He should not play straight eighth notes or dotted eighths followed by sixteenths. The members of the rhythm section should establish whether they are going to play on top of the beat, behind the beat, or right on the beat. Once there is a cohesive rhythm section, the drummer and lead trumpet player should work together in leading the ensemble. These players are the rhythmic and dynamic force of the band, much like the first trumpet and timpani are in an orchestra. The lead trumpet sets the musical pace for the rest of the ensemble, and the drummer should interpret the music in the same manner.

Playing musically with a big band

Playing musically means performing in such a way that your instrument becomes an integral, unobtrusive part of the music, which is a challenge on drums because they can be loud, and they are easily over-played. A player needs sound technique so that he doesn't worry about executing what he hears. He needs a good understanding of dynamics, phrasing, rhythm interpretation, and reading. Without this background he may be afraid to play, and fear spells disaster: over playing, rushing, inappropriate fills, everything but music.

First, a drummer should know the musical attributes of his set. The basic drum set has four voices: soprano (snare), alto (tom-tom), tenor (floor tom), and bass (bass drum). These are analogous to the same four voices within the ensemble. A drummer should use the voices in his set to complement and contrast the four basic voices of the ensemble. For example, if the lead trumpet ended a phrase on a high C, the note would best be complemented and supported by the snare, not the bass drum, keeping the drum sound in the same timbre.

Timbre must be accompanied by the appropriate duration of the notes and the right kind of accent (or lack of accent). How many times have you heard an ensemble play:

and the drummer is playing:

That isn't musical. The drummer should be playing short-sounding instruments such as snare drum or closed hi-hat.

Dynamics seem to be the nemesis of younger players. Playing softly often means dragging, and playing loudly will find a drummer rushing. This will change as a player gains experience through playing and practice, and as he explores the wide range of dynamics possible on his drums. Dynamic range and tempo control will also improve if a drummer practices his technical exercises at all dynamic levels.

Phrasing correctly is an obvious point, but so many times it is overlooked. If a chart is built of ten-bar phrases, that is the way a drummer should interpret it. Yet, some drummers constantly phrase in 2-, 4-, or 8-bar segments, delineating each segment with a bass drum kick and cymbal crash. One should be able to phrase in any length.

Style is also often overlooked. This happens when you hear a drummer playing *La Fiesta* as though he were playing *String of Pearls*. Stylistic awareness comes from listening to the music from different eras until you know how the different kinds of music were played.

Chart reading and interpretation

The average drum chart, particularly at the junior high and high school level, is a crude map of music. About all it shows is the form of the piece. Dynamic markings are seldom present, and if the chart is designated as being in "swing time," the young drummer is instructed to play the following measure throughout the chart:

If it is in another style, the young player is given cryptic instructions at the top of the chart like, "play with a bossa-rock-funk-gospel feel." That kind of direction makes it hard for anyone to play musically.

A drummer should be able to read a chart fast. Once the form is familiar and crucial accents, dynamics, and kicks are known, the chart should be put away and the drummer should then begin listening and interpreting what is happening rhythmically and melodically in the main lines.

Fills and solos

A fill is not the same as a solo. A fill is played for the benefit of the ensemble. It sets up the band's entrance, acts as a bridge between phrases, or begins or ends a phrase. (It is not the place for a drummer to show-off). It should sound like part of the music, retaining the same dynamic and rhythmic character as the music the band has played or will play. Of course, there are always exceptions. A drummer may have to make the transition to double time, to another time signature, or to a different rhythmic style.

All fills lead into an ensemble entrance that is either on the beat or off the beat. The drummer can help the ensemble by setting up an entrance with a fill that has the same feel to it.

A drummer's solos should also sound as if they are part of the piece. He can do this by following the structure of the chart, such as AABA, or he can use rhythmic and melodic motives found in the chart. There is nothing more unmusical than a drummer playing a solo using practice room licks and stickings that have no relation to the chart.

Every serious drummer should listen to the following bands and learn technique from their drummers: Chick Webb (his own big band); Joe Jones (early Count Basie); Sam Woodyard (Duke Ellington); Louis Bellson (Duke and his own big band); Dave Tough (early Woody Herman); Jake Hanna (Woody Herman); Rufus Jones (early Maynard Ferguson); Peter Erskine (Maynard Ferguson); John Von Ohlen (Stan Kenton); Mel Lewis (Gerry Mulligan's big band); Mel Lewis (Thad Jones-Mel Lewis Big Band); Buddy Rich; and Gene Krupa (Benny Goodman).

There are no short cuts, no magic exercises, and no formulas to learning how to listen and play musically in a big band. There is only hard work. But there are rewards, too, like being part of an organization of sixteen individuals who play as one. ■

Percussion Solos and Studies

Don R. Baker

The new music of this past year looked generally better than last year's and seemed to have at least one or two good works in each area. Even though there is more mallet/keyboard literature, there still seems to be too many impractical drum set technique books and a remaining large void in original mallet/keyboard solos for junior and senior high school players.

F. Michael Combs' *Percussion Manual,* published by Wadsworth, is an excellent reference text for the music educator. It has a clear and concise text and the thorough appendix is extremely valuable. It includes recommended methods, solos, recordings, and dealers' and distributors' addresses, and almost half the book is devoted to snare drum. Obviously written for a college instrumental methods percussion class, it could be of some use in a high school percussion situation.

Mallet/Keyboard

The Marimba Goes Baroque, arranged by Linda Loren Pimentel is a collection of works by J.S. Bach and others. The pieces vary in length and difficulty. An experienced four-mallet performer will find these challenging and rewarding. Duets, solos, and marimba-accompanying-marimba pieces using two-, three-, or four-mallet playing are included. The works are clean, legible, and well-edited for 4- or 4-1/3-octave marimba. The collection is available from Permus Publications.

Csárdás by V. Monti, another piece from Permus Publications, has been arranged by James Moore for marimba, xylophone, or vibes. The work is an excellent training piece to develop fast two-mallet technique and slow legato three-mallet style. It is long enough to be used for contest or recital, and the accompaniment is very easy.

William J. Schinstines' *Castor and Pollux* published by Kendor, is a relatively short duet in rondo form. The duet is designed for building technique but offers little in developing good musicianship. The total range is two-and-a-half octaves, and it is fun for high school performance or college sight reading.

Permus Publications has another work for mallet/keyboard instruments that may interest the more advanced player. *Marie* by Geary Larrick is written for marimba or vibes, but there are no pedaling instructions. The piece is in rag style, and four mallet independence is required.

Mary and Wally Barnett have again come out with a nice series of very easy mallet and snare drum solos with piano accompaniment. All are part of Belwin-Mills' *Contemporary Band Course.* The pieces are short, about a page long, and use a melodic concept to teach phrasing. They are clear and legible to read with an easy piano accompaniment. *Swiss Chocolate* contains triplets and requires double stops. Rolls for snare drum are open, rudimental style. These pieces are fun to play and are good supplemental solos for beginner's motivation and first recital. *Swiss Chocolate, Waltz from "Coppelia,"* and *Nutcracker Melodies* are for mallet percussion, and *A Horse of a Different Color, George M. Cohan Medley* and *Hum Drum* are for snare drum.

Drum Set

The books labeled 1, 2, and 3 in Dennis G. Rogers' *Solo Studies* for drum set, a publication of Southern Music Company, do not indicate the usual easy-to-difficult level; all are generally very difficult for the high school student and very challenging for the proficient college drummer. The music is for a typical five-piece drum set but is written in an unconventional score order. The solos are actually based on the snare drum rudiments.

A Volume of Instruction for the Drum Set is written and published by Steve Faulkner. It is written for a standard four-piece drum set, notated in standard vertical order without a cymbal line. Five sections – containing coordination patterns, stick control and independence studies, and basic beats – progress from very simple to very difficult material.

Jim Piekarczyk's *The Drumset Exerciser,* published by Opus, is another technique book for a four-piece drum set. The book is designed as an "endurance conditioner," and it does this very well. The text is clear, informative, and offers several good suggestions on practicing. The book is layed out well, progresses normally, and is a good guide for educators.

C.L. Barnhouse has added two new drum set solos by Larry Snider to its New Dimensions Series: . . .*to Rock for Admiral Shunk* and *Rondo for Drumset.* Rondo is in swing style and the former is obviously in rock style. Good independence and around-the-drum coordination are necessary. Both solos are based on melodic and musical phrasing, but they still contain exciting rhythmic appeal. Moderate in length, both could be played by a good junior high or senior high school student. These two solos are worthy additions to our literature not only because they are musically oriented but because they are written for todays "in" five-piece set.

Snare Drum

Evocation No. 2, a Kendor publication by William J. Schinstine, is a difficult work for the advanced snare drummer. It is not too long and could be useful contest material. It has good dynamic contrast and rhythmic interest, but it's very asymetrical, loaded with meter changes and rhythmic abstractions. This piece is a mental monster but fun and challenging.

Paul Moore's *Percussion Method* published by Ludwig, includes a cassette tape of piano accompaniments and rhythm exercises, available separately. There is, of course, the intonation prob lem while playing with pitched instruments on tape. This book is layed out very well, clear in text, printing, and notation. Two unusual advantages are the index and a very thorough contents chart; these are often left out of educational methods. The basic rhythmic pedagogy starts with sixteenth notes and progresses to longer values, like eighth-notes, quarter-notes, half-notes, and dotted figures. Concert or rudimental rolls may be taught using Moore's notation and descriptions, even though the tape has only rudimental-style rolls. Most importantly, the book progresses by lessons with mallet/keyboard instruction included, thus making the method a total approach to percussion. Moore also includes instruction for bass drum, cymbals, multiple percussion, and score reading. The selection of melody etudes is not as linear as it should be for beginners, because beginners don't play skips well. I like the book very much and look forward to using it with beginning students.

Timpani

Two Episodes by Jared Spears, a Barnhouse publication, is a two-movement work for two timpani of 29" and 26" at the high school level. The performers must play on the bowls of the timpani, on the butt ends of the sticks, and use half- and whole-step glissandi.

Soundings, a Kendor publication by Douglas Igelsrud, requires a set of four timpani with the middle two having pedals. The piece is not very long, and tuning problems are challenging. It sounds like an etude for the college student.

William J. Schinstine has added some new works and etudes to his solo collection *The Developing Solo Timpanist,* published by Southern. The music requires two to four timpani with some added percussion. Difficulty runs from very easy to advanced high school level. This book is a good progressive collection for learning timpani techniques, some of which are beyond the traditional playing manner. This solo collection is also a good buy for your money.

Multiple Percussion

Excursion, an MCA Music publication by Robert Staren, was written for the Brooklyn (N.Y.) Music Society. It requires two timpani, three bongos, two temple blocks, and a wood block. Players must make 2, 3, and 5 divisions of the beat and several meter changes with a variety of different sticks, dynamics, and timpani pitches. The piece has a spatial sound quality with very little continuity.

Mezcládo by Tómas White is published by Barnhouse and requires wind chimes, suspended cymbal, two cowbells, and timbales. With work on the rhythms any high school student can play this piece, but the last section is unclear whether the performer should continue the free solo ad lib or play the rhythms as written. I see no point in notating what is basically a written-out Latin improvisation for a typical timbale set with wind chimes. A student with a good sense of Latin beats would do just as well improvising.

Jared Spears has written three solos for multiple percussion, *Trilogy for Solo Percussionist, Introduction and Furioso,* and *Promenade,* published by Barnhouse. *Trilogy* is in three movements, the first for snare drum and two tom toms, the second for mallet instrument, and the third for five temple blocks. This is playable by most junior high students. *Introduction* requires four tom toms and two suspended cymbals. It's a nice work for the junior high level, but the player needs good legato style on drums as well as energetic technique. *Promenade,* for snare drum, three tom toms, and suspended cymbal, is slightly more challenging but well worth the student's effort. Spears writes excellent literature at different levels for public school use, and any of these three could be used for contest, but I strongly recommend *Promenade.* ■

1980 - 1981

582	From Marching Band to Concert Hall	Frank Shaffer	January
583	Percussion Means More Than a Snare Drum	Anna Watkins	February
585	Triangle Performance Technique	Edward P. Asmus	March
586	Developing Concert Snare Drum Technique	Robert McCormick	April
588	A Cymbal Symposium	Kenneth L. Neidig, *et al.*	May
592	Expert Advice for Percussion Students	Gordon Peters, Tony Ames and Fred A. Wickstrom, Jr.	May
595	The Top Ten Ensemble Works	David P. Eyler	May
599	Directory of Timpanists and Percussions in American Symphony Orchestras		May
600	Teaching Mallet Instruments to Beginners	Mario Gaetano	May
602	Percussion Recordings	Don R. Baker	May
604	Organizing a Percussion Ensemble	Walter C. Schneider	May
607	Teaching Musicianship to Percussionists	David W. Vincent	May
608	A Rotating Schedule for the Percussion Section	Milton Nelson	May
609	Teaching Accessory Percussion Instruments	Garwood Whaley	May
611	Substitute Percussion Instruments	James McKinney	July
612	Audition Solos for First-Year Percussionists	William J. Schinstine	August
613	Survey of Marching Percussion Materials	Jay A. Wanamaker	September
615	African Rhythms for American Percussionists	Phil Faini	October
618	Rudimentary Awakening	Gene Bardo	November
619	Percussion Literature	Don R. Baker	December
621	Beginning Four-Mallet Playing	Mario A. Gaetano, Jr.	January
623	Percussion Maintenance and Repair	Don R. Baker	February
626	Warm-Up for Young Percussionists	Paul P. Brazauskas	March
627	Two-Mallet Keyboard Fundamentals	Frank Shaffer, Jr.	April
629	Marching Mallet Percussion	Lauren Vogel	May
631	International Drum Rudiment Proposal	Jay A. Wanamaker	July
632	Field Position and Drill Ideas for the Marching Percussion Section	Kevin Lepper	September
634	Adjudicating the Marching Percussion Section	Sherman Hong	October
637	Interval Study on Mallet Percussion Instruments	Linda Pimentel	November

From Marching Band to Concert Hall

Frank Shaffer

When marching season is over and concert season rolls around, members of the percussion section grow restless because most concert band percussion parts can't compete with the flash and fanciness of a halftime show's percussion feature. However, an organized percussion ensemble can serve as a bridge between the football field and the concert hall, helping percussionists understand the importance of the accessory instruments, keyboard percussion instruments, and timpani; and by performing these compositions, students can realize the importance of all the percussion instruments as color in the concert band. Moreover, the increasing number of solo and ensemble contests gives percussion ensembles important performance goals.

The compositions selected for listing here use only the standard percussion instruments found in most schools. They will help keep interest alive in the percussion section after marching band season passes, and they will make the transition to concert season easier and more musically rewarding for your percussionists.

Three Brothers by Michael Colgrass is published by Music for Percussion and requires nine players. The instrumentation is bongos, snare drum, four timpani (shared by two players), cowbell, maracas, tambourine, suspended cymbal, and three tom-toms.

Students especially enjoy this selection's Latin-style second section, in which each instrument has a brief solo. This piece is a very effective contest selection and though challenging, it is not beyond the abilities of most high school students. A tri-tom set could be used for the three tom-toms part. And while it does not sound quite the same, the second timpani part could be played on two marching bass drums or low tom-toms if your school does not have four timpani. The only change which must be made in this arrangement is that the first timpani (third line in the score) must play the glissando and the pedaling part of Timpani 2 from letters E to F.

Nonet by Jack McKenzie is published by Music for Percussion and needs eight players. Its instrumentation includes bongos, small conga or small tenor drum, large conga or large tenor drum, guiro and bass drum, cowbell and tam-tam, suspended cymbal, maracas and claves, four tom-toms, marimbula or four temple blocks, and tom-tom.

While not as challenging as *Three Brothers,* this is an effective piece with a percussion section in which good, average, and beginning players are mixed. Four of the eight parts are of medium difficulty, but the others are relatively easy. The marimbula part could be played on a xylophone if temple blocks are not available, and a low-pitched cymbal could be substituted for tam-tam.

A La Nañingo by Mitchell Peters requires five or ten players and is published by the composer. The selection's instrumentation is two cowbells, suspended cymbal, and triangle (Player 1); bongos and snare drum (Player 2); three tom-toms and tambourine (Player 3); three timpani and two temple blocks (Player 4); and bass drum and wood block (Player 5).

This piece alternates between $\frac{6}{8}$ and $\frac{3}{4}$ in an ABA form with a coda. Performers trade solos with each other. While directors may encourage students to make the instrument changes required in multiple percussion set-ups, it would be possible to have five different players perform on the instruments required in the piece's B section, thus involving more players. Tri-tom sets could be used for the three tom-toms, and two more wood blocks could serve as temple blocks.

Little Suite by Kenneth Krause is published by Music for Percussion and requires six players. Its instrumentation includes three timpani, snare drum, bells and xylophone, bass drum, gong, wood block, ratchet, and suspended cymbal.

This three-movement piece ("Fanfare," "Waltz," and "Finale") will give your high school marching keyboard players a workout; parts for the other performers are fun, too. A deep suspended cymbal can substitute for gong.

Piece for Percussion, composed and published by Mitchell Peters, requires at least four players, or as many as eight performers. The instrumentation is snare drum, xylophone (Player 1); three tom-toms, bells, and castanets (Player 2); three timpani (Player 3); three temple blocks, bass drum, tambourine, triangle, suspended finger cymbal, and chimes (Player 4).

This is a very effective piece if taken at the proper tempo (very fast ♩=180) and if dynamics are closely observed. A chordal section for xylophone requires basic knowledge of four-mallet technique. Neither the bell nor the chime part is difficult, and a second set of bells or a bell lyre could substitute for chimes. More than four players could perform this piece, especially if they were assigned to the Player 4 part, but these extra performers would be left counting rests for long periods. Another person could also be used to play castanets and bells in the Player 2 part, and three wood blocks could be used instead of temple blocks.

Study in $\frac{5}{8}$, composed and published by Mitchell Peters, requires four players. The instrumentation is snare drum, and tambourine (Player 1); suspended cymbal and small tom-tom (Player 2); two timpani and castanets (Player 3); and bass drum, large tom-tom, and field drum (Player 4).

The challenge of this piece is its odd meter. The work is most effective with a minimal number of instruments played by the specified, four performers. The composer specifies tom-toms in standard drumset sizes. To involve more players, directors may assign more than one student to each part of *A La Nañingo* or *Piece for Percussion,* but this piece will not work well that way.

Three Pieces for Percussion Quartet by Warren Benson is published by G. Schirmer for four players. The instrumentation is two snare drums, field drum, bass drum, suspended cymbal, triangle, wood block, castanets (machine preferable), small and large tom-toms, milk bottle, and gong.

This long-time favorite in three short, contrasting movements still appeals to high school students. It makes musical use of stick clicking, playing on different areas of a cymbal, and alternating use of tips and butts of sticks with exciting results. Alternating rhythmic figures between three and four instruments provides an interesting variety of timbres. A good milk bottle substitute is a one liter, or quart size soft drink bottle. The glass is thick enough to avoid breakage when struck to produce the sound. Snare drums need to be pitched at least a major second apart, if two of the same size are used.

African Sketches by J. Kent Williams is published by Ludwig Music and requires four players. The selection's instrumentation is high tom-tom, two medium tom-toms, low tom-tom, three tuned drums, log drum, guiro, two cowbells, and maracas.

Don't let the several exotic instruments here keep you from performing this challenging, exciting piece. The three contrasting movements feature syncopated African-style rhythms. The high tom-toms could be parade or tenor drums; and a floor tom-tom, from a drum set tuned low, would be a good low tom-tom. In addition, a pair of bongos and a snare drum with snares off would be a good substitute for the three tuned drums. Two wood blocks or two temple blocks can't compare with the sound of a log drum, but they would be acceptable substitutes if a log drum is unavailable. A seasoned two-by-four board, cut in various lengths and suspended on a frame, also makes a good log drum substitute when played with hard yarn or rubber mallets.

Housemusic for Percussion, for four players, was composed and published by Stanley Leonard. Its instrumentation is bells, two tambourines, wood block, two tom-toms, castanets, triangle, and tam-tam.

This piece features an odd-metered first movement, a second-movement duet for tambourine and tam-tam, and a spirited third-movement allegro. This selection is effective and not extremely difficult. Special effects include the use of triangle beaters and wire brushes while playing the tam-tam. ■

February, 1980

Percussion Means More Than a Snare Drum

Anna Watkins

Most elementary percussion students are given instruction on snare drum. While snare drum training is an excellent way to begin, anyone who has heard bands and orchestras knows you need more than a snare drum in the percussion section.

Each of the percussion instruments has its own playing techniques that should be taught separately. I give my students lessons on different instruments each session and include etudes or percussion parts from compositions to show how the techniques are used. Here are some sample lessons.

Bass Drum

• (Begin with your bass drum heads loose enough so you have a good bass drum sound.) Using a large bass drum beater, strike different areas of the drum head moving slowly from the edge toward the center. Listen for the different timbres. As you move toward the rim, you will hear more of the upper partials sounding. Find the areas of the head where you hear a typical bass drum sound.

• Using different pairs of beaters (bass drum roll beaters, timpani mallets, snare drum sticks, vibe or marimba mallets), play a single stroke roll just fast enough to keep a continuous sound. Because the bass drum head is large and vibrates slowly, allow time for the head to recover before striking it again in the roll.

• Play notes at various dynamic levels and try different methods of muffling: use one hand, both hands, another bass drum beater pressed against the head, and the technique of hugging the drum. Find out how much muffling is necessary to stop the sound.

• Practice playing correct note values. There should be a noticeable difference between 𝅗𝅥 𝅗𝅥 and ♩ 𝄽 ♩ 𝄽 .

Triangle

• Unless the part is extremely difficult or you need to make a quick change to another instrument, hold the triangle in front of you at eye level so you can watch the music and the conductor at the same time.

• Use different sizes of triangle beaters, nails, welding rods, etc. and listen for the various sounds they make.

• Practice muffling the triangle with the little finger while holding the clip holder with the other fingers of the same hand.

• Suspend the triangle with two clips and play with a matched pair of beaters.

• Play on the side opposite the opening and on the lower leg of the triangle. A triangle should not sound any specific pitch, so find the striking spot where you can hear the most overtones.

Tam-Tam or Gong

• Warm up or prime the tam-tam or gong before you strike it. Because it is a large instrument which vibrates slowly, you must start it vibrating quietly with the fingers or the beater before you play it so it will sound on time.

• Play on different areas. Move slowly from the edge toward the center listening for the different timbres. Find the combination of bright and dark sounds that gives you a balanced, typical sound.

• Practice playing rolls using bass drum beaters and vibe mallets.

Tambourine

• Hold the tambourine at eye level.

• Practice using different parts of the hand to strike the tambourine: fingertips, fist, palm, and knuckles.

• Play on different head areas.

• Learn to play different kinds of rolls: shake rolls, thumb rolls, yarn mallet rolls on the edge with the tambourine placed on the trap table cushioned with a towel.

• Practice different playing techniques: play fast articulated passages with mallets; place the tambourine on the knee and play with both hands; or alternate striking between knee and fist.

Suspended Cymbal

• Find the three basic playing areas: edge, bow, and dome (cup or bell). Listen for the different tone qualities from bright to dark, resonant to dry, and find the areas where the cymbal "speaks" faster. Sometimes you will need to prime the cymbal before playing.

• Play with yarn marimba mallets, snare drum sticks, and brushes.

• Scrape lightly across the ridges with a small triangle beater, coin, rattan handle of a mallet, brushes, or brush handle.

• Play a one-handed roll with the cymbal placed between two mallets or with the separated wires of a brush.

Crash Cymbals

• (Before picking up the cymbals the students should learn proper striking angle and position using just their hands.) Keep the cymbals close together in the set position before the crash. When you crash the cymbals, the outer edges should be almost, but not quite, together. (If the edges are exactly together the cymbals produce a "whoof" sound.)

• When you strike the two cymbals together, try to get the full plate of both cymbals to sound so you will hear the maximum number of partials.

• For different dynamic levels keep the cymbals the same distance from each other but use different amounts of energy in your stroke. Moving the cymbals farther apart increases the possibility of getting a "whoof" sound.

• For a sustained crash continue the follow-through motion holding the cymbals up so they don't touch anything. To damp the cymbals pull them quickly against your sides.

Learning to play keyboard percussion instruments and timpani requires in-depth study, but your students should know a few basic playing techniques.

Timpani

• Learn the ranges of drums. (Be sure your drums are tuned to the proper ranges and the heads are in tune with themselves.)

• Learn to tune by intervals. Begin by using only the 29-inch and the 26-inch drums, and practice tuning these two drums a perfect fifth apart and then a perfect fourth apart.

• Choose the correct playing spot for a full, resonant tone. This is about three inches from the rim, but don't use a ruler to find it, use your ears.

• Practice damping exercises such as repeated half note-half rest patterns followed by shorter note values.

Keyboard Percussion

• Keep the hands low when playing xylophone, marimba, bells, or vibraphone by using wrist action and not arm movement.

• Learn to play equally well with both hands by practicing alternate sticking on scales and chord patterns.

• Do not allow the mallet to linger on the bar because this kills part of your sound. Exaggerate the up part of the stroke.

In general tell your students not to waste motion in their playing. They should learn to move quickly, silently, and gracefully. After your students have learned basic techniques, encourage them to use different playing areas, mallets, and muffling for a variety of sounds.

One or more of the following recommended text and reference books can be used as guides:

Combs, F. Michael, *Percussion Manual,* Wadsworth.

Denov, Sam, *The Art of Cymbal, Playing,* Adler (Belwin).

Goldenberg, Morris, *Modern Method for Snare Drum with a Guide for the Artist Percussionist,* Chappell.

Morales, Humberto and Henry Adler, *How to Play Latin-American Rhythm Instruments,* Belwin Mills.

Payson, Al, *Techniques of Playing Bass Drum, Cymbals and Accessories,* Payson Percussion Products.

Price, Paul, *Technique and Exercises for Playing Castanets, Triangle and Tambourine,* Music for Percussion. ■

March, 1980

Triangle Performance Technique

Edward P. Asmus

Playing the triangle is an often overlooked area of percussion performance. The instrument has been struck by everything from the back end of a bass drum beater to a heavy railroad spike. Such misuse is not deerved because the triangle is capable of producing beautiful sounds. Unfortunately, many players lack a good foundation in triangle technique and have no concept of how to produce a good triangle tone.

Two general schools of thought exist on what the tone of a triangle should be. One school maintains that the triangle should produce a relatively pure sound that is centered in character and lacks an abundance of overtones. The second school describes a well-produced triangle tone as a shimmer that has an abundance of overtones.

The centered triangle tone is rather easily produced and can be achieved at many locations over the surface of the instrument. The tone rich in overtones is more difficult to achieve because there are relatively fewer locations at which it can be produced. However, the triangle sound rich in overtones does have some distinct advantages. If you were able to "freeze" the sound of a band or orchestra at a moment where the triangle played and the sound spectrum of this moment were analyzed, you would find that the frequencies inherent in this slice of complex sound would cluster in harmonically related frequencies determined by the scoring of the work. This clustering of sound leaves open gaps of frequencies. A triangle tone rich in overtones has a greater potential for filling these gaps because it produces an abundance of harmonically unrelated frequencies. The centered sound, on the other hand, has a substantially greater probability of being masked by the ensemble-produced harmonic clusters because its sound is focused into relatively few frequency domains. Also, because the proper triangle tone has a limited dynamic range, the overtone-rich triangle sound has greater potential for being perceived by the listener; it does not have to be over-played for it to be heard.

Selecting an Instrument

The triangle, like any musical instrument, varies in quality from instrument to instrument. The best way to select a triangle with the capacity for producing a rich, sonorous tone is to com pare as many triangles as possible until an appropriate instrument is found.

The kind of beater used will affect the tone produced. The instrument's limited dynamic range results in a corresponding limited range of appropriate beater weights. The beater must be of sufficient weight to set the triangle into vibration at a level adequate to produce the desired sound rich in overtones. However, it must not be so heavy as to over-play the instrument and surpass the instrument's dynamic capacity.

The triangle clip is used by most performers to support the triangle. This clip, which resembles a strongly constructed metal clothespin, can be found in most hardware stores. Two loops of 25- to 30-pound-test monofilament fishing line are draped from the clip. The loops are formed so the inner loop supports the triangle and the outer loop acts as a safety guard if the first loop fails.

Playing Position

The triangle clip is supported on the tops of the tips of the thumb and first finger so that the remaining three fingers can be used to muffle the instrument.

The player should position the triangle so the open end is opposite the playing hand. All notes that aren't rolled should be sounded by striking the inside of the lowest tine at a distance of one-fourth its length from the closed corner. All rolls are produced inside the top corner approximately 1/2 to 3/4 of an inch from the apex of the triangle.

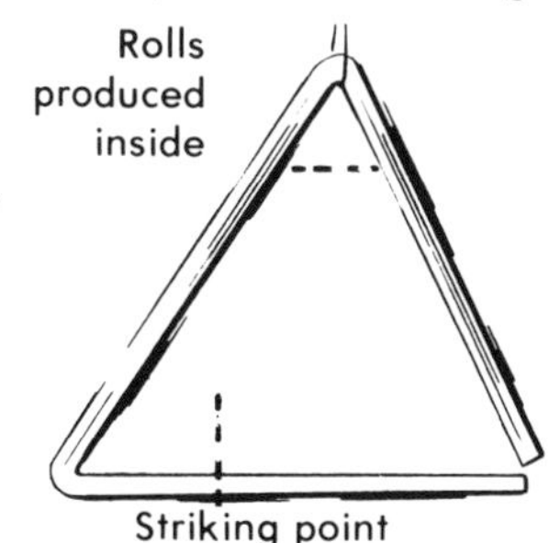

The triangle beater is held with a relaxed, delicate grip between the thumb and first finger. The beater must be able to rebound naturally from contact with the triangle after a tone is initiated.

Striking the Instrument

With the beater held properly, the triangle is struck with the playing hand held below the bottom tine, which means that the beater strikes at an angle on the upper outside edge of the tine. Here is the secret to producing an overtone-rich sound. If the instrument is struck with the hand at a position even with the lower tine, contact is made with the top inner portion of the tine only, which results in a centered sound that lacks overtones.

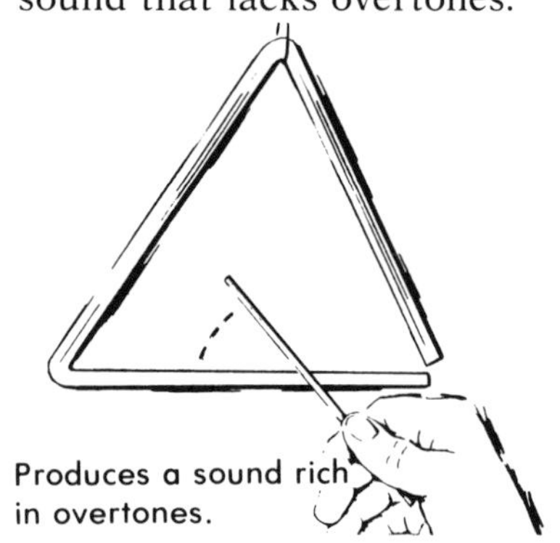

Produces a sound rich in overtones.

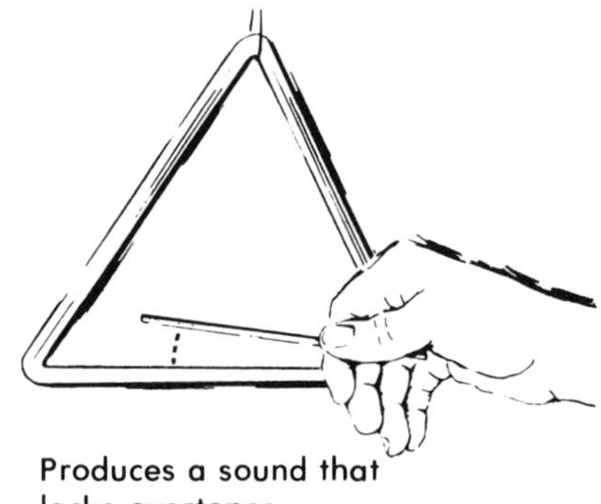

Produces a sound that lacks overtones.

A roll is created by striking the two side tines with a rapid alternating movement of the wrist. To produce a roll with a rich overtone quality, the triangle must be struck with the playing hand to the right or left of the triangle's center. In this position the triangle contacts both side tines at an angle, without sacrificing the evenness of a roll.

In very fast passages it may be necessary to suspend the triangle with two clips attached to a music stand; the clips suspend the triangle from each corner. The player uses two identical beaters, one in each hand, and generally plays on the closed tine of the triangle, depending on the tone he wants to produce.

Vibrato

Triangle vibrato is an effect that can be used to significantly enhance the musicality of the triangle sound. It is produced by placing the three lower fingers of the playing hand, held together forming a small wall, between the two side tines of the triangle. The entire hand then fans in a horizontal manner using the upper arm and keeping the wrist rigid while limiting movement at the elbow as much as possible. This somewhat robot-like movement is used for two reasons: it generates the greatest movement of air around the triangle; and it keeps the triangle beater, supported by the thumb and first finger, from inadvertently contacting the instrument.

The triangle is an instrument capable of truly artistic performance, and all many players need is a fundamental knowledge of sound production and technique on the instrument. ■

April, 1980

Developing Concert Snare Drum Technique

Robert McCormick

Helping students develop their concert snare drum technique is an area we often neglect. For instance, one of the most difficult problems of students is learning to relax while controlling the muscles. This skill is as important to the percussionist as it is to the athlete; yet many young players tend to grasp the sticks too tightly because they have not learned how to hold the sticks with a relaxed grip that allows for a natural rebound stroke and encourages a musical tone instead of a "noisy" sound. So teaching students to hold drum sticks loosely enough to work with the natural forces of gravity lets them play more musically with increased stick control.

Similarly, students are often taught to keep the right little finger wrapped tightly around the stick. While this works well in rudimental drumming, it hinders the freedom of motion needed for proper phrasing in concert performance. A similar problem occurs with the left-hand, "palm-up" grip; the middle finger placed firmly around the stick tends to limit the necessary freedom of motion.

It is important to supervise the beginner's snare drum grip carefully. Even though using the arms plays a significant role in snare drum finesse, emphasize wrist strokes with the young player. This emphasis is necessary because the students tend to lock their wrists and use only their forearms.

Most important is that the student be comfortable with his grip; so the teacher should allow for minor variations in either the matched or traditional grip. A good general rule is that if the grip does not appear to be hindering execution, it is probably acceptable. There are almost as many slight variations of holding the sticks as there are fine players. Remember that supervision is needed to insure freedom of motion, relaxation, correct angles, and stroke, but too much supervision can make the student tense.

The teacher should also tell students to think legato-style when playing basic strokes, because even though staccato-style playing is occasionally used, the association of a flowing legato line with basic strokes will usually result in the student's playing a more musical sound.

Furthermore, too many players limit themselves to a tight, sharp stroke that can hinder musical expression, so students should think of the stick bringing the wrist up effortlessly, instead of thinking that the wrist brings the stick up, as is often taught. Actually, both notions can be used in practice: the first idea will help develop sound-quality and phrasing, while the second will help muscle development.

Dynamic control is another common problem. Most percussionists spend their time practicing at the *mp* to *f* level, but it would be beneficial for them to spend a certain amount of time practicing as soft as possible and as loud as possible. A favorite exercise of mine is to play a *ppp* buzz roll for approximately two minutes, then crescendo gradually to *fff* for two minutes. The exercise is completed by gradually returning to the *ppp* level. This same exercise can also be played with flams, drags, and single strokes.

Teach students to use a longer stroke for loud passages and a shorter stroke for soft passages. Many young players tend to use a short stroke when playing loud, and this action results in an undesirable sound. Even when playing soft passages, the best sound and control can be achieved by working with the natural rebound. The students can demonstrate this technique by playing an identical *ff* passage first with a long stroke, then with a short stroke. (Any passage will work.) The results of this exercise show the student the difference between a musical sound and a forced noisy quality.

There are a number of outstanding books available to help students develop snare drum technique. *Stick Control* by George L. Stone is often referred to as the Bible of drumming technique, and *Encyclopedia for Snare Drum* by Forrest Clark offers a complete study of single strokes, drags, flams, and rolls. Of course, serious study must include more than technique so I use musical etudes in *Portraits in Rhythm*, by Anthony Cirone, and *Advanced Snare Drum Studies*, by Mitchell Peters.

Artistic repertoire is another vital area of concert snare drum study, and two especially worthwhile books in this category are *Modern School for Snare Drum* by Morris Goldenberg, which offers the percussion parts to a number of important works, and *The Logic of It All* by Anthony Cirone and Joe Sinai, which offers a number of insights into interpreting the orchestral repertoire.

Learning concert snare drum repertoire is perhaps the most important and most overlooked of all facets of study. In this area the student best learns to use his imagination, develop interpretive abilities, and perform musically. Learning repertoire also helps the student develop ensemble skills, which cannot be taught with an etude book. Listening to and practicing repertoire helps the student learn the difference between an accompaniment *forte*, a solo *forte*, and how to blend in an orchestra. This method of study works successfully from the elementary to the advanced level, and it will also work on any other percussion instrument. In order to develop a well-rounded musician, repertoire study should include not only listening to orchestral music, but also listening to jazz and avant-garde chamber literature.

The following list offers a few suggestions on what pieces could be studied in the standard orchestral snare drum repertoire.

Bartók – *Concerto for Orchestra*
Berlioz – *Hungarian March*
Bernstein – *Symphony #2 ("Age of Anxiety")*
Bloch – *Schelomo*
Borodin – *Polovtzian Dances*
Debussy – *Nocturnes*
Debussy – *Iberia*
Honneger – *Pacific 231*
Kodaly – *Harry Janos Suite*
Nielsen – *Concerto for Clarinet*
Nielsen – *Symphony #5*
Prokofiev – *Lt. Kije Suite*
Prokofiev – *Peter and the Wolf*
Prokofiev – *Symphony #5*
Ravel – *Bolero*
Ravel – *La Valse*
Ravel – *Rhapsodie Espagnol*
Ravel – *Daphnis and Chloe*
Rimsky-Korsakov – *Capriccio Espagnol*
Rimsky-Korsakov – *Scheherezade*
Schuman, William – *Symphony #3*
Shostakovich – *Symphony #1, #5, #7*

A student or class could listen to one of the works on the list, and then be assigned to answer the following questions. How loud was the snare drum within the context of the orchestra? How was the snare drum tuned – high, medium, or low? Did the drum have a wire-snare or a gut-snare sound? How did the drummer phrase a particular passage? How much crescendo or diminuendo was used during a particular passage? How closed were the snare drum rolls, flams, and drags? Were any accents used that are not written in the part? Did the composer use percussion during a particular passage for rhythmic reinforcement, color, or other reason? Then the students could play along with the recording.

Developing concert snare drum technique this way helps players listen more critically and become more musical concert snare drummers. ■

A Cymbal Symposium

with Bobby Christian Bill Crowden Sam Denov and Brian Shlim

conducted by Kenneth L. Neidig

(Denov) There are many choices, but just three basic types: French, Viennese, and Germanic. The French are the thinnest, the Viennese are a little thicker,and the Germanic are the heaviest. All are available in various diameters. I use two pair of French (19" and 22"), and three suspended cymbals (17", 19", and 21") for about 80% of my playing with the Chicago Symphony.

How do you go about choosing a pair of cymbals?
(Denov) Usually I go to the factory and ask for a stack of the type and size I want. Then I suspend each from a knotted rope and hit them with a vibraphone mallet (designed for striking metal – don't use a timpani mallet; they're designed for striking skin), I watch the movement of the metal, looking for uniform vibration. I want a cymbal that has good action all around its surface, and I like a dark tone quality, with good sustaining power. I need plenty of overtones because the cymbals must match any tonality the orchestra plays in, so I rule out cymbals that have only one clearly defined pitch. After I have picked out a large number of cymbals that sound good individually I start matching them up, choosing two that are at least a minor third apart in their basic pitch area. I mix them up until I find some that work well together. After I've narrowed it down to four to six pairs I'll try one against another, and interchange some of the mates.

Can you describe the sound you are looking for?
(Denov) No, it's something that exists in my head and I have to hear it. I can't describe it in words. If I wrote to the factory and tried to describe the cymbal, I'd never get exactly what I want. I have to go and pick it out in person; that's the only way I can tell. However, the factory people know what I like and they are able to save me a tremendous amount of time. They can just give a cymbal one tap and tell if I should consider it or not.

Let's say you're a budget-squeezed director in a small town and you can only afford one pair of cymbals. What do you buy?
(Denov) I'd go for the 19" French. Because they're thin, even the 19" pair is not so heavy; almost anyone can handle them.

How about suspended cymbals on a low budget?
(Denov) Unfortunately you'll need at least two French. What's good for the light and delicate situation is just not going to be big enough for the tremendous volumes. If you have to start a roll *pp* and build to *fff*, no one instrument can do it. I often use a 17", 19", 21" in tandem, moving from one cymbal to the other during the roll. The sound of a cymbal is so sustained that you can very easily glide from one cymbal to the other without any break. Also you can get a good quality sound with a great variety of overtones by hitting two different-sized suspended cymbals at the same time.

You've talked only about the French. When do you use the Viennese or Germanic?
(Denov) For more heavily orchestrated music with a big volume of sound you have to cut through – Germanic for Wagner's "Ride of the Valkyries," for example. For good general use I would stick with the French or Viennese.

Now Bobby, suppose we have the same tight-budget situation for the set drummer in the school stage band.

(Christian) I'd see that he gets a good 17" ride cymbal, and a 20". For the high hat that would be used in a conventional school stage band I'd suggest 14" medium on top and heavy on the bottom. For a rock combo you need heavier equipment.

One cymbal can sometimes be used for many things. For example, if you strike a ride cymbal in the area about three inches from the cup you get all the high sounds; so if you want to imitate the sound of two cymbals, start playing at the edge and for the big climax hit it about 2½ inches away from the cup. In this way a drummer on a limited budget can get by with fewer cymbals; but it's nice to have more. Because I do such a variety of work in the recording studios, I have about 35 different cymbals.

Do you use the same process to pick out cymbals that Sam does?

(Christian) I only hit about three or four, because they all start to sound alike.

(Denov) That's right. They all start out completely different, but after a while your mind gets boggled. After about 30 minutes, I'll usually take a break and come back to it again.

Do you ever try them out in the hall?

(Denov) Very often we do. No matter where you try them out it's important to work with a colleague so you can listen to the cymbals from a distance.

Can you trust that the way someone else plays the cymbals will be close enough to the way you will play them?

(Denov) He may not play them exactly the way I do, but I'll still be able to tell the difference in the quality of the cymbals.

(Christian) It's a lot like sitting next to a good cello player and hearing scraping and raspy sounds, but getting further away and enjoying a gorgeous full-bodied tone.

Can you describe the sound you are listening for?

(Denov) From a distance it's even harder to put your finger on it, but I know a good sound when I hear it.

I think we need to talk about how you get a good sound in your ear.

(Denov) Experience is the only way and it takes a long time. There are no shortcuts, nothing to replace years of hearing a great variety of sounds in many different situations.

(Christian) I agree 100%

Do records help?

(Denov) No, you can't depend on recorded sound because it's so artificial, adjusted so much. The best way is to go to live performances.

Of any major symphony?

(Denov) You can't go too far wrong, even though you'll find cymbal players in some of those orchestras who have never studied cymbals and have had to learn the hard way. Most of them do very well, and occasionally one will develop into a really first-class artist.

Would you care to name some?

(Denov) No, I might leave someone out.

Bobby, are there any set drummers who are especially noted for their work with cymbals, people we should listen to in order to get a good sound in our ears?

(Christian) Buddy Rich, of course; Harold Jones; in fact most of the big-name drummers have been around long enough to know how to get a good sound from the cymbals.

But aren't there some drummers who do more melodic things with cymbals as opposed to those who concentrate more on the drum heads?

(Christian) yes, there are. Carmine Apice is a great cymbal player. He likes to move all over, but he does it with good taste and he still keeps time. The drummer with "The Who" was marvelous. The trio drummers like Ed Thigpen, Joe Morello, and Dave Tough did a lot of nice things.

Sam, would you suggest some particular symphonic compositions to look for on a live program if you want to hear some good cymbal playing?

(Denov) That I can say more about. One of the most expressive works for cymbals is Debussy's *La Mer* — different effects, crescendos, diminuendos. And the notation of the piece leaves a lot to the cymbal player's imagination, so he has an opportunity to interpret, which you can't do very much on the other percussion instruments. So if you want to hear some good cymbal playing, go hear a live performance of *La Mer*. Other compositions with lots of cymbal playing, most of it loud, are *Scheherezade*, the finale to Tchaikovsky's Fourth Symphony, and *Romeo and Juliet*. When you hear an orchestra play these pieces you can tell very quickly if the cymbal player is good or not so good.

Bill, I'm sure you probably get a lot of the same questions about cymbals over and over from customers who come into your store---

(Crowden) Yes, most of them are searching, but they try not to let me know how little they know, so I have to be careful. For example, when someone says "I'm looking for a 15" cymbal," I usually ask them what they want to use it for. Often the answer is "Well, I was thinking of a ride cymbal." So I very cautiously guide them into considering something a little larger, because I know the 15" will crack when used as a ride cymbal. Or their answer may be, "I'm going to use it as my sustaining cymbal and I want to hear my stick go ping,

ping, ping." So I guide them to a heavier cymbal that will give them a lot of ping. The more information I can get from a drummer on how he wants to use a cymbal, the more I can help; but I have to pull it out of him.

What are some of the questions you're likely to ask in the process?

(Crowden) What type of music are you playing? How large a group do you have? Are there any amplifiers? Are you a jobbing drummer? Do you move around a lot? Are you often on a stage with curtains and carpets? Do you ever record? Do you play outside fair dates? That approach has worked a lot better for me than asking musical questions like, "Do you want something in E♭? Or would E be better?"

I usually ask drummers to think of their cymbals as a carpenter thinks of his tools and I tell them, "If you're going to drive a big nail (big band) you need a big hammer; and if you try to drive a big nail with a little hammer you'll break it."

Do you see a lot of broken cymbals?

(Crowden) They bring them to us in a paper bag. And most breakage is because of improper choice of equipment.

(Christian) I have never broken a cymbal in all my years of playing, and some of the cymbals I own are 50 years old.

(Denov) I never have broken a cymbal either.

How do you know what the capacity of a cymbal is? Where are its outer limits?

(Denov) That's another thing you learn only from experience.

Are there signs when you're getting to the edge?

(Denov) Yes, the sound starts to break up.

Like when a car is going too fast and it starts to shake?

(Denov) Exactly. The sound quality changes and you make a mental note of the point and don't go beyond it with that cymbal. That's why I use two suspended cymbals so often, switching during a crescendo. Cymbals will break when abused.

(Shlim) Carelessness is a major cause. Students will lay them on the rehearsal room floor and someone else steps on them, or they're knocked off a table. This abuse shows up maybe 3-6 months later when they break and the director wonders why. You have to love your cymbals and take care of them like any other instrument.

What are some common misconceptions about cymbals?

(Crowden) The first is the dictionary definition — "a brass plate. . ." Obviously Mr. Webster was not a drummer. Actually most cymbals are made from an alloy of copper, tin, silver, and other elements; the material is considered to be a form of bronze.

(Shlim) People get a lot of wrong ideas because they don't know the manufacturing process. Some cymbals are made by stamping them out of a sheet of metal, but one of the dangers of the process is that the metal is stretched under tons of pressure and the stress can cause internal breakage that will show up later. At the Zildjian factory they use a different process. First they prepare their alloy, cast it into small discs (like oversized pancakes), and allow them to cool. Then the discs are heated and put through a rolling mill, perhaps as many as 25 times depending on the diameter and thickness desired. This step produces a thin, wavy plate that is then flattened by a hammer, and trimmed to a circle. Next the center hole is punched and the cup formed. After that, the disc goes through three hammering sessions (for as long as 90 minutes each time) to form the characteristic bowed shape. Cymbals are not "spun out" as some people believe; the shallow striations ("grooves") are cut into the surface using a high speed lathe and a sharp cutting tool. They are then aged before being tested, graded, and sometimes paired.

Does a cymbal change with age?

(Denov) My theory is that the manufacturing process — especially the hammering — continues as the cymbal is played, and a "played-in" cymbal will always sound better.

Does only good come from age?

(Denov) There is a point when they become fatigued, but with proper playing and care, that's a long way down the road. There was recently a sale in New York of cymbals used by the man who played in the Philadelphia Orchestra under Stokowski, and some of them went for over $500. What beautiful instruments.

Can you hurt cymbals by cleaning them?

(Denov) I'd hate to tell you how infrequently I shine my cymbals. Any cleaner is going to be somewhat abrasive and that will wear down the striations and the cymbal will start to sound like the "earth" cymbals [those that are removed from the manufacturing process before the grooves are cut in]. A little soap and water is enough. I remember when I was in the Navy they wanted brilliantly polished cymbals so we would take them to the machine shop and use jeweler's rouge and a buffing wheel. It made them completely smooth. The cymbals looked great, but were ruined for playing. They had such a definite pitch you wouldn't believe it.

What about holders for hand cymbals?

(Denov) Never use the wooden holders that are clamped to the cymbal. They ruin the sound and exert pressure on the metal that will lead to cracks. I don't even like the big wool pads because they absorb too much of the sound; although they are useful in marching bands where comfort may be more important than musicality. I recommend leather pads and rawhide straps.

I've seen adhesive tape used on the underside of a cymbal. What's that all about?

(Christian) They're trying to kill some overtones in order to improve the sound of the cymbal.

(Shlim) Too many times a student will see a professional drummer with tape here and there and he'll go home and put it on the same place on his cymbals, not even knowing why.

(Denov) You'll never see a symphony cymbal player with any of that. Actually these people are experimenting to try to improve the sound of a cymbal, when what they should be doing is looking carefully to find the proper cymbal to begin with.

(Crowden) Yes, I run into the experimenters all the time. A fellow will come in the store and say, "I don't like the sound of this cymbal; will you put rivets in it for me?" I try to explain that the rivets will add a sizzle effect but they won't change the basic sound of the cymbal, and if I put rivets in, all he will have is a cymbal he doesn't like that now has rivets in it. Another "solution" people request is to cut down the size of a cymbal, and those conversations go like this:

"Why do you want it cut down?"

"I don't like the sound of it."

"What don't you like?"

"It just rings too much; I've tried tape but that doesn't work."

"Well maybe you just don't like the sound of this cymbal."

"I guess that could be."

"Maybe we'd better try to find you a cymbal you do like because cutting this one down will not change the basic sound."

(Shlim) These stories just emphasize the fact that you must pick the right cymbal, and have it in the right hands.

(Christian) Yes, the individual player is so important. It's like a top-level wind instrument player who can take almost any old horn and make it sound good.

Are you saying that cymbal quality doesn't matter, that it's all in the performer? Isn't there something intrinsic there that will sound, even when it's struck by the worst amateur?

(Denov) What we're saying is that no one can take a bad cymbal and make it sound OK; but a decent cymbal can be enhanced by the way it is played. And it is possible for a poor player to make a good cymbal sound bad.

How should school band and orchestra directors buy cymbals?

(Crowden) Having a large selection to choose from is important. If you're looking for a 20″ ride cymbal, for example, you should have a minimum of six cymbals to pick from. Sometimes I'll get a call from a drummer who says, "Bill, I'm looking for a 20″ and I'll need it in a couple of weeks. Call me when you have 12."

And that's a reasonable request?

(Crowden) Sure, that's very reasonable. I'll tell him, "I have a shipment coming in on the 24th." Also a shop that does a large volume or deals regularly with well-known performers can call the factory and ask them to pick out a pair of cymbals "like Sam Denov uses," and they are able to make a selection that at least gets in the ball park.

So the director almost has to deal with a specialty drum shop, then, doesn't he?

(Shlim) Right, the typical music store can't carry a large stock, and the one pair of cymbals in the small store probably came through a jobbing house, and who knows whether the pair is matched or not.

(Denov) Of course you can always get lucky. The one cymbal in that little store may be the one you have been looking for.

(Christian) Yes, the search for the Holy Grail. All drummers are looking for it, and it may be sitting right on that little guy's shelf.

Crowden) The important thing is to get the cymbal that is right for the use you want to make of it. I ask set drummers who are looking for a new cymbal to bring in the others they already have because I want to hear what the marriage of sound needs to be.

What about cymbal instruction? You all believe it's necessary. Where can you get it?

(Shlim) Schools have specialist instructors come in for the trumpets and flutes and other instruments; and many schools are close enough to a symphony orchestra that they could get a cymbal specialist. Why, just one hour with someone like Sam Denov or Bobby Christian could provide all the basics of cymbal playing, and that's what so many students and directors need.

(Christian) I think Sam's book on cymbals [*The Art of Playing the Cymbals*, Henry Adler, New York, 1963] should be in every high school. It has excellent photos, diagrams, and clear explanations of every aspect of cymbal playing.

(Denov) I tried to cram in as much information as possible, but the book does not have exercises or excerpts. It just has the basic things to do in order to produce a good sound on the cymbals.

Obviously there is a lot still to be done with cymbals. It seems clear that there is a need for percussionists to engage in specialized study of the instrument; music dealers could probably help school directors and stimulate business at the same time by sponsoring cymbal clinics similar to the one you have presented; and the field of cymbal methods, studies, and excerpts seems to be wide open.

Thank you very much, gentlemen. I believe the last paragraph of Sam's book would be a fitting conclusion to our discussion:

"The cymbalist's capabilities of coloring the organization's tone are almost without equal in any other individual performer. The fact that he, almost without question, can *ruin* a performance more readily than any other individual should alone serve to illustrate his importance. As time and music progress the cymbalist may evolve as one of the most important positions in any musical organization and as such will attract more people to investigate and study the art of playing the cymbals." ■

Expert Advice for Percussion Students

from
Gordon Peters, Tony Ames, and Fred A. Wickstrom, Jr.

Grip

Ames: I recommend the matched grip for students because of its versatility. Once you become a multiple percussionist, you'll be expected to play everything. Because many of the mallet instruments require that you use a matched grip, it's a lot easier to stay with that grip overall than to switch back and forth from one method to the other.

Peters: The controversy of matched grip versus rudimental grip can be resolved only by the individual percussion player, according to his specific needs. It is good to be familiar with both grips, but what really matters is what ultimately works best for you. For either grip, the most important thing is that it be firm but relaxed. Gripping the stick should feel natural and there should be no tension in the wrist or arm. If you feel comfortable with your present grip and can achieve good sound on the instrument, I recommend that you keep it.

Wickstrom: In playing snare drum I use mostly the traditional grip. I've played it since I was five years old, and still seem to get more power from it than from matched grip, which I've only played about 12 years. However, I find myself switching to matched grip for softer playing and when I play the snare drum as part of a drumset or another multiple percussion setup.

Rolls

Ames: I've developed what I believe is a "foolproof" method for learning rolls. It's amazing. Some students can master a good-sounding roll in only a month. Since we have learned that smooth rolls are made up of triplets, the best way to learn a roll is to practice triplets with the sticks bouncing three times for every hand movement.

Starting slowly, let the sticks bounce three times just to get the feel of it. Then increase the speed gradually. Work for clarity and precision, but stay relaxed. Once you become tense, all anyone will hear is the strokes — and you'll strain your wrists as well. To master the technique, you can build all sorts of little exercises for yourself using three strokes per stick.

Peters: The function of a roll on any percussion instrument is to sustain the sound of the initial stroke. If one hand does not match exactly what the other hand does — such as lifting one stick higher, or moving one wrist faster — the result will be an uneven sound. To help eliminate any inconsistency, first isolate the problem and then exaggerate it in both hands, one at a time. In this way you will become more conscious of executing identical motions in both hands. Also, your ear should tell you if your roll is producing an even sound or not, and for this reason a tape recorder can be extremely helpful in evaluating your practicing and in detecting unevenness of sound in rolls.

Rhythm

Ames: To improve your rhythm, always subdivide beats. When you play eighth-notes, count sixteenths. It is very helpful and makes for great precision in all your playing. It noticeably improves accuracy in ritards and accelerandos. Sometimes students aren't convinced that there is any difference between "almost right" and "absolutely right." But there is a difference, and the problems created by "almost right" rhythm become painfully obvious in a group where each player is a little bit inaccurate.

Wickstrom: I like to use the metronome for instruction and practice. It can be used in many different ways, such as tapping quarter, eighth, or sixteenth notes. To develop an internal rhythmic pulse, set the metronome to only the downbeat of each measure. For jazz I'll use the metronome clicking two beats to a measure, the second and fourth. I ask the student to think of it as a drummer's high hat. Learning to read rhythmic notation is important, right from the beginning.

Versatility

Ames: I strongly urge getting plenty of experience playing many different instruments in a variety of styles because the percussion field is currently highly competitive. The more you play, the better your chances will be.

Peters: You've got to be absolutely first class on all the percussion instruments if you want more doors open to you in the professional music business. I was accepted into the band at West Point even though they had too many drummers — not because I was a superstar drummer, but because I was versatile. They gave me the job because they needed a percussionist who could also play marimba and timpani. If you limit yourself to only those instruments you can play well, you also limit yourself to fewer job opportunities in the percussion field.

Wickstrom: A percussionist today can be either a musician capable of performing on a wide variety of instruments in divergent areas or can be a virtuoso on one instrument in one field. The choice is ultimately each performer's; background in all areas of percussion as a young player will give you the basis to make intelligent choices and to re-direct goals in performance throughout your life. I personally believe every percussionist should have some knowledge of snare drum, timpani, mallet keyboard percussion, and drumset.

Timpani

Peters: A good ear is essential for the timpanist. In fact, the ability to hear true harmonic intervals is the primary requisite for playing timpani because the intonation of the drums must be exact. The timpanist should learn to tune the drum with one reference pitch (from a tuning fork or from the tuning note of a band or orchestra) and then change pitches intervallically from that initial pitch. To check the exactness of your tuning, hum the desired pitch into the drum: when it resonates back the loudest, the intonation is as good as you can get it. I don't approve of electronic tuning devices because they become a crutch for the ear.

The best playing area on the timpani head is generally about one-third of the distance from the rim of the drum to the center of the head. While playing, I prefer to sit on a stool because pitch changes can be made more efficiently.

Wickstrom: I began playing timpani by using the flat-handed matched grip identical to what I use on snare drum — referred to by many as the German style. Gradually I changed to a thumbs-up or thumbs-almost up position, often called the French grip. I find that in playing timpani with this thumbs-up position the stick comes up off the head as far as with the flat grip and in addition there's a certain wrist snap on impact that actually helps you take the stick off the drum.

I divide timpani lessons into technique, reading, repertoire (solo and ensemble), and of course, tuning. Tuning is a big part of timpani playing. Mallet study, piano study, and singing all help with timpani tuning and help develop your musicianship.

Mechanical knowledge of the instrument is invaluable. I play timpani in the Florida Philharmonic, and I try to get to every concert a half-hour early to check the drums. I make sure they haven't been jarred, the posts are all in tune, and everything is functioning.

Snare Drum

Wickstrom: I believe there are two ways to develop technique on the snare drum: through work on rudiments and rudimental solos, and through using multiple bounce methods, such as *Stick Control* by George Lawrence Stone. I start a beginning student with a multiple bounce roll: I use it 99 percent of the time I play. But I won't neglect the double-bounce rudimental roll, either.

Playing the snare drum is important for developing your hands for all percussion playing. Practice pads are helpful for working on your hands, but you can't develop a snare drum sound with a pad so it's important to practice on the drum as well.

Mallet Percussion

Ames: For four-mallet percussion, work on broken chords in all keys with four mallets starting slowly and gradually increasing speed when possible, but without sacrificing accuracy. You can make up all sorts of exercises. For example, in C major, play C and G in the left hand with E and C in the right. Roll the chord, playing in a 1-2-3-4 pattern. Then try 1-3-2-4 or 1-4-2-3, and so forth. Proceed through all keys, major and minor.

After practicing the exercises, play easy keyboard music such as simple Bach chorales and other pieces that highlight the vertical quality of four-mallet playing in really difficult technical passages, you'll be able to use two mallets and then return to the four when you can.

It's important to learn about chords and harmonic progressions for improvising on vibes and marimba. Also, I recommend using a good etude book written for any instrument to help increase your musicality along with your technique.

Peters: Technical studies are important for the mallet player. When you play scales and arpeggios in practice, not only do you develop your technique but you also learn to recognize their occurrence in the music you play. Mallet players should have a balance between technique and sight-reading ability. Weak sight-reading can be strengthened only by doing a lot of it. When I was a student, playing duets with someone who read better than I did was an invaluable aid in improving my sight-reading. A book I recommend to mallet players is Pasquale Bona's *Rhythmical Articulation* (Carl Fischer), an excellent collection of studies to improve your phrasing and basic musicianship.

Wickstrom: There are many ways to hold mallets when playing marimba, bells, vibes, and xylophone. Fundamentally, in holding four mallets there are three principal techniques: the traditional or scissors grip, the Musser grip, and the Burton grip. I use the Burton grip in most of my playing but teach all three. Detailed descriptions and illustrations of these grips are in front of Volume II of my *Keyboard Mastery for Mallet Percussion.*

I start a mallet lesson with technical exercises, including traditional scales and arpeggios. Next we work on reading, including sight-reading and re-reading for speed and accuracy. Taking a simple thing and playing it very fast is a good way to improve your sight-reading. Morris Goldenberg's book *Modern*

School for Xylophone, Marimba, and Vibraphone is good for a student past the beginning stages. Also, Bartok's *Mikrokosmos* for piano are excellent. Because they're written for young pianists, there are no large stretches for the hand and therefore no big leaps on the marimba. A good follow-up to that book is the Louis Moyse *Little Songs for Beginning Flutists*. The piano accompaniment gives the percussionist a chance to work with another instrument. "Music Minus One" records are also good for this purpose.

Another suggestion is to learn to read in all clefs, not just the treble clef. It will facilitate your reading and later "on the job" transpositions.

Double-stop playing is another important part of the lesson plan. One of the best books on this subject is Al Payson's *Double Stops for Mallet Instruments*.

I think every part of the lesson should use all four mallets, even if it's only for striking and rolling triads and other easy things. Creative Music Publishing has some good books by Bobby Christian and the Rubank *Intermediate Method* for marimba is good. Guitar music and two-part Bach piano music works well. Other good books that demonstrate this mallet technique are David Friedman's *Vibraphone Technique* and *The Solo Marimbist*, Vols. I and II by James L. Moore and Linda Pimental.

Accessories

Peters: The accessory instruments are probably the most neglected area of percussion playing. Inexperienced players often assume that they can play a bass drum, tambourine, triangle, and similar instruments if they can simply read the part. But it takes as much practice to play a cymbal crash correctly as it does to play a snare drum roll evenly. Take the time to experiment with each of the accessory instruments, playing as many articulations (staccato, legato, roll, etc.) as possible, pianissimo to fortissimo. Look to your percussion teacher and/or band director for advice. Two books that can be very useful in strengthening your playing on accessory instruments are Al Payson's *Techniques of Playing Bass Drum, Cymbals, and Accessories* (Payson Products, Inc., 2130 Glenview, Park Ridge, Illinois) and Morris Goldenberg's *Modern School for the Snare Drum* (Chappell).

Additional Books

Ames: Two helpful background works that I recommend for every percussionist are James Blades' *Percussion Instruments and Their History* (Praeger) and Emile Richards' *The World of Percussion* (Gwyn Publications, Box 5900, Sherman Oaks, California). Two exercise books I suggest are John Bergamo's *Style Studies* (Music for Percussion) and Delecluse's *Complete Method for Vibraphone* (2 vols., Leduc).

Wickstrom: A good rudimental book for snare drum is *Odd-Meter Rudimental Studies* by Mitch Peters; I especially like one piece, "The Downfall of Paris," which is written in $\frac{5}{8}$. For reading notation, *Teaching Rhythm* by Joel Rothman is very good and more thorough than any other book I've used with beginners. The book goes through all combinations of quarter and eighth notes and rests before moving on to anything else.

Final Advice

Ames: Playing with others will build your confidence and prepare you for different situations. And if you're at ease, others will feel comfortable with you. Try to do as much ensemble playing as you can — there's no substitute for it.

Listen to other musicians perform things you are working on. For example, if you're playing a Bach violin partita with mallets, listen to some violinists play it and compare phrasing. Or if you're doing a keyboard work by Bach, listen to Glenn Gould at the piano and compare interpretation. Those are the things that distinguish a really good musician from an ordinary one.

Peters: Listening is the single most important aspect of musicianship. The ear must be the ultimate guide. Whether practicing or performing, a player must listen to himself and constantly evaluate the sound he hears.

Wickstrom: I think piano study is basic for anybody going into a music school. You need it for theory and harmony classes and it's required as a secondary instrument. The more proficient you can become in high school, the better off you'll be in college. In general, the best type of experience for us all is playing, and it's playing with other people that counts. The most successful people coming into the university are those who played in everything in high school. They were in marching band, concert band, jazz band, and symphony orchestra. ■

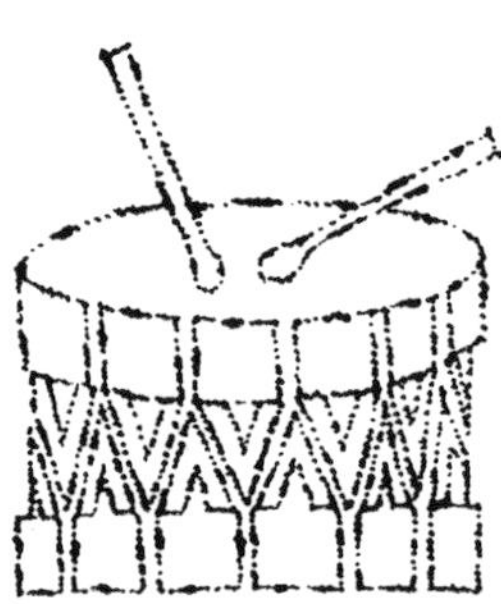

The Top Ten Ensemble Works

David P. Eyler

Many teachers and students do not have the opportunity to make an in-depth study of available solo and ensemble literature before selecting works for concerts and contests. It is difficult to find suitable music for any all-percussion study, so teachers often unintentionally restrict percussion students to those experiences available only through participation in the full band or orchestra. Percussion ensemble performances, however, provide members of the ensemble with the opportunity to take a starring role at a concert and also become more familiar with all the percussion instruments.

The section entitled "Programs" in the Percussive Notes Magazine, the publication of the Percussive Arts Society, is the best published source for keeping up on the solo and ensemble literature being played. During the three-year period from summer 1976 to summer 1979, 801 percussion ensemble performances were reported by performing groups ranging from junior high school to the collegiate level.

The following are the 10 most frequently performed percussion ensemble compositions during that period. These compositions were analyzed for the number of performers, difficulty of parts, performance time, instrumentation, pedagogical uses, audience receptivity, and special performance problems. I have graded each ensemble based on a scale from I (very easy) to VI (difficult).

Difficulty Level	(No. of (Performances)	Title and Composer (No. of Players)	Publisher
V	(75)	*Toccata for Percussion Instruments,* Carlos Chavez (6)	Belwin Mills
VI	(56)	*Gainsborough,* Thomas Gauger (5)	Southern
IV	(55)	*October Mountain,* Alan Hovhaness (6)	C.F. Peters
IV	(53)	*Swords of Moda-Ling,* Gordon Peters (8)	Franks Drum Shop
V	(48)	*Three Brothers,* Michael Colgrass (9)	Music for Percussion
IV	(48)	*Overture for Percussion Ensemble,* John Beck (8)	Kendor
V	(43)	*Encore in Jazz,* Vic Firth (7)	Fischer
V	(43)	*Sabre Dance,* Khatchaturian/Moore (3-7+)	Permus
VI	(36)	*Suite for Percussion,* William Kraft (4)	Belwin Mills
V	(35)	*Jazz Variants,* John Beck (8)	Boston Music

Toccata

Carlos Chavez completed his *Toccata* in 1942, but it was neither published nor performed until 1948. Now it has become the most frequently performed percussion ensemble in the repertoire. It requires six performers and the following instrumentation: player I — Indian drum, glockenspiel (with hard mallets), small Indian drum (tom-tom could be substituted); player II — side drum (snare drum), xylophone, Indian drum (may be the same instrument shared with player I), tenor drum; player III — side drum, suspended cymbal; player IV — tenor drum, chimes, one maraca, suspended cymbal; player V — 3 timpani, small gong; player VI — bass drum, large gong.

A characteristic of the majority of Chavez' compositions is the combination of the so-called orchestral percussion instruments with those indigenous to Latin America.

Chavez provides detailed performance instructions. His concern with the pitch of the drum instruments is evident, and there are explanations on stick selection and positioning of the drums.

The *Toccata* is in three uninterrupted movements, each exploring a different timbre. In the first movement Chavez uses a wide range of membrane instruments, the second movement uses only the metallic and wooden melodic instruments (glock, xylophone, etc.), and the final section has predominant sounds of the membrane instruments combined with the short wooden sounds of the maracas and claves and metallic sounds produced on the cymbal and glockenspiel.

Counting is extremely important. Chavez often writes a succession of uninterrupted eighth notes that move from one player to another.

The *Toccata* takes about 14 minutes to perform. Movements are $\frac{3}{4}$, $\frac{8}{8}$, and $\frac{2}{2}$, respectively, with a tempo change only in the last movement. The bar percussion parts are not technically difficult and should pose few problems. The timpanist does not need to change pitches during any movement.

Instrumentation of the *Toccata* is suitable to

most school situations. Any single movement selected from this work would make an excellent contest selection.

Gainsborough

The *Gainsborough For Percussion Quintet* by Tom Gauger may be one of the best compositions written specifically for percussion ensemble. The work is in three movements, basically fast-slow-fast, and requires about 15 minutes to perform.

A principal reason for the grade VI difficulty level is the need for two very competent mallet performers, both of whom must be capable of playing four-mallet technique. Player I needs marimba, vibraphone and triangle while the second performer is assigned to marimba, bass drum, orchestra bells, and vibraphone (the same instrument shared with player I). Instruments needed for the other three players are: player III – snare drum, gong, orchestra bells, chimes and two tom toms; player IV – four timpani and a triangle; and player V – a bass drum with attached cymbal, crash cymbals, suspended cymbal, and gong.

The best set-up I have found is to place the two primary mallet performers at the front of the ensemble, with the other three performers behind them.

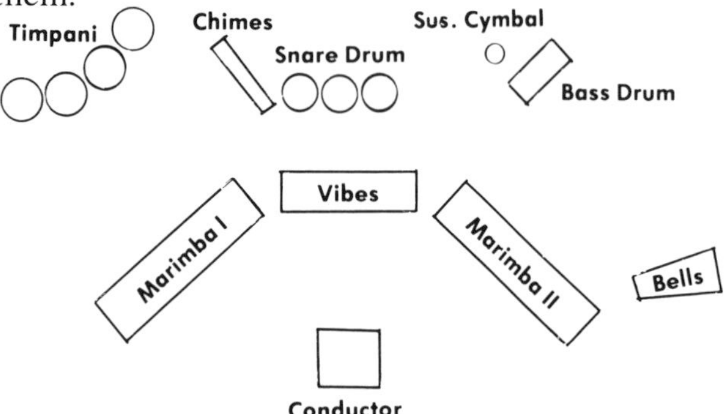

The timpanist must make several tuning changes within each movement, but ample time is allowed. In the first and third movements player V must play the bass drum with attached cymbal, a rare technique in contemporary performance. Players II and V can use the same bass drum; however, a fast change would be required of player II.

The first movement of *Gainsborough* is written in $\frac{9}{8}$ (♩.=100). In one section some players are in $\frac{9}{8}$ while the others are in $\frac{3}{4}$, but this hemiola effect is easy to accomplish. Movement two, marked "slow, hesitant," has a very lyrical solo recitative by the vibraphone over a sustained marimba chord. It is basically in a $\frac{4}{4}$ meter that can be subdivided so the eighth note provides the pulse. The third movement, marked "presto ($\bullet$ =180)," is in a fast $\frac{2}{4}$ with some $\frac{3}{8}$ measures injected.

This work is one of the most rewarding pieces written for percussion and is highly recommended for a group with capable players.

October Mountain

Alan Hovhaness' *October Mountain* is a suite of five movements requiring six performers. The instrumentation is as follows: player I – marimba (4 octaves from C4 to C6); player II – glockenspiel, marimba (may be the same instrument used by player I); player III – two timpani; player IV – giant tam tam, player V – tenor drum, bass drum, one timpani (low F♯); player VI – bass drum, tenor drum, (may be the same instruments used by player V) and gong. In order for this double use of instruments to work effectively certain players must set-up together (players I & II, V & VI).

There are no written performance instructions accompanying the score; Hovhaness does not stipulate mallet types or the sizes of drums to be used.

Throughout this piece the melodic material is based on the modal scales, a characteristic of Hovhaness' compositional technique. Each movement provides its own material with no single theme being used throughout the work.

The first movement opens with a solo recitative consisting of random rhythmic groupings of various durations. The short, non-metrical introduction leads to a metrical passage in $\frac{2}{4}$, closing this short movement.

All movements in the work are relatively short. Ostinato rhythms in irregular meter are combined into ensemble effects of regular meter in the second, fourth, and fifth movements. The only movement that may cause a few problems is the third which is mostly a dialogue between the marimba and glockenspiel and opens in $\frac{17}{16}$ meter with a solo marimba.

Although rolls are not indicated on the mallet part, they should be added to the longer notes played on the marimba. Avoid rolls on the glockenspiel.

The two-bar percussion parts are only moderately difficult and should pose few problems for most junior and senior high school percussionists. For use in a contest or concert, a movement or two could be performed.

October Mountain is a very solid, well-constructed ensemble. Its instrumentation is practical for almost any performing situation, whether it be a contest or a feature on your next band or orchestra concert.

Swords of Moda-Ling

Like Hovhaness' *October Mountain, Swords of Moda-Ling* by Gordon Peters is an excellent work for teaching musicianship to your percussion students. This serious and rewarding work uses the full gamut of bar percussion instruments, as well as piano. This composition was written for eight or nine players with the following instrumentation: orchestra bells, vibraphone, xylophone, chimes, piano, four timpani, snare drum, wood block, marimba, triangle, temple blocks, bass drum, gong, and suspended cymbal. The marimba and vibraphone parts are optional; if no marimba is available, the marimba part, which uses only four pitches, can be played on temple blocks.

The *Swords of Moda-Ling* has an oriental flavor similar to the modal quality of *October Mountain. Swords* exploits the very high metallic sounds of the percussion instruments. Brass mallets are called for on the orchestra bells and chimes while plastic mallets are to be used on the xylophone and suspended cymbal. Peters gives explicit directions on the types of sticks and mallets to be used (e.g. "small wood mallets," "triangle beater on cymbal," etc.). He even calls for three different pairs of sticks to be used on the timpani. Peters also offers an instrumental set-up that will work well for most groups.

The basically chordal piano part in this selection is not terribly difficult; however, the very widespread chords (five notes in one hand) require the performer to have rather large hands.

After a brief introduction, the first section contains ostinato passages with the piano carrying the main melody. Gradually each part decrescendos, then fades away so that only the piano remains. A short piano cadenza leads into the second section of the piece where the roles are reversed from the first section: the piano plays the ostinato while the bar instruments, using very hard mallets, carry the melody. Before a short coda, a brief pause occurs during which the director has the option of asking the mallet keyboard players to sequentially *ad. lib.* a short cadenza-like passage, each ending on a D as their final note, prior to returning to the printed part; or he may elect to go directly to the coda if improvisation presents a problem for the group.

During the nine-measure coda, the bells, vibraphone, and xylophone players must sustain four-note chords with an equal number of mallets. The rest of the piece requires only two-mallet technique for the bar instrument performers.

This work will make a definite contribution to the musicianship training of the young percussionist. Although written entirely in common time, the strength of the composition is its emphasis on exploring the elements of music (melody, harmony, rhythm, and dynamics).

Three Brothers

Three Brothers by Michael Colgrass is an ensemble for the percussion section that has limited access to melodic percussion instruments; because there are none used. Nine players are required, each one responsible for a single instrument with the exception of the two timpanists, who must play two timpani each.

The score specifies the use of timpani in F and C (one player), timpani in C and D (second player), bongos, snare drum, cow bell, maracas, tambourine, suspended cymbal and three tom toms.

The title, *Three Brothers*, refers to the bongos, snare drum, and first timpani players who carry the main solo lines throughout the piece as the other instruments provide accompaniment.

Three Brothers begins with a fast $\frac{4}{4}$ (♩=132) which serves as an introduction to the cut-time (𝅗𝅥=96) section at measure 21. Most of the piece is in alla breve and has a "jazz-like" feel throughout. Each player must be very accurate in executing his part because the parts fit together like a puzzle. Accents are also very important, and all the parts are at about the same level of difficulty. This is one of the few non-melodic percussion ensembles that is interesting for both the players and the audience.

Suite For Percussion

Suite For Percussion by William Kraft is a quartet in five movements. Kraft, one of the foremost composers of percussion music today, has written a suite that is well-constructed and very musical. The instrumentation is as follows: player I – bongos, glockenspiel, tambourine, song bells, flexitone; player II – two snare drums (high and

Overture For Percussion Ensemble

The *Overture For Percussion Ensemble* by John Beck is one of the new, exciting additions to the percussion ensemble literature. The number of performances this work has received since its publication is overwhelming, perhaps partly because it provides easy listening for the audience.

The *Overture's* playing time is approximately three and a half minutes, which makes it very suitable for contests or festivals. The publisher has given it a grade V, but I believe a less-advanced group could handle the work with few problems.

The instrumentation is as follows: player I – orchestra bells; player II – chimes and suspended cymbal; player III – marimba; player IV – vibraphone and xylophone; player V – gong and roto-toms (four concert toms could be substituted); player VI – snare drum; player VII-tenor drum; player VIII – four timpani.

This percussion octet is scored well for the ensemble. The four-mallet technique required of the players make these parts the most challenging. However, both parts are in a four-note chordal style of reasonable difficulty. One suggestion which might help if there are more players available, or if the mallet players are less advanced, would be to divide the four notes among two players (one player could take the top two notes, etc.).

The opening of the *Overture* contains sustained chords in the melodic percussion while the timpani plays the melodic line. The chimes soon join the timpani with a countermelody before starting a contrasting section in $\frac{4}{4}$ ($\frac{8}{8}$). This jazz-like section, which can be counted in either of those two meters, uses a basic pulse of two dotted-quarter notes followed by a single quarter note for each measure. After a full development section the *Overture* returns to the first theme followed by a climactic finish with a short timpani cadenza.

Aiding in the excitement of the *Overture* are the high sounds of the melodic percussion. The bells, vibes, and marimba are all rolling full chords at a *forte* dynamic level. The tempo, allegro (♩=132), and the common time meter help make the piece relaxing for both players and listeners. The syncopation adds a touch of swing to the piece.

The melodies, harmonies, and rhythms are consonant and make the *Overture* an excellent training piece.

Encore In Jazz

Vic Firth's *Encore In Jazz*, a percussion septet, has become a standard in the percussion ensemble repertoire. The two mallet percussion parts (marimba and vibraphone) are perhaps the most challenging of all the parts. Both require only two mallets for each performer, but each features rapidly moving passages.

The instrumentation is as follows: a set of four timpani; three drums of different sizes; vibraphone and Indian drum; marimba and cowbell; bongos; a single conga drum; and a dance drum set. The entire piece has a jazz feel with two distinct sections: one in medium tempo (𝅗𝅥 = 100) and one in a very fast tempo (𝅗𝅥 = 144) with a slow coda in four (♩ = 84). There are many solo and soli passages for the non-melodic instruments. There is also a substantial amount of interplay between the parts which often creates some ensemble problems requiring careful rehearsal.

Although the marimba and vibraphone parts are the most difficult, they should lie within the capabilities of most high school percussionists. The limited range required of these two instruments makes the piece suitable for most school situations. The timpani part requires no tuning changes except for a glissando and a few changes on one drum in the last four bars.

The set-up suggested by Firth works quite well in most instances. The mallet percussion instruments should always be placed in the front of the ensemble. One problem that often occurs in this piece, as well as in other similar pieces, is that the melodic instruments are covered by the sound of the heavier non-melodic instruments, so be careful to balance the ensemble. A procedure that often works successfully is to add another player to the mallet parts.

Sabre Dance

Aram Khachaturian's *Sabre Dance*, arranged by James Moore, is one of the most exciting works ever written or arranged for percussion ensemble. It may be performed by as few as three players using only the mallet percussion instruments; two timpani and small tam tam (or substitute a large suspended cymbal); and a drum set. One wooden (marimba or xylophone) and one metal (bells, vibes, or chimes) instrument will suffice for the bar instrument part. The addition of parts IV through VII (tambourine, triangle, three concert tom toms, and large tam tam) and employing several players on the bar percussion part will create a much fuller sound and a more exciting performance.

Be careful that the timpani and drum set do not over-balance the bar percussion instruments. This is especially important if only one player is assigned to the mallet instruments. This selection can be adapted to fit the needs of any particular group because you can use as few as three players or as many as are available. The mallet part requires only two-mallet technique, but the double stops (two notes played simultaneously) must be played very rapidly. For maximum speed and clarity, less-advanced players may divide the double stops.

Most of the parts are about the same level of difficulty except for the mallet part. The main problem will be one of ensemble precision. Tempo will depend on the capabilities of the members of your group, although the fastest controllable tempo is preferred. The eighth note remains constant throughout the piece.

Sabre Dance has a great deal of audience appeal and will make a very exciting concert opening or finale.

low), glockenspiel, bass drum, E temple bell, bongos; player III — field drum, tenor drum, vibraphone, low cow bell, temple bell; player IV — bass drum, four tuned gongs, tam tam, and hand drum. The instrumentation of the work presents a problem, but some substitutions can be made.

The first movement is scored for bongos, two snare drums, field and tenor drums, and a bass drum. This "Fanfare" begins with a slow andante (♩ = 72) introduction, then jumps right into a moderato (♩ = 100) to complete the movement. The meter is 4/4 with an occasional 3/4 measure. The short fanfare uses no bar instruments yet melody is present. Pieces for drums alone such as these (and *Three Brothers* discussed earlier) can help develop a percussionist's awareness of melody without using mallet instruments.

The second movement incorporates all of the bar instruments listed before as well as the tuned gongs. Mixed meters are throughout.

"Ostinatos," the third movement, is entirely in 6/8 meter. Tambourine, snare drum, field drum, and bass drum are used. The snare and field drum parts call for brushes while thumb rolls are included on the tambourine.

The fourth movement, "Toccata," like the "Fanfare," makes no use of the bar instruments or gongs. It is entirely in cut-time with a few tricky rhythms. The last movement uses all the instruments not previously presented (song bells, temple bell, etc.).

Some movements of this work are not nearly as difficult as others. If there is a time factor, or if instrumentation is limited, you can extract one or two of the movements. This *Suite* is definitely a valuable piece of literature for the percussion ensemble, either in whole or part.

Jazz Variants

Jazz Variants by John Beck will provide a dynamic finale to any concert. Its popular sound and rhythms are exciting for listener and performer alike. Beck scored his work for eight players with the following instrumentation: player I — vibraphone; player II — marimba; player III — bells and tambourine; player IV — chimes, bell tree (or wind chimes), guiro, triangle and bongos; player V — suspended cymbal, cow bell, bass drum, tambourine and conga drum; player VI — bell tree (same as player IV), tambourine, bongos and four tom toms; player VII — four timpani; player VIII — drum set (with two tom toms). He is very explicit as to the sticks and beaters to be used (for example, marimba: four M-1 mallets, two M-2 mallets and four M-8 mallets). I do not agree that it is necessary to use a particular brand name mallet (M-8 stands for the Musser number eight model) because there are so many fine mallets of comparable quality on the market today. The composer is really asking for a certain type of sound to be produced and that is what the percussionist should try to achieve.

Other special instructions are excellent. The vibraphone player is asked to "bend the pitch" in his part and is given explicit directions for doing so. Beck also notes that the eighth notes are to be played "evenly in the rock section" and "as triplets in the jazz section," a distinction often overlooked by the director and performer.

As the title suggests, this ensemble is in a jazz style; however the first section is played with the even eighth note feeling of rock. The vibraphone opens the piece with several short cadenzas over a sustained chord. At the end of the vibe cadenza the marimba plays a three-measure solo bass line (written in bass clef) followed by a lead-in fill by the drum set. From here the work grows with energy until the climactic finish.

This composition is written in a style familiar to more students, and is, or should be, well within the grasp of most high school ensembles.

The syncopated rhythms may cause a few problems at first, but a good drum set player can really complement the rest of the ensemble with tasty kicks and fills. The bar percussion parts all call for two mallets except for a very brief section in the marimba.

The instruments needed for *Jazz Variants* are all basic to the modern percussion section except possibly the bell tree. I recommend setting up the ensemble with the bar instruments toward the front if possible. There is some potential for balance problems in this work, especially when there are fewer bar instruments than rhythm instruments playing. This is another piece in which some of the mallet parts could be doubled in order to strengthen the sound. The performance time of the work is about nine minutes, which makes it a perfect piece for recital or contest. ■

May, 1980

Directory of Timpanists and Percussionists in American Symphony Orchestras

Atlanta Symphony
Paul Yancich, *Timpani*
Jack Bell, *Principal*
William Wilder *(Assistant Timpani)*
Eugene Rehm

Baltimore Symphony
Dennis Kain, *Timpani*
Christopher Williams, *Acting Principal*
Robert Kennick, *Co-Principal*
Leo Le Page

Boston Symphony
Everett Firth, *Timpani*
Arthur Press, *Assistant Timpani*
Charles Smith
Thomas Gauger
Frank Epstein

Buffalo Philharmonic
Jesse Kregal, *Timpani*
Lynn Harbold
John Rowland

Chicago Symphony
Donald Koss, *Timpani*
Gordon Peters, *Principal*
Sam Denov
Albert Payson
James Ross

Cincinnati Symphony
Eugene Espino, *Timpani*
William Platt, *Principal*
Richard Jensen
Edward Wuebold

Cleveland Orchestra
Cloyd Duff, *Timpani*
Richard Weiner, *Principal*
Joseph Adato
Robert Matson
Donald Miller

Dallas Symphony
Kalman Cherry, *Timpani*
Vernon Ewan
Doug Howard
Ronald Snyder

Denver Symphony
Edward Small, *Timpani*
William Roberts
Paul Dolby
Tim Pfannenstiel

Detroit Symphony
Salvatore Rabbio, *Timpani*
Robert Pangborn, *Principal*
Norman Fickett
Ray Makowski
Sam Tundo

Honolulu Symphony
Richard Kashanski, *Timpani*
Lois Russell, *Principal*
Robert DeMello
Wayne Yabiku

Houston Symphony
David Wuliger, *Timpani*
James Simon, *Principal*
Fraya Fineberg

Indianapolis Symphony
Thomas Akins, *Timpani*
Donald Morehead, *Principal*
Paul Berns
Art Schildbach

Kansas City Philharmonic
David S. Gross, *Timpani*
Vincent Bilardo, *Principal*
Gaylon Umbarger, *Assistant*
Thomas H. Plaster

Los Angeles Philharmonic
William Kraft, *Co-Principal*
Mitchell Peters, *Co-Principal*
Walter Goodwin
Charles DeLancey

Louisville Symphony
James Rago, *Timpani*
John Pedroja, *Principal*
Peggy Stephens

Milwaukee Symphony
Tele Lesbines, *Timpani; Principal Percussion*
Joseph Conti
Linda Raymond
Thomas Wetzel, *Assistant*

Minnesota Orchestra
Jack Moore, *Timpani*
Marvin Dahlgren, *Principal*
Paula Culp
Elliot Fine

National Symphony
Fred Begun, *Timpani*
F. Anthony Ames, *Principal*
Charles Wilkinson *(Assistant Timpani)*
Kenneth Harbison

New Orleans Philharmonic
Douglas Cade, *Timpani*
Leland Beach, *Principal*
David DeGroot

New York Philharmonic
Roland Kohloff, *Timpani*
Walter Rosenberger, *Principal*
Elden Bailey
Morris Lang *(Associate Timpani)*

North Carolina Symphony
John Feddersen, *Timpani*
Richard Motylinski, *Principal*
Kenneth Whitlow *(Assistant Timpani)*

Oklahoma Symphony
John Bannon, *Timpani*
Tom Maguire, *Principal*
Dan Armstrong
Richard Gipson
Scott Myers

Oregon Symphony
Paul Salvatore, *Timpani*
Niel De Ponte, *Principal*
Steve Lawrence
Christine Perry

Philadelphia Orchestra
Gerald Carlyss, *Timpani*
Michael Bookspan, *Timpani; Percussion*
Alan Abel
Anthony Orlando
William Saputelli

Pittsburgh Symphony
Stanley S. Leonard, *Timpani*
John Soroka, *Principal (Associate Timpani)*
Gerald Unger, *Assistant*
William Schneiderman
Edward I. Myers

Rochester Philharmonic
John Beck, *Timpani*
William L. Cahn, *Principal*
Ruth Cahn

St. Louis Symphony
Richard Holmes, *Timpani*
Richard O'Donnell, *Principal*
John Kasica
Thomas Stubbs

San Francisco Symphony
Barry Jekowsky, *Timpani*
Thomas Hemphill, *Principal*
Anthony Cirone
Lloyd Davis
Peggy Lucchesi

Seattle Symphony
Meyer Slivka, *Timpani*
Randolph Baunton, *Principal*
Howard Gilbert
Ronald Johnson

Syracuse Symphony
Herbert Flower, *Principal*
Ernest Muzquiz
Douglas Igelsrud *(Timpani)*
Michael Bull
Raymond Elwood

Utah Symphony
Robert Lentz, *Timpani*
Craig Fineshriber, *Principal*
Don H. Main
Keith Guernsey
Michael Cottam

May, 1980

Teaching Mallet Instruments to Beginners

Mario Gaetano

The diversity of percussion sounds in compositions is growing larger, particularly with the increased use of mallet percussion instruments. Here are some suggestions to help you decide which instruments to purchase, and when and how to begin students on mallet instruments.

Every high school concert band percussion section should have at least a xylophone, one set of orchestra bells, and a set of tubular chimes if you want your band to perform with the instrumentation that the majority of contemporary band literature calls for. The xylophone should be portable, easy to transport, and mounted on a sturdy frame with casters. A range of 3½ octaves from F4 to C8 is ideal. I recommend the synthetic wood xylophones because even though the synthetic material does not have the earthy, natural sound of rosewood, it has many advantages for public school use. The bars of the instrument are almost impossible to dent or chip. They produce a brilliant sound characterized by high overtones, and they will never go out of tune, even in extreme temperatures. With proper care and maintenance, a xylophone with synthetic wood bars will last indefinitely. The xylophone should never be played with brass mallets or drum sticks; use only rubber and plastic mallets.

Orchestra bells should have steel bars, which are strong and durable. Steel bars also project sound well. Purchase orchestra bells with a strong case for protection, and buy an adjustable orchestra bell stand to accommodate players of different heights. A 2½-octave set from G5 to C8 is ideal. Provide the students with a variety of mallets made of rubber, plastic, and brass.

Chimes should have a range of 1½ octaves from C5 to C6, and they should be mounted on a sturdy frame with a damper pedal and casters. Players can produce a rich, warm tone if they use a rawhide chime mallet; however, many times a more brilliant, biting, carillon-like sound is desired, and only a plastic hammer can produce that quality. Plastic hammers are inexpensive and can be purchased at any hardware store. With either hammer, be certain that students play only on the crown (top) of each tube.

Students should begin lessons on mallet percussion instruments as soon as they comfortable with basic snare drum concepts and techniques. The trend in percussion education is to employ the matched grip for snare drum playing and then transfer this grip to all areas of percussion. When a student begins percussion study in the elementary school and shows potential and interest, he should begin branching out into the mallet and timpani areas upon reaching the junior high level.

Try to stress the importance of complete percussion playing to your students. Emphasize to any college-bound individuals that music schools will not accept a percussion student who does not have some experience in all areas. Inform your students of orchestra concerts in the area or on tele-

vision, percussion ensemble concerts, and percussion clinics so that they may see how versatile and well-rounded the contemporary percussionist has become.

Beginning study of mallet instruments should include technical, reading, and melodic studies. When beginning the student on orchestra bells or xylophone, I suggest starting with medium soft rubber mallets with flexible, fiberglass shafts. These mallets provide a faster rebound and aid the students greatly when they learn to play rolls.

Mallets should be held between the thumb and the first joint of the index finger, with the other fingers wrapped lightly around the mallet shaft. The wrists should be as relaxed as possible; they do all the up and down movement, not the arms. The back of the hand should always be facing upwards, and the mallets should leave the bar as soon as they strike, as if to draw the tone out of the bar.

Make up scale and arpeggio exercises for your students. Below are some scale studies I recommend students practice in all keys. The student should start each exercise with the left hand. With a few exceptions always keep the left hand above the right during chromatic passages.

There are numerous useful books available. Here are a few I can recommend for public school use:

Method Books for Technical Study

Kraus, Phil, *Modern Mallet Method,* Volume I, Belwin Mills.

Goldenberg, Morris, *Modern School for Xylophone, Marimba, and Vibraphone,* Chappell.

Feldstein, Sandy, *Learning to Play Keyboard Percussion,* Alfred.

Method Books for Reading and Melodic Study

Whaley, Garwood, *Fundamentals Studies for Mallets,* J.R. Publications.

Feldstein, Sandy, *Mallet Student,* Belwin Mills.

Schaefer, F., *Xylophone and Marimba Method,* Belwin Mills.

Marching Mallet Instruments

The number of marching band mallet instruments varies proportionally with the size of the percussion section and the size of the band. For instance, a percussion section of 8 to 12 musicians is generally used in a band of 60 to 100 players, and this size section should use at least a set of marching bells. A larger band with a bigger percussion section should add a xylophone.

Marching bells should have a range of 2½ octaves from G5 to C8 and they should be made of steel for maximum durability and sound projection. I recommend using a set of horizontally-carried bells with an adjustable harness instead of a vertical bell lyre. The sound projection is superior with horizontally-carried bells and the student can easily transfer technique from the marching bells to the concert band's set of orchestra bells. Use hard rubber and plastic mallets to play contrasting textures on marching bells.

A marching xylophone should have a range of 2½ octaves from C5 to G7. The xylophone should also have individually-tuned resonators, made of synthetic material. Brilliant sound projection and perfect intonation regardless of outdoor weather conditions make the synthetic material superior in this case. Plastic or hard rubber mallets should be used, depending on the composition being performed. Both the xylophone and the bells should be mounted on lightweight frames with adjustable shoulder harnesses. ■

Percussion Recordings

Don R. Baker

Many percussion recordings are available that can be useful as reference or teaching examples.

The reference category includes the Clinician Series on Golden Crest Records. The *Percussion* album is a recording of Saul Feldstein's clinic on percussion ensemble instrument selection, balance, timbre, etc. Examples are drawn from the elementary to high school level, and his discussion of techniques and musicianship is extremely valuable to the educator and student. A copy of the script would have been advantageous, but this record is still an absolute must for educators and university libraries.

In the same series, Tom Brown's *Vibist* is an excellent recording on which he discusses the technical aspects of vibraphone playing, such as mallet stroke, damping, pedaling, voicing, and chording. The record features several works in jazz style. There is no printed copy of the narration.

Music Minus One offers a similar teaching aid for the vibraphonist, but the company also offers the familiar play-along concept with its recordings. *For Vibists Only-A Blues Method* and *Good Vibrations, A "Pop" Method* feature vibe artist Shelly Elias.

If you are looking for snare drum performance examples of contest rudiments, seek out the *26 Standard American Drum Rudiments,* played by the long time National Rudimental Champion Frank Arsenault. All 26 rudiments are played slow to fast with excellent execution. There are bands of selected older rudimental solos, which may be more interesting to the novice.

If you are looking for examples of modern rudimental notation or cadences, try the tapes available through McCormick's, sound sheets from publishers, or listen to the drum lines on the *Drum Corps International Championship* recordings that offer some of the finest snare drum playing in the world.

Recently, Latin Percussion has been developing educational recordings that include discussions and performances on the typical Latin instruments. The records include *Understanding Latin Rhythms, Volume I* and *Understanding Latin Rhythms, Volume II - Down to Basics.* There is an accompanying manual that details the musical examples and text. Volume I leans heavily on performing groups and emphasis on style, while Volume II stresses basic playing techniques. This series is most advantageous for the high school or college student, and it provides the most needed exposure to the proper sound of each instrument because many teachers cannot play or do not know the correct sound of open tones, slap, etc. These records are also valuable as a teaching aid for playing jazz or Latin style.

Drum Solos Volumes I, II, and *III,* also from Latin Percussion, are the play-along type, featuring top professionals who play solos and accompaniment with congas, bongos, timbales, and full rhythm section. The recordings are an extension of the learned basics from Latin Percussion's *Understanding Latin Rhythms.* Volume I begins with a refresher on the clave patterns, and Side A contains the rhythm section with different drum solos on four tunes. Side B contains only the rhythm section of those previous tunes and allows the student to play along with the record. Volumes II and III are much the same but the solos are more complex.

Drum set methods rarely have companion recordings, even though this is almost a requirement for good listening and improvisation study. Most educational records available for study center around jazz or jazz/rock styles. Music Minus One offers the most diverse series of recordings, which develop both small group and big band playing and include special techniques like brush work, independence, chart-reading, and style-playing. These records deal more with basic techniques rather than playing along with a large band. *Sit-In,* for example, has a 40-page booklet that includes technique development, chart-reading, and the written out version as played by Jim Chapin. This particular album is in swing style; others include Dixieland, Beatles music, be-bop, etc. Chapin has edited several excellent Music Minus One recordings, and all are worth consideration by the combo percussionist.

A relatively new series, emphasizing big band charts, has been edited so you can buy the complete band version, or individual records "minus one" player. This selection allows the director and the student to hear the whole band while the student can take the "minus one" record home for practice. A drum set chart is included in the jacket, in the common abbreviated manuscript style. The chart, *2+2=5,* for example, is challenging for most high school students, but also for the college player. This recording contains good rhythmic development in odd meters like $\frac{7}{4}$, $\frac{1}{4}$, $\frac{5}{4}$, and $\frac{7}{2}$. While other stage band series use more common time signatures, these recordings are excellent play-along exercises that develop improvisation, chart-reading, and good musicianship.

Alfred has a fine method book/record set called *Drum-Set Artistry,* featuring Roy Burns. Each piece has a technique and training preface in the accompanying book. The charts are included, and the listener may follow along to hear how Burns executes the parts. This set does not provide a recording without the drummer, so it is much like any other record except you can see the actual chart along with the extra repeats minus a few cues. This set is like the new collection of charts titled *It's Time* (Kendor) that are published in one bound set; all are on the Thad Jones-Mel Lewis Orchestra recordings.

In the classical and symphonic style, Music Minus One offers two albums: *Stravinsky: The Soldiers Tale* and *Classical Percussion.* Arthur Press has put together the wide variety of famous percussion excerpts for the three-record boxed set, *Classical Percussion.* This excellent set is well edited, both with and without the percussion part included. The accompanying booklet provides useful graphics with verbal explanations of performance techniques for all the typical orchestral percussion instruments. Even though there are some performance errors, this is the best performance set of recordings available of its kind, and it is a must for any school library or percussion teacher's studio.

Solo and Ensemble Works

The Ohio State University Percussion Ensemble, directed by James L. Moore, has put together an album with a variety of works from popular and jazz styles to the more serious *Toccata for Marimba and Percussion Ensemble* by Robert Kelly. The recording includes difficulty levels from junior high through college. Generally, this record is a very enjoyable first album to purchase for an overview of percussion ensemble literature.

F. Michael Combs, director of the University of Tennessee-Knoxville Percussion Ensemble, has a pressing with a collection of works from popular to contemporary. This recording also includes music for junior high through college level, and it contains three of the same works performed on the Ohio State University recording.

Another recording on the Mark label, *The Percussionist,* featuring Theodore Frazeur, emphasizes solo pieces. There is one percussion ensemble cut, but the strength of the record lies in the educational music selected for several instruments — triangle through multiple percussion on one side and all mallet/keyboard solos on the other side. All the solo literature can be played by high school or younger students. This disc is a required recording for all educators to hear a wide variety of good classical percussion with functional works for students.

Golden Crest Records offers *Warren Benson Presents Percussion,* which includes selections of percussion ensemble literature by many composers. Arrangements and original works have been included from diverse difficulty levels. Although the recording has been around for a while, it is valuable for listening, and some of the works are still available in published form.

Another older record is Golden Crest's *Conflict* by Phil Kraus, with six works for a percussion ensemble of three or more players. Most works are playable by high school students. This record is surely worth using as a laboratory listening record.

Percussion at Fredonia has six ensemble works that include the futuristic sounds of Varese and the more appealing programmatic work by Stabile. All are examples of good literature for percussion, but generally are too difficult for high school performance.

Because most recordings are of published scores, they lack the spontaneous creativity of improvised performances. *Repercussion Unit* has put together an ensemble that will fascinate students. Their energetic recording combines jazz/rock, modern noise instruments, and classical writing. Under the musical direction of John Bergamo, the group performs on junk, gold mining pans, conduit pipes, vibes, synthesizer, and other instruments to make a cluster of beautiful "noises" producing melody, harmony, flow, direction, and exciting programmatic works. ■

DISCOGRAPHY

Classical Percussion, Arthur Press, percussionist, Music Minus One MMO 4065.

Clinician Series-Percussion, Saul Feldstein, percussionist and conductor, Golden Crest Records CR 1005.

Clinician Series-Vibist, Tom Brown, vibist, Golden Crest Records CR 1012.

Concepts in Percussion-Ohio State University Percussion Ensemble, James L. Moore, director, Mark Records MES 35747.

Conflict, Phil Kraus, director, Golden Crest Records CR 4004. Drum Corps International Recordings, Volumes I-V (Available from Drum Corps International, P.O. Box 192, Villa Park, Illinois.)

Drum-Set Artistry, Roy Burns, drums, Alfred (No issue number).

Drum Solos Volume I, Produced by Martin Cohen, Latin Percussion Ventures LPV 445.

Drum Solos Volume II, Produced by Martin Cohen, Latin Percussion Ventures LPV 450.

Drum Solos Volume III, Produced by Martin Cohen, Latin Percussion Ventures LPV 451.

For Vibists Only - A Blues Method, Shelly Elias, vibraphonist, Music Minus One MMO 4076.

Good Vibrations, A "Pop" Method, Shelly Elias, vibraphonist, Music Minus One MMO 4077.

New Sounds of Percussion-University of Tennessee-Knoxville Percussion Ensemble, F. Michael Combs, conductor, Fleetwood BMC 511.

Percussion at Fredonia, Theodore C. Frazeur, director, State University of New York at Fredonia APD 075S.

The Percussionist, Theodore Frazeur, percussionist and director, Robert Marcel, piano, Mark Records MRS 37070.

Repercussion Unit, John Bergamo, musical director, Robey Records ROB #1.

Sit-In, Jim Chapin, drums, Music Minus One MMO 4004.

Stravinsky: The Soldier's Tale, Music Minus One MMO 78.

The 26 Standard American Drum Rudiments and Selected Solos, Frank Arsenault, snare drum, Ludwig #2.

2+2=5, Towson State College Jazz Ensemble, Music Minus One MMO 2048.

Understanding Latin Rhythms - Volume I, Martin Cohen, producer, Latin Percussion Ventures LPV 337.

Understanding Latin Rhythms - Volume II - Down to Basics, Martin Cohen, producer, Latin Percussion Ventures LPV 422.

Warren Benson Presents Percussion, Ithaca Percussion Ensemble under the direction of Warren Benson, Golden Crest Records CR 4016.

Organizing a Percussion Ensemble

Walter C. Schneider

Developing a percussion ensemble in the middle or junior high school helps students learn proper percussion playing concepts on a wide variety of percussion instruments. The group also allows you to feature percussion students as soloists, playing music written especially for percussion; to develop ensemble playing, emphasizing teamwork rather than competition; and to develop ensemble feeling for playing in larger groups, like marching and concert bands.

One obstacle many directors first find in starting an ensemble is acquiring equipment; but many times both the director and the students can find substitutes. (Substitute percussion instruments that I've used appear below.) Do not be afraid to borrow equipment, either. Much of the percussion equipment is not used at the high school after marching band season, so you might borrow instruments from them. Remind your high school colleagues that they will have a better percussion section in a few years if you do borrow the instruments. Coordinate your concerts so you can use extra equipment from the high school in addition to the middle school equipment.

Choosing music is usually not a problem if directors look at the catalogs of publishers with percussion ensemble listings. Find music listed for more than four players or music that suits the number of players in your percussion section. Remember to pick percussion ensemble pieces, not drum ensembles. There is older literature of drum ensemble music, which requires only older traditional instruments like snare drums, bass drum, and cymbals. Percussion ensemble music should have at least one mallet part, a timpani part, and parts for other pitched and non-pitched instruments. Selections I can recommend appear below.

In order to develop a strong percussion group, rotate players on every piece so that each learns mallets, timpani, drums, and traps. Start your players on the instrument they play best, then gradually switch them to instruments on which they are less proficient. Soon you will have percussionists, not just bell players or snare drummers. Follow this organizational plan in larger mixed ensembles, too, emphasizing the total percussionist at all times.

Staging the ensemble can be a problem, because during a concert the audience wants to see the ensemble. Set up as far forward on stage as possible, and plan to have the group perform either first on the program or after intermission, so you can use pre-concert or intermission time to set up equipment and instruments. Mallet instruments should be in front, flanked on the sides by small, softer-sounding trap instruments such as wood blocks, triangle, etc. Place higher-pitched drums such as snare drum and bongos behind the mallets, and position the larger, more visual instruments, like bass drum, timpani, gong, and cymbals, behind the higher-pitched drums. Your audience may appreciate a few brief remarks about the compositions to be performed; and you can describe musical forms, motives, and unusual instruments in program notes. I have found that if audiences are unfamiliar with percussion, these remarks and program notes help them to understand the music and increase their enjoyment of the concert.

During the dress rehearsal take time to practice the set-up and movement from piece to piece. Observe and organize movement, but try to leave the instruments in the same place. Let the performers move from one instrument to another. Sample rugs (1′ x 1½′) placed on a flattened music stand make functional trap tables for small instruments and sticks. Do not allow students to place instruments, sticks, or mallets on the floor.

The performance should emphasize precision, ensemble playing, dynamics, and musicianship. Remember that percussion instruments have a wide dynamic range, so draw your student's attention to this. Also, pauses and endings in the music should involve all the musicians and instruments in a total visual freeze. In this respect, observe the rests at the end of many compositions, too.

When you establish your percussion program, you may have more players than available parts. Many percussion ensembles have individual parts that call for two or more instruments to be played simultaneously by one player, or the part requires the player to switch from one instrument to another. In these instances you can assign more than one player to a part, each person playing one instrument of the part. A director can often switch a pianist to a mallet instrument because the keyboards of both instruments are similar. In order to balance the keyboard parts dynamically, a bell part can be doubled with vibraphone or xylophone, thus using more players. Occasionally you can double other parts if players adjust their dynamics.

Participating in the percussion ensemble will not only enhance your students' music education, but this experience will improve their sight-reading, advance their technique, make them more aware of nuances in all music they play, and provide the feeling of togetherness that they will need in concert and marching band performance. The effects of this experience take time to cultivate, so start early, in the middle or junior high school. The rewards surely outweigh the effort.

Instrument Substitutions for Percussion Ensemble Use

Agogo bells — two small lengths of automobile exhaust pipe (different lengths) or two small cowbells.
Almglocken — clay flower pots
Anvil — small suspended square of metal, small section of railroad track, heavy metal or steel pipe, or automobile brake drum.
Bell tree — glissando on orchestra bells, or wind chimes.
Bongos — two tunable practice pads with inner mutes removed.
Cabasa (afuché) — maracas.
Celeste — bells played with medium rubber mallets.
Claves — wood block played with medium rubber mallets.
Conga Drum — floor tom tom.
Cowbell — one- or two-quart sauce pan.
Field Drum — snare drum with pitch lowered.
Finger cymbals — very small triangle (perhaps used in elementary school).
Gong — large suspended cymbal played with soft mallet near the edge.
Japanese Temple Gongs — stainless steel mixing bowls.
Marimba — xylophone played in lower register with medium-soft yarn mallets.
Orchestra Bells — marching glockenspiel or resonator bells.
Temple blocks — various pitched woodblocks, coconut shells hollowed out and struck on a flat, wood surface.
Timbales — two different pitched snare drums with snares off, or two tom toms.
Timpani — large drum with one head tuned carefully to same pitch at each tension rod.
Tom-toms — tuned parade drums with batter bottom heads and snares removed.
Trap table — music stand turned horizontal to flat position with a small sample rug placed on top.
Triangle — bell of suspended cymbal played with light drumsticks.
Triangle holder — a #1A clamp available in many hardware stores. Drill two holes in the clamp and thread it with gut violin string or covered bell wire.
Vibraslap — güiro.
Whip — two pieces of thin wood board hinged together.

Middle School Percussion Ensemble Selections

Abel, Alan. *Tom-Tom Foolery*, Carl Fischer, 4 players. Three different-pitched tom-toms and two timpani. A rousing drum ensemble program opener. Grade II.

Anslinger, Walter. *Percussion on the Prowl*, Pro Art, at least 7 players. Triangle, bass drum, chimes, suspended cymbal, gong, bongos, tambourine, 4 tom-toms, snare drum, and 4 timpani. An interesting piece that explores the tone colors of the percussion instruments used. Grade III.

Christian, Bobby. *Dakota*, Creative Music, 7-9 players. Bells, cymbals, xylophone (requires 3 mallets), sleigh bells, tambourine, 4 tom-toms, parade drum, 2 timpani, bass drum, and suspended cymbal. Sounds like American Indian music. Grade III.

Christian, Bobby. *March of the Toy Dolls*, Creative Music, 6-8 players. Bells, triangle, xylophone, temple blocks, parade drum, rachet, triangle, snare drum, 2 timpani, suspended cymbal, and bass drum. Typical mechanical-sounding music with rachet and meter changes. Mallets parts require 3 and 4 mallets. Grade III.

Christian, Bobby. *Teen, Tam, Tum*, Creative Music, 5-6 players. Bells, triangle, tambourine, castanets, snare drum, 2 timpani, and suspended cymbal. Easiest of the three pieces by this composer. This piece has a swing beat, and the bell part is very easy. Good selection to introduce playing without strict time and rubato. Cymbal and bass drum on Part IV should be divided to avoid an awkward instrument change. Grade II.

Davis, Thomas L. *Bossa Novacaine*, C.L. Barnhouse, 6-7 players. 2 mallet parts, 2 timpani, suspended cymbal, claves, and bongos. A Bossa Nova, as the title implies. Use bells on mallet I and xylophone on mallet II, and add a student to play maracas with the suspended cymbal part for a more Latin flavor. Good piece for training syncopation. Grade III.

Davis, Thomas L. *Three Four All*, C.L. Barnhouse, 6 players. Bells, 2 timpani, suspended cymbal, snare drum, triangle, and woodblock. As the title implies, this piece has a hemiola-jazz-waltz feeling. Light and happy, this selection makes a good choice as a final program selection. Grade III.

Davis, Thomas L. *Waltz for Swingers*, Creative Music, 6-7 players. Mallet, 2 timpani, suspended cymbal snare drum, tambourine, and wood block. Use brushes on the snare drum part; double the mallet parts on xylophone, bells, and vibes; and use medium rubber mallets on the wood block part. Grade II.

Farberman, Harold. $\frac{6}{8}$ *Dance*, Belwin Mills, 6 players. Bells, xylophone or marimba, snare drum, or tenor drum, suspended cymbal, bass drum, and 2 timpani. Slow tempo makes this selection easier than it first appears. Good for sight-reading. Grade I.

Farberman, Harold. *Latin Ostinato*, Belwin Mills, 6-8 players. Bells, marimba and xylophone, maracas, claves, cowbell, bongos, wood block, and 2 timpani. Use plastic mallets for bells, and if you have no marimba, use medium yarn or rubber mallets on xylophone to obtain a marimba-like sound. Trap parts may be shared. Grade II.

Farberman, Harold. *Percussion Sleigh Ride*, Belwin Mills, 6 players. Bells, xylophone, sleigh bells, triangle, snare drum, and timpani. Easy, cute but short composition for first-year players. Keep the snare drum down in volume. Grade I.

Firth, Vic. *Roll-Off Rhumba*, Carl Fischer, 7-11 players. 2 timpani, maracas, snare drum, 2 wood blocks, parade drum, tambourine, bongos, conga drum, castanets, cymbals, and bass drum. This piece features bongos. Have the student play them with rattan mallet handles, or fingers if he use proper bongo technique. Substitute floor tom-tom if conga drum is unavailable. Grade II.

Firth, Vic. *Six Little Indians*, Belwin Mills, 9 players. 2 timpani, triangle, tambourine, snare drum, field drum, wood block, crash and suspended cymbals, bass drum, and gong. Easy piece with no mallets required. Substitute another large cymbal if gong is unavailable, and lower a snare drum's pitch for field drum. Grade I.

Frock, George. *Fanfare*, Southern, Double percussion trio of 6 players. Bells, vibes, chimes, bongos, 2 tom-toms, tenor and bass drums, 2 Pyrex bowls, and 2 flower pots. This selection is useful for introducing graphic notation. Complete directions are included by the composer, so don't shy away from this composition. Place the bowls on a toweled trap table. Knot and rope the pots from the inside, and hang them upside down, suspended from a rack or sousaphone stand. Play the pots with soft yarn (yellow) mallets. Grade III.

Heim, Alan. *Fanfare for Percussion*, Music for Percussion, 5 players. Snare drum, tom-tom, crash cymbals, bass drum, and 2 timpani. A good program opener and excellent to teach mixed meter. Grade III.

Hopkins, Matthew. *Statement for Percussion*, Elkan-Vogel (Presser), 5 players. Snare drum, tenor drum, bass drum, xylophone, vibraphone, suspended cymbal, and 2 timpani. Interesting piece to program during the middle of your concert. Changes in meters and tempos require much rehearsal. Xylophone part at the end of the piece is challenging but not difficult; beware that the score is crowded and not complete. Vibe part could be played on bells with medium rubber mallets. Grade II.

Kinyon, John. *Ensembles for Young Performers*. Alfred. Snare drum, bass drum, wood block, triangle, cymbals, and bells. A collection of short pieces for elementary or beginning ensembles. Grade I.

Kraus, Kenneth. *Little Suite for Percussion*, Music for Percussion, 5-6 players. 3 timpani, bells, xylophone, snare drum, bass drum, and gong. Set in 3 movements, "Fanfare," Waltz," and "Finale," the first two movements seem too short. Provide time for the timpanist to tune between movements or have a fourth drum available tuned to E. "Finale" should start with the timpanist using wood sticks – a fast change is required, but using reversing sticks should solve this problem. Have the student reverse mallets – felt at rehearsal number 19, returning to wood at 38. The gong sounds particularly effective in this piece, so it may be worth renting a gong if you can't borrow one. Grade III.

Missal, Joshua. *Hoe-Down for Percussion*, Music for Percussion, 7 players. Hi Hat, wood block, 2 tom-toms, bass drum with cymbal or crash cymbals, xylophone, bells, timpani, snare drum, and piano. The "boom-chuck" piano part keeps this selection moving and one of your pianist/mallet players will be happy to return "home" in this fun and rousing percussion ensemble program closer. This selection of percussion parts require the students to count carefully. Grade III.

Schinstine, William. *Metallic Mystique*, Southern, 6 players. All metal instruments: high and low triangle; vibes or bells; finger cymbals; 5 automobile brake drums; suspended cymbal scraped with coin and played with snare drum sticks; and tambourine. Typical tinkling, bell-like writing. The 5 brake drums provide unusual programming with great audience appeal. Your local junk yard probably has a wide variety of different-pitched brake drums. Involve your students in removing the rust and painting them. A few school desks with small rugs make functional trap tables for the cumbersome brake drums. Have your students play them with medium hard rubber mallets, and be sure that the audience can see the brake drums and the players clearly. Grade III.

Schinstine, William. *Scherzo for Percussion*, Southern, 7 players. Tambourine; snare, field, and bass drums; suspended and crash cymbals; and 2 timpani. Keep the tempo up in this light, happy piece. No keyboard instruments are required. Grade II.

Spears, Jared. *Scamper*, C.L. Barnhouse, 5 players. 4 tom-toms, snare drum, bass drum, triangle, suspended cymbal, wood block, and 2 timpani. This selection is a fast-moving, rousing program opener. Grade III.

Thamm, Duane. *Rolling Progress*, Creative Music, 7 players. Bells, snare drum, timpani, triangle, suspended cymbal, bass drum, xylophone, and parade drum. A straight-forward easy ensemble selection for second-year students, but the publisher should print both mallet parts together in the score. Grade II.

Thamm, Duane. *Sonic Boom*, Creative Music, 5-6 players. Bells, snare drum, timpani, suspended cymbal, triangle, and bass drum. In $\frac{5}{4}$ time. The mallet part, in 5 flats, can be shared. Grade II.

Volz, Edward. *Prelude and Allegro*, Bourne, 5-6 players. Snare drum, tambourine, 4 tom-toms, 2 timpani, suspended cymbal, triangle, gong, and bass drum. Part IV can be shared. This piece has some meter changes. A good program opener or closing number with no mallet parts. Tambourine part and snare drum can be shared in Part II in several places. Grade II.

Whaley, Garwood. *Introduction and March*, Kendor, 7 players. Chimes, xylophone, gong, bells, 4 timpani, triangle, 2 tom-toms, suspended cymbal, and bass drum. A full-sounding piece. Put your strongest mallet player on the xylophone part. Grade III. ■

Teaching Musicianship to Percussionists

David W. Vincent

The incentive for improving percussion student musicianship must come from the director. Teach students by example and by actual instruction to pay close attention to dynamics, phrasing, articulation, pitch, and timbre, as well as to match the quality of their sound to that of the ensemble. Esprit de corps, an important factor in any ensemble's musical life, can be especially helpful in molding the percussionists into a unit that plays musically.

Here are some other ideas to help your percussionists become better musicians.

• Give the principal player a copy of each score being performed. In this way he can answer questions concerning assignment of parts. The extra score is also a useful guide for the timpanist to learn how to find pitches to check tuning while the ensemble plays, although this technique should be used only after the student has secure pitch discrimination.

• Teach your students to refrain from overplaying percussion instruments, which have a much wider dynamic range than strings and winds. The idea, "Percussion is loud" probably comes from the boisterous playing that is much too common.

• Teach your students to play common percussion figures correctly. One such figure is a suspended cymbal roll with a crescendo, notated below.

Many players increase the volume too quickly, thus reaching the peak of the crescendo too soon and destroying its effect. To achieve an exciting effect, the cymbal player should leave one-third to half the crescendo for the fourth beat. In no case should the crescendo peak before the first beat of the second measure.

• Instruct your percussionists to play the same phrasing as other band or orchestra sections playing similar figures, as in the following choices for a common figure.

• Be sure percussionists phrase and place accents appropriately. While playing a part that repeats, such as bass drum and cymbals in a march, phrasing with the ensemble will add immeasurably to the musical effect. A well-placed accent often makes the difference between a routine rendering of a piece and a sparkling performance. To hear excellent recorded examples of this kind of sparkling performance, listen to Frederick Fennell's Eastman Wind Ensemble march recordings on Mercury Records.

• Teach your cymbal player to watch the bass drum beater to coordinate the attack of the two instruments, eliminating the flam effect common in many percussion sections.

• The beater, stick, or mallet used to strike the instrument is the first component of articulation, and percussionists should have a variety of these tools to choose from. To select the proper implement for a particular passage, consider the work's overall style and character as well as the specific passage. For example, a fast and rhythmically complex timpani part sounds better with harder mallets; however, choose the softer of two possibilities whenever possible because hard mallets produce more contact sound and less tone than soft mallets.

Rolls

• Legato sounds on percussion instruments are attained by using rolls. Many percussionists develop fine snare drum rolls and then try to apply the same technique to timpani and keyboard mallet instruments; but there are additional considerations when rolling on instruments other than snare drum. Timpani and keyboard rolls are slower than snare drum rolls. A roll, the long tone of a percussion instrument, should be no faster than necessary to create a legato sound.

• Consider the pitch range of each drum to play the best-sounding roll. In general, as the pitch of the part rises on keyboard instruments, the roll speed should increase; and as the pitch rises within the range of the timpani, the roll speed should also increase. Thus, the same pitch would have different roll speeds on different-size timpani. The volume factor is quite natural; as the volume increases, so does the roll speed.

• Teach your percussionists to adjust their roll speeds according to the intensity of a phrase. Just as the string player varies the speed of his vibrato, increasing it for more intensity, so should a percussionist increase roll speed for more intensity within a phrase.

• When rolling from one surface to another, the sound must be continuous. Teach your students to keep the motion of the hands steady and use the arms to move to the new surface. The larger the distance between surfaces, the greater the chance that the initial stroke on the new surface will be too hard and produce an unwanted accent. To solve the problem, play the initial stroke of the roll on the new surface softer than the general volume of the passage.

Tuning

Even though percussionists often tune timpani diligently, they sometimes disregard tuning the other drums. Adjusting equal tension at each rod around the rim will put a drum in tune with itself; but it is equally important to consider the relative pitch of the drum and its relationship to other drums in the section. Teach your percussionists that tuning drums is as important as tuning any wind or string instrument. The snare drum should be at the highest pitch, the tom-toms in the middle, and the bass drum at the bottom of the tuning range.

The Right Instrument

• Choose a suitable instrument for each particular use. Having the right basic sound is almost as important as playing the correct notes. For example, imagine *The Stars and Stripes Forever* with a piccolo snare drum (lacking full-bodied tone) or the Finale of Tchaikovsky's Fourth Symphony with 22-inch cymbals (too large to control); yet performances with inappropriate instrument choices occur much too frequently.

• Choose the correct-size timpani. Select one on which the notes of a passage are in the timpani's mid-range. This choice produces maximum tone because higher pitches in a drum's range require tighter heads, which do not vibrate as freely; and lower pitches on a timpani require looser heads, which vibrate too freely.

Finally, extraneous noise is unmusical, so teach your percussionists to eliminate careless percussion sounds, such as foot-tapping, throwing sticks on a music stand, or dropping instruments and sticks during performances. Playing tambourine is one such problem because keeping the instrument quiet while it is not actually being played is difficult. Moving the tambourine from normal playing position to resting it on the knee must be carefully worked out in practice so that this movement produces no extra sounds.

When you teach your percussionists to make each musical sound while listening and being aware of all other sounds that occur in the ensemble, musicianship in the percussion section will improve, thus increasing the overall quality of the entire ensemble. ■

May, 1980

A Rotating Schedule for the Percussion Section

Milton Nelson

For many years I have had more drummers than are needed at one time in the concert band. Because I want all of them to participate, I've tried leaving it up to them to take turns playing, but have discovered that a few members of the section do all the playing while the rest sit and do their homework. I've also tried assigning specific pieces to each player, but too often players are left out on days when their pieces weren't rehearsed and they didn't learn all the band's repertoire for the year.

To solve the problem I devised a rotating schedule that lists what instrument a student should play on a given day. With this system my students learn to play all the percussion instruments and participate in some way every day. The only time I depart from the schedule is preceding a concert, when I assign each student to an instrument for each piece on the program. After the concert it's back to the schedule.

The numbers on the chart represent the days of the month. Each drummer's assignment is easy to determine by finding the date and moving down the column to his name. Weekends, holidays, and extra days are skipped in each month; and the rotation takes as many days as there are students in the percussion section. The reserve member plays any extra instruments called for in the score, or fills in for an absent player.

Rotating Schedule

KEY: S.D. I - snare drum I
S.D. II - snare drum II
Cym - cymbals
B.D. - bass drum
Timp - timpani
Acces - triangle, etc.
Res - reserve

	1 8 15 22 29	2 9 16 23 30	3 10 17 24 31	4 11 18 25	5 12 19 26	6 13 20 27	7 14 21 28
Smith	S.D. I	Res	Acces	Timp	B.D.	Cym	S.D. II
Jones	S.D. II	S.D. I	Res	Acces	Timp	B.D.	Cym
Hayes	Cym	S.D. II	S.D. I	Res	Acces	Timp	B.D.
Morgan	B.D.	Cym	S.D. II	S.D. I	Res	Acces	Timp
Fitch	Timp	B.D.	Cym	S.D. II	S.D. I	Res	Acces
Gordon	Acces	Timp	B.D.	Cym	S.D. II	S.D. I	Res
Williams	Res	Acces	Timp	B.D.	Cym	S.D. II	S.D. I

May, 1980

Teaching Accessory Percussion Instruments

Garwood Whaley

"Hold the triangle above the music stand. Don't hide the instrument. Cymbal player, you must make the cymbals resonate; let the entire cymbal ring."

If you have attended a high school regional or all-state band rehearsal recently, you have probably heard the conductor give similar instructions to the percussion section. Why is it necessary for a conductor to teach elementary performance skills to advanced students? Most directors would be embarrassed if a guest conductor had to teach woodwind and brass players how to hold their instruments in order to produce an acceptable sound. Yet, most directors don't seem concerned when a visiting conductor spends precious rehearsal time teaching fundamental skills to the percussion section.

Many student percussionists are unable to play accessory instruments such as triangle, tambourine, castanets, and cymbals. This problem stems from the fact that most conductors are wind players who lack the knowledge to teach the fundamental techniques of accessory playing. Even knowledgeable directors and percussion specialists spend little time on accessory instruments; instead they emphasize the "big 3": snare drum, mallets, and timpani. Studying these instruments is important because they provide both musical and technical challenges. However, almost all wind band literature calls for accessory percussion; thus, students also need to develop specialized techniques and concepts of sound for the basic accessory instruments.

To compound this problem

further, most percussion auditions at the high school level, including those for regional and all-state bands, usually do not require performance on accessory instruments. Prepared music and sight reading are usually required only for snare drum, mallets, and timpani. Calling for students to perform prepared audition pieces on percussion accessories is a logical first step in assuring competence on these instruments.

Recently, students auditioning for Virginia's District Ten Regional Band were directed to prepare an audition piece composed for snare drum, cymbals, tambourine, triangle, and bass drum. Most of the students who auditioned had never played accessory parts that required the use of idiomatic techniques. Students had to learn these techniques by seeking assistance from their directors, taking private lessons, and reading about them in percussion publications. Several band directors also had to learn or review these techniques. One director decided to take private lessons so he would be able to demonstrate the necessary techniques for his students.

The audition piece became a catalyst that stimulated learning. Most of the students who auditioned were able to perform the piece effectively, and several students performed the work with a high degree of musicality.

The audition procedure called for students to develop fundamental techniques on several accessory percussion instruments. The benefits of the procedure indicate that percussion auditions should include performance on accessory instruments as standard practice.

The accompanying audition piece requires students to arrange instruments in order to move smoothly from one to the other while accurately counting measures of rest. The specialized techniques necessary to perform this piece include tambourine thumb rolls and rapid fist-to-knee playing; triangle rolls and grace notes; bass drum rolls with two beaters; cymbal crashes, short articulations, and muffling; and controlled musical snare drum playing. I encourage the use of accessory percussion instrument audition materials. You may want to use the following solo for your next percussion audition. ■

Regional High School Band Percussion Audition Piece

Substitute Percussion Instruments

James McKinney

When a group does not have and cannot borrow the instrument called for in a score, substitutions are sometimes possible. Here is a list of suggested alternatives for percussion instruments that may not be in your storage cabinet. The required instrument appears first, in italic type.

Instruments with Wood-like Sounds

Wood block. Play the rim of a snare drum (snares off) or the rim of a bass drum with the butt ends of the sticks, or play temple blocks with hard rubber mallets.

Temple blocks. Play different-pitched wood blocks or the rims of differently-tuned snare and tenor drums. Place the wood blocks on foam rubber or on a carpet scrap, and play them with medium rubber mallets.

Claves. Play a high-pitched wood block with a hard wood beater.

Vibra slap. Play a ratchet by slowly rotating the handle.

Piccolo wood block. Play claves with a larger one (in diameter) striking a smaller one.

African claves. These claves have a very low sound, so use a medium-sized temple block or a large wood block, and a medium rubber mallet.

Güiro. Cut notches into a snare drum stick or a large dowel; scrape it across the rim of a snare drum with the snares on.

Tubo. Play two maracas in one hand.

Whip. Play a snare drum rim shot and strike a wood block at the same time or slap two small boards together.

Cabasa. Play two maracas in one hand.

Marching machine. Use bamboo wind chimes, and let the ends of the different lengths of bamboo strike a tom-tom head.

Instruments with Metal Sounds

Anvil. Use a large triangle or a large pipe. Place one leg of the triangle on the center of a large timpani, and strike the triangle with a heavy metal beater. The echo from the timpani bowl gives the effect of an anvil.

Crotales (antique cymbals). Play orchestra bells with brass mallets.

Finger cymbals. Use small triangles. If two pitches are called for, use two triangles played with metal beaters.

Bell tree. Scrape a thin metal beater across one or two sets of brass wind chimes.

Gong. Play a tam tam or a large cymbal with yarn mallets. Produce a flam by striking the cymbal on opposite sides near the edge.

Hi-hat. Use crash cymbals. Have one percussionist play the part while another closes the cymbals on beats two and four.

Cowbell. Play on the cup of a suspended cymbal with a hard rubber mallet or with a snare drum stick.

Ago-go bells. Play two different-sized cowbells with rubber mallets and allow them to ring.

Drum Substitutes

Timpani. Use bass drum or low tom-toms. Tune low, and don't try to produce the exact required pitch.

Bongos. Use two snare drums, tighten the heads more than usual, and play with small sticks.

Congas. Use tom-toms tuned lower than usual, and play them with timpani mallets.

Concert tom-toms. Play different-tuned concert snare or field drums with the snares off.

Timbales. Use two different-pitched snare drums with the bottom (snare) heads removed, and play with thin snare drum sticks.

Piccolo snare drum. Play a regular snare drum with the heads tuned very tightly.

Keyboard Percussion

Chimes. Use orchestra bells or vibraphone (motor off) and play the written note at the same time as a note one octave lower. If there is not room to add the lower note, add a note one octave higher.

Marimba. On a xylophone play the written marimba notes down one octave, using the softest mallets that can still produce a sound.

Vibraphone. Play the part on bells with the softest mallets that allow the part to be heard.

Xylophone. On a marimba play the written xylophone notes one octave higher and use hard rubber mallets.

Celeste. On a vibraphone play the part as written, using rubber mallets. The part might have to be played up an octave if it is written in the lower range. ■

Audition Solos for First-Year Percussionists

William J. Schinstine

Many directors need audition material for young percussionists; but selecting appropriate music can be time-consuming, and even the percussion specialist has difficulty choosing from the volume of material available.

The following list of solos is appropriate for students who have completed percussion training in an average elementary school band program. I have selected five solos for each of the three categories: snare drum, keyboard mallets, and timpani.

SOLOS

Snare Drum Solos

Flim Flam, Tom Brown, Kendor, $1.00.

This single sheet solo in $\frac{2}{4}$ time has 76 measures containing quarter and eighth notes, rolls, flams, and no repeats.

Three Plus Two from *Snare Drum Music,* Roy Burns and Saul Feldstein, Alfred, $2.50.

Simple rhythms in an alternating time signature of $\frac{3}{4}$ and $\frac{2}{4}$ identify this solo which uses the edge, middle, and center of the snare drum. The solo also uses snares on and off. Other similar solos of varying difficulty are included in the book.

The High-Stepper, Floyd O. Harris, Ludwig Music, $1.50.

This solo in march style and $\frac{2}{4}$ time is well within the technical abilities of upper elementary students. It uses quarter, eighth, and sixteenth notes and rests, plus flams and a wood block.

Repetivio, Fred M. Hubbell, Kendor, $1.00.

Varying dynamics are effective in this single sheet solo. Half, quarter, eighth, and sixteenth notes and several lengths of rolls are included. Time 1:30.

March Mac from *Little Champ First Year Drum Solos,* William J. Schinstine, Southern, $2.50.

This solo march in $\frac{4}{4}$ time contains short and long rolls, flams, first and second endings, repeats and various note values from whole to eighth. Available with piano accompaniment or recording of accompaniment.

Keyboard Mallet Solos

Valse Bluette from *Three Ballads,* Drigo, arr. Tom Brown, Kendor.

The piano accompaniment is available with this two-mallet waltz for marimba or vibes, which is also within bell range. This suite also contains a simple solo, *Liebestraum* by Liszt, if a student can handle simple three mallet technique.

In a Spanish Garden, William H. Hill, Kjos, $1.00.

This single sheet solo with piano accompaniment in $\frac{4}{4}$ time moderato can be played on any keyboard percussion instrument. The clear notation lies within a range of a tenth.

Adagio from *Master Solos Intermediate Level,* W. Mozart, arr. by Peter Magadini, Hal Leonard, $3.95 or $9.95 with cassette.

A cassette tape of the accompaniment and of a performance is included with this very simple two mallet work with piano accompaniment. The book contains innovative concepts and materials and interesting solos in each of the other areas of percussion.

Gymnopedie from *Solos for the Percussion Player,* Erik Satie, arr. by John O'Reilly, G. Schirmer, $7.95.

This very easy but quite satisfying solo could be played on any keyboard percussion instrument. A piano accompaniment is included.

Skater's Waltz from *Music for Marimba,* E. Waldteufel, arr. Art Jolliff, Rubank, $2.00.

This two mallet work with piano accompaniment uses some double stops and can be played on small keyboard instruments.

TIMPANI SOLOS

March from *Master Solos Intermediate Level,* J.S. Bach, arr. by Peter Magadini, Hal Leonard, $3.95, $9.95 with cassette.

Peter Magadini has made a good arrangement for a very simple timpani part to go with the Bach piece. The piano accompaniment is included, and the cassette tape contains a performance and a separate accompaniment part.

Pauken Parade, William J. Schinstine, Southern.

Two timpani are required for this solo in regular march form with no pitch changes or difficult rhythms. Printed in single sheet form or as part of the collection, *Tymp Tunes.*

Solos #6 and #9 from *The Developing Solo Timpanist,* William J. Schinstine, Southern, $7.50.

Solo #6 is a simple $\frac{4}{4}$ piece with rolls and no pitch changes, and #9 has alternating measures of $\frac{2}{4}$ and $\frac{3}{4}$ with rolls, sixteenth notes, and no pitch changes.

Solo #1 from *Musical Studies for the Intermediate Timpanist,* Garwood Whaley, JR Publications, $3.50.

Very easy rhythms of whole, half, quarter, eighth, and sixteenth notes make up this work. It includes two simple pitch changes with ample time to make them.

COLLECTIONS

The following collections contain a large variety of solos and some etude material as well. Those by Pimentel, Moore, and Akins include the more progressive and challenging literature.

Snare Drum

Drum Along, Harr and Buchtel, Kjos, $1.50, $2.50 piano accomp., $3.00 record, $5.50 complete.

Snare Drum Duets, Don Gilbert, HaMar Percussion Pub., $2.95.

Keyboard Mallets

Mallet Soloist, Saul Feldstein, Belwin, $1.25.

Basic Training Course for Keyboard Percussion, John Kinyon, Alfred, $1.50.

Bach for Marimba, James L. Moore, ed., Kendor, $4.00.

Bar Percussion Notebook, Linda Lorren Pimentel, Permus Publications, $4.00.

The Solo Marimbist Vol. I, Linda Lorren Pimentel, Permus Publications, $5.00.

Fundamental Studies for Mallets, Garwood Whaley, JR Publications, $4.00.

Timpani

The Musical Timpanist, Thomas N. Akins, Kendor, $7.50.

Studies for Timpani, Siegfried Fink, N. Simrock, $12.00. ■

September, 1980

Survey of Marching Percussion Materials

Jay A. Wanamaker

With the increasing interest in corps style percussion, a number of corps style features, cadence books, textbooks, method books, and films have appeared on the market over the past two years. This survey includes the title, author, publisher, cost, grade level, and a brief annotation of these materials.

Instrumentation is generally consistent throughout most features and cadences, which usually includes snares, timp-tom trios, four tuned bass drums, bells, xylophone, and from one to four cymbal parts depending on the particular arrangement. Auxiliary percussion instruments have been discussed in each annotation.

Marching Percussion Textbooks

Championship Auxiliary Units, Robert E. Foster, Jay A. Wanamaker, Bob Duffer, Kraig Cowles, Alfred, 256pp., $14.95. The "Contemporary Marching Percussion Ensemble" portion of the book (pages 9-83) is broken into separate sections on instrumentation, technique, visual effects, field presentation, examples of scoring, and administration. A number of photographs demonstrate proper teaching techniques and visual effects. This book is a starting point for developing a corps style marching percussion ensemble.

Developing Corps Style Percussion, Mike Cahill, Hal Leonard, 32pp., $5.95. This is primarily a collection of 22 exercises for a corps style percussion ensemble.

Developing the Corps Style Percussion Section, Larry Snider, Barnhouse, 32pp., $9.00. The book contains information on size of band vs. number of percussionists and tuning concepts. It includes 20 exercises plus pictures of correct technique.

Percussion Section: Developing the Corps Style, Sherman Hong and Jim Hamilton, Band Shed, 80pp., $14.95. This text deals with instrumentation, tuning procedures, staging, and scoring suggestions. Technical hints are given on all the instruments; and technical exercises, illustrations, and photographs are also included.

Marching Percussion Ensemble Method Books

Corps Style Drumming for the Intermediate Drummer, Roger B. Willis, Studio P/R, 38 pp., $6.95. This method book is designed for the intermediate corps style drummer, and deals with technique, rudiments, and exercises for snare, tri-toms, and tonal bass drums.

Precision Marching Percussion Ensemble Method, Robert Buck, Alfred, Teacher's Book 62pp., $5.95, Student's Book 32pp., $2.00. The teacher's book covers equipment, individual technique, development of segments and ensembles, and custom arranging. The student's book is concerned with individual technical development on the various instruments in the ensemble. The two books should be used together.

Marching Percussion Method, Will Rapp, Jenson, Conductor's Manual $9.95, Manual with cassette tape $16.95, 113pp., Snare Drum Book, Triple Tom Book, Bass Drum Book, Cymbal Book, and Keyboard Percussion Book $3.95 each, book and cassette $9.95. The Conductor's Manual deals with instrument selection, tuning procedure, basic technique, timing, and warm-up exercises. Each instrument book contains exercises along with information on how to develop a uniform style. The exercises are performed on the cassette tape.

Marching Percussion Ensemble Features

Battle Fatigue (Joshua), arr. by Michael J. Cahill, Hal Leonard, $12, Grade IV. Mallet parts are on an easy level while snare drummers are required to perform buzz rolls, rim shots, and quarter-note triplet figures.

Can Can, Offenbach/Jay A. Wanamaker, Alfred, Grade III (recording included). This series features convertible scoring concepts along with a performance guide that includes technical and visual suggestions. Kazoos are used for humming the melody along with off-beat hand claps. Cymbal effects include forming cymbal trees and patty-cake cymbal crashes. Police whistle, cowbell, and ratchet are also used.

Corps Style Percussion Special, "The Hustle," "New York, New York," "Dance Macabre," and "Joy," Warner Bros., $25.

"The Hustle" (disco version), McCoy/Ron Watson, Grade III. This series includes performance instructions along with diagrams of instrument placement. Auxiliary percussion instruments include two bass drum parts, flexatone, and optional timpani.

"New York, New York," Bernstein/Ron Watson, Grade III. This arrangement includes tempo changes and suggestions for visual effects. Auxiliary percussion instruments include police whistle, and optional timpani.

"Dance Macabre" by Saint-Saens, and "Joy" by Bach, arr. by Marty Hurley, Grade IV. Visual effects include snare drummers twirling sticks and tri-toms performing cross sticking patterns. Auxiliary percussion instruments include triangle, finger cymbals, and optional timpani.

Cumana, Allen/Will Rapp, Jenson, $15, Grade V. Snare drummers perform fake notes and play on different snare drums while timp-tom trios are featured performing cross-sticking patterns and sixteenth-note triplets. An optional bongo part is included.

Gypsy Fantasy (Based on Bizet's Carmen) arr. by Will Rapp, Jenson, $15, Grade V. This arrangement uses a number of complex snare drum rudiments and includes optional marimba and vibraphone parts.

I've Been Working, arr. by Michael J. Cahill, Hal Leonard, $12, Grade V. This feature is an arrangement of "I've Been Working on the Railroad" that includes a number of complex snare drum parts. Mallet parts are easy.

Mexican Hat Dance, Patrichala/Jay A. Wanamaker, Alfred, $10, Grade III (recording included). The arrangement features cymbalists performing with tambourines and snare drummers performing stick clicks. Auxiliary percussion include claves, two pitched woodblocks, slide whistle, and siren whistle.

Muppet Show, Theme From, Henson and Pottle/Will Rapp, Jenson, $15, Grade III. Kazoos are used on the melody. Auxiliary percussion includes triangle, slide whistle, wood-block, kazoo, cowbell, gong, and optional timpani.

Night on Bald Mountain, Mussorgsky/Jay A. Wanamaker, Alfred, $10, Grade IV (recording included). Visual effects include bass drum dips, cymbalists lying down, snare drummers playing on different snare drums, and optional bass drum head stands. Mallet parts are difficult.

Parade of the Wooden Toy Soldiers, MacDonald and Jessel/Will Rapp, Jenson, $12, Grade IV. Snare drummers perform a number of visual effects including stick clicks, stick beats (tap sticking), along with a number of drags, ratamacues, and six-stroke rolls. Auxiliary percussion includes ratchet, slide whistle, triangle, woodblock, and police whistle.

Pop (Pop Goes the Weasel), arr. by Michael J. Cahill, Hal Leonard, $12, Grade V. This feature is very similar to the 1969 rendition of the Boston Crusader's percussion feature of "Pop Goes the Weasel." Scored for advanced snare drumming with easy mallet parts.

Russian Sailor's Dance, Gliere/Will Rapp, Jenson, $15, Grade IV. This arrangement has snare drummers performing split parts while timp-tom players perform effects such as scraping cymbals with triangle beaters. A molto ritard slows to quarter-note equals 72, then accelerates to 186 for the finale.

Sabre Dance, Khachaturian/Will Rapp, Jenson, $12, Grade V. The snare drum segment performs a number of complex rudiments and variations. Bass drummers are instructed to use hard and soft mallets at appropriate sections for dynamic contrast.

Trepak (from the Nutcracker), Tchaikovsky/Will Rapp, Jenson, $12, Grade IV. This work features the cymbalists performing on tambourines using a knee and fist technique.

Turkey in the Straw, arr. by Michael J. Cahill, Hal Leonard, $12, Grade V. This arrangement features a number of complex snare drum parts and easy mallet parts.

William Tell, Rossini/Jay A. Wanamaker, Alfred, $10, Grade IV (recording included). Visual effects include tap sticking, horse gallops, cone head movement, snare drummers playing on different drums, and use of black Lone Ranger masks.

Percussion Features with Marching Band

Percussion Destruction, Jay A. Wanamaker and Robert E. Foster, Alfred, $16, Grade IV. This features the marching percussion ensemble performing various two- and four-bar breaks.

Visual effects include cymbalists skipping, snares strumming, and a surprise ending.

Percussion Discussion, Robert E. Foster and Jay A. Wanamaker, Shows Inc., $15, Grade IV. This disco chart features the percussion section in a drum set kind of function rather than a rudiment approach. Visual effects include snares kneeling, cymbalists lying down, and bass drum dips.

Cadence Books

Corps Style Cadences Set No. 1, Will Rapp, Jenson, $18, Grade III-V. A total of five graded cadences with auxiliary percussion including cowbell, tambourine, and police whistle.

Corps Style Cadences Set No. 2, Will Rapp, Jenson, $12, Grade IV-V. A total of six graded cadences with auxiliary percussion including tambourine, cowbell, and agogo bells.

Corps Style Cadences for the Contemporary Marching Percussion Ensemble, Jay A. Wanamaker, edited by Jim Petercsak, Award Music Co.(Music Sales), $15, Grade III-V. Scored for two bass drums and does not include mallet parts. Included are "Chop Builder" exercises which contain ensemble warm-ups and individual exercises emphasizing triplets, sixteenth notes, flam rudiments, and roll exercises.

Corps Style Street Beats, Michael J. Cahill, Hal Leonard, $15, Grade IV-V. Cadences include "March of the Gangly Men," "Brothers and Mothers," "Tom Foolery," and "Sneaky Pete."

Total Marching Percussion Book I, Larry Snider, Barnhouse, $7, Grade III-V. Scored for two bass drums and does not include mallet parts. Contains a total of 25 cadences with one copy of the score and no parts. Auxiliary percussion include tambourine, cowbell, and ratchet.

Total Marching Percussion Book II, Larry Snider, Barnhouse, $8, Grade III-IV. Scored for two bass drums. Contains a total of 20 cadences with one copy of the score and no parts. Auxiliary percussion include triangle, cowbell, tambourine, and metal shaker.

Marching Percussion Films

Building the Individual, Precision Drumming, Part 1, "Instant Learning Series," McCormick's. Featuring Rob Carson, 12 minutes, $145. Rob Carson demonstrates a number of rudiments including long roll, buzz roll, paradiddles, flams, single and double drags, and ratamacues. Warm-up exercises, back sticking, tap sticking, and finger control exercises are also presented.

Building the Section, Precision Drumming, Part 2 "Instant Learning Series," McCormick's. Featuring Fred Sanford and the Santa Clara Vanguard Percussion Section, 12 minutes, $145. This film covers the techniques used in performing the instruments in a marching percussion ensemble while stressing control and timing. Each section is featured while performing warm-ups and dexterity drills.

Championship Marching Percussion "How to Series," McCormick's. Featuring Larry McCormick and the Santa Clara Vanguard Drum and Bugle Corps, 14 minutes, $145. A good portion of this film was made at a live clinic and stresses three basic movements in precision drumming: stroke, tap, and grace notes. Various instruments of the ensemble are discussed regarding implements, tuning, dimensions, and sound projection. ■

African Rhythms for American Percussionists

Phil Faini

It seems strange that in the music of "primitive" societies we find rhythm to be in a higher state of development than in the more advanced Western European culture, where for centuries rhythm has been organized over a relatively simple metric base divisible by two or three. The reason is that with the advent of polyphony, western composers focused their attention on harmony, counterpoint, and orchestration, leaving rhythm in a more primitive state of development. In the music of many of the primitive societies the so-called tyranny of the bar line is abdicated and the monotonous repetition of the simple duple or triple meters is replaced with asymetric rhythms or polyrhythms. A typical example of this practice is an asymetric thythm in a children's clapping song from Rhodesia.

or the use of the polyrhythm 2:3 which is achieved by the grouping of six pulses into three groups of two or two groups of three.

These are but two rudimentary examples of the type of rhythmic organization used in African music. Also, tempos in African music move at a brisk pace (♩=288) and the African musician is often called upon to play interlocking rhythms:

Player I

Player II

or

Learning to play these rhythms increases individual precision and develops better ensemble playing. The following techniques can be used to teach the American percussionist a feel for African polyrhythms.

2:3, or African Hemiola is played on a pair of gourd shakers (maracas) or with drum sticks on a set of two high- or medium-pitched drums (bongos or timbales):

Example 1

𝅗𝅥. = 72-96

B R L R

R R R

L L

R = right hand

L = left hand

B = both hands together (like a flat flam)

The sticking may be reversed to ♩♫♩ (B L R L) which results in three in the left hand and two in the right.

Fluctuating single line rhythm moves between $\frac{3}{4}$ or $\frac{6}{8}$ meter depending on phrasing or accent. This can be played with drum sticks on a high tom-tom:

Example 2

A war dance called "Otole" from the Acholi tribe of northern Uganda uses African Hemiola. The microrhythmic part of the dance can be played on two high tom-toms (8" and 12") by two players using the butt end of snare drum sticks in order to produce a full drum sound. If notated in a traditional western rhythmic style it would be played as follows:

Example 3

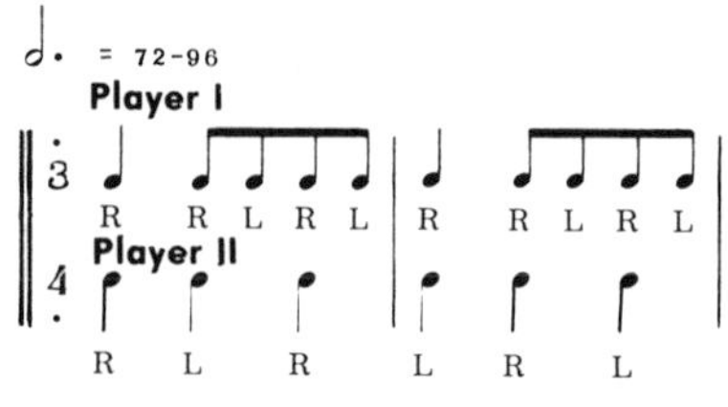

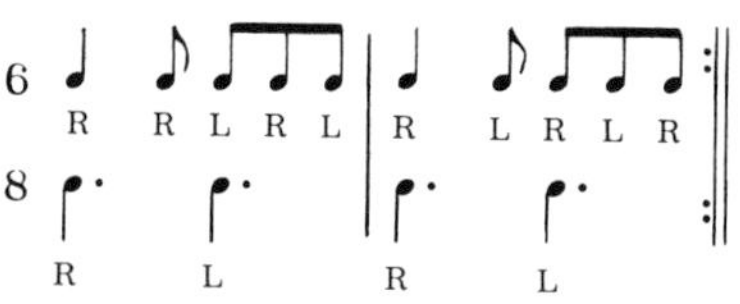

The African drummers, however, would tend to play example 3 as a polyrhythm in the following manner:

Example 4

A good practice exercise would be to alternate playing examples 3 and 4.

The macrorhythmic part of the dance is played with felt mallets on two low pitched tom-toms (14" and 16") or a low tom-tom and a bass drum. Here it is notated in a unison style:

Example 5

Example 6

Notated in a polyrhythmic style it looks like this:

The preceding music examples can be scored as an ensemble:

Example 7

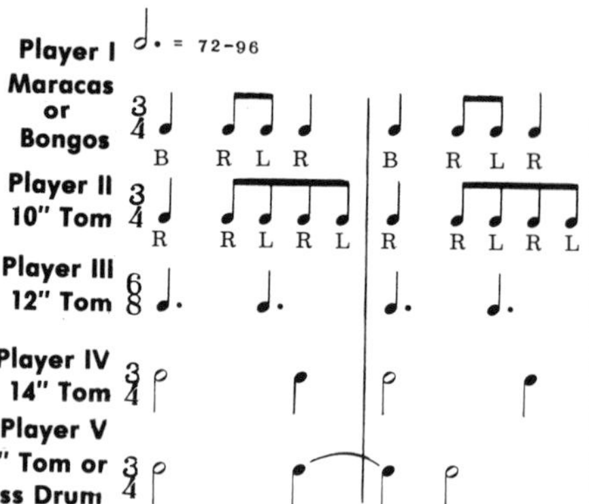

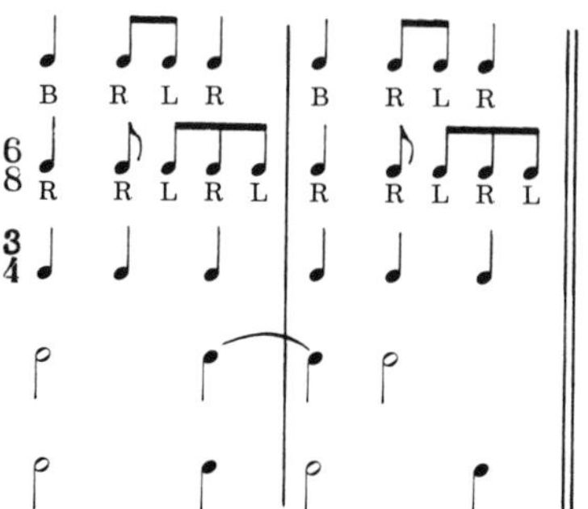

Instruments

African instruments are now available in the U.S. from various percussion specialty companies. Having authentic instruments is certainly desirable, but not a prime requisite, because the African musician does not hesitate to use substitute instruments. I have even seen an African use a five gallon square metal can to play a background ostinato rhythm that was originally performed on a hollowed out section of a log. To make intelligent substitutions one needs to know the original instrument's pitch (high or low), function (background or solo), and usual playing technique (stick or hand). With the variety of drums available today — all sizes and ranges of tom-toms, bass drums, hand drums, as well as congas, quintos, tumbas and bongos — the choice of a substitute western instrument is not difficult. Idiophone and rattle substitutions are also not difficult because we have a variety of bells, scrapers, maracas, and other shakers to choose from. The only exception is the "hour glass" drum, which is a highly specialized West African pressure drum with extreme flexibility of pitch range and performance technique.

The following list shows substitute instruments for some East and West African drums, which are classified as to pitch, function, and technique.

East Africa
Nankasa (high, background, stick) — use 12" tom
Engalabi (high, solo, hand) — use quinto (small congo)
Bakisimba (medium, background and solo, hand) — use tumba (large conga) or 16" tom
Mpunyi (low, background, hand) — use 22" bass drum with soft beater.

West Africa
Petia (High, background, stick) — use 12" tom
Akukua (high, background, stick) — use 10" tom
Apentemma (medium, background and solo, hand) — use conga
Atumpan (low, solo, stick, played in pairs) — use 23" and 25" timpani, or 20" and 24" bass drums

Technique

The African drummer is very particular about sound production. He achieves a variety of sounds from his drums through the use of various hand techniques: center strokes that sound deep and muted through the use of a cupped hand; ringing sounds on the edge of a drum produced by a quasi rim shot technique; muted finger taps; and sharp, raucous finger and hand slaps used for accentuation. These are the same techniques used on conga and bongo drums today. Latin American gourd shakers and maracas also use the same techniques as their African counterparts. The agogo bells and cuíca drums from Brazil use the same techniques as the double gongs and friction drums found in Africa. Because the hand drumming techniques of the South American conga and bongo drums have their ptototypes in Africa, students who study African drumming also gain additional understanding and technique that serves them well in playing jazz, as well as Latin-style concert arrangements.

Music

There are now three types of music available for performance: transcriptions of African music, original compositions based on African music, and Latin American compositions with an African influence.

Folk Songs of Ghana, by J.H. Kwabena Nketia (Oxford University Press) includes transcriptions of African dances. Melodies and texts are given for the songs, as well as a complete score for the drum ensemble used to accompany the singing. Voices are not necessary for performance as the drum rhythms will stand alone. The book contains extensive descriptions of each dance, including a discussion of instruments, tempos, rhythms, variations, playing techniques, and function of each drum. The author also discusses the polyrhythmic relationship of the instruments, including numerous examples of the various styles of solo passages used. All of this information facilitates the proper performance of these dances and provides an insight into African drum polyphony.

African Songs and Rhythms for Children, by W.K. Amoaku (B. Schott's Sohne) is written in the Orff-Schulwerk tradition for educators who want to introduce their students to the musical traditions of other countries, but it also includes complete drum ensemble scores.

Michael Udow's *African Welcome Piece* (University of Miami Music Publications) includes rhythms from three different styles of African dances plus a chorus. The instrumentation calls for traditional western percussion instruments such as tom-toms, timbales, snare drums, bongos, timpani, and a steel drum or two pairs of agogo bells. Although the piece uses western instruments, it captures the style, spirit, and sound of African drumming and is excellent on a concert program.

The Ritmicas of Amadeo Roldán (Southern Music) contains South American rhythms that are derivitives of African style rhythms and use traditional Latin American percussion instruments. Many Central and South American dances use instruments and rhythms with African origins. For example, the Brazilian Samba uses the cuíca — a friction drum similar to the types found in Africa, and the berimbau, which is derived from the African musical bow.

Sikyi — a youth dance from Ghana in West Africa (example 8) can be played on substitute western instruments: (1) small cow-bell; (2) maracas, both held in the same hand; (3) medium cowbell; (4)(5) bongos, H=high, L=low; (6) tumba or 20" bass drum (soft beater), O=open, D=dampen; (7) 12" tom (sticks), X=press stick on head to raise pitch; (8) conga or 16" tom (soft mallet), O=open, D=dampen; (9) conga or 18" tom (soft mallet), O=open, D=dampen.

Parts 4 and 5 were originally written for the "hour glass" drum but a high and low pitch from a pair of bongos on two small toms works just as well. Parts 8 and 9 can be played on the same size drums if the one used for part 9 is lower in pitch.

Example 8

In over a decade of performing African music I have found that it has exceptional audience appeal. The music is fresh, exciting, and commands the attention of both young and old. It broadens the musical experience of the player and listener alike, and aids in the development of the performer's rhythmic sophistication and precision, which is essential to good ensemble performance. I encourage music educators to augment their programs with the vital and moving spirit of African music. ■

November, 1980

Rudimentary Awakening

Gene Bardo

I have become aware of a trend that I think is detrimental to students: people claiming that one need not study rudiments in order to play drums. These naysayers have been with us for a long time. Almost without exception they are not very good drummers, and are able to play only the relatively simple literature of the orchestra or they may be capable of handling a stint in a rock or pop band. The only problem is that in some instances the people who are preaching this anti-rudimental line are teaching percussion at the college level.

Of course, it is possible to play drums and not study rudiments. It is also possible to play violin and not study scales and arpeggios, but if you approach the violin on a note-by-note basis, progress is painfully slow. Any piece of music can be analyzed as either part of a scale or an arpeggio, so if you study all scales and arpeggios, when you read a piece of music it is merely a matter of identifying what old familiar pattern is called for at any given instance.

The same idea holds true for snare drum. There are a finite number of patterns that can be performed on a drum. Because most of these patterns are very fast, the only way to perfect them is by practicing them slowly at first, gradually increasing the speed until playing tempo is reached. Then the eye sees the pattern, the mind recognizes it, and the conditioned reflex allows the hands to reproduce the pattern on the drum.

What is the value of rudimental training? In a letter from my one-time friendly competitor (in school band and drum corps) John Beck, who is now teaching percussion at Eastman, he says that rudiments make excellent training exercises for wrist and arm but should never be studied as an end in themselves. I agree with the statement; but suggest that if you have mastered the rudiments you are in the position of not worrying about technique when you play and thus are able to concentrate on the musical values. In short, a thoroughly trained rudimental drummer can read anything at tempo, and at sight. After all, shouldn't that be the goal of any training program?

Another value of rudimental training is its effect on ensemble playing. Sanford Moeller, in *The Moeller Book,* which is to an older generation of percussionists what the Arban book is to trumpeters, writes that a competent drum section can be created only from people who have practiced their various strokes in the same precise manner, so that when they play as an ensemble, it will sound as one person.

When only one man is playing percussion in a group (a jazz band, for example), section precision is not needed. The problem is that this same player is sometimes called on to play in an all-percussion ensemble or a concert band. This past season in the Saginaw Eddy Band (see article in *The Instrumentalist,* April, 1980), we had to find a replacement for one of our five-man percussion section for 3 concerts. It was very difficult to find anyone to fill the vacancy, and when we finally did settle on someone, the results were not too successful. The fellow had great trouble playing precisely. This is not to fault him because he is very talented. He simply has not had the opportunity to learn to play in an ensemble, and this I attribute to his lack of rudimental training.

In your enthusiasm for keyboard mallet and all the other exotic forms of percussion, do not slight the lowly snare drum in your teaching. There are a lot of drummers about, but only a few masters of the instrument. Rudimental instruction is still the best way to reach the fullest potential of your students. ■

Percussion Literature

Don R. Baker

Mallet/Keyboard Instruments

This has been an excellent year for mallet literature. Most all of the music is worthwhile and encompasses a good spectrum of styles from jazz to contemporary. More transcriptions for mallet instruments have appeared by Scott R. Meister, *Celebrated Menuet* and *Spanish Dance* (Ludwig). These are not as appealing as some of his other transcriptions but they will work well for intermediate students. One fine collection of xylophone solos designed for the very young beginner with piano and percussion accompaniment by Colin Evans is *Fun With Xylophone* (Paxton). Orff style instruments can be used to play these simple works, and well-designed teacher rehearsal techniques are included.

For the beginning four mallet student a fun yet musically developed collection of works has been edited or composed by Linda Lorren Pimentel. The *Linda Lorren Pimentel's Bar Percussion Notebook Vol. II* (Permus) develops the student's technique through creative "problem solving" situations using a bass and treble clef approach similar to piano pedagogy. Select volume I and II of the *Notebook* before her *Solo Marimbist* volume I and II because her *Notebooks* seem more musically attractive and more reasonable in difficulty. A warm, lyrical work for four mallet marimba, *Compassion* (Permus) by Lorraine Goodrich Irvin is a good change-of-pace, but look out for those octaves. For something more popular, turn to William J. Schinstine's, *Gee, I May Be Late* (Kendor) for some four mallet jazz with marimba accompaniment. Something more difficult would be *Two Pieces* by Murray Houliff (Southern) which includes "Mountain Song" and "Rosewood Forest" for four mallet marimba.

For the advanced marimbist, *Casper's Dance* by Murray Houliff (Kendor) is not at all a problem of difficulty like most of his earlier works. There is independence of the mallets required but more in a homophonic than a contrapuntal style.

College students will enjoy Tilo Medek's *Zur Unzeit Erblühtes* (Edition Wilheim Hansen, Magnamusic-Baton) for four mallet marimba written one octave lower than it sounds in a style similar to Hank Badings.

A must for all developing four mallet students is the well-illustrated and technically explained method by the now famous marimba artist, Leigh H. Stevens. *Method of Movement for Marimba* (Marimba Productions) is divided into two sections: grip movement; and 590 exercises for developing stroke, independence, and rolls for the marimba. This is Stevens' own approach, and a significant one.

A new marimba ensemble series with music arranged by Ruth Jeanne and James Moore is for four to six players and ranges from easy to moderately difficult works. Many times the players can double up on one of a variety of instruments, although the pieces will fit more comfortably on four separate marimbas. The works are good reading and training pieces, and they would also be appropriate for light programming at the college level or for music camps. All copies are done in good hand manuscript except *Toccata in D Minor*. The arrangements include: *Ronda Ala Turk, Toccata in D Minor, Ave Maria, Farandole, Prelude, Rondo, Air, Galloping Comedians, Can Can, The Mill, Staccato Etude, Moment Musical, Marimba, Espani Cani* and *La Cumparsita*. (Permus).

Bon Vivant (Ludwig) by Jacques Dont, edited by Scott Meister, is a mallet trio with piano accompaniment that includes at least two marimba and one xylophone. This short work will be moderately easy for high school students.

Bill Molenhof has a collection of works for piano and vibes plus five works for marimba and vibes: *Vibes-Piano Duos* and *Quiet Celebration, Song for the New Year, Saturday's Child Sings a Hopeful Song, One Notch Higher, Busy Signal* (Kendor). All difficult, for advanced high school or college performers, the works use four mallets, and a plastic recording of the marimba/vibes duets is included. The *Quiet Celebration* and *Saturday's Child* seem particularly appealing for their homogeneous tone quality.

Drum Set

A very basic, simple method for

the unschooled drummer is Peter Magadini's *Learn to Play the Drum Set* (Hal Leonard). Very simple techniques, basic styles, and practice routines are discussed. I recommend this book for the student who progresses slowly or the average student who will proceed through the book very quickly. Hats off to the artist. The cover is one of the most attractive on the market.

For the more advanced drummer an excellent collection of modern set solos by well-known artists has been transcribed by Fred Gruber. All solos can be heard on the indicated recordings. *Contemporary Drum Solos* (Hal Leonard) has limited use, but it fills a needed area in drum set listening.

Ralph Humphrey has a fresh new book out called *Even in the Odds* (C.L. Barnhouse) that deals with odd meters and rhythms for the drummer in both jazz and rock styles. There are recordings listed of the examples and plenty of "chop buster" exercises. The really outstanding feature in the book is the section on using East Indian rhythm systems on drum set — a first in print — even though drummers have used them for years.

Kendor Music has published four new works of Murray Houliff's for a four piece drum set. All needed, all good, all fun, all a challenge, and a welcome collection for the student: *Philly, Ain't It Rich!, Just for the "Funk" of It,* and *Samba-Ly.*

Multiple Percussion

This important area received little attention this year. The new work by Martin Gümbel, *Uberschreitungen* für Schlagzeug solo (edition Moeck), will need German translation and contemporary music playing experience. Recommended for college students where modern equipment is available.

Timpani

Two new works are available for the advanced timpanist, both written for or by John Beck of the Eastman School of Music. Beck's own work requires four timpani and a player with a good ear plus good pedal technique. The first movement of *Three Episodes for Timpani* (Kendor) requires a piano and use of sympathetic vibrations to enhance timbral effects. The last movement is overly simplistic compared to the rest of the movements. Consider Beck's other works first as this is primarily a bag of tricks for timpani. Samuel Adler's *Canto IX* (Ludwig) in five movements was written for John Beck and includes the use of six roto toms, five timpani, a tambourine, five cymbals, and three pieces of cloth. This is definitely for the professional player and contemporary music listener due to its abstract nature and the unwarranted amount of time needed to retune almost all the drums between movements. A very personalized solo not readily useful for the general public.

The *Timpanist Etudes Bk. I* by Steve Kastuck (Multi-Media Productions) contains almost all the typical problems of modern timpani playing. The etudes do not progress from easy to more difficult but from etudes for two to four drums. Because of the significant tuning and graphic notation used in this book it is primarily designed for advanced high school students or college percussionists. There is no text or explanation of the graphics, so some have no logical meaning. There are printing errors, but the manuscript is very clean.

Snare Drum

If you are looking for a book to answer your questions about concert roll development, Gary Olmstead's, *The Snare Drum Roll* (Permus) is a must. This is a reader's guide and not a method book but it is an excellent approach to concert roll playing which should be considered by all directors and their students.

For those of you who remember the progressive rudimentalist, Charlie Wilcoxon, his solos and books have been reissued by Ludwig. Be sure to consider these rudimental swing style methods: *The All-American Drummer, Modern Rudimental Swing Solos for the Advanced Drummer,* and the sing-along, *Drumming plus Hummin' A Tune.* But if you're looking for a good up-to-date corps style solo that thrives on sticking dexterity, then consider Jeffry P. Funnell's *Corps-Dially Yours* (Kendor).

Phil Perkins has been developing a series of what he calls, "a logical approach to," in this case snare drum. Both volumes I and II are published by Logical Publications and have some problems with practicality. The theoretical approach may seem "logical" but in reality it does not fit the general music trends in public schools. Volume I could be used for any instrument as it is just an additive process of rhythms and dynamic changes. Nothing is particularly idiomatic to the snare drum. Volume II suddenly throws rolls, flams, and drags at the reader within a short period of time. All those phases need slow maturing in easy rhythm steps before bounding into more challenging rhythms, so use supplemental teaching aids for a broader development. Perkins' *Logical Approach to Rhythmic Notation* is similar to Joel Rothman's excellent book on *Teaching Rhythm* (Music for Percussion) and either one should be used weekly in heterogeneous ensembles for learning duple and triple meters.

Snare drum methods generally do not include multiple percussion etudes or solos but Michael LaRosa's *Contemporary Drum Method* (Somers) does. There is no discussion of where to play on the drum but both traditional and matched grips are covered. The etudes progress normally from quarter notes to the end with triplets and drags. There is little material on each new concept, usually two or three pages, and this does not give the student time to reinforce these new elements. Also, the book has only two pages of 3/4 time, and all the rest is in duple meter. The roll discussion is only in rudimental style (open, double stroke) and lacks preface exercises for the etudes. Use of this book would require outside materials and supplemental exercises.

Siegfried Fink's, *Kreuzpunkte* (Schott) is a trio for non-specific percussion instruments. There is an exercise section for the trios but the African-like rhythms are not fully developed for performance. The cost ($7) seems high for the little originality in the music and the easy access to African recordings which would produce the same ideas.

Percussion Section: Developing the Corps Style (The Band Shed/ Eagle Press) by Sherman Hong and Jim Hamilton has a good marching guide for the high school drum line. The material is basic and not as complex as some modern corps lines, making it practical for the smaller school or a less advanced section. The music examples of scoring are few and a large portion of the section covers dance rhythms. ■

Beginning Four-Mallet Playing

Mario A. Gaetano, Jr.

If a young percussion student wants to pursue a career in music and study at the university level he must be well prepared in all areas of percussion. One area that calls for extra preparation for college-bound percussionists is mallet-keyboard performance. Many schools now require auditions in this area and some expect previous four-mallet study. Here are some of the most frequently asked questions I hear from students and band directors concerning four-mallet playing.

• *When should a student start playing four mallets?* A student should begin four-mallet playing as soon as basic techniques and an overall familiarity with the instrument are acquired through two-mallet playing. His lessons after that point should include both two- and four-mallet exercises, studies, and sight-reading. Although both types of playing use similar concepts and disciplines, there are many differences. Equal practice time must be spent in both areas.

• *What grip should I use?* There are three basic grips. In the traditional cross-stick grip, the mallets are held so the handle of the inner mallet crosses over the handle of the outer mallet. The thumb and the first finger are placed between the mallets and used to spread the mallets open. The outer mallet comes in contact with the first joint of the first finger while the inner mallet touches the thumb at the base of the thumb nail. The third and fourth fingers hold the mallets in the palm of the hand where they cross and are used to bring the mallets together. Thus, there are two opposing forces at work: the thumb and the first finger in one direction and the third and fourth fingers in another direction. Play the instrument with the palms facing down. The cross-stick grip is the most popular because of its simplicity in mallet manipulation. The disadvantage of this grip is that individual mallet independence is not at a maximum because both mallets are touching each other; when one moves, the other also moves in the opposite direction (see photo).

Cross-stick grip

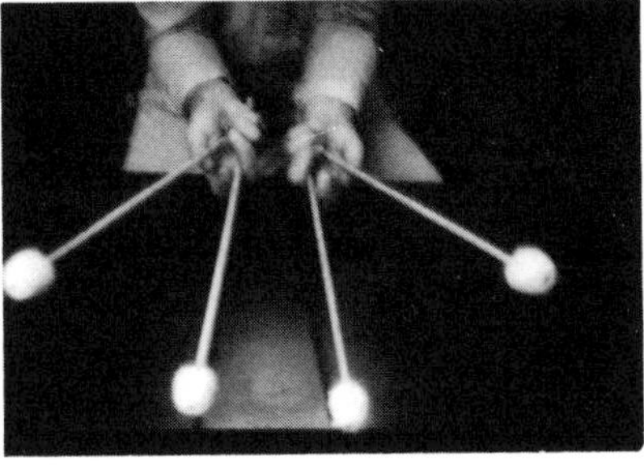

The Burton grip is also a cross-stick grip, but this time the handle of the outer mallet crosses over the handle of the inner mallet. The third and fourth fingers are used along with the thumb and first finger in spreading the mallets open. (Students may have a dexterity problem in using the third and fourth fingers to aid in opening the mallets). The second finger is used to stabilize the outer mallet. This grip offers an advantage when playing two-mallet passages because the unused mallet is secured in the hand with no excess movement. The mallets of the right hand usually remain open at a 90 degree angle so the outer mallet attacks the bars straight up and down, rotating over the inner mallet with no side-to-side motion. Again, the palms face down in playing position, and because the mallets cross one another, mallet independence is not at a maximum. This grip seems to work best when playing jazz vibes where two-mallet passages are frequent and the melody is usually in the outermost mallet (see photo).

Burton grip

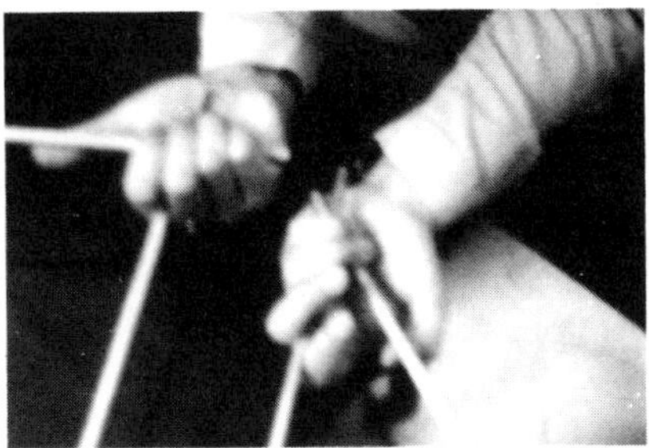

In the Musser grip, each mallet is held in a different part of the hand. The outer mallet is held securely by the third and fourth fingers at the end of the mallet shaft, while the inner mallet is held between the thumb and first finger. The shaft of the inner mallet rests on the first joint of the first finger with the end of the handle securely placed in the ball of the hand. The thumb rests lightly on top. In using this grip, the thumb nail should be pointing up at all times. It will take the student long hours of practice to develop both parts of the hand working independently, but experts agree that in the long run this grip offers a maximum amount of independence and control (see photo).

Musser grip

Choosing a grip should be a joint decision by the student and teacher with the long-term goals and objectives of the student taken into consideration.

• *What method books are available for four-mallet playing?* Below is a cross-section of the most popular method books as well as beginner through high school solo collections.

Method Books

Developing Four Mallet Technique, Marj Holmgren, Studio 4 Productions.

Four Mallet Studies, Gary Burton, Creative Music.

Four Mallet Technical Studies, Garwood Whaley.

Graded Reading Exercises for Four Mallets, Max Neuhaus, Music for Percussion, Inc.

Mallet Technique for Bass and Treble Clef/Book II, Sandy Feldstein, Belwin.

Method of Movement for Marimba, Leigh Stevens, Marimba Productions.

Modern Mallet Method Vol. 3, Phil Kraus, Henry Adler.

Solo Collections

Mallets in Mind, Tom Brown, Kendor Music.

78 Solos for Marimba Vol. 2, Art Jollif, Belwin.

Solos for the Vibraphone, Ian Finkel, G. Schirmer.

Solo Marimbist Books I and II, Linda Pimental, Permus Publications.

• *What are some exercises that develop four-mallet playing?* The following exercises are categorized into four areas: all four mallets striking the bars at once; rapid interval change exercises; exercises that develop independence; exercises combining rapid interval changes with independence.

Any of the three grips can be used, but certain factors must always be considered that will help the student get the best results. They are: • The exercises should be practiced first at an extremely slow tempo, then slowly increased in speed, but never so fast that control is lost.

• The student should get in the habit of moving immediately from one playing position to the next no matter how slow the tempo. • The arms should always be relaxed, with the majority of movement coming from the wrists. • In the exercises that use four mallets striking at once the four mallets should all strike the instrument at precisely the same time with equal volume. Do not roll. • Avoid striking nodal points of the bars. When playing on the accidentals, the mallets should strike the center of the bar or the nearest end. • The mallets should bounce off the bars with the effect of drawing the tone out of the instrument.

The exercises should be played in all major keys, and the mallets are numbered as follows:

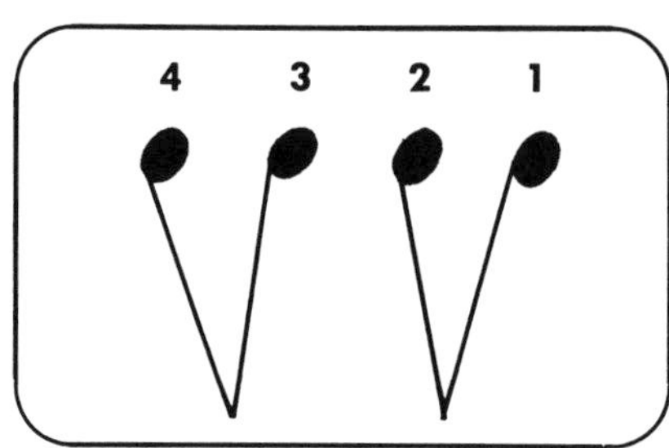

All four mallets striking the bars at once

Exercise 1.

Exercise 2.

Exercise 3.

Rapid interval change exercises

Exercise 1.

Exercise 2.

Exercise 3.

Exercise 4.

Exercise 5.

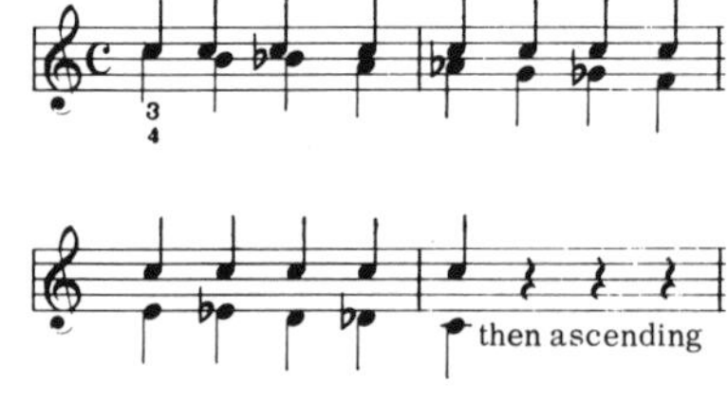

February, 1981

Percussion Maintenance and Repair

Don R. Baker

Percussion instrument care is an often neglected area of a percussionist's or music educator's background. Periodic care of percussion instruments will prolong their life and prevent major repairs. The following guidelines will not give you all the procedures for care and repair, but they will touch on those that seem to occur most often.

Experience is the best teacher, so get involved by doing. No one can say how tight a snare drumhead should be. It's all relative so listen, feel the head, then play the surface. Tear a drum apart yourself. It is not nearly as complicated as a flute. Just be active. Foster this same kind of involvement in your students by having a cleaning party some evening. Your students will have more respect for their instruments when they have to do the work themselves. Supply the rags, cleansers, and tools, and teach them how to use them. Once the maintenance system is established, the upper classmen should be assigned to teach the new students. Be sure everyone has experience maintaining each group of percussion instruments before leaving high school.

In general, check heads, snares, straps, and screws periodically. Touch them up with dusting and a little polish every three or four months, although you will want to polish them before each marching performance or competition. All drums (except timpani), cymbals, and accessories should be completely torn down and recleaned once a year, preferably at the beginning of the school year. I also recommend a complete cleaning of the marching equipment at the end of the season before it is stored. Then set the heads and snares at medium tension. In addition, it is always better to travel or move equipment in cases specifically designed for the instrument.

Drums: Snare drum, bass drum, tom-tom, roto tom, etc.

Care: Periodically clean the heads, shell, and chrome with a dry cloth. Soiled batter heads should be cleaned occasionally with window cleaner or mild soap and water; just be sure to remove any residue of soap. Do not let the water creep down between the collar and counter hoop. Stands should be cleaned with moist or dry cloth. Dry and shine them immediately if you are using a moist cloth.

Repair: Remove the heads and lug casings. Dust out the inside of the shell, file or sandpaper the edge of the shell if it is rough or splintered, and clean the outer shell with a damp cloth. If there is a pearl finish, use window cleaner. Clean out lug nuts with a pipe cleaner or swabs and remove old grease from the lugs. Clean chrome lug casings, hoops and the snare release with a mild application of chrome cleaner, leave it on for a minute, and then remove it with a soft cloth. Remount lugs and the snare release and tighten the inside screws securely. If the casings were buzzing before repairing, stuff some light foam around the springs in the lug case (sometimes tape is sufficient). Mount new and used heads with the manufacturer's emblem away from the playing area, and then add the counterhoops. Add a very small amount of petroleum jelly or lug lubricant to the last four or five threads of the lug screw, then place the screw through the hoop ears and into the lug nut. Make a few turns to secure the screw.

Bring down all the lug screws until you just feel tension on the hoop and you eliminate wrinkles. Then start making half turns in a pattern as given below, decreasing the degree of rotation as the tension nears the correct tension of the head. The correct balance is achieved primarily by feel. Some degrees of rotation will be more or less to compensate for irregular tension of the head and bent hoops.

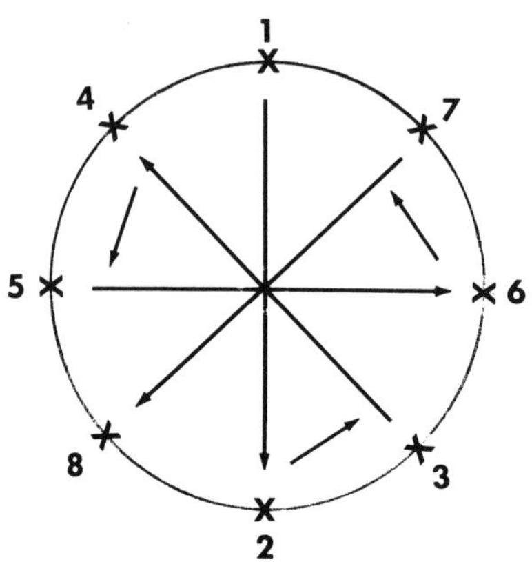

Strike the head 1½" to 3" in from each lug point. Bring the high pitches down to the overall sound, then bring all the lugs up in sequence until the correct tension is achieved. This may be a long process, because as you turn one screw it affects all screw points but predominantly the point straight across and the immediate next door neighbors. Balance the head to the best of your ability, leave it overnight, and return the next day for a final tuning.

All newly mounted heads should only be played with moderate power. The head will be settling for four to eight days, but after that point you can retension the heads to their proper position and they should stay in this area for some time.

Snare Drum

Care: Follow the same steps as above, and in addition adjust the tension on the snares as needed and check the tone control. Snare tension should not be too loose (snares will have a rattling sound when struck loudly) or too tight (snares will have a chocked sound when struck softly). The muffler or tone control should just touch the head to take out unwanted "ring." The muffler should not make a bulge on the head surface.

Repair: Pulled or overly stretched individual snares should be cut off with wire cutters near the mount. Gut snares may often stretch completely out, so re-soak in room temperature water, re-mount, and let them dry at moderate tension. If the snare does not conform to the rest of the snares, you should replace it. Replace worn cord suspensions with nylon or heavy cotton fiber, or in some cases you can use heavy-duty plastic tape. Be sure snares are centered on the head and the snare bed.

Pearl shells may be reglued and clamped or rope tensioned. Old paint or faded pearl can now be easily replaced with new pearl through several available commercial kits. Warped or seriously bent shells must be replaced, and bent or warped hoops should be replaced.

Snare release: when remounting snares or suspension cords, be sure tension screws are in their middle range so flexibility of tension can be taken into account.

Tension rods: stripped threads may be rethreaded by a local music dealer or hardware store, but bent rods should be replaced.

Tone controls or mufflers: wrap tape around buzzing springs and replace the felt muffler by gluing and not riveting.

Stands: replace rubber sleeves when they are worn so the drum is not scratched. Flaking chrome must be finely sandpapered then touched-up with a sealant or clear nail polish.

Bass Drum Stands

Swivel and suspended mounted bass drum stands must be oiled and hex nuts tightened. Rubber bands or elastic suspension parts should be replaced if they are worn or dried out.

Cymbals

Care: Dust them periodically and store them in a dry area.

To clean cymbals soak them overnight completely submerged in room temperature water with a mild soap added. Remove them from the tub and while they are still moderately wet add commercial cymbal cleaner (or Zud, Brasso, etc.) to one surface. Rub with paper towels in a circular direction with the grooves. Do not rub against the grain. Let them be until the cleanser becomes chalky, then remove any excess cleanser with a damp towel. Do not keep rubbing with dirty towels, replace them often. If the cymbal does not come clean, repeat this step after wetting the cymbal again. Take a soft cloth and wipe clean the inner valleys of the grooves, staying with the grain. Use only the clean areas of the rag. Then spray window cleaner on the cymbal surface and use the softest cloth to wipe out the last bit of tarnish from the grooves. Again, use only the clean areas of the rag. Flip the cymbal and repeat the process. Then dry and hand rub the cymbal until it is polished.

Repair: For cracked cymbals,

begin by drilling a small hole at the end of a crack with a high-speed drill, which will keep the crack from spreading. If the cymbal buzzes from the two edges rubbing together, take a fine edged file and file out the crack. If the crack is on the edge, cut a "V" toward the drilled hole with a hacksaw, and then file the edges.

Inside-out cymbals should be fixed by having one person place his knee in the underside of the cup and pulling the outside edge while another person pushes from the top side of the cymbal, making a four point contact. Force the buckle out. Remember, once a cymbal has buckled, it will become increasingly easier to buckle a cymbal during playing.

Replace the leather straps after every few years of heavy use. They should remain supple and strong and be tied with a square knot.

Replace any worn suspended cymbal stand pads and metal washers. Rubber sleeves can be cut from surgical tubing to insulate the cymbal from the threaded rod.

Gongs

Little care is needed except to clean the surface with window cleaner and cloth and replace the suspension cord with gut or Venetian blind cord. Cracks should be repaired in the same manner as cymbal cracks. Stands should be checked periodically for loose bolts.

Timpani

Care: Before each rehearsal or performance, wipe the head clean with a soft cloth (like flannel) and be sure to recover the head after each use. Do not place covers on the floor. Static electricity will pick up any dirt and this will be transferred to the head.

Repair: Heads are mounted as described under drums, but balancing and tuning is even more critical. One difference lies in the collar. The timpani head and bowl edge must be lubricated with lanolin or cork grease. (I find vaseline sloppy, paraffin tacky, and powder too dry.) In an emergency, attach the extension nozzle to a can of WD-40 and spray under the collar where the squeak is occurring.

Bring the head up to the bottom pitch of its pitch range before attempting any other kind of spring tension or clutch adjustment.

Oil moving mechanical parts and use petroleum jelly on the lug screw between the cap screw and where it comes into contact with the counter-hoop. Other squeaks, buzzes, and rattles are idiomatic to the drum. Try oil, tape, and sponge rubber to prevent these unwanted noises.

Severe dents in copper or copper alloy bowls should be taken out. Remove the head and take a rubber hammer (used to replace hub caps) and gently tap out the dent working from the edge of the dent to the middle). Blocking on the outside will be beneficial. Other problems such as broken suspension arms, bent hoops, levers, or toe piece, should be repaired or replaced only by a qualified person.

Mallet/Keyboard Instruments

Care: Keep hands off the bars and pipes as much as possible, wipe them clean with a dry cloth periodically, and dust the frame and oil the wheels.

Repair: Orchestra bells should be cleaned with chrome cleaner, and all worn felt, rubber grommets and suspension cord should be replaced as needed.

Clean vibraphone bars with an aluminum cleaner and then wipe them dry. Oil the motor and rotating vibrato shaft periodically. Irregular vibrato is generally due to a slipping belt; replace it if necessary. If the damper bar is packed down, it may be fluffed (evenly) with a needle point, or it may need to be replaced. Replace a worn suspension cord. If a pedal slips, check for a stripped screw, then check all other screws as they have a tendency to loosen with use of the pedal. Re-glue the pedal cushion shock.

Remove chimes pipes and clean them with chrome cleaner. Replace any worn suspension cord with Venetian blind cord or tightly woven nylon cord. When remounting the pipe, be sure the suspension cord is tight enough so the striking cap is suspended above the mounting bracket in an even line. Damper felt can be replaced or re-glued. Check the chimes pedal in the same manner as those on a vibraphone.

Bars on a marimba and xylophone should be cleaned with a moist cloth and dried immediately. Synthetic bars may have a mild soap applied to them, but abrasive use can remove painted surfaces. Vacuum out the resonator tubes with a nozzle type vacuum sweeper but be careful not to bump the resonator plug. Any worn rubber grommets, suspension cords, and felt should be replaced.

All bars or pipes will need to be retuned eventually after several years of use. This should be done only by a qualified serviceman. You can send individual bars or octaves or complete keyboards to the tuner. Just state the pitch calibration or, if this is unknown, you will need to send more than one bar along for pitch reference. Cracked bars must be replaced.

Accessories

Care: General maintenance of small accessories is nominal. In general they should be stored properly and cleaned with a dry or moist cloth.

Repair: Broken heads on tunable tambourines can be replaced in the same manner as drum heads. Tacked or glued on heads must be taken off, tacks removed, and the rim and edge sanded. Order a replacement head three inches wider than the diameter. Soak it in room temperature water until it is pliable. Put white glue (Elmers) on the top edge of the shell and along the sides. Place the head over the shell, put a large rubber band around the head, and pull the head under the rubber band until it is evenly taut. Let the head dry slowly, remove the rubber band; and cut off the excess head about 3/4" from the edge of the shell. Jingles and pins can be replaced or reset while the head is off.

Wood blocks, temple blocks and guiro can crack and pull apart. Be sure all of the crack is found, then put a very strong "super" wood glue between the parts, force them together, and maintain pressure on the area either by clamps or rubber bands. When dry, sand the excess glue away. This process does not guarantee retention of the original sound quality. If it works you have saved money, if not, you must replace the already broken instrument.

For a thorough explanation of mallet and timpani stick making and repair, see Arthur Press' book, *Mallet Repair* (Belwin Mills).

The following equipment includes the tools, cleansers, and miscellaneous parts I use or recommend for cleaning and repairing percussion instruments.

Tools

Necessary: 3/16" bit screwdriver; 3/8" bit screwdriver; Phillips screwdriver; nut driver set; wire cutters; 6" pliers; 6" Crescent wrench; knife; masking tape; fine sandpaper; white glue (Elmers); mole skin; wood "super" glue; large rubber band.

Additional: needle nose pliers; file; punch; rubber hammer; rubber bands; 4" Crescent wrench; hacksaw, 7" vise-grip; drill with bits; pipe wrench, scissors; hex wrench.

Miscellaneous Replacement Parts: string for snare drum; gut for gong; Venetian blind cord – chimes; cymbal stand pads; cymbal stand rubber grommet; miscellaneous nuts and bolts; yarn; needle and thread; piano felt, unwaxed dental floss.

Cleansers

Necessary: old clothes; cymbal cleaner (Brasso, Zud); vacuum sweeper; chrome cleaner (Brasso); household oil (3 in 1); petroleum jelly (Vaseline); window cleaner (Windex); lubricant (WD-40); rags (medium heavy duty and very soft); paper towels; pipe cleaner or swabs (Q-Tips).

Additional: Liquid Wrench; rust remover (Naval Jelly); glue; paint remover. ■

March, 1981

Warm-Up for Young Percussionists

Paul P. Brazauskas

As music educators we are very concerned about proper warm-up for our young instrumentalists, especially the brass and woodwind players. What about the young percussionist? Why do we insist on strict procedures for instrumental players and often exclude the percussion section from a truly good warm-up? The percussionist's hands are his embouchure and must be developed in the same way as the muscles, lips, tongue, and teeth of the wind players. The hands of the percussionist are trained right from the beginning levels of instruction, and good warm-ups should be an on-going part of his development.

The young percussionist sees and hears popular corps style playing in the local high school band or on TV, and wants to play the same way. Unfortunately he doesn't realize the amount of warm-up time that precedes a performance, probably because he's never been taught anything about warm-up.

A good performance cannot take place without preparation. Here are my suggestions for a daily warm-up routine.

1. Practice the following warm-up individually or as a section drill using bass drums, cymbals, snare drums, timpani, and accessory instruments. The keyboard instruments can use scales, intervals (3rds, 4ths, 5ths, and octaves), and arpeggios.

2. Practice with a metronome, first setting it at ♩=60. Work to develop smoothness and evenness. After mastering the warm-up procedure, increase the tempo until you reach ♩=120.

3. Tap your foot and count out loud.

4. If possible practice in front of a mirror so you can watch your hands, wrists, stick height, and position without having to look down all the time.

Daily Warm-Up Routine

Repeat each line 10 times.

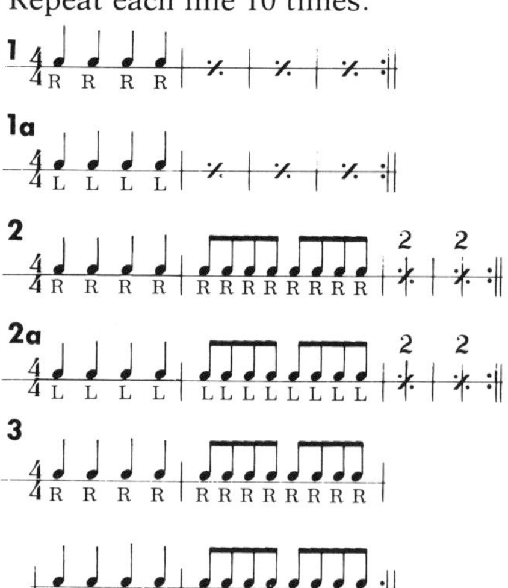

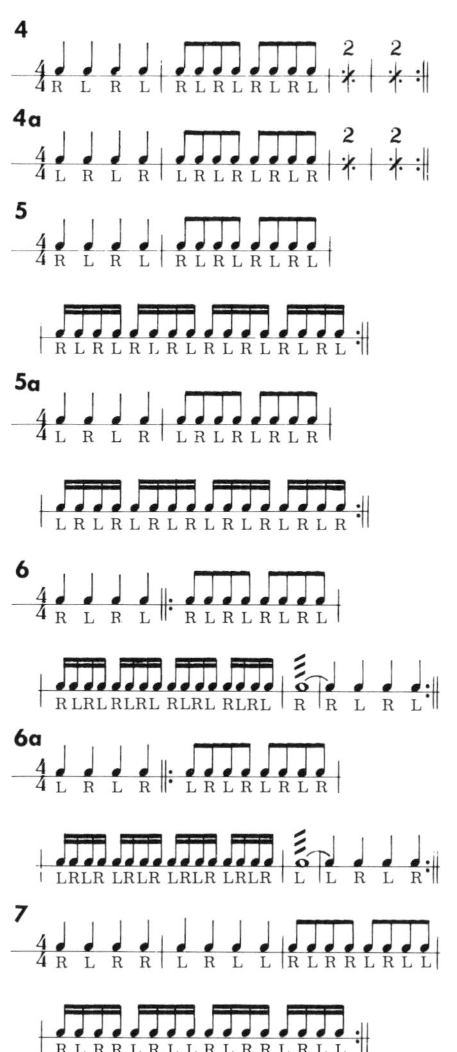

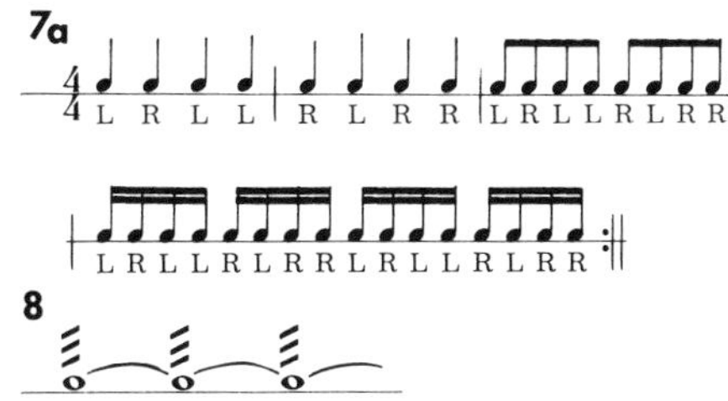

5. Dynamic levels are not indicated; they have been left to the discretion of the teacher and the student. Warming-up softly (mp) will help develop muscle control.

6. There are no accents. All notes are to be considered even, without any pulsations.

Long roll for one minute. Do the double stroke (rudimental) roll for one minute, then the multiple bounce (concert) roll for one minute.

Most beginner and intermediate percussionists claim to be either right handed or left handed, so naturally one hand will be weaker than the other. Teachers should stress the importance of developing both hands equally. A small rubber ball that the student can hold in the palm of his hand and squeeze with his fingers will help develop muscles.

Below are some exercises to help develop the weaker hand of a young percussionist. Again start slowly at first and listen for evenness. Use the metronome as suggested in the previous warm-up drills, although the settings may vary according to the need of the individual. The mirror will be useful here too.

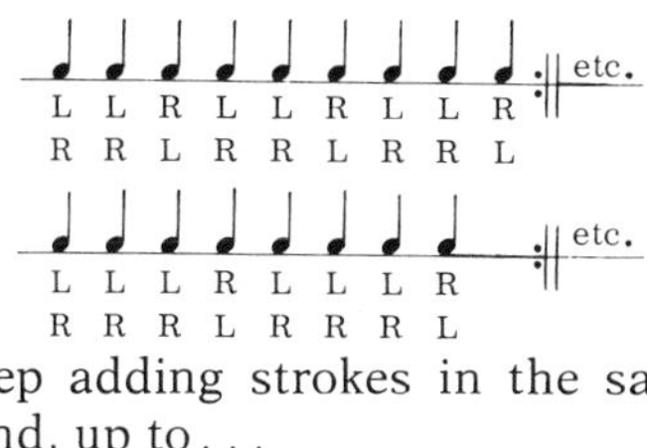

Keep adding strokes in the same hand, up to . . .

Once the student has learned the continuity of this drill, he can attempt to play it without stopping between each line. Again, don't push the student for speed. Once accuracy, smoothness, and evenness are developed through diligent daily practice, speed will come easily, almost naturally.

There are many good warm-ups published for bands with percussion parts that fit in with the woodwind and brass parts; they serve their purpose well. The examples I've used are for warm-up before the group starts as well as for the development of the individual player. ■

April, 1981

Two-Mallet Keyboard Fundamentals

Frank Shaffer, Jr.

Drummers are continually being encouraged to become percussionists by gaining skill on keyboard percussion instruments. For aspiring percussionists without a keyboard background, there are six basic two-mallet skills which must be mastered: major and minor scales, chromatic scale, playing in octaves, rolls, arpeggios, and doubling technique.

Major and Minor Scales

In teaching the major and minor scales, good tone production habits must be emphasized. Place the two mallets on the keyboard instrument and tell the student to pick them up. He should hold the mallet between the thumb and third joint of the first finger (the joint right below the finger nail). Wrap all other fingers around the mallet and have the palms of the hands facing downward. Because the wrist is used primarily to move the mallet up and down, and the arm moves the mallet from note to note, have your student play a C major scale for one octave in half notes with only one hand, then the other. Using a $\frac{4}{4}$ time signature, emphasize that on counts one and three the wrist snaps to strike the note, and on counts two and four the arm moves the wrist to the next scale degree.

Example 1

Have the student play the C scale in quarter notes, up two octaves and back, beginning with the left hand

and alternating hands. Then have the student play the C scale down two octaves and back beginning with the right hand.

Example 2

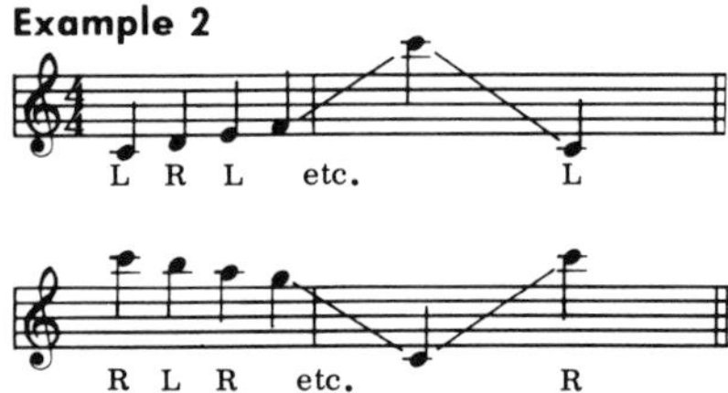

This technique gives the student an opportunity to discover all the possibilities for sticking scale passages rather than always starting with the right hand. Stress the need to keep the hands close to the keyboard for accuracy. While the ideal sound comes from the center of the bar, accidentals may be played on the very edge of the bar for speed when necessary.

When playing most major scales, the right and left hands take turns playing the accidentals. The hand that occupies the top position (closer to the accidentals) or the bottom position (in the center of the natural bars) depends on each scale's particular problems. In going up the D major scale, place the left hand on top since it will play the F♯ and C♯. When moving from C♯ into the second octave of the scale, the hands switch positions and the right hand ends up on top. The same problem occurs between B♭ and C♯ in the D minor scale.

Example 3

A student who understands that most scales have these obstacles and practices these switch positions will progress rapidly. A simple exercise to practice switch positions is illustrated in example 4, for B♭ major and D major. Alternate beginning the scale with the right and then the left hand.

Example 4

Chromatic Scale

The same basic hand movements used in playing example 4 make the two breaks in the chromatic scale relatively easy to master. Practice the two switch positions continuing to work for a smooth sound in chromatic passages.

Example 5

Start on the bottom note of the instrument with either left or right hand and go all the way to the top in triplet rhythm and return. Then start with the other hand and repeat the procedure.

Playing in Octaves

After learning major and minor scale forms, a student can be challenged by having him practice the exercises illustrated in examples 6a through 6d. Practice harmonic minor scales in single notes with a different rhythm pattern each day for one week (6a and 6b are two suggestions). During that same week play the melodic minor scales in octaves. The following week switch and play harmonic minor scales in octaves and melodic minor scales using different rhythms in single notes. The octave exercises may be done for two octaves instead of one if a four octave instrument is available.

Example 6a

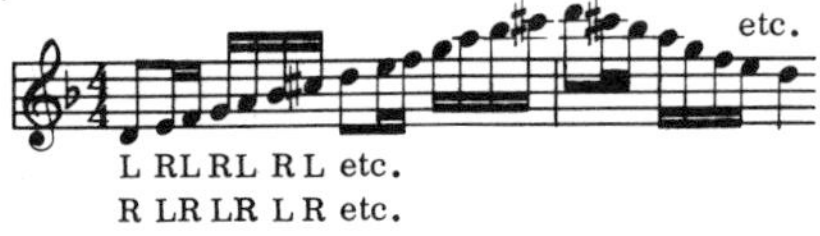

Example 6b

Example 6c

Example 6d

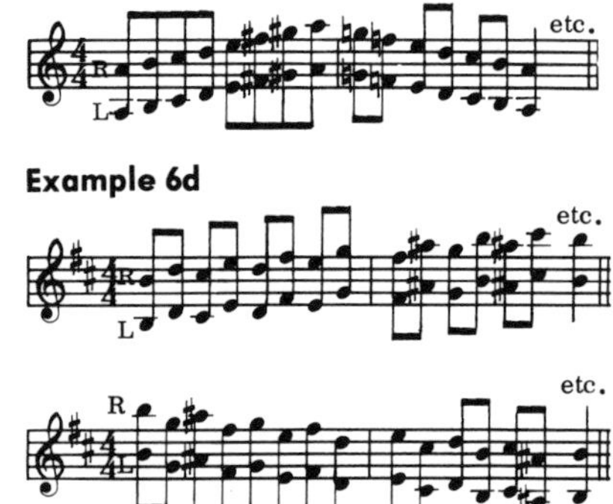

Rolls

Two rhythmic exercises for developing a roll will help a student maintain this important technique.

Example 7

Have the student concentrate on obtaining a non-articulated legato sound, increasing the speed by relaxing his wrist and finger muscles. Use a slow speed for the first few days and gradually increase it while using a relaxed grip. The rhythms melt into a roll. A one note legato roll can be easily mastered.

Example 8

The movement from natural bars to accidental bars (E to F♯ and B to C♯) can be done one of two ways: (1) move both hands to the center of the accidental bar, choosing one hand to lead the way; or (2) move one hand to the center of the accidental bar and the other hand to the edge closest to the natural notes. Example 9 illustrates these two possibilities.

Example 9

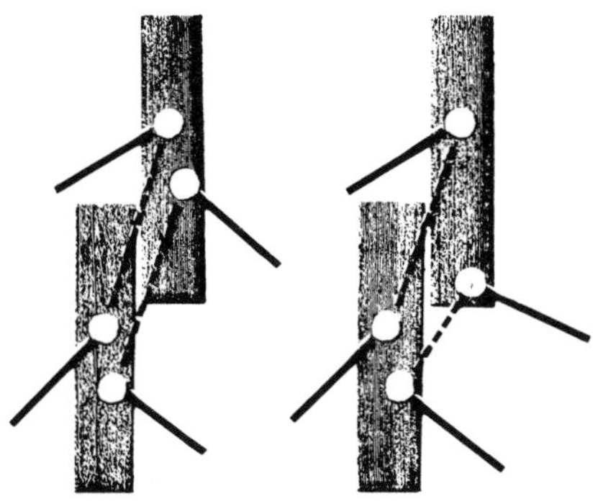

Additional roll studies may be found in the beginning of Goldenberg's *Modern School for Xylophone, Marimba,* and *Vibraphone,* pages 9-12. Good musical examples to further develop this technique are in Mitchell Peter's *Sonata Allegro* for marimba and piano and Peter Tanner's *Sonata for Marimba and Piano.*

Arpeggios

Students can easily master arpeggio technique if each chord position is isolated and practiced individually using triplets. The left hand begins when going up and the right begins when coming back down.

Example 10

Switch positions in various chords are more easily understood this way. After several weeks of practicing chords in this way, try the standard four note arpeggio form going from one position of the chord to the next.

Example 11

Practice chords in the following order: major, minor, dominant seventh, minor seventh, diminished seventh, and augmented chords. It is probably best to begin with the easier chord types in all keys, then add the next more difficult one.

Doubling Technique

Doubling technique makes awkward passages easier to perform and needs to be included in daily practice after other basic skills have been learned. Example 12 practiced in three stages makes doubling smooth and easy.

Example 12

Repeat each set of four scale notes four times for a week, then repeat each set for two times the next week. Once on each four note set going up the scale slowly will be enough by the third week. Gradually increasing the speed and adding other keys as time permits will produce a smooth doubling technique that should sound almost like single sticking.

After all of these exercises have been mastered, devise a daily warm-up routine. Use major scales up and back with the left hand one day and down and back with the right hand the next day. Octaves can be practiced using one of the minor scale forms while another minor scale form can be played in single alternating style. Add the chromatic scale and one of the roll exercises in several keys. As time permits continue playing arpeggios and the doubling exercise in as many keys as possible at least every other day. These fundamental exercises will help make a percussionist more comfortable in learning to play mallet keyboard instruments. ■

May, 1981

Marching Mallet Percussion

Lauren Vogel

In recent years the marching percussion section has expanded to include most of the instruments found in a standard concert band setting. In addition to the basic snare drums, bass drums, cymbals, multi-toms, and timpani, more drum corps and marching bands have added the melodic percussion family, consisting of bells, xylophones, marimbas, and vibes. No longer is the percussion solo just a drum break – it can be an entity in itself, made up of melodies, harmonies, and counterpoint.

There are two major manufacturers of marching mallet percussion in today's market: Deagan (a division of Slingerland Drum Company), and Musser (a division of Ludwig Industries). Both companies produce the four types of melodic percussion instruments now used.

Bells are usually considered the soprano of the marching quartet. The 2½ octave range extends from G3 to C6, sounding two octaves higher than written.

The Deagan 1576 Marching Bells are made of steel and weigh 23½ pounds (excluding the carrier). The Musser M-69 Marching Bells are also of steel and weigh 25 pounds. Their M-65 Aluminum Marching Bells weigh less (18 pounds), yet they project and carry outdoors as well as the others. The aluminum produces a clear, bell-like tone that is not blurred by overtones.

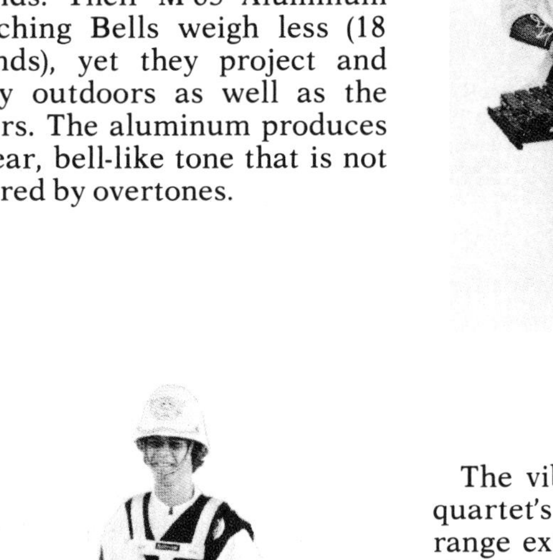

Bells

The alto of the quartet is the marching xylophone. The 2½ octave range extends from C4 to G6, and sounds one octave higher than written. The Deagan 877 Marching Xylophone (without resonators) has Klyperon bars and weighs 28 pounds. The Musser M-67 Marching Xylophone (with resonators – also available without resonators as the M-66) has Kelon bars and weighs 28 pounds. The resonators enhance projection outdoors.

The marimba acts as the tenor of the quartet. The 2+ octave range extends from C4 to D6 in the Deagan model and to C6 in the Musser model, sounding as written. The Deagan 678 Marching Marimba is made of Klyperon and weighs 36¾ pounds with an arched set of resonators. The Musser M-63 Marching Marimba is made of Kelon and weighs 38 pounds with resonators.

Marimba

The vibraphone serves as the quartet's bass. The 2+ octave range extends from F3 to G5 in the Deagan model and to C6 in the Musser model, also sounding as written. The Deagan 578 Marching Vibes, with aluminum alloy bars, arched resonators, and a battery-operated motor and pack, weighs 36 pounds. The Musser M-64 Marching Vibraphone has aluminum bars, resonators, battery-operated motor, and weighs 40 pounds. Both manufacturers' models come with a damper bar to increase versatility.

Vibraphone

Mallet selection for the marching keyboards is very important, because inappropriate ones will not produce a good tone and could damage the instrument. Mallet handles should be made of plastic or wood dowels (rattan handles lose their firmness outdoors).

Bells and xylophones are usually played with hard plastic mallets; however, hard rubber mallets will carry and offer a new sound. During rehearsals rubber mallets may be substituted for the plastic ones to save both the player's ear and the keyboard. Show mallets may be used during final practices and actual performances as well as any time the ensemble balance is being checked.

The marimba should never be played with hard plastic mallets – they will crack the bars. Use hard rubber mallets to create a good sound; for a more legato effect, wrapped mallets (thin yarn or cord over a fairly hard core) may be used.

The traditional vibe sound is produced by using wrapped mallets, though rubber mallets may also be used. Never use hard plastic.

To provide versatile sound on the field carry several different types of mallets in addition to those to be used as spares. Mallets should not be stored by suspending them between bars as this reduces playing range. Instead, small mallet bags (which can be hand-made) should be tied to the carrier.

On the field the keyboard quartet is usually placed near the front sideline in an arc around the 50-yard line. This position aids sound projection into the stands. Because the keyboards usually have a different part than the drums, they are kept together within the larger percussion section; they should never be too far from the drums as distance can cause problems. Also an alert timpani player who is close enough can use the keyboards for pitch reference.

Scoring for the keyboard quartet takes extra thought and imagination. Often these instruments double a woodwind line and their unique sound is lost. They are capable of carrying the melody themselves or playing a contrapuntal line. They can also outline harmonic progressions in interesting rhythmic patterns, or fill in empty spots with their fascinating color. The quartet should never be scored in unison. Use different lines and avoid parallels.

Band directors in smaller schools with limited budgets usually cannot afford the luxury of having all four keyboards. The bells and xylophone are considered standard, and the next instrument to be purchased is usually the marimba, adding new color and fullness of sound. Vibes cost quite a bit more and are usually added last. Try not to duplicate instruments before one of each type has been purchased.

Marching mallets are only one facet of the ever-expanding marching percussion section, but a very exciting aspect because the section can now present a complete musical texture – melody, harmony, and rhythm. ■

July, 1981

International Drum Rudiment Proposal

Jay A. Wanamaker

In 1933 during the American Legion National Convention in Chicago drummers from all parts of the country met to discuss methods of drumming and drum instruction. The group selected 13 rudiments they believed all drummers should know because these rudiments taught valuable sticking patterns and led to an orderly progression for development of physical control, coordination, and endurance. The "essential 13" were used as a test for membership in the Thirteen Club, organized for the promotion of rudimental drumming by the National Association of Rudimental Drummers (N.A.R.D.). In later years 13 additional rudiments were combined with the original 13, forming the Standard 26 American Drum Rudiments.

Why Revise The Standard Twenty-Six?

One year ago the Marching Percussion Committee of the Percussive Arts Society began a revision and standardization of the present list of rudiments. The reasons for revising the list were:

• The current list is not logically ordered nor are the rudiments grouped by families such as rolls, flams, and drags.

• There is a need for a more advanced notational system. A number of rudiments are not interpreted as they are notated; for example, the interpretation of grace note rudiments varies between concert and rudimental styles.

• There is a need for increasingly advanced rudimental patterns designed to challenge today's percussionists.

Each committee member submitted his suggestions concerning what merited inclusion in this revised list of rudiments, and a comprehensive list was presented at the committee's meeting at the Percussive Arts Society International Convention in San Jose on November 15, 1980. At that time the list was further revised.

Those committee members who developed the International Drum Rudiment Proposal were: Jim Campbell, Montana State University; Rob Carson, Remo, Inc.; Sherman Hong, University of Southern Mississippi; Marty Hurley, Phantom Regiment Drum and Bugle Corps; Mike Kumer, Duquesne University; James Mallen, Drum Corps International Judge; Bill McGrath, New York Federation of Contest Judges; William F. Ludwig, Jr., Ludwig Industries; James Petercsak, P.A.S. President, Crane School of Music; Will Rapp, Millersville State College; Fred Sanford, Ludwig Industries; Dan Spaulding, Guardsmen Drum and Bugle Corps; George Tuthill, Sky Ryders Drum and Bugle Corps; Larry Vanlandingham, P.A.S. First Vice-President, Baylor University; Jay A. Wanamaker, Alfred Publishing Co., Inc.

Selected Comments

The following comments by committee members provide some background and rationale for the revision.

Bill McGrath: "I have always thought the rudiments should be grouped in some manner. . .six stroke roll and triplet roll; hallelujah, it's about time!"

Marty Hurley: "Three Swiss rudiments should be added: tap flam, Swiss triplets and pataflafla. The buzz roll should definitely be added [and] should follow immediately after the open roll, so that music educators will see a clear difference. None of the original rudiments should be deleted."

Mike Kumer: "To eliminate ambiguity between rudimental and concert percussionists, I feel we should change the term 'ruff' to 'drag.' Most orchestral percussionists use this term already. In order to follow in a logical continuation, the single drag should be changed to drag tap and double drag changed to double drag tap."

George Tuthill: "I feel rolls should be taught in two basic meters: binary and ternary. For instance, a five-stroke roll can be played as a triplet roll or as a binary roll."

William F. Ludwig, Jr.: "My father always stressed a standardized listing of drum rudiments to be established as the supreme system of proper drum education. The Standard 26 Rudiments as listed today were laid out by him and Gus Moeller in the 1930s in many Sunday afternoon sessions in our Evanston home. I was a youth of eight at the time and I vividly recall these two great gentlemen standing around the padded mahogany dining room table with their practice pads, their snakewood sticks, and their long, black cigars going over and over the Strube as well as the Bruce & Emmett, drum methods of 60 years earlier.

"Bear in mind that all the drum companies will be switching their literature and rudimental sheets over to the P.A.S. rudiments when a final vote is taken someday. So you have an awesome task which may well leave an imprint on the music world for 100 years or more!"

Your Response Is Needed

In the following list, notation is included only for newly added rudiments; notation for all rudiments will appear when the new adoptions are made. Variations between rudimental and orchestral notation will also be notated. John Beck of the Eastman School of Music heads a committee that will determine the correct notation of the orchestra rudiments. All roll rudiments will be broken down into binary and ternary pulsations. This collection of rudiments should be considered a list rather than a sequential method of study.

The Percussive Arts Society would like your response concerning the adoption of the International Drum Rudiments. Please examine the following list and send your comments and suggestions to Jay A. Wanamaker, c/o Alfred Publishing Co., Inc., 15335 Morrison Street, Sherman Oaks, California. ■

Proposed International Drum Rudiments

I. ROLL RUDIMENTS

- A. Single Stroke Roll
  - Single Stroke Four
  - Single Stroke Seven
- B. MULTIPLE BOUNCE ROLL (buzz, orch. press)
- C. DOUBLE STROKE OPEN ROLLS
  - Double Stroke Roll
  - Five Stroke Roll
  - Six Stroke Roll
  - Seven Stroke Roll
  - Nine Stroke Roll
  - Ten Stroke Roll
  - Eleven Stroke Roll
  - Thirteen Stroke Roll
  - Fifteen Stroke Roll
  - Triplet Stroke Roll

II. COMBINATION SINGLE AND DOUBLE STROKE RUDIMENTS

- Single Paradiddle
- Double Paradiddle
- Triple Paradiddle
- Single Paradiddle-diddle

III. DOUBLE GRACE NOTE RUDIMENTS

- Drag
- Single Drag Tap (single drag)
- Double Drag Tap (double drag)
- Lesson 25
- Single Dragadiddle
- Drag Paradiddle No. 1
- Drag Paradiddle No. 2
- Single Ratamacue
- Double Ratamacue
- Triple Ratamacue

IV. FLAM RUDIMENTS

- Flam
- Flam Accent
- Flam Tap
- Tap Flam
- Flamacue
- Flam Paradiddle
- Single Windmill Stroke
- Flam Paradiddle-diddle
- Pataflafla
- Swiss Army Triplets
- Flam Drags

DESCRIPTION OF LESS COMMON RUDIMENTS

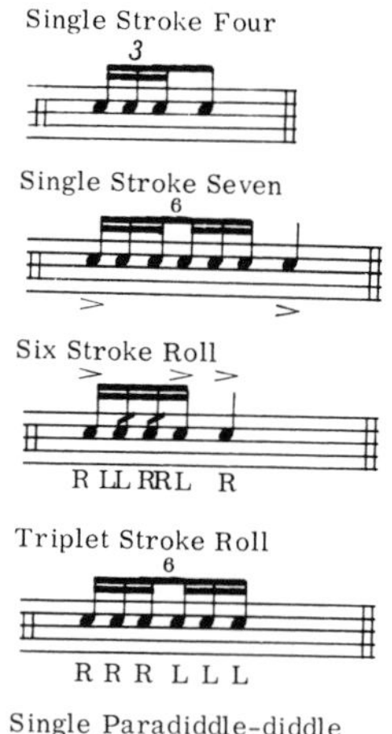

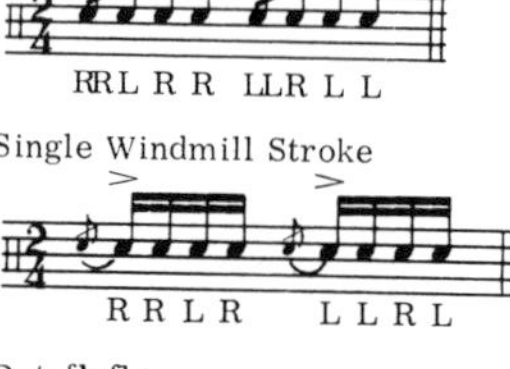

September, 1981

Field Position and Drill Ideas for the Marching Percussion Section

Kevin Lepper

The percussion section can make or break any marching band's performance. By keeping some basic concepts in mind the percussion section cannot only be part of a band's drill but also continue to be the rhythm center for the band. Placing the percussion section on the field should take minimal time and effort, but it requires careful planning by the band director. Overall criteria to consider for a drill are:

- What kind of music is being played? (intense, relaxed, building, fading)
- What forms fit this music? (angular-more intense, curved-flowing)
- Where do you want the rhythmic center?
- Where do you want the audience to focus its attention?
- Where have you come from and where are you going?

With these ideas in mind, percussion field placement is relatively simple. The section must complement the band's form while serving as the pulse center of the band. If these two concepts are realized, you minimize the problems of band and percussion being out of phase ("phasing"), percussion drills being unrelated to the rest of the band, and the music not fitting the drill.

A director must keep in mind the following restrictions and capabilities of the percussion section:

- When the entire section is playing, the individual percussionist cannot hear the band.
- Percussion equipment restricts some of the player's movement. Therefore, as a section, the percussion should not be expected to cover as much distance as other band members.
- Drums are less directional than wind instruments.
- The more experienced the section, the farther you can spread them apart; the less-experienced section needs to hear the other people. However, this doesn't always mean block percussion.
- The instruments themselves can be used as linking items. The popular white drums in a line against dark uniforms form a wall, which can be used to define forms, images, etc.

Before going into more depth with drill and field position, here's a general list of trends in effective percussion positioning:

Loud Sections

Don't mask any sound — all voices have to be placed where they will project. If you must mask, score unisons.

For punches or accents don't play behind the horns.

Mallets and timpani should be out in front if you want them to be heard.

Tubas, sousaphones, or electric bass should be very close to the percussion section so the percussionists can hear chord changes. You want a tight, jazz band style section.

Bass drum heads should be facing the audience for projection

Keep instrument sections together; try not to split bass drums or timp-toms.

Soft Sections

Files will make your section's sound disappear or at least diminish.

Files also make your section visually smaller.

If mallets are in front and aren't playing, they should move so they do not take the spotlight when tacet.

Cymbal spins catch the eye. Make sure you are using them to point to the proper area.

Percussion Features

Percussion should be near the sideline so they are spotlighted.

Highlight the soloing section:

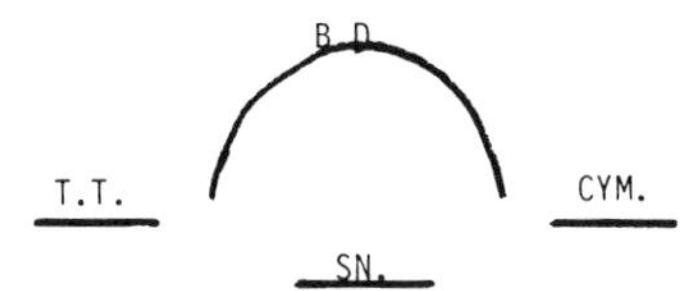

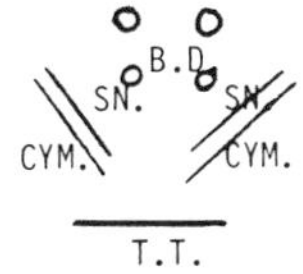

Rotate the highlighted section if needed; this can be accomplished by a kneel, by stepping out of the spotlighted section, or by pointing to that section.

Many band directors write the percussion drills last and, therefore just fit them into the show. The practice commonly produces a block percussion section that just moves up and down the 50-yard line; but it does have its good points because the rhythmic center is all together; the drill should be easy enough to perform while playing; and it's easy to set up and execute.

Now, let's look at its problems: all instruments except the snares will always be "masked;" all forms must include a block on the 50-yard line; enthusiasm in the percussion section is lacking because they feel left out and not capable of doing anything else; and it usually does not depict what the music is expressing.

Therefore, here are some drills where the percussion considerations that were listed before are incorporated.

Loud Sections

Percussion voices are exposed:

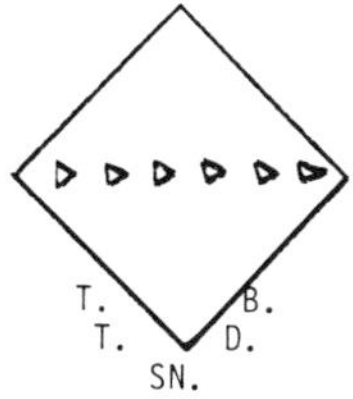

Percussion connects the band both visually and rhythmically:

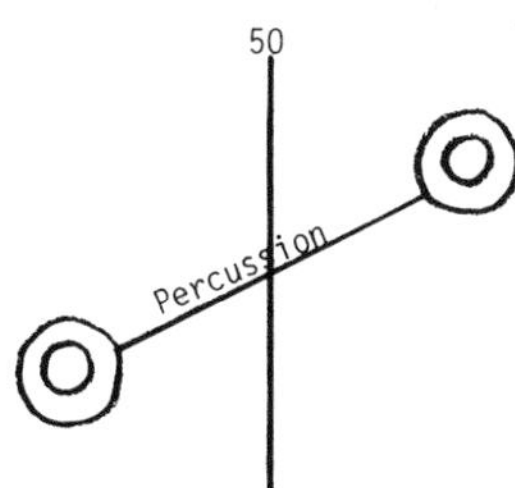

Percussion players covering down opposite each other for density and projection:

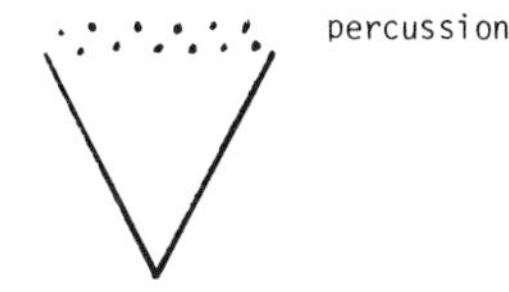

Soft Sections

Percussion is used behind the horns for a masking effect; mallets are with the percussion section, not out front; snares are filed for a diminished sound:

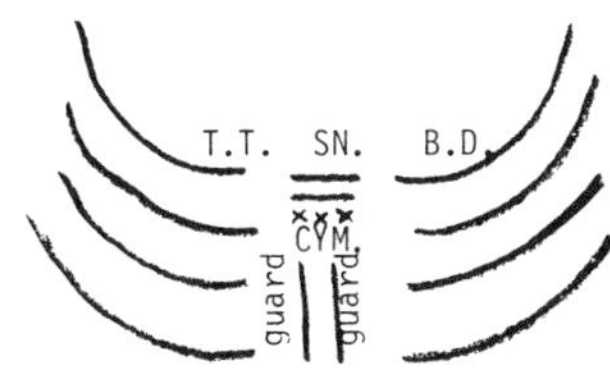

Percussion are in files for a diminished sound and visual quality:

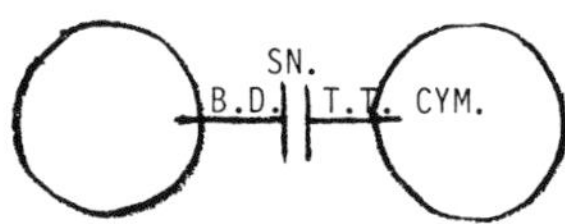

Percussion players are masked by horns:

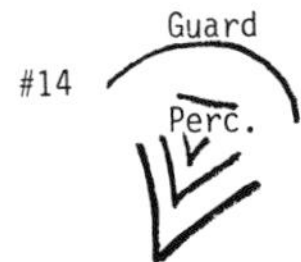

Notice how these percussion section placements contribute to the drill while still keeping the percussion in a section.

The final problem area is cluttering. In an example from an actual drill everyone was as close as possible to the next person and the whole form was close to the sideline. As you can see, the quartet of soloists was heard but was not easily seen:

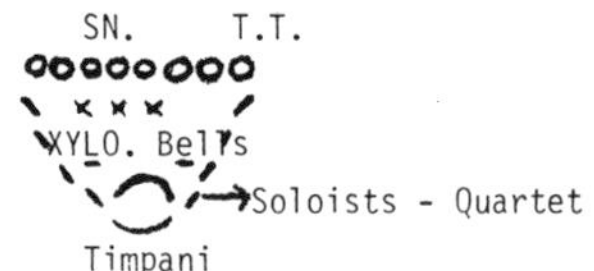

The audience only sees a mass of bodies and instruments. In order for this form to work, it needs to be seen as an audience sees it – at an angle. Elongation of the form gives it life but it takes up one and a half to two times the initial space:

Another common form of cluttering is caused by grouping the percussion section into small circles. On paper this looks fine, but on the field you again get the mass look. Uniforms, drums, and carriers distort the effect. With just three dots spread out you have a hard time defining a circle; with five you come closer; with twelve you're there:

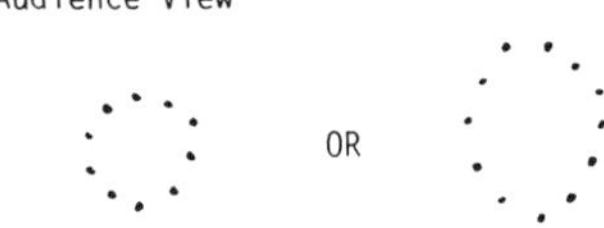

Now, since we have looked at some of the numerous possibilities for drill writing and field placement of the percussion, let's go one step further. Let's look at an easy drill move that will take you from a soft building passage to a hard driving section in 8 to 16 counts:

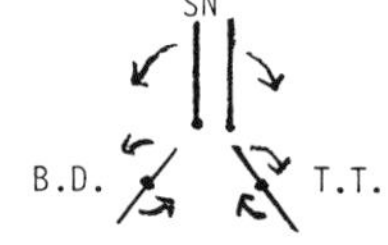

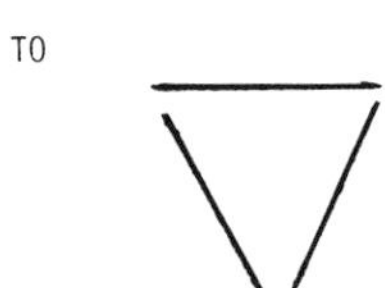

The snares are in files and they pivot off the front person. The bass drums and timptoms use the center of their line as the pivot point. Visually, this movement, if done correctly, will appear to be confusion and then pop – your form appears.

The percussion section is very important to your musical and visual program. Keep working with them so your program develops to its potential. ■

October, 1981

Adjudicating the Marching Percussion Section

Sherman Hong

The trend towards better adjudicated marching band competitions has probably reached every state in the union. This trend, along with the widespread influence of drum corps competitions and styles of shows, has led to a keen awareness of marching percussion sections – what they should do, what they can do, and what they do.

Numerous competitions now feature separate adjudicators for auxiliary units and drumlines; consequently, band directors are more concerned with how their percussion sections play, sound, and appear. The inevitable question directors ask is "what does the percussion judge look for?" Although the answers vary from contest to contest, and from judge to judge, most adjudicators look for a technically and musically sound performance.

Most marching percussion adjudication sheets are too general and have not been revised to meet the more demanding percussion performance requirements. A form similar to the example printed here would be helpful because it enables the adjudicator to comment on both the musical and technical aspects of a performance.

Recording Errors

When an error of execution is made, the adjudicator uses a letter from the key, pointing out which segment of the section made the error; and by using one column per composition, he is able to point out the errors in each piece of music. In the final column the errors are added together and then subtracted from the total points allowed for execution.

Caption	Music I	Music II
Attacks	SSBST	TTBS

Music III	No. Ticks
SSBSC	14

Suppose at the end of the performance there were a total of 35 ticks. Subtract the number of tick points (35 ticks) from total execution ticks allowed (100) to get the points credited for execution:

100 ticks possible
− 35 ticks
———
65 credited

Because 1 tick = .1 point, 65 is then equal to 6.5 points credit.

Drum and bugle corps make extensive use of the tick system; a D.C.I. judge is extensively trained and experienced, having developed the correct ear and sight for "ticking."

Execution Captions

1. Attacks — Is the section or segments of the section attacking together?

2. Releases — Is the section or segments of the section releasing together? A common problem occurs with the release of rolls.

3. Taps/Strokes — Are stickings the same height and are they played with the same patterns?

4. Rolls — Are rolls played with the same pulse (time)? The same type of rolls should be used by all at the same volume.

5. Sextuplets — Although this could be judged within captions 3 and 6, they are used frequently and require separate captions.

6. Flams/Drags — Are the stickings the same height and are they equally "open" or "closed"? Are the flams "popped"?

7. Phasing — Is the section playing with a unified beat and pulse, or are certain segments slightly ahead or behind? The most obvious phasing problems occur in unison rhythmic patterns of 16th notes (♬♬), sextuplets (³♬ ³♬), and double stroke rolls.

8. Balance — Does the section sound as a unified whole with the timbre of each instrument blending and balancing with others? The most common balance problems occur with bass drums. A well-tuned bass drum line has the power to over-

DRUM LINE
ADJUDICATION

School ______________________ Rating ____________

Score ____________

EXECUTION
(10 points)

	Music I	Music II	Music III	Music IV	Music V	No. Ticks
Attacks						
Releases						
Taps/Strokes						
Rolls						
Sextuplets						
Flams/Drags						
Phasing						
Balance						
Tempi						
Visuals/Rimshots, etc.						
Carriage						
Mark Time/Instrument Position						
Staging						
Execution Errors						
1 tick = .1 point / Points of Credit						

Key:
- S = snare drum
- TT = timp-tom
- T = tenor
- B = bass drum
- C = cymbal
- M = mallets
- N = timpani
- ta = tambourine
- tm = timbali
- A = accessories

CREDIT: Exposure to Error 3 pts.
Tuning 2 pts.
Musicality 5 pts.

Execution _____ of 10 pts.

Exposure to Error _____ of 3 pts.

Tuning _____ of 2 pts.

Musicality _____ of 5 pts.

TOTAL _____ of 20 pts.

Comments:

Adjudicator ______________________

balance the entire section or band. Strangely enough, snare drums often need to play louder, simply because they do not project as well as timp-toms or bass drums. Many additional problems with balance can be attributed to improper staging.

9. Tempi – Does the section maintain proper tempo? Because a good marching unit plays music of varying styles and tempi, the percussion section must not only keep good time, but also produce the proper style (jazz, Latin, swing, etc.). A marching unit usually drills or moves during the music; the percussion must unify the whole.

10. Visuals, Rimshots, etc. – Are the visuals together and in context with the music? This caption can include body movements, stick flashes, back-sticking, and other techniques designed to add visual and auditory appeal. A common problem is an emphasis on visuals that distract from the music.

11. Carriage – Does the section move together smoothly, and does it look and move as a unit?

12. Mark Time/Instrument Position – Is there a unified mark time? Is everyone carrying their instrument in a position conducive to proper performance techniques? Are instruments played properly?

13. Staging – Is the section arranged to produce the best balanced sound and best picture? For example, if the mallet keyboards are scored melodically, are they placed so they can be heard? Because of the nature of these instruments, it is best to have the keyboards in front of the drums.

Credit Captions

These points are added to the execution scores:

1. Exposure to Error – Are the parts written or played by the section challenging? Do the parts require a variety of techniques?

2. Tuning – Are the instruments tuned to produce the best sounds?

3. Musicality – Does the section play with good dynamics, contrasts, tempo changes, etc. that enhance the music? Do the percussion parts fit the music?

The ten point credit captions are intended to reward a section, helping to balance any execution errors. Many percussion sections will play easy drum parts with few execution problems; however, another section of equal ability will play more demanding parts where mistakes have a greater chance to occur. The second section should receive a higher "Exposure to Error" score than the first; the final scores should be relatively balanced. Some adjudicators feel there should be an equal balance of points between the execution and the exposure to error. If this fits your locality better, balance the system with equal numbers, raising or lowering the total point system accordingly.

The second and third credit captions should also be used to reward a musically aware section. Because there will probably be only one percussion judge, ask him to include comments on the percussion section's general effect.

I have found this adjudication sheet to be functional in both contests and festivals. In contests, trophies are often awarded to the best percussion section. This type of score sheet enables the adjudicator to base his award on the evidence of points. For the festival competition which awards ratings (superior, I, excellent II, etc.), the adjudicator can devise a scale that enables him to use numerical standards. For example, he can state that scores of 17 and above produce a superior and 14 to 16.99 rate an excellent; the judge can encourage percussion sections as he points out their execution mistakes as well as crediting their strengths. The comment section is for specifics and allows the adjudicator to give advice.

This sheet is not foolproof because it is impossible for one judge to hear and record all the errors in a performance. However, it is helpful to band directors and their percussion sections in pointing out the who, what, and when of errors. Each caption is important to a good percussion section and should make students more aware of what they can do musically and with good execution. In fact, a high scoring marching percussion section produces individual members who become more conscientious, flexible, and musical in their concert percussion performances. ■

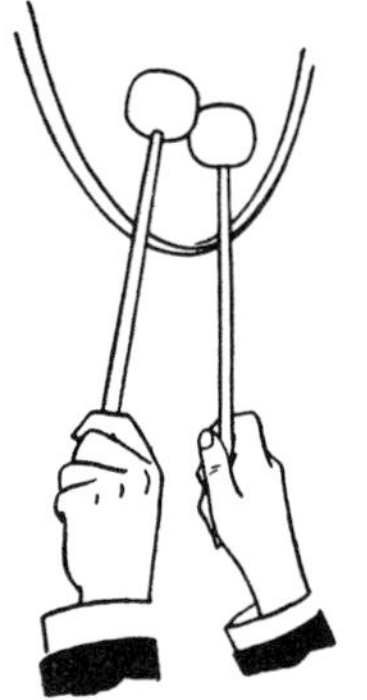

Interval Study on Mallet Percussion Instruments

Linda Pimentel

Interval study may be the most important area of technical concentration for the beginning mallet percussionist. Recognizing intervals rather than just single notes is the first step toward reading complete melodic sentences. Interval reading is also the key to quickly grasping chord voicings and contrapuntal movements.

Most original mallet percussion literature, both solo and ensemble, has been written in the 20th century and is full of chromaticism, so I have beginners practice chromatic intervals by their first or second lesson. The student percussionist who can play the examples in this article will build his technical skills while experiencing a variety of literature.

The intervals of a fourth and fifth are popular in mallet percussion music, are easy to visualize on the instruments, and are comfortable to play with two mallets in each hand. After the student has learned to pick out the chromatic scale, the first exercise (example 1a) should be practiced by ear. While he is holding two mallets in his weaker hand, usually the left, have the student play the chromatic fifths, repeating the exercise for reinforcement and added security. He needs to practice firmly, using a good wrist stroke. As soon as he has become secure, have him add the stronger hand, (example 1b) at the octave. Later, he can practice 1c and 1d.

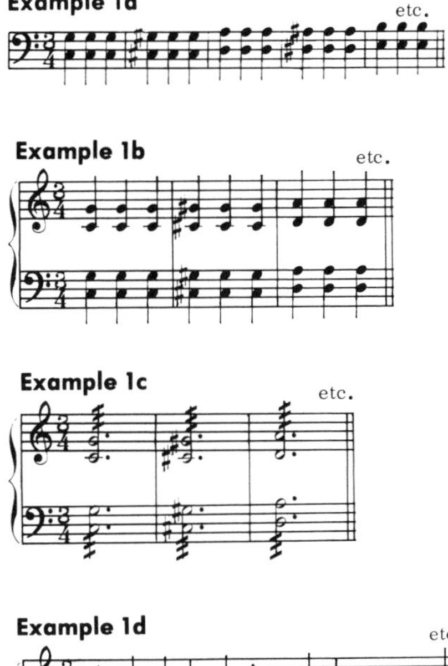

During the past decade, mallet percussionists have moved toward performing with four (more rarely six) mallets in both solo and ensemble situations. Beginning students learn from the start to manipulate all four mallets independently. In two-mallet playing, the trunk of the performer's body acts as an axis from which the two arms flex in a flow of alternating patterns. When each of the four mallets is used independently, the elbow and the shoulder become the balancing axis, with the hand and forearm rotating in a motion similar to opening and closing a jar lid.

Example 2 shows some of the patterns that a student can practice using the interval of a fifth to develop mallet independence. Meanwhile, the same patterns can be practiced using the interval of a fourth (example 3), and later students can study the more complex thirds and sixths (example 4). Eventually he will stack these into various chord combinations and include diatonic practice as well (example 5).

Example 2. Exercises for developing the interval of a fifth.

Example 3. The interval of a fourth.

Example 4. An exercise for sixths.

Example 5. Chord combinations and diatonic exercises.

The student can apply these skills to an array of attractive beginning and intermediate music. "Kumbaya" (Pimentel, *Bar Percussion Notebook Vol. 1,* Permus Publications), contains parallel fifths to produce a contemporary sound.

Composer and percussionist Mitchell Peters has written many excellent student pieces. "Undercurrent" (Peters, Mitchell Peters), uses smoothly moving fourths.

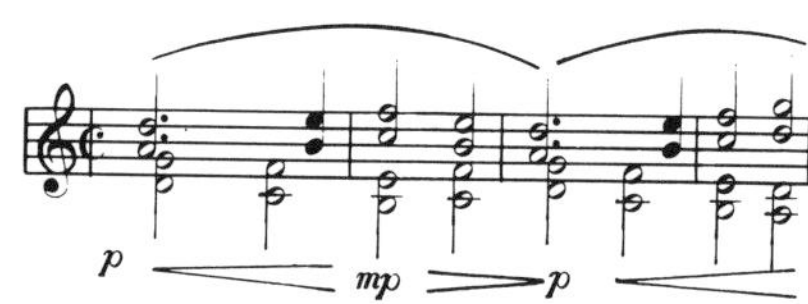

Fourths are melodically traced and embellished in "Concertino" (Frock, Southern Music Company).

"Strolling in the Sunshine" (Pimentel, *Bar Percussion Notebook Vol. II,* Permus Publications), uses simultaneous patterns of fifths in the left hand and fourths in the right hand.

"Yellow After the Rain" (Peters, Mitchell Peters), is one of the percussionists' favorite intermediate level pieces. This excerpt contains alternations of double fifths and includes a passage that moves downward in whole tones.

Thirds and sixths are combined very simply in "Flying" (Pimentel, *Bar Percussion Notebook Vol. I,* Permus Publications). The beginner could play each measure as a block chord, rolling or repeating each chord three times, before practicing the composition.

Pairs of thirds mingle delightfully in "Reel" (Pitfield, *Sonata,* C.F. Peters).

A repeated rhythm pattern shifts subtly as thirds and fourths group in different combinations in "Romp" (Boo, *Pieces of R,* Permus Publications).

The "Rosewood Forest" (Houilif, *Two Pieces,* Southern Music Company), contains thirds, fourths, and fifths moving in both parallel and contrary motion.

Fifths and sixths are paired between the hands in "Streams and Beams" (Brown, *The Vibe Player's Method,* Ludwig Industries).

In "Daybreak" (Chapman, Music for Percussion, Inc.), a flowing melody is combined with a tritone accompaniment.

Chromaticism combined with fourths and fifths accentuate the rhythms in "Elegy" (Stout, Studio 4 Productions).

In "Antique Folk Dance #2" (Pimentel, *Bar Percussion Notebook No. II,* Permus Publications), thirds are unusually combined.

In the first three measures, the thirds move upward diatonically against the pedal point G. In the fifth and sixth measures they become tenths, and in the ninth and tenth measures they are surrounded by a leaping octave.

The beginning percussionist who thoughtfully practices these four mallet interval studies and at the same time develops a repertoire based on the musical examples will be building technical skills while experiencing a variety of literature, in a balanced, thoughtful manner. ■

1982-1983

Drum Set Exercises

James McKinney

I have been experimenting with various ways of helping my students retain more of what they practice on the drum set. This project has led to the use of what I call "multiple variations" for each textbook page of music. Some of these ideas may work for you; I have found that they help achieve the delicate balance between boredom and repetition in drumming.

The illustration is an example of the exercises printed in numerous drum set books; the rest of the article describes how I use them.

Typical Snare Drum Exercises

1. Use both swing feel eighth-notes and straight or rock eighth-notes on the snare drum.

Swing eighths =

Rock eighths =

2. Keep a swing feel going on the ride cymbal with the right hand ( ) and then play the illustrated rhythms on the snare drum with the left hand. At this point it might be helpful to have the student write out both lines to see how they are aligned:

Measure 1 =

Right Hand

Left Hand

The combined sound is:

R L T T R T R

(R = right hand; L = left hand; T = together)

For variety, play one time through on the snare drum, next time through on the small tom-tom, then all the way through on the large tom-tom.

3. Add the bass drum on counts 1 and 3 and the hi-hat on counts 2 and 4 while playing both the swing cymbal rhythm and the rhythmical exercise. At this point most people are ready to go on to the next exercise. However, try the following ideas before you turn the page.

4. While keeping the ride cymbal going, add the hi-hat and snare drum on beats 2 and 4 and play the written exercise with the bass drum.

5. Keep the ride cymbal going and add the snare drum on beats 2 and 4, the bass drum on 1 and 3, and play the written exercises with the hi-hat. This exercise has challenged my best set players.

6. Now try to keep the swing beat going (ride cymbal, rhythm, bass drum on beats 1 and 3, hi-hat on 2 and 4), and play all of the quarter-notes on the snare drum and all of the eight-notes on the small tom-tom.

This idea is almost endless. Play the quarter-notes on the snare drum and the eighth-notes on the bass drum or vice versa. Play the quarter-notes on the small tom-tom and the eighth-notes on the large tom-tom.

7. Play continuous triplets on the snare drum and let the written rhythm serve as accents:

Measure 1 =

Variations are possible by putting all of the accents on the small or large tom-tom or bass drum. You could also assign certain beats to a drum: place beat 1 accents on the small tom-tom, beat 2 accents on the large tom-tom, beat 3 accents on the floor tom-tom, and beat 4 accents on the snare drum.

8. Go through the exercise and circle notes at random. Now assign a certain drum to each circled note and another drum to each uncircled note.

After practicing these eight variations, the fun can really begin.

• Because the measures line up vertically, play the exercise (using the variations) going straight down each column. First play measures 1, 5, 9, 13, 17 and then go down the second column with measures 2, 6, 10, 14, 18. And of course continue down the third and fourth columns as well.

• Play two measures of each line: measures 1-2, 5-6, 9-10, etc.

• Play the exercise at a diagonal: measures 1, 6, 11, 16; then measures 17, 22, 27, 32.

Practicing this way helps develop eye-hand coordination. I have found that after going through exercises using this method, the student is much more comfortable in reading a page of regular music. There is also a bonus. Because the multiple lines are not written out, a student's thinking process is challenged to remember which notes are to be played on which drum. It takes an extra amount of concentration.

Of course, the point of practicing these patterns for long periods of time is to prepare a set drummer to recognize them immediately the next time he is faced with sight-reading a chart. I hope it works for your students; it has certainly helped mine. ■

February, 1982

The Interpretation of Rolled Notes in Mallet Instrument Performance

John Raush

In music written for the mallet instruments, especially marimba and xylophone, the roll is a technique of singular importance because it provides the only means of playing *legato.* Rolled passages are annoyingly unmusical if all rolls are played with identical attacks, releases, and volume. Rolled notes are sustained musical sounds that must be shaped by the movement of the melodic line, the contour of a phrase, and the phrase ending.

The speed of rolls may be varied for the purpose of expressing tension or relaxation. Normally, a soft roll is played with a short stroke and a relatively slow mallet speed; however, if stroke height is kept at a minimum with rapid mallet speed, the result is a soft but tense-sounding roll. As rolls become louder, they require longer strokes, and a slight increase in mallet speed to maintain a finely-textured sound. Students should be encouraged to practice *forte* and *fortissimo* rolls to develop the wrist strength and accuracy demanded at those volumes.

Roll Attacks

Teachers should encourage students to think of rolls as sustained sounds in the musical fabric, rather than mechanical functions that are performed in the same mold. This concept will help avoid many of the bad roll habits that are associated with attacks and releases.

The initial stroke of a roll is the most important one. Although it must establish the appropriate volume, it should never be so heavy that the result is a *forte-piano* effect. For the beginning mallet player, rolls should include the types pictured here:

Example 1

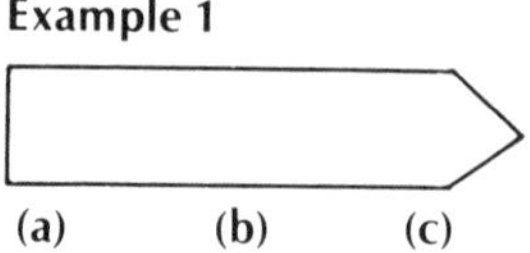

(a) (b) (c)

Example 2

Example 3

In example 1, important features are a clean attack (a); an even volume resulting from a controlled series of alternated strokes (b); and an unaccented, tapered release (c). Example 2 represents the sound of a clean attack, as in the first example, but also of detached, accented rolls at moderate to fast tempos: . Rolls written as have a clean attack plus a continuous, even volume giving the note more breadth and are represented in example 3.

Legato rolls contribute some of the greatest obstacles to the young mallet player. A common bad habit caused by the difficulty of moving rapidly from one bar to another, is accenting the initial stroke of each roll. Rolls need to be connected smoothly, with no audible breaks when changing bars. The initial stroke of each roll should be no louder than the remainder of the strokes in it. Two factors that may contribute to the difficulty of moving from one note to another without breaking the roll or accenting each attack include using a roll speed that is faster than necessary, and using a grip that is not kept absolutely relaxed.

It is important for a student to develop the knack of leading with either his left or right hand with equal ease when rolling from one bar to another. The actual decision of which hand moves first, or leads, is a matter of which mallet is closest to the next note, and common sense.

Examples 4 and 5 use pictographs that show a roll with a heavily accented attack, and a roll with an accented release.

Example 4

Example 5

Crescendo and Diminuendo Rolls

Playing evenly-paced *crescendo* and *diminuendo* rolls is no easier than playing unrolled *crescendos* and *diminuendos*. Have a student watch his strokes gradually lengthen in a *crescendo* and shorten in a *diminuendo*. Good *crescendo* and *diminuendo* rolls can be seen as well as heard.

When playing a *diminuendo* roll, be particularly careful that stick height does not drop prematurely. If it does, a *forte-piano* sound, as represented in example 6, will result. To avoid this problem, play the first few strokes of the roll with the same intensity as the first stroke, followed by strokes that gradually decrease in length. The desired *diminuendo* roll is represented in example 7.

Example 6

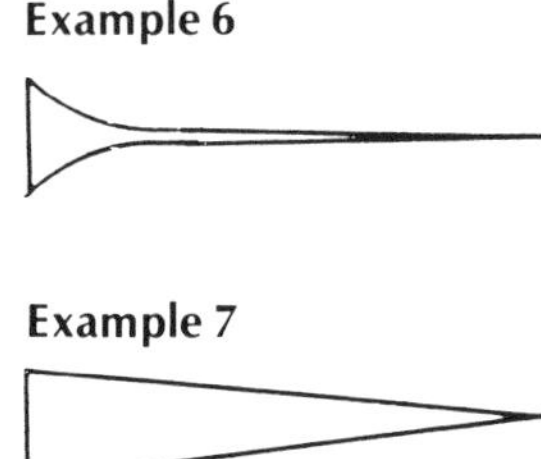

Example 7

Roll Releases

An annoying trait frequently heard in mallet performances is a strong accent placed on the final stroke of a rolled note, without regard to its rhythmic position. Although the last stroke of a roll, found as an upbeat in example 8, does receive an accent, the rolls in example 9 must be terminated delicately. Accents on the eighth-notes would distort the rhythm.

Example 8

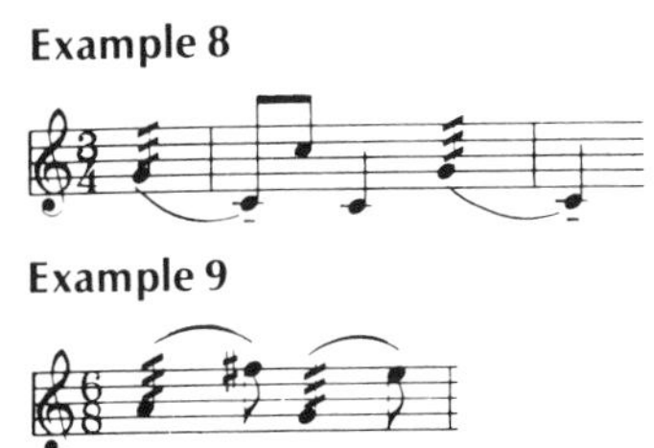

Example 9

In the case of detached rolls in example 10, the final stroke on each note should be unapparent. To achieve this, have the student play the last stroke more softly than any of the preceding strokes, so the rolls sound as represented in example 11.

Example 10

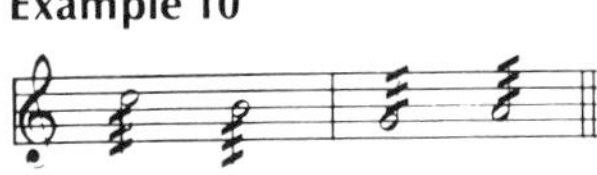

Example 11

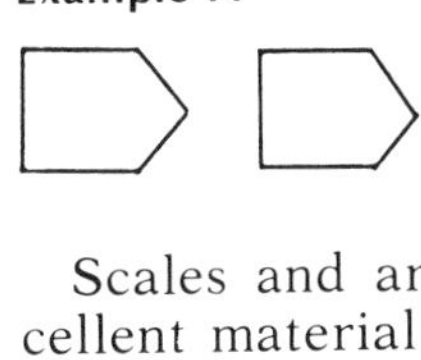

Scales and arpeggios are excellent material for students to practice roll skills required in mallet performance. In the following exercises *crescendos* and *diminuendos* can be added as suggested, and rolls can be played detached ( ), accented ( ), or *legato*. Giving shape to rolled notes, and executing them with the correct attacks and releases will add greatly to the musicianship of a performance providing added satisfaction to the student and listener as well. ■

Roll Exercises

Writing Effective Percussion Parts

Kevin Lepper

If you are a band director or percussion instructor whose section needs to learn a lot of music in a short period of time, this information is for you. Even if your group presents the same show all year, the ground rules for scoring marching percussion will make your section musically effective with a minimum amount of effort.

The marching percussion section's main function is to produce a solid, stylistically correct rhythmic center for the band. Most directors believe this concept is more difficult to accomplish than it actually is. The two basic schools of percussion thought are to either play a pattern throughout a piece or to change the pattern in every measure.

These two techniques are direct opposites. The band director who presents a new show every week can combine them for material that is easy to teach, easy to learn, effective, and provides a foundation for musical productions.

Before writing any parts, a director must know:

1. The ability level of every section in the group
2. The style of the music
3. The sections of the music that will be performed
4. The impact points of the music

A recording of the arrangement, with correct dynamics and tempos, should be used when teaching the parts. An instructor should make sure the percussionists can sing the music's melodic line to help them play their parts effectively.

Pattern Playing

Advantages

Easy to teach
Easy to learn
Sounds full
Provides a solid foundation for the band

Disadvantages

Boring to hear
Boring to play
Does not take into account musical changes

Changing the Pattern

Advantages

Exciting to play
Exciting to hear
Challenges the student
Takes into account musical changes, breaks, and solos
Provides a solid foundation for the band

Disadvantages

Difficult to teach
Difficult to learn
Time-consuming to teach
Time-consuming to learn

Rehearse the percussion section by following this plan:

1. Play one phrase of the recorded arrangement
2. While students mark time, have them sing the melody
3. Repeat steps 1 and 2 until everyone knows the melody
4. Play the parts to the phrase while marking time
5. Play the parts with the music
6. Repeat steps 4 and 5 until everyone has a good feeling for the melody and their part, even though some notes may be wrong

A three-minute tune will take approximately 30 minutes to one hour to learn. Remember to help the percussion section by having their music ready, with dynamics and tempos marked, when the rest of the band receives their parts. It is always nice to read a part rather than having to learn it by rote.

Here are some basic concepts for scoring each instrumental group:

Snares are the soprano voice of the section. They are your busiest players and can perform the fastest and clearest.

Timp-toms provide a middle voice that can double the snares. They function as moving lines, counter-lines, or double the bass drum accents. Timp-toms add body by playing the rhythm of the second and third trumpets or the second alto sax. These players usually carry accessories such as tambourine, triangle, etc.

Bass drums are the foundation of the section and usually play with the other basses. One is playing almost all the time to give pulse to the music. Unison writing must be simple and the playing level of each instrumentalist must be considered when writing the parts. Try to march and play each part yourself.

Cymbals are used as a ride cymbal and hi-hat for snares. When used as a hi-hat, the "ssssit" sound of opening and closing the cymbal is hard to achieve on the field and should be used sparingly. Ride cymbal and hi-hat effects are softer than loud crashes.

Bells and xylophone cut through the overall band sound. Do not overuse these instruments; they become annoying if they are playing all the time.

General scoring concepts to remember when writing for a percussion section include alternating the drum sound with the cymbal sound, using cross accents between the various instruments, and changing the feel and texture of the scoring at a section change. Write busy or strong patterns to create more intensity and fill in the parts at the end of the phrase. Score rhythms with the band or opposite the band, being careful not to over-score or under-score. Use the band's texture and intensity as a guide to writing percussion parts that will be in proper balance.

Playing a pattern and filling it in with simple kicks describes the Count Basie style scoring in the following examples. I have my percussionists keep time, then kick in at the musically appropriate place, without getting too fancy. This concept works. For each style of music there is a list of suggested titles, in some cases followed by a suggested percussion part.

Classical: "William Tell Overture," "1812 Overture," "Can Can," and "Star Wars." This style lends itself well to group accents (example 1, measure 4) and gives a nice moving feel or gallop beat. The bass drum lines in this example are good for a stationary feel. To end the piece, score the bass drums in eighth-notes, similar to timpani scoring at the end of a symphony, to create tension and excitement. Don't write busy parts for classical numbers.

Latin: "Legend of a One-Eyed Sailor," "Land of Make Believe," "Echano," "Temptation," and "Late in the Evening." Latin is the hardest style for percussionists to grasp, and therefore the band usually has problems too. Difficulties include playing the rhythms too straight or square, trying to play too much, and not playing with a tension-versus-release style. A good Latin percussionist can play the same pattern through an entire piece without letting it become boring.

Score the bass drums to follow the rhythm of the bass line. Accessory percussion instruments may be used, but don't let them become overbearing. Tambourines, cabasas, shakers, etc., usually play sixteenth-notes; cowbell plays a simple pattern; samba whistles, police whistle, flexatone, vibraslap, etc., can be used occasionally for special effects. Have the snare drummers play a pattern on the snare or cymbal and snare. When scoring the hi-hat, indicate whether it should be loose or tight.

A good lead-in to ensemble parts uses sixteenth notes with a *crescendo* for one measure. This effect increases intensity while fitting the end of a phrase and builds to a note to kick.

In the scored Latin piece of example 2, note the change in texture and instrumentation at each section. Because the same rhythm is repeated or changed slightly, the sound is kept interesting without the need of asking the player to learn a new beat.

The introduction to many Latin songs consists of a soloist ad-libbing over a sustained percussion chord. For more action than just random cymbal splashes, have the wood block or cowbell played slowly, getting faster, then slowing down again. This process should take three to five seconds.

Latin material is scored using two common techniques. Cross-accents are characterized by having one instrument play an accent and another answer it. In pyramid writing, instruments are added every two bars, similar to the Baroque fugue, to provide color and depth.

Country-Western: "Yakety Sax" and "In America." Straightforward, simple styling works best in country-western writing. Avoid scoring that becomes too busy.

Country Western

Rock: "Ease on Down the Road," "Theme From Rocky," "Dancin' Queen," "Chase Medley," "Sir Duke," "Hot Stuff," and "Chump Change." When scoring rock music, bass drums can either play the set bass drum part or help kick a rhythm. Be sure to check all the parts for playability. In the example, bass drum 2 has to play both the band part plus kick with other bass drums. This player will be unable to feel both parts because they are close together. The crisp rhythm will sound cluttered. A simplified version of the rhythm corrects this situation.

Rock

Cluttered bass drum with kick

Simplified part

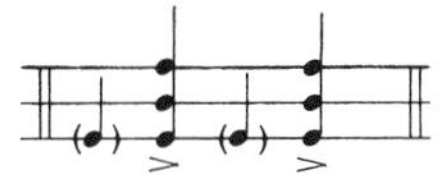

The marching bass drum 1 will notice that trying to play the next line is difficult. The rhythm becomes playable by giving the percussionist a downbeat on which to start or end.

Bass Drum Line

Too hard to play and march

Corrected version

Try playing these rhythms in order to understand the players' problems. It may save the rock number in your show.

Rock has many texture changes. In example 3, the ensemble plays two bars and then a soloist and a drum fill take over. Notice during the fill how only one dampened bass drum is used. The timp-toms share the fill and the snares hit the accents on cymbals. A cowbell on quarter-notes sets a rock feel nicely. Also, tambourines, shakers, and cabasas on sixteenth-notes help with an off-the-beat pattern. For a quick solo, try a measure of sixteenth-notes with accents in the snare drum.

If the phrase keeps gaining intensity, as in example 4, fill in the timp-tom line and simplify the bass drum with only the necessary unisons.

Fast swing: "Fascinatin' Rhythm" and "New York, New York." The rhythms ♪. ♬, ♩♪ (3), or ♫ are usually played the same way (♩♪ 3) in swing. Be sure everyone plays them together. Make the breaks or fills easy, clear, and with a definite beginning and end. Cymbals are usually played near the bell for a "pingy" jazz sound. The bass drum parts resemble walking bass lines, and timp-toms fill in for snares or double accents.

For a quick beat, use the pattern of the swing beat in the low drums, mimic the horn rhythm before a solo, or try *crescendo* triplets. Split up these three ideas and your solos will sound full of variety. For a rock effect in the shout chorus use heavy accents on beats two and four.

Slow swing: "Harlem Nocturne" and "Blues." Use a splashy cymbal sound, played near the edge for slow swing styles. Also, have snares play hard rim shots on beats two and four. The shuffle pattern is usually used, and the phrase endings lend themselves to triplet *crescendos.*

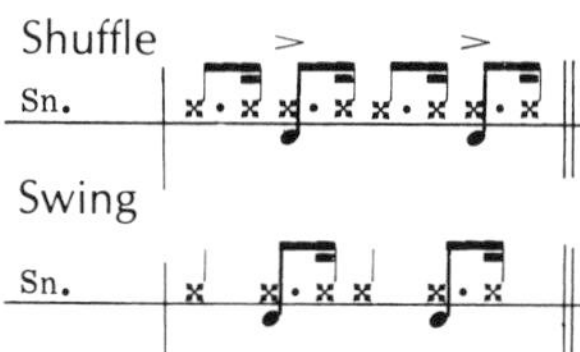

Slow rock (big ending): "The Way We Were," "I Write the Songs," "Climb Every Mountain," "Send in the Clowns," "Brian's Song," and "My Way." A cross-section of this music generally resembles the format in example 5: first phrase – soloist; first phrase repeat – soloist plus accompaniment; second phrase – color change, rhythm change, transition to ending; *maestoso* ending – long note, melody bolero feel. A closer look at the percussion scoring shows it consists of three patterns and kicks. In the bolero rhythm the quarter-note triplet in the second bar is easy to achieve.

Now that most of the styles of music you'll encounter have been covered briefly, try writing some effective percussion parts for your group. Listen to what your percussionists have to say because they will offer some of the best ideas. This approach to percussion writing gives you the control to enhance the style being played, to provide a solid, varied foundation for the band, and to do it with a minimum amount of time and effort in both arranging and rehearsal. ■

Example 1 Classical

♩ = 140
Band, Sn., T.T., B.D., Cym.
p crescendo
ff all accented
all accented

Example 2 Latin Sketch

♩ = 172
Band, Sn., T.T., B.D., Cym.
Introduction — *mf*
Song proper — *mf*
Tambourine 16's
Cowbell
Lead into ensemble — *fp* crescendo
to Sn.

Band, Sn., T.T., B.D., Cym. — *ff* — *f* — etc.
Tambourine 16's
One sn. Cowbell

Example 3 Rock with texture changes

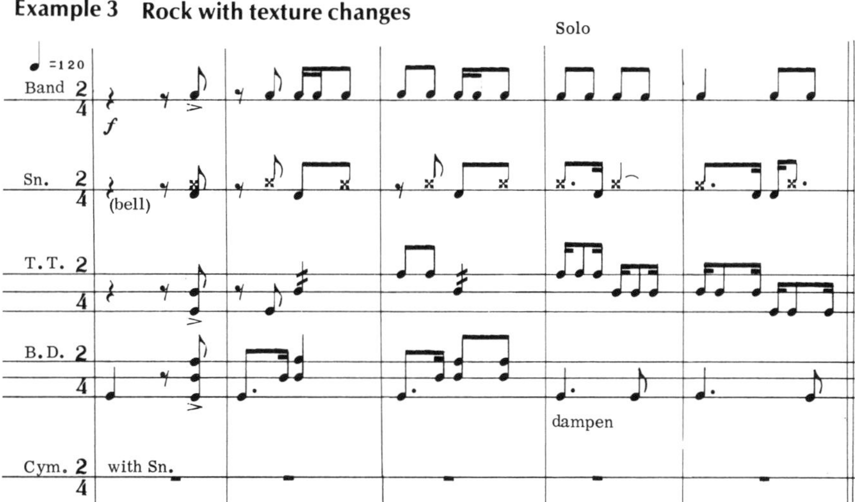

Example 4 Scoring that gains intensity

Example 5 Slow closer with light rock to bolero

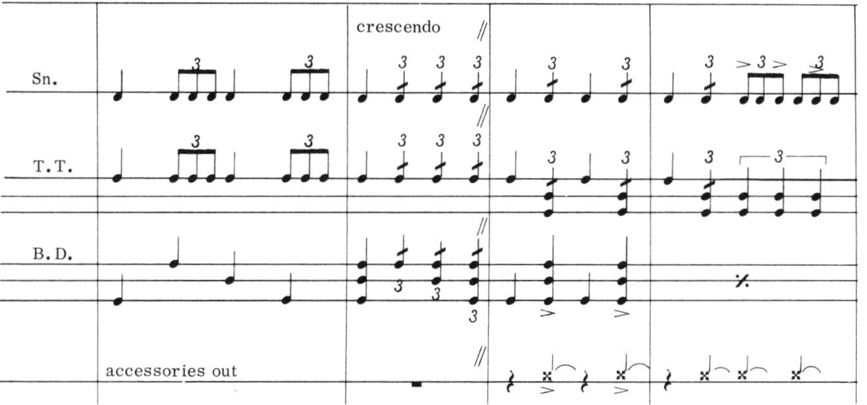

The High School Percussion Ensemble

Anna Watkins

For most high school students "percussion ensemble" means the preparation of a piece for the annual solo and ensemble festival. If the music is chosen carefully and rehearsals are designed to develop fine ensemble playing, students can gain the ability to play as a unit, whether it is to be used for further percussion ensemble playing or for band, orchestra, or chamber music.

I like to precede the rehearsal of any printed music with what I call ensemble games. I have the players face each other in a circle, each with one drum. We begin with one designated player playing eight 8th notes, followed in time by the next person to the right, continuing the pattern around the circle as many times as desired. The effect should be continuous 8th notes at a constant dynamic level; but it is not as easy as it sounds. Using the same procedure, we then have the first player begin at pianissimo and each consecutive player play slightly louder to achieve a gradual crescendo. Then we try diminuendo.

In the next variation on the games a designated player begins by playing a 4-beat pattern which is immediately repeated by the others in unison. Then the next person to the right plays a different 4-beat pattern to be imitated by the others, and continues around the circle. For the first attempts at this game I ask that they avoid rolls and accents. If at anytime the group loses the pattern or beat, the next player plays straight quarter notes to get them back together. The variations on the games are limited only by the students' own technique and creativity. My students' initial reaction was negative, but they grew to enjoy the games more as they played them each week. I was especially delighted when I saw them using ensemble games as a welcoming ceremony for a new member of the group.

Those who are familiar with the Colgrass *Percussion Music* will see how ensemble games lead into the performance of the imitative passages in the music, especially the cascading 16th note patterns in the first and fourth movements. Identical unison playing should be stressed in this work along with scrupulous adherence to the dynamic markings. In rehearsing the first movement section from rehearsal letter B to C I have discovered what may be at least a temporary cure for the inability to count when confronted with rolls. First we rehearse the section without rolls, playing it at least three or more times so students become aware that a line of 16th and 8th notes is shared among all the parts. When we add the rolls, players are asked to count correctly and not allow the rolls to obscure the line.

Solo entrances in the second movement are tricky and should be rehearsed separately at first. Everyone must have a clear understanding of the alternating meters (4 and 5). I recommend counting out loud in the first rehearsals, especially from rehearsal letter J through K. In the third movement we practice paired rhythms first so the players get a feel for playing with a partner.

Prelude and Allegro by Edward Volz combines several types of ensemble playing: solo with accompaniment, "shared lines" (two or more parts in hocket style), and unison playing. There is a lively, syncopated tambourine part in the Prelude, and the timpani and tom-toms are featured with jazzy solos in the Allegro. Be sure to drill the unison passages. To rehearse the hocket parts, write the composite rhythms on a chalkboard or on large cards so the whole group can first read and play them in unison before playing the parts as written. Even then you may want to have one player continue to play the composite rhythm.

Three Pieces for Percussion Quartet by Warren Benson is a set of short pieces which has much to offer the beginning percussion ensemble. "Allegretto" uses dynamic contrast and makes effective use of silence. Some individual parts contain difficult-looking rhythms which are isolated 16th notes that combine into straightforward composite rhythms. The imitative section in the middle uses jazzy syncopated rhythms and provides an excellent opportunity to point out principal and subordinate lines. In the first rehearsal of this section have the students play only their solo lines. "Scherzino" is marked "fast, playfully" and is really fun to play. The interplay of parts is quite clever and there is an interesting shift of meters at the end of the piece. This one must be precise; use a metronome. "Fughetta alla Siciliana" is the most rudimental of the three Benson quartets and the most difficult technically with challenging snare drum, field drum, and tom-tom parts. The meter changes must be explained carefully and rehearsed thoroughly.

Three Asiatic Dances by George Frock is a good introduction to exotic Eastern music. It requires some subtle playing for delicate atmosphere contrasted with aggressive, fast, and loud playing in the final movement. The softer moments in this piece should convince the audience that percussion can be beautiful, and your students will enjoy displaying their musicianship on this work. Yarn-covered or felt mallets will help the players to play softly with control in the first movement, "Temple Dance." In the second movement ("Po Chung and Te Chung"), be sure to indicate tempo changes clearly and rehearse these transitions separately. This composition is most effective when the directions at the end of the second movement are followed "Attacca-Segue." To make the beginning of the last movement even more startling in performance I have doubled the bass drum and tom-tom parts. The soft sections in this movement are a brief but necessary contrast in this predominately loud dance, titled "Sacrifice." Rehearse them separately along with the transitions from loud to soft. Maintain or increase the dynamic level at the ending for the best effect.

A La Samba by Mitchell Peters is fun to play and is a good introduction to typical Latin percussion playing with lots of ostinato rhythms. Every player gets a solo, and the whole group must be aware of each solo to make the piece work dynamically. I recommend memorizing this one. Solos may be varied slightly once the players know the structure of the piece. This is an excellent opportunity for teaching techniques on Latin percussion instruments. Trading parts in rehearsal would be helpful in this regard. Be sure that your group understands *Da Capo*.

In choosing ensemble pieces to perform, explore possibilities for instrument substitution before rejecting a number because you don't own the exact instruments listed in the score. Different sizes of student-owned drums could combine into sets of tom-toms, for example. Use your imagination, but be guided by the type of sound and pitch relationships indicated on the score. If the work has several movements, don't put it aside because you can't play the whole work; simply choose the movements you can play well, and let that be your performance.

Whenever there are rhythms which are imitated in sequence by every member of the group, the players should set up in order so they can hear each other better and the audience can follow the line visually as well as aurally. Rehearsal and performance set-ups should be consistent. Diagrams will help to set up quickly and prevent forgetting needed instruments. If a player uses more than one pair of mallets or sticks, they should be indicated on the part in pencil. Use a trap table or towel-covered music stand to hold the sticks.

I believe it is necessary for each ensemble member to be aware of the total effect of the music, not just the one part he is playing. We often tape record rehearsals so students can listen to themselves; and if a professional recording of the work is available, I have them listen to that. Sometimes when a number is almost ready for performance, I ask the students to trade parts on a certain section, rotating until everyone has played every part.

The following graded selected list includes pieces already discussed in this article, plus other percussion ensembles that are often performed at the high school level. The ensembles listed will serve as a good basis for technical as well as musical performance experiences.

Composer	Title & Number of Players	Level of Difficulty	Publisher
Benson	Allegretto (4)	II	G. Schirmer
	Scherzino (4)	II	G. Schirmer
	Fughetta alla Siciliana (4)	III	G. Schirmer
Benson	Trio for Percussion (3)	IV	Music for Percussion
Chavez	Toccata (6)	IV	Belwin-Mills
Cirone	Triptych (4)	V	Cirone
Colgrass	Inventions on a Motive (4)	IV	Music for Percussion
Colgrass	Percussion Music (4)	III	Music for Percussion
Firth	Encore in Jazz (7)	IV	Carl Fischer
Frock	Three Asiatic Dances (6)	III	Southern Music
Handel/Moore	"Allegro" from Water Music (4)	II	Permus
Handel/Moore	Bourree (4)	II	Permus
Haydn/Moore	Trio Sonata No. 1 (3)	III	Permus
Hovhaness	October Mountain (6)	IV	C.F. Peters
Joplin/Moore	The Entertainer (4)	III	Permus
Khachaturian/ Moore	Sabre Dance (3 - 7)	II	Permus
Kraft	Suite for Percussion (4)	III	Belwin-Mills
Kraft	Theme and Variations (4)	II	Western Intl.
O'Reilly	Three Episodes (5)	III	G. Schirmer
Peters	A La Samba (6)	III	Mitchell Peters
Schiffman	Musica Battuta (7)	III	Schirmer
Tull	Sonatina (4)	IV	Boosey & Hawkes
Volz	Prelude and Allegro (5)	II	Bourne
Williams	African Sketches (4)	III	Ludwig

New Music, Sounds, and Approaches in Percussion Literature

Part I

Don R. Baker

This past year has been a productive one for percussion literature. Many empty spots, especially in the areas of rototom, conga, and timpani literature, are now filled. Publishers and authors should be congratulated on their fine work and productivity. Instructors are starting percussionists earlier in all areas, and these methods reflect their need for new music, sounds, and approaches in percussion literature.

Snare Drum

Contest Solos for the Young Snare Drummer (Kendor) by Murray Houllif presents 12 unaccompanied pieces for beginning and early junior high students. The solos combine regular phrase structures and rhythms with the sound of brushes and rims that make the music delightful. Drumming rudiments include simple rolls, flams, and easy drags. The students' greatest challenge will be in reading and playing passages with both hands at once. The clear and large notation is appropriate for beginners. These solos are a grateful addition to the percussion library.

Flam-It-All, Follow Me (grade levels 1 and 2), *7-Down, Snare Force,* and *Space Race* (grade level 3) are by Thomas A. Brown (Kendor). Each book focuses on different playing techniques. *Flam-It-All* concentrates on flams and dynamic contrast; *Follow Me* uses easy meter changes and center and edge imitation playing; *7-Down* focuses on the seven-stroke roll; and *Snare Force* centers on the paradiddle. *Space Race* offers musical contrast in material that is not rhythmically difficult. Innovative writing on the rim, edge, center, and with snares on or off provides a technical challenge. Brown has edited the solos, offering introductory remarks to help players focus on the technical skills in each piece.

Three Festival Solos and *Recital Suite for Solo Snare Drum* (Kendor) are by William J. Schinstine. Besides using conventional rhythms, the solos offer practice in meter changes, dynamic contrast, and roll control. The first collection is for grades 1 and 2. *Recital Suite,* marked grade 6, is for the mature player; however, the first movement lacks musical continuity and flow. The second movement uses a mirror image of its theme and has an interesting rhythmic touch. It won second prize in the 1980 Percussive Arts Society Composition Contest.

Kitten Kaboodle, Poppycock, Up Beat Pete's Suite, Whodunit, and *March for a Different Drummer* are written and arranged by Wally Barnett; and *That's Tough* is composed by E.L. Masoner (Belwin-Mills). Listed in progressive order of difficulty, each solo includes a simple piano accompaniment. *Kitten Kaboodle* is in $\frac{3}{4}$ and uses only quarter notes. *Poppycock* and *That's Tough* have simple flams, eighth notes, and accents. *Up Beat* contains three short movements and has flams and sixteenth notes. *Whodunit* uses snares on and off plus playing on the rim. *March* is done in rudimental style with open rolls. The piano accompaniments add musical interplay and shaping to the phrases.

There are some problems with Morris Lang's *The Beginning Snare Drummer* (Lang Percussion Company). This rudimental method does not develop fundamental rhythms well enough before introducing exercises with mixed rhythms. There is no discussion on grips, and the material on flam and drag technique development is inadequate. Each lesson ends with a series of exam questions, yet some of the questions are not answered until the next assignment. Many written explanations will need additions from a teacher. Useful aspects of this method include extensive use of the accents and clear explanations of music fundamentals (text references, counting, sticking, contemporary time signatures, and duets). The method proceeds rather fast on ties and syncopation, and it includes a good approach in lining up similar rhythms that are written in different notations.

Primary Handbook for Snare Drum (Meredith) by Garwood Whaley is a good beginning text for young players. This comprehensive book includes contemporary meters, multiple percussion, and a refreshing new approach to the rudiments – they are identified as American, Swiss, or contrived. Two areas that need revision are the notation for introducing rolls and the lack of discussion of dotted rhythms. The approach to right-hand grip is somewhat unorthodox and can be misleading; I suggest teachers check another source.

Garwood Whaley's *Solos and Duets for Snare Drum* (Meredith) is a collection of works for the intermediate or moderately advanced player. The text is divided into musical material that is written either with or without rolls, flams, or ruffs. The compositions use a variety of musical idioms, and there are a few solos for multiple percussion. Each solo begins with a preliminary study that focuses on difficult passages. This collection would serve as good supplementary or contest material.

Ron Fink (Fink Publishing Company) has finally compiled his snare drum exercises into book form. *Chop Busters* is a volume of warm-up patterns that develop coordination, accuracy, speed, dynamics, and rhythm recognition. The exercises are listed by meter: $\frac{2}{4}$, $\frac{6}{8}$, $\frac{3}{4}$, $\frac{4}{4}$, $\frac{2}{2}$, and $\frac{12}{8}$. All have tempo marking challenges. However, there does not seem to be a logical sequence in the development of rhythms or stickings; and most of the exercises are written in notation that is more difficult to understand than necessary. Some of the hand manuscript is messy but readable. The experienced player will find this collection rewarding.

Sight Reading and Audition Etudes for Snare Drum (Fink Publishing Company) by Ron Fink is a collection of progressive material for the high school and college level student. Though inconsistent in quality, the etudes present attractive literature. The manuscript is legible, and some parts call for playing on different areas of the drum.

Corps-Dially Yours (Kendor) by Jeffrey P. Funnell is a corps style *tour-de-force* snare drum solo. The tempo marking combined with the sticking make this solo almost impossible to play. At a more reasonable tempo (around ♩ =120), the work will still sound effective and be playable by skilled performers.

Prestidigitation (C.L. Barnhouse) by J. Michael Roy is a rudimental piece for the high school drummer. This musically versatile composition is long enough for contest use, and includes some meter changes.

The *Corps Style Snare Drum Dictionary* (Alfred) by Jay A. Wanamaker is a handy book with exercises, special effects, and short solos using American and Swiss rudiments that go beyond the standard 26. Many of the illustrations are taken from the author's well-used *Championship Auxiliary Units.* There are some excellent practice exercises for each rudiment; however, the solos are too compact and offer little musical development. The technical exercises are effective and to the point. This book is a valuable resource for the marching snare drummer.

Drum Set

Waltz Duo and *Rock Duo* (Kendor) by Murray Houllif are a treat to play and a nice addition to drum set literature. Although both are short, the high school level player can sink his hands into some nice figures around the drums (a four-piece set is required). *Rock Duo* is especially well composed. The music is written so the parts are not cluttered with sounds or rhythms, and there is good variety and technical challenge as well. Highly recommended.

Ron Fink's *Drum Set Suite* (Fink Publishing Company) is a collection of three pieces that fit nicely together. The composer makes good use of the tonal combinations in a four-piece set. Extensive use of sixteenths and triplets plus rim shots, cymbal colors, syncopations, and meter changes make this a nice study for fun or contest.

Contemporary Drumset Solos (Kendor) by Murray Houllif is written for the contemporary drummer and incorporates advanced independent playing. The styles include swing, be-bop, Latin, fusion, and funk rock as well as rudimental playing. Melodic tom techniques are used. These solos are suitable for recital, contest, and jury examinations.

Brushfire (R and W) by Willis F. Kirk is the most thoroughly written method for brushes to date. The text assumes the player has some degree of proficiency and can play basic dotted rhythms. Circle diagrams that represent each beat are used; however, a few rhythms are not properly lined up and some are written incorrectly. Advanced brush techniques and single and double stroke rolls in $\frac{5}{4}$ time are used, and seven brush-style solos are included.

Today's Sounds for Drumset (Kendor) by Murray Houllif is a method to help develop a variety of rhythms on the four-piece drumset. Although the rhythms are broken down by lessons and never become too advanced, the writer assumes the player has had some playing experience. The text includes fill examples and shows how to use them in typical phrase structures.

Studies for the Contemporary Drummer (Hansen House) by John Xepoleas and Warren Nunes includes a soundsheet for rock and jazz study. Standard exercises and beats for rock, jazz, reggae, and Latin as well as a suggested listening discography are included. This volume of compact, no frills exercises, with pages for student creativity, is part of a series for guitar, bass, piano, and improvisation techniques.

Drum Time and Space (Centerstream) by Pat Carlucci is another basic method on drumming fundamentals, from stick holding to dotted rhythms, that incorporates the drum set. The matched grip is incorrectly introduced – even the following page has the same mirror image marked "wrong way." The beginning material has good, repetitive basic patterns, but the sixteenth note rhythms lack sufficient musical exercises. ■

New Music, Sounds, and Approaches in Percussion Literature

Part II

Don R. Baker

Conga

The *Basic Introduction to Playing the Conga Drum* (Gon Bops of California) by Paul Lopez includes two cassette tapes and a small instruction manual. Series I presents two basic rhythms on the tapes; the material is written so it can be played on one or two drums with variations. The tapes are excellent. They imitate the basics of beginning lessons and provide practice rhythms as well as an accompaniment by a five-piece rhythm section. Each is well-narrated by the author.

Conga Drumming (Congeros) by Jerry Daraca is a thorough and well-illustrated text for conga playing. This method offers conga history as well as a variety of styles including soul, disco, reggae, and rock. The accompanying cassette, which is excellently recorded, contains rhythm, practice drills, and ensembles for each style. The text is complete and exciting, with a touch of phonetics for each of the Latin terms. This is a good method for the college student who has little conga experience. A truly professionally-packaged and well-conceived method.

RotoToms

RotoTom Technique (Carl Fischer) by Vic Firth is a complete text on rototom history, equipment, ranges, etc. The title is misleading because the book is almost exclusively a collection of progressive etudes, written in a style similar to Firth's *The Solo Timpanist.* There are several etudes that could serve as solos if they were longer. The studies cover two to six drums, a wide variety of meters, rhythm groups, dynamics, and styles. The text is unique: it is written in four languages. This volume is a good addition for the experienced player or as supplemental etude or solo material for the progressing multiple percussionist.

RotoTom Solos for the Melodic Drummer (Southern) by William J. Schinstine provides percussion solos for three, four, and seven rototoms. It is a mixed collection of music, with some pieces being extension-of-technique exercises. Most of the solos are one page long, and a few have pitch changes. One work is in treble clef, an obvious mistake. The material is for the young college student or advanced high school player.

Timpani

The timpanist should also consider the *RotoTom Technique* collection by Vic Firth (discussed under *RotoToms*) as a valuable addition to instrument range and etude material.

The Well-Tempered Timpanist (Belwin-Mills) by Charles Dowd is the only timpani book of its kind: it offers computer permutations. The text includes 770 technical studies for two to six timpani and has a nice section on cross-rhythms. Dowd strives for musical phrases and optional sticking within each study. Where Saul Goodman's ever-so-popular *Modern Method for Timpani* is lacking in technical exercises, this volume makes up for it, acting as a good supplement. Not only is this book current, it anticipates the future technical demands of the modern timpanist. I recommend it.

The *Primary Handbook for Timpani* (Meredith) by Garwood Whaley is an excellent beginning method for young players with two timpani. The well-explained text progresses logically in dealing with fundamental playing techniques and presenting clear diagrams. The tuning exercises are not related to most current timpani literature but they are manageable. The descriptions of strokes and rolls are clear, and the author provides a creative approach to executing the staccato stroke. The last 13 pages contain effective and musical solos. Whaley seems to have a natural flair for teaching and writing for timpani.

Fred Begun has written a collection of *Twenty-One Etudes for* Timpani (Meredith). The challenging etudes (solos) are designed primarily for the advanced player. They are rhythmically and technically demanding, and the music includes several tuning changes with some passages of pure pedaling. An annotation of each etude describes important lines, possible trouble spots, position, and type of sticks. When five drums are needed, the commonly-used 25" is added. This is a well-designed text and a good addition to the timpanist's repertoire.

Timpani Tuning Etudes (Fink Publishing Company) by Ron Fink is primarily a tuning book written for advanced players who use two to five drums. The material is often contrived and more technically than musically oriented. The review copy had some blank pages.

Mallets and Keyboards

Primary Handbook for Mallets (Meredith) by Garwood Whaley is a well-designed, systematic approach to learning mallet and keyboard instruments. The method contains technical studies, rote memorization, reading studies, four-mallet techniques, and duets for a student who has already had some playing experience. The text progresses too fast for a young beginner, but it is appropriate for a more mature student.

Wally Barnett has several beginning solos for mallets or keyboards (bells) that have piano accompaniment: *The Glens of Wicklow, Caterpillars and Butterflies, A Walk Through Kalamazoo, Scrumpy* (Mary Barnett, collaborator), *The Musical Clock,* and *The Ash Grove* (Belwin-Mills, First Division Band Method). The piano accompaniments are simple, solos are one page long, the keys are easy, rhythms include simple dotted notes and eighths, the range is limited, and the music is programmatic in nature. The first three are for beginners, and the second three are only slightly more challenging.

Simple Solos for Mallets (Kendor) by Thomas A. Brown are beginning mallet or keyboard solos. Each is one page long, clearly printed, and written in a popular dance style. They are well-edited and marked for rolls or pedaling (two mallets only). These would be attractive for intermediate and high school students. In contrast, Brown's *The Solo Vibist* (Permus) includes short works using two to four mallets, incorporating folk, classical, and programmatic styles. Some pages are crowded; but the printing is clear and well-edited for sticking, dampening, and pedaling. These are excellent supplemental solos for the intermediate and high school player.

Contest Solos for the Young Mallet Player (Kendor) by Murray Houllif is a collection of easy two-mallet solos in Latin, jazz, rock, and march styles. They are one to two minutes in length and use simple dotted rhythms, eighth notes, and traditional harmony. Only "Lou's Blues" requires reading triplets. This is another attractive supplemental set for the experienced beginner.

A Witch's Brew, Grand Ballroom, Waltz, Mallet Magic, and *Whispering Woods* (Kendor) are unaccompanied mallet or keyboard solos by William J. Schinstine. The *Brew* and *Woods* require a four octave marimba and four-mallet technique. *Woods* is short but offers the greatest musical interest.

Christmas tunes rarely show up in percussion literature as solos, let alone as duets. However, this year two collections were published (Kendor). *Merry Mallet Christmas Favorites,* arranged by Murray Houllif, is a solo collection that varies from moderate to difficult in ability level. Two to four mallets are needed, and styles from traditional block chords to contemporary counterpoint are used. The melodies are uncluttered and clearly recognizable. *Christmas for Two,* arranged by Lloyd Conley, presents ten duets that have a barrage of gimmicks that spice up the works. They are playable and will be attractive to junior or senior high players (two mallets only).

Armand Russell has written *Rondo* and *Fantasia,* two easy xylophone solos with simple piano accompaniments (HaMaR Percussion). There are no rolls, the rhythms are straightforward, and the harmony in *Fantasia* is contemporary in nature.

First Suite from 12 Light Dances (Southern) by Gerald M. Walker is for two to four mallets on marimba. There is good style contrast in each of the five dances. Left and right independence is needed, and often the left hand accompanies the right. A four octave marimba is required to play these colorful little pieces for high school or college level performers.

Songs for Vibes (Fink Publishing Company) by Ron Fink is a collection of six songs each having a woman's name as the title. Four mallets are required. All the tempo markings are slow, giving the works a lyrical style. Well-notated and edited for vibes, any combination of the songs could be used in a recital.

A Dancer at Heart (Kendor) by Bill Molenhof is a marimba solo with piano. It does not seem as well written as the composer's other works. At first glance the piece does not look difficult, but the tempo marking of ♩ =126, along with the four required mallets, makes it challenging. The work is written in a quasi-syncopated, jazz-rock style with the piano serving as an integral part of the musical line.

Soliloquies and Celebrations (C.L. Barnhouse) by Jared Spears is a solo for the advanced player on four-mallet marimba. The work has contrasting sections of strong pulse and lyricism, as well as traditional and spatial notation. It is recommended for an experienced player who is developing speed and independence in his playing. Spear's *Caccia Caper* (C.L. Barnhouse), also for marimba, is easier and requires only two mallets. There is good contrast between the allegro and the adagio expressivo sections. Both works require a four octave marimba.

14 Jazz-Rock Duets (Kendor) by John LaPorta are really duets in the key of C that have also been transcribed for other instruments. The jazz-rock sound is convincing. The duets are for high school level players or above, and the music helps fill a void in the mallet and keyboard literature.

Lyric Suite for flute and marimba (Southern) by Michael Horvit is for college level performers and requires four mallets and a four octave marimba. The music contains good two and four mallet interplay with meter changes, key changes, and contrasting styles. The marimba serves primarily as an accompaniment to the flute; however, both parts are challenging and similar in difficulty. It is an attractive work for a recital.

Percussion Duo (C.F. Peters) by Charles Wuorinen is written for one percussionist (using marimba and vibes) and one pianist. It is a difficult, contemporary work for the advanced college player or professional. ■

Tips for Good Cymbal Playing

Paul Brazauskas

Too many percussion students feel as though anyone can play the cymbals, so they'd much rather perform the more demanding snare drum parts than to get stuck on the cymbals. Unfortunately, some of this attitude comes from directors who feel the same way. Actually the cymbals can be quite challenging and artistically satisfying when played well. There is little specialized teaching material and the cymbal information in the typical beginning band method is sketchy at best. The following information has been useful to me in my work with young players.

Equipment

Cymbal equipment includes a pair of hand cymbals, a suspended cymbal, straps, cymbal pads for marching, a pouch or bag, polish, a soft cloth (bath towel size), and a good stand. Too often hand cymbals are too big for both the player and the ensemble. The idea that "bigger is better" isn't true. Grade school or junior high percussionists shouldn't use anything larger than a pair of 17-inch cymbals. The choice of tone color is up to the director. A pair of hand cymbals should be a long-term investment, so choose them wisely and carefully.

Sling shot cymbal straps are popular, easy to use, and don't have to be tied. The strap, which has a small pocket sewn on it, is threaded through the cymbal and a marble-sized ball bearing is placed in the pocket. Because the ball bearing is larger than the hole in the cymbal's dome, the strap can't back out. This system eliminates the problems associated with a loose cymbal knot. Check the straps for cracks and weaknesses periodically and replace them when they are worn.

Clean cymbals produce the maximum amount of tone with the best clarity. I suggest first washing them with soap and water to get dirt out of the grooves, and then using a commercial cymbal polish to add a final luster to the instrument.

Store the cymbals in a pouch or bag after each rehearsal or when they are transported. A bag with a zipper is easy to use and helps protect the instrument from dirt and scratches.

Gripping Cymbals Correctly

For concert playing students should grip the cymbal straps in the palms of their hands, rather than put their hands through the strap loops. Players should also be discouraged from using cymbal pads. They have a tendency to muffle the tone. When marching, however, players should put their hands through the straps to make carrying the cymbals easier. I also suggest using lamb's wool pads for parades because they make playing more comfortable for a youngster's hands.

Playing Styles

For ease in playing and a better performance, have students hold the cymbals properly. In concert work a player should position the cymbals at an angle, almost like hi-hat cymbals, holding his lower arm close to his body, a little above his waist. This position helps the player support the bottom cymbal and provides control and stability for rapid muffling (dampening) and swift crashes. The bottom cymbal is held still while the percussionist moves the top one, using a quick, boxing jab-like motion. The movement is easy for a student to see because it happens in front of him. Teaching students to move both cymbals so they meet somewhere in mid-air produces poor attacks and air-pockets. The musical result will be discouraging. Because the student can see between the two cymbals, he becomes aware of the relationship between distance and dynamic level. The position also allows for a better view of the music and the director.

When marching, students should hold the cymbals straight up and down. Again, the player holds one cymbal still while he moves the other one, and any showy movements are made after the attack.

Cymbal Crashes

Often students complete crashes by holding the cymbals up in the air. This effect may extend from a director's instructions, an attempt to project the sound over the ensemble, or a desire to be dramatic. Unfortunately, in this position the cymbals rest on the player's hands and the tone dies away rapidly. If pads are on the cymbals, the tone deteriorates even faster. After a crash the percussionist should suspend the cymbals by their straps and then use his body to dampen the tone at the appropriate time. This technique allows the entire cymbal to vibrate freely with little resistance. Because all the overtones are heard the tone has better quality and projection.

Suspended Cymbal Technique

The suspended cymbal is easier to play than a pair of cymbals. I like to use a 20-inch thin-crash model. It responds quickly and is a good general-purpose instrument for grade school and junior high ensembles. A large cymbal is acceptable because the student doesn't have to hold it. It may be struck with a drum stick, triangle beater, or a pair of yarn wound mallets with rattan handles (never use timpani mallets). This cymbal can also be scraped with a coin or struck on the edge, in the center, or on the dome (bell) to get a variety of tonal effects.

To get a good crash sound, strike the suspended cymbal with a glancing stroke. This movement eliminates the hard, explosive sound that results from a straight downward hit.

When rolling, use single strokes and keep the mallets on opposite edges of the cymbal. This position provides a quicker response and gets more of the cymbal vibrating.

A plastic sleeve protects the center hole of the suspended cymbal by keeping the cymbal from rubbing against the metal mount. If the plastic wears through, replace it at once or a crack may develop in the cymbal, and you'll end up with a much larger expense.

Practice Material

Good material for the beginning cymbalist is limited and hard to find, but you can make up exercises to help students develop playing technique. Your players should keep these points in mind:

- Muffle (dampen) the cymbals on rests.
- Use the whole cymbal, not just the edge, when playing softly.
- When practicing, count out loud or tap a foot, and practice with a metronome.

Establish a tempo of ♩=60 and have your students start with these patterns, varying the dynamic level as each exercise is repeated.

1. Sustain a whole note and then rest for four beats; repeat four times.
2. Sustain a half note and then rest for two beats; repeat four times.
3. Play the pattern of whole note, half note, half note, rest for four beats; repeat the pattern four times.
4. Play four quarter notes and then rest for four beats; repeat four times. Continue by practicing the following exercises:

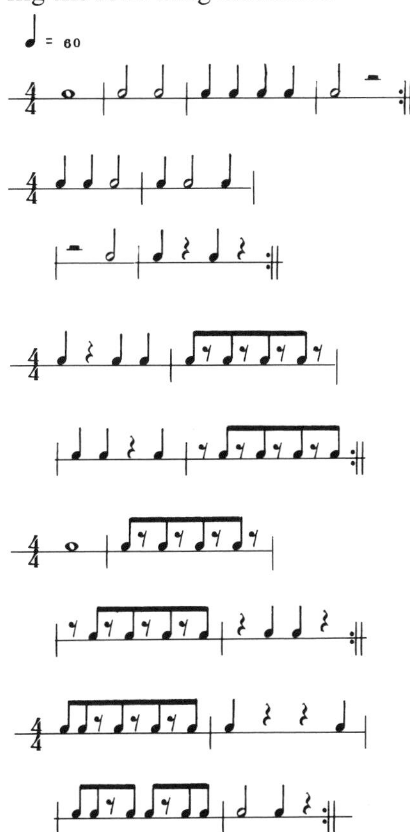

Directors should emphasize the importance of good cymbal playing to their percussionists as well as offer them interesting parts. When correct cymbal techniques are expected, students will work harder to improve their performing skills and meet the challenges of playing their parts well. ■

September, 1982

Percussion Readiness: The Director's Resources

Don R. Baker

Good organization, which helps day-to-day problem solving, is a necessary asset in handling the percussion section. I have found that a percussion resource file, which is supplemented with resource guides, can easily help answer many questions, such as:

- Who has checked out the snare drum?
- What is a good percussion ensemble work for my students?
- What can I do when the timpani pedal keeps moving forward?
- How should I prepare the end-of-the-year reports?

Having resources on hand can save time and limit frustration, thus allowing more time for creative music making with students.

Here I offer the following suggestions for organizing a percussion resource file (which may be adapted to other instrumental groups) and titles for developing a personal library of percussion reference guides.

Instrument Information

I keep my filing system simple, being careful not to overfile for fear of not finding anything. A series of general information folders helps in collecting tips about percussion instruments (such as education aids, magazine articles, handouts, repair and maintenance guides), as well as contests, camps, and public relations material.

Concert Snare Drum: include information on concert drumming techniques, buzz roll charts, beginning snare drum guides, performance techniques, flam execution, etc.

Rudimental Snare Drum: outdoor percussion playing, rudiment chart, open roll chart, execution height, head tension, etc.

Mallet/Keyboard: playing and teaching techniques, selection of mallets, four-mallet techniques, etc.; with a separate file for jazz vibraphone.

Timpani: timpani performance, ear-training exercises, ranges, mallets, etc.

Accessories: information about all types of accessory instruments including Latin percussion.

Drum Set (Jazz/Rock Ensemble): drum set playing, styles, set-ups, exercises, articles, charts, record lists, etc.

Marching Percussion: include all aspects of marching percussion except rudimental snare drum, plus general articles on field placement, warm-ups, etc.

General Information

Percussion Ensemble: recommended ensemble lists, pedagogical aids, programs.

Contests: Keep an up-to-date list of state and district contests, their rules and regulations, plus performance lists. This folder should also include rules for marching percussion, and M.T.N.A.

Public Relations: Maintain a current list of your percussion students. If they perform as an ensemble maintain a record of their appearances and have publicity pictures ready for future playing dates. Keep a list of addresses for publicity mailing purposes. It should include radio stations, newspapers, P.T.A.s, and music supervisors.

Camps: Have a folder of camps just for percussionists. Dates, audition procedures, and addresses are important. Check *The Instrumentalist's* "Directory of Summer Music Camps, Clinics, and Workshops" every spring.

Student Objectives: This folder should include section leader responsibilities and criteria for grading students, plus assignment sheets to divide up parts and responsibilities in the percussion section. Keep misunderstandings to a minimum by writing everything down.

College Auditions: Include articles on preparing for an audition, audition lists, repertoire, and college and scholarship information.

Instrument Inventory: This information can be kept on a master list or on card files, listed by instrumental group or as individual entries for each instrument. Include the instrument's manufacturer, model number, serial number, purchase date, identifying characteristics (color), size, and school number. Include a check-out section for inventory, repair, and student assignments. Be sure all instruments are engraved or stenciled to identify school ownership.

Students: This file contains student evaluation information which can be useful for consultations. It should not be made available to students. It should contain general information about each student and have sections for exam results, placement scoresheets, solo and ensemble performances, contest involvement, section responsibility, names of private teachers, and yearly summaries or evaluations. It is important to be objective about each student's progress. The information will be helpful for conferences, or when writing resumes for college bound music students.

Music

Use two filing systems to help organize music: a legal-size file is necessary for storing scores and parts, and a small 4x6 card file is useful to catalog the compositions.

Some directors file by assigning all works a catalog number and then posting the numbers on 4x6 card files which are filed by composer. I prefer filing ensembles by composer; and solos and methods by subject area (snare drum, timpani, mallet/keyboard, multi-percussion/accessories), then by composer. Mark the ensemble folders with the number of players needed to perform the work. The corresponding file card should include not only reference information, but performance problems and how to solve them, historical information, the last performance date, and if the music was recorded.

Taping a data page to the inside cover of the score, and then filing the music by composer can omit a separate card file and save time. The information sheet should include instrument performance problems, number of players, last peformance, set-up diagrams for the multiple percussion parts, and historical information.

Miscellaneous

Programs: Use a binder to keep programs for easy reference and memorabilia.

Private Teachers: A list of private teachers, their phone numbers, and costs per lesson is helpful to have on hand.

Percussion Ensemble Performance Dates: This folder should include upcoming contest dates and scheduled community performances, plus the names of interested people for performance outlets. If you want to get your local Lions Club to buy a marimba, this file should be full of community names and meeting dates.

Help-Line: Keep the addresses and phone numbers of percussionists you can trust for quick and reliable information. Also, don't be afraid to call a local university percussion teacher for advice. This list should include local music dealers and percussion repair shops as well.

Manufacturers and Publishers: Some directors lump manufacturers and publishers together, listing them alphabetically. Others prefer two separate files, one for each category.

Reference Guides

College Percussion Texts: One of the most important references you own is the percussion text you used in college, because it represents your personal, first-hand experience with percussion. Another good reference guide is *Teaching Total Percussion* (Parker Publishing Company) by Kenneth Mueller. It tells how to develop curriculum, pedagogy, and musicianship, and answers everyday organizational problems; but it is difficult to find. Two good general methods are F. Michael Combs' *The Percussion Manual* (Wadsworth Publishing Company) and *Percussion in the School Music Program* by Al Payson and Jack McKenzie (Payson Percussion Products). These books are good general coverage guides which include chapters on specific areas of percussion, lists of ensembles, manufacturers, and instrument recommendations.

Solo and Ensemble Literature for Percussion: The most complete listing of all published percussion solos and ensembles is printed by the Percussive Arts Society. The solo works are grouped by instrument and the ensemble information includes the number of players needed. This listing is being updated and is scheduled to be ready by the fall of 1982.

Percussive Arts Society: All directors should belong to the Percussive Arts Society, because it offers a wealth of percussion information and supports percussion pedagogy and performance throughout the world. The organization publishes six issues per year of magazines which include valuable articles, up-to-date products, fix-it guides, ensemble programs (including junior and senior high school level material), plus detailed inforamtion about areas of percussion. The cost of joining is $10.00.

Percussion Dictionary: I recommend Morris Lang and Larry Spivack's *Dictionary of Percussion Terms* (Lang Percussion Company). It is a small, concise, and useful dictionary for orchestral literature.

Composer Biography: A dictionary that includes band and contemporary composers is a must for every school. The revised edition of *Band Music Notes* by Norman Smith and Albert Stoutamire (Kjos West) gives program note material, and the publisher has granted readers permission to use the information on their printed programs. I suggest libraries purchase dictionaries like Baker's *Biographical Dictionary of Musicians,* sixth edition, by Nicolas Slonimsky (Schirmer Books) and the *Dictionary of Contemporary Music* by John Vinton, editor (E.P. Dutton and Company).

The Percussion Anthology (The Instrumentalist Company): This volume is a collection of excellent articles which have been selected from 31 years of material published in *The Instrumentalist.* It is a necessary supplement to a director's library because the articles focus on the practical side of public school percussion teaching and playing.

Having a percussion resource file and good reference guides is an organized and flexible way to keep information at hand. They are helpful and time-saving for directors who are busy with the daily workings of a teacher's life. ■

October, 1982

Timpani Fundamentals: Rolls

Bill Wiggins

The timpani roll has two basic functions in an ensemble: it supplies tonal support and adds to dramatic effects. The sustained sound of a timpani offers a tonal cushion over which layers of musical texture can be added. The instrument can reinforce the harmony as well as add a distinct color and deep resonance to the music.

The dramatic effect of a timpani roll is well known. Anyone who has ever attended a stage show or watched a televised awards presentation has heard the familiar sequence: Timpani: sforzando...diminuendo... pianissimo..."And now ladies and gentlemen..." This is one of the most over-used effects around, of course; but it does get your attention. Reversing the dynamics for a piano to forte effect is also commonly used. There are more subtle occasions for dramatic timpani rolls. For example, in the fourth movement of Tchaikovsky's Symphony No. 4 at the Tempo I, the timpani provides a transition into the coda. And finally there is the ubiquitous big ending – bells up, trumpets ablaze, drums rolling – when the effect is enhanced by a well-executed timpani roll.

Unlike the snare drum with its staccato sound that requires frequent stick attacks to give the illusion of a sustained tone, the timpani sound decays more slowly, requiring fewer contacts in the same time span to produce a sustained effect. It is common for many beginners to damage the instrument's tone quality and pitch. The strokes must be controlled – allowing the drum to ring between each blow – to produce a beautiful legato sound with undistorted pitch. Students should be taught that "speed kills."

Several factors influence the speed of the roll. Head tension is an important consideration because producing a sustained sound on a slack head requires less speed than on a tight one. Teach beginning students to listen to the drum's tone when they are rolling and to adjust the head tension and roll speed to achieve the most satisfying sound. Volume and speed do not go hand in hand on the timpani. The easiest way for a player to get more volume is to move the hands at a slower rate while increasing the stroke size. Raise the hands slightly to allow for greater stick travel and move the sticks in a broad arc at an angle perpendicular to the head's surface. The frenetic "hit it as hard as you can" approach does not produce a beautiful sound.

Tempo is also important in determining the roll's speed, especially in rhythmic passages where rolls are mixed with single strokes. At faster tempos fewer strokes should be used; and for slower tempos more strokes should be added, with their spacing kept constant. Players should avoid crowding strokes together to force a roll to end on a certain hand. In fact, subtracting a stroke usually produces a more musical effect.

It is often necessary for the player to calculate an exact rhythm to play in a quasi-rudimental fashion, providing the roll with an underlying rhythmic foundation. This consideration is not always borne out in practice. I have seen too many accomplished snare drummers disregard rhythmic concerns when playing rolls on timpani. This may be partly due to vague notation. For example, the commonly used tremolo sign, tr~~ , is not specific; it only suggests rapid motion. The other roll indication, , can be misinterpreted as an abbreviation for . Though this figure is rhythmic, it may not result in the most desirable sound. For the timpanist these symbols simply indicate a sustained sound without a specific pulse.

My experience shows that a triple subdivision of the pulse is often satisfactory for varying lengths of rolls at different tempos. Substitution of for in lengthy sustained passages opens up the instrument's sound by allowing more time for the drum to ring between blows. This modification, combined with a relaxed grip, produces a much freer sound. For playing on a head with lower tension and/or soft volume, I recommend . (Grip and stick choice – lengthy topics in themselves – have a significant effect on the sound of the roll.)

Rolling From Drum to Drum

Rolls that pass from drum to drum, either ending with a single stroke or continuing on in an unbroken fashion, present a special problem for players at all levels. The most desirable sound for a continuous passing roll, unless otherwise indicated, is one where no bump is heard at the moment of the pass, only a pitch change. To develop this skill I have found it helpful to practice rolls using an asymmetrical rhythmic base, such as a group of five notes: . The rhythm should be practiced slowly at first, beginning with the right hand on the right hand drum. A sixth stroke with the left hand moves the pattern to the left drum. As smoothness and grace are achieved, the tempo is increased. The same procedure develops the opposite maneuver from left to right, by reversing the sticking. When the two patterns are combined, they produce an unbroken passing roll.

Gripping the Mallet

A player's grip will affect the sound of both the roll and a single stroke. Though most performers prefer a thumbs-up position, the thumb's angle is less important than finger placement. All the fingers should contact the stick for maximum control. There should be minimal tension at the fulcrum, with tension distributed to the third and fourth fingers; and the butt of the stick should not project beyond the heel of the palm for proper leverage. Thus, the stick is held with the hand, not the fingers alone.

The stick's movement should come from a twisting forearm/wrist motion, with a pronounced lift following each stroke. Using the fingers should be delayed until a comfortable forearm/wrist stroke is developed. This motion, combined with the player's relaxed upper body, arms, and shoulders, will greatly enhance the timpani's overall sound.

The condition of the timpani head and the type of sticks used also affect the timpani's sound. A poorly maintained head which is dirty, nicked, dented, or out of tune will never produce the resonance that is important for a beautiful timpani sound, much less be in tune with any other instrument.

The choice of sticks – hard, medium, or soft – will influence the sound. As a general rule I feel that large, fluffy sticks should be avoided for normal playing because they tend to muffle the sound, especially when rolling. The student should avoid relying on soft sticks to produce a smooth roll, and concentrate on even strokes and controlled speed to produce a sustained tone. Harder sticks are the better choice in passages where articulated rhythms are mixed with sustained tones. The player can then use sticks with firmer heads for clarity and concentrate on relaxing his hands to produce a smooth sounding roll. Naturally, if the passage is entirely rhythmic or entirely legato, sticks appropriate for those characteristics should be used.

Many schools of thought exist regarding the best approach to timpani playing. Each is backed by professionals who have years of playing experience. The techniques I have described come from my teaching and performing background; however, I have no doubt these ideas will continue to evolve. Constant self-awareness and an openness to new concepts are essential to anyone who wishes to develop musically. ■

October, 1982

I Feel It!

Tim Lautzenheiser

"Drums, shut up. How can I explain this drill to the band when you are pounding on those things?"

Sound familiar? Have you ever said (yelled) it?

What is one supposed to do with the drum section when trying to teach the band the drill routines?

If you keep them with the band they get bored and just waste time.

If you send them to the band room they will not be available when you're ready to add them (not to mention what might happen there without some supervision).

If you send them to another part of the rehearsal field to practice, the sound bleeds over so badly that no one can hear.

If you don't let them do anything, you are losing valuable rehearsal time for them and, inevitably, it's the percussion parts that need the work.

There may not be any perfect solution, but perhaps this story will give you part of the answer.

Scene I

As a percussionist in both high school and college, I found that most of my marching band experience was spent not playing. There are still vivid memories of trying to practice my part quietly on the edge of the drum head, only to be quickly reminded of my bad manners and told "your chance will come." Of course when the spotlight did go on, none of us could come close to executing the unrehearsed parts; therefore another lecture followed concerning the irresponsibility and lack of musicianship of the drum section. It was a test of my patience and reasoning. I often wondered how any band director could be so insensitive.

Scene II

The reality of the band directing world arrived as 150 eager young college students gathered before me to learn the first show of the season. It wasn't until the second day of band camp that I grabbed my trusty bullhorn and, in the style of any respected leader, blurted out that profound phrase: "Drummers! Will you *please* put those sticks away and act like musicians." It was one of those times when I would have given anything if everyone had been momentarily deaf. I'll never forget those stares of amazement from the percussion section; it was as if their best friend had ended a long and endearing relationship.

Scene III

We were in the final stages of rehearsal and in the middle of some very intense drill changes. In the background the drums were attempting to practice their parts "softly," as I had instructed them. I recognized the paradox of asking the section to "punch-kick-accent-lift-pop" and then telling them to practice softly. A fine drummer feels the part; but the proper physical action and reaction can only be sensed when rehearsed at performance volume. It was absurd; still, I had tested every feasible solution and could find nothing that worked.

After three unsuccessful attempts to shout instructions to the woodwinds, I ran back to the drums, planted myself firmly in front of them, assumed my famous band director glare, and accidentally blundered onto a suggestion that not only solved the problem, but had far-reaching effects:

"If you can't play quietly on those drums, then I suggest you pound out the parts on each other."

I did a smart about-face and headed back to the band. We went on with rehearsal and the glorious silence served to expedite all the problem solving. After an hour of unusually quiet environment, I called for the percussion section to join us. I expected a musical wreck or one of the traditional "we'll show you" boycotts; but it was the surprise of a lifetime. They played better than ever before.

Following the rehearsal the section headed in my direction. Instead of the protests that I was certain were coming, they thanked me for the great suggestion and enthusiastically promised bigger and better things for the future with this new sure-fire method.

Finale

It wasn't until the next day during a private lesson that the explanation became clear. This student told me that when the section members stood in a circle and played on each other's backs, they felt how the person behind them was interpreting the part – which accents received the most attention, when a player leaned on a phrase, etc.

It's not often one can kill two birds with one stone – solve a noise level problem and strengthen a section.

I guarantee the formula if you will sell the players. You must get them past wanting to do bodily injury to one another before you'll see the improvement. Believe me, it's well worth those first few giggles of astonished embarrassment.

Epilogue

I have used this same rehearsal idea when wind instrument players are making rhythmic errors. Rather than tiring embouchures, ask the players to sing the passage while tapping it out on the shoulder of their neighbor. The results will shock you. ■

November, 1982

Teaching the Vibraphone

Mario A. Gaetano

The vibraphone, an instrument similar to the xylophone and marimba, requires special playing skills because of its damper pedal. When purchasing a vibraphone for school use, music directors should look for a three octave instrument with wide aluminum alloy bars. Other features to consider are a variable-speed motor, a swivel foot pedal, a damper bar with adjustable tension, a fiber case, and a drop cover; portable instruments are the most convenient.

Vibraphone mallets are different from those used on the marimba or xylophone. It's best to purchase sets of four mallets at one time. They should be made of nylon cord or thin yarn, wrapped tightly around a hard rubber core with either rattan or fiber glass shafts. I recommend fiber glass styles for beginners because they are flexible, balanced, and will not warp. Never use plastic, brass, or hard rubber mallets because they may dent the vibraphone's bars. Also, avoid using marimba mallets. They are made from coarse natural yarn which is loosely wrapped and has a tendency to produce too much contact sound on metal bars. Leading mallet instrument manufacturers will often have an excellent line of mallets to choose from.

The vibist should develop technical facility with four mallets from the start, because the majority of solo pieces for vibraphone are unaccompanied and call for four mallets. Also, the multi-voice sonorities in contemporary concert band literature and the comping chord figures in jazz charts require four-mallet technique.

Four-Mallet Grips

I recommend two grip styles for four-mallet playing. (They are not necessarily the same grips used on the marimba and other mallet instruments.) The first is called a cross-stick grip. The inner mallet shaft crosses over the outer one, and the thumb and the first finger are placed between the mallets to spread them open. The outer mallet comes in contact with the first joint of the first finger while the inner mallet touches the thumb at the base of the thumb nail. The third and fourth fingers hold the mallets in the palm of the hand where they cross and are used to bring the mallets together. Thus, two opposing forces are at work: the thumb and first finger move in one direction and the third and fourth fingers go in another. The instrument is played with palms facing down. This cross-stick grip is popular because it is easy to use and gets students playing in a relatively short time.

Cross-stick grip

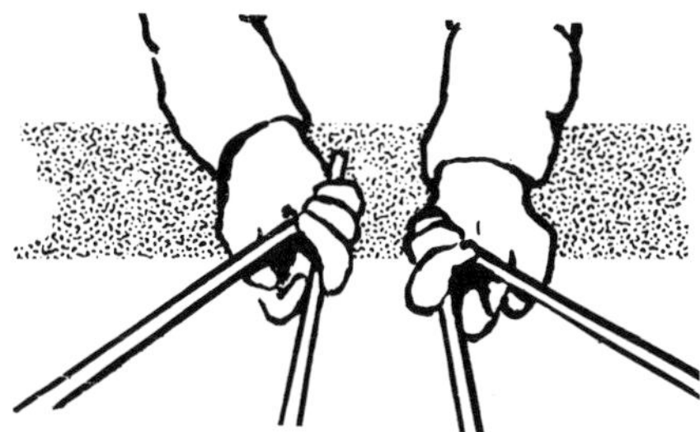

The Burton grip is also a cross-stick grip; however, this playing style requires the outer mallets to cross over the inner ones. The third and fourth fingers are used along with the thumb and first finger in spreading the mallets open, and the second finger acts to stabilize the outer mallet. This grip requires more dexterity than the first cross-over style, but it offers an advantage when playing two-mallet passages because the unused mallet is held securely with no excess movement. Again, the palms are held face down for playing. The mallets of the right hand usually remain open at a 90 degree angle so the outer mallet attacks the bars straight up and down, rotating over the inner mallet. The grip seems to work best in playing jazz vibes where two-mallet passages frequently occur in improvised solos.

Burton grip

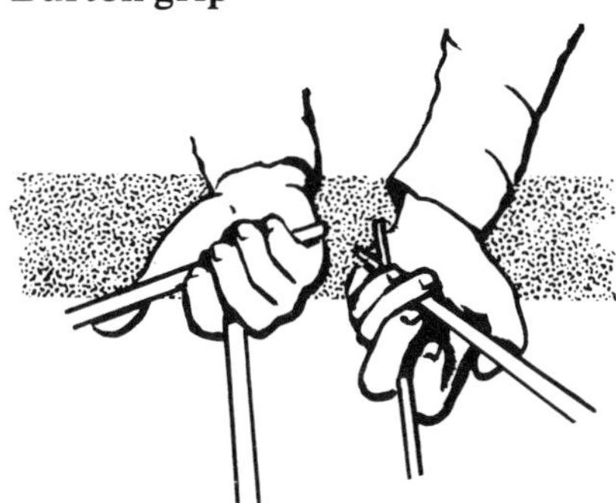

The following technical exercises are divided into two large categories; they represent only a sampling of the beginning exercises that are available for students. The first set can be used to develop technique with any mallet instrument; the vibist doesn't need to worry about using the damper pedal. The second set of exercises is designed for the vibist to help develop pedaling and dampening skills.

The exercises should be practiced at a slow tempo that is gradually increased, but never to a point where control is lost. The student should get into the habit of moving immediately from one playing position to the next no matter how slow the tempo. The majority of playing movement should come from the wrists while the arms are relaxed. The mallets should bounce off the bars with the effect of drawing the tone out of the instrument. When playing accidentals strike the edge or the center of the bar, and avoid the bars' nodal points. Rolls should not be used with any of these exercises.

The mallets are traditionally numbered in this manner:

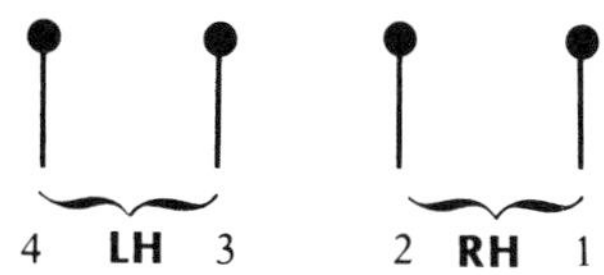

Exercises for Xylophone, Marimba, and Vibraphone

Strike the bars with all four mallets at once to produce a uniform attack, and play these exercises in all major and minor keys.

Exercise 1

Exercise 2

Exercise 3

Exercise 4
Play ascending and descending

Exercise 5
Play ascending and descending

Practice the following exercises to develop independent sticking. Again, play the exercises in all major and minor keys.

Exercise 6

Exercise 7

Exercise 8

Exercise 9

Dampening Techniques for Vibraphone

Practice dampening by following the arrows, ↑ ↓, which represent the direction of the pedal. Again, play in all major and minor keys.

Exercise 1

Exercise 2

Exercise 3

Exercise 4

Exercise 5

Exercise 6

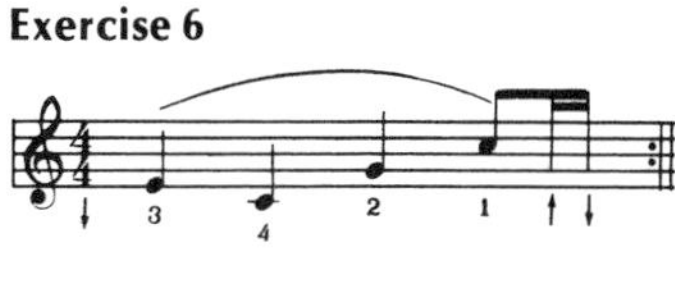

Exercise 7

To dampen the vibraphone using mallets, practice the following exercises with the pedal down. A mallet in one hand dampens the notes marked with an "x," while the other plays the exercise. The action between the two hands should occur simultaneously. Try to dampen without creating any additional sounds. Practice these exercises first with the left hand doing the dampening, then the right; use all major and minor keys, in ascending and descending motion.

Exercise 9

Exercise 10

Pedaling Demarcations

Composers use a variety of methods to notate pedaling. The most popular style, as in this excerpt from *Suite for Solo Vibraphone* by Alexander Lepak (Windsor), consists of a line below the notes to be pedaled.

Often a composer uses *Ped.* to indicate when the pedal is down and an asterisk to show when it is up, as in this example from *Five Episodes* by Michael Smolanoff (Seesaw).

Another method involves using an asterisk followed by a dotted line. The asterisk denotes the pedal down until the dotted line ends. This excerpt from *Catapault* by Gary Burton (Creative Music) shows this type of notation.

Chord Comping

In a jazz ensemble the vibraphone takes on a role similar to that of the guitar or piano in comping chord figures. The vibist can create rich harmonies by adding notes to basic chords. Generally, in major triads, players can add the 6th, 7th, 9th, or raised 11th to the chord. In minor triads, the 7th, 9th, or natural 11th may be added. Dominant seventh chords can be altered by adding the 9th, raised 11th, or 13th. When the vibist adds these color tones to chords, he has to delete other notes to accommodate his four mallets. As a general rule he can remove either the root or fifth from a chord. Also, notes are never doubled — it wastes the use of a mallet.

A simple repeating rhythmic pattern, which requires little use of the pedal (except for slow ballads), can be used to comp chord figures. The player should experiment with rhythmic patterns, fitting them to the style of the arrangement and the rest of the rhythm section as well. Here is an example of a typical blues progression.

Recommended Method Books

Vibes for Beginners, Phil Kraus (Adler Inc.).

Jazz Phrasing for Mallets, John Rae (Adler Inc.).

Developing the School Jazz Ensemble (Vibes), John LaPorta (Berklee Press).

Play Vibes, Julius Wechter (Adler, Inc.).

Four Mallet Studies, Gary Burton (Creative Music).

The Vibes Players Method, Tom Brown (Kendor Music).

Introduction to Jazz Vibes, Gary Burton (Creative Music).

Practical Improvisations, Bob Tilles (Belwin-Mills).

Vibraphone Technique, David Friedman (Berklee Press).

Solo Collections

Solos for the Vibraphone Player, Ian Finkel (G. Schirmer Inc.).

Solo, Gary Burton (Creative Music).

Mallets in Mind, Tom Brown (Kendor Music). ■

an interview with

Peter Erskine

Sue Bradle

Peter Erskine, at 28, has known for 22 years that he wanted to be a jazz drummer. He began playing when he was four and had made up his mind by the time he was six. His single-mindedness and talent brought him to the attention of such well-known musicians as Stan Kenton, Maynard Ferguson, and the members of "Weather Report;" and his continued success has gained a place for him among today's top jazz drummers.

You started playing drums at a pretty early age.

Yes, I was four years old. My dad is a psychiatrist, but he had played bass, so he had an interest in helping me musically. I always wanted to be a jazz musician. I can also remember always wanting more drums. I lived near Atlantic City, New Jersey, and as a kid I remember wanting to have drums that stretched from Atlantic Avenue to the Boardwalk – that's about three city blocks.

I know you started going to the Stan Kenton Summer Jazz Clinics when you were young. How did that come about?

My mom got me into the camp. My drum teacher had mentioned to her that it was too bad I wasn't older because I could go to this great new summer jazz clinic. She decided to give it a try anyway, telegrammed the camp, and they accepted me; but when I got there they didn't want to let me stay. I had just turned 7 and their policy was not to take students under 14. I got a chance to play for Stan and the others in the clinic, and they let us stay, maybe because my parents and I had come all the way from New Jersey to Indiana. In any case this started an annual trip for the family. For a week every summer we packed up and traveled to one of the jazz camps.

Did you learn a lot from the clinics?

Sure, I was young and impressionable, and getting to be around Kenton's whole band and people like Alan Dawson, it's more than inspiring. It was incredible.

I'm really thankful my parents let me be a part of that. They still gave me time to play baseball, but I was a shabby baseball player. I really just wanted to be a jazz musician.

It must have been a real kick for you to then be asked to play in Kenton's band when you were 18.

When he called me, it was out of the blue. I was in college and playing legit music as well as jazz, but I decided to go with Stan's band.

You started playing drums at a pretty early age.

Yes, I was four years old. My dad is a psychiatrist, but he had played bass, so he had an interest in helping me musically. I always wanted to be a jazz musician. I can also remember always wanting more drums. I lived near Atlantic City, New Jersey, and as a kid I remember wanting to have drums that stretched from Atlantic Avenue to the Boardwalk – that's about three city blocks.

I know you started going to the Stan Kenton Summer Jazz Clinics when you were young. How did that come about?

My mom got me into the camp. My drum teacher had mentioned to her that it was too bad I wasn't older because I could go to this great new summer jazz clinic. She decided to give it a try anyway, telegrammed the camp, and they accepted me; but when I got there they didn't want to let me stay. I had just turned 7 and their policy was not to take students under 14. I got a
learning how to relax when I play, which affects my touch on the instrument. I'm getting a better sound out of the instrument

and not having to work quite so hard. You know, you should only have to hit or blow into an instrument so hard. If you do this too much, then I think it becomes self-defeating.

I used to like playing with a lot of energy and really working out, but you've got to balance that kind of playing with playing an instrument intelligently. It's something you learn as you establish more rapport with your instrument over the years.

I've also learned a lot from Zawinul (Josef Zawinul, keyboardist in "Weather Report") about how to move when I play. I used to hunch my shoulders when I played, which was a dead give-away for tension, and I wasn't aware of it. When Zawinul heard something that didn't sound right, he would look over, see my shoulders, and he knew I was tensed up.

Once he told me about it, I started looking in the mirror and then I could see what I looked like. I began taking advantage of gravity in my playing. The natural laws apply to everything in playing whether it's on a trumpet or a snare drum. I began to rely less on my strength as my calling card in drumming and more on my musicality, making the music I was playing more interesting.

How did your thinking change?

It's like learning a language. As your vocabulary grows, you learn subtleties and nuances and you work with space and delivery of your words – you don't have to scream the same thing over and over. That's not the greatest analogy, but learning to play more musically is along those same lines. You choose your notes more intelligently.

A good word to young musicians is that you should avoid playing corny music. Sometimes I'll hear musical quotes that are clever, but if someone plays "Old McDonald Has a Farm" in the middle of a piece, that's dumb. That's a waste of notes.

So you shouldn't always think that if a musical phrase worked for another drummer, it will work for you.

Definitely. We all go through a period of heavy influence, and that's important, it's natural and good, as long as a player reminds himself every now and then that he is still growing. You only want to sound like somebody else in order to figure out how they got the phrase that they did, and then you should move on.

You said this happened to you when you were listening to Max Roach.

Yes, my teacher gave me some Max Roach and Buddy Rich albums. Buddy was an influence, too, but I always felt a little more kinship with the bebop generation, with drummers Art Blakey, Max Roach, and Alvin Jones.

It is really important to listen to early drummers and get acquainted with the history of the music you are playing. Not only should you know the history of the music but you should also know the musical concepts behind the styles. Here's what I mean: I've heard a lot of sax sections in high school bands that sound terrible. They're lousy. They have no concept of phrasing, and they haven't heard how lead altos should sound or how sax sections should swing. But who can blame them if they haven't heard it?

Listening is important because by hearing and imitating you can then go beyond. Otherwise, you'll be trying to make up years of time in your own exploration. We're really very fortunate because we have the availability of so much music, both contemporary and historical. It sounds corny, but kings had to listen to whatever band they had in the castle, but we can throw anything on the record player.

Who should jazz musicians be listening to?

Listen to the whole spectrum of the history. Go back before swing drumming, and even before Gene Krupa. Then when you play you know where what you are playing originated.

Drummers should especially listen to bebop drummers. This playing is the foundation for most of the modern music today that has anything to do with jazz. You just can't pick up with Steve Gadd, Jackie DeJohnette, and Bill Cobb. These are exciting and important drummers, but you've also got to go back and listen to the people they were listening to in order to create their style.

I know you attended Interlochen and Indiana University, so you've been mixing classical and jazz playing in your career. Has knowing classical playing techniques helped your drumming in any way?

As a matter of fact, on Jaco's (Jaco Pastorius, bass player with "Weather Report") new album we play an excerpt from Alan Hovaness' Second Symphony, "Mysterious Mountain." I'm playing timpani and most of the musicians on that cut are from the Los Angeles Philharmonic. It was fun to get a chance to do the kind of playing again that I had done in college.

Having a kind of classical sensibility has helped my playing without going too far and getting too schooled or trained or rigid. It helps in your touch on the instrument, and just the knowledge of the music helps too. If you know Stravinsky or Varese, then you know what it's like to really wail.

You've studied with a lot of people

throughout your career. Is there anything they told you that you still remember today and has made a different in your playing?

It's funny, some of the things you remember aren't so much about playing, but more about a philosophy of playing. I do remember one thing that George Gaber told me. He said never be afraid to turn down a gig. Music is vital and important, but also leave enough time for growth in other areas of your life. If you are spending eight hours a day practicing, you may not be learning much. I remember seeing people in college who would spend hours in the practice rooms, and their playing wouldn't improve that much. Quality rather than quantity is important — you could spend one hour of time practicing intelligently, then go do something else, and you'll be better off for it.

Do you do any special practicing now?

No, but I still try to watch my hands. My technique gets a little sloppy sometimes, then I have some drumming exercises I work on — just basic things to keep the fingers, wrists, and arms fairly limber. I always work at not having any part of my body lock up, to play as relaxed as I can.

Any advice for our readers on how they can become better musicians?

I've already made the points about quality, practice versus quantity practice and listening to all kinds of music; in addition you should also have fun when you play. At the same time, if it really means something to you, go all the way with your music. Even if you're not going to become a professional musician, give it all you've got, because it's so gratifying when you put that much into it.■

Peter Erskine began his professional career as a jazz drummer at the age of 14. He studied with Alan Dawson, Ed Soph, Billy Dorn, and George Gaber, attended the Interlochen Arts Academy and began his studies at Indiana University.

Erskine became a member of "Weather Report," a top jazz group, which in the '70s had honors from magazines like *down beat, Record World, Cash Box,* Japan's *Swing Journal,* and Europe's *Jazz Forum.* He plays on their Grammy Award winning album, *8:30.*

Living in New York City since March, Erskine spends most of his playing time with the groups "Steps" and "The Word of Mouth Band." His other professional time is devoted to representing Yamaha as a clinician, writing music and recording. Some of his own tunes will be featured on the album, *Peter Erskine.* It was recorded live and is scheduled to be released in January 1983.

Discography

With Stan Kenton —
Kenton Plays Chicago
Fire, Fury, and Fun
National Anthems of the World
7.5 on the Richter Scale
Birthday in Britain

With Maynard Ferguson —
Conquistador
New Vintage
Carnival

With "Weather Report" —
Mr. Gone
8:30
Night Passage
Weather Report

With Various Artists —
Bobby Hutcherson — *Un Poco Loco*
George Cables — *Cables Vision*
Joe Farrell — *Sonic Text*
Joni Mitchell — *Mingus*
Michel Clombier — *Michel Clombier*
Michael Maineri — *Wanderlust*

His Own Album (scheduled for a January 1983 release) —
Peter Erskine

New Percussion Solos and Methods

Don R. Baker

Snare Drum

False Images (Kendor) by Eric J. White was the winner of the 1980 Percussive Arts Society composition contest. This challenging snare drum solo uses different playing locations, brushes, rim shots, and muffling techniques. One spot in the music calls for double-stick rim shots, yet at the same time, a stir with a brush – three hands must be required. Polyrhythms abound, so beware.

Drum Method, Modern Rudimental Swing Solos for the Advanced Drummer, Wrist and Finger Stroke Control for the Advanced Drummer, The Junior Drummer, and *The Drummer on Parade* (Ludwig) by Charlie Wilcoxon are reprints of the composer's books now under a new publisher. Because of the differences in the type, a player can easily see the editing by Robert Matson in two of the works. Although *The Drummer on Parade* is outdated, the *Drum Method* and *Junior Drummer* combine to add a drum set/marching swing style to the snare drum pedagogy. *Wrist and Finger Stroke Control,* a useful method, is still a favorite of many teachers.

Power Plus (Southern) by Donald K. Gilbert is a collection of advanced snare drum solos that contain unusual meter signatures. Though the author suggests that players make modifications in dynamics, these changes may be needed only in a few solos to enhance the musical value of the work. There is a short commentary on important points or problems for each solo. This collection will be useful for high school or college level players.

Multiple Percussion

Energy Suite (Barnhouse) by Jared Spears is in three movements. The first requires a suspended cymbal, snare drum, and three tom-toms; the second, a mallet/keyboard instrument; and the third, a snare drum and three tom-toms. This moderately simple yet effective piece is well designed for the young and intermediate player. I recommend it for recitals or contests.

Monolog No. 11 (Carl Gehrmans Musikförlag, available through Boosey & Hawkes) by Erland van Koch is a multiple percussion solo using four mallet/keyboard instruments, four timpani, six skin-covered instruments, and four metal ones. The theme and variations are introduced by the timpani followed by a statement from a four mallet marimba section. The work is moderately difficult and playable by high school or college percussionists.

Rag Music (Alphonse Leduc) by Eugene Bozza is a multiple percussion solo with piano accompaniment using five timpani, four mallet/keyboard instruments, seven skin-covered, four metal, and seven wood instruments. The solo is written in the typical Paris Conservatory of Music style with the score order of timpani, mallets, and percussion, creating notation that is spread out and often difficult to read. There are some difficult ensemble problems between piano and percussion along with meter changes in the score. The mallet part requires four mallet technique and good two mallet dexterity; two cadenzas are written out. This work would serve as a college jury exam or recital solo piece.

Two Pictures for Solo Percussion and Orchestra (Wimbledon) by Phillip Lambro is a two movement concerto that was written at the request of Saul Goodman. Another version of this work is available for solo percussionist and two pianos by the same publisher. It is a difficult work requiring a vast array of percussion instruments: snare drum, four timpani, three piccolo timpani, Peking gong, two octave crotales, three suspended cymbals, field drum, wood block, piccolo snare drum, two sets of brass wind chimes, three tuned toms, and cymbal tree. There is no suggested set-up. The mallet changes are difficult and the 28" timpani must have a range of a seventh. The timpani part, which has many pedal changes, is often interspersed with the sounds of other melodic instruments. The orchestra edition requires celesta, harp, and piano. However, the generally thin scoring creates more of a texture than it does a melodic or contrapuntal line. Obviously the two piano version is similar; but I feel it loses, to some extent, the timbral quality and angularity that the orchestral scoring offers. The two piano set comes with a solo percussion part and two piano scores, and the music is clear to read. This is a challenging and mature work for percussion and should be considered only by advanced college percussionists or professionals.

Drum Set

Advanced Techniques for the Modern Drummer Vol. II (Chapin) by Jim Chapin is truly a work of art. Though the price is high ($50) the well designed mechanical aspects offered by this large ring-binder text are remarkable: windowed exercises, variable accent pages, and overlays that can be positioned in four directions. The detailed text includes such topics as polyrhythms, independence, warm-ups, listening, and many playing styles (jazz, rock, samba, bossa nova, etc.). This book is not for the average player, but for the serious, dedicated student who wishes to develop independence on the drum set. Though the amount of material is enormous and may be overwhelming to the young percussionist, advanced students should use it as a guide and teachers can make use of the parts that pertain to their students' individual needs.

Two Sketches (Kendor) by Eric J. White is the winner of the 1980 Percussive Arts Society composition contest. The drum set solo requires a regular four-piece set plus cowbell. The work is divided into two movements. The first is in a fast swinging $\frac{4}{4}$ with motivic ideas throughout, lots of syncopation, and three beats played against four. The second movement is a funk style solo in $\frac{7}{4}$ with an open solo ad lib section. The first movement has a better design and is rhythmically more exciting than the second. This piece is worth preparing by the advanced high school or college student who has good command of independence and reading ability on drum set.

Mallet Keyboard

Contemporary Mallet Duets (Permus) by Murray Houllif is a collection of seven duets for the advanced performer. Any three octave F-F mallet instrument will work, however, no pedaling is marked for vibraphone. The composer has used several contemporary writing styles in these short but challenging works that require two and four mallets. The music is both rhythmically and melodically interesting, and I find the selections worth playing.

Musical Marimba Solos (Permus) by William Schinstine is written for a four octave marimba and played with two or four mallets. Technical challenges, however, are more of a concern on the two mallet solos than on the ones using four mallets. These generally tonal works vary in style from traditional to contemporary. They fill a need for the high school and early college student in that they suit the instrument well and are slightly longer than the typical short solos often found in collections. If the director selects the rest of the publisher's Complete Series, the student will have an excellent array of styles and literature for the two primary mallet instruments, the marimba and the vibraphone.

Contemporary Solos for Vibraphone and Marimba (Belwin-Mills) by Gitta Steiner are, for the most part, short and difficult works. Some selections, however, are long enough for contest and student recitals, and a few are playable by high school students. The music is rich in contemporary harmonic color and requires a C-C marimba, an F-F vibraphone, and four mallet playing. Pedaling indications are not marked.

Estudio No. 5 and *Estudio No. 6 para Marimba* (Permus) by Murray Houllif are four mallet solos for the advanced marimbist. *No. 5* offers the greater challenge in mallet independence, yet *No. 6* requires the easy execution of one-handed rolls. Both have good musical development and clear notation. If you like the well-known Musser *Etudes* then *Estudio No. 5* should be added to your repertoire.

Fantasia (Southern) by Michael Lang is a moderately difficult marimba duet for the high school or college student. The themes and rhythms are of limited interest in this short work. Two mallets are required.

Aaron and *Le Mammouth Débonnaire* (Alphonse Leduc) by Francois Dupin are short xylophone works with piano accompaniment. Both pieces require only two mallets and are easy to moderate in their technical demands. However, playing with the piano will offer a greater ensemble challenge to the xylophonist.

Mist (Kendor) by Murray Houllif is a short programmatic work for the three octave vibraphone. The music requires easy to moderate four mallet techniques, and the pedaling indications are clear. The repetitious nature of this work makes playing it easier for the performer.

Methode Rapide pour Xylophone — Deuxième Cahier-Etudes Complementaires (Alphonse Leduc) by Francois Dupin is a collection of complementary studies for Dupin's *Rapid Tutor, Book I.* There are only 14 etudes and five are transcriptions designed for the moderately advanced two mallet player. The text is in French, English, German, and Spanish. The etudes would be useful as supplemental material to other method books.

New Works for New Times (Kendor) by Bill Molenhof is a collection of six difficult solos for the vibraphone. The pieces require four mallets, polyrhythmic reading, improvisation, and a good understanding of contemporary jazz style. Some of the works are recorded on the album *Beach Street Years*; this book I recommend only for the advanced jazz vibist.

William J. Schinstine has added two more books containing Christmas tunes to our literature: *Carols and Drums* and *Ten Christmas Carols for Two Marimbas* (Kendor). The first is written in an easy playing level for snare drum and a melody instrument. It is a special collection, the only one of its kind, and should be of interest to music educators. *Ten Christmas Carols* comes with two scores and is written for two marimbas (either four octave or four-and-a-third octave instruments). Two mallet playing is required, but some four mallet work is used for dance rhythms and swing. The music is scored with typical pop arranging techniques, and these pieces range from moderate to advanced in their ability requirements.

Music for Mallet Percussion Ensemble (Ludwig) is a collection of three works arranged by James Moore and David Eyler for any combination of mallet percussion instruments or other sonorities such as flute, bass, etc. They are easy works and excellent for a beginning ensemble. The collection, which comes with a score and parts, is easy to read.

Timpani

Raga No. 1 (Wimbledon) by William Cahn is a timpani solo for four drums. Though tuned to G, B♭, C♭, and G, the 29" (28") drum must be able to reach the range of a sixth as it glissandos to other pitches. Cahn uses a type of bongo rim shot on the timpani that I avoid because it can damage the instrument's rim and collar. The piece is effective rhythmically and has a South Indian improvisational sound. The printing is clear, but the explanatory notes could be rearranged and more performance notes would be helpful. Also the music has no double bar at the end. This is a moderately difficult solo that is worth trying.

Le Roi Igor (Alphonse Leduc) by Francois Dupin is a short, slow timpani solo for three timpani and piano. There are no tuning changes and musical interest lies mostly in the rhythm. The work is playable by a high school student and the piano part is of moderate difficulty.

The Artiste Sonata (No. 6) (Kendor) by William J. Schinstine is written for four pedal timpani and is a difficult solo. The three movements offer a wide variety of musical interest: the first requires independence and timbral playing; the second is slow but uses melodic pedal changes; but the third, written in an upbeat jazz style, is too fast for rhythmic clarity with its quick pedal changes. The work is well edited for page turns, cross-sticking, and pedaling.

Additional Material

Percussion for Music Educators, Teaching and Techniques (Jackson Publications) by Douglas Jackson is a book for the prospective music educator who is taking a percussion methods course. Because the text lacks sufficient detail and moves slowly, I do not recommend it for applied students. The material is presented clearly in outline form and the number of musical exercises are more than ample. Additionally, the section on multiple percussion and the repertoire/manufacture listings are also valuable. However, the outdated marching percussion section, a lack of attention of jazz-rock styles in the drum set, and the need for detail concerning some performance techniques are apparent weaknesses in the text. Percussion teachers could fill out these points for their students.

One important area, which methods of this type either omit or discuss insufficiently, is that of percussion related problems such as the selection of students, part organization, equipment breakdown, and solving basic musicianship problems.

All-State Solo Percussion Series (Somers) by Alexander Lepak includes six solos, two each, for the snare drum, timpani, and mallet/keyboard. The snare drum and timpani solos require dynamic control and contain a variety of rhythmic figures. The selections would work well as etude material for auditions or all-state competitions. The timpani etudes call for two pedal timpani, and the music is scored with meter changes. The mallet/keyboard solos are difficult to play and I do not suggest them for auditions at the high school level. Each solo may be purchased separately or as a set.

Solos for Schools (Thompson) by Robert Hughes is a collection of graded solos for Canadian schools. Each work focuses on a technical problem that is particular to the instrument, and accompaniments are playable by a small percussion ensemble. All the snare drum material is rudimental in nature. The grade of difficulty varies from beginning through junior high levels.

Audition Etudes (Meredith) by Garwood Whaley is a graduated collection of 14 etudes each for snare drum, timpani, mallet/keyboard, and multiple percussion. The selections can be used for evaluation, sight-reading, or auditions. The level of the material progresses from beginning studies through high school grade selections; however, tuning changes are not used for timpani and there are no four mallet pieces for the high school player. The multiple percussion etudes are more like typical large ensemble excerpts and would make particularly useful audition material. As usual, Whaley's texts are well conceived and demonstrate an understanding of the needs of modern percussionists. I hope state contest and audition committees look at this collection for use in their festivals. ■

Mallet Keyboard Sight-Reading

Jeff B. Smith

Sight-reading ability can increase productivity, relieve performance tension, and result in more efficient use of practice time. By using the following approach, performing mallet keyboard music at sight can become a reflexive skill that is fast and accurate.

Perception

Students must first be able to recognize notes, key signatures, and two to four beat rhythmic passages at a glance. I suggest flash cards, a commonly-used educational tool that effectively speeds up the ability to recognize symbols. A full set of cards containing key signatures, note values, bass and treble clef notes, and a variety of rhythms can be made easily on ruled 3 x 5 cards with groups of five printed lines darkened to represent the staff.

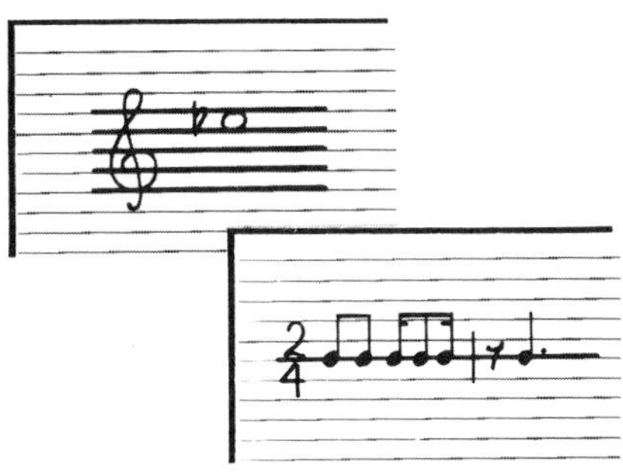

When first using the cards, have students respond with the name of the note, the key signature, or count out the rhythm. Gradually increase the speed at which you flash the cards and add those that have notes on leger lines and longer or more complex rhythm patterns. Although simply having students glance at a piece of music is a possible alternative to using flash cards, teachers will lose the control that cards offer – being able to review material or move on to more difficult concepts.

Interpretation

To help students apply their knowledge I select pitches at random; then, with a metronome providing a steady beat, I say the name of a pitch on one beat and have the student play it on the next. An octave numbering system that designates A=440 as octave 4 is easy to learn and easy to say:

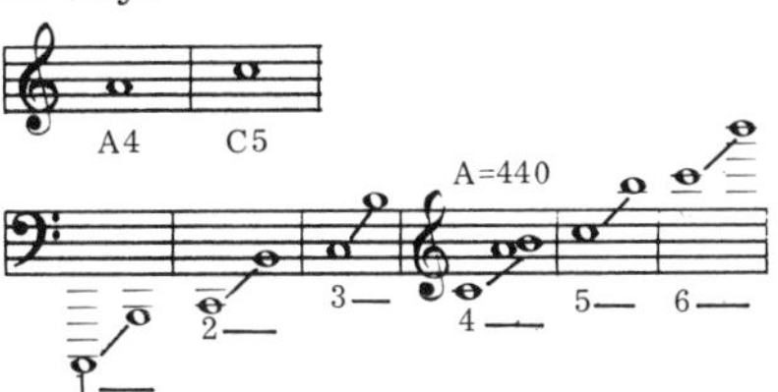

With the teacher saying the names of the notes, the student can keep his eyes on the instrument and become increasingly familiar with the keyboard, learning the distance mallets have to travel between notes.

To help a student develop a mental image of the keyboard, ask him to look over a simple melody and imagine the mallets playing it. The picture in his mind must be clear and formed without hesitation. This kind of practice away from the instrument is as essential as real practice on the instrument, especially in the early stages of learning to sight-read. The student's intentions must be clear before he can carry out musical ideas accurately.

Execution

The percussionist must be able to read the music, see the instrument, and watch the conductor. To do all of this at the same time he must develop peripheral vision. Aiming the eyes about six inches above the keyboard will help. The eyes should not travel from note to note, but rather see the overall playing area, using the black notes as landmarks. Wide peripheral range is much more important than quickly-moving eyes.

Being able to look ahead in the music provides the time to make decisions and preparations regarding sticking, dynamics, accidentals, tempo changes, and key changes. A simple method for training the eyes to look ahead a beat or more is to cover up the music one count before it should be played (again the 3 x 5 card can be used, this time as a moving cover). This technique helps eliminate the tendency to read one note at a time. Reading from flash cards with one or two beat melodic fragments on them is also good practice.

Suggestions for Practice

Begin practicing by using a metronome with the tempo set as slow as necessary to play the music at a constant pace. This will help keep the eyes moving on when you make a mistake, because stopping is much more costly than missing a note. Accuracy can take years of practice to develop, but musical flow and continuous playing can be learned in the early stages on an instrument. Find the most difficult passage, determine a safe speed for playing it, and use that tempo throughout.

Practice on all the keyboard instruments; each has its own

technical demands and special problems. On the marimba and vibraphone the bar widths vary over the range of the keyboard. The vibraphone requires facility with the pedal. The xylophone and glockenspiel have narrow bars requiring accurate mallet placement. When playing the chimes, the music is placed well below the playing area between the performer and the instrument, while the line of vision to the conductor is off to one side. The percussionist must be able to adjust to all these differences between instruments.

Material for Two-Mallet Reading

Many mallet method books can be used for sight-reading; but music for other instruments also works well. Here are some books you can probably borrow from other players or teachers:

335 Selected Melodious Progressive and Technical Studies for French Horn, by Max Pottag and Albert Andraud (Southern).
Forty-Two Studies or Caprices for Violin by Kreutzer (G. Schirmer).
Advanced Method for Flute by H. Voxman (Rubank).
Melodious and Progressive Studies for Flute by Andersen, Garibalki, Koehler, and Terschak, revised by Robert Cavally (Southern).
Arban's Complete Conservatory Method (for Trumpet) by J.B. Arban, edited by E.F. Goldman and Walter Smith (Carl Fischer).

Sight-reading of duets and ensembles is also excellent practice, and many wind instrument duets adapt easily for mallet use.

Double Stop and Four Mallet Sight-Reading

The drill techniques for two mallet sight-reading development can be applied to double stop and four mallet reading skills. I suggest using flash cards with two, three, and four note chords and two line rhythmic passages.

It's best to read chords from the bottom voice to the top voice, a note at a time. After picturing the chord's position on the keyboard, the student should move the mallets to that position and play the chord. The tempo must be as slow as is necessary to follow the procedure of perception-execution. Drill and practice will increase speed. It's best to avoid forming the chord on the keyboard one note at a time; it will slow progress. I suggest rolling or stopping the chords in eighth or sixteenth note subdivisions. Doing this keeps the mallets in position for the length of the chord and it is easier to move quickly and simultaneously to the next one. Using only peripheral vision when practicing four mallet arpeggios and spreading exercises will help students broaden their visual range.

Material for Four Mallet Reading

Mallet Technique for Bass and Treble Clef, Book II by Sandy Feldstein (Belwin).
Multiple Mallet Studies for Marimba edited by Ramon Meyer (HaMaR).
Graded Reading Exercises for Four Mallets by Max Neuhaus (Music for Percussion).
Progressive Studies in Double Stops for Mallet Instruments by Al Payson (Music for Percussion).
Four-voiced chorales and hymns (edit as necessary).
Easy piano pieces (edit as necessary).

Sight-reading skills require frequent practice. Recognition drills must be practiced so a rarely-encountered leger line or rhythm will not slow the reading process. Occasionally teachers should run a 3 x 5 card across the music to be sure students are still reading ahead. Students should maintain peripheral vision by practicing technical studies without looking at the keyboard. Sight-reading is too valuable a skill; it must not be allowed to deteriorate, but should be a regular part of every percussionist's practice schedule. ■

Percussion Accessories You Can Make

James McKinney

With the rising cost of percussion accessories and shrinking school budgets, I have found that I can save money by making some of the accessory equipment used by the percussion section. The following items are functional and inexpensive; they can be made by any novice handyman, without power tools. If you can't find the time to make accessories, talk to a student who would be interested in helping out with such a project, or ask the shop teacher to consider making them as a class project.

Triangle Clamps

Instead of buying triangle clamps, purchase gluing clamps at a hardware store. Those made by Stanley are produced in a variety of sizes at a fraction of the cost of regular triangle clamps. Because these clamps have holes drilled in them, you just need to add cord or fish line to hold the triangle. As a bonus, most of the clamps come with rubber tips to help eliminate the extra noise that can occur when the clamp is attached to an oversized stand.

Triangle Beaters

Cold rolled-steel rods, purchased at a hardware store, make good triangle beaters. The rods, which are 36 inches in length, come in a variety of diameters. I have made some with 1/4 inch and 5/16 inch diameters. First cut the rods to the desired length (at least eight inches) with a hacksaw, then smooth the sharp ends with a file. Buy a length of clear flexible plastic tubing with inside diameters of 1/4 inch and 5/16 inch to use as handles. Slide the tubing over the last four inches of the rod and the job is complete. You'll have a great set of triangle beaters that cost very little.

Güiro Scratcher

Almost every director loses the güiro scratcher before he can get the güiro from the display case to the band room. For an easy substitute use chopsticks. They are cheap, plentiful, and do a great job.

Cowbell Beater

A length of 5/8 inch diameter dowel rod at least 10 inches long will do the trick for a new cowbell beater. Wrap most of the dowel with tape, using a little or a lot, depending on the desired degree of hardness you want in the sound.

Crash Cymbal Straps

Strong and durable cymbal straps can be made from two inch wide nylon web. Buy at least 24 inches of webbing for each cymbal so you can double the strap over and have enough excess to tie the ends under the cymbal. If you want the equivalent of lamb's wool pads for the cymbals, try using buffing pads.

Cymbal Stand Repair

It's easy to lose parts from suspended cymbal stands – the wing nut, felt washers, or the sleeve that keeps the cymbal from vibrating on the metal post. You can buy wing nuts from the hardware store by the dozen. While you're there, ask the clerk for felt washers, which are often stocked in a variety of sizes. Surgical tubing 1/4 inch in diameter can work as the protective sleeve. If your hardware store doesn't carry it, try a pharmacy.

Timbale Sticks

To make timbale sticks, try using 5/16 inch diameter dowel rods cut to about 16 inches. They will last longer if they are sanded and finished with varnish or shellac.

Timpani Beaters

Make timpani beaters from 5/8 inch diameter wood dowels or aluminum tubing. After cutting the dowels to 15 inch lengths, tightly wrap 3/4 inch masking tape around one end. Continue to wrap the masking tape until a good sized head is formed on the dowel. Dip the masking tape into a can of clear varnish, then hang the beater upside down until it dries. Repeat this dipping process once. You now have a good mallet for tom tom work or full timpani playing. To make the mallet softer, cover it with a layer or two of hobby felt, and cover the felt with moleskin, a foot-care product available in drugstores.

If you are a serious hobbyist, try covering the mallets with 100% wool cast felt, the kind used in casts for broken bones. The felt can be purchased at a surgical supply store. You can experiment with covering the heads or follow directions in *Mallet Repair* by Arthur Press (Belwin Mills).

Bass Drum Beater

Following the directions for timpani beaters, you can make a bass drum beater by using two inch masking tape instead of the 3/4 inch size. You can wrap the handles with plastic tape or duct tape or simply stain them without putting any tape on.

Tambourines

To perform fantastic thumb rolls on the tambourine, apply a two inch wide semi-circle of skateboard surfacing material to the head of the instrument. This sandpaper-like material has a sticky backing and is put on skateboards so riders won't slip off; it is also used to provide traction on boats and stairs.

Anvil

The next time your ensemble performs an arrangement of the "Anvil Chorus," use an old brake drum from a car to get the proper anvil-like sound. A large piece of metal pipe or a portion of railroad track will also do the job.

Slapstick

For a great slapstick that is louder than any you can buy, join two sections of two by four inch boards, each about two feet long, with a strap hinge. Attach screen door handles near the ends of the boards so students won't smash their fingers as they play. The instrument will outlast most store-bought models.

Snare Drum Sticks

Corps style drumsticks are hardly more than a wood dowel that is 5/8 inch in diameter, with one end tapered. To make your own, buy a dowel and have students sand down the bottom third of the stick. I suggest using hardwood dowels because the sticks will last longer than the ones made of soft wood. Sticks made this way work well and cost considerably less than those purchased in accessory shops.

James McKinney

With a little experimenting, I have made some good quality, long-lasting percussion accesories. I have fun while saving money, and have found a new hobby as well. ■

May, 1983

Re-Defining Rudiments

George Tuthill

It is clear that learning rudiments should be part of every percussionist's training. The real question, however, is what are the rudiments? The subject was discussed at length when a Percussive Arts Society committee* met to combine the 26 standard American rudiments commonly used around the world in order to create a more complete catalog for use by students.

Dictionary definitions of the word "rudiment" always include something about it being the first principle of a subject. One of the first rudimental encounters for most students has been the long roll, perhaps the most difficult technique to perfect and the source of much frustration for students and teachers. In learning to play the long roll in the traditional way (starting slowly and gradually increasing to optimum speed in one smooth progression) the beginner usually encounters gaps in the rhythmic flow. Playing the roll smoothly requires the ability to pass through technique changes, suggesting that the long roll is really a combination of basic strokes and threfore not a "rudiment" after all.

Given these facts, it is possible to formulate a system of teaching based on note values and sticking patterns that combine to form the sound patterns commonly referred to as rudiments. This type of system provides an approach to teaching basic percussion that can be used by a teacher whose primary background is not in the percussion area. There are teaching methods presently in use that deal with two, three, or four basic strokes. The system presented here uses four strokes. Also, some systems use strokes of various heights, such as drag and tap strokes which are different levels of the four basic strokes used here.

A discussion of style and stick grip has been purposely avoided because this approach can work with any basic technique (wrist, arms, finger control, or any combination of these). Students should play all of the exercises in a notated framework at various tempos. By practicing in this manner, players will be learning to apply the sound patterns to written material at all times.

Basic Strokes

Bounce stroke. Direct the stick down to the drum head and then let the wrist follow the natural rebound of the stick back to the top of its arc. At this point the stick should be pushed back down. A smooth continuous motion should be used, as though bouncing a ball.

BOUNCE STROKE

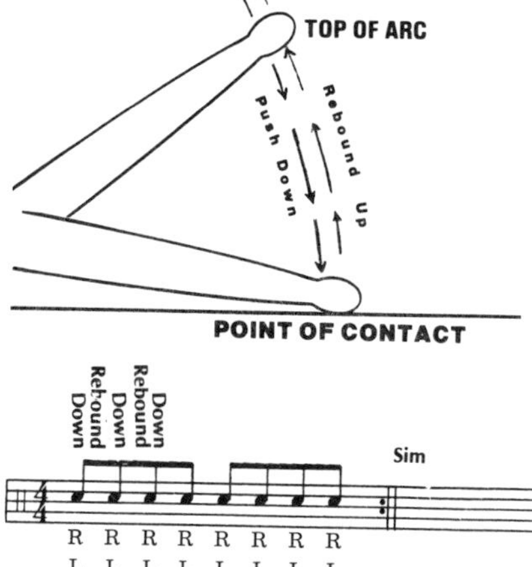

Downstroke. The stick is moved down to the drum head and allowed to rebound only about one inch.

DOWN STROKE

Turn stick down allowing it to rebound about one inch.

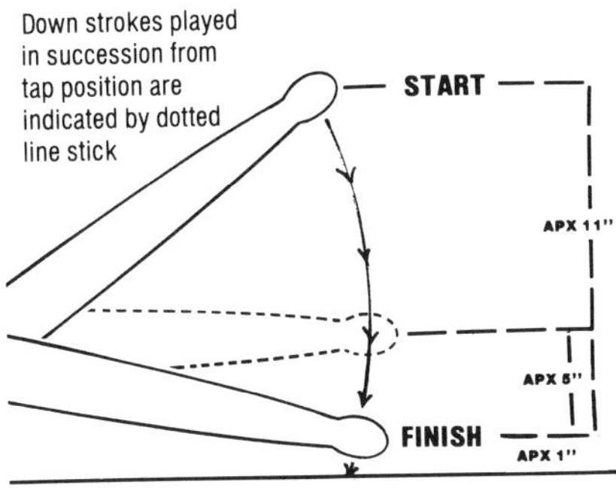

Upstroke. Start with the stick about one inch from the drum head and play with the feeling that the tone is being pulled from the head in the same manner timpani are played.

UP STROKE

Feel as though the up stroke is being pulled out of the head

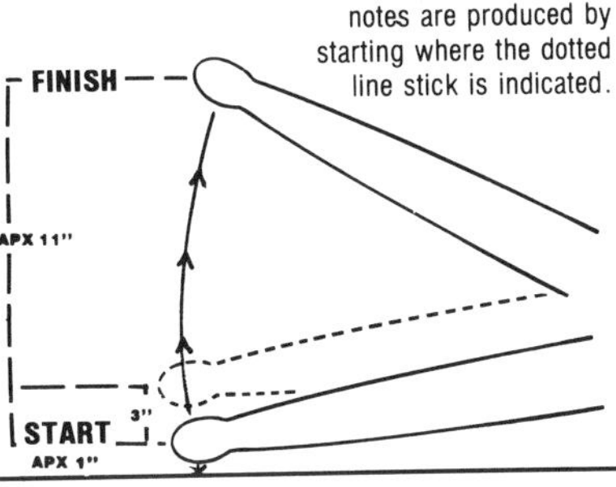

Multiple bounce stroke. Basically a downstroke that is allowed to bounce at a low level, creating a series of taps close together that are controlled by the fingers.

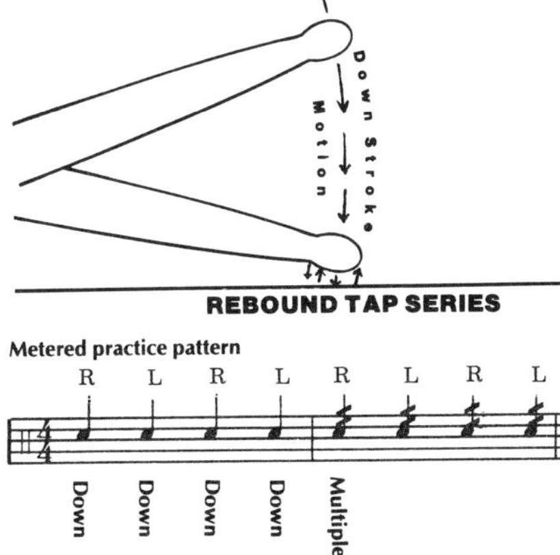

Sticking Patterns

Students who learn these four basic strokes can begin to play simple rhythms by using various sticking patterns. The tempo will determine the type of stroke to use.

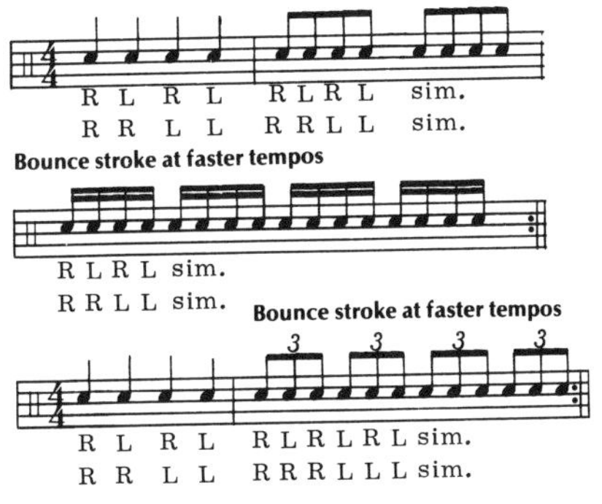

After learning the basic note values, the player should develop the ability to change sticking patterns within a given notation. This kind of practice will help him understand rudimental construction.

In exercise 6a the student plays 16th notes, changing from single to double strokes. Every paradiddle rudiment sticking is contained in the exercise, as shown in example.

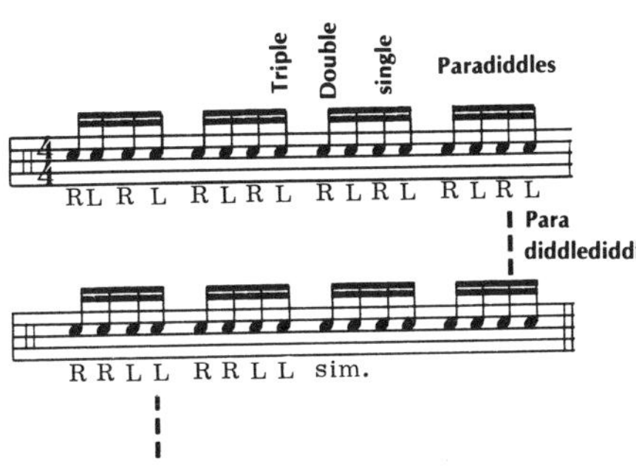

After mastering this exercise, each paradiddle can then be developed separately while maintaining a metric value.

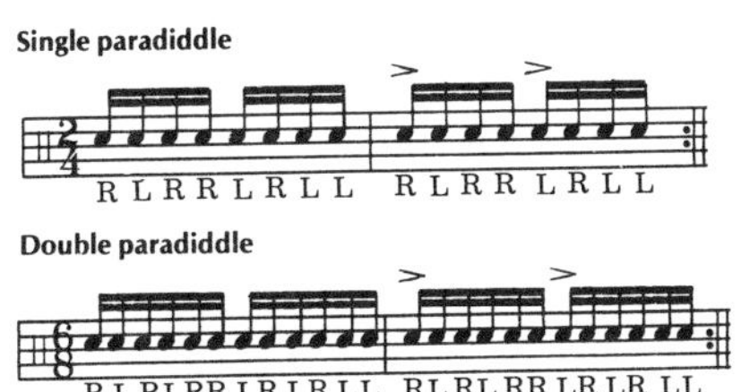

Rolls

To play a roll the student must learn to play either double or multiple bounce strokes with one downstroke motion.

When playing double strokes the second tap is actually accomplished with the fingers. Students who perfect the double or multiple bounce can go on to learn the pulsation patterns that are used to frame rolls of various durations.

These patterns enable students to understand how to fit rolls to musical notation. If desired, traditionally numbered rolls can then be correlated to frame patterns.

Grace Notes

Grace note rudiments are taught as a combination of basic strokes. To play a flam (♪♩), one hand plays an upstroke while the other plays a downstroke.

RIGHT FLAM

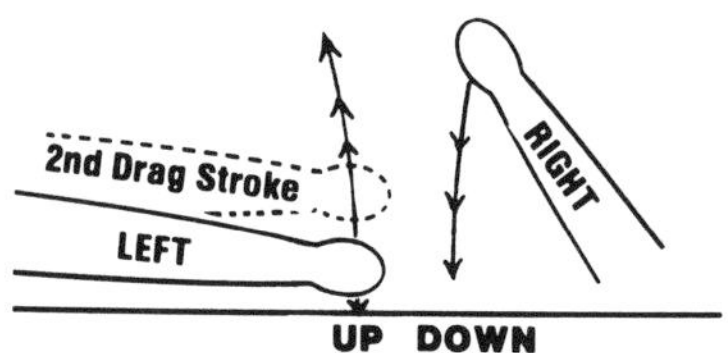

LEFT FLAM

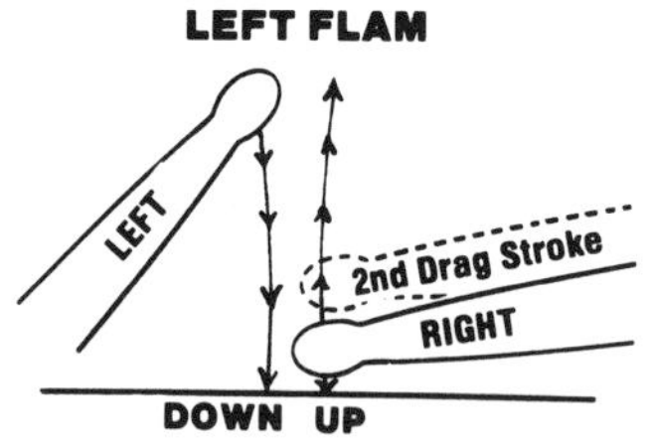

To play flam: one hand plays an up stroke while the other plays a down stroke. The procedure is reversed to play on alternate hand.

I suggest teaching the drag either as two low level upstrokes (see example 3) followed by a downstroke,

or as two 32nd notes inside a framework of 16ths in the same manner we teach double stroke rolls.

This method, commonly referred to as corps style, works well with marching percussion because it produces the metered grace notes that help achieve uniform interpretation.

Combining Techniques

By using the 16th note pattern and the 32nd note doubling technique, you can form many rudiments from one basic pattern.

Lesson 25

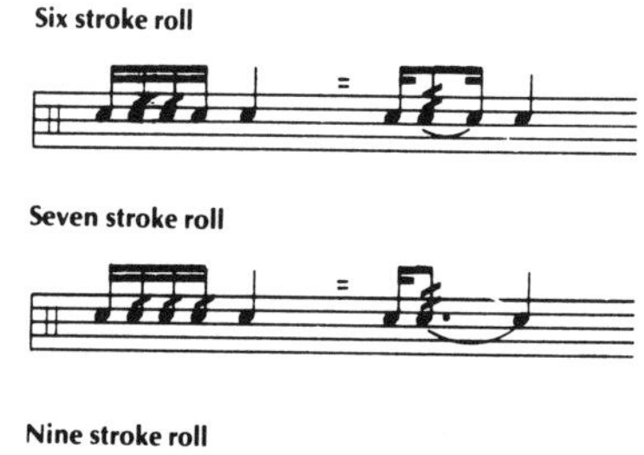

It's now possible to learn more difficult patterns by combining basic techniques and patterns.

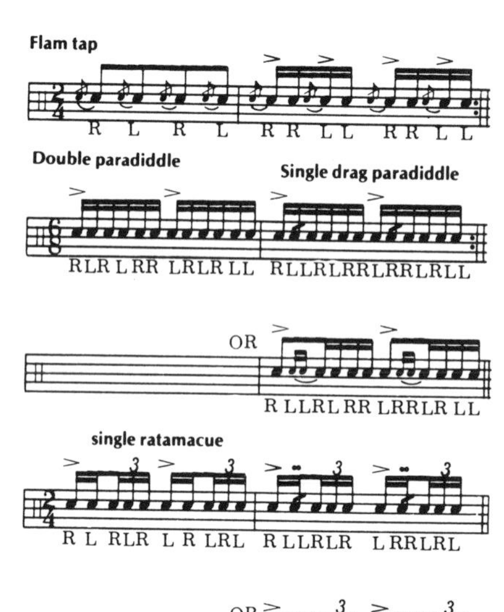

The following exercises will help improve mental and physical control, making it easier to master traditional rudiments.

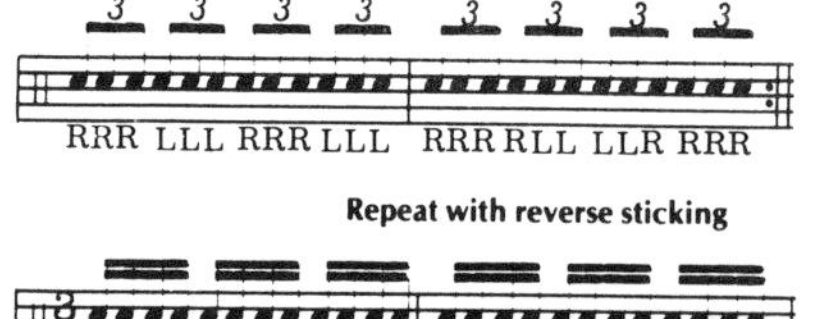

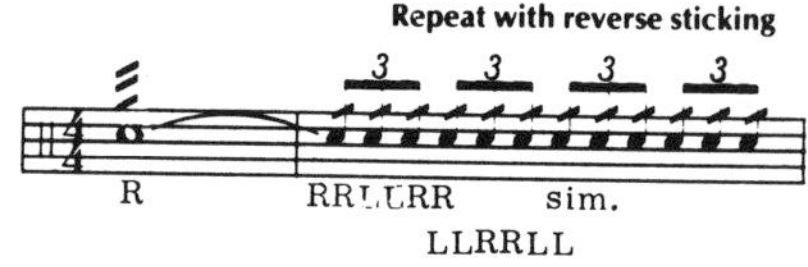

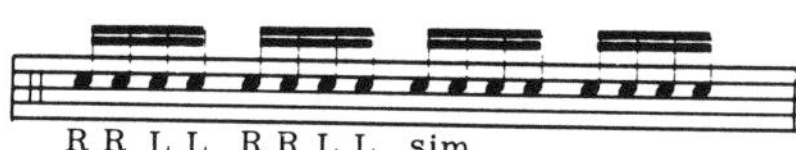

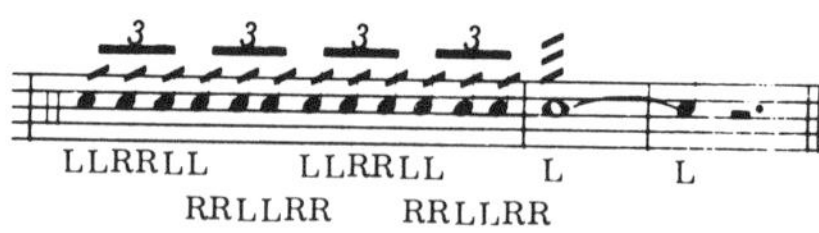

These exercises are only a small part of a system that can develop rudimental techniques in an efficient manner. Because all traditional rudiments can be broken down into basic patterns, the advantage of the system described here is that the player can learn the patterns in a metered context, rather than in the isolation of traditional rudiment study. This concept makes it easier for the student to apply the traditional rudiments to all types of playing. ■

*P.A.S. International Drum Rudiment Committee: John Beck, James Campbell, Rob Carson, Anthony Cirone, Sherman Hong, William F. Ludwig, Jr., Charles Owens, James Petercsak, Fred Sanford, Dan Spaulding, George Tuthill, Larry Vanlandingham, Jay Wanamaker.

Maintaining Concert Percussion Equipment

George Frock

Because of the increased use of percussion instruments in school music programs, directors need to be able to maintain equipment rather than replace it and strain the budget. The following information should help instructors care for the existing equipment and keep it in good performing condition.

Timpani

The standard set of timpani consists of four drums: 32", 29", 26", and 23". Because the timpani's head gets pounded out at the playing spot and stretched with constant pedaling, teachers should replace the heads each year. After removing the head, first dust the inside of the bowl, then sand the bowl's edge with emery cloth or fine steel wool. Next wipe a thin layer of parafin or Gulf wax around the edge. You can install a new head by performing the next seven steps:

• Center the head so that the overlap is even around the bowl.

• Carefully place the counterhoop over the head.

• Dip the tension screws in some type of lug lubricant.

• Pull the tension screws down to the point you can finger-tighten each one.

• With the pedal in its mid range, slowly bring the head to its playing range by turning the screws carefully in this order:

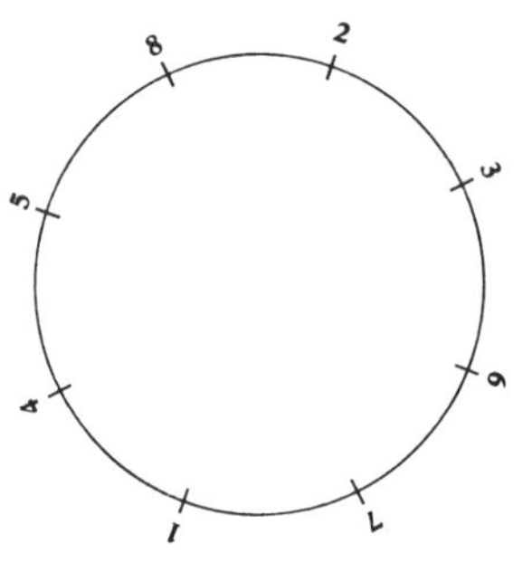

• When the head is sounding in its playing range, tap at each post and make any adjustments necessary to produce a clean tone that is free of out-of-tune "beats." By placing the ear near the head and tapping softly with a mallet, the overtone of a fifth should be fairly strong and even.

• If possible let the head "seat" for at least 24 hours before playing it.

To keep the heads in peak condition, students should observe several points to help in the daily care of the instrument.

• Wipe the heads free of fingerprints and dust with a towel or cloth after each playing session.

• Cover the heads with heavy cardboard or wood covers when they are not in use.

• Keep the pedals in a mid to upper range position when the timpani are not being played.

• Cover the drums with full length drop covers to keep dust from collecting around the mechanical and moving parts.

Orchestral Bells

With very little care, a set of orchestra bells should stay in excellent condition. Directors, however, should be aware of a problem: students who perform a high percentage of parts with brass tip bell mallets. This type of mallet will greatly reduce the instrument's playing life. Hard rubber and plastic mallets produce a warm sound as well as keep damage to a minimum. Here are some general maintenance suggestions that should be helpful.

• Clean the bars with fine steel wool and polish them with glass wax at least every four months.

• Adjust any felt that is so worn the bars produce too much box sound.

• Re-glue the case or support bars if needed.

Xylophone/Marimba

The xylophone and marimba have bars made of rosewood or keylon, for which the care is the same. As with orchestra bells, a hard mallet will do more damage to the bars than one which is not as dense. For regular care I suggest some routine maintenance steps:

• Apply a thin coat of a non-abrasive wax to the bars at four to six month intervals.

• Regularly check all support posts and straighten any that are touching the bars.

• Make sure the support string is taut and replace it when worn.

• Keep the instruments covered when they are not in use to keep dust from getting in the resonators.

Vibraphone

Vibraphone bars, which are made chiefly of aluminum, should always be played with mallets that are wound with yarn or chord. Players should avoid using rubber mallets (they spot and deface the bars) and plastic or brass mallets (they will dent the bars). Here are some tips for the routine care of the vibraphone:

• Occasionally wipe the bars with a thin coat of glass wax.

• Check and straighten the support pins so that they don't touch the bars. Re-insulate the support pins with felt or soft rubber if needed.

• Keep a spare belt pully on hand to replace the old one when worn.

• Spray any moving parts that click or squeak with WD40.

• Oil the motor if the directions say to.

• Keep the instrument covered when not in use.

Chimes

Problems with the chimes often occur with either the instrument's support strings (wires) or the dampening system. It's important to observe how the dampening system connects to the pedal and carefully replace any worn felt. Because chime tubes are extremely heavy, they rapidly wear out the support strings. Most chimes made today are supported on cable that can be replaced by the manufacturer. However, in an emergency, heavy gauge picture wire will work if it is attached with a metal clamp available from hardware stores. The chime tubes will retain their glossy luster if fingerprints are cleaned after each use and the instrument is occasionally cleaned with glass wax. One end of the chime mallet should be covered with moleskin or chamois cloth to produce a softer attack sound for piano levels of performance.

Snare Drums and Tom-Toms

Snare drum and tom-tom heads should be changed at least once each year by following the same steps used for the timpani. The snare mechanism should be cleaned and oiled, and the snare string checked. To eliminate an after-buzz in the snare drum's sound, clip off any snare strands that hang below the others. It is important for directors to be aware of the types of physical conditions that create poor tone quality. For example, I feel that internal mufflers tend to create a dead tone; and pushing too hard against the batter head makes the drum's tone lifeless and the head difficult to play on. To reduce drum ring, make a muffler out of a ring of chamois cloth that is about the size of a silver dollar and place it on the batter head. To protect drum heads and keep them dust-free between rehearsals, cover them with a head-sized disc of cardboard, plus a towel.

Cymbals and Gongs

Although cymbal polishes will work on cymbals and gongs, regularly scheduled maintenance, accomplished by brushing the instruments with laundry detergent and water, will save money, maintain the instrument's luster, and avoid a waxy build-up. It's important to always clean the instruments by hand because buffing or polishing machines can reduce tone grooves and alter the sound of the cymbal. Directors should replace the gong's suspension cord at regular intervals, never taking a chance that a worn cord will make it through the next performance. I suggest using such materials as leather shoe strings, nylon rope or cord, and gut strings.

Stands and Hardware

If players are taught to properly use drum and cymbal stands, there is no reason for the equipment to wear out. I've noticed that young players have a tendency to adjust the drum stand's position by placing their hands on the drum, and then twisting both the drum and stand at the same time. Because stands are designed with a friction tension plate, twisting the stand breaks the friction and causes it to fall. It's important to teach students to either reach down and turn the entire stand or free the friction plate — you'll keep the stand for years. Over-tightening the thumb screw is another problem. I have seen too many students use snare drum sticks as a wrench, tightening thumb screws to the point where the threads break. If you have a stand that is this mistreated, make it safe from falling by placing a small radiator hose clamp just above the base.

The only parts of a snare stand that tend to wear with age are the rubber insulation strips on the wings of the cradle. I suggest replacing them with pieces of rubber tubing to reduce rattles between the counter-hoop and the stand. Such tubing can be purchased from a medical supply outlet, or obtained from physicians or hospitals; tubing that is 12 inches long should last several years.

Players should keep a watchful eye on the felt insulation pads and the insulation tube on cymbal stands because the two items insure against rattles. It is a good idea to keep a good supply of felt discs, washers, and thumb screws on hand as these small items are easily lost. Cymbal washers may be purchased from a music store, but fender washers from an auto or hardware store work just as well. Plastic tubing from the hardware store makes for excellent insulation and will last much longer than rubber tubing.

Accessory Instruments

Most damage to accessory instruments occurs when students play them with a mallet or stick that is too hard. A good solution to this problem is to have players strive for a warm sound by using soft mallets whenever possible. Because most accessory instruments are inexpensive, they should be replaced when damaged.

It's important to check triangle clips and replace any worn string with a strong-test fishing line. I suggest using two strings to provide a back-up in case one breaks.

You can replace the gut on castanets with small strips of gut or elastic. Those fortunate enough to have some old calf timpani heads can use them to replace worn out tambourine heads. Be sure to soak the skin before tacking it on the shell of the tambourine. Then cover the instrument with a plastic bag so the skin will dry slowly.

The continuous care of equipment eliminates the last minute need for special repairs and unexpected problems, whether right before an important concert or a daily rehearsal. By maintaining percussion equipment, directors not only extend the playing life of the instruments, but save the money needed to replace them. ■

The Percussion Ensemble – A Director's Best Friend

James Lambert

In the not-too-distant past, members of the percussion section held little prestige and many directors even regarded them as marginal musicians. Also, compositions for band usually needed a dual difficulty rating system: brass and woodwinds, grade 5; percussion, grade 2. Because many daring, innovative concert band composers and conductors have challenged both the talents and sounds of the percussion choir, members of this ensemble, once considered troublemakers, are now thought of as musical trouble-shooters.

This change in attitude was brought about by such noteworthy band compositions as H. Owen Reed's *La Fiesta Mexicana*, Vaclav Nelhybel's *Trittico*, and Karel Husa's *Music for Prague, 1968*. The music served to inspire a 20th-century renaissance in percussion performance attitudes and equipment demands, plus performance problems and possible solutions. No longer could band directors spend 95% of their rehearsal time with the brass and woodwinds and the remaining 5% with the percussion section. The average needs of the percussion section changed dramatically to include a significant amount of keyboard percussion (xylophone, vibraphone, and marimba) in addition to the orchestra bells and chimes. The musical demands in these compositions created a necessity for band directors to improve their teaching skills, which in turn forced college music departments to re-design percussion education curriculum.

This growth has not only affected the concert band director but has also brought a change in the marching band director's attitude toward the percussion section. Because of the drum and bugle corps' influence, marching percussion sections now include tuneable bass drums in graduated pitch sizes, multi-tom setups, xylophone, vibes, and timpani, as well as the traditional snare drum, cymbals, and accessory percussion. The greater performance demands of the new percussion ensemble require educators to know more about these specialized instruments and the teaching techniques needed to instruct their students.

Special Rehearsals

Directors can schedule percussion ensemble rehearsals before school, during lunch, and after school, or during the regular band rehearsal when an assistant director or percussion instructor can be present. I suggest the following approach for a percussion ensemble rehearsal.

1. *Warm-up or technical exercises* (10 minutes). Begin with basic percussion technique that includes snare drum warm-up exercises (incorporating rudiments) coordinated with keyboard percussion, timpani, and accessory percussion exercises. Unfortunately, the percussion section is often overlooked in the typical band warm-up.

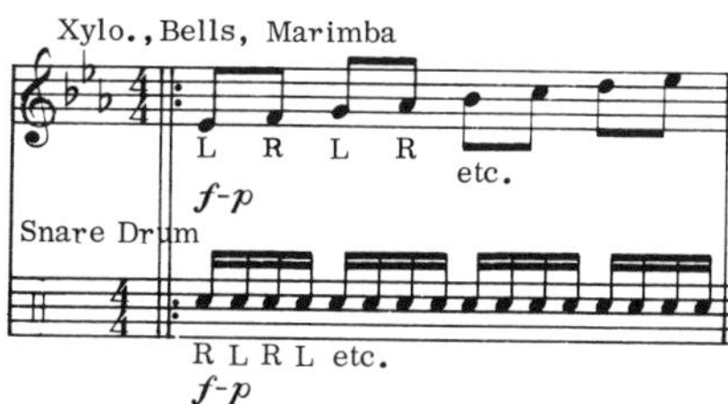

R L R L R L etc.
R L R L R L

(Transpose each exercise to all major keys)

2. *Rehearse band music* (10-15 minutes). Drill on the performance problems at hand is next. During regular rehearsals directors should identify difficult areas in the score by jotting problems down as they occur. Some typical notes might be:

- Work on precision with those who have similar vertical rhythms.
- Point out balance in sound between the different instruments (for example, xylophone and bells not being overshadowed by the snare drums and bass drums).

Try making a video or audio recording of the rehearsal – it will help you and the students to become aware of the places that need improvement.

3. *Practice percussion ensemble literature* (25-30 minutes). The most rewarding portion of the rehearsal should be preparing a percussion ensemble com-

position. Band directors can select them by using their state's suggested listing or reviewing the Percussive Arts Society ensemble listing (available by sending $10 to 214 West Main Street, Urbana, Illinois). The compositions should complement the repertoire of the concert band so that in a concert or contest setting selections played by the groups would offer a variety of instrumental combinations.

Ensemble Suggestions

Jared Spears' *Bayport Sketch* (Barnhouse) is an excellent high school percussion ensemble. The composer uses a combination of keyboard percussion (xylophone, bells, marimba, vibes, and chimes) contrasted with membrane percussion (timpani, snare drum, and two tom-toms). Mitchell Peters integrates the marching band percussion instruments in a setting of *March of the Eagles* (Mitchell Peters). This work is scored for two timpani, two tom-toms, snare drum, bass drum, and cymbals, and is playable by junior high percussion ensembles. A challenging, yet well-accepted composition for percussion ensemble is Thomas Brown's *Particles* (Southern). This three-movement suite has a charming third movement, "Simple Samba," scored for six performers on vibes, marimba, xylophone (also tambourine and bells), drum set, chacollo, and conga drum (also chimes). These three compositions demonstrate the variety of styles in percussion ensemble literature. By sampling, rehearsing, and performing ensembles such as these, the musical skills of percussionists will be increased and the band director will be able to select even more challenging concert or marching band literature.

If the director makes full use of the percussion ensemble, students will become more aware of timbral combinations, increase their sensitivity to dynamics and articulations, have a better perception of musical structure, form and phrasing, as well as develop the feeling of section unity that can help motivate other members of the band. Because of the percussionists' increased musical stature, the band director will have more freedom in assigning percussion parts and can begin to rely on the section as a rehearsal tool, making the percussion ensemble one of his best friends. ■

November, 1983

Preparing for Percussion Auditions

Rich Holly

Serious percussion students who are planning to audition for all-state or similar organizations need to prepare for the event mentally, physically, musically, and technically. The following suggestions can help players develop an approach to getting ready for such a performance.

Select Music

All-state committees often have their own literature lists from which players select music for the audition. However, students living in states where this method is not used should choose music that reflects their strengths. For example, the percussionist who is not comfortable performing a long, rapid series of flam-taps should avoid a work with that type of phrase, even if he thinks the music will eventually sound good. It's important to consider the audition as a performance, letting the adjudicator see and hear proficient playing in order to rate the audition as objectively as possible.

Review Musical Directions

Once the work is selected, a player's first job is to analyze the music. After finding a comfortable chair in a quiet spot, study such indications as tempo and volume directions, *accelerando* and *ritardando* markings, and style information. This type of advanced mental preparation helps students understand the music before they spend practice time on learning the notes.

Strive for Consistency

Next look for phrases that are repeated. Such places not only lead to an understanding of the music's structure, but also act as checkpoints for consistency in performance. A snare drum excerpt shows how this idea works. After a four measure introduction, the first phrase of the composition appears:

Players should review the music for this phrase – it may appear either in full or part – and perform the rhythm with the same sticking pattern whenever it occurs.

Plan Dynamic Levels

Before practicing, take a few minutes to consider the music's dynamic ranges. Play a series of 16th-notes, MM=112-120, at all dynamic levels from *pianissimo* to *fortissimo*. When practicing it's easier to anticipate the volumes to strive for at all dynamic markings. The *mezzoforte* in the middle of the work should be the same dynamic level as the *mezzoforte* in the beginning.

Rhythmic Accuracy

Although most keyboard percussionists and timpanists begin training on snare drum, rhythm is often the largest problem in their performances. Using a snare drum or drum pad, these players should take the time to go over troublesome spots and check them for rhythmic accuracy. It's also possible to locate poorly executed rhythms by listening to tape recordings of practice sessions. Some of the problems most often encountered involve dotted rhythms, short-valued rests, and holding longer-valued notes. If you have a problem with these rhythms, sing them a few times with careful consideration for the correct lengths of note and rest values. The following example shows several rhythms along with their common incorrect interpretations.

The Instruments

Auditions usually provide keyboard instruments and timpani at the performance site. However, I suggest that keyboard percussionists investigate to see what specific instruments will be available. If a player is accustomed to a brand and model that is not available, he should consider bringing his own instrument, or the school's, to the audition – it offers more insurance for a successful performance. However, although it's important to be comfortable at an audition, players should weigh the following requirements involved with moving a large instrument:

• Know the procedure for dismantling and setting up the instrument.

• Check the frame to make sure it is solid. If the frame seems weak, it will need to be reinforced.

• Replace any weak cord that runs through the bars.

• Correct any rattles or creaks in the instrument.

• Check the bars for correct tuning.

Because few audition sites provide snare drums, students should bring their own instrument or one from school. As with keyboard instruments, the snare drum should be in the best possible condition for an audition. An old and pitted batter head should be replaced; and a dirty head, otherwise in good shape, can be cleaned with mild soap and warm water. Players can also polish the shell of the drum and adjust the snares and snare strainer for optimum sound. It's also important to check the snare drum stand, making sure it's in good condition and that the height can be adjusted for a comfortable performance.

In the audition use sticks and mallets that are as new as possible. A five-year-old pair of sticks that look and respond as though new, certainly would be acceptable. However, if a favorite pair of marimba mallets look more like Raggedy Ann and Andy, they will need to be replaced. I suggest using any sticks or mallets purchased for the audition for at least two to four weeks before the audition date in order to become comfortable with them.

Advice for the Performer

At the audition, it's in the player's best interest to dress nicely and comfortably. Remember, the adjudicator is looking for a musician to represent a school and state in front of hundreds of people in a public performance. Being well-dressed shows the adjudicator a concern for good taste, and dressing comfortably allows the musician to concentrate on the performance – not the hot, tight sports coat.

Act with confidence (but not overly so), and do your best to be pleasant at the audition. Ideally, the adjudicator should remember each musician not only as a performer, but as a person as well. Here are some more quick tips for the audition.

• Use correct posture to give the performance a professional look.

• Lay sticks and mallets on a music rack that is covered with a towel so you can quickly exchange mallets in going from one instrument to another.

• Release the snares on the snare drum before proceeding to other instruments.

• Use a pitch pipe or tuning fork to eliminate running to a keyboard instrument.

• Bring your own stool to sit at the timpani while performing.

These steps are only part of the process of preparing for a successful all-state audition. Because there is no substitute for professional guidance, I suggest seeking the help of a band director, and, if possible, enrolling in private lessons. Most importantly, students should design and follow a method of preparation, being careful to address all musical aspects during practice sessions. The resulting audition should prove to be a rewarding musical experience for the performer, the adjudicator, and those in attendance at the festival as well. ■

Solos and Studies for Percussion

James Lambert

This year's collection of percussion music is heavily weighted in the grade 4-5 difficulty level, but spread throughout many categories, including a relatively large number of compositions for keyboard percussion and concert percussion ensemble.

Each work is discussed individually, with grade level, instrumentation, price, and publisher included.

Snare Drum

Solo Suite for Snare Drum by Robert McCormick (HaMar) is a three-movement, unaccompanied snare drum solo. The selection features contrasting styles as indicated by the titles: "Swing," "Tango," and "Bravura." The first movement is scored with brushes exclusively while the second makes use of the rim and rim shot sounds. The third movement is more march like in character. The selection makes a nice solo for a contest. Grade 5.

Master Technique Builders for Snare Drum, compiled and edited by Anthony Cirone (Belwin), gives players the chance to try out the daily practice routines used by 21 professional percussionists. The artists represented include John Beck, Louie Bellson, Joe Morello, Al Payson, Mitchell Peters, and Ed Soph. $5.95.

Artistic Snare Drum Solos With Piano Accompaniment by Myron D. Collins (Highland Music), contains 10 different works that are all accessible to the young percussionist. Grades 2-3.

Timpani

Partita by Carlos Chavez (G. Schirmer) is a difficult unaccompanied timpani solo that requires six instruments. An additional 29-inch timpani is needed to perform this four-movement composition. The movements are entitled "Praeludium," "Sarabande," "Allemande," and "Giga." Grade 6. $12.50.

Classic-African by Joseph Aiello (HaMar) is an unaccompanied timpani solo requiring four instruments. The scoring makes use of special techniques such as double-stops and includes the need to rapidly change the sticks from their normal striking ends to the butt ends. Sudden meter changes add to the complexity of this grade 5 solo for the advanced high school timpanist.

Multiple Percussion

The Multiple Percussionist by Julia Fraser (Barnhouse) is a solo collection that includes 15 compositions with a variety of percussion instruments for the solo multiple percussionist (unaccompanied). The material also offers a recommended set-up for each solo, a glossary of percussion instruments, information for appropriate mallet selection, and helpful hints to prepare students for a variety of set-ups in orchestra or band music. Grades 3-5. $10.

Music for Solo Percussion by Larry Barnes (Southern), a three-movement work, requires the single percussionist to perform the following instruments: claves, wood blocks, temple blocks, small suspended cymbal, tom-toms, vibraphone, maracas, xylophone, and small tam-tam. Distinct notation makes this grade 5 composition accessible to the advanced high school percussionist. $4.

The Performing Percussionist Solo Album by James Coffin (Barnhouse) is a collection that includes 16 works, from snare drum solos to multiple percussion. Set-up diagrams are included for the multiple percussion compositions. Grades 2-4. $7.50.

Drum Set

Drum Set Principles by Paul Humphrey (Alfred) is unique in that a cassette tape accompanies the written text. The cassette contains the beats and patterns found in the book as well as all of the charts in their original recorded versions. This format allows the student to play along with Humphrey and a group of all-star musicians. Divided into two sections, the book also has an introduction on drum facts, such as muffling drums for recording. Section one deals with 12 different styles plus accents; section two contains lead sheets for drum set performance. A grade 4-5 ability is needed for adequate understanding of this text. $12.95.

Concert Percussion Ensemble

The Young Lions by William Schinstine (Southern), a percussion sextet, is an excellent selection for the junior high percussion ensemble. The instrumentation calls for players on high snare drum, low snare drum, small crash cymbals, bass drum, two timpani, and keyboard percussion (bells, xylophone, marimba, or vibes, which may be doubled). This ensemble is a good additior to the contest repertoire for young percussionists. Grade 2. $4.

Fire by Pete O'Gorman (Barnhouse) is a grade 3 percussion quartet scored for snare drum, timbales, three tom-toms, and small bass drum. This composition will serve the needs of junior high directors as they motivate young percussion ensembles. $5.

Rat Race by William Schinstine (Kendor) is a novelty percussion quartet scored with the following instrumental requirements: first player – woodblock, whistle, xylophone, snare drum; second player – snare drum, bells, xylophone, claves, crash cymbals, suspended cymbal; third player – crash cymbals, suspended cymbal, bass drum, maracas, bird whistle; fourth player – four timpani. Only one xylophone is needed, as it can be shared between players one and two. Although this composition is short (two-and-a-half minutes), it demands accurate timing for a comic effect and an organized set-up, which is designed by the composer. This percussion ensemble is great fun and pure entertainment. Grade 4. $6.

Celebrating Christmas With Percussion arranged by Thomas Brown (Kendor) is designed for percussion quintet with electric bass (or string bass). The following instrumentation is required: first player – bells and tambourine; second player – vibes and triangle; third player – marimba; fourth player – marimba, suspended cymbal, and triangle; fifth player – chimes, timpani, snare drum, temple blocks, suspended cymbal, and sleigh bells. Some four-mallet technique is required of both marimba players, but the remaining parts are not as difficult. The arrangement includes "Joy to the World," "Silent Night," "We Wish You a Merry Christmas," and "Jingle Bells." Grade 4. $12.

William Tell Overture by Rossini arranged by Murray Houliff (Kendor) requires the following instrumentation for a percussion sextet: first player – bells and tambourine; second player – xylophone and woodblock; third player – two timpani; fourth player – snare drum; fifth player – cymbals; sixth player – bass drum. This arrangement of Rossini's galop theme (à la Lone Ranger) is good for contest, pops concerts, or student audiences. The duration of the work is approximately three minutes. Grade 4. $8.

Overture for Hans N. Feet by William Schinstine (Kendor) is a novelty piece that requires four musicians or any group of musicians in multiples of four. It uses knee slapping, hand clapping. finger snapping, foot tapping, and vocal sounds. No director can complain about not having the instruments for this ensemble, because all he needs are four rhythmically sophisticated, fun-loving percussionists (or musicians who always wanted to be in a percussion ensemble). The performance duration is two-and-a-half minutes. Grade 4. $3.50.

Blues and Chaser by Jared Spears (Southern) is a terrific percussion ensemble which is scored for eight players on the following instruments: orchestra bells, xylophone, marimba, tambourine and chimes, vibes, four timpani, three tom-toms, and drum set. This ensemble is a superb example of what the concert percussion ensemble can do in a jazz or swing style. Not only is the selection good for contests, it makes a great addition to the jazz ensemble or pops concert. Grade 5. $12.50.

Five Short Pieces by Donald Miller (Ludwig) is scored for five percussionists on the following instruments: first player – crash cymbals, claves, xylophone, two suspended cymbals; second player – bells, marimba, bongos; third player – snare drum, tam-tam, triangle, temple blocks; fourth player – field drum, bass drum, four tom-toms; fifth player – five timpani, maracas, chimes. The composition is well-suited for the advanced high school percussion ensemble, and because the performance duration is six-and-a-half minutes, directors can use the complete work at a contest. Grade 5. $12.95.

Keyboard Percussion Solos and Ensembles

Solos:

Donald Miller has transcribed Claude Debussy's *First Arabesque* for vibraphone and piano, and *Second Arabesque* for marimba and piano (Ludwig). This sample of Impressionism allows the keyboard percussionist to experience Debussy's characteristic writing style. Two-mallet technique is required for both of these grade 4 arrangements. $5.95 each.

Suite Mexicana by Keith Larson (Southern) is for unaccompanied marimba. Written in three contrasting movements (fast, slow, fast), the work requires four-mallet technique; and the two-mallet roll is combined with the four-mallet roll in the second movement. None of the movements is long, making this grade 4 composition accessible for the high school keyboard percussionist. $2.

Contemporary Marimba Solos by Bill Molenhof (Kendor) is a collection of original compositions that reflect the composer's unique jazz-fusion style on the marimba. The solos are entitled "An American Sound," "Between Two Minds," "Learning," "Sandwich Papers," "P.B.," "New Hope," and "At Home In My Heart." This collection is excellent for the percussionist who is interested in the possibilities of jazz-rock on unaccompanied marimba. Grades 5-6. $6.

Prelude by Kevin Hiatt (HaMar) is an unaccompanied four-mallet marimba solo that alternates between E major and E minor. The performer's primary concerns will be for independent mallet control as well as roll control. This grade 5 composition is definitely for the advanced high school percussionist or the player who is entering college.

The Whirlwind, the xylophone solo by Joe Green, has been edited and arranged by William Schinstine (Southern) for either xylophone or marimba and piano accompaniment. This selection, which demands technical fluency with two mallets, is characteristic of the flashy xylophone compositions that survived the vaudeville era. Joe Green's works are always crowd-pleasers. Grade 5. $3.50.

Etudes in Contemporary Style by Murray Houliff (Southern) offers 12 etudes that are excellent keyboard percussion technique exercises for two-mallet skills. The use of non-traditional tonal and rhythmic schemes make the difficulty ratings in the grade 5 and 6 arena. $4.50.

Ensembles:

Ave Verum by W.A. Mozart, arranged by Ruth Jeanne (Permus) is a beautiful adaptation of the famous melody. Although scored for four marimbas, two instruments will suffice if players one and three perform on the same marimba and players two and four on the other. The music is not technically demanding, but it does require the choice of soft mallets and careful attention to phrase control through smooth, even rolls. Grade 2. $5.

La Llorona (Mexican Folk Song) arranged by Ruth Jeanne (Permus) is scored for players on one xylophone and three marimbas (one player may use vibes); optional parts are for bass and guitar. However, the arrangement can be performed on as few as three instruments if players two and four share the same marimba. This three-and-a-half minute composition is a marvelous way to introduce the high school percussionist to rondo form, D minor, and the character of the Mexican marimba band. Grade 3. $7.

Little Fugue in G Minor by J.S. Bach, arranged by James Moore (Permus) for marimba ensemble requires four performers, each on their own instrument. This arrangement is a great way of introducing the high school or college percussionist to J.S. Bach's contrapuntal style. Grade 4. $9.

Maple Leaf Rag by Scott Joplin, arranged by Murray Houliff (Permus), is the traditional Joplin rag adapted for three marimbas and drum set. The grade 5 difficulty of this composition is a result of the explicit style and exact precision demanded of the three marimba performers. $5.

Nine Kabalevsky Pieces have been transcribed by Donald Miller for two marimbas (Ludwig). These pieces, considered as standard in the repertoire of student pianists, now are available for percussionists to perform in a duet format. Any one of them would be great at a contest or could add to any light concert atmosphere. Grades 3-4. $10.

Marching Percussion

Chop Builders by Jay A. Wanamaker (Alfred) includes a full score with parts for bells, xylophone, snare drum, timp-tom trio, tonal bass drums, and cymbals. Suggested alternatives to this full instrumentation are given by the composer. As the title suggests, the selections are dexterity warm-up exercises for the full marching percussion ensemble. Once memorized, the exercises (Triplets," "Hugga-Dugga-Brrr," "Mega Roll," "Flim-Flam," and "Bossa Fever") allow percussionists to devote attention to sound projection and technique. The performance levels of these exercises include grades 3-5. As an additional benefit, "Bossa Fever" can function as a nice change-of-pace marching percussion cadence. $25.

Corps Style Cadences by Jay Wanamaker (Alfred) is scored for the same instrumentation as *Chop Builders*. Here, the four marching percussion cadences vary in style from the march-like quality of "Main Street Strut" to a samba, "I.T." Also included is an adaptation of *Entry of the Gladiators* called "Circus, Circus" and one of Southern Cal's Trojan Marching Percussion cadences, "Triplets." These cadences are well written and playable by most high school marching percussion sections (bell and xylophone parts are doubled). Grades 3-4. $25.

Four Mexican Dances by Jay Wanamaker (Alfred) includes a full score and separate parts for bells, xylophone, snare drum, timp-tom trio (with maracas, cowbell, woodblock, triangle), tonal bass drums (with ratchet, cowbell, siren, whistle), and cymbals. The four traditional Mexican folk tunes, which are arranged for marching percussion, include "La Cucaracha," "Chiapanecas," "La Raspa," and "Mexican Hat Dance." Although the subtitle states that this work is "for the young marching percussion ensemble," I feel the music will take a relatively high level of performance maturity to control this excellent grade 4 percussion feature. $25. ■

1984-1985

Sonata for Timpani — The Composer's Concept

John Beck

Composer and percussionist John Beck wrote Sonata for Timpani *for jazz virtuoso Steve Gadd's senior recital at the Eastman School of Music in 1968. Beck, who received both his Bachelors and Masters degrees from Eastman, now heads the school's percussion department, conducts the Eastman Percussion Ensemble, and is timpanist with the Rochester Philharmonic Orchestra. He has recorded on the CRI, Turnabout, Mark, and Heritage labels, and is second vice-president of the Percussive Arts Society.*

Sonata for Timpani consists of three solo movements, each with a contrasting musical style: "Mysteriously," "Jazz-Like," and "Fast." Although the movements may be played separately, the musical ideas in the composition become clear when all movements are played as one work. This grade 6 solo requires a mature player of high school or college level ability, and lasts approximately 9:30 minutes.

First Movement

The first movement is based on a diminished seventh chord, F♯-A-C-E♭, a tonality often associated with mystery. Requiring soft timpani mallets, the score indicates a slow tempo, ♩=58, except for a brief four measure section of ♩ = 184. Rolls are the predominant technique in this section where it is vitally important that they be smooth and well connected.

Double stop rolls (rolling on two drums at once) are used and should be started together as if playing two keys on a piano. Practice these rolls until you are not aware of the individual mallets on each drum. This technique is possible with soft timpani mallets, but much more difficult with harder ones.

There is frequent use of bowl playing (striking the side of the timpani bowl with the mallet), which needs to be practiced so that each bowl makes a full tone.

Play the main rhythmic figure, on both the timpani head and bowl.

Although the dynamics are generally soft, *crescendos* and accents must be played with a sense of drama.

Smooth rolls, good intonation, and good dynamic contrast are

essential to a successful performance of this movement.

Second Movement

The second movement, "Jazz-Like," is based on a theme and variations format on the pitches F-C-D-F. The movement should be practiced with a metronome using general timpani mallets. Play the theme with smooth, flowing lines as though you were a horn player.

Following the theme is a jazz-like variation reminiscent of a walking string bass line. Play this section as though you were a bass player in a jazz combo.

Two measures of snare drum-style rim shots follow.

The drum idea leads to a jazz chorus that is played with the hands and fingers.

The bass line returns, the theme is stated once more, and the movement ends with sounds reminiscent of many big band charts.

More Practicing Hints

In this movement the term "jazz-like" does not mean jazz style where all eighths are played ♩♪ (3). Here, eighth notes are to be played straight. However, by feeling a double time eighth-note pulse, much like a drummer playing hi-hat on the second eighth of every quarter note, the timpanist can produce jazz-like results.

To capture this feeling, which is essential to the movement, it would be helpful to practice with someone playing a drum set in double time.

Play the section using hand claps and fingers with conviction. The hand clapping must be firm and sonorous; practice the part trying to get a full rich sound.

The finger section, a double time solo chorus as in a jazz piece, is technically difficult. To produce the best sound, strike the drum with the index finger, using the weight and force of the hand, much like bongo playing. If getting volume is a problem, try using all the fingers, being careful not to produce a heavy sound. Stand or lean forward on the timpani stool to play this section. It's difficult to use a normal playing position without the added length of the timpani mallets. Try to maintain the tempo of ♩ = 100 throughout this movement because if the tempo increases, the finger section is impossible to play and the movement develops a restless feel rather than the relaxed jazz-like feel. As always, maintain good dynamic contrast.

Third Movement

The third movement, "Fast," is marked ♩ = 138/152/ ♪ = ♪ throughout, and is the *tour de force* for the performer. Hard timpani mallets are required. The main theme, using the pitches E-C-D-E, is based on a Latin American rhythmic figure.

To give the rhythm a more "legit" feel it is coupled with a $\frac{3}{8}$ measure throughout the movement.

Practice the theme until the $\frac{4}{4}$ - $\frac{3}{8}$ combination becomes natural. A break in the rhythmic pattern occurs for a brief seven-measure section in $\frac{12}{8}$ using a *hemiola* between two drums.

Another section requires *glissandi* from E2 to as high as the drums will go releasing on an E3.

This passage also requires that a scale be played over four drums.

The most technically difficult section requires a steady, continuous 16th note pattern at a soft dynamic level with *forte* accents played on various drums. For a good performance, this technique requires extra practice, beginning at a slow tempo, to maintain all the dynamics.

The movement ends with a restatement of the theme and concludes with a flourish of notes, one *glissando,* and a final *sfz* on E2.

Set the 30-inch drum so that it produces an E2 when the heel of the pedal is on the floor. This procedure works well for standard spring tension pedals, but it cannot be used on Dresden timpani where the player must rely on his ear or the feel of the pedal for an exact pitch.

By following these suggestions and with careful practice and attention to detail, the timpanist will be able to give a satisfying and enjoyable performance of this work. ■

March, 1984

Conga Technique

Brian R. Kilgore

The beginning Latin percussionist must master fundamental hand positions in order to produce the four basic sounds of the congas in a musical and authentic manner. Once these sounds can be properly executed, the player can learn typical Latin rhythms.

The beginning player will need at least two instruments. Four good brands are Latin Percussion, Slingerland, Valje, or Gon Bop. Considering the heavy use and rough handling the instruments receive in high schools and colleges, it is better to use the more durable fiberglass congas rather than wooden ones. Although the fiberglass sound is not quite as warm, they do have the power to cut through a big band sound. Congas which have tacked or synthetic heads should be avoided, as well as those with conical sides, because they do not produce an authentic sound. Barrel shaped drums are best.

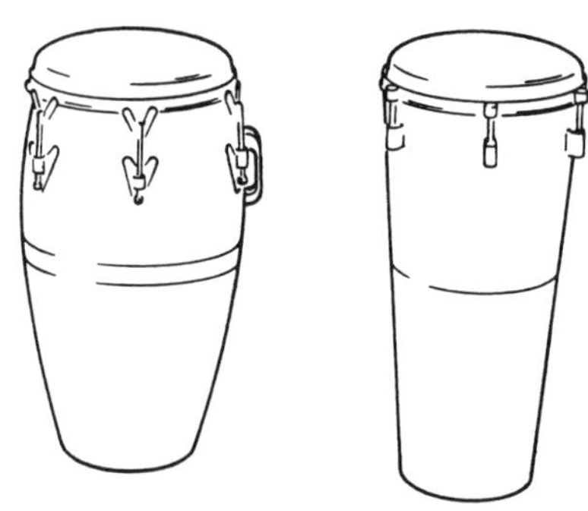

Congas are easiest to play when tuned to a pitch in the drum's midrange. If the heads are too loose it will be difficult to get slaps to sound clearly. However, if the heads are too tight the open tones will sound choked. The interval between the drums should sound from a minor third up to a perfect fourth depending on the drum sizes. When tuning, all tension rods should be adjusted evenly to keep the counterhoops level and to give the heads a consistent sound over the entire surface.

Playing Positions

The correct playing position is with the larger drum, the tumba, on the player's right and the smaller drum, the conga, on the left. The student may either sit or stand while playing the drums; however, if he chooses to stand he should use the manufacturer's stand for the conga and not a sling. A sling puts the drum at an awkward angle and makes playing difficult for someone learning the basic hand positions. When played while sitting, the conga should be held between the knees and tilted away from the player. The tumba rests flat on the floor.

Open Tone

The open tone is one of the most characteristic sounds produced on the congas and utilizes as much sustaining ability as the instrument has. The open tone is produced by hitting the head with just four fingers of the right hand, not the palm, and allowing the hand to bounce off immediately to achieve maximum resonance. The entire surface of all four fingers held firm and flat should strike the head from the edge of the drum simultaneously. A player with small hands may have to move the hand more towards the center to get a full sound. There should be no space between the fingers and the hand should point towards the center of the drum, not to the side. When practicing open tones, the student should strive for the fullest, most resonant sound possible.

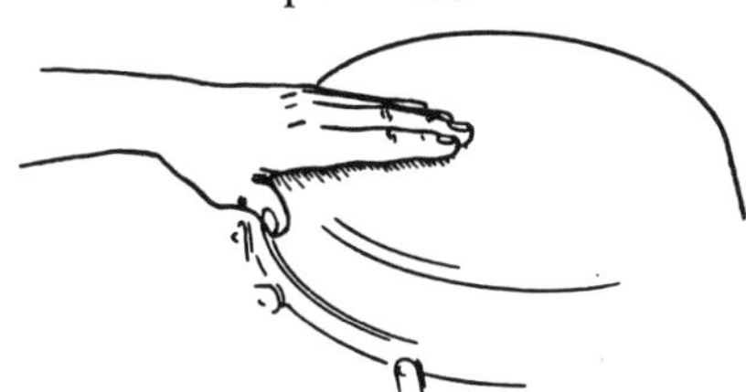

The Slap

The slap, also called the pop, is the most difficult sound to develop. The right hand position is similar to that used for the open tone except that it is slightly cupped allowing only the fingertips to touch the head, with the hand about an inch more towards the center.

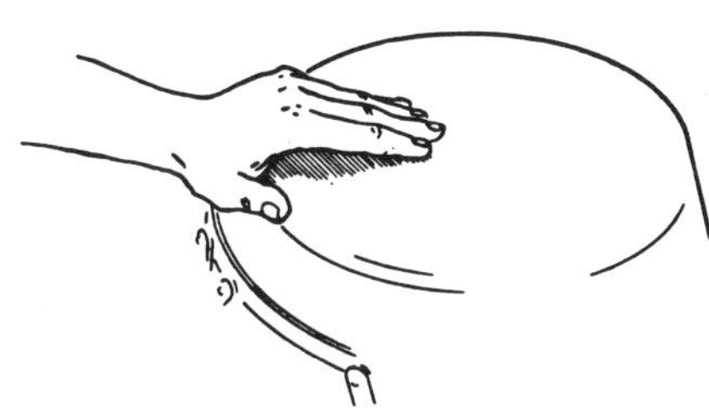

To get a decent sound, the wrist must snap towards the head in a whip-like fashion at the same time that the forearm swings toward the head.

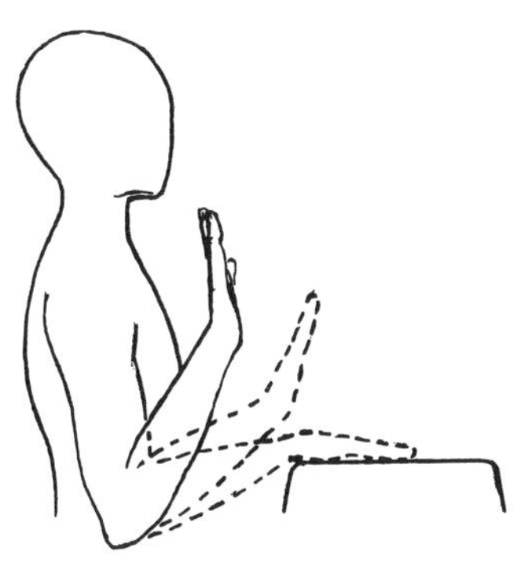

Unlike the open tone, the fingers press down on the head for a brief moment after striking it. Care should be taken not to cup the hand too much, or to cup the fingers towards the side of the drum.

Usually the slap, which doesn't have to be played loud to have the characteristic sound, is played with the right hand while the left hand rests on the far side of the head to dampen any after ring.

Bass Tone

The bass tone is produced by striking the drum in the center of the head with the lower half of the left hand palm, while holding the fingers up.

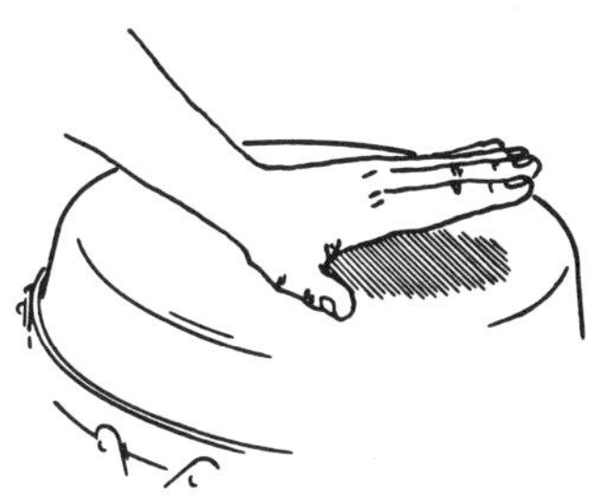

The hand remains on the head but does not press down. The sound should be a deep and resonant boom.

Finger Tone

The finger tone often follows a bass tone and serves more to fill in eighth note spaces and give smoothness to certain rhythms rather than act as a sound by itself. After playing a bass tone the left hand rocks forward so that the fingers hit the drum head producing a muffled thud.

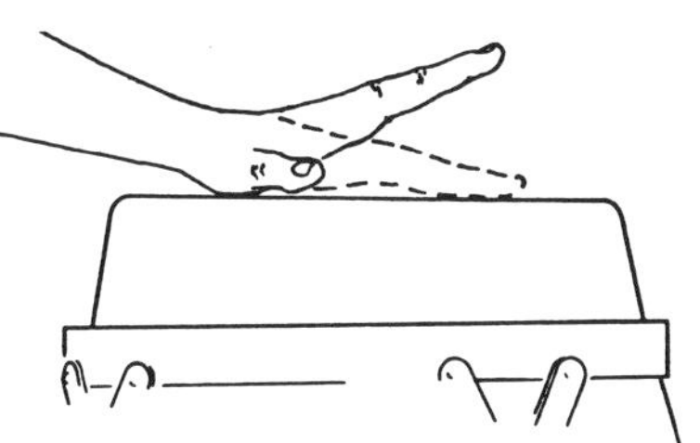

If the following note by the right hand is an open tone, the left hand should be lifted off the head to let the tone ring clearly. If the following tone is a slap, the hand should stay on the head to damp any after ring.

Exercises

When practicing the following exercises the player should strive to make a distinction between each of the four sounds. Starting at a slow comfortable tempo, the player can increase the speed as he progresses. The ability to play these exercises in $\frac{6}{8}$ as well as $\frac{4}{4}$ will prepare him for patterns commonly used in conga solos.

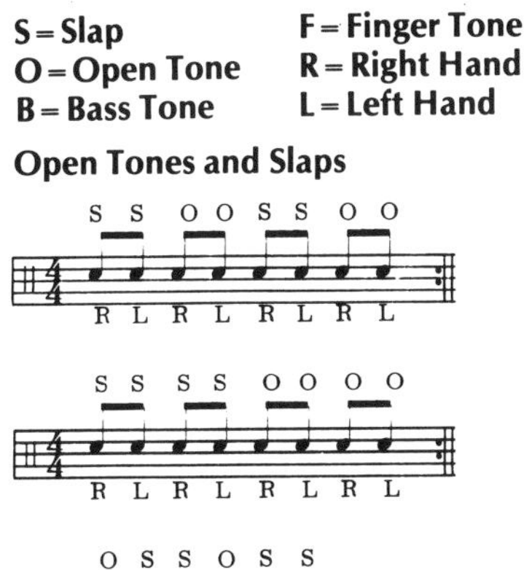

Open Tones, Slaps, Bass Tones, and Finger Tones

Once the player has mastered each of the basic conga drum sounds with each hand he is ready to start playing rhythms. If utilized in a tasteful and musical manner, these conga patterns can add a new dimension to any jazz band performance. For most of the Cuban patterns presented here each hand stays in the same area of the drum. The right hand playing slaps and open tones stays positioned at the edge of the drum, while the left, playing bass and finger tones, stays near the center.

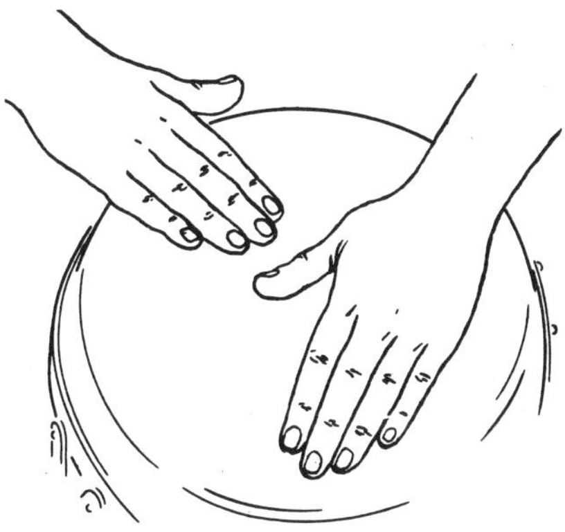

Many of these patterns utilize a rebound following a slap to act as a finger tone. For this sequence the right hand is held in the same position as a slap, but the fingers do not press down on the head.

Cha Cha

The *cha cha* is one of the most common Cuban rhythms used in the United States today and can be adapted for use in many other styles of music. To achieve an authentic sound it must be played with a hard driving quarter-note feel. The slaps should be strong, but not overpowering.

B = Bass Tone
F = Finger Tone
S = Slap
R = Rebound
O = Open Tone

For the variation, finger tones are replaced by slaps in the left hand. By playing the bass tone closer to the edge of the drum the hand is drawn back then rocks forward to execute the slap. The variation is more driving than the standard *cha cha* pattern.

Mambo

The *mambo* is similar to the *cha cha* except that it is played at a faster tempo. As with the *cha cha* the feel of this rhythm should be hard and driving.

The difficulty with the *mambo* variation lies in keeping precise rhythmic placement of the open tone on the "and" of two in the second bar. The rhythmic placement must be smooth and consistent with the rest of the pattern.

Samba

The *samba* is one of the most important rhythms from Brazil. While congas are not traditionally used for a *samba,* they can be effectively adapted by being played with a light, floating, 16th-note feel. The player should stay with one pattern or phrase and keep time leaving the solo fills to the drummer.

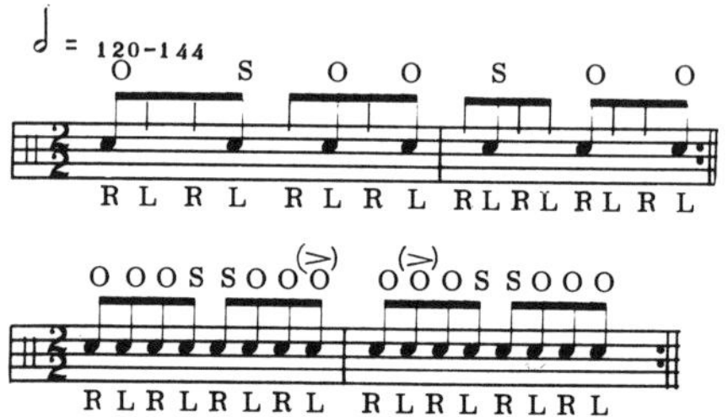

Jazz

Congas are not traditionally used on jazz tunes, but they can enhance a performance with careful and tasty playing. The main problem is making the conga swing in a light way. The slaps and open tones on two and four should be at a normal volume; but the bass and finger tones on one and three should be barely audible, if at all.

Funk

Congas are commonly used in funk and other styles of popular music. When playing the following patterns, the player should rhythmically place all 16th notes equally.

Bolero

The *bolero* (not to be confused with the classical *bolero* in $\frac{3}{4}$) can be an effective accompaniment to a pop-rock ballad. Because *boleros* are usually slow, however, it can be difficult to hold the tempo steady and play the eighth notes evenly.

Although most of these rhythms were originally used as accompaniment to a specific dance, it is possible to adapt them to various styles of music. When adapting these rhythms the player should base whatever pattern he uses on what the bassist and drummer are doing. For example, if both musicians are playing eighth-note rhythms, the conga player will want to play an eighth-note pattern such as the *cha cha* or *bolero.* Also, the length of phrases of all three players should be consistent, and the conga pattern should adapt to the overall feeling and phrasing of the chart. For example, in order to use a *cha cha* on a *bossa nova* it has to be played with a much lighter feel.

By experimenting the conga player can discover which patterns fit with certain kinds of music. Although there are no hard and fast rules, he must use his ears. If it sounds good and fits, then it is right.

Two exceptional recordings of some conga rhythms are *Understanding Latin Rhythms Vol. I* (which comes with an instructional booklet), produced by Latin Percussion Inc., and *Agora* by Paulinho da Costa, produced by Pablo Records. ■

Illustrations by Mark Kilgore.

TYPES of TUNES (with examples)

RHYTHMIC PATTERNS	POP-ROCK BALLAD (Feelings)	SAMBA (Copacabana)	FUNK (Brickhouse)	ROCK (What a Fool Believes)	JAZZ (Killer Joe) (Moondance)	BOSSA-NOVA (Girl from Ipanema)	MAMBO (Malagueña)	CHA-CHA (Oye coma va)
CHA-CHA	X			X		X		X
MAMBO		X	X	X			X	
SAMBA		X	X					
SWING					X			
FUNK			X	X				
BOLERO	X					X		

Editing Overwritten Percussion Parts

Paul Brazauskas

Band directors carefully select new pieces by checking the music's key and time signatures, range for cornets and clarinets, and difficulty of the horn and tuba parts. Unfortunately, many directors don't check the music for the percussion section. Often these parts, especially in concert literature, are overwritten or don't fit with the material scored for the other instruments. Editing such overwritten percussion parts can improve the sound of the band and give less experienced students a chance to perform more music and learn while playing alongside the more advanced musicians in the percussion section.

Helpful Hints

To edit percussion parts, I work from the conductor's score so that the revised part will fit in with the rest of the ensemble. Start by removing some of the grace notes; arrangers often use them to lengthen percussion tones or broaden the drum sound. Having fewer grace notes makes the part playable by less experienced students.

The following examples were edited because students either had trouble with the part, or because the part didn't fit with the rest of the music being played.

Remember that editing a part doesn't mean rewriting it. Try not to get carried away and change every measure.

Young percussionists need to be able to perform alone, in small ensembles, and in the school's band or orchestra. We should make every effort to be sure that inexperienced players have as much opportunity to succeed as possible. Editing overwritten percussion parts is one way we can help. ■

Common Errors in Snare Drum Playing

Dan Spalding

A snare drummer's goal is twofold: (1) to play with perfect evenness in both volume and rhythm, and (2) to produce a sound quality that is clear, precise, and musical. My observations of young players in festivals and concerts reveal common errors that stand in the way of this goal. Most can be corrected with proper guidance.

The sticks are not matched. It is impossible to play the drums evenly when each stick is a different weight, size, and density. When purchasing sticks, check the pitch of each one by dropping it on a hard floor. Also, listen for the sound quality the sticks produce by playing on a pad or other hard surface. If the sticks come paired in a plastic bag that the salesman won't let you open, go to another store. If that isn't possible, buy several pairs at a time and match them up at home.

The sticks are too small or too large. When playing on a standard 5½" or 6½" x 14" concert snare drum, use medium-size sticks that have strong shoulders, such as the 2B or Vic Firth General Purpose models. Inexperienced players overplay the drum with 3S sticks left over from marching season, while set drummers often use sticks that are too thin to produce a good round tone.

The sticks do not hit in the same spot. Nothing changes tone more drastically than sticks striking the drumhead in different places. Most playing should be done in the center, even at *piano* levels. However, when a situation requires moving toward the edge, make sure that each stick is the same distance from the rim. This position insures a consistent tone quality from right to left. You also get a consistent response by placing the drum so the snares are on a line between 12 and 6 o'clock, then moving the sticks up and down between these two points.

Proper playing area and snare drum set up

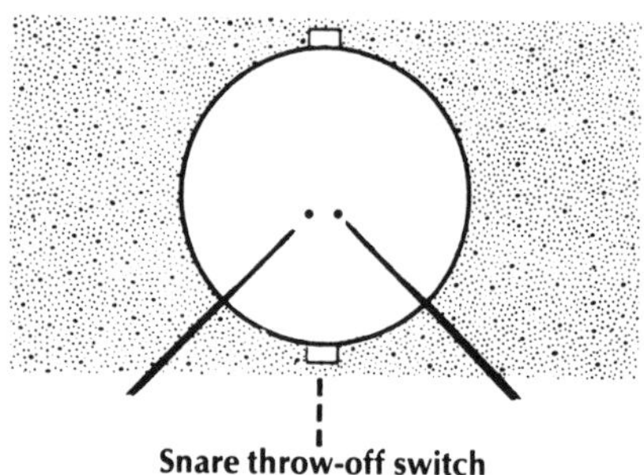

The sticks project at different angles. This problem is usually typical of traditional grip players who fail to tilt the drum properly. Always adjust the drum to accommodate your grip, not vice versa. Make sure that both sticks strike a direct blow even if this means tilting the drum as much as 45 degrees. Players who use the matched grip should not tilt the drum at all.

The snares are too loose. Young drummers invariably loosen the snare tension to help cover up lumpy buzz roll technique. Doing this may help the roll sound, but unfortunately, all the other articulations are affected; the sound becomes "mushy" and the rhythms are indistinguishable. To avoid this problem, loosen the snares just below the tension point where the drum begins to sound choked so that the sound is dry and crisp. A tight bottom head will also help shorten the response.

The tone control (mute) is too tight. A drum's unwanted ring is best controlled by having the felt lightly touch the head. Any more pressure makes the mute less effective. If the mute is not enough to stop any unwanted ring, a billfold or handkerchief placed on the head near the edge usually works well.

Heads are too loose or tension is uneven. It is important to make sure that the tension around each head is even, otherwise the full tone of the drum is inhibited. When replacing a head, finger tighten all the tension rods as much as possible, then tighten them with the key by going around the head, using full or half turns. Be sure to keep track of the starting and ending point of each turn. Next, fine tune the head by lightly tapping at each lug to listen for the pitch; make adjustments accordingly. In most cases, you won't have to make too many changes. Generally, concert snare drums sound and respond best when pitched high. Keep this in mind, especially if you use a snare from a drum set, because these snares are usually kept at a lower pitch in order to obtain "fat" sounding backbeats.

All of these common errors are related to use of the equipment. When they are corrected, the player will be able to concentrate on the music and snare drum technique without any unnecessary handicaps. ■

Is It Live or Is It a Drum Machine?

Dave Black

The digital drum machine, a drum set in a box, is the latest of the computerized devices to have a profound effect on contemporary music and the recording industry. Played by controlling slides, pushing buttons, and turning knobs, these machines offer a variety of features that make their use practical by percussionists and non-percussionists alike.

Machines on the Market

Though the features of these machines vary according to price (the more expensive ones have more to offer), you'll find most of them reproduce the following:

- bass drum, snare drum, open hi-hat, closed hi-hat, cymbals, and hand clap sounds
- pre-set rhythmic patterns
- any newly programmed rhythmic pattern
- any rhythmic pattern in perfect time

For example, the new Dr. Rhythm from Boss is a portable workshop drum machine that has a graphic readout designed for easy programming. The sounds can be programmed into 32 different rhythmic patterns, which can be combined into two complete songs of 128 measures each. Its suggested retail price is $240.

The TR-909 Rhythm Composer produced by RolandCorp is a more expensive drum machine. It offers two dynamic levels that can be programmed on the bass, snare, hi-hat, and all tom sounds; and accent, flam, and shuffle effects can be added. The sounds can be arranged into 96 programmable patterns that can be grouped into songs on four memory tracks. The memory capacity of this machine is 1,792 notes, and the equipment will interface with other synthesizers. The suggested retail price is $1,200.

The LinnDrum is getting the most attention of all the drum machines. The first of its kind, the LinnDrum is being used by such artists as Michael Jackson, Billy Joel, Lionel Richie, Jeff Pocaro, and Harvey Mason, to name a few. Because it uses actual digitally recorded drum sounds, percussionists say this machine has the most authentic sound on the market. Even with a price tag of several thousand dollars, many players are using the LinnDrum.

In addition to backing up other musicians, the drum machine has other uses. It's possible to program a pattern, one element at a time at a slow tempo, then play back the pattern at a tempo that would be difficult or impossible for a drummer to execute. Also, players can study and develop more difficult patterns on the drum machine using slow tempos, then reproduce them on a conventional drum set.

A Significant Question

Because many writers, artists, and producers are now using drum machines, players view this equipment as a tool and consider its use as a skill necessary for the job. However, many drummers are asking, "Will the drum machines put me out of work?" One answer is found in remembering that drum machines can't program themselves – a person needs to do that; and although anyone can program a drum machine, the professional drummer has the ability to make it sound the most authentic.

There is, however, a market where the drum machine may replace the percussionist – the jingle market. Because many jingles are only a few seconds long, often with only the lyrics or orchestration changed when used again, a studio could hire a drummer to record a number of patterns that could be used over several years.

Pros and Cons

The drum machine's ability to keep perfect time can be seen both as an advantage or a disadvantage depending on the musical requirements of the job. Because dance music requires a steady, unwavering beat, the drum machine is the perfect choice, whereas a drummer would play with some irregularity in the beat. (For example, the LinnDrum is used in Irene Cara's *Flash Dance.*) The disadvantage is that many drummers don't care for the metronome-like feel of such perfect time because it eliminates any chance for interplay between musicians. In fact, professional drummers are known to "move the notes around" in a bar so there is never a feeling of perfect time. The human touch just cannot be programmed into a machine. The lack of personality and energy is a big complaint about drum machines, and a further reason why they will never entirely replace the live performer.

It's unlikely that a single product like the drum machine will completely change the music industry, but if such a machine can be used to help the musician expand and enhance his ideas, then its use is essential. ■

Marching Percussion Rehearsal Techniques

Barry D. Bridwell

While the band director discusses clarinet fingerings and trumpet phrasing with the rest of the marching band, the percussion players usually become bored, lose concentration, and hence, make little progress. If you're a band director and have never scheduled a percussion sectional because you don't know where to begin, keep reading.

Get Organized

Before the sectional rehearsal, decide what it is you want to accomplish during the hour and write it down. Except for the beginning of the season when the main focus is on fundamentals, my rehearsal plan usually looks like this:

Warm-ups	:05
Timing exercises	:10
Patterns	:10
Main target	:30
Final run-through	:05
Total	:60

Be sure to take a watch or clock to rehearsal, and stick with your schedule. Your players will appreciate your efficiency and feel more compelled to concentrate.

Warm-ups

Players who attempt to warm up by playing complex patterns at blazing fast tempos are defeating the purpose of preparing mentally and physically for rehearsal, not to mention risking such injuries as pulled muscles and severe cramps. Warm-ups should be simple drills, and the following two exercises make good warm-ups for several reasons:

- They are playable by any level of percussionist.
- They can be taught by rote quickly.
- The entire section, except the cymbals, can play them in unison.
- Their simplicity allows the players to concentrate on such aspects as grip, stick angle, stick height, etc.

Multiple stroke exercise. Start out playing eight measures in succession with each hand, then four measures, two, one, then one-half. Because there is a tendency to speed up the tempo each time the number of strokes per hand is diminished, the director may have to conduct a few bars at each changing point. However, you should try to minimize your conducting and let the players feel the time. Save your motions to cue changes in tempo, dynamics, patterns, etc.

Single stroke exercise. The most basic coordination problem – hand to hand alternation – is encountered here. Count off a tempo and ask the section to maintain it at a moderate volume for at least 30 seconds. Then test the players' alertness by having them change tempo without changing the dynamic level, and vice versa. You can cue dynamic changes by raising or lowering your hand, or you may want to try a number system, such as this one:

1 – as soft as possible with control
2 – soft
3 – general playing volume
4 – loud
5 – as loud as possible with control

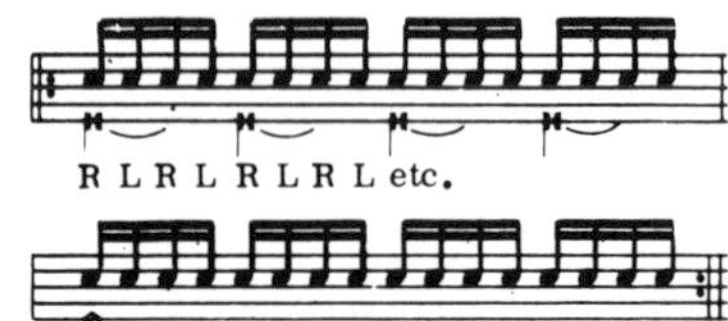

As your section improves, make the warm-ups more challenging by adding accents to the patterns and letting the cymbals play on the accents.

Be careful not to use up too much of the clock with the warm-ups, and allow 20-30 seconds after each one for players to stretch their finger muscles.

Timing Exercises

Timing exercises teach percussion players to feel subdivisions as a section. A good exercise to begin with is a whole note exercise used by Fred Sanford. Play through the exercise a few times with the whole section in unison, then split into segments and play the exercise as a round (snares start off, two measures later toms begin, then basses). The overlapping rhythms make each player aware of his own tendency to rush or drag the tempo.

After the whole note exercise, begin to focus on problems common to each instrument. Snare drummers and tom players need to work on various rudiments such as double-stroke rolls, paradiddles, drags, and sextuplets. Mallet players should practice scales, *arpeggios*, and double-stops; and bass drummers and cymbalists need to practice playing tonal parts, where each player is responsible for one pitch, in a melodic line.

Although there are a number of good books with section exercises for drumlines, you may find it more helpful to write your own and teach them by rote. Begin by writing a short snare drum exercise of two to four measures in length and incorporate one of the rudiments. Double this part in the toms and add pitches. For the bass drums and cymbals, write a simple melodic part using ascending or descending lines. Then find a scale or *arpeggio* that fits into the rhythmic scheme for the mallets.

Teaching by rote requires patience. Rehearse one group at a time. Sing the snare drum part and have the players perform it at a slow speed. Check to see if their sticking is uniform and accurate. Gradually increase the tempo. Next, do the same for players on the toms. Have the students play their part entirely on one drum at first, changing to another drum on each repetition. Only when they have succeeded in mastering the rhythm should you allow them to play rhythms and pitches.

Mallet players usually have no problem learning timing exercises, but bass drummers and cymbalists almost always do, partly because they fail to see the importance and excitement of their roles. To encourage some enthusiasm, get the whole section into the act. Split the section into as many units as you have bass drums and have them clap the bass drum rhythms as a group. The snare drummers always get a charge out of this activity, and everyone will welcome the chance to take the instruments off for a while.

Repeat this entire procedure with each timing exercise you write. Make sure that for each group, you focus only on one technical problem at a time so that the players can devote their full attention to mastering that technique. As a result, your percussionists will be able to execute the particular technique correctly when they encounter it in a musical situation.

Patterns

Once you have established a repertoire of timing exercises, combine them to create different patterns. Start with two exercises, alternating between them without pausing. When the pattern is mastered add another exercise. Before you know it your section will have a fairly lengthy pattern memorized to accompany the band's daily scale warm-ups.

Main Target

At the beginning of the season, spend the entire sectional rehearsal working on warm-ups, timing exercises, and patterns. Once fundamentals begin to solidify, however, you will need to spend most of the rehearsal working on music, solos, and cadences. To make more efficient use of this "main target" portion of the rehearsal, prepare the section members for the required techniques by covering them in the timing exercises and patterns. For example, if the selection you are working on requires a variety of paradiddle patterns, work those same patterns into the timing exercises.

Learning New Music

When working on a new chart concentrate on learning the rhythm first. Have each tom player perform on one drum, and have each bass drummer play the entire bass drum part. Next, focus on getting the proper pitches, then add dynamics and phrasing. Only after the musical aspect of performing begins to take shape should you think about the visual aspect. When everyone has learned the rhythms, pitches, dynamics, and visuals, you are ready for polishing.

If at all possible, split the section into smaller groups when working on music. Perhaps your section leader is capable of rehearsing the snares and toms. If so, send them off to another location for a few minutes. Then you can concentrate more on the remaining players. The smaller the group the more you can accomplish.

Final Run-Through

Always reserve a few minutes

before dismissal time for a final run-through. This should be a time of intense performance-level concentration. Announce the selection to your players and allow them a few seconds to prepare themselves mentally, then call them to attention. Wait until there is perfect silence and no movements, then count off the selection. After they finish, make sure they freeze at attention until you give them the at-ease.

This portion of the rehearsal can do wonders for your section's morale, pride, and confidence. You may even wish to set aside one tape for "percussion sectionals" and record the run-throughs each time. This procedure enables both you and the students to evaluate progress. Before dismissing the section, tell the players how you feel about what was accomplished, especially if you were pleased.

Obviously there are more steps involved in staging a successful marching percussion sectional than have been included here, but these exercises and suggestions are a good place to start.

Below is a list of supplementary materials that may help you in putting together a first-rate drumline.

Recommended Method Books

Corps Style Warm-ups, Jay A. Wanamaker (Alfred). Progressive series of warm-up exercises for high school or college ensemble. Instrumentation includes bells, xylophone, snare, multi-toms, bass drums, and cymbals, but exercises are written in such a way that some parts may be omitted. Designed to precede every rehearsal and performance.

Developing Corps Style Percussion, Michael J. Cahill (Hal Leonard). Seventeen full ensemble exercises (snare, tri-toms, four bass drums, cymbals, and mallets), plus five exercises for snares only. Includes coaching tips that could be helpful for an inexperienced conductor. Recommended for high schools who do not have a percussion instructor.

Marching Percussion Method: An Ensemble Approach, Will Rapp (Jenson). Excellent approach to teaching rudimental style through full ensemble warm-ups and timing exercises. Includes several one- and two-measure patterns, plus longer street-beat type patterns. Each exercise is preceded by helpful hints, and the book is filled with illustrations on grips, carriage, tuning, etc. Written for snares, tri-toms, four bass drums, cymbals, and mallets, the book is appropriate for intermediate and advanced players.

Percussion Section: Developing the Corps Style, Sherman Hong and Jim Hamilton (Eagle Press). Excellent manual for the band director or section leader which includes information on tuning, maintenance, purchasing, staging, scoring, and visuals, in addition to the proper method of teaching individual and ensemble technique. Exercises are included for snare, tri-toms, bass drums, cymbals, mallets, timpani, and accessories, as well as full ensemble.

Films

Championship Marching Percussion, McCormick's "How-to Series." This film, featuring Larry McCormick and the Santa Clara Vanguard Drum and Bugle Corps, spotlights the ingredients in a championship marching percussion section, as well as discussing the three basic movements used in precision drumming. 14 minutes.

Building the Section, McCormick's "Instant Learning Series." This film features Fred Sanford and the Santa Clara Vanguard Percussion Section as it focuses on the techniques involved with playing each of the instruments in the marching percussion section. ■

September, 1984

Even Percussionists Can Be Musicians

Lance Haas

Many band directors are plagued by a lack of musicianship from members of the percussion section. Because snare drum solo literature for junior high and high school students often consists of nothing more than a series of rhythmic patterns designed to develop sticking technique, these players spend much of their time just pounding out rhythms. As a result their ability to interpret music is severely limited. A possible alternative is to provide these students with snare drum music that inspires musical interpretation.

A Musical Solo

Three Dances for Solo Snare Drum by Warren Benson (Chappell & Co., distributed by Hal Leonard) is one of the best pieces I have found that provides percussionists with a musical snare drum solo. It contains a wealth of material that requires a sensitive and thoughtful interpretation. For example, in the third movement the players must hit the sticks together in what resembles a chromatic scale. This requirement alone makes selecting the sticks a critical issue, because just any pair will not do. Players will need to check the sticks for resonance and choose the ones with the best tone quality. Such a judgment requires a musical decision on the part of the students. Here are some of the musical elements that *Three Dances* has to offer.

The First Movement

Because the piece is programmatic in nature, the title of each movement suggests the composer's intent and provides some interpretive clues. "Cretan Dance," the first movement, is based on the music used to accompany traditional dancers who leap in and out between two long wooden clappers that are controlled by kneeling members of the dance troop. The $\frac{5}{4}$ meter provides a rhythmic structure that suggests this action.

This movement requires drum sticking that alternates between the center and the edge of the instrument's surface, with the player developing both tone qualities. Practicing the technique can help cure a major problem among snare drummers, the "piano-edge" syndrome – moving to the edge of the drum for all musical passages marked *piano* or *pianissimo*. Because the edge of the drum offers a unique sound, the area should be used only when it is specifically requested by the composer, and not for each softly indicated passage in every score.

The Second Movement

Titled "Fox Trot," a dance usually performed by a man and woman duo, this movement gives players a chance to develop independent sticking. Using the idea of a canon, the player's left hand directly imitates his right hand after four measures of playing.

For teaching purposes, I call the right hand the leader (as in a dance duo) and the left hand the follower. Choosing the mallets coincides with a correct interpretation because the right hand plays with a wooden stick for a louder sound and the left hand uses a brush to get a softer quality. In this movement, students can play the eighth notes with a swing feel, ♫ = ♩𝄾♪ (triplet), to provide a more authentic fox trot style. style.

The Third Movement

"Fandango" is scored with a principal theme that suggests the heel tapping of a Spanish dancer. It uses an unusual technique that involves striking one stick on the other while still using the snare drum head to imply a castanet sound.

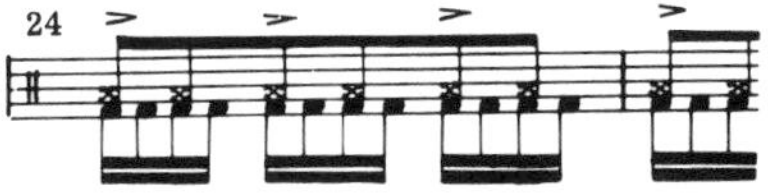

The climax of the movement, however, is achieved by players simply striking the sticks together, squeezing them to dampen the resonance and then gradually loosening the grip to increase it. The pitch is also controlled by changing the striking position from the center of the sticks to the tip area. If the final three measures of the movement are played carefully, the resulting chromatic scale effect offers a truly climactic ending.

Three Dances for Solo Snare Drum is just one example of music that gives percussionists a chance to be musicians. Using such selections gives students a reason for developing interpretive skills and techniques on the snare drum rather than just pumping out rhythmic patterns. ■

October, 1984

New Trends in Rudimental Snare Drumming

Jay Wanamaker

The percussion world is experiencing new trends in snare drumming. Because of the influence of drum and bugle corps, a virtuoso style of drumming has emerged that includes traditional, Swiss, and contemporary rudiment styles, as well as multiple and odd time signatures and visual effects. A new "bible" of drum rudiments, the *International Drum Rudiments List,* from the Percussive Arts Society, plus standardized notation for drum rudiments have also contributed to the trend. Being familiar with the language of today's rudimental drumming is important for every percussionist. It is what differentiates the championship style of Frank Assenault in the 1950s from that of Rob Carson in the 1980s.

Swiss Rudiments

As the forerunner of several American rudiments, Swiss rudiments have become quite popular and are often used when substituting sticking patterns.

Tap flams (inverted flam tap). Similar to the traditional flam tap (R R L L), tap flams have a tendency to produce a heavier sound that creates more flow.

Tap Flam

(Music examples from the *Corps Style Snare Drum Dictionary* by Jay Wanamaker, published by Alfred)

To gain facility in each hand, I suggest practicing the right and left hand rhythms of a rudiment separately. Practice tap flams by performing three consecutive strokes off of one hand to build the technique that is needed to perform the rudiment.

Tap Flam Practice

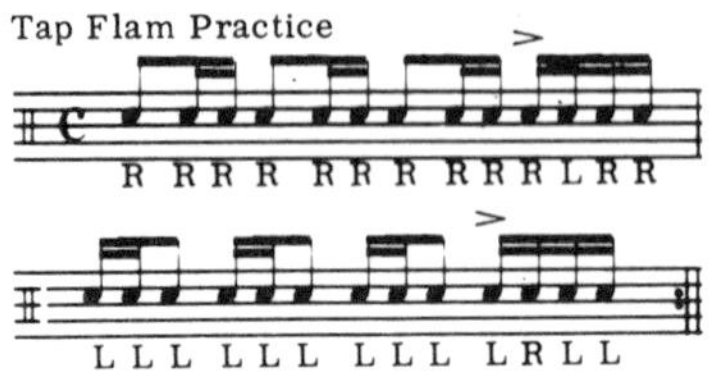

This approach also works well with flam taps.

Pataflaflas. Perform pataflaflas singularly, off a flam, doubled, or connected with a flam paradiddle.

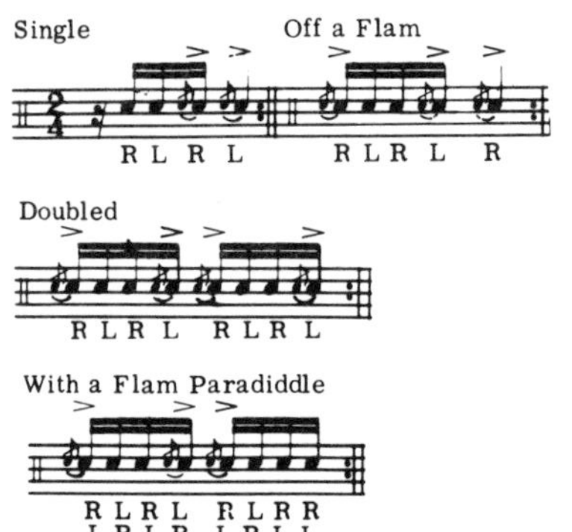

Swiss Army Triplets. As the most common Swiss rudiment in America, Swiss triplets are often substituted for flam accents (RLR LRL) because they are much easier to perform at quick tempos.

Swiss Triplet

Dragadiddles. These rudiments are actually paradiddles (RLRRLRLL) played with a double stroke in place of the accent.

Windmills. These strokes are often used as substitutes for flam paradiddles (RLRR LRLL), because they are easier to perform at quick tempos.

Berger Lesson 25. Identical to the standard Lesson 25 rudiment (R LLR LR LLR L) this rudiment contains a variation in sticking.

Berger Lesson 25

Flammed Rolls. Placing the flam on the attack of a roll is a common practice in the Swiss style.

Flammed Nine Stroke

Rolls

The majority of rolls played in a rudimental solo are performed as double stroke open rolls. Arrangers use slashed 16th notes (32nd notes) rather than grace notes to indicate the double strokes (RR L RR L). It is a method of notation that has become common practice in recent rudimental performance. Multiple bounce rolls (buzz rolls) are now notated with a "z" through the stem: .

Triplet Rolls. Often performed in $\frac{6}{8}$ meter, the triplet roll requires a triple pulsation, not the double pulsation commonly found in $\frac{4}{4}$ meter.

Tap Rolls. Used to initiate and accent the beginning of a roll, tap rolls are performed by placing a single stroke accent at the beginning of the roll.

Six Stroke Rolls. A form of a tap roll, the six stroke roll begins with a tap and ends with a tap.

Notation

Interpretation

Triple Stroke Rolls. Recently added to the rudiment list, the triple stroke roll is performed by playing three single strokes on each hand. Initially, I suggest using one wrist turn while bouncing the following two strokes.

Triple Stroke Rolls

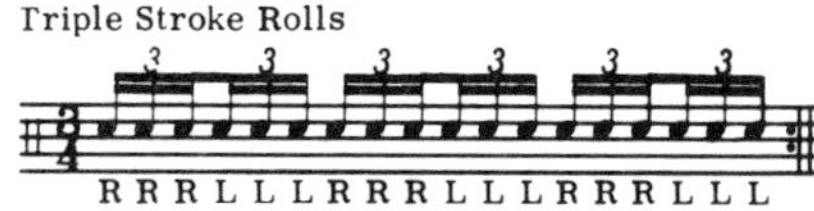

Visual Effects

A number of visual effects are

used in rudimental solos. It is not uncommon to find works that call for such visuals as twirling, throwing, and flipping the drum sticks.

Back Sticking (B.S.). To accomplish back sticking, turn the drum stick so that the butt end strikes the drum head. Rotate each stick in a clockwise direction until the butt end strikes the playing surface. You can successfully use both matched and traditional grips for this effect.

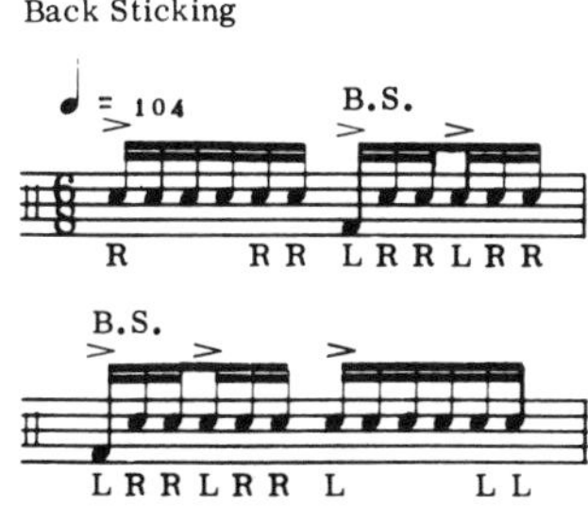

Tap Sticking (T.S.). Perform this effect by striking the shoulder of the right stick against the shoulder of the left stick, about six inches above the drum head.

Stick on Stick (S.O.S.). Execute stick on stick by clicking the shoulder of the right stick against the shoulder of the left stick in front of your chest.

Stick Shots. Perform stick shots by striking the right stick on top of the left stick while the left stick rests on both the drum and the rim. You can raise and lower the left stick from the rim in order to produce varied effects.

Rim Shots. Strike the drum head so that the drum stick contacts the rim three to four inches from the tip, while the tip of the stick simultaneously strikes the drum. To perform double rim shots strike both hands simultaneously, as for the rim shot, to obtain additional volume.

Rim Click (R.C.) With the left palm holding the shoulder of the stick in the center of the drum head strike the rim with the butt end of the same stick. Rim clicks are commonly used to imitate a clave-like sound when performing a bossa nova or any other Latin rhythm.

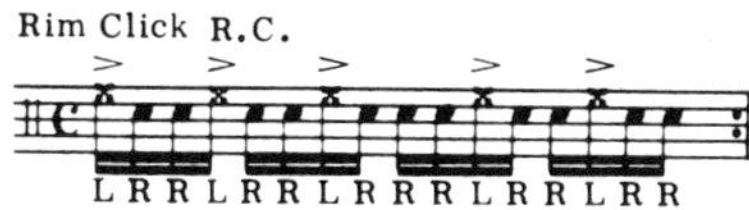

Solos

I recommend the following list of rudimental snare drum solos for advanced high school percussionists.

Championship Corps Style Contest Solos, Wanamaker (Alfred)
Chop Buster, Wanamaker (Potsdam)
Corps-Dially Yours, Funnell (Kendor)
Punctuality, Varner (Permus)
Snare Drum Solo, Tuthill (Music for Percussion)
Snare Drum Solo No. 1, Petercsak (Music for Percussion) ■

Screening Prospective Percussionists

by Dennis Koehler

Too often we look at our junior high or high school percussion section and wonder how certain students ever got started on percussion. Some of them cannot march in step with the music and simply cannot play certain basic rhythms.

The time to wonder about these students is not in high school but at the beginning, before they start to learn percussion. A simple test at the beginning can save years of disappointment and embarrassment for the director and the students.

I use a short test to help measure the coordination and rhythmic ability of prospective percussion students. The first part of this test deals with coordination of hands and feet, while the second part measures the ability to perceive, retain, and play back rhythms. The test (reproduced here) evaluates each skill and serves as a guide for later instructions to each student.

Coordination

When taking the test, students need to tap hard so there is no doubt about the placement of each beat. Steps 1-3 are basic; students who cannot accomplish these three will have difficulty learning any percussion instrument. Check coordination of foot and hand with the click of the metronome and whether the student understands right and left, follows instructions the first time, and keeps time with his foot without having to look at it.

When explaining steps 4-7, keep the terminology simple. For example, in step 4, tell the student: "Tap the hand twice for every time the foot taps once." When demonstrating you may also wish to count "1-2, 1-2" or "1 and, 2 and." If the student makes it to step 7, explain that 2 against 3 can be done as "together, one and one."

Those who can do every step fairly well definitely have enough coordination to begin the study of a percussion instrument.

Rhythm Repeats Test

I usually tap my hand on the desk and ask the student to do the same. Make sure the student understands that you will tap each rhythm only once. Try to play each pattern without any accents, as a shift of emphasis can change the level of difficulty.

As with any diagnostic test, you should not expect a student to make a perfect score in order to qualify; many people can have rewarding experiences with less than genius-level natural talent. ■

Percussion Test

Student's Name__________ Class-Period__________

COORDINATION: Students should tap a minimum of 8 counts with the metronome set at 80.

	Good	Fair	Poor	Not At All
Step 1: right foot & right hand together				
Step 2: left foot & left hand together				
Step 3: either foot & alternate hands (LRLR)				

The director explains & demonstrates each step before the student attempts it

Step 4: Tap quarter notes with either foot & eighth notes with the right hand				
Step 5: Tap quarter notes with either foot & triplets with the right hand				
Step 6: Tap quarter notes with either foot & sixteenth notes with the right hand				
Step 7: Tap quarter notes with either foot, eighth notes with the left hand & triplets with the right hand				

RHYTHM REPEATS: The director taps each rhythm once and the student taps it right back (by ear).

1.				
2. ¢				
3. ¢				
4.				
5.				
6.				

Additional Comments:__________

Recommendation:__________

Other Test Results:__________

International Drum Rudiments

Percussive Arts Society

All rudiments should be practiced: *open* (slow) to *close* (fast) to *open* (slow) and/or at an even moderate march tempo.

I. ROLL RUDIMENTS

A. SINGLE STROKE ROLL RUDIMENTS

1. SINGLE STROKE ROLL *

2. SINGLE STROKE FOUR

3. SINGLE STROKE SEVEN

B. MULTIPLE BOUNCE ROLL RUDIMENTS

4. MULTIPLE BOUNCE ROLL

5. TRIPLE STROKE ROLL

C. DOUBLE STROKE OPEN ROLL RUDIMENTS

6. DOUBLE STROKE OPEN ROLL *

7. FIVE STROKE ROLL *

8. SIX STROKE ROLL

9. SEVEN STROKE ROLL *

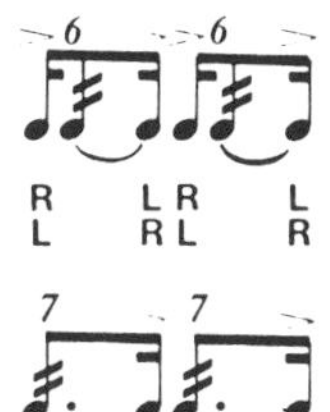

10. NINE STROKE ROLL *

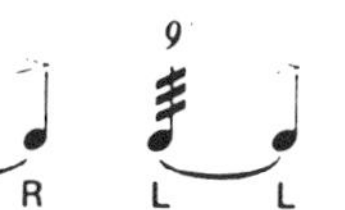

11. TEN STROKE ROLL *

12. ELEVEN STROKE ROLL *

13. THIRTEEN STROKE ROLL *

14. FIFTEEN STROKE ROLL *

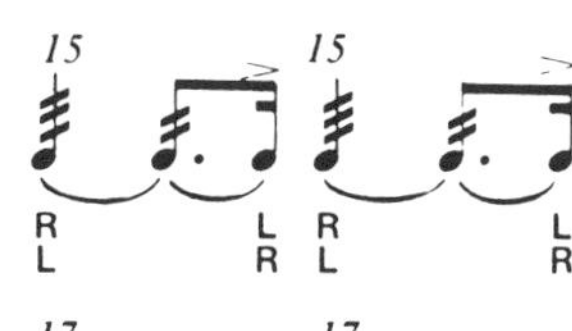

15. SEVENTEEN STROKE ROLL

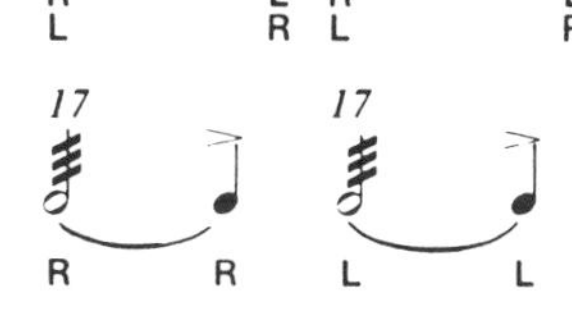

II. DIDDLE RUDIMENTS

16. SINGLE PARADIDDLE *

17. DOUBLE PARADIDDLE *

18. TRIPLE PARADIDDLE

19. SINGLE PARADIDDLE-DIDDLE

*These rudiments are also included in the original Standard 26 American Drum Rudiments.

III. FLAM RUDIMENTS

20. FLAM *

21. FLAM ACCENT *

22. FLAM TAP *

23. FLAMACUE *

24. FLAM PARADIDDLE *

25. SINGLE FLAMMED MILL

26. FLAM PARADIDDLE-DIDDLE *

27. PATAFLAFLA

28. SWISS ARMY TRIPLET

29. INVERTED FLAM TAP

30. FLAM DRAG

IV. DRAG RUDIMENTS

31. DRAG *

LL R RR L

32. SINGLE DRAG TAP *

33. DOUBLE DRAG TAP *

34. LESSON 25 *

35. SINGLE DRAGADIDDLE

36. DRAG PARADIDDLE #1 *

37. DRAG PARADIDDLE #2 *

38. SINGLE RATAMACUE *

39. DOUBLE RATAMACUE *

40. TRIPLE RATAMACUE *

Fortissimo to Pianissimo — A Percussionist's Dilemma

Larry White

One of the more difficult assignments for a percussionist to face is a musical passage calling for an immediate drop from a dynamic level of *fortissimo* to one marked *pianissimo*. Whether performing on snare drum, xylophone, or timpani, or any instrument of the percussion family struck with a mallet, one basic premise has to be understood: all dynamics on these instruments need to be controlled by stick or mallet height. So many drummers, when approached with this problem, head for the rim when playing snare, or move their mallets to the nodal point on a xylophone or marimba bar. This solution does indeed lower the dynamic level, but it also diminishes the quality and timbre of sound. Learning to control the mallet during a sudden drop from loud to soft is a process that needs to be practiced.

Suppose a snare drummer is faced with the following passage:

Both examples illustrate an immediate change from *ff* to *pp*, with no *decrescendo* or *diminuendo* indicated by the composer. In judging of various contests on the high school and symphonic levels, I have witnessed players attempting the change in dynamics by using a quick *diminuendo* or *crescendo* to reach the new level — but not accomplishing this until after the fact. To make sure, in example 1, that the last 16th note in the first measure is *ff* and beat one in the second measure is *pp*, I suggest the following sticking:

In other words, use a paradiddle RLRR for the fourth beat, with the RR giving the player ample time to quickly position the left stick a half-inch off of the rim, ready and waiting to begin measure two at *pp*. With practice, this concept works very well and enables the player to keep the flow of the rhythm intact. The problem of alternating dynamic levels frequently can be solved this way:

Here, with both sticks striking the same spot on the head, the player's right hand represents "loud" and is positioned accordingly above the drum, while his left hand represents "soft" and stays about one inch off the head through the passage. Again, control of the weaker hand and thus the dynamic level can be achieved through practice, ideally in front of a mirror.

For the mallet instruments, especially the xylophone, immediate dynamic control happens through much the same technique. Where, because of the contour of a particular phrase, a double-sticking is inappropriate, the player should practice "digging in" with the last two strokes and leave his mallets a half-inch off the bar in preparation for the ensuing *pp* section:

Where appropriate, single sticking of a particularly soft passage with the mallet no more than an inch above the bar is most effective at achieving the desired drop from *fortissimo* to *pianissimo*, following a loud alternated pattern:

Going from *ff* to *pp* on the timpani can usually be achieved through lowered mallet height, but with timpani, muffling of the loud passage is necessary and presents problems:

Here, the player treats the quarter-note on beat three as an eighth note, followed by a quick muffle on the second half of three with the left hand, effectively killing the sound before the ensuing *piano* level in the second measure. Another, but less recommended method would have the muffling occur in place of beat one in the second measure, and then playing beat two softly:

Whether on snare drum, xylophone, or timpani, playing dynamic drops from loud to soft is possible through many of the techniques described above. For today's percussionist, achieving the dynamic change musically, is the ideal to strive for. ■

March, 1985

A Drag is Not a Diddle

Sherman Hong

The January, 1985 issue contained a listing of forty rudiments approved by the Percussive Arts Society International Rudiments Committee. As a member of that committee, I can assure your readers that we approached the compilation of new and traditional rudiments with a great deal of thought and discussion. Because our committee was composed of concert percussionists and teachers, marching percussion instructors, and industry educational specialists, we were able to discuss and consider varied approaches to notation, interpretation, and execution of rudiments. Not all opinions or thoughts were reflected in the final listing; however, we did compromise in most cases.

The list published in *The Instrumentalist* is only a partial representation of the complete listings. For a more complete understanding of snare drum rudimental expectations (fundamental stick control), I recommend that interested teachers and players obtain a copy of *International Drum Rudiments* (Alfred Publishing Company), compiled by Jay Wanamaker and Rob Carson. That publication reflects our concerns with both rudimental and concert snare drum technical executions.

The book expresses a pedagogical concern that the listing is a collection of rhythmic and sticking patterns grouped into four families: rolls, diddles, flams, and drags. It was our expectation that teachers and students should learn those rudiments or patterns applicable to their performance situations and levels. For example, a junior high band student would find few applications of the "pataflafla" or "inverted flam tap" in his educational environment; yet another junior high person who plays in a drum corps would be expected to perform those.

I would like to discuss some concerns I have with a few of the notated and interpretation suggestions in the book. There were some alternate notations of rudiments which, I feel, create problems for those who have students that play in both concert and marching groups. The prime problem arises with notation and interpretation of double and triple grace notes. In the traditional rudimental and concert sense, grace notes should be executed at a playing height of approximately ½" to 1" above the drum head. The resultant volume level would be *pianissimo* to *mezzo-piano*. In the execution of drags or ruffs, the dynamic interpretation would then be

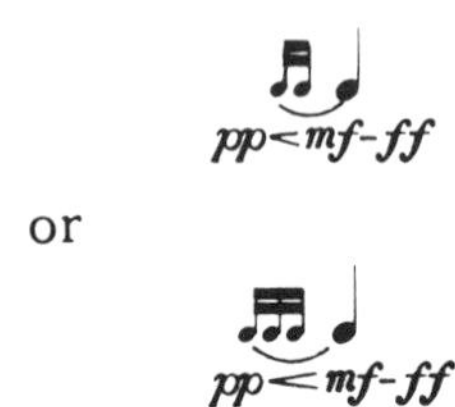

This interpretation, in my opinion, is valid for concert and traditional rudimental performance. The alternate notation given can easily be misinterpreted. For example, the four-stroke ruff

is listed in rudimental interpretation as

That notation does not relate to the traditional interpretation;

rather, what is notated is the corps style interpretation. Note that in corps style notation, the grace notes become precisely timed singlets played at a tap level or above; thus, the rhythm and nuance are completely different from traditional interpretation. Another example is seen in rudiment 34, the lesson 25

The alternate notation given is

Proper dynamic illustration would show a difference in resultant timing and sound pattern:

as opposed to

The error is notating the grace notes as diddles (double taps). The second patern is easier for a marching snare drum section to time and execute precisely; however, the rhythmic interpretation has been changed completely.

Another case in point is the dragadiddle

Instead of a drag, what is expected to be played is a diddle so perhaps it should be called a diddle-ly-diddle

Such syllabification works in quickly producing the proper nuance and rhythmic interpretation. To help my own students learn the proper sound of the rudimental patterns, I use a general rule: diddles are double taps played *mezzo forte* or louder; grace notes are always played at a *pianissimo* to *mezzo piano* level. Remember a drag is a drag, not a diddle!

What I stress is that we cannot make traditional interpretation of rudiments fit corps style interpretations in all cases. In my teaching and judging experiences, I have heard many students who cannot properly interpret traditional rhythmic patterns using flams, drags, and ruffs. Conscientious students and teachers must become aware of the differences in notation and interpretations utilized in concert and corps style settings. Both styles are valid and should be learned. A versatile, educated snare drummer is vital in concert and marching environments.

April, 1985

Percussion Solos and Studies, Part III

James Lambert

Keyboard Percussion Solos

Southern Special Marimba Solos by William J. Schinstine, is a collection of 27 solos that range from grade 2 to grade 5 (Southern Music). Most of the solos are short (one per printed page) and most are for two-mallet technique. A few solos call for three- and four-mallet technique, however. Schinstine prefaces the music by relating that "an honest attempt has been made to create these solos in a variety of keys, meters, and styles." This is an extraordinary bargain for 27 solos, all unaccompanied. $4.

Through Harry Breuer's *Mallet Solo Collection* percussionists can become acquainted with such ragtime favorites as "Back Tack," "Bit O' Rhythm," "Happy Hammers," "On the Woodpile," "Powder Puff," "Encore Elise" (a spoof of Beethoven's "Für Elise"), and the "1908 Rag" (Alfred). Breuer is one of America's all-time great xylophone composers and performers, and the selections were all composed in the heyday of xylophone-ragtime, 1920-30. The printing is excellent and a piano accompaniment is included along with a brief biography of Breuer. This solo collection is highly recommended for either advanced high school or college-level percussionists. Grade 4-5. $9.95.

In the collection *Mallets in Wonderland,* Victor Feldman has composed/arranged 10 works for unaccompanied vibraphone. "The music," says Feldman, "has a multiple purpose." Those include giving vibraphonists a broader repertoire of styles; enabling the player to practice with a guitar or bass accompaniment (chord symbols are provided); improving four-mallet technique; and opening up the musician's ears to many voicing options on vibes. This is an excellent vibes collection for the avid, advanced four-mallet percussionist. Grade 5. $8.

Scherzo for Xylophone and Piano by Marta Ptaszynska, is a single-movement composition in a three-part form (fast-slow-fast). The xylophone melody is somewhat angular, which when combined with the lively piano part, makes this three-minute work a challenge for the intermediate to advanced high school keyboard percussionist. Only two-mallet technique is required of the xylophonist. Grade 4. $3.

Departure to... is an unaccompanied work for vibraphone by Ed Saindon. It is an excellent composition for the young high school percussionist who needs an intermediate-level contest or solo piece (Ed Saindon). The work requires basic four-mallet technique along with damping techniques. Grade 4.

Solfeggio in C Minor by C.P.E. Bach is an adaptation for solo marimba that provides a technical challenge for the performer of a 4½ octave marimba. Continuous subdivisions in simple meter give this work a typically Baroque quality, while making the advanced high school player aware of linear harmonic control. Grade 4. $2.

Donald Miller has done an excellent job of transcribing two of Claude Debussy's piano works to a setting for vibraphone and piano accompaniment (Ludwig Music). *First Arabesque* is a single-movement Impressionistic piece that contains stylistic moods. Pedal markings and stick-damping require more than just a first glance; however, only two-mallet technique is necessary. The piano accompaniment is equally well written. Grade 5. $5.95. Also for vibraphone with piano accompaniment, *Second Arabesque* is an excellent composition for the intermediate-advanced high school keyboard percussionist to become more familiar with the Impressionistic style. It also requires two-mallet technique. Grade 4. $5.95.

The Whirlwind by Joe Green is a ragtime xylophone solo scored with an accompaniment by three marimbas (Southern Music). The title makes an obvious comment regarding the difficulty of this march-form novelty by one of America's keyboard percussion kings. Grade 4. $6.

Abmiram is a suite of four dances for the advanced high school marimba performer (Permus). Titled "Morning Procession," "Supplication," "Pantomime," and "Ritual and Dance," the selection requires four-mallet technique in each movement. Grade 5. $6.

Ed Saindon's *Solace* for unaccompanied vibraphone is especially well suited to the highly motivated high school or junior college keyboard percussionist (Saindon). The work is published in two versions – one abbreviated, and the other extended. The shorter version is solid grade 4 material, while the extended version is grade 5. Fluency in four-mallet technique is required.

Essence by Thomas Brown is a three-minute, unaccompanied vibraphone solo for the moderately-advanced, four-mallet keyboard percussionist (Southern Music). The work is in a single movement in $\frac{12}{8}$ meter, with the suggested sticking clearly marked. This solo, which would be well-suited for undergraduate college percussionists, demonstrates the composer's challenging, yet accessible writing for vibraphone. Grade 5. $2.

Marta Ptaszynska's *Four Preludes for Vibraphone and Piano* is for the college percussionist who is seeking a seriously composed vibraphone work for a recital (Belwin-Mills). This four-movement composition (slow-fast-slow-fast) makes four-mallet demands in the second movement; the remaining movements are difficult but possible with two mallets. The piano accompaniment is a true complement to the vibraphone. Grade 5. $5.

Mario Gaetano's unaccompanied vibraphone solo, *Song of the Libra*, is a single-movement work that requires moderate four-mallet technique (Music for Percussion). A six-part composition that extends for 10 pages, the music has several changes in tempo, meter, and style that will make it challenging for the college percussionist. Grade 5.

Fantaisie à la Neige by Eyichi Asabuki is a theme with four variations, an introduction, and finale (Alfred). The work is in seven sections and scored for marimba and piano. It includes primarily two-mallet technique for the marimba; however, the unaccompanied second variation requires three-mallet technique. Contrasting compound and simple meters are used to create interest in a composition that extends for seven pages. Grade 5. $10.

Octave Etude No. 2 for marimba by Lorraine Irvin, is a two-page etude that requires four-mallet technique (Alfred). Although the music is largely comprised of tertial, 16th-note, arpeggiated figures, the music's dynamic demands add to a feeling of perpetual motion. Sticking suggestions are clearly marked. Grade 5.

Snare Drum Solos and Collections

Championship Corps-Style Contest Solos by Jay Wanamaker includes seven excellent rudimental snare drum solos that incorporate new rudiments, patterns, and visual effects (Alfred). The solos are titled "Fourth of July," "Main Street Strut," "Spirit of Sanchez," "Drum Corps on the March," "Hurricane," "Crazy Army," and "Bridgemen." Each is two pages in length and clearly printed. The solos contain meter changes, timbral variety, and special stick effects. Also included in the publication are the ten additional international rudiments as adopted by the Percussive Arts Society. (See *The Instrumentalist*, January 1985, pp. 74-75.) Wanamaker's solos are certain to become a part of the rudimental solo repertoire of the 1980s. Grades 4-5. $3.95.

Speed Trap is a duple compound meter, unaccompanied snare drum solo by Mark Spede (Permus). This is an effective solo that will develop the high school snare drummer's awareness of rudimental accents, rolls, and stickings within compound meter. The composition's only weakness is that a suggested tempo is not given. *Speed Trap* should find a home in the snare drum contest repertoire. Grade 4. $2.50.

David Eyler's *Watching the Time Go By* is an unaccompanied snare drum solo with changing meters (Permus). It is an excellent pedagogical composition for high school percussionists to perform successive meter changes – $\frac{2}{4}$ to $\frac{6}{8}$ to $\frac{5}{8}$ to $\frac{9}{8}$. Effective dynamics, tempo markings, accents, and rudiments add to a work that would also make good sightreading material for contests because of its moderately difficult challenge. Grade 4. $2.

Contrasts by James Sewrey is subtitled, "Four Short Episodes for the Concert Snare Drum" (Hal Leonard). A preface explains such techniques as playing on the rim, playing positions on the drum head, stick clicks, and measured or multiple bounced rolls, all of which should be correctly used in order to achieve timbral variety. The four movements, "Fanfare," "Ostinato," "Scherzo," and "Marche," should enable the advanced junior high or intermediate high school percussionist to grow musically as well as technically. Grade 4. $3.

Donald Miller's *Four Marches* is a suite of four unaccompanied compositions: "Quickstep March," "Solemn March," "Military March," and "Double-Time March" (Ludwig Music). Any single march is not all that difficult, but the four grouped together gives this composite work a higher difficulty rating. Tempo variations set the mood for each piece, and stickings, measurements of rolls, and dynamics are clearly marked. Any one of these marches would be an excellent high school contest snare drum solo, or the suite would be appropriate for recital material. Grade 5. $3.50.

Joel Leach's *The Olympians* is a solid intermediate unaccompanied, rudimental snare drum solo (Alfred). The rudiments are five, nine, and seventeen-stroke rolls, flams, flamacues, and flam taps. There are also a couple of back stickings to add some variety to the accents. This is a good snare drum solo for an eighth or ninth grade percussionist who is studying rudimental snare drum technique. Grade 3. $1.50. *The Yearling*, also by Joel Leach is a good solo for the first year student percussionist (Alfred). Technical demands are limited and the piece's length makes it suitable to memorize. Grade 3. $1.50.

Ensemble Literature

The current publications for percussion ensembles are in three classifications: serious percussion compositions, "pop" percussion compositions, and original or arranged classical works for keyboard percussion ensembles. Directors should expose their students to the many stylistic, musical opportunities that these works afford. The specific percussion instruments required for each composition are noted; and, remember, in many instances of the keyboard percussion ensembles, performers can double on instruments.

Serious Percussion Ensembles

Written in three movements that are published separately, *Suite for Percussion* by Frank Erickson is scored for essentially the same instrumentation in each movement with only minor changes for auxiliary percussion (Belwin-Mills). The percussion parts require six players on bells, snare drum, bass drum, and two timpani (29" and 26"); auxiliary percussion calls for triangle and suspended cymbal throughout, maracas for movement two, and tambourine and wood block for movements one and three. Frank Erickson has done a good job of making reasonable rhythmic demands for this junior high percussion work. Movement one, "Sonatina," is moderately fast and in D minor; movement two, "Nocturne," is at a slower tempo in $\frac{3}{4}$ in the key of E♭; "Rondo," movement three, is a fast $\frac{2}{4}$ rondo in A♭ major. Effective dynamic markings help make this suite a rewarding musical experience for the young percussion ensemble. Grade 3. Each movement, $4 for score and parts.

Michael Boo's *Three Percussion Moods* is a suite of three vignettes for five or more percussionists (Ludwig Music). The following percussion are required: part 1 — xylophone (may be doubled by marimba or vibe); part 2 — snare drum, slide whistle, two wood blocks, suspended cymbal; part 3 — three pitched tom-toms; part 4 — bass drum, cowbell, triangle; part 5 — three timpani, bird whistle (optional). The three movements — "Waltz," "March," and "Rag" — offer stylistic contrasts to give students the opportunity to blend sounds in a variety of entertaining ways. The movements were composed using seven-measure phrases that add extra musical interest. This composition is a good selection for the elementary- to intermediate-level percussion ensemble. Grade 3. $9.95.

Seven Modal Miniatures for flute and percussion by Karl Ahrendt (Ludwig Music) requires the following percussion: movement one — tam-tam (with mallet and brush); movement two — glockenspiel; movement three — tambourine; movement four — vibraphone (two-mallet technique); movement five — temple blocks; movement six — bongos; movement seven — cymbal and snare drum. Ahrendt says of this work: "Each of these miniatures is written in a different mode, and each features a different percussion instrument. In the middle section of the last miniature, the flute plays actual bird calls which I heard near my home." The complete work is suitable for recitals; individual movements would be well within the technique of mature high school performers. Grade 4. $8.95.

Vocalise for marimba and flute by Wilbur Chenowith, arranged by C. Smith and R. Gipson, is a duet that is well suited to blending the timbres of both instruments (OU Percussion Press). The middle register of the flute is combined primarily with the lower register of the 4⅓ octave marimba. The marimbist must have intermediate four-mallet technique and be able to execute a right-handed rotary roll, as well as be a sensitive accompanist to the flutist. This selection would be an excellent addition to a college percussion recital. Grade 4. $6.

Tom O'Connor's *The Winding River* (Barnhouse) requires the following instruments: player one — marimba; player two — vibes; player three — snare drum and temple blocks; player four — four tom-toms; player five — suspended cymbal and gong; player six — two timpani (29" and 26"). The two keyboard percussion parts are scored with two-mallet technique. This fast, single-movement rondo effectively combines and contrasts the selected instruments. There are excellent variations in accent placement, and the use of timbral changes (the timpanist striking the bowls; the tom-tom performer playing on the rims) adds interest to the composition. This is a superb work for the high school percussion ensemble, one that I highly recommend. Grade 4. $8.

Zeke, by Tim Wray, is a snare drum duet that is rudimental in nature and contains multiple-bounced rolls (Barnhouse). Combined with accented variations, this single-movement work is well suited for two high school drummers in need of a good contest duet. Grade 4. $2.50.

Five Short Pieces for Percussion Quintet by Donald Miller (Ludwig Music) requires the following instruments: crash cymbals, bongos, snare drum, field drum, four timpani, claves, xylophone, guiro, marimba, slapstick, five temple blocks, wood block, castanets, bells, tam-tam, bass drum, maracas, chimes, triangle, tom-toms, and two suspended cymbals. Because each of the five movements calls for a different combination of instruments, each percussionist should plan a well-organized setup. Both the xylophone and marimba performers will need four-mallet technique in movement four. Rapid changes in meter as well as instrument changes make this ensemble better suited for college percussionists; however, an advanced high school percussion ensemble could perform the work. Grade 5. $12.95.

Introduction and Rondo by Elliot A. Del Borgo (Southern) is scored for the following instruments: player one – orchestra bells, snare drum, large suspended cymbal; player two – gong, wood block, two bass drums; player three – sizzle cymbal, three suspended cymbals, four tom-toms, xylophone; player four – vibraphone, field drum, claves; player five – marimba, bongos; player six – chimes, four timpani, temple blocks. The *Introduction* is written to highlight the vibraphone, chimes, bells, and marimba (four-mallet technique required), with accompaniment by the suspended cymbal, gong, and tom-toms. The *Rondo* is scored with the initial theme played with rhythmic imitation through the snare drum, field drum, and tom-toms. The second portion of the music is primarily wood percussion – claves, xylophone, wood block, temple blocks, and marimba – accompanied by snare drum. A return to the opening drum sounds of the first theme is followed by a third theme of metallic percussion sounds – gong, vibraphone, suspended cymbal, bells. A repeat of the second theme and the first theme is followed by a coda that features the four timpani and four tom-toms. This advanced percussion ensemble would be appropriate for mature and musically sophisticated high school percussionists or for a college percussion ensemble. I highly recommend the work. Grade 5. $12.5C.

Diptych No. 2 by Gordon Stout is for a marimba soloist plus seven percussionists and one pianist (OU Percussion Press). The following instruments are required: player one – bells, five temple blocks; player two – chimes; player three – vibes; player four – piano, celeste; player five – four timpani; player six – three triangles, suspended cymbal; player seven – piccolo snare drum, regular snare drum, field drum; player eight – finger cymbal with metal beater, bass drum, and two low tom-toms. Commissioned by the University of Oklahoma Percussion Ensemble, the work is dedicated to John Beck, professor of percussion at the Eastman School of Music. Stout wrote this marimba solo for his own technique; it is a bear! The music is for only the advanced college or professional percussion ensemble. Scored as a single movement in a slow-fast-slow form, the work has modern harmonies and changing meters. it is well worth the time investment required for a performance. Congratulations Gordon Stout and the OU Percussion Press. Grade 6. $30.

"Pop" Percussion Ensemble

Matthias Schmitt has composed an original work, *Cabo Frio Bossa Nova*, for two keyboard percussion instruments (vibraphone and marimba) with conga and triangle accompaniment (Zimmermann Musikverlag, G. Schirmer). Four-mallet technique is necessary for the marimbist, with two-mallet technique required for the vibraphonist. This Latin pop tune is ideal for any light concert setting. The musical demands are such that the marimba part could be divided between two percussionists, making this work very accessible for the high school percussion ensemble. Grade 4.

Country Variations by Jared Spears (Barnhouse) requires the following instruments: player one – orchestra bells; player two – xylophone; player three – marimba; player four – three timpani and bass drum; player five – four tom-toms; player six – snare drum. Here is the familiar folk tune, "Arkansas Traveler," presented as a theme and four variations. The variation styles include a waltz, rudimental march, bossa nova, and a swing. This is an excellent composition to teach high school styles, and the music would be a percussionists the differences in fun-filled addition to a light concert setting. Grade 4. $9.

Scott Joplin's *The Entertainer* has been arranged by Matthias Schmitt for a percussion quintet of four keyboard percussion – glockenspiel, xylophone, vibraphone, and marimba – and accessory percussion – a skeletal drum set (bass drum, hi-hat, snare drum), triangle, and two wood blocks (Zimmermann Musikverlag, G. Schirmer). The combination of the keyboard percussion makes this arrangement appealing, and only the marimbist requires four-mallet technique. The printing of the five parts and score is very clear. This arrangement is ideal for a pops program. Grade 4.

Lovely Lady by Thomas Brown

is in Belwin-Mills' Percussion Pops Series. The following instruments are needed: player one — bells; player two — vibes; player three — marimba (four-mallet technique required); player four — marimba (two-mallet technique required); player five — chimes and timpani (one drum, 26"); player six — accessory percussion (finger cymbals, triangle, bell tree); player seven — drum set; player eight — bass. This jazz waltz is a mellow composition that could be used alone or combined with Brown's *Mardi Gras* or *Windfall* for contrast. *Lovely Lady* is an excellent teaching tool for its stylistic demands and is well suited for the intermediate high school percussion ensemble. Grade 4. $10.

Siegfried Fink has arranged Scott Joplin's stop-time, two-step *Ragtime Dance* to have the bass part in the 4½ octave marimba and the melody-accompaniment divided between the xylophone and vibraphone (Zimmermann Musikverlag, G. Schirmer). Four-mallet technique is required of the marimbist, while two-mallet technique is necessary for the xylophone and vibraphone performers. The accessory percussion consists of bass drum, snare drum, splash cymbal, wood block, triangle, cowbell, and mouth siren. This composition is well-suited to moderately-advanced high school percussionists or to a college percussion ensemble. Grade 4.

Snows of la Serena by Thomas Brown (Belwin-Mills) requires the following players: player one — vibes; player two — marimba; player three — marimba; player four — suspended cymbal, bell tree, cowbell, tambourine, bells, and timpani; player five — gong, chimes, and claves; player six — drum set; player seven — string bass. An optional synthesizer producing a "wind effect" is suggested or the ensemble members can "imitate the wind by hissing softly." The work begins with the "wind effect" in the introduction followed with a Mexican-sounding folk melody in $^{12}_{8}$ in the keyboard percussion. A section in $^{9}_{8}$ is highlighted by an opportunity for keyboard percussionists with a brief use of three-mallet technique. This composition is a good choice for the intermediate high school percussion ensemble. Grade 4. $10.

Another work by Thomas Brown, *Windfall*, requires six percussionists plus string bass. Player one — xylophone (or upper register of the marimba, one octave higher); player two — vibes and flexatone; player three — marimba; player four — bongos and chocallo; player five — snare drum, tom-tom, afuchi; player six — drum set; player seven — string bass. A moderately laid-back rock tune, the work highlights special effects, sudden silences, and extended vamps. Excellent dynamic demands contrast the formal sections of the piece. Particularly effective is the use of dynamics in the ending, which almost fades away before a syncopated stinger is added. Only two-mallet technique is required for the keyboard percussionists. Perhaps a publisher's oversight was the omission of the last page of the conductor's score in the review copy. Aside from this *faux-pas*, Tom Brown's *Windfall* is another entertaining work in Belwin-Mills' Percussion Pops Series that is well-suited to the intermediate high school percussion ensemble. Grade 4. $12.50.

Mardi Gras by Thomas Brown, is scored for six percussionists and electric bass (Belwin-Mills). Player one — chocallo and vibes; player two — claves and marimba; player three — guïro and marimba; player four — drum set; player five — timbales and three cowbells; player six — congas and bongos; player seven — electric bass. The vibist and two marimbists convey the happy melodies in this lively samba, along with the sophisticated, stylistic technique of the drum set and bass players. The keyboard percussionists will need intermediate four-mallet technique. This is a fun-filled, entertaining composition that can be performed by an intermediate-advanced high school percussion ensemble. I highly recommend the work. Grade 5. $10.

Original or Arranged Classical Works

Richard Gipson has carefully adapted the 17th-century art song, *Lasciatemi Morire*, by Claudio Monteverdi for marimba ensemble (OU Percussion Press). Here is an effective composition that can be performed on as few as four marimbas; however I believe it would sound best on five separate instruments. Access to the instruments will probably limit the performance of this beautiful composition to college percussion ensembles. I highly recommend the piece. Grade 3. $10.

In *Classic Duets for Marimba*, William J. Schinstine has arranged 11 familiar compositions by ten composers — Hummel, J.S. Bach, Beethoven, Schumann, Byrd, Handel, Kabalevsky, Khatchaturian, Shostakovich, and Prokofieff (Almitra). The collection is an excellent source of keyboard percussion duets for junior high or high school marimbists who are seeking material for special contests or concerts. These works offer excellent sight-reading material and are a good resource for the styles of the composers represented. Grades. 3-4. $6.

Adagio from Symphony No. 3 by Camille Saint-Saëns has been arranged by Richard Gipson for multiple marimbas (OU Percussion Press). The arranger has suggested that the eight marimba parts be performed on four marimbas. Phrasing, proper mallet selection, and blend are the important principles that can be learned from this beautiful movement. Grade 4. $12.

Schlagzeug Klassisch (the title means simply *Percussion Classical*) is a duet for vibraphone and marimba, arranged by Martin Kruger, of the five-movement suite by Karl Ditters von Dittersdorf originally for viola and cello (Zimmermann Musikverlag, G. Schirmer). The five movements are "Allegro moderato" (a sonata allegro form), "Minuetto 1" (with trio), "Adagio," "Minuetto 2" (with trio), "Theme with Five Variations." This work is accessible to moderately-advanced high school percussionists. Two-mallet technique is predominant with the exception of suggested three-mallet technique on the third variation of movement five. Grade 4. $12.

Michael Boo's *First Suite for Marimba Quartet* may be performed on two, three, or four marimbas (Ludwig Music). The composer suggests that "parts one and three, and two and four share instruments. Mallets should be graduated in hardness so the melody line predominates." The first movement, "Song for My Mother," is written without key signatures in F major, $\frac{4}{4}$ meter. "Hymn," the second movement is in $\frac{4}{4}$, in a contemporary sounding G major. "Rejoice," the finale movement, is in $\frac{3}{4}$, in straightforward C major. No single movement of the suite is lengthy, however, each one is musically sophisticated. The music is appropriate for either the high school keyboard percussion ensemble or as an addition to a college percussion ensemble concert. I highly recommend this selection. Grade 4. $6.95.

W.A. Mozart's beautiful *Rondo in D* adapts easily to the marimba ensemble, and William Schinstine has transcribed and arranged this work with careful attention (Southern). This piece would be well-suited to four moderately-advanced high school keyboard percussionists or to the college marimba quartet. Grade 4. $4.

Suite for Keyboard Percussion for four marimbas is a three-movement work by Joseph Westley Slater commissioned by the University of Oklahoma Percussion Ensemble (OU Percussion Press). Written in modern harmonies, the sophisticated first movement is a dance that uses changing meters ($\frac{9}{8}$, $\frac{8}{8}$, $\frac{7}{8}$) before settling down to a regular $\frac{6}{8}$. The changing meters do not get in the way of the musical content. The second movement is chorale-like, and the composer suggests much *rubato*. The third movement is fugal with the subject containing changing meter accentuations. A *stretto-coda* leads to an exciting marimba quartet finish. This composition is best suited for the college marimba ensemble; however, advanced high school marimbists could perform it. Except for three-mallet technique required in the second marimba part, movement three, two-mallet technique is used exclusively. OU Percussion Press has done a splendid job in the clearly printed score and parts. Grade 5. $20.

Two Movements for Mallets II by William Steinhort is another of several works commissioned by the University of Oklahoma Percussion Ensemble, Richard Gipson, director, and published by OU Percussion Press. Scored for seven keyboard percussionists and one optional bass marimbist, the work calls for glockenspiel, xylophone, two vibraphones, three marimbas (one which is 4⅓ octaves), and an optional bass marimba. Movement one, "Prelude," begins in a chorale fashion before moving to an aria-like melody and accompaniment. "Scherzo," movement two; opens in $\frac{3}{8}$, then moves to continuous meter changes with 20th-century harmonic-melodic techniques. This work is superb for the mature college percussion ensemble. Grade 5. $30. ■

April, 1985

Teaching Quintuplets and Septuplets

John R. Raush

Band directors frequently plead for improved musicianship among the members of the percussion sections. Unfortunately, developing basic skills among these students is often taken for granted, with training methods concentrating only on patterns in simple duple and triple divisions of the beat. These books neglect two irregular note-groups — quintuplets and septuplets — which are often found in contemporary percussion literature.

Quintuplets and Septuplets as Subdivisions of One Beat

Students should learn to play quintuplet and septuplet note-groups with the same confidence and ease as duple, triple, and quadruple subdivisions of the beat.

First, in a series of evenly-spaced, repeated notes, have the student set off groups of five or seven notes by accenting the first note of each group, following the sequence of sticking patterns indicated in the example, using non-alternating sticking first. Note that when playing with a hand-to-hand pattern, the sticking of the initial note of each group alternates:

Second, student and teacher play five-note or seven-note groups on alternate beats with the student eliminating any spaces between note-groups and striving to make all notes as similar in length and volume as possible:

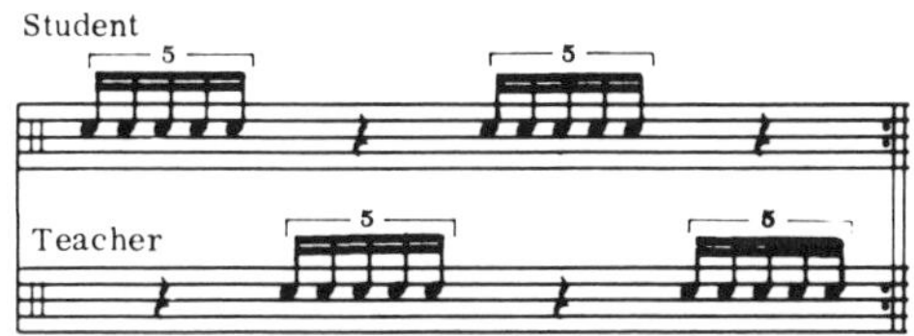

Third, juxtapose subdivisions of quintuplets and septuplets with all other subdivisions of the beat from two to eight. This will help the student develop the important facility for changing, on a beat-to-beat basis, from fives or sevens to other beat subdivisions. Teacher and student alternate playing single note-groups as follows:

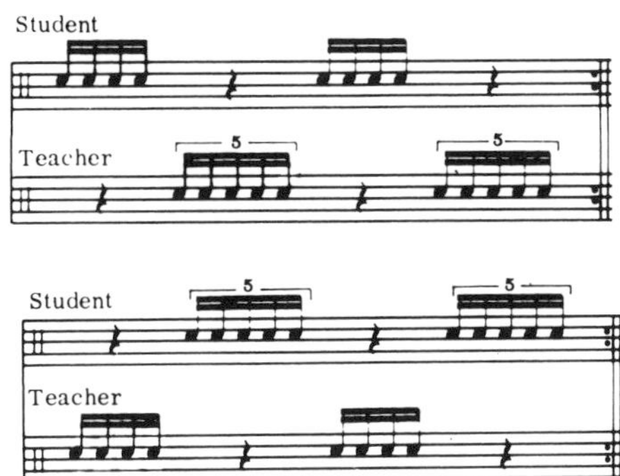

Next, each person plays two successive note-groups:

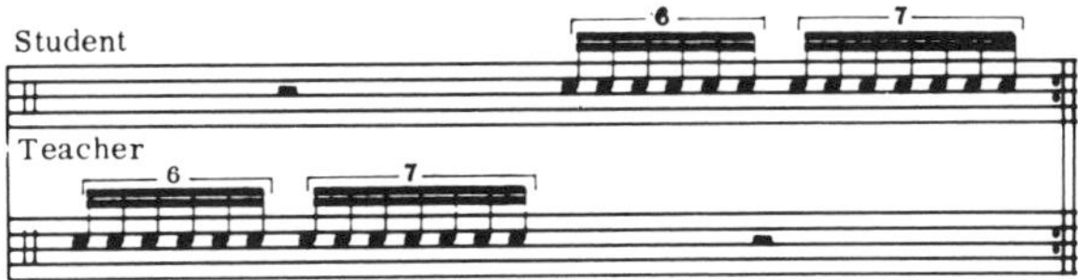

Practice juxtaposing subdivisions of quintuplets and septuplets with all other subdivisions of the beat from two to eight, and practice as indicated in the preceding example. Remind students to listen carefully to make sure they give all notes in the irregular groups the same length. Avoid playing fives sounding

or sevens sounding

Quintuplets and Septuplets in Unequal Rhythm Groups

Perhaps the most difficult problem involving quintuplets and septuplets results from using these figures in unequal rhythm groups. This occurs in contrapuntal writing using different rhythms in each line

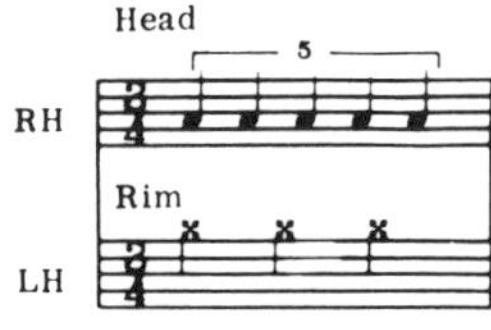

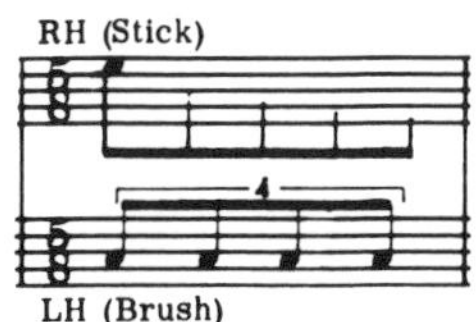

(© *Eric White,* False Images *for solo snare drum, Kendor, 1981)*

and in situations in which fives or sevens are written against a conflicting metric unit.

© *Michael Colgrass,* Fantasy-Variations for Eight Chromatic Drums and Percussion Sextet, *Music for Percussion, Inc., 1973)*

In exercise 1, the most frequently encountered unequal units with quintuplet and septuplet note-groups have been notated so that they can be practiced while counting in duple, triple, or quadruple subdivisions of the beat.

Play each line in the next exercise alone, counting the subdivisions aloud. To help differentiate the two conflicting rhythms, play each line on a different playing surface, for example, with one hand on the rim and the other on the drum head. Play both lines simultaneously, at a very slow tempo, counting aloud.

Exercise 1

Five against two

Five against three

Five against four

Seven against two

Seven against three

Seven against four

RH
LH
1e&a 2e&a 3e&a 4e&a 5e&a 6e&a 7e&a 1e&a 2e&a 3e&a 4e&a 5e&a 6e&a 7e&a

Now play and memorize the following composite rhythms

Five against two

Five against three

Five against four

Seven against two

Seven against three

Seven against four

Once again, play through exercise 1. This time, however, substitute the beats of a metronome for the written quarter notes. Begin with a comfortable tempo and gradually increase speed to m.m. =200.

Use exercise 2 to provide practice for situations in which quintuplets or septuplets are played against two, three, or four beats. A metronome is set to beat the quarter notes, and the student should use hand-to-hand sticking. In the second measure of each example, notes in parentheses can be struck silently on the leg as a preliminary step to eliminating them completely in the final measures.

Exercise 2

Five against two

Five against three

Five against four

Seven against two

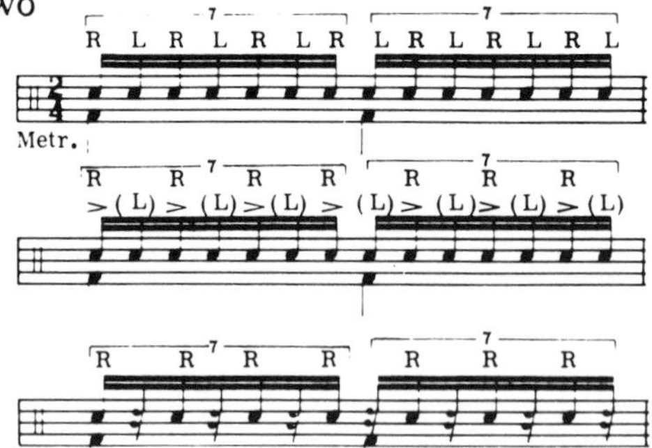

Seven against three

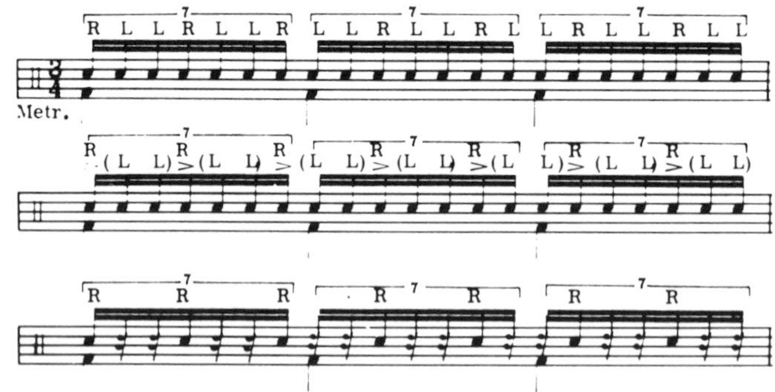

Seven against four

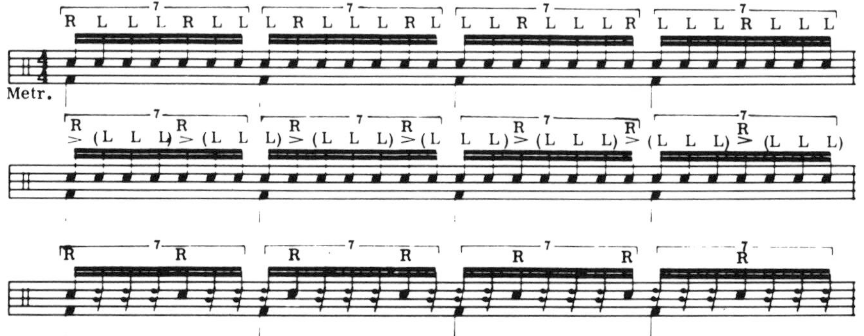

A good indication of whether a student has mastered the unequal note-groups presented here is the following test. Have him play, by memory, the last measures of exercise 2 against the beat of the metronome, without the benefit of the first two warm-up measures. If he has mastered the pattern, he should be successful on the very first attempt. ■

Playing Rudiments Musically

Sherman Hong

I have found that the simplest way to help beginning percussion students develop basic technique is not only to develop motor facility, but also to work simultaneously with mental and auditory skills. For example, in the beginning stages of learning to execute single strokes (first slowly and then rapidly), students usually play with too much tension and with an unsteady beat. However, the student who sings the rhythms he or she plays produces a rhythmically correct performance with less tension in the technique. It is an approach to teaching and learning that can be highly successful.

Single Strokes

When teaching basic single-stroke patterns, have the student sing the rhythm in a *legato* fashion:

du du du du

Then ask him to sing the rhythm and play the pattern simultaneously. The resulting sound will be more resonant and flowing, and because the player uses his muscles more naturally, the tone is less tense. If you desire a more intense or *staccato* sound, ask the student to sing different syllables:

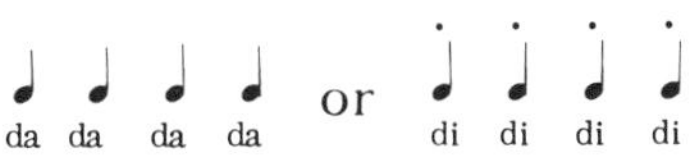

da da da da or di di di di

As a result of singing, the muscles being used naturally become firmer and thus change the color of the sound. The next step in producing a musical drummer is to have the student mentally sing the syllables that he plays and listen carefully to the sounds. In this first lesson, a student should be able to change timbre on a drum through active singing and mental concentration.

Flams

Before teaching rolls, I prefer to teach alternate and separate hand control at varied dynamics. For example, my students produce the flam by alternating their hands, one at a *pianissimo* volume and the other louder. As easy as this appears, producing this rudiment properly requires a great deal of effort. The stick producing the grace note is quite frequently played too loudly or is accented.

The quickest way to approach executing the flam ( ) with the use of syllables is to have the student first say either the word "flam" or "plum," and then play an imitation of it. The "f" in flam or the "p" in plum represents the grace note of the flam and the "lam" or "lum" indicates the primary stroke:

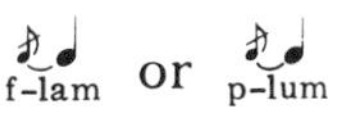

f-lam or p-lum

After saying the words, notice how softly and quickly you say the "p" and "f." If the student imitates the sound of the words as he sings and plays this pattern, he will play and phrase the flams he produces properly.

Diddles

At this point, I teach the paradiddles. The single paradiddle consists of two alternate strokes followed by one diddle (double stroke) played by one hand:

R L R R L R L L

Too often students play the diddle with an uneven rhythm and a volume that varies with the alternate strokes.

Teaching the student to say "paradiddle" in a rhythmically even fashion can ease the transition between playing single and double strokes. I start with the idea that "pa" and "ra" are two different syllables and relate them to two alternate strokes; the "diddle," however, comes from one word so one hand plays it. Have the student simultaneously say the syllables and play the pattern:

Pa-ra-did-dle

Your beginner will immediately perform the paradiddles evenly, fairly quickly, and the double stroke will be at the proper volume and rhythm. Once you point out these facts to the student, suggest that he mentally sing the syllables as he plays.

Use the same approach in teaching the double paradiddles or flamadiddles. For the double paradiddles the player sings "para-para-diddle":

pa-ra-pa-ra-did-dle
R L R L R R

and for the flamadiddles he sings "flamadiddle":

f-lam-a-did-dle

Rolls

Next, the student is ready to learn double stroke rolls. Remembering that the word "diddle" refers to double strokes, instruct the student to sing and play hand-to-hand diddles evenly and quickly. The slur marks indicate units of phrasing:

I advocate the student sing the exercises in a scale-like fashion because the sounds he produces will be more resonant and musical, and his muscles will have less tension.

The student should then practice exercises that form six and eight beat phrases as a prerequisite to playing rolls of greater duration.

After the student performs these rolls with some speed as well as with an even pulse and volume, teach him numbered rolls — 5, 7, 9, 13, 17 stroke rolls. These rolls, which give the student an understanding of attacks and releases, can also be taught using syllables and singing. I suggest you use an outline similar to this one:

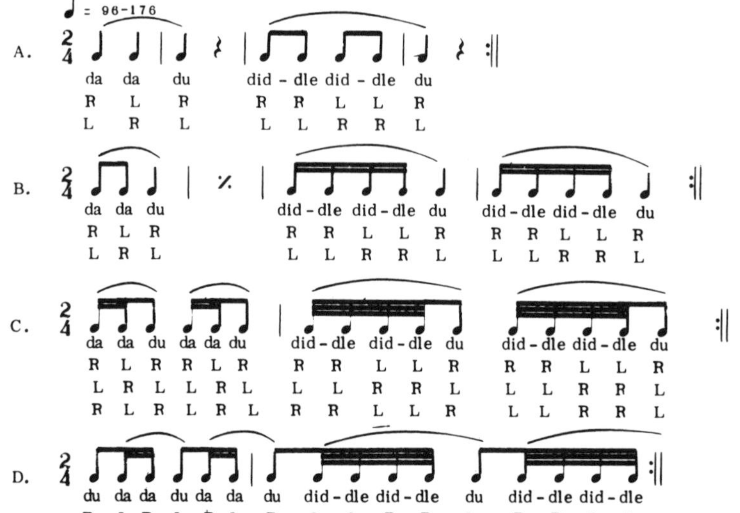

I also advocate that students sing these patterns to a scale passage. Exercise B can be executed in the following manner:

The student who practices this way produces sounds that are more resonant and musical; in other words, he plays a natural *crescendo* from low to high notes and rolls have direction as well.

Accents are not given here because they are easier to add when indicated in the music, rather than eliminated from material that is practiced. For an accented note, change the syllable to fit the sound desired. The following examples illustrate two different accents and intensities.

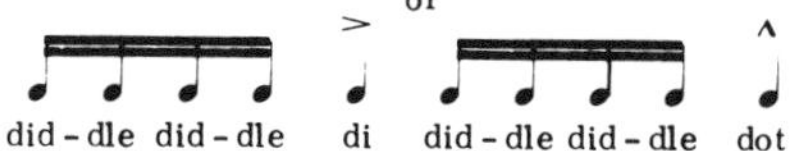

The second accent ( ) has more intensity and breadth. By simply changing one syllable in the singing pattern, the drummer can play three different endings to the roll.

Other Rudiments

Each rudiment has a particular phrasing. For example, one of the most misphrased and misplayed rudiments is Lesson 25, in which the percussionist plays two grace notes softly, with a *crescendo* to the primary stroke:

R LL R L LL R L R

Because of the frequent use of diddles in corps-style drumming and because the grace notes are difficult to time correctly, many play this rudiment as a diddle pattern:

R LL R L

The corps-style influence apparently causes many to play the grace notes as diddles, equal in volume to the primary stroke, similar to a Baroque interpretation of the embellishment. Lesson 25, however, is normally interpreted in the Romantic style; the grace notes are softer; they are not given durational values equivalent to the primary note; and they most frequently are slurred to the primary note.

To produce the proper phrasing, try using the following syllables:

da dr-ag - a dr-ag- a - da

The "dr" relates to the grace notes, the "ag" to the first 16th note, and the "a" relates to the second 16th. There is a natural *crescendo* from the first to last sound of the word "drag." Students must be aware of this fact to produce the proper phrasing.

Another rudimental pattern often interpreted incorrectly is the ratamacue:

It is frequently played with incorrect phrasing:

Again students frequently play the grace notes as diddles, playing them too soon. To produce the proper phrasing, have the student either say or sing the word "ratamacue," and the phrasing becomes evident:

Remember: a drag is not a diddle!

Syllables can be applied to all other rudiments; however, teachers should choose words or syllables that emulate the correct phrasing. For example, although the flam accent,

does not have a name that sounds like the pattern, teachers can devise a word, such as "flam-a-la," to fit the sound:

fl am-a-la fl am-a-la
R L R L R L

A commonly used rudiment not on the standard American list, that is notated the same as the ratamacue, is the Swiss army triplet.

Note how changing syllables changes the sound of the pattern.

The use of syllables when combined with singing makes students more aware of correct phrasings and rhythms when executing rudiments. It is an approach that incorporates the entire being – the mind, the voice, the muscles – to make music learning more relevant to the performer. This type of study will lead to performing rudiments in a musical manner and that will carry over into all areas of percussion performance. ■

May, 1985

Percussion Solos and Studies

James Lambert

Timpani Solos and Collections

Timpani Audition Solos by William Schinstine is a collection of 12 solos that are divided into three sections: two drum solos, three drum solos, and four drum solos (Kendor). In the preface Schinstine suggests that "players will find the solos useful on student recitals. It is also very possible to use them as sightreading material for contests." These solos are well written, and every high school band/orchestra library should have this book for its student percussionists. Grades 3-4, $6.

Robert McCormick's *Fanfare Variations for Solo Timpani* is a four minute, unaccompanied composition for four timpani (Kendor). Sounding mostly in D minor, the work opens and closes with the same theme, and there are four variations to complement it. The music is for an intermediate-advanced high school timpanist or it can be used as audition material for college percussionists. Grade 5. $2.

Triptych Motif by John Beck is a single movement, unaccompanied timpani solo for four drums (Kendor). This is an excellent composition; however, the grade of 5-6 should not frighten high school timpanists. The syncopated quintuples that are the qualifying factor for the higher rating are in a section of the work that may be cut. The solo is not only reduced in length from five minutes to a little more than three minutes, it also becomes easier. There are a couple of mallet changes between medium mallets and wooden ones, but there are no pitch changes. This is an excellent high school timpani solo for advanced players or young college percussion students. Grades 5-6. $2.

Percussion Methods

The Virtuoso Drummer by James Morton is a method specifically for snare drum technique (Mel Bay). The volume contains three parts: "Fundamental Technique," "Hand-to-Hand Coordination," and "Ambidexterity." A final section offers a recommended daily workout for the snare drummer. The exercises presented will assist those learning strict rudimental technique and concert snare drum technique. $4.95.

Mitchell Peters' *Hard Times* is a collection of 20 difficult etudes for solo snare drum (Mitchell Peters). The technical demands of each etude relate to changing meters ($^{6}_{16}$ to $^{4}_{16}$ to $^{5}_{16}$), as well as uncommon, asymmetrical rhythms (four against three in $\frac{5}{8}$ meter). The performance of these etudes demands mental and musical sophistication as well as superb manual technique. This collection will challenge the finest percussionist, and any one of the etudes would be excellent snare drum audition material. Grade 6. $8. ■

A Little Exercise for Two-Mallet Keyboard Percussion

Richard C. Gipson

You may think that perhaps every possible technical exercise for keyboard percussion has been written, with all combinations of sticking, notes, and rhythms exhausted. For keyboard percussionists, however, finding the most valuable technical exercises is especially important, given the abundance of possibilities. The ideal exercise is simple to learn, simple to remember, and continuously beneficial. It helps you get warmed up, reminds you of what you need to think about, and generally keeps your playing on the right track. My ideal exercise, adapted from George Lawrence Stone's book "Mallet Control," covers most of the technical concerns that face students who are working to develop basic two-mallet technique.

In playing two-mallet percussion, the musician is concerned with

- Stance
- Body position
- Grip/wrist interaction
- Stroke
- Mallet placement

The student works to make sure all these technical aspects of playing are correct, and then has to hit the right bar as well.

By using this simple technical exercise a student can concentrate on one single aspect of playing at a time or a combination of them. The exercise should be played slowly at first, keeping the pace of the 16th note constant from beginning to end. Quicken the 16th note only when you can play the entire exercise well at the slower tempo. Strive for a continuous stroke and a relaxed movement when encountering each new scale degree. When transposed, the exercise provides a number of uniquely new problems for the percussionist to solve. ■

The Role of Percussion in Marching Ensembles

Thomas Hannum

Along with improvements in the quality of percussion arrangements, instructors, and performers, the role of the percussion section in drum corps and marching bands has changed drastically in the past three to four years. The most obvious development has been the initiation of a front percussion ensemble, the "pit," to complement the traditional use of snares, multi-tenors, bass drums, and cymbals.

Two Types of Sections

In essence there are two basic elements of the modern marching percussion section: the front percussion ensemble (those who play stationary instruments off the front sideline), and the battery percussion segment (those who march with instruments). Although the battery segment is still developing and changing, its typical instrumentation includes 8-10 snare drums, 4-6 multi-tenors, 5 bass drums of graduated size and pitch, and 5-6 pairs of hand cymbals. While difficult to coordinate, it is not uncommon for any players on these instruments to change to others in order to achieve the desired musical effect.

On the other hand, as instructors realized that stationary equipment enabled one performer to play more than one instrument, directors expanded the front ensemble to contain virtually any percussion instrument. In short this group is now thought of as a percussion ensemble on the front sideline. Typical instrumentation includes one or more of the following: concert grand marimba, vibraphone, xylophone, orchestra bells, pedal timpani, crotales, mounted concert toms, various gongs and hand cymbals, a drum set, and a trap station that contains an assortment of suspended cymbals and special effects instruments. Usually six to eight people are responsible for playing these instruments.

Reasons for Change

The reasons that marching percussion has developed so rapidly are simple. First, the diversity of musical styles being performed by drum corps and marching bands has grown to include classical, jazz, rock, pop, and contemporary to name a few. In addition to performing original compositions, directors often program arrangements from concert band and symphonic wind band literature, jazz band libraries, and orchestral scores. All these styles of music require a variety of percussion instruments to accurately interpret the composer's intentions.

Secondly, there is a significant increase in the number of well-educated percussionists who are now active as marching ensemble instructors and performers. As composers and arrangers explore the capabilities of each instrument, musical demands on the players have increased and playing techniques that are more demanding are commonplace.

Finally, percussion manufacturers are paying more attention to the needs of marching percussion ensembles and have instituted promotional programs as well as research and development projects to improve the visibility, quality, and marketing of their products. As a result, drum corps and marching band directors can purchase instruments to accommodate the needs of the music.

Programming

From a musical standpoint the percussion section functions as an integral voice within the entire ensemble, at times supporting the brass and at other times acting as the lead or solo voice. The percussion should always remain within the context of the musical production as it develops from beginning to end. For example, all the percussion features for the Garfield Cadets (1983 and 1984 Drum Corps International World Champions) are contained within a composition. They are not separate entities that tend to interrupt the flow of the program, either aurally or visually. After all, the goal of every marching ensemble is to blend each and every element of the group so as to produce a pleasing balance between hearing the music and seeing the marching.

For the past several years, the Garfield Cadets have used music that is symphonic in nature. The program in 1983 featured a concert band piece, *Rocky Point Holiday* by Robert Nelson, with the remainder of the show consisting of selections from Leonard Bernstein's *Mass*. Last year, directors based the entire presentation on *West Side Story*, another Bernstein work chosen because of the versatility it offered the percussion ensemble.

Visually speaking, the directors of the Garfield Cadets have a philosophy that is the same as any successful Broadway producer's — use the entire stage to heighten the effect of the production. The field is a stage that should be used to its fullest extent.

Guidelines for Arrangements

Directors who arrange parts for marching percussion ensemble should follow these guidelines for their work. First, remember that the single most important feature of arranging for the marching percussion ensemble is the coordination of the battery and front elements. The battery's contribution is mostly rhythmic, whereas the front ensemble's is primarily melodic and harmonic. Take care to determine when the percussion ensemble is the lead voice and when it functions in a supporting role, as well as when the battery or front segments act as the lead or supporting voice. By scoring the percussion with these points in mind, the arranger helps the entire musical ensemble, including the wind instruments, to reach its maximum potential.

The following list offers criteria to help arrangers develop a complete and thorough score:

1. *Idiomatic Interpretation* — Accurately portray the style of the chart. No longer do drummers simply play cadence-like patterns to provide a solid pulse for the ensemble
2. *Tempo/Pulse Control* — The consistent control of tempos and pulse is a primary consideration for cohesive ensemble performance. Be aware of the density of parts at fast tempi.
3. *Melodic and Harmonic Support* — Determine the lead and support parts in the front ensemble prior to writing.
4. *Dynamic Contrast* — Be aware that certain parts are easier to perform at certain volume levels. The use of different playing areas on the drum head, keyboard, and cymbal can increase dynamic control.
5. *Contouring of Phrases* — Make all phrasing concepts consistent throughout the entire ensemble.
6. *Accents* — Achieve accents by one of two methods: the number of players scored for a given note value; the increase in playing heights of the mallets.
7. *Tuning/Intonation* — Tune the ensemble before playing to ensure that each voice will be heard clear-

ly. Intonation for timpani and keyboard depends on scoring, the accuracy of the stroke in the striking area, and the condition of the instruments.

8. *Articulation* — The length of articulated sound — *staccato, tenuto, legato* — should be consistent throughout the musical ensemble. Give special consideration to instruments with sustaining qualities (dampening techniques help to determine articulation).

9. *Explore Timbral Effects* — Alter the timbre of the ensemble by striking different playing areas, incorporating dampening techniques, and experimenting with a variety of voicing combinations.

10. *Ensemble Blend and Balance* — After working out the mechanics of the music, be aware of the blend and balance between the percussion instruments and between the percussion and wind instruments.

For the Reader and the Fan

For those interested in becoming more familiar with marching percussion, I recommend reading some of the following related material and viewing marching ensemble competitions.

- *Pearl-A-Diddle* — each edition has a column highlighting current aspects of the marching idiom.
- *Percussive Notes* — a publication of the Percussive Arts Society that entertains a variety of topics in "Percussion on the March."
- *Modern Percussionist* — a relatively new magazine published by Modern Drummer that features a marching percussion article in each issue.
- *Drum Corps World* — a weekly paper that provides a complete schedule of upcoming events and competition results from all regions of the United States and Canada.

For viewing audiences, Drum Corps International presents its Championships in Madison, Wisconsin, August 14-17. Here the top 48 corps from the United States and Canada square off in a series of competitions that culminate with the final event on the evening of August 17 when the 12 best corps go head-to-head to determine who is the best in the world.

Yes, the role of the marching percussion ensemble is changing. If seeing is believing, give it a try.■

September, 1985

Tuning Tips for Marching Drums

Jay Wanamaker

One of the biggest problems marching band directors face is that of tuning the drums. Marching drums are a special breed of instrument and they require special attention in tuning them. The following tips are for marching snares, multi-toms, and tuned bass drums. Each drum is assigned a specific pitch only as a point of reference. In the beginning use these pitches until you find the ones that work best for you.

Snare Drums

Pitch. Tune the batter head of the 14" snare drum to D5 and the snare a minor third lower to B4. It is important to tune all the batter heads in the snare drum section to the same pitch, as well as all the snare heads.

Gut Snares. Tune each gut individually by using a banjo-style tuning method. Place two small wooden dowels between the snare head and the gut snares. Use a screwdriver to adjust the snares at the butt plate as you pluck each gut. Adjust the tension by tuning each screw clockwise to tighten the snares, or counter-clockwise to loosen them. Strive to tune each gut to a uniform pitch (14" gut snares tune to about G3). If the gut snares become subjected to moisture, apply a water repellent spray (Scotch Guard) directly to the snares.

Snare Strainer. Adjust the strainer after you tune the individual gut snares. Set the vertical snare adjustment so that the snares lay firmly against the edge of the shell (bearing edge). As you tighten the snares with the horizontal snare adjustment, the snares will become brighter (higher sounding) until that point when there is too much tension, and a choked, darker sound results. Try to attain a crisp, articulate, high-pitched snare sound.

Muffling. No additional muffling is required.

Recommended Size. 14" x 12"

Multi-Toms

Pitch. When tuning multi-toms strive for a dry, high-pitched, clean sound with the interval of a minor third between each tom. Tune all toms of the same size to the same pitch, and avoid mixing trios with quad combinations. Recommended pitches:

6" - A♭5
8" - F5
10" - D5
12" - B4
13" - G♯4
14" - F4
16" - D4

Drum Heads. Pin-stripe heads are

recommended.

Muffling. No additional muffling is required.

Recommended Sizes:
Trio - 10", 12", 14"
Quad - 10", 12", 13", 14"
Quint - 6", 10", 12", 13", 14"

Tuned Bass Drums

Pitch. Strive for a round, warm, true-centered pitch when tuning bass drums. It is best to tune the basses a minor third apart, remembering to tune both heads of the drum to the same pitch. Recommended pitches:
22" - G3
24" - E3
26" - C#3
28" - A#2
32" - G2

Drum Heads. Smooth white bass drum heads are recommended.

Muffling. Use additional muffling to reduce overtones and unwanted ringing. Weather stripping with self-adhesive provides muffling for the bass drum when you attach it to the inside of the drum hoop. Place the foam rubber portion of the weather stripping against the edge of the drum head. Use the amount of weather stripping that is proportional to the drum head size. For instance, the 28" bass should contain weather stripping around the entire hoop, while the 22" bass should have it one quarter of the way around. Experiment with this idea to find the best muffling for your bass drums.

Recommended Sizes. Number of drums:
6 - 20", 22", 24", 26", 28", 32"
5 - 22", 24", 26", 28", 32"
4 - 22", 24", 26", 28"
3 - 24", 26", 28"
2 - 24", 28"
1 - 28"

- Always use a criss-cross tuning procedure to make sure that every drum head is in tune with itself.
- Change the drum heads when necessary, and tune the drums on a daily basis.
- Maintain a constant interval of a minor third from the highest to the lowest drums.
- Most marching drums are not pitched high enough and, therefore, have a low, tubby sound that does not project well.

For a snappy sound from your marching band, give some extra attention to the drums. By keeping these instruments in good tune you'll improve their projection and avoid that tubby sound when it's time for the marching drums to solo. ■

1986-1987

721	Timpani: Improving Sound	Robert M. McCormick	April
722	Marching Tonal Base Drums	William Guegold	June
723	Percussion Section Considerations	Ray Wifler	July
724	Can You Play Glockenspiel?	Jeanine Smith	December
726	Sticking Revisited	David R. Vose	April
727	Timpani Sizes and Ranges	John J. Papastefan	June
729	Snare Drum Tips	Charles Holmes	August
731	Triangular Considerations	Lynn Glassock	September
732	Build a Percussion Storage Cabinet	Norman Weinberg	October
734	Aim High for Your Percussion Section	Mark Ford	December
737	Percussionists Are Musicians	Jesse Pearl	October

Timpani: Improving Sound

Robert McCormick

How does the timpanist create a beautiful tone? Although acoustics, bowl design, kinds of sticks or mallets used, stylistic nuances, and technical facility influence sound, the first step towards attaining a beautiful tone is to ensure that the drums are in good repair and playing condition. Not even the finest professional can play with a beautiful tone on drums that are out of tune with themselves. Timpanists use a method known as truing to tune a drumhead with itself.

1. Remove the old head and clean the edge (lip) of all dust and debris. Place a light coat of lubricant along the edge and wipe it clean with a cloth. The lubricant remaining on the edge should eliminate unwanted squeaks from the head while tuning.
2. Place the new head on the drum and add the counterhoop. (The Remo Company has printed a line on their timpani heads for best placement.) At this time make sure that the head and counterhoop are equally distant and diametrically placed around the edge.
3. Tighten the rods with the fingers as much as possible. To bring the drum into playing range turn the key the same number of times at all tension points.
4. Strike around the edge of the drum at each tension area and listen for uniformity of pitch and resonance. If one spot sounds particularly clear in the fundamental, try to match the other rods to it. Because the vibrations of the head tend to move across the drum, the best approach is to tune by matching tones at opposite points, rather than tuning clockwise or counterclockwise around the drum.
5. If you do not get results the first time, don't worry. Allow the head a few days to break in and adapt to the contour of the bowl. If the drum still does not meet expectations, return to step four.

Influencing Tone

When discussing the concept of good tone with students, compare the many bowl designs to the sounds they produce. For example, the flat bottom timpani used in European orchestras is associated with a darker tone, while the parabolic or round bottom timpani played in most American orchestras tends to make the timpani sound brighter and the vibrations last longer.

The choice of stick or mallet also influences tone and varies greatly from professional to professional. Generally speaking, the softer stick is less percussive and has less contact sound; it offers a beautiful, warm, full-bodied tone. Harder sticks are needed to bring out various degrees of articulation and color that may not be possible with the softer mallet. The acoustics of the performance hall can also influence the choice of stick and the type of stroke used. Timpanists in recording sessions often use a harder mallet than when playing live.

Most timpanists interchange a variety of sticks to create stylistic nuances. Experimenting with different mallets should help the director and student decide which mallets to use for a particular passage. Consider the following excerpt from Beethoven's Symphony No. 1. Because clear articulation is important, choosing a harder stick will help the timpanist articulate the passage distinctly and the tone of the timpani will blend with the detached triplets of the accompanying violin part.

The contrabasses and contrabassoons double the *expressivo e legato* passage from Brahms' Symphony No. 1. To achieve a round and full tone, start with a general purpose or softer cartwheel-style mallet and, most important, remember that the quality of sound is enhanced by the style and length of the stroke. A slower, long motion using the natural rebound of the head fits the style of the Brahms' passage, while a firm grip with a short, fast wrist stroke suits the style of the passage from Beethoven's Symphony No. 1.

Whether the student uses a French-style grip (i.e., holding the stick with the first two fingers, thumbs facing up) or a German grip (i.e., similar to the matched snare drum grip), he should remember that the hands should remain flexible. If the freedom of motion of the stick is inhibited or too much finger and hand are wrapped tightly around the stick, the player chokes the tone and creates a noisy sound.

Playing area and the angle of the stroke are common problems in developing a good tone. Unless otherwise indicated by the composer, the sticks should always strike the head the same distance from the edge – usually two to four inches depending on the drum size and quality of the desired sound. The angles of the sticks as well as the relative position of the hands to the drum should be consistent. Especially noticeable in cross-sticking passages, placing one mallet higher than the other yields an inconsistent sound.

The timpanist who is familiar with the concepts of good tone production can perform with the artistic decision and imagination that creates interest for listeners. Most important, instructors should correct deficiencies in the student's playing and reinforce correct techniques regularly. ■

June, 1986

Marching Tonal Bass Drums

William Guegold

Many bands are including a timpani-like effect in their marching ensembles by using multiple-tuned bass drums, an idea that has been around for quite some time. Most competing marching bands as well as many non-competing groups now use them. Two to six drums of various sizes and pitches are included in most sections.

Though marching percussion sections now enjoy the increased timbres these drums bring, several problems have developed from using them. The active parts written for the section require great skill from the players and, at the same time, carrying the larger drums has resulted in a good deal of physical strain for students. These factors have often caused directors to select players solely on the basis of the students' physical characteristics. When players are selected only because they can carry the instrument, the section lacks basic musical stability. Getting several players to think as one is another problem. What directors are asking is the equivalent of having four or five people play the timpani part in concert band ensembles.

Several innovations are helping directors deal with these problems. First of all, percussion manuacturers are beginning to market lightweight drums that allow smaller students to manage the instruments. Some companies have even designed carriers that hold a stacked group of instruments, so that one person can carry more than one drum at a time. One student can carry three drums, with a more practical number being two. Using a cart to transport a bass drum is not new. After all, who has not seen the World's Largest Bass Drum at Purdue?

Height is a major drawback with the stacked units because players often have difficulty seeing over the larger drums, let alone a stacked set. Balance can also be a problem because increased height can lead to some footing problems on a wet field.

A solution developed at my high school is the use of a cart carrying all four of the band's tonal bass drums. One student plays all four drums, thus eliminating the inherent problems in a "bell choir" type of section.

Now my school's bass drum section is more balanced and the students' precision has increased tremendously. I had the choice of either using one cart assistant to move the unit about the field or grounding the entire unit in the sideline pit area. This frees two to four players for other roles in the percussion section. Having opted for the grounded unit in the pit, I keep all mallets, auxiliary percussion, timpani, and the bass drum unit in the sideline area. To answer the question of phasing and ensemble precision, I place skilled people on each of these instruments and demand that each keep an attentive eye on the field commander. By using the grounded bass drum with a single player, I have been able to give the band music that presents an even greater variety of percussion color in our musical performances.

A multiple-tuned bass drum unit played by a single player might not solve all your marching percussion problems, but it may help those of you who have smaller bands or a limited number of skilled players. ■

Percussion Section Considerations

Ray Wifler

During 11 years of conducting a community band and working to develop it into a sensitive concert ensemble, I have found the percussion section to be the most difficult to organize and staff with capable players. Musical considerations such as section size, instrumentation, and balance, and various aspects of organization including part assignment, maintaining music folders, and transporting instruments are all vital to developing a good percussion section.

While the classic percussion section of earlier bands had only three players – snare, bass and cymbals, and timpani – recent compositions and arrangements clearly require a larger section. Six players can cover the parts in most music, but where economics is a factor, bands may have to get along with four or five. Performing with a smaller section requires careful score study to determine which parts can be cut.

It is important to have an accurate timpani tuner and a mallet player who can execute difficult xylophone parts, as well as a set player who is familiar with the many different styles needed for swing, pop, and jazz music. Combining the talents of two or more players, however, is no substitute for the drive and unifying ability of one good set player. Using a string bass, bass guitar, or amplified string bass also helps when playing these styles, although with amplified instruments be sure to find the correct tone and balance with the rest of the band.

The bass drum sound is often inconsistent in community bands either because a nonpercussionist is given the job, or because poor quality instruments and inappropriate equipment are used. Provide the section with a large bass drum with low (loose) tuning and a quality mallet to help create a consistent sound. Producing a tone that is sufficiently low and resonant with a lightweight mallet is difficult. The Payson mallets by Ludwig, for example, make it much easier to get a good sound on bass drum. You will need an L-308 for most playing and a pair of L-309 for rolls.

The percussion section should also have a field drum and a concert snare. Make sure the field drum is tuned to produce a distinctly different sound from the snare. In addition, at least two pairs of cymbals are required: a smaller pair for marches and rapidly moving parts where a quick response is needed, and a larger pair for other parts. For the large pair I prefer light cymbals, such as those marked "French" which produce little attack and many overtones. If you can afford a third pair, a large, heavy set should be purchased. At least two suspended cymbals are part of the necessary equipment, one small and light, the other large and heavy. Also, orchestral bells are far superior to marching bell lyra and are well worth the expenditure. Most bell parts sound best when played with small brass mallets, but plastic mallets are desirable for some *piano* parts.

The percussion can easily overpower wind players and cause them to force. Consequently, the entire band sound becomes distorted; the brass sound often becomes strident, dominated by the trumpets and trombones and except for the piccolo and high range clarinets, the woodwinds get buried. Consider the dynamic dynamics will make the grand moments all the more grand.

More than any other section, percussionists need a leader who not only assigns parts, but also organizes the music and is responsible for equipment. As an alternative, our band has recently created the position of assistant conductor, and among his responsibilities are leading the percussion section and assisting in it when necessary. Because the extent of organization needed in the percussion section often cannot be completed during rehearsal time, remuneration for the leader's services may be in order.

For efficiency, continuity, and accuracy in performance, written-out part assignments should be prepared before rehearsals, keeping in mind the players' strengths and weaknesses as well as preferences. While this time-consuming task can be done by the conductor, it may be better to delegate it to the section leader. If so, the section leader should remain in close communication with the conductor so he is aware of any variation in personnel or programming.

The high visibility of the percussion section can be an added attraction for the audience during concerts or it can make your band look like a group of bumbling amateurs. Again, organized part-assignments as well as a carefully planned layout of the instruments are required for players to move about the stage easily.

Percussion music folders are another problem area, especially during the summer months when the band may have as many as 50 selections in the folders at once. Three folders marked snare, bass, and cymbals; timpani; and, auxiliary work best with the music filed alphabetically. At one time we used an expansion folder in which all the parts were stored, but we have found the three-folder system to be more accessible for our group.

Timpani writing in current styles frequently requires three or four drums. Even though this poses transportation problems, the drums are necessary. Furthermore, one drum has to be very large (32 inches) to adequately handle the lowest pitches with clarity. Similarly, the xylophone and tubular chimes are a problem to move, but both instruments add distinctive color to the band. The best and easiest way to move a xylophone is to leave it fully assembled. Given the right vehicle, an assembled instrument takes only a little more room than an unassembled one.

We solved our problems with moving instruments by purchasing an older, 16-foot camping trailer and gutting it, except for one closet that we use for storing extra uniforms. A vehicle like this can easily haul all the percussion instruments, sound equipment, music boxes, and almost anything else that is needed. Braces, floor stops, and tie-downs can also be added so that the instruments do not move around while being transported.

Because the percussion section has many organizational needs, I often refer to it as a band within a band. Experience has shown me, however, that the extra time it takes to select the proper equipment, find a responsible section leader, work on balance between the percussion and the rest of the band, and create smooth choreography among the members of the section is rewarded not only in musical results, but also in your players' satisfaction and pride. ■

December, 1986

Can You Play Glockenspiel?

Jeanine Smith

Ah, community bands! My first experience in one was at best a case of trial and error. Eight years ago, on a snowy January night, 12 of us showed up in the band room at a local junior high school for the first rehearsal of the Noank-Mystic Community Band. Ever since then, I've been hooked.

A lone lawyer toting a well-used drum with three missing snares represented the fledgling percussion section of our ensemble. By the band's third rehearsal, I was handed a pair of brass mallets and introduced to the glockenspiel. As a pianist who knew nothing about percussion or the glockenspiel, I was greatly relieved to see that the instrument resembled a piano keyboard. Percussion music proved to be considerably more enigmatic. Each measure of music was tightly printed in a half inch or less of space, with the part containing many repeat signs and lots of rests. There were no sharps or flats. I was horribly confused by the mysterious symbols denoting the various beats. Without the help of familiar phrase markings and chord patterns to guide me I was sure I would lose my place.

Tearfully, I drove home from that rehearsal and phoned Constance Coghlan, a percussionist I had seen and heard in local concerts. Coghlan, principal percussionist with the U.S. Coast Guard Band, invited me to her studio the following week. She showed me how to hold the mallets, ding the triangle, and strike the tambourine. I learned how to coax a variety of dynamics from an oversized concert bass drum, and we went over the fine points of playing the suspended and crash cymbals.

My training didn't stop there. I attended concerts presented by the U.S. Coast Guard Band with its outstanding percussion section and jotted down whatever I saw — the placement of players, stickings, types of mallets used, timpani dynamics. Later I studied snare drums with a local teacher to learn stick technique. At age 45, I felt out of place with the teenagers carrying drumsticks in their hip pockets, but I persevered.

Our director chose section leaders based on players' availability and the amount of time they had spent with the band. I qualified for the job; now I needed to know what a section leader did. Eagerly I pored over back issues of *The Instrumentalist*, joined the Percussive Arts Society, and got in touch with area school band directors. I received valuable playing advice and learned about the resources available for obtaining instruments. I brought home conductor's scores and percussion music folders, spread them on the living room floor, and made instrument assignments or rearranged parts when necessary.

Through time the section's mallet supply and auxiliary instrument inventory grew. We purchased woodblocks, triangles, tambourines, and jingle bells. A local basketball coach who played trumpet donated a police whistle, and volunteers made sandpaper blocks and supplied an anvil (two lead pipes with a rawhide cord attached). To carry the school-owned timpani, xylophone, and bass drum to concerts, a 1970 red pick-up was pressed into service. My section attended percussion seminars, made it our business to be on the band's set-up crew, and participated in the music selection committee, making sure that the special needs of our section were known.

Every community band needs capable percussion players, and my experience is proof that ensembles can train their own. Any section will reflect the particular strengths of the players, but snare, bass drum, and cymbals are essential instruments. As our director once said, "Everything else is gravy." A good set drummer who can cover snare, bass drum, cymbals, and a number of auxiliary instruments is a boon to the ensemble. So is a keyboard player who can manage bells, xylophone, and chimes. A third player may be needed to handle the timpani.

Even the most organized community band percussion section cannot escape Murphy's Law. For us, the night before the band's annual Christmas concert, the all-important chimes disappeared. Phone calls made by anxious players helped to locate the instrument, and it was in place only a half-hour before curtain. During one summer program a strong sea breeze blew the drummer's music folder upside down and against a nearby fence, sending two young players scrambling to find the next tune to be played from the scattered parts. The week before a recent winter concert, the set drummer heard about a college seminar he needed to attend and announced he would not be playing. (The director had planned a program of Broadway show tunes around the drummer.) The two of us who remained covered most of the drumbells, cymbal, and auxiliary parts. We even came up with a floorslap made of an old broom trimmed with a tambourine, small cowbells, and a dozen wooden drapery rings for clatter on one of the tunes.

In my years with the band, I have crashed cymbals at the wrong time, become hopelessly lost in the music, and played bells where none were written. I have dropped a triangle during a quiet arrangement of *I Saw Three Ships* and tried the patience of many a conductor. I know the exuberance of playing before a crowd of 50,000 people waiting for Fourth of July fireworks and the quiet thrill of having an audience of two while practicing the timpani.

Now the Noank-Mystic Community Band numbers 40 musicians and the percussion section has three players. We rotate the responsibilities of section leader by concert. Rehearsals are held in the local high school's large band room, and considerably more instruments are available to us than just the first snare drum of eight years ago.

Through the band I entered the world of percussion, made friends among musicians at all levels of ability, and developed confidence in my skills as a musician and a person. Though musicians make up the band, it truly takes a community to build a community band. ■

Stickings Revisited

David R. Vose

Percussion teachers and beginning players often wonder what sticking method to use. Even professional percussionists who know of numerous sticking combinations often hesitate when asked about sticking methods for beginners. The following suggestions are designed for teaching stickings on the snare drum.

The system is based on four-note groupings such as four quarter notes, four eighth notes, or four sixteenth notes. For a line of quarter notes and quarter rests in 4/4 meter, beats one and three are played with a right-hand stroke and beats two and four are played with a left-hand stroke. The first example shows the result when this method is used during a simple line of quarter notes and quarter rests:

When playing eighth notes, play the downbeats with a right-hand stroke and the upbeats with a left-hand stroke. When combining quarter notes and eighth notes, the sticking method of the smallest value prevails, as shown:

If "one e and a" is used to count sixteenth notes, the "one" and the "and" should be played with a right-hand stroke and the "e" and "a" should be played with a left-hand stroke. Any beat unit containing at least one sixteenth note will be considered a sixteenth grouping — ♫, ♫, ♫, for example. Continuing this approach with all groupings of four notes eliminates students' fears when seeing multiple beams. The following example shows the parallel between the various rhythms and their stickings:

This method also helps to develop coordination and clarify the relationship of different note values. Because most beginning snare drummers do not read pitches (which helps other instrumentalists visualize rhythm divisions) the stickings help to reduce the chance of getting lost during active passages.

The method used for groupings of three notes (triplets, or triple meters) is slightly different. When playing three consecutive notes, start with a right stroke and alternate.

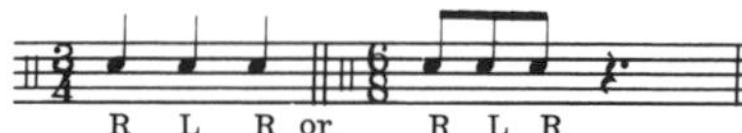

When the rhythm is two notes and a rest, play a right-hand stroke, then left, regardless of which two beats the notes fall on.

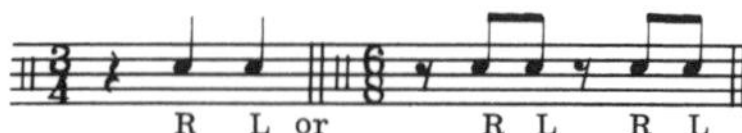

For a single note, if it is on beat one, play it with a right-hand stroke; but if it is on beat two or three, play it with a left-hand stroke.

When the stickings do not fall into place exactly as the rules are stated, simply follow your natural inclinations.

Consistency in sticking is important in playing evenly. In the common eighth and two sixteenth rhythm, the right hand should consistently play two eighth notes per beat while the left hand plays one note per beat. R RL R RL . A consistent approach is also important in achieving speed. Often, playing fast is thought to be a matter of the physical ability of moving the hands quickly. With the exception of extremely fast passages, however, it is proper stick motion — which is more a mental than a physical process — that improves speed. To test this idea, try playing the eighth and two sixteenth rhythm at a tempo of ♩= 184. You might find this difficult. Now play continuous eighth notes all with the right hand at the same tempo. Now play continuous quarter notes all with the left hand again at the ♩= 184 tempo. Did either hand have difficulty playing that fast? Because you probably did not experience difficulty, you can see why the challenge is in how you put the stroke motions together; not in the quickness of the hand motions.

When playing multiple strokes, such as rolls and multiple grace notes, stickings are based on hand motions instead of individual strokes. The same sticking methods discussed earlier will apply:

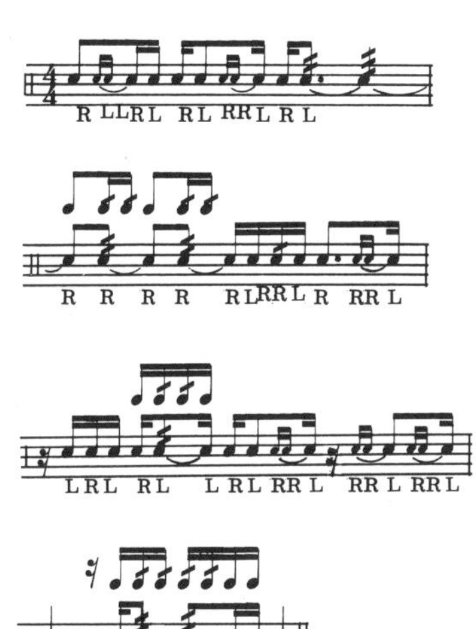

June, 1987

Timpani Sizes and Ranges

John J. Papastefan

For many years, a pair of timpani with stadard diameter sizes of 28 and 25 inches or 29 and 26 inches was the norm. Today, a set of at least four timpani has become essential to perform the music written for advanced high school level students and beyond. Timpanists need a minimum of four drums, measuring 32, 29, 26, and 23 inches, to meet the range requirements of the music they perform with good tone quality.

A pair of timpani will produce all of the notes found within the octave F2 to F3. By adding a drum 20 inches in diameter to the four sizes listed above it is possible to extend the upper register of the group of timpani to C4. Adding more timpani to the basic pair gives a player flexibility in choosing the instrument for the required pitches; it also reduces the number of tuning changes needed during the course of a composition.

Why is such flexibility important? Because so many orchestral works call for timpani parts with extended ranges. *La Création du Monde* by Darius Milhaud requires D4 and F♯4; *The Rite of Spring* by Stravinsky calls for B3, and several other composers, including Copland, Kabalevsky, and Kodály, require A3 in their works.

Many compositions in the solo literature also require five or more timpani. For example, *Sensemayá* by Silvestre Revueltas requires timpani tuned to G♭2, B2, F3, G3, and A♭3. The Sonata for Piano and Percussion by Peggy Glanville Hicks calls for timpani tuned to G2, A2, B2, E3, and B3. Several timpani concertos, including those by Werner Thärichen, Sam Raphling, and Robert Parris, also require five drums. If enough composers and arrangers write for four or more timpani, this number will eventually become the norm rather than the exception.

As early as 1930 Percival Kirby recommended the use of five timpani measuring 30, 28, 26, 24, and 22 inches, "for those who desire to produce really artistic results" (*The Kettle-Drums*). Resonance, depth, and tone color can be enhanced by using five timpani of 32, 29, 26, 23, and 20 inches; in addition, the 12-inch span between the largest and smallest sizes offers a greater degree of flexibility and better tone quality than the 8-inch span suggested by Kirby. According to Gordon Peters, principal percussionist of the Chicago Symphony Orchestra, the best timpani sizes for professional use are 32, 29, 26, 23, and 21 inches, and include pedals, rather than one of the other pitch changing mechanisms (*The Drummer: Man*). The 21-inch size is indeed a rarity in the United States; substituting the 20-inch size for the 21-inch timpani is more consistent with 3-inch gradations and further, sounds less stuffy in the pitches located above C4. Some timpanists, however, prefer the 21-inch, believing it has a fuller sound.

The 28- and 25-inch pair of timpani was developed much earlier than the other sizes now in use. This pair can be used interchangeably with the 29- and 26-inch pair, which was introduced around 1960. However, the 29- and 26-inch diameters produce better tone quality throughout the entire range of each drum, and particularly at the extreme ends of the range.

The size of a timpani refers to the bowl diameter, which is measured in inches. The range of a drum varies with the make and model and can be quite wide, but the best quality sound is generally obtained within a perfect fifth. Ranges for the five sizes recommended here are as follows:

The black notes indicate the range in which the best tone quality can usually be achieved. The timpani can be tuned to the ranges shown by the white notes, but achieving good tone quality is less certain. Tone quality within these ranges will vary among different makes and models of timpani.

Directors, players, and arrangers should not assume that each note within these traditional ranges sounds equally good. Every timpani (like every piano or other instrument) is slightly different. To determine which notes sound best, begin by experimenting with each drum, then plan a tuning strategy accordingly. The range of each drum may be extended slightly in either direction, especially when playing on top-quality plastic mylar heads, but the resulting pitches will not have the same quality as the notes within the standard ranges.

Once a player has developed the ability to identify and sing intervals, he should be capable of tuning the timpani. With your heel, press the pedal of each drum all the way down to the position of lowest pitch. At the same time gently press on the center of the head with the heel of the hand. This seems to iron out the head and yield more accurate tuning. Be sure that this bottom, or home base, note is the appropriate lowest pitch for the particular drum being tuned. Using a pitch pipe, tuning fork, or other reliable pitch source, fine-tune the drum to the correct note, using the tuning lugs. It is absolutely essential that the head be in tune with itself, which means that the pitch is identical at each tuning lug. Only then will the pitch be true and the tone resonant.

Once the drum is tuned to the base pitch, the pedal is used to change the pitch as needed. Gently strike the drum and, slowly and as silently as possible, increase the tension on the head by pushing down on the pedal until the desired pitch is reached. Always approach the pitch from below, as this seems to settle the head most effectively and result in more accurate intonation. If you move past the desired pitch be sure sure to "heel down" the pedal as described above, time permitting.

The quality of tone at the extreme high or low range of any timpani is usually rather poor. Optimal sound and beauty of tone are obtained around mid-range and slightly above. For maximum resonance, pitches in the high register of any size drum are best played on the next smaller size in the set. For example, the note D3 can be played on a 28- or 29-inch drum with fine plastic heads and modern pedal mechanisms, but it will not have the reverberation of the D3 played on a 25- or 26-inch drum.

The bottom note on a timpani is comparable to an open string of an orchestral string instrument and should be avoided, if possible, unless specifically designated. Notes at or near the bottom of the range tend to be less distinct in pitch and rhythm. Pitches at the top of the range sound constricted, "pinched," and lack projection. Plastic heads can enable the player to obtain one or two extra notes at either end of the range, although the tone quality at these extremes leaves much to be desired in the way of clarity and resonance.

On some occasions, composers call for artificial tuning – tuning a timpani to a pitch lower or higher than its normal tuning note. For example, tuning the 23-inch drum to C3 rather than to the usual D3. This technique is analogous to *scordatura*, the abnormal tuning of a string instrument in order to obtain unusual chords, facilitate difficult passages, or change tone color. Avoid using this tuning alteration consistently; such a change affects the balanced action mechanism in some timpani, causing pitches to go sharp by themselves. This practice can also be confusing to the timpanist who relies on the basic (bottom) tuning note to serve as his home base. This is particularly true of the inexperienced timpanist who may be used to pushing the pedal to the floor to get a certain pitch, a factor to be remembered when scoring for student or other amateur ensembles.

Drums manufactured at both ends of the timpani range have increased the available scope and quality of pitches. For example, a 32-inch timpani not only produces a fuller, more resonant F2 and E♭2, but a clear and true sounding D2 and even C2. The timpani method books by Saul Goodman and Friese and Lepak advise using a 32-inch drum, or a specially made larger size, to ensure good tone quality and intonation for notes in the vicinity of C2.

For high notes, a 21-inch or the more available 20-inch timpani, sometimes referred to as a piccolo timpani, will reach B3 and C4 with relative ease. Although the sound of these notes may be tight and not overly resonant, the pitch will be true and clear. Special sizes, such as 15-

and 14-inch timpani, which can reach D4 and F#4, respectively, with a clear vibrant sound, are available. However, these unusual sizes are difficult to find outside professional orchestras. Timpani smaller than the 23-inch and larger than the 32-inch sizes are occasionally used in conservatory and professional orchestras; but it is best for a composer to avoid writing for these sizes unless he is commissioned by a particular ensemble that owns the less common ones.

Selecting the number and sizes of drums for a timpani section can be confusing. With some experimentation and examination of the type of pieces the group will be playing, timpani can be chosen and tuned to obtain the best sound in all ranges required. ■

August, 1987

Snare Drum Tips

Charles Holmes

Young percussionists often experience problems with tension, which interferes with stick control. Your students' inability to relax and control the sticks can cause them to play rolls, flams, ruffs, and other rudiments poorly.

Stick control is primarily responsible for the sound a drummer produces. In attempting to compensate for a lack of it young drummers often tighten their grip and squeeze the sticks, producing tension in the hands, arms, shoulders, and back.

You can begin to promote good stick control by helping your students learn the correct grip. The most important aspect of the grip is correct use of the thumb and fingers. Whether you teach rudimental or matched grip, students should let the sticks do the work.

In matched grip only the thumb and the index finger actually grip the stick. The thumb should be placed on the inside of the stick rather than on top of it.

The other fingers should curve loosely around the stick to help control it, floating or riding with the stick as it moves.

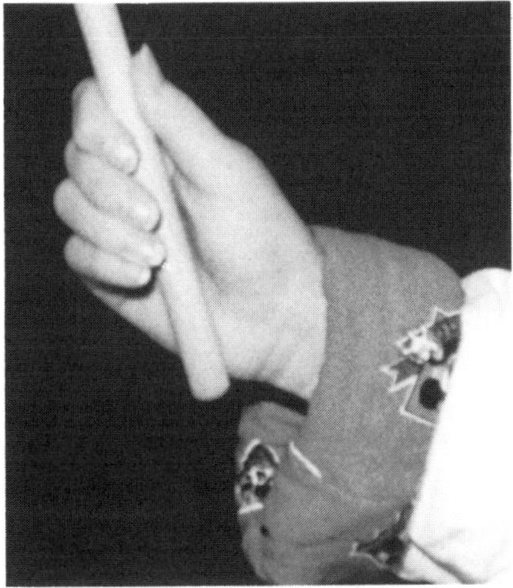

If the other three fingers actually grip the stick, they will restrict its ability to bounce.

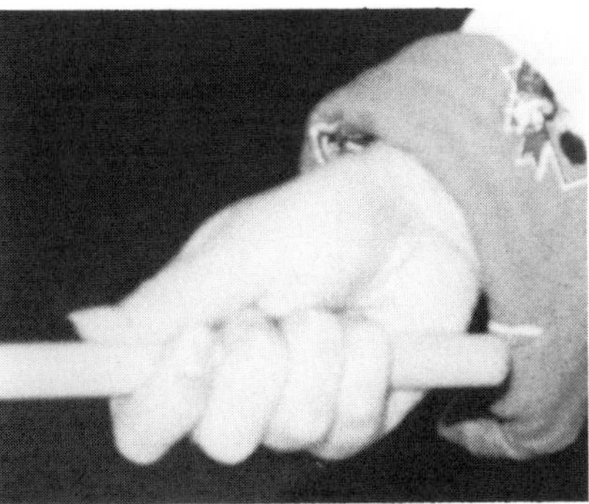

In the rudimental grip the right hand functions just as it does when using matched grip, but the left hand is quite different. The muscles between the thumb and the index finger, not the fingers themselves, grip the stick. The thumb should be straight, not bent over the stick, and only the index finger should be placed over the stick, not the middle finger. This helps to ensure maximum rebound of the stick.

French grip, the method of playing matched grip with the thumbs on top of the stick instead of on the side, is best suited to timpani playing.

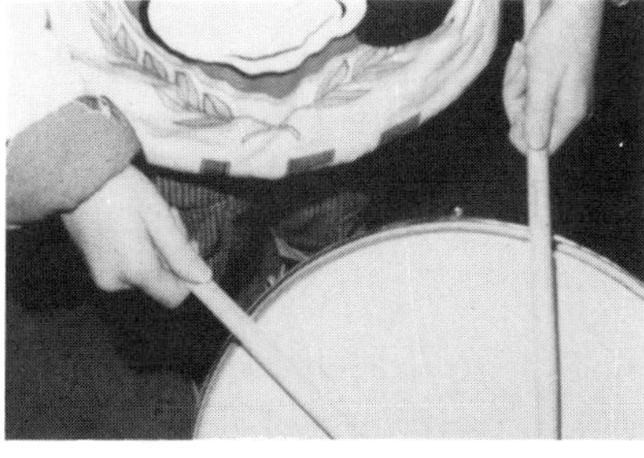

It is inappropriate for snare drum playing because it doesn't permit adequate use of the muscles and joints in the back of the wrist. It is also a poor choice for drum set playing because it doesn't allow lateral movement around the set. An additional drawback to the French grip is that it can cause thumb blisters, because snare drum and set players use more downward pressure than timpani players. A more comfortable and practical grip to use is the thumb on the side of the stick.

The "stick flick" is a good exercise to help drummers gain control of their middle, ring, and little fingers. The fingers of both hands can be exercised by holding the stick with the tip pointing up and using the fingers to flick or pivot the stick. This exercise helps to develop dexterity in the fingers; it will loosen up the forearm muscles as well.

Good posture is also essential for endurance. In school concert bands, where drummers stand, it is essential that they stand erect and distribute their weight evenly between the feet. Novice drummers often do not take time to adjust the height of their

Student drummers often depend on their band director to tell them what size sticks to buy. Frequently they are told to buy size 2B, but these sticks are often too long and heavy for young drummers, and this contributes to stick control problems.

Have your drummers experiment with sticks of different lengths and weights. Encourage them to try 5A, 7A, or SD4 (Vic Firth). They need to find a stick that fits the hand and feels comfortable. Direct your students to a local drum shop if possible; specialty shops often carry stick sizes that are unavailable in regular music stores.

Relaxing while performing is important to all musicians, but it is especially important to drummers because they use their hands and wrists to produce sound. When a student plays snare drum, he uses most of the muscles in the upper body; and when he plays a drum set, he uses all the muscles from the neck down. The ability to relax not only improves performance but also increases a drummer's stamina.

snare drums properly; if the drum is too low they have to stoop to play it.

Have them adjust the drum to about belt height.

Drum set players in stage bands also experience posture problems. Encourage them to sit with the back straight. A curved spine contributes to tension and fatigue. The drum throne should be adjusted so that it is not too high. The center of gravity should be in the hips – not in the feet and legs. This allows freer use of the legs, which results in better coordination and independence of the limbs. Whether playing snare drum or drum set, the elbows should be kept close to the body to avoid upper-body tension.

Rudiments are to drummers what scales are to wind players. Most directors require their drummers to know at least the first 13 of the 26 rudiments. The four rudiments that beginning drummers should learn first are the long roll, the five-stroke roll, the nine-stroke roll, and the flam. These are the ones most commonly found in concert band music at the middle-school level.

Rudiments develop technique as well as speed. Young drummers have a tendency to play rudiments too fast, often exceeding the speed at which they can control the sticks, which causes the upper-body muscles to tighten up. Encourage your students to work for precision rather than speed. Speed comes gradually through relaxation of the upper-body muscles. The more relaxed a drummer is, the more speed he will achieve. Impress upon your drummers that speed is not instantly attainable; it is developed over a long period of time along with maturity.

Percussion remains a mystical area to many band directors, but it needn't be. The nature of the instruments and the number of students involved often make it difficult to give young percussionists the individual attention they need. Make it a point to get to know percussion as well as you know the other sections of your band. You and your band will be well rewarded. □

Triangular Considerations

Lynn Glassock

While the triangle is a familiar instrument in every band, few directors understand what factors are important in producing a satisfactory triangle sound. First, the triangle needs to be capable of producing a long-ringing collection of upper partials with an absence of any definite pitch. Inexpensive triangles are often made of metals other than steel or have small diameters that make them unacceptable for concert use. Most triangles range in size from four to ten inches. In general the small sizes produce lighter, more delicate sounds. Ideally a concert band or orchestra should have at least two triangles, one in the eight- to ten-inch range and another in the four- to six-inch range.

What holds the triangle is another important element that is sometimes overlooked. The cord used to suspend the triangle should be a very thin yet strong material, such as gut or nylon. A thick cord will dampen the tone considerably. If there is any question about the strength of the cord being used, a longer, heavier auxiliary loop can be attached in case the thin one breaks. The holder should also have a clamp that will allow it to be attached to a music stand.

The beater(s) should be seven to ten inches in length and also made of steel. It is best to have several matched pairs of beaters ranging from 1/16th inch to 5/16th inch in diameter. This will aid the performer in obtaining the desired tone and dynamics. Other types of beaters (such as wood) should only be used when called for in the score.

Once the triangle, holder, and beater are taken care of, the remaining ingredient is the playing technique. This includes how to hold the triangle, how and where the beater makes contact, and whether the resulting sound should ring or be muffled.

When the music allows sufficient time, the triangle should be held rather than attached to a music stand. This will allow better eye contact with the instrument, the music, and the conductor; and the sound will project better if the triangle is held above the stands, chairs, and performers. The holder should rest on the thumb and second finger (which forms a C) and the index finger should be placed on top for a more secure grip. The remaining two fingers are used for muffling when needed.

Just as the sound varies, from one triangle to another, every triangle is capable of producing a variety of different sounds. The amount and type of overtones produced depend on the spot and the angle at which the beater strikes the triangle. When played as in the first example, the triangle will produce the fewest number of overtones and will produce a fairly definite pitch.

This is probably the sound least desired by most professional percussionists. Changing the point of impact and the angle, as in the next example, produces a more diffuse sound with higher overtones.

Striking the bottom leg of the triangle at a 45-degree angle, as shown in the third example, will

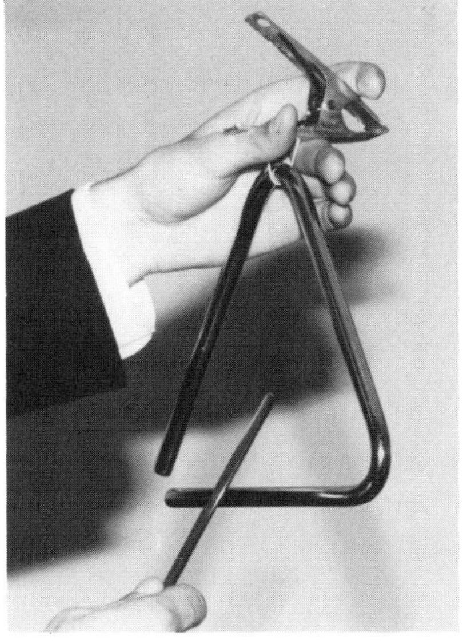

produce a wide range of overtones, including lower ones not commonly found at most other angles. Playing vertically near the corner of the bottom leg, as in the last example, will produce a variety of high-pitched overtones somewhat similar to the sound produced in the second example.

Experimenting with different locations and angles is very helpful in finding the best sound for each particular situation.

Rolls are performed by rapidly moving the beater between two adjacent legs of the triangle. Dynamics can be controlled by the distance the beater moves (the closer to the corner, the shorter the stroke and therefore the softer the sound), and by the size of the beater. Two beaters are sometimes used to play rolls and passages too fast to be played with one hand. In these cases, of course, the triangle cannot be held. It is sometimes advantageous to use two clips (one in each corner) to attach the triangle to a music stand.

As is the case with many other percussion instruments, the written notation does not always accurately represent the length of time the triangle should ring. The next example shows two common ways of letting the performer know that the triangle should not be muffled. The three notes in the example following, however, may or may not correctly represent the length of time the triangle should ring.

This is not a question of the performer (or director) overruling a composer's wishes, but a musical decision, because many percussion parts are not written correctly with respect to ring time.

If the composer has used the L.V. (let vibrate) or half tie in some situations, then it is likely that an unaltered note of short duration should be taken literally. If, on the other hand, these notations are not used, the overall musical context must be considered in determining if and when the instrument should be muffled.

In such cases, it is probably better to assume that the sound should diminish naturally (no muffling) unless it is musically distracting. To save time and avoid confusion in later rehearsals, proper notation should be added to the parts that are unclear.

A good triangle sound has no single most important element. Bringing together the correct combination of equipment and playing techniques can be accomplished without great expense of time or money. With a little care, the triangle can add a touch of color that will be an asset to any organization. □

October, 1987

Build a Percussion Storage Cabinet

Norman Weinberg

As most band and orchestra directors know, small percussion instruments present a unique storage problem. These instruments have the nasty habit of walking away to parts unknown, or at best, hiding themselves in places where you wouldn't think to look. Here is a small, space-saving cabinet that may solve a lot of these problems for you and make your life a little more organized.

We have used such a cabinet at Del Mar College for five years now, and nothing has been lost or misplaced. The cabinet attaches to the wall, keeping your

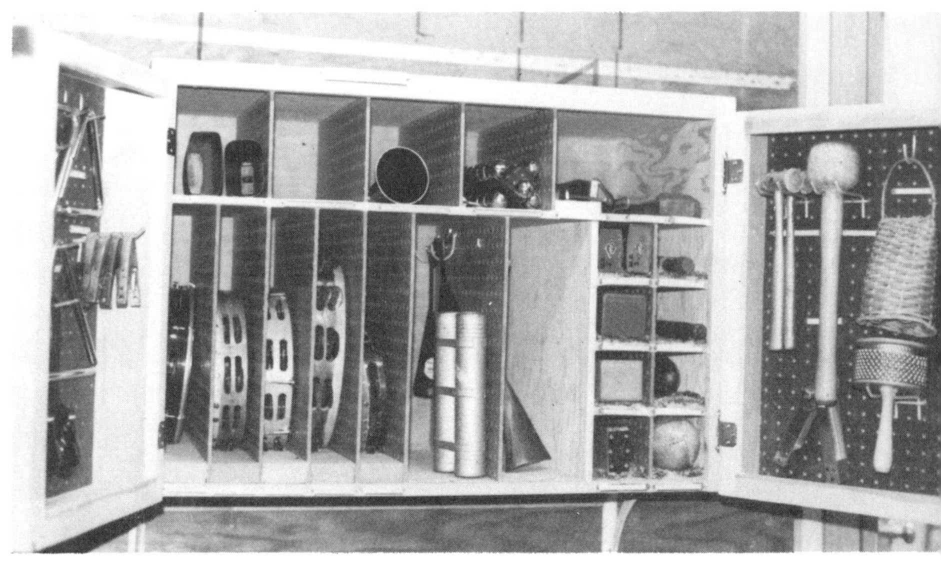

valuable floor space free for other storage. The body of this cabinet will hold five tambourines, bass drum and gong mallets, four woodblocks, castanets, whip, cowbells, sound effects, and Latin percussion instruments. The "shadow-box" style pegboard doors permit storage of many smaller instruments that can hang from hooks.

In the following drawings, the thick lines indicate ¾" plywood and the thin lines ¼" pegboard. Measurements for thick lines are from side to side, and measurements for thin lines are from center to center.

If you don't have much experience with woodworking or the proper tools for a straight cut, you may want to have the lumber company cut the pieces for you. It will be easier for them if you first take the time to draw a pattern of how the various pieces fit onto the standard sheet of plywood. After all the pieces are cut, it is a good idea to put the cabinet together on the floor without glue or screws, just to make sure that all the parts fit together properly.

The pegboard dividers should be set into ¼" deep grooves on the top, bottom, and shelf supports to prevent warping. It is important to make careful measurements before using the router to cut these grooves. After cutting the grooves and assembling the cabinet, use the wood glue to set the dividers into place.

List of Materials:

A) One and one-half sheets (4' x 8') of ¾" plywood, cut into:

3 pieces	18" x 36"	top, bottom, middle support
4 pieces	18" x 24"	sides and door fronts
3 pieces	18" x 8¾"	small shelf
3 pieces	18" x 3½"	small shelf supports
1 piece	18" x 4"	small shelf support
4 pieces	4" x 18"	door spacer
4 pieces	4" x 24"	door spacer

If you desire a back on this cabinet, add an additional piece of 24" x 36". This back will require an extra half-sheet of plywood.

B) One sheet (4' x 8') of ¼" pegboard, cut into:

2 pieces	18" x 24"	door
6 pieces	18" x 5½"	large storage dividers
4 pieces	18" x 7"	medium storage dividers
3 pieces	18" x 4"	small storage dividers
1 piece	18" x 4½"	small storage divider

C) Additional lumber:

4 pieces	1" x 1" x 18"	door pegboard spacer
4 pieces	1" x 1" x 24"	door pegboard spacer
4 pieces	1" x 2" x 18"	door lip
4 pieces	1" x 2" x 24"	door lip

D) Tools and extra parts:

Wood glue, clamps for gluing, screws, router, screwdriver (power type is recommended), four heavy-duty hinges, two large heavy-duty supports (this cabinet is heavy!), and pegboard hooks of various sizes.

"SHADOW-BOX" DOORS CUTAWAY VIEW

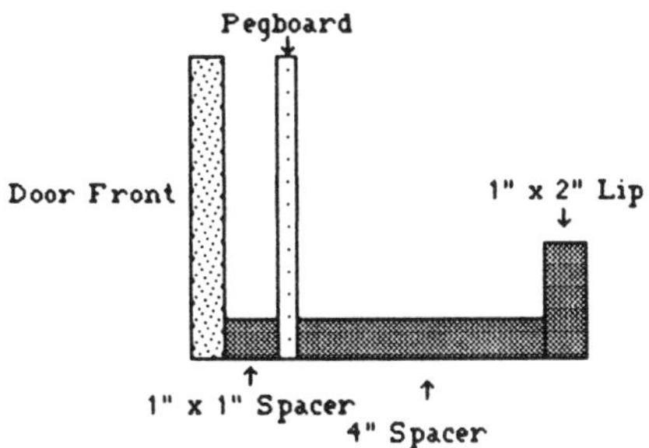

The "shadow-box" style doors go together in the following way: The piece of ¾" plywood is on the outside of the door. Attached to this is a window frame of 1" x 1" lumber, which provides a

"SHADOW-BOX" DOORS EXPLODED VIEW

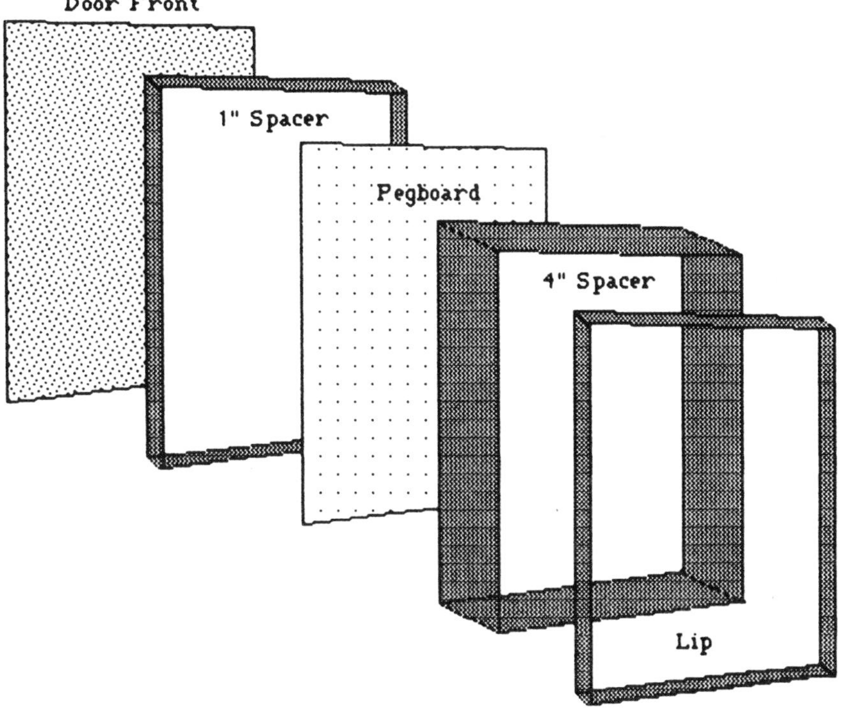

space behind the pegboard so that the hooks can be inserted properly. The pegboard (also 18" x 24") goes on top of this window frame. Next comes the 4" window frame, which acts as a door spacer so the instruments that hang from the pegboard are positioned inside the door (a little like a refrigerator door). The last piece of this door is another window frame of 1"x 2" lumber used as a lip around the entire door.

After you have assembled the cabinet and both doors, all that remains is to attach the doors with the hinges and mount the entire cabinet on the wall. Of course, the dimensions can be altered to fit your individual small instrument inventory.

The biggest advantage of this cabinet is that the students can find what they need quickly. Another plus is that you can tell at a glance if any instrument is missing before the cabinet is closed. If security is a big problem, a hasp-type lock can be added to the doors and unlocked only during rehearsals or performances. This cabinet is not expensive to build — about $50.00 in materials — and you might even convince your school woodworking class to build it for you. □

WALL MOUNTED STORAGE CABINET — SIDE VIEW

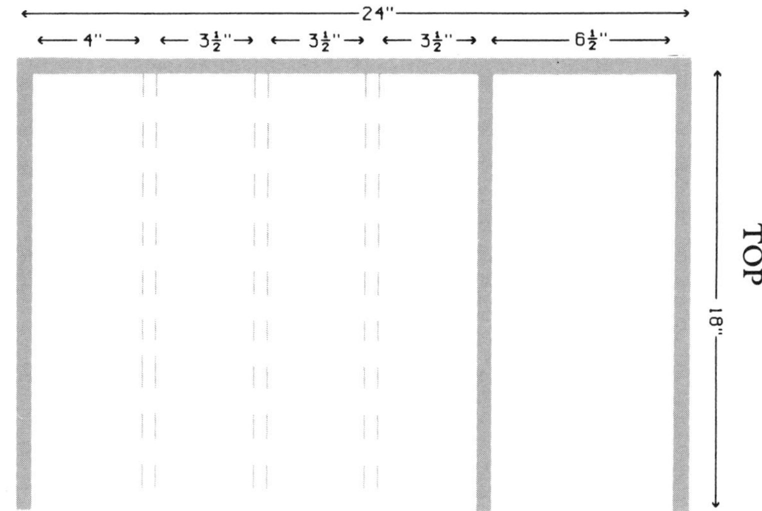

WALL MOUNTED STORAGE CABINET — FRONT VIEW

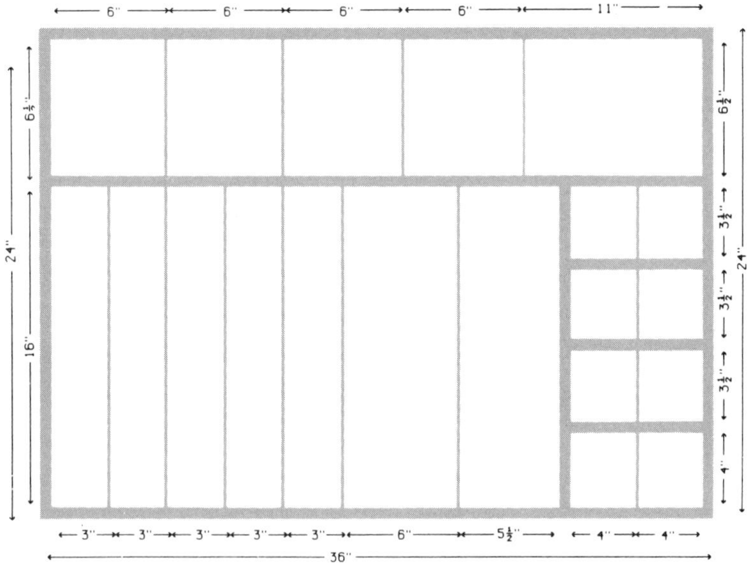

December 1987

Aim High for Your Percussion Section

BY MARK FORD

A particular problem faces most high school band directors each year: What is the best way to encourage the musical growth of the 10 to 20 drummers who have just completed marching band season and now stand in the back of the band room with little to do by comparison?

The scenario is the same in most schools. For three or more months the director relies on the percussion section to control tempo, add excitement to the show, and lead the group in executing features on the field. As members of the concert band, however, percussionists perform literature that requires them to play only occasionally; and what is worse, these students may have to compete with each other to play certain works if there are more percussionists than parts. This can quickly divide a section that only weeks before functioned as a cohesive unit.

The first step to a successful start of the concert band season is to raise your expectations of the percussionists in your ensemble. Often it is the director who encourages drummers to participate in outside musical activities, yet this same person will turn around and say, "I know my percussionists won't do any of these things. I don't know what's the matter with them." Though you may believe you are encouraging them, students will sense whether this is your true attitude. If you expect more from the percussionists and make your musical goals clear, the students in turn will expect more of themselves.

Spend time with the percussion section, either as a group or individually with one-on-one lessons. Becoming more closely involved will give you insight into how the students are progressing individually. Regular master classes run by you or by a percussion instructor can help students master band literature or other special problems. Invite guest percussionists from local symphonies or colleges to illustrate playing techniques on different instruments or demonstrate how to select mallets for varying sounds and styles.

These group sessions also present a good opportunity for students to visit local colleges to hear percussion recitals or to attend clinics featuring professional percussionists at local drum shops. Often these clinics and concerts are free to the public.

Attending master classes, along with receiving the director's advice, often encourages students to take private lessons. By becoming familiar with snare drum, mallets, or timpani in these lessons students develop a better understanding of rhythm, harmony, and melody, making it possible for them to perform a broader range of repertoire.

The experience of performing is vital to the young percussionist's development. Though there are plenty of ways to arrange occasions for the high school percussionist to perform, the most enjoyable for the student and audience alike is the percussion ensemble. Playing in an ensemble benefits students more than solo work because it requires them to interact with other musicians. While offering the opportunity to perform on different instruments, it increases the player's knowledge of styles of literature and most important, builds students' confidence for future performances. Rehearsals of small ensem-

Selected Music for High School Percussion Ensemble

BY GUY REMONKO

One of the band director's most difficult jobs is selecting music for the percussion ensemble that is both playable and enjoyable, while using the available number of players and instruments. The following five compositions represent time-tested, quality works in a variety of styles and difficulty levels that will help develop the two most important aspects of percussion ensemble performance: rhythmic precision and sensitivity to color.

(E3) FUGUE, Philip Faini. Instrumentation: xylophone, bells, chimes, marimba, four timpani, five tom-toms, snare drum, triangle, cymbals. Six players are required.

This is a great piece for developing ensemble listening habits, sensitivity to color, and tone production concepts in a newly organized or inexperienced ensemble. The subject statements are easily heard and followed as they pass through the ensemble. The keyboard parts can easily be memorized if necessary and played with only two mallets. Modulation, countersubjects, augmentation, diminution, thematic fragmentation, dynamic contrast, and changing textures are used to create a musical piece that really swings. (Accura Music)

(E3) THE SWORDS OF MODA-LING, Gordon Peters. Instrumentation: piano, bells, xylophone, marimba, vibraphone (optional), chimes, four timpani, temple blocks, snare drum, bass drum, suspended cymbal, tam-tam, triangle. Nine players are required, including piano and optional vibraphone.

An Oriental mood best describes this unique composition. Modality, pointillism, changing textures, various colors, and maximum melodic use of the percussion instruments all contribute to the style of the composition. This is a single-movement work containing four sections: a slow introductory theme in the piano punctuated by pointillistic interruptions in the percussion; an "Allegro" based on a dialogue between timpani and keyboard percussion; a piano chorale; and a thickly textured "Piu Allegro." As the piece builds, the composer creates a gamelan-like cushion of sound by layering repeated four-note motives in groups of instruments.

If your percussion inventory does not include a marimba, the composer sanctions using temple blocks in place of all marimba parts. This and other suggested alterations are supplied with the score. (Dallas Percussion, 1613 Temple Terrace, Wilmington, Delaware, $31.50)

(E4) SUITE FOR PERCUSSION, William Kraft. Instrumentation: two snare drums, field snare, tenor drum, bass drum, bongos, tambourine, hand drum. Four players are required.

The three movements in this suite present creative drum writing that really cooks. Albles often function like master classes in which players learn specific techniques and concepts that they can transfer to concert band or orchestra.

Plan performances for the percussion ensemble according to the students' performing ability. Nothing is worse than rehearsing one or two selections for three or four months, then only performing once. Try to arrange a chamber recital, either at school or at a local civic club meeting, including the percussion ensemble and other chamber groups from the concert band.

Another excellent performance opportunity exists in solo and ensemble festivals where the group can be evaluated. The Percussive Arts Society initiated a "High School Percussion Ensemble Contest" in 1985, which many state chapters are continuing, either as a contest or a festival. If you are interested in starting a percussion ensemble but are unsure of the literature, either contact a percussion instructor at a local college or write the Percussive Arts Society (214 West Main Street, Urbana, Illinois). Either source should be able to provide a list of ensemble literature appropriate for students.

Other opportunities to perform include tryouts for all-regional or all-state band and orchestra. These solo tryouts are valuable because each student has to prepare and perform material without the aid of other musicians or a conductor. Of course students usually enlist the help of the band director or private instructor to prepare the music.

The student who studies privately may be asked to perform

though traditional melodic instruments are not used, each movement takes on melodic implications resulting from the pitches of the various graduated drums coupled with a somewhat pointillistic compositional style.

The "Ostinatos" movement, famous for its use of brushes, requires a horizontal sweeping technique rather than a sticklike vertical technique. The demanding tambourine part calls for thumb rolls and use of the knuckles. This movement also contains one of the best bass drum parts ever written. (Mills Music, $7.50)

(E4) MUSIC FOR PIECES OF WOOD, Steve Reich. Instrumentation: five pair of claves. Five players are required.

Minimalism and the African concept of playing cross-rhythms are the precepts behind this crafty composition. The piece is in three sections, each with a different meter: $\frac{6}{4}$, $\frac{4}{4}$, and $\frac{3}{4}$. Each section develops as follows: The composer states and repeats a simple, inactive rhythm, then gradually adds notes until the pattern becomes active. At this point a pattern evolves and becomes an accompaniment to the next entrance. This continues until all players are repeating their individual patterns, and suddenly all the patterns are the same. The individual rhythms are not very complex, but when combined, produce a highly complex fabric. This piece will definitely improve each player's sense of precision and time feel. After students understand the concept behind the work, they will be able to practice the piece without a conductor. (Universal Edition, $15)

(E5) GAINSBOROUGH, Thomas Gauger. Instrumentation: vibraphone, two marimbas, bells, chimes, four timpani, two tom-toms, snare drum, bass drum with attached cymbal, gong, hand cymbal, suspended cymbal. Five players are required.

If you have two outstanding mallet players, this three-movement work is the perfect showcase for their talents. Both mallet parts require technique in solid, block chord performance and hand-to-hand four-mallet playing. The majority of the block chord passages are easily executed because of the use of parallel chords. This exciting contemporary work contains effective tonal writing achieved by tertian and quartal voicings, modality, interesting textures, and extensive interplay between parts. This piece is easy to prepare, because of a rather transparent texture that uses the battery to create rhythmic drive, while fulfilling thematic functions.

Whereas the first and third movements use the two marimbas as "workhorses," the slow second movement uses vibe-marimba pairing. The natural lyrical and sustaining qualities of the vibe, supported by rolled marimba chords and a delicate accompaniment in the percussion, establish a pensive mood, which contrasts the first and third movements. (Southern Music Company)

Compositions for percussion ensemble reflect influences from many parts of the world: Africa, Latin America, Indonesia, India, Turkey, and Europe. These influences are present not only in the instruments themselves, but also in the rhythmic structures, scales, textures and colors, and other compositional devices used by composers of percussion art music. Band directors have the opportunity to expose high school percussionists to many types of music while maintaining high standards of quality. Performing this music just might inspire students to study privately and strive for higher musical goals. □

in a master class with other of his teacher's students. Here is another opportunity for percussion ensemble members to hear and see other students perform, then evaluate their own abilities.

Evaluating a percussionist's musicality is difficult to do in a short period of time. Many directors have had success by breaking down yearly goals for the percussion section into playoffs every six weeks for a grade or evaluation. These playoffs can include prescribed levels of technique on snare drum, mallets, and timpani, as well as sightreading. When held consistently these events give students the incentive to learn specific musical skills. Beginning the school year with a playoff to establish the materials and concepts to be evaluated gives the students an idea of what to expect. If you have a percussion instructor on your staff, discuss with him the percussion section's goals for the year.

What should directors expect from high school percussionists? You can only expect as much in return as you offer. Set high goals for your players, and with your help they'll reach them. □

October 1987

Percussionists Are Musicians

– Jesse Pearl Miami, Florida

Percussionists add accents, punch, and excitement to music, but somewhere in their training, they must also come to accept the chore of being patient producers of dull, monotonous, carefully balanced rhythmic patterns. The percussion section should be the most respected group in the entire ensemble, yet band and orchestra directors often do not appreciate it. Perhaps instructors need to take a closer look into the scope, sequence, and circumstances that go into training these players.

Begin by asking yourself a few questions: Do you give the percussion section as much time as other sections? Do you put your percussion section into a group with another family of instruments, then ignore the players to the point where discipline becomes a problem? Have you ever considered the fact that percussionists need to learn two clefs and the techniques of performing on many instruments in the same time span as musicians concentrating on one instrument? If your answers show that the percussion section is a problem for you, consider making a change. Try creating a special class for these young musicians.

A year of training at the junior high or middle school level in a class of no more than 20 candidates will produce a section of about 12 students who can be grounded in the basics of rudiments, rhythms, sticking techniques, keyboard, bass clef (for reading timpani music), and treble clef (for glockenspiel parts). They should also learn musicianship, so as to develop into a cooperative section with no discipline problems. The eight or so students who do not succeed with this training will drop the program or switch to another instrument. Don't worry; the effort will not have been wasted. No matter what instrument they eventually play, students will benefit from this disciplined approach to playing rhythms.

When I offered summer percussion classes, I invited other instrumentalists to join, too. This strengthened their rhythmic acuity and gave them an appreciation of the percussionist's role. Those who elected to continue with percussion studies in the fall term helped to familiarize the new students with the class routine.

Part of the instruction was devoted to the care and appreciation of the instruments. By taking instruments apart, then lubricating and reassembling them, students gained a greater understanding of their value. When we left school to perform at other locations, students insisted on carting their own equipment. They knew the tone qualities and mechanical conditions of the timpani, snare, bass drum, cymbals, and so on, and did not want to trust to luck the instruments borrowed at other locations.

For the first semester of school students trained on pads, using heavy, thick sticks to develop the wrists. Using pads helped make it possible to hear over the sound of practicing. (Pads also expose uneven sticking and sloppy rhythms.) The next semester, class members took turns at the snare, as the other instruments were introduced. Through such training students accomplished the transition to the instruments with respect, eliminating the unnecessary abuse that can occur when players are unfamiliar with performing techniques.

Specializing on one instrument, either during the training period or when the student plays in an ensemble, is a definite no-no. If all percussionists regularly play all instruments and cover all parts while working up an arrangement, then in the event of a missing musician, the conductor will not be uncomfortable, nor will the precision of the ensemble suffer.

Students allowed equal training opportunities can achieve the excellence and self-reliance necessary for a performing organization. These are the people who will elect to further their studies privately, who will enhance the high school groups, and who will go on to college scholarships and finally into the profession.

Remember, percussionists are musicians, too; they deserve to be trained.

1988-1989

Putting Electronic Percussion into Perspective

BY LARRY RHODES

Despite the protests of many classical musicians, Harvey Warner, percussionist of the Nashville Symphony, considers electronic percussion as respectable an instrument as any. "To a great extent, today's advent of electronic percussion is no different from the development of the first crude drum of ages past," says Warner, who put in some time as a 1960s rock and jazz fusion trapset player before becoming a classical percussionist. En route to holding positions as music librarian and principal percussionist of the Nashville Symphony, the Ohio native also studied under Mike Rosen at Oberlin Conservatory and Don Miller and Richard Weiner of the Cleveland Orchestra.

"The percussion synthesizer or, more specifically, the electronic drumset, will most likely be this era's addition to the percussion instrument family," adds Warner. "As serious 20th-century percussion performers, we need not only to understand how these instruments were developed, but also to consider all possibilities or contexts for their use to realize their potential.

"Actually, the use of electronics in music began about the end of World War II, with the tape recorder. Music composed with this instrument used two types of sound: concrete or natural sounds, and sounds generated by electronic means. Composers would manipulate the sound by slowing down the tape, speeding it up, or by splicing to organize these sounds into a composition."

Warner points out that Walter Carlos's performances of *Switched-On Bach* on the Moog synthesizer during the '60s introduced the masses to electronic music. Shortly after the release of these recordings, there was an album called *Switched-On Nashville*, which exposed the new technology to an even broader audience.

During the '70s electronics took on a greater role in new music, according to Warner. Computers were used to sequence electronic instruments. The machines became the performers, analyzing the formulas that make up music or reaching conclusions about a composer's initial work. With the '80s the electronic specialization of individual instruments made them more accessible to musicians, not just to composers or acousticians. Nowadays, according to Warner, the advent of MIDI adds unlimited timbre to a musician's toolbox, giving performers a boundless ability of sound creation.

"The pop music market is now flooded with electronic sounds and instruments," says Warner. "At some point in the near future, courses that address MIDI sequencing, sampling, and basic computer science will have to be included in college curricula to prepare young percussion students for the job market. Because of improvements in sound quality, electronic drums are being used, both in solo performances and in ensemble playing with symphony orchestras."

Warner points out that electronic percussion has even attracted enough attention to merit a grant from the National Endowment for the Arts to commission Dave Felder to compose a concerto for electronic percussion and orchestra. This work, to be completed in 1988, will be performed in New York, Michigan, and California.

Pearl International also sponsored previews of five works for solo electronic and acoustic percussion at the 1987 International Percussion Symposium in St. Louis, featuring Warner. The composers and their works were: a composition for synthetic brass and electronic percussion by Kenneth Schermerhorn, conductor and music director of the Hong Kong and Nashville Symphony Orchestras; a work for sequenced strings, electronic percussion, trombone, vibes, and congas by Larry Borran, principal trombonist of the Nashville Symphony; a composition by Kent State electronic music instructor Frank Wiley for magnetic tape with acoustic and electronic percussion, which was played through speakers surrounding the audience to create octaphonic sound; a piece by University of Illinois composition instructor Paul Zahn that satirizes the use of electronics; and an electronic piece by Denver Symphony timpanist Bill Hill.

Warner had already been personally involved in percussion electronics through a series of Nashville Symphony Chamber Ensemble and young peoples' concerts, performing Frederick Zehem's Concerto for Percussion and Orchestra. For the realization (translation of written music into electronic jargon) of the piece, Warner used the Pearl Syncussion-X electronic percussion system. The performance incorporated some 210 sound colors, all based on specifications in the score by the composer.

"This was the first time that electronic drums were used as a solo or concerto instrument," says Warner. "The historical importance of these concerts is that they prove that this new instrument is capable of presenting a complete musical idea."

To the purists who question the use of electronic instruments as substitutes for acoustic ones, Warner makes these points:

• Difficult passages may be adjusted when using electronic drums so that easier sticking patterns can be used, expanding technical possibilities and allowing performers more virtuosity.

• The amount of electronic percussion already heard in popular music has accustomed the ears of the average audience member to the sound.

• Electronic drum sounds in a concerto give a better "sound print" when played with acoustic orchestral instruments, because acoustic drums tend to sound more like accompaniment than a solo instrument.

• Travel and setup time for electronic drums (including tuning) is less than that of acoustic drums.

"As the 20th century draws to a close, we will continue to see improvements in the sounds of and compositions for electronic percussion," predicts Warner. "These instruments could very well move out of the techno-pop realm and into the symphony hall."

Warner also believes that electronics has a validity in the classroom beyond the aspect of preparation for the job market. He has already used his Apple II computer system, a major part of his percussion setup, to store the various parts of compositions such as *African Sketches* by J. Kent Williams. This allows the

Harvey Warner

individual student to learn his part in an ensemble by playing along with the computer in a sort of "Music-Minus-One" fashion.

Warner has also used his computer in a similar way to program sequenced orchestral accompaniment on a floppy disk for the Bach violin concerto that has become a popular transcription for mallet instruments among junior high and high school students. This allows students to become accustomed to the timbres of a full orchestral accompaniment, which would be impossible practicing with a piano.

Warner believes that from classroom to concert hall electronics is destined to become an important link in the evolution of percussion. Although the limited repertoire of works written for this medium is a drawback for students interested in exploring electronic percussion, Warner says some recent compositions are worth checking out. *Within the Vortex* by Frank Wiley incorporates a normal battery of percussion instruments, magnetic tape, and a set of electronic quad pads. William Hill's *Five Primitive Chants* uses acoustic drum set, marimba, timpani, vibes, and a set of eight electronic drum pads played with a four-mallet technique.

"There are other pieces in which composers have used electronic drum sounds," says Warner, "but they are achieved either with computer or magnetic tape. In performing all the pieces I have mentioned it is important to remember that the setups are very involved. You must have all your instruments set up in a particular order to execute a passage, because these machines can sometimes have minds of their own. You have to give some thought to things like the number of tracks to be used, the type of boards, and so forth."

One instrumentalist Warner knows wishes the technology of his instrument were still growing, lamenting the fact that there have been no new developments in it in the past 200 years. "All I have to say to percussionists is that the technology of our instrument is growing. We just need to open our minds and our ears to realize it." □

April 1988

The Ultimate Metronome

BY NORMAN WEINBERG

Although the metronome was originally invented to provide a type of yardstick to more accurately specify tempos, educators have used it for many years to help develop their students' rhythmic accuracy. Most musicians have used a metronome at one time or another, but are often hampered by its restrictions. Now, there is an educational tool that can solve your rhythmic problems. It is called a drum machine; I call it the ultimate metronome.

Before anyone gets the wrong idea, let me say that I do not believe that learning to play with rhythmic accuracy and control results in a mechanical performer. Years ago Warner M. Hawkins said it very well in the October 1908 edition of *Etude*:

> The saying that a too-constant employment of absolute time in study is productive of mechanical playing is as ridiculous as it is ungrounded. I have never known a person having either a natural or acquired positive sense of time to have difficulty in executing the most delightfully regular ritards and accelerandos; on the other hand an artistic performance of these effects is almost impossible in the hands of a deficient timekeeper.

The author works with student Anthony Perez on the ultimate metronome

In February 1986 I received a grant from Del Mar College to investigate the educational value of electronic percussion instruments. Though my work deals primarily with percussion students, the techniques I have developed with the ultimate metronome can be used by students of any instrument or voice.

If you could design a metronome that would do everything you could hope for, what features would you want? Features included in some of the more advanced standard metronomes today should be part of your new machine. You would want it to click in different subdivisions of the beat, and you would probably want these clicks to sound in different tones so that the ear could easily hear the differences. A few metronomes now have a feature that allows for less common divisions of the beat, such as five or seven clicks per beat level. It is even possible to find a metronome that can place seven beats in a measure.

While all of these features are great ideas, you could add some features that are not available in the standard metronome. One handy item would be a reverse metronome. To use it you would tap twice, and the time between these taps would immediately convert into beats per minute. A feature like this gives you the chance to instantly calculate performance speed. Would you have any use for a metronome that could perform an accelerando or ritardando? Of course, the changes in speed would have to be adjustable so that they could be either perfectly smooth or change in their rate of movement, slowing down more quickly towards the end.

Though some metronomes allow for seven beats in a measure, why not consider a machine that would perform 10 or 11 beats per bar? The ability to perform in meters of any length would be a great expansion of this feature. On the subject of less common meters, the ultimate metronome would be able to indicate less common subdivisions within meters, such as $\frac{9}{8}$ meter in 3+3+3, 2+2+2+3, 3+2+2+2, and so on. No metronome available today can be set for mixed meters. This is perhaps the biggest drawback of all in trying to use a metronome in contemporary literature.

The drum machine that I use as my ultimate metronome is the E-Mu Systems SP-12. Like all other drum machines, it has a variety of sounds that are built into the unit's permanent memory. Some drum machines have more sounds than others, but all come with enough different sounds to serve a variety of needs. The SP-12 contains 24 different sounds, which can be altered in pitch, dynamic volume, and amount of decay.

Using these variations, it is possible to create hundreds of different sound combinations to build any type of sound relationship between measure speed, beat speed, and a variety of subdivision speeds. It is even possible to determine the relative duration of your clicks. In other words, a cowbell, which has a short sound (a small window of the beat), would require that your attack points be more exact. An electronic snare drum sound, which has a longer duration (a wider window of the beat), would allow slightly more leeway in the placement of notes. These subtle changes can be of use when the performer desires a slightly different feel to the meter. A wider window can accommodate playing a little ahead or behind the beat.

Once you've determined the type and quality of sound to use for a metronome pattern, the next step is to program the pattern into the machine. Different brands of drum machines program in different ways, the two most common approaches being real-time and step-time. Real-time means playing the buttons at the exact time that you want the machine to record the sounds. To make this job easier, all real-time machines have some type of "auto correct" feature that cleans up slight rhythmic problems made during this recording process. Step-time is more like a freeze frame video. You bring the machine to a specific point within the measure, play the sound that you want to record, then continue to repeat the process until you complete the pattern.

Using these programming techniques, you can program any type of measure that you desire. A bar of $\frac{17}{16}$ or $\frac{11}{8}$ is just as easy to set up as a measure of common time. On the SP-12 you simply key in the upper number (the choices are from 1-99) and the lower number (the choices are 2, 4, 8, 16, and 32). The next step is to determine how many different measures of the pattern you want the machine to play. If the metronome pattern you write is going to be repeated over and over, you only need one pattern; but if you want to have it change a bit, then consider a two-measure pattern. In addition to programming measures that have less common meters, you can easily program more common meters that have different subdivisions. A measure of $\frac{4}{4}$ that is phrased as 3+2+3 can be easily demonstrated by using different sounds for the stronger and weaker portions of the measure.

Most drum machines allow the user to create many different patterns (up to 100 or more), then save them for future use. How they are saved varies with the different brands of machine, but the most common ways to save patterns are by off-loading them on to a cassette or computer disc. Once these patterns are saved, the working memory inside the machine can be erased to create even more patterns. To return to patterns that you developed last week or even last year, reverse the off-loading process by placing the data back into the internal memory of the drum machine. This allows you to program just about any type of measure that you want, assign it to different memory locations, and get it back in a matter of minutes. Using a reference chart to keep track of sequences helps you know where certain patterns are located.

All drum machines allow the user to combine patterns into a performance called a "song," which is nothing more than a set of directions that tell the machine to play a series of patterns by chaining them together. This feature of connecting individual patterns allows the ultimate metronome to perform mixed meters. For example, if pattern number 50 is in $\frac{7}{8}$ meter

Sequence Chart

Sequence Name________________

Storage Location________________

1	26	51	76
2	27	52	77
3	28	53	78
4	29	54	79
5	30	55	80
6	31	56	81
7	32	57	82
8	33	58	83
9	34	59	84
10	35	60	85
11	36	61	86
12	37	62	87
13	38	63	88
14	39	64	89
15	40	65	90
16	41	66	91
17	42	67	92
18	43	68	93
19	44	69	94
20	45	70	95
21	46	71	96
22	47	72	97
23	48	73	98
24	49	74	99
25	50	75	00

with a phrasing of 3+2+2, and pattern number 24 is in $\frac{4}{4}$ meter with quarter-note triplets, then these two different patterns can be connected. These songs can be programmed to either repeat for a specified number of times, or play one time through the song and then stop.

In this example, only two measures were chained together to form the song. In reality songs can be made up of several hundred measures so that an entire work or etude can be programmed and placed into memory along with the patterns. Song number 1 might be the "Triumphal March of the Devil" from Stravinsky's *The Soldier's Tale*, while song number 46 could be the "Dance Sacrale" from *The Rite of Spring*. Keep in mind that all the patterns and songs programmed can be performed at any tempo between 40 and 240 beats per minute. All the data, including tempo changes, accents, and use of different pitch levels and instruments, will remain the same. If you have programmed an increase of 15 beats per minute over 4 measures, the machine doesn't care if the original speed is 88 beats per minute or 128 beats per minute. This makes it possible to begin study of a passage at a slower tempo and then increase the speed until you achieve the desired performance tempo.

You may even decide to go one step further with your ultimate metronome. With a device as sophisticated as a drum machine, you could even program the entire written rhythm of the piece. Most musicians know that when playing with a metronome, they can make small adjustments so that the beats fall with the sound of the click while the subdivisions may wobble around a bit. When the complete rhythm is sounded on the metronome, you will be able to hear any weaknesses or discrepancies in time and tempo with a much finer degree of accuracy. In addition to playing along with the work you or your students can listen to a perfect rhythmic performance.

With all of these possibilities, you might think that a drum machine is difficult to program and that to use anything this sophisticated would take you hours and hours to learn. Let me just say that programming a drum machine to play a song is not at all as difficult as programming a computer to perform a program. Yes, it takes some learning, but you can be setting up your metronome patterns in a matter of hours. It's important to ask yourself at what point does the time expended to learn the system pay off in relation to what the machine can do.

Computers have already been accepted by educators to help with ear training, theory, and even the charting of marching band shows. The drum machine – a rhythm computer – just may be the first piece of equipment to help students in areas of performance where past technology has proven to be incomplete. I have found the ultimate metronome to be a valuable addition to my studio for both me and my students. □

Managing the Percussion Section

BY CORT McCLAREN

Percussionists sometimes act as if they were in a world of their own, and no wonder. Isolated at the back of the room, they face difficulties – and temptations – unlike those of other musicians. It is possible, though, to guide percussionists to high standards of musicianship and to cure them of the gum chewing, giggling, and other disruptive behavior that thrives four rows away from the conductor. Devising a plan for percussionists to follow as they set up, warm up, rehearse, and leave the room takes time; but the results are gratifying.

Setup

Each percussionist should get into the habit of putting the percussion area in order before rehearsal begins. This includes arranging instruments, as well as removing and folding timpani and keyboard percussion covers. Chairs, stands, and trap tables also should be put in place.

Setup can be a simple procedure if you assign each percussionist a specific job, no matter how small or seemingly insignificant. Place a list of these jobs on a chart and post it in an obvious place near the rehearsal area so everyone in the section can see it. Each individual should fulfill his setup assignment before the rehearsal begins, then return the same item to its original location after rehearsal.

Percussion Setup Assignments

Larry: Bass drum cover, mallet stand for B.D., B.D. mallets
Mike: Timpani cover, mallet stand, throne, key, mufflers, clean timpani heads
Scott: Music stands for all instruments, unlock and lock cabinet
Pam: Crash cymbals and table, mallet stand for snare, suspended cymbal and stand
John: Covers, mallet stands, clean keyboard instruments with a soft cloth
Sue: Accessories needed for each composition, trap table

Use the same percussion setup every day so that all of the musicians in the ensemble develop a sense of organization and neatness. You'll find that your percussionists will soon become upset if anyone fails to treat this space with respect. Ask other students to stay away from this area, even to the point of keeping horn cases out of the way; it is difficult to maneuver when objects or people are constantly in the way.

Using another chart, assign a storage area for all instruments, stands, and chairs. Label each item and its place in the storage area so that there is no question as to where it belongs or who is assigned to taking it out and putting it away. If an instrument or piece of equipment is missing or stored improperly, you can easily look at the chart to see where the instrument should be and who is responsible for putting it there. Reassign setup responsibilities every now and then so that all students learn how to manage the various instruments.

Warm-Up

Warming up is important for all musicians, including percussionists. Developing good tone quality, flexibility, intonation, balance, blend, and nuance is as important for drummers as it is for trumpet and clarinet players. Use this precious time judiciously so percussionists feel they are an important part of the ensemble. It is the first step in achieving a positive attitude.

Develop a rotating schedule, assigning each player to a specific instrument during the full ensemble warm-up. Drummers need to learn to play several instruments, so provide them with opportunities to perform on all the basic percussion instruments – snare drum, timpani, keyboard percussion, and accessory instruments. Post the assignments in an area easily seen by the section, and make sure that everyone participates.

A common complaint about having percussionists warm up with the rest of the ensemble is that it becomes difficult for the director and other musicians to listen for balance and intonation. If this is true, you may need to assess the nature of the percussion warm-up. For example, what patterns are being played? Are the percussionists playing too loudly? If you cannot hear the ensemble properly when percussionists are included in the warm-up, then I would assume that it is also impossible to play in tune while rehearsing or performing. Expect percussionists to play with the same finesse as flutists, oboists, or any other musician.

The Rehearsal

If you were to ask your percussionists about what it's like to play in a band or orchestra, they would likely answer resoundingly, "Boring." After all, consider what percussionists do during ensemble rehearsals: sit for extended periods of time with nothing to perform; play occasionally; or worse, never play at all. Percussionists

Rotating Warm-Up Schedule

	Larry	Mike	Scott	Pam	John	Sue
Mon	Xylo	Xylo	Snare	Snare	Timp	Acc Insts
Tues	Xylo	Xylo	Snare	Snare	Timp	Acc Insts
Wed	Snare	Snare	Xylo	Xylo	Acc Insts	Timp
Thurs	Snare	Snare	Xylo	Xylo	Acc Insts	Timp
Fri	Acc Insts	Timp	Snare	Snare	Xylo	Xylo

often complain of never getting to play important parts or of having to fight the upperclassmen for even the smallest part. Once a student has a part, it may be one that allows for little musical growth and development.

It's easy to say, "That's the way it is; you should get accustomed to sitting idle and counting rests for long periods of time." In a professional setting this undoubtedly is true; but the role of a band or orchestra director is to develop young musicians to their fullest capacity by providing them with as many activities as possible. In short, percussionists need to play as many instruments as possible as often as possible. There should be no such thing as a bass drummer, a snare drummer, or a timpanist.

One way to get more percussionists involved is to double parts. Use several snare drummers, especially during rehearsals; if you demand the ultimate musicianship from each player, you can easily control the volume. Add keyboard percussion parts by doubling woodwind or brass instruments, or write an original part for keyboard percussion. This is an unexplored area that has tremendous potential for brave composers interested in developing better percussionists while expanding the possibilities of color in school ensemble music. Finally, add accessory parts that complement the nature of the music being played. No composition is so sacred that directors should require the majority of the percussion section to sit idly while a select few do the playing.

Assign each player to specific parts for each musical selection by developing a chart that lists the compositions and the names of the students who will play. To be effective, percussionists should rotate instruments, giving each person a chance to develop appropriate technique on all the basic instruments. For example, a student may play timpani on one composition, snare on another, and triangle on still another. This procedure takes a little time, but the payoff is worth the effort.

Departing

At the end of every rehearsal students should return the percussion area to its original appearance. The students responsible for setup at the beginning of the rehearsal should return all instruments and equipment to the storage cabinets and drawers, making sure to lock them.

Allow time for percussionists to put equipment away in a neat and orderly fashion. If you continue the rehearsal until after the bell rings, expect to find instruments and accessories dropped in a corner or improperly stored. With practice, it takes about two minutes for everyone to replace items and fulfill their responsibilities.

By organizing the percussion section, you've taken the first step toward ensuring that these students will develop as first-rate musicians. Dividing the rehearsal into four segments and planning goals for each one is just the start of developing your percussionists' musicianship to the fullest extent. □

December 1988

Humorous Effects from the Percussion Section

BY LEONARD B. SMITH

One composer who called for a wide variety of drum traps and effects in his music was John Philip Sousa. For example, he required 20 different percussion effects in his suite *At the Movies.* Sousa biographer Paul Bierley located another example of Sousa's percussion scoring in a delightful article in the *New York Evening World,* April 24, 1918. It was titled, "Blame it on John Philip Sousa. 'Trap Drummer' in Band Now Plays 76 Instruments. Drummer's Life is One Slam Bang After Another."

The story involved Sousa's recently composed march *The Volunteers.* His idea was to musically depict the effect of a shipbuilder's riveting machine. Naturally the man to operate such a contrivance would be the trap drummer. Sousa took his new march to the Hippodrome Theatre to have it played by a big band at a benefit for the war fund. The band was eager to play it, but the ensemble's leader admitted he was stumped by the demand for the riveting effect.

"Our drummers are not trap drummers," he told Sousa. "They play drums only."

"That's all right," replied the March King. "I'll see Jimmy." Sousa asked that James T. Lent, the tall, thin, sorrowful-looking man who played trap drums for the Hippodrome orchestra, be summoned. Jimmy came and listened.

"That's easy," he offered. "I'll fix up an effect."

Jimmy did, and thus the trap drummer's riveter came into being. "It took a little thought," he said. "I got an electric motor, put a little wheel on it, and attached a sheet of iron for the other piece to hit. After that I turned on the juice and the riveting began in great shape. That riveter I call Trap No. 76, because I had been using 75 before Mr. Sousa called for it. It will have to be used whenever *The Volunteers* is played or the punch of the march will be lost."

My own experience with *The Volunteers* has been equally amusing. When we recorded it, the percussion section used a hand-operated siren, which sounds quite effective on the recording. The mallet on wood block comes

through, as does the anvil. We tried the riveting machine, but it did not pick up well at all. When it was loud enough to be recorded, it made a sound that would cause anyone to believe the record was defective.

As it was, I received a letter from one purchaser who explained he was sure an emergency medical unit or ambulance had been outside the auditorium because, as he said, he could hear the siren. He also admonished us in no uncertain terms to be more careful in the future.

Sousa's *U.S. Field Artillery* march has another interesting effect: three accented chords in measures 17 and 25. The Sousa Band used gunshots (blanks, of course) to highlight the accents on the second go-round of the trio. We always did it that way with the Goldman Band, and I do it with my band today.

I recall Gus Helmecke, the famous bass drummer of the Sousa and Goldman Bands, telling us of a time when he played that march with the Sousa Band. A stagehand had rigged up three fake ducks in the scenery. A split second after the three shots were heard, three ducks came down, plop-plop-plop, at the front of the stage, followed by a scattering of feathers.

I recounted this anecdote to some colleagues at the Blossom Music Festival last summer. Sure enough, during the concert, right after the gun shots, three scrawny rubber chickens hit the stage, plop-plop-plop.

Here are some of Sousa's more interesting admonishments and instructions to percussion players:

"Bass drum on hoops" (*Easter Monday on the White House Lawn*)

"Cymbal to imitate an electric riveting machine" (*The Volunteers*)

"Clinking of stone cups" (*Last Days of Pompeii*)

"Drum on shell" (*Beau Ideal, Jack Tar*)

"Gong or cymbal hit with a stick" (*Golden Star*)

"Imitate wood shoe" (*Free Lance*)

"Mallet striking wood imitating chopping of trees" (*White Man*)

"With martial ardor" printed on all parts (*The Lambs*)

"Shout 'Right, left' " (*Right-Left*)

"Shout 'Hurrah, hurrah' " (*Sheridan's Ride*)

"This should be played on the bass drum with sticks made of a number of thin iron rods tied together" ("Greek National Air" in *International Congress*)

I do remember using an effect when the Detroit Concert Band recorded *The National Game*, the title of course referring to baseball. In the interlude strain before the last trio, you hear the crack of a bat hitting the baseball. Though the idea was not one of Sousa's, I believe he would have approved. □

October 1988

Respect Your Percussionists

by Rod McIntyre

Percussionists frequently encounter negative attitudes on the part of band directors, who cite a general lack of technique, musical sensitivity, and fundamental skills on the part of the percussion section. Are the students really to blame? Percussionists certainly can be expected to attain a level of musicianship comparable to that of their brass and woodwind counterparts, but such an expectation is realistic only when they receive equal attention and instruction.

Rather than continuing the misdirected quest to determine what is wrong with percussionists, perhaps music educators should scrutinize their approaches to teaching them. Counterproductive methods and procedures have become so commonplace that cause-and-effect relationships between the way percussionists are taught and the manner in which they respond go unrecognized.

Music educators first need to realize that there is nothing inherently unmusical about percussionists; it is instead a series of oversights on the part of teachers that produces most of the unwanted results. Many directors fail to appreciate the degree of skill required to play each percussion instrument proficiently and musically. Without the same guidance given wind players, percussionists inevitably will be plagued by deficiencies.

Rehearsals often alienate percussionists by minimizing their musical involvement. Warm-up exercises either fail to include the percussion section or merely provide percussionists with something to do that has no actual musical purpose. Comments directed to the percussion section during rehearsals are likely to be limited to the correction of rhythmic figures or the adjustment of dynamic levels, with no evaluation of tone quality, phrasing, or stylistic interpretation. Given no objective other than hitting an instrument at the proper time, it should come as no surprise that most percussion students are capable of doing little more.

The following suggestions are only a few of many that can help prevent the problems in the percussion section.

Approach the percussion section in the same manner that you approach the other sections of the band, and afford your percussionists the same degree of respect and consideration you give the other sections. Any student is more likely to succeed if he enjoys rehearsals.

Start percussionists on mallet instruments, either exclusively or in combination with other percussion instruments. Playing mallet instruments helps percussionists learn aural and reading skills that they would not necessarily pick up by playing percussion instruments of indefinite pitch. It also lets them enjoy the added incentive of learning to play melodies, as well as teaching them to approach all percussion instruments in a more musical way.

As much as possible, select music that allows each member of the percussion section to participate actively. Even when sight-reading, decide in advance how you want to assign the percussion parts. This will help to avoid the problem of students getting locked into playing certain instruments. Wind players are not expected to determine how to distribute parts; don't ask this of the percussionists.

Just as it does for wind players, the warm-up provides an excellent opportunity to percussionists to improve their playing. If necessary write a warm-up specifically for the percussion section. This would not consume much rehearsal time, and if it's reasonable for the percussionists to wait for the wind players to warm up, the reverse is equally true.

Remember that the percussionists

in your ensemble are musicians, just like the wind players. Treat them with the same respect, give them the same high-quality training, and the results may surprise you.

May 1989

The Care and Feeding of Young Drummers

by Barbara Prentice with Julie Sutton

Back when I was in college, in what my son refers to as the Dark Ages, I attended a medium-sized school in west Texas. Tech had a great band and a fairly large music department; the faculty included the usual theory and music history profs and private studio teachers, including several wind and brass specialists. There was, however, no percussion instructor, so I received my training on drums from my trumpet-playing band director. All of us would-be band directors learned how to decipher those crazy percussion hieroglyphics called flams and ruffs, and we practiced feverishly every day from Haskell Harr's books.

Armed with this knowledge I started my teaching career in a small farming community where cotton was the topic of conversation at the local cafe, and the organist at the First Baptist Church and I were the only ones in town who knew how to read music. There, during my first 10 years of band directing, all the beginners were lumped into one large class of winds, brass, and percussion. The drummers suffered the most from this arrangement. Oh, they could read rhythm well enough to perform any band music we attempted at grade 3 and lower, but I had to teach those tricky parts (like the third movement of *La Fiesta Mexicana*) by rote. The timpanists always scored at all-region tryouts because of the ear training exercises, but the snare drummers never fared well. All of the percussion solo and ensemble comment sheets were filled with remarks like "lacks dynamic contrast, work on flams and rolls, etc."

Then I moved into a large metropolitan school district where my junior high scheduled the beginning percussionists alone in their own separate class, taught by the high school director (a real drummer) with whom I team-taught. By November these 12-year-olds were playing better than any seniors I'd had in my old high school band. Their rolls sounded like a buzz saw, not like a BB loose in a box car.

I began to sit in on Ron's class and learned the STUB theory: everything a snare drummer plays is a Stroke, Tap, Upstroke, or Bounce. As a college student in percussion class I had concentrated on playing the rhythm; now I was learning to play the snare drum. For the first time in my life, I could play a decent flam because I realized that those two notes were completely different kinds of strokes. That's what makes the flam sound, not two notes being played almost together. Incredible.

In a few years I took over the duties of teaching that percussion class and started devising my own strategies for developing snare drummers. I attended clinics, dogged my drummer friends for exercises, and took lessons at North Texas State University. This fall a student teacher from North Texas was assigned to my school, a percussionist, with whom I am writing this article. Julie has added material to exercises I already used, and has clarified to me exactly why these exercises work so well.

First, let me give some background information about how I teach all my beginning band classes. I subscribe to the Shinichi Suzuki theory of teaching the instrument first and music reading later. When a child first handles his brand new instrument it feels awkward, even uncomfortable. He needs to learn how to hold it properly, how to care for it, how to breathe, all of those things. So for the first weeks, months even, I teach my classes by rote, with no books. We concentrate on instrument carriage, posture, hand position, embouchure, air speed – all the fundamentals. I play and the students echo back to me.

I've discovered that if you train the muscles to do their jobs correctly first, the posture, carriage, and hand position can become automatic and will remain correct later on when the student begins to concentrate on reading the music. Once the eye gets into the act, it seems that all the brain power is directed to that task, focusing entirely on what the eye is seeing. These youngsters have a difficult enough time concentrating on one thing. It's foolish to complicate matters by giving them ten things to worry about.

In percussion class I emphasize correct form, stick angle, stick height, hand position, and matching sounds from right to left hand. These exercises begin when the students know the grip, understand quarter notes, and can throw a stroke. We work on the first exercise for most of the year. Initially we concentrate on creating even sound, even rhythm, and full wrist extension. Later, we use this exercise, which we call 8,4,2,1, as a physical and mental warmup. The primary function is to develop the muscles and to gain a modicum of stick control. Remember, we do these by rote, not by reading.

Red Rum teaches the concept of accents and taps. The accents should use full extension of the wrists and both accents should be the same height. As the teacher you must constantly correct accent heights, because the students almost always play the second accent lower than the first. To help precision in a large class tell the students to listen to each other and match the taps. If the taps are together, the accents will take care of themselves. Volume is determined by stick height (among other things). Use this as a yardstick p=1", mp=2", mf=3, f=4", ff=5-6"; an accent calls for full extension.

4's, 2's twice, 1's four times is a standard accent exercise with multiple benefits. Later you can vary this exercise to help bounces (diddle control), to develop rolls, and eventually as a flam exercise. Students must concentrate to define the accent. Contrasting the stick height between accents and taps helps achieve this. Again, precision will improve if you advise students to listen to each other and line up the taps.

First do the exercise with this sticking.

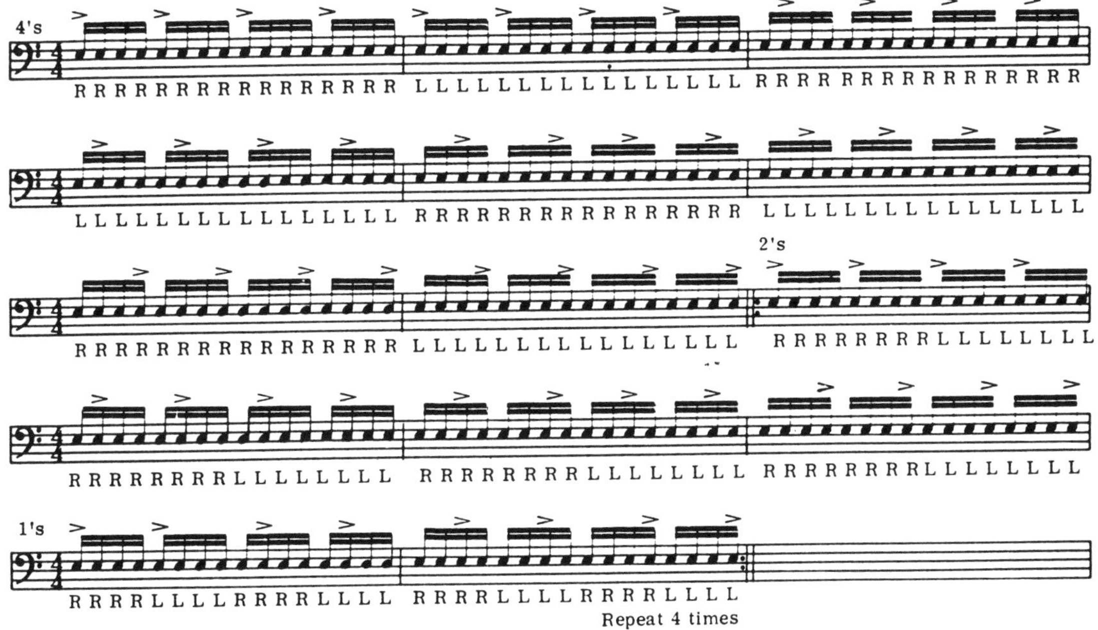

Then change and alternate the sticking.

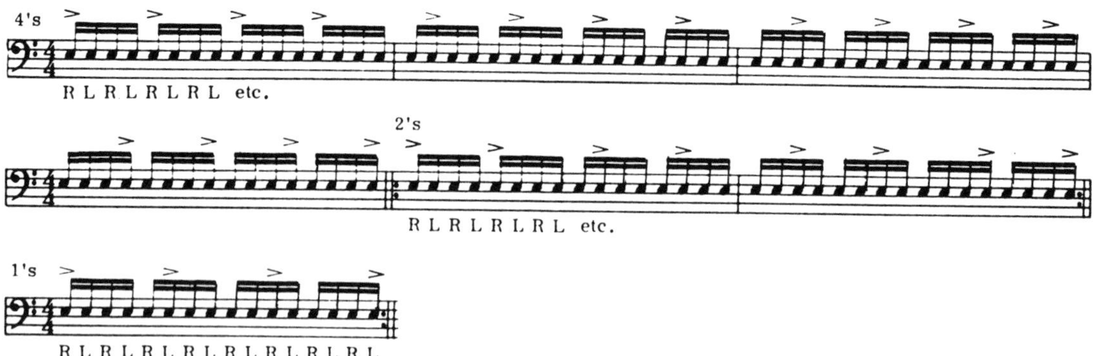

Irish Spring develops consistency of the diddle. Because this exercise employs a stroke followed by a bounce, you should remind students to listen to make sure the second sound is the same volume as the first. The wrists should be fairly relaxed. Tell the student to let the stick do the work. Play twice in each hand.

Dr. Marcus Welch, a physician who treats adolescents with learning disabilities and other school-related problems, once confided to me that if a child ever admits that a class was interesting, you should pat yourself on the back. When teachers assign repetitious work designed to drill a new concept, students are bored. We band directors and percussion teachers have a built-in problem here, because so much of what young drummers do is training their muscles, gaining control, and establishing muscle memory. The only way they'll ever learn to play snare drum is to practice things over and over, to get the motions coordinated. Besides, the great teacher Suzuki says "Remember one thing – repetition. If one has learned a thing, it has to be thoroughly mastered by repeating it again and again. One must practice more until it is natural and easy."

The trick, then, is to disguise those repetitive exercises, to vary them and intersperse other exercises designed to promote additional growth and good habits. Switch from stick control exercises to rolls to accents. Include mental practice and concentration games. Have students drop out when they make a mistake; have all but one play air drums while that single soloist performs on a line or exercise.

Roll Exercises

We start teaching rolls early, in the second or third week, concentrating first on the concept of one hand motion and two sounds. When a student can perform 40 bounces in a row (in each hand) with no mistakes, he is ready to begin roll exercises.

Our warm-up roll exercise is the two-count roll, a skeleton (hand motions of the roll) on the first two beats followed by two counts of bounces. Work for fluidity, evenness of sound (volume) in tap to bounce and from right to left hand.

The four-count roll is simply double the length. *See example #1 below.*

Add-a-count roll has a two-beat check pattern (the skeleton as above), followed by a roll, each a beat longer than the last one. First of all, make sure your students understand the exercise; it can be confusing. You can take this as far as you want; we've gone up to 24 counts on a roll. *See example #2 below.*

Roll timing – the check pattern inserted helps to stabilize rhythm and encourage a steady tempo. It also allows beginning students to think ahead to the upcoming pattern. Later, for intermediate students, take out the check pattern. This one is great for concentration.

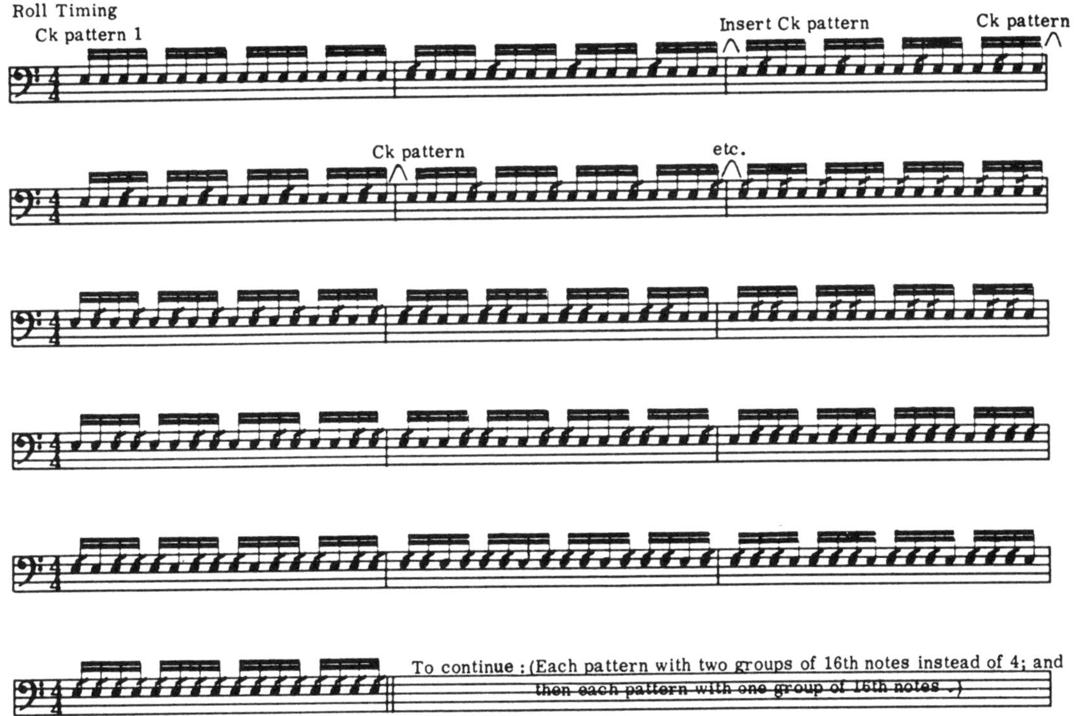

In all of these roll exercises, realize that the greater the number of drummers, the messier the rolls will sound. Counteract this by insisting that the students match tempo on the check pattern. Once they can line up those 16th notes, the rolls will improve, I promise. Another tip is for you to hear each child on rolls each day. Have the class play the *roll du jour* (exercise of the day), then call on one player to perform it, followed immediately by the entire class, then the next student alone, followed by the whole group, with no pause between performances. As the players improve, have them play in pairs, matching speed and volume.

4's, 2's, and 1's, as written earlier can be instantly transformed into a roll practice by replacing the accents with bounces or diddles. Caution the students against accenting the diddles, though.

Accent Exercises

My long-range goal is to have percussionists who can read accent patterns, rather than drummers who learn a rhythm and add accents to it at a later time. 4's, 2's, and 1's merely trains the muscles, and youngsters need variety in the accents to become readers. Because most elementary snare methods include very few accent exercises, a supplemental page like this is necessary.

Guarantee

There is no guarantee that every child that learns these exercises will become a Mitch Markovitch or William Ludwig. However, assuming your young drummers are intelligent, rhythmic, and coordinated, they can make phenomenal progress. These exercises have helped my students play well, be successful at solo competitions, come out on the top of the heap at auditions for regional honor bands, and enjoy their playing. □

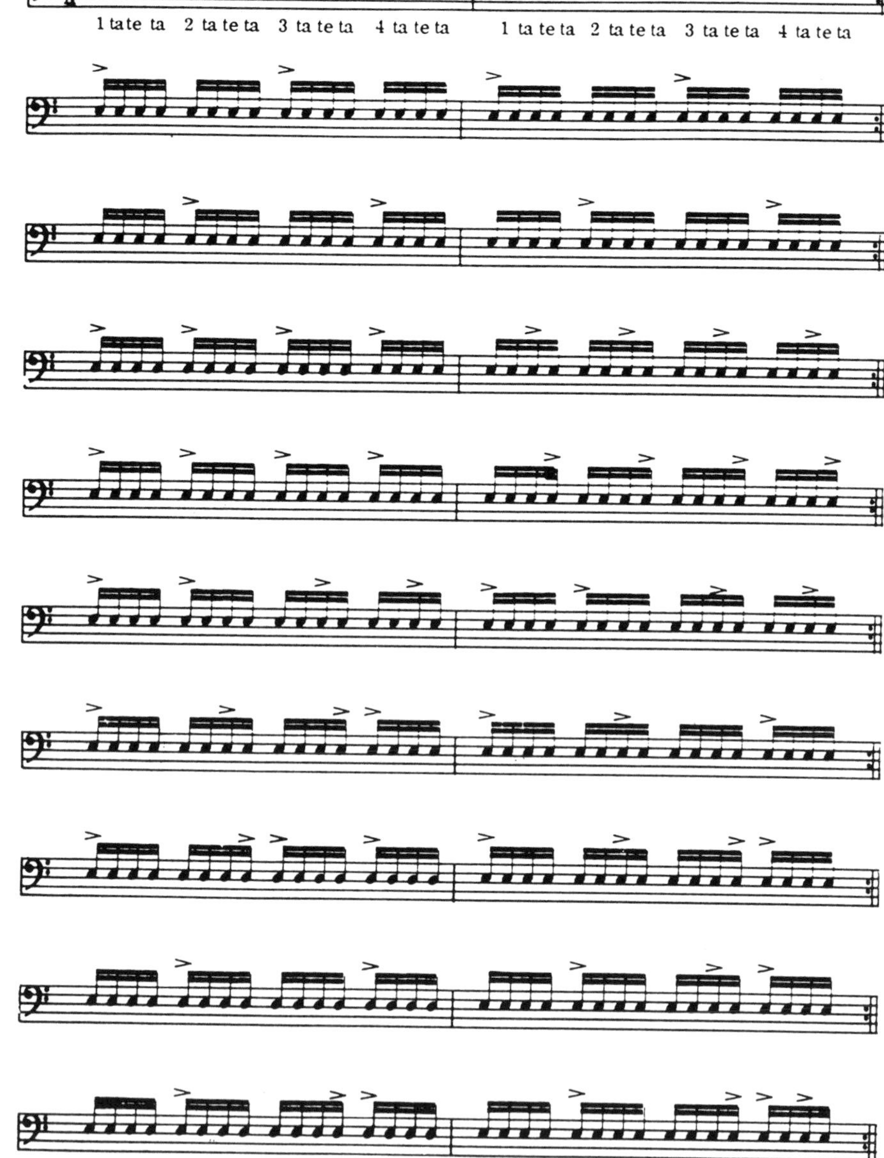

Judging Marching Percussion

by Sherman Hong

High school and university band directors frequently are asked to serve as adjudicators for marching band competitions, and are sometimes called on to comment on the percussion. Because of their limited knowledge of the subject, nonpercussionists feel uneasy and unqualified to comment beyond general "you're too loud" or "careful of the tempo" remarks. Although nonpercussionist judges are not expected to give detailed analysis and criticism, using the following suggestions can help the generalist make helpful suggestions.

Bear in mind the primary function of a percussion section: to keep time; accent rhythms; add color; provide transitions between sections of changing styles, tempos, or timbres; perform needed solos as the band restages; and enhance the visual appeal of the ensemble.

Specific functions of the instruments:

- Snare drums keep time for the band. They relate in timbre to the high wind parts (usually the first melodic parts and rhythmically strengthen these parts.
- Bass drums in various sizes and tunings relate rhythmically, tonally, and texturally to low winds such as tubas and third trombones. Drums that are not overly dampened add bottom resonance to wind chords.
- Cymbals are used primarily to add brilliance and color to climaxes. Ride

cymbal patterns emphasize timing and add style; crashes and rolls help fuse sections of the band; and the instrument in general adds color.

• Mallet keyboards relate to harmonic, melodic, or contrapuntal wind voicings or drum solos. Be aware of the timbre produced by different octaves of the keyboards. Bear in mind, too, that bells and vibes don't sound alike; neither do bells and xylophones or marimbas. Keyboard colors should correlate with wind timbres; for example, a rolled high-octave xylophone part does not blend well with a mid-voiced trombone solo.

• Timpani are used to enhance harmonic movement, blend parts, play chords, or produce mid- to low-voiced melodies.

• Accessories are used to enhance a particular musical style, for pure color, or to blend parts. Commonly used accessory instruments include triangles, suspended cymbals, cowbells, maracas, tambourines, concert toms, bass drums, and bongos. Other effects include bird whistles, whistles, and castanets. A word of warning: make sure that the instruments used are needed and that they enhance or indicate a particular musical style. You should comment if a band uses timbale in a non-Latin piece of music. Just because a band has the equipment doesn't mean it has to be used.

After you have become familiar with and used the above guidelines, check the following points:

Technical fundamentals

Observe if battery players (snare drums, timp-toms, or bass drums) have uniform grip and stroking techniques; listen for uniformity of segment sounds (single patterns, appoggiaturas, rolls, accents, and uniform volumes) and overall tone quality.

Ensemble timing

There should be defined concepts of beat, pulse, and tempo within each segment and as an ensemble; make sure percussion and winds agree. On-field battery players often must alter their own timing slightly to synchronize with winds; inflexible percussion sections come across as having incorrect timing.

Lapses in ensemble timing frequently are caused by lapses in concentration in extended roll passages, after periods of rests, and at ends of phrases. Check the timing between on-field battery and sideline percussion. Contrary to what percussionists are told (to follow the drum major's beat) sideline percussionists often should ignore him and listen to the band for correct ensemble timing. Percussionists tend to rush simple patterns, such as eighth or sixteenth notes.

Attacks and releases

Listen for uniform timing on attacks, especially after any period of rests. Roll passages of several beats or more frequently are slowed just before release; conversely, non-rolled patterns tend to be slightly rushed, especially if they occur at the end of a crescendo.

Dynamic control

Because it is more difficult to play either very softly or very loudly, percussion sections usually play moderately soft to moderately loud dynamics. Percussionists need to be aware of their dynamic balance with the band in relation to band staging and scoring. Percussionists usually play solo drum breaks within a composition too softly.

Phrasing

Listen for correlation of dynamics and phrasing with winds; observe if drum soli incorporate dynamic contrasts, texture changes, and other musical nuances. Drum soli should communicate a message, not simply function as filler.

Projection and blend

Size and tuning of each instrument are the primary factors in projection and blend. Be aware that bass drums project more than other battery instruments and are highly directional. Timp-toms are often pitched so high that their timbres are masked. Other factors to consider are staging in a drill, mallet or stick selections, textures in scoring, and ranges being used by mallet keyboard instruments or timpani.

Variety in writing

Each segment should have varied technical and musical demands; too frequently, arrangements are oriented toward the snare drum. Key and texture changes in wind scoring should be reflected in percussion writing. Also consider whether accessory instruments are used effectively.

Style and interpretation

Contemporary marching bands can incorporate a wide variety of music; such variety necessitates comments about how successfully the band performs the styles. A few things to check:

• Rhythms — interpretation of eighth notes, syncopations, stylistic percussion fills or lead-ins, style of the drum soli, use of the ride and crash cymbals.

• Timp-toms — tend to overplay in jazz-rock tunes.

• Bass drums — tonal bass drums can be strong purveyors of style; use of walking bass (jazz, swing), rock, or Latin bass lines help determine the success of a band arrangement.

• Accessory instruments — should be idiomatic of the style performed; for example, cowbells and tambourines are not idiomatic to a straight jazz tune.

Thanks to the positive influence of drum and bugle corps and the availability of better teaching and arrangements, marching percussion sections have improved so much that a judge should view them as percussion ensembles. Just as any judge would discuss musicality, articulation, tone, balance, blend, and style in relation to winds, so, too, should he comment on these factors when judging percussion. When it's your turn to judge, make every effort to evaluate the percussion section on the same high plane as the rest of the ensemble. □

The Mallets Make a Difference

by John Papastefan

By his choice of mallets a timpanist controls the quality of sound he produces. A good timpanist will own anywhere from six to twenty pairs of different mallets, and a musically sensitive player will experiment with a passage in rehearsal to determine which mallets produce the best sound. While beginning wind players can use standard-issue mouthpieces, timpani mallets are best chosen by the timpanist right from the start. Inexperienced student players will need to experiment until they learn to distinguish the appropriate sound. Personal preference is important, though the choice of mallets can depend on the type of timpani and membranes, acoustics in the performing area, and the interpretive intent of the conductor.

The Percussive Arts Society has designated four abbreviations for composers to use in identifying the mallets to be used in their scores: H – staccato effects, articulated passages; M – normal playing; S – legato playing, Wood – special effects.

In addition, composer Vaclav Nelhybel devised a system to indicate the degree of hardness of mallets. In order to avoid confusing certain of these indications with dynamics, he placed them inside parentheses and used a relative scale that is somewhat different from that of conventional dynamic indications:

(ss) – very soft
(s) – soft
(m) – medium
(h) – hard
(hh) – very hard

Although the system is relative (an extra hard mallet for the xylophone is certainly not the same as for timpani, for example) it suggests to the player the sound quality that the composer intended. Of course, these indications will only begin to make sense to the young player when he develops an awareness of the variety of sounds that can be extracted from the same instrument with different mallets.

The all-purpose mallet is appropriate for most types of general playing; it is soft enough to produce a beautifully full, round tone, but it is firm enough for the attacks and rhythmic clarity needed in the contemporary repertoire. This type of mallet is constructed from a hard inner core, sometimes wrapped with cord. It is covered with one or more tightly wound layers of fine-grade felt, such as split piano damper felt, affixed so as to eliminate the seam on the striking surface of the mallet head. The varying degrees of hardness depend on the number of felt coverings attached.

The staccato mallet (also known as normal staccato) consists of a slightly smaller ball and one or two layers of somewhat harder felt than the general purpose mallet. This mallet is excellent for the rhythmic definition and light staccato playing required in the classical repertoire, particularly in Mozart and Haydn symphonies. The staccato mallet is vital for projecting rhythms in the contemporary repertoire. It is ideally suited to recording because it produces a concise sound without the objectionable boom.

The ultra staccato stick, with a small-headed ball of hard felt, produces an articulated sound surpassed in clarity only by that produced by the wood ball timpani stick. Timpanists often select the ultra staccato stick for recording and for creating unblemished, rhythmical articulation, especially on low notes. It is useful in passages such as the Scherzo from Mendelssohn's *A Midsummer Night's Dream* and the third movement of Rimsky-Korsakov's *Scheherazade Suite*, both of which call for rhythmic clarity. The ultra staccato mallet works well when one player is required to play multiple percussion but has no opportunity to change sticks; it also serves as an emergency vibraphone or marimba mallet.

The wood ball mallet is a special effects stick that both romantic and contemporary composers frequently request. Wood sticks produce optimum definition, creating a hard, clattering sound well suited to rhythmical passages in recording. A wood stick is usually made by turning it out of one solid piece of wood to eliminate the two-piece construction of a ball glued to the stick shaft.

The cartwheel mallet is intended for soft, velvety rolls and legato strokes. It is particularly well suited for obtaining maximum richness of sound. The core of the stick is a medium-hard felt covered with a layer of soft piano damper felt. Some companies manufacture a core that is not flat, but slightly convex to allow the stick to produce a round sound. Exceptionally effective on low note rolls, the cartwheel mallet produces a soft roll on any note of the timpani range. For sustained solo rolls, especially at pianissimo, this mallet is capable of eliciting the optimum beauty of tone. The cartwheel mallet is appropriate, though the composer did not request it, for the long F♯ roll in the first movement of Tchaikovsky's Symphony No. 6 and the soft roll in the coda of his Symphony No. 4.

Finally, there is a custom stick similar to the general purpose mallet except that the former is slightly larger and heavier. Because it is capable of great volume and powerful attacks, it must be employed with discretion, for it can be overpowering. The custom mallet works well for some compositions of Brahms, Wagner, Bruckner, and Mahler that call for a heavier sound.

The combined effects of large or small contact areas and soft or hard mallet heads.

For full, sustained, legato sounds a softer ball type of stick will give the desired sound. For rhythmic clarity, a hard stick will produce clearer definition. According to British composer Reginald Smith-Brindle, when a soft mallet strikes a *timpano* (singular of the plural *timpani*), its head gives, spreading momentarily, but just long enough to impede vibrations of short wavelength. Because high overtones are smothered before they have a chance to sound, only the fundamental and lower harmonics are heard, resulting in mellow, deep timbres.

Mallets with hard heads have less give, sometimes none at all. Thus high overtones vibrate freely when a hard-headed mallet strikes the head, and a relatively bright sound is produced.

If a mallet has a large contact area, high overtones will not sound. Conversely, a mallet having a small contact area, such as one with a thin shaft and a small, hard head, will produce high overtones in a marked degree, and possibly render lower sounds almost inaudible. Soft mallets tend to have large contact areas, hard mallets smaller contact areas, so these two factors normally reinforce each other.

The timpanist should use sticks one degree harder than those that may sound suitable to him, because the articulation will sound somewhat less pronounced to the listener than to the timpanist. Joel Leach of California State – Northridge stipulates that timpanists follow this rule particularly when recording. Varying the point of contact will also produce a marked impression of the pitch rising and falling. Playing closer to the rim produces a sharper tone, while playing further toward the center creates a flatter tone. One thing is certain: when a player uses a hard stick to achieve rhythmic clarity, he sacrifices tone quality. Vic Firth, timpanist of the Boston Symphony Orchestra, has noted that it is important for the composer, and ultimately the player or conductor, to determine which is more important in a particular passage – rhythm or sound.

Timpani are capable of producing an array of sounds through the use of various types of sticks, mallets, and other striking instruments. As you can see, many factors can affect a player's decision to choose a particular pair of mallets for a certain musical passage. That is why beginning and professional players, as well as conductors, need to experiment continually. With the many options available today, a player can choose the right equipment for any musical situation. □

Suggested Reading

Guide to Teaching Percussion, 4/e. Harry R. Bartlett and Ronald A. Holloway (William C. Brown Company)

Contemporary Percussion, Reginald Smith-Brindle (Oxford University Press)

The Logic of it All, Anthony J. Cirone and Joe Sinai (Cirone Publications)

New Music Notation, David Cope (Kendall/Hunt)

Percussion Symposium, Vic Firth (Carl Fischer)

"Some Thoughts on Timpani and Intonation." Ted Frazeur (NACWPI Journal, Volume 18, Number 3)

Timpani, Percussion Education Series Number 12. George Frock (Selmer-Premier)

Percussion Manual for Music Educators, Joel Leach (Henry Adler)

"Percussion Notation," Vaclav Nelhybel (*The Instrumentalist*, June, 1975)

Standardization of Percussion Notation, Percussive Arts Society (the Percussive Arts Society) □

1990-1991

Practicing the Snare Drum

by John J. Papastefan

Most beginning drummers learn a rudimental approach to playing the snare drum. Though appropriate for rudimental solos, drum corps, and marching band, this method does not necessarily prepare the player to handle demanding percussion parts found in contemporary compositions. It's preferable to seek a broader approach to teaching snare. Too often the rudimental style is used to the exclusion of all else.

To start you need a practice pad mounted on an adjustable stand or a snare drum with a Gladstone pad on a stand; a music stand; a well-lighted and well-ventilated room in which to practice; a reliable metronome; general purpose sticks, such as Firth SD-1; and a copy of *Stick Control* by George L. Stone, along with one other substantial method book such as *Modern School for Snare Drum* by Morris Goldenberg. The Gladstone pad is named after its designer, Billy Gladstone, of Radio City Music Hall fame. Made of pure rubber with an embedded steel plate beneath the raised center, it provides two playing surfaces. A vacuum cavity holds the pad firmly in place on the batter head. This type of pad is ideal because it allows sensitive snare response while reducing volume during practice.

Usually students begin with the right-hand lead system, using the right hand on all strong pulses. This system is popular because most beginners naturally play strong pulses with the right hand and weak pulses with the left; however, this will only prepare students to play snare drum, not other percussion instruments. Ultimately students need to develop and strengthen both hands.

Using the matched grip avoids the somewhat unnatural left-hand position of the traditional grip. This factor alone will enable the beginning player to progress more quickly and efficiently than with the traditional grip, and teachers won't have to devote time to making corrections of the left hand.

When the player uses the matched grip the snare drum or practice pad should be parallel to the floor. Because the grip for both sticks is the same as the right hand of the traditional method, there is no need to tilt the drum. The top of the drum should be a few inches below belt height.

Another point in favor of the matched grip is that the muscular skills learned transfer to the other percussion instruments. It is easy to adapt the matched grip to the drum set, especially the new popular melodic tom-tom setups. Today's percussionist is often expected to play a wide variety of instruments well, and most find the matched grip more versatile for multi-instrument performance.

The traditional grip evolved as a result of the snare drum originally being carried on a sling. With the advent of newer devices designed to carry the marching drum level, there is little need for the traditional grip. Many drum corps and marching bands equipped with such harnesses now use the matched grip.

Most students who plan to become professional players practice at least four hours each day, more at the college or conservatory level. Although it is a good idea to practice as often as possible, I recommend the following minimum guidelines: grade school/junior high – 45 minutes per day; high school – 1 hour per day; college and beyond – 2 hours per day. It is not wise to suddenly embark on long and intense practice sessions; it is better to increase the length of practice sessions by one-quarter to one-half hour each day until the desired number of hours have been reached.

Some musicians prefer to practice early in the day when they are fresh, while others prefer to practice late in the day or at night when there are fewer distractions. At a university or conservatory students often have to squeeze in practice sessions when the facilities and instruments are available, not at their own convenience.

Many players put in practice time without understanding the purpose. To realize optimum value from practice time, you should set realistic goals and encourage students to take every opportunity to hear great players, both live and on recordings, to develop aural and visual images of how a fine player performs. A player who assesses his weaknesses benefits most from practice. Whether the problem is sound, facility, or sight-reading, he needs to consider how the music he is currently studying relates to these problems.

The ideal practice session consists of a warm-up period, technical work, solo and ensemble literature, sight-reading, and a cool-down period to relax before ending.

Teach students to focus only on the task at hand while practicing. Remind them to check and double check to make sure that mistakes do not creep in. Often it is more difficult to unlearn mistakes that have been practiced for a period of time. Students often learn pieces badly because they are impatient, so caution them not to play passages any faster than they can be played well. Instead of assigning a long piece to be learned all at once, divide it into sections. Ask students to count aloud. Finally, as it sometimes happens, do not let them become discouraged if they cannot play something as well today as they could yesterday.

The original purpose of the metronome was to provide a reference with which tempos could be accurately measured and specified. Practicing with a metronome has been criticized by some musicians as encouraging mechanical playing, while others maintain that only through discipline can freedom evolve. To acquire acute control of rhythm, with all its nuances, a percussionist, of all musicians, needs to understand the subtle use of metronome technique.

Using a metronome lets the player set an absolute tempo (number of beats per minute); it can also guide him through learning complex rhythms. Because percussionists are expected to have flawless rhythm and the ability to hold steady tempos, using the metronome during practice is essential. Performance problems related to rushing or dragging can be virtually eliminated by using a metronome for all practice sessions.

To use the metronome for teaching tempo memory, turn on the metronome and have the student begin to play a composition, then turn it off. Later during the playing at presumably uniform tempo, check the tempo and tell the student exactly how much the tempo has drifted. Just as some musicians can acquire a sense of absolute or nearly absolute pitch, so musicians can acquire a sense of absolute or nearly absolute tempo.

In addition to the metronome, you can use other teaching and learning aids as the need arises. To learn the symphonic repertoire, have the student play the percussison part along with a record. The conventional record turntable allows you to lift the tone arm and repeat certain passages over and over. Whether students purchase Music Minus One albums or create this homemade variant, the practice works well.

Use a tape recorder or video camera to record lessons and practice sessions, then play back to listen, analyze, and critique the student's ability. Practicing with a tape recording of the piano accompaniment to a solo or recital piece helps the student become more familiar with the piano accompaniment and learn exactly how his part fits with the rest of the music. When a videocamera is available, you can record not only how the student sounds, but also how he looks, an important aspect of performance. By viewing the videotape, you can readily recognize any physical problems in the set-up or playing technique. A number of instructional videotapes made by outstanding professionals are also available for the students' viewing.

Understanding styles of drumming is also an important aspect of practicing. It is unfortunate to hear a drummer play eighth notes in strict fashion if the composer has indicated that a syncopated style is to be used. It is just as unfortunate as well as annoying to hear a drummer give a free syncopated interpretation to eighth notes if a literal rendition was indicated.

The best method of gaining control and improving technique on various drumming styles is to play them in ensembles that employ them most frequently. Orchestral snare drumming requires a player to attain the control demanded to play a wide variety of dynamics. The most difficult passages are the soft, rapid series of strokes and the *pianissimo* roll, especially when these occur as solos. Students should practice these two problem techniques on the drum rather than on the practice pad. The ultimate goal of practice is to be able to play a passage at any dynamic level and any speed without losing control.

Training the muscles, eyes, ears, and minds of young players requires enormous amounts of repetitive drill in order to achieve the best results. Unfortunately, some young people who are victims of the immediate gratification syndrome lack the necessary discipline to become truly good performers. There simply is no shortcut for the methodical, logical, and gradual development of one's playing ability over a period of time.

Suggested Reading

Guide to Teaching Percussion, 4/e. Harry R. Bartlett and Ronald A. Holloway (William C. Brown Company)

Why Rudiments Are No Longer Enough. James Coffin (Premier Stick Tips, No. 5)

Teaching Percussion. Gary D. Cook (Schirmer)

The Fine Art of Practice. Karen Ervin (Ludwig)

Metronome Technique. Frederick Franz (Franz)

Some Thoughts on Practicing. Lloyd S. McCausland (Remo)

"Variations on Stick Control." Joe Morello (*Modern Drummer*, October, 1989)

"A Realistic Look at the Matched Grip." (*Modern Drummer*) □

August, 1990

The Concert Snare Drum Roll

by Lance Haas

Most young drummers do not know how to play a concert roll correctly. Using the same stick motion as a military or rudimental roll, they press the sticks into the drum head, rather than let them bounce, producing a buzz roll. When students attempt to play these rolls they adjust their hand speed to the tempo of the piece, which is the same thing they would do with a military roll. For example, in 4/4 time at a tempo of ♩ =120, the following roll played in military style would result in a 17-stroke roll.

The wrist and arm make a total of nine movements, creating a subrhythm to produce the roll.

Beginning drummers often perform this concert roll with nine accented pulse beats, the same amount of arm movement they would use in a rudimental roll. Concert rolls have no audible pulse and should flow evenly from beginning to end, the same as a held note on a wind instrument.

Students should understand the difference between a concert roll and a military roll. In a military roll the stick bounces only once with each stroke, and each stick hits the drum head two times. Because each stroke is limited to one bounce, military rolls can actually be measured; a 17-stroke roll should have exactly 17 hits in it. In rudimental rolls the term stroke is a misnomer, and there are really only 9 strokes, 8 of them with a bounce and then the last one stops the roll action with a single tap. In a concert roll the bounces are unlimited; the objective is to allow the sticks to bounce as often as possible with each stroke. A concert roll cannot be measured, and it is virtually impossible to tell how many times each stick bounces.

As with all aspects of snare drumming, players should begin with the proper grip, holding the stick between the thumb and first finger with the thumb on the side and the first finger curled around the stick, cradling it in the first joint. The back three fingers should curve toward the stick but not touch it. If the back fingers touch the stick it will not bounce freely. The palms should face the floor, but avoid the hammer grip, which has the knuckles turned to the floor.

It helps to teach the military and the concert roll simultaneously because if the military roll is learned first, students often develop a tight, uneven concert roll. If students learn the concert roll first, they usually have an uncontrolled and poorly played military roll. By learning the two rolls simultaneously, students develop both correctly; I introduce them at the first lesson.

Begin a concert roll by finding the sticks' balance point or fulcrum so the stick will bounce freely for several beats instead of falling dead on the drum head. Student players should work on each hand separately without attempting to put the roll together. The goal is to get as many bounces as possible, letting the sticks do the work. Alternate strokes slowly, keeping the sticks bouncing freely, increasing the tempo of alternating strokes until a roll develops.

I follow the same procedure for introducing a military roll. If a student has trouble producing a bounce, he is not recoiling the stick far enough. Lift the stick by flexing the wrist so that the palm faces the direction of the drum; then snap the wrist downward, causing the stick to bounce off the head in reaction. Without this recoil there can be no bounce. To stop the stick from bouncing further, squeeze it lightly with the back three fingers. In a concert roll leave the stick on the head with the wrist down. Concert rolls require much less recoil, and the feeling should be that of placing the sticks on the head rather than hitting the head with them. In a concert roll the sticks do the work, but in a military roll the player does.

To get a smooth texture in concert rolls, replace the idea of buzzing a military roll with the subrhythm concept. Stick motion should not speed up or slow down to adjust for musical tempos as it would in a military roll, but the subrhythm varies with the tempo of the piece and the rate of arm movement will be almost the same every time. The following are examples of the same notated roll played with different subrhythms.

played at ♩ =80 will have a subrhythm of

played at ♩ =120 will have a subrhythm of

played at ♩ =152 will have a subrhythm of

Look for the underlyn.g subrhythm when playing concert rolls to maintain a smooth effect.

Students often play a concert roll *fortissimo* by buzzing a military roll as loudly as possible. It is physically impossible to play a *fortissimo* concert roll.

Drummers often do not understand *piano* and *pianissimo* playing, and use the edge of the drum for soft concert rolls, moving the sticks in to the center to increase volume. Discourage this kind of playing because it produces an obvious change in tone color. Although a conductor may request it, the composer who wants it will probably notate it. (See "Even Percussionists Can Be Musicians," *The Instrumentalist*, September 1984.)

A well-tuned snare drum will create a beautifully resonant roll even at the softest volume when the player uses the proper area of the drum head's playing surface. As band directors we often criticize wind players because their tone becomes thin at the lower dynamic levels, yet many of us teach snare drummers to create a thin tone on soft volume rolls. If you teach military and concert rolls together and with the correct grip, and explain the subrhythm in a concert roll and how to count strokes in a military roll, there will be no buzz of misunderstanding among your players. □

October, 1990

Training Student Percussionists

by Douglas R. Overmier

Too often we relegate students who can't delineate pitch or coordinate wind instrument fingerings to the percussion section; the opposite should be true. Because today's percussion literature is technically demanding and not consistent in notation, only a perceptive student with genuine desire should be a candidate for percussion training. Students who have had previous experience with piano or training in Orff or Dalcroze methods have some grasp of the concepts of duration and intensity, and learn percussion techniques faster. Simple tests with rote playing, singing intervals, and improvising rhythms help evaluate students.

Beginning method books play an important role in developing young percussionists. Look for books that present material in a logical order, that emphasize musicianship, illustrate concepts, and offer an element of unpredictability. Repetition encourages memorization, but it does little to develop sight-reading. *Fundamental Studies for Snare Drum* by Garwood Whaley and *Vic Firth's Drum Method, Book I* by Vic Firth are clear, easy-to-read, and contain these qualities for snare study. Most band instrumental methods contain adequate exercises for beginning mallet instruction, and you can supplement them with elementary flute, oboe, and piano books.

One approach to percussion instruction is to teach basic snare drum techniques first before going on to the other instruments. This way students master stroke, motion, fulcrum, and tone with the snare, then transfer these concepts to mallets and the rest of the percussion instruments. Another approach is to teach keyboard and matched grip techniques simultaneously, giving equal amounts of attention to each instrument at every lesson. Regardless of which approach you use, make sure students fully understand all the previously studied material. Incorporate some repair techniques, literature, and history of percussion instruments into each student's training, and point out differences in style and interpretation when listening to recordings with him.

To produce well-trained percussionists rehearse both the full ensemble as well as classes with similar instruments. Although scheduling restrictions may make it difficult, try working with beginning percussionists separately, monitoring their individual technique and performance problems.

Timpani training is a practical application of a few mastered fundamentals and should come only after the student demonstrates consistent grip, stroke, tone, and a good ear for intervals. Start ear training while working on mallet instruments.

Encourage students to study privately with an instructor who teaches all aspects of percussion training; drum set study alone is not enough, nor is learning rudiments. Often a student who studies privately will share his knowledge with other members of the section, but whether your percussionists study privately or not, you can help them by emphasizing the need for individual practice, which develops self-discipline and provides time for problem solving. Involved parents play a part in this, too. Parents who show interest about consistent practice, even if they have no musical background, help their children keep abreast of their lessons.

Playing in a percussion ensemble is a good way for students to develop musicianship and a feel for percussion performance. It also enhances their technique on a variety of instruments.

Require each percussionist to purchase sticks and mallets. Place the financial burden on the student and he will break fewer sticks. Beginning percussion students should own one pair of sticks (Vic Firth Generals, 2B or equivalent), a pair of plastic bell mallets (also usable on xylophone), a pair of yarn marimba mallets for general playing range, a pair of general purpose timpani mallets, a drum key, and a case or stick bag suitable for containing all of the above. Junior high school students should augment this with a second, lighter weight drum stick (5A, Vic Firth Bolero or equivalent) and a pair of brushes. Encourage them to invest in another pair of hard timpani mallets and an additional pair of keyboard mallets.

Every high school percussionist should own two or three pairs of sticks for marching band and other ensemble work; one soft and one hard pair of timpani mallets; one pair of yarn or marimba mallets for general range of performance on the vibe, marimba, or low end of the xylophone; one pair of hard rubber or plastic mallets for xylophone or bells; three pairs of various weight triangle beaters; two triangle clips; a pair of brushes; a tuning fork or pitch pipe; and a mallet bag to carry it all. The serious percussion student should also purchase hand-held percussion instruments — cowbell, woodblock, guiro, triangle, and maocca.

Numerous books and pamphlets contain information on the minimum instrumentation for elementary, junior high, and high school percussion sections. Contacting the educational resource divisions of the Ludwig Division of the Selmer Company or Yamaha and requesting information will yield a plethora of material.

Training Existing Percussion Sections

Just as you decipher harmonies, form, and counter melodies in the wind parts, you can analyze the role of percussion instruments in providing rhythm, dynamics, articulations, colors, special effects, and stating and developing themes. Keeping time is not solely a function of the percussion section; it is everyone's responsibility.

Rarely do percussion parts specify sizes, materials, or types of mallets or sticks, and every composer uses different percussion symbols. For example, an x by one composer may mean a choked cymbal, while to another composer it represents a triangle stroke. Players have to listen to the ensemble for cues as to length and color.

Just as different textures and styles call for different techniques in wind performance, the same is true in the percussion section. A trained percussionist will need a variety of sticks and mallets in the same piece, so a trap table should be near each player. Placing a music stand in a horizontal position and covering it with a cloth or piece of carpet will prevent sticks from rolling off and will muffle any extraneous noises from changing from one pair to another.

Rehearsal Techniques

Each day incorporate the percussion section into the warm-up phase of the rehearsal. In the beginning warm-up, assign an instrument to each member of the section. Two or three persons may perform on a marimba or xylophone at one time. The bass drummer could provide tempo and accents while snare drummers add rhythmic accompaniment or subdivisions. Mallet players provide harmony, which is useful in checking intonation with the rest of the ensemble, and the suspended cymbals can heighten climaxes to make chorales and scales more interesting, while timpanists play scales and cadences with the band. In the middle of the warm-up have the players switch to a new instrument and continue.

Getting players into the routine of setting up all of the instruments before rehearsal saves time and confusion, and posting the rehearsal schedule for the week helps keep the section organized. Copy the entire score for the percussion section so that the players can grasp the scheme of the piece. Let them see what you see, and instruct them to write in and follow all the directions you give to the wind players. Every performance suggestion made to the winds is applicable to the percussion section. A chorale sound requires the section to strive for long, sustained tones, and conversely, you will not get a clean sound if the entire ensemble plays staccatto unisons, and the bass drummer allows the drum to ring between attacks.

Try to find band literature that contains many percussion parts. A single part will often require one player to perform on several instruments at different times. Giving the responsibility of each instrument to different players involves more personnel, and doubling existing parts or the high woodwind parts on mallet instruments gives everyone something to play.

If the majority of your band's literature uses only a few percussionists, organize a separate percussion group to work on ensemble literature during rehearsals. A student teacher, parent, alumni, or trusted student could run those rehearsals, and even with limited instrumentation there is enough literature that includes accessories, homemade instruments, or instruments that the students own.

Concert and rudimental playing are two different styles. Rudimental playing is characteristically open and dry with little harmonic ring from the drum. Ruffs, drags, and rolls are metronomically measured and clearly articulated with the musician playing every stroke over the center of the head where little ring occurs. Concert style playing is generally performed off-center to allow a more full tone and ring from the drum with rolls that are pulse-free and smooth without audible subdivision.

To produce consistent tone the player should use single hand repetition, which is more accurate than alternating patterns. This is similar to the differences between single and double tonguing. Playing doubled strokes (RRLL) in unison with wind players who are single tonguing will produce a less consistent sound than if the drummer plays the pattern in alternation or one-handed. Students should not attempt every pattern with one hand, but easier, less technical passages will be clean and consistent this way.

Good percussion sections develop gradually through consistent musical and technical guidance. By providing that guidance to your young percussionists, you will produce players to meet the musical and technical demands of today's literature. □

November, 1990

Teaching Accessory Percussion

by Jeff Brown

Developing technique on bass drum, cymbals, and triangle seems simple but is as important as snare drum technique. The characteristic sound of the concert bass drum is a sustained sound with few overtones and should not be confused with the thudlike sound of the bass drum in a drum set. Although concert bass drum heads are not tuned to a specific pitch, the playing side should be slightly higher in pitch than the other side. Avoid tuning the drum to a recognizable pitch that will be a chord tone in some keys and dissonant in others; find a pitch that will blend well in all situations.

The exact center of the drum produces dark tones that have an attack-like quality to the sound, which players can use to good advantage in dramatic passages. The best playing area is slightly off center of the head because at the edge of the head the tone becomes brighter and thinner and the ringing and resonance are harder to control.

The sound of the bass drum should be a sustained tone; students tend to dampen the heads too much so encourage them to dampen according to the style of the music. When dampening is appropriate it is best done on the playing side with a soft cloth in the free hand. When music should have less bass drum sound, dampen the playing side with your knee and the opposite side with your hand.

A bass drum that is 36 inches in diameter with a shell depth of 14 or 16 inches is good for concert playing. Among several types of stands, the best is the kind that tilts the drum, but a stand should support the instrument firmly and not rattle.

Select bass drum beaters with enough head weight to produce a full dark tone. Beaters with small heads and little weight tend to produce thin, bright tones.

Grip the mallet at a point along the shaft where there is the greatest control; wrap the fingers firmly but not tightly around the shaft of the mallet keeping a relaxed wrist and the palm facing the drum head, and place the thumb on top of the shaft pointed toward the head. A direct stroke is preferable to a glancing stroke because the head weight of the mallet helps to produce a dark tone and makes more efficient use of the arm motion. Because keeping the mallet pressed to the head muffles the tone, allow it to remain in contact as briefly as possible.

Perform rolls using two matched mallet heads on opposite sides of the same head. Double-headed mallets produce inferior sound even in the hands of experienced players. Tilt the drum slightly; because of the resonant tone of the bass drum, the roll should be slower than with other drums. In fact, fast rolls on the bass drum tend to stifle the sound rather than enhance it.

In selecting crash cymbals for concert band or orchestra, consider the sound you want. There are three thicknesses of cymbals – thin, medium, and heavy (sometimes known as French, Viennese, and German). Thin cymbals produce many overtones, little sense of pitch, and sounds that peak quickly. Heavy cymbals have fewer overtones, more discernible pitch, and more of a clang sound. A well-developed program needs all three thicknesses in either 16 or 18 inch diameters. Marching band cymbals generally do not make good concert cymbals.

For a crash, place the fingers under the strap next to the dome of the cymbal so that the thumb is on top and perpendicular to the cymbal. Do not put your hands inside the straps because you need to be able to put the cymbals down or pick them up quickly. To execute a crash, stand with the feet apart, one slightly in front of the other, distribute the weight evenly between both feet, and follow these steps: hold the cymbals at a slight angle to the body with the lighter cymbal on top, move the cymbals apart in opposite directions, and bring the cymbals together for the crash, being sure that one to three inches of the top edge of the bottom cymbal are visible. To prevent air lock keep the edges of the cymbals off center.

At the moment of contact strike the bottom edges of the cymbal just before the top edges come together. Then bring the cymbals apart in the same order – bottom edges first, then the top.

If crashes occur in succession, repeat the process, keeping the same cymbal always on top; do not alternate. If there is no note following the crash, then the performer should follow through with the crash by turning both hands inward allowing the cymbals to face the floor. Allow as little contact as possible between yourself and the cymbals to enable the cymbals to vibrate freely.

The dynamic level of the crash is controlled by the force of the attack, the angle of the cymbals in relation to each other, and the angle of the cymbals in relation to the performer. Because you strike the cymbals harder for a louder crash, the distance between the cymbals before the crash becomes greater. Prepare for the longer distance so that the attack will not be late.

For soft crashes the angle of the cymbals in relation to one another should be narrow. To increase the dynamic level, widen the angle between the cymbals.

The angle of the cymbals in relation to the performer also helps control the dynamic level. Soft crashes are easier to perform if you hold the cymbals in a vertical position. As the dynamic level increases, hold the cymbals more near the horizontal. This way gravity will assist in making the crash louder.

To choke the cymbals, bring them against the chest or stomach after a crash. Knowing when to choke the cymbals can be difficult because notation for cymbal parts often tells the performer more about when to play than how long to hold the sound. When the length of the choke is not indicated, listen to the other instruments in the band and match the length of the crash to the ensemble. To execute the choke in forte-piano crashes, choke one cymbal and allow the other to vibrate.

For a legato effect allow the cymbals to remain briefly in contact with each other after an attack. This technique is easiest to perform at soft dynamic levels when the distance between cymbals is short and the force of the attack not so great. As the dynamic level increases this technique becomes more difficult.

Two other cymbal techniques are what I term swish, and the two-plate roll. To execute the swish, scrape the inside of one cymbal with the edge of the other. You can perform this most conveniently on the suspended cymbal. For the two-plate roll move the cymbals in a circular motion against one another. This is a difficult technique because it requires that the circular motion be consistent. The edges of the cymbals must not align or they will airlock.

As with the crash cymbals, choose the suspended cymbal giving consideration to where you will perform it and the sound you want. Large diameter cymbals produce more volume, and thick cymbals have fewer overtones. A good first choice for a suspended cymbal is an 18 inch medium or medium-thin instrument.

Mount the cymbal on a stand or suspend it from a crook by a strap. If mounted, be certain that points of contact between the cymbal and stand are well-insulated by a piece of felt to prevent unwanted vibrations. Adjust the stand so that the cymbal is parallel to the floor and at a comfortable height for the player. Medium yarn marimba mallets work best on the suspended cymbal.

To perform single strokes strike the cymbal with both mallets on opposite sides of the cymbal at the same time. This technique causes the cymbal to respond quickly.

The most common technique for the suspended cymbal is the roll, executed by alternating single strokes on opposite sides of the cymbal. Because the cymbal sound decays slowly, the speed of the roll should not be too fast. A frequent misconception is that the player should roll faster to crescendo; however, the reverse is more exact. To crescendo strike the cymbal harder and slow the alternation of the hands. Determine the speed of your roll by the decay time of the tone and by the desired dynamic level.

There are many special effects that you can create with the suspended cymbal. Scraping a coin, a wire brush, or a triangle beater across the cymbal from the center toward the outside edge produces swish sounds. A coin taped to a cymbal that is allowed to vibrate creates a sizzle when the cymbal is struck. A violin bow pulled across the edge of the cymbal offers a unique display of sound. The player's imagination and willingness to experiment can produce many new forms; and while some techniques may be more appropriate than others, the only technique that is never acceptable is one that causes damage to the instrument.

Triangles range in size from 4 to 10 inches. Some of the most popular brands are Alan Abel, Danmar, Grover, Latin Percussion, Stoessel, and SpectraSound. A good choice for a first triangle is the 6 inch Alan Abel. A well-equipped school percussion section should include the 4, 6, and 8 inch sizes. Avoid purchasing thin triangles because they do not have a wide dynamic range and tend to have an easily distinguishable pitch. Also avoid aluminum triangles, whose tone quality is inferior to steel triangles.

Pitch is not as important in triangle selection as is the timbre. Obtain a triangle whose tone contains many overtones; such a triangle generally lacks definite pitch and as a result will not interfere with the pitch center of other instruments.

A steel beater produces the characteristic sound of the triangle. Other beaters such as snare drum sticks, brushes, xylophone and bell mallets, and marimba mallets will produce special effects.

SpectraSound and Stoessel are good choices for commercial triangle beaters, though you can make beaters from steel rods available at most hardware stores. The student should have several sizes of beaters in matched pairs.

To mount your triangle, you can purchase spring clips either through music dealers or at hardware stores. Drill two holes about one inch apart in one side of the clip, then attach two loops of plastic fishing line through the two holes. One of the loops sould be slightly larger than the other to act as a safety if the smaller loop breaks. Suspend the triangle from the smaller of the two loops close to the clip but without allowing it to touch either the clip or the player's hand.

How you hold the triangle has a great deal to do with producing a characteristic sound as well as controlling the natural movements of the instrument. To gain control and make dampening easier, ask students to hold the triangle in the following way: form a C with the thumb and second finger of the left hand. (Left-handed students should use their right hand); rest the clip on the C with the open end of the triangle on the left; rest the index finger of the left hand on top of the clip to keep it firmly in place; raise the triangle to nose level so that the conductor is visible just above the triangle.

The single stroke is the most common technique in triangle playing, and many factors affect its sound: the size of the beater and instrument and the force of the stroke; also the place where the triangle is struck, the angle of attack in relation to the plane of the triangle, and the point of contact on the beater. The two most accepted playing spots on the triangle are the bottom side approximately two-thirds of the distance from the opening, and near the top on the side opposite the opening. Remember that repeated single stroke notes will sound consistent only when all factors are the same for each stroke.

For passages too fast to be played by one hand, clip the triangle to a stand and use two beaters. You can suspend the instrument from a single clip and play on opposite sides of the top corner or suspend the triangle upside down from two clips with the open corner at the bottom and play on the opposite side.

To perform a roll rapidly alternate

strokes on the inside of either of the closed corners. To crescendo move the beater further away from the corner so that the beater covers more distance.

To execute a choke, the hand that holds the triangle suddenly stops it from vibrating after a traditional free stroke, producing a unique effect.

Striking the triangle while it is muffled produces a clank sound. Students can also shade their strokes by playing in different areas of the triangle, varying the amount of muffling used as well as the angle of the beater in relation to the plane of the triangle.

To create a vibrato place the striking hand in front of the triangle between the listener and the triangle and fan it rapidly back and forth, being careful not to touch the triangle. Another technique is to rotate the hand holding the triangle with a twisting motion of the wrist to produce the vibrato. In both of these methods the object is to interfere with the sound waves by disturbing the air around the triangle.

With the bass drum, the cymbals, and the triangle, as with many other instruments, there is no one way to play. Encourage students to be sensitive to varying musical interpretations so they realize that the sound used in one passage may not be appropriate in others. Once players take the time to master the basic techniques, they will develop an awareness of the many sounds they can create. □

November 1990

A History of American Drumming

by William F. Ludwig, Jr

In the morning of April 19, 1775 William Diamond strapped on his drum, stepped onto the village commons, and sounded the alarm of the American Revolution. Later that morning British troops fired on the 69 volunteers he summoned, but Diamond escaped, and his drum is now in a Boston museum. Two-and-one-half months later drummers on both sides beat cadences to steady the troops as they closed for battle on Bunker Hill.

The drums gave order to the chaos of the battlefield. In the din of musket and cannon fire the drummers sounded calls that could be heard by the troops. While the human voice penetrates only a few hundred yards, the sound of the drum carries for a quarter to half mile. George Washington insisted that at least one drummer be assigned to every marching unit to provide the cadence to move the men in an orderly fashion. He used the drum to set the time of camp activities throughout the day. The first of these distinctive calls was "Reveille," which drummers performed as soon as they could see a tree at 1,000 paces in the early morning light.

With a marching tempo of only 90 steps per minute, drummers fashioned intricate patterns called fillings between the beats. Today these fillings appear in many modern percussion books as paradiddles, flam accents, and double drags. These early cadences were the beginning of our present rudimental system and were written with left-hand strokes with stems pointing up while stems for right-hand strokes pointed down. Drummers played all hollow notes pianissimo, solid ones fortissimo, and solid notes with a slash mezzo fortissimo. Slowly American drummers perfected the new notation of the calls and cadences and passed them through the regiments of the growing Continental Army.

George Frederick von Steuben, an aristocratic Prussian whom Washington made Inspector General to the Continental Army, ordered a drum factory set up in Philadelphia and three artisans produced 399 military rope drums for regimental drummers. By contrast, however, one ship sailing from England provided the British with 760 drums.

The Drummer of Valley Forge

The Revolutionary War barrel drums were enormous by today's standards and had shells measuring 18 inches by 17 inches across, and an overall height of 22 inches to provide maximum volume. Constructed of solid beechwood or maple panels, drum shells were soaked in water and then steamed and bent into their circular shape. The two-inch-high hoops were of half-inch thick straight-grained maple to withstand the rigors of field use, and drum heads were tanned calfskin, while the snare or lower head was tanned from unborn calfskin. Lamb gut snares provided a crisp sound and action but were affected by weather and humidity changes unless heavily shellacked. Drum sticks of this period were thick and heavy. When squeezed down by the drummer, leather tugs around the shell applied tension to both heads simulatneously. This method of tightening both drum heads at once persisted into the mid-19th century when J. Dermond developed independent tensioning. Spare sash cord was braided to hang below the drum for decoration, but drummers often used it to replace frayed and worn segments of the regular tensioning cord. Because taut skin heads often cracked with changes in temperature or humidity, drummers relaxed the rope tensioning whenever the drum was not in use.

In section 21 of his field manual, von Steuben ordered all large bodies of troops to form three separate camps in the event of a surprise night attack. The three camps were a minimum of a half mile apart, and drummers soon developed a system of calling back and forth before "Taps" with a series of continuous five- ten- and eleven-stroke rolls. A drummer in one camp would begin playing the first section of "Three Camps" followed by the second section played by the drummer in the next camp. Both drummers waited for the drummer in the third camp to check in. If a British drummer familiar with the piece broke in, the Americans would know it by the style of his drumming and sound the alarm. Still in use today, "Three Camps" is a marvelous solo that shows the solid nature of the rudimental system.

When leaving or entering camp, companies and regiments marched to drum cadences, but in open country drummers released the tension from their drum heads and carried their instruments by the ceremonial sash cords until marching into the next campsite when they resumed playing cadences.

Von Steuben's infantry manual of 1778 prescribed drum and fife practice from 10:00 a.m. until 1:00 p.m. each day in camp. Young drummers taught by older hands memorized dozens of calls and cadences until they could be played on demand of the commanding officer. At dawn's first light the duty drummer sounded "Drummer's Call," which was the signal for all company drummers to report to the regiment and sound enmasse "Reveille" at dawn. "Officer's Call" and "Breakfast Call" soon followed. For dinner call fifers and drummers sounded "Roast Beef," so named because the army issued each

infantryman a slab of raw beef to cook on the end of a pointed stick. For today's drummer "Roast Beef," with its double drags, is an excellent exercise. The last call of the day was "Taps." Six evenly spaced slow taps, the first *f*, the second *p*, were repeated twice. Thus, from sun up to sun down the drum governed every moment of the field soldier's day.

Drums and fifes were an integral part of the surrender ceremony at Yorktown. "Yankee Doodle," originally invented by the British fifers and drummers as a derisive song for the bumpkins of the American colonies, was tauntingly played by the Americans as the British troops threw their guns to the ground.

In the War of 1812 drummers controlled the loading and firing of artillery batteries. After each volley a cloud of smoke enveloped the cannoneers and they could not see the artillery's controlling officer. To avoid confusion drummers rolled loudly until ordered to stop by the artillery officer lowering his saber. Upon hearing the roll cease, the artilleryman fired a round. If drummers resumed rolling the men reloaded the cannon and waited for the roll to stop before firing again. If there were no drum roll after a round was fired, the troops moved the battery to another location.

In the first 90 days of the Civil War, drummers, fifers, and bands paraded to attract volunteers in a form of recruitment termed marching to the drum because enlistees often signed the Papers of Fidelity on a drum head. All Northern States sent musical units with their enlistees. Neither their uniforms nor musical instruments matched, but eventually the Department of War standardized both, settling on a rope-tensioned field snare 12 inches deep by 15 inches in diameter. The Revolutionary War's barrel drum was abandoned because the marching cadence increased to over 100 steps per minute in the 50 years separating the wars, and drummers wanted a more manageable field drum with a crisp, higher-pitched sound. Jos. Rogers & Son, the J.W. Pepper Co., and other Union drum manufacturers produced 64,000 eagle drums, each emblazoned with the Great Seal of the United States.

At the War's beginning drummers were adults, but as the conflict dragged on and casualties mounted, they were ordered from musical units to serve as combat troops. Young boys who had left their homes to follow the army and perform camp duties soon enlisted as drummers and received uniforms. These camp followers became skilled in rudimental proficiency because their light duties allowed for several hours of practice each day. Their newly achieved status, however, lost its glamour on the battlefield: many young drummers broke rank and ran in the heat of combat leaving their units without a means of communication. To avoid this officers sometimes tied young drummers to their braided sashes and dragged them into battle. By the end of the War both sides had used drummers younger than 10 years of age.

Replica of a Revolutionary War field drum

During the War over-the-shoulder slings gradually replaced neck slings, and drummers carried their instruments against their left leg; this allowed the right hand, which is usually stronger, to bring the bead of the stick flat against the head. If the stick came down at too

The Battle of Bunker Hill

much of an angle it would split the head with the tip of the bead.

Drummers always marched to the right in the front rank alongside the officer and the color bearer. All three were prime targets for enemy sharpshooters who could stop an infantry's advance by knocking out any one of them. Without the sight of the colors or the sound of the drum, an attack would falter. In an average advance across 500 yards, 6 or 7 color bearers would be shot, but another soldier would immediately pick up the colors and restore the forward momentum.

This was the first war in which camp entertainment consisted of fifers and drummers performing popular tunes and playing the troops to sleep each night. Official reviews and parades were popular in this era; there were long periods between campaigns in which drummers and fifers provided pageantry for the popular parades and when the War was finally over, 250,000 soldiers marched down Pennsylvania Avenue to the cadence of eagle drums.

With the demobilization of the Civil War armies, the U.S. Government formed large cavalry regiments to protect the westward-bound wagon trains. With the use of a bugle a cavalry soldier could sound signal calls while still controlling his mount. Thus, the drum, which was the instrument of choice within the ranks of armies for centuries, was displaced by the compact little horn. By 1868 the drum became the instrument of pure entertainment that it is today.

Because the government allowed returning Civil War veteran drummers to keep their instruments, thousands of small community bands and dance orchestras formed. A dance drummer of this time would set his snare drum on a chair in front of him (the snare drum stand was not invented yet) and place his bass drum at a right angle to it. He'd tap the bass drum with his snare stick on the down beat and his snare on the after beats on polkas, waltzes, quadrilles, and standard $\frac{2}{4}$ marches. This arrangement worked well as long as the dance music remained fairly straightforward.

On February 1, 1887 George R. Olney changed all this by patenting the first bass drum foot pedal. Drummers were now free to use both hands for snare performance. Following Olney's breakthrough came a number of devices that transformed the drum from a military instrument to one used for entertainment. Olney's bass drum pedal, E.E. Fry's throw-off snare drum strainer, wire brushes by L. Allis & A.R. Wines,

Barrel drum from the Revolutionary War

and the low-boy sock cymbal pedal invented by dixieland drummer Vick Berton show particular genius and have changed the way we use percussion instruments.

The development of the bass drum pedal enabled one man to perform the function of three players combining bass, snare drum, and cymbals all under one command. Small groups of five players gathered around the new setup of drums and performed marches, polkas, and waltzes to the steady beat of one drummer instead of three. Bass drum stabilizers soon made an appearance and eventually took the form of small spurs attached to the drum's lower counterhoop. Until their development a bass drum would roll over on its side if accidentally touched in the wrong place.

Another primary invention of the mid-19th century was the development of the first separate tension drum, which enabled drummers to control the tension on the heads independently of each other. The first patent for this instrument was issued on February 3, 1863 to J. Dermond. His invention consisted of nothing more dramatic than fastening two cut-down rope tension drums together allowing separate tension applications to the batter head as well as the tender snare head. These separate tensioned drums arrived too late for use in the Civil War, but afterwards the J.W. Pepper Drum Co., one of America's earliest full-production drum manufacturers, replaced the rope of the Dermond separate tension drum with metal rods and added slotted tension screws. Later a simple center stud in the shell was threaded on each end to receive tension screws. This was the most direct application for tensioning and variations of this model are produced today.

A year after Berton's invention of the low-boy sock cymbal, Barney Walberg of Worcester, Massachusetts added a 32-inch tube extension and brought the cymbals up to their present hi-hat position. At the time of the invention cymbals had a deep-cupped shape resembling the profile of a formal dress high hat. This last development gave us the drum set that we still use today.

Prior to 1927 all movies were without sound, and theater owners employed musicians to accompany the action on the flickering screen. Drummers brought their drums and contraptions, soon shortened to traps, to do this. A single movie of that era could call for as many as 120 different sound effects from the drummer, who carried the massive array in a steamer trunk. Often drummers would trade sound effects with one another to balance their inventory.

Most movie houses supplied the public with six shows each day, and because the projectionists had to rewind a reel of film by hand before they could start another one, live performing acts were featured between each movie. Percussionists' work never stopped; at the end of a week's run, they spent an all-night session lining up sound effects for the following week's bill and learning every leg kick, rim shot, and sound effect for live acts. Of course, with the introduction of talking movies in the late 1920s, live acts at movie houses came to an end.

America's history in the early years was guided by the development of drums. I doubt that armies could have marched and fought without the indispensable aid of the drum and those drummer boys of long ago. Then as now, we applaud the drum's importance on history's musical stage. □

Teaching the Seven Fundamental Rudiments

by Bruce Roberts

Rudiments are to percussionists what scales are to wind players, yet often teachers neglect to emphasize rudimental techniques. The 7 essential rudiments provide a foundation for the remaining 33. Single-stroke rolls, multiple-bounce rolls, and double-stroke open rolls, ranked one, two, and three, comprise the three stroke types; all other rudiments are an extension or combination of these three basics. Each rudiment should be performed in the standard open-closed-open style (sometimes referred to as "slow-accelerate-decelerate") and should last from 60 to 90 seconds. Students should play with a relaxed grip.

The single-stroke roll is the fundamental rudiment that forms the basis of the remaining 39 rudiments.

Strive for even velocity and rhythm. The height of the drum stick and the playing area of the head influence velocity; problems arise if one stick, usually the one in the weaker hand, is lower than the other. Practicing the following exercise while watching stick height in a mirror will help players improve the weak hand. Play on the same spot for consistent velocity and timbre.

Students will develop an even rhythm by listening to the silent or dead spaces between strokes; this inverted way of listening helps students play evenly in an accelerating or decelerating passage.

Musical sprints help students build speed if they play eight notes alternating hands, using a fast, lifting stroke (piston stroke) after a relaxed, fast downward stroke.

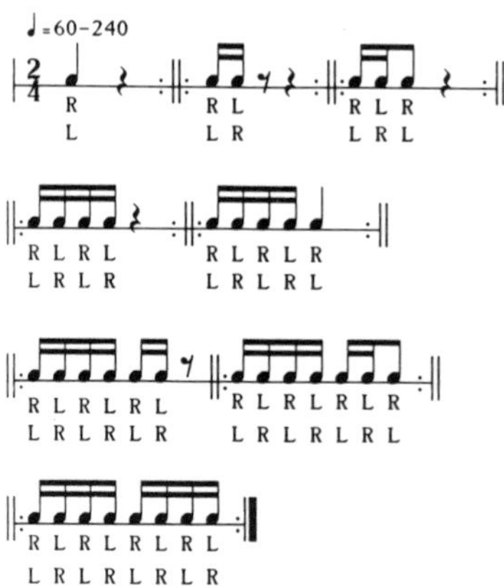

The multiple-bounce roll, sometimes called a closed, buzz, concert, or orchestral roll, is similar to the single-stroke roll but uses a slight tension from the third, fourth, and fifth fingers while increasing the velocity of the downward stroke a little. Students should listen for the same number of buzzes from each hand. Begin by playing a relaxed single-stroke, leaving the wrist in the down position until all bounced strokes gradually stop; by using a relaxed pivot point, or fulcrum, between the thumb and index finger, the tip of the stick will bounce freely. Once leaving wrists in the down position a little longer is learned, add an upstroke before all bounced strokes stop, regulating the number of bounces per hand by applying slight tension with the third, fourth, and fifth fingers while executing the down stroke by pulling fingers inward toward the palm. On up strokes, relax the tension in preparation for the next stroke, repeating this exercise 100 times a day with each hand.

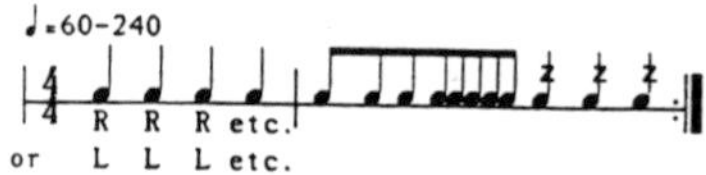

The multiple-bounce stroke in the first measure is an extension of the single stroke; in the second measure play the same number of strokes from beat to beat and from hand to hand and velocity of the multiple-bounce stroke increases or decreases the number of successive bounces, both of which are beneficial in performing various styles of music.

When multiple-bounce strokes are consistent, perform the multiple-bounce roll as a rudiment: imitate the single-stroke roll, playing in a slow-accelerate-decelerate style, listening for the same number of bounced strokes per hand. When there are no variances in velocity or rhythm, decelerate, listening for the silent spaces between strokes.

A second way to perform a multiple bounce roll is in a slow, smooth, and sustained roll while varying the dynamic from pianissimo to fortissimo and back by moving from the edge of the drum to the center or by regulating the stick height in the same area of the head (pianissimo = one inch; fortissimo = six inches). Concentrate on even velocity and rhythm while listening for the same number of multiple-bounced strokes per hand.

pp < ff > pp
edge center edge

The double-stroke open roll, perhaps the most difficult to master, consists of two notes produced in equal volume by the same hand. Execute the first note from the wrist in the same manner as a single-stroke roll; the difficulty lies in producing the second note. Long gone are the days of "hit once, let it bounce once" without precise placement of the second stroke. Instead, players should place the second notes of a double stroke (sometimes called a diddle) as precisely as the first.

Beginning with a stick approximately eight inches above the drum surface, let your wrist fall, so the tip of the stick travels to the head of the drum surface. Once the stick rebounds, keep your wrist in the down position having a relaxed pivot point between thumb and index finger. While the wrist remains down, the stick rebounds upward and the third, fourth, and fifth fingers pull inward towards the palm and force the stick back to the drum head; this action involves no wrist motion. After the second stroke, the wrist returns to the upper position in a relaxed, lifting motion. This entire process usually lasts less than half a second.

To play a double-stroke open roll as in a rudiment, begin slowly, using two wrist motions for each note of the double stroke in slow tempos, essentially performing two single strokes and avoiding a fast double-stroke spacing when performing the rudiment in a slow tempo. When the speed increases so two wrist motions are no longer possible, convert to one wrist motion and use the third, fourth, and fifth fingers to produce the second stroke of the double stroke. The point at which this happens varies from player to player; but when the change is made, increase the speed of the double stroke and concentrate on the first note of every double stroke while listening to rhythmic evenness between strokes.

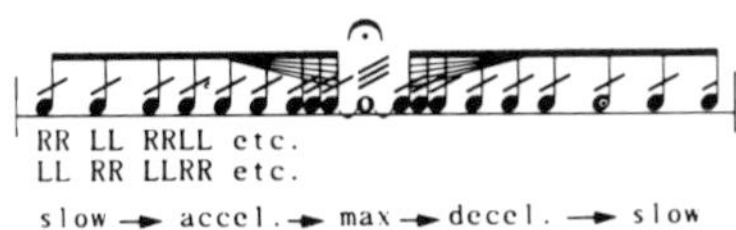

The five-stroke roll normally contains two double strokes followed by an accented single stroke; a concert or orchestral version consists of two multiple-bounce strokes followed by an accented single stroke.

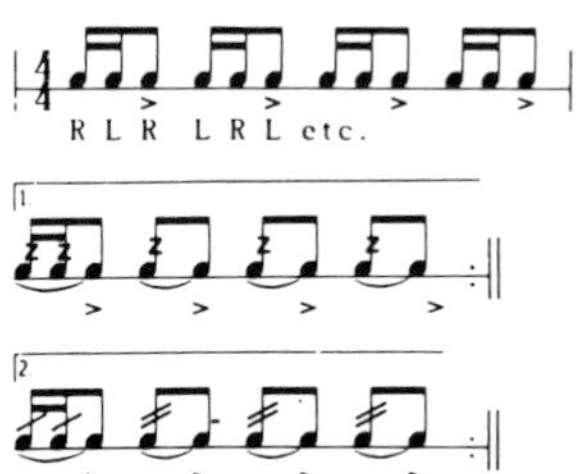

To effectively play a five-stroke roll, analyze and execute the roll base, which is sometimes called the fundamental.

Once the underlying rhythm is consistent in tempo, substitute either double strokes or multiple-bounce strokes for a rudimental or concert-style five-stroke roll; the principles used in performing the double-stroke or multiple-bounce stroke rudiments apply to any double-stroke rudiment.

When performing the five-stroke roll as a rudiment, use a mixture of duple and triple subdivisions to effect a smooth acceleration and deceleration, and use two double strokes followed by an accented single stroke rather than using the orchestral version. To produce the second note use two wrist motions in slow tempos, and a wrist-finger combination in faster tempos.

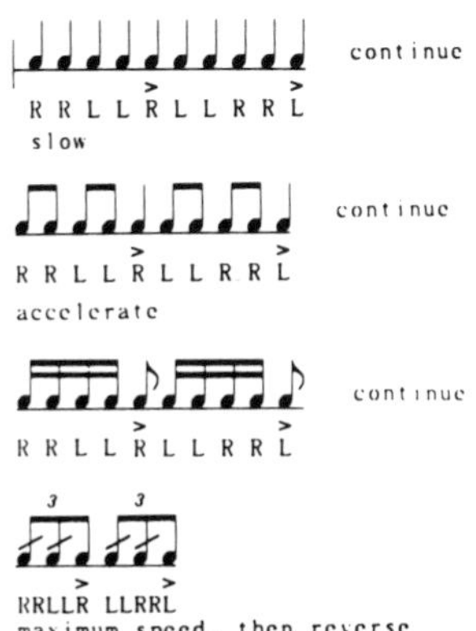

The paradiddle, as the name suggests, is a combination of two single strokes followed by a double stroke, and is useful for changing stick directions and easing movement on such percussion instruments as timpani, keyboard, or multiple percussion setups. The rudiment uses a combination of down, up, and neutral stick heights: the up stroke, a variation of the basic percussion stroke, begins with the tip of the stick in a low position of approximately three to four inches; drop the tip of the stick straight down toward the head and immediately raise the stick tip to a higher position of six to eight inches. For a down stroke, reverse the procedure and begin at a high position of six to eight inches and allow the stick to rebound to a level of three to four inches, pulling the third, fourth, and fifth fingers in as the stick rebounds. A neutral stroke starts and ends at the same basic percussion stroke level. Practice at a slow tempo until all stroke directions become ingrained.

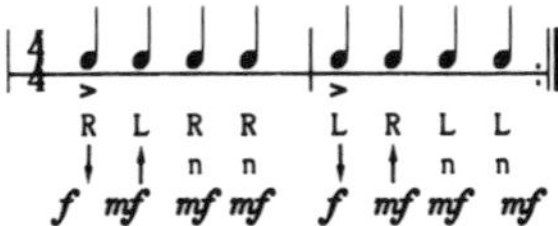

To build speed and improve stick height, isolate the rhythm of each hand from a series of successive, alternating flams.

To build speed, focus on the single stroke aspect of the paradiddle, then substitute a diddle on the upbeat eighth note.

Finally, perform the paradiddle as a rudiment, using a slow-accelerate-decelerate style for 60 to 90 seconds.

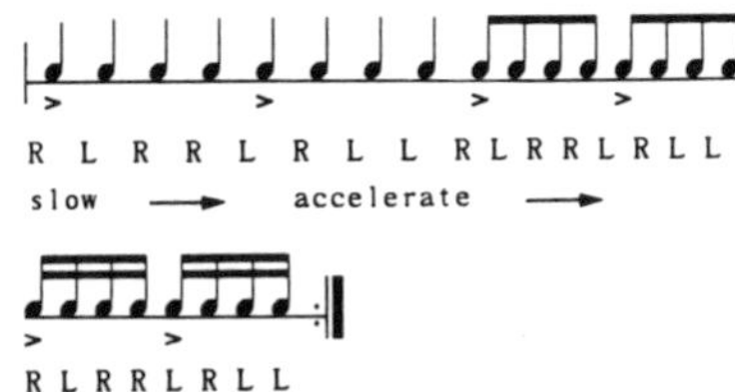

Many of the same concepts that apply to flams also pertain to drags (formerly called ruffs), both of which are alternating successions of down and up strokes. To visualize this, isolate either the right or left hand in a series of flams.

1R rL 1R rL | 1. R r R r | 2. l L l L

Using one hand and rounding off the grace note to the nearest quarter note, concentrate on the technique of alternating up and down strokes. As each hand performs this alternating succession, the only difference is that the hands are displaced by one beat: while the right hand plays a down stroke, the left hand performs an up stroke. The drag uses this same principle, replacing the grace note with a double stroke.

To control the rebound of down strokes pull the third, fourth, and fifth fingers in towards the palm, and immediately relax in preparation for the next stroke. When learning the technique, exaggerate high and low stick positions from one inch to approximately eight inches; as speed increases, the distance lessens. The exercise improves accent control.

To apply these principles to the rudiment, play slowly and concentrate on the opposite positions of up and down strokes. Place the primary note on the beat with the grace note preceding it. The space should be close enough that the two strokes sound like the word flam; if it sounds like fa-lam the spacing is too much.

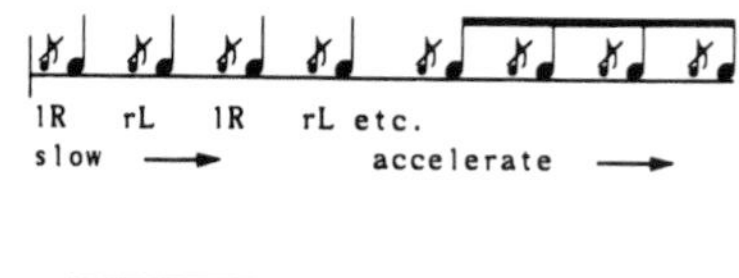

maximum speed, then reverse

The only difference between the two rudiments is the spacing of the grace notes. The double stroke should be close enough to the primary note that it sounds as one unit, yet the spacing should be rhythmically consistent; when executing the drag as a rudiment, strive for a duple subdivision throughout.

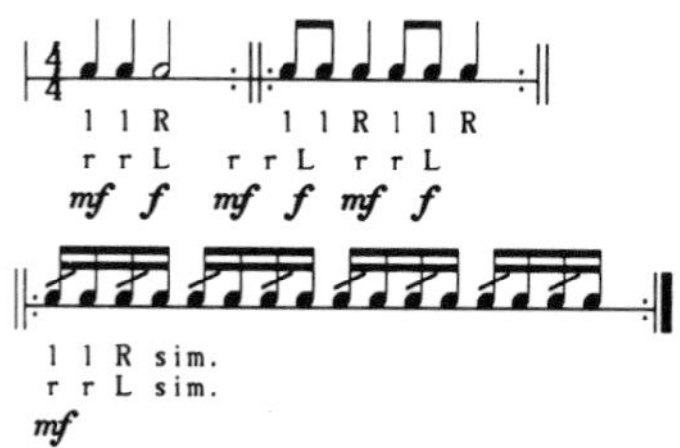

After learning the double stroke grace notes in strict rhythm, perform the drag as a rudiment, using a slow-accelerate-decelerate style.

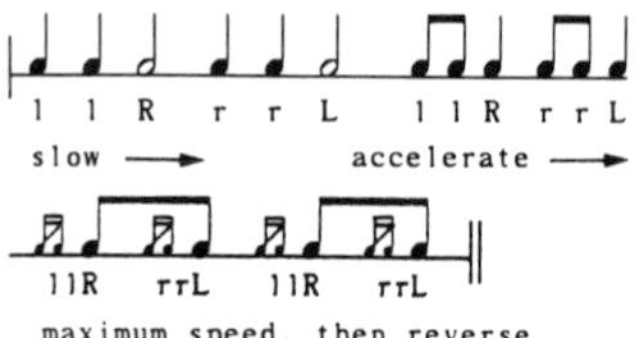

The seven essential rudiments are the basis for the remaining 33 rudiments, but as in all things musical, it takes many years to practice and master them. □

June 1991

Marimba and Xylophone Sight-Reading

by Steve Hemphill

Although teachers and performers agree sight-reading is a necessary skill for xylophone and marimba players, young players are weak at this. A relaxed grip and stroke; quick, controlled eye movements to and from the keyboard; and a good feel for intervals, patterns, and sequences are all important sight-reading skills; ear training helps in recognizing pitches and intervals.

Begin by gripping the mallets with relaxed fingers, keeping wrists loose so they follow the mallet handle movements. Mallets should be free enough to move between fingers and the outside base pad of the palm and pivot between the thumb and forefinger. The backs of the hands should face up so mallets immediately return to their original positions when playing lifted, full strokes. Think of the wrist and finger movements used in sustaining pitches with a relaxed single-stroke roll.

Although many players alternate between gripping the mallets loosely with the fingers for rolled passages and gripping them tightly, striking from the wrist, for others, it is better to concentrate on only one technique when learning to play marimba and xylophone; using only one grip allows better control of the mallets and increases note accuracy.

Keep fingers loose and relaxed for agility in playing, much like a boxer dances on his toes, ready to side-step a punch. Contrast this with a boxer's lazy, flat-footed approach or a percussionist's tight grip that doesn't lend itself to quick, lateral movements. Mallet technique with finger control not only allows for sudden sideways movement, but it also reduces unnecessary elbow pivoting when combined with side-to-side wrist movements.

Place the music stand near the area of the keyboard where most playing occurs. Position the stand high enough so players are not tempted to look at the keyboard too often.

To develop a feel for the keyboard without looking at it, imagine playing an even roll on the C bar of a marimba. If you move to one side at a steady rate of speed, a C major scale results. Of course, this lateral movement has to be proportionate to the speed of the roll to produce a scale in which all note values are equal.

Apply this concept by rolling on the C bar with eyes closed, and after several seconds, play diatonically up to G, then return back to C, noting which mallet moves first. Once comfortable playing this five-note pattern, extend the scale to a full octave, still with eyes closed. If you play a note twice or skip one, adjust your side-to-side motion. Practicing major and minor scales without looking at the keyboard helps to accurately measure intervals with hands and wrists, and frees the eyes for reading music.

Before practicing a new piece, mark points in the music where a look at the keyboard is absolutely necessary, and glance down only at those places. Bounce the eyes back and forth, much like pianists who take quick mental snapshots of the keyboard and return their eyes immediately to the music. Rather than focusing on one keyboard note, use a non-focused glance and take in groupings of sharp and flat bars as reference points. Focusing on one note makes it necessary to search for the current measure and beat when returning to the music, but if the eyes bounce to the keyboard and back, they automatically return to the right spot.

Reading note-to-note is slow, inefficient, and tedious. Increase reading speed and comprehension by identifying groups of notes as diatonic or chromatic passages, motives, intervals, or arpeggios. Help beginners' sight-reading by covering two notes ahead of the one sounding with a three-by-five inch index card, which makes students read ahead; they will immediately understand forward eye motion.

Just as French horn players negotiating the closely spaced upper partials of their instruments have to hear a pitch before producing it, so too should keyboard percussionists hear pitches before they play them. Much 20th-century percussion literature lacks an obvious tonal center and diatonic scale passages; in this music the ear distinguishes between correct and incorrect pitches with no time for the player to look at the keyboard.

When working with young marimba and xylophone players, include sight-reading in all daily practice sessions; use other treble clef instruments' method books for additional material. Have students start by sight-reading for 10 minutes each day and make sure they do some of this with a metronome. As they advance, acquaint them with the works of Telemann, Haydn, Handel, Mozart, Quantz, Scarlatti, and Bach, all of which will challenge their sight-reading abilities and musicianship. □

August 1991

Beginning Percussion Ensembles

by Robert Reely

One solution to a junior high director's dilemma of keeping young percussionists from getting bored is a percussion ensemble, which teaches students a variety of instruments and increases their musical skills. Ensembles will challenge percussionists who master concert band literature faster than woodwind and brass players.

A major obstacle to forming percussion ensembles is finding a free period during the school day when all percussionists are available. Directors may also feel overwhelmed by the number of concerts and other appearances the band makes; at the high school level a student-led rehearsal can ease time pressures on the director, but the director should plan the session in detail. If regular percussion ensemble rehearsals or sectionals cannot be arranged, having one just before a performance will improve the quality of the concert. During a full band rehearsal, a director may not have time to ascertain whether a mistake is occurring; but in a sectional there is time to dissect difficult passages with individual players without embarassing them by identifying an error in front of a larger group. To stimulate hard work, replace chair try-outs with ensemble tests, grading the group as a whole and emphasizing teamwork. It's worth the effort to find a local percussionist who can rehearse your ensemble during school hours.

Without fail, either a surplus or a shortage of players exists. A shortage limits repertoire, but don't hesitate to rewrite parts so one player can cover additional music. With careful planning and instrument placement, a player can often cover two parts, depending on the music. Recruit wind players with rhythmic skills for auxiliary instruments, and those who play piano can cover mallet parts. However, don't take all mallet parts away from snare drummers, who should learn keyboard percussion.

Directors who are not percussionists may be uncomfortable with a percussion ensemble, but its musical aspects parallel those of a band. Strive for resonant sounds on each instrument and read percussion methods or talk with professional players for mallet choices because mallets are a prime factor in producing tone colors. Work for even strokes on all instruments, and do not allow a player's right hand to strike harder than the left. Use a metronome for steady tempo, especially in passages with crescendos. Adjust balance so all parts can be heard and phrase as you would with wind instruments.

Well-organized rehearsals allow the percussion to improve both as a member of a larger ensemble and as an independent unit. The sessions should cover a variety of challenges including difficult areas in band music, percussion ensemble pieces, and technical exercises. The opportunity to practice challenging passages from band pieces is vital; many directors experience frustration as wind players impatiently wait for percussionists to master a difficult rhythm. Solving these problems with the percussion section alone permits the larger ensemble to progress more rapidly. Learning percussion ensemble pieces breeds enthusiasm among students and provides an opportunity to improve technique. Allow some time in each rehearsal for improvisation, which encourages creativity and awareness of tone colors without reading music.

After learning several ensemble works, find as many performance opportunities as possible. Parents rarely get to hear children play in ensembles because performances are limited to contests. Feature percussion ensembles at band concerts or schedule programs dedicated to solo and ensemble literature, including woodwind and brass players. Share the importance of percussion ensembles and educate audiences by demonstrating less familiar percussion instruments.

Two important factors influence staging: the area available and the program. If possible, position an ensemble where all members and their instruments are visible. If room permits, a semi-circle works well because the players can see each other and the director. Otherwise, place mallet instruments in front, flanked by small percussion instruments like woodblocks and triangle. Place higher-pitched drums such as snare drums and bongos behind the mallets, and position larger, more visual instruments like bass drum, timpani, gong, and cymbals behind the high-pitched drums. Also consider the program and experiment with set-ups. Performers with many rhythmically similar passages or important interactions should be close together. This will help young players with rhythmic stability and understanding learn how individual parts fit into a whole.

Although organizing and maintaining an active percussion ensemble requires planning and time, the results make the effort worthwhile. Versatile percussionists with musical sensitivity and reading and technical skills are welcome additions to any band.

Percussion literature for young ensembles is readily available, and these are some recommended works for young players:

Bossa Novacaine by Thomas L. Davis (Barnhouse). For six players, this syncopated Bossa Nova uses two mallet parts, claves, bongos, two timpani, and suspended cymbal.

Chinese Laundry Man by Harold F. Prentice (Southern Music). With parts for two snare drums, tom-tom, cymbals, bass drum, sand paper, woodblock, and gong, six players are ideal for this entertaining and relatively easy novelty piece.

Country Variations by Jared Spears (Barnhouse). Employing six players on bells, xylophone, marimba, three timpani, bass drum, four tom-toms, snare drum, and optional field drum, these variations on a well-known melody may be out of the reach of many young ensembles because of their length (132 measures). Strong players are required for all parts.

Drum Tunes, Vol. 1 by Schinstine and Hoey (Southern). The tunes contain solos, duets, and ensembles in progressive order of difficulty, beginning with easy and ending with more difficult exercises involving syncopation, 16th notes, flams, ¢, and $\frac{6}{8}$ times.

Drum Tunes, Vol. 2 by Schinstine and Hoey (Southern). This book examines march form, auxiliary percussion instruments, flamacues, paradiddles, drags, and $\frac{3}{8}$ and $\frac{6}{8}$ times and is a nice multi-percussion solo.

Encounter by Thomas O'Connor (Barnhouse). For five players on four tom-toms, snare drum, suspended cymbal, woodblock, tambourine, bass drum, triangle, and two timpani, it is an enjoyable work for good second-or third-year ensembles.

Lafayette by Maxine Lefever (Southern). This percussion quintet for two snares, three tom-toms, suspended cymbal, and bass drum is an introduction for young ensembles to $\frac{6}{8}$ time.

Mosaics by Jared Spears (Barnhouse). Spears wrote this percussion sextet for snare drum, four tom-toms, tambourine, woodblock, suspended cymbal, bass drum, triangle, and two timpani.

Percussion Instrument Substitutions

Antique cymbals – orchestra bells with brass mallets

Anvil – small suspended square of heavy metal or steel pipe

Bell tree – glissando across orchestra bells or wind chimes with a triangle beater

Bongos – two snare drums with heads tightened more than usual and played with small sticks

Cabasa – maracas

Celeste – bells played with rubber mallets

Castanets – woodblock

Chimes – orchestra bells in octaves with brass mallets

Congas – tom-toms tuned low and played with timpani mallets

Cowbell – strike bell of cymbal with hard rubber mallet or snare stick

Field drum – snare drum with pitch lowered

Finger cymbals – small triangle

Gong – large suspended cymbal played with yarn mallets near the edge

Hi-hat – crash cymbals

Marimba – xylophone played an octave down from written marimba notes, with yarn mallets

Ratchet – rudimental roll on shell of bass drum

Temple blocks – differently pitched woodblocks

Timbales – two differently pitched snare drums with snares off or two tom-toms

Timpani – bass drum or low tom-toms

Tom-toms – two differently pitched snare drums with snares off or marching tri-toms or quad-toms

Triangle – bell of cymbal with light drumsticks

Vibraphone – orchestra bells played with yarn mallets

Whip – two pieces of thin board hinged together

Woodblock – shell of bass or snare drum

Xylophone – marimba played an octave above written notes using hard rubber mallets

Percussion Ensembles for Young Performers by John Kinyon (Alfred). Parts are for snare drum, bass drum, suspended cymbal, triangle, woodblock, tambourine, and bells. This is an easy collection appropriate for beginners, and coincides with woodwind and brass books in the same series.

Quint Capers by Maxine Lefever (Southern). A percussion quintet for two snares, triangle, suspended cymbal, and bass drum, it is within reach of a first-year ensemble. Syncopated sections need special attention.

Rudimental Rock and Rolls by Duane Thamm (Creative Publications). The quintet for two snares, tenor drum, suspended cymbal, and bass drum requires steady rhythm and mastery of various 16th-note combinations.

Scamper by Jared Spears (Barnhouse). An ensemble piece for five players on four tom-toms, snare drum, bass drum, triangle, suspended cymbal, woodblock, and two timpani, this is similar in scope to O'Connor's *Encounter*.

Suite for Percussion by Acton Ostling (CPP Belwin). Ostling scored the suite for four players, four movements: "March for Membranes" (concert snare, field snare, small woodblock, large woodblock, and temple blocks), "Dance O'Woods" (snare sticks, small woodblock, large woodblock, and temple blocks), "Metallics" (triangle, suspended cymbal, large suspended cymbal, and bells), and "Finale" (each player on three instruments).

Whole-Tone Fantasy by Thomas O'Connor (Barnhouse). This is a six-player ensemble piece for xylophone, vibes, optional bells, snare drum, four tom-toms, triangle, suspended cymbal, and bass drum. □

September, 1991

Percussion on the March

by Marty Province

Training a marching percussion line should begin as early as possible, over the summer or in the dead time between the last spring concert and *Pomp and Circumstance*. During the season each student should play daily warm-up exercises, as should the full group at every rehearsal, even when it seems that the music and drill will never be learned in time for the first game. My drummers rehearse for two hours, twice weekly, and spend twenty minutes of each rehearsal on warm-up exercises. I find they learn the music more quickly when we take time out for the basics.

Repetitive and simple daily exercises will improve muscle control while students concentrate on grip, stick height, and playing spot. Students should practice this pattern daily, fifteen minutes with each hand.

Start slowly (♩=80), increasing speed (♩=200), and repeat with the left hand. Such repetitive patterns will develop muscles while introducing odd meters, perhaps from music on the next program. Dave Brubeck's music is a source of syncopated warm-ups.

Unsquare Dance

Blue Rondo a la Turk

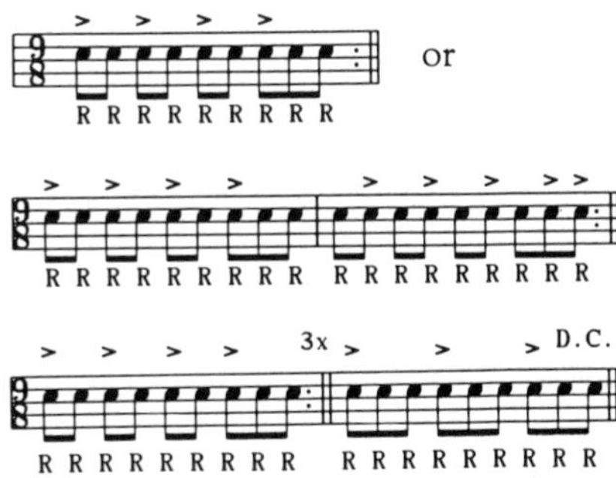

As with the first example, start slowly and gradually speed up for fifteen minutes each hand. Cymbal players can play with sticks on the cymbals or play chunks on the accented notes.

Many drum lines do not begin together or play in unison; they could improve on both problems by using the following exercise, playing one note per measure but on a different beat each time. Students should bring their sticks up together on the half beat before striking the drum, so they think "and-one" or "up-down."

Play the exercise slowly because entering together is difficult in slower tempos. Have students start by standing in a circle facing in, counting aloud to mark time, eventually facing away and counting silently.

After practicing initial attacks, the line should play clean single strokes on the following exercise with every rhythmic pattern used in a marching show. Mallet players can play the same pattern on any individual note or play the suggested scale pattern. A cymbal pattern is included, but it may vary with the number of players in the group.

All drums

repeat in all keys

When students learn this basic exercise, substitute any of the following patterns for the bracketed rhythms.

The easiest way to play accents is with a different type of preparation, bringing the stick up higher. Still, players' stick heights should be uniform, and they should not rush the accents. In example 1 the exercises can be played in unison or with the alternate parts for multi-toms and mallets. Drummers may also practice rim shots on accented beats.

Finally, drum lines should learn to play double strokes or rolls cleanly. The right- and left-hand roll progressions in example 2 cover doubles in varying numbers of strokes, beginning on either hand.

Variations on roll progressions include playing the check pattern only once followed by measures 2, 4, 6, and 8; repeating measures 1-2, 3-4, 5-6, and 7-8; and repeating only measures 2, 4, 6, or 8 until each roll is clean. Bass drum, mallet, and cymbal players are included in example 3 below. Drummers on multi-toms may play the same patterns as the snares or those in the following exercise.

The combinations for further exercises are limitless. Using shifting accents the following permutations are possible.

Doubles instead of accents

Double all unaccented notes

Double note following each accent

Double note before each accent

Example 1

S.D. T.T. Quad. B.D.

T.T. alt.

Quad.

Mall. alt.

R L R L R L R L   R L R L R L R L

etc.

Speed up and Repeat

Repeat in all keys

These warm-ups and exercises are starting points any director, percussionist or not, can use to improve a drum line. Proper grip, stroke technique, stick height, and playing spot should be controlled and checked during the warm-up routine. In addition to improving percussion technique, warm-up exercises can address specific weaknesses. When there is a difficult passage in a show, isolate it and incorporate it into the warm-up. Encourage students to write warm-ups of their own; usually when given the opportunity they will make up fine exercises to help the percussion line progress and mature. □

Example 2
Right Hand
check pattern
3 stroke roll
1
R L R L R L R L R L R L R L R L
2
R L R L R L R L etc.
check pattern
5 stroke roll
3
4
check pattern
7 stroke roll
5
6
check pattern
long roll
7
8
Speed up and Repeat
Left Hand
check pattern
3 stroke roll
1
R L R L R L R L R L R L R L R L
2
R L R L R L R L R L R L R L R L
check pattern
5 stroke roll
3
4
check pattern
7 stroke roll
5
6
check pattern
long roll
7
8
Speed up and Repeat
Example 3
T.T. R L R L R L R L
R L R L R L R L etc.
Quad. R L R L R L R L
R L R L R L R L etc.
B.D. R R R R
R R R R R R R R
Cym.
Mall. R L R L R L R L
R L R L R L R L
Speed up and Repeat
R L R R L R R L R R L R
R L R L R L R L R L R L R L R L
R L R L etc .
Repeat in all keys

1992-1995

Disruptive Percussion Sections

by Kerry Hart

Few have heard of a band program where the percussion section is the most well-behaved section of the ensemble. When band directors talk about discipline, attitude, and responsibility problems in their ensembles, the percussion section is often at the top of the most troublesome list.

The rest of the band seldom has to be told to put their folders away after band rehearsals; no matter how many times drummers are admonished there will inevitably be a percussion folder on a music stand as the class hurries out the door at the bell. After a concert at least one percussion part will be missing when music is collected. The portion of band rooms most often left in disarray is the percussion section. It's the percussion section that delays giving the downbeat for the next number, and often even after taking extra time to get ready we discover that an important piece of percussion equipment is still missing after the band is well into rehearsing the piece. The list could go on to include unnecessary noise during rehearsals, tardiness, unreliability, and a lack of dedication to the ensemble.

After 17 years as a band director, I have run the gamut from analyzing to solving problems with percussion sections. It is common knowledge among band directors that certain personality types are attracted to specific instruments, and I even changed recruiting strategies with beginning bands, placing promising flute and French horn players on percussion. It didn't work. Somewhere along the way all were corrupted and turned into unruly drummers.

I ascertained that percussionists are as intelligent as any other student musician, so there had to be other reasons for the recurrent problems. Gradually I came to view one cause as the director's attitude toward percussionists and drummers as problem children who are vying for attention because they felt neglected. I came up with several things that we can do to minimize discipline problems in the percussion section.

The physical distance between the podium and the percussion section becomes a psychological distance as well. It is easier to feel close to first chair flutists and clarinetists because they are right next to us at every rehearsal, and these students feel the proximity. Percussionists are always in the back of the room, and are the only ones without assigned seating. The physical set-up alone makes the drummers feel removed from the conductor and the rest of the band.

The first challenge is to make drummers feel needed and wanted. Assigned seating is not possible but assigning parts to individual percussionists for every selection is. Parts should be rotated so each student plays all percussion instruments. Assigning parts makes musical sense and gives students a sense of purpose and reduces discipline problems. Another inherent problem is the literature. Percussion parts are usually so different and removed from the other band parts that percussionists feel separated from the band on a musical level. If percussionists are taught to play musically, they understand their role in the band. Because the percussion parts are so different, implement percussion ensembles early in beginning bands and orchestras.

Unlike other band members, percussionists do not own their instruments. Other players come to a rehearsal, assemble instruments, and later clean them. Drummers walk into a rehearsal at the sound of the bell, knowing that some of the equipment is already set up while the balance is in cabinets, but none of it belongs to them. Directors can foster a sense of propriety in percussionists by assigning each student to care for and set up particular items, rotating responsibilities over time. As students learn responsibility for the equipment, so also will their behavior improve.

Because many directors were never percussionists, their knowledge of technique may be limited and few can adequately demonstrate how to blend different colors and sounds on percussion instruments. Students become

acutely aware of such ignorance. Many conductors make the mistake of trying to conceal their deficiencies. One conductor tried to show his expert knowledge by requesting a different sound from the timpani. After trying every available timpani mallet to achieve the director's desired effect the student went back to his original mallets and played louder. "That's it," said the director. "Use these mallets."

Credibility is sometimes lost on the professional level as well, as when a well-known guest conductor rehearsed a major symphony orchestra and was dissatisfied with the cymbal crash. After the percussionist crashed every pair of cymbals with several variations in crash styles, the conductor still was not satisfied. Frustrated and angry, the percussionist brought a pair of trash-can lids into rehearsal the next day. The conductor stopped the orchestra after hearing the crash, looked at the percussionist, and said: "Bravo! That's exactly what I wanted."

Percussionists lose concentration on the music when it contains more rests than any other part, a not uncommon occurrence. The usual symptom of this is disruptive behavior. Correspondingly because percussionists have had time to study their parts but instead used the time being disruptive, directors are less tolerant of a drummer's mistake. If a flute player misses one note in a series, he may receive praise for improving. If a triangle player misses a note after 52 measures of rest, the director may become upset while the percussionist silently seethes at the double standard for error. Certainly the difficulty in correctly playing the note is different, but the error stemmed from not concentrating, which in turn may be attributable to the director. Every conductor has repeatedly rehearsed a section, stopping just before the percussion entrance while the percussionists patiently counted through the material each time without ever playing. When the director finally continues on, this is the time the counting stops and the entrance is missed, and a blow-up results. Conductors can anticipate this result by telling percussion (and other) players to relax until the part is worked out. The odds are that when the percussionists join the group again, they will concentrate well.

The physical distance between the podium and the percussion section is unavoidable but directors can decrease the psychological distance by working with the percussion section individually and as a group outside of rehearsals. There are frequent woodwind and brass sectionals but usually few for percussionists. When drummers receive attention, they will reciprocate in rehearsals. The solution to percussion section problems stems from understanding what causes students to misbehave. By using common sense to determine this cause, a director will earn their respect and enhance their sense of dedication and responsibility. □

June, 1992

Teaching Snare Techniques

by Barry Bridwell

Teaching snare drum can be frustrating for many band directors because the playing techniques are so different from those of wind instruments, and some are overlooked or not fully developed in method books.

Right Hand Lead System

A good method for teaching beginners is using the right hand lead system, which teaches counting, sight-reading, steady tempos, and playing with a consistent sound. This concept is not new, but few band directors know about it because most modern band methods omit it.

In this system the right hand plays the strong beats and the left hand the weak beats. Using the same sticking for specific rhythms produces a consistent sound. With quarter-notes the right hand plays beats 1 and 3, and the left hand 2 and 4.

With 8th-note divisions, the right hand plays on the beat, and the left hand plays off the beat.

R L R L R L R L R L L R R L
R R L R L R L L R L

To demonstrate 16th-note rhythms use the following:

1 1 e + a 2 (e + a)
R L R L R

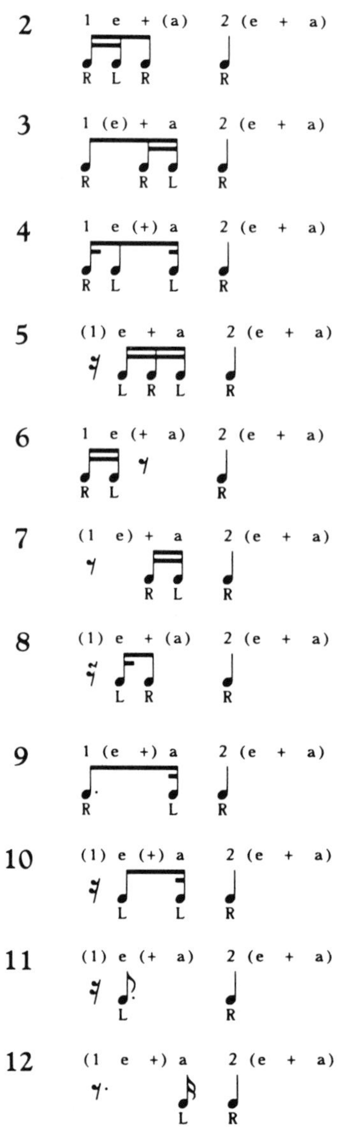

Teach each of the 12 simple rhythms separately then in succession. Later vary the order so students read rather than memorize rhythms. Encourage students to pat their right foot on all downbeats and say counting syllables out loud while playing. Once familiar with these 12 rhythms, students can recognize them within longer passages.

1 e(+)a 2 e + a 3(e)+ a 4 e +(a)
R L L R L R L R R L R L R
#4 #1 #3 #2

Follow this approach until students can analyze complex rhythms, and encourage them to write and analyze their own patterns. After using this method for a while students will begin to understand how rhythm works.

Flams

Flams are difficult for young drummers to understand because they have two parts, a grace-note stroke and a regular stroke, which are written as different-sized notes. The two strokes do not occur simultaneously, but students should perceive them as one unit.

To explain the flam sound, have students say the word flam; the whispery f is the grace-note and the emphatic LAM is the main note. Playing the notes too far apart produces fa-LAM with each note heard separately. Playing both at the same time sounds like fAM, often called a flat flam because striking the drum in two places at once prevents the head from vibrating freely.

The key to flams is controlling the stroke height. Because the two notes should be different volumes, players hold the sticks at different heights.

Beginners should exaggerate this by holding the grace-note stick one inch above the head, and the other stick 10-12 inches above. Both sticks move downward simultaneously, with the stick closest to the head hitting first at a softer volume. Do not lift the grace-note stick before beginning the downward motion; this results in a flat or inverted flam where the grace-note falls after the main note and sounds like LAMf.

Alternating flams is a difficult skill that many beginning band books introduce too early. Executed properly, a ten-inch rebound follows the one-inch grace-note, and a one-inch rebound the ten-inch stroke. Rebound height is normally less than stroke height, so this feels unnatural.

Students should practice right- and left-hand flams separately to gain rebound control. Flams are right- or left-handed depending on which hand plays the main note.

LR LR LR LR

Continue with left-hand flams.

RL RL RL RL

Once students master both flams, begin the challenge of alternating them.

LR LR LR LR | RL RL RL RL

LR LR LR | RL RL RL

LR LR RL RL

LR RL LR RL

Practice these exercises slowly, allowing time to change stick positions between right- and left-hand flams; stress the importance of proper stick heights and simultaneous downward motion.

Developing Speed

Nothing impresses young players as much as speed; they want to emulate players with the fastest fingers and hands. Runners build up speed through windsprints, focusing on short distances and channelling energy into short bursts. The same approach works with drumming.

For fast, single-strokes develop speed in each hand separately, then combine them.

RRRRRR | LLLLLL

RR R RR R | LL L LL L

RR R LL L

RLRL R RLRL R | LRLR L LRLR L

RLRL R RLRL R | LRLR L LRLR L

RLRL R LRLR L

Play the first note of each group with a wrist motion, and subsequent notes with finger control. Use a metronome and gradually increase the tempo. When students gain finger control, expand the exercise to more complicated patterns.

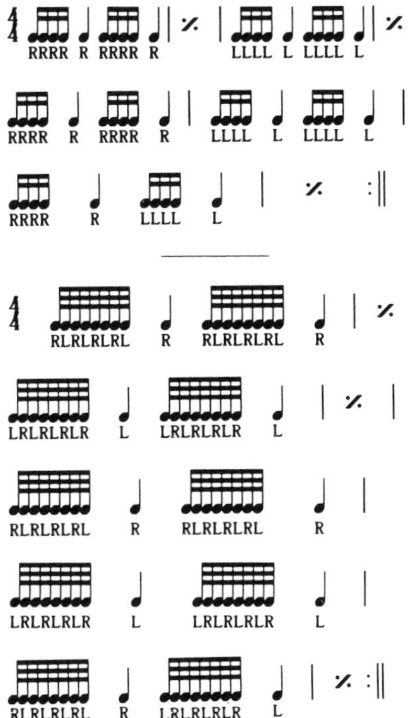

Further expansion is possible, but doing so would develop endurance rather than speed.

Concentrate on small rhythmic units, so muscles work in short bursts with time between to relax and recover. A metronome is a valuable tool in developing speed, because it measures consistency and progress. By teaching students these concepts in a logical sequence, they will steadily improve. □

Cymbal Seminar

by Mitchell Peters and Dave Black

Good cymbal technique adds enormous power, dynamic contrast, and color to an ensemble, but too often percussionists focus on the big three – snare drum, mallets, and timpani – and neglect cymbals and other accessory instruments.

The basic techniques of cymbal playing are important, but in the long run what counts is that your cymbal playing sounds good. Never be afraid to experiment or adjust technique to find a more comfortable and effective way to play. Beginning students should learn the fundamental cymbal techniques at all dynamic levels using one pair of cymbals instead of changing from a small pair for soft dynamics to a larger pair for louder dynamics. A basic pair is eighteen-inch cymbals of medium weight. Younger players should use a smaller size for easy handling.

In concert cymbal playing the foundation of it all is having a good solo cymbal crash. Nothing accentuates an exciting passage as well as a brilliantly executed cymbal crash. What constitutes a good cymbal sound is subjective, but good-quality cymbals are an excellent starting point. The goal is to get each cymbal to vibrate fully.

The concept behind getting a good crash is minimizing the initial contact (impact) sound and focusing on a full and resonant tone after the contact. Think more in terms of playing legato than of playing percussively.

There are two widely used basic crashes, each named for the motion of the strong hand. Some performers use an upward motion with the strong hand, and others prefer a downward motion. Whichever motion a player uses the weak hand moves in the opposite direction. The right hand will be referred to here as the strong hand.

Relaxation is the key to a good sound, and this starts with the grip. Do not put hands through the loop of the straps, but grasp the strap close to the bell of the cymbal using the top of the first joint of the index finger and the flat fleshy part of the thumb (see illustrations). By gripping the straps firmly and not too close to the bell of the cymbal, the cymbals will ring freely. Use the thumb lightly on the bell to guide and control the cymbal during fast passages, but the thumb should not be on the bell when the cymbals are crashed for maximum resonance.

Leather or rawhide straps are the best. The cymbal knots are important to prevent the thongs of the strap from coming undone and slipping through the hole of the cymbal. If the thongs are long enough, tie them again directly on top of the first knot

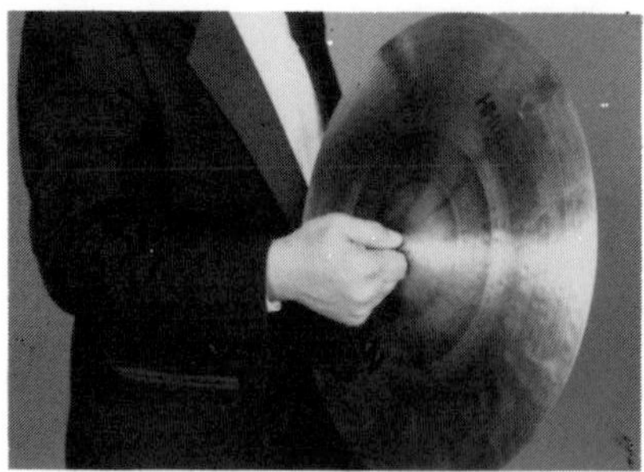

for added security. The diagram illustrates the standard method for tying the cymbal knot; check the knots frequently because they occasionally become lose.

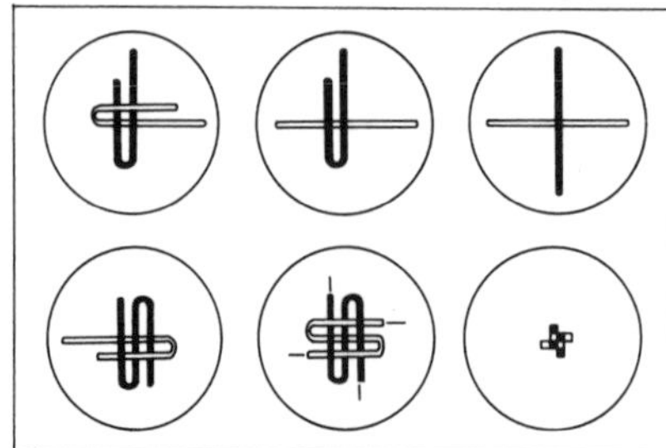

Cymbal pads are not recommended but if used they should be small and not inhibit vibration.

For young or beginning players the basic one-hand crash with upward motion is a good starting point. One-hand means only one hand is in motion until the cymbals meet, after which both are in motion. This enables beginning cymbal players to focus on the motion of the strong hand and on the angle at which the cymbals come into contact. The result is a clean, resonant sound. When this motion is comfortable, add the preparatory motion of the other hand.

Begin by placing the cymbals together in the proper position. This position will serve as a memory lock when the cymbals actually meet.
Keep the top of the cymbals just below eye level to avoid blocking the music and the conductor. Tilt the cymbals slightly to the left with the right cymbal about a half to one inch lower than the left cymbal. It is important that the cymbals do not meet concentrically or an air pocket will

form and produce a dead or flat-sounding crash.

Drop the right cymbal slightly below and away from the left. With the left cymbal stationary, strike the right cymbal against it in a glancing blow, moving inward and upward at the same time. The right cymbal should strike the left cymbal at an angle with the top of the cymbals meeting first, then follow through with the rest of the cymbal. The effect is similar to a flam.

The angle of the cymbal and spacing of the flam will vary depending on the volume of the crash. The flam should always be subtle (closed) and not heard as two separate attacks.

The angle between the cymbals will be wider for loud crashes and will decrease as the volume gets softer. For soft crashes the cymbals will be almost parallel to each other. The distance between the cymbals also varies with the volume. For soft crashes the distance between the plates will be small, and become greater as the volume of the crashes increases.

The follow-through is important, and when the cymbals make contact the player should focus on separating the cymbals by continuing the upward motion of the right hand and moving the left hand downward bringing the cymbals to approximately shoulder height and spreading them so the overtones ring freely. Spreading the cymbals will produce a brighter sound, while keeping them together will result in a darker sound.

All motions from the start of the crash through the strike and the follow-through should be relaxed and continuous. With repeated cymbal strokes, the player cannot place the cymbals together each time.

After developing control of the right hand, players can enhance the sound of the crash by adding the preparatory motion of the left hand. Start with the cymbals together in the contact position and drop the right hand and raise the left hand up slightly; move the cymbals in opposite directions, the right hand up and the left hand down. Make contact with the cymbals in the same manner as with the one-handed crash. For higher-volume crashes, the added motion of the left hand produces a bigger sound.

Because cymbals ring a while following a crash, players will often dampen the sound by bringing the edges against their chest.

Dampening

Buttons and objects in the player's pockets may create extraneous sounds when the cymbals come in contact with them. In a series of crashes the cymbals are usually not dampened between notes. These are the technical foundations of cymbal playing, and with practice and experimentation players will adjust to ways that are the most comfortable and produce the desired sounds. □

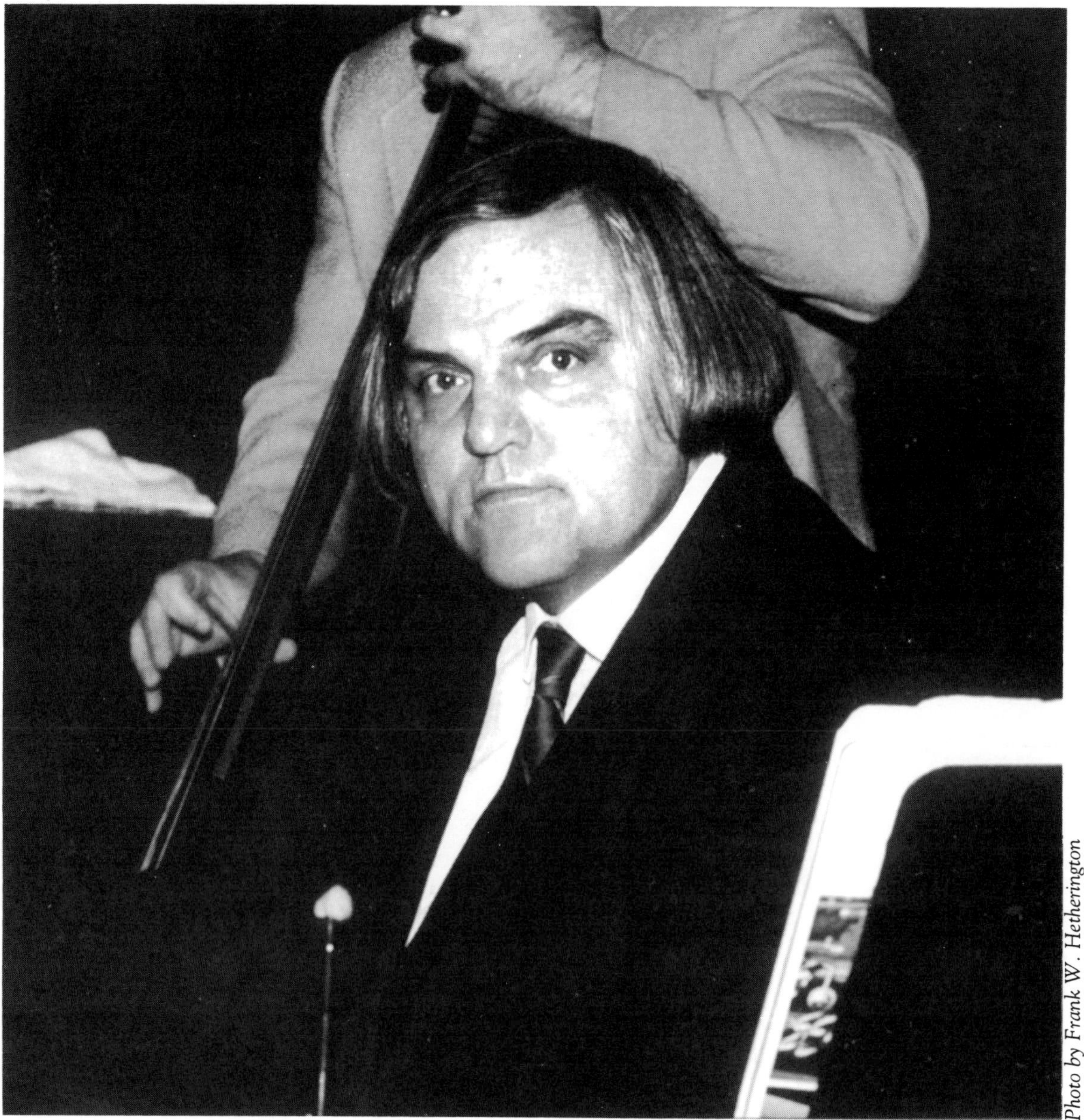

Photo by Frank W. Hetherington

Drumming With Distinction

Von Ohlen Keeps Rollin'

by Heather Pettit

It is difficult to find a jazz musician as content with his life as John Von Ohlen. He has transformed his experiences in music into what he wanted – almost without fail. From his student days with a local big band to his final tours with Stan Kenton, Von Ohlen has maintained his ideal of playing only acoustic jazz without becoming a relic when the popularity of the road bands ended. He used that juncture to pursue a parallel career as a member of the jazz faculty at the University of Cincinnati, College-Conservatory of Music. This in turn opened up musical horizons in Cincinnati where he quickly found himself fronting the big band at the Blue Wisp jazz club, performing with a newly formed faculty jazz ensemble, and gathering some local musicians into a combo that plays weekly at a popular restaurant. He frequently gives clinics and plays short tours with big bands; most recently with Mel Torme in Japan. With strong beliefs John Von Ohlen has successfully held back the tide of change.

What training prepared you for a career as a big band drummer?

From my earliest musical experiences I played in a big band. Growing up in Indianapolis, I took trombone lessons from Bob Phillips, whose students played in a big band once or twice a week. Though I started on trombone and piano, I wanted to play drums and at 17 a friend gave me his new Gretsch drumset when he joined the Navy; I spent six months practicing.

After a year at North Texas State University, I went on the road with Ralph Marterie, who helped me learn the fine points of dance band drumming, which is a little different than playing flat out in a jazz band. To keep people's feet moving when they start dancing, I immediately switch to a two-beat or two-step. Dance music is still based on a two-beat feeling, even rock and roll.

When drafted I played in an Army group that performed for servicemen, then returned to playing shows around Indianapolis. These activities don't look like much on a resume, but I learned from the gigs and played with all the great singers on the circuit. I didn't want to play behind singers because I was into bebop and straight-ahead jazz, but I learned the ins and outs of making them sound good.

In 1966 my career as a big band drummer started to take off, first with Billy Maxted's Manhattan Jazz Band and in 1967 with Woody Herman. I really cut my teeth in Woody's band because it was loaded with fine musicians, but I had another motive for staying with him. My goal was to break into the studio scene in Hollywood or New York, and working in Woody's band for a couple of years proved that I had what it took to play there. However, the studio scene rapidly changed from swing to rock during that period, so I ended up back in Indianapolis nursing my wounds over an interrupted career. After about a year a friend finally signed me on with Stan Kenton.

Did the Kenton band have as much fun as they seemed to?

When Stan came to town, it was an event. I had a ball with him because he was such a loose leader; you could just about do anything. He filled me with all the confidence I could ever want. Stan only told me a few things that he didn't like. One was that he could not stand it when a drummer hit a cymbal with a brush but I never understood this until I started teaching and fronting bands. The other thing was that I hit the bass drum too hard; he told me the band wasn't a drum and bugle corps.

Stan was the perfect leader. I didn't like some of the things he was into, but he believed in them. Sometimes when the band really started swinging, he would try to get me to do something to thwart it, such as superimposing another time signature over the band to break it up. I don't think he liked it much when I just sat back there and let it swing; but my policy is, if it's swinging, let it alone.

Many big band leaders supported music education through clinics and master classes. Now that you are teaching and playing, how do you view jazz education?

I had misgivings about the workshops given by Kenton's younger band members. There is an old Oriental saying that you shouldn't teach until you are 50, and it may be correct. Young players think they know everything. They may play great, but teaching is another ballgame. Many people probably got erroneous information through those clinics.

Now that I am older, I feel comfortable with a university teaching position, but the University of Cincinnati is different because it has a jazz faculty member on each instrument in order to give students lessons with the legit players and jazz players as well. It is surprising how many schools with jazz programs do not even have a jazz drum instructor.

After four years in high school and four years in college learning to play jazz, what happens to students after graduation?

That's a hard question to answer. Everything seems to have its time, and perhaps the time of the road bands is past. In the 1890s every town had a concert and marching band, but you rarely hear about such things today. Those bands are in schools now and have gone from being oom-pah-pah groups to great concert bands. When I was on the road, that was how the young players got their education. Most of the great players didn't go to college, but went directly on the road with a band. Today, big band jazz is in the schools. There are more big bands now than ever before, and even among those that are not professional, many play at that level. Having big bands in the schools is healthy because in that atmosphere groups can take chances and try out experimental music. They are not dependent on making money and can pull an unusual piece out of the library, learn it, and play it for an appreciative audience.

The big question, though, is what all these players will do. This question reminds me of a dilemma from my high school days: I was the drum major in the marching band and loved it, but was heartsick after realizing there was nowhere for me to apply this skill after graduation. This is an extreme example of what happens to young jazz musicians. Though the state of affairs changes all the time big bands will not return to the popularity of the 1930s and 1940s, yet there are many towns with committed players and great groups. The vast numbers of players graduating from schools today should make it surprisingly easy to organize a high quality, marketable band. New York has quite a few young players making records and doing well. The same can be said about Chicago, where there are eight or nine bands, but it is certainly different from the days when there was a definite field out there you could prepare to enter. Unfortunately, for musicians hungry to play, school is often the best place today.

What qualities do you listen for when auditioning students?

I have students play in different styles, such as an old Kansas City shuffle and a simple swing beat, but the most important skill is keeping time. What I want to hear is very basic; I'm not impressed by a lot of speed. It's fun to watch a fast drummer but that's not my criterion. If they can keep time on a simple, basic beat, they can master a more difficult one. A good swing feel is difficult to teach; it is something you are born with. Most big bands in schools play in swing and rock styles, but there are few drummers who really swing, and the bottom line in big band playing is for the drummer to swing.

The syncopation of jazz music is different than any other style. Triplets are the base of a swing feel rather than straight eighth notes. Rock or funk beats are generally straight eighths,

whereas a swing beat is broken up into triplets.

By coming off those triplets you enter an entirely different world of rhythm from rock style. In the 1950s when I was growing up, rock and roll hadn't really hit it big yet. There was Bill Haley's and a few other groups, but most players came from old blues bands and still used a swing or shuffle beat. Some of the drummers from that time had not been very successful playing swing, but when the eighth-note rock feeling hit, those same drummers sounded pretty good. I think the eighth-note beat is easier to comprehend and play because it's so straight and dictatorial; it's either black or white. The triplet pulse is more subtle and loose and a lot of drummers don't understand that.

Another difference between jazz and rock drumming is shading. A rock drummer produces the same amount of volume with each of his limbs; the volume in the bass drum is the same as in the right or left hand. In jazz the bass drum is often soft, almost inaudible, whereas the hands can be strong. Beyond that, there are different volumes in each hand, so it's hard to teach shading to someone who has played nothing but rock. The shading is what makes jazz work, whereas rock drums are in your face all the time.

Through early intervention teachers can correct some of the problems drummers encounter. Everybody knows what drums are supposed to sound like, but sitting down and producing the right effect is something else. I encourage band directors to attend my clinics. In fact, I find this preferable because the real problem in schools, high schools especially, is that most band directors were schooled in classical music but took over a program that included a jazz band. They're good with horn players and teach them all the right things, but don't know what to tell the drummer. All they know is when it doesn't sound right or is too loud. Most directors who do not play drums are uncomfortable and unsure of how to instruct jazz drummers. Students want to learn how to fix a problem to improve the sound of the group, but the same director who is confident with the horns is not capable of helping the drummer. My broad experience lets me speak from the perspective of a drummer, horn player, and conductor, so I can fix problems quickly by teaching directors little tricks to tell the drummer.

What equipment changes should drummers be aware of when switching from combo to big band to rock drumming?

In the past you didn't need any different equipment, but today the different kinds of music necessitate changes. Equipment is often based on whether the group is electric or acoustic rather than its size. When players cross over to an electric band the basic set up changes. This doesn't mean another drum set, but different heads or cymbals to cut through the electronics. In acoustic drumming cymbals are the most important part of the set and currently are made to play too loudly. The cymbal companies seem to make cymbals that cut, and that is what acoustic groups should avoid. Cymbals should blend and melt into the horns. Band directors often accuse drummers of playing cymbals too loudly, but it's not really their fault. What are they supposed to do, sit back there and pull punches? You need to be able to touch the cymbal with a nice relaxed stroke, but with today's cymbals, it is difficult to keep the sound from being too loud. If I knew of anyone making cymbals that do not cut, I would buy them right now.

It is possible to work a combo and a big band with the same equipment, though I tune the drums a little differently. In a big band I tune them very low, like dark cymbals, because I tend to hit them hard. By making them sound dark, I can go ahead and hit them hard and it doesn't get in the way. This works for me, but a light drummer might want a little brighter equipment that penetrates more.

I don't see any reason to use much extra equipment. A couple of extra drums or cymbals beyond the basic set is all that is needed. It was a fad in the 1950s to use two bass drums, but few players used them effectively. Dave Black, Duke Ellington's drummer, was the only player I ever admired who used two basses, the second one serving as a tom-tom. He even made up fills that incorporated it but rock drummers just play straight beats as fast as they can. It is also important to remember that if both your feet are tied up playing bass drum, you are left with nothing to cover the hi-hat. Hi-hat is not integral to rock drumming but it plays a big part in jazz.

A side consideration about more equipment is that it often is impractical to lug another piece around. Young players look with admiration at big sets, but I remind them that most of the players using this multitude of equipment have roadies to help them set it up, tear it down, and move it. I always hated moving equipment, so this is a big factor to me. You have to be at the gig an hour early and stay an hour after everyone else has gone, all for the same money.

What are the primary things you listen for in a group?

In a combo the players have much more freedom, especially the drummer. That's the idea. True improvisational jazz usually comes from small groups. It's set up that way; you just play. The drummer's function in a small group is still to keep time but also to augment the soloist. If the soloist is strong, play strongly and support him; when he backs off, accompany and interact. In addition to simply keeping time, the group should swing. A lot of drummers interact well but they don't swing. Keep in mind Duke Ellington's famous expression, "It don't mean a thing if it ain't got that swing." In small groups it is important to be flexible and keep your ears wide open for everything going on.

In a big band there is less freedom, and the drummer's specific role is probably to be the ensemble's best musician because controlling the group is his responsibility. It took me a long time to understand that. Players can gain this control in one of two ways. The first is the Buddy Rich style of "follow me or else." It was effective for Buddy because he used the band as accompaniment to his playing. When I began playing with bands I tried adopting this approach, dominating them and forcing them to come with me, maybe against their musical will. On the opposite side, there is someone like Mel Lewis. He and Buddy were good friends but quite different in controlling their bands. Mel played softly but had complete control; he just held the band in his hands loosely. That's the way I operate now. It is a more subtle form of control that takes more experience to develop.

The drummer is also responsible for anticipating and coloring everything the band does. With 15 people creating 15 ideas, the drummer should take charge. Take dynamics, for example. When the band starts a decrescendo out of a loud passage, the drummer should already be soft before it happens. If the band has played softly and wants to get some excitement going, the drummer has to start that excitement before the band comes in. Young drummers should become familiar with the sounds they can make and how to use them to complement the horn parts. I was lucky because I intuitively had the drums organized mentally and knew what sound best supported a certain chord or sound.

If the trombones are punching a low bark, I wouldn't hit a rim shot. It would be more appropriate on the bass drum, and certain chords require different cymbal sounds. Drummers can color the whole band and control it in every way. Bands have two leaders: the leader and the drummer, though the lead trumpet shapes the phrasing.

How do you work on making the rhythm section a cohesive unit?

Dizzy Gillespie claimed that the bass player was the key to the band, not the drummer, and if the one you want is not available, don't even start the band. I completely agree with Dizzy; because without a good bass player, the drummer is dead. The only way to get a feel is through him. The drummer and the bass player are like a married couple. I always told one of my favorite bass players, Lynn Seaton, that if he were a woman I'd marry him; we fit like a glove. I have had good luck with most of the bass players in Cincinnati, on the road with Woody Herman that was not the case. I just could not play with his bass player. He was a wonderful guy and a fine player, but we just didn't fit. The bass player is the pulse of the band, and the drummer needs this to set up the right groove.

How important is playing by ear and with records?

Playing with records is the second best way to learn; the best is on a band stand, on the firing line. Play with records that feel good to you and keep playing them to instill good time. Learning to play in good time becomes second nature only through practice and repetition. Playing with records is fun and makes good sense for any musician. On the trombone I played the section parts and pretended that I was part of the group.

Taping your performances for future study is another recommendation. By listening to the tape it is easy to find out if your time wasn't making it and to take steps to fix it. In drumming there are some basic skills that have to be there before a performer can reach the level of art. Taping gives you a chance to review basic skills critically and to practice changes until you are satisfied.

I am disputing a belief held by many drummers, but I do not feel that playing with a metronome is a good method. I just do not see the value of having student drummers sit in a practice room with one little tick-tock going, so when they arrive at a big band rehearsal where there are 15 different tick-tocks competing, they don't know what to do. Playing with records is a far superior way to practice.

How do you use drumset parts?

Woody Herman often told me to get my nose out of the book; drum parts are guides to insanity. They are not very useful because composers do not know what to write. With a straight-ahead big band chart, I like to have the lead trumpet or trombone part; it helps that I used to play trombone. With one of these parts I can see the shape of the line that the static bunch of notes on the drum part don't indicate. If the trumpet section plays a string of eighth notes that starts out low, goes high in the middle, and back down low, you'll see that and know how to shape it.

Through repetition and study I work out what to do and rarely vary how I play a chart. I hate to say that because it doesn't sound spontaneous, but it is similar to an actor performing the same part every night for three years. It's always the same part, but with good material, something with depth, a performer can dive into it deeper. Good drummers may sound as though they are improvising, but in big band drumming, the parts, including the fills, are often carefully worked out. This can cause problems when I am a guest with another group. I prefer not to do charts I know well, like those long, epic Kenton charts, because I played those charts for so long and have them all worked out to fit Stan's group. Invariably I do the same things, no matter what the band does. It's like being programmed to do it that way. Sometimes it is better for me to sightread a new piece instead of one I know well. Leaders don't understand this and want to call attention to my past experience by playing something made famous by another group. More often than not, the result is disastrous.

Do you feel there are any particular strengths or weaknesses in young drummers today?

I don't think today's drummers are better, just different. Every generation has great players. There are certain aspects older players had that I almost never hear in young drummers, but the older ones came out of a different day. They played with a space and simplicity that might not be necessary, but I would sure like to hear them more. On the other hand, young drummers are able to cross-over into different styles. Older players could never have done that; they just played one way. Drummers today are interested in playing everything.

One particular problem that young drummers have is playing with little variation in volume, something brought on by amplification, especially of the bass. Before bass players plugged in, they were seldom too loud and bands could easily get soft and play naturally. When the bass is too loud and pushing all the time, the drummer tends to crank the volume up too much. By unhooking the bass and playing acoustically, bands can return to softer, more natural playing.

I made the choice to stay with acoustic music. Even if there was no market for it, it is what I love to do. There will always be drummers who want to play many different kinds of music, including electronic, computer drums, everything. I'm behind them all the way because there is nothing wrong if you love what you are doing; I just don't want to do it. Quincy Jones once said he was afraid of purists. If that makes him happy, fine, but I like being a purist. That makes me happy. □

Hampton Virtually Invented the Vibes

Reflections of Lionel Hampton

by Bob Laber

Benny Goodman had just achieved prominence in 1936 when he discovered Lionel Hampton in Culver City, California. Hampton had led a band and played the drums and vibraphone. This was a new instrument, sometimes called a vibraharp. Goodman promptly invited Hampton to record "Moonglow" and "Dinah" with the Goodman trio. This August 19, 1936 recording was the first for the Benny Goodman Quartet and Hampton joined the Goodman band in New York that November. With this Lionel Hampton was catapulted to international fame.

Although he didn't invent the vibraphone, Hampton effectively did so by introducing the instrument to the world six years before meeting Goodman. By 1930 Hampton had achieved some recognition as a drummer with the Les Hite band in Los Angeles. He was billed as the world's fastest drummer. Louis Armstrong heard the young Lionel and invited him to a recording session at the N.B.C. studios in Los Angeles. During that session the two men discovered a vibraphone in the studio, and Armstrong asked Hampton to play something. As a boy Lionel had developed a formidable mallet technique on xylophone. Hampton approached the vibraphone and tried a slow introduction to "Memories of You," a new Eubie Blake ballad, lightly outlining chords and figures behind Armstrong's solo. After that day, the vibes would be associated with jazz, and both were inexorably linked with Lionel Hampton.

Gary Burton observed recently that, "Every new instrument has a trial period. It was Hampton who really established the vibraphone. Even today, people will come up to me after a concert and compare my playing in some way to Lionel's. I know they're paying me the ultimate compliment. Non-musicians will sometimes ask what instrument I play. When I tell them the vibes, they don't always know what I mean so I add, 'like Lionel Hampton,' and they understand." Burton also noted that, "Jazz history has associated Hampton primarily with the Goodman days when a whole genre of music was popularized. That's a disservice to Hampton. He really broke through that. His real role was to become a star, and since then he's even broken through his jazz star identity to become a cultural icon."

Lionel Hampton was an innovative, original improvisational artist playing an unusual instrument when he joined Goodman. His 1989 autobiography, *Hamp*, states, "By the time I joined Benny, I had developed my style, and it really hasn't changed much since. With my background as a drummer, it made sense for me to drum on the vibraharp. Something I did that was unique was to make use of silences – I used long rests between phrases, and that made for some high drama." The book notes that during the Goodman years, Hampton learned augmented 5ths and minor 9ths.

During Hampton's years with Goodman, 1937-1940, he could call R.C.A. and set up a session whenever he had something to record, and he asked the best and most influential musicians of the day to take part in these sessions. He held 23 impromptu sessions, many of which are available on *Lionel Hampton: Hot Mallets, Vol. 1* (Bluebird 6458-2RB). The most historically important of these recordings, "Hot Mallets," took place in September 1939. The session players included Benny Carter on alto sax; Coleman Hawkins, Chu Berry, and Ben Webster on tenors; Clyde Hart on piano; Charlie Christian on guitar; Milt Hinton on bass; Cozy Cole on drums; and Dizzy Gillespie on trumpet.

Hampton recalls that Dizzy Gillespie, a relative newcomer, was included in this all-star session. "I had played with this young trumpet player and thought that he ought to be recorded, so I set up a session with R.C.A. and brought him down. Some say that recording was the first bebop record."

By the 1950s Hampton filled his vibraphone solos with weaving whole tone scale fragments, intricate interval sequences, carefully perfected rhythmic devices, and bebop-inspired riffs and melodic lines. In talking about these developments in his style, Hampton offered only a modest explanation. "I always just played what I felt. When I listen to recordings, I'm surprised to hear things I didn't even know I was doing at the time. See, I have a wonderful imagination, and God gave me the talent to just make my hands do it. I was listening to a recording just the other day called *Lionel Hampton Live in Vienna Vol. 1*. It was recorded in 1954. I'm surprised by a lot of the stuff that's on there."

In 1953 Hampton first took his band on extensive European tours, and he was one of the first American band leaders to do so. In his autobiogra-

Hampton, Phil Moore, Louis Armstrong, and Danny Kaye, 1948

The Louis Armstrong Orchestra in 1930

phy Hampton explained that "...after [World War II], most popular jazz in the U.S. was small combo jazz. Over in Europe, there was a big outcry for American big bands."

For the first tour he assembled a powerhouse group of exciting young players. The trumpet section included Clifford Brown, Art Farmer, high-note specialist Walter Williams, and a recent Berklee graduate, Quincy Jones. Others were Jimmy Cleveland, trombone; Gigi Gryce, alto sax; Alan Dawson and Curley Hammer on drums; bassist Monk Montgomery; pianist George Wallington; and Billy Mackel on guitar. Quincy Jones also arranged music for the band. Although the band made no studio recordings, a newly issued C.D. captures a performance in Sweden (*Oh, Rock*, Natasha Imports, NI 4010).

While listening to a slow vibraphone solo on the *Live in Vienna* C.D. Hampton sat with his eyes closed for several choruses, then raised his left index finger and commented: "Here I'm mixing augmented chords and diminished chords. I wouldn't think about doing that. It was just what I felt I wanted to play there." As the recording continued Hampton gave the names of players and chuckled over musical quotations in solos. Hampton's solo work on the *Live in Vienna* recording is mesmerizing, and the band is tight, swinging, and powerful.

Hampton's early recordings, particularly with Goodman, established his jazz credentials and a name that attracted audiences. These were his obvious stock and trade when he left Goodman in the fall of 1940 to organize a band of his own. His ability to spot young talent and his flair for showmanship produced the first of a long line of wailing young bands that introduced exciting new players. Some of the graduates of Hampton bands are alto saxophonist Marshall Royal; tenors Hershal Evans and Illinois Jacquet; baritone saxophonist Charlie Fowlkes; trumpeters Snooky Young, Joe Newman, Joe Wilder, and Clark Terry; trombonists Benny Powell and Al Grey; and singer Joe Williams. All started with Hampton and moved on to Count Basie. Other future stars in the Hampton bands were alto saxophonist Earl Bostic; tenors Dexter Gordon, Arnett Cobb, and Johnny Griffin; trumpeters Cat Anderson, Ernie Royle, and Jimmy Nottingham; and singers Dinah Washington, Betty Carter, and Aretha Franklin.

Listening with Hampton one afternoon to the Shearing-sound treatment of "September In the Rain" on the *Live in Vienna* recording reminded me of some of the innovators who worked with Hampton. In the 1940s pianist and arranger Milt Buckner developed the block-chord style of playing that was adopted by George Shearing's popular quintets of the late 1940s and 50s. This style can be heard on the April 2, 1947 recording of "How High The Moon," available today on an excellent reissued collection, *The Best of Lionel Hampton*, of his Decca recordings between 1942 and 1950. This album (now on M.C.A. 2-4075) includes the "Mingus Fingers," by the innovative young bass player, Charlie Mingus. The same album has a September 1946 cut of "Cobb's Idea," which displays another of Hampton's influential tenor soloists of the 1940s, Arnett Cobb. There's a May 1945 recording of "Blow Top Blues" with one of Hampton's most important vocal discoveries, Dinah Washington, and two 1950 recordings featuring another distinctive, though less well-known Hampton singer, Jimmie Scott. He is heard on several ballads in this collection, backed by a rhythm section that by 1950 included a Hammond organ.

Hampton was the first to use the electronic organ and the electric bass in a big band. According to legend, bassist Monk Montgomery found an electric bass guitar in Hampton's instrument inventory, and Hampton suggested using it with the band. Hampton confirmed that this story was accurate. "Yes," he said, "I go by the bass line when I solo, and I wanted it louder so I could hear it better."

For his biggest hit, "Flying Home," Hampton along with John Hammond persuaded jazz's first important electric guitarist, Charlie Christian, to join the legendary Benny Goodman Sextet. The Sextet recorded "Rose Room" in 1939 with "Flying Home" on the flipside. This jazz classic became Hampton's signature song for the next 50 years. When the Hampton band recorded it on May 26, 1942, it was the group's first hit and made a star of tenor man Illinois Jacquet. The Jacquet approach to tenor solos was copied by rhythm and blues groups of the late 1940s and by rock groups of the 1950s.

It was part of the Hampton style for him to twirl drum sticks or jump up and down to excite a crowd. Gunther Schuller observed in his book, *The Swing Era,* that Hampton "is like Armstrong, one of the old school, where the entertainer role is always prominent, perhaps even primary."

Even in the early 1930s in California, Hampton understood the power of showmanship. When he left Goodman to form a band, Hampton became one of the most demonstrative performers of the swing era, dancing on tom-toms or parading around the room twirling drumsticks. In the all-out finale for his shows the brass section formed a long line while the tenors wailed choruses on "Flying Home." These antics rarely missed with audiences, but alienated many jazz fans and critics.

Proof that Hampton understood audiences is found on his apartment walls, which hold personal notes and official citations from four U.S. presidents plus honorary degrees from a half-dozen universities. Besides his music there is always a ready smile and an eagerness that even today belie his 86 years. When asked why the big bands of the 1940s disappeared, Hampton paused and commented, ". . . because the big boys [Goodman, Shaw, Miller, and the Dorseys] began dropping off the scene; the other bands didn't really know how to operate. They couldn't read a crowd. Many couldn't present themselves well and put on a good show or they didn't have good discipline and rules of operation. That's why the big bands lost their audience."

Lionel Hampton still packs concert halls around the world and can bring an audience to its feet in appreciation of his particular brand of jazz: a concoction of craft and bombast; naiveté and sophistication, humor and spirituality. These disparate elements have thrived in Hampton's music over the years because Hampton is an original. He not only forged an identity playing an unusual musical instrument, but actually invented a personal style of presenting musically interesting and exciting concerts. Few artists can make that claim. □

Lionel Hampton and Dizzy Gillespie. (Photos courtesy of Lionel Hampton Jazz Festival and Virginia Wicks)

Challenging Percussionists

by Bruce Dalby

New directors are frequently unprepared to teach percussion instruments. Every director knows that many problems associated with percussion sections stem from unchallenging parts, but it is not possible to give a demanding snare part to every player on every piece; someone has to play bass drum and triangle. A harried director often relies on more talented students to cover difficult parts and relegates others to less difficult parts. These students tend to fall farther behind in performance skills and sometimes develop behavior problems.

Beginning Instruction

Method books for beginning ensembles include parts for a variety of percussion instruments but have few technical and rhythmic challenges. Each student should learn snare drum and mallet skills, which take years to perfect. Mallet players learn pitches as well as rhythms and become better sight-readers. Primary method books challenge most beginning players, but advanced mallet students might play some exercises from an oboe book. Other students could practice intermediate snare drum techniques.

Developing skills on snare drum and mallets is important and worthy of doubling some parts during rehearsals. Don't hesitate to have several students play snare drum parts while another plays a xylophone using the oboe part. Leave out the auxiliary parts, such as woodblock, and let students learn them at the last minute after practicing a more interesting part in rehearsals.

Intermediate Instruction

The excitement of first-year band may give way to frustration in the second and third years if parts are boring and repetitive. Idle percussionists may develop behavior problems or drop out. Unfortunately, directors sometimes give little thought to the best way to use the percussion section during warm-ups. Musical figures that challenge wind players may be dull and tedious for drummers. While other students learn new scale fingerings, percussionists often play little more than quarter and eighth notes.

Intermediate woodwind and brass players should develop scale technique by starting on different notes, rather than simply running up and down from tonic to tonic.

Grade three bands should be able to play this exercise up to step five in B♭, A♭, and C major at ♩ =92 or better. All instruments except horns can play in these keys without switching octaves. Some percussionists should play this exercise on melody instruments with the winds while others practice advanced snare drum techniques.

Corps-style percussion sections practice the roll pyramid, an exercise that develops mastery of every combination of rolled and non-rolled sixteenth notes in a given beat. The nine easiest permutations of the roll pyramid correspond with the nine scales of the above exercise. The first eight patterns include combinations of one or two sixteenth notes in each beat rolled, and the ninth variation is a 65-stroke roll for four beats. This exercise challenges middle and junior high school percussionists, even those who study privately. After mastering these nine patterns, players should practice more difficult variations of the roll pyramid.

For variety have snare drummers practice rudiments or roll patterns while the winds play long tone scales. Constant repetition develops precision, consistency, and endurance. While one student plays a slow scale on timpani, another might keep time on a drumset. Encourage students to learn different drumset styles to develop versatility.

Mallet players should practice scales with two, four, or eight notes or a single-stroke roll on each note. More advanced students might learn a series of rolled chords on each note of a scale in all keys. Students may use Leonard B. Smith's *Treasury of Scales* and learn voicings for each chord. This exercise is too difficult for most students, but advanced players will find it challenging.

Many directors continue with the same method book series for two or three years. The third and fourth books of most series have fun unison passages for winds that develop rhythmic and technical precision and are adaptable for percussionists.

This excerpt from book four of the *First Division Band Method* is a variation on *Battle Hymn of the Republic* written in unison. The written bass and snare drum parts provide a standard rhythmic accompaniment appropriate for students who do not play basic patterns well. Somewhat more advanced students should single-tap the rhythm of the melody on snare drum while mallet players read from the oboe book.

If single-tapping rhythms is too easy for advanced snare drummers, they should read from a flute, clarinet, or oboe book and play rolls for any note longer than an eighth note. The roll should be one eighth-note less than each note value with eight strokes per count and a tap on the final eighth note. Quarter notes become 5-stroke rolls, dotted quarters 9-stroke rolls, and half notes 13-stroke rolls and so on. Advanced students find this exercise challenging and will benefit from practicing this way. The crisp eighth notes at the end of each roll will help the entire ensemble play with more precision.

Advanced Instruction

High school groups typically spend less time on exercises and training materials than do younger ensembles. While working on advanced literature conductors will rarely double percussion parts for the sake of building technique. Although students perfect difficult percussion techniques during marching season, many original band works and a majority of transcriptions have little for the percussion section to do. Students may learn how their parts contribute to the overall performance of a work, but this maturity does not develop playing skill.

Directors should plan programs that allow percussionists to prepare one or two pieces with an emphasis on their section in exchange for sitting patiently during the slow movement of a Holst suite. Much contemporary band literature is appropriate; *Symphonic Movement* by Nelhybel is an excellent composition with advanced parts for an entire percussion section. Percussionists might hold sectional rehearsals or prepare a work written for percussion ensemble while the winds work on the introduction to *Elsa's Procession to the Cathedral.* These practices foster maturity, independence, leadership, and initiative.

Unfortunately, there is a limited supply of excellent works with worthwhile percussion parts. Many pieces with extensive percussion have dubious musical value; others offer little challenge. The musical sophistication of a clave/tambourine part rarely equals that of the easiest wind part. Three cymbal crashes may earn the same pay in a professional orchestral as a thousand clarinet notes but cannot pay the same educational dividends in a school ensemble.

Accordingly, directors should limit percussion sections to four or five well-trained players. Use students from other sections for pieces that call for more musicians; wind players read well and can play simple percussion parts capably. Playing bass drum might be a novel and educational experience for a flute player; it is too simple for a good percussion student. Many high school directors have little control over middle school programs, but having too few percussionists is preferable to having many who never play. □

Scale Exercise with Snare Drum Part (Roll Pyramid)

1st 16th note
2nd 16th note
3rd 16th note
4th 16th note
1st & 2nd 16th notes
3rd & 4th 16th notes
1st & 3rd 16th notes
2nd & 4th 16th notes

Battle Hymn Variation

21 stroke 5 stroke 5 stroke 5 stroke 29 stroke 5 stroke
21 stroke 5 stroke 5 stroke 29 stroke
21 stroke 5 stroke 21 stroke 5 stroke 13 stroke
9 stroke 5 stroke 5 stroke 5 stroke 5 stroke
21 stroke 5 stroke 5 stroke 29 stroke 21 stroke
21 stroke 5 stroke 5 stroke 17 stroke 5 stroke 21 stroke
13 stroke 5 stroke 5 stroke 9 stroke 13 stroke 5 stroke
5 stroke 5 stroke 5 stroke 5 stroke 5 stroke 5 stroke 5 stroke

Advice for Future College Drummers

by Steve Houghton

It seems that many students would like to become drummers when they start out in a school band. It looks like so much fun to be in the back row, and the drummer gets to hit things. Whatever the reasons, there are many students who take up the drums but never finish. Often the problem is that students have to become percussionists, which generally turns off a student who just wants to play drumset.

In fact, many students never really get to study the drumset with the way school music programs are set up, other than with the jazz band, if the school has one. Percussion ensembles are one solution, but the basic problem is that drumset simply does not fall within the traditional educational circle, so many students drop out because the concert band is not relevant to what students see on television or hear on the radio.

A director with limited percussion background may simply give students instructions to play faster, simpler, or louder, but these suggestions do little to help young drumset players, who are often confused and frustrated. This is the time when it is important for students to develop good skills as an instrumentalist. I was fortunate to have a private teacher who stressed the importance of learning all percussion instruments, not just drumset. He also forced me to study piano at an early age, although I did not recognize at the time how fortunate I was.

One of the difficult aspects of learning to play drums is to develop coordination through an organized practice routine instead of merely banging away without set goals. Inexperienced players tend to practice what they already do well and lack the discipline to work on the areas they do not understand or have not mastered.

The study of drumset can be divided into the basic areas of technique, style, reading/interpretation, and soloing. When these are practiced on a regular basis, the student will develop into a musical drummer. The fundamental technical skills include coordination and independence of hands and feet, endurance, and speed. It is always best if technical exercises incorporate reading skills and style. There are a number of books that develop good snare drum technique: *Master Studies for Snare Drum* by Joe Morello, *Stick Control* by George Lawrence Stone, *Accents on Accents* by Marvin Dahlgren, *Syncopation* by Ted Reed, and *Alfred's Beginning Snare Drum Method* by Dave Black. *Alfred's Beginning Drumset Method* by Sandy Feldstein and *Drum Sessions* by Peter O'Gorman are good remedial drumset books, while *Essential Techniques For Drumset* by Ed Soph, *Advanced Techniques* by Jim Chapin, and *Technique Patterns* by Gary Chaffee are useful to develop advanced technique.

Students may also watch demonstration videos, such as *Hand Development Technique* by Henry Adler, *Speed, Power, Control, Endurance* by Jim Chapin, and *The Drumset: A Musical Approach* by Ed Soph, to learn good technique through example. Students should relate the techniques learned, such as a ride cymbal grip, to actual music by playing with a recording.

Many drumset players have limited reading and interpretive skills as they enter college. When a drummer has difficulty reading a drum chart, it is usually the basic rhythms that cause problems. These basic rhythms can be found in snare drum music. A percussionist should understand several concepts when reading charts: setups, fills, section figures, ensemble figures, and articulation. To prepare for college, students should read as many different types of drum parts as are available, including the music from school musicals, jazz choir, or a civic pops band. The more varied the reading material, the better equipped the drummer will be to play with an advanced ensemble.

Students will find useful snare drum reading exercises in Benjamin Podemski's *Standard Snare Drum Method*, Louie Bellson's *Modern Reading Text*, Anthony Cirone's *The Orchestral Snare Drummer*, Garwood Whaley's *Basics in Rhythm* and *Primary Handbook for Snare Drum*, Charles Wilcoxin's *The All-American Drummer*, and Michael Lauren's *Understanding Rhythm*. Helpful drumset reading books include *Studio and Big Band Drumming* by Steve Houghton, *Syncopated Big Band Figures* by Jake Hanna, *Drumset Reading* by Ron Fink, *Big Band Primer* by Ed Soph, and *Mel Bay's Stage Band Drummers Guide* by John Pickering. To receive extra instruction on chart reading students should watch the videos *Drummers Guide To Reading Drum Charts* by Steve Houghton, *Drum Chart Reading* by Hank Jaramillo, and *Playing, Reading, and Soloing with a Band* by Greg Bissonette.

Keeping up with the current styles of playing is a challenge because they change on a regular basis. Even so, there are four basic styles that make up the foundation of popular music: jazz, rock, country, and Latin. Within these four categories there are endless subcategories: in jazz there is medium swing, up tempo swing, shuffle, bebop, Dixieland, and contemporary jazz; in rock there is pop, heavy metal, rap, funk, techno, and fusion; in country there is bluegrass, gospel, and country-rock; and in Latin under Afro-Cuban there is mambo, songo, cha-cha, rumba, and guaguanco, and under Brazilian there is samba, bossa-nova, and baion. To remain current with all of these styles is difficult at best. Most students have poor listening habits and later regret not developing listening skills at a younger age. Listening is the only way to build a broad concept of the music that is pertinent to a professional drumset player. Although there are thousands of recordings to choose from, students should start by listening to Woody Herman, Count Basie, Thad Jones, and Bob Florence for the big band sound; Irakere, Eddie Palmieri, Poncho Sanchez, Mongo Santamaria, Tito Puente, and Paquito D'Rivera for Latin recordings; Bill Evans, Miles Davis, John Coltrane, and Cannonball Adderley to hear swing; and Yellowjackets, Pat Metheny, Spyro Gyra, and David Sanborn to study fusion.

Once students identify the various styles available, encourage them to try two new beats or styles a week. Instead of simply working with skills they al-

Studio and Big Band Drumming *by Steve Houghton, ©1985 C.L. Barnhouse Co.*

ready have learned, students should develop the discipline to work on new skills. After listening to a new style, ask students to perform it either with a play-along track or with a live rhythm section. Entering college freshmen should understand the common styles of Latin, swing, rock, fusion, and their subcategories.

It is important for students to develop soloing skills beyond trading fours. Contemporary drumset solos use a variety of formats, so a drummer should explore challenging solos in different forms. Solo studies should include trading twos, fours, eights, and whole choruses in different styles and at different tempos; soloing over melodies, forms, kicks, vamps, and harmonic rhythms; transition solos with a change in tempo; and open solo (in time). Students should also develop a strong sense of time, which means being capable of playing in time with the appropriate style either on the beat, behind the beat, or ahead of the beat. Students should count rhythms and rests accurately without a metronome or conductor. To improve this area, practice with a metronome or program a drum machine to play for four bars then rest for four bars. It also helps to sing, memorize, and play the tunes from fake books and lead sheets of popular hits.

Students who prefer to play the drumset should still learn the technical skills to play mallets, timpani, and auxiliary instruments. Keyboard knowledge and piano training is a valuable tool for musicianship, sight-reading, and note identification. Set drummers may choose to experiment with drum machines, sequencers, samplers, and M.I.D.I. programs to get ahead in their field. By incorporating various aspects of drumset performance into practice sessions, students should develop the skills to advance to the college level.

Recommended Books on Style
Advanced Funk Studies by Rick Latham
Afro-Cuban Grooves for Bass and Drums by Lincoln Goines
Afro-Cuban Rhythms for Drumset by Frank Malabe
The Beat, The Body, The Brain by Skip Hadden
Brazilian Percussion Manual by Dan Sabanovich
Brazilian Rhythms For Drumset by Duduka Fonseca
Essential Styles Books 1 and 2 by Steve Houghton
Future Sounds by David Garibaldi
The Salsa Guide Book by Rebeca Mauleon

Recommended Videos on Style
Advanced Funk Studies by Rick Latham
Afro-Caribbean Rhythms by Chuck Silverman
The Contemporary Rhythm Section – Drums by Steve Houghton
From R&B to Funk by Earl Palmer
New Orleans Drumming by Herlin Riley
Timekeeping – 2 by Peter Erskine ☐

Biographies

This biographical information is current as of the date shown in parentheses.

Alan Abel
(January 1952) President of the American Drummers Association and prominent authority, writer, lecturer, and professional drummer. Performed with the late Glenn Miller, the Columbus (Ohio) Symphony, and David Rose. Three years in the Army Air Force as percussionist with Moss Hart's "Winged Victory," which toured the U.S. and the South Pacific. Assistant director Ohio State Fair Boys Band, Director of percussion at Arrowhead Music Camp for the past five years, holds two VFW drumming championships. Graduate of Ohio State University.

Tony Ames
(May 1980) Timpanist with the National Symphony Orchestra in Washington, D.C.

Tony Applebaum
(January 1975) Instructor of percussion instruments and director of the preparatory winds and percussion department at Northwestern University. Received his B.M.E. and M.M. degrees from Northwestern. Performs all styles of music with various performing organizations in the Chicago area including the Grant Park and Chicago Symphony Orchestras.

Edward P. Asmus
(March 1980) Percussionist and former band director in Kansas City, Kansas. Assistant professor of music at State University of New York at Buffalo.

Harold B. Bachman
(September 1962) Trained at the North Dakota Agricultural College and the VanderCook College of Music (Chicago). Taught in North Dakota and Minnesota and served in World War I in the 116th Engineer Band. Organized and conducted Bachman's Million Dollar Band and served as band director at the University of Chicago. After serving in World War II, accepted a position at the University of Florida as Professor of Music and Director of Bands. Recently retired to do guest conducting and clinic work.

Donald R. Baker
(September 1983) The contributing editor for the Percussion Clinic section of *The Instrumentalist.* Teaches at the University of North Carolina, Greensboro and has taught percussion at Western Michigan University. Holds degrees in music education from the University of Michigan and Indiana University of Pennsylvania.

Gene Bardo
(November 1980) Currently one of five percussionists in the Saginaw Eddy band, was a Curtis graduate and a member of the Jacksonville and St. Petersburg symphonies before becoming the owner of the WKYO radio station that broadcasts to the Detroit, Michigan area.

Wallace Barnett
(December 1962) A graduate of Phillips University in Enid, Oklahoma, holds master's degree from Millikin University. Has served on the music faculty of the Decatur (Illinois) public schools for fifteen years. Is now Director of Instrumental Music at Eisenhower High School (Decatur) and an Instructor in Woodwinds at Millikin University. Has studied television production and direction at the University of Southern California and toured with the Hanna Concert Company as a mallet percussionist throughout North America.

John Beck
(February 1984) Head of the percussion department at Eastman School of Music, conducts the Eastman Percussion Ensemble, and is timpanist with the Rochester Philharmonic Orchestra. He has recorded on the CRI, Turnabout, Mark, and Heritage labels, and is second vice-president of the Percussive Arts Society. He holds degrees from Eastman.

James R. Beckham
(October 1974) Instructor of music theory and percussion at Weber State College in Ogden, Utah.

Fred Begun
(April 1960) Timpanist of the National Symphony, Washington D.C. Attended the Juilliard School of Music where he studied timpani with Saul Goodman. Has been a faculty member of Catholic University of America.

Louis Bellson
(June 1962) Louis Bellson has played with dance bands led by Ted FioRito, Benny Goodman, Tommy Dorsey, Harry James, and Duke Ellington. During World War II he played in a service and was a member of the Norman Granz *Jazz at the Philharmonic* group. Has written many works in jazz and other idioms and since 1954 has led both a combo and large band of his own.

Sidney Berg
(January 1952) Director of band and orchestra in Maury High School and assistant to the director of music of the Norfolk, Virginia public schools. Now in his eighth season as tympanist with the Norfolk Symphony Orchestra, has served as guest director at the Virginia Band Camp for four summers.

Joe Berryman
(February 1955) Band director and percussionist in Itta Bina, Mississippi.

John C. Bircher, Jr.
(March 1972) Member of the faculty at the University of South Carolina where he conducts the percussion ensemble. Also teaches percussion in the Columbia (South Carolina) City Schools.

Dave Black
(April 1993) Noted percussionist and author in Los Angeles.

Sue Bradle
(September 1983) Holds music education degrees from the University of Illinois and is a former associate editor of *The Instrumentalist.*

Gene A. Braught
(January 1971) Director of Bands at the University of Oklahoma where he also teaches conducting, band administration, and applied percussion. Holds a B.A. degree from Simpson College, a M.S. from Drake University, and the D.M. from Southern College of Fine Arts.

Paul Brazauskas
(April 1984) Adjudicator for the Texas All-State Percussion All-State Band since 1977 and has written percussion solo and ensemble material published by Kjos. He holds bachelor and master degrees in music education from VanderCook College of Music.

Barry D. Bridwell
(January 1992) A D.M.A. candidate in percussion performance at the University of North Texas and a free-lance musician in Spartanburg, South Carolina.

Mervin Britton
(May 1970) Teaches percussion and theory at Arizona State University. Authored *Creative Approach to the Snare Drum* and Timpani Tuning and is a columnist for the Percussive Arts Society publication. Has served as percussion editor of the NACWPI *Bulletin.*

Jeff Brown
(November 1990) Assistant band director at Jones County Junior College in Ellisville, Mississippi where he also teaches percussion and theory. He holds degrees from Delta State University and has 15 years of teaching experience in public schools and colleges in Mississippi.

Merrill Brown
(February 1977) Professor of music at the University of Toledo. In addition to teaching in the Iowa public schools for 10 years, has taught at Carthage College and Dakota State College. Holds a Ph.D. from the University of Iowa.

Theodore D. Brown
(February 1973) Has taught percussion in public schools and at Wisconsin State University, Stevens Point. Professional experience includes work with the Boston Civic Orchestra, the Toledo Symphony, and the Green Bay Symphony. Currently a doctoral student at the University of Michigan.

Thomas Brown
(April 1974) Professor of music at the College of Saint Rose in Albany, New York. Artist-clinician for the Ludwig Drum Company and *down beat* magazine as well as percussion editor for the magazine *Brass and Percussion.*

Robert Buck
(September 1979) Teaches at Pasadena City College and is associate director and percussion instructor of the Official Tournament of Roses. In addition to being a lecturer and clinician, is an adjudicator for Drum Corps International.

Robert W. Buggert
(June 1958) Percussion instructor and head of graduate studies in music at the University of Wichita, as well as timpanist in the Wichita Symphony. Taught formerly at the University of Michigan and at VanderCook School of Music. Publications include numerous method books, solos, and ensembles.

Roy Burns
(May 1972) Staff artist for Rogers Drums and is active as a clinician throughout the country. Has played with numerous professional bands and for many national T.V. shows.

Wayne E. Charles
(August 1979) Free-lance writer and musician who lives in Trinidad, West Indies.

Bobby Christian
(May 1980) Experienced percussionist now working in Chicago recording studios and leading his big band.

Anthony Cirone
(June 1969) Assistant professor of music at San Jose State College and director of the school's percussion ensemble. Holds bachelor's and master's degrees from Juilliard School of Music and has had several works for percussion published. Now principal percussionist and assistant timpanist with the San Francisco Symphony.

Jay Collins
(February 1967) Assistant professor of music at Wisconsin State University, Whitewater, teaching percussion, percussion ensemble, percussion technique, and music appreciation. Has a B.M. from the University of Miami and M.A. from Eastern Carolina College. A member of the Percussive Arts Society, he is also state chairman if NACWPI and a member of the CBDNA.

F. Michael Combs
(September 1974) Percussion instructor at the University of Tennessee in Knoxville and timpanist with the Knoxville Symphony Orchestra. Active as an adjudicator and clinician.

John M. Crawford
(May 1961) Writes as a representative of the University of Texas Longhorn Band.

Bill Crowden
(May 1980) Owner and manager of Drums, Ltd., a drum specialty shop in Chicago.

Patrick Crowley
(January 1978) Music director at J.T. Morgan Academy, Selma, Alabama.

Paula Culp
(November 1966) Timpanist with the Metropolitan Opera National Company. Holds a B.M.E. from Oberlin College Conservatory of Music, an M.M.E. from Indiana University, and studied at the Mozarteum in Salzburg, Austria.

Bruce Dalby
(September 1994) Assistant professor of music at the University of New Mexico, where he teaches courses in music education and directs the jazz program. He has ten years of experience in the public schools of Idaho and New Mexico. Dalby received a bachelor's degree from Utah State University and master's and doctorate degrees from the University of Illinois at Urbana-Champaign.

Thomas L. Davis
(February 1958) Graduate of Northwestern University and the U.S. Naval School of Music in Washington, D.C. After four years in Navy bands, returned to Northwestern University where he is presently doing graduate work, is assistant in the band department and director of the university percussion ensemble.

Serge de Gastyne
(September 1962) After service in the French underground came to America to study music at the University of Portland and at the Eastman School of Music. Then joined the Air Force Band as a composer-arranger and has had some of his major works performed by many of the nation's outstanding symphony orchestras.

Ron Delp
(February 1975) Performer, composer, and director of the Applied Music School in Tampa, Florida.

Sam Denov
(May 1980) In his tenth year as cymbalist of the Chicago Symphony Orchestra, is a former member of the Pittsburgh Symphony Orchestra and the San Antonio Symphony. Has had professional experience in miscellaneous commercial engagements, radio, television, and recordings. Is a clinician for the A. Zildjian Company and a judge in the Chicago Public High School Percussion Solo Contests.

Jeffrey M. Dire
(September 1977) Has taught percussion at all levels, and is active as a performer and adjudicator. Holds degrees from DePaul University and Northwestern University.

James Dutton
(September 1950) Teaches at the American Conservatory in Chicago. Has achieved significant success as a soloist and teacher.

Karen Ervin
(March 1978) Active as percussion recitalist and clinician. Has won international competitions and made several recordings. Teaches at California State University, Northridge.

David P. Eyler
(May 1980) Principal percussionist of the Baton Rouge Symphony Orchestra, teaches at Louisiana State University.

Phil Faini
(October 1980) Professor of music at West Virginia University where he teaches percussion and African music. Has made two trips to Africa to study and his percussion ensemble was selected by the United States Department of State for a ten nation tour of South America.

Frederick Fairchild
(October 1977) Teaches percussion at the University of Illinois where he is an assistant professor of music and university bands. Has served as timpanist and percussionist at the United States Naval Academy Band and is presently principal percussionist of the Champaign-Urbana Symphony Orchestra. Holds degrees from the University of Illinois.

Saul Feldstein
(October 1968) Assistant professor of music at the State University College at Potsdam, New York, and president of the Percussive Arts Society. Conducts the Percussion Ensemble and is co-conductor of the Symphony Band at the College.

Ron Fink
(December 1975) Ron Fink is coordinator of percussion on the music faculty at North Texas State University. A graduate of the University of Illinois, has taught in public schools and at Northern Illinois University. Also performs professionally in the Fort Worth area.

Vic Firth
(April 1976) Timpanist with the Boston Symphony Orchestra.

Neal L. Fluegel
(January 1963) Received his bachelor's degree from Arizona State University and was a member of the Phoenix, Arizona Symphony Orchestra for three seasons. After teaching high school for two years he now is a master's candidate at the University of Southern Illinois where he is assistant to the band director.

Mark Ford
(December 1987) He is the coordinator of the percussion program at East Carolina University in Greenville, North Carolina. He recently taught at Middle Tennessee State University, where his percussion ensemble won first place in the Tennessee P.A.S. College Percussion Ensemble contest.

George Frock
(September 1983) Professor of percussion at the University of Texas at Austin and timpanist in the Austin Symphony Orchestra. Founder-conductor of the University of Texas Percussion Ensemble, holds degrees from University of Illinois and University of Kansas.

Mario A. Gaetano
(November 1982) Percussion instructor at Western Carolina University in Cullowhee, North Carolina. Received his degrees from the State University of New York at Potsdam and East Carolina University.

John Galm
(January 1968) Percussion instructor at the University of Colorado. Holds B.M. and M.M. degrees from Eastman School of Music and is completing his Ph.D. at the Catholic University of America.

Donald K. Gilbert
(March 1977) Active percussion adjudicator and assistant professor of music at Louisiana State University. Holds degrees from Eastman School of Music, Michigan State University, and the University of Michigan.

Richard C. Gipson
(June 1985) Teaches percussion and conducts the percussion ensemble at the University of Oklahoma (Norman).

Lynn Glassock
(September 1987) Associate professor at the University of North Carolina at Chapel Hill where he teaches percussion and theory. He is active as a performer and clinician.

Saul Goodman
(May 1953) Has been with the New York Philharmonic Symphony since 1926 when he became solo tympanist. He is instructor of tympani and percussion at the Juilliard School of Music, the School of General Studies at Columbia, and the Montreal Conservatory of Music. Has played for radio, films, television and has recorded for Victor, Columbia, and Decca.

William Guegold
(June 1986) Director of bands at Crestwood High School in Mantua, Ohio. He holds music degrees from Capital University and Kent State University, where he is completing a Ph.D. in education.

Lance Haas
(August 1990) Holds degrees from the University of Wisconsin at Madison, teaches at Wilmot (Wisconsin) High School, and operates Drumit Publications.

Thomas Hannum
(August 1985) Assistant marching band director at the University of Massachusetts in Amherst and percussion program director of the Garfield Cadets Drum and Bugle Corps.

Lewis Harlow
(June 1967) Educated at Harvard and as recipient of the Payne Award, continued his studies in Paris. Has supervised instrumental music in grade school in New England and directed adult community bands.

Haskell Harr
(June 1973) Nationally recognized as a leading pioneer in percussion work in the public schools. He had a long career as a professional percussionist and teacher. His percussion instruction books are widely known and used.

Kerry Hart
(January 1992) Associate professor of music and Chairman of the Music Department at Adams State College, Alamosa, Colorado. She has been a band director at both the public school and college level.

William Sebastian Hart
(June 1963) Founder and director of the Gettysburg Symphony Orchestra. Member of the faculty of Peabody Conservatory, Baltimore. Received a bachelor's degree from Johns Hopkins University, a Ph.D. from California Golden Gate University, and a D.M. from Allen University, Columbia, South Carolina.

Alyn Heim
(November 1967) Music director at Manchester Regional High School in New Jersey. A graduate of Juilliard, also has an M.A. in music education from Columbia University Teachers College. Authored several drum books and is a former member of the Houston Symphony.

Steven Hemphill
(June 1991) Teaches percussion at Florida State University where he is currently completing his doctorate. He has taught at the University of Wyoming and holds degrees from the Eastman School of Music.

Fred Hinger
(March 1961) Has been a member of the Philadelphia Orchestra for the past twelve years, being first percussionist from 1948 to 1950 and timpanist from then to the present. He is a faculty member of the Curtis Institute of Music.

Richard Hochrainer
(February 1972) Professor of percussion instruments at the Vienna Academy of Music and the author of *Etüden für Timpani,* volumes 1 and 2 and *Ubungen für kleine Trommel.* Recently retired as principal timpanist of the Vienna Philharmonic and Vienna State Opera Orchestras.

Rich Holly
(November 1983) Received degrees in percussion performance from the State University of New York at Potsdam and East Carolina University. He is instructor of percussion studies at Northern Illinois University in DeKalb and a member of the audition/contest committee for the Percussive Arts Society.

Charles Holmes
(August 1987) Band director at Chinook Middle School in Bellevue, Washington. He holds bachelor's and master's degrees from the University of Wisconsin-Milwaukee.

Sherman Hong
(September 1989) Professor of music at the University of Southern Mississippi. He teaches percussion, music education, and concert band. He is a member of D.C.I. and D.C.M. judging associations.

Steven Houghton
(April 1995) Studied at the University of North Texas and performed with various groups including the big bands of Woody Herman, Bob Florence, Frank Mantooth, and Doc Severinsen. He frequently performs jazz and symphonic percussion as a clinician at festivals and colleges and serves as the national percussion chairman for the International Association of Jazz Educators. Houghton is a board member of the Percussive Arts Society. The Contemporary Rhythm Section series is his most recent publication.

Bob Houston
(May 1978) Percussion instructor at East Texas State University and an active clinician. Has performed with the Dallas Symphony Orchestra and the Fort Worth Symphony.

Doug Howard
(October 1979) Graduate of Bethany College in Lindsborg, Kansas and has done graduate work at the University of Wichita. While in the service played in Army bands in Italy and Korea. Taught for four years in the Gypsum (Kansas) public schools and currently is at the Buhler (Kansas) Grade School.

Mark Johnson
(February 1976) Assistant professor of percussion and music literature at Michigan State University in East Lansing. Graduate of the University of Illinois and former member of the San Antonio Symphony, is the timpanist with the Santa Fe Opera during the summer.

Ronald Johnson
(December 1972) Assistant conductor of the wind orchestra at California State University, Northridge.

Larry C. Jones
(March 1979) Instrumental music teacher at Mattawan, Michigan. Also active as a percussion teacher and adjudicator.

Dennis Kahle
(May 1974) Formerly percussion instructor at the University of Pittsburgh and is presently percussionist/composer at the Center for the Creative and Performing Arts in Buffalo, New York. Chairman of the committee on avant-garde percussion literature and techniques for the Percussive Arts Society.

Brian R. Kilgore
(March 1984) A member of Bill Watrous's Refuge West Big Band. A graduate of California State University Northridge, he has studied hand percussion with Alex Acuña and Jerry Steinholtz.

Donald F. Knaack
(January 1974) Former percussionist in the Louisville Orchestra. Served as a graduate assistant in percussion at the University of Louisville and percussion soloist with the U.S. Military Academy Band at West Point. Currently free-lancing in New York City.

Roy C. Knapp
(January 1948) President of Knapp School of Percussion, Chicago, Illinois.

Dennis Koehler
(January 1985) Band director of the Taft (Texas) Junior High School. He received his bachelor's degree from St. Mary's University of San Antonio and his master's degree from Southwest Texas State University.

Roland Kohloff
(September 1963) Timpanist with the San Francisco Symphony and Opera Orchestras. Head of the percussion department at San Francisco State College, and is leader of the San Francisco Percussion Ensemble. Received the performer's diploma from the Juilliard School of Music, where he studied with Saul Goodman. Has played with the Aspen Festival Orchestra and the Goldman Band.

Kenneth C. Krause
(October 1964) Band director at Southwest High School, Atlanta, Georgia. Holds bachelor's and master's degrees from Northwestern University. Former member of the Atlanta Symphony and with the Grant Park Symphony of Chicago. Has also performed with the Chicago Symphony.

Bill Kreutzer
(October 1972) Formerly a teacher in the public schools of western Kansas now fulfilling a two-year military obligation as a bandsman/percussionist in the U.S. Army.

Bob Laber
(July 1994) Assistant superintendent for curriculum and administration in the Darien, Connecticut public schools. From 1972-78 he was director of performing and creative arts for the Arlington, Massachusetts public schools and has worked extensively in the commercial and educational music industries.

Michael B. Lamade
(September 1958) Graduate of Syracuse University presently teaching percussion at Ohio University, Athens and a graduate assistant in music education.

James Lambert
(May 1985) Assistant professor of music and director of percussion studies at Cameron University in Lawton, Oklahoma. He holds degrees from Baylor University, the University of North Carolina, and the University of Oklahoma and serves as the Contributing Editor to the Percussion Clinic for *The Instrumentalist.*

Geary Larrick
(June 1972) Member of the faculty at the University of Wisconsin, Stevens Point. Holds a B.S. degree from Ohio State University, M.M. from the Eastman School of Music, and is presently a doctoral candidate at the University of Colorado. Formerly a member of the Baltimore Symphony Orchestra and the American Wind Symphony, has also performed with the Rochester Philharmonic and has recorded with the Eastman Wind Ensemble.

Arved M. Larsen
(May 1949) Writes from Florida State University, Tallahassee.

Tim Lautzenheiser
(October 1982) Executive director of Marching Bands of America. Received his degrees from Columbia Pacific University, Ball State University, and the University of Alabama.

Paul Lawrence
(November 1976) Music instructor at the Bedford (Ohio) elementary schools. Holds M.A. from Ohio State University.

Joel T. Leach
(March 1969) Assistant professor of percussion and music theory at Texas Technological College in Lubbock, Texas. Received the bachelor and master of education degrees from Michigan State University. Taught in the junior high system in Lansing and was instructor of percussion at Michigan State. Has been an adjudicator at solo and ensemble festivals and a percussion clinician.

Hoyt F. LeCroy
(June 1977) Has served as percussion instructor and associate director of bands at the college level, and as music supervisor of the Coweta County (Georgia) school system. Currently a doctoral candidate at the University of Southern Mississippi.

Jack Lee
(March 1954) Director of bands at the University of Arizona. Earned degrees at Ohio State University and served as supervisor of music in the public schools of Worthington, Ohio and served as assistant conductor at the University of Michigan.

Maxine Lefever
(December 1968) Percussion instructor and assistant to the director of bands at Purdue University and directs the summer music and twirling camps there. Holds degrees from Western State College in Colorado and Purdue, and is serving as secretary-treasurer of the N.B.A.

Kevin Lepper
(March 1982) Received degrees from New Mexico State University and has taught at marching band camps and arranged for marching bands.

David Levine
(May 1979) Percussion instructor at the University of California at Santa Barbara. Member of the California Percussion Ensemble and an active clinician and performer in the Los Angeles area.

Rey Morgan Longyear
(October 1961) Graduate of Los Angeles State College with a master's degree from the University of North Carolina, and a doctorate from Cornell University. Associate professor of percussion and musicology and coordinator of counseling in music at Mississippi Southern College.

William F. Ludwig, Jr.
(November 1990) Formerly president of Ludwig Industries, the Musser Marimba Company, and a co-founder of the W.F.L. Drum Company currently is a consultant to the Selmer Company. This article has been excerpted from his regular slide lecture, "A History of Percussion."

William F. Ludwig, Sr.
(June 1982) Founder and president of the Ludwig Drum Company. Professional musician and founder of the National Association of Rudimental Drummers.

David Maker
(October 1965) Former student of Bill Moffitt at Michigan State University teaching and studying at the University of Connecticut.

Betty Masoner
(June 1971) Holds B.S. and M.S. degrees from Bemidji State College, presently music director at Gonvick (Minnesota) public School.

Paul T. Mazzacano
(December 1970) Assistant professor of percussion and director of jazz studies at Texas Tech University . Holds B.M. and M.M.E. degrees from DePaul University and makes numerous appearances as a clinician and adjudicator.

Frank McCarty
(June 1975) Composer and performer in the field of contemporary music. Former student of Ingolf Dahl, Robert Erickson, Pauline Oliveros, and Ken Gaburo currently an Assistant Professor of Composition at the University of Pittsburg.

Larry McCormick
(October 1967) Author of several percussion pulications and a noted percussion clinician. Board member of the Percussive Arts Society, holds a bachelor's degree from the University of Illinois and master's from the University of Arkansas.

Robert M. McCormick
(April 1986) Associate professor of music at the University of South Florida, principal percussionist with the Florida Orchestra, and drummer with the university's Faculty Jazz Group. His compositions, published by G. Schirmer, Kendor, Studio 4, and Belwin, have been performed at major universities throughout the United States.

Rod McIntyre
(October 1988) Graduate student at the University of Kansas.

Jack McKenzie
(May 1961) Assistant professor in the School of Music at the University of Illinois. Conductor of the Illinois Percussion Ensemble. Former National Secretary of the National Association of College wind and Percussion Instructors and now President of the new Percussion Composers and Authors League. Holds bachelor's and master's degrees.

James R. (Jim) McKinney
(January 1977) Associate director of bands and percussion instructor at South Dakota State University in Brookings. Taught at the University of Arkansas and Friends University in Wichita, Kansas. An experienced free-lance percussionist, he is currently chairman of the North and South Dakota Chapters of the Percussive Arts Society.

Edward M. Metzenger
(March 1950) Timpanist with the Chicago Symphony Orchestra.

Ramon Meyer
(December 1967) Assistant professor of percussion at the Florida State University, Tallahassee. Holds Ph.D. in theory and has been percussionist with the Louisville Orchestra and the Cincinnati Symphony Orchestra.

Jerrold M. Michaelson
(April 1978) On the staff at Northern Michigan University, Marquette.

James L. Moore
(February 1961) Percussionist with the Indianapolis Symphony Orchestra. During military service was percussion instructor at the U.S. Naval School of Music in Washington. Holds bachelor's and master's degrees from the University of Michigan.

Vincent B. Mottola
(June 1959) Administrative assistant and personnel manager of the Northwestern University bands. Previously was a percussionist with the Navy Unit Band, and with the Charleston and South Carolina Symphony Orchestras.

Jerome Mouton
(September 1969) Assistant professor of music at the Inter-American University in San German, Puerto Rico. Holds a B.M.E. from the University of Southwestern Louisiana and an M.M. from Louisiana State.

Bill Muehler
(October 1958) After study in high school toured with various bands until establishing his own drum studio in Joliet, Illinois. Teaches privately and rehearses drum ensembles for bands throughout northern Illinois and has made recordings and played on radio.

Joe Barry Mullins
(January 1953) Assistant professor of music and director of band at Northeast Louisiana State College, Monroe. Earned his B.M. at Southwestern in Memphis, Tennessee, and his M.M. at Peabody in Nashville. An experienced high school and college band director, has frequently served as contest judge, festival director, and clinic conductor.

Kenneth L. Neidig
(September 1983) Editor of *The Instrumentalist* since 1970. Earned degrees at Murray (Kentucky) State University and the University of Kentucky. Taught instrumental music in the public schools for 15 years, played in U.S. Army bands, and has written three books for the Prentice-Hall organization.

Vaclav Nelhybel
(June 1975) Czech-born American composer, lecturer, clinician, and guest conductor throughout the country.

Milton Nelson
(May 1980) Instrumental music specialist for the Akron Public Schools and instrumental music director in Innes Junior High School.

Arthur E. Neumann
(March 1958) Consulting engineer in the Chicago, Illinois area.

Fred William Noak
(September 1956) Timpanist, composer, and music educator trained at the Dresden Conservatory. Broad professional experience includes the Dresden Opera Orchestra, the Vienna State Opera, the Salzburg Festivals, and the Cincinnati Symphony Orchestra. Presently timpanist with the New York Metropolitan Opera Orchestra.

John P. Noonan
(September 1960) Has taught at Illinois Wesleyan University in Bloomington for many years and owns his own store there. Original editor of the Percussion Clinic in *The Instrumentalist* through Volume VI.

H.E. Nutt
(December 1953) Secretary of VanderCook College of Music and Dean of the faculty. Formerly taught science and music in the Chicago public schools. Cofounder of the Mid-West Band Clinic and has been active in educational research.

Rees Olson
(September 1968) Music supervisor of the Centralia (California) School District, and teaches elementary music methods at the University of California, Irvine. Holds a Ph.D. from Indiana University.

Acton Ostling
(April 1955) Graduate of Ithaca and director in Endicott, New York. Studied with J. Burns Moore and spent three seasons with the Conway Concert Band. Has authored methods for percussion.

Douglas Overmier
(October 1990) Director of bands and percussive studies at Concord College in Athens, West Virginia and holds degrees in percussion from Ohio University.

John J. Papastefan
(February 1990) An associate professor of music and director of percussion studies at the University of South Alabama, Mobile.

Al Payson
(February 1970) Percussionist with the Chicago Symphony Orchestra. A graduate of the University of Illinois, began his professional career with the Louisville Symphony. Clinician for the Ludwig Drum Company.

Jesse Pearl
(October 1966) Instrumental music teacher in the Dade County (Florida) public schools. Received his bachelor of music and master of music degrees from the University of Miami where he was a member of the band and symphony orchestra. Was a member of the 5th All-American Bandmaster's Band under the direction of Morton Gould.

Russell Peck
(September 1978) Graduate of the University of Michigan and composer. Has taught composition at Northern Illinois University, Eastman School of Music, and is currently on the faculty at the School of the Arts, Winston-Salem, North Carolina.

Charles Perry
(October 1963) Has worked with numerous dance bands, jazz bands, and show bands and recorded for Capitol, Columbia, RCA Victor, Decca, and Mercury. Has conducted seminar-workshops for students and teachers at the University of Indiana, Southern Methodist University, and Michigan State University. Has authored several drum books.

G. David Peters
(January 1978) Head of the PLATO Music Project at the University of Illinois, where he is a member of the School of Music faculty. Holds a B.M.E. degree from the University of Evansville and M.S. and Ed.D. degrees from the University of Illinois.

Gordon Peters
(May 1980) A graduate of Northwestern University and Eastman School of Music, was active in the founding of the Percussive Arts Society serving as the first president. Principal percussionist of the Chicago Symphony Orchestra and administrator/conductor of the Chicago Civic Orchestra, the training orchestra of the Chicago Symphony.

Mitchell Peters
(April 1993) Principal timpanist and percussionist in the Los Angeles Philharmonic.

Heather Pettit
(July 1993) Received degrees from the University of Cincinnati College-Conservatory of Music and Northern Kentucky University and taught instrumental music for ten years. She is a free-lance horn player and an assistant editor of *The Instrumentalist.*

Mark Petty
(October 1978) Percussion instructor and arranger for the Cavaliers Drum and Bugle Corps of Chicago.

James Piekarczyk
(November 1979) Teaches at Thornton Community College in South Holland, Illinois.

Linda Pimentel
(November 1981) Clinician for the Ludwig Drum Company. Formerly taught percussion at Ohio State University, now teaches at the University of Lethbridge in Alberta, Canada.

Ralph R. Pottle
(December 1962) Head of the Department of Fine Arts, Southeastern Louisiana College. Received bachelor's degree from the New Orleans Conservatory, and master's from Louisiana State University and Teacher's College, Columbia University. Holds Ph.D. from Peabody College for Teachers, Nashville. Member of many professional organizations, author, and lecturer throughout the country.

Harrison Powley
(February 1972) Faculty member at Brigham Young University. Holds B.M. and M.A. degrees from the Eastman School of Music where he is a candidate for the Ph.D. degree. Studied with Professor Hochrainer at the Vienna Academy as a Fulbright scholar.

Barbara Prentice
(May 1989) Director of bands at Boles Junior High School in Arlington, Texas and a consulting editor of *The Instrumentalist.*

Paul Price
(March 1953) Assistant professor of music at the University of Illinois. Graduate of the New England Conservatory of Music with a master's degree from the Cincinnati Conservatory of Music. Serves as conductor of the University of Illinois Percussion Ensemble.

Marty Province
(September 1991) Director of bands at Wake Forest University in Winston-Salem, North Carolina.

Joe M. Pullis
(October 1971) Twice state drumming champion of Arkansas, six times state champion in Texas, and National Rudimental Drumming Champion of the United States in 1957.

John R. Raush
(April 1985) Instructor of percussion in the school of music at Louisiana State University in Baton Rouge and timpanist of the Baton Rouge Symphony Orchestra.

H. Owen Reed
(April 1968) Well-known composer, professor of music and chairman of graduate composition at Michigan State University.

Robert Reely
(August 1991) Holds degrees from Harding University in Searcy, Arkansas, and is currently band director at Paragould Junior High School in Paragould, Arkansas.

LaVerne Reimer
(October 1973) Director of bands and head of the music department at York Community High School (Elmhurst, Illinois). Holds bachelor's and master's degrees from Northwestern University.

Guy Remonko
(December 1988) Associate Professor of Percussion at Ohio University's School of Music in Athens.

Larry Rhodes
(January 1988) Has been a freelance writer on music and entertainment for 14 years. His publications include articles in *Modern Drummer.*

Marvin Rosenberg
(September 1961) Band director at Midwood High School, Brooklyn, New York, and assistant conductor of the All-City High School Orchestra of the New York Public Schools. Holds bachelor's and master's degrees from the Manhattan School of Music and has extensive experience as a professional performer.

James J. Ross
(April 1965) Member of the Chicago Symphony and its Percussion Ensemble. Graduate of the New England Conservatory of Music and has performed under Fritz Reiner and Eugene Goosens with the Cincinnati Symphony, under Pierre Monteux with the San Francisco Symphony, and under Fritz Reiner and William Steinberg with the Pittsburgh Symphony.

Thomas D. Rossing
((May 1976) Professor of physics at Northern Illinois University, has taught courses in musical acoustics and established an acoustics laboratory. Director of a church choir, singer, and performer on clarinet and recorder.

Bruce Roberts
(March 1991) Received degrees from the University of Arkansas and has taught in the Arkansas Public Schools and the University of Arkansas.

James Salmon
(September 1967) Professor of percussion instruments at the University of Michigan and the author of several percussion texts. Holds bachelor's and master's degrees from the University of Michigan.

Fred Sanford
(June 1975) Program director and instructor for the Alberta (Canada) All-Girl Drum and Bugle Corps. Also instructs the championship Santa Clara Vanguards drum line.

Richard P. Scherer
(November 1951) Director of the high school and municipal bands in Fairmont, Minnesota. Studied percussion with E.W. Weflen and Henry Denecke, Minneapolis Symphony Orchestra. Holds B.S. from Mankato (Minnesota) Teachers College and University of Minnesota.

William J. Schinstine
(August 1980) Prolific author of over 300 published works, methods, and percussion ensembles, now owns and operates the S. & S. School of Music in Pottstown, Pennsylvania. Taught instrumental music in the Pottstown public schools for 27 years.

Walter C. Schneider
(May 1980) Director of bands in the Tenafly, New Jersey public schools.

Richard Schory
(April 1960) Educational and advertising director for the Ludwig Drum Company. As a percussion performer has played with the Chicago Symphony Orchestra, the Air Force Command Band, and various other groups. Active as a clinician throughout the country.

Frank Shaffer, Jr.
(January 1978) Assistant professor of percussion and theory at Memphis State University. Timpanist of the Memphis Symphony and Memphis Opera Orchestras, and has performed extensively with rock, jazz, theater, and commercial groups. Holds degrees from Duquesne and Yale Universities.

Brian Shepard
(April 1979) Senior at the University of Kansas majoring in percussion.

Brian Shlim
(May 1980) Representative of Schilke Music Products and serves as a marketing consultant for the Zildjian Cymbal Company.

Emil Sholle
(January 1958) Member of the Cleveland Symphony Orchestra and has performed with the staff orchestra at radio station WHK, Cleveland. Has conducted the band and orchestra at Northfield (Ohio) High School and teaches at the Hruby Conservatory of Music in Cleveland as well as the Currier Music Center in Cleveland Heights. Has authored percussion texts.

Carolyn Reid Sisney
((April 1969) Teaches and performs on the marimba and vibraphone in her own studio and teaches at Bradley University. Received a bachelor of music education from Bradley and an M.M.E. from Northwestern University.

Robert Slider
(March 1959) Band instructor in the public schools of Joliet, Illinois, formerly at Donovan, Illinois. Has a bachelor's degree from Indiana University and a master's from VanderCook College.

Jeanine Smith
(December 1986) Director of publicity for the Noank-Mystic (Connecticut) Community Band.

Jeff B. Smith
(March 1983) Percussion instructor at Humboldt State University in Arcata, California. Holds degrees from Baylor University and the University of Illinois and gives clinics on mallet keyboard instruments.

Leonard B. Smith
(December 1988) Music director of the Detroit Concert Band, a position he has held for 42 years. An advocate of bands and band music, he has been a member of *The Instrumentalist's* Board of Advisors since June 1973.

Hugh Soebbing
(December 1977) Has played percussion professionally in various bands, orchestras, dance bands, and shows since 1940. Presently professor of percussion at Quincy (Illinois) College and directs the jazz ensemble there.

Dan Spalding
(May 1984) Assistant professor of music at Stephen F. Austin State University in Nacogdoches, Texas. He received his bachelor's and master's degrees from Northwestern University where he studied with Terry Applebaum and Glenn Steele.

Charles L. Spohn
(December 1955) Graduate of the Arthur Jordan College of Music and of Ohio State University. Has taught at the preparatory, intermediate, and college levels including Ohio State. Director of the ROTC Regimental Band, Assistant Director of the Marching and Concert Bands, and percussionist with the Columbus Symphony.

Donald Stanley
(February 1969) Assistant professor of music at Mansfield (Pennsylvania) State College, teaching low brass and percussion. Holds B.S. and M.A. from Ohio State University. Also conducts the marching and symphonic bands, the brass choir, and the percussion ensemble.

Julie Sutton
(May 1989) Received a B.M.E. from the University of North Texas. A percussionist, she teaches at Oakland High School and LaVergne High School in Tennessee as well as at Middle Tennessee State.

Nicholas Tawa
(November 1963) Music director at Beverly (Massachusetts) High School. Received bachelor's degree from Harvard University, master's degree from Boston University and is currently a candidate for the Ph.D. at Harvard.

Bob Tilles
(March 1967) Chairman of the percussion department of the School of Music of DePaul University in Chicago. Has appeared on radio and television and is on the staff of Columbia Broadcasting in Chicago. Has written several books on percussion and composed ensembles and solo works.

David A. Tobias
(November 1965) Director of the concert and marching bands at Oak Crest High School (New Jersey). Received his B.S. from Lebanon Valley College, Pennsylvania and his M.A. at Teachers College, Columbia University where he taught for two years.

George Tuthill
(May 1983) Clinician and product development consultant for the Slingerland Drum Company. Percussion consultant for the Hal Leonard Publishing Company, program coordinator for the Sky Ryders Drum and Bugle Corps, and a member of the Percussive Arts Marching Percussion Committee.

Michael Udow
(January 1976) Principal percussionist with the Santa Fe Opera, as well as being a composer and an instrumental designer. Currently is artist in residence at the University of Illinois where he is a doctoral candidate.

Ronald F. Vernon
(September 1976) Assistant professor of percussion at the University of Mississippi.

David W. Vincent
(May 1980) Assistant professor of percussion and theory at East Tennessee State University, Johnson City.

Lauren Vogel
(May 1981) Vice-president of the Texas chapter of the Percussive Arts Society and has played with the Dallas Symphony Orchestra, the Dallas Ballet Orchestra, and the Dallas Civic Symphony. Marched marimba and bells with the Phantom Regiment Drum and Bugle Corps of Rockford, Illinois.

David R. Vose
(April 1987) Percussion instructor at the Berklee College of Music and a clinician for the Ludwig Drum Company. He is the author of *The Developing Drummer.*

Jay Wanamaker
(September 1985) Market development manager of percussion and a staff clinician for Yamaha International Corporation in Grand Rapids, Michigan.

Anna Watkins
(April 1982) Instructor of percussion at the Flint Institute of Music and the University of Michigan. Received her degrees from Bowling Green State University and Michigan State University.

Norman Weinberg
(April 1988) Associate professor of music at Del Mar College in Corpus Christi, Texas and principal percussionist of the Corpus Christi Symphony Orchestra. He holds music degrees from Indiana University.

Garwood Whaley
(May 1980) Percussion instructor at the Catholic University, Washington, D.C., and director of music at Bishop Ireton High School, Alexandria, Virginia. Graduate of the Juilliard School of Music, has done doctoral study at Catholic University.

Charles L. White
(February 1964) Timpanist in the Los Angeles Philharmonic Orchestra for 43 years and the author of a percussion book.

Larry White
(February 1985) Assistant director of bands and instructor of percussion at the University of Texas at El Paso where he instructs percussion majors, the percussion and marimba ensembles, and directs the marching band, basketball band, and the university symphony band. He is timpanist with the El Paso Symphony.

Lawrence White
(March 1960) Former member of the Boston Symphony Orchestra. Was also a faculty member of the Boston University College of Music and of the New England Conservatory, receiving his bachelor's and master's from the latter. After serving as staff percussionist at WGN in Chicago, teaches in the public schools of Glencoe, Illinois.

David Whitwell
(December 1972) Conductor of the wind orchestra at California State University, Northridge.

Fred A. Wickstrom, Jr.
(May 1980) Principal percussionist in the Florida Philharmonic and a music faculty member at the University of Miami.

Ray Wifler
(July 1986) Professor of music and chairman of the music department at Marion College in Fond du Lac, Wisconsin and the music director of the Fond du Lac Community band for the past 11 years. He holds a Ph.D. in music education from Michigan State University.

Bill Wiggins
(October 1982) Timpanist for the Nashville Symphony and artist/teacher of timpani and percussion at Vanderbilt University's Blair School of Music. Studied at George Peabody College.

Raymond Willard
(June 1979) Graduate of Ithaca College now teaching instrumental music at North Adams (Massachusetts) Middle School.

C.B. Wilson
(November 1973) Executive Assistant to the Dean at the Cleveland Institute of Music. Holds a Ph.D. in musicology from Case Western Reserve University and has taught in all fields of music.

Jack Witmer
(October 1973) Director of Choirs at York Community High School in Elmhurst, Illinois.

Martin Zyskowski
(July 1979) Associate professor of percussion at Eastern Washington University at Cheney.

Index of Articles by Title

Index of Articles by Category

Accessory Instruments and Miscellaneous Percussion

Acoustics

Bass Drum - Instruments and Playing

Contests and Auditions

Ensembles

Equipment

General

Instrument Construction, Care, and Repair

Jazz/Stage Band

Latin Percussion

Literature and Instruction Materials

Mallet Percussion - Instruments and Playing

Marching Band

Multiple Percussion

Musicianship

Notation

Rudimental Drumming

Snare Drum - Instruments and Playing

Stick Grip

Sticking

Teaching

Timpani (Tympani) - Instruments and Playing

Tuning

Index of Articles by Author

The author column lists the author and subject of an article; thus articles by and about Fred Sanford can be located under his name to facilitate locating materials. Many titles have been shortened in the indices.